Excel 2002 Bible

John Walkenbach and Brian Underdahl

Wiley Publishing, Inc.

Excel 2002 Bible

Published by
Wiley Publishing, Inc.
909 Third Avenue
New York, NY 10022
www.wiley.com

Copyright ©2001 by Wiley Publishing, Inc.,
Indianapolis, Indiana

Published simultaneously in Canada

Publishing, Inc., is not associated with any product or vendor mentioned in this book.

For general information on our other products and services or to obtain technical support, please contact our Customer Care Department within the U.S. at 800-762-2974, outside the U.S. at 317-572-3993, or fax 317-572-4002.

Wiley also publishes its books in a variety of electronic formats. Some content that appears in print may not be available in electronic books.

Library of Congress Cataloging-in-Publication Data:

Library of Congress Control Number: 2001090745
ISBN: 0-7645-3583-8

Manufactured in the United States of America
10 9 8 7 6 5 4 3
1B/QW/RS/QS/IN

Credits

Acquisitions Editor
Jill Byus Schorr

Project Editor
James H. Russell

Development Editor
Darren Meiss

Technical Editor
Kristen Tod

Copy Editor
Rich H. Adin

Project Coordinator
Regina Snyder

Graphics and Production Specialists
Amy Adrian, John Greenough, Gabriele
McCann, Kristin Pickett, Betty Schulte

Quality Control Technician
Andy Hollandbeck

Proofreading and Indexing
TECHBOOKS Production Services

About the Author

John Walkenbach is the author of more than two dozen spreadsheet books. Visit his Web site at http://www.j-walk.com.

Brian Underdahl is the well-known, best-selling author of nearly 60 computer books including several current titles from Hungry Minds: *Pocket PCs For Dummies, Internet Bible, 2nd Edition, Teach Yourself Windows 2000 Professional*, and *Teach Yourself Office XP*.

Brian spends most of his time at the keyboard writing about personal computing. When he finds the time, he enjoys taking in the view from the home he and his wife Darlene built in the mountains 2,000 feet above Reno, Nevada. He tries to find the time to attend Mensa meetings whenever possible, and has become a fairly decent gourmet cook in recent years, too.

Preface

Thanks for purchasing the *Excel 2002 Bible*. Our goal in writing this book is to share with you some of what we know about Excel, and in the process make you more efficient on the job.

The book contains everything that you need to know to learn the basics of Excel and then move on to more advanced topics at your own pace. We present many useful examples as well as loads of dynamite tips and slick techniques that I've accumulated over the years.

Is This Book for You?

The *Bible* series from Hungry Minds is designed for beginning, intermediate, and advanced users. This book covers all the essential components of Excel and provides clear and practical examples that you can adapt to your own needs.

In this book, we've tried to maintain a good balance between the basics that every Excel user needs to know and the more complex topics that will appeal to power users. As someone who've used and taught about spreadsheets for many years, we realize that almost everyone has something to learn. Our goal is to make that learning an enjoyable process.

Software Versions

This book was written for Excel 2002 (also known as Excel 9), but much of the information also applies to Excel 2000 and to Excel 97. If you use a version prior to Excel 97, you'll find that a significant portion of this book does not apply. The earlier versions of Excel are drastically different from the current version.

Conventions This Book Uses

Take a minute to scan this section to learn some of the typographical and organizational conventions that this book uses.

Excel commands

In Excel, as in all Windows programs, you select commands from the pull-down menu system. In this book, such commands appear in normal typeface. An option available under a particular menu is indicated after an ⇨ symbol, as in "Choose File ⇨ Print to print your document."

Filenames, named ranges, and your input

Input that you make from the keyboard appears in bold. Named ranges may appear in a code font. Lengthy input usually appears on a separate line. For instance, we may instruct you to enter a formula such as the following:

```
="Part Name: " &VLOOKUP(PartNumber,PartList,2)
```

Key names

Names of the keys on your keyboard appear in normal type. When two keys should be pressed simultaneously, they are connected with a plus sign, like this: "Press Alt+E to select the Edit menu." Here are the key names as we refer to them throughout the book:

Alt	down arrow	Num Lock	right arrow
Backspace	End	Pause	Scroll Lock
Caps Lock	Home	PgDn	Shift
Ctrl	Insert	PgUp	Tab
Delete	left arrow	Print Screen	up arrow

Functions

Excel's built-in worksheet functions appear in uppercase, like this: "Enter a SUM formula in cell C20."

Mouse conventions

We assume that you're using a mouse or some other pointing device. You'll come across some of the following mouse-related terms:

✦ **Mouse pointer:** The small graphic figure that moves onscreen when you move your mouse. The mouse pointer is usually an arrow, but it changes shape when you move to certain areas of the screen or when you're performing certain actions.

✦ **Point:** Move the mouse so that the mouse pointer is on a specific item: for example, "Point to the Save button on the toolbar."

✦ **Press:** Press the left mouse button once and keep it pressed. Normally, this is used when dragging.

✦ **Click:** Press the left mouse button once and release it immediately.

✦ **Right-click:** Press the right mouse button once and release it immediately. The right mouse button is used in Excel to pop up shortcut menus that are appropriate for whatever is currently selected.

✦ **Double-click:** Press the left mouse button twice in rapid succession. If your double-clicking doesn't seem to be working, you can adjust the double-click sensitivity using the Windows Control Panel icon.

✦ **Drag:** Press the left mouse button and keep it pressed while you move the mouse. Dragging is often used to select a range of cells or to change the size of an object.

What the Icons Mean

Throughout the book, you'll see special graphic symbols, or icons, in the left margin. These call your attention to points that are particularly important or relevant to a specific group of readers. The icons in this book are as follows:

This icon signals the fact that something is important or worth noting. Notes may alert you to a concept that helps you master the task at hand, or they may denote something that is fundamental to understanding subsequent material.

This icon marks a more efficient way of doing something that may not be obvious.

We use this symbol when a possibility exists that the operation we're describing could cause problems if you're not careful.

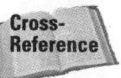

This icon indicates that a related topic is discussed elsewhere in the book.

How This Book Is Organized

Notice that the book is divided into seven main parts, followed by an appendix.

QuickStart — This part gives you a fast start with the fundamentals of Excel 2002, and shows you some of the things that are new in this version.

Part I: Getting Started With Excel — This part consists of six chapters that provide back-ground about Excel. These chapters are considered required reading for Excel newcomers.

Part II: Working with Formulas and Functions — The chapters in Part III cover everything you need to know to become proficient with performing calculations in Excel.

Part III: Enhancing Your Excel Workbooks — The chapters in Part IV cover topics that make your work look better: formatting, charts, and pictures. In addition, you learn how to use the powerful array features to make "impossible" calculations easy.

Part IV: Analyzing Data with Excel — The broad topic of data analysis is the focus of the chapters in Part V. Users of all levels will find some of these chapters of interest.

Part V: Using Advanced Excel Features — This part consists of seven chapters dealing with topics that are usually considered advanced. Many beginning and intermediate users may find this information useful as well.

Part VI: Programming Excel with VBA — Part VII is for those who want to customize Excel for their own use or who are designing workbooks or add-ins that are to be used by others. It starts with an introduction to programming, and provides in-depth coverage of UserForms, add-ins, toolbars, and menus.

Appendix — The appendix consists of supplemental and reference material that may be useful to you.

How to Use This Book

This book is not intended to be read cover-to-cover. Rather, it's a reference book that you can consult when . . .

✦ You're stuck while trying to do something.

✦ You need to do something that you've never done before.

✦ You have some time on your hands, and you're interested in learning something new.

The index is comprehensive, and each chapter typically focuses on a single broad topic. If you're just starting out with Excel, we recommend that you read the first few chapters to gain a basic understanding of the product, and then do some experimenting on your own. After you become familiar with Excel's environment, you can refer to the chapters that interest you most. Some users, however, may prefer to follow the chapters in order.

Don't be discouraged if some of the material is over your head. Most users get by just fine using only a small subset of Excel's total capabilities. In fact, the 80/20 rule applies here: 80 percent of Excel users use only 20 percent of its features. However, using only 20 percent of Excel's features still gives you lots of power at your fingertips.

Contents

• •

Part II: Working with Formulas and Functions   117

Part III: Enhancing Your Excel Workbooks   **249**

Part V: Using Advanced Excel Features   507

Chapter 25: Creating and Using Worksheet Outlines 509

Chapter 26: Linking and Consolidating Worksheets 523

Getting Acquainted with Excel

Excel 2002 is a very powerful and capable program, but unless you understand the basics of using Excel, you won't get much out of it. This chapter introduces you to the basics of Excel so that you can begin to make use of the most popular spreadsheet program available. We will show you the important elements of the Excel screen so that you can get a quick idea of what's going on. Then we will show you how to move around in Excel. Then, we will start your adventure with Excel by having you do something useful with just a couple of minutes of work. Last, we introduce you to the new features we feel will have the greatest impact as you use Excel 2002.

If you're an experienced Excel user you'll probably find that most of the material in this chapter is a review of things you already know. If so, you may want to just quickly skim through it to refresh your memory and then move on to the more advanced chapters that follow. Remember, though, that even the most experienced of us can sometimes use a reminder about some of the basics that we have forgotten.

Understanding Files

You won't get too far without understanding the basic concept of files. Every computer program uses files, and a good understanding of how to manage files stored on your hard drive will make your job easier. This chapter discusses how Excel uses files and what you need to know about files to use Excel.

A *file* is an entity that stores information a disk. A hard disk is usually organized into directories (or folders) to facilitate the organization of files. For example, all the files that comprise Excel are stored in a separate folder on your computer. Files can be manipulated in several ways. They can be copied, renamed, deleted, or moved to another disk or folder. These types of file operations are usually performed by using the tools in Windows (although you also can perform these operations without leaving Excel).

Understanding Excel

Excel is an electronic *spreadsheet* — a program that you use to perform various types of calculations on your PC. For example, you might create a set of calculations in Excel to help you determine how long it will take to recover the extra costs you would incur if you refinanced your home mortgage to take advantage of a lower interest rate. Or you might use Excel to calculate the amount of gravel necessary to create a new driveway. That's the real beauty of a multitalented program such as Excel — you can use it in thousands of different ways that are limited only by your imagination.

When you see Excel for the first time, it's easy to be a little intimidated by all of the different elements that make up the window. Don't be put off by this — you'll soon see that the Excel screen really isn't all that difficult to understand after you learn what the various pieces do.

Figure QS-1 shows you the more important bits and pieces of the Excel screen. As you look at the figure, refer to Table QS-1 for a brief explanation of the items shown in the figure.

Table QS-1		
Parts of the Excel Screen That You Need to Know		
Item #	**Name**	**Description**
1	Active cell indicator	This dark outline indicates the currently active cell (one of the 16,777,216 cells on each worksheet).
2	Close button	Clicking this button closes Excel or the workbook (depending on which Close button you click). If you have any unsaved files, you're prompted to save them.
3	Column headings	Letters ranging from A to IV — one for each of the 256 columns in the worksheet. After column Z comes column AA, which is followed by AB, AC, and so on. After column AZ comes BA, BB, and so on until you get to the last column, labeled IV. You can click a column heading to select an entire column of cells.
4	Formula bar	When you enter information or formulas into Excel, they appear in this line.

Item #	Name	Description
5	Horizontal scrollbar	Enables you to scroll the sheet horizontally.
6	Maximize/ Restore button	Clicking this button increases the workbook window's size to fill Excel's complete workspace. If the window is already maximized, clicking this button "unmaximizes" Excel's window so that it no longer fills the entire screen.
7	Menu bar	This is Excel's main menu. Clicking a word on the menu drops down a list of menu items, which is one way for you to issue a command to Excel. You can drag the Menu bar to any side of the window or even make it free-floating if you like.
8	Minimize button	Clicking this button minimizes Excel's window (or the workbook, depending on which Minimize button you click) and displays it in the Windows taskbar.
9	Row headings	Numbers ranging from 1 to 65,536 — one for each row in the worksheet. You can click a row heading to select an entire row of cells.
10	Sheet tabs	Each of these notebook-like tabs represents a different sheet in the workbook. A workbook can have any number of sheets, and each sheet has its name displayed in a sheet tab. By default, each new workbook that you create contains three sheets.
11	Status bar	This bar displays various messages, as well as the status of the Num Lock, Caps Lock, and Scroll Lock keys on your keyboard.
12	Tab scroll buttons	These buttons let you scroll the sheet tabs to display tabs that aren't visible.
13	Task Pane	This pane enables you to quickly select from sets of related tasks — such as opening an existing workbook or starting a new workbook.
14	Task Pane selector	Clicking here enables you to select from different task panes so you can open workbooks, use the Office Clipboard, or search your workbook.
15	Title bar	All Windows programs have a title bar, which displays the name of the program and holds some control buttons that you can use to modify the window.
16	Toolbars	The toolbars hold buttons that you click to issue commands to Excel. Some of the buttons expand to show additional buttons or commands.
17	Vertical scrollbar	Lets you scroll the sheet vertically.

Task Pane selector

Close button

Maximize/Restore button

Minimize button

Active cell indicator

Task Pane

Column headings

Title bar   Menu bar   Toolbars   Formula bar

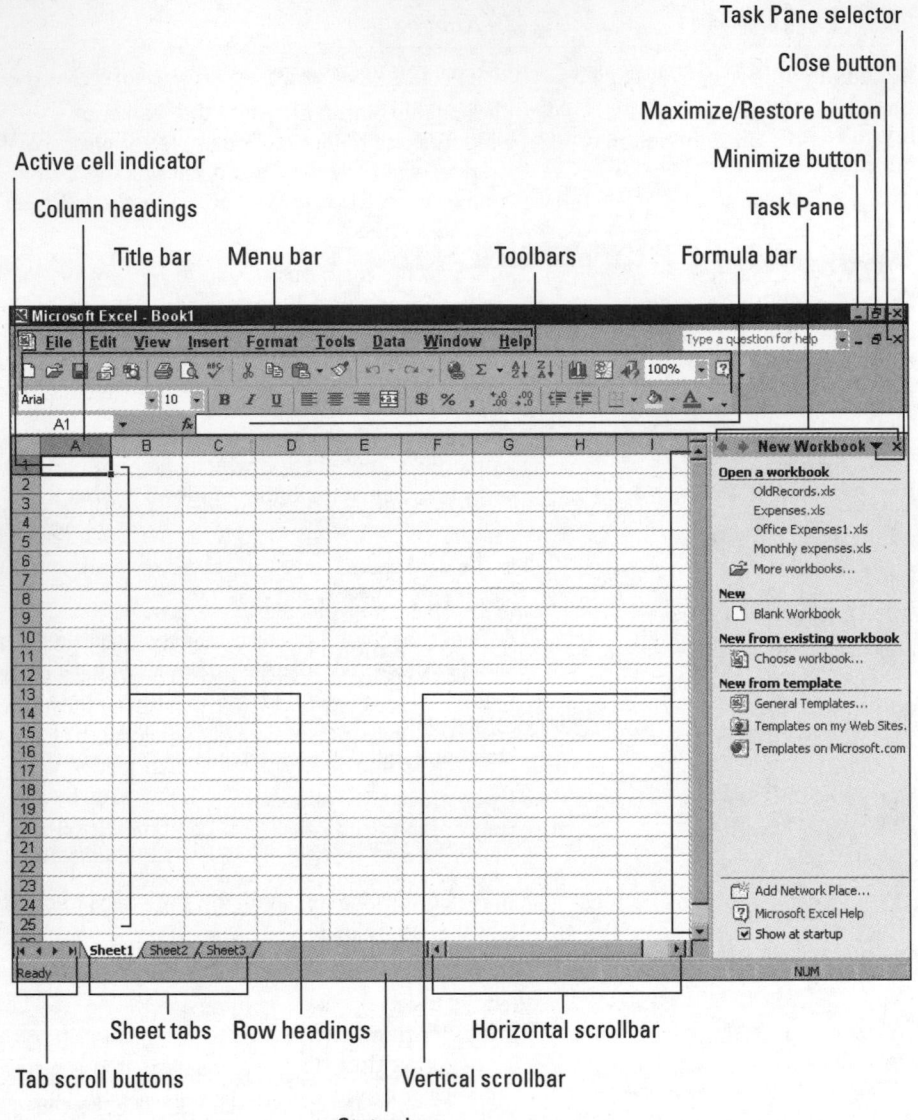

Sheet tabs   Row headings   Horizontal scrollbar

Tab scroll buttons   Vertical scrollbar

Status bar

Figure QS-1: The Excel screen has several very useful elements that you will use often.

Navigating Through Excel

Because you'll spend lots of time working in Excel, you need to understand the basics of navigating through workbooks and how best to use Excel's user interface. If you're an experienced Windows user, some of this information may already be familiar to you, so this is your chance to learn even more.

Using Excel's menus and toolbars

Excel is designed to take orders from you. You give these orders by issuing commands. In many cases, you can choose how to issue a particular command. For example, if you want to save your workbook to disk, you can use the menu (the File ⇨ Save command), a shortcut menu (right-click the workbook's title bar and click Save), a toolbar button (the Save button on the Standard toolbar), or a shortcut key combination (Ctrl+S). The particular method you use is up to you.

The following sections provide an overview of several important methods of issuing commands to Excel.

Using menus

Excel, like all other Windows programs, has a menu bar located directly below the title bar (see Figure QS-2). This menu bar is always available and ready for your command. Excel's menus change, depending on what you're doing. For example, if you're working with a chart, Excel's menus change to give you options that are appropriate for a chart. This all happens automatically, so you don't even have to think about it. Opening the menu is quite straightforward. Click the menu that you want to open, and it drops down to display menu items. Click the menu item to issue the command. To issue a menu command from the keyboard, press Alt and then the menu's hot key. The hot key is the underlined letter in the menu; for example, F is the hot key for the File menu. After you open the menu, you can press the appropriate hot key for a command on the menu. For example, to issue the File ⇨ Print command, press Alt, press F, and then press P.

Some menu items lead to an additional submenu; when you click the menu item, the submenu appears to its right. Menu items that have a submenu display a small triangle. For example, the File ⇨ Send To command has a submenu, which is shown in Figure QS-2. Excel's designers incorporated submenus primarily to keep the menus from becoming too lengthy and overwhelming to users.

Tip   Sometimes, you'll notice that a menu item appears grayed out. This simply means that the menu item isn't appropriate for what you're doing. Nothing happens if you select such a menu item.

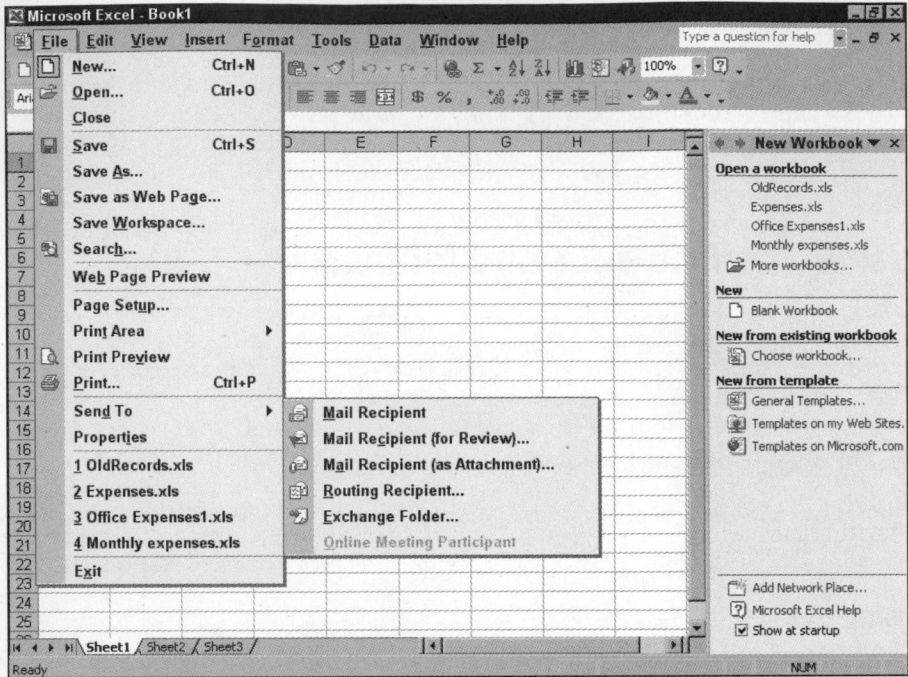

Figure QS-2: When you click an Excel menu, you gain access to the commands that tell the program what you want to do.

Menu items that are followed by an ellipsis (three dots) always display a dialog box. Menu commands that don't have an ellipsis are executed immediately. For example, the File ⇨ Open command results in a dialog box, because Excel needs more information about the command. The File ⇨ Print Preview command doesn't need a dialog box, so Excel performs this command immediately.

Tip

In Excel you can move the menu bar to a new location, if you prefer. To move the menu bar, just click the set of vertical gray dashes at the left side of the menu bar and drag it to its new location. You can drag the menu bar to any of the window borders or leave it free-floating.

Using shortcut keys

Some menu items also have shortcut keys associated with them. For example, the File ⇨ Save command's shortcut key combination is Ctrl+S. As you use Excel, you'll find that learning the shortcut keys for commands you use often can save you a lot of time.

The best way to learn the shortcut keys is typically to watch for them on Excel's menus. The most useful ones display next to the menu item when you open the menus.

Changing Your Mind

Just about every command in Excel can be reversed by using the Edit ⇨ Undo command. Select Edit ⇨ Undo after issuing a command in error, and it's as if you never issued the command. You can reverse the effects of the last 16 commands that you executed by selecting Edit ⇨ Undo more than once.

Rather than use Edit ⇨ Undo, you may prefer to use the Undo button on the toolbar. If you click the arrow on the right side of the button, you can see a description of the commands that can be reversed. The Redo button performs in the opposite direction of the Undo button: Redo repeats commands that have been undone.

Using shortcut menus

Besides the omnipresent menu bar, Excel features a slew of shortcut menus. A shortcut menu is context-sensitive—its contents depend on what you're doing at the time. Shortcut menus don't contain every relevant command, just those that are most commonly used for whatever is selected. You can display a shortcut menu by right-clicking just about anything in Excel.

As an example, Figure QS-3 shows the shortcut menu (also called a context menu) that appears when you right-click a cell. The shortcut menu appears at the mouse-pointer position, which makes selecting a command fast and efficient. The shortcut menu that appears depends on what is currently selected. For example, if you're working with a chart, the shortcut menu that appears when you right-click a chart part contains commands that are pertinent to what is selected.

Tip   You can select a group of cells before you right-click to apply the same command to the entire selection.

Using toolbars

Excel includes convenient toolbars that provide another way of issuing commands. In many cases, a toolbar button is simply a substitute for a menu command. For example, the Copy button is a substitute for Edit ⇨ Copy. Some toolbar buttons, however, don't have a menu equivalent. One example is the AutoSum button, which automatically inserts a formula to calculate the sum of a range of cells. Toolbars can be customized to include menu commands as well as buttons.

To learn what the toolbar buttons do, you can hold the mouse pointer over a toolbar button (but don't click it). A small box appears that tells you the name of the button. Often, this provides enough information for you to determine whether the button is what you want.

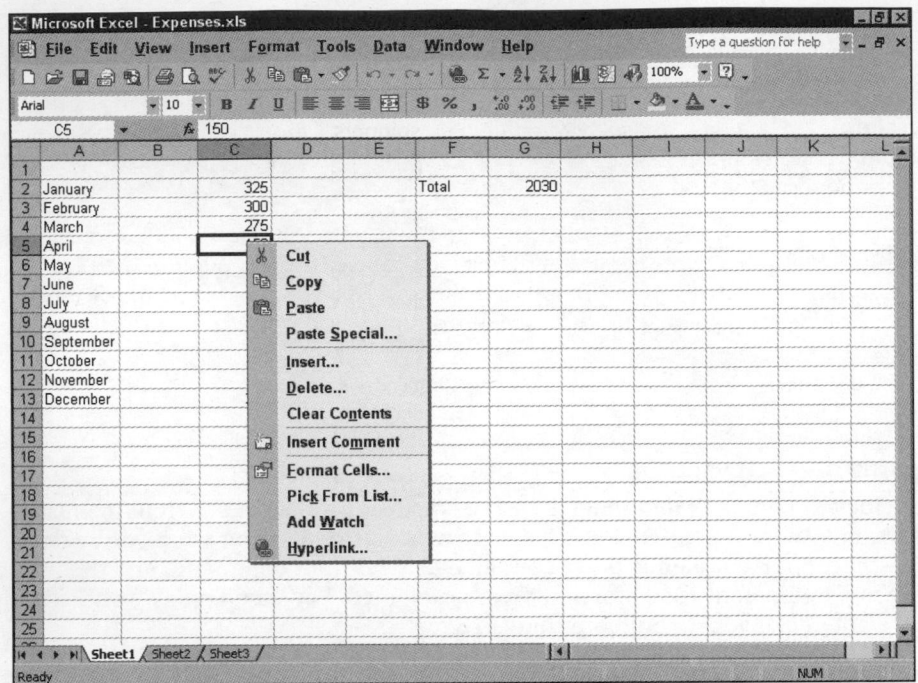

Figure QS-3: Click the right mouse button to display a shortcut menu with the commands that you are most likely to use.

Tip

For context-sensitive help on a menu command or toolbar button, choose the Help ⇨ What's This? command (or press Shift+F1). The mouse pointer turns into an arrow with a question mark beside it. Now, click any menu command or toolbar button, and Excel displays a description of the item. The command itself won't be issued when you click a menu item or toolbar button as long as the mouse pointer includes the question mark.

Table QS-2 lists many of Excel's more useful built-in toolbars.

Table QS-2 Excel's Most Useful Built-In Toolbars	
Toolbar	**Use**
Standard	Issues commonly used commands
Formatting	Changes how your worksheet or chart looks
Borders	Adds borders around selected areas
Chart	Manipulates charts

Toolbar	Use
Drawing	Inserts or edits drawings on a worksheet
Forms	Adds controls (buttons, spinners, and so on) to a worksheet
Formula Auditing	Identifies errors in your worksheet
Picture	Inserts or edits graphic images
PivotTable	Works with pivot tables
Protection	Controls what types of changes can be made in your worksheet
Reviewing	Provides tools to use workbooks in groups
Text to Speech	Provides tools to read aloud cell contents
Web	Provides tools to access the Internet from Excel
WordArt	Inserts or edits a picture composed of words

Hiding or showing toolbars

By default, Excel displays two toolbars (named Standard and Formatting). You have complete control over which toolbars are displayed and where they are located. In addition, you can create custom toolbars, made up of buttons that you find most useful.

To hide or display a particular toolbar, choose View ⇨ Toolbars, or right-click any toolbar. Either of these actions displays a list of common toolbars (but not all toolbars). The toolbars that have a check mark next to them are currently visible. To hide a toolbar, click it to remove the check mark. To display a toolbar, click it to add a check mark.

Moving toolbars

Toolbars can be moved to any of the four sides of Excel's window, or they can be free-floating. A free-floating toolbar can be dragged onscreen anywhere that you want. You also can change a toolbar's size simply by dragging any of its borders. To hide a free-floating toolbar, click its Close button.

Note

When a toolbar isn't free-floating, it's said to be docked. A docked toolbar is stuck to the edge of Excel's window and doesn't have a title bar. Therefore, a docked toolbar can't be resized.

To move a toolbar (docked or free-floating), click and drag anywhere on the background of the toolbar (that is, anywhere except on a button). When you drag it toward the window's edge, it automatically docks itself there. When a toolbar is docked, its shape changes to a single row or single column.

Moving around a worksheet

You'll be spending a lot of time moving around your worksheets, so it pays to learn all the tricks.

Every worksheet consists of rows (numbered 1 through 65,536) and columns (labeled A through IV). After column Z comes column AA; after column AZ comes column BA, and so on. The intersection of a row and a column is a single cell. At any given time, one cell is the active cell. You can identify the active cell by its darker border, as shown in Figure QS-4. Its address (its column letter and row number) appears in the Name box. Depending on the technique that you use to navigate through a workbook, you may or may not change the active cell when you navigate.

Tip   The row and column headings of the active cell are displayed in bold — making it easy to identify the active cell.

The name box indicates the address of the active cell

The darker row and column headings indicate the active cell intersection

The formula bar shows the contents of the active cell

	A	B	C	D	E	F	G	H	I	J	K	L
1												
2	January		325									
3	February		300									
4	March		275									
5	April		150									
6	May		125									
7	June		75									
8	July		55									
9	August		55									
10	September		70									
11	October		140									
12	November		185									
13	December		275									
14			2030									

Microsoft Excel - Expenses.xls

C14   =SUM(C2:C13)

Sheet1 / Sheet2 / Sheet3 /

The active cell has a dark border

Figure QS-4: The active cell is the cell with the dark border — in this case, cell C14.

Navigating with your keyboard

As you probably already know, you can use the standard navigational keys on your keyboard to move around a worksheet. These keys work just as you would expect: the down arrow moves the active cell down one row, the right arrow moves it one column to the right, and so on. PgUp and PgDn move the active cell up or down one full window (the actual number of rows moved depends on the number of rows displayed in the window).

Tip

You can scroll through the worksheet without changing the active cell by turning on Scroll Lock. This can be useful if you need to view another area of your worksheet and then quickly return to your original location. Just press Scroll Lock and use the direction keys to scroll through the worksheet. When you want to return to the original position (the active cell), press Ctrl+Backspace. Then, press Scroll Lock again to turn it off. When Scroll Lock is turned on, Excel displays SCRL in the status bar at the bottom of the window.

The Num Lock key on your keyboard controls how the keys on the numeric keypad behave. When Num Lock is on, Excel displays NUM in the status bar, and the keys on your numeric keypad generate numbers. Most keyboards have a separate set of navigational keys located to the left of the numeric keypad. These keys are not affected by the state of the Num Lock key.

Table QS-3 summarizes all the worksheet movement keys available in Excel.

Table QS-3 Excel's Worksheet Movement Keys	
Key	*Action*
Up arrow	Moves the active cell up one row
Down arrow	Moves the active cell down one row
Left arrow	Moves the active cell one column to the left
Right arrow	Moves the active cell one column to the right
PgUp	Moves the active cell up one screen
PgDn	Moves the active cell down one screen
Alt+PgDn	Moves the active cell right one screen
Alt+PgUp	Moves the active cell left one screen
Ctrl+Backspace	Scrolls to display the active cell
Up arrow*	Scrolls the screen up one row (active cell does not change)

Continued

Table QS-3 *(continued)*	
Key	**Action**
Down arrow*	Scrolls the screen down one row (active cell does not change)
Key	Action
Left arrow*	Scrolls the screen left one column (active cell does not change)
Right arrow*	Scrolls the screen right one column (active cell does not change)

* With Scroll Lock on

> **Tip**
>
> If you know either the cell address or the name of the cell that you want to activate, you can get there quickly by pressing F5 (the shortcut key for Edit ⇨ Go To). This command displays the Go To dialog box. Just enter the cell address in the Reference box (or choose a named cell from the list), press Enter, and you're there.

Navigating with your mouse

Navigating through a worksheet with a mouse may be even easier than navigating using your keyboard. To change the active cell by using the mouse, click another cell; it becomes the active cell. If the cell that you want to activate is not visible in the workbook window, you can use the scrollbars to scroll the window in any direction. To scroll one cell, click either of the arrows on the scrollbar. To scroll by a complete screen, click either side of the scrollbar's scroll box. You also can drag the scroll box for faster scrolling.

> **Tip**
>
> If you have a Microsoft IntelliMouse (or a compatible wheel mouse), you can use the mouse wheel to scroll vertically. The wheel scrolls three lines per click at the default rate. Also, if you click the wheel and move the mouse in any direction, the worksheet scrolls automatically in that direction. The more you move the mouse, the faster the scrolling. If you prefer to use the mouse wheel to zoom the worksheet, select Tools ⇨ Options, click the General tab, and then place a check mark next to the option labeled Zoom on roll with IntelliMouse.

Using the scrollbars or scrolling with your mouse doesn't change the active cell. It simply scrolls the worksheet. To change the active cell, you must click a new cell after scrolling.

Working with Excel's windows

The files that Excel uses are known as workbooks. A workbook can hold any number of sheets, and these sheets can be either worksheets (a sheet consisting of rows and columns) or chart sheets (a sheet that holds a single chart). A worksheet is what people usually think of when they think of a spreadsheet. You can open as many Excel workbooks as necessary at the same time—although most people use one workbook at a time.

Tip   When more than one Excel workbook is visible at the same time, you can drag-and-drop information between the open workbooks.

Figure QS-5 shows Excel with four workbooks open, each in a separate window. One of the windows is minimized and appears near the lower-left corner of the screen (when a workbook is minimized, only its title bar is visible). Worksheet windows can overlap, and the title bar of one window is a different color. That's the window that contains the active workbook.

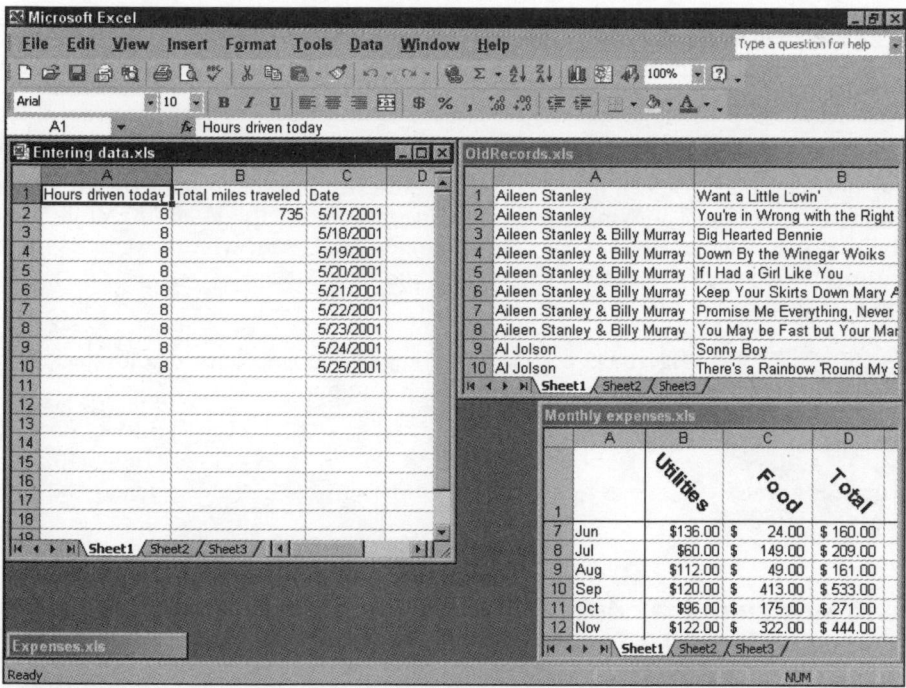

Figure QS-5: You can open several Excel workbooks at the same time.

The workbook windows that Excel uses work much like the windows in any other Windows program. Excel's windows can be in one of the following states:

✦ **Maximized:** Fills Excel's entire workspace. A maximized window does not have a title bar, and the worksheet's name appears in Excel's title bar. To maximize a window, click its Maximize button.

✦ **Minimized:** Appears as a small window with only a title bar. To minimize a window, click its Minimize button.

✦ **Restored:** A nonmaximized size. To restore a maximized or minimized window, click its Restore button.

If you work with more than one workbook simultaneously (which is quite common), you have to learn how to move, resize, and switch among the workbook windows.

Moving and resizing windows

To move a window, click and drag its title bar with your mouse. If you want them to, the windows can extend off the screen in any direction.

To resize a window, click and drag any of its borders until it's the size that you want it to be. When you position the mouse pointer on a window's border, the mouse pointer changes shape, which lets you know that you can now click and drag to resize the window. To resize a window horizontally and vertically at the same time, click and drag any of its corners.

Note You cannot move or resize a workbook window if it is maximized. You can move a minimized window, but doing so has no effect on its position when it is subsequently restored.

If you want all of your workbook windows to be visible (that is, not obscured by another window), you can move and resize the windows manually, or you can let Excel do it for you. The Window ⇨ Arrange command displays the Arrange Windows dialog box, shown in Figure QS-6. This dialog box has four window-arrangement options. Just select the one that you want and click OK.

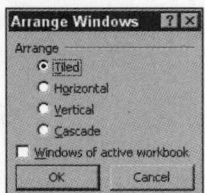

Figure QS-6: Use the Arrange Windows dialog box to quickly arrange all open workbook windows.

Switching among windows

At any given time, one (and only one) workbook window is the active window. This is the window that accepts your input, and it is the window on which your commands work. The active window's title bar is a different color, and the window appears at the top of the stack of windows. To work in a different window, you need to make that window active. There are several ways to make a different window the active workbook:

✦ Click another window, if it's visible. The window you click moves to the top and becomes the active window.

✦ Press Ctrl+Tab to cycle through all open windows until the window that you want to work with appears on top as the active window. Shift+Ctrl+Tab cycles through the windows in the opposite direction.

✦ Click the workbook icon in the Windows Taskbar.

✦ Click the Window menu and select the window that you want from the bottom part of the pull-down menu. The active window has a check mark next to it. This menu can display up to nine windows. If you have more than nine workbook windows open, choose More Windows (which appears below the nine window names).

Tip

Most people seem to prefer to do most of their work with maximized workbook windows. This enables you to see more cells and eliminates the distraction of other workbook windows getting in the way.

When you maximize one window, all the other windows are maximized, too (even though you don't see them). Therefore, if the active window is maximized and you activate a different window, the new active window is also maximized. If the active workbook window is maximized, you can't select another window by clicking it (because other windows aren't visible). You must use either Ctrl+Tab, the Windows taskbar, or the Window menu to activate another window.

Tip

You also can display a single workbook in more than one window. For example, if you have a workbook with two worksheets, you may want to display each worksheet in a separate window. All the window-manipulation procedures described previously still apply. You use the Window ⇨ New Window command to open a new window in the active workbook.

Closing windows

If you have multiple windows open, you may want to close those windows that you no longer need. To close a window, simply click the Close button on the title bar.

When you close a workbook window, Excel checks whether you have made any changes since the last time you saved the file. If not, the window closes without a prompt from Excel. If you've made any changes, Excel prompts you to save the file, before it closes the window.

Working with dialog boxes

Many Excel commands display dialog boxes. For example, all menu items that end with an ellipsis (three dots) display a dialog box. A dialog box is simply Excel's way of getting more information from you. For example, if you choose View ⇨ Zoom (which changes the magnification of the worksheet), Excel can't carry out the command until it finds out from you what magnification level you want.

Tip Although a dialog box looks like just another window, it works a little differently. When a dialog box appears, you can't do anything in the workbook until the dialog box is closed. In other words, you must dismiss the dialog box before you can do anything. If the dialog box obscures an area of your worksheet that you need to see, simply click the dialog box's title bar and drag the box to another location.

When a dialog box appears, you make any necessary choices in the dialog box by manipulating the controls. When you're finished, click the OK button (or press Enter) to continue. If you change your mind, click the Cancel button (or press Esc) and nothing further happens — it's as if the dialog box never appeared.

Understanding dialog box controls

Most people find working with dialog boxes to be quite straightforward and natural. The controls usually work just as you would expect, and they can be manipulated either with your mouse or directly from the keyboard.

Figure QS-7 shows the most common dialog box controls. Table QS-4 describes these controls and a few others you may encounter.

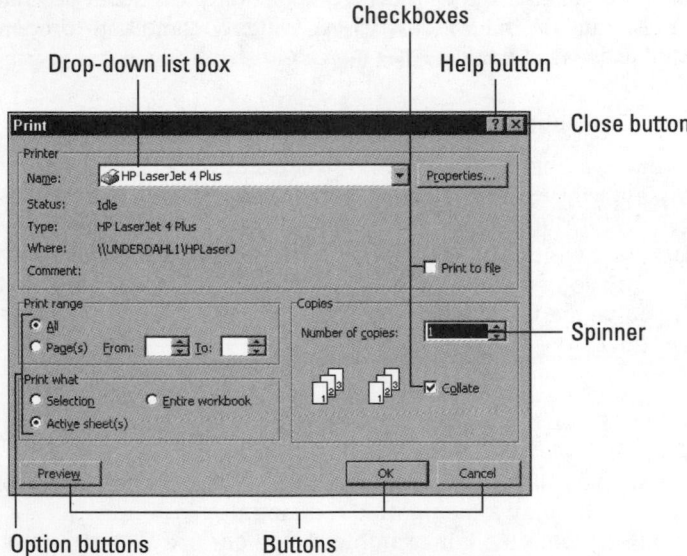

Figure QS-7: Use the dialog box controls to enter information and control the dialog box.

Table QS-4 Common Dialog Box Controls	
Name	*Description*
Buttons	A button control is about as simple as it gets. Just click it and it does its thing. Pressing the Alt key and the button's underlined letter is equivalent to clicking the button.
Option buttons	Option buttons are sometimes known as radio buttons because they work like the preset station buttons on an old-fashioned car radio. Like those car radios, only one option button at a time can be "pressed." When you click an option button, the previously selected option button is unselected. Option buttons usually are enclosed in a group box, and a single dialog box can have several sets of option buttons.
Check boxes	A check box control is used to indicate whether an option is on or off. Unlike option buttons, each check box is independent of the others. Clicking a check box toggles it on and off.
Range selection boxes	A range selection box enables you to specify a worksheet range by dragging inside the worksheet. A range selection box has a small button that, when clicked, collapses the dialog box to make it easier for you to select the range by dragging in the worksheet.
Spinners	A spinner control makes specifying a number easy. You can click the arrows to increment or decrement the displayed value. A spinner is almost always paired with an edit box. You can either enter the value directly into the edit box or use the spinner to change it to the desired value.
List boxes	A list box control contains a list of options from which you choose. If the list is longer than will fit in the list box, you can use its vertical scrollbar to scroll through the list.
Drop-down boxes	Drop-down boxes are similar to list boxes, but they show only a single option at a time. When you click the arrow on a drop-down box, the list drops down to display additional choices.

Navigating dialog boxes

Navigating dialog boxes is generally very easy—you simply click the control you wish to activate.

Although dialog boxes were designed with mouse users in mind, you can also use the keyboard. Every dialog box control has text associated with it, and this text always has one underlined letter (a hot key or accelerator key). You can access the control from the keyboard by pressing the Alt key and then the underlined letter. You also can use Tab to cycle through all the controls on a dialog box. Shift+Tab cycles through the controls in reverse order.

Tip
When a control is selected, it appears with a darker outline. You can use the spacebar to activate a selected control.

Using tabbed dialog boxes

Many of Excel's dialog boxes are "tabbed" dialog boxes. A tabbed dialog box includes notebook-like tabs, each of which is associated with a different panel. When you click a tab, the dialog box changes to display a new panel containing a new set of controls. The Options dialog box, which appears in response to the Tools ⇨ Options command, is a good example. This dialog box is shown in Figure QS-8; it has 13 tabs, which makes it functionally equivalent to 13 different dialog boxes.

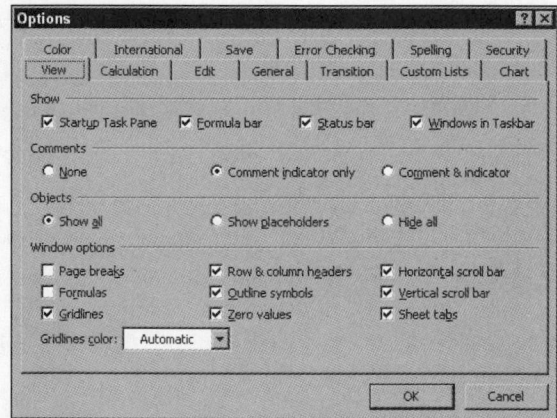

Figure QS-8: Use the dialog box tabs to select different functional areas in the dialog box.

Tabbed dialog boxes are quite convenient, because you can make several changes in a single dialog box. After you make all of your setting changes, click OK or press Enter.

Tip
To select a tab by using the keyboard, use Ctrl+PgUp or Ctrl+PgDn, or simply press the first letter of the tab that you want to activate.

Quickly Creating Your First Excel Worksheet

The remainder of this chapter is an introductory session with Excel. If you've never used Excel, you may want to follow along on your computer to get a feel for how this program works.

For this example you'll create a simple but useful worksheet that calculates loan payments. You can use this type of worksheet for many different purposes such as figuring out what the payments would be on a new car, a boat, or your dream house. So, even though the example is easy to follow, you'll end up with an Excel worksheet you can really use.

Getting started on your worksheet

To begin, open Excel and make certain that you have a blank worksheet showing (if you've been playing around with Excel, just click Blank Workbook in the task pane to get a fresh start).

You begin by entering some headings into the worksheet. While these aren't absolutely necessary for the worksheet to function properly, you will find that the headings help you to use the worksheet — especially when you want to reuse the worksheet later. Here's how to begin:

1. If it isn't already there, move the cell pointer to cell A1 by using the direction keys. The Name box displays the cell's address.

2. Enter **Loan Amount** into cell A1. Just type the text and then press Enter. Depending on your setup, Excel either moves the cell pointer down to cell A2 or the pointer remains in cell A1.

3. Move the cell pointer to cell A2, type **Interest Rate**, and press Enter.

4. Move the cell pointer to cell A3, type **Term**, and press Enter.

5. Move the cell pointer to cell A4, type **Payment**, and press Enter.

Entering your data

In this stage, you simply enter the values for each of the items needed to calculate the loan payments. In this case, you can use some numbers that might be typical if you were buying a new car.

1. Move the cell pointer to cell B1, type **$25,000**, and press Enter. We'll assume you're borrowing $25,000 toward the new car.

2. Move the cell pointer to cell B2 and enter **8%** and press Enter.

3. Move the cell pointer to cell B3 and enter **60** and press Enter. In this case we'll assume you're applying for a 60-month loan. You could also enter 5 to represent the term as 5 years, but as you'll soon see, doing so would add an additional complication to the formula you need to enter. At this point, your worksheet should look like Figure QS-9.

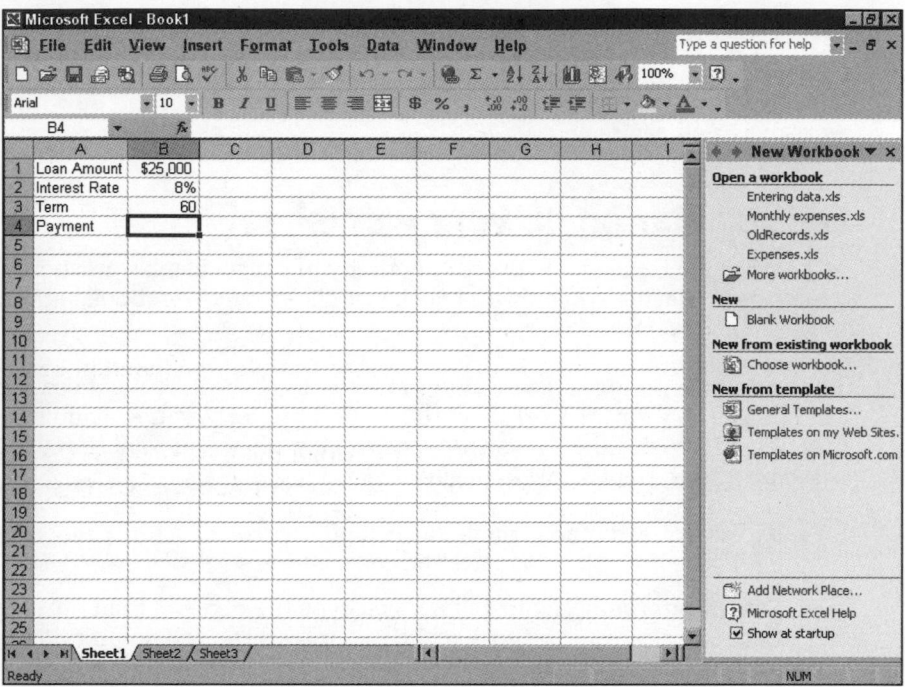

Figure QS-9: Your worksheet is ready for a formula.

Creating a formula

So far, what you've done has been fairly mundane. In fact, you could accomplish the same effect with any word processor. In this stage, you take advantage of the power feature of a spreadsheet: formulas. You next create a formula to calculate the monthly loan payment. In this case you use one of Excel's built-in functions to do the calculation.

1. Move the cell pointer to cell B4.

2. Click the Insert Function button (it is just to the left of the formula bar and looks like *fx*. Clicking this button opens the Insert Function dialog box shown in Figure QS-10.

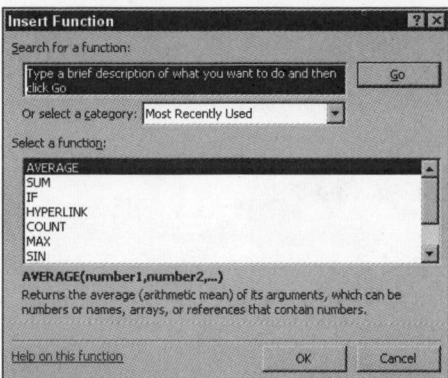

Figure QS-10: Use the Insert Function dialog box to select the correct function for your formula.

New Feature

3. Enter **Calculate a loan payment** in the Search for a function box. This tells Excel what you want to accomplish with your formula.

4. Click the Go button. Excel determines that the PMT function is the function you need (see Figure QS-11). From the description shown in the dialog box, it appears that this function will indeed serve your purpose.

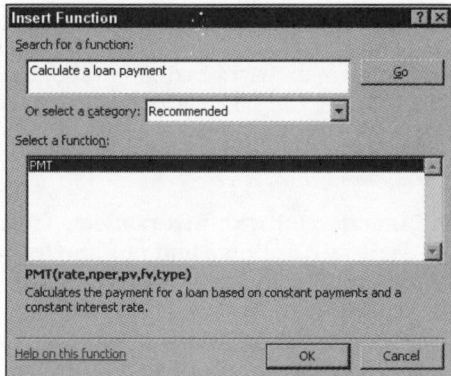

Figure QS-11: After you describe what you want to do, Excel suggests the function(s) that best suit your needs.

5. Click OK, which enters the PMT function into your worksheet and opens the Function Arguments dialog box shown in Figure QS-12. You use this dialog box to tell Excel where to find the information necessary to calculate your answer. This information is known as the *function arguments*.

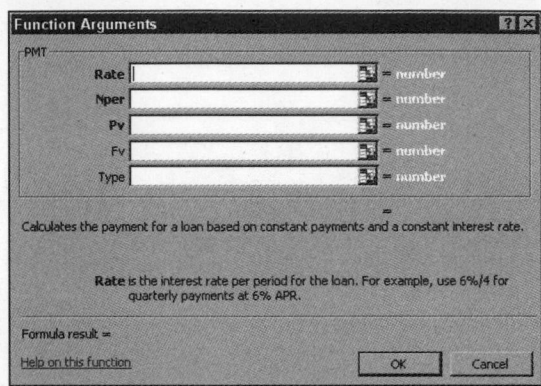

Figure QS-12: Use this dialog box to fill in the necessary details for the calculation.

6. Click in the Rate box and then click cell B2 to enter the address of the cell into the box. Because the payments are monthly but the interest rate is an annual rate, you need to enter **/12** (which divides the rate by 12) immediately following the B2 to express the interest rate as a monthly rate.

7. Click in the Nper box and then click cell B3 to enter the address of the cell into the box. If you had entered the term as years instead of month in cell B3, you would have had to add *12 following the B3 to adjust the loan period.

8. Click in the Pv box and then click cell B1 to enter the address of the cell into the box. This is the amount of the loan.

9. Click OK to enter the completed function into your worksheet. The remaining two function arguments, Fv and Type, are optional and not needed in this case (required arguments appear bold in the list of function arguments).

At this point, your worksheet looks like Figure QS-13. To demonstrate that this is an actual "live" formula, try changing one or two of the values in the first three rows. You'll see that the cell with the formula changes also. In other words, the formula is recalculating and displaying new results using the modified data.

 **Note** You've probably noticed that Excel is showing the loan payment as a negative amount. This is simply because Excel's financial functions require loan amounts to be entered as negative numbers. In this case, you can correct the confusion by editing the formula to place a minus sign in front of the Pv argument (so B1 becomes -B1); or you can add a minus sign in front of the function name (PMT); or you can simply ignore the "error" because you know that the bank really isn't going to pay you $506.91 each month when you're borrowing the money from them.

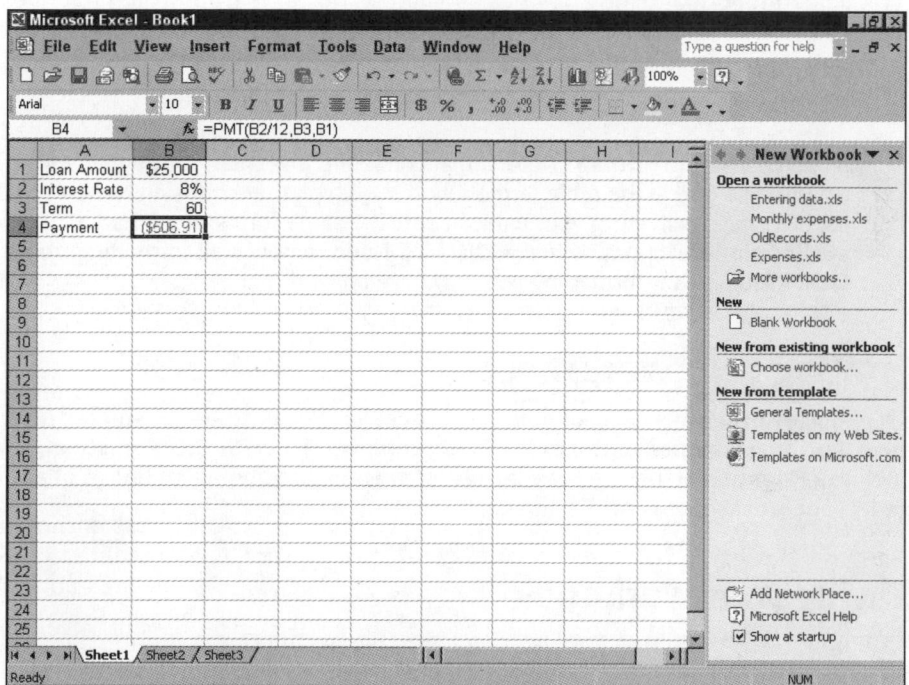

Figure QS-13: Your worksheet is now completely functional and ready to use.

Making your worksheet look a bit fancier

Your worksheet works just fine, and you can easily change any of the numbers to calculate the payments on different types of loans. If you want to make it look a bit fancier, though, you can use Excel's automatic formatting feature to spiff up the table a bit. Changing the formatting won't affect the way Excel calculates the results, but it can make your worksheet look a little more professional.

If you want to try out some formatting, follow these steps:

1. Move the cell pointer to any cell in the table (it doesn't matter which one because Excel will figure out that table's boundaries).

2. Click the Format menu; it drops down to display its menu items.

3. Select AutoFormat from the list of menu items. Two things happen: Excel determines the table boundaries and highlights the entire table, and it displays the AutoFormat dialog box.

4. The AutoFormat dialog box has 16 "canned" formats from which to choose (plus one called "None" that removes all formatting). Click the table format that you want to apply.

5. Click the OK button. Excel applies the formats to your table.

Caution

If you choose the Format ⇨ AutoFormat command and then decide that you don't want to use one of the table formats, you may think that choosing None from the list of formats will return your worksheet to the same formatting it had before you applied an AutoFormat. Actually, choosing None removes all formatting from the table including any formatting you may have applied manually.

Printing your worksheet

Excel makes printing a copy of your worksheet very easy to do (assuming that you have a printer attached and that it works properly). To print the worksheet, just click the Print button on the Standard toolbar (this button has an image of a printer on it). The worksheet is printed using the default settings.

Saving your workbook

Until now, everything that you've done has occurred in your computer's memory. If the power should fail, all would be lost, so it's time to save your work to a file. Call this workbook **My first workbook**.

1. Click the Save button on the Standard toolbar. The Save button looks like a disk. Excel responds with the Save As dialog box (see Figure QS-14).

2. In the box labeled File name, enter **My first workbook** and then either click Save or press Enter.

Excel saves the workbook as a file. The workbook remains open so that you can work with it some more.

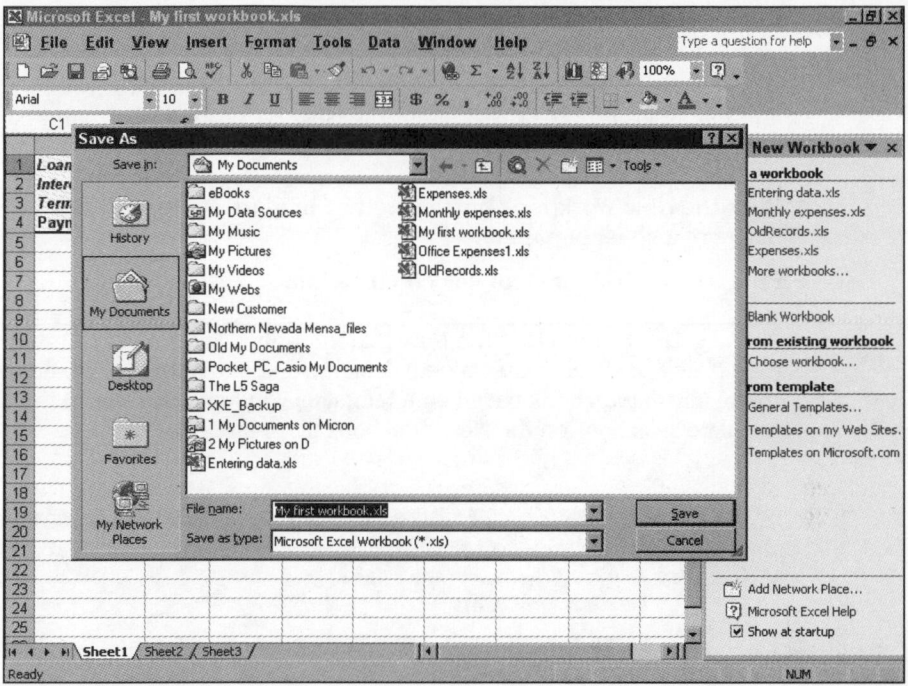

Figure QS-14: You need to save your workbook so that you can reopen it and use it in the future.

Learning the Essentials of Excel's Files

This section describes the operations that you perform with workbook files: opening, saving, closing, deleting, and so on. As you read through this section, remember that you can have any number of workbooks open simultaneously, and that at any given time, only one workbook is the active workbook. The workbook's name is displayed in its title bar (or in Excel's title bar if the workbook is maximized).

Creating a new workbook

When you start Excel, it automatically creates a new (empty) workbook called Book1. This workbook exists only in memory and has not been saved to disk. By default, this workbook consists of three worksheets named Sheet1, Sheet2, and Sheet3. If you're starting a new project from scratch, you can use this blank workbook.

There are several ways by which you can create a new workbook:

New Feature

  ✦ Use the File ➪ New command (which opens the New Workbook task pane) and click one of the selections in the New Workbook task pane (see Figure QS-15).

  ✦ Click the New Workbook button on the Standard toolbar (this button has an image of a sheet of paper).

  ✦ Press the Ctrl+N shortcut key combination.

Tip

Pressing Ctrl+N or clicking the New button on the Standard toolbar bypasses the New dialog box and creates a new default workbook immediately. If you want to create a new workbook based on a template, you must use one of the New from template selections on the New Workbook task pane.

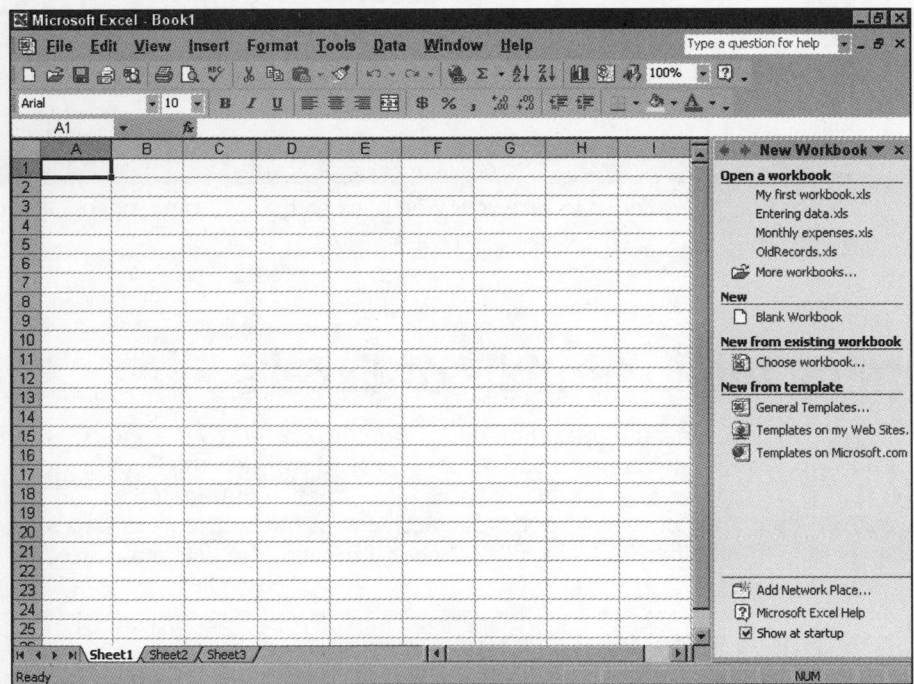

Figure QS-15: The New Workbook task pane enables you to quickly open an existing workbook or to create a new one.

If you select General Templates from the New Workbook task pane, Excel displays the Templates dialog box. This is a tabbed dialog box that enables you to choose a template for the new workbook. If you don't have any custom templates defined, the General tab displays only one option: Workbook. Clicking this gives you a plain workbook. Templates that are included with Excel are listed in the Spreadsheet Solutions tab. If you choose one of these templates, your new workbook is based on the selected template file.

Cross-Reference

Templates are discussed later in Chapter 6.

Opening an existing workbook

You'll no doubt find that you'll often want to open a workbook that you've saved on your computer. The following are some of the ways to open a workbook that has been saved on your disk:

✦ Select the file you want from the list at the top of the New Workbook task pane.

✦ Select the workbook you want from the list at the bottom of the File menu.

✦ Use the File ⇨ Open command.

✦ Click the Open button on the Standard toolbar (the Open button has an image of a file folder opening).

✦ Press the Ctrl+O shortcut key combination.

The last three of these methods display the Open dialog box shown in Figure QS-16.

Tip

To open an existing Excel workbook without first opening Excel, simply open the workbook file you want from the My Documents folder or from your Windows desktop. Windows will automatically open Excel when it opens the workbook file.

To open a workbook from the Open dialog box, you must provide two pieces of information: the name of the workbook file (specified in the File name field) and its folder (specified in the Look in field). Click Open, and the file opens. You also can just double-click the filename to open it.

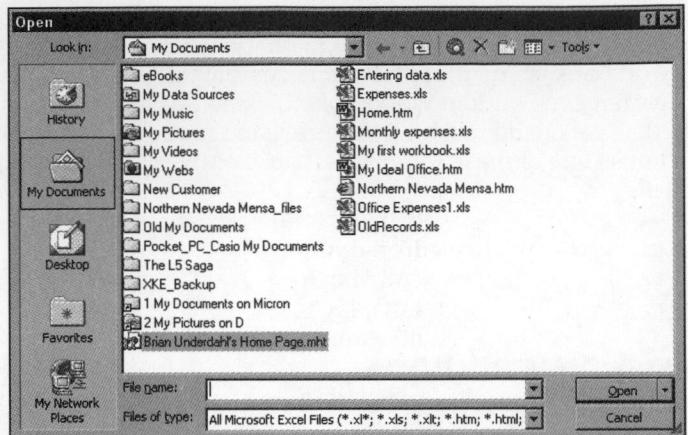

Figure QS-16: Use the Open dialog box to open any of your Excel workbook files.

The Open button is actually a drop-down list. Click the arrow and you see the additional options:

✦ **Open:** Opens the file normally.

✦ **Open Read-Only:** Opens the selected file in read-only mode. When a file is opened in this mode, changes cannot be saved to the original filename.

✦ **Open as Copy:** Opens a copy of the selected file. If the file is named budget.xls, the workbook that opens is named Copy of budget.xls.

✦ **Open in Browser:** Opens the file in your default Web browser.

 ✦ **Open and Repair:** Opens the file after a crash and recovers from any damage that may have resulted from the crash.

 You can hold down the Ctrl key and select multiple workbooks. When you click OK, all the selected workbook files will open.

Right-clicking a filename in the Open dialog box displays a shortcut menu with many extra choices. For example, you can copy the file, delete it, modify its properties, and so on.

Selecting a different location

The Look in field is actually a drop-down box. Click the arrow, and the box expands to show your folders. You can select a different drive or directory from this list. The Up One Level icon (a file folder with an upward arrow) moves up one level in the folder hierarchy.

Choosing to open a different type of file

At the bottom of the Open dialog box, the drop-down list is labeled Files of type. When this dialog box is displayed, it shows All Microsoft Excel Files (and a long list of file extensions). This means that the files displayed are filtered, and you see only files of that type. In other words, you see only standard Excel files.

If you want to open a file of a different type, click the arrow in the drop-down list and select the file type that you want to open. This changes the filtering and displays only files of the type that you specify.

Choosing your file display preferences

The Open dialog box can display your workbook filenames in several different styles. You control the style by clicking the View icon and then selecting from the drop-down list. The View icon is located in the upper-right section of the Open dialog box just to the left of the Tools button. The style that you choose is entirely up to you.

Using the Tools menu

Clicking the Tools menu, listed last in the upper-right section of the Open dialog box, displays a shortcut menu. The following are the menu items displayed and what they do:

✦ **Search:** Opens a new dialog box that enables you to search for a particular file.

✦ **Delete:** Deletes the selected file(s).

✦ **Rename:** Enables you to rename the selected file.

✦ **Print:** Opens the selected file, prints it, and then closes it.

✦ **Add to Favorites:** Adds to your Favorites directory a shortcut to the selected file.

✦ **Add to "My Places":** Adds a shortcut to the selected file to your My Network Places folder.

✦ **Map Network Drive:** Displays a dialog box that enables you to map a network directory to a drive designator.

✦ **Properties:** Displays the Properties dialog box for the selected file. This enables you to examine or modify the file's properties without actually opening it.

Opening Workbooks Automatically

Many people find that they work on the same workbooks day after day. If this describes you, you'll be happy to know that you can have Excel open specific workbook files automatically whenever you start Excel.

The XLStart folder is located within the Microsoft Office folder. Any workbook files (excluding template files) that are stored in this folder open automatically when Excel starts. If one or more files open automatically from this folder, Excel won't start up with a blank workbook.

You can specify an alternate startup folder in addition to the XLStart folder. Choose Tools í Options and select the General tab. Enter a new folder name in the field labeled At startup, open all files in. After you do that, when you start Excel, it automatically opens all workbook files in both the XLStart folder and the alternate folder that you specified.

Saving and closing your workbooks

When you're working on a workbook, it's vulnerable to day-ruining events, such as power failures and system crashes. Therefore, you should save your work to disk often. Saving a file takes only a few seconds, but re-creating hours of lost work takes many hours.

Excel provides four ways to save your workbook:

✦ Use the File ⇨ Save command

✦ Click the Save button on the Standard toolbar

✦ Press the Ctrl+S shortcut key combination

✦ Press the Shift+F12 shortcut key combination

If your workbook has already been saved, it's saved again using the same filename. If you want to save the workbook to a new file, use the File ⇨ Save As command (or press F12).

Tip

If your workbook has never been saved, its title bar displays a name such as Book1 or Book2. Although Excel enables you to use these generic workbook names for filenames, it's not recommended. Therefore, the first time that you save a new workbook, Excel displays the Save As dialog box to let you provide a more meaningful name.

The Save As dialog box is similar to the Open dialog box (see Figure QS-17). Again, you need to specify two pieces of information: the workbook's name and the folder in which to store it. If you want to save the file to a different folder, select the desired folder in the Save in field. If you want to create a new folder, click the Create New Folder icon in the Save As dialog box. The new folder is created within the folder that's displayed in the Save in field.

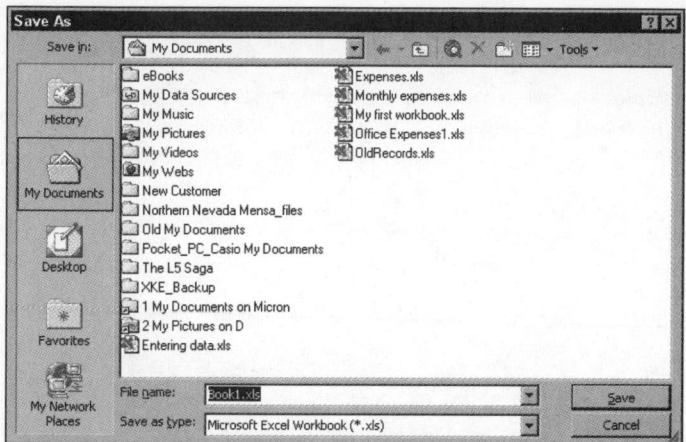

Figure QS-17: Use the Save As dialog box to save or rename your Excel workbook files.

After you select the folder, enter the filename in the File name field. You don't need to specify a file extension—Excel adds it automatically, based on the file type specified in the Save as type field. If a file with the same name already exists in the folder that you specify, Excel asks whether you want to overwrite that file with the new file. Be careful with this, because you can't recover the previous file if you overwrite it.

Caution Remember that saving a file overwrites the previous version of the file on disk. If you open a workbook and then completely mess it up, don't save the file! Instead, close the workbook without saving it, and then reopen the good copy on disk.

When you're finished with a workbook, you should close it to free the memory that it uses. You can close a workbook by using any of the following methods:

✦ Use the File ➪ Close command

✦ Click the Close button in the workbook's title bar

✦ Double-click the Control icon in the workbook's title bar

✦ Press the Ctrl+F4 shortcut key

✦ Press the Ctrl+W shortcut key

If you've made any changes to your workbook since it was last saved, Excel asks whether you want to save the workbook before closing it.

Tip To close all open workbooks, press the Shift key and choose File ➪ Close All. This command appears only when you hold down the Shift key while you click the File menu. Excel closes each workbook, prompting you for each unsaved workbook.

File-Naming Rules

Excel's workbook files are subject to the same rules that apply to other Windows files. A file-name can be up to 255 characters, including spaces. This enables you to give meaningful names to your files. You can't, however, use any of the following characters in your file-names:

\ (slash)

? (question mark)

: (colon)

* (asterisk)

" (quote)

< (less than)

> (greater than)

| (vertical bar)

You can use uppercase and lowercase letters in your names to improve readability. The file-names aren't case-sensitive—My 2002 Budget and MY 2002 BUDGET are equivalent names.

Setting the file-saving options

The Save As dialog box has a drop-down menu labeled Tools. When you click this menu, one of the options displayed is labeled General Options. Selecting this item displays the Save Options dialog box, shown in Figure QS-18. This dialog box enables you to set the following options:

- ✦ **Always create backup:** If this option is set, the existing version of the workbook is renamed as a BAK file before the workbook is saved. Doing this enables you to go back to the previously saved version of your workbook.

- ✦ **Password to open:** If you enter a password, the password is required before anyone can open the workbook. Passwords can be up to 15 characters long and are case-sensitive. Be careful with this option, because it is impossible to open the workbook (using normal methods) if you forget the password.

- ✦ **Password to modify:** This option enables you to specify a password that will be required before changes to the workbook can be saved under the same file-name. Use this option if you want to make sure that changes aren't made to the original version of the workbook.

- ✦ **Read-only recommended:** If this option is checked, the file can't be saved under its original name. This is another way to ensure that a workbook file isn't overwritten.

✦ **Advanced:** Clicking this button enables you to select the type of encryption that is used to protect your workbook. Depending on your security needs, different encryption methods may provide superior protection.

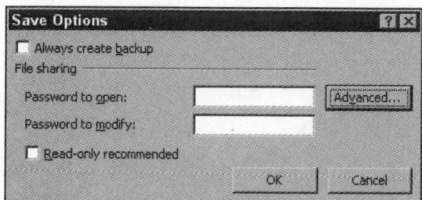

Figure QS-18: Use the Save Options dialog box to protect your Excel workbook files with passwords or backup copies.

Setting the workbook summary information

When you save a file, Excel saves some additional information about the file, too. This information includes items such as the title, author, and statistics about the file. You can view this information and modify some of it using the workbook's Properties dialog box. You can access the Properties dialog box for the active workbook at any time by selecting File ⇨ Properties from the menu. In addition, you can view the properties of a workbook from the Open dialog box. Right-click the file in which you're interested and choose Properties from the shortcut menu.

The Properties dialog box has five tabs:

✦ **General:** Displays general information about the file — its name, size, location, date created, and so on. You can't change any of the information in this panel.

✦ **Summary:** Appears by default when you first save the file. It contains nine fields of information that you can enter and modify. You can use the information in this panel to locate workbooks quickly that meet certain criteria.

✦ **Statistics:** Shows additional information about the file and can't be changed.

✦ **Contents:** Displays the names of the sheets in the workbook, arranged by sheet type.

✦ **Custom:** Can be quite useful if you use it consistently. Basically, it enables you to store in a sort of database a variety of information about the file. For example, if the workbook deals with a client named Smith and Jones Corp., you can keep track of this bit of information and use it to help locate the file later.

Using Template Files

No one likes to do a lot of unnecessary extra work. You may be able to save your-self quite a bit of work by using a template instead of always creating a new work-book from scratch. A template basically is a worksheet that's all set up with formulas, ready for you to enter data.

You can use one of the templates that are included with Excel, find additional templates on the Web, or create your own templates. When you click General Templates on the New Workbook task pane, you'll find that the Spreadsheet Solutions tab of the Templates dialog box includes several useful templates.

 **Tip**   When you open a new workbook based on the template, you save the workbook to a new file. In other words, you don't overwrite the template.

 **Cross-Reference**   See Chapter 6 for information on creating and using templates.

Protecting Your Work

Nothing is worse than spending hours creating a complicated Excel workbook only to have it destroyed by a power failure, a hard disk crash, or even by human error. Fortunately, protecting yourself from these disasters is not a difficult task.

Earlier in the chapter, you learned how to make Excel create a backup copy of your workbook when you save the file. That's a good idea, but it certainly isn't the only backup protection you should use. If a file is truly important, you need to take extra steps to ensure its safety. The following are several backup options for ensuring the safety of individual files:

✦ Keep a backup copy of the file on the same drive. This is essentially what happens when you select the Always create a backup option when you save a workbook file. Although this offers some protection if you create a mess of the worksheet, it won't do you any good if the entire hard drive crashes.

✦ Keep a backup copy on a different hard drive. This assumes, of course, that your system has more than one hard drive. This offers more protection than the preceding method, because the likelihood that both hard drives will fail is remote. If the entire system is destroyed or stolen, however, you're out of luck.

✦ Keep a backup copy on a network server. This assumes that your system is connected to a server on which you can write files. This method is fairly safe. If the network server is located in the same building, however, you're at risk if the entire building burns down or is otherwise destroyed.

✦ Keep a backup copy on a removable medium. This is the safest method. Using a removable medium, such as a floppy disk or tape, enables you physically to take the backup to another location. So, if your system (or the entire building) is damaged, your backup copy remains intact.

 Excel, like all of the applications in Office 2002, has the capability to recover the workbook that was in use at the time of a crash. When you reopen Excel after a crash, the program presents you with a list of workbooks that were recovered so that you can choose which copies to save. This feature is not, however, a substitute for keeping a backup copy of important workbook files.

New Usability Features

Without any doubt, it's very important for applications such as Excel to be easy to use. An extremely powerful computer program would be useless if people couldn't figure out how to use the program. Excel 2002 incorporates a number of features designed to make the program far easier and more intuitive to use. Here are our picks of the features we think will help you use Excel 2002.

Task panes

Excel 2002 uses *task panes* to make it far simpler for you to do several common tasks. Figure QS-19 shows the New Workbook task pane that appears when you first open Excel.

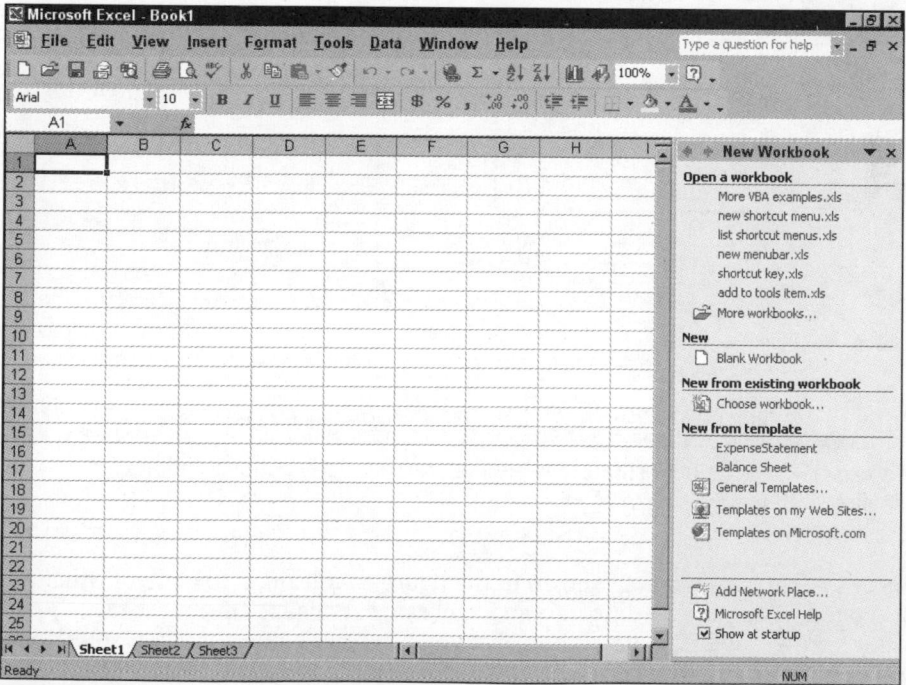

Figure QS-19: The new Excel task panes enable you to easily access the tools you need for a number of common tasks such as opening workbooks.

As the figure shows, the New Workbook task pane makes it easy for you to select an existing workbook or to create a new workbook. The task panes gather a set of related options into one place so you don't have to go searching to find what you need.

In addition to the New Workbook task pane, Excel 2002 includes task panes for the Clipboard, for searching your workbooks, and for working with clip art.

Smart tags

Excel 2002 has a feature called *smart tags* that greatly simplify many tasks. Figure QS-20 shows an example of a smart tag that is available when you copy and paste data.

Figure QS-20: The new smart tags enable you to quickly choose options for dealing with many aspects of your data.

In this case, the smart tag shown in the figure enables you to control which options are used when pasting data into an Excel range. Because the smart tags appear after you've added the data, they give you a second chance if you wanted something other than simply pasting the data as is.

Excel 2002 has a number of smart tags you can use. For example, if you add a stock symbol to a worksheet, you'll be able to use a smart tag to automatically update the ticker price for that security. Other smart tags help with filling ranges and error checking in formulas.

Speech technology

Excel 2002 can both speak and listen. If you've always wanted to control your computer by talking to it, or have your computer automatically write down your words, you'll find these features built into your new copy of Excel.

Although a bit less futuristic, Excel's ability to speak may be of even more use to you. By using the Tools ➪ Speech commands, you can instruct Excel to read aloud the data in selected ranges. This feature might be very handy in a number of scenarios — such as verifying the accuracy of data after you've entered it into a worksheet.

Unmerge in a click

Excel's Merge and Center feature has long been a handy way to combine data from several cells into a single block that spans several columns. Now Excel 2002 makes this feature even better by making it just as easy to unmerge the merged cells simply by clicking the Merge and Center button again.

Improved Web queries

It's clear to almost anyone who has used the Internet that there's an awful lot of very useful information available on the Web. Previous versions of Excel have had the ability to use Web queries to obtain data from the Web, but the process was far from simple. In Excel 2002 you will find that creating a Web query so that you can use Web-based data has become a simple point-and-click operation.

Managing links

Links to external workbook data have long been a very useful way to consolidate information from various sources. Unfortunately, managing those links has sometimes been a slightly frustrating task. Excel 2002 takes some large steps forward in this area. Figure QS-21 shows the new Edit Links dialog box that includes important options — such as the ability to break links and to change the startup prompt — to solve problems that plague users whose workbooks include external reference formulas.

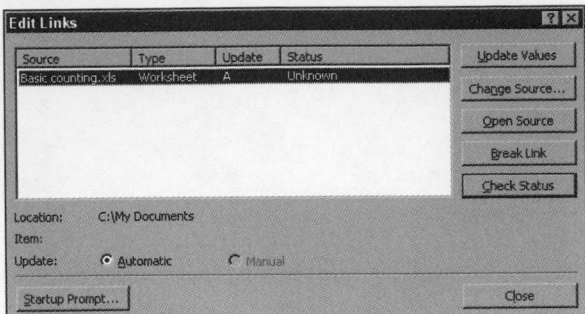

Figure QS-21: The new Edit Links dialog box gives you far more control over external references.

Improvements in Formulas and Functions

Entering formulas and using functions can be quite confusing. Even the most experienced Excel users will sometimes find themselves trying to remember the correct syntax for a function, or even trying to determine which function will produce the desired result. Excel 2002 has several improvements to help out — whether you're an experienced spreadsheet jockey or just starting out.

ScreenTips for functions

Want to use a function but can't remember the order of the arguments? Excel 2002 now includes pop-up tips that show you the arguments, and it even provides a link you can click if you need more help instantly.

The Function Wizard recommends functions

Don't you envy those people who always seem to know the difference between the AVERAGE and the MODE functions? Well, even if you don't, you'll still appreciate the bit of extra help Excel 2002 now offers when you need to create a formula. As Figure QS-22 shows, the Insert Function dialog box now includes a box where you can tell the Function Wizard what you'd like to accomplish. Once you've entered the description, the Function Wizard will present you with a list of the most likely suspects so your choice will be much easier.

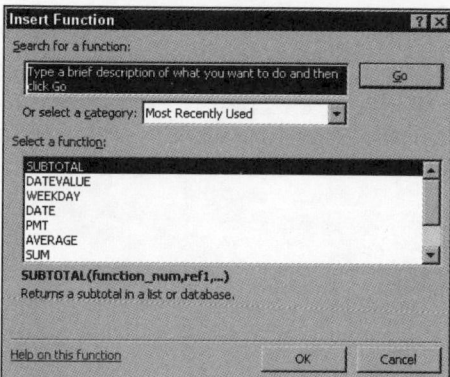

Figure QS-22: The Insert Function dialog box can now help you find the correct function to suit your needs.

Watch window

If you've ever tried to keep track of the results of a formula while you made changes elsewhere in an Excel workbook, you'll really appreciate the new Watch Window toolbar in Excel 2002. This toolbar enables you to track specified cells no matter where you roam in your workbooks. Figure QS-23 shows an example of the Watch Window.

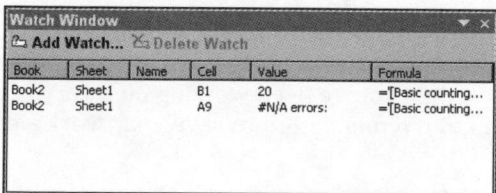

Figure QS-23: You can use the Watch Window to easily see what's going on in specified cells as you move around your workbooks.

More AutoSum options

Excel's AutoSum feature makes it very easy to quickly sum a group of values. Now that feature has been improved to make it easier to select a function other than SUM. The AutoSum button in Excel 2002 now includes a drop-down list so you can choose an alternate function.

Formula evaluator

Excel 2002 now makes it easier for you to determine the values of nested functions. By using the Formula evaluator, you can see the various parts of a nested formula evaluated in the order the formula is calculated. This makes it far easier to figure out what's going wrong when a formula doesn't seem to be working quite right.

Improved Security for Your Data

Nothing on your computer is more important than your data. Excel 2002 takes great strides forward in helping you to protect that data.

Increased protection against macro viruses

Macro viruses can be a huge threat not only to your Excel workbooks, but to all the other data on your PC as well. Unfortunately, VBA — Visual Basic for Applications — is one of the tools that cretins often use to create macro viruses.

Excel 2002 recognizes this threat and takes a couple of important steps to reduce it to a more manageable level. First, the default security setting now prevents you from accidentally opening an Excel workbook that might contain macro viruses. Second, you can install Excel 2002 without installing VBA — thus totally eliminating the macro virus threat.

Document recovery and safer shutdown

Computers sometimes crash, and when they do it seems like they choose the worst possible time to do so. For example — when you've been working on a very complex workbook for hours and haven't quite remembered to save your work along the way.

If your system crashes while you're working with Excel 2002, all is not lost. First, Excel automatically saves copies as you work, and second, it recognizes that a workbook might not be completely lost even if some of your work can't be saved. When you open Excel after a crash, you're given the opportunity to recover any workbooks that were open at the time of the crash.

Office safe mode

Finally, if Excel 2002 encounters the same problem several times when you are starting the program, it may offer to start up in *safe mode* so that you can complete your work and correct the problem. For example, if you attach an add-in and discover that it is incompatible with Excel 2002, safe mode gives you the option to remove the add-in and prevent future problems.

✦   ✦   ✦

Getting Started with Excel

This part is intended to give you a quick start with Excel 200, where we show you how to get down to work with Excel and get comfortable with the fundamentals of using Excel effectively. Here you'll see how to make use of all the basics that are so important to every Excel user. If you've used Excel (or even a different spreadsheet program) in the past, much of this information may seem like review. Even so, we're certain you'll find quite a few tricks and techniques covered in this part that will make your life with Excel a whole lot easier.

If you're new to Excel you should probably check out the Quick Start chapter that comes before this part, which will have you up and using Excel in no time. Even if you've used Excel, you'll probably want to have a quick look through the later sections of the Quick Start, where we tell you about some of the most important new features in this release.

Entering and Editing Worksheet Data

Every Excel worksheet needs some type of data if it is going to be of any use to anyone. Excel doesn't treat all data equally, so it's important to understand the differences between the different types of data you can use in an Excel worksheet, and how those differences can affect your results. In this chapter, We show you what you need to know about entering, using, and modifying data in your worksheets.

Understanding the Types of Data You Can Use

An Excel workbook can hold any number of worksheets, and each worksheet is made up of a large number of cells. When you place data into a worksheet, you place that data into one or more of the cells. A cell can hold any of three basic types of data:

+ Numerical values
+ Text
+ Formulas

In addition to data, a worksheet also can hold charts, maps, drawings, pictures, buttons, and other objects. These objects actually reside on the worksheet's *draw layer,* which is an invisible layer on top of each worksheet.

Excel's Numerical Limitations

You may be curious about the types of values that Excel can handle. In other words, how large can numbers be? And how accurate are large numbers?

Excel's numbers are precise up to 15 digits. For example, if you enter a large value, such as 123,123,123,123,123,123 (18 digits), Excel actually stores it with only 15 digits of precision: 123,123,123,123,123,000. This may seem quite limiting, but in practice, it rarely causes any problems.

Here are some of Excel's other numerical limits:

Largest positive number: 9.9E+307

Smallest negative number: −9.9E+307

Smallest positive number: 1E−307

Largest negative number: −1E-307

These numbers are expressed in scientific notation. For example, the largest positive number is "9.9 times 10 to the 307th power."

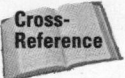

The draw layer is discussed in Chapter 15. This chapter is concerned only with data that you enter into worksheet cells.

Understanding numerical values

Numerical values represent a quantity of some type: sales, number of employees, atomic weights, test scores, and so on. Values that you enter into cells can be used in formulas or can be used to provide the data that is used to create a chart. Values also can be dates (such as 6/26/2002) or times (such as 3:24 a.m.).

Excel can easily manipulate numbers and can display them in many different formats. Later in this chapter, in "Improving Worksheet Appearance by Formatting Cells," you'll see how different format options can affect the display of numerical values.

Understanding text entries

Most worksheets also include nonnumeric text in some of their cells. You can insert text to serve as labels for values, headings for columns, or instructions about the worksheet. Text that begins with a number is still considered text. For example, if you enter an address such as 1425 Main St. into a cell, Excel considers this to be text rather than a value.

Text is often used to clarify what the values in a worksheet mean. In most cases, the text is more important to someone viewing the worksheet than it is to Excel, because the text makes it easier for the viewer to determine which numerical values are which — Excel knows what the values represent from the way they are used in formulas.

Understanding formulas

Formulas are what make a spreadsheet a spreadsheet. Excel enables you to enter powerful formulas that use the values (or even text) in cells to calculate a result. When you enter a formula into a cell, the formula's result appears in the cell. If you change any of the values used by a formula, the formula recalculates and shows the new result.

Formulas can be simple mathematical expressions, or they can contain some of the powerful functions that are built into Excel. Figure 1-1 shows a typical Excel worksheet with values, text, and formulas. Note that we added some additional text in column C to make the worksheet a little easier to understand.

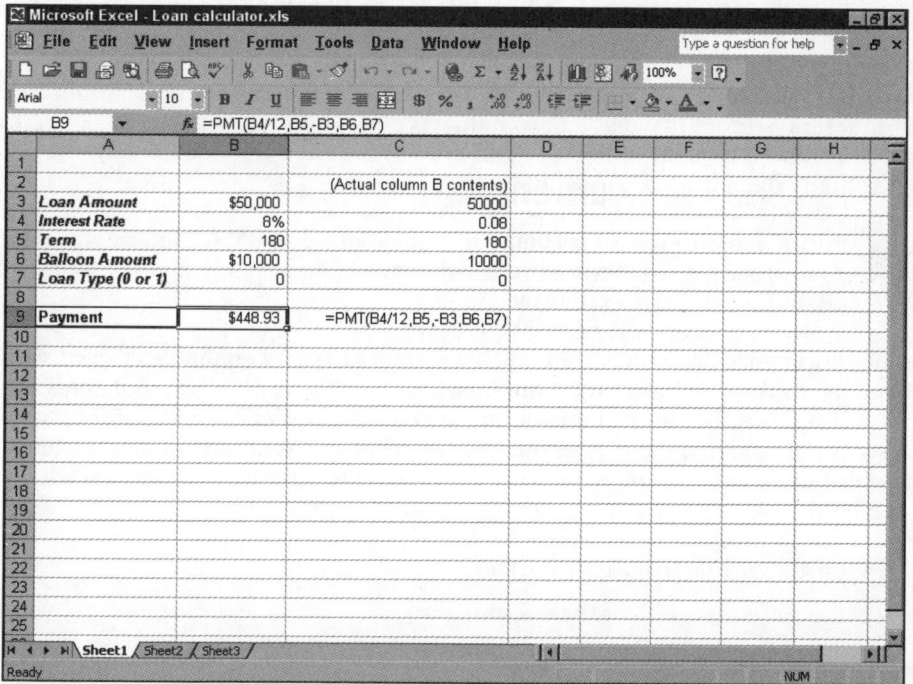

Figure 1-1: You can use numbers, text, and formulas to create useful Excel worksheets.

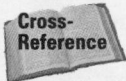
You'll learn much more about formulas in the chapters in Part 3.

Entering Text and Values into Your Worksheets

Entering text and numerical values into a cell is quite easy. Just move the cell pointer to the appropriate cell to make it the active cell, enter the value, and then press Enter. The value is displayed in the cell and also appears in Excel's formula bar. You can, of course, include decimal points and dollar signs when entering values and dollar signs, along with plus signs, minus signs, and commas. If you precede a value with a minus sign or enclose it in parentheses, Excel considers it to be a negative number.

Sometimes, a value won't be displayed exactly as you entered it. For example, if you enter a very large number (one with a large number of digits), it may be converted to scientific notation. Notice, however, that the formula bar displays the value that you entered originally. Excel simply reformats the value so that it fits into the cell. If you make the column wider, the number is displayed as you entered it.

Entering text into a cell is just as easy as entering a value: activate the cell, type the text, and then press Enter. A cell can contain a maximum of about 32,000 characters — more than enough to hold a typical chapter in this book. Even though a cell can hold a huge number of characters, you'll find that it's usually not possible to actually display all of these characters.

If you type an exceptionally long text entry into a cell, the characters appear to wrap around when they reach the right edge of the window, and the formula bar expands so that the text wraps around.

What happens when you enter text that's longer than its column's current width? If the cells to the immediate right are blank, Excel displays the text in its entirety, appearing to spill the entry into adjacent cells. If an adjacent cell is not blank, Excel displays as much of the text as possible (the full text is contained in the cell; it's just not displayed). If you need to display a long text string in a cell that's adjacent to a nonblank cell, you can take one of several actions:

✦ Edit your text to make it shorter

✦ Increase the width of the column

✦ Use a smaller font

✦ Wrap the text within the cell so that it occupies more than one line

✦ Use Excel's "shrink to fit" option (see Chapter 5 for details)

 **Note**   As you'll learn in Chapter 5, Excel's text alignment options can also affect how text that is too long to fit the column width is displayed. For example, Figure 1-2 shows several examples where the same text has been stored in several cells in column C, but different text alignment options were used to format the cells.

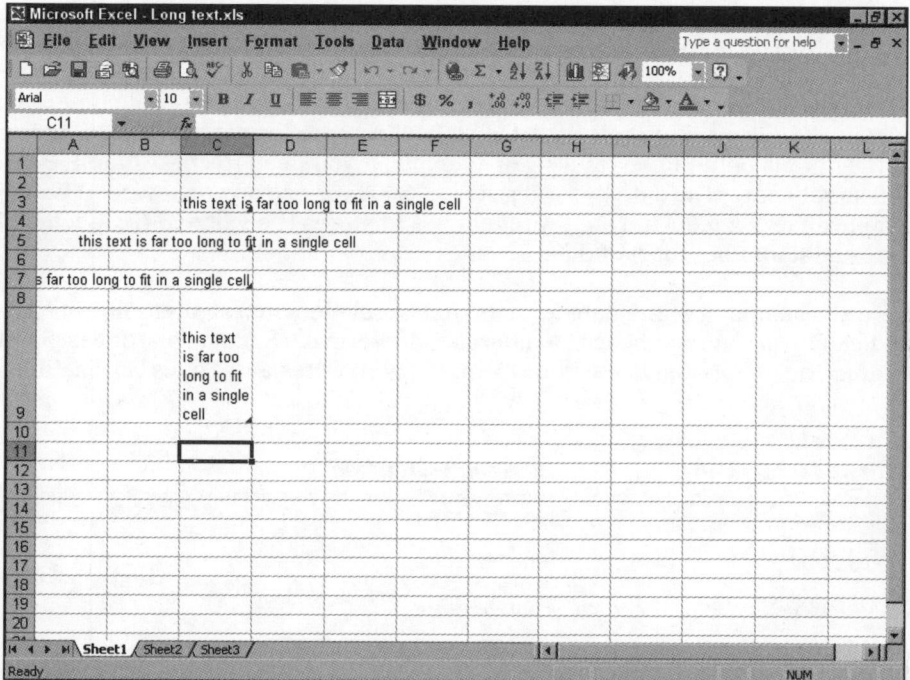

Figure 1-2: All of this text was entered into cells in column C, but different alignment options change how the text appears in the worksheet.

Entering Dates and Times into Your Worksheets

Excel treats dates and times as special types of numeric values. Typically, these values are formatted so that they appear as dates or times because humans find it far easier to understand these values if they appear in the correct format.

Entering date values

If you work with dates and times, you need to understand Excel's date and time system. Excel handles dates by using a serial number system. The earliest date that Excel understands is January 1, 1900. This date has a serial number of 1. January 2, 1900, has a serial number of 2, and so on. This system makes it easy to deal with dates in formulas. For example, you can enter a formula to calculate the number of days between two dates.

Most of the time, you don't have to be concerned with Excel's serial number date system. You can simply enter a date in a familiar date format, and Excel takes care of the details behind the scenes. For example, if you need to enter June 1, 2002, you can simply enter the date by typing June 1, 2002 (or use any of several different date formats). Excel interprets your entry and stores the value 37408 — which is the date serial number for that date.

Here is a sampling of the date formats that Excel recognizes. After entering a date, you can format it to appear in a different date format. (Such formatting is covered later in the chapter, in the section "Working with Dates and Times" in Chapter 10.)

Entered into a Cell	Excel's Interpretation
6-26-02	June 26, 2002
6-26-2002	June 26, 2002
6/26/02	June 26, 2002
6/26/2002	June 26, 2002
6-26/02	June 26, 2002
June 26, 2002	June 26, 2002
Jun 26	June 26 of the current year
June 26	June 26 of the current year
6/26	June 26 of the current year
6-26	June 26 of the current year

Note   Excel is rather smart when it comes to recognizing dates that you enter, but it's not perfect. For example, Excel does not recognize any of the following entries as dates: June 1 2002, Jun-1 2002, and Jun-1/2002. Rather, it interprets these entries as text. If you plan to use dates in formulas, make sure that the date you enter is actually recognized as a date; otherwise, your formulas will produce incorrect results.

Avoid Century Surprises

Be careful when entering dates by using two digits for the year. Excel has a rather arbitrary decision point in interpreting your entries. Two-digit years between 00 and 29 are typically interpreted as 21st century dates. Two-digits years between 30 and 02 are interpreted as 20th century dates. For example, if you enter 12/5/28, Excel interprets your entry as December 5, 2028. But if you enter 12/5/30, Excel sees it as December 5, 1930. To avoid any surprises, it's a good practice to simply enter years using all four digits.

Tip   After you enter a date, check the formula bar. If the formula bar displays the date as text, Excel didn't interpret the date that you entered as a date. If the formula bar displays your entry in a format like mm/dd/yyyy, Excel correctly interpreted your entry as a date.

Entering time values

When you work with times, you simply extend Excel's date serial number system to include decimals. In other words, Excel works with times by using fractional days. For example, the date serial number for June 1, 2002, is 37408. Noon on June 1, 2002 (halfway through the day) is represented internally as 37408.5 because the time fraction is simply added to the date serial number to get the full date/time serial number.

Again, you normally don't have to be concerned with these serial numbers (or fractional serial numbers, for times). Just enter the time into a cell in a recognized format.

Here are some examples of time formats that Excel recognizes:

Entered into a Cell	Excel's Interpretation
11:30:00 am	11:30 a.m.
11:30:00 AM	11:30 a.m.
11:30 pm	11:30 p.m.
11:30	11:30 a.m.

The preceding samples don't have a day associated with them. You also can combine dates and times, however, as follows:

Entered into a Cell	Excel's Interpretation
6/1/02 11:30	11:30 a.m. on June 1, 2002

Changing the Way Dates Are Interpreted

It's actually Windows—not Excel—that determines how two-digit dates are interpreted. If you want to change the sliding 100-year window so that two-digit dates are interpreted differently, you'll need to change a setting using the Windows Control Panel. Note, however, that this changes the way two-digit years are interpreted for all the Windows programs—not just Excel. Here's how to make the change:

1. On the Windows Start menu, select Settings ➪ Control Panel.

2. Double-click the Regional Settings or Regional Options icon (depending on your version of Windows), and then click the Date tab. (If you do not see the icon, click View all Control Panel options.)

3. In the box labeled When a two-digit year is entered, interpret as a year between, change the upper-limit for the century (see figure). As you change the upper-limit year, the lower-limit year automatically changes.

4. Click OK to close the dialog box.

You can change the sliding window used to interpret two-digit dates using the Windows Control Panel.

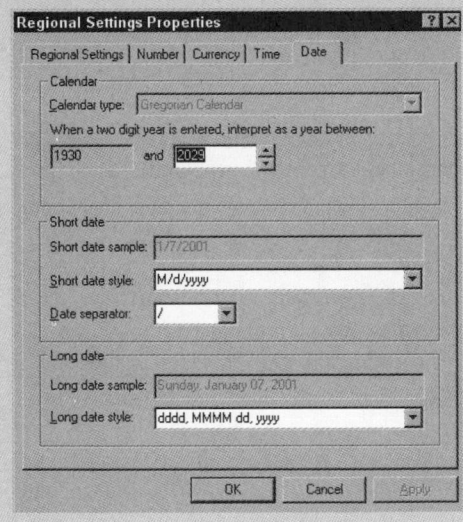

Modifying and Editing Information

Not surprisingly, you can change the contents of a cell after the fact. After you enter a value or text into a cell, you can modify it in several ways:

✦ Erase the cell's contents

✦ Replace the cell's contents with something else

✦ Edit the cell's contents

Erasing the contents of a cell

To erase the value, text, or formula in a cell, just click the cell and press Delete. To erase more than one cell, select all the cells that you want to erase, and then press Delete. Pressing Delete removes the cell's contents, but doesn't remove any formatting (such as bold, italic, or a different number format) that you may have applied to the cell.

For more control over what gets deleted, you can use the Edit ➪ Clear command. This menu item has a submenu with four additional choices:

✦ **All:** Clears everything from the cell

✦ **Formats:** Clears only the formatting and leaves the value, text, or formula

✦ **Contents:** Clears only the cell's contents and leaves the formatting

✦ **Comments:** Clears the comment (if one exists) attached to the cell

Replacing the contents of a cell

To replace the contents of a cell with something else, just click the cell and type your new entry, which replaces the previous contents. Any formatting that you previously applied to the cell remains in place and is applied to the new content.

Tip   You can also replace cell contents by dragging-and-dropping or by pasting data from the Clipboard. In both cases the cell formatting will be replaced by the format of the new data (unless you use the Edit ➪ Paste Special command or the Paste Options button to choose to paste the data without altering the destination format).

Editing the contents of a cell

If the cell contains only a few characters, replacing its contents by typing new data usually is easiest. But if the cell contains lengthy text or a complex formula, and you need to make only a slight modification, you probably want to edit the cell rather than re-enter information.

When you want to edit the contents of a cell, you can use one of the following ways to enter cell-edit mode:

✦ Double-click the cell. This enables you to edit the cell contents directly in the cell.

✦ Press F2. This enables you to edit the cell contents directly in the cell.

✦ Activate the cell that you want to edit and then click inside the formula bar. This enables you to edit the cell contents in the formula bar.

You can use whichever method you prefer. Some people find it easier to edit directly in the cell; others prefer to use the formula bar to edit a cell. All of these methods cause the formula bar to display two new icons. The X icon cancels editing, without changing the cell's contents (Esc has the same effect). The Check Mark icon completes the editing and enters the modified contents into the cell (Enter has the same effect).

When you begin editing a cell, the insertion point appears as a vertical bar, and you can move the insertion point by using the direction keys. You can add new characters at the location of the insertion point. You also can use the mouse to select characters while you're editing a cell. Just click and drag the mouse pointer over the characters that you want to select.

Learning some handy data entry techniques

You can simplify the process of entering information into your Excel worksheets and make your work go quite a bit faster by using a number of very handy tricks. The following sections show you how to save both time and work entering data into Excel worksheets.

Limiting entries to specific types of data

One very useful data entry technique is to limit data entry errors by specifying the type of data that a cell or range should hold. For example, you might develop a spreadsheet that has an input cell that is used in a formula. This particular cell might require a value between 1 and 12 to produce valid results in the formula — for example, if you were calculating a date and needed to make certain the user entered a valid month number. You can use the data-validation feature to display a message if the user enters a value that does not fall between 1 and 12.

To set up data validation, select the cell or range of cells that you want validated, and then choose Data ➪ Validation. Excel displays the Data Validation dialog box, with its three tabs (see Figure 1-3).

✦ Click the Settings tab and specify the type of data that the cell should contain. The dialog box changes, depending on your choice in the Allow box.

✦ Click the Input Message tab and specify a message that will appear when the cell is selected (optional). The message appears from the Office Assistant (if it's displayed) or in a small pop-up box.

✦ Click the Error Alert tab and specify the message that will appear in a dialog box if invalid data is entered (optional).

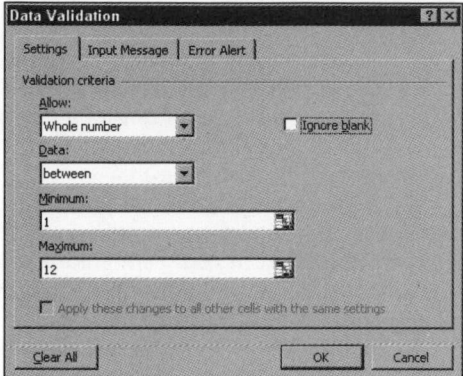

Figure 1-3: You can use data validation to ensure that the correct type of data is entered into the worksheet.

You can set up data validation for as many cells as necessary.

Caution Excel's data validation isn't foolproof. The validation does not occur if the user pastes invalid data into a cell that is set up for validation.

Automatically moving the cell pointer after entering data

By default, Excel automatically moves the cell pointer to the next cell down when you press the Enter key after entering data into a cell. To change this setting, choose Tools ➪ Options and click the Edit tab (see Figure 1-4). The check box that controls this behavior is labeled Move selection after Enter. You can also specify the direction in which the cell pointer moves (down, left, up, or right).

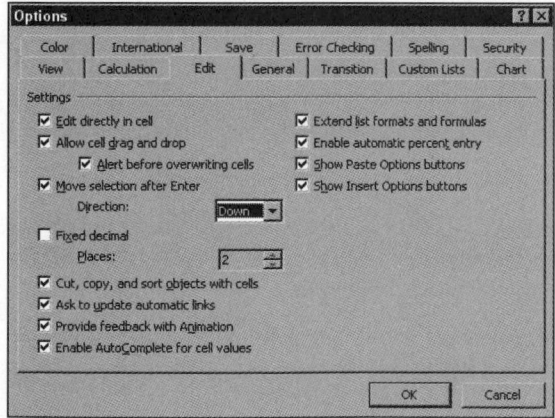

Figure 1-4: You can use the Options dialog box Edit tab to select a number of very helpful input option settings.

Using arrow keys instead of pressing Enter

Instead of pressing the Enter key when you're finished making a cell entry, you also can use any of the direction keys to complete the entry. Not surprisingly, these direction keys send you in the direction that you indicate. For example, if you're entering data in a row, press the right-arrow (→) key rather than Enter. The other arrow keys work as expected, and you can even use PgUp and PgDn.

Caution   If you use a direction key while you are entering or editing a formula, Excel may assume that you want to enter a cell reference instead of completing the entry. If you see a moving border around the cell after you press a direction key, Excel is attempting to interpret the key as a cell reference. Press Esc to cancel the reference.

Selecting a range of input cells before entering data

Here's a tip that most Excel users don't know about: If you select a range of cells, Excel automatically moves the cell pointer to the next cell in the range when you press Enter. If the selection consists of multiple rows, Excel moves down the column; when it reaches the end of the selection in the column, it moves to the first selected cell in next column. To skip a cell, just press Enter without entering anything. To go backward, press Shift+Enter. If you prefer to enter the data by rows rather than by columns, press Tab rather than Enter.

Using Ctrl+Enter to place information into multiple cells simultaneously

If you need to enter the same data into multiple cells, Excel offers a handy shortcut. Select all the cells that you want to contain the data, enter the value, text, or formula, and then press Ctrl+Enter. The same information will be inserted into each cell in the selection.

Entering decimal points automatically

If you need to enter lots of numbers with a fixed number of decimal places, Excel has a useful tool that works like some adding machines. Select Tools ⇨ Options and click the Edit tab. Check the check box labeled Fixed decimal and make sure that it's set for the correct number of decimal places for the data you need to enter. When the Fixed Decimal option is set, Excel supplies the decimal points for you automatically. For example, if you enter 12345 into a cell, Excel interprets it as 123.45 (it adds the decimal point). To restore things back to normal, just uncheck the Fixed Decimal check box in the Options dialog box. Changing this setting doesn't affect any values that you have already entered.

Caution   The fixed decimal places option applies to the entire area of all worksheets — not just a selected range of cells. If you forget that this option is turned on you can easily end up entering incorrect values.

Using AutoFill to enter a series of values

Excel's AutoFill feature makes it easy to insert a series of values or text items in a range of cells. It uses the AutoFill handle (the small box at the lower left of the active cell). You can drag the AutoFill handle to copy the cell or automatically complete a series.

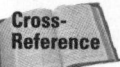

Cross-Reference　To learn more about AutoFill, see Chapter 4.

Using AutoComplete to automate data entry

Excel's AutoComplete feature makes it very easy to enter the same text into multiple cells. With AutoComplete, you type the first few letters of a text entry into a cell, and Excel automatically completes the entry, based on other entries that you've already made in the column. Besides reducing typing, this feature also ensures that your entries are spelled correctly and are consistent.

Here's how it works. Suppose that you're entering product information in a column. One of your products is named Widgets. The first time that you enter Widgets into a cell, Excel remembers it. Later, when you start typing Widgets in that same column, Excel recognizes it by the first few letters and finishes typing it for you. Just press Enter and you're done. It also changes the case of letters for you automatically. If you start entering widget (with a lowercase w) in the second entry, Excel makes the w uppercase, to be consistent with the previous entry in the column.

Tip　You also can access a mouse-oriented version of AutoComplete by right-clicking the cell and selecting Pick from List from the shortcut menu. Excel then displays a drop-down box that has all the entries in the current column, and you just click the one that you want.

If you find the AutoComplete feature distracting, you can turn it off on the Edit tab of the Options dialog box. Remove the check mark from the check box labeled Enable AutoComplete for cell values.

Entering the current date or time into a cell

If you need to date-stamp or time-stamp your worksheet, Excel provides two shortcut keys that do this for you:

✦ **Current date:** Ctrl+; (semicolon)

✦ **Current time:** Ctrl+Shift+; (semicolon)

Caution　When you use either of these shortcuts to enter a date or time into your worksheet, Excel enters a static value into the worksheet. In other words, the date or time that is entered does not change when the worksheet is recalculated. Generally, this is probably what you want, but you should be aware of this limitation.

Forcing text to appear on a new line within a cell

If you have lengthy text in a cell, you can force Excel to display it in multiple lines within the cell. Use Alt+Enter to start a new line in a cell.

Note   When you add a line break, Excel automatically changes the cell's format to Wrap Text (see "Improving Worksheet Appearance by Formatting Cells" later in this chapter). But unlike normal text wrap, your manual line break forces Excel to break the text at a specific place within the text. This makes it possible for you to exercise more precise control over the appearance of the text than if you rely on automatic text wrapping.

Tip   To remove a manual line break, open the text in the cell for editing and press Delete when the insertion point is located at the end of the line that contains the manual line break. You won't see any symbol to indicate the position of the manual line break, but the text that follows it will move up when the line break is deleted.

Entering numbers with fractions

If you want Excel to enter a fraction into a cell, leave a space between the whole number and the fraction. For example, to enter the decimal equivalent of 6⅞, enter 6 7/8, and then press Enter. When you select the cell, 6.875 appears in the formula bar, and the cell entry appears as a fraction. If you have a fraction only (for example, ⅛), you must enter a zero first, like this: 0 1/8—otherwise Excel will likely assume that you are entering a date. When you select the cell and look at the formula bar, you see 0.125. In the cell, you see ⅛.

Simplifying data entry using a form

Many people use Excel to manage simple spreadsheet databases in which the information is arranged in rows. Excel offers a simple way to work with this type of data through the use of a data entry form that Excel can create automatically. Figure 1-5 shows an example of this.

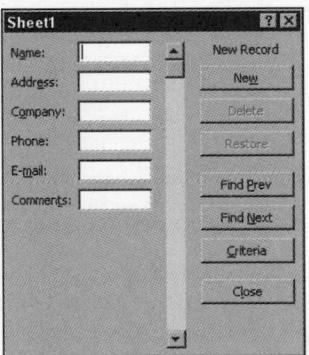

Figure 1-5: Excel's built-in data form can simplify many data entry tasks.

To use a data entry form, you must arrange your data so that Excel can recognize it as a spreadsheet database. Start by entering headings for the columns in the first row of your data entry range. You can always erase these entries later if you don't need them. Excel needs headings for this command to work, however. Select any cell in the header row and choose Data ➪ Form. Excel asks whether you want to use that row for headers (choose OK). Excel then displays a dialog box similar to the one shown in the figure. You can use Tab to move between the text boxes and supply information. When you complete the data form, click the New button. Excel enters the data into a row in the worksheet and clears the dialog box for the next row of data.

Cross-Reference   To learn more about using data forms, see Chapter 20.

Using AutoCorrect for shorthand data entry

You can use Excel's AutoCorrect feature to create shortcuts for commonly used words or phrases. For example, if you work for a company named Consolidated Data Processing Corporation, you can create an AutoCorrect entry for an abbreviation, such as cdp. Then, whenever you type cdp, Excel automatically changes it to Consolidated Data Processing Corporation.

You can customize the AutoCorrect feature by using the Tools ➪ AutoCorrect Options command. Check the option labeled Replace text as you type, and then enter your custom entries (Figure 1-6 shows an example). You can set up as many custom entries as you like. Just be careful not to use an abbreviation that might appear normally in your text.

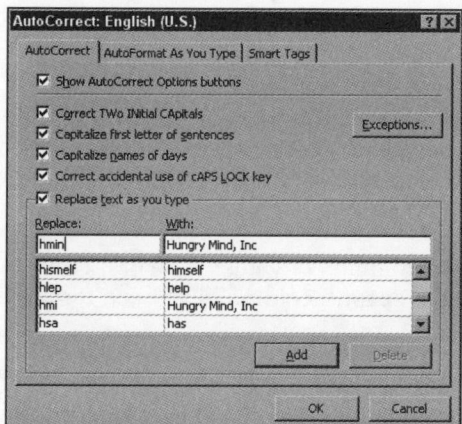

Figure 1-6: AutoCorrect allows you to create shorthand abbreviations for text you enter often.

Tip   Excel shares your AutoCorrect list with other Office applications. Any AutoCorrect entries you created in Word will also work in Excel.

Improving Worksheet Appearance by Formatting Cells

Without formatting, values in an Excel worksheet can be very difficult to understand. Formatting displays values in a form that is more recognizable so that you don't have to guess about what those values represent. For example, if you encounter a cell that displays $25,000.00 in a worksheet, you probably won't have any difficulty recognizing the entry as a numeric value representing a specified amount of money. Likewise, values formatted as dates, times, percentages, and so on are much easier to understand than raw numbers that don't provide any clues to their meaning.

Formatting an Excel worksheet can encompass far more than simply applying numerical formats to numbers. You can also change the alignment, font, or several other attributes to make your worksheets easier to understand.

In the following sections you'll see how to use many of Excel's formatting options to quickly improve the appearance of your worksheets.

See Chapter 5 for more information on the complete range of formatting options that are available using the Format ➪ Cells command.

Remember that the formatting you apply works with the selected cell or cells. Therefore, you need to select the cell (or range of cells) before applying the formatting.

Improving understanding by formatting numbers

Values that you enter into cells normally are unformatted. In other words, they simply consist of a string of numerals. Typically, you want to format the numbers so that they are easier to read or are more consistent in terms of the number of decimal places shown.

Figure 1-7 shows a worksheet that has two columns of values. The first column consists of unformatted values. The cells in the second column have been formatted to make the values easier to read.

If you move the cell pointer to a cell that has a formatted value, you find that the formula bar displays the value in its unformatted state. This is because the formatting affects only how the value is displayed in the cell—not the actual value contained in the cell.

Using Automatic number formatting

Excel is smart enough to perform some formatting for you automatically. For example, if you enter 12.2% into a cell, Excel knows that you want to use a percentage format and applies it for you automatically. If you use commas to separate thousands (such as 123,456), Excel applies comma formatting for you. And, if you precede your value with a dollar sign, the cell will be formatted for currency.

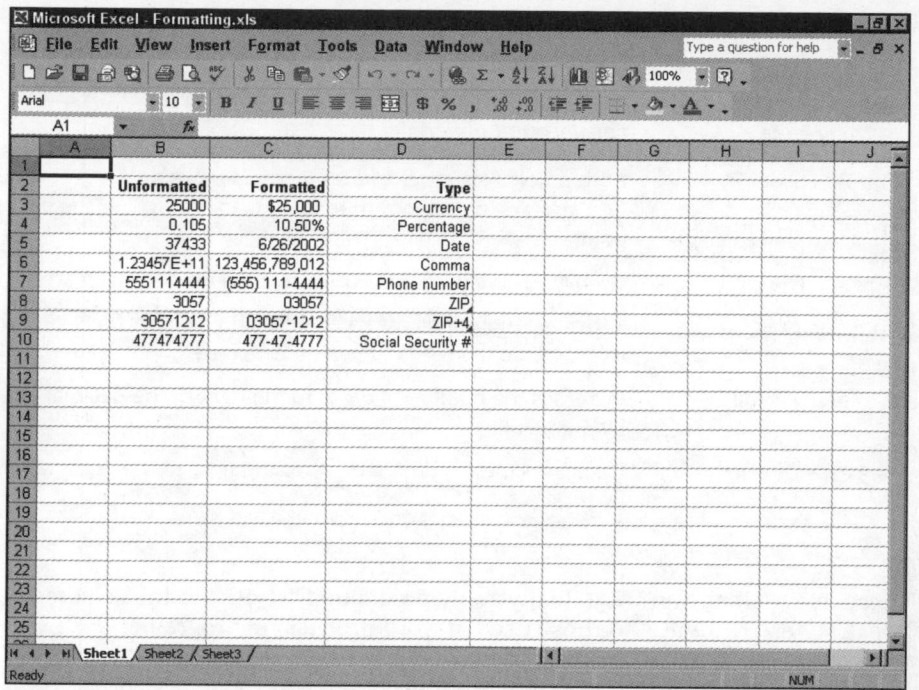

Figure 1-7: Use numeric formatting to make it easier to understand what values in the worksheet represent.

Tip A handy feature in Excel makes it easier to enter percentage values into cells. Select Tools ➪ Options, and click the Edit tab in the Options dialog box. If the check box labeled Enable automatic percent entry is checked, you can simply enter normal value into a cell formatted as a percent (for example, 12.5 for 12.5%). If this check box is not checked (the default setting), you must enter the value as a decimal (for example, .125 for 12.5%).

Cross-Reference See "Entering Dates and Times into Your Worksheets" earlier in this chapter for information on formats that Excel automatically recognizes as date entries.

Formatting numbers using the toolbar

The Formatting toolbar contains several buttons that let you quickly apply common number formats. When you click one of these buttons, the active cell takes on the specified number format. You also can select a range of cells (or even an entire row or column) before clicking these buttons. If you select more than one cell, Excel applies the number format to all the selected cells. Table 1-1 summarizes the formats that these Formatting toolbar buttons perform.

Table 1-1
Number-Formatting Buttons on the Formatting Toolbar

Button Name	Formatting Applied
Currency Style	Adds a dollar sign to the left, separates thousands with a comma, and displays the value with two digits to the right of the decimal point
Percent Style	Displays the value as a percentage, with no decimal places
Comma Style	Separates thousands with a comma and displays the value with two digits to the right of the decimal place
Increase Decimal	Increases the number of digits to the right of the decimal point by one
Decrease Decimal	Decreases the number of digits to the right of the decimal point by one

These five toolbar buttons actually apply predefined "styles" to the selected cells. These styles are similar to those used in word processing programs.

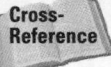 **Cross-Reference** Chapter 5 describes how to modify existing styles and create new styles.

Formatting numbers using the Format Cells dialog box

In some cases, the number formats that are accessible from the Formatting toolbar are just fine. More often, however, you want more control over how your values appear. Excel offers a great deal of control over number formats through the use of the Format Cells dialog box. Figure 1-8 shows this dialog box. For formatting numbers, you need to use the Number tab.

There are three ways to bring up the Format Cells dialog box. Start by selecting the cell or cells that you want to format and then do the following:

✦ Select the Format ➪ Cells command.

✦ Right-click and choose Format Cells from the shortcut menu.

✦ Press the Ctrl+1 shortcut key.

The Number tab of the Format Cells dialog box displays 12 categories of number formats from which to choose. When you select a category from the list box, the right side of the tab changes to display appropriate options. For example, Figure 1-8 shows how the dialog box looks when you click the Number category.

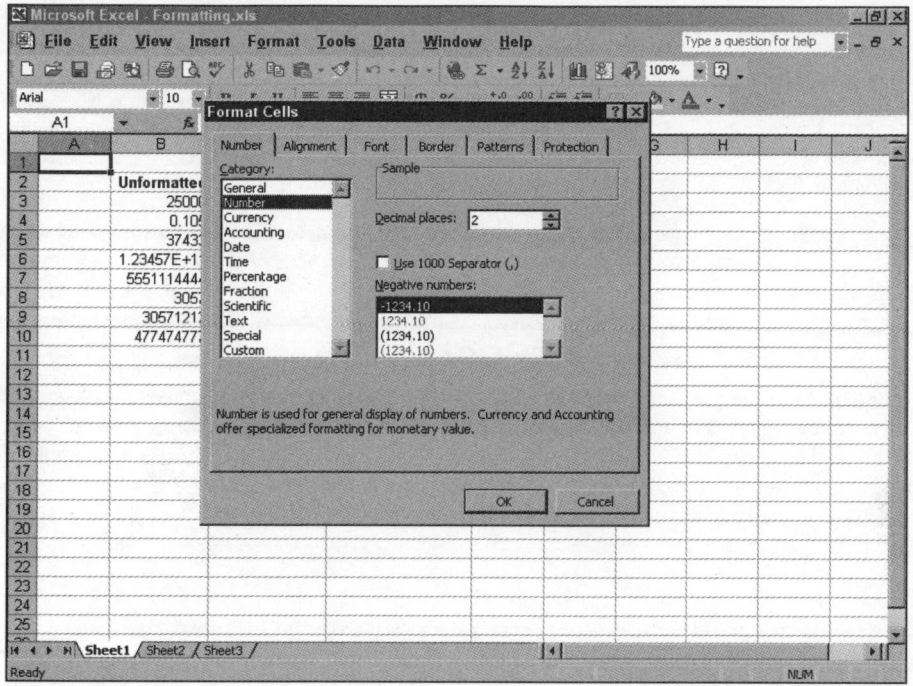

Figure 1-8: When you need more control over number formats, use the Format Cells dialog box.

The Number category has three options that you can control: the number of decimal places displayed, whether to use a thousand separator, and how you want negative numbers displayed. Notice that the Negative numbers list box has four choices (two of which display negative values in red), and the choices change depending on the number of decimal places and whether you choose to separate thousands. Also, notice that the top of the tab displays a sample of how the active cell will appear with the selected number format. After you make your choices, click OK to apply the number format to all the selected cells.

Caution   Selecting the Precision as displayed option changes the numbers in your worksheets to permanently match their appearance onscreen. If you want to select this option, all worksheets will use the same setting.

Cross-Reference   ROUND and other built-in functions are discussed in Chapter 8.

When Numbers Appear to Add Up Incorrectly

Applying a number format to a cell doesn't change the value — only how the value appears in the worksheet. For example, if a cell contains .874543, you might format it to appear as 87%. If that cell is used in a formula, the formula uses the full value (.874543), not the displayed value (.87).

In some situations, formatting may cause Excel to display calculation results that appear incorrect, such as when totaling numbers with decimal places. For example, if values are formatted to display two decimal places you may not see the actual numbers that are used in calculations. But because Excel uses the full precision of the values in its formula, the sum of two values may appear to be incorrect.

Several solutions to this problem are available. You can format the cells to display more decimal places. You can use the ROUND function on individual numbers and specify the number of decimal places Excel should round to. Or you can instruct Excel to change the worksheet values to match their displayed format. To do this, choose Tools ➪ Options, select the Calculation tab, and then check the Precision as displayed check box.

The following are the number-format categories, along with some general comments:

✦ **General:** The default format; it displays numbers as integers, decimals, or in scientific notation if the value is too wide to fit in the cell.

✦ **Number:** Enables you to specify the number of decimal places, whether to use a comma to separate thousands, and how to display negative numbers (with a minus sign, in red, in parentheses, or in red and in parentheses).

✦ **Currency:** Enables you to specify the number of decimal places, whether to use a dollar sign, and how to display negative numbers (with a minus sign, in red, in parentheses, or in red and in parentheses). This format always uses a comma to separate thousands.

✦ **Accounting:** Differs from the Currency format in that the dollar signs always line up vertically.

✦ **Date:** Enables you to choose from several different date formats.

✦ **Time:** Enables you to choose from several different time formats.

✦ **Percentage:** Enables you to choose the number of decimal places and always displays a percent sign.

✦ **Fraction:** Enables you to choose from among nine fraction formats.

✦ **Scientific:** Displays numbers in exponential notation (with an E): 2.00E+05 = 200,000; 2.05E+05 = 205,000. You can choose the number of decimal places to display to the left of E.

✦ **Text:** When applied to a value, causes Excel to treat the value as text (even if it looks like a value). This feature is useful for items such as part numbers.

✦ **Special:** Contains four additional number formats (Zip Code, Zip Code +4, Phone Number, and Social Security Number).

✦ **Custom:** Enables you to define custom number formats that aren't included in any of the other categories. Custom number formats are described in the next section.

Tip   If a cell displays a series of pound signs (such as ##########) , it means that the column is not wide enough to display the value in the number format that you selected. Either make the column wider or change the number format.

Adding your own custom number formats

Sometimes you may want to display numerical values in a format that simply isn't included in any of the other categories. If so, the answer is to create your own custom format.

Excel gives you much flexibility in creating custom number formats. You construct a number format by specifying a series of codes that represent the desired format. You enter this code sequence in the Type field after you select the Custom category on the Number tab of the Format Cells dialog box. Here's an example of a simple number format code:

    0.000

This code consists of placeholders and a decimal point and tells Excel to display the value with three digits to the right of the decimal place. Here's another example:

    00000

This custom number format has five placeholders and displays the value with five digits (no decimal point). This is a good format to use when the cell will hold a ZIP code (in fact, this is the code actually used by the ZIP Code format in the Special category). When you format the cell with this number format and then enter a ZIP code such as 06604, the value is displayed with the leading zero. If you enter this number into a cell with the General number format, it displays as 6604 (no leading zero).

Tip   To use an existing format as the basis for building your new custom format, first select the existing format in its own category and then click the Custom category at the bottom of the Format Cells dialog box's Category list. Doing so places the selected format code into the Type box so you can modify it for your own use.

If you scroll through the list of number formats in the Custom category in the Format Cells dialog box, you see many more examples. Most of the time, you can use one of these codes as a starting point, and only slight customization will be needed.

Excel also enables you to specify different format codes for positive numbers, negative numbers, zero values, and text. You do so by separating the codes with a semicolon. The codes are arranged in the following structure:

```
Positive format; Negative format; Zero format; Text format
```

The following is an example of a custom number format that specifies a different format for each of these types:

```
[Green]General;[Red]General;[Black]General;[Blue]General
```

This example takes advantage of the fact that colors have special codes. A cell formatted with this custom number format displays its contents in a different color, depending on the value. In this case, positive numbers are green, negative numbers are red, zero is black, and text is blue.

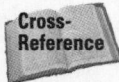

Cross-Reference   If you want to apply cell formatting automatically, such as text or background color, based on the cell's contents, a better solution is to use Excel's Conditional Formatting feature. This feature is discussed in Chapter 5.

Table 1-2 lists the formatting codes available for custom formats, along with brief descriptions. These codes are described further in Excel's online help.

Table 1-2 Codes Used to Create Custom Number Formats	
Code	**Comments**
General	Displays the number in General format
#	Digit placeholder
0 (zero)	Digit placeholder
?	Digit placeholder
.	Decimal point
Code	Comments
%	Percentage
,	Thousands separator
E- E+ e- e+	Scientific notation
$ - + / ( ) : space	Displays this character
\	Displays the next character in the format

Code	Comments
*	Repeats the next character, to fill the column width
_	Skips the width of the next character
"text"	Displays the text inside the double quotation marks
@	Text placeholder
[color]	Displays the characters in the color specified
[COLOR n]	Displays the corresponding color in the color palette, where n is a number from 0 to 56
[condition value]	Enables you to set your own criteria for each section of a number format
m	Displays the month as a number without leading zeros (1–12)
mm	Displays the month as a number with leading zeros (01–12)
mmm	Displays the month as an abbreviation (Jan–Dec)
mmmm	Displays the month as a full name (January–December)
d	Displays the day as a number without leading zeros (1–31)
dd	Displays the day as a number with leading zeros (01–31)
ddd	Displays the day as an abbreviation (Sun–Sat)
dddd	Displays the day as a full name (Sunday–Saturday)
yy or yyyy	Displays the year as a two-digit number (02), or as a four-digit number (2002)
h or hh	Displays the hour as a number without leading zeros (0–23), or as a number with leading zeros (00–23)
m or mm	Displays the minute as a number without leading zeros (0–59), or as a number with leading zeros (00–59)
s or ss	Displays the second as a number without leading zeros (0–59), or as a number with leading zeros (00–59)
[ ]	Displays hours greater than 24, or minutes or seconds greater than 60
AM/am/A/a/PM/pm/P/p	Displays the hour using a 12-hour clock; if no AM/PM indicator is used, the hour uses a 24-hour clock

Note   Custom number formats are stored with the worksheet. To make the custom format available in a different workbook, you must copy a cell that uses the custom format to the other workbook.

Figure 1-9 shows several examples of custom number formats. Studying these examples will help you understand the concept and may give you some ideas for your own custom number formats.

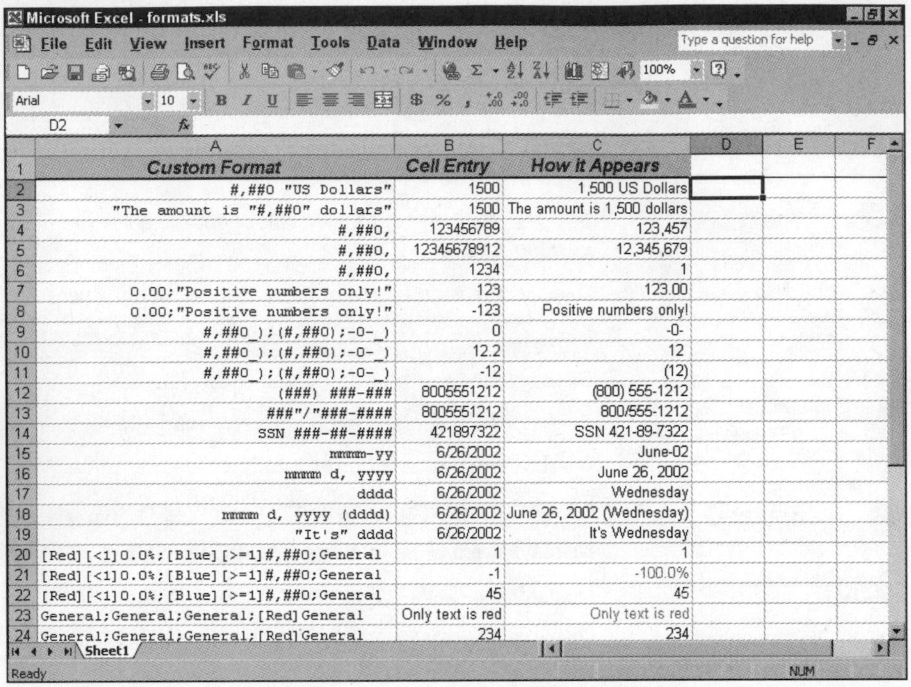

	A	B	C	D	E	F
1	*Custom Format*	*Cell Entry*	*How it Appears*			
2	#,##0 "US Dollars"	1500	1,500 US Dollars			
3	"The amount is "#,##0" dollars"	1500	The amount is 1,500 dollars			
4	#,##0,	123456789	123,457			
5	#,##0,	12345678912	12,345,679			
6	#,##0,	1234	1			
7	0.00;"Positive numbers only!"	123	123.00			
8	0.00;"Positive numbers only!"	-123	Positive numbers only!			
9	#,##0_);(#,##0);-0-_)	0	-0-			
10	#,##0_);(#,##0);-0-_)	12.2	12			
11	#,##0_);(#,##0);-0-_)	-12	(12)			
12	(###) ###-####	8005551212	(800) 555-1212			
13	###"/"###-####	8005551212	800/555-1212			
14	SSN ###-##-####	421897322	SSN 421-89-7322			
15	mmmm-yy	6/26/2002	June-02			
16	mmmm d, yyyy	6/26/2002	June 26, 2002			
17	dddd	6/26/2002	Wednesday			
18	mmmm d, yyyy (dddd)	6/26/2002	June 26, 2002 (Wednesday)			
19	"It's" dddd	6/26/2002	It's Wednesday			
20	[Red][<1]0.0%;[Blue][>=1]#,##0;General	1	1			
21	[Red][<1]0.0%;[Blue][>=1]#,##0;General	-1	-100.0%			
22	[Red][<1]0.0%;[Blue][>=1]#,##0;General	45	45			
23	General;General;General;[Red]General	Only text is red	Only text is red			
24	General;General;General;[Red]General	234	234			

Figure 1-9: You can create your own custom formats when you need to display values in a special way.

✦   ✦   ✦

Essential Spreadsheet Operations

◆ ◆ ◆ ◆

In This Chapter

Understanding Excel
worksheet essentials

Controlling your view

Manipulating the
rows and columns

◆ ◆ ◆ ◆

Whenever you work with Excel, you are working with worksheets. Understanding the basics of using and manipulating worksheets will make using Excel far easier for you. This chapter shows you how to take control of your worksheets so that you will be more efficient using the program.

Learning the Fundamentals of Excel Worksheets

In Excel, each file is called a *workbook* and each workbook can contain one or more *worksheets*. You may find it helpful to think of an Excel workbook as a notebook and worksheets as pages in the notebook. As with a notebook, you can activate a particular sheet, add new sheets, remove sheets, copy sheets, and so on.

By default, Excel automatically creates three worksheets in each new workbook. Even if you seldom use more than one worksheet, these extras worksheets can be handy. In later sections in this chapter, you'll learn how you can add, delete, hide, or move worksheets.

Let's have a look at the many handy operations that you can perform with worksheets.

Making a worksheet the active sheet

At any given time, one workbook is the active workbook, and one sheet is the active sheet in the active workbook. To activate a different sheet, just click its sheet tab, located at the bottom of the workbook window. You also can use the following shortcut keys to activate a different sheet:

✦ **Ctrl+PgUp:** Activates the previous sheet, if one exists.

✦ **Ctrl+PgDn:** Activates the next sheet, if one exists.

If your workbook has several sheets, all tabs may not be visible. You can use the tab-scrolling buttons (see Figure 2-1) to scroll the sheet tabs. The sheet tabs share space with the worksheet's horizontal scrollbar. You also can drag the tab split box to display more or fewer tabs. Dragging the tab split box simultaneously changes the number of tabs and the size of the horizontal scrollbar.

Tip   When you right-click any of the tab-scrolling buttons to the left of the worksheet tabs, Excel displays a list of all sheets in the workbook. You can quickly activate a sheet by selecting it from the list.

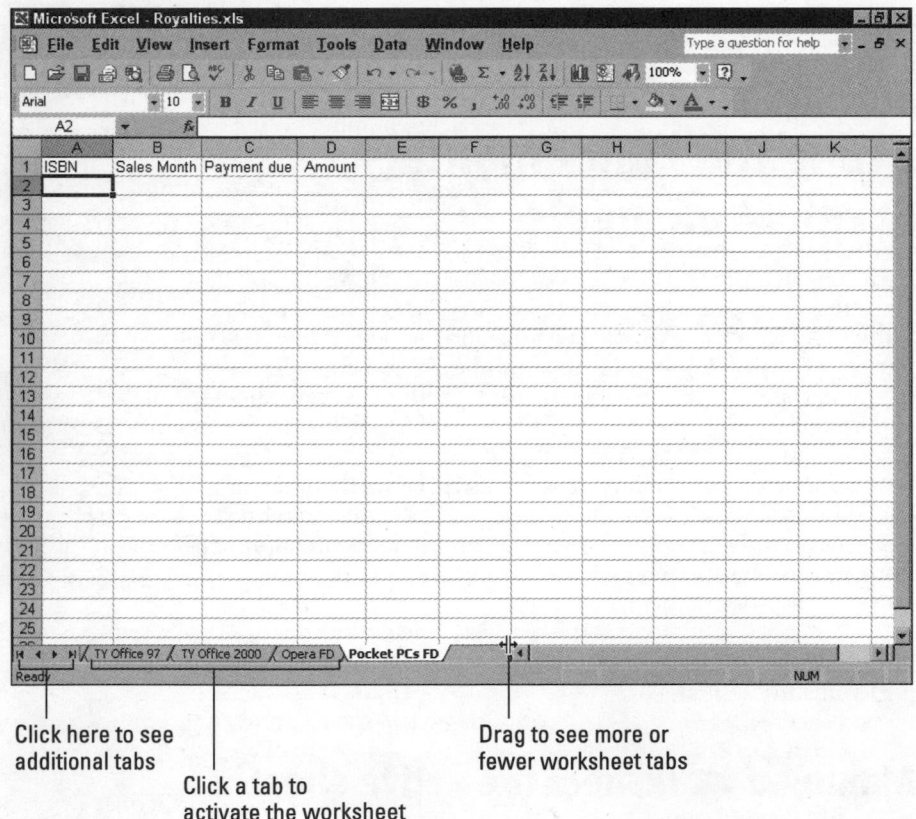

Figure 2-1: Use the tab controls to activate a different worksheet or to see additional worksheet tabs.

Adding a new worksheet to your workbook

Worksheets can be an excellent organizational tool. Instead of placing everything on a single worksheet, you can use additional worksheets in a workbook to separate various workbook elements logically. For example, if you have several products whose sales you track individually, you might want to assign each product to its own worksheet and then use the top worksheet page to consolidate your results.

The following are three ways to add a new worksheet to a workbook:

✦ Select the Insert ➪ Worksheet command.

✦ Press Shift+F11.

✦ Right-click a sheet tab, choose the Insert command from the shortcut menu, and then select Worksheet from the Insert dialog box.

When you add a new worksheet to the workbook, Excel inserts the new worksheet before the active worksheet, and the new worksheet becomes the active worksheet.

 Tip To insert more than one worksheet at a time, hold down the Shift key and click a range of worksheet tabs. When you issue the command to insert a worksheet, Excel will add as many worksheets as the number of worksheet tabs you selected before issuing the command.

Deleting a worksheet you no longer need

If you no longer need a worksheet, or if you want to get rid of an empty worksheet in a workbook, you can delete it in either of two ways:

✦ Select the Edit ➪ Delete Sheet command.

✦ Right-click the sheet tab and choose the Delete command from the shortcut menu.

If the worksheet contains any data, Excel asks you to confirm that you want to delete the sheet. If you have never used the worksheet, Excel deletes it immediately without asking for confirmation.

 **Tip** You can delete multiple sheets with a single command by selecting the sheets that you want to delete. To select multiple sheets, press Ctrl while you click the sheet tabs that you want to delete. To select a group of contiguous sheets, click the first sheet tab, press Shift, and then click the last sheet tab. Then, use either method to delete the selected sheets.

 **Caution** When you delete a worksheet, it's gone for good. This is one of the few operations in Excel that can't be undone.

Tip   If you often find yourself adding or deleting worksheets when you begin a new workbook, you can change the default number of worksheets that Excel creates in new workbooks. To do so, select Tools ⇨ Options, select the General tab, and then change the Sheets in new workbook setting to whatever setting you prefer. Figure 2-2 shows this dialog box.

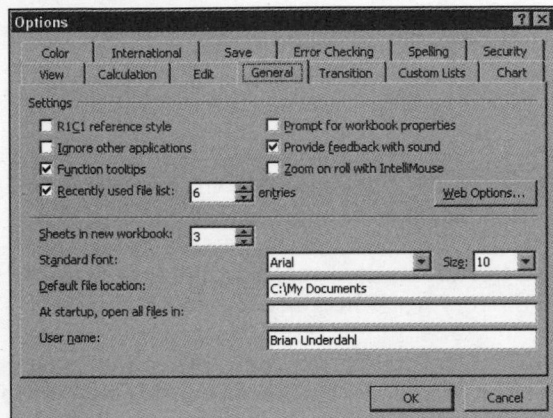

Figure 2-2: Use the Options dialog box to control the number of worksheets that appear in new workbooks.

Changing the name of a worksheet

The default names Excel uses for worksheets — Sheet1, Sheet2, and so on — aren't very descriptive. If you don't change the worksheet names it can be a bit hard to remember where to find things in multiple-sheet workbooks. That's why providing more meaningful names for your worksheets is usually a good idea.

To change a sheet's name, use any of the following methods to begin:

✦ Choose Format ⇨ Sheet ⇨ Rename.

✦ Double-click the sheet tab.

✦ Right-click the sheet tab and choose the Rename command from the shortcut menu.

After you have done one of the above actions, Excel highlights the name on the sheet tab so that you can edit the name or replace it with a new name.

Tip   To edit the worksheet name rather than to replace it completely, it's usually easiest to double-click the sheet tab, and then click within the name where you want to make a change.

Sheet names can be up to 31 characters, and spaces are allowed. However, you can't use the following characters in sheet names:

:   colon

/   slash

\\   backslash

?   question mark

*   asterisk

Caution   Although Excel lets you use square brackets in a worksheet name, you should avoid doing so because it can cause problems with formulas that use external links.

Tip   Remember that a longer worksheet name results in a wider tab, which takes up more space onscreen. Therefore, if you use lengthy sheet names, you won't be able to see very many sheet tabs without having to scroll.

Rearranging your worksheets

You may want to rearrange the order of worksheets in a workbook. If you have a separate worksheet for each sales region, for example, arranging the worksheets in alphabetical order or by total sales might be helpful. You may want to move a worksheet from one workbook to another (to move a worksheet to a different workbook, both workbooks must be open). You can also create copies of worksheets.

You can move or copy a worksheet in the following ways:

✦ Select the Edit ➪ Move or Copy Sheet command to display the Move or Copy dialog box.

✦ Right-click the sheet tab and select the Move or Copy command (this also displays the same Move or Copy dialog box).

✦ Click the sheet tab and drag it to its desired location (either in the same workbook or in a different workbook) to move the worksheet. When you drag, the mouse pointer changes to a small sheet, and a small arrow guides you.

✦ Click the sheet tab, press Ctrl, and then drag it to its desired location (either in the same workbook or in a different workbook) to copy the worksheet. When you drag, the mouse pointer changes to a small sheet with a plus sign on it.

Tip   You also can move or copy multiple sheets simultaneously by selecting them by pressing Ctrl as you click the sheet tabs.

Dragging is usually the easiest method, but if the workbook has many sheets, you may prefer to use the Move or Copy dialog box. This dialog box is shown in Figure 2-3, and it enables you to select the workbook and the new location.

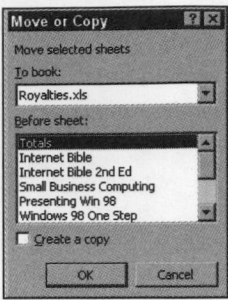

Figure 2-3: Use the Move or Copy dialog box to move or copy worksheets in the same or another workbook.

If you move or copy a worksheet to a workbook that already has a sheet with the same name, Excel changes the name to make it unique. For example, Sheet1 becomes Sheet1 (2).

Note   When you move or copy a worksheet to a different workbook, any defined names and custom formats also get copied to the new workbook.

Hiding and unhiding a worksheet

If you want to, you can hide worksheets that are in your workbooks. Hiding a worksheet may be useful if you don't want others to see it, or if you just want to get it out of the way. When a sheet is hidden, its sheet tab is also hidden.

Tip   Hiding a worksheet may prevent casual users from viewing or changing important information in a workbook.

To hide a worksheet, choose Format ➪ Sheet ➪ Hide. The active worksheet (or selected worksheets) will be hidden from view. Every workbook must have at least one visible sheet, so Excel won't allow you to hide all the sheets in a workbook.

To unhide a hidden worksheet, choose Format ➪ Sheet ➪ Unhide. Excel opens a dialog box that lists all hidden sheets. Choose the sheet that you want to redisplay and click OK. You can't select multiple sheets from this dialog box, so you need to repeat the command for each sheet that you want to redisplay.

Tip   To more fully protect a workbook from unauthorized changes, use the Tools ➪ Protection menu commands. These commands give you several options in deciding how much access other users will have to the worksheets in your workbooks.

Controlling the Worksheet View

As you add more information to a worksheet, you may find that it gets more difficult to navigate and locate what you want. Excel includes a few options that enable you to view your sheet, and sometimes multiple sheets, more efficiently. This section discusses a few additional worksheet options at your disposal.

Viewing worksheets in multiple windows

Sometimes, you may want to view two different parts of a worksheet simultaneously — perhaps to make it easier to reference a distance cell in a formula. Or, you may want to examine more than one sheet in the same workbook simultaneously. You can accomplish either of these actions by opening a new view to the workbook, using one or more additional windows.

To create and display a new view of the active workbook, choose Window ➪ New Window.

Tip   If the workbook is maximized when you create a new window, you may not even notice that Excel has created the new window, but if you look at the Excel title bar you'll see that the workbook title now has :2 appended to the name. Select Window ➪ Arrange and choose one of the options in the Arrange Windows dialog box to display the open windows.

Excel displays a new window with the active workbook, similar to Figure 2-4. Notice the text in the windows' title bars: OldRecords.xls:1 and OldRecords.xls:2. To help you keep track of the windows, Excel appends a colon and a number to each window.

A single workbook can have as many views (that is, separate windows) as you want. Each window is independent of the others. In other words, scrolling to a new location in one window doesn't cause scrolling in the other window(s). This also enables you to display a different worksheet in a separate window.

You can close these additional windows when you no longer need them. For example, clicking the Close button on the active window's title bar closes the active window but doesn't close the other windows.

Tip   Multiple windows make it easier to copy information from one worksheet to another. You can use Excel's drag-and-drop procedures to do this.

Splitting the worksheet window into panes

If you prefer not to clutter your screen with additional windows, Excel provides another option for viewing multiple parts of the same worksheet. The Window ➪ Split command splits the active worksheet into two or four separate panes. The split occurs at the location of the cell pointer. You can use the mouse to drag the individual panes to resize them.

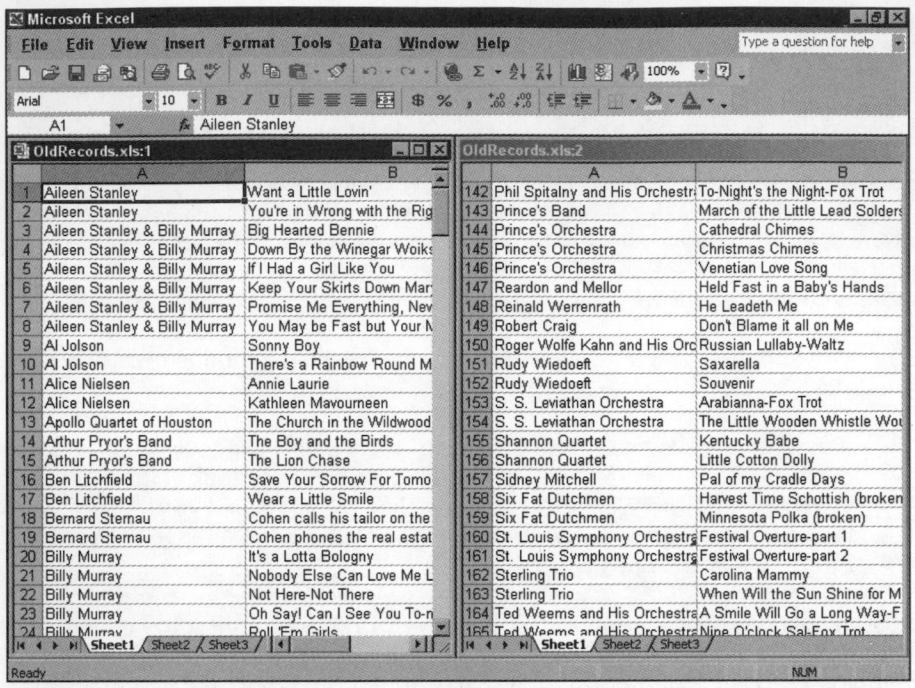

Figure 2-4: Use multiple windows to view different sections of the workbook at the same time.

Figure 2-5 shows a worksheet split into two panes. Notice that row numbers aren't continuous. In other words, splitting panes enables you to display in a single window widely separated areas of a worksheet. To remove the split panes, choose Window ➪ Remove Split.

Another way to split and unsplit panes is to drag either the vertical or horizontal split bar. These bars are the small rectangles that normally appear just above the top of the vertical scrollbar and just to the right of the horizontal scrollbar. When you move the mouse pointer over a split bar, the mouse pointer changes to a pair of parallel lines with arrows pointing outward from each line. To remove split panes by using the mouse, drag the pane separator all the way to the edge of the window, or just double-click it.

Keeping the titles in view by freezing panes

If you set up a worksheet with row or column headings, it's easy to lose track of just where you are when you scroll to a different location in the worksheet. Excel provides a handy solution to this problem: freezing panes. This keeps the headings visible while you are scrolling through the worksheet.

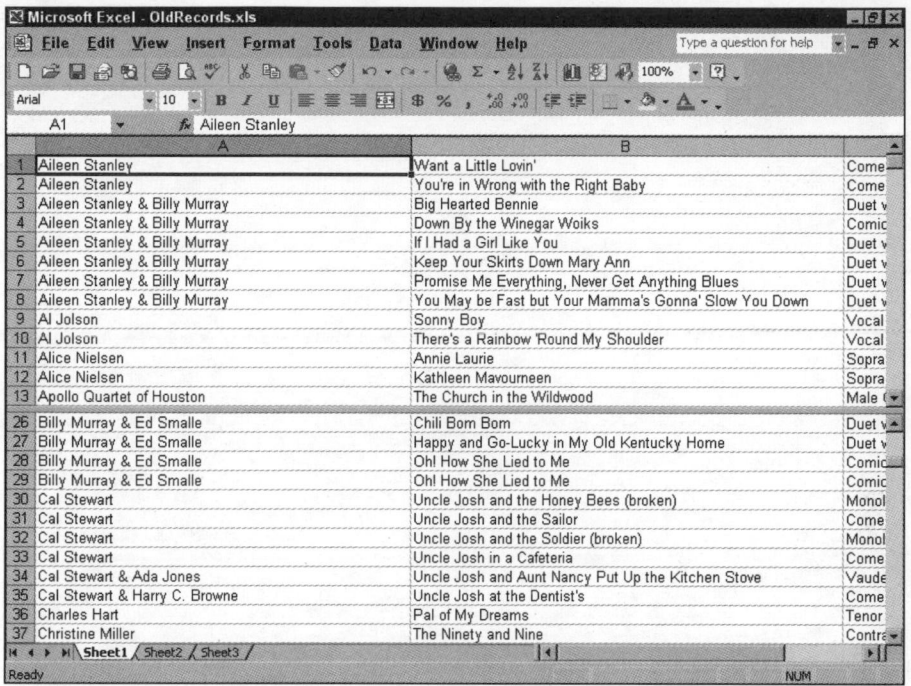

Figure 2-5: You can also split the worksheet window to view different areas of the worksheet at the same time.

To freeze panes, start by moving the cell pointer to the cell below the row that you want to remain visible as you scroll and to the right of the column that you want to remain visible as you scroll. Then, select Window ➪ Freeze Panes. Excel inserts dark lines to indicate the frozen rows and columns. You'll find that the frozen row and column remain visible as you scroll throughout the worksheet. To remove the frozen panes, select Window ➪ Unfreeze Panes.

Figure 2-6 shows the worksheet from Figure 2-5, but with frozen panes. In this case, row 1 and column A are frozen in place, and we have scrolled down and to the right to locate some information while keeping the column titles and the column A entries visible.

Tip

If you press Ctrl+Home while the worksheet has frozen panes, the cell selector moves to the top-left unfrozen cell. You can move into the frozen rows or columns using the direction keys or your mouse.

Microsoft Excel - OldRecords.xls

File   Edit   View   Insert   Format   Tools   Data   Window   Help   Type a question for help

Arial   10   B   I   U

C50   Violin Solo

	A	C	D	E
1	Artist	Description	Label	
50	Eddy Brown	Violin Solo	Columbia	
51	Eddy Brown	Violin Solo	Columbia	
52	Edgar A. Guest	Recitation	Victor	
53	Edgar A. Guest	Recitation	Victor	
54	Elliot Shaw	Baritone with orchestra	Victor	
55	Ernest Hare	Baritone Solo	Domino	
56	Ferera and Franchini	Hawaiian Guitars	Banner	
57	Frank Crumit	Orchestra	Victor	
58	Frank Crumit	Comedian with clarinet, ukulele and guitar	Victor	
59	Frank Crumit	Orchestra	Victor	
60	Frank Crumit	Tenor with Guitar and organ	Victor	
61	Frank Crumit	Tenor with orchestra	Victor	
62	Frank Crumit	Comedian with ukulele and piano	Victor	
63	Frank Crumit	Tenor with piano and ukulele	Victor	
64	Frank Crumit	Comedian with violin and piano	Victor	
65	Frank Crumit	Tenor with orchestra	Victor	
66	Frank Crumit	Tenor with Guitar and organ	Victor	
67	Frank Crumit	Comedian with violin, guitar and ukulele	Victor	
68	Frankie Carle	Piano	Columbia	
69	Frankie Carle	Piano	Columbia	
70	Fred Hughes	Tenor Solo	Columbia	
71	Fred Hughes	Tenor Solo	Columbia	
72	Gene Austin	Tenor with violin, cello and piano	Victor	
73	Gene Austin	Comedian with ukulele	Victor	

Sheet1   Sheet2   Sheet3

Ready   NUM

Figure 2-6: By freezing certain columns and rows, they remain visible while you scroll the worksheet.

Zooming in or out for a better view

Excel enables you to zoom in or out to scale the size of your worksheets. Normally, everything you see onscreen is displayed at 100 percent. You can change the "zoom percentage" from 10 percent (very tiny) to 400 percent (huge). Using a small zoom percentage can help you to get a bird's-eye view of your worksheet, to see how it's laid out. Zooming in is useful if your eyesight isn't quite what it used to be and you have trouble deciphering tiny type. Figure 2-7 shows a window zoomed to 10 percent and a window zoomed to 400 percent.

You can easily change the zoom factor of the active worksheet by using the Zoom tool on the Standard toolbar. Just click the arrow and select the desired zoom factor as shown in the figure. Your screen transforms immediately. You can also type a zoom percentage directly into the Zoom toolbox. If you choose Selection from the list, Excel zooms the worksheet to display only the selected cells (useful if you want to view only a particular range).

Tip   Zooming affects only the active worksheet, so you can use different zoom factors for different worksheets.

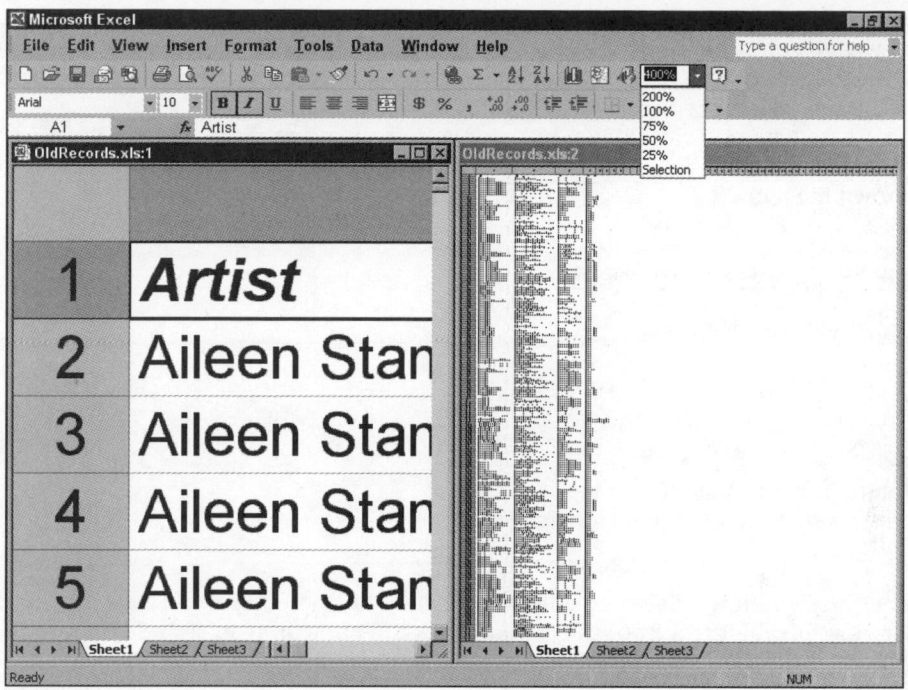

Figure 2-7: You can zoom in or out for a better view of your worksheets.

If your worksheet uses named ranges (see Chapter 4), you'll find that zooming your worksheet to 39 percent or less displays the name of the range overlaid on the cells. This is useful for getting an overview of how a worksheet is laid out.

You can also set the zoom percentage by using the View ➪ Zoom command. This command displays the Zoom dialog box, where you can select an option or enter a value between 10 and 400.

Excel contains separate options for changing the size of your printed output (use the File ➪ Page Setup command). See Chapter 3 for details.

Saving your view settings

If you create a number of different worksheet views for different purposes, you may want to save those view settings so that you can easily recall them without going through all of the necessary setup steps each time you want to use the same view. To save your view settings, create a *named* view.

A named view includes settings for window size and position, frozen panes or titles, outlining, zoom factor, the active cell, print area, and many of the settings in the

Options dialog box. Optionally, a view can include hidden print settings and hidden rows and columns. If you find that you're constantly fiddling with these settings and then changing them back, using named views can save you lots of effort.

To create a named view, begin by setting up the view settings the way you want them. Then select View ➪ Custom Views to display the Custom Views dialog box shown in Figure 2-8.

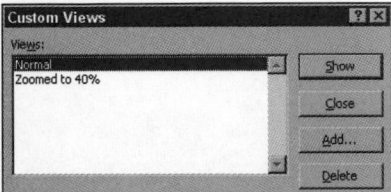

Figure 2-8: Use the Custom Views dialog box to save or select named view settings.

The Custom Views dialog box displays a list of all named views. To select a particular view, just select it from the list and click the Show button. To add a view, click the Add button and provide a name. To delete a named view from the list, click the Delete button.

Working with Rows and Columns

Rows and columns make up an Excel worksheet. Every worksheet has exactly 65,536 rows and 256 columns. These values are fixed, and you can't change them. This section discusses some worksheet operations that involve rows and columns.

Note   Although Excel worksheets always have 65,536 rows and 256 columns, there is an interesting if not altogether useful anomaly that occurs if you save a workbook as a Web page. Excel worksheets that are saved as Web pages and then are opened in a Web browser seem to have an unlimited number of rows and columns. Unfortunately, because there is no way for you to add anything in the extra rows or columns (Excel can't even see the extras), the extra rows and columns are pretty much useless.

Inserting rows and columns

Although the number of rows and columns in a worksheet is fixed, you can still insert and delete rows and columns if you need to make room for additional information—perhaps to include additional items in a calculation, for example. These operations don't change the number of rows or columns. Rather, inserting a new row moves down the other rows to accommodate the new row. The last row is simply removed from the worksheet if it is empty. Inserting a new column shifts the columns to the right, and the last column is removed if it's empty.

Note

If the last row (row 65,536) is not empty, you can't insert a new row. Similarly, if the last column (column IV) contains information, Excel won't let you insert a new column. Attempting to add a row or column displays the dialog box shown in Figure 2-9.

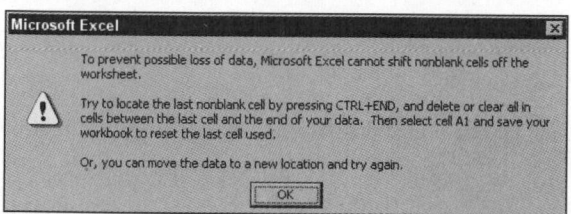

Figure 2-9: You can't add a new row or column if doing so would move nonblank cells off the worksheet.

To insert a new row or rows, you can use any of the following techniques:

✦ Select an entire row or multiple rows by clicking the row numbers in the worksheet border. Select the Insert ⇨ Rows command.

✦ Select an entire row or multiple rows by clicking the row numbers in the worksheet border. Right-click and choose Insert from the shortcut menu.

✦ Move the cell pointer to the row that you want to insert and then select Insert ⇨ Rows. If you select multiple cells in the column, Excel inserts additional rows that correspond to the number of cells selected in the column and moves the rows below the insertion down.

The procedure for inserting a new column or columns is the same, but you use the Insert ⇨ Column command.

You also can insert cells, rather than just rows or columns. Select the range into which you want to add new cells and then select Insert ⇨ Cells (or right-click the selection and choose Insert). To insert cells, the other cells must be shifted to the right or shifted down. Therefore, Excel displays the dialog box shown in Figure 2-10 to learn the direction in which you want to shift the cells.

Deleting rows and columns

You may also find that it's necessary to delete rows or columns in a worksheet. For example, if you lay out a worksheet and then discover that you can't print the entire active area on a single sheet of paper without shrinking the type to the point where it is too small to read comfortably, deleting empty rows or columns may enable you to print the report without needing a magnifying glass to read it.

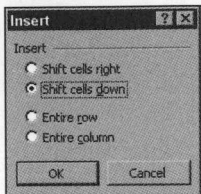

Figure 2-10: You can insert partial rows or columns using the Insert dialog box.

To delete a row or rows, use any of the following methods:

✦ Select an entire row or multiple rows by clicking the row numbers in the worksheet border and then select Edit ➪ Delete.

✦ Select an entire row or multiple rows by clicking the row numbers in the worksheet border. Right-click and choose Delete from the shortcut menu.

✦ Move the cell pointer to the row that you want to delete and then select Edit ➪ Delete. In the dialog box that appears, choose the Entire row option. If you select multiple cells in the column, Excel deletes all selected rows.

Deleting columns works the same way. If you discover that you accidentally deleted a row or column, select Edit ➪ Undo (or Ctrl+Z) to undo the action.

Caution

Excel doesn't warn you if the rows or columns you intend to delete contain important information, nor if those rows or columns are referenced in any formulas. It's a good idea to save the workbook before you delete rows or columns.

Changing column widths and row heights

Excel normally adjusts column widths and row heights automatically to best display any information you enter into cells in the row or column. Sometimes, though, you may need to make these adjustments manually to suit your needs. For example, rather than allowing column widths to grow to fit extremely long entries, you may prefer to only display the first part of those entries in order to control the width of a printed report. Or you may want to increase a row's height to make a table's headings stand out from the table's data.

Excel provides several different ways to change the widths of columns and the height of rows.

Changing column widths

Column width is measured in terms of the number of characters of a *fixed pitch font* that will fit into the cell's width. By default, each column's width is 8.43 characters.

This is actually a rather meaningless measurement because most of the fonts you will use are *proportional fonts*—the width of individual characters varies; for example, the letter *i* is much narrower than the letter *W.*

Tip   If pound signs (#) fill a cell that contains a numerical value, then the column's width isn't wide enough to accommodate the information in the cell. Widen the column to solve the problem. For the most part, however, Excel automatically adjusts column width as you enter information.

There are several ways to change the width of a column or columns; they are listed next. Before you change the width, you can select multiple columns, so that the width will be the same for all selected columns. To select multiple columns, either click and drag in the column border or press Ctrl while you select individual columns. To select all columns, click the Select All button in the upper-left corner of the worksheet border (or press Ctrl+A).

✦ Drag the right-column border with the mouse until the column is the desired width.

✦ Choose Format ➪ Column ➪ Width and enter a value in the Column Width dialog box.

✦ Choose Format ➪ Column ➪ AutoFit Selection. This adjusts the width of the selected column so that the widest entry in the column fits. If you want, you can just select cells in the column, and the column is adjusted based on the widest entry in your selection.

✦ Double-click the right border of a column header to set the column width automatically to the widest entry in the column.

Tip   To change the default width of all columns, use the Format ➪ Column ➪ Standard Width command. This displays a dialog box into which you enter the new default column width. All columns that haven't been previously adjusted take on the new column width.

Caution   After you manually adjust a column's width, Excel will no longer automatically adjust the column to accommodate longer entries.

Changing row heights

Row height is measured in points (a standard unit of measurement in the printing trade—72 points is equal to 1 inch). The default row height depends on the font defined in the Normal style. Excel adjusts row heights automatically to accommodate the tallest font in the row. So, if you change the font size of a cell to 20 points, for example, Excel makes the column taller so that the entire text is visible.

You can set the row height manually, however, by using any of the following techniques. As with columns, you can select multiple rows.

✦ Drag the lower row border with the mouse until the row is the desired height.

✦ Choose Format ➪ Row ➪ Height and enter a value (in points) in the Row Height dialog box.

✦ Double-click the bottom border of a row to set the row height automatically to the tallest entry in the row. You also can use the Format ➪ Row ➪ AutoFit command for this.

Changing the row height is useful for spacing out rows and is sometimes preferable to inserting empty rows between lines of data.

Hiding rows and columns

If necessary, you can hide rows and columns. This may be useful if you don't want users to see particular information or if you need to print a report that summarizes the information in the worksheet without showing all the details.

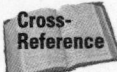

Cross-Reference   Chapter 26 introduces another way to summarize worksheet data without showing all the details — outlining.

To hide rows or columns in your worksheet, select the row or rows that you want to hide and then choose Format ➪ Row ➪ Hide. Or, select the column or columns that you want to hide and then choose Format ➪ Column ➪ Hide.

Tip   You also can drag the row or column's border to hide the row or column. Drag the bottom border of a row upward or the border of a column to the left.

A hidden row is actually a row with its height set to zero. Similarly, a hidden column has a column width of zero. When you use the arrow keys to move the cell pointer, cells in hidden rows or columns are skipped. In other words, you can't use the arrow keys to move to a cell in a hidden row or column.

Unhiding a hidden row or column can be a bit tricky, because selecting a row or column that's hidden is difficult. The solution is to select the columns or rows that are adjacent to the hidden column or row (select at least one column or row on either side). Then, select Format ➪ Row ➪ Unhide or Format ➪ Column ➪ Unhide. Another method is to select Edit ➪ Go To (or its F5 equivalent) to select a cell in a hidden row or column. For example, if column A is hidden, you can press F5 and specify cell A1 (or any other cell in column A) to move the cell pointer to the hidden column. Then, you can use the appropriate command to unhide the column.

✦   ✦   ✦

Printing Your Work

L ike it or not, reports printed on paper are still with us and likely will be around for a long time. Many of the worksheets that you develop with Excel can easily serve as printed reports. You'll find that printing from Excel is quite easy, and that you can generate attractive, well-formatted reports with minimal effort. In addition, Excel has many options that provide you with a great deal of control over the printed page so that you can make your printed reports even better. These options are explained in this chapter.

Printing a Report as Quickly as Possible

If you simply want to print a copy of a worksheet with no fuss and bother, Excel provides you with a very simple and easy way to do so. The Print button on the Standard toolbar is a quick way to print the current worksheet, using the default settings. Just click the button, and Excel sends the worksheet to the printer. If you've changed any of the default print settings, Excel uses the new settings; otherwise, it uses the following default settings:

+ Prints the active worksheet (or all selected worksheets), including any embedded charts or drawing objects.

+ Prints one copy.

+ Prints the entire worksheet.

+ Prints in portrait mode.

+ Doesn't scale the printed output.

+ Uses 1-inch margins for the top and bottom and .75-inch margins for the left and right margins.

✦ Prints with no headers or footers.

✦ For wide worksheets that span multiple pages, it prints down and then across.

You can change any of these default print settings.

When you print a worksheet, Excel prints only the active area of the worksheet. In other words, it won't print all four million cells — just those that have data in them. If the worksheet contains any embedded charts or drawing objects, they also are printed (unless you have modified the Print Object property of the object).

Tip   To quickly determine the active area of the worksheet, press Ctrl+End to move to the last active cell in the worksheet. The active area is the area between cell A1 and the last active cell.

Cross-Reference   If you create a workbook based on a template, the template may contain different default print settings. Templates are discussed in Chapter 6.

Adjusting Your Print Settings for Better Results

Although simply clicking the Print button may produce acceptable results in many cases, you'll probably find that a little tweaking of the print settings can often improve your printer reports.

You adjust Excel's various print settings in two different dialog boxes:

✦ The Print dialog box (accessed either by the File ➪ Print command or by pressing Ctrl+P).

✦ The Page Setup dialog box (accessed by the File ➪ Page Setup command). This is a tabbed dialog box with four tabs.

Both of these dialog boxes have a Preview button that previews the printed output onscreen.

Cross-Reference   See "Previewing Reports Before Printing" later in this chapter for more information on using the print preview feature.

Adjusting the settings in the Print dialog box

You use the Print dialog box to select which printer you wish to use, to choose what part of the worksheet you want to print, to specify the number of copies you want, and to access the properties settings for your printer. After you select your print settings, click OK from the Print dialog box to print your work.

Tip
Clicking OK in the Print dialog box without adjusting any settings is the equivalent of clicking Excel's Print button.

Figure 3-1 shows the Print dialog box; the following sections describe the settings in this dialog box.

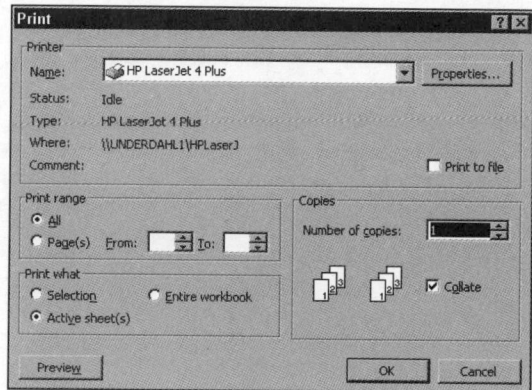

Figure 3-1: Use the Print dialog box to select a printer or choose what will print.

Choosing your printer

The Printer section of the Print dialog box enables you to choose which printer you wish to use as well as to access the settings that are specific to the selected printer.

Before printing, it's a good idea to make sure that you have selected the correct printer (applicable only if you have access to more than one printer). You can select the printer from the Name drop-down list. This section of the dialog box also lists information about the selected printer, such as its status and where it's connected.

Note
If you want to adjust the printer's settings, click the Properties button to display a property box for the selected printer. The exact dialog box that you see depends on the printer. The Properties dialog box lets you adjust printer-specific settings such as the print quality and the paper source. In most cases, you won't have to change any of these settings, but you should be familiar with the settings that you can change.

After you print a worksheet, Excel displays dashed lines to indicate where the page breaks occur. This is a useful feature, because the display adjusts dynamically. For example, if you find that your printed output is too wide to fit on a single page, you can adjust the column widths (keeping an eye on the page-break display) until they are narrow enough to print on one page.

Using a Printer You Don't Have

If you need to print a report on a printer that is not currently attached to your PC or which is unavailable on your network, you can send the report to a print file. You will need to make certain that you have installed the correct printer drivers for the printer, which you do by using the Add Printer icon in the Printers folder (click the Windows Start button and choose Settings ⇨ Printers to open this folder).

When you check the Print to file check box, Excel stores the output in a file, prompting you for a filename before printing. The resulting file will not be a standard text file. Rather, it will include all the printer codes that are required to print your worksheet. You can save the file and then send this file to your printer at a later time. This technique is also useful if you want to e-mail a print file to someone so that they can print the report on their printer—even if they don't have Excel on their PC.

To actually use the print file, you need to copy the file to the printer at the command prompt. The following is an example of the command you would use (assuming that you saved the file to drive A: using the name Report.prn and that your printer is connected directly to your PC on printer port 1):

```
COPY  A:\REPORT.PRN  /B  PRN
```

Tip   If you don't want to see the page breaks displayed in your worksheet, use Tools ⇨ Options to open the Options dialog box, click the View tab, and remove the check mark from the Page Breaks check box.

Specifying what you want to print

Sometimes you may only want to print a part of the worksheet rather than the entire active area. Or you may want to reprint selected pages of a report without printing all of the pages. You can make both of these types of selections in the Print dialog box, too.

The Print What section of the Print dialog box lets you specify what to print. You have three options:

- ✦ **Selection:** Prints only the range that you selected before issuing the File ⇨ Print command.

- ✦ **Active sheet(s):** Prints the active sheet or sheets that you selected (this is the default). You can select multiple sheets by pressing Ctrl and clicking the sheet tabs. If you select multiple sheets, Excel begins printing each sheet on a new page.

- ✦ **Entire workbook:** Prints the entire workbook, including chart sheets.

You can also select File ⇨ Print Area ⇨ Set Print Area to specify the range or ranges to print. Before you choose this command, select the range or ranges that you want to print. To clear the print area, select File ⇨ Print Area ⇨ Clear Print Area.

If your printed output uses multiple pages, you can select which pages to print by indicating the number of the first and last pages to print in the Print Range section. You can either use the spinner controls or type the page numbers in the edit boxes.

To check the printer properties before you print a long report, you may want to use the Print Range selection to specify a single page. That way you'll be able to see the actual printer output without wasting a lot of test sheets.

Printing multiple copies of a report

If you need to print multiple copies of a report, it's far easier to issue the print command one time and let your PC make certain you get the correct number of copies.

To select the number of copies to print, use the Number of copies spin control. Simply enter the number of copies you want and then click OK to print them.

If you are printing multiple copies of a report, make certain that the Collate check box is selected. If you choose this option, Excel prints the pages in order for each set of output. If you're printing only one page, Excel ignores the Collate setting.

Many printers — especially laser printers — allow your PC to specify the number of copies to print rather than requiring your PC to send the same print job multiple times. Needless to say, this is far more efficient and enables you to do other things with your PC while the printer is managing the print job.

Adjusting the Page Setup settings

For more control over how your reports print, you may need to adjust the settings that are found in the Page Setup dialog box. Using the Page Setup dialog box, you can control page layout settings, adjust the margins, create headers and footers, and adjust several worksheet appearance settings. Choose File ⇨ Page Setup to open the Page Setup dialog box; Figure 3-2 shows the Page tab of the Page Setup dialog box.

Selecting your page appearance settings

You use the Page tab of the Page Setup dialog box to control several options that can greatly affect the appearance of your printed report. The Page tab options enable you to control these settings:

✦ **Orientation:** Choose either Portrait (tall pages) or Landscape (wide pages). Landscape orientation is useful when you have a wide range that doesn't fit on a vertically oriented page.

✦ **Scaling:** You can set a scaling factor manually or let Excel scale the output automatically to fit on the number of pages that you specify. Scaling can range from 10 percent to 400 percent of normal size. If you want to return to normal scaling, enter 100 in the box labeled % normal size.

Tip

If your report is just a little too large and spills over onto extra pages, you can shrink the printout just enough to fit the desired number of pages by using the option labeled Fit to.

✦ **Paper size:** This setting enables you to select the paper size that you're using. Click the box and see the choices. Remember, though, that you must also load the selected size of paper into your printer.

✦ **Print quality:** If the installed printer supports it, you can change the printer's resolution, which is expressed in dots per inch (dpi). Higher numbers (resolutions) represent better print quality, but higher resolutions may take longer to print.

✦ **First page number:** You can specify a page number for the first page. This is useful if the pages that you're printing will be part of a larger document and you want the page numbering to be consecutive. Use Auto if you want the beginning page number to be 1 or to correspond to the pages that you selected in the Print dialog box. If you're not printing page numbers in your header or footer, this setting is irrelevant.

Tip

The Options button opens the Properties dialog box for your printer so that you can adjust the printer settings. If you selected a nonstandard paper size, you may be able to use this dialog box to specify an alternate paper tray if your printer supports this feature.

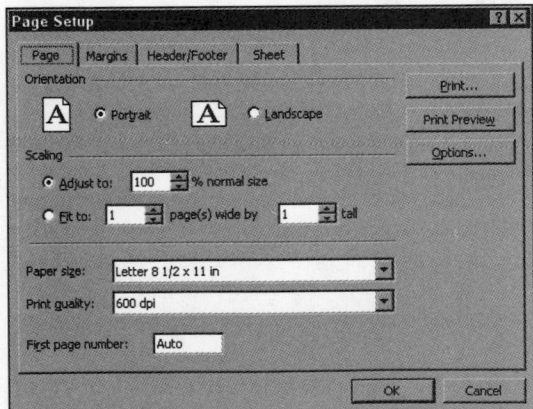

Figure 3-2: Use the Page Setup dialog box to choose a number of important appearance options.

Adjusting the report margins

Margins are the unprinted areas along the sides, top, and bottom of a printed page. You can control all four page margins from the Margins tab of the Page Setup dialog box, shown in Figure 3-3. (See the "Changing print settings while previewing" section later in this chapter where we discuss how to view and edit page breaks in Print Preview.)

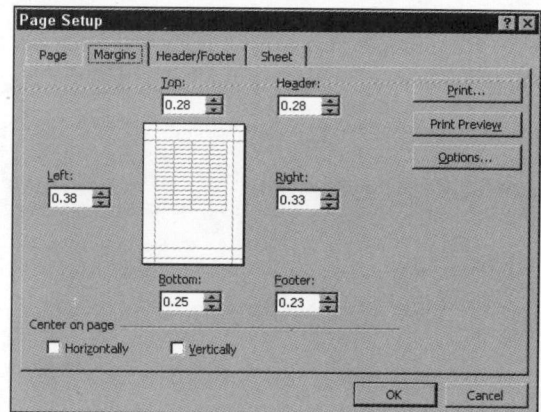

Figure 3-3: Use the Margins tab to control the amount of unprinted area around your report.

To change a margin, click the appropriate spinner (or you can enter a value directly).

Note The Preview box in the center of the dialog box is a bit deceiving, because it doesn't really show you how your changes look in relation to the page; rather, it displays a darker line to let you know which margin you're adjusting.

Caution Most printers cannot print to the very edge of the paper. If you specify a print margin that is too small for your printer, it's likely that some of the text in your report will simply not appear in the printout.

In addition to the page margins, you can adjust the distance of the header from the top of the page and the distance of the footer from the bottom of the page. These settings should be less than the corresponding margin; otherwise, the header or footer may overlap with the printed output.

Normally, Excel aligns the printed page at the top and left margins. If you would like the output to be centered vertically or horizontally, check the appropriate check box in the section of this tab labeled Center on page.

Cross-Reference You also can change the margins while you're previewing your output — ideal for last-minute adjustments before printing. Previewing is explained later in this chapter.

Adding a header or footer to your reports

A header is a line of information that appears at the top of each printed page. A footer is a line of information that appears at the bottom of each printed page. You can align information in headers and footers at the left margin, in the center of the header or footer, and at the right margin. For example, you can create a header that prints your name at the left margin, the worksheet name centered in the header, and the page number at the right margin. By default, new workbooks do not have any headers or footers.

The Header/Footer tab of the Page Setup dialog box appears in Figure 3-4. This dialog box displays the current header and footer and gives you other header and footer options in the drop-down lists labeled Header and Footer.

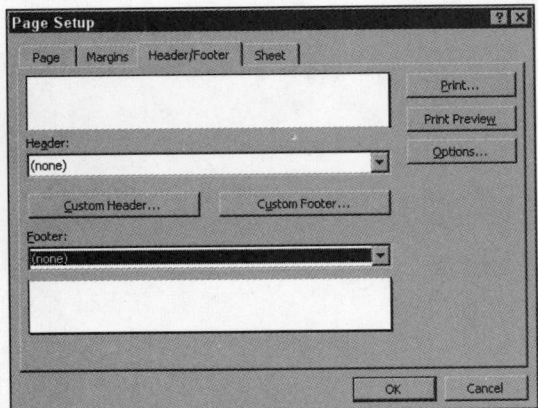

Figure 3-4: Use the Header/Footer tab to add headers or footers to your report.

When you click the Header (or Footer) drop-down list, Excel displays a list of predefined headers (or footers). If you see one that you like, select it. You then can see how it looks in the sample header or footer area. If you don't want a header or footer, choose the option labeled (none) for both the Header and Footer drop-down list boxes.

If you don't find a predefined header or footer that is exactly what you want, you can define a custom header or footer. Click the Custom Header or Custom Footer button, and Excel displays a dialog box like the one shown in Figure 3-5.

This dialog box enables you to enter text or codes in each of the three sections. To enter text, just click in the section and enter the text. To enter variable information, such as the current date or the page number, you can click one of the buttons. Clicking the button inserts a special code. The buttons and their functions are listed in Table 3-1.

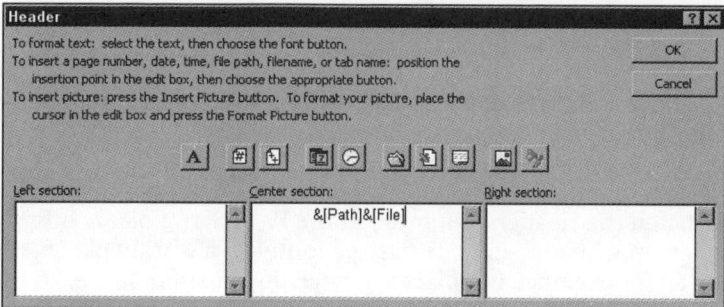

Figure 3-5: If none of the predefined headers or footers is satisfactory, you can define a custom header or custom footer.

Table 3-1
Custom Header/Footer Buttons and Their Functions

Button	Code	Function
Font	Not applicable	Lets you choose a font for the selected text
Page Number	&[Page]	Inserts the page number
Total Pages	&[Pages]	Inserts the total number of pages to be printed
Date	&[Date]	Inserts the current date
Time	&[Time]	Inserts the current time
Path and filename	&[Path]&[File]	Inserts the workbook's complete path and filename
File	&[File]	Inserts the workbook name
Sheet	&[Tab]	Inserts the sheet's name
Insert Picture	Not applicable	Enables you to add a picture
Format Picture	Not applicable	Enables you to change the picture's settings

You can combine text and codes and insert as many codes as you like into each section. If the text that you enter uses an ampersand (&), you must enter the ampersand twice (because Excel uses an ampersand to signal a code). For example, to enter the text Research & Development into a section of a header or footer, enter Research && Development.

You also can use different fonts and sizes in your headers and footers. Just select the text that you want to change and then click the Font button. Excel displays its

Fonts dialog box so that you can make your choice. If you don't change the font, Excel uses the font defined for the Normal style.

Tip   You can use as many lines as you like. Use Alt+Enter to force a line break for multiline headers or footers.

After you define a custom header or footer, it appears at the bottom of the appropriate drop-down list on the Header/Footer tab of the Page Setup dialog box. You can have only one custom header and one custom footer in a workbook. So, if you edit a custom header, for example, it replaces the existing custom header in the drop-down list.

Unfortunately, you can't print the contents of a specific cell in a header or footer. For example, you might want Excel to use the contents of cell A1 as part of a header. To do so, you need to enter the cell's contents manually — or write a macro to perform this operation.

Setting the sheet printing options

The Sheet tab of the Page Setup dialog box (shown in Figure 3-6) contains several additional options. Each option is described in the sections that follow.

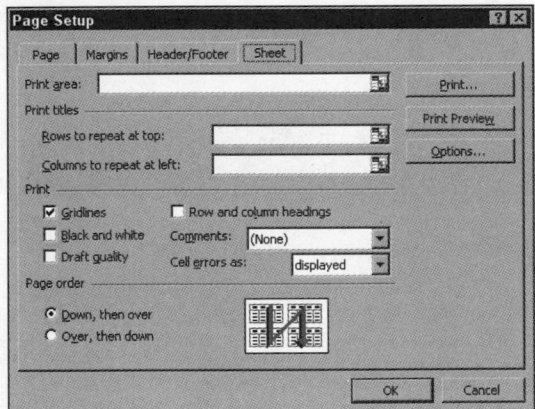

Figure 3-6: Use the Sheet tab to select the final page setup options.

Choosing the print area

The Print area box lists the range defined as the print area. If you select a range of cells and choose the Selection option in the Print dialog box, the selected range address appears in this box. Excel also defines this as the reference for the Print_Area name.

If the Print area box is blank, Excel prints the entire worksheet. You can activate this box and select a range (Excel will modify its definition of Print_Area), or you can enter a previously defined range name into the box.

Printing row and column titles

If your worksheet is set up with titles in the first row and descriptive names in the first column, it can be difficult to understand data that appears on printed pages where those titles do not appear. To resolve this problem you can choose to print selected rows or columns as titles on each page of the printout.

Row and column titles serve pretty much the same purpose on a printout as frozen panes do in navigating within a worksheet. See Chapter 2 for more information on freezing panes.

Don't confuse print titles with headers; these are two different concepts. Headers appear at the top of each page and contain information such as the worksheet name, date, or page number. Print titles describe the data being printed, such as field names in a database table or list.

You can specify particular rows to repeat at the top of every printed page, or particular columns to repeat at the left of every printed page. To do so, just activate the appropriate box and select the rows or columns in the worksheet. Or, you can enter these references manually. For example, to specify rows 1 and 2 as repeating rows, enter 1:2.

In the old days, users often were surprised to discover that print titles appeared twice on the first page of their printouts. This occurred because they defined a print area that included the print titles. Excel now handles this automatically, however, and doesn't print titles twice if they are part of the print area.

You can specify different print titles for each worksheet in the workbook. Excel remembers print titles by creating sheet-level names (Print_Titles).

Choosing optional elements in the printout

The section labeled Print contains several options:

✦ **Gridlines:** If checked, Excel prints the gridlines to delineate cells. If you turn off the gridline display in the worksheet (in the View tab of the Options dialog box), Excel automatically removes the check from this box for you. In other words, the default setting for this option is determined by the gridline display in your worksheet.

✦ **Black and white:** If checked, Excel ignores any colors in the worksheet and prints everything in black and white. By taking advantage of this option, you can format your worksheet for viewing on your monitor and still get readable print output.

✦ **Draft quality:** If checked, Excel prints in draft mode. In draft mode, Excel doesn't print embedded charts or drawing objects, cell gridlines, or borders, which reduces the printing time.

✦ **Row and column headings:** If checked, Excel prints the row and column headings on the printout, enabling you to identify easily specific cells from a printout.

✦ **Comments:** Excel prints cell notes by using the option that you specify: None, At the end of the sheet, or As displayed on sheet.

✦ **Cell errors as:** Excel prints errors that appear in the cells option that you choose from the drop-down list. This can be useful if you want to print a copy of a worksheet but don't want any errors to stand out in the printout.

Selecting the page printing order

The final option on the Sheet tab specifies how Excel should print the pages if the printout won't fit on a single page. You can choose to print the pages top to bottom or side to side.

Cross-Reference See "Selecting Your Page Appearance Settings" earlier in this chapter for information on shrinking the printout to fit on fewer pages.

Controlling where pages break in your printouts

If you print lengthy reports, you know that it's often important to control the page breaks. For example, you normally wouldn't want a row to print on a page by itself. Fortunately, Excel gives you superb control of page breaks.

As you may have discovered, Excel handles page breaks automatically. After you print or preview your worksheet, it even displays dashed lines to indicate where page breaks occur. Sometimes, however, you'll want to force a page break—either a vertical or a horizontal one—so that the report prints the way you want it to. For example, if your worksheet consists of several distinct areas, you may want to print each area on a separate sheet of paper.

Forcing a page break to appear where you want it

To insert a horizontal page break line, move the cell pointer to the cell that will begin the new page, but make sure that you place the pointer in column A; otherwise, you'll insert a vertical page break *and* a horizontal page break. For example, if you want row 14 to be the first row of a new page, select cell A14. Then, choose Insert ➪ Page Break. Excel displays a dashed line to indicate the page break.

To insert a vertical page break line, move the cell pointer to the cell that will begin the new page, but in this case, make sure that you place the pointer in row one. Select Insert ➪ Page Break to create the page break.

Removing page breaks you've added

To remove a manual page break, move the cell pointer to the first row beneath (or the first column to the right) of the manual page break and then select Insert ➪ Remove Page Break (this command appears only when you place the cell pointer adjacent to a manual page break).

Tip

To remove all manual page breaks in the worksheet, click the Select All button (or press Ctrl+A), and then choose Insert ➪ Remove Page Break.

Cross-Reference

See "Previewing Reports Before Printing" later in this chapter to see how to get an overview of the page breaks in the worksheet.

Preventing certain cells from appearing in print

If have a worksheet that contains confidential information, you may want to print the worksheet, but not the confidential parts. There are several techniques that you can use to prevent certain parts of a worksheet from printing:

✦ When you hide rows or columns, the hidden rows aren't printed.

✦ You can effectively hide cells or ranges by making the text color the same color as the background color.

✦ You can hide cells by using a custom number format that consists of three semicolons (;;;).

✦ You can mask off a confidential area of a worksheet by covering it with a rectangle object. Click the Rectangle tool on the Drawing toolbar and drag the rectangle to the proper size. For best results, you can make the rectangle white with no border.

Cross-Reference

If you find that you must regularly hide data before you print certain reports, consider using the custom views feature to create a named view that doesn't show the confidential information. See "Creating Custom Views of Your Worksheet" later in this chapter for more information.

Previewing Reports Before Printing

When you're creating a report, it's not necessary to waste a lot of time and printing supplies to fine-tune all of the print settings. It's far better to use Excel's print preview feature to display an image of the printed output on your screen. This is a handy feature that enables you to see the result of the options that you set, before you actually send the job to the printer.

Viewing the print preview

Several ways exist to preview your document:

✦ Select the File ➪ Print Preview command.

✦ Click the Print Preview button on the Standard toolbar. Or, you can press Shift and click the Print button on the Standard toolbar (the Print button serves a dual purpose).

✦ Click the Preview button in the Print dialog box.

✦ Click the Print Preview button in the Page Setup dialog box.

Any one of these methods changes Excel's window to a preview window, similar to that shown in Figure 3-7.

The preview window has several buttons along the top that you can use to control the process:

✦ **Next:** Displays an image of the next page.

✦ **Previous:** Displays an image of the previous page.

✦ **Zoom:** Zooms the display in or out. This button toggles between the two levels of zooming that are available. You also can simply click the preview image to toggle between zoom modes.

✦ **Print:** Sends the job to the printer.

✦ **Setup:** Displays the Page Setup dialog box, so that you can adjust some settings. When you close the dialog box, you return to the preview screen, so that you can see the effects of your changes.

✦ **Margins:** Displays adjustable columns and margins, which are described in the next section.

✦ **Page Break Preview:** Displays the worksheet in Page Break Preview mode.

✦ **Close:** Closes the preview window.

✦ **Help:** Displays help for the preview window.

Changing print settings while previewing

If you discover that the print preview window points out potential problems with your printed report, you can make some changes directly in the print preview window. That way, you'll be able to see the effect of those changes.

When you click the Margins button in the preview window, Excel adds markers to the preview that indicate column borders and margins (see Figure 3-8). You can drag the column or margin markers to make changes that appear onscreen.

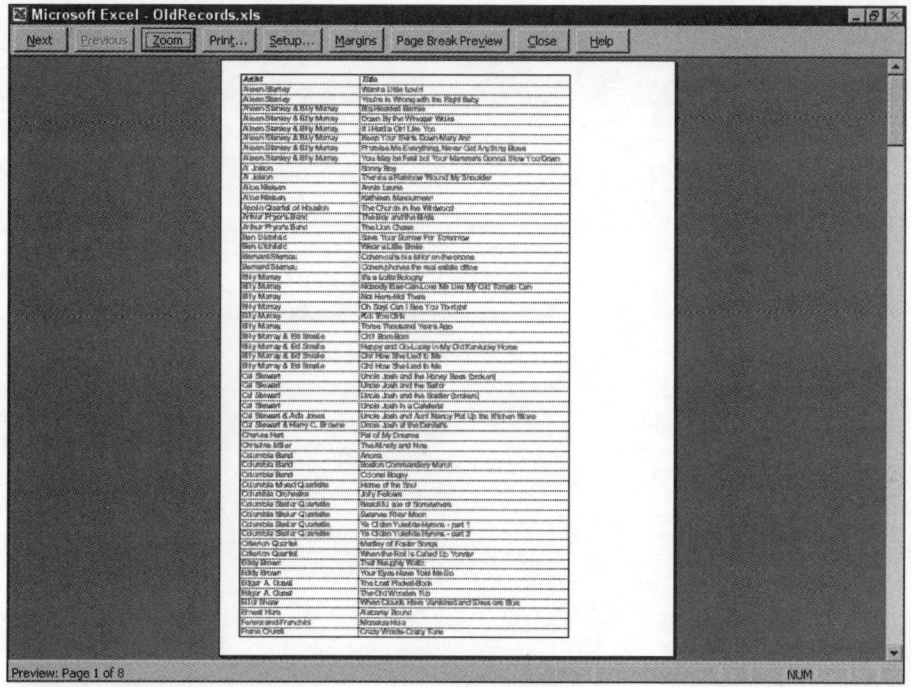

Figure 3-7: Use the Print Preview command to save paper by previewing the printed output.

For example, if you print a worksheet and discover that Excel is printing the last column on a second page, you can adjust the column widths or margins in the preview window to force all the columns to print on a single page. After you drag one of these markers, Excel updates the display so that you can see what effect it had.

When you make changes to the column widths in the preview window, these changes also are made in your worksheet. Similarly, changing the margins in the preview window changes the settings that appear in the Margins tab of the Page Setup dialog box.

Viewing the page break overview

The print preview window shows you how the individual pages of the report will appear, but it can be a little difficult to visualize just how the overall print job will break down into pages. For this overview, you might want to view your worksheets in Page Break Preview mode.

To enter Page Break Preview mode, choose the View ➪ Page Break Preview command or click the Page Break Preview button in the print preview window. The worksheet display changes, and you can see exactly what will be printed and where the page breaks occur as shown in Figure 3-9.

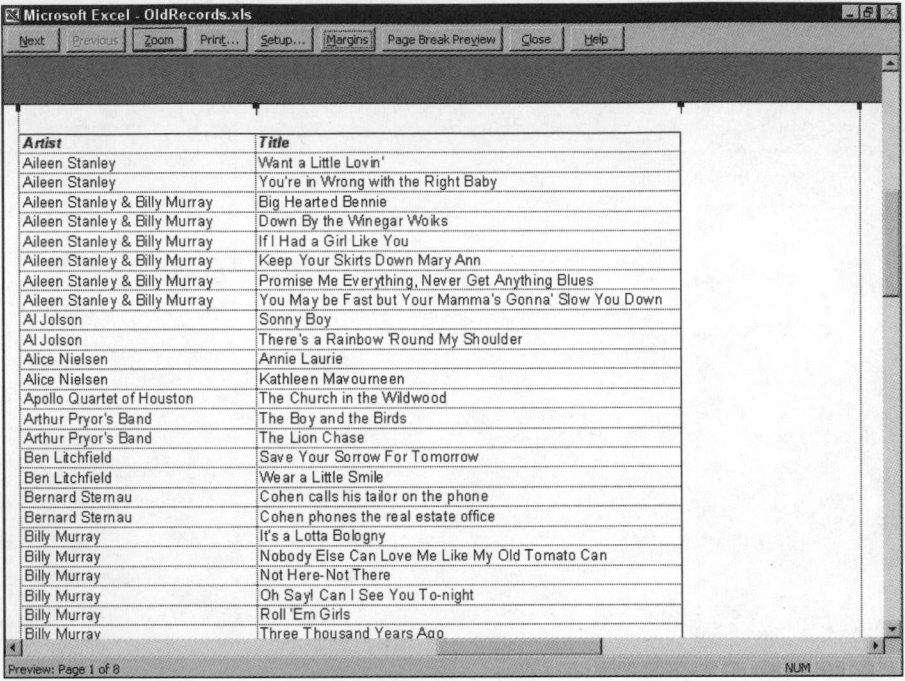

Figure 3-8: You can adjust column widths or margins directly from the print preview window (the window is zoomed in to better show the markers).

When you enter Page Break Preview mode, Excel

✦ Changes the zoom factor so that you can see more of the worksheet

✦ Displays the page numbers overlaid on the pages

✦ Displays the current print range with a white background; nonprinting data appears with a gray background

✦ Displays all page breaks

When you're in Page Break Preview mode, you can drag the borders to change the print range or the page breaks. When you change the page breaks, Excel automatically adjusts the scaling so that the information fits on the pages, per your specifications.

Tip   In Page Break Preview mode, you still have access to all of Excel's commands. You can change the zoom factor if you find the text to be too small.

To return to normal viewing, select the View ➪ Normal command.

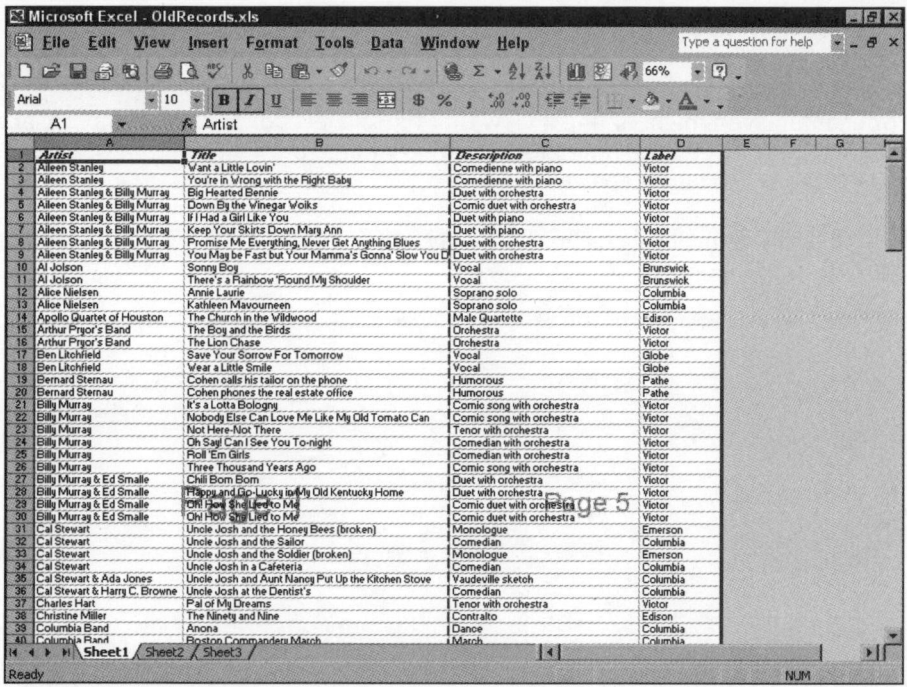

Figure 3-9: Page Break Preview mode gives you a bird's-eye view of your worksheet and shows exactly where the page breaks occur.

Creating custom views of your worksheet

If you need to create several different reports from the same Excel workbook, you may find that setting up the specific settings for a report can be a tedious project. An excellent way to simplify the process is to create custom-named views of your worksheets that include the proper settings for each report.

The custom views feature enables you to give names to various views of your worksheet, and you can quickly switch among these named views. A view includes settings for the following:

✦ Print settings, as specified in the Page Setup dialog box (optional)

✦ Hidden rows and columns (optional)

✦ Display settings, as specified in the Options Display dialog box

✦ Selected cells and ranges

✦ The active cell

✦ Window sizes and positions

✦ Frozen panes

For example, you might define a view that hides a few columns of numbers, another view with a print range defined as a summary range only, another view with the page setup set to landscape, and so on.

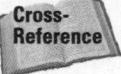

Cross-Reference To learn more about creating custom views, see Chapter 2.

✦   ✦   ✦

Working with Cell Ranges

As you use Excel worksheets, you must deal with cells
and ranges virtually constantly. Understanding how
best to manipulate cells and ranges will save you time and
effort. This chapter discusses a variety of techniques that you
can use to work with cells and ranges.

Understanding Excel's Cells and Ranges

A cell is a single element in a worksheet that can hold a value,
text, or a formula. A cell is identified by its address, which
consists of its column letter and row number. For example,
cell D12 is the cell in the fourth column and the twelfth row.

A group of cells is called a range. You designate a range
address by specifying its upper-left cell address and its lower-
right cell address, separated by a colon.

Here are some examples of range addresses:

C24	A range that consists of a single cell
A1:B1	Two cells that occupy one row and two columns
A1:A100	100 cells in column A
A1:D4	16 cells (four rows by four columns)
C1:C65536	An entire column of cells; this range also can be expressed as C:C
A6:IV6	An entire row of cells; this range also can be expressed as 6:6
A1:IV65536	All cells in a worksheet

Excel's Alternate Cell Address Notation

Typically, you reference cells by their column letter and row number (cell D16, for example). However, Excel gives you a choice in this matter. You can select Tools ➪ Options (General tab) and then choose the R1C1 reference style option. After selecting this option, the column borders in your worksheets are displayed as numbers rather than letters. Furthermore, all cell references in your formulas use this different notation.

The numbers in the brackets refer to the relative position of the reference. For example, R[–5]C[–3] specifies the cell that's five rows above and three columns to the left. On the other hand, R[5]C[3] references the cell that's five rows below and three columns to the right. If the brackets are omitted, it specifies the same row or column: R[5]C refers to the cell five rows below in the same column.

Selecting ranges

To perform an operation on a range of cells in a worksheet, you must select the range of cells first. For example, if you want to make the text bold for a range of cells, you must select the range and then click the Bold button on the Formatting toolbar (or, use any of several other methods to make the text bold).

When you select a range, the cells appear highlighted in light gray. The exception is the active cell, which remains its normal color. Figure 4-1 is an example of a selected range in a worksheet.

You can select a range in several ways:

✦ Use the mouse to drag, highlighting the range. If you drag to the end of the screen, the worksheet will scroll.

✦ Press the Shift key while you use the direction keys to select a range.

✦ Press F8 and then move the cell pointer with the direction keys to highlight the range. Press F8 again to return the direction keys to normal movement.

✦ Use the Edit ➪ Go To command (or press F5) and enter a range's address manually into the Go To dialog box. When you click OK, Excel selects the cells in the range that you specified.

Tip   As you're selecting a range, Excel displays the number of rows and columns in your selection in the Name box (located on the left side of the formula bar). As soon as you finish the selection the Name box reverts to showing the address of the active cell.

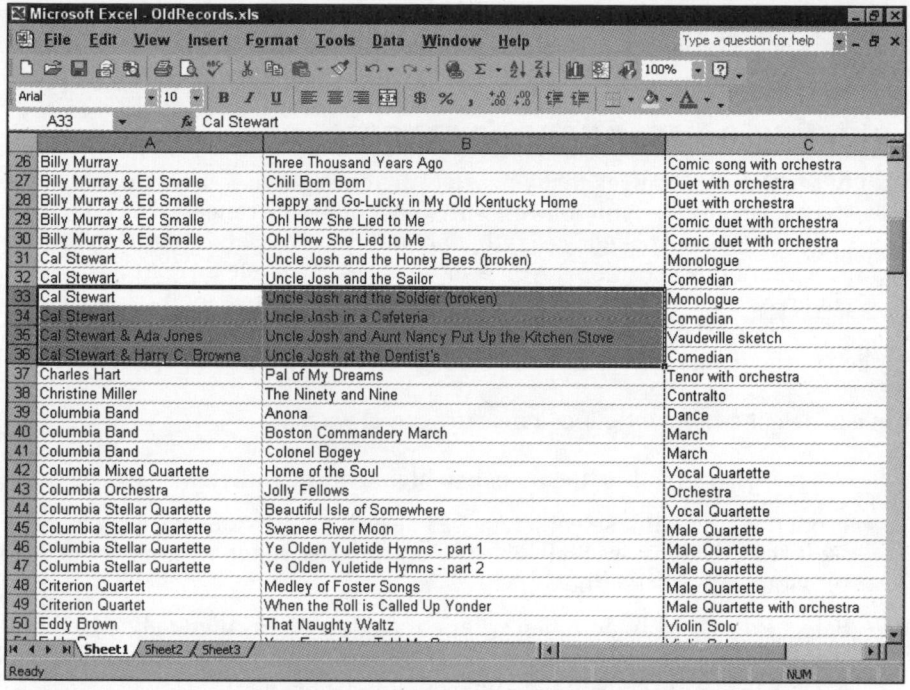

Figure 4-1: When you select a range, it appears highlighted, but the active cell within the range is not highlighted.

Selecting complete rows and columns

In addition to selecting a limited range of cells, you may have occasion to select an entire row or column. For example, you may want to apply the same numeric format or the same alignment options to an entire row or column. You can select entire rows and columns in much the same manner as you select ranges, as follows:

✦ Click the row or column border to select a single row or column.

✦ To select multiple adjacent rows or columns, click a row or column border and drag to highlight additional rows or columns.

✦ To select multiple (nonadjacent) rows or columns, press Ctrl while you click the rows or columns that you want.

✦ Press Ctrl+spacebar to select a column. The column of the active cell (or columns of the selected cells) is highlighted.

✦ Press Shift+spacebar to select a row. The row of the active cell (or rows of the selected cells) is highlighted.

Press Ctrl+A to select all cells in the worksheet, which is the same as selecting all rows and all columns.

Selecting noncontiguous ranges

Most of the time, the ranges that you select are contiguous — a single rectangle of cells. Excel also enables you to work with noncontiguous ranges, which consist of two or more ranges (or single cells) that are not next to each other. This is also known as a multiple selection. If you want to apply the same formatting to cells in different areas of your worksheet, one approach is to make a multiple selection. When the appropriate cells or ranges are selected, the formatting that you select is applied to them all. Figure 4-2 shows a noncontiguous range selected in a worksheet.

You can select a noncontiguous range in several ways:

✦ Press Ctrl as you drag the mouse to highlight the individual cells or ranges.

✦ From the keyboard, select a range as described previously (using F8 or the Shift key). Then press Shift+F8 to select another range without canceling the previous range selections.

✦ Select Edit ➪ Go To and then enter a range's address manually into the Go To dialog box. Separate the different ranges with commas. When you click OK, Excel selects the cells in the ranges that you specified.

Noncontiguous ranges differ from contiguous ranges in several important ways. One obvious difference is that you cannot use drag-and-drop methods to move or copy noncontiguous ranges.

Selecting multisheet ranges

In addition to two-dimensional ranges on a single worksheet, ranges can extend across multiple worksheets to be three-dimensional ranges.

Suppose that you have a workbook set up to track expenses by department. A common approach is to use a separate worksheet for each department, making it easy to organize the data. You can click a sheet tab to view the information for a particular department.

Figure 4-3 shows a workbook that has four sheets, named Totals, Marketing, Operations, and Manufacturing. The sheets are laid out identically. The only difference is the values. The Totals sheet contains formulas that compute the sum of the corresponding items in the three departmental worksheets.

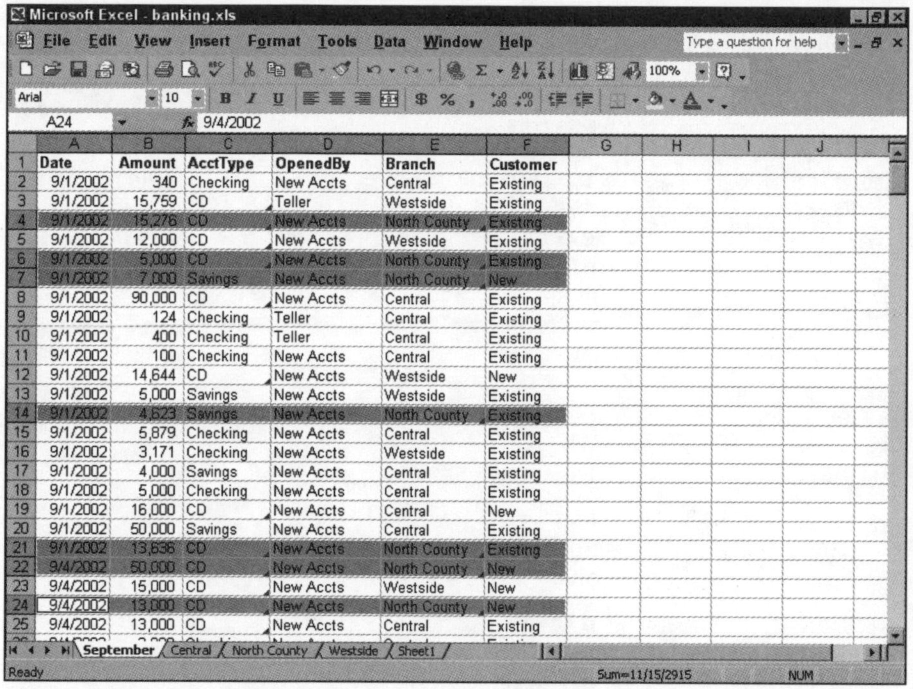

	A	B	C	D	E	F
1	Date	Amount	AcctType	OpenedBy	Branch	Customer
2	9/1/2002	340	Checking	New Accts	Central	Existing
3	9/1/2002	15,759	CD	Teller	Westside	Existing
4	9/1/2002	15,276	CD	New Accts	North County	Existing
5	9/1/2002	12,000	CD	New Accts	Westside	Existing
6	9/1/2002	5,000	CD	New Accts	North County	Existing
7	9/1/2002	7,000	Savings	New Accts	North County	New
8	9/1/2002	90,000	CD	New Accts	Central	Existing
9	9/1/2002	124	Checking	Teller	Central	Existing
10	9/1/2002	400	Checking	Teller	Central	Existing
11	9/1/2002	100	Checking	New Accts	Central	Existing
12	9/1/2002	14,644	CD	New Accts	Westside	New
13	9/1/2002	5,000	Savings	New Accts	Westside	Existing
14	9/1/2002	4,623	Savings	New Accts	North County	Existing
15	9/1/2002	5,879	Checking	New Accts	Central	Existing
16	9/1/2002	3,171	Checking	New Accts	Westside	Existing
17	9/1/2002	4,000	Savings	New Accts	Central	Existing
18	9/1/2002	5,000	Checking	New Accts	Central	Existing
19	9/1/2002	16,000	CD	New Accts	Central	New
20	9/1/2002	50,000	Savings	New Accts	Central	Existing
21	9/1/2002	13,636	CD	New Accts	North County	Existing
22	9/4/2002	50,000	CD	New Accts	North County	New
23	9/4/2002	15,000	CD	New Accts	Westside	New
24	9/4/2002	13,000	CD	New Accts	North County	New
25	9/4/2002	13,000	CD	New Accts	Central	Existing

Figure 4-2: Excel enables you to select noncontiguous ranges, as shown here.

The worksheets in the Department Budget Summary workbook aren't formatted in any way. If you want to apply number formats, for example, one (not so efficient) approach is simply to format the values in each worksheet separately. A better technique is to select a multisheet range and format the cells in all the sheets simultaneously. The following is a step-by-step example of multisheet formatting, using the workbook shown in Figure 4-3.

1. Activate the Totals worksheet.
2. Select the range B2:F6.
3. Press Shift and click the sheet tab labeled Manufacturing. This selects all worksheets between the active worksheet (Totals) and the sheet tab that you click—in essence, a three-dimensional range of cells (see Figure 4-4). Notice that the workbook window's title bar displays [Group]. This is a reminder that you've selected a group of sheets and that you're in Group edit mode.
4. Click the Comma Style button on the Formatting toolbar. This applies comma formatting to the selected cells.
5. Click one of the other sheet tabs. This selects the sheet and also cancels Group mode; [Group] is no longer displayed in the title bar.

Microsoft Excel - Department Budget Summary.xls

File   Edit   View   Insert   Format   Tools   Data   Window   Help

B2   135000

	A	B	C	D	E	F	G	H	I	J	K
1		Quarter 1	Quarter 2	Quarter 3	Quarter 4	Year Total					
2	Salaries	135000	139050	143221	147517	564788					
3	Travel	14000	14420	14852	15297	58569					
4	Supplies	5500	5665	5834	6009	23008					
5	Facility	18000	18540	19096	19668	75304					
6	Total	172500	177675	183003	188491	721669					

Totals \ Marketing / Operations / Manufacturing /

Figure 4-3: This workbook is laid out identically on each worksheet.

Excel applied comma formatting to all of the values in the selected sheets.

Tip   When a workbook is in Group mode, any changes that you make to cells in one worksheet also apply to all of the other grouped worksheets. You can use this to your advantage when you want to set up a group of identical worksheets, because any labels, data, formatting, or formulas you enter will automatically be added to the same cells in all of the grouped worksheets.

In general, selecting a multisheet range is a simple two-step process: select the range in one sheet and then select the worksheets to include in the range. To select a group of contiguous worksheets, you can press Shift and click the sheet tab of the last worksheet that you want to include in the selection. To select individual worksheets, press Ctrl and click the sheet tab of each worksheet that you want to select. If all the worksheets in a workbook aren't laid out the same, you can skip the sheets that you don't want to format. When you make the selection, the sheet tabs of the selected sheets appear in reverse video, and Excel displays [Group] in the title bar.

Tip   To select all sheets in a workbook, right-click any sheet tab and choose Select All Sheets from the shortcut menu.

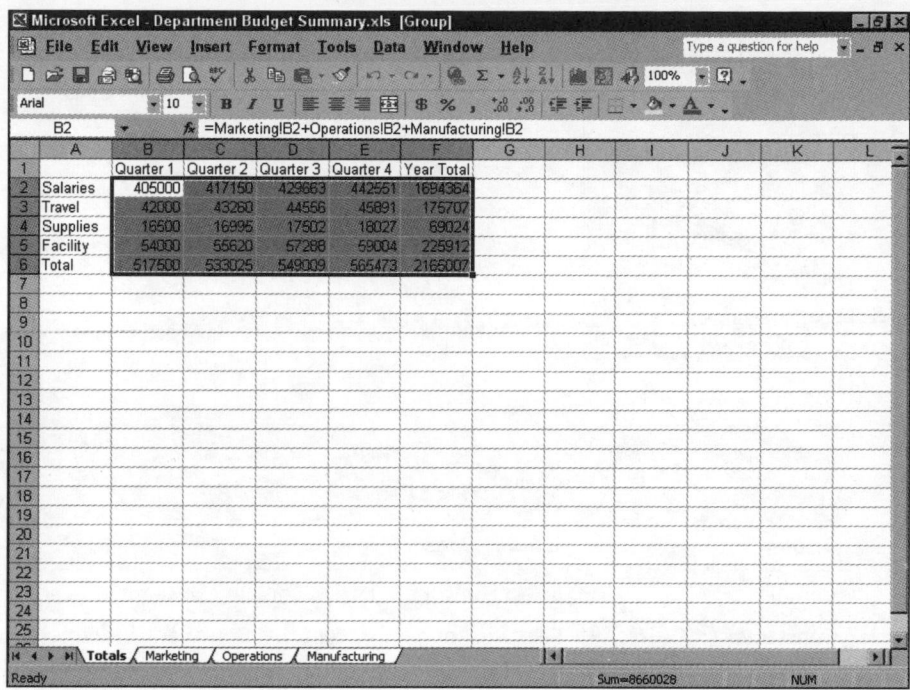

Figure 4-4: Place Excel in Group mode with a three-dimensional range of cells selected to apply the same formatting to the entire range at once.

Selecting special types of cells

As you use Excel, you'll probably find yourself wondering how you can locate specific types of cells in your worksheets. For example, wouldn't it be handy to be able to locate every cell that contains a formula, or perhaps all of the cells whose value depends on the current cell? Actually, Excel does provide an easy way to locate these and many other special types of cells. You do this by choosing Edit ➪ Go To to display the Go To dialog box and then clicking the Special button to display the Go To Special dialog box, shown in Figure 4-5.

After you make your choice in the dialog box, Excel selects the qualifying subset of cells in the current selection. Usually, this results in a multiple selection. If no cells qualify, Excel lets you know with the message No cells were found.

Tip

If you bring up the Go To Special dialog box with only one cell selected, Excel bases its selection on the entire active area of the worksheet.

Table 4-1 offers a description of the options available in the Go To Special dialog box. Some of the options are very useful.

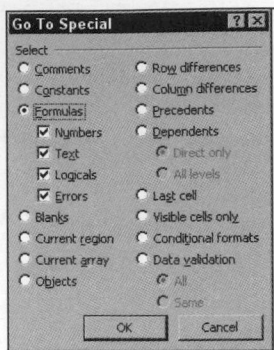

Figure 4-5: Use the Go To Special dialog box to select specific types of cells.

Table 4-1 **Select Special Options**	
Option	**What It Does**
Comments	Selects only the cells that contain cell comments.
Constants	Selects all nonempty cells that don't contain formulas. This option is useful if you have a model set up and want to clear out all input cells and enter new values. The formulas remain intact. Use the check boxes under the Formulas option to choose which cells to include.
Formulas	Selects cells that contain formulas. Qualify this by selecting the type of result: numbers, text, logical values (TRUE or FALSE), or errors.
Blanks	Selects all empty cells.
Current Region	Selects a rectangular range of cells around the active cell. This range is determined by surrounding blank rows and columns.
Current Array	Selects the entire array.
Objects	Selects all graphic objects on the worksheet.
Row Differences	Analyzes the selection and selects cells that are different from other cells in each row.
Column Differences	Analyzes the selection and selects the cells that are different from other cells in each column.
Precedents	Selects cells that are referred to in the formulas in the active cell or selection. You can select either direct precedents or precedents at any level.
Dependents	Selects cells with formulas that refer to the active cell or selection. You can select either direct dependents or dependents at any level.

Option	What It Does
Last Cell	Selects the bottom-right cell in the worksheet that contains data or formatting.
Visible Cells Only	Selects only visible cells in the selection. This option is useful when dealing with outlines or an auto-filtered list.
Conditional Formats	Selects cells that have a conditional format applied (using the Format ⇨ Conditional Formatting command).
Data Validation	Selects cells that are set up for data entry validation (using the Data ⇨ Validation command). The All option selects all such cells. The Same option selects only the cells that have the same validation rules as the active cell.

Tip

When you select an option in the Go To Special dialog box, be sure to note which suboptions become available. For example, when you select Constants, the suboptions under Formulas become available to help you further refine the results. Likewise, the suboptions under Dependents also apply to Precedents, and those under Data Validation also apply to Conditional formats.

Copying or Moving Ranges

Few worksheets are ever perfect when they are first created. You'll often find yourself copying or moving information from one place to another. Fortunately, Excel makes copying or moving ranges of cells very easy. Here are some common things you might do:

✦ Copy a cell to another cell.

✦ Copy a cell to a range of cells. The source cell is copied to every cell in the destination range.

✦ Copy a range to another range. Both ranges must be the same size.

✦ Move a range to another range.

Tip

The primary difference between copying and moving a range is the effect of the operation on the source range. When you copy a range, the source range is unaffected. When you move a range, the contents are removed from the source range.

Note

Copying a cell normally copies the cell contents, any formatting that is applied to the original cell (including conditional formatting and data validation), and the cell comment (if it has one). When you copy a cell that contains a formula, the cell references in the copied formulas are changed automatically to be relative to their new destination.

Copying or moving consists of two steps (although shortcut methods exist, as you'll see later):

1. Select the cell or range to copy (the source range) and copy it to the clipboard. To move the range instead of copying it, cut the range rather than copying it.

2. Move the cell pointer to the range that will hold the copy (the destination range) and paste the clipboard contents.

Caution   When you paste information, Excel overwrites any cells that get in the way without warning you. If you find that pasting overwrote some essential cells, choose Edit ➪ Undo (or press Ctrl+Z).

Because copying (or moving) is used so often, Excel provides many different methods. We discuss each method in the following sections. Because copying and moving are such similar operations, I'll only point out any important differences between the two.

Copying by using toolbar buttons

Clicking the Copy button transfers a copy of the selected cell or range to the Windows clipboard and the Office clipboard. After performing the copy part of this operation, select the cell that will hold the copy and click the Paste button.

Tip   If you click the Copy button more than once before you click the Paste button, Excel automatically displays the Office Clipboard toolbar.

If you're copying a range, you don't need to select an entire range before clicking the Paste button. You need only activate the upper-left cell in the destination range.

If you want to fill a range with the copied values, Excel uses the following methods to determine what to do:

✦ If you select a single cell as the destination, Excel will paste a complete copy of the range you copied into as many cells as you originally copied.

✦ If you select a destination range of more than one cell, but with fewer cells than the source range, Excel will still paste the entire range of cells you copied — even though this will extend beyond the selected destination range.

✦ If the selected destination range matches the size of the source range, it will be completely filled by the copy.

✦ Finally, if you select a destination range that is larger than the source range, Excel will repeat the source range entries as many times as necessary to fill the destination range.

Understanding the Office Clipboard

Whenever you cut or copy information from a Windows program, Windows stores the information on the Windows clipboard, which is an area of memory. Each time that you cut or copy information, Windows replaces the information previously stored on the clipboard with the new information that you cut or copied. The Windows clipboard can store data in a variety of formats. Because Windows manages information on the clipboard, it can be pasted to other Windows applications, regardless of where it originated.

Office has its own clipboard, the Office clipboard, which is available only in Office programs. Whenever you cut or copy information in an Office program, such as Excel, the program places the information on both the Windows clipboard and the Office clipboard. However, the program treats information on the Office clipboard differently than it treats information on the Windows clipboard. Instead of replacing information on the Office clipboard, the program appends the information to the Office clipboard. With multiple items stored on the clipboard, you can then paste the items either individually or as a group. You'll learn how the Office clipboard works later in this chapter.

Copying by using menu commands

If you prefer, you can use the following menu commands for copying and pasting:

✦ Edit ➪ Copy copies the selected cells to the clipboard. (Use Edit ➪ Cut to move.)

✦ Edit ➪ Paste pastes the clipboard contents to the selected cell or range.

✦ Right-click the range and select Copy (or Cut) from the shortcut menu to copy the selected cells to the clipboard.

✦ Right-click and select Paste from the shortcut menu to paste the clipboard contents to the selected cell or range.

Copying by using shortcut keys

The copy and paste operations also have shortcut keys associated with them:

✦ Ctrl+C copies the selected cells to both the Windows and Office clipboards.

✦ Ctrl+X cuts the selected cells to both the Windows and Office clipboards.

✦ Ctrl+V pastes the Windows clipboard contents to the selected cell or range.

Tip   These shortcut keys also are used by most other Windows applications.

Copying by using drag-and-drop

Excel also enables you to copy or move a cell or range by dragging. Be aware, however, that dragging and dropping does not place any information on either the Windows clipboard or the Office clipboard.

Tip   The drag-and-drop method of moving or copying does offer one big advantage over the copy and paste method — Excel warns you if a drag-and-drop operation will overwrite existing cell contents.

To copy using drag-and-drop, select the cell or range that you want to copy and then move the mouse pointer to one of its four borders. When the mouse pointer turns into an arrow pointing up and to the left, press Ctrl; the mouse pointer is augmented with a small plus sign. Then, simply drag the selection to its new location, while you continue to press the Ctrl key. The original selection remains behind, and Excel makes a new copy when you release the mouse button. To move using drag-and-drop, don't press Ctrl while dragging.

Tip   If the mouse pointer doesn't turn into an arrow when you point to the border of a cell or range, you need to make a change to your settings. Select Tools ➪ Options, click the Edit tab, and place a check mark on the option labeled Allow cell drag and drop.

Copying to adjacent cells

Often, you'll find that you need to copy a cell to an adjacent cell or range. This type of copying is quite common when working with formulas. For example, if you're working on a budget, you might create a formula to add the values in column B. You can use the same formula to add the values in the other columns. Rather than re-enter the formula, you can copy it to the adjacent cells.

Excel provides some additional options on its Edit menu for copying to adjacent cells. To use these commands, select the cell that you're copying and the cells that you are copying to (see Figure 4-6). Then, issue the appropriate command from the following list for one-step copying:

> ✦ Edit ➪ Fill ➪ Down (or Ctrl+D) copies the cell to the selected range below.
>
> ✦ Edit ➪ Fill ➪ Right (or Ctrl+R) copies the cell to the selected range to the right.
>
> ✦ Edit ➪ Fill ➪ Up copies the cell to the selected range above.
>
> ✦ Edit ➪ Fill ➪ Left copies the cell to the selected range to the left.

None of these commands places information on either the Windows clipboard or the Office clipboard.

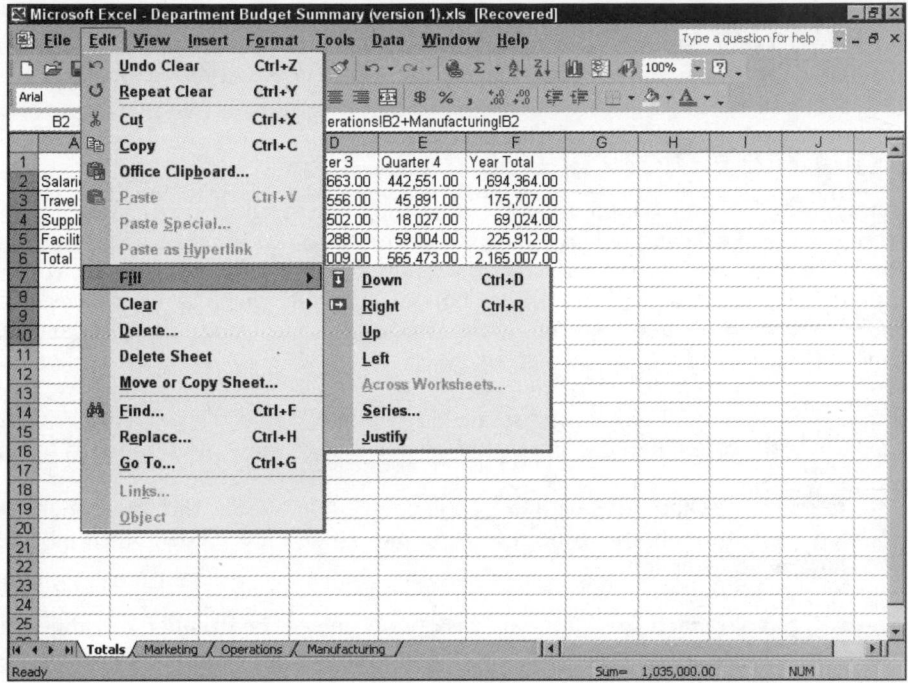

Figure 4-6: Use the Edit ➪ Fill commands to copy cell contents to adjacent cells.

Tip

You also can use AutoFill to copy to adjacent cells by dragging the selection's fill handle. Excel copies the original selection to the cells that you highlight while dragging. For more control over the AutoFill operation, drag the fill handle with the right mouse button. AutoFill doesn't place any information on either the Windows clipboard or the Office clipboard.

Copying a range to other sheets

The copy procedures described previously also work to copy a cell or range to another worksheet, even if the worksheet is in a different workbook. You must, of course, activate the other worksheet before you select the location to which you want to copy.

Excel offers a quicker way to copy a cell or range and paste it to other worksheets in the same workbook. Start by selecting the range to copy. Then, press Ctrl and click the sheet tabs for the worksheets to which you want to copy the information (Excel displays [Group] in the workbook's title bar). Select Edit ➪ Fill ➪ Across Worksheets, and a dialog box appears that asks what you want to copy (All, Contents, or Formats). Make your choice and then click OK. Excel copies the selected range to the selected worksheets; the new copy will occupy the same cells in the selected worksheets as the original occupies in the initial worksheet.

Caution Be careful with the Edit ⇨ Fill ⇨ Across Worksheets command, because Excel doesn't warn you if the destination cells contain information. You can quickly overwrite lots of information with this command and not even realize it.

Using the Office clipboard to paste

As mentioned earlier, whenever you cut or copy information in an Office program, such as Excel, you can place the information on both the Windows clipboard and the Office clipboard. When you copy information to the Office clipboard, you append the information to the Office clipboard instead of replacing what is already there. With multiple items stored on the Office clipboard, you can then paste the items either individually or as a group.

To use the Office Clipboard, you first need to open it. Select View ⇨ Task Pane to open the task pane. Then use the task pane selector to view the Clipboard task pane.

Tip To make the Office Clipboard task pane open automatically, click the Options button near the bottom of the task pane and choose the Show Office Clipboard Automatically option.

After you have opened the Clipboard task pane, select the first cell or range that you want to copy to the Office clipboard and copy it by using any of the techniques described earlier. Repeat this process, selecting the next cell or range that you want to copy. As soon as you copy the information, the Office clipboard task pane shows you the number of items that you've copied and a brief description (see Figure 4-7). The Office clipboard will hold up to 24 items.

When you're ready to paste information, select the cell into which you want to paste information. To paste an individual item, click it in the Clipboard task pane. To paste all the items that you've copied, click the Paste All button.

You can clear the contents of the Office clipboard by clicking the Clear All button.

The following items about the Office clipboard and its functioning are worth special noting:

✦ Excel pastes the contents of the Windows clipboard when you paste either by clicking the Paste tool on the Standard toolbar, by choosing Edit ⇨ Paste, by pressing Ctrl+V, or by right-clicking to choose Paste from the shortcut menu.

✦ The last item that you cut or copied appears on both the Office clipboard and the Windows clipboard.

✦ Pasting from the Office clipboard places that item on the Windows clipboard. If you choose Paste All from the Office Clipboard toolbar, you paste all items stored on the Office clipboard onto the Windows clipboard as a single item.

✦ Clearing the Office clipboard also clears the Windows clipboard.

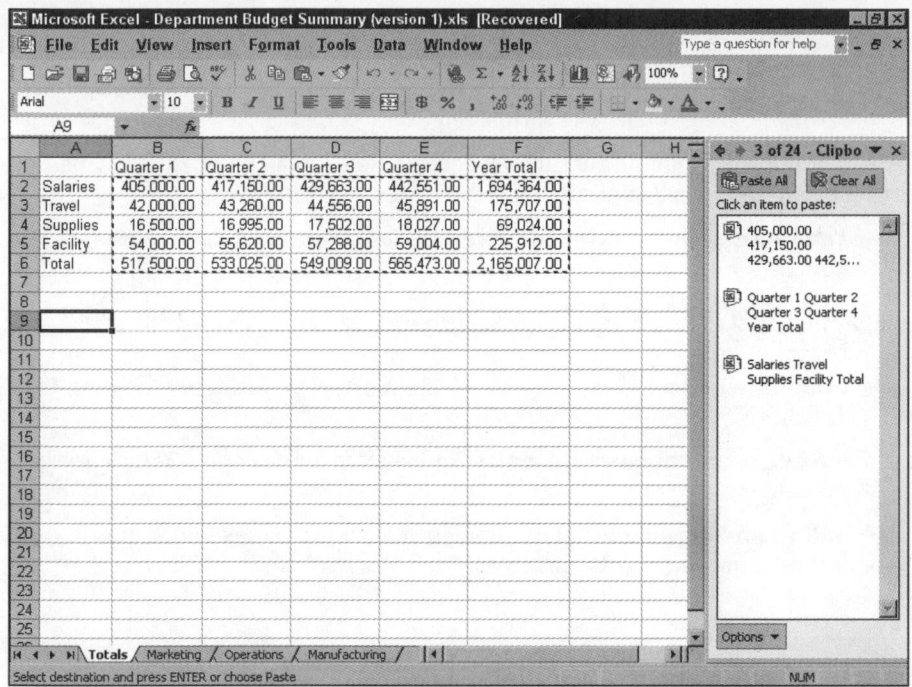

Figure 4-7: Use the Clipboard task pane to copy and paste multiple items.

Pasting in special ways

You may not always want to copy everything from the source range to the destination range. For example, you may want to only copy the current values of formulas rather than the formulas themselves. Or you may want to copy the number formats from one range to another without overwriting any existing data or formulas. To control what is copied into the destination range, you use the Edit ➪ Paste Special command — a much more versatile version of the Edit ➪ Paste command. Figure 4-8 shows the Paste Special dialog box that appears when you select this command. This dialog box has several options, which are explained in the following list. (You can also right-click and select Paste Special to display this dialog box.)

Tip

For the Paste Special command to be available, you need to copy a cell or range to the clipboards (using Edit ➪ Cut won't work).

✦ **All:** Equivalent to using the Edit ➪ Paste command. It copies the cell's contents, formats, and data validation from the Windows clipboard.

✦ **Formulas:** Only formulas contained in the source range are copied.

✦ **Values:** Copies the results of formulas. The destination for the copy can be a new range or the original range. In the latter case, Excel replaces the original formulas by their current values.

✦ **Formats:** Copies only the formatting.

✦ **Comments:** Copies only the cell comments from a cell or range. This option doesn't copy cell contents or formatting.

✦ **Validation:** Copies the validation criteria so the same data validation will apply.

✦ **All except borders:** Copies everything except any borders that appear in the source range.

✦ **Column widths:** Copies column width information from one column to another.

✦ **Formulas and number formats:** Copies all formulas and numeric formats, but no values.

✦ **Values and number formats:** Copies all current values and numeric formats, but not the formulas themselves.

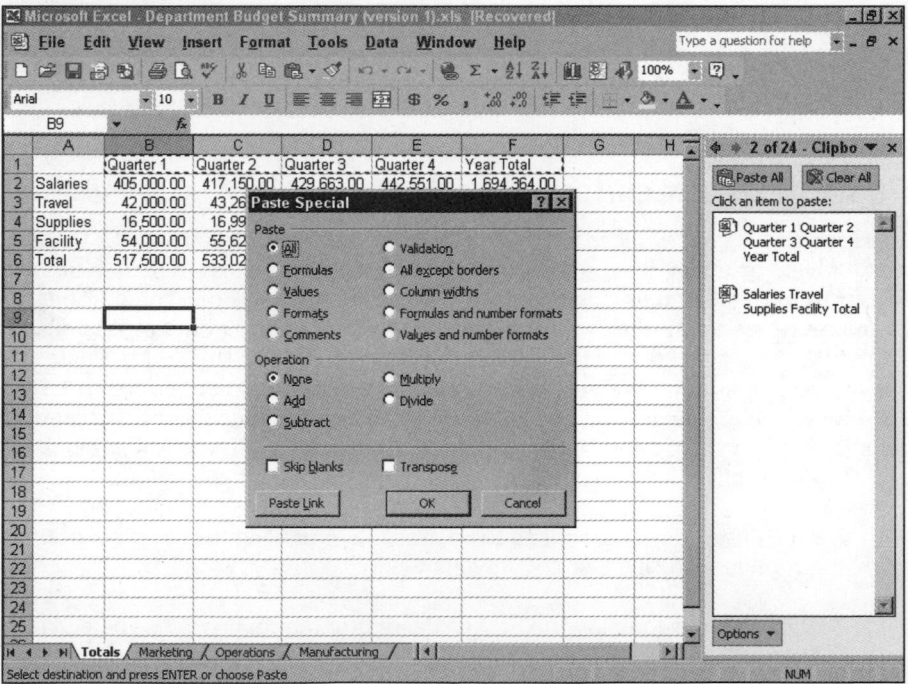

Figure 4-8: Use the Paste Special dialog box to control what is copied from the source to the destination range.

Performing mathematical operations without formulas

The option buttons in the Operation section of the Paste Special dialog box let you perform an arithmetic operation. For example, you can copy a range to another range and select the Multiply operation. Excel multiplies the corresponding values in the source range and the destination range and replaces the destination range with the new values.

Skipping blanks when pasting

The Skip Blanks option in the Paste Special dialog box prevents Excel from over-writing cell contents in your paste area with blank cells from the copied range. This option is useful if you're copying a range to another area but don't want the blank cells in the copied range to overwrite existing data.

Transposing a range

The Transpose option in the Paste Special dialog box changes the orientation of the copied range. Rows become columns and columns become rows. Any formulas in the copied range are adjusted so that they work properly when transposed. Note that this check box can be used with the other options in the Paste Special dialog box. Figure 4-9 shows an example of a horizontal range that was transposed to a vertical range.

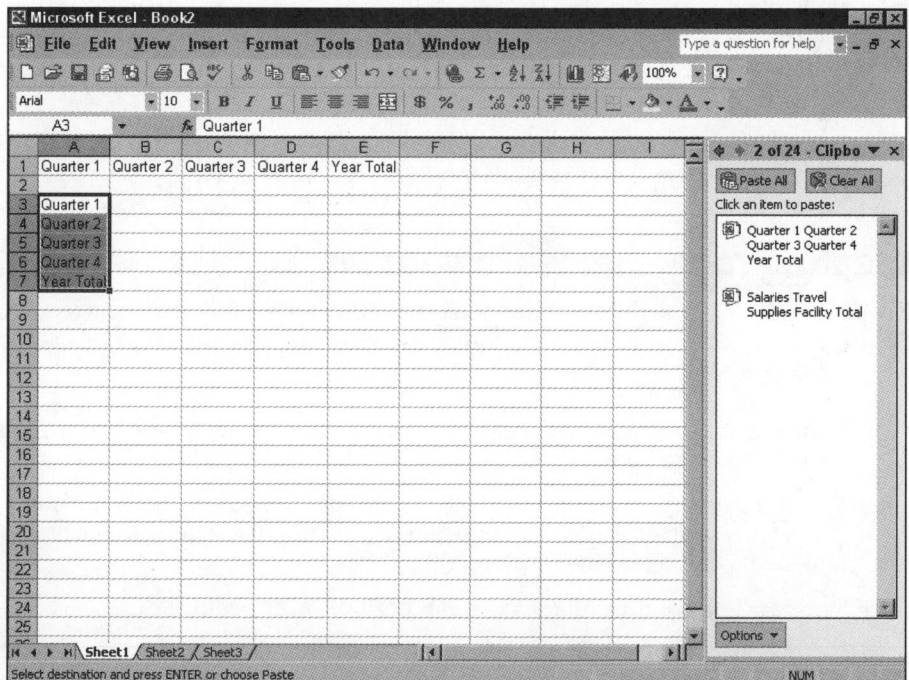

Figure 4-9: Transposing a range changes the orientation as the information is pasted into the worksheet.

Tip   If you click the Paste Link button in the Paste Special dialog box, you create an active link to the source range. This means that the destination range will automatically reflect changes in the source.

Using Names to Work with Ranges

Dealing with cryptic cell and range addresses can sometimes be confusing (this becomes even more apparent when you deal with formulas, which are discussed in Chapter 7). Fortunately, Excel enables you to assign descriptive names to cells and ranges. For example, you can give a cell a name such as Interest_Rate, or you can name a range JulySales. Working with these names (rather than cell or range addresses) has several advantages:

✦ A meaningful range name (such as Total_Income) is much easier to remember than a cell address (such as AC21).

✦ Entering a name is less error-prone than entering a cell or range address.

✦ You can quickly move to areas of your worksheet either by using the Name box, located at the left side of the formula bar (click the arrow to drop down a list of defined names) or by choosing Edit ➪ Go To (or F5) and specifying the range name.

✦ Creating formulas is easier. You can paste a cell or range name into a formula by using the Insert ➪ Name ➪ Paste command, by selecting a name from the Name box, or simply by typing the name.

✦ Names make your formulas more understandable and easier to use. A formula such as =Income–Taxes is more intuitive than =D20–D40.

Creating range names in your workbooks

Excel provides several different methods that you can use to create range names. Before you begin, however, you should be aware of some important rules about what is acceptable:

✦ Names can't contain any spaces. You might want to use an underscore character to simulate a space (such as Annual_Total).

✦ You can use any combination of letters and numbers, but the name must begin with a letter. A name can't begin with a number (such as 3rdQuarter) or look like a cell reference (such as Q3).

✦ Symbols, except for underscores and periods, aren't allowed.

✦ Names are limited to 255 characters, but you should keep names as short as possible, yet still meaningful and understandable.

Excel also uses a few names internally for its own use. Although you can create names that override Excel's internal names, you should avoid doing so. To be on the safe side, avoid using the following for names: Print_Area, Print_Titles, Consolidate_Area, and Sheet_Title.

To create a range name, start by selecting the cell or range that you want to name. Then, select Insert ⇨ Name ⇨ Define (or press Ctrl+F3). Excel displays the Define Name dialog box, which is shown in Figure 4-10.

Type a name in the box labeled Names in workbook (or use the name that Excel proposes, if any). The active or selected cell or range address appears in the box labeled Refers to. Verify that the address listed is correct and then click OK to add the name to your worksheet and close the dialog box. Or, you can click the Add button to continue adding names to your worksheet. If you do this, you must specify the Refers to range either by typing an address (make sure to begin with an equal sign) or by pointing to it in the worksheet. Each name appears in the list box.

Tip   A faster way to create a name is to use the Name box (to the left of the formula bar). Select the cell or range to name and then click the Name box and type the name. Press Enter to create the name (you must press Enter to actually record the name; if you type a name and then click in the worksheet, Excel won't create the name). If a name already exists, you can't use the Name box to change the range to which that name refers. Attempting to do so simply selects the range.

The Name box is a drop-down list and shows all names in the workbook. To choose a named cell or range, click the Name box and choose the name. The name appears in the Name box, and Excel selects the named cell or range in the worksheet.

You may have a worksheet that contains text that you want to use for names for adjacent cells or ranges. For example, you might want to use the text in column A to create names for the corresponding values in column B. Excel makes this very easy to do.

To create names by using adjacent text, start by selecting the name text and the cells that you want to name (these can be individual cells or ranges of cells). The names must be adjacent to the cells that you're naming (a multiple selection is allowed). Then, choose Insert ⇨ Name ⇨ Create. Excel displays the Create Names dialog box, shown in Figure 4-11. The check marks in this dialog box are based on Excel's analysis of the selected range. For example, if Excel finds text in the first row of the selection, it proposes that you create names based on the top row. If Excel didn't guess correctly, you can change the check boxes. Click OK, and Excel creates the names.

Note   If the text contained in a cell would result in an invalid name, Excel modifies the name to make it valid. For example, if a cell contains the text Net Income (which is invalid for a name because it contains a space), Excel converts the space to an underscore character. If Excel encounters a value or a formula where text should be, however, it doesn't convert it to a valid name. It simply doesn't create a name.

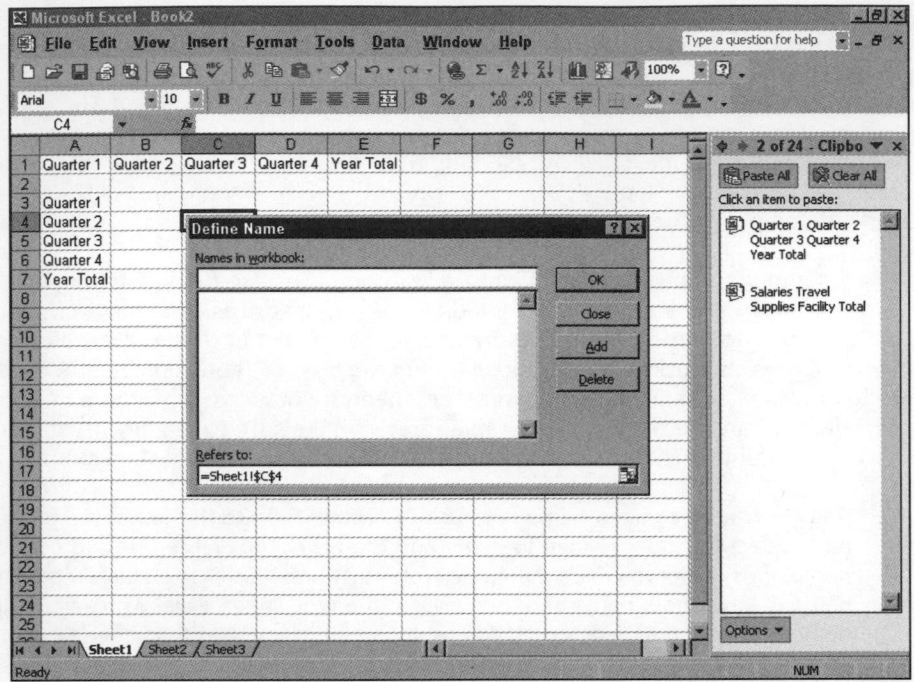

Figure 4-10: Create names for cells or ranges by using the Define Name dialog box.

Caution

If the upper-left cell of the selection contains text and you choose the Top Row and Left Column options, Excel uses that text for the name of the entire data excluding the top row and left column. So, before you accept the names that Excel creates, take a minute to make sure that they refer to the correct ranges.

Creating a table of range names

After you create a large number of range names, you may need to know the ranges that each name defines, particularly if you're trying to track down errors or document your work. Excel lets you create a list of all names in the workbook and their corresponding addresses. To create a table of names, first move the cell pointer to an empty area of your worksheet—the table is created at the active cell position and will overwrite any information at that location. Use the Insert ➪ Name ➪ Paste command (or press F3). Excel displays the Paste Name dialog box, shown in Figure 4-12, which lists all the defined names. To paste a list of names, click the Paste List button.

Modifying existing range names

You may discover that the range names you have created don't completely fill your needs. For example, you may have created a range name that refers to a single cell but should actually refer to a group of cells. Or perhaps you have a large number of range names in the workbook that you no longer need.

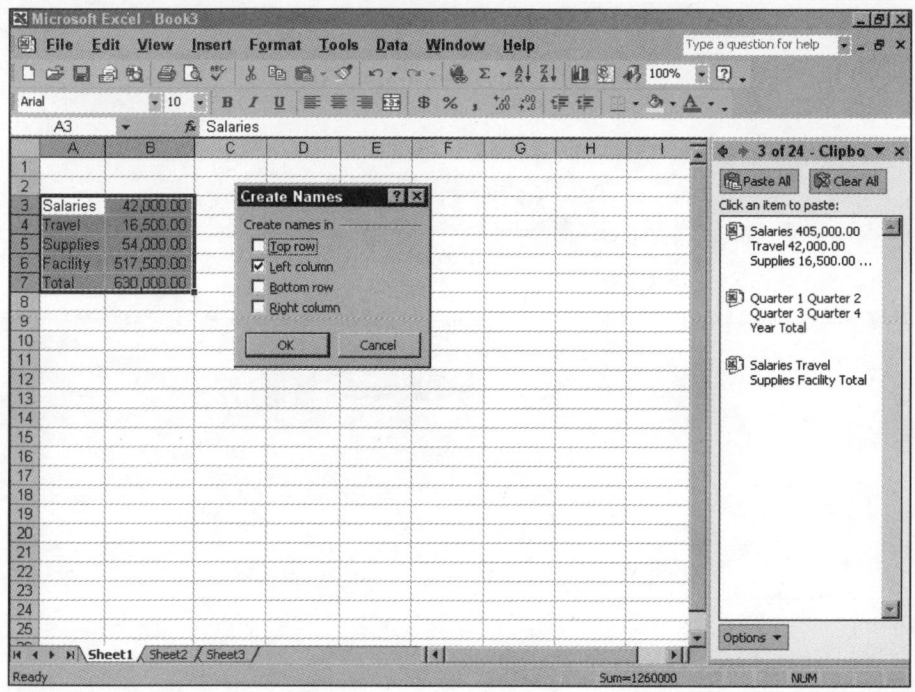

Figure 4-11: Use the Create Names dialog box to name cells using labels that appear in the worksheet.

Redefining names

If you want to change the cell or range to which a range name refers, start by selecting Insert ➪ Name ➪ Define to display the Define Name dialog box. Click the name that you want to change and then edit the cell or range address in the Refers to edit box. If you want to, you can click the edit box and select a new cell or range by pointing in the worksheet.

Deleting names

If you no longer need a defined name, you can delete it. Deleting a range name does not delete information in the range.

To remove a range name, choose Insert ➪ Name ➪ Define to display the Define Name dialog box. Choose the name that you want to delete from the list and then click the Delete button.

Caution

Be extra careful when deleting names. If the name is used in a formula, deleting the name causes the formula to become invalid (it will display #NAME?). However, deleting a name can be undone, so if you find that formulas return #NAME? after you delete a name, select Edit ➪ Undo to get the name back.

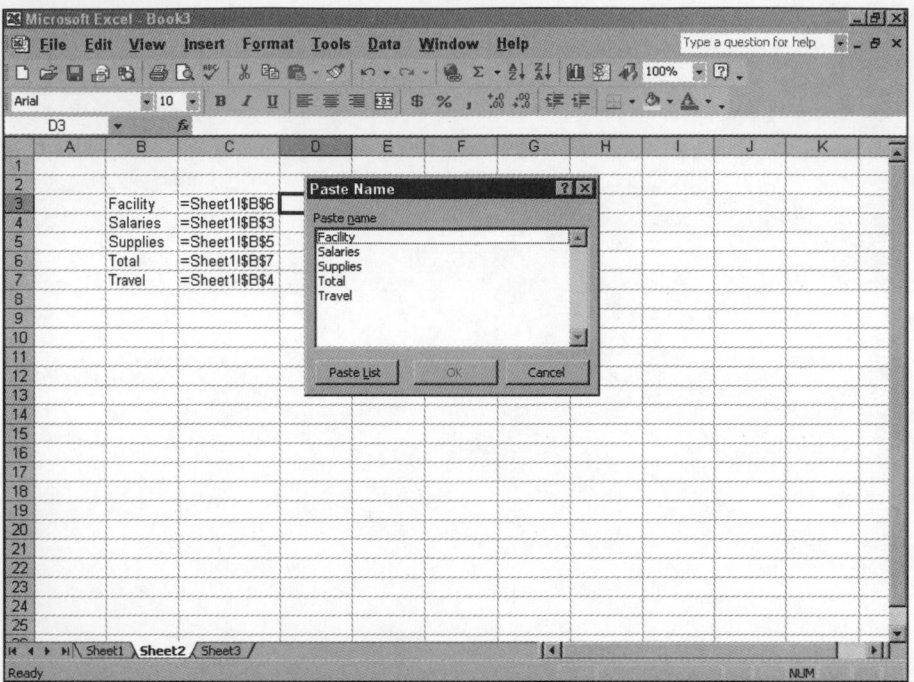

Figure 4-12: Use the Paste Name dialog box to add a list of range names to the worksheet.

If you delete the rows or columns that contain named cells or ranges, the names contain an invalid reference. For example, if cell A1 on Sheet1 is named Interest and you delete row 1 or column A, Interest then refers to =Sheet1!#REF! (that is, to an erroneous reference). If you use Interest in a formula, the formula displays #REF.

Adding Notes to Cells

Large, complex worksheets can be difficult to understand. Sometimes it can be helpful to have some documentation that explains certain elements in the worksheet. One very handy way to do so is to add comments to cells. This feature is useful when you need to document a particular value. It's also useful to help you remember what a formula does.

To add a comment to a cell, select the cell and then choose Insert ➪ Comment (or Shift+F2). Excel inserts a comment that points to the active cell, as shown in Figure 4-13. Initially, the comment consists of your name. Enter the text for the cell comment and then click anywhere in the worksheet to hide the comment.

Cells that have a comment attached display a small red triangle in the upper-right corner. When you move the mouse pointer over a cell that contains a comment, the comment becomes visible.

Tip   Select Tools ⇨ Options and click the View tab to control how cell comment indicators are displayed. You can turn off these indicators if you like.

If you want all cell comments to be visible (regardless of the location of the cell pointer), select View ⇨ Comments. This command is a toggle; select it again to hide all cell comments. To edit a comment, activate the cell, right-click, and then choose Edit Comment from the shortcut menu.

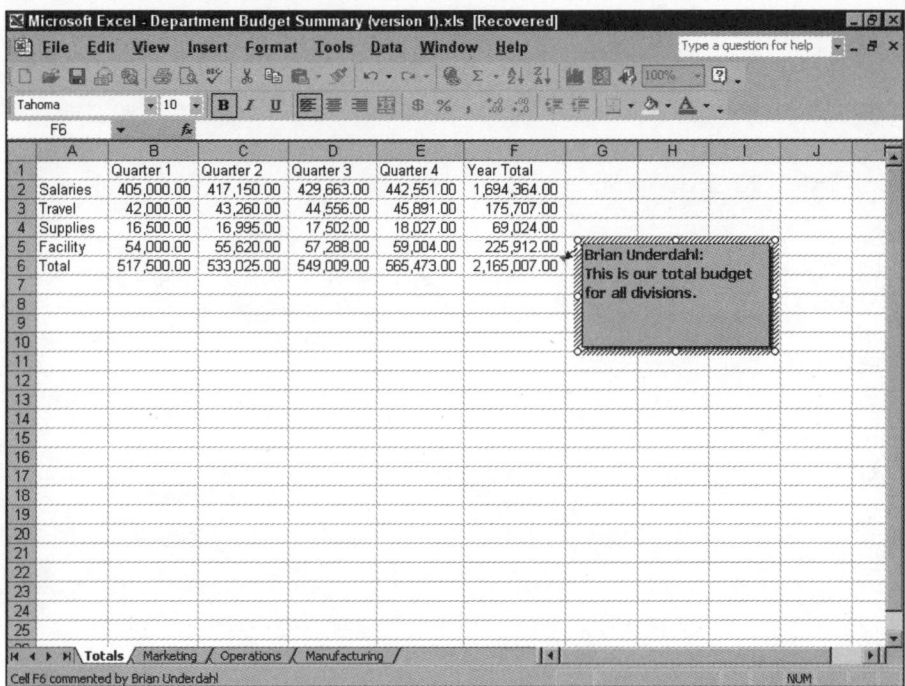

Figure 4-13: You can add comments to cells to help clarify important items in your worksheets.

Tip   You can use the Reviewing toolbar to navigate between the comments in the worksheet.

To delete a cell comment, activate the cell that contains the comment, right-click, and then choose Delete Comment from the shortcut menu.

✦   ✦   ✦

Worksheet Formatting

Formatting is like the icing on a cake—it may not be absolutely necessary, but it sure makes the end product a lot tastier. In an Excel worksheet, formatting serves to make information look a lot more interesting and can even make it easier for other people to understand the worksheet's purpose.

 This chapter covers stylistic formatting. To learn more about using numeric formats, see Chapter 1.

How Formatting Can Improve Your Worksheets

The stylistic formatting that you apply to worksheet cells doesn't affect the actual content of the cells. Rather, you should use stylistic formatting with the goal of making your work easier to read or more attractive. In this chapter, you learn about these types of formatting:

✦ Using different type fonts, sizes, and attributes

✦ Changing the way the contents of cells are aligned within cells

✦ Using colors in the background or foreground of cells

✦ Using patterns for cell background

✦ Using borders around cells

✦ Using a graphic background for your worksheet

Stylistic formatting isn't essential for every workbook that you develop—especially if it is for your own use only. On the other hand, it only takes a few moments to apply some simple formatting, and, once applied, the formatting will remain in place without further effort on your part. Figure 5-1 shows how even simple formatting can significantly improve a worksheet's readability.

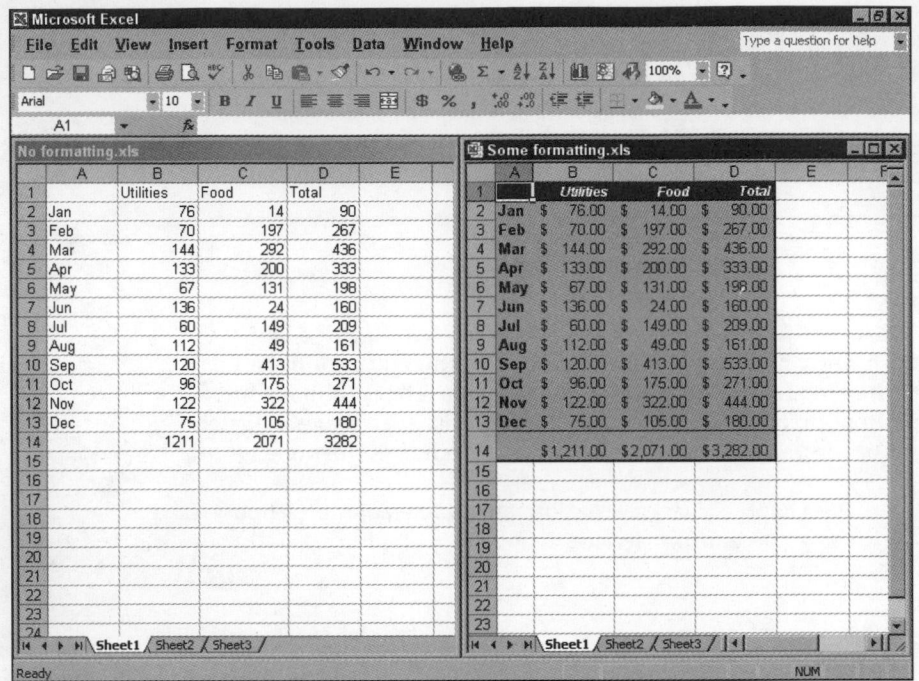

Figure 5-1: In just a few minutes, some simple formatting can greatly improve the appearance of your worksheets.

Getting to Know the Formatting Tools

When you want to apply formatting to your worksheets, you can use either of Excel's formatting tools — the Formatting toolbar or the Format Cells dialog box. Generally, using the toolbar is faster but the dialog box offers more options.

Using the Formatting toolbar

The Formatting toolbar provides quick access to the most commonly used formatting options. Normally this toolbar is docked immediately below the Standard toolbar, but you can drag it to any other edge of the Excel window or even make into a floating toolbar as shown in Figure 5-2.

Cross-Reference To learn more about using the Formatting toolbar to apply numeric formats, see Chapter 1.

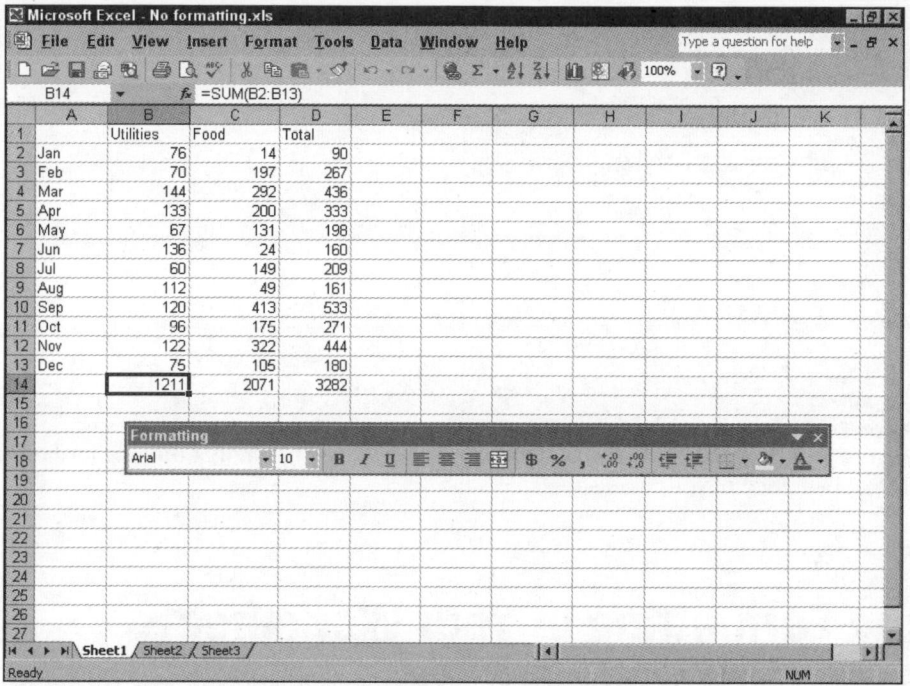

Figure 5-2: The Formatting toolbar contains many tools that you can use to apply formats to your worksheets.

In many cases, this toolbar may contain all the formatting tools that you need. But some types of formatting require that you use the Format Cells dialog box. This chapter covers the finer points of stylistic formatting, including options not available on the Formatting toolbar.

Using the Format Cells dialog box

Throughout this chapter you'll use the Format Cells dialog box to apply different formatting options. This is a tabbed dialog box (see Figure 5-3) from which you can apply nearly any type of stylistic formatting (as well as number formatting). The formats that you choose in the Format Cells dialog box apply to the cells that you have selected at the time.

After selecting the cell or range to format, you can display the Format Cells dialog box by using any of the following methods:

✦ Choose the Format ➪ Cells command.

✦ Press Ctrl+1.

✦ Right-click the selected cell or range and choose Format Cells from the short-cut menu.

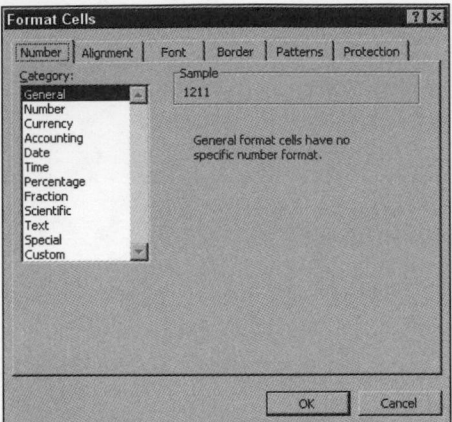

Figure 5-3: The Format Cells dialog box gives you many additional options for fine-tuning the appearance of your worksheets.

Using Formatting in Your Worksheets

No matter what anyone tries to tell you, choosing and applying stylistic formatting to Excel worksheets is not an exact science. Just as different people like different types of music or art, different people will also have differing opinions on what constitutes a good-looking worksheet. Therefore, in the following sections we stick to telling you how to select and apply formatting—it's up to you to choose the options you like the best.

Tip   Stylistic formatting applies to any text that appears in the selected cells—no matter whether the text represents simple text labels or the results of formulas.

Playing around with different fonts

You can use different fonts, sizes, or attributes in your worksheets to make various parts stand out, such as the headers for a table. You also can adjust the font size to make more information appear on a single page.

Cross-Reference   Reducing the font size so that your report fits on a certain number of pages isn't always necessary. Excel has a handy "fit to" option that automatically scales your printed output to fit on a specified number of pages, which is discussed in Chapter 3.

By default, the information that you enter into an Excel worksheet uses the 10-point Arial font. A font is described by its typeface (Arial, Times New Roman, Courier New, and so on) as well as by its size, measured in points (there are 72 points in

1 inch). Excel's row height, by default, is 12.75 points. Therefore, 10-point type entered into 12.75-point rows leaves a small amount of blank space between the characters in adjacent rows.

Tip If you have not manually changed a row's height, Excel automatically adjusts the row height based on the tallest text that you enter into the row.

The default font is the font specified by the Normal style for the workbook. All cells use the Normal style unless you specifically apply a different style. If you want to change the font for all cells that use the Normal style, you simply change the font used in the Normal style by following these steps:

1. Choose the Format ⇨ Style command. Excels displays the Style dialog box.

2. Make sure that Normal appears in the Style name drop-down box and click the Modify button. Excel displays the Format Cells dialog box.

3. Click the Font tab and choose the font and size that you want as the default.

4. Click OK to return to the Style dialog box.

5. Click OK again to close the Style dialog box.

The font for all cells that use the Normal style changes to the font that you specified. You can change the font for the Normal style at any time.

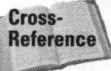 **Cross-Reference** See "Using Named Styles for Easier Formatting" later in this chapter for more information on what you can do with styles.

If you plan to distribute a workbook to other users, you should stick with the standard fonts that are included with any version of Windows. If you open a workbook and your system doesn't have the font with which the workbook was created, Windows attempts to use a similar font. Sometimes this works, and sometimes it doesn't. To be on the safe side, use only the following fonts if you plan to share your workbook with others:

✦ Arial

✦ Courier New

✦ Symbol

✦ Times New Roman

✦ Wingdings

Use the Font and Font Size tools on the Formatting toolbar to change the font or size for selected cells. Just select the cells, click the appropriate tool, and then choose the font or size from the drop-down list. You can see samples of the fonts when you open the Font list box on the Formatting toolbar (see Figure 5-4).

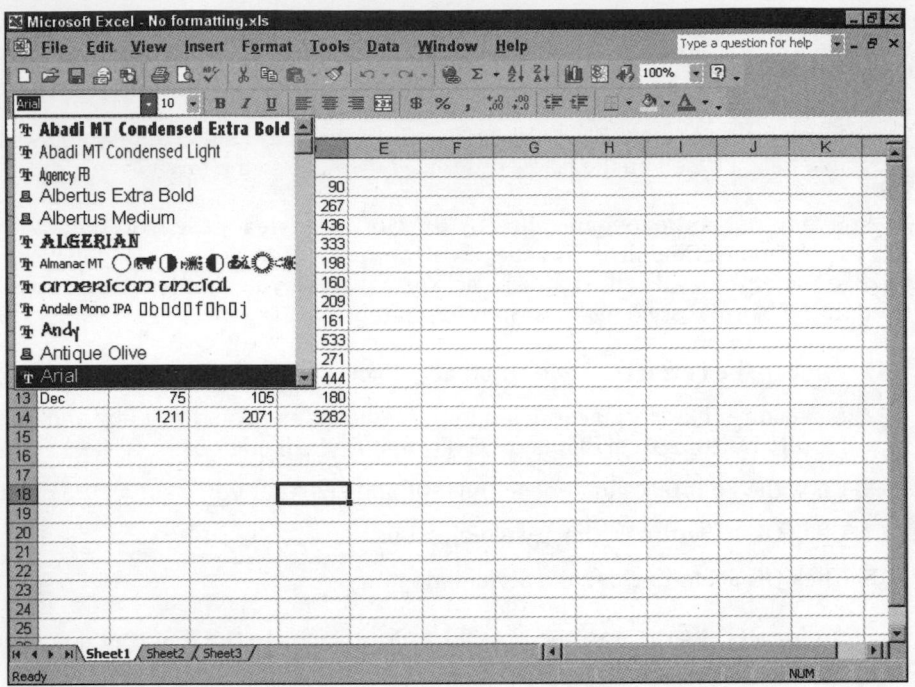

Figure 5-4: Excel shows you samples of each font to make it easier for you to select the font you really want.

You also can use the Font tab in the Format Cells dialog box to choose fonts, as shown in Figure 5-5. This tab enables you to control several other attributes of the font from a single dialog box and preview the font before you select it. Notice that you also can change the font style (bold, italic), underlining, color, and effects (strikethrough, superscript, or subscript). If you click the check box labeled Normal Font, Excel displays the selections for the font defined for the Normal style.

Figure 5-6 shows several different examples of font formatting. In this figure, the gridlines were turned off to make it easier to see the underlining. Notice in the figure that Excel provides four different underlining styles. In the two non-accounting underline styles, only the cell contents are underlined. In the two accounting underline styles, the entire width of the cells is always underlined.

If you prefer to keep your hands on the keyboard, you can use the following shortcut keys to format a selected range quickly:

✦ **Ctrl+B:** Bold

✦ **Ctrl+I:** Italic

✦ **Ctrl+U:** Underline

✦ **Ctrl+5:** Strikethrough

These shortcut keys act as a toggle. For example, you can turn bold on and off by repeatedly pressing Ctrl+B.

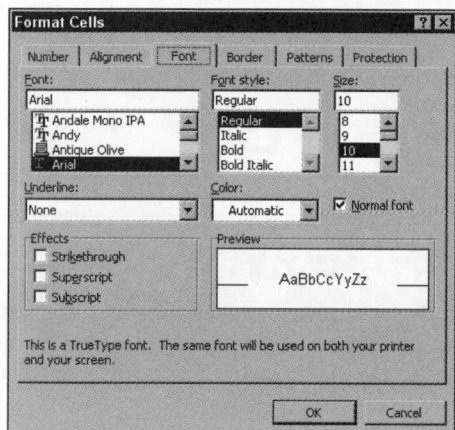

Figure 5-5: The font tab of the Format Cells dialog box gives you many additional font attribute options to choose.

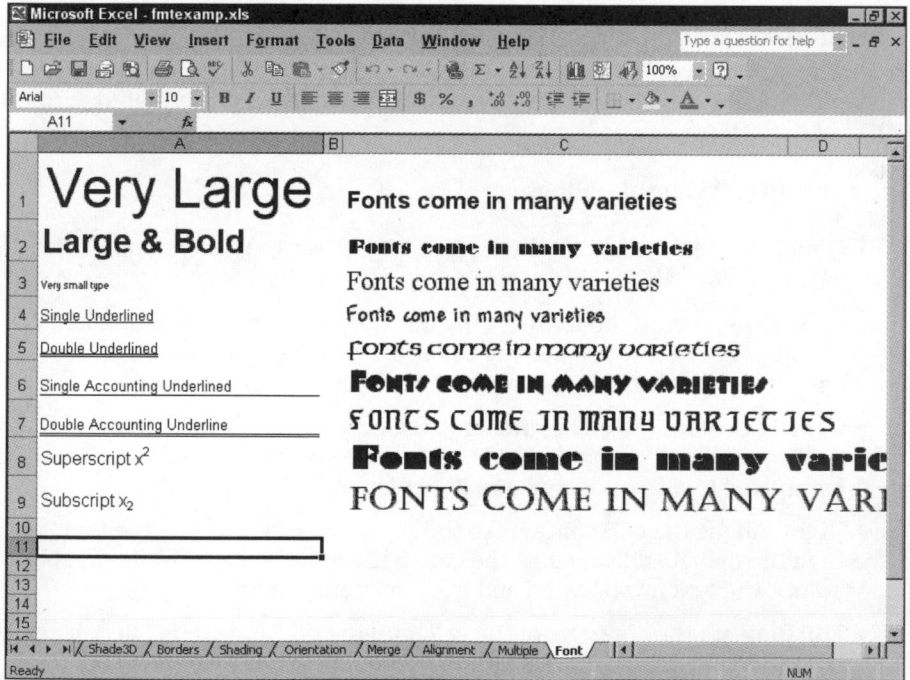

Figure 5-6: You can choose many different font formatting options for your Excel worksheets.

Using Multiple Formatting Styles in a Single Cell

If a cell contains text, Excel also enables you to format individual characters in the cell. To do so, switch to Edit mode (double-click the cell) and then select the characters that you want to format. You can select characters either by dragging the mouse over them or by pressing the Shift key as you press the left- or right-arrow key. Then use any of the standard formatting techniques. The changes apply to only the selected characters in the cell. This technique doesn't work with cells that contain values or formulas.

Changing the way text aligns in worksheet cells

Spreadsheet programs have always used the rather odd convention of aligning numbers to the right of a column and text to the left of the column. Fortunately, you don't have to accept this strange-looking arrangement because Excel gives you a whole range of options for aligning cell contents. You can align the contents of a cell both vertically and horizontally.

Figure 5-7 shows some examples of cells formatted with the various horizontal and vertical alignment options. The figure also shows the Alignment tab of the Format Cells dialog box.

Choosing horizontal alignment options

The horizontal alignment options are the alignment options that you're most likely to use. These options control the way the cell contents are distributed across the width of the cell (or cells).

The horizontal alignment options are

- ✦ **General:** Aligns numbers to the right, aligns text to the left, and centers logical and error values. This option is the default alignment.

- ✦ **Left:** Aligns the cell contents to the left side of the cell. If the text is wider than the cell, it spills over to the cell to the right. If the cell to the right is not empty, the text is truncated and not completely visible.

- ✦ **Center:** Centers the cell contents in the cell. If the text is wider than the cell, it spills over to cells on either side, if they are empty. If the adjacent cells aren't empty, the text is truncated and not completely visible.

- ✦ **Right:** Aligns the cell contents to the right side of the cell. If the text is wider than the cell, it spills over to the cell to the left. If the cell to the left isn't empty, the text is truncated and not completely visible.

- ✦ **Fill:** Repeats the contents of the cell until the cell's width is filled. If cells to the right also are formatted with Fill alignment, they also are filled.

- ✦ **Justify:** Justifies the text to the left and right of the cell. This option is applicable only if the cell is formatted as wrapped text and uses more than one line.

✦ **Center across selection:** Centers the text over the selected columns. This option is useful for precisely centering a heading over a number of columns.

✦ **Distributed:** Distributes the text evenly across the selected column.

Choosing vertical alignment options

The vertical alignment options typically aren't used as often as the horizontal alignment options. These settings are really only useful if you have adjusted row heights so they are considerably taller than normal.

The vertical alignment options are

✦ **Top:** Aligns the cell contents to the top of the cell.

✦ **Center:** Centers the cell contents vertically in the cell.

✦ **Bottom:** Aligns the cell contents to the bottom of the cell.

✦ **Justify:** Justifies the text vertically in the cell; this option is applicable only if the cell is formatted as wrapped text and uses more than one line.

✦ **Distributed:** Distributes the text evenly vertically in the cell.

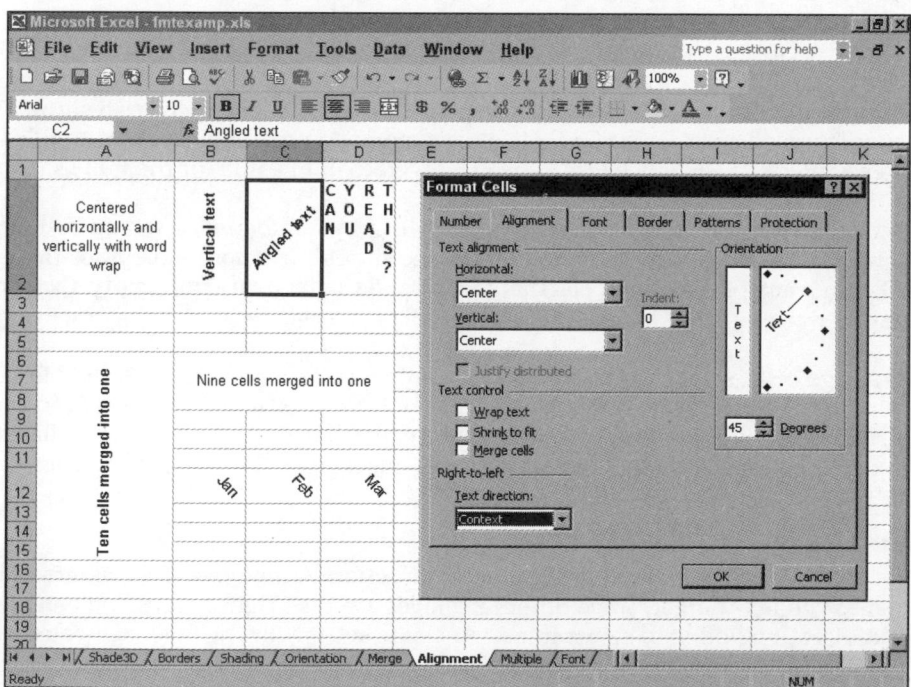

Figure 5-7: Use the Alignment tab to choose text alignment options for your Excel worksheets.

Wrapping or shrinking text to fit the cell

If you have text that is too wide to fit the column width but don't want that text to spill over into adjacent cells, you can use either the Wrap text option or the Shrink to fit option to accommodate that text — depending on your needs.

The Wrap text option displays the text on multiple lines in the cell, if necessary. Use this option to display lengthy headings without having to make the columns too wide, and without reducing the size of the text.

Excel includes a Shrink to fit option, which reduces the size of the text so that it fits into the cell without spilling over to the next cell.

Tip   If you apply wrap text formatting to a cell, you can't use the shrink-to-fit formatting.

Merging worksheet cells to create additional text space

If you enter text that is too wide to fit the column width, the text will spill over into adjacent cells — but only if those adjacent cells are empty. If someone later adds something to one of the "empty" cells, your carefully crafted titles can suddenly appear truncated. But even if you don't encounter this problem, you still can run up against the problem of trying to display a title across several worksheet rows. Excel simply does not extend text across rows of cells. The answer to both of these problems is to merge the adjacent cells so that you can treat them as a single cell.

When you merge cells, you don't combine the contents of cells. Rather, you combine a group of cells that occupy the same space into a single cell. Figure 5-8 shows two sets of merged cells. Range C3:G3 has been merged into a single cell that holds the table's title. Range B5:B9 has also been merged to hold a title for the table's rows.

You can merge any number of cells, occupying any number of rows and columns. However, the range that you intend to merge should be empty, except for the upper-left cell. If any of the other cells that you intend to merge are not empty, Excel displays a warning.

To merge cells, select the cells that you want to merge and then click the Merge and Center tool on the Formatting toolbar. The only way to "unmerge" cells is to use the Format Cells dialog box. Select the merged cell(s), open the Format Cells dialog box, and, on the Alignment tab, remove the check from the Merge cells box.

Controlling the text direction

Not all languages use the same character direction. Although most Western languages run left-to-right, some other languages are read right-to-left. You can use the Text direction option to select the appropriate setting for the language you use.

Note   Changing the text direction setting won't have any affect unless you have the proper language drivers installed on your PC. For example, you must install Japanese language support from the Office CD-ROM to use right-to-left text direction Japanese characters.

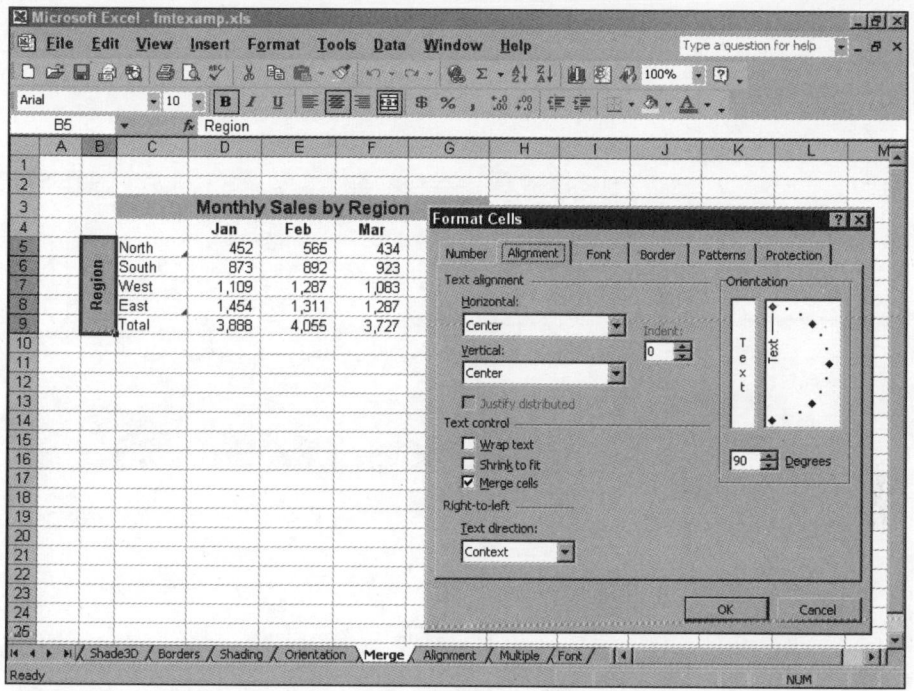

Figure 5-8: Merge worksheet cells to make them act as if they were a single cell.

Displaying text at an angle

Another way to create a visual impact is to display text at an angle so that the text does not appear horizontally in the cell. You can display text horizontally, vertically, or specify an angle between 90 degrees up and 90 degrees down.

To change the orientation, select the cell or range, open the Format Cells dialog box, and select the Alignment tab. Use the gauge to specify an angle between –90 and +90 degrees.

Figure 5-9 shows an example of text displayed at a 45-degree angle.

Tip   In addition to using the Degrees spin control, you can drag the orientation pointer to the angle you want.

Using colors and shading to enliven your worksheets

Excel provides the tools to create some very colorful worksheets. You can change the color of the text or add colors to the backgrounds of the worksheet cells.

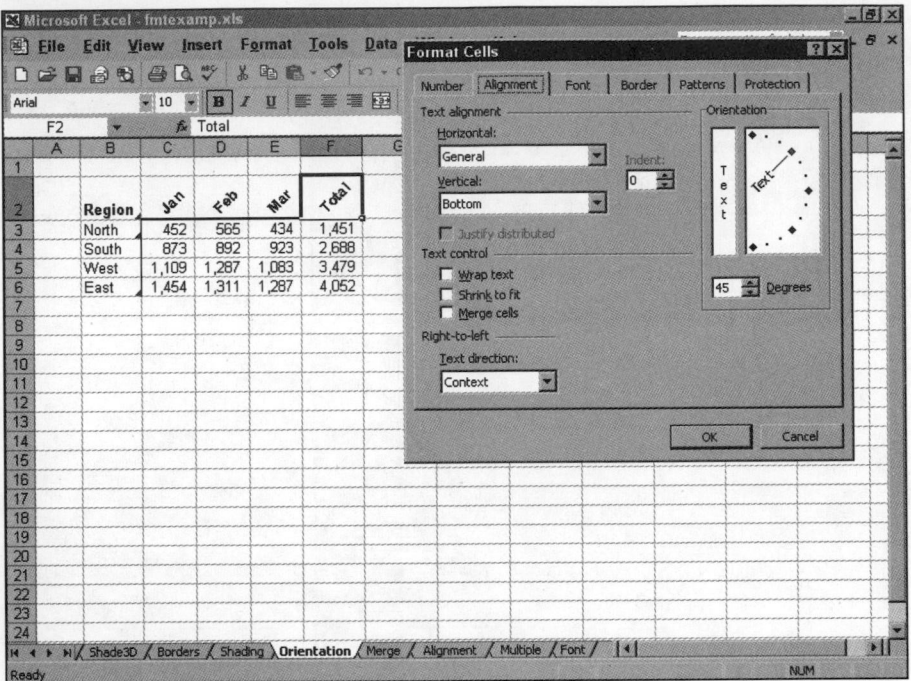

Figure 5-9: Rotate text for additional visual impact.

You control the color of the cell's text in the Font tab of the Format Cells dialog box, and you control the cell's background color in the Patterns tab. You can also use tools on the Formatting toolbar (Font Color and Fill Color) to change the color of these items.

A cell's background can be solid (one color) or consist of a pattern that uses two colors. To select a pattern, click the Pattern drop-down list in the Format Cells dialog box. It expands as shown in Figure 5-10. Choose a pattern from the top part of the box and a second color from the bottom part. The first pattern in the list is "None"—use this option if you want a solid background. The Sample box to the right shows how the colors and pattern will look. If you plan to print the worksheet, you need to experiment to determine how the color patterns translate to your printer.

You might want to use a background color to make a large table of data easier to read. You probably are familiar with computer printer paper that has alternating green-and-white horizontal shading (often referred to as "green bar"). You can use background colors to simulate this effect in Excel. Figure 5-10 shows an example of this.

Tip To quickly hide the contents of a cell, make the background color the same as the font text color. The cell contents are still visible in the formula bar when you select the cell, however.

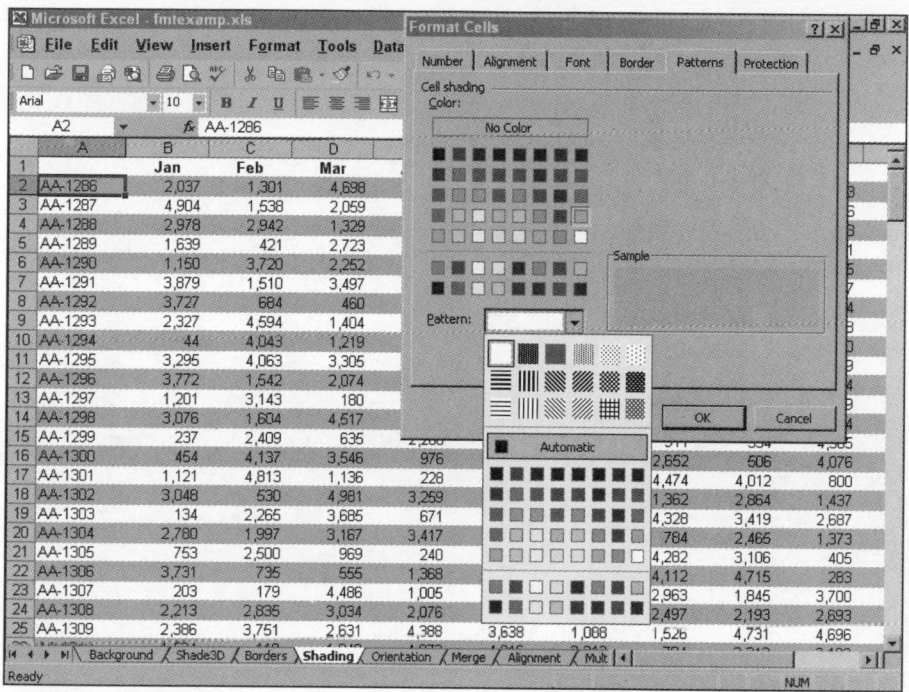

Figure 5-10: Choose a fill pattern and color to add a colored background to worksheet cells.

Adding borders and lines

Borders (and lines within the borders) are another visual enhancement that you can add around groups of cells. Borders are often used to group a range of similar cells or to delineate rows or columns. Excel offers 13 different styles of borders, as you can see on the Border tab in the Format Cells dialog box (see Figure 5-11). This dialog box works with the selected cell or range and enables you to specify which border style to use for each border of the selection.

Before you open this dialog box, select the cell or range to which you want to add borders. First, choose a line style and then choose the border position for the line style by clicking one of the icons.

Notice that the Border tab has three "presets," which can save you some clicking. If you want to remove all borders from the selection, click None. To put an outline around the selection, choose Outline preset. To put borders inside the selection, click Inside preset.

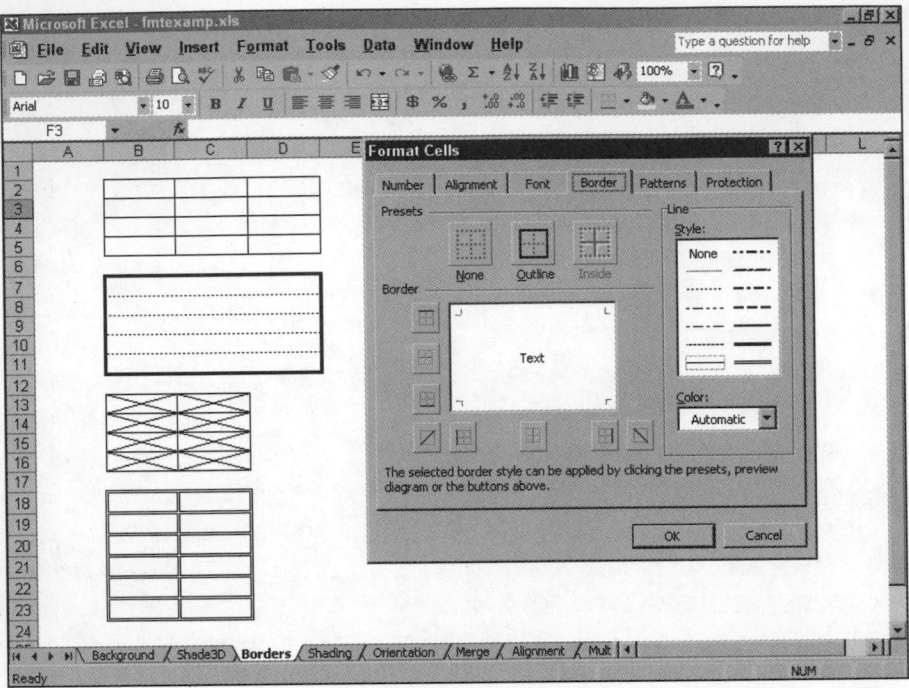

Figure 5-11: Use the Border tab to add lines around and through worksheet cells.

Excel displays the selected border style in the dialog box. You can choose different styles for different border positions; you can also choose a color for the border. Using this dialog box may require some experimentation, but you'll get the hang of it. Figure 5-11 shows several examples of borders in a worksheet.

When you apply diagonal lines to a cell or range, the selection looks like it has been crossed out.

Tip   If you use border formatting in your worksheet, you might want to turn off the grid display, to make the borders more pronounced. Use the View tab of the Options dialog box to do this.

Adding a background image to a worksheet

Excel also enables you to choose a graphics file to serve as a background for a worksheet similar to the wallpaper that you may display on your Windows desktop. The image that you choose is repeated, so that it fills the entire worksheet.

To add a background to a worksheet, choose Format ➪ Sheet ➪ Background. Excel displays a dialog box that enables you to choose a graphics file. When you locate a file, click OK. Excel tiles the graphic across your worksheet (see Figure 5-12). You'll also want to turn off the gridline display, because the gridlines show through the graphic.

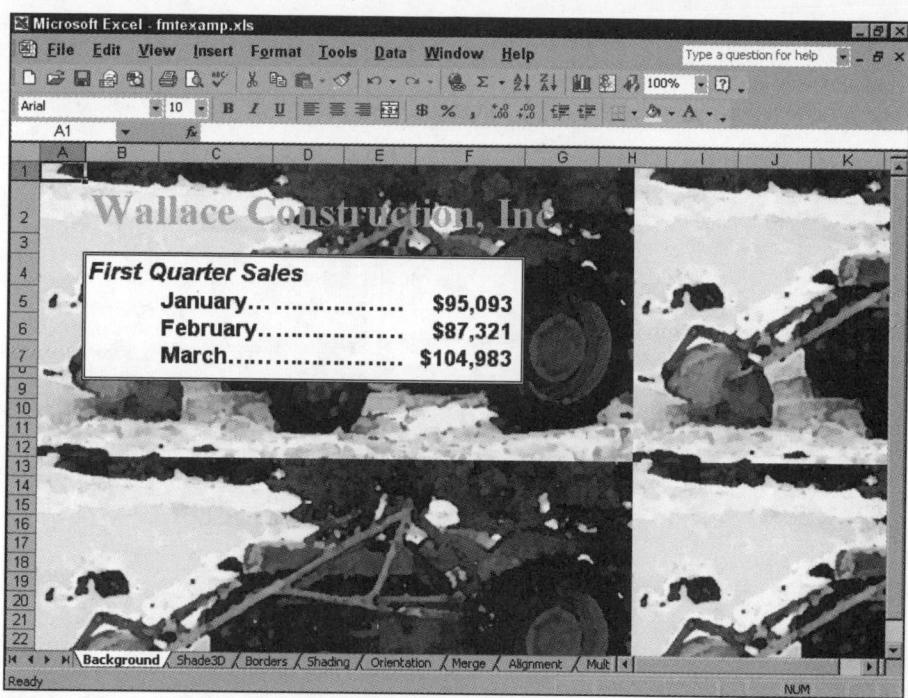

Figure 5-12: You can add almost any image file as a worksheet background image.

Some backgrounds make viewing text difficult, so you may want to use a solid background color for cells that contain text.

The graphic background on a worksheet is for display only — it isn't printed when you print the worksheet.

Using AutoFormat for quick and easy worksheet formatting

So far, I've described the individual formatting commands and tools at your disposal. Excel also has an AutoFormat feature that can automatically perform many types of formatting for you.

To apply an AutoFormat, move the cell pointer anywhere within a table that you want to format; Excel determines the table's boundaries automatically. Then, choose Format ➪ AutoFormat. Excel responds with the AutoFormat dialog box shown in Figure 5-13. Choose one of the 17 AutoFormats from the list and click OK. Excel formats the table for you.

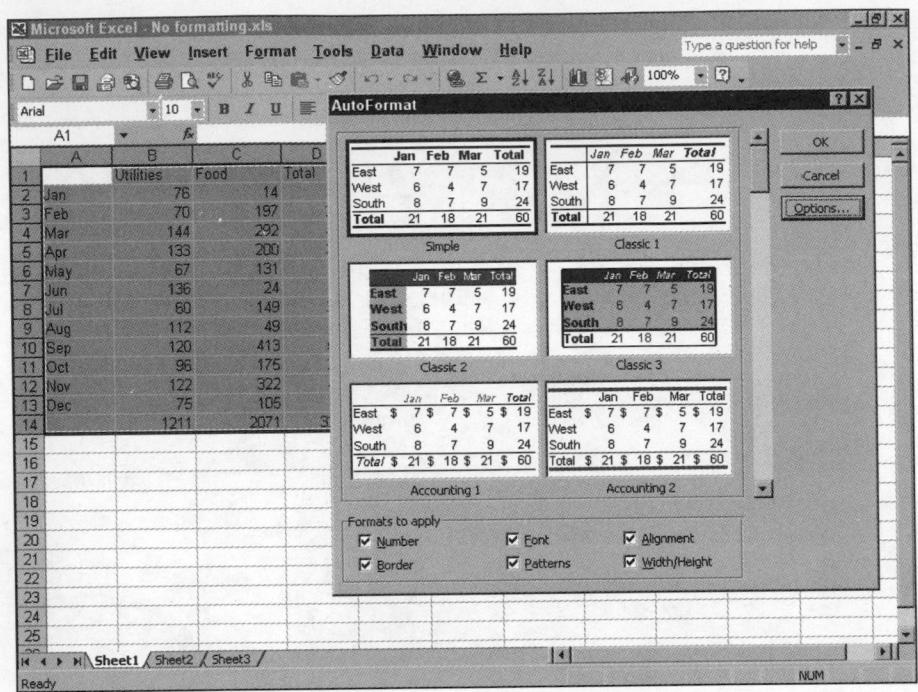

Figure 5-13: Use the AutoFormat dialog box to quickly apply a preset selection of formatting options to your worksheet.

Excel applies AutoFormat rather intelligently. For example, Excel analyzes the data contained in the table and then formats the table to handle items such as subtotals.

Although you can't define your own AutoFormats, you can control the type of formatting that is applied. When you click the Options button in the AutoFormat dialog box, the dialog box expands to show six options that appear at the bottom of Figure 5-13.

Copying Formats by Painting

The quickest way to copy the formats from one cell to another cell or range is to use the Format Painter button on the Standard toolbar (the button with the paintbrush image).

Start by selecting the cell or range that has the formatting attributes you want to copy. Then, click the Format Painter button. Notice that the mouse pointer changes to include a paintbrush. Next, select the cells to which you want to apply the formats. Release the mouse button, and Excel applies the same set of formatting options that were in the original range.

If you double-click the Format Painter button, you can paint multiple areas of the worksheet with the same formats. Excel applies the formats that you copy to each cell or range that you select. To get out of paint mode, click the Format Painter button again (or press Esc).

Initially, the six check boxes are all checked—which means that Excel will apply formatting from all six categories. If you want it to skip one or more categories, just remove the check from the appropriate box before you click OK. For example, if you've already formatted the numbers, you may want to turn off the Number option.

Using conditional formatting to highlight specific values

The formatting options you've seen so far are equal opportunity formatting—the same formatting applies to whatever appears in the formatted cells. Sometimes, though, you may want certain values to really jump out and grab you. For example, suppose you have a small business and you use Excel to keep track of your weekly net profit. Most weeks you have a profit, but every now and then your returns exceed your sales and your business shows a loss for the week. To make these losing weeks stand out, you can use conditional formatting to make the losses show up in bold red characters.

Excel's conditional formatting feature changes cell formats based on the contents of the cell. To apply conditional formatting to a cell or range, select the range and then choose Format ➪ Conditional Formatting. You'll see the Conditional Formatting dialog box shown in Figure 5-14, which enables you to specify up to three conditions for the selected cells.

The condition can be based on either the cell's value or on a formula that you specify (the formula must be a logical formula and return either True or False). Follow these steps to apply conditional formatting:

1. In the first drop-down list, choose either Cell Value Is or Formula Is.

2. If you chose Cell Value Is in Step 1, specify the conditions by using the controls in the dialog box. For example, you can specify between 0 and 100. You can enter values or cell references.

3. If you chose Formula Is in Step 1, specify a reference to the formula. Remember, the formula must return either True or False.

4. Click the Format button and specify the formatting that will be used when the condition is true.

5. If you want to specify another conditional format for the selection, click the Add button. The dialog box expands so that you can repeat Steps 1 through 4 for another condition.

6. When you finish, click OK.

Caution

Conditional formatting is a great feature, but it's not foolproof. If you copy a value and paste it into a cell that has conditional formatting, the formatting will not be applied. In fact, copying a value to a cell that has conditional formatting wipes out the conditional formatting information. In other words, the feature works only for data that is entered into a cell manually or calculated by a formula.

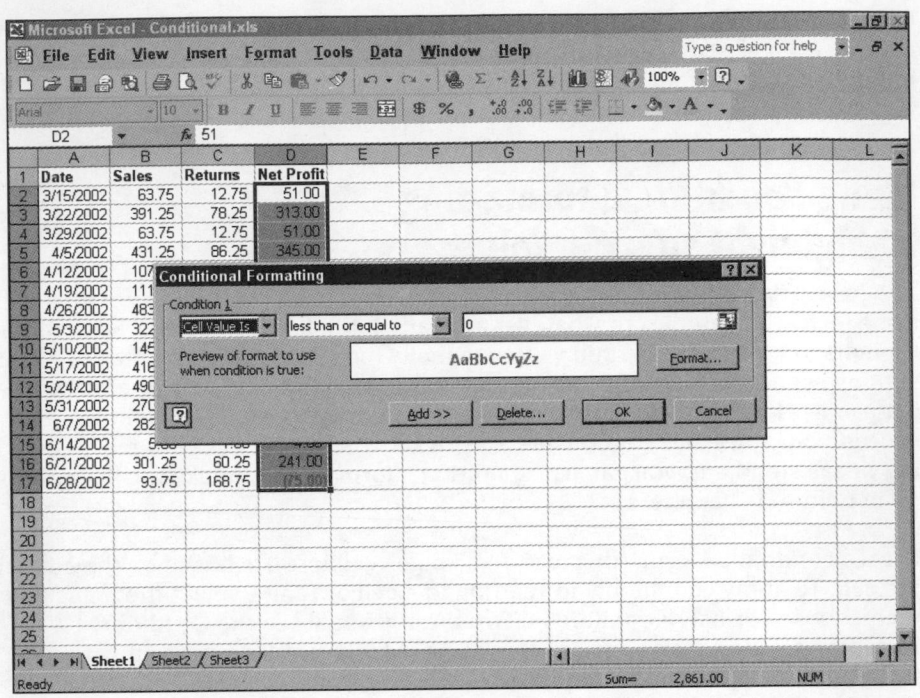

Figure 5-14: Use conditional formatting to make specific types of values much easier to see in your worksheets.

Cross-Reference   See Chapter 1 for information on creating custom numeric formats.

Using Named Styles for Easier Formatting

If you find that you are continually applying the same combination of fonts, lines, and shading in your worksheets, you can save time and effort if you create and use named styles. Named styles apply, in a single step, the formats that you specify, helping you to apply consistent formats across your worksheets.

A style can consist of settings for six different attributes, although a style doesn't have to use all the attributes. You may recognize these attributes; they correspond to the six tabs in the Format Cells dialog box. The attributes that make up a style are

✦ Number format

✦ Font (type, size, and color)

✦ Alignment (vertical and horizontal)

✦ Borders

✦ Pattern

✦ Protection (locked and hidden)

The real power of styles lies in what happens when you change a component of a style; in this case, all the cells that use that named style automatically incorporate the change. Suppose that you apply a particular style to a dozen cells scattered throughout your worksheet. Later, you realize that these cells should have a font size of 14 points rather than 12 points. Rather than change each cell, simply edit the style. All cells with that particular style change automatically.

By default, all cells have the Normal style. In addition, Excel provides five other built-in styles — alll of which control only the cell's number format. The styles that are available in every workbook are listed in Table 5-1. If these styles don't meet your needs (and they probably don't), you can easily create new styles.

	Table 5-1 **Excel's Built-In Styles**	
Style Name	*Description*	*Number Format Example*
Normal	Excel's default style	1234
Comma*	Comma with two decimal places	1,234.00
Comma[0]	Comma with no decimal places	1,234
Currency*	Left-aligned dollar sign with two decimal places	$ 1,234.00
Currency[0]	Left-aligned dollar sign with no decimal places	$ 1,234
Percent*	Percent with no decimal places	12%

* This style can be applied by clicking a button on the Standard toolbar.

Applying styles to your worksheets

There are several different methods that you can use to apply one of the named styles to cells or ranges.

✦ You can use the Currency Style, Percent Style, or Comma Style buttons on the Standard toolbar to attach a particular style to a cell or range. You need to understand that when you use these buttons to format a value, you're really changing the cell's style. Consequently, if you later want to change the Normal style, cells formatted with any of these buttons won't be affected by the change.

✦ You also can apply a style by using the Format ⇨ Style command, which prompts Excel to display its Style dialog box. Just choose the style that you want to apply from the Style Name drop-down list.

If you plan to work with named styles, you might want to make an addition to one of your toolbars. Excel has a handy Style tool available that does not normally appear on any of the built-in toolbars. To add the Style tool to a toolbar (the Formatting toolbar is a good choice), follow these steps:

1. Right-click any toolbar and choose Customize from the shortcut menu. Excel displays its Customize dialog box.

2. Click the Commands tab.

3. In the Categories list box, click Format. The Buttons box displays all available tools in the Formatting category.

4. Click the Style tool (it's a list box labeled Style) and drag it to your Formatting toolbar. If you drag the Style tool to the middle of the toolbar, the other tools move over to make room for it.

5. Click the Close button in the Customize dialog box.

To apply a style by using the Style tool, select the cell or range, open the Style list box, and then choose the style that you want to apply.

Creating your own new styles

In addition to using Excel's built-in styles, you can create your own styles. This can be quite handy because it enables you to apply your favorite formatting options very quickly and consistently.

There are two ways to create a new style: you can use the Format ➪ Style command or you can use the Style tool. To create a new style, first select a cell and apply all the formatting that you want to include in the new style. You can use any of the formatting that is available in the Format Cells dialog box.

After you format the cell to your liking, choose Format ➪ Style. Excel displays its Style dialog box, shown in Figure 5-15. Excel displays the name of the current style of the cell (probably Normal) in the Style Name drop-down. This box is highlighted so that you can simply enter a new style name by typing it. When you do so, Excel displays the words By Example to indicate that it's basing the style on the current cell.

The check boxes display the current formats for the cell. By default, all check boxes are checked. If you don't want the style to include one or more format categories, remove the check(s) from the appropriate box(es). Click OK to create the style.

You also can create a style from scratch in the Style dialog box. Just enter a style name and then click the Modify button to select the formatting.

If you added the Style tool to one of your toolbars, you can create a new style without using the Style dialog box. Just format a cell, click inside the Style tool list box, and then type the name. Using this method, you can't specify which formatting categories to omit from the style, but, as you learn next, you can easily modify an existing style.

Note The Protection option may not seem like it fits in the Style dialog box, but that's where Excel's designers placed it. This option simply controls whether users will be able to modify cells and is only effective if you've also turned on worksheet protection.

Modifying a style to meet your needs

To change an existing style, select Format ⇨ Style to open the Style dialog box. From the Style name drop-down box, choose the style that you want to modify. You can make changes to the check boxes to include or exclude any of the format categories, or you can click the Modify button to display the Format Cells dialog box. Make the changes that you want and click OK. Click OK again to close the Style dialog box. Excel modifies all the cells formatted with the selected style by applying the new formatting.

Tip You also can use the Style tool to change a style. Start by modifying the formatting of a cell that uses the style. Then, click inside the Style tool list box, select the style name, and press Enter. Confirm that you want to redefine the style and to change all of the cells that use the style.

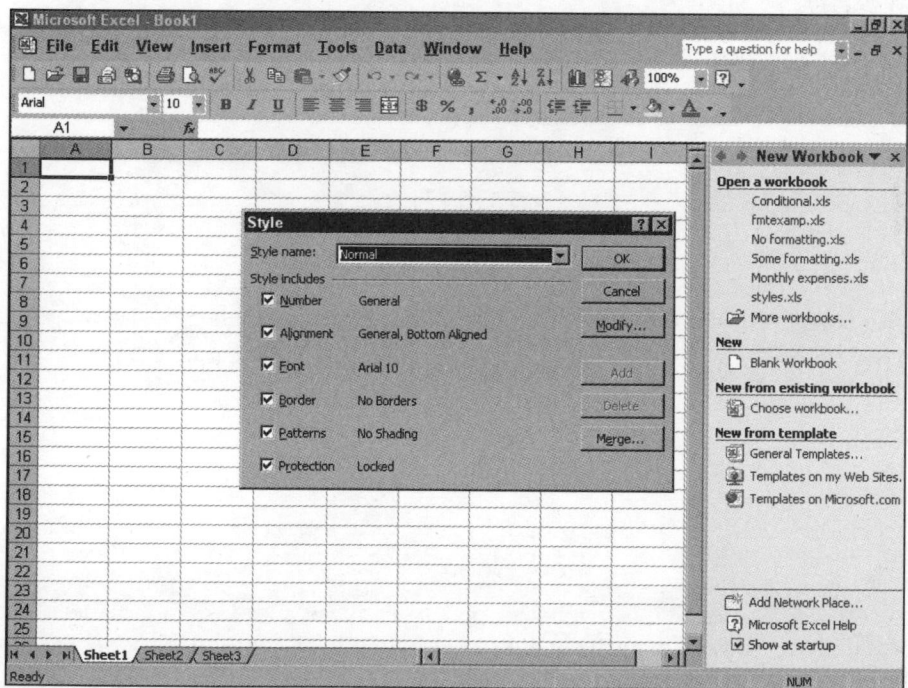

Figure 5-15: You can create your own styles using the Style dialog box.

After you apply a style to a cell, you can apply additional formatting to it by using any formatting method discussed in this chapter. Formatting modifications that you make to the cell don't affect other cells that use the same style.

Merging styles from other workbooks

If you use styles quite often, you probably don't want to go through all of the work to create copies of those styles in each new Excel workbook. A better approach is to merge the styles from a workbook in which you previously created them.

To merge styles from another workbook, open both the workbook that contains the styles that you want to merge and the workbook into which you want to merge styles. From the workbook into which you want to merge styles, choose Format ➪ Style and click the Merge button. Excel displays the Merge Styles dialog box with a list of all open workbooks, as shown in Figure 5-16. Select the workbook that contains the styles you want to merge and click OK. Excel copies styles from the workbook that you selected into the active workbook.

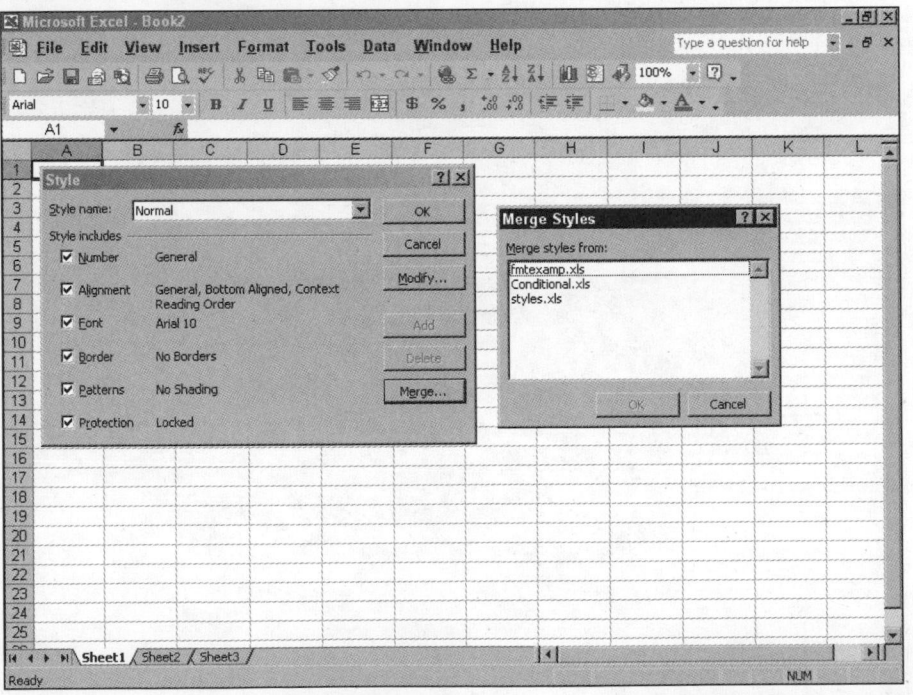

Figure 5-16: You can merge your own styles from other Excel workbooks so you don't have to re-create them.

When you're merging styles, colors are based on the palette stored with the workbook in which you use the style. Therefore, if the two workbooks involved in the merge use different color palettes, the colors used in the styles may not look the same in each workbook.

Tip You may want to create a master workbook that contains all of your custom styles so that you always know which workbook to merge styles from.

Controlling styles with templates

When you start Excel, it loads with several default settings, including the settings for stylistic formatting. If you spend a lot of time changing the default elements, you should know about templates.

Here's an example. You may prefer to use 12-point Arial rather than 10-point Arial as the default font. And maybe you prefer Wrap Text to be the default setting for alignment. Templates provide an easy way to change defaults.

The trick is to create a workbook with the Normal style modified to the way that you want it. Then, save the workbook as a template in your XLStart folder. After doing so, you can select File ➪ New to displays a dialog box from which you can choose the template for the new workbook. Template files also can store other named styles, providing you with an excellent way to give your workbooks a consistent look.

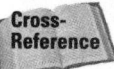

Cross-Reference Chapter 6 discusses templates in detail.

✦   ✦   ✦

Using and Creating Templates

This chapter discusses one of the most useful features in Excel — template files. Templates can be used for a variety of purposes, ranging from custom "fill-in-the-blanks" workbooks to a way to change Excel's defaults for new workbooks or new worksheets.

Even if you only create Excel worksheets for your own use, you'll find templates quite useful. By making your own template files you'll save a lot of time in the future when you want to make use of the same settings, formulas, or even things such as custom number formats you've developed.

Understanding Excel's Templates

A template is essentially a model that serves as the basis for something else. An Excel template is a workbook that's used to create other workbooks. If you understand this concept, you may save yourself a lot of work.

For example, you may always like to use a particular header or footer on your printouts. Consequently, every time that you print a worksheet, you need to select File ➪ Page Setup to add your page header. Although this isn't a lot of work, wouldn't it be easier if Excel simply remembered your favorite page settings and used them automatically?

The solution is to modify the template that Excel uses to create new workbooks. In this case, you modify the template file by inserting your header into the template. Save the template file, and then every new workbook that you create has your customized page settings.

Excel supports three types of templates:

✦ **The default workbook template:** Used as the basis for new workbooks.

✦ **The default worksheet template:** Used as the basis for new worksheets that are inserted into a workbook.

✦ **Custom workbook templates:** Usually, these are ready-to-run workbooks that include formulas, but they can be as simple or as complex as you like. Typically, these templates are set up so that a user can simply plug in values and get immediate results. The Spreadsheet Solutions templates (included with Excel) are examples of this type of template.

Each template type is discussed in the following sections.

Working with the Default Templates

The term *default template* may be a little misleading. In reality, Excel uses its own internal settings — not an actual template file — if you haven't created your own template files to control the default settings. That is, Excel uses your template files to set the defaults for new workbooks or worksheets, but if you haven't created these files Excel is perfectly happy to use its own settings.

Using the workbook template to change workbook defaults

Every new workbook that you create starts out with some default settings. For example, the workbook's worksheets have gridlines, text appears in Arial 10-point font, values that are entered display in the General number format, and so on. If you're not happy with any of the default workbook settings, you can change them.

Making changes to Excel's default workbook is fairly easy to do, and it can save you lots of time in the long run. Here's how you change Excel's workbook defaults:

1. Open a new workbook.

2. Add or delete sheets to give the workbook the number of worksheets that you want.

3. Make any other changes that you want to make, which can include column widths, named styles, page setup options, and many of the settings that are available in the Options dialog box.

   To change the default formatting for cells, choose Format ➪ Style, and then modify the settings for the Normal style. For example, you can change the default font, size, or number format.

4. When your workbook is set up to your liking, select File ➪ Save As.

5. In the Save As dialog box, select Template (*.xlt) from the box labeled Save as type.

6. Enter **book.xlt** for the filename.

Excel will offer the name Book1.xlt. You must change this name to book.xlt if you want Excel to use your template to set the workbook defaults.

7. Save the file in your \XLStart folder.

The \XLStart folder may be located within your C:\Program Files\Microsoft Office\Office folder, in the C:\Windows\Application Data\Microsoft\Excel folder, or in your C:\Windows\Profiles*user_name*\Application Data\Microsoft\Excel folder (where *user_name* is your user name). The exact location depends on the version of Windows you are using.

8. Close the file.

9. Close and then restart Excel (if you skip this step, Excel won't use your new template until the next time you do restart Excel).

You can also save your book.xlt template file in the folder that is specified on the General tab of the Options dialog box in the box labeled At startup, open all files in.

After you perform the preceding steps, the new default workbook is based on the book.xlt workbook template. You can create a workbook based on your template by using any of these methods:

✦ Click the New button on the Standard toolbar.

✦ Press Ctrl+N.

✦ Open Excel without first selecting a workbook to open.

Figure 6-1 is an example of a very simple workbook that resulted from creating a workbook default template file. In this case, we set up the default workbook to have five worksheets and a title in cell A1.

Using the worksheet template to change worksheet defaults

When you insert a new worksheet into a workbook, Excel uses its built-in worksheet defaults for the worksheet. This includes items such as column width, row height, and so on.

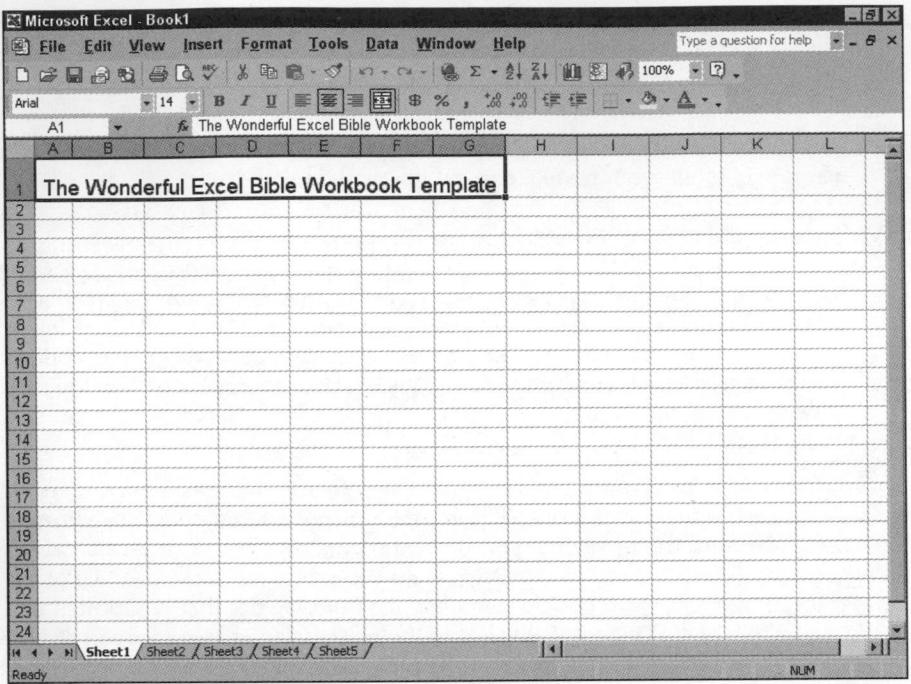

Figure 6-1: After you create a book.xlt template, Excel creates new workbooks that are based on your template.

If you don't like the default settings for a new worksheet, you can change them by following these steps:

1. Start with a new workbook, deleting all the sheets except one.

2. Make any changes that you want to make, which can include column widths, named styles, page setup options, and many of the settings that are available in the Options dialog box.

3. When your workbook is set up to your liking, select File ⇨ Save As.

4. In the Save As dialog box, select Template (*.xlt) from the Save As type box.

5. Enter **sheet.xlt** for the filename.

6. Save the file in your \XLStart folder (or in the folder that is specified on the General tab of the Options dialog box in the box labeled At startup, open all files in).

7. Close the file.

8. Close and restart Excel.

After performing this procedure, all new sheets that you insert with the Insert ⇨ Worksheet command will be formatted like your sheet.xlt template.

When you right-click a sheet tab and choose Insert from the shortcut menu, Excel displays its Insert dialog box (which looks just like the New dialog box). If you've created a template named sheet.xlt, you can select it by clicking the icon labeled Worksheet.

Editing your templates

After you create your book.xlt or sheet.xlt templates, you may discover that you need to change them. You can open the template files and edit them just like any other workbook. After you make your changes, save the file and close it.

Resetting the default workbook and worksheet settings

If you create a book.xlt or sheet.xlt file and then decide that you would rather use the standard default settings, simply delete the book.xlt or sheet.xlt template file — depending on whether you want to use the standard workbook or worksheet defaults — from the XLStart folder. Excel then goes back to its built-in default settings for new workbooks or worksheets.

 **Tip**   You can also rename or move the template files if you'd like to keep them for future use.

Creating Custom Templates

The book.xlt and sheet.xlt templates discussed in the previous section are two special types of templates that determine default settings for new workbooks and new worksheets. This section discusses other types of templates, referred to as workbook templates, which are simply workbooks that you set up as the basis for new workbooks or worksheets.

Why use a workbook template? The simple answer is that it saves you from repeating work. Assume that you create a monthly sales report that consists of your company's sales by region, plus several summary calculations and charts. You can create a template file that consists of everything except the input values. Then, when it's time to create your report, you can open a workbook based on the template, fill in the blanks, and be finished.

You could, of course, just use the previous month's workbook and save it with a different name. This is prone to errors, however, because you easily can forget to use the Save As command and accidentally overwrite the previous month's file.

When you create a workbook that is based on a template, the default workbook name is the template name with a number appended. For example, if you create a new workbook based on a template named Sales Report.xlt, the workbook's default name is Sales Report1.xls. The first time that you save a workbook that is created from a template, Excel displays its Save As dialog box, so that you can give the template a new name if you want to.

A custom template is essentially a normal workbook, and it can use any of Excel's features, such as charts, formulas, and macros. Usually, a template is set up so that the user can enter values and get immediate results. In other words, most templates include everything but the data, which is entered by the user.

Tip   If novices will use the template, you might consider locking all the cells except the input cells (use the Protection panel of the Format Cells dialog box for this). Then, protect the worksheet by choosing Tools ➪ Protection commands.

Saving your custom templates

To save the workbook as a template, choose File ➪ Save As and select Template (*.xlt) from the drop-down list labeled Save as type. Save the template in your Templates folder — which Excel automatically suggests — or a folder within that Templates folder.

If you later discover that you want to modify the template, choose File ➪ Open to open and edit the template.

Tip   Before you save the template, you may want to specify that the file be saved with a preview image. Select File ➪ Properties, and check the box labeled Save Preview Picture. That way, the New dialog box displays the preview when the template's icon is selected.

Ideas for creating templates

This section provides a few ideas that may spark your imagination for creating templates. The following is a partial list of the settings that you can adjust and use in your custom templates:

✦ **Multiple formatted worksheets:** You can, for example, create a workbook template that has two worksheets — one formatted to print in landscape mode and one formatted to print in portrait mode.

✦ **Several settings in the View panel of the Options dialog box:** For example, you may not like to see sheet tabs, so you can turn off this setting.

✦ **Color palette:** Use the Color panel of the Options dialog box to create a custom color palette for a workbook.

✦ **Style:** The best approach is to choose Format ➪ Style and modify the attributes of the Normal style. For example, you can change the font or size, the alignment, and so on.

✦ **Custom number formats:** If you create number formats that you use frequently, these can be stored in a template.

✦ **Column widths and row heights:** You may prefer that columns be wider or narrower, or you may want the rows to be taller.

✦ **Print settings:** Change these settings in the Page Setup dialog box. You can adjust the page orientation, paper size, margins, header and footer, and several other attributes.

✦ **Sheet settings:** These are options in the Options dialog box. They include gridlines, automatic page break display, and row and column headers.

You can, of course, also create complete workbooks and save them as templates. For example, if you frequently need to produce a specific report, you might want to create a template that has everything for the report except for the data you need to enter. By saving your master copy as a template you are less likely to overwrite the original file when you save the file after entering your data.

✦ ✦ ✦

Working with Formulas and Functions

❖ ❖ ❖ ❖

In This Part

Formulas and worksheet functions are essential to manipulating data and obtaining useful information from your Excel workbooks. This part shows you how to create formulas and use functions in your Excel worksheets. You'll learn how to choose the functions that will make creating the formulas you need much easier, and you'll see many useful examples that you can quickly adapt to your own purposes.

❖ ❖ ❖ ❖

Creating and Using Formulas

Formulas are what make a spreadsheet so useful. You use formulas in your Excel worksheets to calculate results from the data stored in the worksheet. When data changes, those formulas produce updated results without extra effort on your part. This chapter introduces formulas and helps you get up to speed with this important element.

Understanding Formula Basics

In many ways, formulas are like just about anything else you might add to an Excel worksheet. To add a formula to a worksheet, you enter it into a cell. You can delete, move, and copy formulas just like any other item of data. Formulas use arithmetic operators to work with values, text, worksheet functions, and other formulas to calculate a value in the cell. Values and text can be located in other cells, which makes changing data easy and gives worksheets their dynamic nature. In essence, you can see multiple scenarios quickly by changing the data in a worksheet and letting formulas do the work.

A formula entered into a cell can consist of any of these elements:

- ✦ Operators such as + (for addition) and * (for multiplication)
- ✦ Cell references (including named cells and ranges)
- ✦ Values or text
- ✦ Worksheet functions (such as SUM or AVERAGE)

A formula can consist of up to 1,024 characters. After you enter a formula into a cell, the cell displays the result of the formula. The formula itself appears in the formula bar when you select the cell, however.

The following lists some examples of formulas:

=150*.05	Multiplies 150 times 0.05. This formula uses only values and isn't all that useful.
=A1+A2	Adds the values in cells A1 and A2.
=Income-Expenses	Subtracts the cell named Expenses from the cell named Income.
=SUM(A1:A12)	Adds the values in the range A1:A12.
=A1=C12	Compares cell A1 with cell C12. If they are identical, the formula returns TRUE; otherwise, it returns FALSE.

Note   Formulas always begin with an equal sign so that Excel can distinguish formulas from text.

Using operators in formulas

Excel lets you use a variety of *operators* in your formulas. Operators are symbols that tell Excel what type of mathematical operation you want the formula to perform.

Table 7-1 lists the operators that Excel recognizes. In addition to these, Excel has many built-in functions that enable you to perform more operations.

Cross-Reference   Functions are discussed in detail in Chapter 8.

Table 7-1	
Operators Used in Formulas	
Operator	**Name**
+	Addition
-	Subtraction
*	Multiplication
/	Division
^	Exponentiation
&	Concatenation
=	Logical comparison (equal to)
>	Logical comparison (greater than)
<	Logical comparison (less than)

Operator	Name
>=	Logical comparison (greater than or equal to)
<=	Logical comparison (less than or equal to)
<>	Logical comparison (not equal to)

You can, of course, use as many operators as you need (formulas can be quite complex). Figure 7-1 shows a worksheet with a formula in cell B5. The formula is

```
=(B2-B3)*B4
```

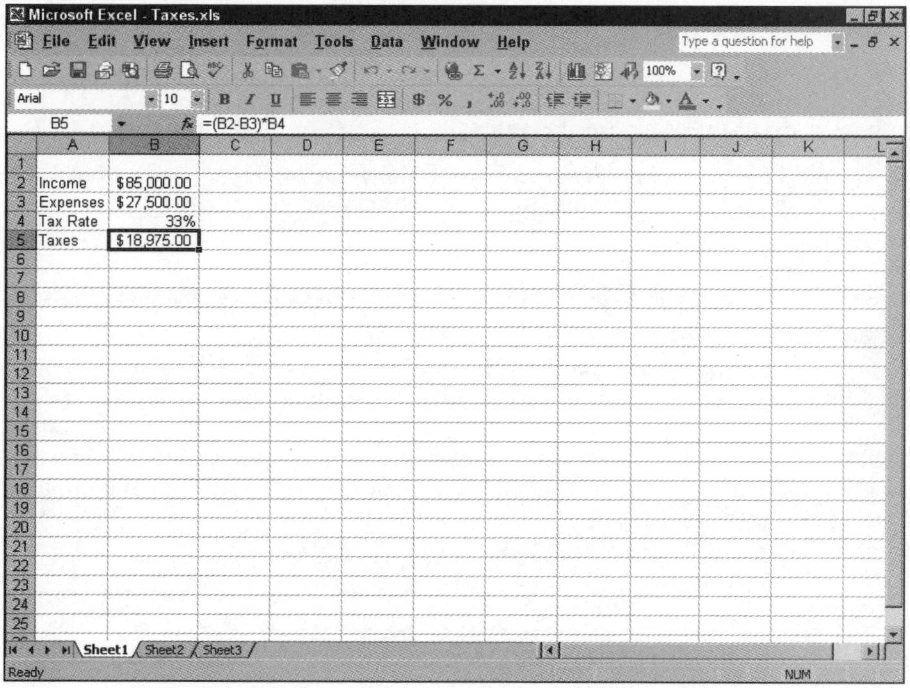

Figure 7-1: You can use operators to create formulas such as this one.

In this example, the formula subtracts the value in B3 from the value in B2 and then multiplies the result by the value in B4. The following are some additional examples of formulas that use various operators.

Formula	What It Does
`="Part-"&"23A"`	Joins (concatenates) the two text strings to produce Part-23A.
`=A1&A2`	Concatenates the contents of cell A1 with cell A2. Concatenation works with values as well as text. If cell A1 contains 123 and cell A2 contains 456, this formula would return the value 123456.
`=6^3`	Raises 6 to the third power (216).
`=216^(1/3)`	Returns the cube root of 216 (6).
`=A1<A2`	Returns TRUE if the value in cell A1 is less than the value in cell A2. Otherwise, it returns FALSE. Logical comparison operators also work with text. If A1 contained Bill and A2 contained Julia, the formula would return TRUE, because Bill comes before Julia in alphabetical order.
`=A1<=A2`	Returns TRUE if the value in cell A1 is less than or equal to the value in cell A2. Otherwise, it returns FALSE.
`=A1<>A2`	Returns TRUE if the value in cell A1 isn't equal to the value in cell A2. Otherwise, it returns FALSE.

Understanding operator precedence in formulas

When Excel calculates the value of a formula, it uses certain rules to determine the order in which the various parts of the formula are resolved. You need to understand these rules if you want your formulas to produce the desired results.

Table 7-2 lists Excel's operator precedence. This table shows that exponentiation has the highest precedence (that is, it's performed first), and logical comparisons have the lowest precedence.

Table 7-2
Operator Precedence in Excel Formulas

Symbol	Operator	Precedence
^	Exponentiation	1
*	Multiplication	2
/	Division	2
+	Addition	3
-	Subtraction	3
&	Concatenation	4

Symbol	Operator	Precedence
=	Equal to	5
<	Less than	5
> ·	Greater than	5

You use parentheses to override Excel's built-in order of precedence. Expressions within parentheses are always evaluated first.

In the earlier example, parentheses are used in the formula to control the order in which the calculations occur. In this case, cell B2 is subtracted from cell B3 and the result is multiplied by cell B4.

```
=(B2-B3)*B4
```

If you enter the formula without the parentheses, Excel computes the wrong answer. Because multiplication has a higher precedence, the cell B3 is multiplied by cell B4. Then, this result is subtracted from cell B2. This isn't what was intended.

The formula without parentheses looks like this:

```
=B2-B3*B4
```

You can also nest parentheses in formulas, which means putting parentheses inside of parentheses. If you do so, Excel evaluates the most deeply nested expressions first and works its way out. Here is an example of a formula that uses nested parentheses.

```
=((B2*C2)+(B3*C3)+(B4*C4))*B6
```

This formula has four sets of parentheses — three sets are nested inside the fourth set. Excel evaluates each nested set of parentheses and then adds up the three results. This sum is then multiplied by the value in B6.

Every left parenthesis, of course, must have a matching right parenthesis. If you have many levels of nested parentheses, it can sometimes be difficult to keep them straight. If the parentheses don't match, Excel displays a message explaining the problem and won't let you enter the formula.

In some cases, if your formula contains mismatched parentheses, Excel may propose a correction to your formula. Figure 7-2 shows an example of the Formula AutoCorrect feature. You may be tempted simply to accept the proposed correction, but be careful — in many cases, the proposed formula, although syntactically correct, isn't the formula that you want.

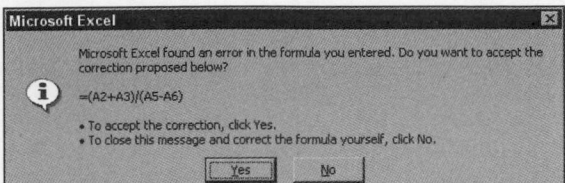

Figure 7-2: Excel's Formula AutoCorrect feature often suggests a correction to an erroneous formula.

Tip   Excel lends a hand in helping you match parentheses. When the insertion point moves over a parenthesis, Excel momentarily bolds it and its matching parenthesis.

Using Excel's built-in functions in formulas

Excel provides a huge number of built-in worksheet functions that you can use in your formulas. These include common functions (such as SUM, AVERAGE, and SQRT) as well as functions designed for special purposes, such as statistics or engineering. Functions can greatly enhance the power of your formulas. They can simplify your formulas and make them easier to read; in many cases, functions enable you to perform calculations that would not be possible otherwise. If you can't find a worksheet function that you need, Excel even lets you create your own custom functions.

Cross-Reference   Excel's built-in functions are discussed in Chapter 8, and Chapter 36 covers the basics of creating custom functions by using Visual Basic for Applications (VBA).

Entering Formulas into Your Worksheets

As mentioned earlier, a formula must begin with an equal sign to inform Excel that the cell contains a formula rather than text. Basically, two ways exist to enter a formula into a cell: enter it manually or enter it by pointing to cell references. Each method is discussed in the following sections.

Entering formulas manually

Entering a formula manually involves, well, entering a formula manually. You simply type an equal sign (=) followed by the formula. As you type, the characters appear in the cell and in the formula bar. You can, of course, use all the normal editing keys when entering a formula.

If you enter a formula, and instead of the result you expect the cell shows a value that begins with a pound sign (#), Excel is telling you that there is an error in the formula. Move the mouse pointer over the Smart Tag that appears next to the cell (see Figure 7-3) to learn more about the error.

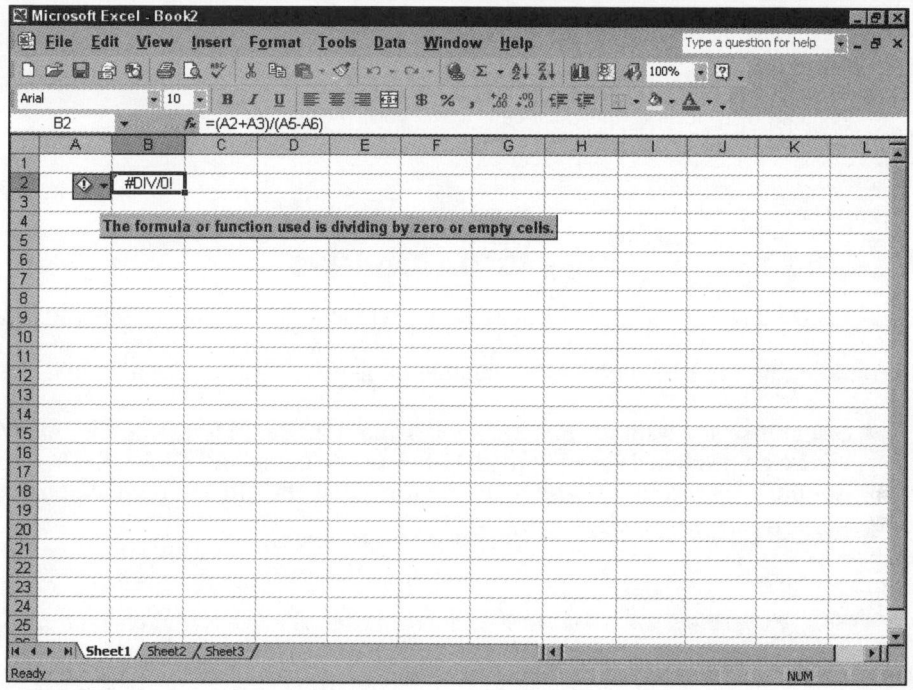

Figure 7-3: Excel's Smart Tags can help you understand errors in formulas you enter.

Cross-Reference

See "Correcting Common Formula Errors" later in this chapter for more on resolving errors in your formulas.

Entering formulas by pointing

Even though you can enter formulas by typing in the entire formula, Excel provides another method of entering formulas that is generally easier, faster, and less error prone. This other method of entering a formula still involves some manual typing, but you can simply point to the cell references instead of entering them manually. For example, to enter the formula =A1+A2 into cell A3, follow these steps:

1. Move the cell pointer to cell A3.

2. Type an equal sign (=) to begin the formula. Notice that Excel displays Enter in the status bar.

3. Press the up arrow twice. As you press this key, Excel displays a faint moving border around the cell, and the cell reference appears in cell A3 and in the formula bar. In addition, Excel displays Point in the status bar.

4. Type a plus sign (+). A solid color border replaces the faint border, and Enter reappears in the status bar.

5. Press the up arrow again. A2 is added to the formula.

6. Press Enter to end the formula.

Tip   You can also point to the data cells using your mouse.

Pasting range names into formulas

If your formula uses named cells or ranges, you can either type the name in place of the address or choose the name from a list and have Excel insert the name for you automatically. You have two ways available to insert a name into a formula:

✦ Select Insert ➪ Name ➪ Paste: Excel displays its Paste Name dialog box with all the names listed (see Figure 7-4). Select the name and click OK. Or, you can double-click the name, which inserts the name and closes the dialog box.

✦ Press F3: This also displays the Paste Name dialog box.

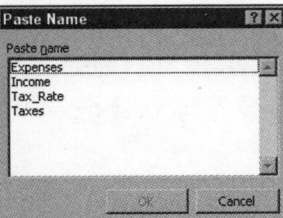

Figure 7-4: You can use the Paste Name dialog box to quickly enter defined names into your formulas.

Editing formulas in your worksheets

You can edit your formulas just like you can edit any other cell. You might need to edit a formula if you make some changes to your worksheet and need to adjust the formula to accommodate the changes. Or, the formula may return an error value and you need to edit the formula to correct the error.

The following are some of the ways to get into cell-edit mode:

✦ Double-click the cell, which enables you to edit the cell contents directly in the cell.

✦ Press F2, which enables you to edit the cell contents directly in the cell.

✦ Select the cell that you want to edit, and then click in the formula bar. This enables you to edit the cell contents in the formula bar.

✦ Click the Smart Tag and choose one of the options for correcting the error (the options will vary according to the type of error in the cell).

While you're editing a formula, you can select multiple characters either by dragging the mouse over them or by pressing Shift while you use the direction keys.

Tip If you have a formula that you can't seem to edit correctly, you can convert the formula to text and tackle it again later. To convert a formula to text, just remove the initial equal sign (=). When you're ready to try again, insert the initial equal sign to convert the cell contents back to a formula.

Understanding How to Use References in Formulas

Nearly all formulas include references to cells or ranges. These references enable your formulas to work with the data contained in those cells or ranges rather than simply with fixed values. That is, if your formula refers to cell A1 and you change the value contained in A1, the formula result changes to reflect the new value. If you didn't use references in your formulas, you would need to edit the formulas themselves to change the values used in the formulas.

Using relative, absolute, and mixed references

When you use a cell (or range) reference in a formula, there are three types of references you can use:

✦ **Relative:** The row and column references can change when you copy the formula to another cell because the references are actually offsets from the current row and column.

✦ **Absolute:** The row and column references do not change when you copy the formula because the reference is to an actual cell address.

✦ **Mixed:** Either the row or column reference is relative, and the other is absolute.

Tip If your formulas reference other worksheets, the sheet reference can also be relative or absolute.

When you create formulas, you need to be able to distinguish between relative and absolute cell references. By default, Excel creates relative cell references in formulas except when the formula includes cells in different worksheets or workbooks. The distinction becomes apparent when you copy a formula to another cell.

Figure 7-5 shows how relative, absolute, and mixed references affect the results when formulas are copied.

Microsoft Excel - References.xls

File Edit View Insert Format Tools Data Window Help   Type a question for help

Arial   10   B I U $ % ,

B15

	A	B	C	D	E	F	G	H	I	J
1		Relative references								
2		2.704545	=(A17+A18)/A19							
3		91.5	=(A18+A19)/A20							
4										
5		Absolute references								
6		2.704545	=($A$17+$A$18)/$A$19							
7		2.704545	=($A$17+$A$18)/$A$19							
8										
9		Mixed references								
10		2.704545	=(A$17+$A18)/A19							
11		63.75	=(A$17+$A19)/A20							
12		42.33333	=(A$17+$A20)/A21							
13		#DIV/0!	=(A$17+$A21)/A26							
14										
15										
16										
17	123									
18	234									
19	132									
20	4									
21	3									
22										
23										
24										
25										

Sheet1 / Sheet2 / Sheet3 /

Ready   NUM

Figure 7-5: You get very different results when you copy formulas that have relative, absolute, and mixed references.

When you copy a formula that uses relative references, Excel doesn't produce an exact copy of the formula; rather, it adjusts the cell references to refer to the cells that are relative to the new formula. Think of it like this: The original formula contained instructions to add the value of two cells 15 and 16 rows down and 1 column to the left and then to divide the result by the value 17 rows down and 1 column to the left. When you copy the cell, these instructions get copied, not the actual contents of the cell. Usually, this is exactly what you want. You certainly don't want to copy the formula verbatim; if you did, the new formulas would produce the same value as the original formula.

Note   When you cut and paste a formula (move it to another location), the cell references in the formula aren't adjusted. Again, this is what you usually want to happen. When you move a formula, you generally want it to continue to refer to the original cells.

Sometimes, however, you *do* want a cell reference to be copied verbatim. Figure 7-5 also shows an example of a formula that contains an absolute reference. In this example, cell B6 contains an absolute reference to each cell. The formula in cell B6 is

```
=($A$17+$A$18)/$A$19
```

Notice that the formula in cell B6 has dollar signs preceding the column letters and the row numbers. These dollar signs indicate to Excel that you want to use an absolute cell reference. When you copy this formula to the cell below, Excel generates the following formula in cell B7:

```
=($A$17+$A$18)/$A$19
```

In this case, the formula wasn't changed, because it used absolute references.

An absolute reference uses two dollar signs in its address: one for the column letter and one for the row number. Excel also allows mixed references in which only one of the address parts is absolute. Cells B10:B13 in Figure 7-5 show the effects of mixed references.

When would you use a mixed reference? Well, imagine that you had a table with interest rates across the top row, and loan amounts along the left column. By using a mixed reference you could create a formula that always referred to the cell in the top row but the same column as the formula for interest rates, and to the left column but the same row for amounts. For example, if the interest rates were in row 1 and the amounts were in column A, you could place the following formula in cell B2:

```
=PMT(B$1,number_of_payments,-$A2)
```

Then when you copied the formula to the rest of the table, the mixed references would produce the desired results.

Changing the types of your references

You can enter nonrelative references (absolute or mixed) manually by inserting dollar signs in the appropriate positions. Or, you can use a handy shortcut: the F4 key. When you're entering a cell reference you can press F4 repeatedly to have Excel cycle through all four reference types.

For example, if you enter =A1 to start a formula, pressing F4 converts the cell reference to =$A$1. Pressing F4 again converts it to =A$1. Pressing it again displays =$A1. Pressing it one more time returns to the original =A1. Keep pressing F4 until Excel displays the type of reference that you want.

Note   When you name a cell or range, Excel (by default) uses an absolute reference for the name. For example, if you give the name SalesForecast to A1:A12, the Refers to box in the Define Name dialog box lists the reference as $A$1:$A$12. This is almost always what you want. If you copy a cell that has a named reference in its formula, the copied formula contains a reference to the original name.

Referencing cells outside the worksheet

Formulas can also refer to cells in other worksheets — and the worksheets don't even have to be in the same workbook. Excel uses a special type of notation to handle these types of references.

Referencing cells in other worksheets

To use a reference to a cell in another worksheet in the same workbook, use this format:

```
SheetName!CellAddress
```

In other words, precede the cell address with the worksheet name, followed by an exclamation point. Here's an example of a formula that uses a cell on the Sheet2 worksheet:

```
=A1*Sheet2!A1
```

This formula multiplies the value in cell A1 on the current worksheet by the value in cell A1 on Sheet2.

Tip

If the worksheet name in the reference includes one or more spaces, you must enclose it in single quotation marks (Excel will do this automatically if you use the point and click method). For example, here's a formula that refers to a cell on a sheet named All Depts:

```
=A1*'All Depts'!A1
```

Referencing cells in other workbooks

To refer to a cell in a different workbook, use this format:

```
=[WorkbookName]SheetName!CellAddress
```

In this case, the workbook name (in square brackets), the worksheet name, and an exclamation point precede the cell address. The following is an example of a formula that uses a cell reference in the Sheet1 worksheet in a workbook named Budget:

```
=[Budget.xls]Sheet1!A1
```

If the workbook name in the reference includes one or more spaces, you must enclose it (and the sheet name) in single quotation marks. For example, here's a formula that refers to a cell on Sheet1 in a workbook named Budget For 2003:

```
=A1*'[Budget For 2003]Sheet1'!A1
```

When a formula refers to cells in a different workbook, the other workbook doesn't need to be open. If the workbook is closed, you must add the complete path to the reference. Here's an example:

```
=A1*'C:\My Documents\[Budget For 2003]Sheet1'!A1
```

Cross-Reference

File linking is discussed in detail in Chapter 27.

Tip To create formulas that refer to cells not in the current worksheet, point to the cells rather than entering the references manually. Excel takes care of the details regarding the workbook and worksheet references. The workbook that you're using in your formula must be open to use the pointing method.

Note If you point to a different worksheet or workbook when creating a formula, you'll notice that Excel always inserts absolute cell references. Therefore, if you plan to copy the formula to other cells, make sure that you change the cell references to relative.

Correcting Common Formula Errors

Sometimes when you enter a formula, Excel displays a value that begins with a pound sign (#). This is a signal that the formula is returning an error value. You have to correct the formula (or correct a cell that the formula references) to get rid of the error display. As noted earlier, Excel often suggests a correction for an erroneous formula.

Tip If the entire cell is filled with pound characters, this means that the column isn't wide enough to display the value. You can either widen the column or change the number format of the cell.

Table 7-3 lists the types of error values that may appear in a cell that has a formula. Formulas may return an error value if a cell to which they refer has an error value. This is known as the ripple effect — a single error value can make its way into lots of other cells that contain formulas that depend on the cell.

Table 7-3 Excel Error Values	
Error Value	**Explanation**
#DIV/0!	The formula is trying to divide by zero. This also occurs when the formula attempts to divide by a cell that is empty.
#NAME?	The formula uses a name that Excel doesn't recognize. This can happen if you delete a name that's used in the formula or if you have unmatched quotes when using text.
#N/A	The formula is referring (directly or indirectly) to a cell that uses the NA function to signal that data is not available.
#NULL!	The formula uses an intersection of two ranges that don't intersect (this concept is described later in the chapter).

Continued

	Table 7-3 *(continued)*	
Error Value	**Explanation**	
#NUM!	A problem with a value exists; for example, you specified a negative number where a positive number is expected.	
#REF!	The formula refers to a cell that isn't valid. This can happen if the cell has been deleted from the worksheet.	
#VALUE!	The formula includes an argument or operand of the wrong type. An operand is a value or cell reference that a formula uses to calculate a result.	

Handling circular references

When you're entering formulas, you may occasionally see a message from Excel similar to the one shown in Figure 7-6, indicating that the formula you just entered will result in a *circular reference*. A circular reference occurs when a formula refers to its own value — either directly or indirectly. For example, you create a circular reference if you enter =A1+A2+A3 into cell A3, because the formula in cell A3 refers to cell A3. Every time the formula in A3 is calculated, it must be calculated again because A3 has changed. The calculation would go on forever.

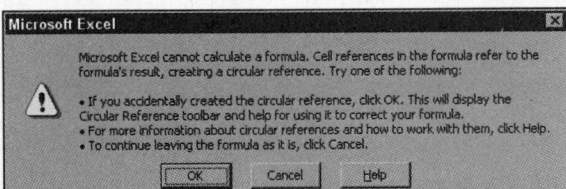

Figure 7-6: If you attempt to create a circular reference, Excel warns you about the potential error.

When you get the circular reference message after entering a formula, Excel gives you two options:

✦ Click OK to attempt to locate the circular reference

✦ Click Cancel to enter the formula as is

Usually, you want to correct any circular references, so you should choose OK. When you do so, Excel displays the Help topic on circular references and the Circular Reference toolbar (see Figure 7-7). On the Circular Reference toolbar, click the first cell in the Navigate Circular Reference drop-down list box, and then examine the cell's formula. If you cannot determine whether the cell is the cause of the circular reference, click the next cell in the Navigate Circular Reference box. Continue to review the formulas until the status bar no longer displays Circular.

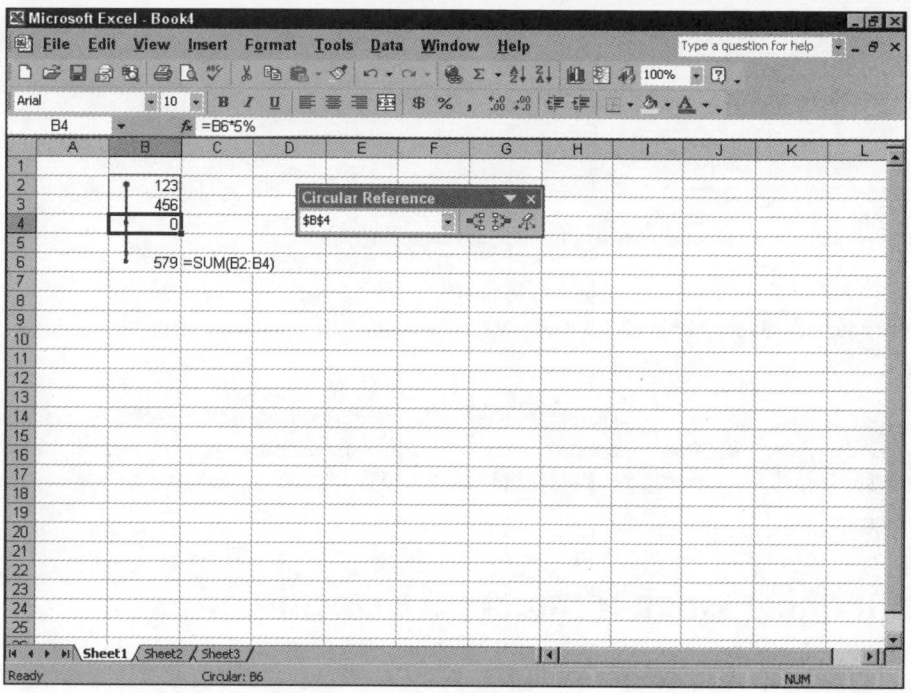

Figure 7-7: You can use the Circular Reference toolbar to investigate the cause of a circular reference.

Tip If Excel does not automatically display the Circular Reference toolbar, select View ⇨ Toolbars ⇨ Circular Reference.

If you ignore the circular reference message (by clicking Cancel), Excel lets you enter the formula and displays a message in the status bar to remind you that a circular reference exists. In this case, the message reads Circular: B6. If you activate a different workbook, the message simply displays Circular (without the cell reference).

Note Excel won't tell you about a circular reference if the Iteration setting is on. You can check this in the Options dialog box (in the Calculation tab). If Iteration is on, Excel performs the circular calculation the number of times specified in the Maximum iterations field (or until the value changes by less than 0.001 or whatever value is in the Maximum change field). In a few situations, you may use a circular reference intentionally. In these cases, the Iteration setting must be on. However, keeping the Iteration setting turned off is best, so that you are warned of circular references. Most of the time, a circular reference indicates an error that you must correct.

Usually, a circular reference is quite obvious and, therefore, easy to identify and correct. Sometimes, however, circular references are indirect. In other words, a formula may refer to a formula that refers to a formula that refers back to the original formula. In some cases, it may require a bit of detective work to get to the problem.

Intentional Circular References

You can sometimes use a circular reference to your advantage. For example, a company has a policy of contributing five percent of its net profit to charity. The contribution itself, however, is considered an expense and is therefore subtracted from the net profit figure. This produces a circular reference.

The Contributions cell contains the following formula:

```
=5%*Net_Profit
```

The Net Profit cell contains the following formula:

```
=Gross_Income-Expenses-Contributions
```

These formulas produce a resolvable circular reference. If the Iteration setting is on, Excel keeps calculating until the Contributions value is, indeed, five percent of Net Profit. In other words, the result becomes increasingly more accurate until it converges on the final solution.

Changing when formulas are calculated

You've probably noticed that Excel calculates the formulas in your worksheet immediately. If you change any cells that the formula uses, Excel displays the formula's new result, with no effort on your part. All this happens when Excel's Calculation mode is set to Automatic. In Automatic Calculation mode (which is the default mode), Excel follows these rules when calculating your worksheet:

✦ When you make a change—enter or edit data or formulas, for example—Excel calculates immediately those formulas that depend on new or edited data.

✦ If Excel is in the middle of a lengthy calculation, it temporarily suspends the calculation when you need to perform other worksheet tasks; it resumes when you're finished.

✦ Formulas are evaluated in a natural sequence. In other words, if a formula in cell D12 depends on the result of a formula in cell D11, Excel calculates cell D11 before calculating D12.

Sometimes, however, you may want to control when Excel calculates formulas. For example, if you create a worksheet with thousands of complex formulas, you'll find that things can slow to a snail's pace while Excel does its thing. In such a case, set Excel's calculation mode to Manual, which you can do in the Calculation tab of the Options dialog box (see Figure 7-8).

To select Manual calculation mode, click the Manual option button. When you switch to Manual calculation mode, Excel automatically places a check in the box labeled Recalculate before save. You can remove the check if you want to speed up file-saving operations.

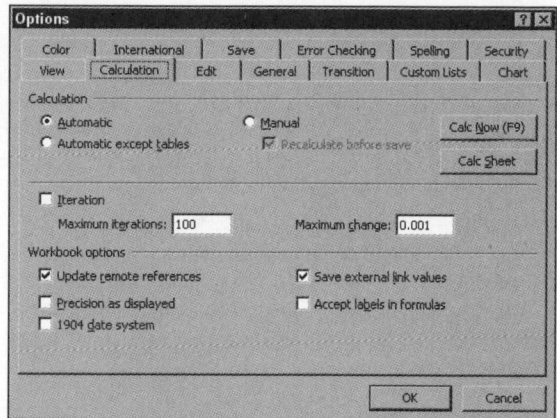

Figure 7-8: You can control when Excel calculates formulas using the settings on the Calculation tab of the Options dialog box.

Tip

If your worksheet uses any data tables (described in Chapter 23), you may want to select the option labeled Automatic except tables. Large data tables calculate notoriously slowly.

When you're working in Manual calculation mode, Excel displays Calculate in the status bar when you have any uncalculated formulas. You can use the following shortcut keys to recalculate the formulas:

✦ **F9:** Calculates the formulas in all open workbooks.

✦ **Shift+F9:** Calculates only the formulas in the active worksheet. Other worksheets in the same workbook aren't calculated.

Note

Excel's Calculation mode isn't specific to a particular worksheet. When you change Excel's Calculation mode, it affects all open workbooks, not just the active workbook.

Using Advanced Naming Techniques

Using range names certainly makes your formulas easier to understand. Excel offers a number of advanced techniques that make using names even more useful. For example, refer back to Figure 7-1. If the worksheet had names defined for these cells, the formula would be a lot more readable. Here's the same formula after naming the cells:

```
=(Income-Expenses)*TaxRate
```

Are you beginning to understand the importance of naming ranges?

Using names for constants

Even many advanced Excel users don't realize that you can give a name to an item that doesn't appear in a cell. For example, if formulas in your worksheet use a sales tax rate, you would probably insert the tax rate value into a cell and use this cell reference in your formulas. To make things easier, you would probably also name this cell something similar to SalesTax.

Here's another way to do it: Choose Insert ➪ Name ➪ Define (or press Ctrl+F3) to bring up the Define Name dialog box. Enter the name (in this case, SalesTax) into the field labeled Names in workbook. Then, click the Refers to box, delete its contents, and replace it with a value such as .075. Don't precede the constant with an equal sign. Click OK to close the dialog box.

You just created a name that refers to a constant rather than a cell or range. If you type =SalesTax into a cell, this simple formula returns 0.075 — the constant that you defined. You also can use this constant in a formula such as =A1*SalesTax.

Tip   A constant also can be text. For example, you can define a constant for your company's name.

Note   Named constants don't appear in the Name box or in the Go To dialog box — which makes sense, because these constants don't reside anywhere tangible. They do appear in the Paste Names dialog box, however, which does make sense, because you use these names in formulas.

Using names for formulas

Just as you can create a named constant, you can also create named formulas. Like named constants, named formulas don't appear in the worksheet.

You create named formulas the same way you create named constants — using the Define Name dialog box. For example, you might create a named formula that calculates the monthly interest rate from an annual rate. Figure 7-9 shows an example of this. In this case, the name MonthlyRate refers to the following formula:

```
=Sheet3!$B$1/12
```

When you use the name MonthlyRate in a formula, it uses the value in B1 divided by 12. Notice that the cell reference is an absolute reference.

Naming formulas gets more interesting when you use relative references rather than absolute references. When you use the pointing technique to create a formula in the Refers to box, Excel always uses absolute cell references, which is unlike its behavior when you create a formula in a cell.

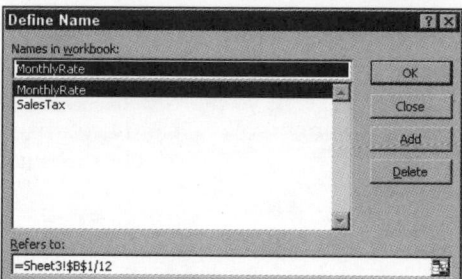

Figure 7-9: Excel lets you give a name to a formula that doesn't exist in a worksheet cell.

For example, if you create the name Power for the following formula

```
=Sheet1!A1^Sheet1!B1
```

make certain that cell C1 is the active cell before opening the Define Name dialog box — this is very important. When you use this named formula in a worksheet, the cell references are always relative to the cell that contains the name. For example, if you enter =POWER into cell D12, cell D12 displays the result of B12 raised to the power of the value contained in cell C12.

Using range intersections

This section describes an interesting concept that is unique to Excel: range intersections. Excel uses an intersection operator — in this case a space — to determine the overlapping references in two ranges. Figure 7-10 shows a simple example. The formula in cell G5 is

```
=B1:B7 A4:E4
```

and returns 90, the value in cell B4 — that is, the value at the intersection of the two ranges.

The intersection operator is one of three reference operators for ranges. Table 7-4 lists these operators.

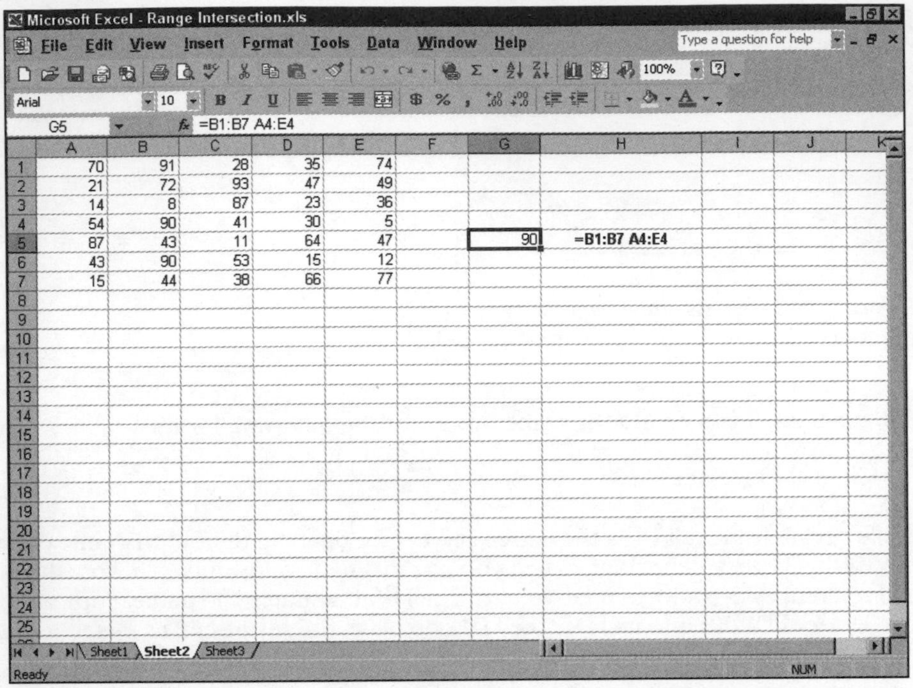

Figure 7-10: You can use a range intersection formula to determine values.

Table 7-4
Reference Operators for Ranges

Operator	What It Does
: (colon)	Specifies a range
, (comma)	Specifies the union of two ranges
(space)	Specifies the intersection of two ranges

The real value of knowing about range intersections is apparent when you use names. Examine Figure 7-11, which shows a table of values. We selected the entire table and then used the Insert ➪ Name ➪ Create command to create names automatically.

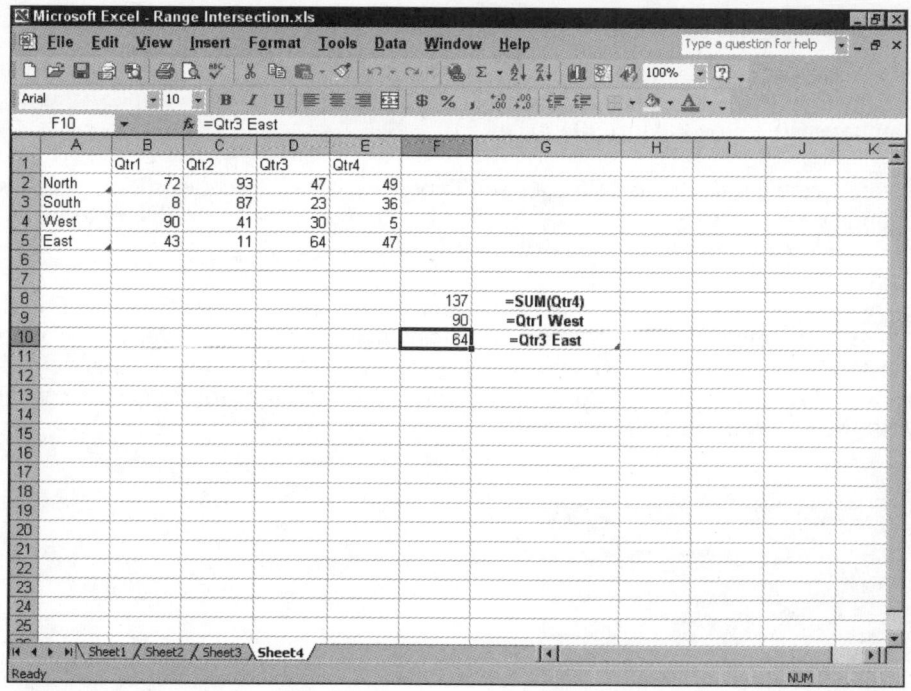

Figure 7-11: When you use names, using a range intersection formula to determine values is even more useful.

Excel created the following names:

North	=Sheet1!$B$2:$E$2	Qtr1	=Sheet1!$B$2:$B$5
South	=Sheet1!$B$3:$E$3	Qtr2	=Sheet1!$C$2:$C$5
West	=Sheet1!$B$4:$E$4	Qtr3	=Sheet1!$D$2:$D$5
East	=Sheet1!$B$5:$E$5	Qtr4	=Sheet1!$E$2:$E$5

With these names defined, you can create formulas that are very easy to read. For example, to calculate the total for Quarter 4, just use this formula:

```
=SUM(Qtr4)
```

But things really get interesting when you use the intersection operator. Move to any blank cell and enter the following formula:

```
=Qtr1 West
```

This formula returns the value for the first quarter for the West region. In other words, it returns the value where the Qtr1 range intersects with the West range. Naming ranges in this manner can help you create very readable formulas.

Applying names to existing references

When you create a new name for a cell or a range, Excel doesn't automatically use the name in place of existing references in your formulas. For example, assume that you have the following formula in cell F10: =A1-A2.

If you define a name Income for A1 and Expenses for A2, Excel won't automatically change your formula to =Income-Expenses. Replacing cell or range references with their corresponding names is fairly easy, however.

To apply names to cell references in formulas after the fact, start by selecting the range that you want to modify. Then, choose Insert ⇨ Name ⇨ Apply. Excel displays the Apply Names dialog box, shown in Figure 7-12. Select the names that you want to apply by clicking them and then click OK. Excel replaces the range references with the names in the selected cells.

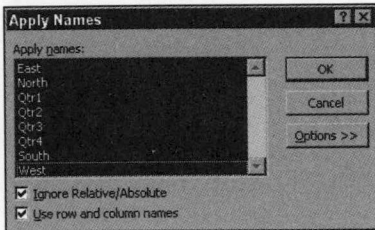

Figure 7-12: You can use the Apply Names dialog box to replace cell or range references with names.

Working with Formulas the Easier Way

There are a number of tricks and techniques that can help you master formulas so that you don't have to work quite so hard to use them. This section shows you a number of these.

Using the formula bar as a calculator

If you simply need to perform a calculation, you can use the formula bar as a calculator. For example, enter the following formula — but don't press Enter:

```
=(145*1.05)/12
```

Using Row and Column Headings as "Names"

You can also use names without actually defining them. Excel lets you use the row and column headers as names in your formulas without first defining the names. For example, in Figure 7-11 you could use the formula

```
=Qtr 2 North
```

without first defining the range names. This technique has several limitations, however. The labels are not "real" names—they don't appear in the Define Name dialog box, nor do they appear in the Name box. For this reason, you can use this method only when the formula refers to cells on the same sheet. The real problem, however, is the inability to document the names. In other words, you can never tell for sure exactly what a name refers to. For that reason, it's usually better to take a few extra seconds and create a "real" range name.

If you press Enter, Excel enters the formula into the cell. But because this formula always returns the same result, you might prefer to store the formula's result rather than the formula. To do so, press F9 and then press Enter. Excel stores the formula's result (12.6875) rather than the formula. This also works if the formula uses cell references.

Making an exact copy of a formula

When you copy a formula, Excel adjusts its cell references when you paste the formula to a different location. Sometimes, you may want to make an exact copy of the formula. One way to do this is to convert the cell references to absolute values, but this isn't always desirable. A better approach is to select the formula in edit mode and then copy it to the clipboard as text. You can do this in several ways. Here's a step-by-step example of how to make an exact copy of the formula in A1 and to copy it to A2:

1. Double-click A1 to get into edit mode.

2. Drag the mouse to select the entire formula. You can drag from left to right or from right to left.

3. Click the Copy button on the Standard toolbar. This copies the selected text to the clipboards.

4. Press Enter to end edit mode.

5. Select cell A2.

6. Click the Paste button to paste the text into cell A2.

You also can use this technique to copy just part of a formula, to use that part in another formula. Just select the part of the formula that you want to copy by dragging the mouse; then, use any of the available techniques to copy the selection to the clipboard. You can then paste the text to another cell.

Formulas (or parts of formulas) copied in this manner won't have their cell references adjusted when they are pasted to a new cell, because the formulas are being copied as text, not as actual formulas.

Tip   You can also convert a formula to text by adding an apostrophe (') in front of the equal sign.

Converting formulas to values

If you have a range of formulas that will always produce the same result (that is, dead formulas), you may want to convert them to values. You can use the Edit ⇨ Paste Special command to do this. Assume that range A1:A20 contains formulas that have calculated results that will never change or that you don't want to change. For example, if you use the @RAND function to create a set of random numbers and you don't want Excel to recalculate the random numbers each time that you press Enter, convert the formulas to values. To convert these formulas to values:

1. Select A1:A20.

2. Click the Copy button.

3. Select Edit ⇨ Paste Special. Excel displays its Paste Special dialog box.

4. Click the Values option button and then click OK.

5. Press Enter or Esc to cancel paste mode.

Using array formulas

Excel supports another type of formula called an array formula. Array formulas can be extremely powerful, because they let you work with complete ranges of cells rather than individual cells. You'll find that you can perform some amazing feats by using array formulas.

For example, if you want to build a table of random numbers, you could enter the =RAND() formula into one cell, copy it to the entire table, and then use Edit ⇨ Copy and Edit ⇨ Paste Special to convert the table into static values. An easier way is to select the entire table, enter =RAND() into the formula bar, and press Ctrl+Enter to enter it as an array formula in the entire table. Then use Edit ⇨ Copy and Edit ⇨ Paste Special to convert the table into static values quickly.

Cross-Reference   Array formulas are discussed in Chapters 17 and 18.

✦   ✦   ✦

Using Worksheet Functions

In Chapter 7, you learned to use basic formulas in Excel. This chapter introduces Excel's built-in functions — which are essentially prebuilt formulas that handle complex calculations easily and simply. By using Excel's functions you can leverage the power of your formulas so that you can get a lot more done with far less work.

Understanding Functions

Functions, in essence, are built-in tools that you use in formulas. They can make your formulas perform powerful feats and save you a lot of time. Functions can do the following:

✦ Simplify your formulas

✦ Allow formulas to perform calculations that are otherwise impossible

✦ Speed up some editing tasks

✦ Allow "conditional" execution of formulas — giving them rudimentary decision-making capability

It might be useful to think of functions in terms of a "black box" that performs a specialized task. You give the function the information it needs, and the function gives you back the answer you want. You don't have to understand *how* the function arrives at the answer — only that it *does* arrive at the answer. You simply have to pick the correct black box — function — and you get the answer you need.

Learning about functions with some examples

A built-in function can simplify a formula significantly. To calculate the average of the values in ten cells (A1:A10) without using a function, you need to construct a formula like this:

```
=(A1+A2+A3+A4+A5+A6+A7+A8+A9+A10)/10
```

Not very pretty, is it? Even worse, you would need to edit this formula if you added another cell to the range. You can replace this formula with a much simpler one that uses one of Excel's built-in worksheet functions:

```
=AVERAGE(A1:A10)
```

Next, look at how using a function can enable you to perform calculations that would not be possible otherwise. What if you need to determine the largest value in a range? A formula can't tell you the answer without using a function. Here's a simple formula that returns the largest value in the range A1:D100:

```
=MAX(A1:D100)
```

Functions also can sometimes eliminate manual editing. Assume that you have a worksheet that contains 1,000 names in cells A1:A1000, and that all the names appear in all uppercase letters, which you would like to change to mixed case; for example, JOHN F. CRANE must appear as John F. Crane. You could spend the next several hours reentering the list — or you could use a formula similar to the following, which uses a function to convert the text in cell A1 to proper case:

```
=PROPER(A1)
```

Enter this formula once in cell B1 and then copy it down to the next 999 rows.

One last example should convince you of the power of functions. Suppose that you have a worksheet that calculates sales commissions. If the salesperson sold more than $100,000 of product, the commission rate is 7.5 percent; otherwise, the commission rate is 5.0 percent. Without using a function, you would have to create two different formulas and make sure that you use the correct formula for each sales amount. Here's a formula that uses the IF function to ensure that you calculate the correct commission, regardless of the sales amount:

```
=IF(A1<100000,A1*5%,A1*7.5%)
```

Figure 8-1 shows some examples of how using Excel's built-in functions can make many calculations far simpler.

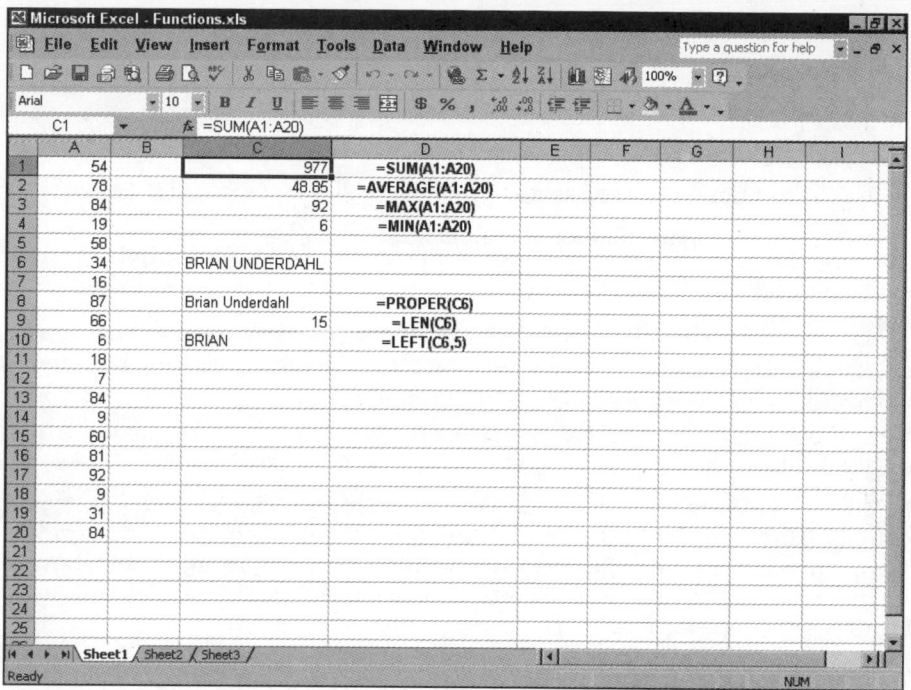

Figure 8-1: Using functions makes it much easier to perform many common calculations.

Learning more about functions

All told, Excel includes more than 300 functions. And if that's not enough, you can purchase additional specialized functions from third-party suppliers, and even create your own custom functions using Visual Basic for Applications (VBA), if you're so inclined.

You can easily be overwhelmed by the sheer number of functions, but you'll probably find that you use only a dozen or so of the functions on a regular basis. And as you'll see, Excel's Insert Function dialog box (described later in this chapter) makes it easy to locate and insert a function, even if it's not one that you use frequently.

Cross-Reference Appendix A contains a complete listing of Excel's worksheet functions, with a brief description of each.

Understanding function arguments

All of Excel's functions share one characteristic: the function name is always followed by a set of parentheses. In most cases, you enter additional information — known as *arguments* — inside the parentheses.

Functions vary in how they use arguments. Depending on the function, a function may use

- ✦ No arguments
- ✦ One argument
- ✦ A fixed number of arguments
- ✦ An indeterminate number of arguments
- ✦ Optional arguments

As an example, the RAND function, which returns a random number between 0 and 1, doesn't use an argument. Even if a function doesn't use an argument, however, you must still provide a set of empty parentheses, like this:

```
=RAND()
```

If a function uses more than one argument, you must separate each argument by a comma. The examples at the beginning of the chapter used cell references for arguments. Excel is quite flexible when it comes to function arguments, however. An argument can consist of a cell reference, a name, literal values, literal text strings, or expressions.

Using names as function arguments

As you've seen, functions can use cell or range references for their arguments. When Excel calculates the formula, it simply uses the current contents of the cell or range to perform its calculations. The SUM function returns the sum of its argument(s). To calculate the sum of the values in A1:A20, you can use

```
=SUM(A1:A20)
```

And, not surprisingly, if you've defined a name for A1:A20 (such as Sales), you can use the name in place of the reference:

```
=SUM(Sales)
```

Help for 1-2-3 and Quattro Pro Users

If you've ever used Lotus 1-2-3 or Quattro Pro, you'll recall that these products require you to type an "at" sign (@) before a function name. Excel's functions do not use the @ before the function name. Still, Excel accepts @ symbols when you type functions in your formulas — but it removes them as soon as you enter the formula.

This accommodation goes only so far, however. Excel still insists that you use the standard Excel function names, and it doesn't recognize or translate the function names used in other spreadsheets. For example, if you enter the 1-2-3 @AVG function, Excel flags it as an error (Excel's name for this function is AVERAGE).

In some cases, you may find it useful to use an entire column or row as an argument. For example, the formula that follows sums all values in column B:

```
=SUM(B:B)
```

This technique is particularly useful if the range that you're summing changes (if you're continually adding new sales figures, for instance).

Tip If you do use an entire row or column, just make sure that the row or column doesn't contain extraneous information that you don't want included in the sum.

Using literal values as function arguments

A literal argument is a value or text string that you enter into a function. For example, the SQRT function takes one argument. In the following example, the formula uses a literal value for the function's argument:

```
=SQRT(225)
```

Using a literal argument with a simple function like this one somewhat defeats the purpose of using a formula. This formula always returns the same value, so it could just as easily be replaced with the value 15. Using literal arguments makes more sense with formulas that use more than one argument. For example, the LEFT function (which takes two arguments) returns the leftmost characters from the beginning of its first argument; the second argument specifies the number of characters. If cell A1 contains the text Budget, the following formula returns the first letter, or B:

```
=LEFT(A1,1)
```

Tip To convert a formula that uses a literal argument into a fixed value, select the formula, and then press F2, F9, and Enter.

Expanding Range References

Many functions contain a range reference as an argument. For example, the function that follows uses the range A10:A20:

```
=SUM(A10:A20)
```

If you add a new row anywhere between rows 10 and 20, Excel expands the formula's range reference for you automatically. If you add a new row between rows 12 and 13, the formula changes to the following:

```
=SUM(A10:A21)
```

In older spreadsheet programs, if you inserted a new row at the top or bottom of the range, the new row would not be included in the range reference.

Using expressions as function arguments

Excel also lets you use expressions as arguments. Think of an expression as a formula within a formula. When Excel encounters an expression as a function's argument, it evaluates the expression and then uses the result as the argument's value. Here's an example:

```
=SQRT((A1^2)+(A2^2))
```

This formula uses the SQRT function, and its single argument is the following expression:

```
(A1^2)+(A2^2)
```

When Excel evaluates the formula, it starts by evaluating the expression in the argument and then computes the square root of the result.

Using other functions as function arguments

Because Excel can evaluate expressions as arguments, you shouldn't be surprised that these expressions can include other functions. Writing formulas that have functions within functions is sometimes known as *nesting* functions. Excel starts by evaluating the most deeply nested expression and works its way out. Here's an example of a nested function:

```
=SIN(RADIANS(B9))
```

The RADIANS function converts degrees to radians — which is the unit used by all of Excel's trigonometric functions. If cell B9 contains an angle in degrees, the RADIANS function converts it to radians, and then the SIN function computes the sine of the angle.

With a few exceptions, you can nest functions as deeply as you need, as long as you don't exceed the 1,024-character limit for a formula.

Entering Functions into Formulas

Of course, Excel's functions are only useful once you enter them into formulas. You can enter a function into a formula either manually or by using the Insert Function dialog box. The following sections describe these two methods.

Entering a function into a formula manually

If you're familiar with a particular function — you know how many arguments it takes and the types of arguments — you may choose simply to type the function and its arguments into your formula. Often, this method is the most efficient.

If you omit the closing parenthesis, Excel adds it for you automatically (if it is possible to do so unambiguously). For example, if you type **=SUM(A1:C12** and press Enter, Excel corrects the formula by adding the right parenthesis.

Tip   If #NAME appears in the cell after you press Enter, Excel does not recognize the name of the function you entered. Most likely this is because you misspelled the function name.

Inserting a function into a formula

The Function Arguments dialog box assists you by providing a way to enter a function and its arguments in a semiautomated manner. Using the Function Arguments dialog box ensures that the function is spelled correctly and has the proper number of arguments in the correct order.

To insert a function, first select the function from the Insert Function dialog box, shown in Figure 8-2. You can open this dialog box by using any of these methods:

✦ Choose the Insert ⇨ Function command from the menu.

✦ Click the Insert Function button (looks like *fx*, just to the left of the Formula bar).

✦ Press Shift+F3.

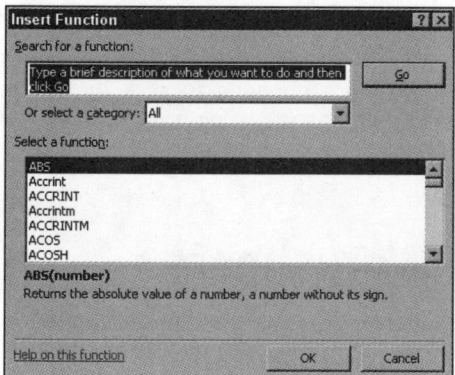

Figure 8-2: Use the Insert Function dialog box to select the correct function for your purpose.

The Insert Function dialog box makes it easy to find the correct function even if you're not quite sure which function you want to use. You simply type a brief description of what you want to do in the Search for a function box and click the Go button. When you do, Excel narrows down the list of functions that are displayed in the Select a function box, enabling you to choose the function that best suits your needs.

The Insert Function dialog box also has a drop-down list of function categories if you'd rather make your own choice. When you select a category, all its functions appear in the box labeled Select a function.

The Most Recently Used category lists the functions that you've used most recently. The All category lists all the functions available across all categories. Use this if you know a function's name, but aren't sure of its category.

When you select a function in the Select a function box, Excel displays the function (and its argument names) in the dialog box, along with a brief description of what the function does.

Tip   As you enter the arguments for a function, the right side of the Function Arguments dialog box shows the current value for each argument, and the lower pane shows the calculated value.

When you locate the function that you want to use, click OK. Excel's Function Arguments dialog box appears, as in Figure 8-3, and the Name box changes to the Formula List box. Use the Function Arguments dialog box to specify the arguments for the function. You can easily specify a range argument by clicking the Collapse Dialog button (the icon at the right edge of each box in the Function Arguments dialog box). Excel temporarily collapses the Function Arguments dialog box to a thin box, so that you can select a range in the worksheet. When you want to redisplay the Function Arguments dialog box, click the button again.

Tip   You can also enter arguments by simply clicking the appropriate argument box in the Function Arguments dialog box, and then selecting the cell or range in the worksheet. When you use this method, there's no need to click the Collapse Dialog button. You can move the Function Arguments dialog box out of your way by dragging it.

Using Functions in Your Worksheets

This section presents examples of formulas that use functions, including the widely used SUM function. It covers all categories listed in the Insert Function dialog box, but not every available function. For more information about a particular function, consult the online Help. For a list of all functions by category, use the Insert Function dialog box.

Cross-Reference   You can also look at the appendix for more functions by category.

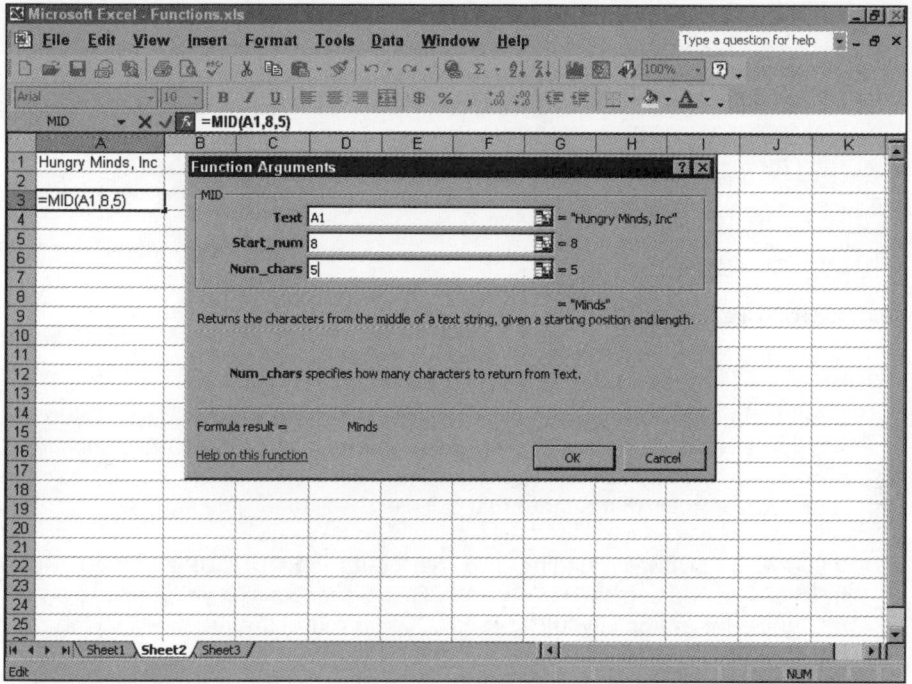

Figure 8-3: Use the Function Arguments dialog box to correctly specify all of the arguments for the function you are entering.

Using the mathematical and trigonometric functions

Excel provides over 50 functions in the Math & Trig function category, more than enough to do some serious number crunching. The category includes common functions, such as SUM and INT, as well as plenty of esoteric functions. Following are a few examples of these functions.

Converting numbers to integers with the INT function

The INT function returns the integer (nondecimal) portion of a number by truncating all digits after the decimal point. The example that follows returns 412:

```
=INT(412.98)
```

Rounding numbers with the ROUND function

The ROUND function rounds a value to a specified digit to the left or right of the decimal point. This function is often used to control the precision of your calculation.

ROUND takes two arguments: the first is the value to be rounded; the second is the digit. If the second argument is negative, the rounding occurs to the left of the decimal point. Here are some examples that show how this works:

=ROUND(123.457,2)	123.46
=ROUND(123.457,1)	123.50
=ROUND(123.457,0)	123.00
=ROUND(123.457,-1)	120.00
=ROUND(123.457,-2)	100.00
=ROUND(123.457,-3)	0.00

Caution   Don't confuse rounding a value with number formatting applied to a value. When a formula references a cell that has been rounded with the ROUND function, the formula uses the rounded value. If a number has been formatted to appear rounded, formulas that refer to that cell use the actual value stored.

Tip   If your work involves rounding, also check out the ROUNDUP and ROUNDDOWN functions. In addition, the FLOOR and CEILING functions let you round to a specific multiple — for example, you can use FLOOR to round a value down to the nearest multiple of 10 (124.5 would be rounded to 120).

Getting the value of π with the PI function

The PI function returns the value of π significant to 14 decimal places. It doesn't take any arguments; it is simply a shortcut for the value 3.14159265358979. In the example that follows, the formula calculates the area of a circle (the radius is stored in a cell named Radius):

```
=PI()*(Radius^2)
```

Finding the sine of an angle with the SIN function

The SIN function returns the sine of an angle. The sine is defined as the ratio between the opposite side and the hypotenuse of a triangle. SIN takes one argument — the angle expressed in radians. To convert degrees to radians, use the RADIANS function (a DEGREES function also exists to do the opposite conversion). For example, if cell F21 contains an angle expressed in degrees, the formula that follows returns the sine:

```
=SIN(RADIANS(F21))
```

Excel contains the full complement of trigonometric functions. Consult the online Help for details.

Obtaining the square root with the SQRT function

The SQRT function returns the square root of its argument. If the argument is negative, this function returns an error. The example that follows returns 32:

```
=SQRT(1024)
```

Tip

To compute other roots, use the POWER function. For example, to find the cube root, enter **1/3** as the second argument — the power argument — for the function.

Summing values using the SUM function

If you analyze a random sample of workbooks, you'll likely discover that SUM is the most widely used function. It's also among the simplest. To calculate the sum of three ranges (A1:A10, C1:10, and E1:E10), you use three arguments, like this:

```
=SUM(A1:A10,C1:10,E1:E10)
```

The arguments don't have to be all the same type. For example, you can mix and match single-cell references, range references, and literals, as follows:

```
=SUM(A1,C1:10,125)
```

Because the SUM function is so popular, you can insert it with just click of the AutoSum button (the one that looks like the Greek letter Sigma) on the Standard toolbar.

Calculating conditional sums using the SUMIF function

The SUMIF function is useful for calculating conditional sums. Figure 8-4 displays a worksheet with a table that shows sales by month and by product. The SUMIF function is used in the formulas in column F. For example, the formula in F2 is

```
=SUMIF(B:B,E2,C:C)
```

SUMIF takes three arguments. The first argument is the range that you're using in the selection criteria — in this case, the entire column B. The second argument is the selection criteria, a product name in the example. The third argument is the range of values to sum if the criteria are met. In this example, the formula in F2 adds the values in column C only if the corresponding text in column B matches the product in column E.

Cross-Reference

You also can use Excel's pivot table feature to perform these operations. Pivot tables are covered in Chapter 21.

Using the text functions

Although Excel is primarily known for its numerical prowess, it has a number of built-in functions that are designed to manipulate text, a few of which are demonstrated in this section.

	Month	Product	Sales		Product Summary		
1	Month	Product	Sales		Product Summary		
2	Jan	Teddy Bear	$450		Teddy Bear	$ 1,329	=SUMIF(B:B,E2,C:C)
3	Jan	Bucket of Paint	$225		Bucket of Paint	$ 1,002	=SUMIF(B:B,E3,C:C)
4	Jan	Tea Bags	$32		Tea Bags	$ 245	=SUMIF(B:B,E4,C:C)
5	Feb	Teddy Bear	$395				
6	Feb	Bucket of Paint	$186				
7	Feb	Tea Bags	$99				
8	Mar	Teddy Bear	$137		Monthly Summary		
9	Mar	Bucket of Paint	$168		Jan	$ 707	=SUMIF(A:A,E9,C:C)
10	Mar	Tea Bags	$22		Feb	$ 680	=SUMIF(A:A,E10,C:C)
11	Apr	Teddy Bear	$347		Mar	$ 327	=SUMIF(A:A,E11,C:C)
12	Apr	Bucket of Paint	$423		Apr	$ 862	=SUMIF(A:A,E12,C:C)
13	Apr	Tea Bags	$92				

(F2 = =SUMIF(B:B,E2,C:C))

Figure 8-4: Use the SUMIF function to return the sum of values that meet specified criteria.

Extracting characters from a string using the LEFT function

The LEFT function returns a string of characters of a specified length from another string, beginning at the leftmost position. This function uses two arguments. The first argument is the string and the second argument (optional) is the number of characters. If the second argument is omitted, Excel extracts the first character from the text. In the following example, the formula returns the letter B:

```
=LEFT("Brian Underdahl")
```

The following formula returns the string Brian:

```
=LEFT("Brian Underdahl",5)
```

Note   Excel also has a RIGHT function that extracts characters from the right of a string of characters and a MID function (described after the next section) that extracts characters from any position.

Finding the length of a string using the LEN function

The LEN function returns the number of characters in a string of text. For example, the following formula returns 9:

```
=LEN("Underdahl")
```

Tip

If you don't want to count leading or trailing spaces, use the LEN function with a nested TRIM function (which trims off leading and trailing spaces). For example, if you want to know the number of characters in the text in cell A1 without counting leading and trailing spaces, use this formula:

```
=LEN(TRIM(A1))
```

Extracting characters from a string using the MID function

The MID function returns characters from a text string. It takes three arguments. The first argument is the text string. The second argument is the position at which you want to begin extracting. The third argument is the number of characters that you want to extract. If cell A1 contains the text Joe Louis Walker, the following formula returns Louis:

```
=MID(A1,5,5)
```

Replacing characters in a string using the REPLACE function

The REPLACE function replaces characters with other characters. The first argument is the text containing the string that you're replacing. The second argument is the character position at which you want to start replacing. The third argument is the number of characters to replace. The fourth argument is the new text that will replace the existing text. In the following example, the formula returns Albert Collins:

```
=REPLACE("Albert King",8,4,"Collins")
```

Finding characters in a string using the SEARCH function

The SEARCH function lets you identify the position in a string of text in which another string occurs. The function takes three arguments. The first argument is the text for which you're searching. The second argument is the string that you want to search. The third argument (which is optional) is the position at which you want to start searching. If you omit the third argument, Excel searches from the beginning of the text.

In the example that follows, assume that cell A1 contains the text John Lee Hooker. The formula searches for a space and returns 5, because the first space character was found at the fifth character position.

```
=SEARCH(" ",A1,1)
```

To find the second space in the text, use a nested SEARCH function that uses the result of the first search (incremented by one character) as the third argument:

```
=SEARCH(" ",A1,SEARCH(" ",A1,1)+1)
```

Converting the case using the UPPER function

The UPPER function converts characters to uppercase. If cell A1 contains the text Lucille, the following formula returns LUCILLE:

```
=UPPER(A1)
```

Note   Excel also has a LOWER function (to convert to lowercase) and a PROPER function (to convert to proper case). In proper case, the first letter of each word is capitalized.

Using the logical functions

The Logical category contains only six functions (although several other functions could, arguably, be placed in this category). This section discusses three of these functions: IF, AND, and OR.

Making decisions with the IF function

The IF function is one of the most important of all functions because it can give your formulas decision-making capability.

The IF function takes three arguments. The first argument is a logical test that must return either TRUE or FALSE. The second argument is the result that you want the formula to display if the first argument is TRUE. The third argument is the result that you want the formula to display if the first argument is FALSE.

In the following example, the formula returns Positive if the value in cell A1 is greater than zero; otherwise, it returns Negative:

```
=IF(A1>0,"Positive","Negative")
```

Notice that the first argument (A1>0) evaluates to logical TRUE or FALSE. This formula has a problem in that it returns the text Negative if the cell is blank or contains 0. The solution is to use a nested IF function to perform another logical test. The revised formula is

```
=IF(A1>0,"Positive",IF(A1<0,"Negative","Zero"))
```

You can nest IF statements as deeply as you need to — although it can get very confusing after three or four levels. Using nested IF functions is quite common, so understanding how this concept works is in your best interest. Mastering IF will definitely help you to create more powerful formulas.

Checking for multiple true values with the AND function

The AND function returns a logical value (TRUE or FALSE) depending on the logical value of its arguments. If all its arguments return TRUE, the AND function returns TRUE. If at least one of its arguments returns FALSE, AND returns FALSE.

In the following example, the formula returns TRUE if the values in cells A1:A3 are all negative:

```
=AND(A1<0,A2<0,A3<0)
```

Checking for any true value with the OR function

The OR function is similar to the AND function, but it returns TRUE if at least one of its arguments is TRUE; otherwise, it returns FALSE. In the following example, the formula returns TRUE if the value in any of the cells — A1, A2, or A3 — is negative:

```
=OR(A1<0,A2<0,A3<0)
```

Using the information functions

The functions in the Information category return a variety of information about cells. Many of these functions return a logical TRUE or FALSE.

Finding a cell's attributes with the CELL function

The CELL function returns information about a particular cell. It takes two arguments. The first argument is a code for the type of information to display. The second argument is the address of the cell in which you're interested.

The example that follows uses the "type" code, which returns information about the type of data in the cell. It returns b if the cell is blank, l if it contains text (a label), or v if the cell contains a value or formula. For example, if cell A1 contains text, the following formula returns l:

```
=CELL("type",A1)
```

If the second argument contains a range reference, Excel uses the upper-left cell in the range.

Note
Excel has other functions that let you determine the type of data in a cell. The following functions may be more useful: ISBLANK, ISERR, ISERROR, ISLOGICAL, ISNA, ISNONTEXT, ISNUMBER, ISREF, ISTEXT, and TYPE.

Table 8-1 lists the possible values for the first argument of the CELL function. When using the CELL function, make sure that you enclose the first argument in quotation marks.

Table 8-1
Codes for the CELL Function Info_Type Argument

Type	What It Returns
Address	The cell's address
col	Column number of the cell
color	1 if the cell is formatted in color for negative values; otherwise, 0
contents	The contents of the cell
filename	Name and path of the file that contains the cell (returns empty text if the workbook has not been saved)
format	Text value corresponding to the number format of the cell
prefix	Text value corresponding to the label prefix of the cell; this is provided for 1-2-3 compatibility
protect	0 if the cell is not locked; 1 if the cell is locked
row	Row number of the cell
type	Text value corresponding to the type of data in the cell
width	Column width of the cell, rounded off to an integer

Finding out about your computer using the INFO function

The INFO function takes one argument—a code for information about the operating environment. In the following example, the formula returns the path of the current folder (that is, the folder that Excel displays when you choose File ➪ Open):

```
=INFO("directory")
```

Table 8-2 lists the valid codes for the INFO function. The codes must be enclosed in quotation marks.

Table 8-2
Codes for the INFO Function

Code	What It Returns
directory	Path of the current folder
memavail	Amount of memory available, in bytes
memused	Amount of memory being used, in bytes

Code	What It Returns
numfile	Number of worksheets in all open workbooks (including hidden workbooks and add-ins)
origin	Returns the cell reference of the top- and leftmost cell visible in the window, based on the current scrolling position
osversion	Current operating system version, as text
recalc	Current recalculation mode—Automatic or Manual
release	Version of Excel
system	Name of the operating environment—mac (for Macintosh) or pcdos (for Windows)
totmem	Total memory available on the system, in bytes

Identifying error values using the ISERROR function

The ISERROR function returns TRUE if its argument returns an error value. Otherwise, it returns FALSE. This function is useful for controlling the display of errors in a worksheet.

Typically, you use the ISERROR function along with the IF function. For example, suppose you have a worksheet that is set up to calculate a percentage by dividing one number by another. If the second number is missing, Excel will return #DIV/0 because dividing by zero is not allowed. You can use the ISERROR function to prevent the #DIV/0 result from appearing in your worksheet. In this case, if cell C2 contains the missing number, you can use the following formula to display a blank cell instead of #DIV/0:

```
=IF(ISERROR(D2/C2),"",D2/C2)
```

Note   Excel offers several other functions that let you trap error values: ERROR.TYPE, ISERR, and ISNA. Also, note that the preceding formula could have used the ISBLANK function to test for missing data.

Using the date and time functions

If you use dates or times in your worksheets, you owe it to yourself to check out Excel's functions that work with these types of values. This section demonstrates a few of these functions.

Cross-Reference   To work with dates and times, you should be familiar with Excel's serial number date-and-time system. Refer to Chapter 1.

Obtaining the current date using the TODAY function

The TODAY function takes no argument. It returns a date that corresponds to the current date—that is, the date set in the system. If you enter the following formula into a cell on June 26, 2003, the formula returns 6/26/2003:

```
=TODAY()
```

Note   Excel also has a NOW function that returns the current system date and the current system time.

Finding a date serial number with the DATE function

The DATE function displays a date serial number based on its three arguments: year, month, and day. This function is useful if you want to create a date based on information in your worksheet. For example, if cell A1 contains 2003, cell B1 contains 12, and cell C1 contains 25, the following formula returns the date serial number for December 25, 2003:

```
=DATE(A1,B1,C1)
```

Determining the day of the month using the DAY function

The DAY function returns the day of the month for a date serial number. If cell A1 contains the date serial number 37798, the following formula returns 26:

```
=DAY(A1)
```

Note   Excel also includes the YEAR and MONTH functions that extract from a date the year part and month part, respectively.

Obtaining a time serial number using the TIME function

The TIME function displays a time based on its three arguments: hour, minute, and second. This function is useful if you want to create a time based on information in your worksheet. For example, if cell A1 contains 8, cell B1 contains 15, and cell C1 contains 0, the following formula returns 8:15:00 AM:

```
=TIME(A1,B1,C1)
```

Finding out the hour using the HOUR function

The HOUR function returns the hour for a time serial number. If cell A1 contains the number .5, the following formula returns 12:

```
=HOUR(A1)
```

Note   Excel also includes the MINUTE and SECOND functions, which extract the minute part and second part, respectively, from a time.

Using the financial functions

The Financial function category includes many different functions that are designed to perform calculations that involve money.

Calculating depreciation

Excel offers several functions to calculate depreciation of an asset over time. The function that you choose depends on the type of depreciation that you use. For example, to calculate straight-line depreciation, you use the SLN function. If the cost, salvage value, and life are in cells A1, A2, and A3, you would use the following formula:

```
=SLN(A1,A2,A3)
```

 Other depreciation functions include DB, DDB, SYD, and VDB. For complete details, consult the online Help system.

Calculating loan payments

Excel offers a broad range of functions for calculating every possible detail about loan payments. For example, to calculate the amount of interest paid on an investment during a specific period, you could use the ISPMT function as in this example:

```
=ISPMT(Rate,Per,Nper,PV)
```

 Many of the payment functions include a *type* argument that is used to specify whether payments are made at the beginning or the end of the period.

The payment functions all use pretty much the same arguments — although the exact arguments that are used depend on the function. To use these functions successfully, you must understand how to specify the arguments correctly. The following list explains these arguments:

✦ **Nper:** Total number of payment periods. For a 30-year mortgage loan with monthly payments, Nper is 360.

✦ **Per:** Period in the loan for which the calculation is being made; it must be a number between 1 and Nper.

✦ **Pmt:** Fixed payment made each period for an annuity or a loan. This usually includes principal and interest (but not fees or taxes).

✦ **FV:** Future value (or a cash balance) after the last payment is made. The future value for a loan is 0. If FV is omitted, Excel uses 0.

✦ **Type:** Either 0 or 1, and indicates when payments are due. Use 0 if the payments are due at the end of the period, and 1 if they are due at the beginning of the period.

✦ **Guess:** Used only for the RATE function. It's your best guess of the internal rate of return. The closer your guess, the faster Excel can calculate the exact result.

Using the lookup and reference functions

The functions in the Lookup and Reference category, some of which are discussed in this section, are used to perform table lookups and obtain other types of information.

Obtaining information from a table with the VLOOKUP function

The VLOOKUP function is useful when you need to use a value from a table, such as a table of tax rates. This function retrieves text or a value from a table, based on a specific key in the first column of the table. The retrieved result is at a specified horizontal offset from the first row of the table.

Figure 8-5 shows an example of a lookup table in range A2:C9. The formulas in cells G4:G8 return the appropriate information for the part by using the lookup table. The formulas are

✦ Cell G4: =VLOOKUP(F4,$A$2:$C$9,2)

✦ Cell G5: =VLOOKUP(F5,$A$2:$C$9,2,TRUE)

✦ Cell G6: =VLOOKUP(F6,$A$2:$C$9,2,FALSE)

✦ Cell G7: =VLOOKUP(F7,$A$2:$C$9,3)

✦ Cell G8: =VLOOKUP(F8,$A$2:$C$9,1)

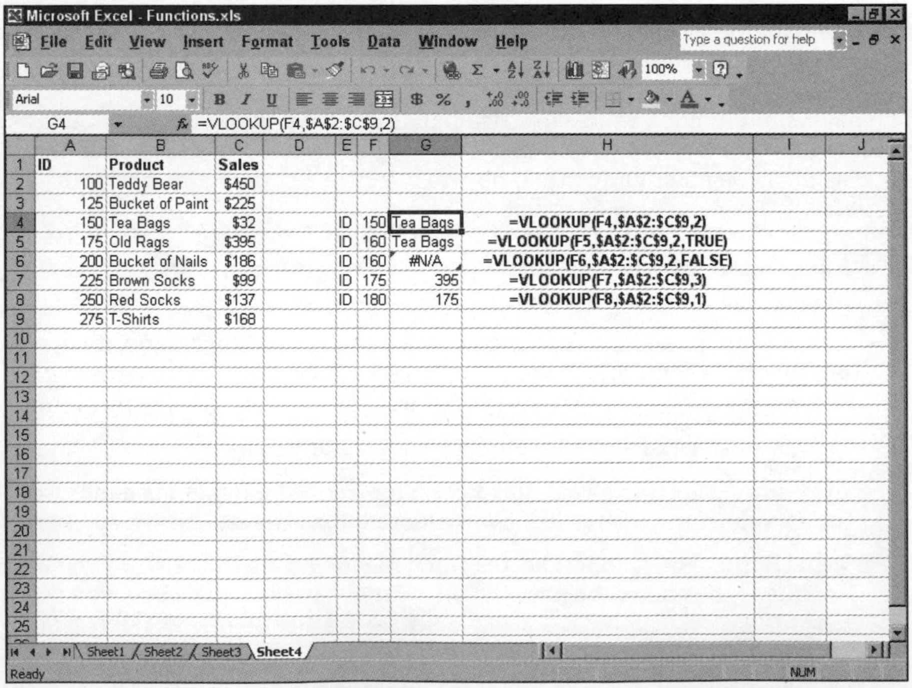

Figure 8-5: Use the VLOOKUP function to find values in a table.

The formulas look up the values in the cells in column F in the first column of the table. They return the values in the column that corresponds to the third argument. The fourth argument tells Excel whether it must find an exact match. If the fourth argument is TRUE (or omitted), Excel returns the next largest value that is less than the lookup value (the values in the first column must be in ascending order). If the fourth argument is FALSE and the value doesn't appear in the table, the formula returns #N/A.

Tip The HLOOKUP function works exactly like VLOOKUP except that it looks up the value horizontally in the table's first row.

Obtaining table values using the INDEX function

The INDEX function returns a value from a range using a row index (for a vertical range), column index (for a horizontal range), or both (for a two-dimensional range). The formula that follows returns the value in A1:J10 that is in its fifth row and third column:

```
=INDEX(A1:J10,5,3)
```

Note The OFFSET function performs a similar function.

Using the statistical functions

The Statistical category contains a huge number of functions that perform various calculations. Many of these are quite specialized, but several are useful for non-statisticians.

Finding the arithmetic mean using the AVERAGE function

The AVERAGE function returns the average (arithmetic mean) of a range of values. The average is the sum of the range divided by the number of values in the range. The formula that follows returns the average of the values in the range A1:A100:

```
=AVERAGE(A1:A100)
```

If the range argument contains blanks or text, Excel doesn't include these cells in the average calculation. As with the SUM formula, you can supply any number of arguments.

Note Excel also provides the MEDIAN function (which returns the middle-most value in a range) and the MODE function (which returns the value that appears most frequently in a range).

Counting occurrences of a specific value with the COUNTIF function

The COUNTIF function is useful if you want to count the number of times that a specific value occurs in a range. This function takes two arguments: the range that contains the value to count and a criterion used to determine what to count. Figure 8-6 shows a worksheet set up to show how many times a product appears in a list. The COUNTIF function is used in the formulas in column E. For example, the formula in E2 is

```
=COUNTIF(A:A,D2)
```

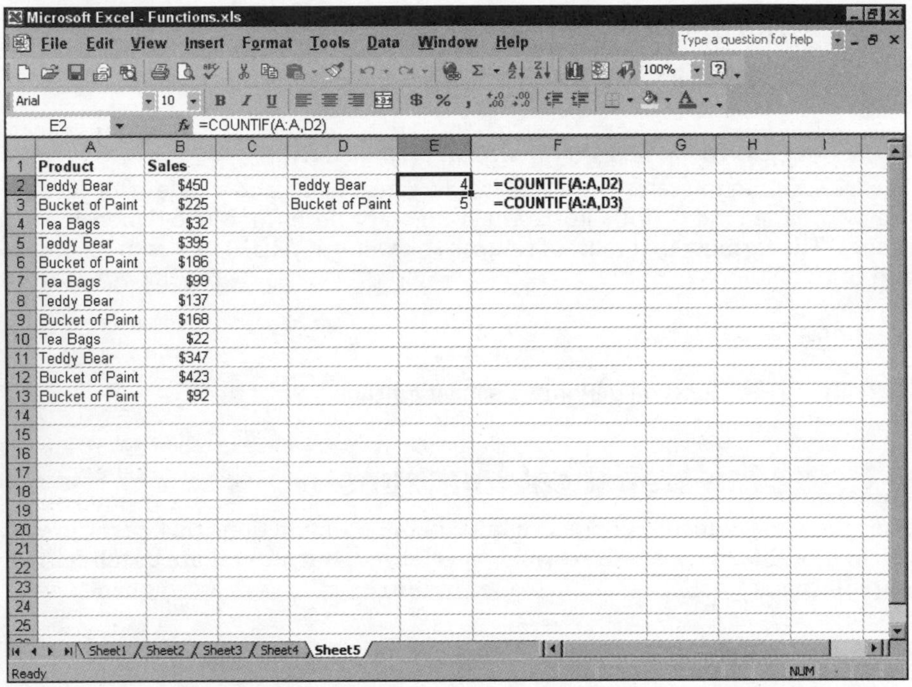

Figure 8-6: Use the COUNTIF function to count specific values in a table.

Notice that the first argument consists of a range reference for the entire column A, enabling you to insert new names easily without having to change the formulas.

Cross-Reference   You also can use the Analysis ToolPak add-in to create frequency distributions. See Chapter 24 for details.

Note   You may also want to use the COUNT, COUNTA, COUNTBLANK, and COUNTIF functions to count specific types of values in a range.

Finding the largest and smallest values

Use the MAX function to return the largest value in a range, and the MIN function to return the smallest value in a range. Both MAX and MIN ignore logical values and text. The following formula displays the largest and smallest values in a range named Data; using the concatenation operator causes the result to appear in a single cell:

```
="Smallest: "&MIN(Data)&" Largest: "&MAX(Data)
```

For example, if the values in Data range from 12 to 156, this formula returns Smallest: 12 Largest: 156.

Note   The MAXA and MINA functions work like MAX and MIN, respectively, but MAXA and MINA don't ignore logical values and text.

The LARGE function returns the *n*th-largest value in a range. For example, to display the second-largest value in a range named Data, use this formula:

```
=LARGE(Data,2)
```

The SMALL function works just as you would expect; it returns the *n*th-smallest value in a range.

Using the database functions

Excel's Database function category consists of a dozen functions that you use when working with database tables (also known as lists) stored in a worksheet. These functions all begin with the letter D, and they all have nondatabase equivalents. For example, the DSUM function is a special version of the SUM function that returns the sum of values in a database that meet a specified criterion. A database table is a rectangular range with field names in the top row. Each subsequent row is considered a record in the database.

To use a database function, you must specify a special criteria range in the worksheet. This type of criteria range is the same one that you use with Excel's Data ➪ Filter ➪ Advanced Filter command.

Cross-Reference   Filtering data is discussed in Chapter 19.

The DSUM function calculates the sum of the values in a specified field, filtered by the criteria table. For example, to calculate the total sales for the North region, enter North under the Region field in the criteria range. Then, enter the following formula into any cell (this assumes that the database table is named Data and that the criteria range is named Criteria):

```
=DSUM(Data,"Sales",Criteria)
```

The formula returns the sum of the Sales field, but only for the records that meet the criteria in the range named Criteria. You can change the criteria, and the formula displays the new result. For example, to calculate the sales for January, enter Jan under the Month field in the Criteria range (and delete any other entries).

If you want to use several DSUM formulas, you can have each of them refer to a different criteria range (you can use as many criteria ranges as you need).

Excel's other database functions work exactly like the DSUM function.

Using the Analysis ToolPak functions

When you begin to feel familiar with Excel's worksheet functions, you can explore those that are available when you load the Analysis ToolPak. This add-in provides dozens of additional worksheet functions.

When you load this add-in, the Insert Function dialog box displays a new category, Engineering. It also adds new functions to the following function categories: Financial, Date & Time, Math & Trig, and Information.

Cross-Reference
The Analysis ToolPak is discussed in Chapter 24. See the appendix for a summary of the Analysis ToolPak functions.

✦   ✦   ✦

Using Functions and Formulas to Manipulate Text

In addition to working with numbers, Excel also has a very comprehensive set of functions that enable you to manipulate text. In this chapter, you learn how to use the text functions to handle both ordinary and advanced text operations.

Manipulating Text by Using Functions

Excel has an excellent assortment of worksheet functions that can handle text. For your convenience, Excel's Insert Function dialog box places most of these functions in the Text category. A few other functions that are relevant to Text appear in other function categories. For example, the ISTEXT function is in the Information category in the Insert Function dialog box.

Tip   For a listing of Text functions, click the Insert Function toolbar button and scroll through the functions in the Text category.

Most of the text functions are not limited for use with text. In other words, these functions can also operate with cells that contain values. Excel is very accommodating when it comes to treating numbers as text and text as numbers.

The examples discussed in this section demonstrate some common (and useful) things you can do with text. You may need to adapt some of these examples for your own use.

Determining whether a cell contains text

In some situations, you may need a formula that determines the type of data contained in a particular cell. For example, you may use an IF function to return a result only if a cell contains text. Excel provides three functions to help you to determine whether a particular cell contains text:

✦ ISTEXT

✦ CELL

✦ TYPE

As you'll see, however, these functions are not always reliable.

Checking cell contents by using the ISTEXT function

The ISTEXT function takes a single argument and returns TRUE if the argument contains text and FALSE if it doesn't contain text. The following formula returns TRUE if A1 contains a string:

```
=ISTEXT(A1)
```

 **Tip**   The ISNONTEXT function works in reverse of the ISTEXT function.

Determining data type with the TYPE function

The TYPE function takes a single argument and returns a value that indicates the type of data in a cell. If cell A1 contains a text string, the following formula will return 2 (the code number for text):

```
=TYPE(A1)
```

 **Caution**   The TYPE function fails when a cell contains more than 255 characters. It returns 16, the code number for an Error value.

Discovering cell properties by using the CELL function

Theoretically, the CELL function should help you to determine whether a particular cell uses the Text format or has an apostrophe prefix. The CELL function's first argument can consist of any of 12 keywords, including format, prefix, or type.

None of these options work as advertised when a number is formatted as Text. For example, if you enter a number into cell A1 and then give it a number format of Text, the following formula returns G, which means Excel considers it formatted using the General format:

```
=CELL("format",A1)
```

Using prefix as the first argument for the CELL function returns an apostrophe if a value is preceded by an apostrophe, but it returns nothing if the cell contains a number and is formatted as Text. Using type as the first argument in the CELL function also yields inconsistent results. For example, if the cell contains more than 255 characters, the function returns v (for value).

Figure 9-1 shows several examples of these functions.

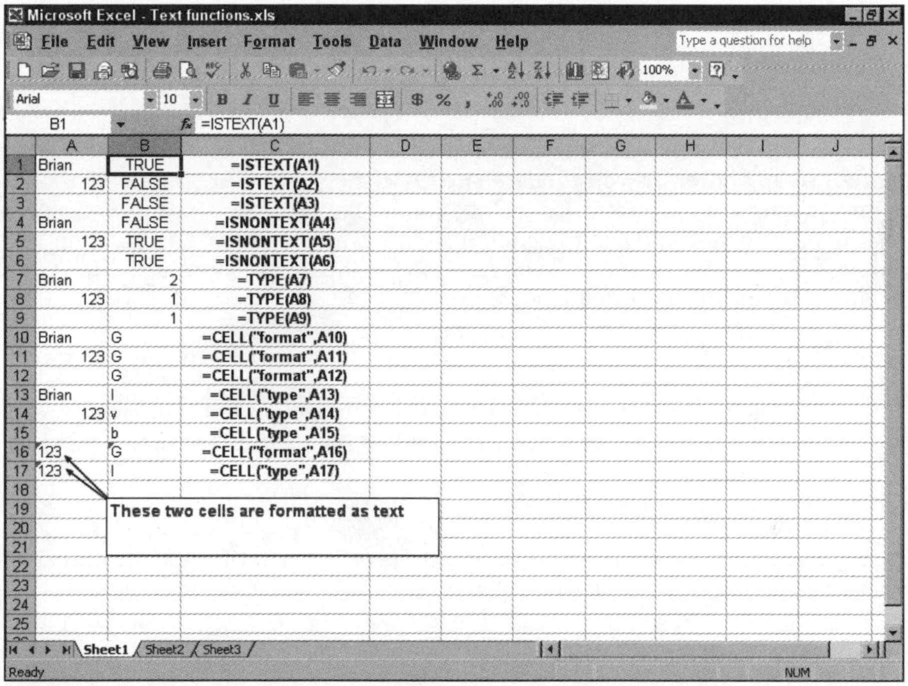

Figure 9-1: These functions can tell you what type of data specified cells contain.

Determining whether two strings are identical

One way to determine whether two cells are identical is to set up a simple logical formula that checks whether the two cells contain the same entry. For example, use this formula to determine whether cell A1 has the same contents as cell A2:

```
=A1=A2
```

Excel is a bit lax in its comparisons when involving text. Consider the case in which A1 contains the word January (initial capitalization) and A2 contains JANUARY (all uppercase). You'll find that the preceding formula returns TRUE, even though the contents of the two cells are not really the same. In other words, the comparison is not case-sensitive.

In many cases, you don't need to worry about the case of the text. But if you need to make an exact, case-sensitive comparison, you can use Excel's EXACT function. The following formula that follows returns TRUE only if cells A1 and A2 contain exactly the same entry:

```
=EXACT(A1,A2)
```

This formula returns FALSE because the first string contains a trailing space:

```
=EXACT("zero ","zero")
```

Combining the contents of two or more cells

If you need to combine text entries from two or more cells — perhaps to build a part number or an address — you concatenate the cell contents. Excel uses an ampersand as its concatenation operator. Concatenation is simply a fancy term that describes what happens when you join the contents of two or more cells. For example, if cell A1 contains the text San Diego, and cell A2 contains the text California, the following formula will return San DiegoCalifornia.

```
=A1&A2
```

Notice that the two strings are joined together without an intervening space. To add a space between the two entries (to get San Diego California), use this formula:

```
=A1&" "&A2
```

Or, even better, use a comma and a space to produce San Diego, California:

```
=A1&", "&A2
```

In the following formula you see a final example of using the & operator. In this case, the formula combines text with the result of an expression that returns the maximum value in Column C.

```
="The largest value in Column C is " &MAX(C:C)
```

Note   Excel also has a CONCATENATE function, which takes up to 30 arguments. This function simply combines the arguments into a single string.

Displaying formatted values as text

You can combine values with text in an Excel worksheet simply by concatenating the text and values. For example, if you place the following formula in cell D1

```
="The net profit is " &B3
```

Excel combines the text string with the contents of cell B3 and displays the result. Note, however, that the numeric value is not formatted in any way. You might want to display B3's contents using a currency number format. Excel's TEXT function enables you to display a value in a specific number format.

Note   Contrary to what you might expect, applying a number format to the cell that contains the formula has no effect because the formula returns a text string, not a value.

Note this revised formula that uses the TEXT function to apply formatting to the value in B3:

```
="The net profit is " & TEXT(B3,"$#,##0.00")
```

This formula displays the text along with a nicely formatted value.

The second argument for the TEXT function consists of a standard Excel number format string. You can enter any valid number format for this argument.

Tip   In addition to using cell references, you can also use functions such as NOW or TODAY with the TEXT function.

If you want to display a number in currency format, you may want to use the DOLLAR function in place of the TEXT function. When you use the DOLLAR function you don't need to remember the correct number format because the DOLLAR function always uses the following number format:

```
$#,##0.00_);($#,##0.00).
```

The DOLLAR function takes two arguments: the number to convert and the number of decimal places to display. If you leave off the second argument, the DOLLAR function defaults to two decimals. So, another way to write the previous formula is

```
="The net profit is " & DOLLAR(B3)
```

Figure 9-2 shows these three different methods of displaying text and numbers.

Repeating a character or string

The REPT function repeats a text string (first argument) any number of times you specify (second argument). For example, the following formula returns HoHoHo.

```
=REPT("Ho",3)
```

Another way to use the REPT function is to pad numbers with asterisks. This is a common security measure (frequently used on printed checks) in which numbers are padded with asterisks on the right. The following formula displays the value in cell A1, along with enough asterisks to make 24 characters total:

```
=(A1 & REPT("*",24-LEN(A1)))
```

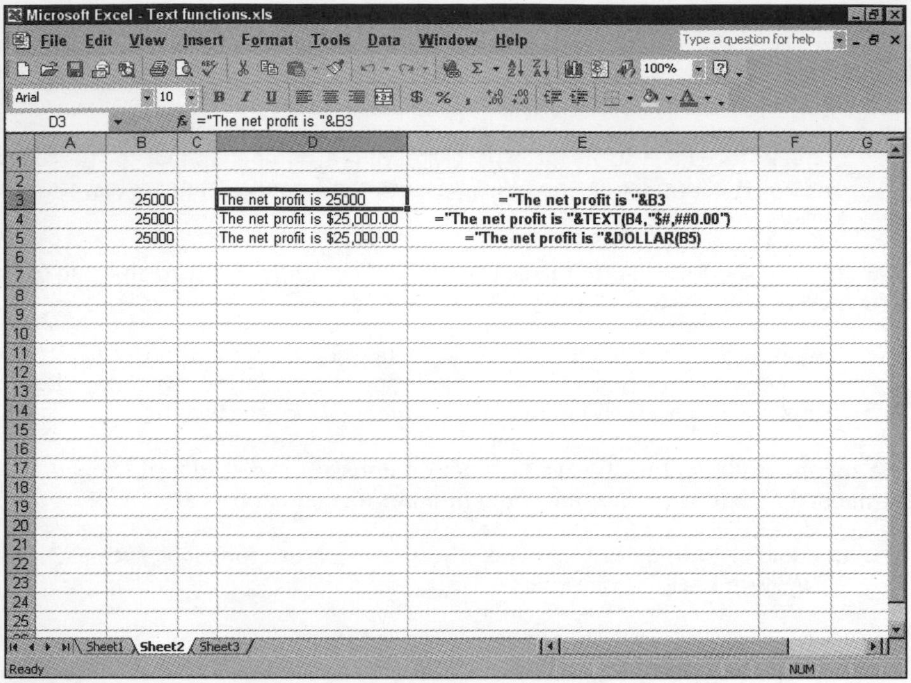

		Microsoft Excel - Text functions.xls				

(spreadsheet screenshot)

Cell D3 formula bar: ="The net profit is "&B3

	A	B	C	D	E	F	G
3		25000		The net profit is 25000	="The net profit is "&B3		
4		25000		The net profit is $25,000.00	="The net profit is "&TEXT(B4,"$#,##0.00")		
5		25000		The net profit is $25,000.00	="The net profit is "&DOLLAR(B5)		

Figure 9-2: Here are several ways to concatenate text and numbers.

Or, if you'd prefer to pad the number with asterisks on the left, use this formula:

```
=REPT("*",24-LEN(A1))&A1
```

The preceding formulas are a bit deficient because they don't show any number formatting. Note this revised version that displays the value in A1 (formatted), along with the asterisk padding on the right:

```
=(TEXT(A1,"$#,##0.00")&REPT("*",24-LEN(TEXT(A1,"$#,##0.00"))))
```

You can also pad a number by using a custom number format. To repeat the next character in the format to fill the column width, include an asterisk (*) in the custom number format code. For example, use this number format to pad the number with dashes:

```
$#,##0.00*-
```

Cross-Reference See Chapter 1 for more information on custom number formats.

Removing excess spaces and nonprinting characters

Often, data imported into an Excel worksheet contains excess spaces or strange (often unprintable) characters. Excel provides you with two functions to help whip your data into shape: TRIM and CLEAN.

✦ **TRIM:** Removes all spaces from its text argument except for single spaces between words.

✦ **CLEAN:** Removes all nonprinting characters from a string. These "garbage" characters often appear when you import certain types of data.

Note   Your PC's operating system has a large influence on the number of characters that can be contained in a font. The CLEAN function may remove some foreign characters in addition to nonprinting ones.

The following example uses the TRIM function. The formula returns Fourth Quarter Earnings (with no excess spaces):

```
=TRIM(" Fourth Quarter Earnings ")
```

Counting the characters in a string

You often need to know the length of a string. The previous examples of padding a number provided a good demonstration of one such use.

Excel's LEN function takes one argument and returns the number of characters in the cell. For example, if cell A1 contains the string "September Sales," the following formula will return 15:

```
=LEN(A1)
```

Notice that space characters are included in the character count.

The following formula returns the total number of characters in the range A1:A3:

```
{=SUM(LEN(A1),LEN(A2),LEN(A3))}
```

Cross-Reference   You will see example formulas that demonstrate how to count the number of specific characters within a string later in this chapter. Also, you may find relevant material in Chapter 11 on counting techniques and Chapter 17 on performing magic with array formulas.

Changing the case of text

A common text-related task is to change the case of text. For example, you might import some address book data and discover that all of the names are in uppercase instead of the more familiar mixed case.

Excel provides three handy functions to change the case of text:

✦ **UPPER:** Converts the text to ALL UPPERCASE

✦ **LOWER:** Converts the text to all lowercase

✦ **PROPER:** Converts the text to "proper" case (The First Letter In Each Word Is Capitalized)

These functions are quite straightforward. The formula that follows, for example, converts the text in cell A1 to proper case. If cell A1 contained the text MR. JOHN Q. PUBLIC, the formula would return Mr. John Q. Public.

```
=PROPER(A1)
```

These functions operate only on alphabetic characters; they simply ignore all other characters and return them unchanged.

Extracting characters from a string

Excel users often need to extract characters from a string. For example, you may have a list of employee names (first and last names) and might need to extract the last name from each cell. Excel provides several useful functions for extracting characters:

✦ **LEFT:** Returns a specified number of characters from the beginning of a string

✦ **RIGHT:** Returns a specified number of characters from the end of a string

✦ **MID:** Returns a specified number of characters beginning at any position within a string

The formula that follows returns the last 10 characters from cell A1. If A1 contains fewer than 10 characters, the formula returns all of the text in the cell.

```
=RIGHT(A1,10)
```

This next formula uses the MID function to return five characters from cell A1, beginning at character position 2. In other words, it returns characters 2 to 6.

```
=MID(A1,2,5)
```

Cross-Reference

See "Searching and replacing within a string" later in this chapter for information on techniques you can use to specify the arguments for these functions.

Replacing text with other text

In some situations, you may need to replace a part of a text string with some other text. For example, you may import data that contains asterisks, and you need to convert the asterisks to some other character. You could use Excel's Edit ➪ Replace command to make the replacement. If you prefer a formula-based solution, you can take advantage of either of two functions:

✦ **SUBSTITUTE:** Replaces specific text in a string. Use this function when you know the character(s) to be replaced but not the position.

✦ **REPLACE:** Replaces text that occurs in a specific location within a string. Use this function when you know the position of the text to be replaced but not the actual text.

The following formula uses the SUBSTITUTE function to replace 2001 with 2002 in the string 2001 Budget. The formula returns 2002 Budget.

```
=SUBSTITUTE("2001 Budget","2001","2002")
```

The following formula uses the REPLACE function to replace one character beginning at position 5 with nothing. In other words, it removes the fifth character (a hyphen) and returns Part544.

```
=REPLACE("Part-544",5,1,"")
```

You can, of course, nest these functions to perform multiple replacements in a single formula.

Tip   You can use the optional instance_number argument with the SUBSTITUTE function to replace the second, third, or so on instance of a string, while leaving the earlier instances untouched.

Searching and replacing within a string

Excel's FIND and SEARCH functions enable you to locate the starting position of a particular substring within a string.

✦ **FIND:** Finds a substring within another text string and returns the starting position of the substring. You can specify the character position at which to begin searching. The FIND function is case-sensitive.

✦ **SEARCH:** Finds a substring within another text string and returns the starting position of the substring. You can specify the character position at which to begin searching. The SEARCH function is not case-sensitive.

Tip   The primary difference between these two functions is that FIND is case- sensitive, whereas SEARCH is not.

The following formula uses the FIND function and returns 7 — the position of the first m in the string. Notice that this formula is case-sensitive.

```
=FIND("m","Big Mamma Thornton",1)
```

The formula that follows, which uses the SEARCH function, returns 5 — the position of the first m (either uppercase or lowercase).

```
=SEARCH("m","Big Mamma Thornton",1)
```

You can use the following wildcard characters within the first argument for the SEARCH function:

  ✦ **Question mark (?):** Matches any single character
  ✦ **Asterisk (*):** Matches any sequence of characters

Tip   If you want to find an actual question mark or asterisk character, type a tilde (~) before the question mark or asterisk.

You can use the REPLACE function in conjunction with the SEARCH function to replace part of a text string with another string. In effect, you use the SEARCH function to find the starting location used by the REPLACE function.

For example, assume cell A1 contains the text Annual Profit Figures. The following formula searches for the word Profit and replaces it with the word Loss:

```
=REPLACE(A1,SEARCH("Profit",A1),6,"Loss")
```

This next formula uses the SUBSTITUTE function to accomplish the same result more efficiently:

```
=SUBSTITUTE(A1,"Profit","Loss")
```

Creating Advanced Text Formulas

The examples in this section appear more complex than the examples in the previous section. But, as you'll see, they can perform some very useful text manipulations.

Counting specific characters in a cell

This formula counts the number of Bs (uppercase only) in the string in cell A1:

```
=LEN(A1)-LEN(SUBSTITUTE(A1,"B",""))
```

This formula works by using the SUBSTITUTE function to create a new string (in memory) that has all of the Bs removed. Then, the length of this string is subtracted from the length of the original string. The result reveals the number of Bs in the original string.

The following formula is a bit more versatile. It counts the number of Bs — both upper- and lowercase — in the string in cell A1.

```
=LEN(A1)-LEN(SUBSTITUTE(SUBSTITUTE(A1,"B",""),"b",""))
```

Counting the occurrences of a substring in a cell

The formulas in the preceding section count the number of occurrences of a particular character in a string. The following formula works with more than one character. It returns the number of occurrences of a particular substring (contained in cell B1) within a string (contained in cell A1). The substring can consist of any number of characters.

```
=SUM(LEN(A1)-LEN(SUBSTITUTE(A1,B1,"")))/LEN(B1)
```

For example, if cell A1 contains the text Blonde On Blonde and B1 contains the text Blonde, the formula returns 2.

The comparison is case-sensitive, so if B1 contains the text blonde, the formula returns 0. The following formula is a modified version that performs a case-insensitive comparison.

```
=SUM(LEN(A1)-LEN(SUBSTITUTE(UPPER(A1),UPPER(B1),"")))/LEN(B1)
```

Expressing a number as an ordinal

You may need to express a value as an ordinal number. For example, Today is the 21st day of the month. In this case, the number 21 converts to an ordinal number by appending the characters st to the number.

The characters appended to a number depend on the number. They exhibit no clear pattern, making the construction of a formula more difficult. Most numbers will use the th suffix. Exceptions occur for numbers that end with 1, 2, or 3 — except if the preceding number is a 1 (numbers that end with 11, 12, or 13). These may seem like fairly complex rules, but you can translate them into an Excel formula.

The following formula converts the number in cell A1 (assumed to be an integer) to an ordinal number:

```
=A1&IF(OR(VALUE(RIGHT(A1,2))={11,12,13}),"th",IF(OR(VALUE(RIGHT
(A1))={1,2,3}),CHOOSE(RIGHT(A1),"st","nd","rd"),"th"))
```

This is a rather complicated formula, so it may help to examine its components. Basically, the formula works as follows:

1. If the last two digits of the number consist of 11, 12, or 13, then use th.

2. If Rule #1 does not apply, then check the last digit. If the last digit is 1, use st. If the last digit is 2, use nd. If the last digit is 3, use rd.

3. If neither Rule #1 nor Rule #2 apply, use rd.

Cross-Reference The formula uses two arrays, specified by brackets. Refer to Chapter 17 for more information about using arrays in formulas.

Figure 9-3 shows the formula in use.

Extracting the first word of a string

To extract the first word of a string, a formula must locate the position of the first space character, and then use this information as an argument for the LEFT function. The following formula does just that:

```
=LEFT(A1,FIND(" ",A1)-1)
```

This formula returns all of the text prior to the first space in cell A1. However, the formula has a slight problem: It returns an error if cell A1 consists of a single word. A slightly more complex formula that checks for the error with an IF function solves that problem:

```
=IF(ISERR(LEFT(A1,FIND(" ",A1)-1)),A1,LEFT(A1,FIND(" ",A1)-1))
```

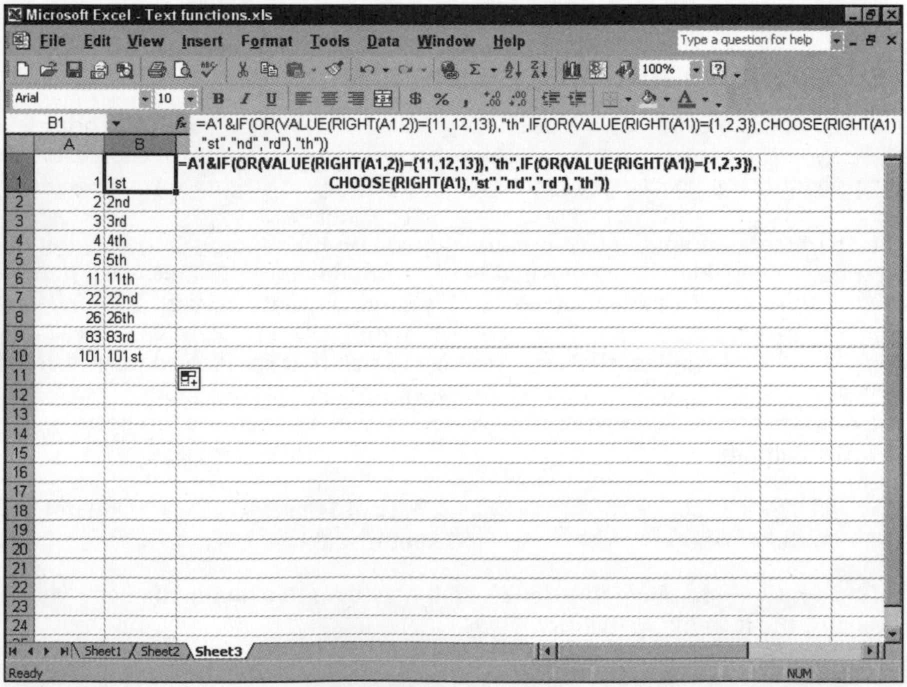

![Microsoft Excel screenshot showing Text functions.xls. Formula bar displays =A1&IF(OR(VALUE(RIGHT(A1,2))={11,12,13}),"th",IF(OR(VALUE(RIGHT(A1))={1,2,3}),CHOOSE(RIGHT(A1),"st","nd","rd"),"th")). Column A and B contain: 1 1st, 2 2nd, 3 3rd, 4 4th, 5 5th, 11 11th, 22 22nd, 26 26th, 83 83rd, 101 101st]

Figure 9-3: This worksheet uses a formula to express a number as an ordinal.

Extracting the last word of a string

Extracting the last word of a string is more complicated, because the FIND function only works from left to right. Therefore, the problem rests with locating the last space character. The formula that follows, however, solves this problem. It returns the last word of a string—all of the text following the last space character:

```
=RIGHT(A1,LEN(A1)-FIND("*",SUBSTITUTE(A1," ","*",LEN(A1)-
LEN(SUBSTITUTE(A1," ","")))))
```

This formula, however, has the same problem as the first formula in the preceding section: It fails if the string does not contain at least one space character. The following modified formula uses an IF function to count the number of spaces in cell A1. If it contains no spaces, the entire contents of cell A1 are returned. Otherwise, the preceding formula kicks in.

```
=IF(LEN(A1)-LEN(SUBSTITUTE(A1," ",""))=0,A1,RIGHT(A1,LEN(A1)-
FIND("*",SUBSTITUTE(A1," ","*",LEN(A1)-LEN(SUBSTITUTE(A1,"
","")))))
```

Extracting first names, middle names, and last names

Suppose you have a list consisting of people's names in a single column. You have to separate these names into three columns: one for the first name, one for the middle name or initial, and one for the last name. This task is more complicated than you may think, because not every name has a middle initial. However, you can still do it.

Note The task becomes a lot more complicated if the list contains names with titles (such as Mr. or Dr.) or names followed by additional details (such as Jr. or III). Although the upcoming formulas will not handle these complex cases, they still give you a significant head start if you're willing to do a bit of manual editing to handle the special cases.

The formulas that follow all assume that the name appears in cell A1.

You can easily construct a formula to return the first name:

```
=LEFT(A1,FIND(" ",A1)-1)
```

Returning the middle name or initial is much more complicated, because not all names have a middle initial. This formula returns the middle name (if it exists). Otherwise, it returns nothing.

```
=IF(ISERR(MID(A1,FIND(" ",A1)+1,IF(ISERR(FIND(" ",A1,FIND
(" ",A1)+1)),FIND(" ",A1),FIND(" ",A1,FIND(" ",A1)+1))-
FIND(" ",A1)-1)),"",MID(A1,FIND(" ",A1)+1,IF(ISERR(FIND
(" ",A1,FIND(" ",A1)+1)),FIND(" ",A1),FIND(" ",A1,FIND
(" ",A1)+1))-FIND(" ",A1)-1))
```

Finally, this formula returns the last name:

```
=RIGHT(A1,LEN(A1)-FIND("*",SUBSTITUTE(A1," ","*",LEN(A1)-LEN
(SUBSTITUTE(A1," ","")))))
```

Figure 9-4 shows the three formulas in action. Remember that you need to do some manual editing to handle names that are more complex, such as those with a title or suffix.

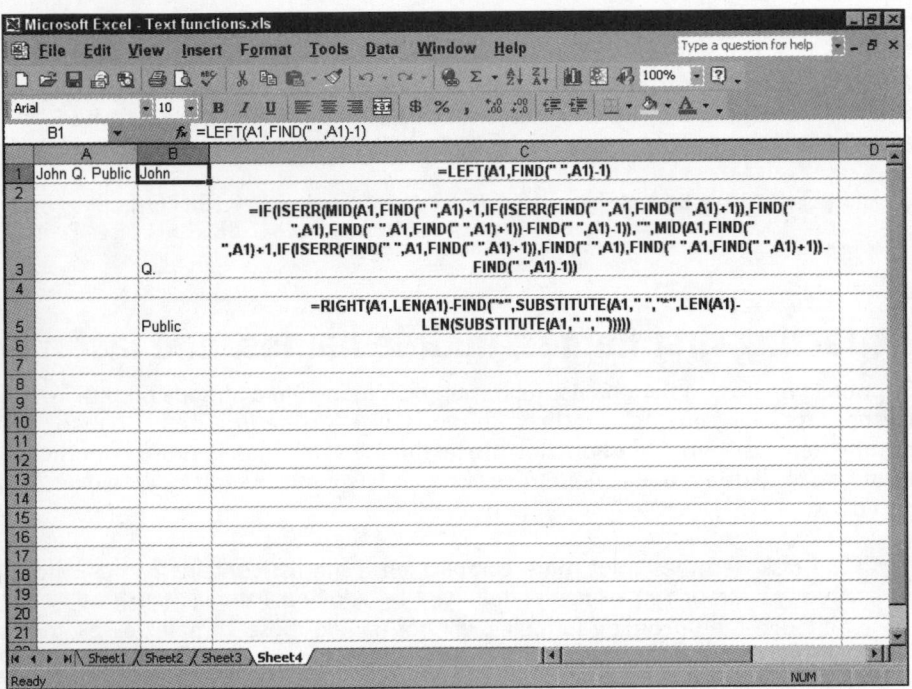

Figure 9-4: This worksheet uses formulas to extract the first name, middle name (or initial), and last name from Column A.

Counting the number of words in a cell

The following formula returns the number of words in cell A1:

```
=LEN(SUBSTITUTE(TRIM(A1),CHAR(32),CHAR(32)&CHAR(32)))-LEN
(TRIM(A1))+1
```

Splitting Text Strings Without Formulas

In many cases, you can eliminate the use of formulas and use Excel's Data ⇨ Text to Columns command to parse strings into their component parts. Selecting this command displays Excel's Convert Text to Columns Wizard—a series of dialog boxes that walk you through the steps to convert a single column of data into multiple columns. See Chapter 18 for more information on importing text into Excel.

The formula works by creating a new string in memory that consists of the original string without any spaces. Then, you subtract the length of this new string from the original string to determine the number of spaces. A value of 1 is added to this result to arrive at the number of words. Notice that the TRIM function eliminates any multiple spaces between words.

✦   ✦   ✦

Working with Dates, Times, and Related Functions

◆ ◆ ◆ ◆

In This Chapter

Understanding how Excel handles dates and times

Working with dates in Excel

Working with times in Excel

◆ ◆ ◆ ◆

You probably use dates and times in your Excel worksheets quite often. Knowing how to best work with them can save you from a lot of wasted effort. This chapter provides the information that you need to create powerful formulas to manipulate dates and times.

Understanding How Excel Handles Dates and Times

This section presents a quick overview of how Excel deals with dates and times. We discuss Excel's date and time serial number system and provide tips for entering and formatting dates and times.

Cross-Reference Other chapters in this book contain additional date-related information. For example, refer to Chapter 11 for counting examples that use dates.

Note Excel supports several different date formats. In this chapter, the dates are formatted according to the United States date format: month/day/year. For example, the date 3/1/2002 refers to March 1, 2002, not January 3, 2002.

Understanding date and time serial numbers

To Excel, a date is simply a number. More precisely, a date is a "serial number" that represents the number of days since January 0, 1900. A serial number of 1 corresponds to January 1, 1900; a serial number of 2 corresponds to January 2, 1900, and so on. This system makes it possible to deal with dates in formulas. For example, you can create a formula to calculate the number of days between two dates.

When you need to work with time values, you simply extend Excel's date serial number system to include decimals. In other words, Excel works with times by using fractional days. For example, the date serial number for June 1, 2001 is 37043. Noon (halfway through the day) is represented internally as 37043.5.

Tip   In Excel, the smallest unit of time is 1/1000th of a second.

Tip   To view a date serial number as a date, you must format the cell as a date. Use the Format Cells dialog box (Number tab) to apply a date format if Excel does not automatically apply the date format.

Excel's Two Date Systems

Excel actually supports two date systems: the 1900 date system and the 1904 date system. Which system you use in a workbook determines what date serves as the basis for dates. The 1900 date system uses January 1, 1900 as the day assigned to date serial number 1. The 1904 date system uses January 1, 1904 as the base date. By default, Excel for Windows uses the 1900 date system, and Excel for Macintosh uses the 1904 date system. Excel for Windows supports the 1904 date system for compatibility with Macintosh files. You can choose the date system from the Options dialog box (select Tools ➪ Options and select the Calculation tab).

Generally, you should use the 1900 date system. And, you should exercise precaution if you use two different date systems in workbooks that are linked together. For example, assume that Book1 uses the 1904 date system and contains the date 1/15/1999 in cell A1. Assume that Book2 uses the 1900 date system and contains a link to cell A1 in Book1. Book2 will display the date as 1/14/1995. Both workbooks will use the same date serial number (34713), but they will be interpreted differently.

An advantage to using the 1904 date system is that it enables you to display negative time values. With the 1900 date system, a calculation that results in a negative time (for example 4:00 p.m. – 5:30 p.m.) cannot be displayed. When using the 1904 date system, the negative time displays as –1:30 (that is, a difference of one hour and thirty minutes). Negative times are still stored correctly in the 1900 date system, but Excel cannot display them.

Note Excel 97 and later versions support dates from January 1, 1900 through December 31, 9999 (serial number = 2958465). Previous versions of Excel support a much smaller range of dates: from January 1, 1900 through December 31, 2078 (serial number = 65380).

Entering dates and times

You can enter a date directly as a serial number (if you know it), but more often you'll enter a date using any of several recognized date formats. Excel automatically converts your entry into the corresponding date serial number (which it uses for calculations) and also applies the default date format to the cell so that it displays as an actual date rather than as a cryptic serial number.

For example, if you need to enter June 1, 2001, you can simply enter the date by typing June 1, 2001 (or use any of several different date formats). Excel interprets your entry and stores the value 37043 — the date serial number for that date. It also applies the default date format, so that the cell contents may not appear exactly as you typed them.

When you activate a cell that contains a date, the formula bar shows the cell contents formatted as a date. It does not display the date's serial number. If you need to find out the serial number for a particular date, format the cell using a nondate number format.

Tip To change the default date format, you need to change a systemwide setting. Access the Windows Control Panel and select Regional Settings. In the Regional Settings dialog box, select the Date tab. The Short date style determines the default date format used by Excel.

Table 10-1 provides a sampling of the date formats that Excel recognizes.

Table 10-1	
Date Entry Formats Recognized by Excel	
Entry	*Excel's Interpretation*
6-1-03	June 1, 2003
6-1-2003	June 1, 2003
6/1/03	June 1, 2003
6/1/2003	June 1, 2003
6-1/03	June 1, 2003
June 1, 2003	June 1, 2003

Continued

Table 10-1 *(continued)*	
Entry	**Excel's Interpretation**
Jun 1	June 1 of the current year
June 1	June 1 of the current year
6/1	June 1 of the current year
6-1	June 1 of the current year

As Table 10-1 shows, Excel is rather smart when it comes to recognizing dates entered into a cell. It's not perfect, however. For example, Excel does not recognize any of the following entries as dates:

✦ June 1 2003

✦ Jun-1 2003

✦ Jun-1/2003

Instead, it interprets these entries as text. If you plan to use dates in formulas, make sure that Excel can recognize the date you enter as a date; otherwise, the formulas that refer to these dates will produce incorrect results.

If you attempt to enter a date that lies outside of the supported date range, Excel interprets it as text. If you attempt to format a serial number that lies outside of the supported range as a date, the value displays as a series of pound signs (##########).

As with entering dates, you normally don't have to worry about the actual time serial numbers. Just enter the time into a cell using a recognized format. Table 10-2 provides some examples of time formats that Excel recognizes.

Table 10-2 **Time Entry Formats Recognized by Excel**	
Entry	**Excel's Interpretation**
11:30:00 am	11:30 a.m.
11:30:00 AM	11:30 a.m.
11:30 pm	11:30 p.m.
11:30	11:30 a.m.
13:30	1:30 p.m.

Because the preceding samples don't have a specific day associated with them, Excel (by default) uses a date serial number of 0, which corresponds to the nonexistent date January 0, 1900. Often, you'll want to combine a date and time. Do so by using a recognized date entry format, followed by a space, and then a recognized time-entry format. For example, if you enter the following text in a cell, Excel interprets it as 11:30 a.m. on June 1, 2001. Its date/time serial number is 37043.4791666667.

```
6/1/2001 11:30
```

When you enter a time that exceeds 24 hours, the associated date for the time increments accordingly. For example, if you enter the following time into a cell, it is interpreted as 1:00 a.m. on January 1, 1900. The day part of the entry increments because the time exceeds 24 hours.

```
25:00:00
```

Similarly, if you enter a date and a time and the time exceeds 24 hours, the date that you entered is adjusted. The following entry, for example, is interpreted as 9/2/2003 1:00:00 a.m.

```
9/1/2003 25:00:00
```

If you enter a time only (without an associated date), you'll find that the maximum time that you can enter into a cell is 9999:59:59 (just under 10,000 hours). Excel adds the appropriate number of days. In this case, 9999:59:59 is interpreted as 3:59:59 p.m. on 02/19/1901. If you enter a time that exceeds 10,000 hours, the time appears as a text string.

Formatting dates and times

Excel gives you a great deal of flexibility in formatting cells that contain dates and times. For example, you can format the cell to display the date part only, the time part only, or both the date and time parts.

You format dates and times by selecting the cells, and then using the Number tab of the Format Cells dialog box, shown in Figure 10-1. The Date category shows built-in date formats, and the Time category shows built-in time formats. Some of the formats include both date and time display. Just select the desired format from the Type list and click OK.

If none of the built-in formats meet your needs, you can create a custom number format. Select the Custom category, and then type the custom format codes into the Type box.

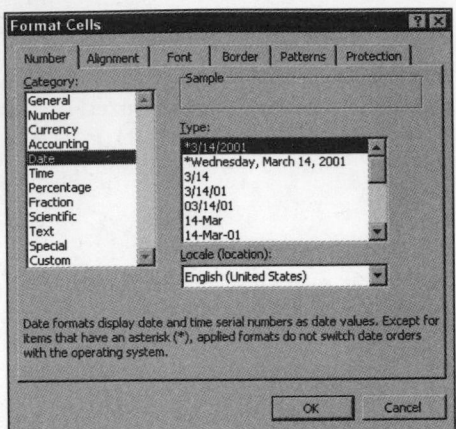

Figure 10-1: Use the Number tab in the Format Cells dialog box to change the appearance of dates and times.

 Tip   A particularly useful custom number format for displaying times is

[h]:mm:ss

Using square brackets around the hour part of the format string causes Excel to display hours beyond 24 hours. You will find this useful when adding times that exceed 24 hours. For an example, see "Summing Times That Exceed 24 Hours," later in this chapter.

Working around Excel's problems with dates

There are, unfortunately, a few date-related problems that you need to be aware of when you work with Excel. None of these problems are insurmountable, but they can have an affect on your results if you aren't aware of them.

Understanding the year 1900 leap-year bug

A leap year contains an additional day (February 29). Although the year 1900 was not a leap year, Excel treats it as such. In other words, when you type the following into a cell, Excel does not complain. It interprets this as a valid date and assigns a serial number of 60.

2/29/1900

How can Excel contain such an obvious bug? The answer is historical. The original version of Lotus 1-2-3 contained a bug that caused it to consider 1900 as a leap year. When Excel was released some time later, the designers knew of this bug, and chose to reproduce it in Excel to maintain compatibility with Lotus worksheet files.

Why does this bug still exist in later versions of Excel? Microsoft asserts that the disadvantages of correcting this bug outweigh the advantages. If the bug were eliminated, it would mess up hundreds of thousands of existing workbooks. In addition, correcting this problem would affect compatibility between Excel and other programs that use dates. As it stands, this bug really causes very few problems because most users do not use dates before March 1, 1900.

Understanding why you can't use pre-1900 dates

The world, of course, didn't begin on January 1, 1900. People who work with historical information using Excel often need to work with dates before January 1, 1900. Unfortunately, the only way to work with pre-1900 dates is to enter the date into a cell as text. For example, you can enter the following into a cell and Excel won't complain:

```
July 4, 1776
```

You can't, however, perform any manipulation on dates recognized as text. For example, you can't change its numeric formatting, you can't determine which day of the week this date occurred on, and you can't calculate the date that occurs seven days later.

Understanding the limitations of two-digit years

You need to exercise caution when entering dates by using two digits for the year. When you do so, Excel has some rules that kick in to determine which century to use.

Two-digit years between 00 and 29 are interpreted as 21st century dates, and two-digit years between 30 and 99 are interpreted as 20th century dates. For example, if you enter 12/5/28, Excel interprets your entry as December 5, 2028. But if you enter 12/5/30, Excel sees it as December 5, 1930.

Caution Older versions of Excel interpreted two-digit years differently, so if you need to share an Excel worksheet with someone who requires an earlier Excel workbook format — perhaps to export data to another program that does not understand the current Excel workbook format — be aware that two-digit years may not be consistent.

To avoid any surprises, you should simply enter all years using all four digits for the year.

Tip You can control the two-digit year window using the Regional Settings applet in the Windows Control Panel. Click the Date tab to change the setting for all Windows programs.

Working with Dates in Excel

Excel has quite a few functions that work with dates, and you can use these functions in your formulas. When you use the Insert Function dialog box, these functions appear in the Date & Time function category.

 **Cross-Reference**   Some of Excel's date functions require that you install the Analysis ToolPak. See Chapter 24 for more information.

Table 10-3 summarizes the date-related functions available in Excel.

	Table 10-3 Date-Related Functions
Function	**Description**
DATE	Returns the serial number of a particular date
DATEVALUE	Converts a date in the form of text to a serial number
DAY	Converts a serial number to a day of the month
DAYS360	Calculates the number of days between two dates based on a 360-day year
EDATE	Returns the serial number of the date that represents the indicated number of months before or after the start date
EOMONTH	Returns the serial number of the last day of the month before or after a specified number of months
MONTH	Converts a serial number to a month
NETWORKDAYS	Returns the number of whole workdays between two dates
NOW	Returns the serial number of the current date and time
TODAY	Returns the serial number of today's date
WEEKDAY	Converts a serial number to a day of the week
WEEKNUM	Returns the week number in the year
WORKDAY	Returns the serial number of the date before or after a specified number of workdays
YEAR	Converts a serial number to a year
YEARFRAC	Returns the year fraction representing the number of whole days between start_date and end_date

Displaying dates in your worksheets

It's often important to be able to display specific dates in a worksheet. In the following sections, you will learn several ways to do this efficiently.

Displaying the current date in your worksheet

The following function displays the current date in a cell:

```
=TODAY()
```

You can also display the date combined with text. The following formula, for example, displays text such as, "Today is Thursday, December 30, 2003."

```
="Today is "&TEXT(TODAY(),"dddd, mmmm d, yyyy")
```

It's important to understand that the TODAY function is updated whenever the worksheet is calculated. For example, if you enter either of the formulas into a worksheet, they will display the current date. But when you open the workbook tomorrow, they will display the current date — not the date when you entered the formula.

Tip   To enter a "date stamp" into a cell, press Ctrl+; (semicolon). This enters the date directly into the cell and does not use a formula. Therefore, the date will not change.

Displaying any date in your worksheet

You can easily enter a date into a cell by simply typing it, using any of the date formats that Excel recognizes. You can also create a date by using the DATE function. The following formula, for example, returns a date comprising the year in cell A1, the month in cell B1, and the day in cell C1.

```
=DATE(A1,B1,C1)
```

The DATEVALUE function converts a text string that looks like a date into a date serial number. The following formula returns 37798, the date serial number for June 26, 2003:

```
=DATEVALUE("6/26/2003")
```

To view the result of this formula as a date, you need to apply a date number format to the cell.

Tip   If you forget to enclose the DATEVALUE argument in quotes, Excel will return an error rather than a date serial number.

Generating a series of dates

Often, you'll want to insert a series of dates into a worksheet. For example, in tracking weekly sales, you may want to enter a series of dates, each separated by seven days. These dates will serve to identify the sales figures.

An efficient way to enter a series of dates that doesn't require any formulas is to use Excel's AutoFill feature. Enter the first date, and drag the cell's fill handle while pressing the right mouse button. Release the mouse button and select an option from the shortcut menu (see Figure 10-2).

Tip   An even faster way to fill a range with a series of dates is to enter the first two dates in the series into the range. Then drag the fill handle and Excel will automatically increment the remaining dates using the same increment.

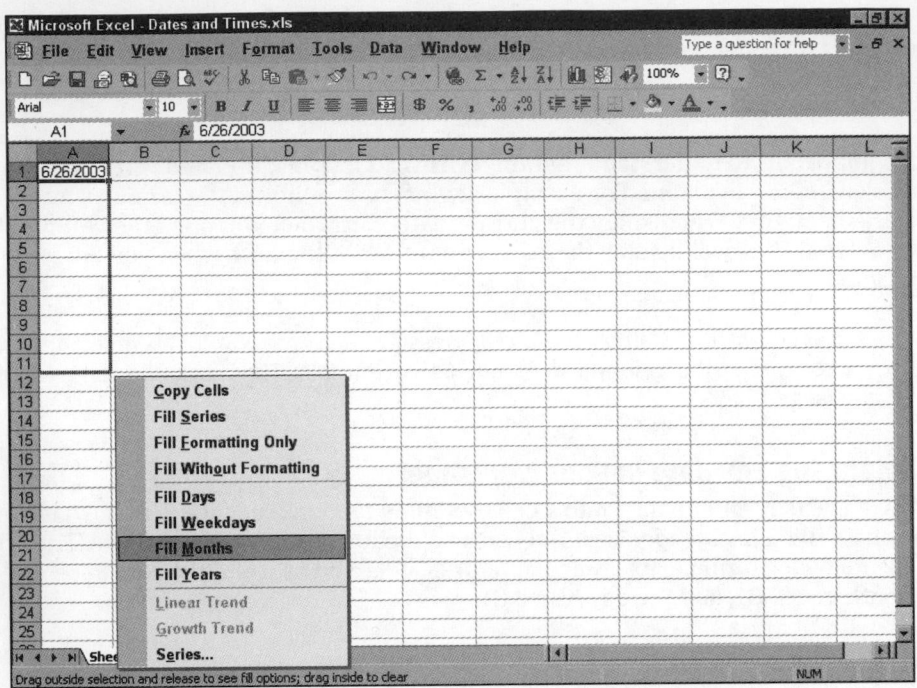

Figure 10-2: Use Excel's AutoFill feature to create a series of dates.

You can also generate a series of dates using formulas. The advantage of using formulas to create a series of dates is that you can change the first date and the others will update automatically. You need to enter the starting date into a cell, and then use formulas (copied down the column) to generate the additional dates.

The following examples assume that you entered the first date of the series into cell A1, and the formula into cell A2. You can then copy this formula down the column as many times as needed.

To generate a series of dates separated by seven days, use this formula:

```
=A1+7
```

To generate a series of dates separated by one month, use this formula:

```
=DATE(YEAR(A1),MONTH(A1)+1,DAY(A1))
```

You can, of course, use any interval you wish between the dates in the series simply by modifying the formula to suit your needs.

Calculating with date values

Many times you'll find a need to calculate using date values. Excel provides many very useful functions and techniques you can use.

Converting unconventional date strings to dates

Often, you may import data that contains dates coded as text strings. For example, the following text represents August 21, 2003 (a four-digit year followed by a two-digit month, followed by a two-digit day):

```
20030821
```

To convert this string to an actual date, you can use a formula such as this one that assumes that the coded data appears in cell A1:

```
=DATE(LEFT(A1,4),MID(A1,5,2),RIGHT(A1,2))
```

This formula uses text functions (LEFT, MID, and RIGHT) to extract the digits, and then uses the extracted digits as arguments for the DATE function. (See Chapter 9 for more info on text functions.)

Calculating the number of days between two dates

A common type of date calculation determines the number of days between two dates. For example, you may have a financial worksheet that calculates interest earned on a deposit account. The interest earned depends on the number of days the account is open. If your sheet contains the open date and the close date for the account, you can calculate the number of days the account was open.

Because dates store as consecutive serial numbers, you can use simple subtraction to calculate the number of days between two dates. For example, if cells A1 and B1 both contain a date, the following formula returns the number of days between these dates:

```
=A1-B1
```

Sometimes, calculating the difference between two days proves more difficult. To demonstrate, consider the common fence-post analogy. If somebody asks you how many units make up a fence, you can respond with either of two answers: the number of fence posts, or the number of gaps between the fence posts. The number of fence posts always remains one more than the number of gaps between the posts.

To bring this analogy into the realm of dates, suppose you start a sales promotion on February 1 and end the promotion on February 9. How many days was the promotion in effect? Subtracting February 1 from February 9 produces an answer of eight days. Actually, the promotion lasted nine days. In this case, the correct answer involves adding 1 to the formula result as in:

```
=EndDay-StartDay+1
```

Calculating the number of workdays between two dates

You may want to exclude weekends and holidays when calculating the difference between two dates. For example, you may need to know how many business days fall in the month of November. This calculation should exclude Saturdays, Sundays, and holidays. The NETWORKDAYS function can help out.

The NETWORKDAYS function calculates the difference between two dates, excluding weekend days (Saturdays and Sundays). As an option, you can specify a range of cells that contain the dates of holidays, which are also excluded. Excel has absolutely no way of determining which days are holidays, so you must provide this information in a range. (See the following sections for more information on calculating dates of holidays.)

Figure 10-3 shows a worksheet that calculates the workdays between two dates. The range D3:D12 contains a list of holiday dates. The formula in cell C14 calculates the workdays between the dates in cells G3 and G4. For this example, the formula in cell C14 is

```
=NETWORKDAYS(G3,G4,D3:D12)
```

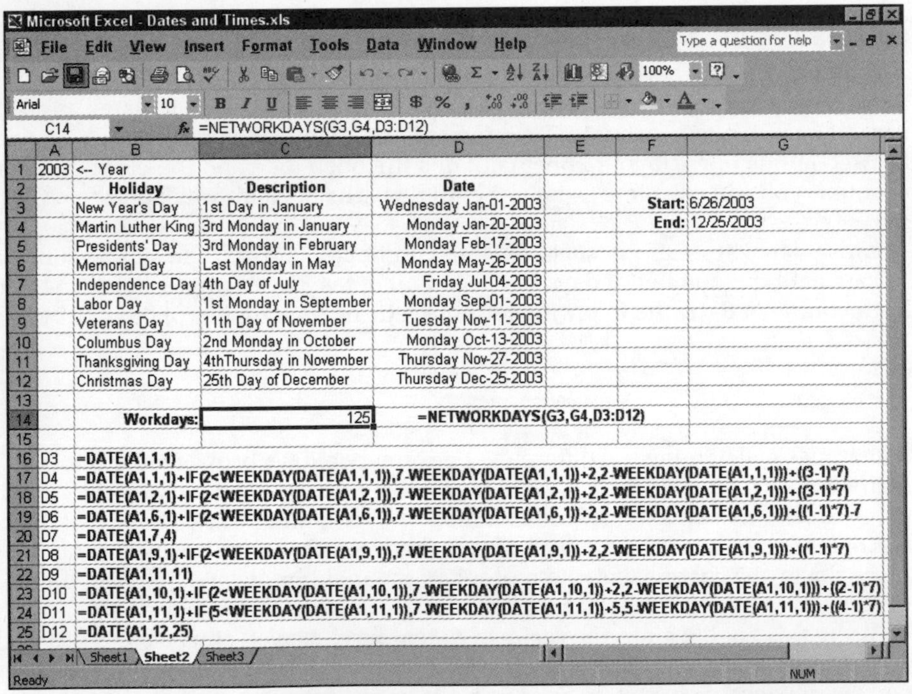

Figure 10-3: Use Excel's NETWORKDAYS function to calculate the number of working days between two dates.

Note   Figure 10-3 also shows the formulas used to calculate the dates of holidays as demonstrated next.

Calculating dates of holidays

Determining the date for a particular holiday can be tricky. Some, such as New Year's Day and Independence Day, are easy, because they always occur on the same date. To enter New Year's Day for a specific year in cell A1, you can enter this function:

```
=DATE(A1,1,1)
```

Other holidays are defined in terms of a particular occurrence of a particular weekday in a particular month. For example, Labor Day falls on the first Monday in September.

Figure 10-3 shows a workbook with formulas to calculate the date for 10 U.S. holidays. The formulas reference the year in cell A1. Notice that because New Year's Day, Independence Day, Veterans Day, and Christmas Day all fall on the same days of the year, the DATE function calculates their dates.

Finding the date of Martin Luther King Jr. Day

This holiday occurs on the third Monday in January. This formula calculates Martin Luther King Jr. Day for the year in cell A1:

```
=DATE(A1,1,1)+IF(2<WEEKDAY(DATE(A1,1,1)),7-WEEKDAY
(DATE(A1,1,1))+2,2-WEEKDAY(DATE(A1,1,1)))+((3-1)*7)
```

Finding the date of Presidents' Day

Presidents' Day occurs on the third Monday in February. This formula calculates Presidents' Day for the year in cell A1:

```
=DATE(A1,2,1)+IF(2<WEEKDAY(DATE(A1,2,1)),7-WEEKDAY
(DATE(A1,2,1))+2,2-WEEKDAY(DATE(A1,2,1)))+((3-1)*7)
```

Finding the date of Memorial Day

The last Monday in May is Memorial Day. This formula calculates Memorial Day for the year in cell A1:

```
=DATE(A1,6,1)+IF(2<WEEKDAY(DATE(A1,6,1)),7-WEEKDAY
(DATE(A1,6,1))+2,2-WEEKDAY(DATE(A1,6,1)))+((1-1)*7)-7
```

Notice that this formula actually calculates the first Monday in June and then subtracts 7 from the result to return the last Monday in May.

Finding the date of Labor Day

Labor Day occurs on the first Monday in September. This formula calculates Labor Day for the year in cell A1:

```
=DATE(A1,9,1)+IF(2<WEEKDAY(DATE(A1,9,1)),7-WEEKDAY
(DATE(A1,9,1))+2,2-WEEKDAY(DATE(A1,9,1)))+((1-1)*7)
```

Finding the date of Columbus Day

This holiday occurs on the second Monday in October. The following formula calculates Columbus Day for the year in cell A1:

```
=DATE(A1,10,1)+IF(2<WEEKDAY(DATE(A1,10,1)),7-WEEKDAY
(DATE(A1,10,1))+2,2-WEEKDAY(DATE(A1,10,1)))+((2-1)*7)
```

Finding the date of Thanksgiving Day

Thanksgiving Day is celebrated on the fourth Thursday in November. This formula calculates Thanksgiving Day for the year in cell A1:

```
=DATE(A1,11,1)+IF(5<WEEKDAY(DATE(A1,11,1)),7-WEEKDAY
(DATE(A1,11,1))+5,5-WEEKDAY(DATE(A1,11,1)))+((4-1)*7)
```

Offsetting a date using only workdays

The WORKDAY function presents the opposite of the NETWORKDAYS function. For example, if you start a project on January 4, and the project requires 10 working days to complete, the WORKDAY function can calculate the date you will finish the project.

The following formula uses the WORKDAY function to determine the date 10 working days from January 4, 2003. A working day consists of a weekday (Monday through Friday).

```
=WORKDAY("1/4/2003",10)
```

The formula returns 37638 — the date serial number for January 17, 2003 (three weekend dates fall between January 4 and January 17).

The second argument for the WORKDAY function can be negative. And, as with the NETWORKDAYS function, the WORKDAY function accepts an optional third argument — a reference to a range that contains a list of holiday dates.

Calculating the number of years between two dates

The following formula calculates the number of years between two dates. This formula assumes that cells A1 and B1 both contain dates.

```
=YEAR(A1)-YEAR(B1)
```

This formula uses the YEAR function to extract the year from each date and then subtracts one year from the other. If cell B1 contains a more recent date than the date in cell A1, the result is negative.

Note that this function doesn't calculate full years. For example, if cell A1 contains 01/01/2003 and cell B1 contains 12/31/2002, the formula returns a difference of one year, even though the dates differ by only one day.

Tip You need to apply the General numeric format to the cell after entering this formula to see the result because Excel automatically applies a Date format to the cell.

Calculating a person's age

A person's age indicates the number of full years that the person has been alive. The formula for calculating the number of years between two dates won't calculate this value correctly. You can use two other formulas, however, to calculate a person's age.

The following formula returns the age of the person whose date of birth you enter into cell A1:

```
=INT(YEARFRAC(TODAY(),A1,1))
```

The following formula, uses the DATEDIF function to calculate an age (see the sidebar, "Where's the DATEDIF Function?"):

```
=DATEDIF(A1,TODAY(),"Y")
```

Determining the day of the week

The WEEKDAY function accepts a date argument and returns an integer between 1 and 7 (1 for Sunday, 2 for Monday, and so on) that corresponds to the day of the week. The following formula, for example, returns 7 because the first day of the year 2000 falls on a Saturday:

```
=WEEKDAY(1/1/2000)
```

The WEEKDAY function uses an optional second argument that specifies the day numbering for the result. If you specify 2 as the second argument, the function returns 1 for Monday, 2 for Tuesday, and so on. If you specify 3 as the second argument, the function returns 0 for Monday, 1 for Tuesday, and so on.

Tip You can also determine the day of the week for a cell that contains a date by applying a custom number format. A cell that uses the following custom number format displays the day of the week, spelled out:

```
dddd
```

Determining the date of the most recent Sunday

You can use the following formula to return the date for the previous Sunday. If the current day is a Sunday, the formula returns the current date:

```
=TODAY()-MOD(TODAY()-1,7)
```

To modify this formula to find the date of a day other than Sunday, change the 1 to a different number between 2 (for Monday) and 7 (for Saturday).

Where's the DATEDIF Function?

You may notice that the DATEDIF function does not appear in the Insert Function dialog box. The DATEDIF function has its origins in Lotus 1-2-3, and Excel provides it for compatibility purposes. To use this function you must always enter it manually.

DATEDIF calculates the number of days, months, or years between two dates. The function takes three arguments: start_date, end_date, and a code that represents the time unit of interest. The following table displays valid codes for the third argument (you must enclose the codes in quotation marks).

Unit Code	Returns
"Y"	The number of complete years in the period.
"M"	The number of complete months in the period.
"D"	The number of days in the period.
"MD"	The difference between the days in start_date and end_date. The months and years of the dates are ignored.
"YM"	The difference between the months in start_date and end_date. The days and years of the dates are ignored.
"YD"	The difference between the days of start_date and end_date. The years of the dates are ignored.

The start_date argument must be earlier than the end_date argument, or the function returns an error.

Determining the nth occurrence of a day of the week in a month

You may need a formula to determine the date for a particular occurrence of a weekday. For example, suppose your company payday falls on the second Friday of each month, and you need to determine the paydays for each month of the year. The following formula will make this type of calculation:

```
=DATE(A1,A2,1)+IF(A3<WEEKDAY(DATE(A1,A2,1)),7-WEEKDAY
(DATE(A1,A2,1))+A3,A3-WEEKDAY(DATE(A1,A2,1)))+((A4-1)*7)
```

The formula in this section assumes that

✦ Cell A1 contains a year

✦ Cell A2 contains a month

✦ Cell A3 contains a day number (1 for Sunday, 2 for Monday, and so on)

✦ Cell A4 contains the occurrence of interest (for example, 1 to select the first occurrence of the weekday specified in cell A3)

If you use this formula to determine the date of the first Friday in June 2000, it returns June 2, 2000.

Note If the value in cell A4 exceeds the number of the specified day in the month, the formula returns a date from a subsequent month. For example, if you attempt to determine the date of the sixth Friday in June (no such date exists), the formula returns the first Friday in July.

Determining the last day of a month

To determine the date that corresponds to the last day of a month, you can use the DATE function. However, you need to increment the month by 1 and use a day value of 0. In other words, the "0th" day of the next month is the last day of the current month.

The following formula assumes that a date is stored in cell A1. The formula returns the date that corresponds to the last day of the month.

```
=DATE(YEAR(A1),MONTH(A1)+1,0)
```

Determining whether a year is a leap year

To determine whether a particular year is a leap year, you can write a formula that determines whether the 29th day of February occurs in February or March. You can take advantage of the fact that Excel's DATE function adjusts the result when you supply an invalid argument — for example, a day of 29 when February contains only 28 days.

The following formula returns TRUE if the year of the date in cell A1 is a leap year. Otherwise, it returns FALSE.

```
=IF(MONTH(DATE(YEAR(A1),2,29))=2,TRUE,FALSE)
```

Note This function returns an incorrect result (TRUE) if the year is 1900.

Working with Times in Excel

Excel, as you might expect, also includes functions that enable you to work with time values in your formulas. This section contains examples that demonstrate the use of these functions.

Table 10-4 summarizes the time-related functions available in Excel. When you use the Insert Function dialog box, these functions appear in the Date & Time function category.

	Table 10-4 Time-Related Functions
Function	**Description**
HOUR	Converts a serial number to an hour
MINUTE	Converts a serial number to a minute
MONTH	Converts a serial number to a month
NOW	Returns the serial number of the current date and time
SECOND	Converts a serial number to a second
TIME	Returns the serial number of a particular time
TIMEVALUE	Converts a time in the form of text to a serial number

Displaying times

Displaying times in Excel worksheets is quite similar to displaying dates. This section describes some useful techniques for working with times.

This formula displays the current time as a time serial number (or as a serial number without an associated date):

```
=NOW()-TODAY()
```

Tip To enter a time stamp into a cell, press Ctrl+Shift+: (colon).

You need to format the cell with a time format to view the result as a recognizable time. For example, you can apply the following number format:

```
hh:mm AM/PM
```

You can also display the time, combined with text. The following formula displays the text The current time is 6:28 PM.

```
="The current time is "&TEXT(NOW(),"h:mm AM/PM")
```

Note Time formulas are updated only when the worksheet is calculated.

You can also create a time by using the TIME function. For example, the following formula returns a time comprising the hour in cell A1, the minute in cell B1, and the second in cell C1.

```
=TIME(A1,B1,C1)
```

 **Note** Like the DATE function, the TIME function accepts invalid arguments and adjusts the result accordingly.

You can also use the DATE function along with the TIME function in a single cell. The formula that follows generates 37638.7708333333, the serial number that represents 6:30 p.m. on January 17, 2003.

```
=DATE(2003,1,17)+TIME(18,30,0)
```

The TIMEVALUE function converts a text string that looks like a time into a time serial number. The following formula returns 0.2395833333, the time serial number for 5:45 a.m.

```
=TIMEVALUE("5:45 am")
```

To view the result of this formula as a time, you need to apply number formatting to the cell. The TIMEVALUE function doesn't recognize all time formats. For example, the following formula returns an error because Excel doesn't like the periods in a.m.

```
=TIMEVALUE("5:45 a.m.")
```

Calculating times

Many worksheets also involve time calculations. You might, for example, want to use an Excel worksheet to calculate the amount owed to employees based on the number of hours they worked. The following sections provide several examples of how you can use Excel's functions to do time calculations.

Summing times that exceed 24 hours

Many people are dismayed to discover that, when you sum a series of times that exceed 24 hours, Excel doesn't display the correct total. Figure 10-4 shows an example. The range B2:B8 contains times that represent the hours and minutes worked each day. The formula in cell B9 is

```
=SUM(B2:B8)
```

As you can see, the formula returns an incorrect total (18 hours, 30 minutes). The total should read 42 hours, 30 minutes.

Unless told otherwise, Excel always displays times as if they comprise part of a day (in other words, limited to 24 hours). As Figure 10-4 also shows, displaying the sum in General format (see cell C9) doesn't solve the problem because the result is the number of days — not hours. To view a time that exceeds 24 hours, you need to change the number format for the cell so that square brackets surround the hour part of the format string. Applying the number format here to cell D9 displays the sum correctly:

```
[h]:mm
```

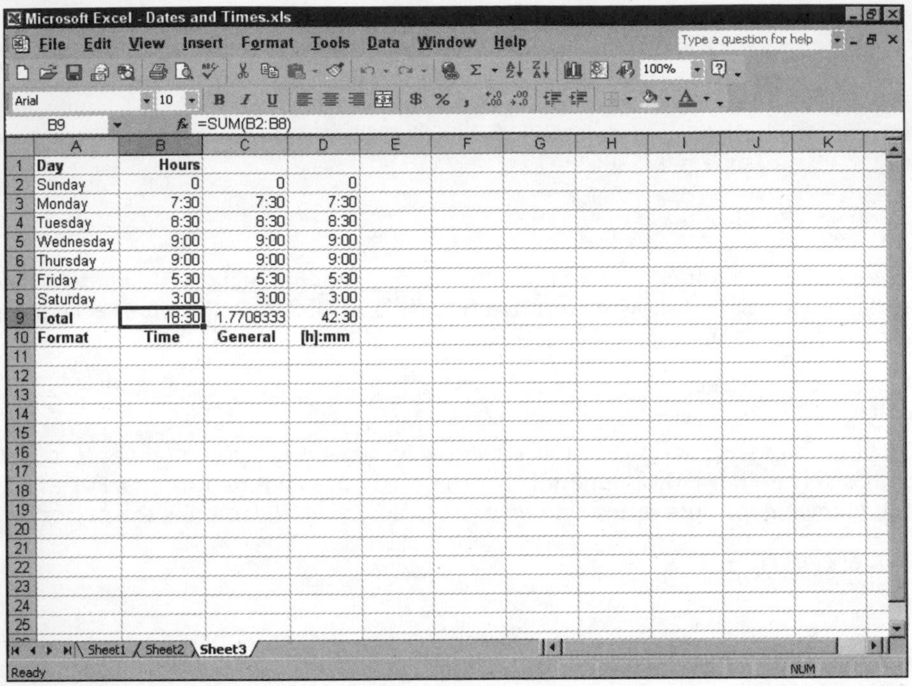

Figure 10-4: Using the SUM function to add a series of times. The answer is incorrect because cell B9 has the wrong number format.

Calculating the difference between two times

Because times are represented as serial numbers, you can subtract the earlier time from the later time to get the difference. For example, if cell A2 contains 5:30:00 and cell B2 contains 14:00:00, the following formula returns 08:30:00 (a difference of 8 hours and 30 minutes).

```
=B2-A2
```

If the subtraction results in a negative value, however, it becomes an invalid time; Excel displays a series of pound signs (########) because a time without a date has a date serial number of 0. A negative time results in a negative serial number, which is not permitted. This problem does not occur when you use a date along with the time.

If the direction of the time difference doesn't matter, you can use the ABS (absolute value) function to return the absolute value of the difference:

```
=ABS(B2-A2)
```

This "negative time" problem often occurs when calculating an elapsed time — for example, calculating the number of hours worked given a start time and an end time. This presents no problem if the two times fall in the same day. But if the work shift spans midnight, the result is an invalid negative time. For example, you may start work at 10:00 p.m. and end work at 6:00 a.m. the next day.

Using the ABS isn't an option in this case because it returns the wrong result (16 hours). The following formula, however, does work.

```
=(B2+(B2<A2)-A2)
```

Another, simpler, formula can do the job:

```
=MOD(B2-A2,1)
```

Converting from military time

Military time is expressed as a four-digit number from 0000 to 2359. For example, 1:00 a.m. is expressed as 0100 hours, and 3:30 p.m. is expressed as 1530 hours. The following formula converts such a number (assumed to appear in cell A1) to a standard time:

```
=TIMEVALUE(LEFT(A1,2)&":"&RIGHT(A1,2))
```

The formula returns an incorrect result if the contents of cell A1 do not contain four digits. The following formula corrects the problem and returns a valid time for any military time value from 0 to 2359.

```
=TIMEVALUE(LEFT(TEXT(A1,"0000"),2)&":"&RIGHT(TEXT(A1,"0000"),2))
```

Converting decimal hours, minutes, or seconds to a time

To convert decimal hours to a time, divide the decimal hours by 24. For example, if cell A1 contains 9.25 (representing hours), this formula returns 09:15:00 (9 hours, 15 minutes):

```
=A1/24
```

To convert decimal minutes to a time, divide the decimal hours by 1,440 (the number of minutes in a day). For example, if cell A1 contains 500 (representing minutes), the following formula returns 08:20:00 (8 hours, 20 minutes):

```
=A1/1440
```

To convert decimal seconds to a time, divide the decimal hours by 86,400 (the number of seconds in a day). For example, if cell A1 contains 65,000 (representing seconds), the following formula returns 18:03:20 (18 hours, 3 minutes, and 20 seconds).

```
=A1/86400
```

Tip   Don't forget to apply a time format to the cells containing the formulas.

Adding hours, minutes, or seconds to a time

You can use the TIME function to add any number of hours, minutes, or seconds to a time. For example, assume that cell A1 contains a time. The following formula adds 2 hours and 30 minutes to that time and displays the result:

```
=A1+TIME(2,30,0)
```

 **Tip**   To fill a range of cells with incremental times, you can also use Excel's AutoFill feature.

Converting between time zones

You may receive a worksheet that contains dates and times in Greenwich Mean Time (GMT, sometimes referred to as Zulu time), which you need to convert to local time. To convert dates and times into local times, you need to determine the difference in hours between the two time zones. For example, to convert GMT times to U.S. Central Standard Time, the hour conversion factor is –6.

 Tip   To find out the correct hour conversion factor, double-click the clock display in the Windows system tray. The time zone setting will show your difference from GMT.

You can't use the TIME function with a negative argument, so you need to take a different approach. One hour equals $\frac{1}{24}$ of a day, so you can divide the time conversion factor by 24, and then add it to the time.

For example, if cell B1 contains the hour conversion factor (–5 hours for U.S. Eastern Standard Time) and cell A4 contains the time you wish to convert, the following formula does the job:

```
=A4+($B$1/24)
```

This formula effectively adds *x* hours to the date and time. If cell B1 contains a negative hour value, the value subtracts from the date and time in column A. Note that, in some cases, this also affects the date.

Rounding time values

You may need to create a formula that rounds a time to a particular value. For example, you may need to enter your company's time records rounded to the nearest 15 minutes. This section presents examples of various ways to round a time value.

The following formula rounds the time in cell A1 to the nearest minute:

```
=ROUND(A1*1440,0)/1440
```

The formula works by multiplying the time by 1440 (to get total minutes). This value is passed to the ROUND function; the result is divided by 1440. For example, if cell A1 contains 11:52:34, the formula returns 11:53:00.

The following formula resembles this example, except that it rounds the time in cell A1 to the nearest hour:

```
=ROUND(A1*24,0)/24
```

If cell A1 contains 5:21:31, the formula returns 5:00:00.

The following formula rounds the time in cell A1 to the nearest 15 minutes:

```
=ROUND(A1*24/0.25,0)*(0.25/24)
```

In this formula, 0.25 represents the fractional hour. To round a time to the nearest 30 minutes, change 0.25 to 0.5, as in the following formula:

```
=ROUND(A1*24/0.5,0)*(0.5/24)
```

Working with non-time-of-day values

Sometimes, you may want to work with time values that don't represent an actual time of day. For example, you might want to create a list of the finish times for a race, or record the time you spend jogging each day. Such times don't represent a time of day. Rather, a value represents the time for an event (in hours, minutes, and seconds). The time to complete a test, for instance, might take 35 minutes and 40 seconds. You can enter that value into a cell as

```
00:35:45
```

Excel interprets such an entry as 12:35:45 a.m., which works fine (just make sure that you format the cell so that it appears as you like). For example, in Figure 10-5 column G uses [hh]:mm:ss to properly display the results.

Tip   When you enter times that do not have an hour component, you must include at least one zero for the hour. If you omit a leading zero for a missing hour, Excel interprets your entry as 35 hours and 45 minutes.

Figure 10-5 shows an example of a worksheet set up to keep track of someone's jogging activity. Column A contains simple dates. Column B contains the distance, in miles. Column C contains the time it took to run the distance. Column D contains formulas to calculate the speed, in miles per hour. For example, the formula in cell D2 is

```
=B2/(C2*24)
```

Column E contains formulas to calculate the pace, in minutes per mile. For example, the formula in cell E2 is

```
=(C2*60*24)/B2
```

Columns F and G contain formulas that calculate the year-to-date distance (using column B), and the cumulative time (using column C). The cells in column G are formatted using the following number format (which permits time displays that exceed 24 hours):

```
[hh]:mm:ss
```

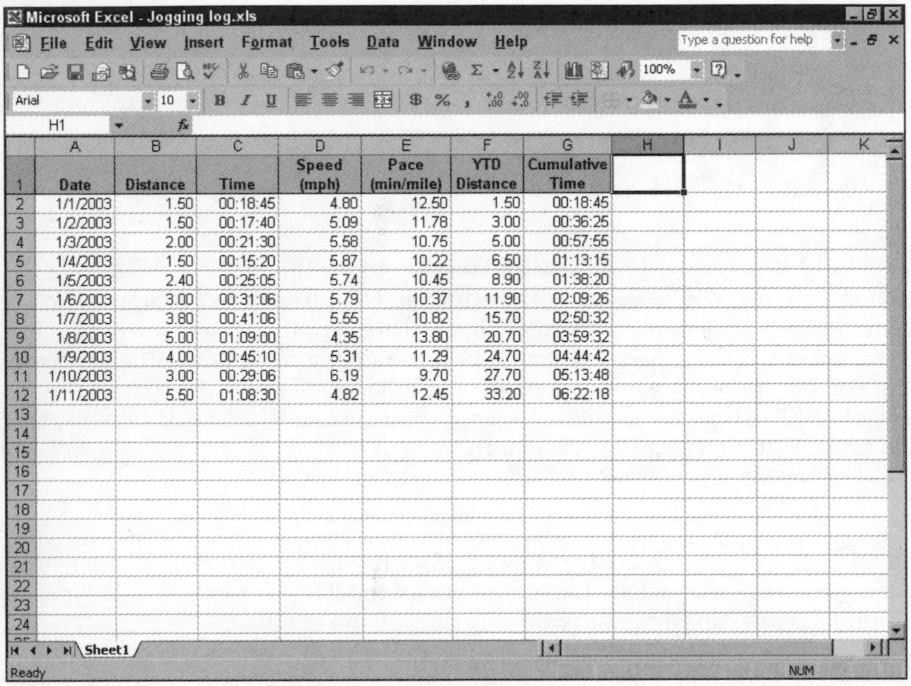

Date	Distance	Time	Speed (mph)	Pace (min/mile)	YTD Distance	Cumulative Time
1/1/2003	1.50	00:18:45	4.80	12.50	1.50	00:18:45
1/2/2003	1.50	00:17:40	5.09	11.78	3.00	00:36:25
1/3/2003	2.00	00:21:30	5.58	10.75	5.00	00:57:55
1/4/2003	1.50	00:15:20	5.87	10.22	6.50	01:13:15
1/5/2003	2.40	00:25:05	5.74	10.45	8.90	01:38:20
1/6/2003	3.00	00:31:06	5.79	10.37	11.90	02:09:26
1/7/2003	3.80	00:41:06	5.55	10.82	15.70	02:50:32
1/8/2003	5.00	01:09:00	4.35	13.80	20.70	03:59:32
1/9/2003	4.00	00:45:10	5.31	11.29	24.70	04:44:42
1/10/2003	3.00	00:29:06	6.19	9.70	27.70	05:13:48
1/11/2003	5.50	01:08:30	4.82	12.45	33.20	06:22:18

Figure 10-5: This worksheet uses times not associated with a time of day.

✦ ✦ ✦

Creating Formulas That Count and Sum

C ounting and summing are two common spreadsheet operations. Excel provides a large number of tools that you can apply to many different types of these tasks. This chapter shows you the techniques you need to know to handle virtually any counting or summing need in your Excel worksheets.

Understanding Basic Counting Techniques

Counting is one of the first things we learn as children. It's no wonder then that we tend to take for granted the complexities that counting can involve. For example, if you ask a young child to tell you how many red balls are sitting on a table, you probably don't even consider that your question involves more than a simple count. First, you've asked the child to only include balls — and no other round objects — and second you've indicated that any balls that aren't red should be ignored. It's important to understand that adding in these qualifiers — criteria — makes for a much more complex task. When you ask Excel to count items, you need to be aware that these same types of complexities exist, and that you need to correctly instruct Excel so that you obtain the answer you expect.

Generally, a counting formula returns the number of cells in a specified range that meet certain criteria. A summing formula returns the sum of the cells in a range that meet certain criteria. The range you want counted or summed may or may not consist of a worksheet database.

Table 11-1 lists Excel's worksheet functions that come into play when creating counting and summing formulas. If none of the functions in Table 11-1 can solve your problem, it's likely that an array formula can come to the rescue.

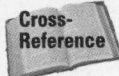

Cross-Reference   See Chapters 16 and 17 to learn more about arrays.

Table 11-1 Excel's Counting and Summing Functions	
Function	**Description**
COUNT	Returns the number of cells in a range that contain a numeric value
COUNTA	Returns the number of nonblank cells in a range
COUNTBLANK	Returns the number of blank cells in a range
COUNTIF	Returns the number of cells in a range that meet a specified criterion
DCOUNT	Counts the number of records in a worksheet database that meet specified criteria
DCOUNTA	Counts the number of nonblank records in a worksheet database that meet specified criteria
DEVSQ	Returns the sum of squares of deviations of data points from the sample mean; used primarily in statistical formulas
FREQUENCY	Calculates how often values occur within a range of values, and returns a vertical array of numbers; used only in a multicell array formula
SUBTOTAL	When used with a first argument of 2 or 3, returns a count of cells that comprise a subtotal; when used with a first argument of 9, returns the sum of cells that comprise a subtotal
SUM	Returns the sum of its arguments
SUMIF	Returns the sum of cells in a range that meet a specified criterion
SUMPRODUCT	Multiplies corresponding cells in two or more ranges, and returns the sum of those products
SUMSQ	Returns the sum of the squares of its arguments; used primarily in statistical formulas
SUMX2PY2	Returns the sum of the sum of squares of corresponding values in two ranges; used primarily in statistical formulas
SUMXMY2	Returns the sum of squares of the differences of corresponding values in two ranges; used primarily in statistical formulas
SUMXMY2	Returns the sum of the difference of squares of corresponding values in two ranges; used primarily in statistical formulas

Figure 11-1 shows a shortcut method of viewing information about a selected range. The AutoCalculate feature displays information about the selected range in the status bar. Normally, the status bar displays the sum of the values in the selected range. You can, however, right-click the AutoCalculate display to bring up a menu with some other options. If you select Count, the status bar displays the number of nonempty cells in the selected range. If you select Count Nums, the status bar displays the number of numeric cells in the selected range.

The following sections demonstrate the use of a number of Excel's counting functions to count the number of cells in a range that meet specific criteria. Figure 11-2 shows a worksheet that uses formulas (in column E) to summarize the contents of range A1:B10 — a 20-cell range named Data. The formulas are described in the following sections.

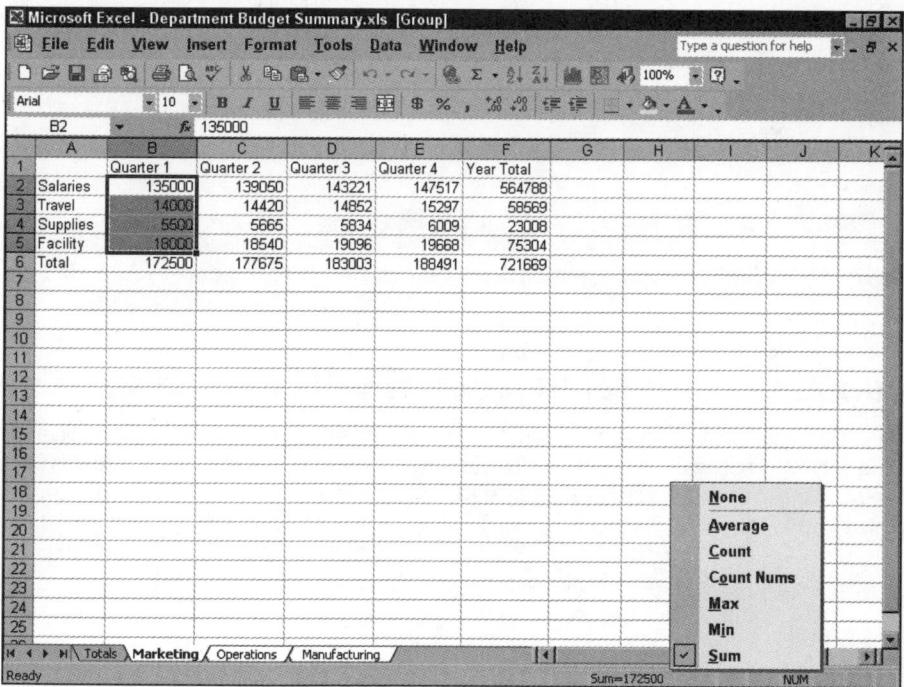

Figure 11-1: You can view summary information about a range without using formulas.

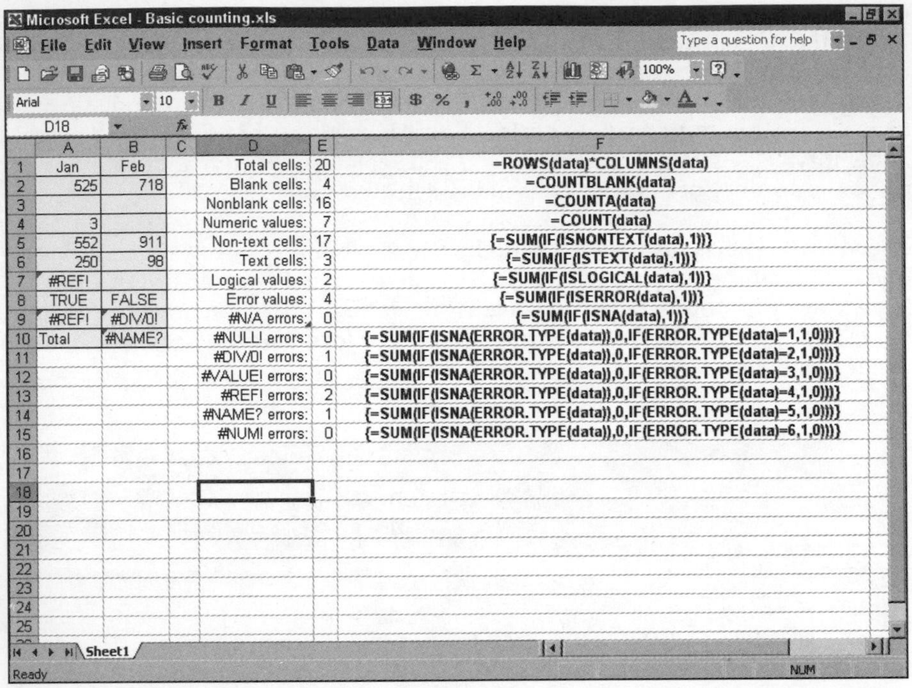

Figure 11-2: These formulas demonstrate various counts of the data in A1:B10.

Counting the total number of cells in a range

To get a count of the total number of cells in a range, use the following formula. This formula returns the number of cells in a range named Data. It simply multiplies the number of rows (returned by the ROWS function) by the number of columns (returned by the COLUMNS function).

```
=ROWS(Data)*COLUMNS(Data)
```

Counting blank cells in a range

To determine how many blank cells are in a range (named Data in this example), you can use the following formula:

```
=COUNTBLANK(Data)
```

The COUNTBLANK function also counts cells containing a formula that returns an empty string. For example, the following formula returns an empty string if the value in cell A1 is greater than 5. If the cell meets this condition, then the COUNT-BLANK function counts that cell.

```
=IF(A1>5,"",A1)
```

Array Formulas

Many of the examples in this chapter consist of array formulas. An array formula, as explained in Chapter 16, is a special type of formula. You can spot an array formula because it is enclosed in brackets. For example

```
{=Data*2}
```

When you enter an array formula, don't type the brackets. Instead, press Ctrl+Shift+Enter (not just Enter) and Excel inserts the brackets for you.

In most cases, you can use the same formula as a standard formula — as opposed to an array formula — to return information about a single cell. The advantage of using an array formula is that a single array formula can return information about an entire range.

Note The COUNTBLANK function does not count cells that contain a zero value, even if you uncheck the Zero values option in the Options dialog box (select Tools ➪ Options, and then click the View tab).

Tip You can also use the COUNTBLANK function with an argument that consists of entire rows or columns.

Counting nonblank cells in a range

The following formula uses the COUNTA function to return the number of nonblank cells in a range named Data:

```
=COUNTA(Data)
```

The COUNTA function counts cells that contain values, text, or logical values (TRUE or FALSE).

Counting numeric cells in a range

To count only the numeric cells in a range (named Data in this example), use the following formula:

```
=COUNT(Data)
```

Cells that contain a date or a time are considered to be numeric cells. Cells that contain a logical value (TRUE or FALSE) are not considered to be numeric cells.

Counting nontext cells in a range

The following array formula uses Excel's ISNONTEXT function, which returns TRUE if its argument refers to any nontext cell (including a blank cell). This formula returns the count of the number of cells not containing text (including blank cells) in a range named Data:

```
{=SUM(IF(ISNONTEXT(Data),1))}
```

Counting text cells in a range

To count the number of text cells in a range, you need to use an array formula. The array formula that follows returns the number of text cells in a range named Data.

```
{=SUM(IF(ISTEXT(Data),1))}
```

Counting logical values in a range

The following array formula returns the number of logical values (TRUE or FALSE) in a range named Data.

```
{=SUM(IF(ISLOGICAL(Data),1))}
```

Counting error values in a range

Excel has three functions that help you determine whether a cell contains an error value:

✦ **ISERROR:** Returns TRUE if the cell contains any error value (#N/A, #VALUE!, #REF!, #DIV/0!, #NUM!, #NAME?, or #NULL!)

✦ **ISERR:** Returns TRUE if the cell contains any error value except #N/A

✦ **ISNA:** Returns TRUE if the cell contains the #N/A error value

You can use these functions in an array formula to count the number of error values in a range. The following array formula, for example, returns the total number of error values in a range named Data:

```
{=SUM(IF(ISERROR(Data),1))}
```

Depending on your needs, you can use the ISERR or ISNA function in place of ISER-ROR.

If you would like to count specific types of errors, you can use the COUNTIF function. The following formula, for example, returns the number of #DIV/0! error values in the range named Data:

```
=COUNTIF(Data,"#DIV/0!")
```

Cross-Reference Excel's Pivot Tables provide another way to count and sum worksheet information. See Chapter 21 for information on using Pivot Tables.

Using Advanced Counting Formulas

Most of the basic examples presented previously represent functions or formulas that perform conditional counting. The advanced counting formulas that are presented next represent more complex examples for counting worksheet cells, based on various types of criteria.

Counting values using the COUNTIF function

Excel's COUNTIF function is very useful for single-criterion counting formulas. With this function you can specify a condition that must be met in order that the cell will be included in the count.

The COUNTIF function takes two arguments:

✦ **Range:** The range that contains the values that determine whether to include a particular cell in the count

✦ **Criteria:** The logical criteria that determine whether to include a particular cell in the count

Table 11-2 lists several examples of formulas that use the COUNTIF function. These formulas all work with a range named Data. As you can see, the criteria argument is quite flexible. You can use constants, expressions, functions, cell references, and wildcard characters (* and ?).

Table 11-2
Example Formulas That Use the COUNTIF Function

Formula	What It Returns
=COUNTIF(Data,12)	The number of cells containing the value 12
=COUNTIF(Data,"<0")	The number of cells containing a negative value
=COUNTIF(Data,"<>0")	The number of cells not equal to 0
=COUNTIF(Data,">5")	The number of cells greater than 5
=COUNTIF(Data,A1)	The number of cells equal to the contents of cell A1
=COUNTIF(Data,">"&A1)	The number of cells greater than the value in cell A1
=COUNTIF(Data,"*")	The number of cells containing text
=COUNTIF(Data,"???")	The number of text cells containing exactly three characters
=COUNTIF(Data,"budget")	The number of cells containing the single word budget (not case-sensitive)

continued

Table 11-2 *(continued)*	
Formula	**What It Returns**
=COUNTIF(Data,"*budget*")	The number of cells containing the text budget anywhere within the text
=COUNTIF(Data,"A*")	The number of cells containing text that begins with the letter A (not case-sensitive)
=COUNTIF(Data,TODAY())	The number of cells containing the current date
=COUNTIF(Data,">" &AVERAGE(Data))	The number of cells with a value greater than the average
=COUNTIF(Data,">" &STDEV(Data)*3)	The number of values exceeding three standard deviations above the mean
=COUNTIF(Data,3)+ COUNTIF(Data,-3)	The number of cells containing the value 3 or −3
=COUNTIF(Data,TRUE)	The number of cells containing logical TRUE
=COUNTIF(Data,TRUE)+ COUNTIF(Data,FALSE)	The number of cells containing a logical value (TRUE or FALSE)
=COUNTIF(Data,"#N/A")	The number of cells containing the #N/A error value

Counting cells using multiple criteria

In many cases, your counting formula will need to count cells only if two or more criteria are met. These criteria can be based on the cells that are being counted, or based on a range of corresponding cells.

Figure 11-3 shows a simple worksheet with the examples in this section. This sheet shows sales data categorized by Month, SalesRep, and Type. The worksheet contains named ranges that correspond to the labels in row 1.

Using AND criteria to select cells

An AND criterion counts cells if all specified conditions are met. A common example is a formula that counts the number of values that fall within a numerical range. For example, you may want to count cells that contain a value greater than 0 and less than or equal to 12. Any cell that has a positive value less than or equal to 12 will be included in the count.

 Note   The words AND and OR don't actually appear in these formulas — rather, you use mathematical operators as shown in the following examples to create the AND or OR conditions.

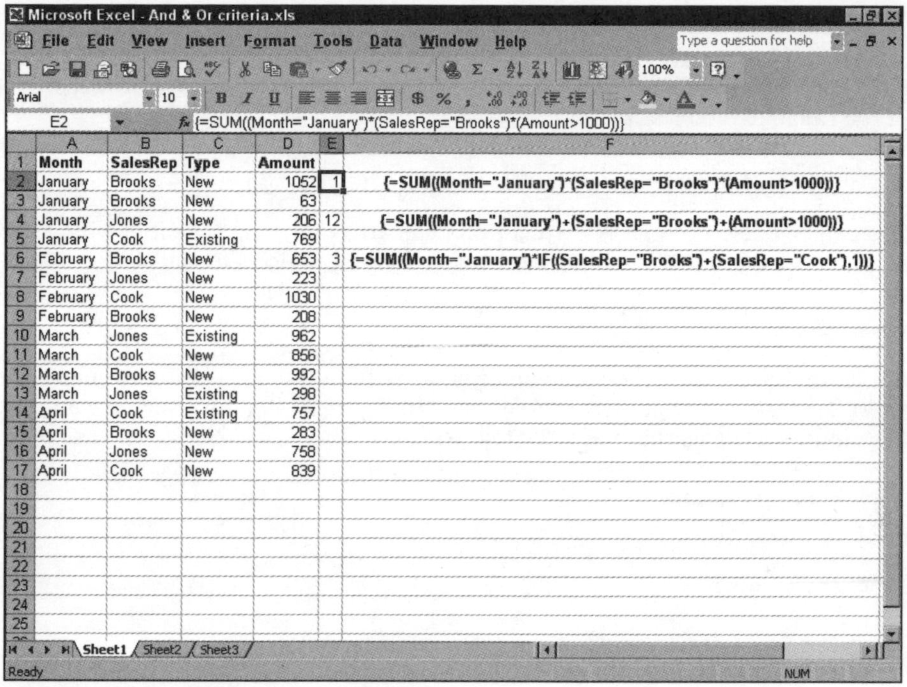

Figure 11-3: This worksheet demonstrates various counting techniques that use multiple criteria.

This sort of cell counting requires an array formula. The array formula that follows returns the count of the number of cells in a range named Data that are greater than 0 and less than or equal to 12:

```
{=SUM((Data>0)*(Data<=12))}
```

Sometimes, the counting criteria will be based on cells other than the cells being counted. You may, for example, want to count the number of sales that meet the following criteria:

✦ Month is January, and

✦ SalesRep is Brooks, and

✦ Amount is greater than 1000

The following array formula returns the number of items that meet all three criteria:

```
{=SUM((Month="January")*(SalesRep="Brooks")*(Amount>1000))}
```

Using OR criteria to select cells

To count using an OR criterion, you can sometimes simply use multiple COUNTIF functions. The following formula, for example, counts the number of 1s, 3s, and 5s in the range named Data:

```
=COUNTIF(Data,1)+COUNTIF(Data,3)+COUNTIF(Data,5)
```

You can also use the COUNTIF function in an array formula. The following array formula, for example, returns the same result as the previous formula:

```
{=SUM(COUNTIF(Data,{1,3,5}))}
```

But if you base your OR criteria on cells other than the cells being counted, the COUNTIF function won't work. Refer back to Figure 11-3. Suppose you want to count the number of sales that meet the following criteria:

✦ Month is January, or

✦ SalesRep is Brooks, or

✦ Amount is greater than 1000

The following array formula returns the correct count.

```
{=SUM(IF((Month="January")+(SalesRep="Brooks")+(Amount>1000),1)
)}
```

Combining AND and OR criteria

You can combine AND and OR criteria when counting. For example, perhaps you want to count sales that meet the following criteria:

✦ Month is January, and

✦ SalesRep is Brooks, or SalesRep is Cook

This array formula returns the number of sales that meet the criteria.

```
{=SUM((Month="January")*IF((SalesRep="Brooks")+(SalesRep="Cook"
),1))}
```

Counting the most frequently occurring entry

Excel's MODE function returns the most frequently occurring value in a range. Figure 11-4 shows a worksheet with values in range A1:D20 (named Data). The formula that follows returns 5 because that value appears most frequently in the Data range:

```
=MODE(Data)
```

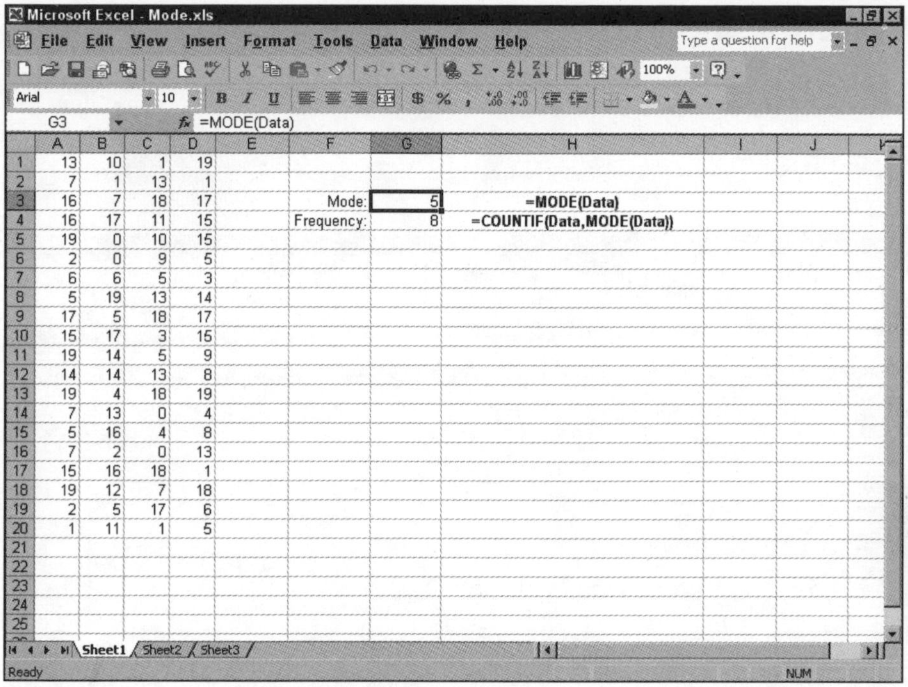

Figure 11-4: The MODE function returns the most frequently occurring value in a range.

To count the number of times the most frequently occurring value appears in the range (in other words, the frequency of the mode), use the following formula:

```
=COUNTIF(Data,MODE(Data))
```

This formula returns 8, because the modal value (5) appears eight times in the Data range.

The MODE function works only for numeric values. It simply ignores cells that contain text. To find the most frequently occurring text entry in a range, you to need to use an array formula such as the following:

```
{=INDEX(Data,MATCH(MAX(COUNTIF(Data,Data)),COUNTIF(Data,Data),0
))}
```

To count the number of times the most frequently occurring item (text or values) appears in a range named Data, use the following array formula:

```
{=MAX(COUNTIF(Data,Data))}
```

Counting the occurrences of specific text

The examples in this section demonstrate various ways to count the occurrences of a character or text string in a range of cells. Figure 11-5 shows a worksheet used for these examples. Various text appears in the range A1:A10 (named Data); cell B1 is named Text.

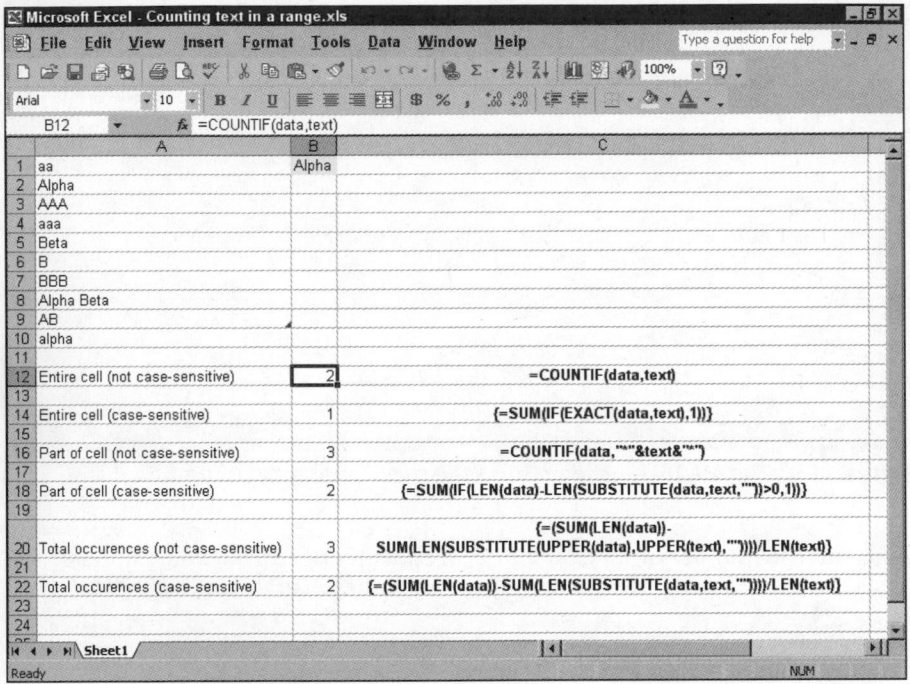

Figure 11-5: This worksheet demonstrates various ways to count text in a range.

Matching the entire cell contents

To count the number of cells containing the contents of the Text cell (and nothing else), you can use the COUNTIF function. The following formula demonstrates:

```
=COUNTIF(Data,Text)
```

For example, if the Text cell contains the string "Alpha," the formula returns 2 because two cells in the Data range contain this text. This formula is not case-sensitive, so it counts both "Alpha" (cell A2) and "alpha" (cell A10). Note, however, that it does not count the cell that contains "Alpha Beta" (cell A8).

The following array formula is similar to the preceding formula, but this one is case-sensitive:

```
{=SUM(IF(EXACT(Data,Text),1))}
```

Matching partial cell contents

To count the number of cells that contain a string that includes the contents of the Text cell, use this formula:

```
=COUNTIF(data,"*"&Text&"*")
```

For example, if the Text cell contains the text Alpha the formula returns 3, because three cells in the Data range contain the text alpha (cells A2, A8, and A10). Note that the comparison is not case-sensitive.

If you need a case-sensitive count, you can use the following array formula:

```
{=SUM(IF(LEN(Data)-LEN(SUBSTITUTE(Data,Text,""))>0,1))}
```

If the Text cells contain the text Alpha, the preceding formula returns 2 because the string appears in two cells (A2 and A8).

Counting all occurrences in a range

To count the total number of occurrences of a string within a range of cells, use the following array formula:

```
{=(SUM(LEN(Data))-
SUM(LEN(SUBSTITUTE(Data,Text,""))))/LEN(Text)}
```

If the Text cell contains the character "B," the formula returns 7 because the range contains seven instances of the string. This formula is case-sensitive.

The following formula is a modified version that is not case-sensitive.

```
=(SUM(LEN(Data))-
SUM(LEN(SUBSTITUTE(UPPER(Data),UPPER(Text),""))))/LEN(Text)
```

Counting the number of unique values

Another useful counting task is to determine the number of unique values in a range. The following array formula returns the number of unique values in a range named Data:

```
{=SUM(1/COUNTIF(Data,Data))}
```

To understand how this formula works, you need a basic understanding of array formulas. (See Chapter 16 for an introduction to this topic.) In Figure 11-6, range A1:A12 is named Data. Range C1:C12 contains the following array formula (entered into all 12 cells in the range):

```
{=COUNTIF(Data,Data)}
```

The array in range C1:C12 consists of the count of each value in Data. For example, the number 100 appears three times, so each array element that corresponds to a value of 100 in the Data range has a value of 3.

Range D1:D12 contains this array formula:

```
{=1/C1:C12}
```

This array consists of the inverse of each value in the array in range C1:C12. For example, each cell in the original Data range that contains a 200 has a value of 0.5 — $\frac{1}{200}$ — in the corresponding cell in D1:D12.

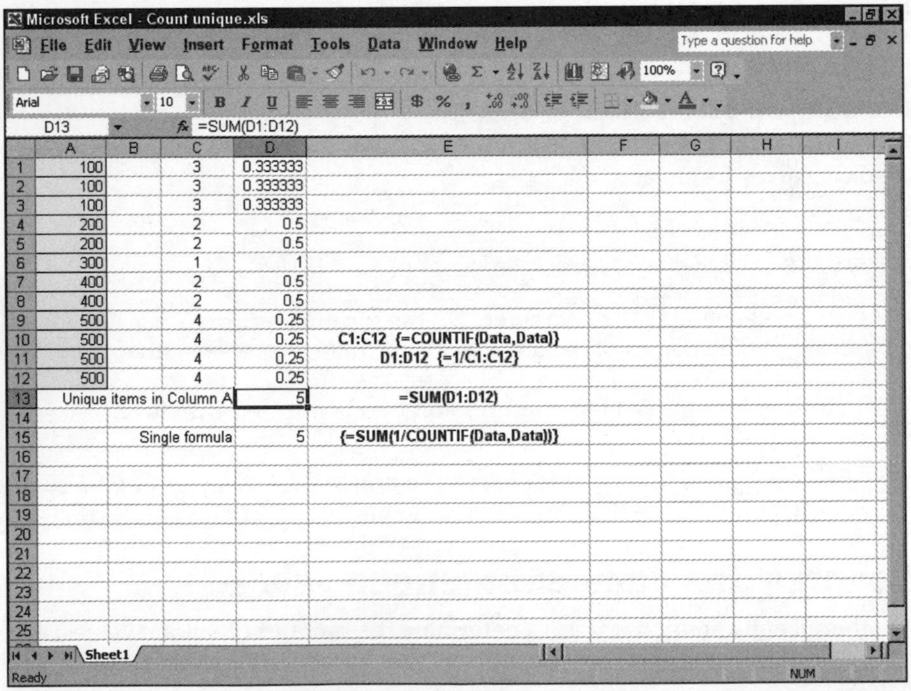

Figure 11-6: This worksheet uses an array formula to count the number of unique values in a range.

Summing the range D1:D12 gives the number of unique items in Data. The array formula presented at the beginning of this section essentially creates the array that occupies D1:D12, and sums the values.

This formula has a serious limitation: If the range contains any blank cells, it returns an error. The following array formula solves this problem:

```
{=SUM(IF(COUNTIF(Data,Data)=0,"",1/COUNTIF(Data,Data)))}
```

Cross-Reference

To create an array formula that returns a list of unique items in a range, refer to Chapter 17.

Creating a frequency distribution

A frequency distribution basically comprises a summary table that shows the frequency of each value in a range. For example, an instructor may create a frequency distribution of test scores. The table would show the count of As, Bs, Cs, and so on. Excel provides a number of ways to create frequency distributions. You can

✦ Use the FREQUENCY function

✦ Create your own formulas

✦ Use the Analysis ToolPak add-in

Cross-Reference

If your data is in the form of a database, you can also use a pivot table to create a frequency distribution. See Chapter 21 for more information.

Using the FREQUENCY function

Using Excel's FREQUENCY function presents the easiest way to create a frequency distribution. This function always returns an array, so you must use it in an array formula entered into a multicell range.

Figure 11-7 shows some data in range A1:E20 (named Data). These values range from 1 to 500. The range G2:G11 contains the bins used for the frequency distribution. Each cell in this bin range contains the upper limit for the bin. In this case, the bins consist of 1–50, 51–100, 101–150, and so on. See the sidebar "Creating Bins for a Frequency Distribution" to discover an easy way to create a bin range.

To create the frequency distribution, select a range of cells that correspond to the number of cells in the bin range (in this case, cells H2:H11). Then, enter the following array formula:

```
{=FREQUENCY(Data,G2:G11)}
```

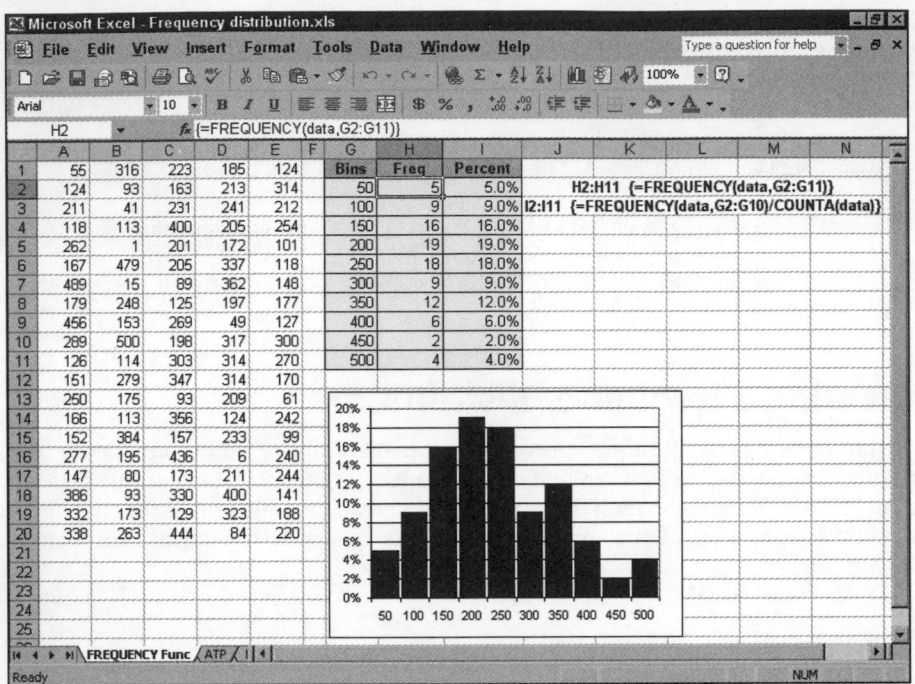

Figure 11-7: You can use a frequency distribution to determine how the values in a range are distributed.

The array formula enters the count of values in the Data range that fall into each bin. To create a frequency distribution that consists of percentages, use the following array formula (in cells I2:I11):

```
{=FREQUENCY(Data,G2:G10)/COUNTA(Data)}
```

Figure 11-7 shows two frequency distributions — one in terms of counts, and one in terms of percentages. The figure also shows a chart (histogram) created from the frequency distribution.

Using formulas to create a frequency distribution

Figure 11-8 shows a worksheet that contains test scores for 50 students in column B (the range is named Grades). Formulas in columns G and H calculate a frequency distribution for letter grades. The minimum and maximum values for each letter grade appear in columns D and E. For example, a test score between 80 and 89 (inclusive) qualifies for a B.

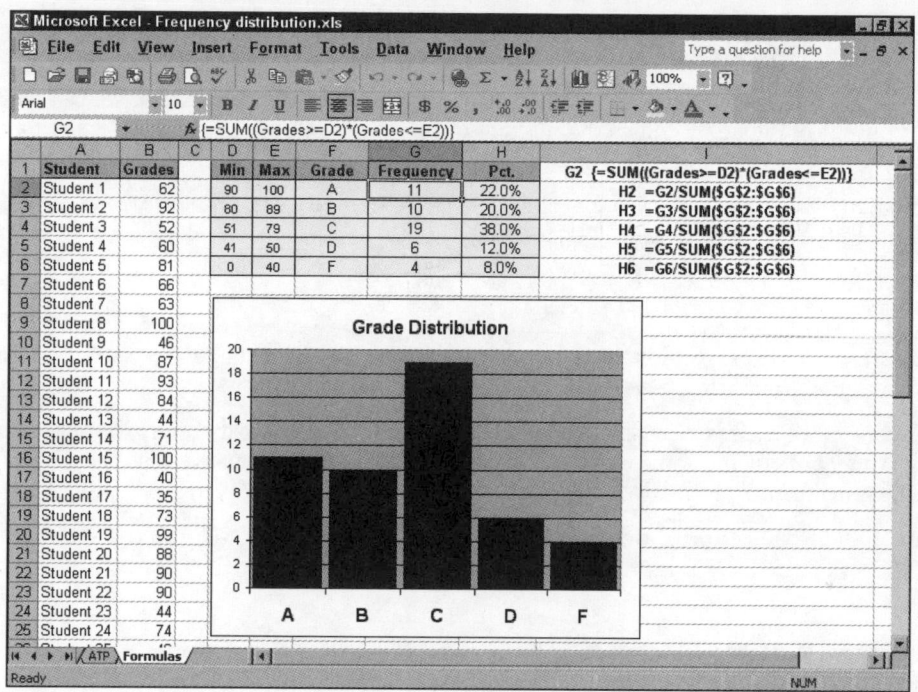

Figure 11-8: You can use formulas like this to create a frequency distribution.

The formula in cell G2 (shown here) is an array formula that counts the number of scores that qualify for an A:

```
{=SUM((Grades>=D2)*(Grades<=E2))}
```

This formula was copied to the four cells below G2.

Caution Make certain that you create the array formula in cell G2 and then copy it to cells G3:G6. If you attempt to create a single array formula in G2:G6, you will get incorrect results.

The formulas in column H calculate the percentage of scores for each letter grade. The formula in H2, which was copied to the four cells below H2, is

```
=G2/SUM($G$2:$G$6)
```

Using the Analysis ToolPak to create a frequency distribution

After you install the Analysis ToolPak add-in, you can use the Histogram option to create a frequency distribution. Start by entering your bin values in a range. Then, select Tools ➪ Data Analysis to display the Data Analysis dialog box. Next, select Histogram and click OK to display the Histogram dialog box shown in Figure 11-9.

Creating Bins for a Frequency Distribution

When creating a frequency distribution, you must first enter the values into the bin range. The number of bins determines the number of categories in the distribution. Usually, each bin represents an equal range of values.

To create 10 evenly spaced bins for values in a range named Data, enter the following array formula into a range of 10 cells:

```
{=MIN(Data)+(ROW(INDIRECT("1:10"))*
(MAX(Data)-MIN(Data)+1)/10)-1}
```

This formula creates 10 bins, based on the values in the Data range. The upper bin will always equal the maximum value in the range.

To create more or less bins, use a value other than 10 and enter the array formula into a range that contains the same number of cells. For example, to create five bins, enter the following array formula into a five-cell range:

```
{=MIN(Data)+(ROW(INDIRECT("1:5"))*(MAX(Data)-MIN(Data)+1)/5)-1}
```

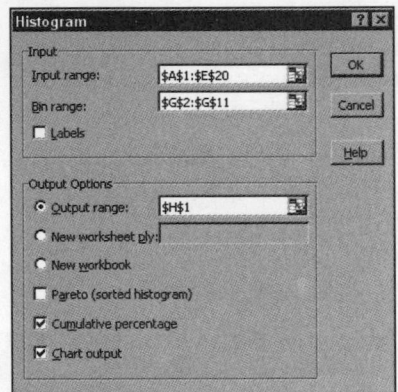

Figure 11-9: You can also use the Analysis ToolPak's Histogram dialog box to create a frequency distribution.

Specify the ranges for your data (Input Range), bins (Bin Range), and results (Output Range), and then select any options. Figure 11-10 shows a frequency distribution (and chart) created with the Histogram option.

Caution

Note that the frequency distribution consists of values, not formulas. Therefore, if you make any changes to your input data, you need to rerun the Histogram procedure to update the results.

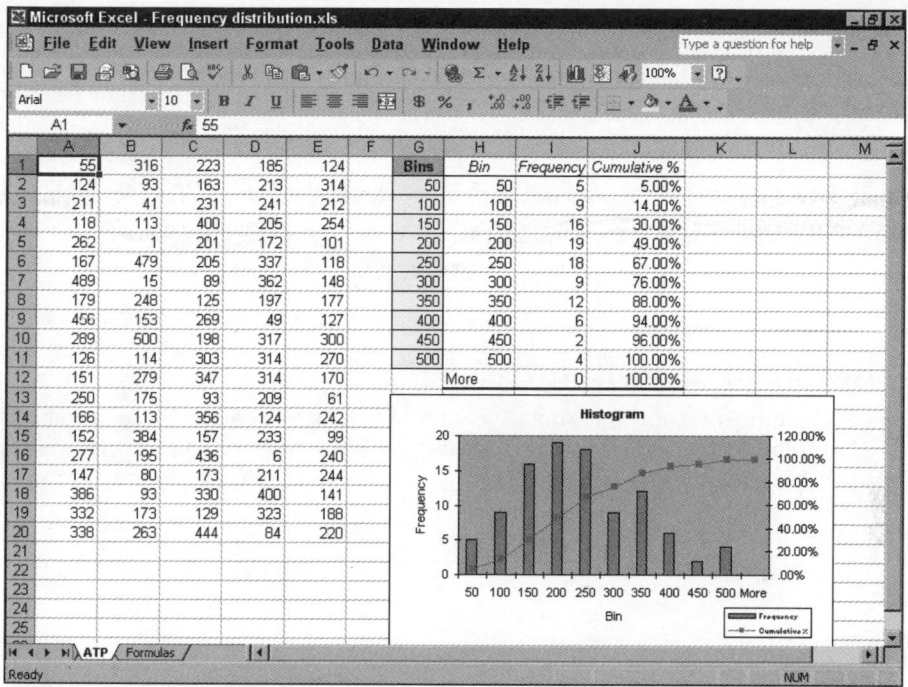

Figure 11-10: Here is a frequency distribution and chart generated by the Analysis ToolPak's Histogram option.

Understanding Basic Summing Techniques

The examples in this section demonstrate how to perform common summing tasks using formulas. The formulas range from very simple to relatively complex array formulas that compute sums using multiple criteria.

Summing all cells in a range

It doesn't get much simpler than this. The following formula returns the sum of all values in a range named Data:

```
=SUM(Data)
```

The SUM function can take up to 30 arguments — the largest number of arguments that any Excel function can accept. The following formula, for example, returns the sum of the values in five noncontiguous ranges:

```
=SUM(A1:A9,C1:C9,E1:E9,G1:G9,I1:I9)
```

You can use complete rows or columns as an argument for the SUM function. The formula that follows, for example, returns the sum of all values in column A. If this formula appears in a cell in column A, it generates a circular reference error.

```
=SUM(A:A)
```

The following formula returns the sum of all values on Sheet1. This formula must appear on a sheet other than Sheet1.

```
=SUM(Sheet1!1:65536)
```

Computing a cumulative sum

You may want to display a cumulative sum of values in a range—sometimes known as a "running total." Figure 11-11 illustrates a cumulative sum. Column B shows the monthly amounts, and column C displays the cumulative (year-to-date) totals.

The formula in cell C2 is

```
=SUM(B$2:B2)
```

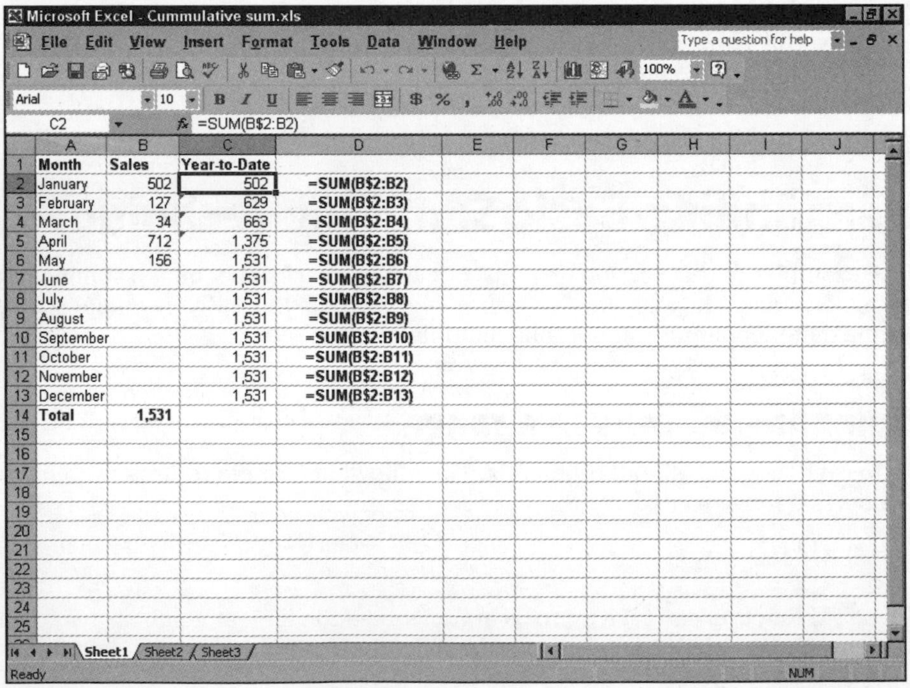

	A	B	C	D
1	Month	Sales	Year-to-Date	
2	January	502	502	=SUM(B$2:B2)
3	February	127	629	=SUM(B$2:B3)
4	March	34	663	=SUM(B$2:B4)
5	April	712	1,375	=SUM(B$2:B5)
6	May	156	1,531	=SUM(B$2:B6)
7	June		1,531	=SUM(B$2:B7)
8	July		1,531	=SUM(B$2:B8)
9	August		1,531	=SUM(B$2:B9)
10	September		1,531	=SUM(B$2:B10)
11	October		1,531	=SUM(B$2:B11)
12	November		1,531	=SUM(B$2:B12)
13	December		1,531	=SUM(B$2:B13)
14	Total	1,531		

Figure 11-11: Simple formulas in column C display a cumulative sum of the values in column B.

Notice that this formula uses a mixed reference. The first cell in the range reference always refers to row 2. When this formula is copied down the column, the range argument adjusts such that the sum always starts with row 2 and ends with the current row. For example, after copying this formula down column C, the formula in cell C8 is

```
=SUM(B$2:B8)
```

You can use an IF function to hide the cumulative sums for rows in which data hasn't been entered. The following modification to the formula would accomplish this:

```
=IF(B2<>"",SUM(B$2:B2),"")
```

Summing the "top n" values

In some situations, you may need to sum the *n* largest values in a range — for example, the top 10 values. One approach is to sort the range in descending order, and then to use the SUM function with an argument that consists of the first *n* values in the sorted range. An array formula such as this one accomplishes the task without sorting:

```
{=SUM(LARGE(Data,{1,2,3,4,5,6,7,8,9,10}))}
```

This formula sums the 10 largest values in a range named Data. To sum the 10 smallest values, use the SMALL function instead of the LARGE function:

```
{=SUM(SMALL(Data,{1,2,3,4,5,6,7,8,9,10}))}
```

These formulas use an array constant comprising the arguments for the LARGE or SMALL function. If the value of *n* for your top *n* calculation is large, you may prefer to use the following formula variation. This formula returns the sum of the top 30 values in the Data range. You can, of course, substitute a different value for 30.

```
{=SUM(LARGE(Data,ROW(INDIRECT("1:30"))))}
```

Using Advanced Conditional Summing

Sometimes the basic summing methods simply won't meet your needs. The following sections describe several advanced techniques that you can use when you need something a bit more powerful.

Finding conditional sums using a single criterion

Sometimes you need to calculate a conditional sum. With a conditional sum, values in a range that meet one or more conditions are included in the sum. This section presents examples of conditional summing using a single criterion.

The SUMIF function is very useful for single-criterion sum formulas. The SUMIF function takes three arguments:

✦ **Range:** The range containing the values that determine whether to include a particular cell in the sum.

✦ **Criteria:** An expression that determines whether to include a particular cell in the sum.

✦ **sum_range:** Optional. The range that contains the cells you want to sum. If you omit this argument, the function uses the range specified in the first argument.

The examples that follow demonstrate the use of the SUMIF function. These formulas are based on the worksheet shown in Figure 11-12. Column F contains a formula that subtracts the date in column E from the date in column D. A negative number in column F indicates payment. The worksheet uses named ranges that correspond to the labels in row 1.

Tip   You can also use the Conditional Sum Wizard to automatically create conditional sums. Use the Tools ⇨ Wizard ⇨ Conditional Sum command to start the wizard.

	A	B	C	D	E	F
						A14 =SUMIF(Difference,"<0")
1	InvoiceNum	Office	Amount	DateDue	Today	Difference
2	AG-0145	Oregon	$5,000.00	3-Apr	6-May	-33
3	AG-0189	California	$450.00	21-Apr	6-May	-15
4	AG-0220	Washington	$3,211.56	30-Apr	6-May	-6
5	AG-0310	Oregon	$250.00	2-May	6-May	-4
6	AG-0355	Washington	$125.50	6-May	6-May	0
7	AG-0409	Washington	$3,000.00	12-May	6-May	6
8	AG-0581	Oregon	$2,100.00	25-May	6-May	19
9	AG-0600	Oregon	$335.39	25-May	6-May	19
10	AG-0602	Washington	$65.00	30-May	6-May	24
11	AG-0633	California	$250.00	1-Jun	6-May	26
12	TOTAL		$14,787.45			36
13						
14	-58	Total past due days				=SUMIF(Difference,"<0")
15	-58	Total past due days (array formula)				{=SUM(IF(Difference<0,Difference))}
16	$8,911.56	Total amount past due				=SUMIF(Difference,"<0",Amount)
17	$8,911.56	Total amount past due (array formula)				{=SUM(IF(Difference<0,Amount))}
18	$7,685.39	Total for Oregon only				=SUMIF(Office,"Oregon",Amount)
19	$7,102.06	Total for all except Oregon				=SUMIF(Office,"<>Oregon",Amount)
20	$250.00	Total amount with due date beyond June 1				=SUMIF(DateDue,">=6/1/2002",Amount)
21	$5,250.00	Total past due amount for Oregon (array formula)				{=SUM((Difference<0)*(Office="Oregon")*Amount)}
22	$5,000.00	Total past due amounts OR amounts for Oregon (array formula)				{=IF((Office="Oregon")+(Difference<0),1,0)*Amount}
23	$5,700.00	Total past due amounts for Oregon and California (array formula)				{=SUM((Difference<0)*IF((Office="Oregon")+(Office="California"),1)*Amount)}
24						
25						

Figure 11-12: This worksheet demonstrates several conditional-summing techniques.

Summing only negative values

The first example demonstrates how to state criteria based on a specified value.

The following formula returns the sum of the negative values in column F. In other words, it returns the total number of past-due days for all invoices. For this worksheet, the formula returns –58.

```
=SUMIF(Difference,"<0")
```

Because you omit the third argument, the second argument ("<0") applies to the values in the Difference range.

> **Note** You can also use the following array formula to sum the negative values in the Difference range:
>
> ```
> {=SUM(IF(Difference<0,Difference))}
> ```

You do not need to hard-code the arguments for the SUMIF function into your formula. For example, you can create a formula such as the following, which gets the criteria argument from the contents of cell G2.

```
=SUMIF(Difference,G2)
```

This formula returns a new result if you change the criteria in cell G2.

Summing values based on a different range

Next is an example in which you use the values in one range to determine which values to include from a second range.

The following formula returns the sum of the past-due invoice amounts (in column C):

```
=SUMIF(Difference,"<0",Amount)
```

This formula uses the values in the Difference range to determine if the corresponding values in the Amount range contribute to the sum.

> **Note** You can also use the following array formula to return the sum of the values in the Amount range, when the corresponding value in the Difference range is negative.
>
> ```
> {=SUM(IF(Difference<0,Amount))}
> ```

Summing values based on a text comparison

You can also use text values as the criteria as shown in this example.

The following formula returns the total invoice amounts for the Oregon office:

```
=SUMIF(Office,"Oregon",Amount)
```

To sum the invoice amounts for all offices except Oregon, use this formula:

```
=SUMIF(Office,"<>Oregon",Amount)
```

Summing values based on a date comparison

Finally, this example shows how to use dates as the selection criteria.

The following formula returns the total invoice amounts that have a due date beyond June 1, 2002.

```
=SUMIF(DateDue,">=6/1/2002",Amount)
```

The formula that follows returns the total invoice amounts that have a future due date (including today).

```
=SUMIF(DateDue,">="&TODAY(),Amount)
```

Notice that the second argument for the SUMIF function is an expression. The expression uses the TODAY function, which returns the current date. Also, the comparison operator, enclosed in quotes, is concatenated (using the & operator) with the result of the TODAY function.

Finding conditional sums using multiple criteria

The examples in the preceding section all used a single comparison criterion. The examples in this section involve summing cells based on multiple criteria. Because the SUMIF function does not work with multiple criteria, you need to resort to using an array formula. Figure 11-12 also shows the examples for the following sections.

Summing values using AND criteria

Suppose you want to get a sum of the invoice amounts that are past due and that are associated with the Oregon office. In other words, the value in the Amount range will be summed only if both of the following criteria are met:

✦ The corresponding value in the Difference range is negative.

✦ The corresponding text in the Office range is "Oregon."

The following array formula does the job:

```
{=SUM((Difference<0)*(Office="Oregon")*Amount)}
```

This formula creates two new arrays (in memory):

✦ A Boolean array @md an array of true or false values @md that consists of TRUE if the corresponding Difference value is less than zero; otherwise, it consists of FALSE

✦ A Boolean array that consists of TRUE if the corresponding Office value equals "Oregon"; otherwise, it consists of FALSE

Multiplying Boolean values results in the following:

```
TRUE * TRUE = 1
TRUE * FALSE = 0
FALSE * FALSE = 0
```

Therefore, the corresponding Amount value returns nonzero only if the corresponding values in the memory arrays are both TRUE. The result produces a sum of the Amount values that meet the specified criteria.

Summing values using OR criteria

Suppose you want to get a sum of past-due invoice amounts or of invoices associated with the Oregon office. In other words, the value in the Amount range will be summed if either of the following criteria is met:

✦ The corresponding value in the Difference range is negative.

✦ The corresponding text in the Office range is "Oregon."

The following array formula does the job:

```
{=IF((Office="Oregon")+(Difference<0),1,0)*Amount}
```

A plus sign (+) joins the conditions; you can include more than two conditions.

Summing values using AND and OR criteria

As you might expect, things get a bit tricky when your criteria consists of both AND and OR operations. For example, you might want to sum the values in the Amount range when the following conditions are met:

✦ The corresponding value in the Difference range is negative.

✦ The corresponding text in the Office range is "Oregon" or "California."

Notice that the second condition actually consists of two conditions joined with OR. The following array formula does the trick:

```
{=SUM((Difference<0)*IF((Office="Oregon")+(Office="California")
,1)*Amount)}
```

✦   ✦   ✦

Creating Formulas That Look Up Values

It's often important for your Excel worksheets to pick the correct values from a table. Excel has several functions that are designed for this purpose, and they are discussed in this chapter. But this chapter also goes much further to show you a number of alternative lookup techniques for those situations in which the standard methods aren't what you need.

Understanding Lookup Formulas

A lookup formula returns a value from a table by looking up another value. A common telephone directory provides a good analogy. If you want to find a person's telephone number, you first locate the name (you "look it up"), and then retrieve the corresponding number.

Figure 12-1 shows a simple worksheet that uses several lookup formulas. This worksheet contains a table of employee data (named EmpData), beginning in row 9. When you enter a name into cell C2, lookup formulas in D2:G2 retrieve the matching information from the table. The following lookup formulas use the VLOOKUP function:

```
D2 =VLOOKUP(C2,EmpData,2,FALSE)
E2 =VLOOKUP(C2,EmpData,3,FALSE)
F2 =VLOOKUP(C2,EmpData,4,FALSE)
G2 =VLOOKUP(C2,EmpData,5,FALSE)
```

Microsoft Excel - Lookup1.xls

File Edit View Insert Format Tools Data Window Help

D2 = =VLOOKUP(C2,EmpData,2,FALSE)

	A	B	C	D	E	F	G	H	I	J	K
1			Last	First	Dept	Ext	Hired				
2			Hustvedt	Morris	Marketing	1320	6/28/1995				
3											
4			D2:	=VLOOKUP(C2,EmpData,2,FALSE)							
5			E2:	=VLOOKUP(C2,EmpData,3,FALSE)							
6			F2:	=VLOOKUP(C2,EmpData,4,FALSE)							
7			G2:	=VLOOKUP(C2,EmpData,5,FALSE)							
8											
9			Last	First	Dept	Ext	Hired				
10			Allen	Bob	Sales	1220	6/26/1994				
11			Alston	Gordon	Operations	1230	10/23/1998				
12			Anderson	Delores	Marketing	1240	4/17/1997				
13			Anton	Dawn	Administration	1250	10/3/1996				
14			Aubol	Wayne	Marketing	1260	11/7/1994				
15			Barich	Tom	Administration	1270	4/15/1999				
16			Boessmann	Alan	Sales	1280	11/20/1998				
17			Drews	Dave	Operations	1290	12/25/1998				
18			Gaudette	Mike	Marketing	1300	9/19/1997				
19			Hollingsworth	Dan	Administration	1310	7/16/1999				
20			Hustvedt	Morris	Marketing	1320	6/28/1995				
21			Immers	Bill	Administration	1330	7/25/1995				
22			Johnson	Paul	Sales	1340	8/28/1995				
23			Jones	Bob	Operations	1350	2/4/1999				
24			Katai	Walt	Marketing	1360	6/30/1994				
25			McKinnies	Charlie	Administration	1370	11/28/1995				

Sheet1 Sheet2 Sheet3

Ready   NUM

Figure 12-1: You can use lookup formulas like those in row 2 to look up the information for the employee name in cell C2.

This particular example uses four formulas to return information from the EmpData range. In many cases, you'll only want a single value from the table, so you use only one formula.

 **Tip**   Remember to name the ranges before you create the lookup formulas. By pre-naming the ranges, Excel will use absolute references for the ranges, making it easier for you to copy the formula.

Creating Basic Lookup Formulas

You can use Excel's basic lookup functions to search a column or row for a lookup value to return another value as a result. Table 12-1 lists and describes these functions.

Table 12-1
Functions Used in Lookup Formulas

Function	Description
CHOOSE	Returns a specific value from a list of values (up to 29) supplied as arguments.
HLOOKUP	Performs a horizontal lookup. Searches for a value in the top row of a table and returns a value in the same column from a row you specify in the table.
INDEX	Returns a value (or the reference to a value) from within a table or range.
LOOKUP	Returns a value either from a one-row or one-column range.
MATCH	Returns the relative position of an item in a range that matches a specified value.
OFFSET	Returns a reference to a range that is a specified number of rows and columns from a cell or range of cells.
VLOOKUP	Performs a vertical lookup. Searches for a value in the first column of a table and returns a value in the same row from a column you specify in the table.

Looking up a value in a column using VLOOKUP

The VLOOKUP function looks up the value in the first column of the lookup table and returns the corresponding value in a specified column of the matching row. The values in the lookup table are arranged vertically. The syntax for the VLOOKUP function is

```
VLOOKUP(lookup_value,table_array,col_index_num,range_lookup)
```

The VLOOKUP function's arguments are

✦ **lookup_value:** The value to be looked up in the first column of the lookup table.

✦ **table_array:** The range that contains the lookup table.

✦ **col_index_num:** The column number within the table from which the matching value is returned.

✦ **range_lookup:** Optional. If TRUE or omitted, an approximate match is returned (if an exact match is not found, the next largest value that is less than lookup_value is returned). If FALSE, VLOOKUP will search for an exact match. If VLOOKUP cannot find an exact match, the function returns #N/A.

Note If the range_lookup argument is TRUE or omitted, the first column of the lookup table must be in ascending order. If lookup_value is smaller than the smallest value in the first column of table_array, VLOOKUP returns #N/A. If the range_lookup argument is FALSE, the first column of the lookup table need not be in ascending order. If an exact match is not found, the function returns #N/A.

The classic example of a lookup formula involves an income tax rate schedule (see Figure 12-2). The tax rate schedule shows the income tax rates for various income levels.

In this example the formula in cell B3 returns the tax rate

```
=VLOOKUP(B2,D2:F7,3)
```

The lookup table resides in a range that consists of three columns (D2:F7). Because the last argument for the VLOOKUP function is 3, the formula returns the corresponding value in the third column of the lookup table.

Note Although the figure shows values in column E, the VLOOKUP formula uses only the values in the first column of the lookup table range when determining which row to use in selecting the return value.

Figure 12-2: You can use VLOOKUP to look up a tax rate.

Note that an exact match is not required. If an exact match is not found in the first column of the lookup table, the VLOOKUP function uses the next largest value that is less than the lookup value. In other words, the function uses the row in which the value you want to look up is greater than or equal to the row value, but less than the value in the next row.

Looking up a value in a row using HLOOKUP

The HLOOKUP function works just like the VLOOKUP function, except that the lookup table is arranged horizontally instead of vertically. The HLOOKUP function looks up the value in the first row of the lookup table and returns the corresponding value in a specified table row of the matching column.

The syntax for the HLOOKUP function is

```
HLOOKUP(lookup_value,table_array,col_index_num,range_lookup)
```

The HLOOKUP function's arguments are

✦ **lookup_value:** The value to be looked up in the first row of the lookup table.

✦ **table_array:** The range that contains the lookup table.

✦ **row_index_num:** The row number within the table from which the matching value is returned.

✦ **range_lookup:** Optional. If TRUE or omitted, an approximate match is returned. If FALSE, HLOOKUP will search for an exact match and returns #N/A if an exact match cannot be found.

Tip

Remember that VLOOKUP searches vertically down a column for a matching value and HLOOKUP searches horizontally across a row for the matching value.

Looking up a value in a row or column using LOOKUP

The LOOKUP function is similar to both VLOOKUP and HLOOKUP, but uses slightly different syntax to specify the function arguments. LOOKUP searches a single-column or single-row table. The syntax for the LOOKUP function is

```
VLOOKUP(lookup_value,lookup_range,result_range)
```

The LOOKUP function's arguments are

✦ **lookup_value:** The value to be looked up in the lookup_range

✦ **lookup_range:** A single-column or single-row range that contains the values to be looked up

✦ **result_range:** The single-column or single-row range that contains the values to be returned

Note Values in the lookup_range must be in ascending order. If lookup_value is smaller than the smallest value in lookup_range, LOOKUP returns #N/A.

Caution LOOKUP always performs an approximate match rather than an exact one. This is the equivalent of omitting the optional range_lookup argument for the VLOOKUP or HLOOKUP functions.

Figure 12-3 shows the tax table again. This time, the formula in cell B3 uses the LOOKUP function to return the corresponding tax rate. The formula in B3 is

```
=LOOKUP(B2,D2:D7,F2:F7)
```

Caution If the lookup values are not arranged in ascending order, the LOOKUP function may return an incorrect value.

Combining MATCH and INDEX for wildcard lookups

The MATCH and INDEX functions are often used together to perform lookups. In many cases, it's advantageous to use MATCH and INDEX together rather than the LOOKUP, HLOOKUP, or VLOOKUP functions because the MATCH function supports wildcard characters for approximate matches. The MATCH function returns the relative position of a cell in a range that matches a specified value. The INDEX function returns a cell value from a range using row and column offsets.

The syntax for MATCH is

```
MATCH(lookup_value,lookup_array,match_type)
```

The MATCH function's arguments are

- ✦ **lookup_value:** The value you want to match in lookup_array, which can include wildcard characters * and ?
- ✦ **lookup_array:** The range being searched
- ✦ **match_type:** An integer (–1, 0, or 1) that specifies how the match is determined

Note If match_type is 1, MATCH finds the largest value less than or equal to lookup_value (lookup_array must be in ascending order). If match_type is 0, MATCH finds the first value exactly equal to lookup_value. If match_type is –1, MATCH finds the smallest value greater than or equal to lookup_value (lookup_array must be in descending order). If you omit match_type, it is assumed to be 1.

Tip When you are specifying the lookup_value for the MATCH function, you can use wildcards. An asterisk (*) matches any characters, and a question mark (?) matches any single character.

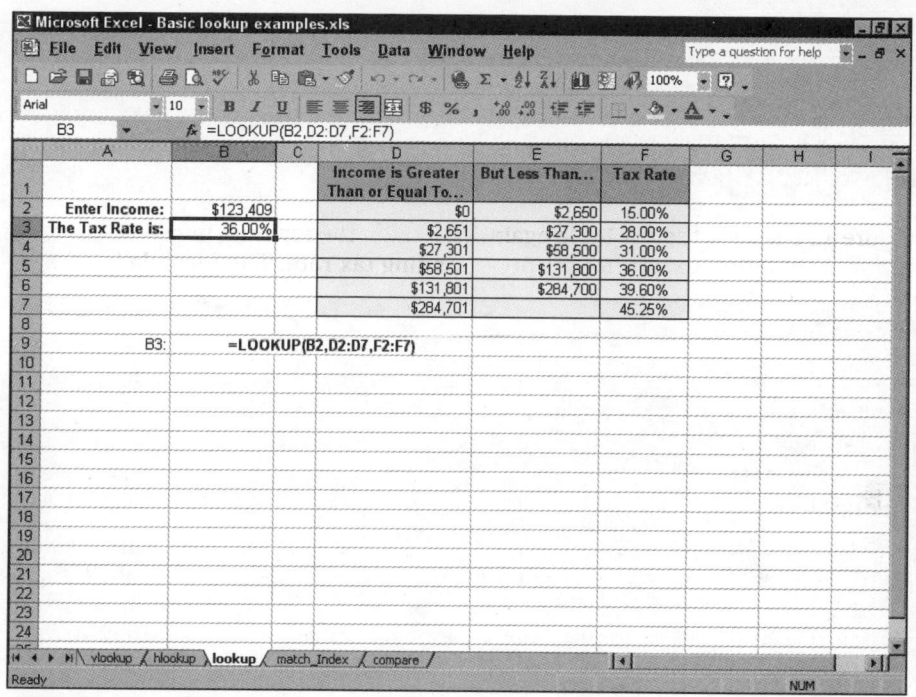

Figure 12-3: You can also use LOOKUP to look up values, but you must specify a range for the third argument.

The syntax for the INDEX function is

```
INDEX(array,row_num,column_num)
```

The INDEX function's arguments are

✦ **array:** A range

✦ **row_num:** A row number within array

✦ **col_num:** A column number within array

Tip   If array contains only one row or column, the corresponding row_num or column_num argument is optional.

Figure 12-4 shows a worksheet that uses INDEX and MATCH to look up values. When you enter a date in cell B1, the following formula (in cell B2) searches the dates in column D and returns the corresponding amount from column F. The formula in B2 is

```
=INDEX(F2:F21,MATCH(B1,D2:D21,0))
```

When a Blank Is Not a Zero

Excel's lookup functions treat empty cells as zeros. If you need to distinguish zeros from blank cells, you must modify the lookup formula by adding an IF function to check whether the length of the returned value is 0. When the looked up value is blank, the length of the value is 0. In all other cases, the length of the returned value is nonzero.

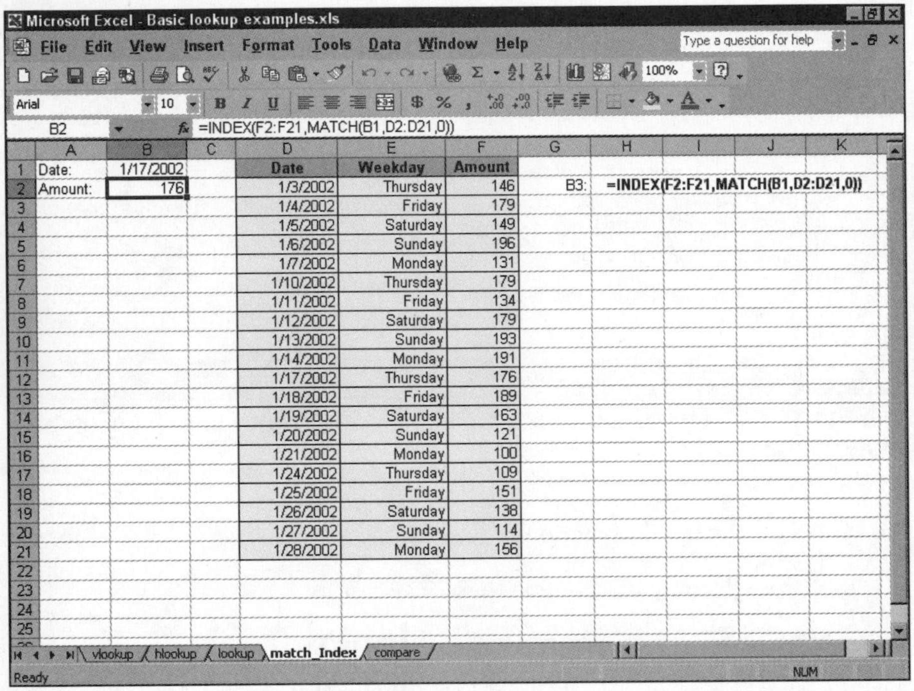

Figure 12-4: You can combine the INDEX and MATCH functions to perform a lookup.

To understand how this works, start with the MATCH function. This function searches the range D2:D21 for the date in cell B1. It returns the relative row number in which the date is found. This value is then used as the second argument for the INDEX function. The result is the corresponding value in F2:F21.

Creating Specialized Lookup Formulas

You can use some additional types of lookup formulas to perform more specialized lookups. For instance, you can look up an exact value, search in another column besides the first in a lookup table, perform a case-sensitive lookup, return a value from among multiple lookup tables, and perform other specialized and complex lookups. The following sections demonstrate ways to adapt Excel's lookup functions to perform these types of lookups.

Looking up an exact value

In some cases, you may want to ensure that an exact match exists between the value to be looked up and the values in the lookup table. VLOOKUP and HLOOKUP don't necessarily require an exact match.

Tip   To look up an exact value only, use the VLOOKUP (or HLOOKUP) function with the optional fourth argument set to FALSE.

When the last argument for the VLOOKUP (or HLOOKUP) function is FALSE, the function returns a value only if an exact match is found. If the value is not found, the formula returns #N/A.

Tip   If the last argument for VLOOKUP is FALSE, the values need not be in ascending order.

If you prefer to see something other than #N/A when the lookup value is not found, you can use an IF function to test for the #N/A result (using the ISNA function) and substitute a different string.

Performing a case-sensitive lookup

Excel's lookup functions (LOOKUP, VLOOKUP, and HLOOKUP) are not case-sensitive. For example, if you write a lookup formula to look up the text budget, the formula considers any of the following a match: BUDGET, Budget, or BuDgEt.

Figure 12-5 shows a simple example. Range B6:B11 is named Range1, and range C6:C11 is named Range2. The word to be looked up appears in cell B1 (named Value).

The array formula that follows is in cell B2. This formula does a case-sensitive lookup in Range1 and returns the corresponding value in Range2.

```
{=INDEX(Range2,MATCH(TRUE,EXACT(value,range1),0))}
```

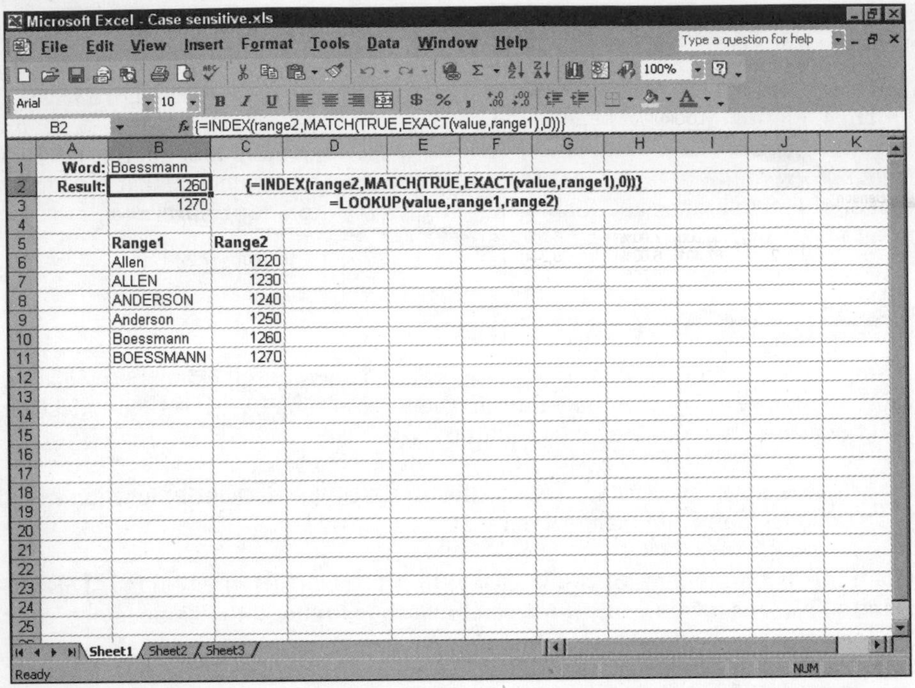

Figure 12-5: You can use an array formula to perform a case-sensitive lookup.

The formula looks up the word Boessmann and returns 1260. The following standard LOOKUP formula returns 1270.

```
=LOOKUP(Value,range1,range2)
```

Choosing among multiple lookup tables

You can, of course, have any number of lookup tables in a worksheet. In some cases, your formula may need to decide which lookup table to use. Figure 12-6 illustrates using multiple lookup tables.

This workbook calculates sales commission and contains two lookup tables: G3:H9 (named Table1) and J3:K8 (named Table2). The commission rate for a particular sales representative depends on two factors: the sales rep's years of service (column B) and the amount sold (column C). Column D contains formulas that look up the commission rate from the appropriate table. For example, the formula in cell D2 is

```
=VLOOKUP(C2,IF(B2<3,Table1,Table2),2)
```

The second argument for the VLOOKUP function consists of an IF formula that uses the value in column B to determine which lookup table to use.

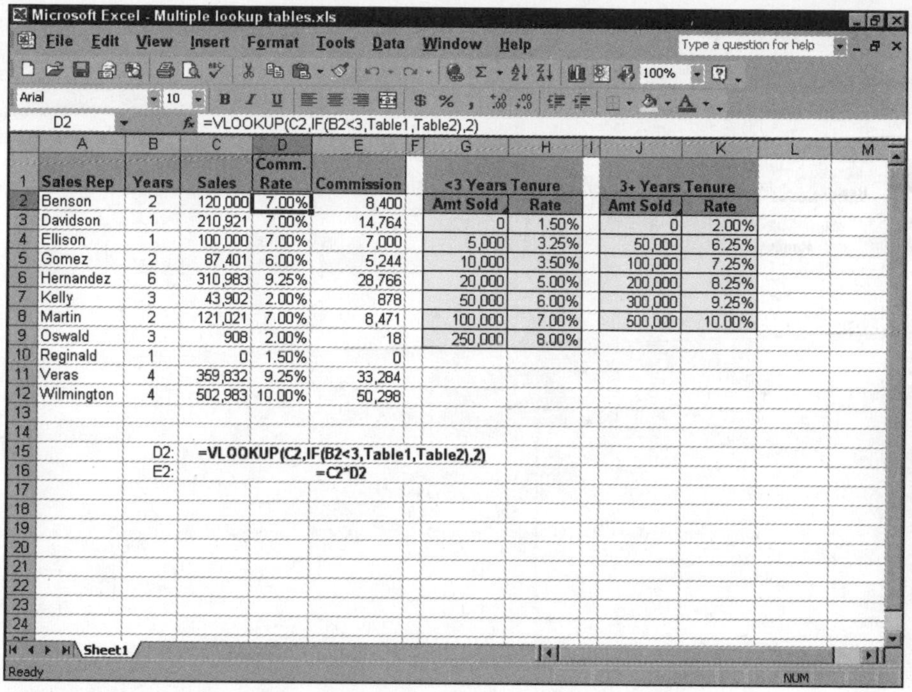

Figure 12-6: You can use multiple lookup tables when necessary.

The formula in column E simply multiplies the sales amount in column C by the commission rate in column D. The formula in cell E2, for example, is

```
=C2*D2
```

Performing a two-way lookup

Sometimes you may need to look up values based on two lookup criteria. For example, you may want to determine sales of a specific product for a particular month. Figure 12-7 shows a worksheet with a table that displays product sales by month. The user enters a month in cell B1 and a product name in cell B2.

To simplify things, the worksheet uses the following named ranges:

Name	Refers To
Month	B1
Product	B2
Table	D1:H14
MonthList	D1:D14
ProductList	D1:H1

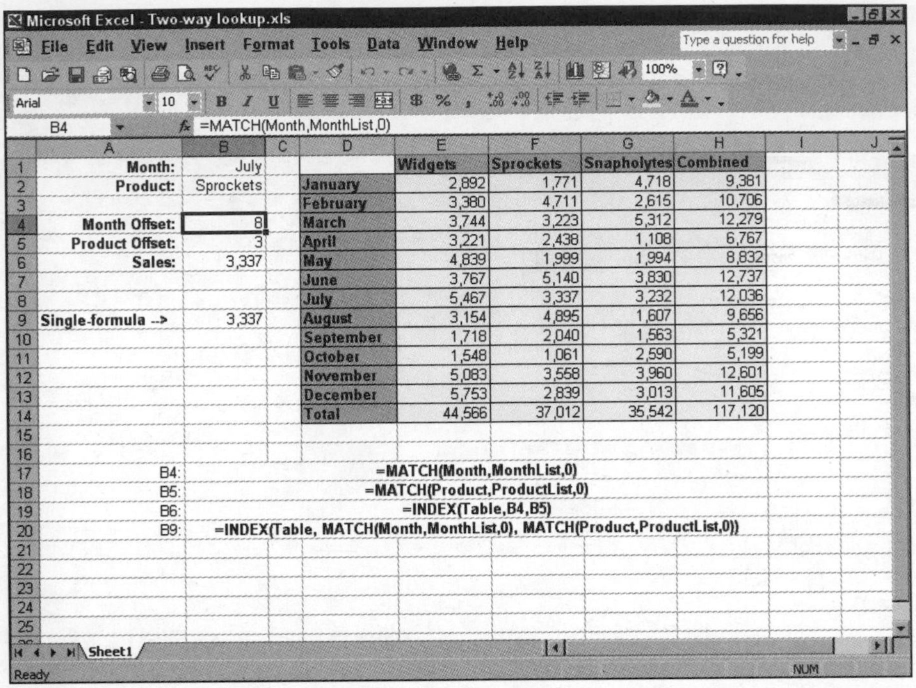

Figure 12-7: You can use the MATCH and INDEX functions to perform a two-way lookup.

The following formula (in cell B4) uses the MATCH function to return the position of the Month within the MonthList range. For example, if the month is January, the formula returns 2 because January is the second item in the MonthList range (the first item is a blank cell, D1).

```
=MATCH(Month,MonthList,0)
```

The formula in cell B5 works similarly, but uses the ProductList range.

```
=MATCH(Product,ProductList,0)
```

The final formula, in cell B6, returns the corresponding sales amount. It uses the INDEX function with the results from cells B4 and B5.

```
=INDEX(Table,B4,B5)
```

You can, of course, combine these formulas into a single formula as shown here:

```
=INDEX(Table,MATCH(Month,MonthList,0),MATCH(Product,ProductList
,0))
```

You can also use the Lookup Wizard add-in to create this type of formula (see Figure 12-8). To open the Lookup Wizard, select Tools ➪ Wizard ➪ Lookup (if the Lookup Wizard is not a menu option, use Tools ➪ Add-Ins to install it).

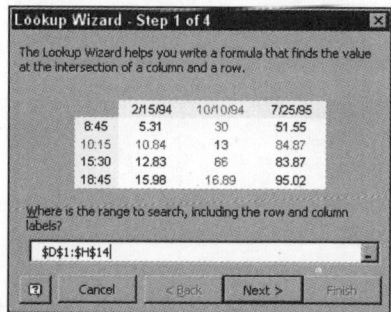

Figure 12-8: The Lookup Wizard can automatically create two-way lookup formulas for you.

Tip

Another way to accomplish a two-way lookup is to provide a name for each row and column of the table. A quick way to do this is to select the table and use Insert ➪ Name ➪ Create. After creating the names, you can use a simple formula, such as = Sprockets July. This formula, which uses the range intersection operator (a space), returns July sales for Sprockets.

Cross-Reference

You may also want to use a Pivot Table to analyze the data. See Chapter 21 for more information.

Performing a two-column lookup

Some situations may require a lookup based on the values in two columns. For example, you might want to locate a phone number based on first and last names, but your table is laid out with separate columns for the first and last name — and you have more than one person with the last name in your list.

Figure 12-9 shows an example using automobile makes and models, and a corresponding code for each. The worksheet uses named ranges, as shown here:

F2:F12	Czode
B1	Make
B2	Model
D2:D12	Range1
E2:E12	Range2

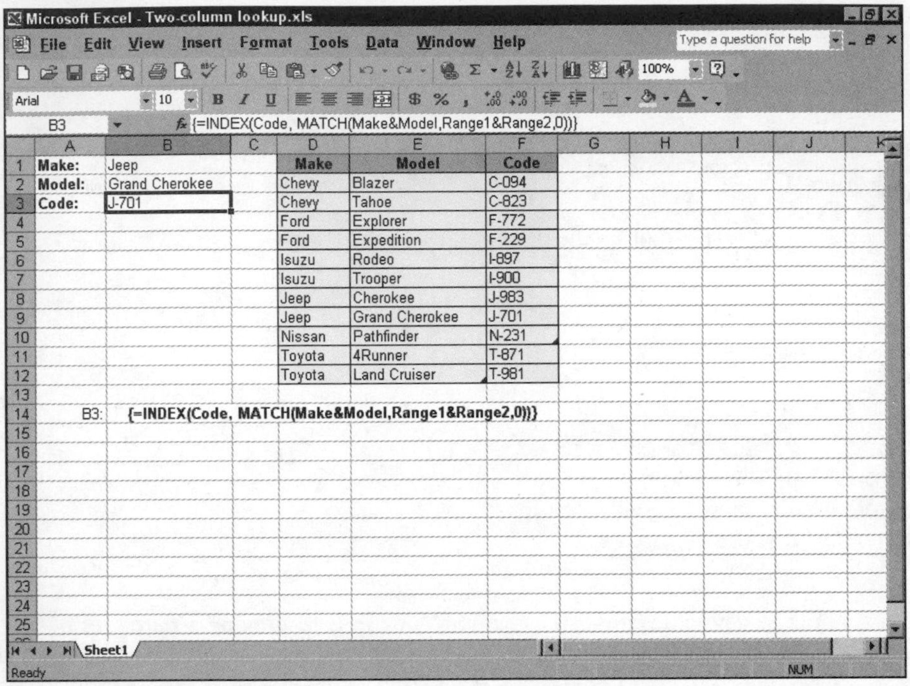

Make:	Jeep		Make	Model	Code
Model:	Grand Cherokee		Chevy	Blazer	C-094
Code:	J-701		Chevy	Tahoe	C-823
			Ford	Explorer	F-772
			Ford	Expedition	F-229
			Isuzu	Rodeo	I-897
			Isuzu	Trooper	I-900
			Jeep	Cherokee	J-983
			Jeep	Grand Cherokee	J-701
			Nissan	Pathfinder	N-231
			Toyota	4Runner	T-871
			Toyota	Land Cruiser	T-981

B3: {=INDEX(Code, MATCH(Make&Model,Range1&Range2,0))}

Figure 12-9: This workbook performs a lookup using information in two columns D and E).

The following array formula displays the corresponding code for an automobile make and model.

```
{=INDEX(Code,MATCH(Make&Model,Range1&Range2,0))}
```

This formula works by concatenating the contents of Make and Model, and then searching for this text in an array consisting of the concatenated corresponding text in Range1 and Range2.

Cross-Reference

To learn more about array formulas, see Chapters 16 and 17.

Determining the address of a value within a range

Most of the time, you want your lookup formula to return a value. You may, however, need to determine the cell address of a particular value within a range. For example, Figure 12-10 shows a worksheet with a range of numbers that occupy a single column (named Data). Cell B1, which contains the value to look up, is named Target.

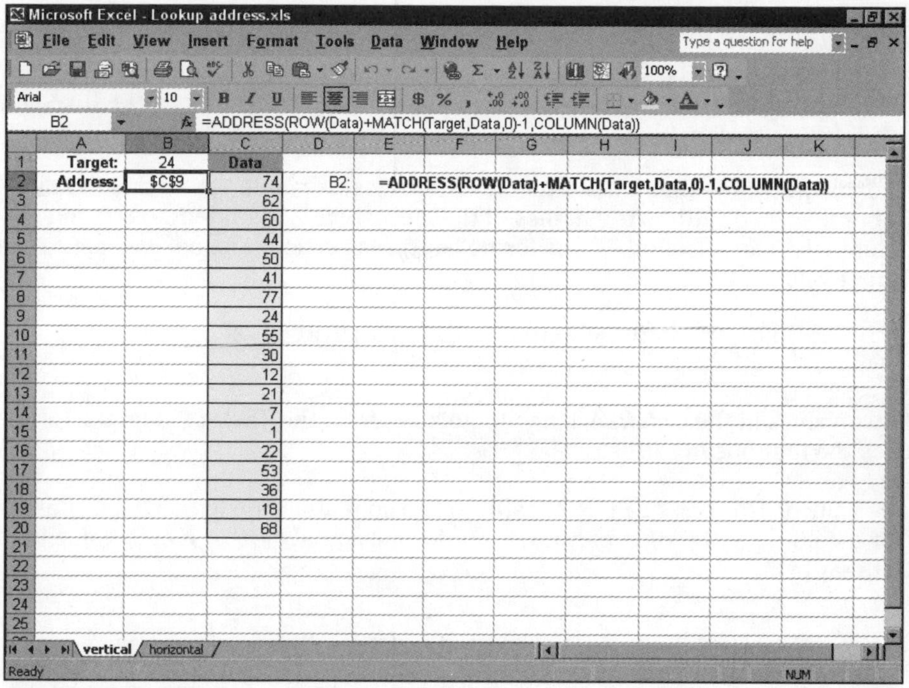

Figure 12-10: You can also determine the cell address of a specific value in a range using lookup techniques.

The formula in cell B2, which follows, returns the address of the cell in the Data range that contains the Target value.

```
=ADDRESS(ROW(Data)+MATCH(Target,Data,0)-1,COLUMN(Data))
```

If the Data range occupies a single row, use this formula to return the address of the Target value:

```
=ADDRESS(ROW(Data),COLUMN(Data)+MATCH(Target,Data,0)-1)
```

If the Data range contains more than one instance of the Target value, the address of the first occurrence is returned. If the Target value is not found in the Data range, the formula returns #N/A.

Looking up a value using the closest match

Sometimes you may need to look up a value based on the closest match. Although VLOOKUP and HLOOKUP can find an approximate match, both will return the value that corresponds to the next largest value that is less than the lookup value. In other words, they'll round up but not down.

Figure 12-11 shows a worksheet that applies a lookup technique that finds the closest match—either higher or lower than the target value. In this worksheet, range B2:B20 is named Data. Cell E2, named Target, contains a value to search for in the Data range. Cell E3, named ColOffset, contains a value that represents the column offset from the Data range.

The array formula that follows identifies the closest match to the target value in the Data range, and returns the names of the corresponding student in column A—the column with an offset of –1. The formula returns Leslie—the one closest to the Target value of 8,025.

```
{=INDIRECT(ADDRESS(ROW(Data)+MATCH(MIN(ABS(Target-Data)),
ABS(Target-Data),0)-1,COLUMN(Data)+ColOffset))}
```

If two values in the Data range are equidistant from the Target value, the formula uses the first one in the list.

The value in ColOffset can be negative (for a column to the left of Data), positive (for a column to the right of Data), or 0 (for the actual closest match value in the Data range).

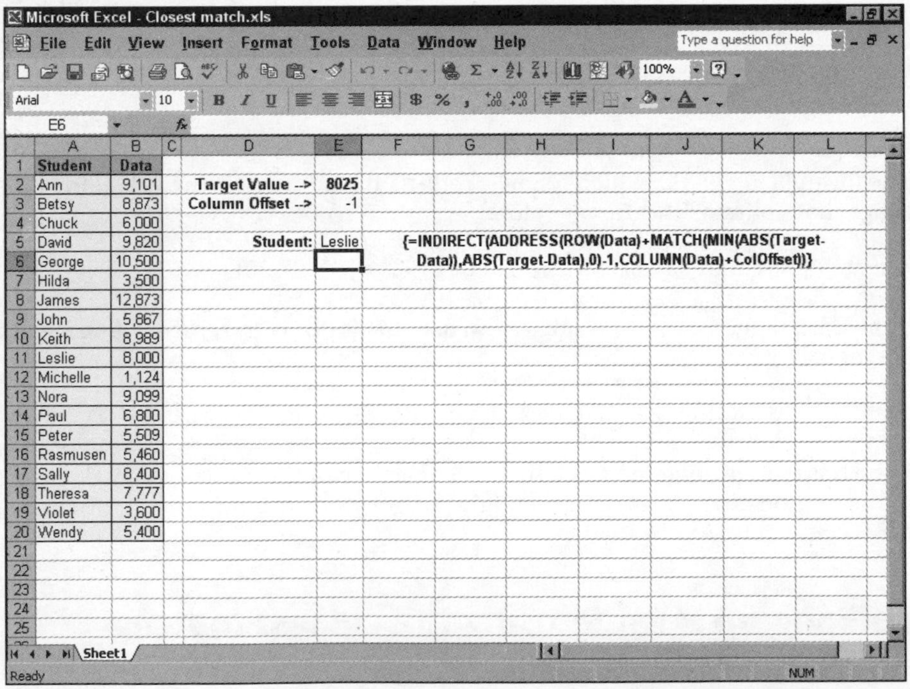

Figure 12-11: This workbook demonstrates how to perform a lookup using the closest match.

Enhancing Your Excel Workbooks

Now that you've learned the basics of using Excel, it's time to move on to some topics that are a bit more interesting. In this part you'll see how to use Excel's advanced graphics capabilities to more clearly display your data, and you'll see how to use some advanced formula techniques to perform seemingly impossible calculations quite easily.

Getting Started Making Charts

To many people, charts — or graphs, if you prefer — are an essential spreadsheet function. For just about as long as there have been PCs and spreadsheets, people have used charts as a means of graphically displaying data.

Excel, of course, has very good chart-making capabilities. In just a few minutes, you can be turning out basic charts that will likely serve your needs quite well. This chapter presents the basic information that you need to know to create charts and to make simple modifications to them.

Understanding Excel's Charts

Charts are a graphical means of making data more understandable. Charts are particularly useful for understanding a lengthy series of numbers and their interrelationships. A chart can help you to spot trends and patterns that would be nearly impossible to identify when examining a range of numbers.

You create charts from numbers in a worksheet. Normally, the data that is used by a chart resides in a single worksheet, but that's not a strict requirement. A single chart can use data from any number of worksheets or even from different workbooks.

When you create a chart in Excel, you have two options for where to place the chart. You can

✦ Insert the chart directly into a worksheet as an object. A chart like the one that appears in the left side of Figure 13-1 is known as an embedded chart.

✦ Create the chart as a new chart sheet in your workbook (see the right side of Figure 13-1). A chart sheet differs from a worksheet in that a chart sheet can hold a single chart and doesn't have cells.

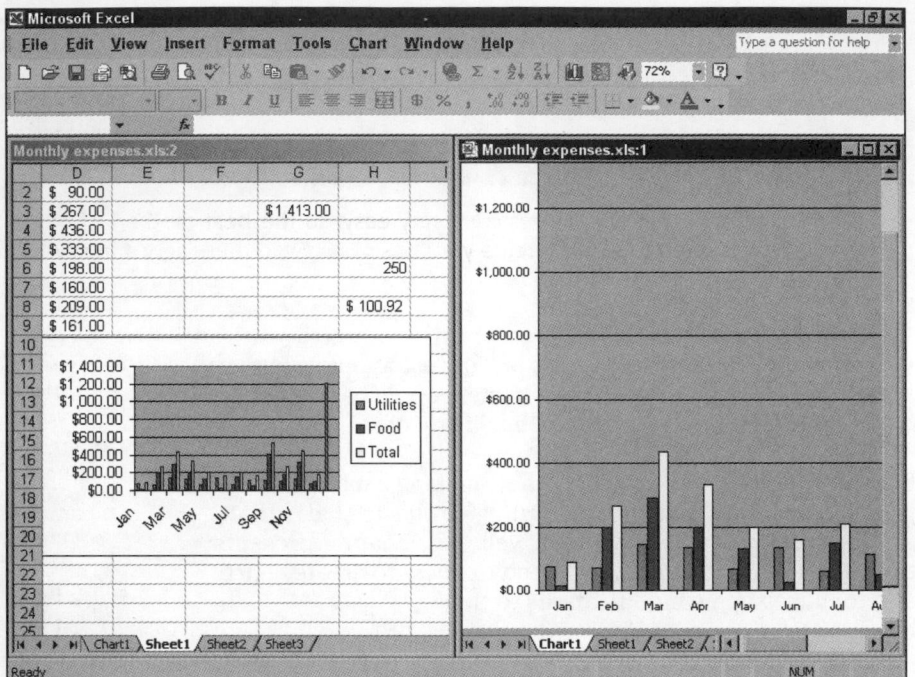

Figure 13-1: A chart can be embedded in a worksheet, or it can appear on a separate chart sheet.

Each method has its advantages, as you'll discover later in this chapter. Regardless of the chart-making option that you choose, you have extensive control over the chart's appearance. You can change the colors, move the legend, format the numbers on the scales, add gridlines, and so on.

Converting a range of numbers into a chart is quite easy, and many people find this aspect of Excel to be rather fun. You can experiment with different chart types to determine the best way to make your case. If that isn't enough, you can make a variety of adjustments to your charts, such as adding annotations, clip art, and other bells and whistles. The real beauty of Excel's charts, however, lies in their connection to worksheet data — if the numbers in your worksheet change, the charts reflect those changes instantly.

Deciding which chart type to use

Excel enables you to create all the basic chart types, and even some esoteric chart types, such as radar charts and doughnut charts. So just how do you decide which type is the best for your needs? Perhaps the best rule is to use the chart type that gets your message across in the simplest way. This may sound simplistic, but the truth is that often there is no one best choice—it really comes down to a matter of personal preference.

See "Choosing the Correct Chart for Your Needs" later in this chapter for a sampling of many of Excel's chart types.

Changing to a different chart type is very easy, so the best method of picking a chart type is often to simply create your basic chart and then view it in several different types until you find the one you like.

Creating your first chart the easy way

If you're new to chart making, you may well wonder how much work is involved in creating a chart in Excel. As you'll see in this section, the whole process can be very simple and easy.

For a quick demonstration of how easily you can create a chart, follow these steps:

1. Enter data to be charted into a worksheet. Typically you want to include several rows and columns of data, as well as labels to indicate what the data represents.

2. Select a cell in the range of data that you entered in Step 1—Excel will automatically determine the size of the range.

3. Press F11. Excel inserts a new chart sheet and displays the chart, based on the selected data. Figure 13-2 shows an example.

In this simple example, Excel created its default chart type (which is a two-dimensional column chart). For more control over the chart-making process, you use the Chart Wizard.

See "Creating Basic Charts" later in this chapter for information on using the Chart Wizard to create charts.

Understanding how Excel handles charts

A chart consists of one or more data series that are displayed graphically. The appearance of the data series depends on the selected chart type. For example, if you create a line chart that uses two data series, the chart contains two lines—each representing one data series. You can distinguish each of the lines by its thickness, color, and data markers. The data series in the chart are linked to cells in the worksheet.

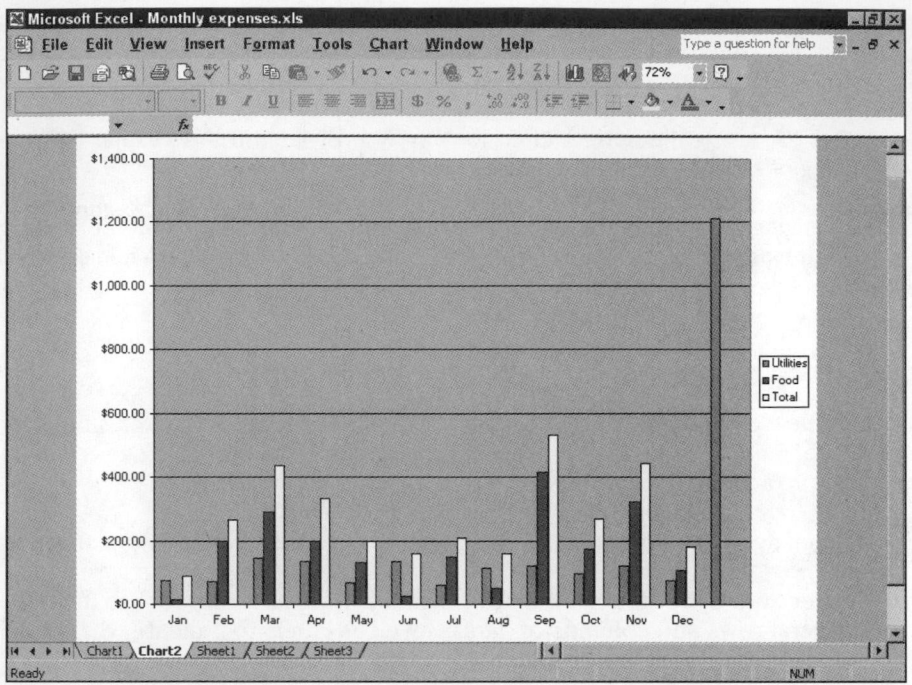

Figure 13-2: Excel can automatically create a chart with almost no work on your part.

You can include a maximum of 255 data series in most charts; the exception is a standard pie chart, which can display only one data series. If your chart uses more than one data series, you may want to use a legend to help the reader identify each series. Excel also places a limit on the number of categories (or data points) in a data series: 32,000 (4,000 for 3D charts). Few users ever run up against this limit.

Charts can use different numbers of axes:

✦ Common charts, such as column, line, and area charts, have a category axis and a value axis. The category axis normally is the horizontal axis, and the value axis normally is the vertical axis (this is reversed for bar charts, in which the bars extend from the left of the chart rather than from the bottom).

✦ Pie charts and doughnut charts have no axes. A pie chart can display only one data series. A doughnut chart can display multiple data series.

✦ A radar chart is a special chart that has one axis for each point in the data series. The axes extend from the center of the chart.

✦ 3D charts have three axes: a category axis, a value axis, and a series axis that extends into the third dimension.

What Is a 3D Chart?

Some of Excel's charts are referred to as 3D charts. This terminology can be confusing because some of these so-called 3D charts aren't technically 3D charts. Rather, they are 2D charts with a perspective look to them; that is, they appear to have some depth.

A true 3D chart has three axes: a value axis (the height dimension), a category axis (the width dimension), and a series axis (the depth dimension).

A chart is not stagnant. You can always change its type, add custom formatting, add new data series to it, or change an existing data series so that it uses data in a different range.

Deciding where to place your chart

Before you create a chart, you need to determine whether you want it to be an embedded chart or a chart that resides on a chart sheet.

Tip   You can easily convert between an embedded chart and one on a separate chart sheet. Choose Chart ⇨ Location and then select the chart location you wish to use. (When you select a chart, a Chart menu replaces the Data menu.)

An embedded chart basically floats on top of a worksheet, on the worksheet's draw layer. As with other drawing objects (such as a text box or a rectangle), you can move an embedded chart, resize it, change its proportions, adjust its borders, and perform other operations.

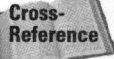

Cross-Reference   Chapter 15 discusses Excel's drawing objects and the draw layer.

To make any changes to the actual chart in an embedded chart object, you must click it to select the chart. Using embedded charts enables you to print the chart next to the data that it uses.

When you create a chart on a chart sheet, the chart occupies the entire sheet. If you plan to print a chart on a page by itself, using a chart sheet is your best choice. If you have many charts to create, you may want to create each one on a separate chart sheet, to avoid cluttering your worksheet. This technique also makes locating a particular chart easier, because you can change the names of the chart sheets' tabs to correspond to the chart that it contains.

Excel's menus change when a chart sheet is active, similar to the way that they change when you select an embedded chart. The Chart menu replaces the Data menu, and other menus include commands that are appropriate for working with charts.

Tip   You can size the chart in a chart sheet according to the window size by using the View ⇨ Sized with Window command. When this setting is enabled, the chart adjusts itself when you resize the workbook window (it always fits perfectly in the window). In this mode, the chart that you're working on may or may not correspond to how it looks when printed.

Creating Basic Charts

You can create both embedded charts and charts on chart sheets with or without the assistance of the Chart Wizard.

Note   Excel always has a default chart type. Normally, the default is a column chart (but you can change this type, as you learn later in the section "Changing the default chart type"). If you create a chart without using the Chart Wizard, Excel creates the chart by using the default chart type. If you use the Chart Wizard, Excel prompts you for the chart type, making the default chart type irrelevant.

Creating a chart with the Chart Wizard

The Chart Wizard consists of four dialog boxes that prompt you for various settings for the chart. By the time that you reach the last dialog box, the chart is usually just what you need.

Selecting your data first

Before you start the Chart Wizard, you may want to select the data to include in the chart. This step isn't necessary, but it makes creating the chart easier for you. If you don't select the data before invoking the Chart Wizard, Excel makes its best guess about what you want to chart — or you can select it in the second Chart Wizard dialog box. When you select the data, include items such as labels and series identifiers (row and column headings).

Tip   The data that you plot doesn't have to be contiguous. You can press Ctrl and make a multiple selection. In this case, Excel uses only the selected cells for the chart.

After you select the data, start the Chart Wizard, either by clicking the Chart Wizard button on the Standard toolbar or by selecting Insert ⇨ Chart. Excel displays the first of four Chart Wizard dialog boxes.

At any time while using the Chart Wizard, you can go back to the preceding step by clicking the Back button. Or, you can click Finish to close the Chart Wizard. If you close the Chart Wizard early, Excel creates the chart by using the information that you provided up to that point.

Don't be too concerned about creating the perfect chart. You later can change, at any time, every choice you make in the Chart Wizard.

Completing Step 1 of the Chart Wizard

Figure 13-3 shows the first Chart Wizard dialog box, in which you select the chart type. This dialog box has two tabs: Standard Types and Custom Types. The Standard Types tab displays the 14 basic chart types and the subtypes for each, and the Custom Types tab displays some customized charts (including user-defined custom charts).

Tip   To get a preview of how your selected chart will appear, hold down the button labeled Press and Hold to View Sample. When you click this button, keep the mouse button pressed.

When you decide on a chart type and subtype, click the Next button to move to the next step.

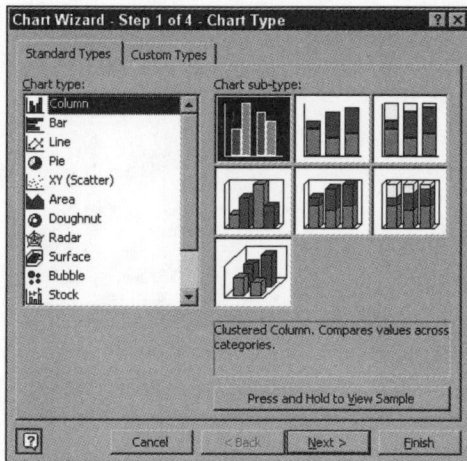

Figure 13-3: Begin by choosing the type of chart you wish to create.

Tip   As you select different chart types and subtypes, read the description below the Chart sub-type box to learn more about your selection.

Completing Step 2 of the Chart Wizard

In the second step of the Chart Wizard, you verify the data ranges and specify the orientation of the data (whether it's arranged in rows or columns). The orientation of the data has a drastic effect on the look of your chart. Usually, Excel guesses the orientation correctly — but not always. You can also select the individual data series settings and add or remove data series from the chart. Figure 13-4 shows the Data Range tab and Figure 13-5 shows the Series tab of Step 2 of the Chart Wizard.

Tip   Excel highlights the data range in the worksheet so that you can verify that the correct range is specified.

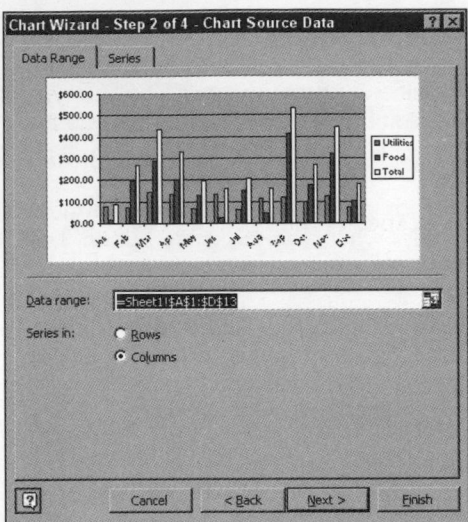

Figure 13-4: Verify that the correct data range and data layout are selected.

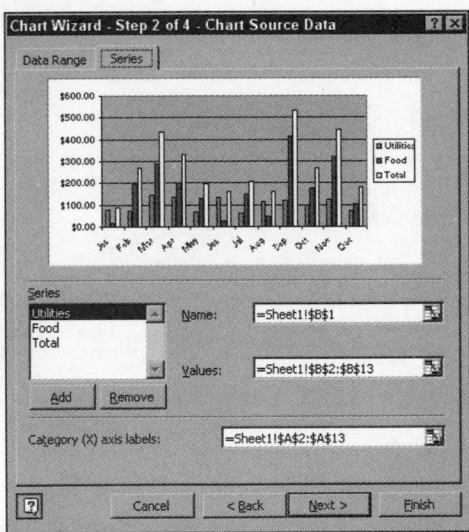

Figure 13-5: If necessary, use the Series tab to control the individual data series used in the chart.

Click the Next button to advance to the next dialog box.

Completing Step 3 of the Chart Wizard

In the third Chart Wizard dialog box, which is shown in Figure 13-6, you specify most of the options for the chart. (The options available depend on the type of chart you selected in Step 1 of the Chart Wizard.) This dialog box has six tabs:

✦ **Titles:** Add titles to the chart

✦ **Axes:** Turn on or off axes display and specify the type of axes

✦ **Gridlines:** Specify gridlines, if any

✦ **Legend:** Specify whether to include a legend and where to place it

✦ **Data Labels:** Specify whether to show data labels and what type of labels

✦ **Data Table:** Specify whether to display a table of the data

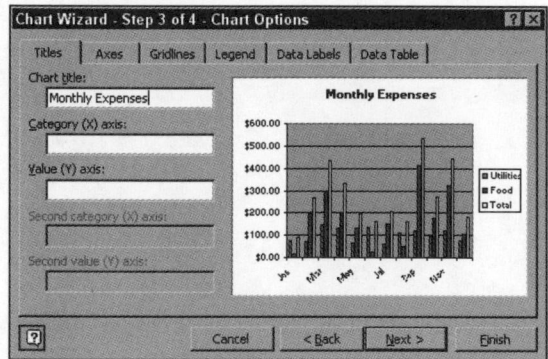

Figure 13-6: Select the options you want to use to enhance your basic chart.

Tip

To learn more about the various options, click the question mark button near the top-right corner of the dialog box and then click the option.

Cross-Reference

You learn more about the chart options in Chapter 14.

After you select the chart options, click Next to move to the final dialog box.

Completing Step 4 of the Chart Wizard

Step 4 of the Chart Wizard, shown in Figure 13-7, lets you specify where to place the chart. Make your choice and click Finish.

Tip

You can enter a name for the new chart sheet rather than accept the default name.

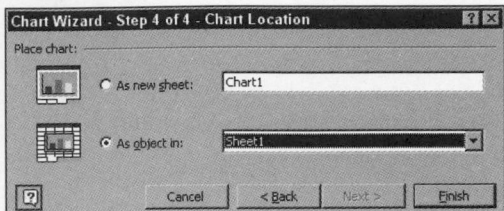

Figure 13-7: Finally, choose the location for your chart.

Tip   You can use the drop-down box to select the destination worksheet if you don't want to place the chart on the currently active worksheet.

Excel creates and displays the chart. If you place the chart on a worksheet, Excel centers it in the worksheet window and selects it.

Understanding the Chart Toolbar

The Chart toolbar appears when you click an embedded chart, activate a chart sheet, or choose View ⇨ Toolbars ⇨ Chart. This toolbar includes nine tools. You can use these tools to make some common chart changes:

- ✦ **Chart Objects:** When a chart is activated, you can select a particular chart element by using this drop-down list.

- ✦ **Format Selected Object:** Displays the Format dialog box for the selected chart element.

- ✦ **Chart Type:** Expands to display 18 chart types when you click the arrow.

- ✦ **Legend:** Toggles the legend display in the selected chart.

- ✦ **Data Table:** Toggles the display of the data table in a chart.

- ✦ **By Row:** Plots the data by rows.

- ✦ **By Column:** Plots the data by columns.

- ✦ **Angle Clockwise:** Displays the selected text at a –45-degree angle.

- ✦ **Angle Counterclockwise:** Displays the selected text at a +45-degree angle.

Excel includes several other chart-related tools that aren't on the Chart toolbar. You can customize the toolbar to include these additional tools, which are located in the Charting category in the Customize dialog box.

 **Note** Excel places colored borders around the data and title ranges whenever the chart is selected. This makes it easier for you to see which data is included in the selected chart — which is especially handy if you have more than one chart in the worksheet.

Creating a chart manually

To create an embedded chart without using the Chart Wizard:

1. Make sure that the Chart toolbar is displayed.

2. Select the data to be charted.

3. Click the Chart Type tool on the Chart toolbar and then select a chart type from the displayed icons (see Figure 13-8).

Excel adds the chart to the worksheet by using the default settings.

 **Tip** To reset angled text to horizontal, click the Angle button again.

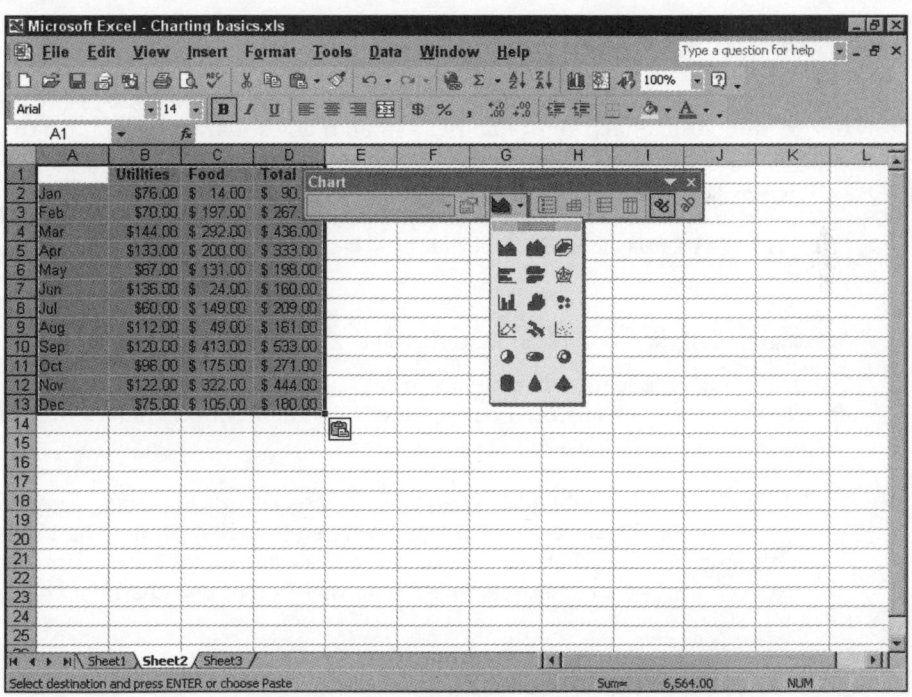

Figure 13-8: Use the Chart Type tool to select a chart type manually.

Making Basic Chart Modifications

After you create a chart, you can modify it at any time. The modifications that you can make to a chart are extensive. This section covers some of the more common chart modifications:

- ✦ Moving and resizing the chart
- ✦ Changing a chart's location
- ✦ Changing the chart type
- ✦ Moving chart elements
- ✦ Deleting chart elements

Other types of chart modifications are discussed in Chapter 14.

Before you can modify a chart, it must be activated. To activate an embedded chart, click it, which also activates the element that you click. To activate a chart on a chart sheet, just click its sheet tab.

Moving and resizing a chart

If you embedded the chart, you can freely move and resize it. Click the chart's border to select the chart; eight handles (small black squares) appear on the chart's border. Drag the chart to move it, or drag any of the handles to resize the chart.

If your chart is on a chart sheet, you can't move or resize it. You can, however, change the way that it's displayed by selecting View ⇨ Sized with Window.

Changing a chart's location

Use the Chart ⇨ Location command to relocate an embedded chart to a chart sheet, or convert a chart on a chart sheet to an embedded chart. This command displays the Chart Location dialog box.

If you select an embedded chart and choose an existing chart sheet as its new location, Excel will ask if you'd like to embed the chart on the chart sheet. If you respond Yes, the chart sheet will contain an additional chart as an embedded object. This is a way to overcome the normal limit of one chart per chart sheet.

Changing the chart type

To change the chart type of the active chart, use either of these methods:

✦ Click the Chart Type button's drop-down arrow on the Chart toolbar. The button expands to show the 18 basic chart types.

✦ Choose the Chart ➪ Chart Type command.

The Chart ➪ Chart Type command displays the dialog box shown in Figure 13-9. This dialog box is the first of the Chart Wizard dialog boxes. Click the Standard Types tab to select one of the standard chart types (and a subtype), or click the Custom Types tab to select a customized chart. After you select a chart type, click OK; the selected chart will be changed to the type that you selected.

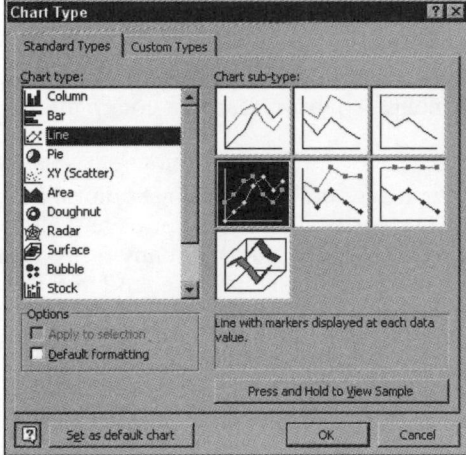

Figure 13-9: You can use the Chart Type dialog box to select a different chart type.

Caution

If you've customized some aspects of your chart, choosing a new chart type from the Custom Types tab may override some or all of the changes that you made. For example, if you add gridlines to the chart and then select a custom chart type that doesn't use gridlines, your gridlines disappear. Therefore, make sure that you're satisfied with the chart before you make too many custom changes to it. However, you can always use Edit ➪ Undo to reverse your actions.

In the Custom Types tab, if you click the User-defined option, the list box displays the name of any user-defined custom formats. If you haven't defined any custom formats, this box shows Default, referring to the default chart type. Changing the default chart type is discussed later in this chapter.

Cross-Reference

Chapter 14 explains how to create custom chart formats.

Moving and deleting chart elements

Some of the chart parts can be moved (any of the titles, the legend, or data labels). To move a chart element, simply click it to select it and then drag it to the desired location in the chart. To delete a chart element, select it and then press Delete.

Tip   To make certain you've selected the correct section of the chart, look at the Chart Objects box on the Chart toolbar. The Chart Objects box identifies the currently selected object.

Making other modifications to your chart

When a chart is activated, you can select various parts of the chart to change. Modifying a chart is similar to everything else you do in Excel. First, you make a selection (in this case, select a chart element). Then, you issue a command to do something with the selection.

You can use the Fill Color tool on the Formatting toolbar to change colors. For example, if you want to change the color of a series, select the series and choose the color that you want from the Fill Color tool. You'll find that many other toolbar tools work with charts. For example, you can select the chart's legend and then click the Bold tool to make the legend text bold.

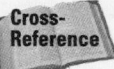

Cross-Reference   See Chapter 14 for more details on modifying charts.

Changing the default chart type

The default chart type is mentioned many times in this chapter. Excel's default chart type is a 2D column chart with a light-gray plot area, a legend on the right, and horizontal gridlines.

If you don't like the look of this chart, or if you typically use a different type of chart, you can easily change the default chart:

1. Select the Chart ⇨ Chart Type command.

2. Choose the chart type that you want to use as the default chart. This can be a chart from either the Standard Types tab or the Custom Types tab.

3. Click the button labeled Set as default chart. You are asked to verify your choice.

Tip   If you have many charts of the same type to create, changing the default chart format to the chart type with which you're working is much more efficient than separately formatting each chart. Then you can create all of your charts without having to select the chart type.

Printing Your Charts

You'll almost certainly want to print many of the charts you create in your Excel worksheets. Printing charts is very easy, although there are some slight differences between printing embedded charts and printing charts that are on chart sheets.

Printing embedded charts is nothing special; you print them the same way that you print a worksheet (see Chapter 3). As long as you include the embedded chart in the range that you want to print, Excel prints the chart as it appears onscreen.

Tip   If you select an embedded chart and then choose File ➪ Print (or click the Print button), Excel prints the chart on a page by itself and does not print the worksheet.

Tip   If you don't want a particular embedded chart to appear on your printout, right-click the chart and choose Format Chart Area from the shortcut menu. Click the Properties tab in the Format Chart Area dialog box and remove the check mark from the Print Object check box.

If you created the chart on a chart sheet, Excel prints the chart on a page by itself. If you open Excel's Page Setup dialog box when the chart sheet is active, the Sheet tab is replaced with a tab named Chart. Figure 13-10 shows the Chart tab of the Page Setup dialog box.

This dialog box has several print size options:

✦ **Use full page:** Excel prints the chart to the full width and height of the page margins. Even though this is the default, this usually isn't a good choice, because the chart's relative proportions may change.

✦ **Scale to fit page:** Expands the chart proportionally in both dimensions until one dimension fills the space between the margins. This option usually results in the best printout.

✦ **Custom:** Prints the chart as it appears on your screen. Select View ➪ Sized with Window to make the chart correspond to the window size and proportions. The chart prints at the current window size and proportions.

The Printing quality options work just like those for worksheet pages. If you choose the Draft quality option for a chart sheet, Excel prints the chart, but its quality may not be high (the actual effect depends on your printer). Choosing the Print in black and white option prints the data series with black-and-white patterns rather than colors.

Tip   Because charts may take longer to print than text, using print preview before you print a chart is a good idea. This enables you to see what the printed output will look like, so that you can avoid surprises.

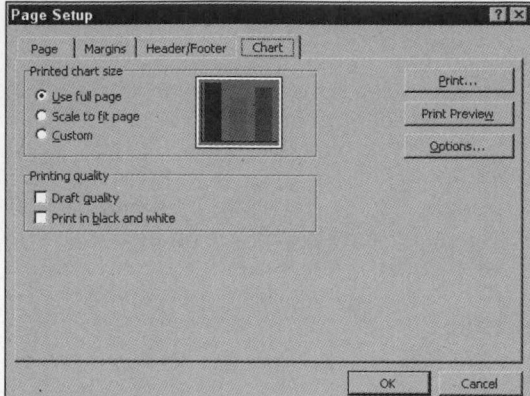

Figure 13-10: You can use the Chart tab of the Page Setup dialog box to select several chart printing options.

Choosing the Correct Chart for Your Needs

Even though choosing the correct chart type is a very subjective choice, the task will be a whole lot easier for you if you have some understanding of the different chart types that are available. For your convenience, this chapter concludes with a discussion of Excel's chart types and a listing of the subtypes for each. This section may help you determine which chart type is best for your data.

Understanding Column charts

Column charts are one of the most common chart types. This type of chart is useful for displaying discrete data (as opposed to continuous data). You can have up to 255 data series, and the columns can be stacked on top of each other. Figure 13-11 shows an example of a Column chart.

Table 13-1 lists Excel's seven Column chart subtypes.

Table 13-1 Column Chart Subtypes	
Chart Type	**Description**
Clustered Column	Compares values across categories.
Stacked Column	Compares the contribution of each value to a total across categories.

Chart Type	Description
100% Stacked Column	Compares the percentage each value contributes to a total across categories.
3-D Clustered Column	Same as a Clustered Column chart but with a perspective look.
3-D Stacked Column	Same as a Stacked Column chart but with a perspective look.
3-D 100% Stacked Column	Same as a 100% Stacked Column chart but with a perspective look.
3-D Column	Compares values across categories and across series.

Understanding Bar charts

A Bar chart is essentially a Column chart that has been rotated 90 degrees to the left. The advantage in using a Bar chart is that the category labels may be easier to read (see Figure 13-12 for an example). You can include up to 255 data series in a Bar chart. In addition, the bars can be stacked from left to right.

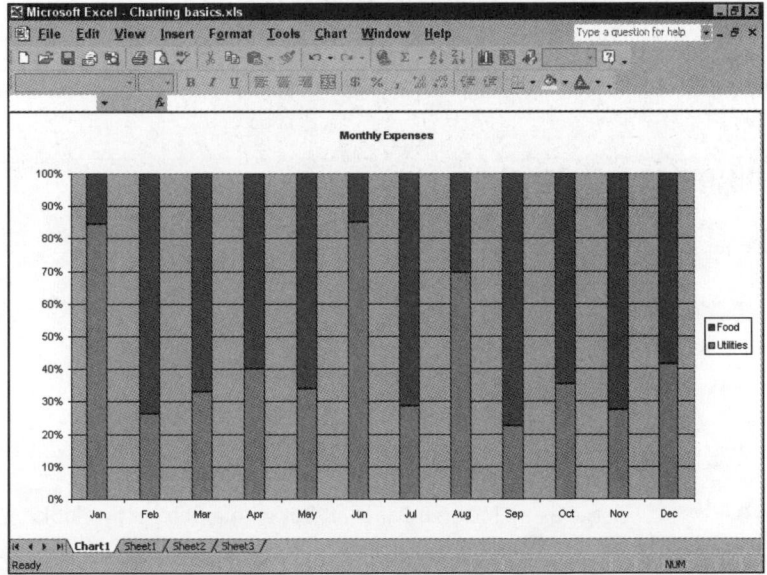

Figure 13-11: This Stacked Column chart displays each series as a percentage of the total.

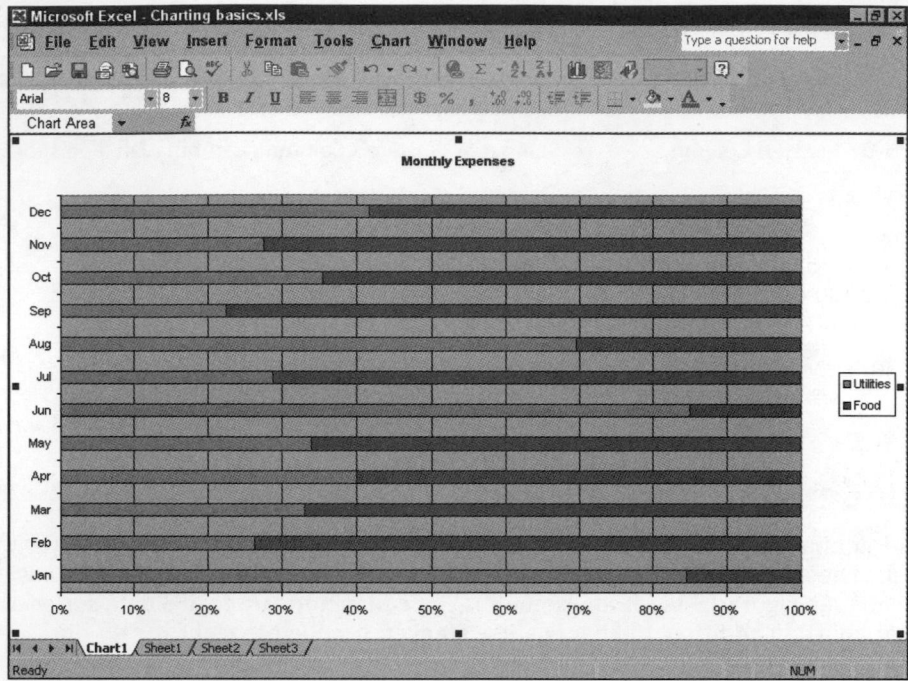

Figure 13-12: A Bar chart may be a good substitute for a column chart.

Table 13-2 lists Excel's six Bar chart subtypes.

Table 13-2 Bar Chart Subtypes	
Chart Type	**Description**
Clustered Bar	Compares values across categories.
Stacked Bar	Compares the contribution of each value to a total across categories.
100% Stacked Bar	Compares the percentage each value contributes to a total across categories.
3-D Clustered Bar	Same as a Clustered Bar chart but with a perspective look.
3-D Stacked Bar	Same as a Stacked Bar chart but with a perspective look.
3-D 100% Stacked Bar	Same as a 100% Stacked Bar chart but with a perspective look.

Understanding Line charts

Line charts are frequently used to plot data that is continuous rather than discrete. For example, plotting monthly expenses as a Line chart may let you spot trends over time. See Figure 13-13 for an example of a Line chart.

Table 13-3 lists Excel's seven Line chart subtypes.

Table 13-3	
Line Chart Subtypes	
Chart Type	*Description*
Line	Displays trend over time or categories.
Stacked Line	Displays the trend of the contribution of each value over time or categories.
100% Stacked Line	Displays the trend of the percentage each value contributes over time or categories.
Line with Data Markers	Same as a Line chart with data markers.
Stacked Line with Data Markers	Same as a Stacked Line chart with data markers.
100% Stacked Line with Data Markers	Same as a 100% Stacked Line chart with data markers.
3-D Line	Same as a Line chart with a 3D visual effect.

Understanding Pie charts

A pie chart is useful when you want to show relative proportions or contributions to a whole. Figure 13-14 shows an example of a Pie chart. A Pie chart can use only one data series.

Tip   You can explode a slice of a Pie chart as shown in Figure 13-14. Activate the chart and select the slice that you want to explode. Then, drag it away from the center.

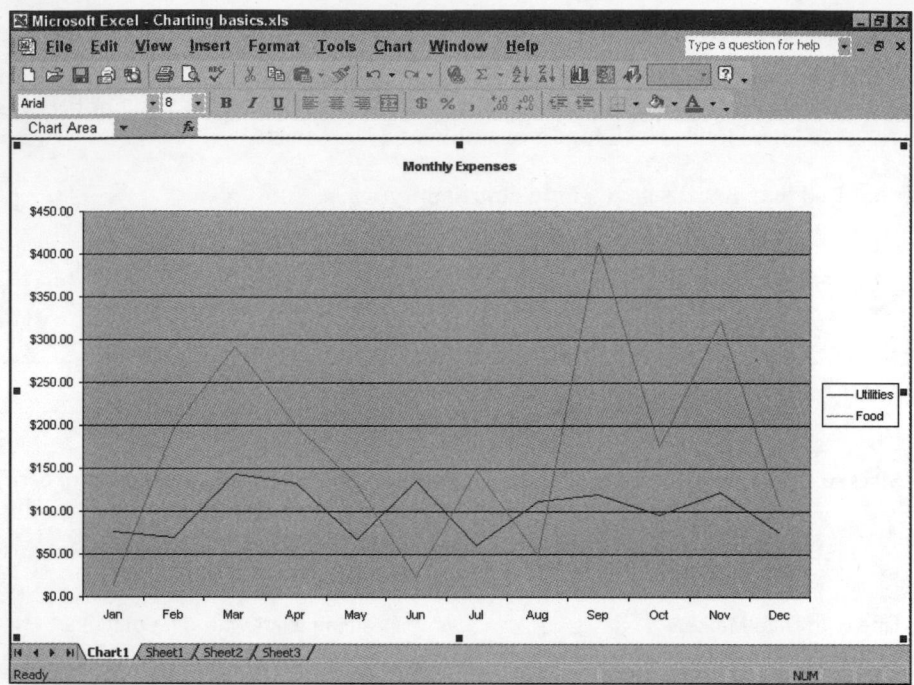

Figure 13-13: A Line chart often can help you spot trends in your data.

Table 13-4 lists Excel's six Pie chart subtypes.

	Table 13-4 **Pie Chart Subtypes**	
Chart Type	**Description**
Pie	Displays the contribution of each value to the total.
3-D Pie	Same as a Pie chart with perspective look.
Pie of Pie	Pie chart with user-defined values extracted and combined into another pie.
Exploded Pie	Same as a Pie chart with one or more slices exploded.
Exploded 3-D Pie	Same as a 3-D Pie chart with one or more slices exploded.
Bar of Pie	Pie chart with user-defined values extracted and combined into a stacked bar.

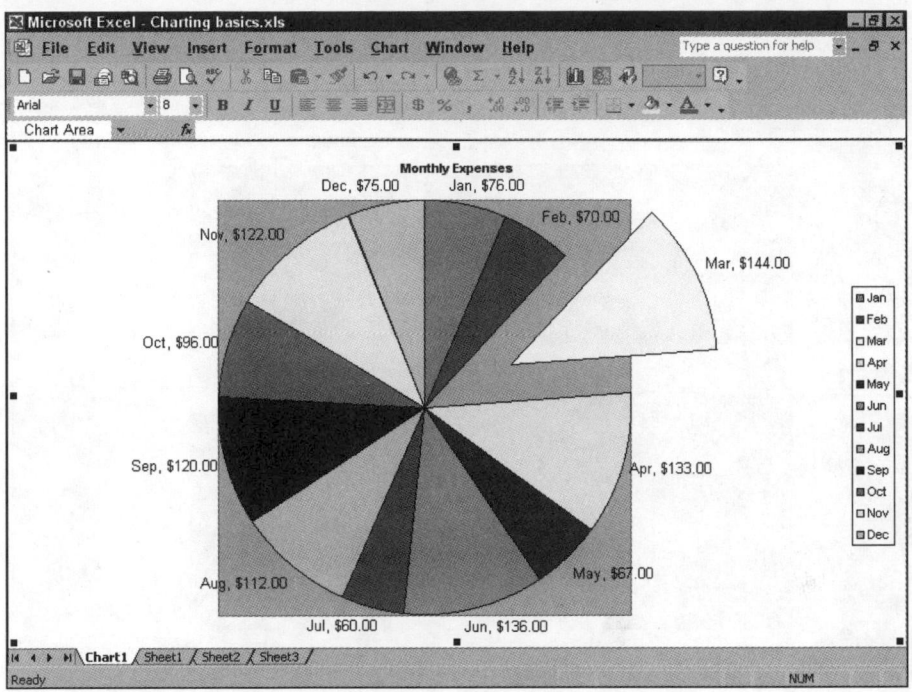

Figure 13-14: A Pie chart emphasizes the proportional contributions to the total.

Cross-Reference The Pie of Pie and Bar of Pie chart types enable you to display a second chart that clarifies one of the pie slices. You can use the Options tab of the Format Data Series dialog box to specify which data is assigned to the second chart. Refer to Chapter 14 for details.

Understanding XY (Scatter) charts

Another common chart type is XY (Scatter) charts (also known as scattergrams). An XY chart differs from the other chart types in that both axes display values (no category axis exists).

This type of chart often is used to show the relationship between two variables. Figure 13-15 shows an example of an XY chart that plots the sine and cosine of a series of angles.

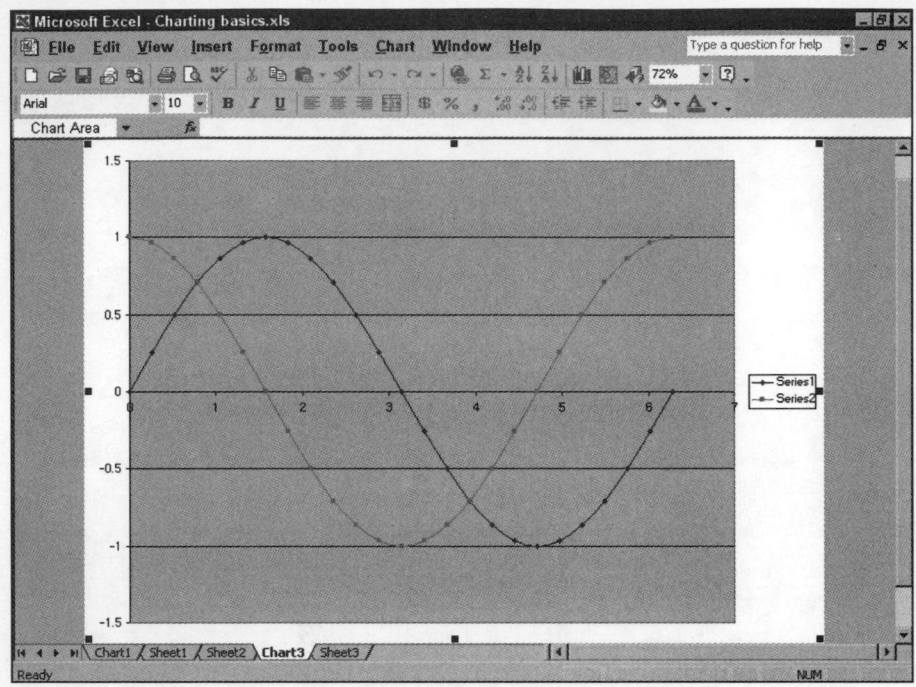

Figure 13-15: An XY chart plots the relationship between two or more variables.

Table 13-5 lists Excel's five XY (Scatter) chart subtypes. All XY charts compare pairs of values.

Table 13-5 XY (Scatter) Chart Subtypes	
Chart Type	*Description*
Scatter	XY chart with markers and no lines.
Scatter with Smoothed Lines	XY chart with markers and smoothed lines.
Scatter with Smoothed Lines and No Data Markers	XY chart with smoothed lines and no markers.
Scatter with Lines	XY chart with straight lines and markers.
Scatter with Lines and No Data Markers	XY chart with straight lines and no markers.

Understanding Area charts

Think of an Area chart as a line chart that has been colored in below the lines. Figure 13-16 shows an example of a Stacked Area chart. Stacking the data series enables you to see clearly the total plus the contribution by each series.

Table 13-6 lists Excel's six Area chart subtypes.

Table 13-6 Area Chart Subtypes	
Chart Type	**Description**
Area	Displays the trend of values over time or categories.
Stacked Area	Displays the trend of the contribution of each value over time or categories.
100% Stacked Area	Displays the trend of the percentage of each value over time or categories.
3-D Area	Same as an Area chart with a perspective appearance.
3-D Stacked Area	Same as a Stacked Area chart with a perspective appearance.
3-D 100% Stacked Area	Same as a 100% Stacked Area chart with a perspective appearance.

Understanding Doughnut charts

A Doughnut chart is similar to a Pie chart, except that it has a hole in the middle. Unlike a Pie chart, a Doughnut chart can display more than one series of data. Figure 13-17 shows an example of a Doughnut chart (the arrow and series descriptions were added manually; these items aren't part of a Doughnut chart).

Notice that Excel displays the data series as concentric rings. As you can see, a Doughnut chart with more than one series to chart can be a little difficult to interpret. Sometimes, a Stacked Column chart for such comparisons expresses your meaning better than a Doughnut chart can express your meaning.

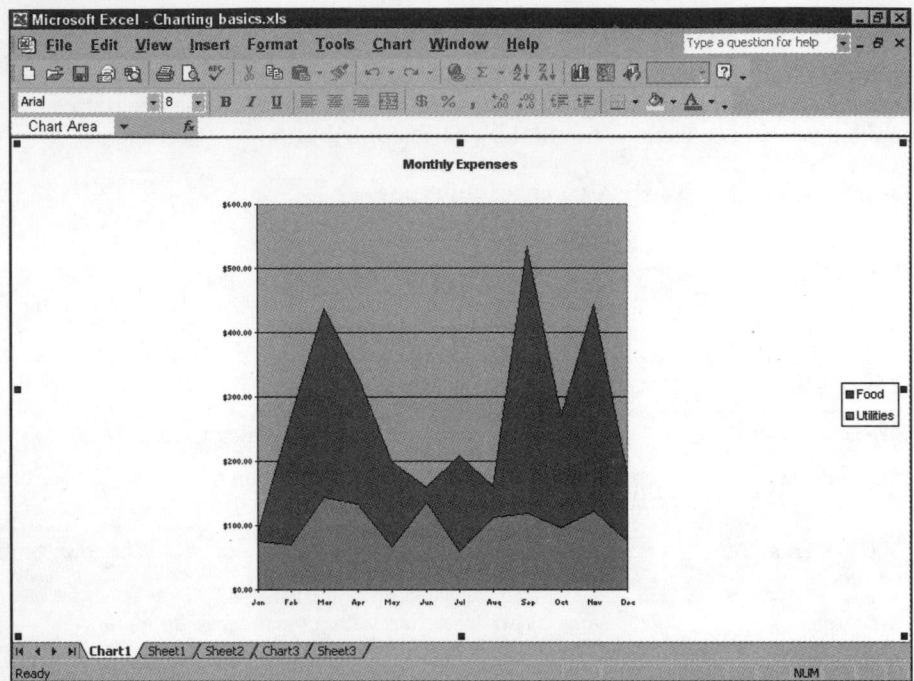

Figure 13-16: An area chart plots the trend of two or more variables.

Table 13-7 lists Excel's two Doughnut chart subtypes.

Table 13-7 Doughnut Chart Subtypes	
Chart Type	**Subtype**
Doughnut	Similar to a Pie chart except that multiple rings plot different data series.
Exploded Doughnut	Doughnut chart with all slices exploded.

Understanding Radar charts

You may not be familiar with Radar charts. A Radar chart has a separate axis for each category, and the axes extend from the center. The value of the data point is plotted on the appropriate axis. If all data points in a series have an identical value, it produces a perfect circle. See Figure 13-18 for an example of a Radar chart.

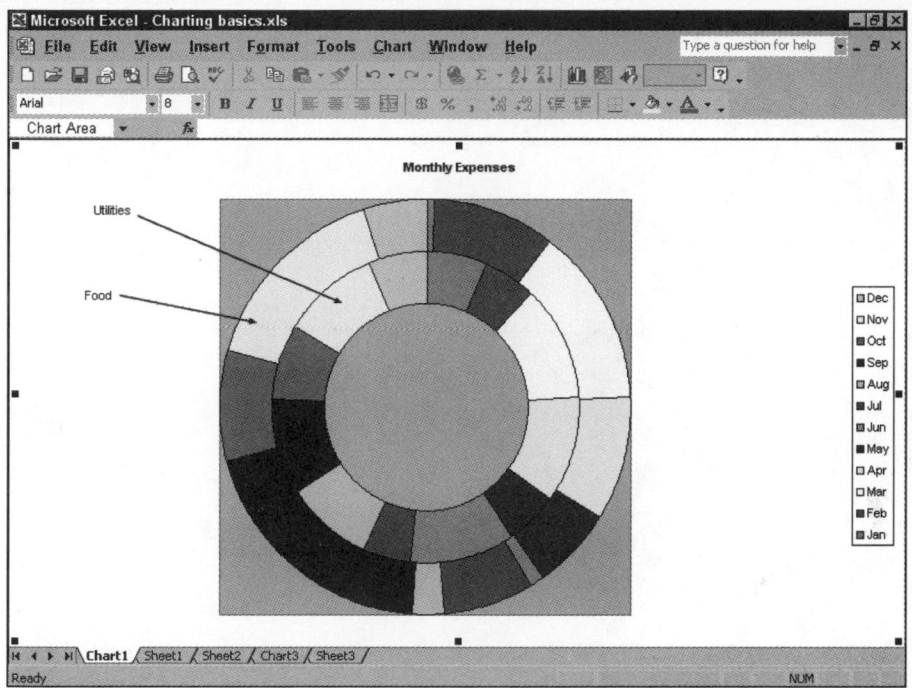

Figure 13-17: A Doughnut chart is similar to a Pie chart except that you can plot more than one data series.

Table 13-8 lists Excel's three Radar chart subtypes.

	Table 13-8
	Radar Chart Subtypes

Chart Type	*Subtype*
Radar	Displays changes in values relative to a center point.
Radar with Data Markers	Same as a Radar chart with data markers.
Filled Radar	Same as a Radar chart with areas colored in.

Understanding Surface charts

Surface charts display two or more data series on a surface. As Figure 13-19 shows, these charts can be quite interesting. For example, you can use a Surface chart to generate a 3D plot of topographical data. Unlike other charts, Excel uses color to distinguish values, not to distinguish the data series.

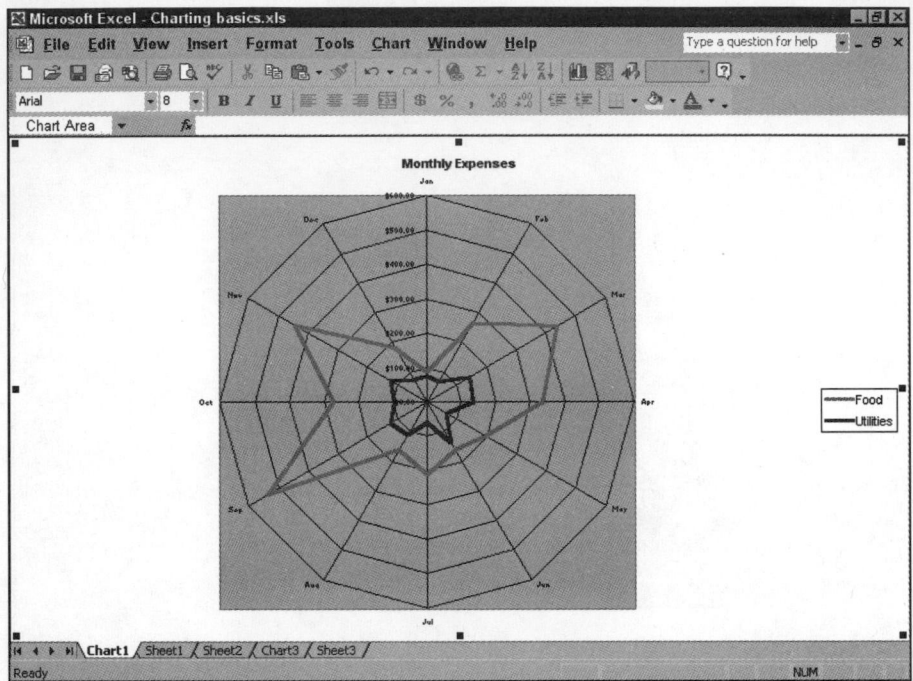

Figure 13-18: A Radar chart plots the data series with increasing values farther from the center point.

 **Tip**

Surface charts often benefit from being rotated. The easiest way to rotate a surface chart is to click one of the walls and then drag the corners.

Table 13-9 lists Excel's four 3D surface chart subtypes.

Table 13-9
Surface Chart Subtypes

Chart Type	Description
3-D Surface	Shows trends in values across two dimensions in a continuous curve.
3-D Surface (wireframe)	Same as a 3-D Surface chart with no colors.
Surface (top view)	Same as a 3-D Surface chart, as viewed from above.
Surface (top view wireframe)	Same as a 3-D Surface chart, as viewed from above, with no colors.

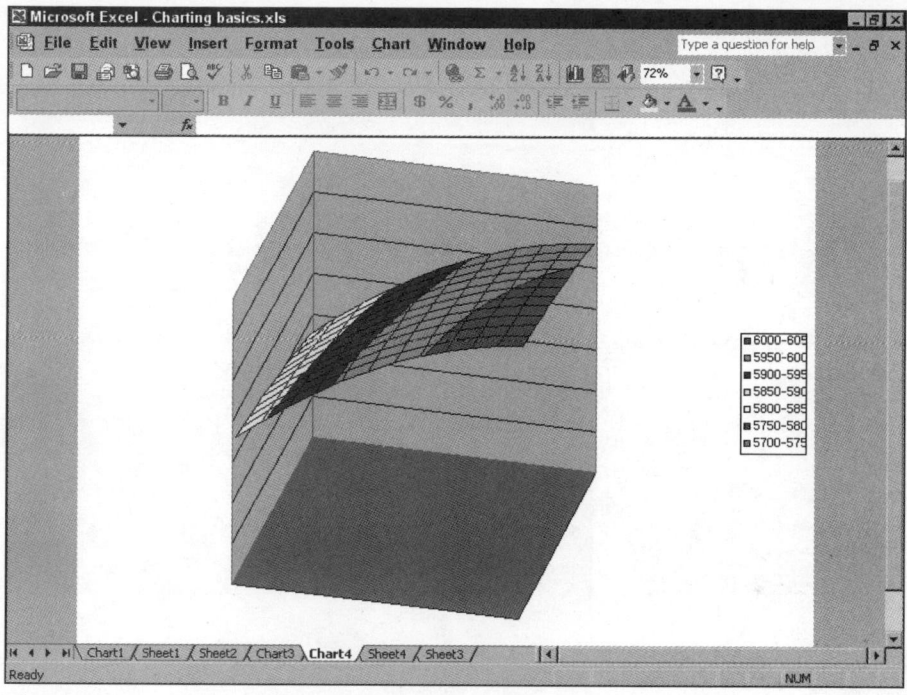

Figure 13-19: A Surface chart plots the data series as a 3-D contour.

Understanding Bubble charts

Think of a bubble chart as an XY (Scatter) chart that can display an additional data series. That additional data series is represented by the size of the bubbles.

Figure 13-20 shows an example of a Bubble chart. In this case, the chart displays the results of a weight-loss program. The y-axis represents the original weight, the x-axis shows the length of time in the program, and the size of the bubbles represents the amount of weight lost.

Table 13-10 lists Excel's two bubble chart subtypes.

Table 13-10	
Bubble Chart Subtypes	
Chart Type	*Subtype*
Bubble Chart	Compares sets of 3 values with the size of the bubble representing the third value.
Bubble with 3-D effect	Same as a Bubble chart with 3-D bubbles.

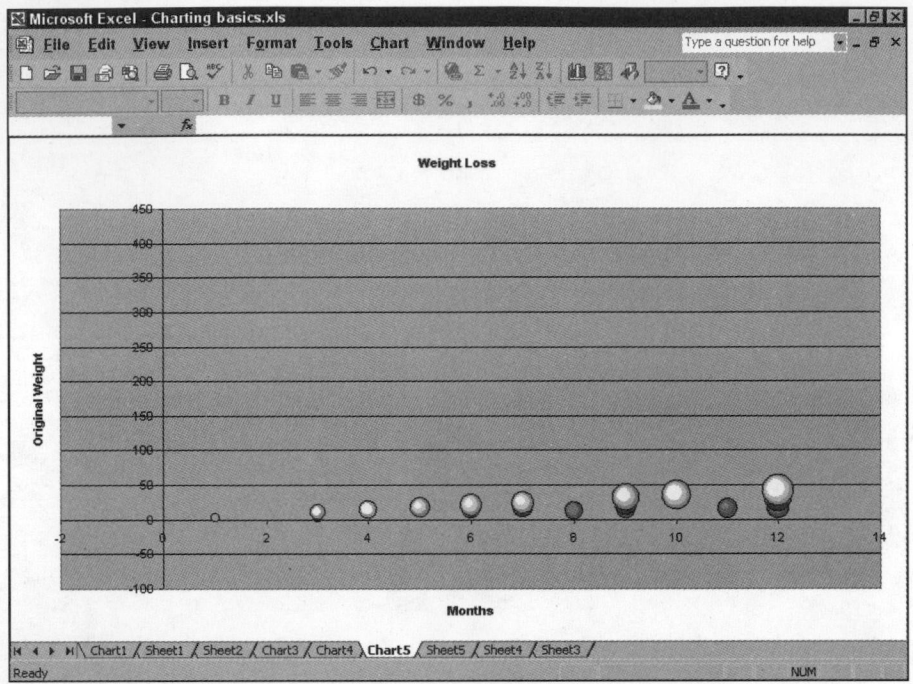

Figure 13-20: A Bubble chart plots the data series as bubbles sized according to value.

Understanding Stock charts

Stock charts are most useful for displaying stock market information. These charts require three to five data series, depending on the subtype.

Figure 13-21 shows an example of a stock chart. This chart uses the Open-High-Low-Close subtype that requires four data series.

Table 13-11 lists Excel's four stock chart subtypes.

Table 13-11	
Stock Chart Subtypes	
Chart Type	**Subtype**
High-Low-Close	Displays the stock's high, low, and closing prices.
Open-High-Low-Close	Displays the stock's opening, high, low, and closing prices.
Volume-High-Low-Close	Displays the stock's volume, high, low, and closing prices.
Volume-Open-High-Low-Close	Displays the stock's volume, open, high, low, and closing prices.

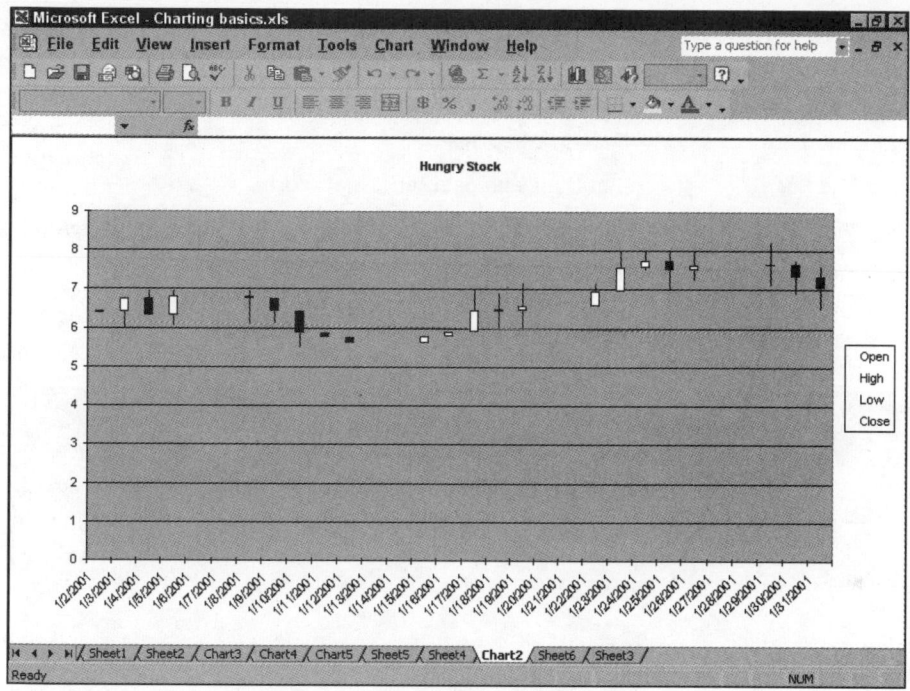

Figure 13-21: A stock chart plots the performance of your stock market investments.

Understanding Cylinder, Cone, and Pyramid charts

These three chart types are essentially the same—except for the shapes that are used. You usually can use these charts in place of a Bar or Column chart.

Figure 13-22 shows an example of a Pyramid chart.

Each of these chart types has seven subtypes, which are described in Table 13-12.

Table 13-12
Cylinder, Cone, and Pyramid Chart Subtypes

Chart Type	Subtype
Clustered Column	Standard Column chart.
Stacked Column	Column chart with data series stacked.
100% Stacked Column	Column chart with data series stacked and expressed as percentages.

Continued

Chart Type	Subtype
Clustered Bar	Standard Bar chart.
Stacked Bar	Bar chart with data series stacked.
100% Stacked Bar	Bar chart with data series stacked and expressed as percentages.
3-D Column	A true 3-D Column chart with a third axis.

Table 13-12 (continued)

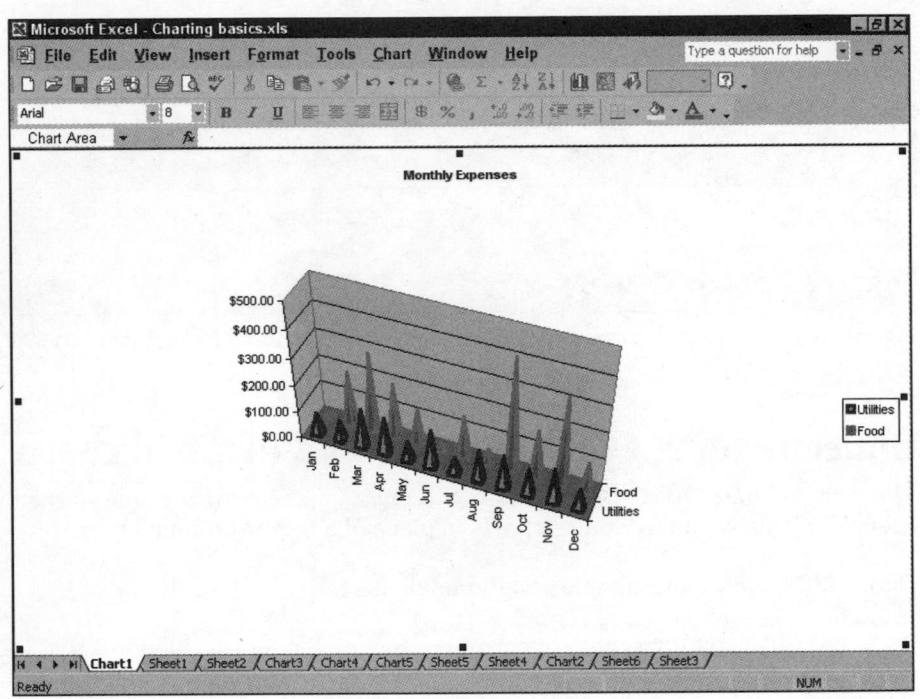

Figure 13-22: A Pyramid chart is essentially a Column chart with a different shape.

✦   ✦   ✦

Learning Some Advanced Charting

The last chapter introduced the basics of charting in Excel. This chapter takes the topic to the next level. You learn how to customize your charts to the maximum, so that they look exactly as you want. You also pick up some slick charting tricks that will make your charts even more impressive.

Understanding Chart Customization

Often, the basic chart that Excel creates is sufficient for your needs. If you're using a chart to get a quick visual impression of your data, a chart that's based on one of the standard chart types usually does just fine. But, if you want to create the most effective chart possible, you probably want to take advantage of the additional customization techniques available in Excel.

Customizing a chart involves changing its appearance, as well as possibly adding new elements to it. These changes can be purely cosmetic (such as changing colors or modifying line widths) or quite substantial (such as changing the axis scales or rotating a 3-D chart). New elements that you might add include features such as a data table, a trend line, or error bars.

Tip Before you can customize a chart, you must activate it. If it is on a chart sheet, do so by clicking its sheet tab. To activate an embedded chart, click the chart's border.

Here's a partial list of the customizations that you can make to a chart:

✦ Change any colors, patterns, line widths, marker styles, and fonts.

✦ Change the data ranges that the chart uses, add a new chart series, or delete an existing series.

✦ Choose which gridlines to display.

✦ Determine the size and placement of the legend (or delete it altogether).

✦ Determine where the axes cross.

✦ Adjust the axis scales by specifying a maximum and minimum, changing the tick marks and labels, and so on. You also can specify that a scale be represented in logarithmic units.

✦ Add titles for the chart and axes, as well as free-floating text anywhere in the chart.

✦ Add error bars and trend lines to a data series.

✦ Display the data points in reverse order.

✦ Rotate a 3D chart to get a better view or to add impact.

✦ Replace line-chart markers with bitmaps.

Before you modify a chart, it's handy to understand the different elements of a chart. The number and type of elements in a chart vary with the type of chart — for example, Pie charts don't have axes, and only 3-D charts have walls and floors.

Modifying a chart is similar to everything else that you do in Excel; first you make a selection (in this case, select a chart element) and then you issue a command to do something with the selection. Unlike a worksheet selection, with a chart selection, you can select only one chart element at a time. The exceptions are elements that consist of multiple parts, such as gridlines. Selecting one gridline selects them all.

Tip You select a chart element by clicking it. The name of the selected item appears in the Name box.

The Chart toolbar, which is displayed when you select a chart, contains a tool called Chart Objects (see Figure 14-1). This is a drop-down list of all the named elements in a chart. Rather than selecting a chart element by clicking it, you can use this list to select the chart element that you want to work with.

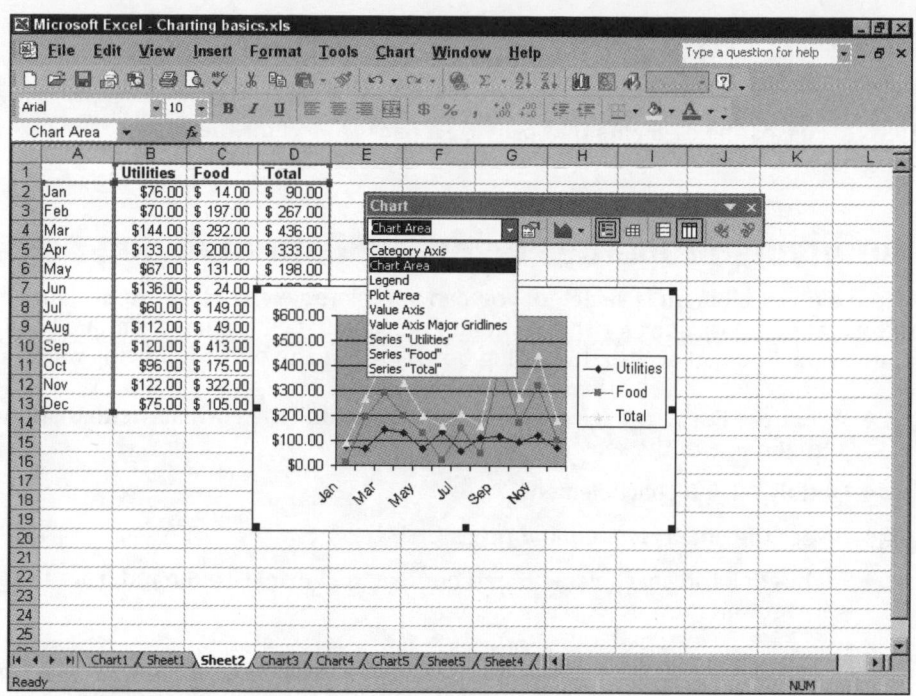

Figure 14-1: The Chart Objects tool in the Chart toolbar provides a handy way to select a chart element.

Tip If the Chart toolbar does not appear when you select a chart, choose View ➪ Toolbars ➪ Chart to display it.

Note Yet another way to select a chart element is to use the keyboard. When a chart is activated, press the up arrow or down arrow to cycle through all parts in the chart. When a data series is selected, press the right arrow or left arrow to select individual points in the series. Excel displays the name of the selected element in the Chart Object tool and highlights the associated item (such as a data series) in the worksheet.

Tip Excel displays the name of each chart element as you allow the mouse pointer to linger briefly over the element.

Changing Basic Chart Elements

As mentioned in the preceding section, a chart consists of many elements. This section discusses the elements that provide a background for the active elements in the chart.

Modifying properties using the Format dialog box

When a chart element is selected, you can access the element's Format dialog box to format or set options for the element. Each chart element has a unique Format dialog box. You can access this dialog box by using any of the following methods:

✦ Select the Format ➪ *selected element* command (the Format menu displays the actual name of the selected part).

✦ Double-click a chart element.

✦ Select the chart element and press Ctrl+1.

✦ Right-click the chart element and choose the Format command from the shortcut menu.

Any of these methods displays a tabbed Format dialog box that enables you to make many changes to the selected chart element. For example, Figure 14-2 shows the dialog box that appears when a data series is selected.

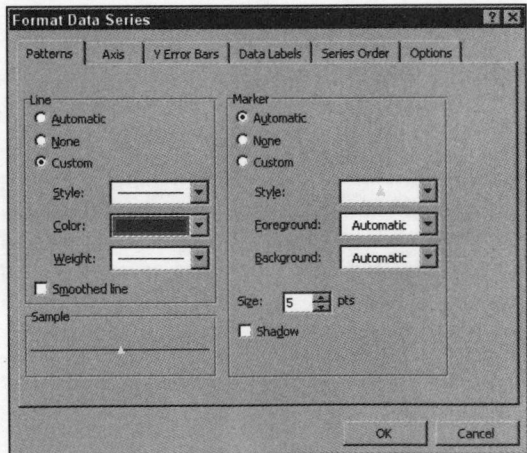

Figure 14-2: Use the Format dialog box to set the properties of a selected chart element.

In the following sections, the details of the various types of chart modifications are discussed in depth.

Modifying the Chart Area

The Chart Area is an object that contains all other elements in the chart. You can think of it as a chart's master background.

The three tabs of the Format Chart Area dialog box and some key points about each are

✦ **Patterns:** Enables you to change the Chart Area's color and patterns (including fill effects) and add a border, if you like.

✦ **Font:** Enables you to change the properties of all fonts used in the chart. Changing the font doesn't affect fonts that you have previously changed, however. For example, if you make the chart's title 20-point Arial and then change the font to 8-point Arial in the Format Chart Area dialog box, the title's font is not affected.

✦ **Properties:** Enables you to specify how the chart is moved and sized with respect to the underlying cells. You also can set the Locked property and specify whether the chart will be printed.

Modifying the Plot Area

The Plot Area is the part of the chart that contains the actual chart. The Format Plot Area dialog box has only one tab: Patterns. This tab enables you to change the color and pattern of the Plot Area and adjust its borders.

Note   When you select a chart element, you'll find that many of the toolbar buttons that you normally use for worksheet formatting also work with the selected chart element. For example, if you select the chart's Plot Area, you can change its color by using the Fill Color tool on the Formatting toolbar. If you select an element that contains text, you can use the Font Color tool to change the color of the text.

Tip   You can resize and reposition the Plot Area by selecting it and then dragging its borders.

Working with chart titles

A chart can have as many as five different titles:

✦ Chart title

✦ Category (X) axis title

✦ Value (Y) axis title

✦ Second category (X) axis title

✦ Second value (Y) axis title

The number of titles that you can use depends on the chart type. For example, a Pie chart supports only a chart title, because it has no axes.

To add titles to a chart, activate the chart and use the Chart ➪ Chart Options command. Excel displays the Chart Options dialog box. Click the Titles tab and enter text for the title or titles (see Figure 14-3).

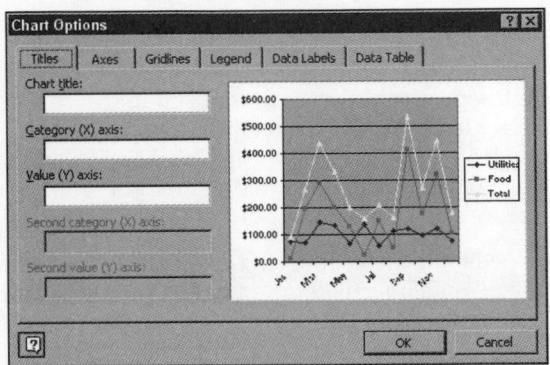

Figure 14-3: Use the Titles tab of the Chart Options dialog box to add titles to a chart.

Tip   You can drag the titles that Excel adds to move them to a different position.

To modify a chart title's properties, access its Format dialog box. This dialog box has the following tabs:

✦ **Patterns:** Change the background color and borders.

✦ **Font:** Change the font, size, color, and attributes.

✦ **Alignment:** Adjust the vertical and horizontal alignment and orientation.

Tip   Text in a chart is not limited to titles. In fact, you can add free-floating text anywhere that you want. To do so, select any part of the chart except a title or data label. Then, type the text in the formula bar and press Enter. Excel adds a Text Box AutoShape that contains the text. You can move the Text Box wherever you want it and format it to your liking.

Working with the legend

A chart's legend consists of text and keys that make it easier to identify the data series. A key is a small graphic that corresponds to the chart's series.

To add a legend to your chart, use the Chart ➪ Chart Options command and then click the Legend tab in the Chart Options dialog box (see Figure 14-4). Place a check mark in the Show legend check box. You also can specify where to place the legend by using the Placement option buttons.

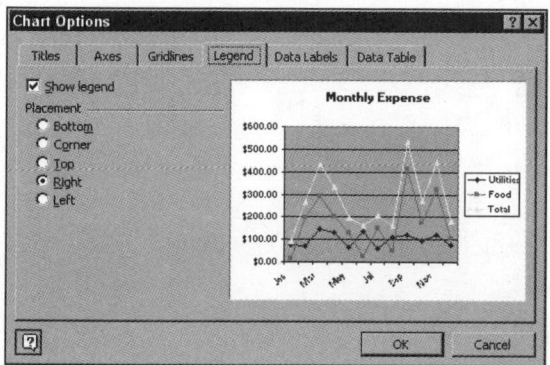

Figure 14-4: Use the Legend tab of the Chart Options dialog box to control the display and placement of the legend that identifies each data series.

The quickest way to remove a legend is to select the legend and then press Delete. To move a legend, click and drag it to the desired location. Or, you can use the legend's Format dialog box to position the legend (using the Placement tab).

You can select individual text items within a legend and format them separately by using the Format Legend Entry dialog box (which has only a single panel: Font). For example, you may want to make the text bold to draw attention to a particular data series.

Tip The Legend tool in the Chart toolbar acts as a toggle. Use this button to add a legend, if one doesn't exist, and to remove the legend, if one exists.

Tip After you move a legend from its default position, you may want to change the size of the Plot Area to fill in the gap left by the legend. Just select the Plot Area and drag a border to make it the desired size.

If you didn't include legend text when you originally selected the cells to create the chart, Excel displays Series 1, Series 2, and so on in the legend. To add series names, choose Chart ➪ Source Data and then select the Series tab in the Source Data dialog box (see Figure 14-5). Select a series from the Series list box, activate the Name box, and then either specify a cell reference that contains the label or directly enter the series name.

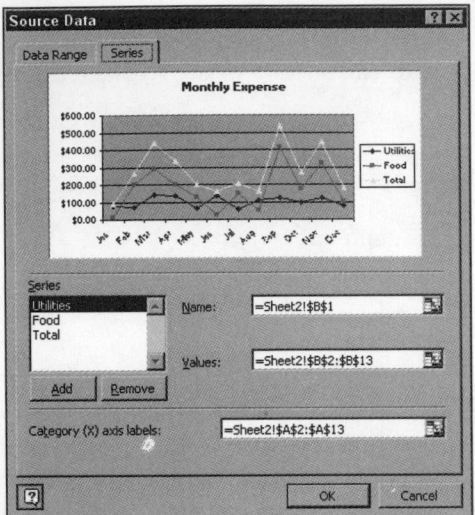

Figure 14-5: Use the Series tab of the Source Data dialog box to change the name of a data series.

Changing the chart gridlines

Gridlines can help you to determine what the chart series represents numerically. Gridlines simply extend the tick marks on the axes. Some charts look better with gridlines; others appear more cluttered. Sometimes, horizontal gridlines alone are enough, although XY charts often benefit from both horizontal and vertical gridlines.

To add or remove gridlines, choose Chart ➪ Chart Options and then select the Gridlines tab. This Chart Options dialog box is shown in Figure 14-6.

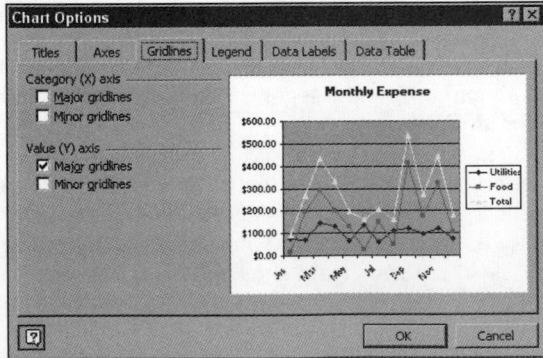

Figure 14-6: Use the Gridlines tab of the Chart Options dialog box to add or remove gridlines.

Each axis has two sets of gridlines: major and minor. Major units display a label. Minor units are located between the labels. You can choose which to add or to remove by checking or unchecking the appropriate check boxes. If you're working with a true 3-D chart, the dialog box has options for three sets of gridlines.

To modify the properties of a set of gridlines, select one gridline in the set and access the Format Gridlines dialog box. This dialog has two tabs:

✦ **Patterns:** Changes the line style, width, and color

✦ **Scale:** Adjusts the scale used on the axis

Cross-Reference   The next section presents an in-depth discussion of scaling.

Modifying the axes

Charts vary in the number of axes that they use. Pie and Doughnut charts have no axes. All 2D charts have two axes (three, if you use a secondary-value axis; four, if you use a secondary-category axis in an XY chart). True 3D charts have three axes. Excel gives you a lot of control over these axes. To modify any aspect of an axis, access its Format Axis dialog box, which has five tabs:

✦ **Patterns:** Change the axis line width, tick marks, and placement of tick mark labels.

✦ **Scale:** Adjust the minimum and maximum axis values, units for major and minor gridlines, and other properties.

✦ **Font:** Adjust the font used for the axis labels.

✦ **Number:** Adjust the number format for the axis labels.

✦ **Alignment:** Specify the orientation for the axis labels.

Because the axes' properties can dramatically affect the chart's look, the Patterns and Scale dialog box tabs are discussed separately, in the following sections.

Modifying the axes patterns

Figure 14-7 shows the Patterns tab of the Format Axis dialog box.

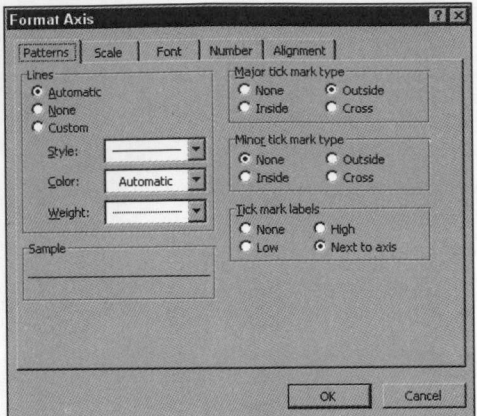

Figure 14-7: Use the Patterns tab of the Format Axis dialog box to control the lines, tick marks, and labels used to identify values.

This tab has four sections:

✦ **Lines:** Controls the line characteristics of the axis (the style, color, and weight of the line).

✦ **Major tick mark type:** Controls how the major tick marks appear. You can select None (no tick marks), Inside (inside the axis), Outside (outside the axis), or Cross (on both sides of the axis).

✦ **Minor tick mark type:** Controls how the minor tick marks appear. You can select the same options as for the major tick marks.

✦ **Tick mark labels:** Controls where the axis labels appear. Normally, the labels appear next to the axis. You can, however, specify that the labels appear High (at the top of the chart), Low (at the bottom of the chart), or not at all (None). These options are useful when the axis doesn't appear in its normal position, at the edge of the Plot Area.

Note   Major tick marks are the axis tick marks that normally have labels next to them. Minor tick marks are between the major tick marks.

Modifying the axes scales

Adjusting the scale of a value axis can dramatically affect the chart's appearance. Manipulating the scale, in some cases, can present a false picture of the data. The actual scale that you use depends on the situation. No hard-and-fast rules exist about scale, except that you shouldn't misrepresent data by manipulating the chart to prove a point that doesn't exist.

Tip   If you're preparing several charts that use similarly scaled data, keeping the scales the same is a good idea, so that the charts can be compared more easily.

Excel automatically determines the scale for your charts. You can, however, over-ride Excel's choice in the Scale tab of the Format Axis dialog box (see Figure 14-8).

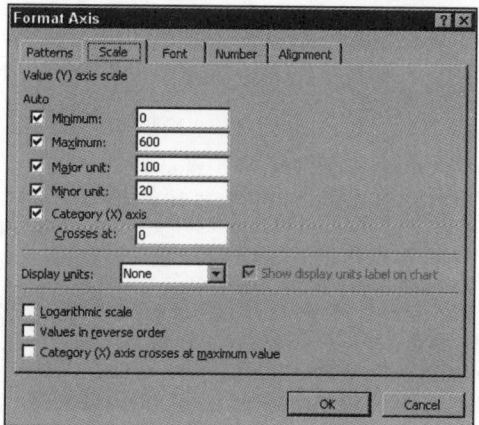

Figure 14-8: Use the Scale tab of the Format Axis dialog box to control the values used on the axis.

Tip

It's often useful to specify a minimum value larger than zero—especially if all of the data values are quite large.

Note

The Scale tab varies slightly, depending on which axis is selected.

This dialog box offers the following options:

✦ **Minimum:** Enter a minimum value for the axis. If the check box is checked, Excel determines this value automatically.

✦ **Maximum:** Enter a maximum value for the axis. If the check box is checked, Excel determines this value automatically.

✦ **Major unit:** Enter the number of units between major tick marks. If the check box is checked, Excel determines this value automatically.

✦ **Minor unit:** Enter the number of units between minor tick marks. If the check box is checked, Excel determines this value automatically.

✦ **Category (X) axis Crosses at:** Position the axis at a different location. By default, it's at the edge of the Plot Area.

✦ **Display units:** Select the unit of measure.

✦ **Show display units label on chart:** Toggles display of the unit on or off.

✦ **Logarithmic scale:** Use a logarithmic scale for the axes. A log scale primarily is useful for scientific applications in which the values to plot have an extremely large range. You receive an error message if the scale includes 0 or negative values.

✦ **Values in reverse order:** Make the scale values extend in the opposite direction. For a value axis, for example, selecting this option displays the smallest scale value at the top and the largest at the bottom (the opposite of how it normally appears).

✦ **Category (X) crosses at maximum value:** Position the axes at the maximum value of the perpendicular axis (normally, the axis is positioned at the minimum value of the perpendicular axis).

Working with Data Series

Every chart consists of one or more data series. This data translates into chart columns, lines, pie slices, and so on. This section discusses most of the customizations that you can perform with a chart's data series.

To work with a data series, you must first select it. Activate the chart and then click the data series that you want to select. In a Column chart, click a column; in a Line chart, click a line; and so on. Make sure that you select the entire series and not just a single point.

Tip   You may find it easier to select the series by using the Chart Object tool in the Chart toolbar.

When you select a data series, Excel displays the series name in the Name box (for example, Series 1, or the actual name of the series), and the SERIES formula in the formula bar. A selected data series has a small square on each element of the series. In addition, the cells used for the selected series are outlined in color.

Many customizations that you perform with a data series use the Format Data Series dialog box, which has as many as seven tabs. The number of tabs varies, depending on the type of chart. For example, a Pie chart has four tabs, and a 3D Column chart has four tabs. Line and Column charts have six tabs, and XY (Scatter) charts have seven tabs. The possible tabs in the Format Data Series dialog box are as follows:

✦ **Patterns:** Change the color, pattern, and border style for the data series. For line charts, change the color and style of the data marker in this tab.

✦ **Axis:** Specify which value axis to use for the selected data series. This is applicable only if the chart has two value axes.

✦ **Y Error Bars:** Add or modify error bars for the Y axis.

✦ **Data Labels:** Display labels next to each data point.

✦ **Series Order:** Specify the order in which the data series are plotted.

✦ **Options:** Change options specific to the chart type.

✦ **Shape:** Specify the shape of the columns (in 3D Column charts only).

✦ **X Error Bars:** Add or modify error bars for the X axis. This is available only for XY charts.

The sections that follow discuss many of these dialog box options.

Deleting a data series

To delete a data series in a chart, select the data series and press the Delete key. The data series is removed from the chart. The data in the worksheet, of course, remains intact.

Note   You can delete all data series from a chart. If you do so, the chart appears empty. It retains its settings, however. Therefore, you can add a data series to an empty chart, and it again looks like a chart.

Adding a new data series to a chart

A common need is to add another data series to an existing chart. You could re-create the chart and include the new data series, but usually, adding the data to the existing chart is easier. Excel provides several ways to add a new data series to a chart:

✦ Activate the chart and select Chart ⇨ Source Data. In the Source Data dialog box, click the Series tab. Click the Add button and then specify the data range in the Values box (you can enter the range address or point to it).

✦ Select the range to add and drag it into the chart. When you release the mouse button, Excel updates the chart with the data that you dragged in. This technique works only if the chart is embedded on the worksheet.

✦ Select the range to add and copy it to the clipboard. Then, activate the chart and choose Edit ⇨ Paste Special. Excel responds with the Paste Special dialog box shown in Figure 14-9. Complete this dialog box to correspond to the data that you selected.

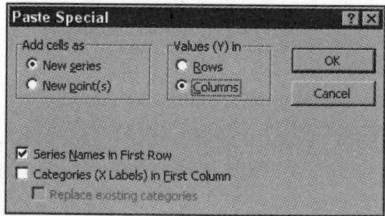

Figure 14-9: Use the Paste Special dialog box to add a new data series to your chart.

Changing data used by a series

You may find that you need to modify the range that defines a data series. For example, you may need to add new data points or remove old ones from the data set.

The following sections describe several ways to change the range used by a data series.

Changing the data range by dragging the range outline

The easiest way to change the data range for a data series is to drag the range outline. This technique works only for embedded charts. When you select a series, Excel outlines the data range used by that series. You can drag the small dot in the lower-right corner of the range outline to extend or contract the data series. Figure 14-10 shows an example of how this looks.

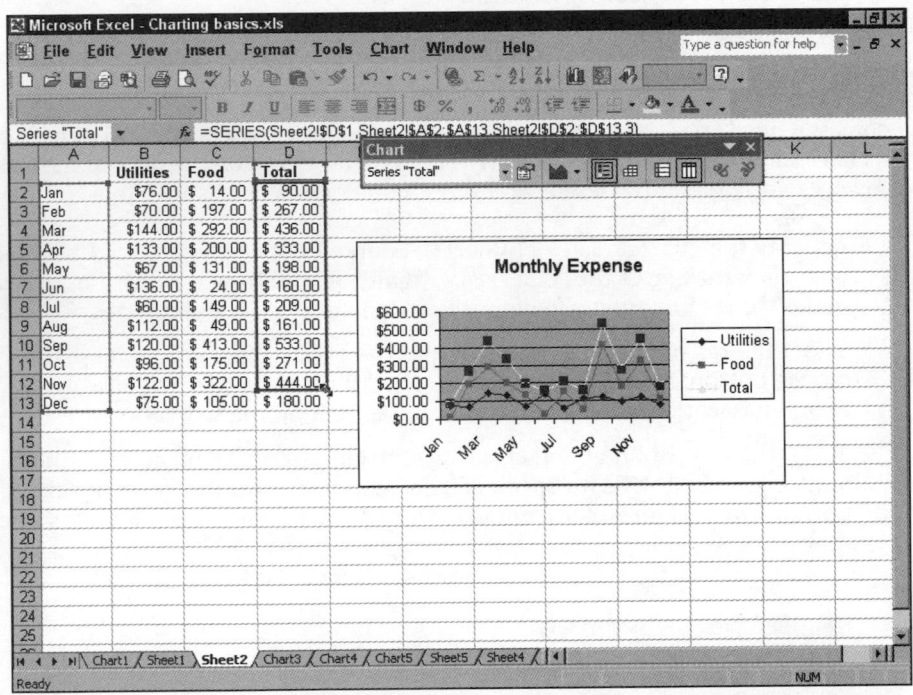

Figure 14-10: To change the range used in a chart's data series, select the data series and drag the small dot at the lower-right corner of the range outline.

Using the Data Source dialog box

Another way to update the chart to reflect a different data range is to activate the chart and select Chart ➪ Source Data. Click the Series tab and then select the series from the Series list box. Adjust the range in the Name box (you can edit the range reference or point to the new range).

Editing the SERIES formula

Every data series in a chart has an associated SERIES formula, which appears in the formula bar when you select a data series in a chart (see Figure 14-11). You can edit the range references in the SERIES formula directly.

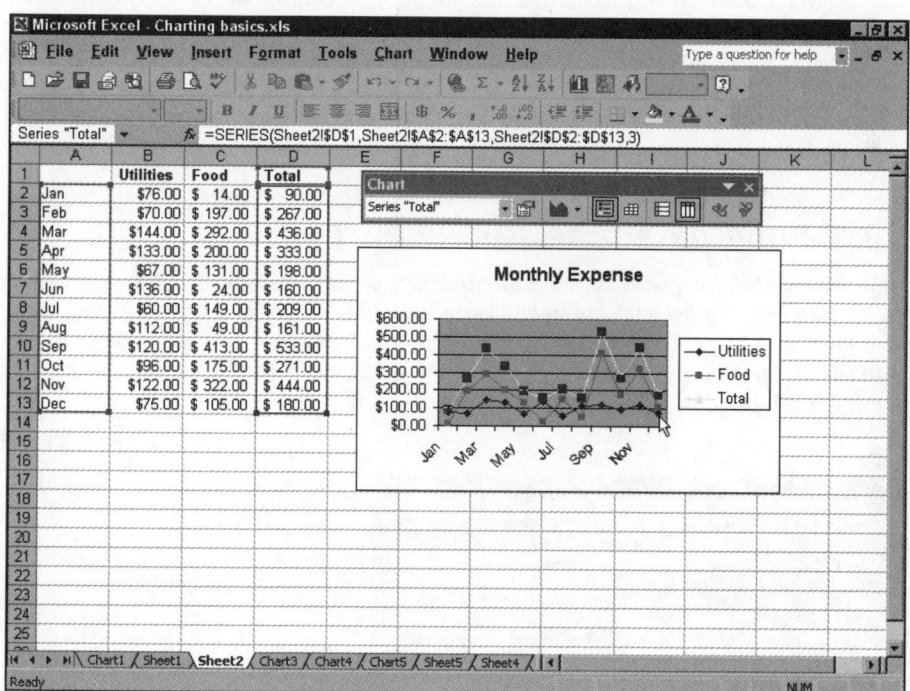

Figure 14-11: When you select a data series, its SERIES formula appears in the formula bar.

A SERIES formula consists of a SERIES function with four arguments. The syntax is as follows:

```
=SERIES(Name_ref,Categories,Values,Plot_order)
```

Excel uses absolute cell references in the SERIES function. To change the data that a series uses, edit the cell references (third argument) in the formula bar. The first and second arguments are optional and may not appear in the SERIES formula. If the series doesn't have a name, the Name_ref argument is missing and Excel uses dummy series names in the legend (Series1, Series2, and so on). If no category names exist, the Categories argument is missing, and Excel uses dummy labels (1, 2, 3, and so on).

Caution   If the data series uses category labels, make sure that you adjust the reference for the category labels also. This is the second argument in the SERIES formula.

Tip   Perhaps the best way to handle data ranges that change over time is to use named ranges. Create names for the data ranges that you use in the chart and then edit the SERIES formula. Replace each range reference with the corresponding range name. After making this change, the chart uses the named ranges. If you add new data to the range, just change the definition for the name, and the chart is updated.

Displaying data labels in a chart

Sometimes, you may want your chart to display the actual data values for each point. You specify data labels in the Data Labels tab of the Chart Options dialog box (see Figure 14-12). This tab has several options. Note that not all options are available for all chart types. If you select the check box labeled Show legend key next to label, each label displays its legend key next to it.

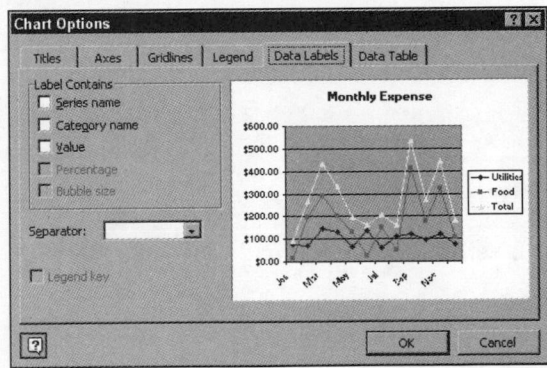

Figure 14-12: Use the Data Labels tab of the Chart Options dialog box to add labels next to the data values.

The data labels are linked to the worksheet, so if your data changes, the labels also change. If you want to override the data label with other text, select the label and enter the new text (or even a cell reference) in the formula bar.

 **Tip** Often, you'll find that the data labels aren't positioned properly—for example, a label may be obscured by another data point. If you select an individual label, you can drag the label to a better location.

Handling missing data

Sometimes, data that you're charting may be missing one or more data points. Excel offers several ways to handle the missing data. You don't control this in the Format Data Series dialog box (as you might expect). Rather, you must select the chart, choose Tools ➪ Options, and then click the Chart tab, which is shown in Figure 14-13.

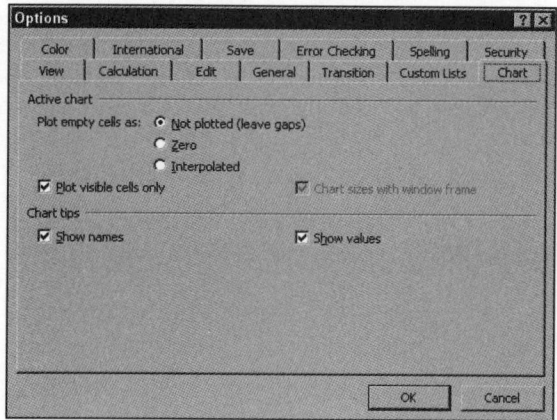

Figure 14-13: Use the Chart tab of the Options dialog box to control the display of missing data values.

The options that you set apply to the entire active chart, and you can't set a different option for different series in the same chart.

The following are the options in the Chart panel for the active chart:

✦ **Not plotted (leave gaps):** Missing data is simply ignored, and the data series will have a gap. This is the default.

✦ **Zero:** Missing data is treated as zero.

✦ **Interpolated:** Missing data is calculated by using data on either side of the missing point(s). This option is available only for Line charts.

Controlling a data series by hiding data

Usually, Excel doesn't plot data that is in a hidden row or column. You can sometimes use this to your advantage, because it's an easy way to control what data appears in the chart. If you're working with outlines or data filtering (both of which use hidden rows), however, you may not like the idea that hidden data is removed from your chart. To override this, activate the chart and select the Tools ➪ Options command. In the Options dialog box, click the Chart tab and remove the check mark from the check box labeled Plot visible cells only.

Cross-Reference   See Chapter 25 to learn about worksheet outlining.

Adding error bars

For certain chart types, you can add error bars to your chart. Error bars often are used to indicate "plus or minus" information that reflects uncertainty in the data. Error bars are appropriate only for Area, Bar, Column, Line, and XY charts. Click the Y Error Bars tab in the Format Data Series dialog box to display the options shown in Figure 14-14.

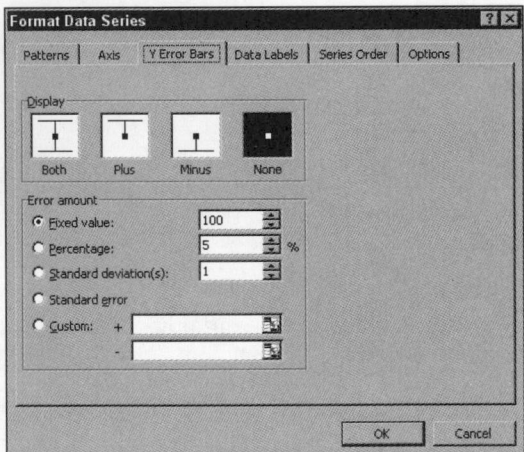

Figure 14-14: Use the Y Error Bars tab of the Format Data Series dialog box to control the display of error bars on your chart.

Tip   A data series in an XY chart can have error bars for both the X and Y values.

Excel enables you to specify several types of error bars:

✦ **Fixed value:** The error bars are fixed by an amount that you specify.

✦ **Percentage:** The error bars are a percentage of each value.

✦ **Standard deviation(s):** The error bars are in the number of standard-deviation units that you specify (Excel calculates the standard deviation of the data series).

✦ **Standard error:** The error bars are one standard error unit (Excel calculates the standard error of the data series).

✦ **Custom:** You set the error bar units for the upper or lower error bars. You can enter either a value or a range reference that holds the error values that you want to plot as error bars.

Adding a trend line

When you're plotting data over time, you may want to plot a trend line that describes the data. A trend line points out general trends in your data. In some cases, you can forecast future data with trend lines. A single series can have more than one trend line.

Excel makes adding a trend line to a chart quite simple. Select Chart ➪ Add Trendline to display the Add Trendline dialog box, shown in Figure 14-15.

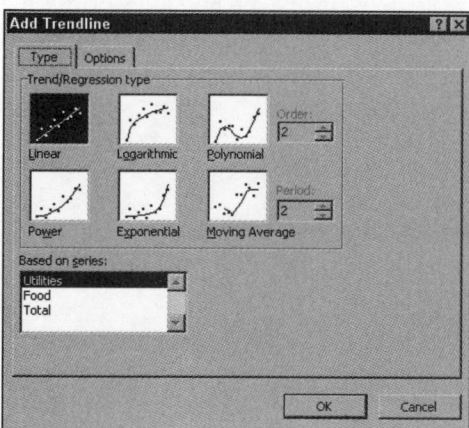

Figure 14-15: Use the Add Trendline dialog box to add a trend line that shows how your data is changing.

The type of trend line that you choose depends on your data. Linear trends are most common, but some data can be described more effectively with another type. One of the options on the Type tab is Moving average, which is useful for smoothing out "noisy" data. The Moving average option enables you to specify the number of data points to include in each average. For example, if you select 5, Excel averages every five data points.

The Options tab of the dialog box enables you to specify a name to appear in the legend and the number of periods that you want to forecast. Additional options let you set the intercept value, specify that the equation used for the trend line should appear on the chart, and choose whether the R-squared value appears on the chart.

Creating Custom Chart Types

You may sometimes feel that Excel's standard charts simply don't express quite the impression that you'd like for your charting needs. If so, you can create your own custom chart types or use one of the existing custom charts.

The first step in designing a custom chart type is to create a chart that's customized the way that you want. For example, you can set any of the colors, fill effects, or line styles; change the scales; modify fonts and type sizes; add gridlines; add a formatted title; and even add free-floating text or graphic images.

When you're satisfied with the chart, choose Chart ➪ Chart Type to display the Chart Type dialog box. Click the Custom Types tab and then select the User-defined option. This displays a list of all user-defined custom chart types.

Click the Add button, which displays the Add Custom Chart Type dialog box, as shown in Figure 14-16. Enter a name for the new chart type and a description. Click OK to add your custom chart type to the list.

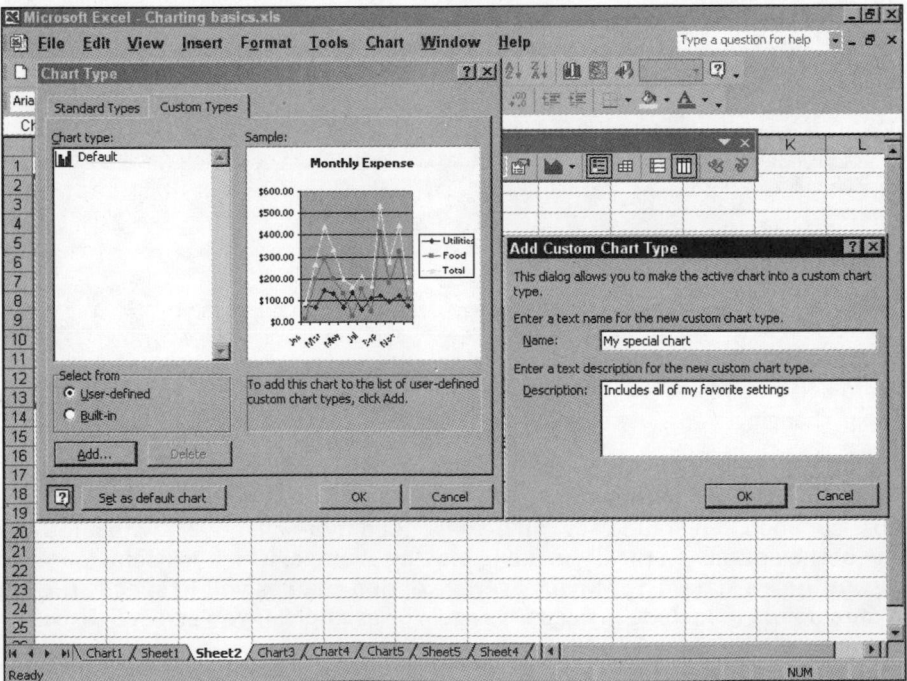

Figure 14-16: Use the Add Custom Chart Type dialog box to add your custom chart settings as a new chart type.

Modifying 3-D charts

All 3-D charts have a few additional parts that you can customize. For example, most 3-D charts have a floor and walls, and the true 3-D charts also have an additional axis. You can select these chart elements and format them to your liking. Generally, 3-D formatting options work just like the other chart elements.

One area in which 3-D charts differ from Excel's 2-D charts is in the perspective — or viewpoint — from which you see the chart. By changing the view angle you can see portions of the chart that might otherwise be hidden, thus making the chart easier to understand.

You can rotate a 3-D chart in one of these two ways:

✦ Activate the 3-D chart and choose the Chart ➪ 3-D View command to display the 3-D View dialog box. You can make your rotations and perspective changes by clicking the appropriate controls. The sample that you see in the dialog box is not your actual chart. The displayed sample just gives you an idea of the types of changes that you're making. Make the adjustments and then choose OK to make them permanent (or click Apply to apply them to your chart without closing the dialog box).

✦ Rotate the chart in real time by dragging corners with the mouse. Click one of the corners of the chart. Black handles appear, and the word Corners appears in the Name box. You can drag one of these black handles and rotate the chart's 3-D box to your satisfaction.

Creating combination charts

A combination chart is a single chart that consists of series that use different chart types. For example, you may have a chart that shows both columns and lines. A combination chart also can use a single type (all columns, for example), but include a second value axis. A combination chart requires at least two data series.

Creating a combination chart simply involves changing one or more of the data series to a different chart type. Select the data series and then choose Chart ➪ Chart Type. In the Chart Type dialog box, select the chart type that you want to apply to the selected series. Figure 14-17 shows an example of a combination chart.

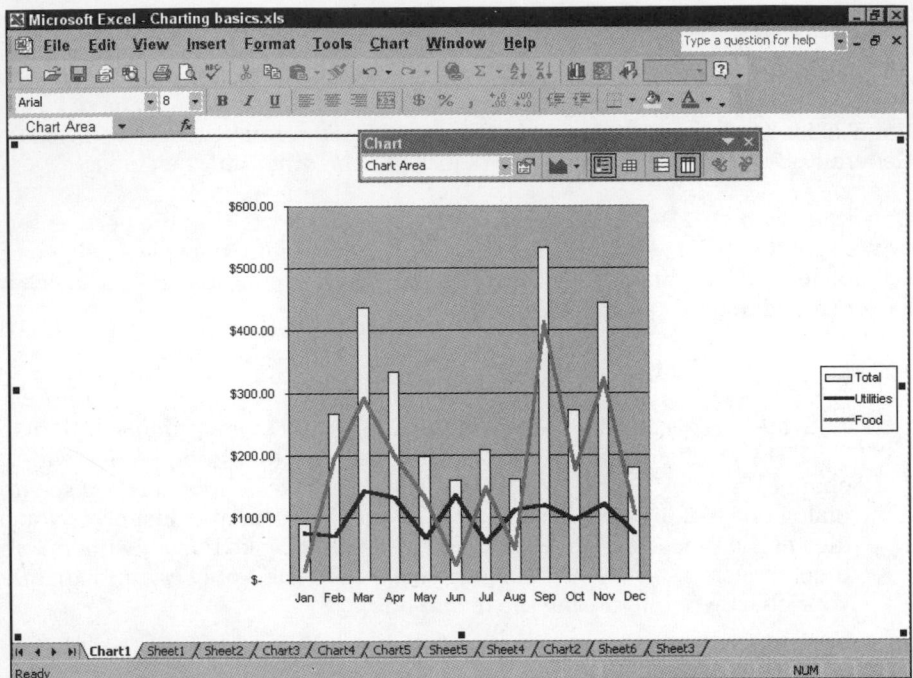

Figure 14-17: You can create a combination chart that uses more than one chart type to display the data.

Note   In some cases, you can't combine chart types. For example, you can't combine a 2-D chart type with a 3-D chart type. If you choose an incompatible chart type for the series, Excel lets you know.

Tip   You can't create combination 3-D charts, but if you use a 3-D Column or 3-D Bar chart, you can change the shape of the columns or bars. Select a series and access the Format Data Series dialog box. Click the Shape tab and then choose the shape for the selected series.

Using secondary axes

If you need to plot data series that have drastically different scales, you probably want to use a secondary scale. For example, assume that you want to create a chart that shows monthly sales, along with the average amount sold per customer. These two data series use different scales (the average sales values are much smaller than the total sales). Consequently, the average sales data range is virtually invisible in the chart.

The solution is to use a secondary axis for the second data series. Because the two axes can have different scales, you can make both data sets visible on a single chart.

To specify a secondary axis, select the data series in the chart and then access the Format Data Series dialog box. Click the Axis tab and choose the Secondary axis option.

Displaying a data table

In some cases, you may want to display a data table, which displays the chart's data in tabular form, directly in the chart.

To add a data table to a chart, choose Chart ⇨ Chart Options and select the Data Table tab in the Chart Options dialog box. Place a check mark next to the option labeled Show data table. You also can choose to display the legend keys in the data table. Figure 14-18 shows a chart with a data table.

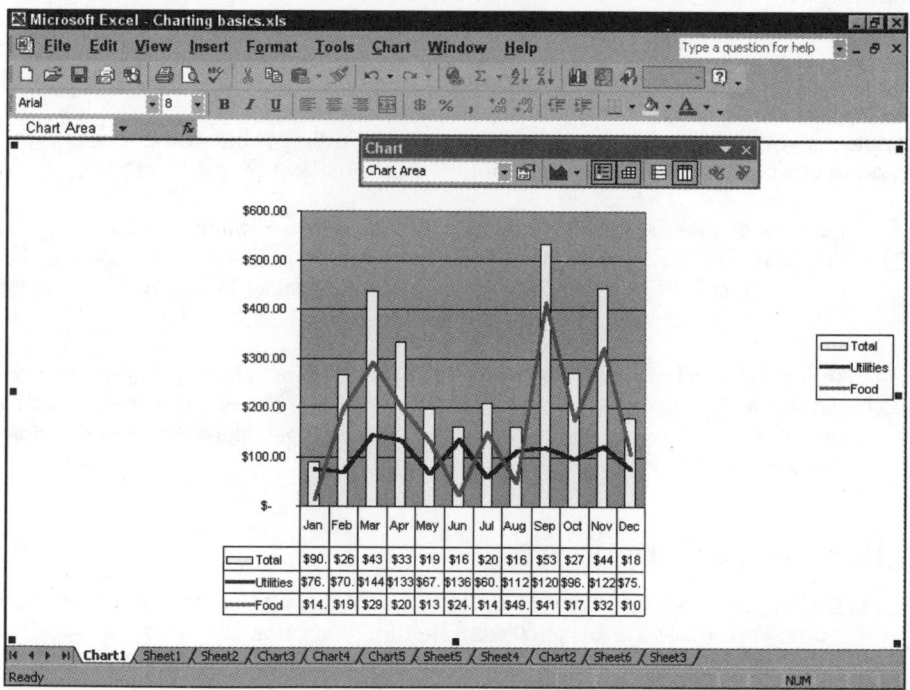

Figure 14-18: You can include a data table to make it easier to understand the values being charted.

To adjust the formatting or font used in the data table, access the Format Data Table dialog box.

Tip If you include the legend keys in the data table you can delete the separate data legend to provide more space for the plot area.

Learning Some Chart-Making Tricks

This section teaches you some interesting chart-making tricks. Some of these tricks use little-known features, and several tricks enable you to make charts that you may have considered impossible to create.

Changing a worksheet value by dragging

Excel provides an interesting chart-making feature that also can be somewhat dangerous. This feature lets you change the value in a worksheet by dragging the data markers on two-dimensional Line charts, Bar charts, Column charts, XY charts, and Bubble charts.

Here's how it works. Select an individual data point in a chart series (not the entire series) and then drag the point in the direction in which you want to adjust the value. As you drag the data marker, the corresponding value in the worksheet changes to correspond to the data point's new position on the chart.

Cross-Reference If the value of a data point that you move is the result of a formula, Excel displays the Goal Seek dialog box (goal seeking is discussed in Chapter 23). Use this dialog box to specify the cell that Excel should adjust to make the formula produce the result that you pointed out on the chart.

Caution This technique is useful if you know what a chart should look like and you want to determine the values that will produce the chart. Obviously, this feature also can be dangerous, because you inadvertently can change values that you shouldn't — so be careful.

Creating picture charts

Excel makes it easy to incorporate a pattern, texture, or graphic file for elements in your chart. Figure 14-19 shows an example of a chart that displays a graphic.

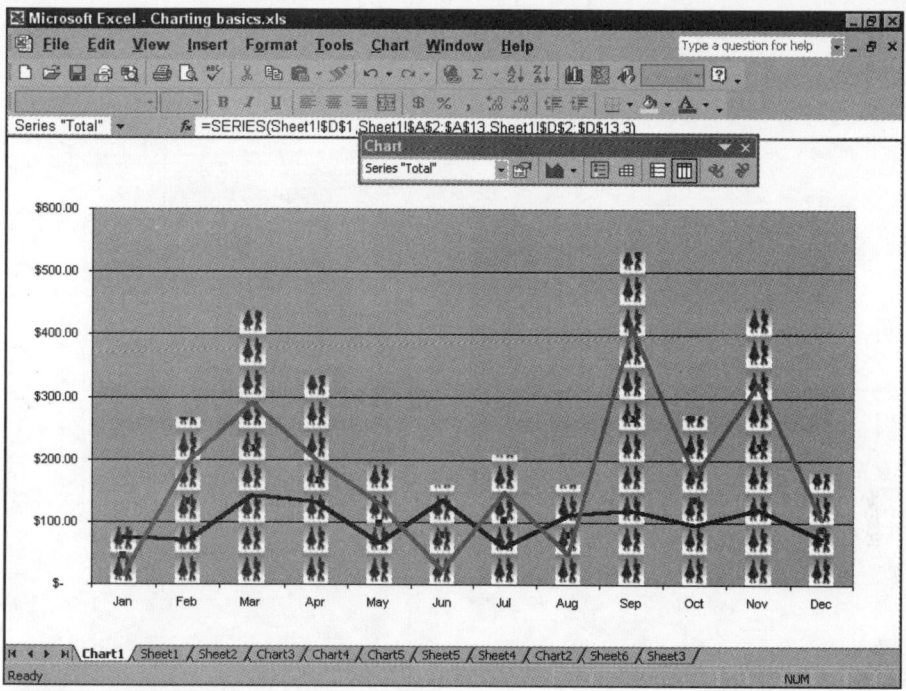

Figure 14-19: You can include graphic images in the columns of a chart.

To convert a data series to pictures, start with a Column or Bar chart (either standard or 3-D). Then, access the chart's Format Data Series dialog box and select the Patterns tab. Click the Fill Effects button to get the Fill Effects dialog box. Click the Picture tab and then click the Select Picture button to locate the graphics file that you want to use. You'll probably find that you need to play around with the settings to make your graphics work out the way you'd like.

Creating comparative histograms

With a bit of creativity, you can create charts that you may have considered impossible with Excel. For example, Figure 14-20 shows a comparative histogram chart. Such charts often display population data.

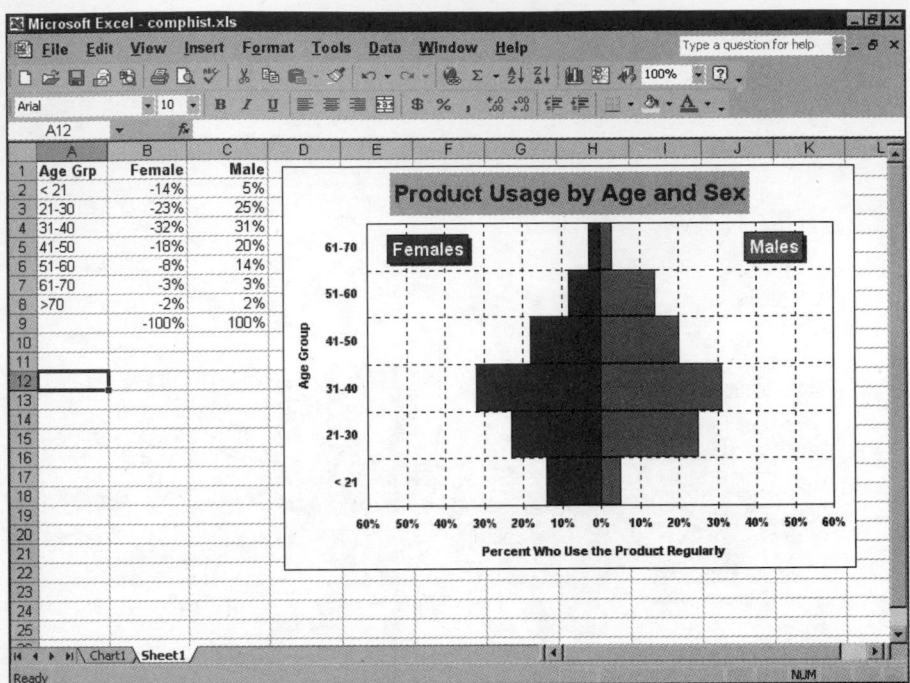

Figure 14-20: With a little ingenuity you can create charts such as this comparative histogram.

Here's how to create the chart:

1. Enter the data as shown in Figure 14-20. Notice that the values for females are entered as negative values.

2. Select A1:C8 and create a 2-D bar chart. Use the subtype labeled Clustered Bar.

3. Apply the following custom number format to the horizontal axis: 0%;0%;0%. This custom format eliminates the negative signs in the percentages.

4. Select the vertical axis and access the Format Axis dialog box. Click the Patterns tab and remove all tick marks. Set the Tick mark labels option to Low. This keeps the axis in the center of the chart but displays the axis labels at the left side.

5. Select either of the data series and then access the Format Data Series dialog box. Click the Options tab and set the Overlap to 100 and the Gap width to 0.

6. Add two text boxes to the chart (Females and Males), to substitute for the legend.

7. Apply other formatting, as desired.

Creating charts that update automatically

If you often need to adjust your data ranges so that your charts plot an updated data range, you might be interested in a trick that forces Excel to update the chart's data range whenever you add new data to your worksheet.

To force Excel to update your chart automatically when you add new data, follow these steps:

1. Create a worksheet similar to the one shown in Figure 14-21.

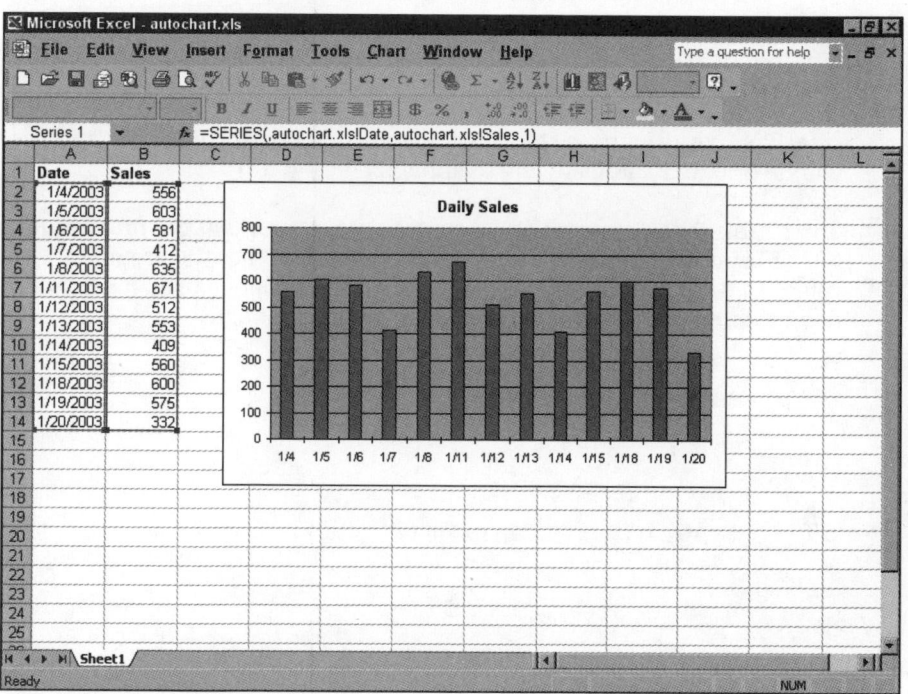

Figure 14-21: This chart is updated automatically whenever you add new data to columns A and B.

2. Select Insert ➪ Name ➪ Define to bring up the Define Name dialog box. In the Names in workbook field, enter Date. In the Refers to field, enter this formula:

```
=OFFSET(Sheet1!$A$2,0,0,COUNTA(Sheet1!$A:$A)-1)
```

3. Click Add. Notice that the OFFSET function refers to the first data point (cell A2) and uses the COUNTA function to get the number of data points in the column. Because column A has a heading in row 1, the formula subtracts 1 from the number.

4. Type **Sales** in the Names in workbook field, and in the Refers to field enter

   `=OFFSET(Sheet1!$B$2,0,0,COUNTA(Sheet1!$B:$B)-1)`

5. Click Add and then OK to close the dialog box.

6. Activate the chart and select the data series. In this example, the formula in the formula bar will read

   `=SERIES(Sheet1!$B$1,Sheet1!$A$2:$A$10,Sheet1!$B$2:$B$10,1)`

7. Replace the range references with the names that you defined in Steps 2 and 4. The formula should read

   `=SERIES(,Sheet1!Date,Sheet1!Sales,1)`

Note   Once you name the workbook, Excel may show the workbook name in the formula.

After you perform these steps, when you add data to columns A and B, the chart will be updated automatically to show the new data.

To use this technique for your own data, make sure that the first argument for the `OFFSET` function refers to the first data point, and that the argument for `COUNTA` refers to the entire column of data. Also, if the columns used for the data contain any other entries, `COUNTA` will return an incorrect value.

✦   ✦   ✦

Enhancing Your Work with Pictures and Drawings

The last two chapters taught you how to add one type of graphical element — charts — to your Excel worksheets. But charts aren't the only way to add some visual interest. In this chapter, you learn how to add some additional graphical elements to make your worksheets even more interesting.

This chapter discusses three major types of images:

◆ Bitmap and line-art graphics imported directly into a workbook or copied from the clipboard

◆ Objects created by using Excel's drawing tools

◆ Objects inserted by using other Microsoft Office tools, such as WordArt and Organization Chart

Using Imported Graphics in Your Worksheets

At times you may feel like dressing up your worksheets by using a graphics image that you imported into Excel. For example, you might be producing a report and would like to include your company logo in the report. Or maybe you want to include some product photos to make it easier for people to understand which products are selling and which ones are just sitting on the shelf.

Excel can import a wide variety of graphics files into a worksheet. You have a choice of methods for importing graphics files. You can

✦ Use the Insert Clip Art task pane to locate and insert an image.

✦ Copy and paste the image by using the Windows clipboard.

✦ Import the image from a digital camera or scanner.

Using the Insert Clip Art task pane to add images

The Insert Clip Art task pane is a new feature in Excel 2002. This task pane makes it easy for you to add images from the Media Gallery and from your own images that you have stored on your PC.

 **Note**
The Insert Clip Art task pane also enables you to open the Media Gallery and work directly in the Media Gallery to locate and insert images. You will likely find, however, that the Insert Clip Art task pane is much easier to use because it acts as a very effective filter for the Media Gallery so that you can more quickly find just the graphic file you need without wading through thousands of images manually.

You access the Insert Clip Art task pane (see Figure 15-1) by selecting the Insert ⇨ Picture ⇨ Clip Art command.

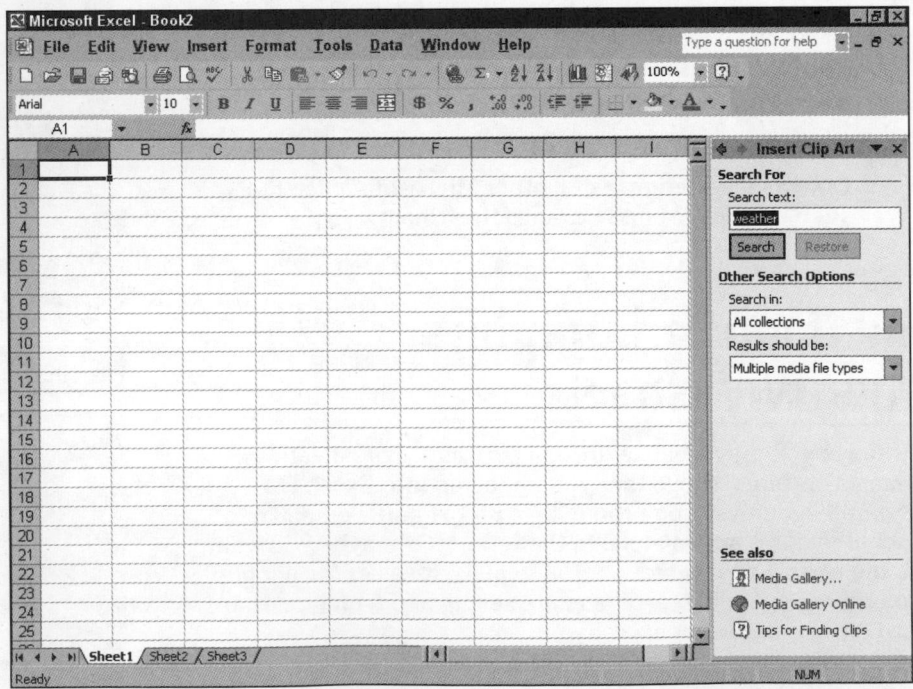

Figure 15-1: The Insert Clip Art task pane enables you to insert pictures, sounds, or video.

To locate an image, enter a search phrase in the Search text box and then click the Search button. The Insert Clip Art task pane will display any graphics that have keywords that match your search phrase.

You can modify your search to limit the results to specific types of images using the Search in and Results should be list boxes. For example, you can open the Results should be list box and limit the search so that only certain formats of clip art are included in the results.

After the Insert Clip Art task pane displays the results, you can choose the specific image that you wish to use. For example, Figure 15-2 shows some clip art images that were selected using "weather" as the search text. To add the image to your worksheet, click the bar that appears along the right edge of the image when the mouse pointer is over the image and choose Insert from the menu.

Tip   If you discover that you often use the same images, select Copy to Collection from the pop-up menu. Then, when you want to use those images in the future, you can limit the search to your collection of favorite images using the Search in list box.

If you select the Insert option, the image is embedded in your worksheet. You can then either select additional images from the Insert Clip Art task pane or close the task pane.

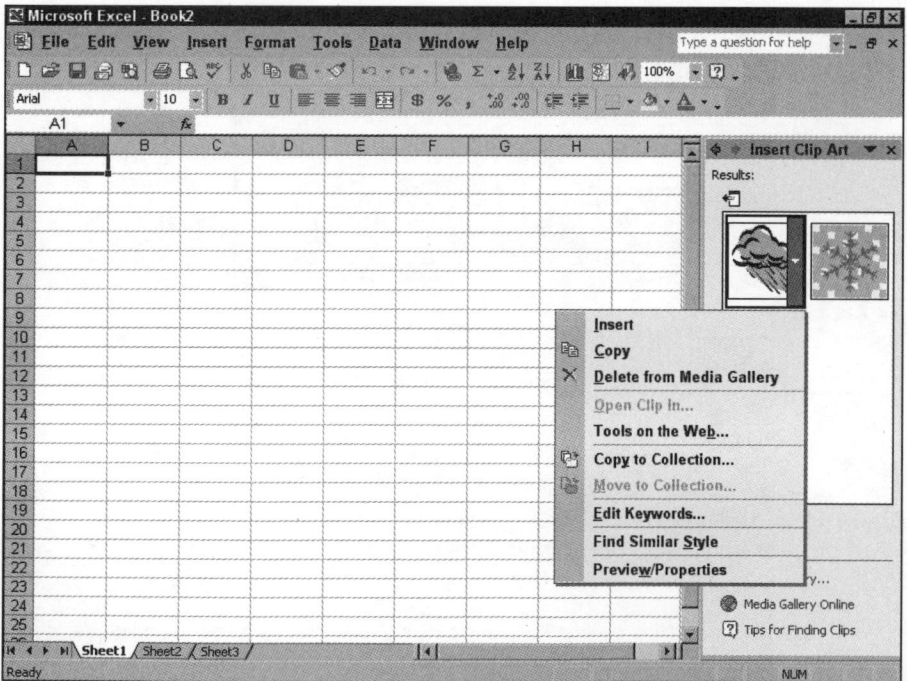

Figure 15-2: The Insert Clip Art task pane displays the images that match your search phrase.

Tip   If you want to use a graphic image for a worksheet's background (similar to wall-paper on the Windows desktop), select Format ➪ Sheet ➪ Background and then select a graphics file. The selected graphics file is tiled on the worksheet. It won't be printed, however.

When an image is selected, Excel displays its Picture toolbar, which contains tools that enable you to adjust the image.

Tip   If you can't find a suitable image, you can go online and browse through the clip art at Microsoft's Web site. In the Insert Clip Art task pane, click the Media Gallery Online button. Your Web browser will be activated, and you can view the images (or listen to the sounds) and download those that you want.

Importing your own graphics files

You can also import graphics files that do not appear in the Insert Clip Art task pane. For example, if you have saved images from your digital camera or scanner, you might want to use some of those images in your worksheets.

If the graphic image that you want to insert is available in a file, you can easily import the file into your worksheet by choosing Insert ➪ Picture ➪ From File. Excel displays the Insert Picture dialog box, shown in Figure 15-3. Select the image you want and click the Insert button to add it to your worksheet.

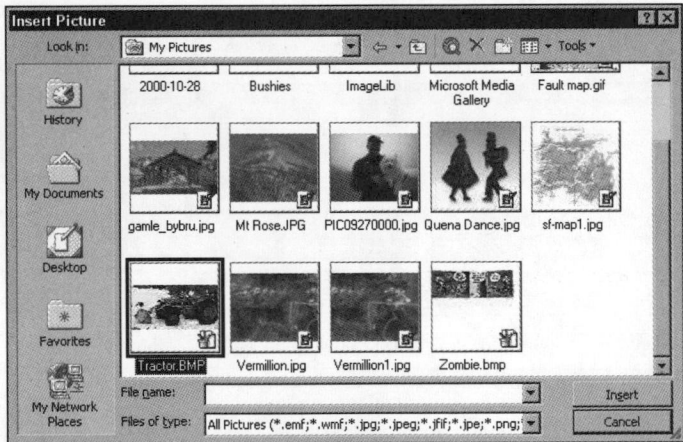

Figure 15-3: The Insert Picture dialog box enables you to insert pictures from your own graphics files.

Tip   If the Insert Picture dialog box does not show previews of the images, click the View button and choose one of the views that previews images.

Adding graphics by using the Clipboard

Another way to import images into an Excel worksheet is by using the Windows Clipboard. This is a useful technique if you have an image that Excel cannot import directly — perhaps because it is in a format that Excel cannot open.

To use the Windows Clipboard, simply copy the image to the Clipboard in whatever program you used to create the image, and then paste it into Excel.

Tip   You can copy the entire screen to the Clipboard by pressing the PrintScreen key, or you can print just the active window (or dialog box) by pressing Alt+PrintScreen.

Importing images from a digital camera or scanner

You can bring in an image directly from a digital camera or a scanner. To use this feature, make sure that your device is connected and set up properly. Then, choose Insert ➪ Picture ➪ From Scanner or Camera. The exact procedure varies, depending on your camera or scanner. For example, Figure 15-4 shows the Capture Pictures from Video dialog box you might see if you have an Intel PC Camera Pro attached to your computer.

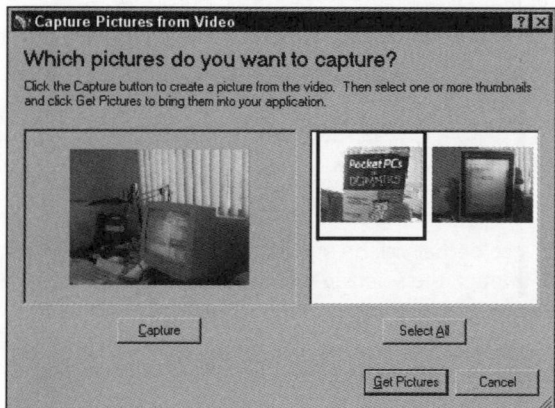

Figure 15-4: You can also import images directly from your scanner or camera.

Modifying pictures after you import them

When you insert a picture on a worksheet, you can modify the picture in various ways by using the Picture toolbar, shown in Figure 15-5. This toolbar appears automatically when you select a picture object. The tools are described in Table 15-1, in left-to-right order on the toolbar.

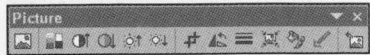

Figure 15-5: You can use the Picture toolbar to modify images you've added to your worksheets.

Table 15-1	
The Tools on the Picture Toolbar	
Tool Name	*What the Tool Does*
Insert Picture from File	Displays the Insert Picture dialog box.
Color	Enables you to change a picture to grayscale, black and white, or a watermark (semitransparent).
More Contrast	Increases the contrast of the picture.
Less Contrast	Decreases the contrast of the picture.
More Brightness	Increases the brightness of the picture.
Less Brightness	Decreases the brightness of the picture.
Crop	Crops the picture. After clicking this tool, drag any of the picture's handles to make the picture smaller.
Rotate Left	Rotates the image 90 degrees counterclockwise.
Line Style	Selects a border for the picture.
Compress Pictures	Reduces the size of images.
Format Picture	Displays the Format Picture dialog box.
Set Transparent Color	Selects a color that will be transparent. Underlying cell contents appear through the selected transparent color. This option is not available for all types of pictures.
Reset Picture	Returns the picture to its original state.

Tip   If you are going to save your worksheets for use on the Web, be sure to use the Compress Pictures tool to reduce the file size so that your Web pages will load more quickly.

Drawing Your Own Graphics

To this point, this chapter has focused on using graphic images from other sources. You can also use the drawing tools built into Excel to create a variety of graphics.

 **Tip** These tools for creating graphics in Excel are also available in the other Microsoft Office applications.

Using the Drawing toolbar

Excel's drawing tools are available on the Drawing toolbar, shown in Figure 15-6. Normally, the Drawing toolbar appears at the bottom of Excel's window, but (as with all toolbars) you can place it anywhere that you like. As you'll see, this toolbar includes more than meets the eye.

Figure 15-6: You can use the Drawing toolbar to create and modify drawings in your worksheets.

 **Tip** Clicking the Drawing tool on the Standard toolbar toggles the Drawing toolbar on and off.

Table 15-2 describes the tools in the Drawing toolbar. The tools are listed in the order in which they appear, from left to right.

Table 15-2		
The Tools on the Drawing Toolbar		
Tool Name	*What the Tool Does*	
Draw	Displays a menu with choices that enable you to manipulate drawn objects.	
Select Objects	Selects one or more graphic objects. If you have several objects and you want to select a group of them, use this tool to drag the outline so that it surrounds all the objects. Click the button again to return to normal selection mode.	
AutoShapes	Displays a menu of seven categories of shapes. Drag this menu to create an AutoShapes toolbar. You also can display the AutoShapes toolbar with the Insert ⇨ Picture ⇨ AutoShapes command.	
Line	Inserts a line.	
Arrow	Inserts an arrow.	
Rectangle	Inserts a rectangle or a square.	
Oval	Inserts an oval or a circle.	

Continued

Table 15-2 *(continued)*

Tool Name	What the Tool Does
Text Box	Inserts a free-floating box into which you type text.
Insert WordArt	Displays the WordArt Gallery dialog box, which enables you to create attractive titles using text. You also can display this dialog box by selecting Insert ➪ Picture ➪ WordArt.
Insert Diagram or Organization Chart	Displays the Diagram Gallery dialog box, which enables you to insert several types of diagrams into your worksheet. You can also display this dialog box with the Insert ➪ Diagram command.
Insert Clip Art	Displays the Insert ClipArt dialog box. You can also display this dialog box with the Insert ➪ Picture ➪ Clip Art command.
Insert Picture From File	Displays the Insert Picture dialog box, which enables you to add images from existing files to your worksheets. You can also display this dialog box with the Insert ➪Picture ➪ From File command.
Fill Color	Select a fill color or fill effect for an object.
Line Color	Select the line color for an object.
Font Color	Select a font color for text objects.
Line Style	Specify the width of the lines in an object.
Dash Style	Specify the style of the lines in an object.
Arrow Style	Specify the arrow style for arrows.
Shadow Style	Specify the type of shadow for an object and settings for the shadow.
3-D Style	Specify the type of perspective effect for an object and settings for the effect.

Drawing AutoShapes

Drawing objects with the AutoShapes tool is quite intuitive. The AutoShapes tool expands to display the following shape categories:

✦ **Lines:** Six styles of lines, including arrows and freehand-drawing capabilities.

✦ **Connectors:** Nine styles of lines designed to indicate connections between other objects. These objects automatically "snap to" other objects.

✦ **Basic Shapes:** Thirty-two basic shapes, including standard shapes, such as boxes and circles, and nonstandard shapes, such as a smiley face and a heart.

✦ **Block Arrows:** Twenty-eight arrow shapes.

✦ **Flowchart:** Twenty-eight shapes suitable for flowchart diagrams.

✦ **Stars and Banners:** Sixteen stars and banners. Stars are handy for drawing attention to a particular cell.

✦ **Callouts:** Twenty callouts, suitable for annotating cells.

✦ **More AutoShapes:** Clicking this button opens the Insert Clip Art task pane and displays various clip art images you can use as AutoShapes.

Click a tool and then drag in the worksheet to create the shape (the mouse pointer changes shape, reminding you that you're in draw mode). When you release the mouse button, the object is selected and its name appears in the Name box (see Figure 15-7).

Tip   Drag the green dot above the center object handle to rotate the object.

Formatting AutoShape objects

You can format the AutoShape objects at any time. First, you must select the object. If the object is filled with a color or pattern, you can click anywhere on the object to select it. If the object is not filled, you must click the object's border.

A Word About the Draw Layer

Every worksheet and chart sheet has as a draw layer an invisible surface that is completely independent of the cells on a worksheet (or the chart on a chart sheet). The draw layer can hold graphic images, drawings, embedded charts, OLE objects, and so on.

Objects placed on the draw layer can be moved, resized, copied, and deleted with no effect on any other elements in the worksheet. Objects on the draw layer have properties that relate to how they are moved and sized when underlying cells are moved and sized. When you right-click a graphic object and choose Format Object from the shortcut menu, you get a tabbed dialog box. Click the Properties tab to adjust how the object moves or resizes with its underlying cells. Your choices are

✦ **Move and size with cells:** If this option is selected, the object appears to be attached to the cells beneath it. For example, if you insert rows above the object, the object moves down. If you increase the column width, the object gets wider.

✦ **Move but don't size with cells:** If this option is checked, the object moves if rows or columns are inserted, but it never changes its size if you change row heights or column widths.

✦ **Don't move or size with cells:** This option makes the object completely independent of the underlying cells.

These options control how an object is moved or sized with respect to the underlying cells.

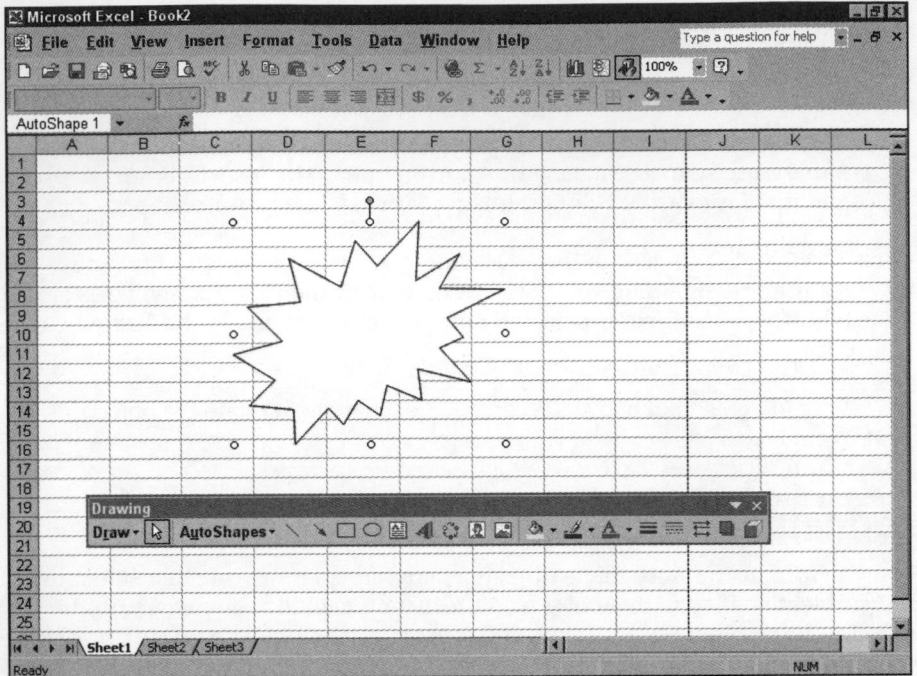

Figure 15-7: You can add AutoShape objects to your worksheets for a quick bit of graphical impact.

Tip   The mouse pointer changes to four arrows pointing outwards when the pointer is in the correct position to select an AutoShape object.

You can make some modifications by using the toolbar buttons — for example, you can change the fill color. Other modifications require that you use the Format AutoShape dialog box. After selecting one or more objects, you can bring up this dialog box by using any of these techniques:

✦ Choose the Format ⇨ AutoShape command.

✦ Press Ctrl+1.

✦ Double-click the object.

✦ Right-click the object and choose Format AutoShape from the shortcut menu.

The Format AutoShape dialog box has several tabs, the number of which depends on the type of object and whether it contains text. Each of these tabs is discussed in the following list.

✦ **Colors and Lines:** Enables you to adjust the colors, lines, and arrows used in the object.

✦ **Size:** Enables you to adjust the size, rotation, and scale of the object.

✦ **Protection:** Determines whether the object is "locked." Locking has no effect, however, unless the worksheet is protected and the Objects option is in effect. You can protect the worksheet with the Tools ➪ Protection ➪ Protect Sheet command.

✦ **Properties:** Determines how an object is moved and sized with respect to the underlying cells.

✦ **Font:** Enables you to apply various font formatting (appears only if the shape contains text).

✦ **Alignment:** Enables you to specify the vertical and horizontal alignment of the text, and choose the orientation (appears only if the shape contains text).

✦ **Margins:** Adjusts the amount of space along the sides of the text (appears only if the shape contains text).

✦ **Web:** If you plan to save your worksheet as a Web page, you can specify some alternative text for the object in this tab. The alternative text appears when the user hovers the mouse pointer over the image in a Web browser.

Changing the order of objects

As you add drawing objects to the draw layer of a worksheet, you'll find that objects are "stacked" on top of each other in the order in which you add them. New objects are stacked on top of older objects.

If you find that an object is obscuring part of another, you can change the order in this stack. Right-click the object and select Order from the shortcut menu. This leads to a submenu with these choices:

✦ **Bring to Front:** Brings the object to the top of the stack.

✦ **Send to Back:** Sends the object to the bottom of the stack.

✦ **Bring Forward:** Brings the object one step higher toward the top of the stack.

✦ **Send Backward:** Sends the object one step lower toward the bottom of the stack.

Grouping objects

Excel enables you to combine two or more drawing objects into a single object, which is known as grouping. For example, if you create a design that uses four separate drawing objects, you can combine them into a group. Then, you can manipulate this group as a single object (move it, resize it, and so on).

To group two or more objects, select all the objects and then right-click. Choose Grouping ➪ Group from the shortcut menu.

Later, if you need to modify one of the objects in the group, you can ungroup them by right-clicking and selecting Grouping ➪ Ungroup from the shortcut menu. This breaks the object into its original components.

Tip   If you have ungrouped a set of objects, you can use the Grouping ➪ Regroup command to add the same set of objects back into the same group.

Aligning objects

When you have several drawing objects on a worksheet, you may want to align these objects with each other. You can either drag the objects (which isn't very precise) or use the automatic alignment options.

To align objects, start by selecting them. Then, click the Draw tool on the Drawing toolbar. This tool expands to show a menu. Select the Align or Distribute menu option, followed by any of the six alignment options: Align Left, Align Center, Align Right, Align Top, Align Middle, or Align Bottom.

Note   Unfortunately, you can't specify which object is used as the basis for the alignment. When you're aligning objects to the left, they are always aligned with the leftmost object. When you're aligning objects to the top, they are always aligned with the topmost object. Alignment in other directions works the same way.

Excel can also "distribute" three or more objects such that they are equally spaced, horizontally or vertically. Select the objects and then click the Draw tool on the Drawing toolbar. This tool expands to show a menu. Select the Align or Distribute menu option, followed by either Distribute Horizontally or Distribute Vertically.

Figure 15-8 shows objects before and after they were aligned to the left and distributed vertically.

Adding shadows and 3D effects

You can apply attractive shadow and 3-D effects to most AutoShapes. Use the Shadow Style and 3-D Style tools on the Drawing toolbar to apply these effects.

To apply either of these effects, select an AutoShape that you've drawn on a worksheet and then click either the Shadow or the 3-D tool. Select an option, and it's applied to the selected shape.

You can adjust the Shadow or 3-D settings by clicking the appropriate tool and then selecting the Shadow Settings or 3-D Settings option. Both of these options display a toolbar that enables you to fine-tune the effect. You'll find that lots of options are available, and they're all quite straightforward. The best way to become familiar with these effects is to experiment.

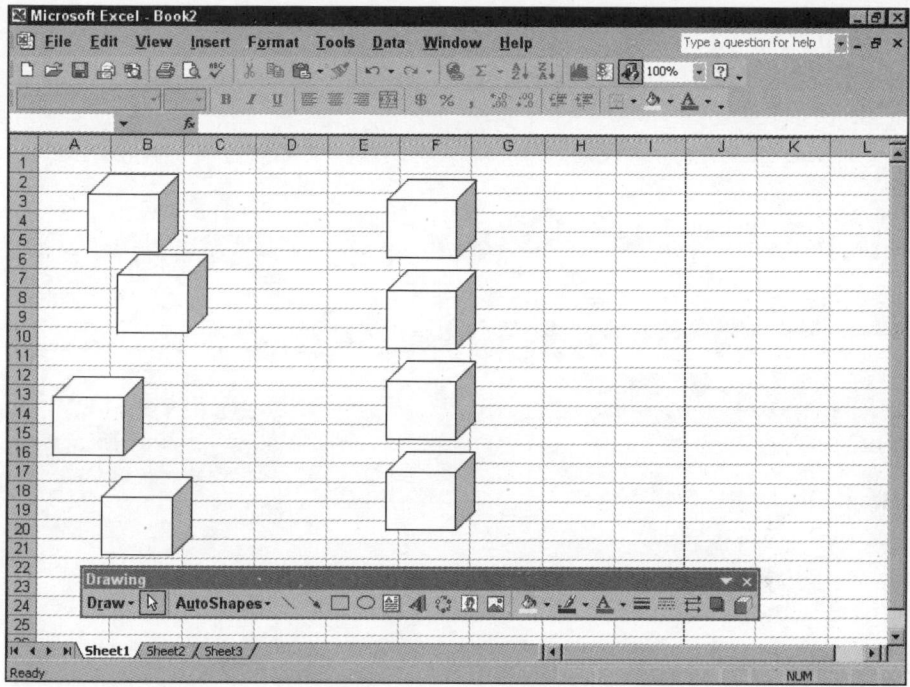

Figure 15-8: You can use the alignment and distribution options to make objects line up for a neater appearance.

Adding a diagram to your worksheet

In addition to basic shapes, Excel has a much more sophisticated tool you can use to add fairly complex diagrams to your worksheets. Figure 15-9 shows an example of a worksheet with an organizational chart diagram added to the worksheet.

To open the Diagram Gallery dialog box, click the Insert Diagram or Organization Chart tool on the Drawing toolbar or select Insert ⇨ Diagram from Excel's menu. Choose the type of diagram to add and click OK. Depending on the type of diagram you add, you will need to fill in a number of text boxes in the diagram object to complete the diagram.

Changing the AutoShape defaults

You can change the default settings for the AutoShapes that you draw. For example, if you prefer a particular text color or fill color, you can set these as the defaults for all new AutoShapes that you draw.

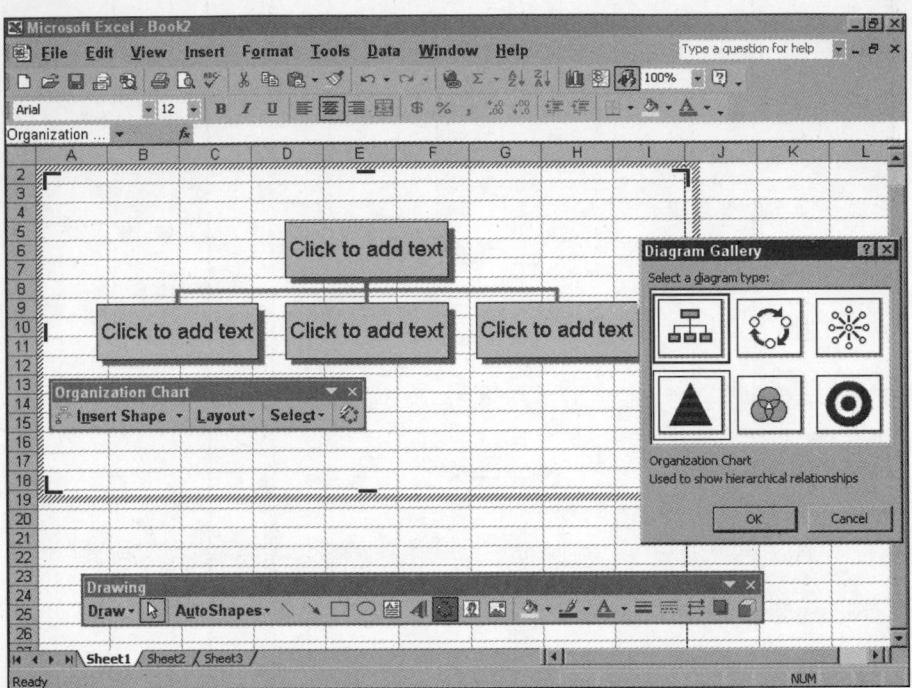

Figure 15-9: You can add several types of diagrams using the Diagram Gallery dialog box.

To change the default settings, create an object and format it as you like. You can change colors, fill effects, line widths and styles, and shadow or 3-D effects. Then, select the formatted object, right-click, and select Set AutoShape Defaults from the shortcut menu. You can also access this command from the Draw tool on the Drawing toolbar (this tool expands to show a menu).

Creating Art from Words by Using WordArt

WordArt is an application that's included with Microsoft Office. You can insert a WordArt image either by using the WordArt tool on the Drawing toolbar or by selecting Insert ➪ Picture ➪ WordArt. Either method displays the WordArt Gallery dialog box (see Figure 15-10). Select a style and then enter your text in the next dialog box. Click OK, and the image is inserted in the worksheet.

When you select a WordArt image, Excel displays the WordArt toolbar. Use these tools to modify the WordArt image. You'll find that you have lots of flexibility with these tools. In addition, you can use the Shadow and 3-D tools to further manipulate the image. Figure 15-11 shows an example of a WordArt image inserted on a worksheet.

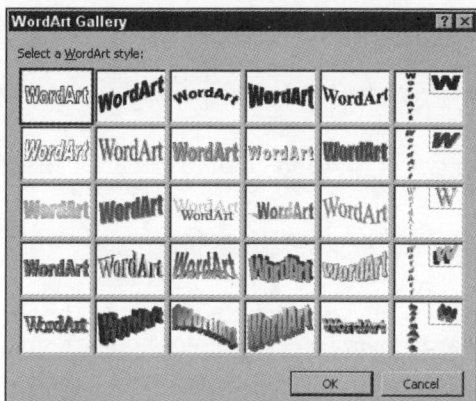

Figure 15-10: Use the WordArt Gallery dialog box to select a general style for your image.

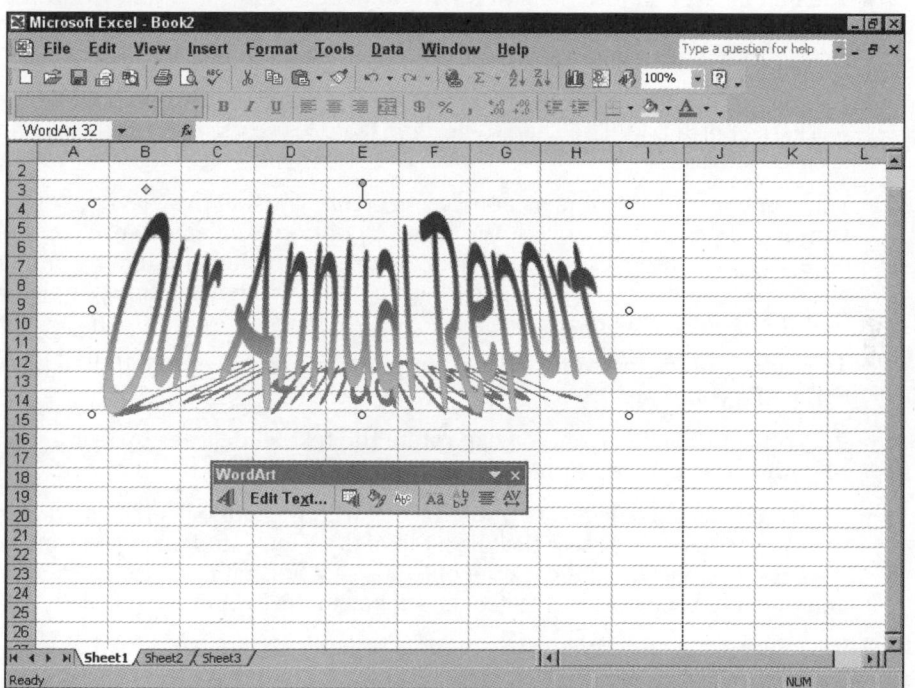

Figure 15-11: You can use WordArt to add text with fancy effects to your worksheets.

Some Useful Drawing Tips

Although drawing objects is quite intuitive, several tips can make this task easier. This section lists some tips and techniques that you should know:

✦ To create an object with the same height and width, press Shift while you draw the object.

✦ To constrain a line or arrow object to angles that are divisible by 15 degrees, press Shift while you draw the object.

✦ To make an object snap to the worksheet row and column gridlines, press the Alt key while you draw the object.

✦ If you press Alt while moving an object, its upper-left corner snaps to the row and column gridlines.

✦ To select multiple objects, press Ctrl while you click them. Or, use the Select Objects tool on the Drawing toolbar to select objects by "lassoing" them.

✦ To select all objects on a worksheet, select Edit ➪ Go To (or press F5) and then click the Special button in the Go To dialog box. Choose the Objects option button and click OK. All objects are selected. Use this technique if you want to delete all objects (select them all and then press Delete).

✦ You can insert text into most of the AutoShapes (the exceptions are the shapes in the Connectors and Lines categories). To add text to a shape, right-click it and select Add Text from the shortcut menu.

✦ You might find that working with drawing objects is easier if you turn off the worksheet grid line. The snap-to-gridline features work, even if the grid lines aren't visible.

✦ You can control how objects appear onscreen by using the View tab of the Options dialog box. Normally, the Show All option is selected. You can hide all objects by choosing Hide All, or display objects as placeholders by choosing Show Placeholders (this may speed up things if you have complex objects that take a long time to redraw).

✦ To copy an object with the mouse, single-click it to select it and then press Ctrl while you drag it.

✦ If an object contains text, you can rotate the text 90 degrees by using the Alignment tab on the Format Object dialog box.

✦ By default, drawn objects are printed along with the worksheet. If you don't want the objects to print, access the Sheet tab of the Page Setup dialog box and select the Draft option. Or, right-click the object, select Format from the shortcut menu, and then uncheck the Print Object check box in the Properties panel.

✦ If you want the underlying cell contents to show through a drawn object, access the Colors and Lines tab in the Format dialog box and then set the Fill option to No Fill. You can also select the Semi-transparent option, which enables you to choose a fill color and have the cell contents show.

✦   ✦   ✦

Introducing Arrays

One of Excel's most interesting (and most powerful) features is its capability to work with arrays in a formula. This chapter introduces the concept of arrays and is required reading for anyone who wants to become a master of Excel formulas.

Understanding Array Formulas

Arrays are a familiar concept to most computer programmers. An array is simply a collection of items that are operated on collectively or individually. In Excel, an array can be one-dimensional or two-dimensional. These dimensions correspond to rows and columns. For example, a one-dimensional array can be stored in a range that consists of one row (a horizontal array) or one column (a vertical array). A two-dimensional array can be stored in a rectangular range of cells. Excel doesn't support three-dimensional arrays.

But, as you'll see, arrays need not be stored in cells. You can also work with arrays that exist only in Excel's memory. You can then use an array formula to manipulate this information and return a result. An array formula can occupy multiple cells, or reside in a single cell.

This section presents two examples of array formulas. One is of an array formula that occupies multiple cells, and the other is of another array formula that occupies only one cell.

Introducing multicell array formulas

Figure 16-1 shows a simple worksheet set up to calculate product sales. Normally, you would calculate the value in column D (total sales per product) with a formula such as the one that follows, and then copy this formula down the column.

```
=B2*C2
```

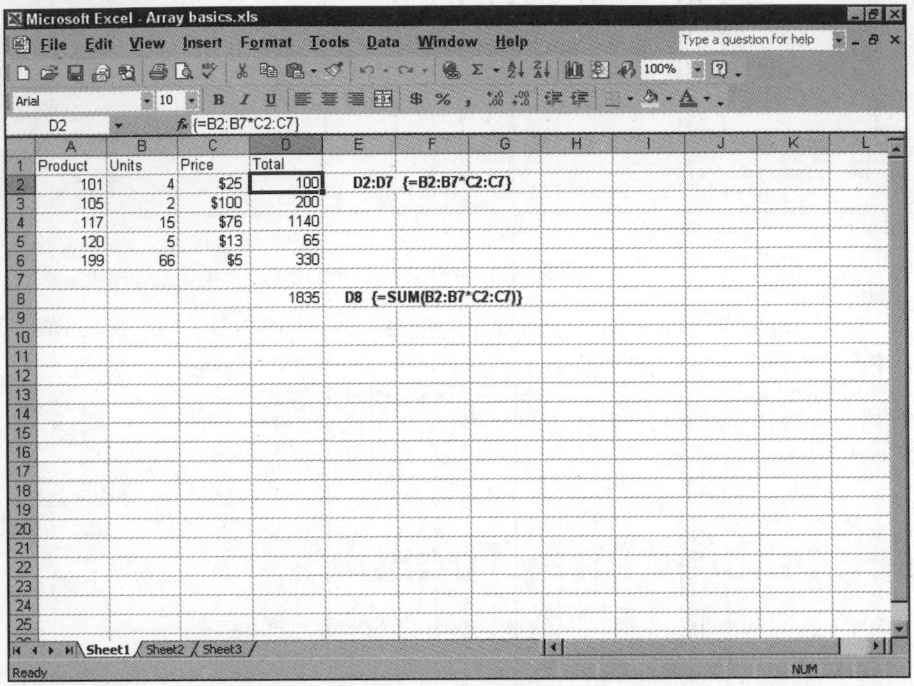

Figure 16-1: The range D2:D7 contains a single array formula that takes the place of six individual formulas.

After copying the formula, the worksheet contains six formulas in column D.

Another alternative uses a single formula (an array formula) to calculate all six values in D2:D7. This single formula occupies six cells and returns an array of six values.

To create a single array formula to perform the calculations, do the following:

1. Select a range to hold the results. In this case, the range is D2:D7.

2. Enter the following formula:

    =B2:B7*C2:C7

3. Press Ctrl+Shift+Enter to enter the formula as an array formula (normally, you press Enter to enter a formula).

The formula is entered into all six of the selected cells. If you examine the formula bar, you'll see the following:

    {=B2:B7*C2:C7}

Excel places brackets around the formula to indicate that it's an array formula.

This formula performs its calculations and returns a six-item array. The array formula actually works with two other arrays, both of which happen to be stored in ranges. The values for the first array are stored in B2:B7, and the values for the second array are stored in C2:C7.

Because it's not possible to display more than one value in a single cell, six cells are required to display the resulting array. That explains why you selected six cells before you entered the array formula.

This array formula, of course, returns exactly the same values as these six normal formulas entered into individual cells in D2:D7:

```
=B2*C2
=B3*C3
=B4*C4
=B5*C5
=B6*C6
=B7*C7
```

Using a single array formula rather than individual formulas does offer several advantages:

✦ It's a good way of ensuring that all formulas in a range are identical.

✦ Using a multicell array formula makes it less likely that you will overwrite a formula accidentally. You cannot change one cell in a multicell array formula.

✦ Using a multicell array formula will almost certainly prevent novices from tampering with your formulas.

Introducing single-cell array formulas

Now, it's time to take a look at a single-cell array formula. Refer again to Figure 16-1. The following array formula occupies a single cell (D8):

```
{=SUM(B2:B7*C2:C7)}
```

You can enter this formula into any cell.

Tip   When you use an array formula, make sure you use Ctrl+Shift+Enter (and don't type the brackets).

This array formula returns the sum of the total product sales. It's important to understand that this formula does not rely on the information in column D. In fact, you can delete the information in column D and the formula will still work.

This formula works with two arrays, both of which are stored in cells. The first array is stored in B2:B7, and the second array is stored in C2:C7. The formula multiplies the corresponding values in these two arrays and creates a new array (which exists only in memory). The SUM function then operates on this new array and returns the sum of its values.

Creating an array constant

The examples in the previous section used arrays stored in worksheet ranges. The examples in this section demonstrate an important concept: An array does not have to be stored in a range of cells. This type of array, which is stored in memory, is referred to as an array constant.

You create an array constant by listing its items and surrounding them with brackets. Here's an example of a five-item vertical array constant:

    {1,0,1,0,1}

The following formula uses the SUM function, with the preceding array constant as its argument. The formula returns the sum of the values in the array (which is 3).

    =SUM({1,0,1,0,1})

Note   When you specify an array directly (as shown previously), you must provide the brackets around the array elements. When you enter an array formula, on the other hand, you do not supply the brackets.

At this point, you probably don't see any advantage to using an array constant. The formula that follows, for example, returns the same result as the previous formula.

    =SUM(1,0,1,0,1)

To see the advantage of using an array constant, look at the following formula that uses two array constants:

    =SUM({1,2,3,4}*{5,6,7,8})

This formula creates a new array (in memory) that consists of the product of the corresponding elements in the two arrays. The new array is

    {5,12,21,32}

This new array is then used as an argument for the SUM function, which returns the result (70). The formula is equivalent to the following formula, which doesn't use arrays:

    =SUM(1*5,2*6,3*7,4*8)

A formula can work with both an array constant and an array stored in a range. The following formula, for example, returns the sum of the values in A1:D1, each multiplied by the corresponding element in the array constant.

    =SUM((A1:D1*{1,2,3,4}))

This formula is equivalent to

```
=SUM(A1*1,B1*2,C1*3,D1*4)
```

An array constant can contain numbers, text, logical values (TRUE or FALSE), and even error values such as #N/A. Numbers can be in integer, decimal, or scientific format. You must enclose text in double quotation marks (for example, "Tuesday"). You can use different types of values in the same array constant, as in this example:

```
{1,2,3,TRUE,FALSE,TRUE,"Moe","Larry","Shemp"}
```

An array constant cannot contain formulas, functions, or other arrays. Numeric values cannot contain dollar signs, commas, parentheses, or percent signs.

Understanding the dimensions of an array

An array can be either one-dimensional or two-dimensional. A one-dimensional array's orientation can be either vertical or horizontal.

Creating one-dimensional horizontal arrays

Commas separate the elements in a one-dimensional horizontal array. The following example is a one-dimensional horizontal array constant:

```
{1,2,3,4,5}
```

To display this array in a range requires five cells in a row. To enter this array into a range, select a range of cells that consists of one row and five columns. Then, enter ={1,2,3,4,5} and press Ctrl+Shift+Enter.

If you enter this array into a horizontal range that consists of more than five cells, the extra cells will contain #NA (which denotes unavailable values). If you enter this array into a vertical range of cells, only the first item (1) will appear in each cell.

Creating one-dimensional vertical arrays

Semicolons separate the elements in a one-dimensional vertical array. The following is a six-element vertical array constant:

```
{10;20;30;40;50;60}
```

Displaying this array in a range requires six cells in a column. To enter this array into a range, select a range of cells that consists of six rows and one column. Then, enter ={10;20;30;40;50;60} and press Ctrl+Shift+Enter.

Creating two-dimensional arrays

A two-dimensional array uses commas to separate its horizontal elements and semicolons to separate its vertical elements. The following example shows a 3×4 array constant.

{1,2,3,4;5,6,7,8;9,10,11,12}

To display this array in a range requires 12 cells. To enter this array into a range, select a range of cells that consists of three rows and four columns. Then, type ={1,2,3,4;5,6,7,8;9,10,11,12} and press Ctrl+Shift+Enter. Figure 16-2 shows how these arrays appear when entered into a worksheet.

Tip   If you enter an array into a range that has more cells than array elements, Excel displays #NA into the extra cells.

Each row of a two-dimensional array must contain the same number of items. The array that follows, for example, is invalid because the third row contains only three items:

{1,2,3,4;5,6,7,8;9,10,11}

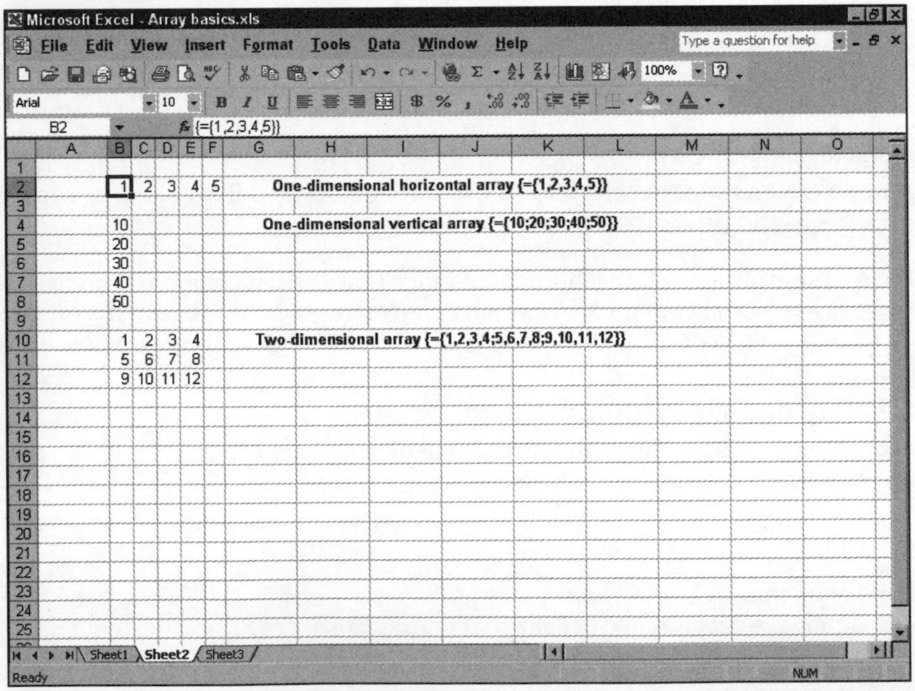

Figure 16-2: Three different types of arrays have been entered into this worksheet.

Naming Array Constants

You can create an array constant, give it a name, and then use this named array in a formula. Figure 16-3 shows a named array being created using the Define Name dialog box. The name of the array is DayNames, and it refers to the following array:

```
{"Sun","Mon","Tue","Wed","Thu","Fri","Sat"}
```

Tip   Technically, a named array is a named formula.

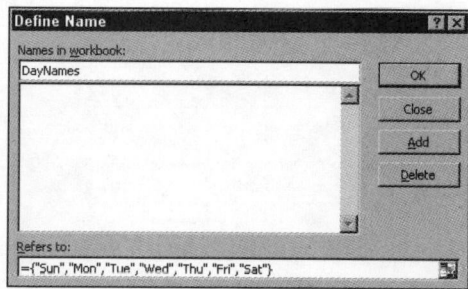

Figure 16-3: You can create a named array constant to use in your formulas.

Notice that, in the Define Name dialog box, the array is defined using a leading equal sign (=). Without this equal sign, the array is interpreted as a text string rather than as an array. Also, you must type the brackets when defining a named array constant; Excel does not enter them for you.

After creating this named array, you can use it in a formula. Figure 16-4 shows a worksheet that contains a single array formula entered into the range A1:G1. The formula is

```
{=DayNames}
```

Note   Because commas separate the array elements, the array has a horizontal orientation. Use semicolons to create a vertical array. Or you can use Excel's TRANSPOSE function to insert a horizontal array into a vertical range of cells (see "Transposing an array," later in this chapter).

You also can access individual elements from the array by using Excel's INDEX function. The following formula, for example, returns Wed, the fourth item in the DayNames array:

```
=INDEX(DayNames,4)
```

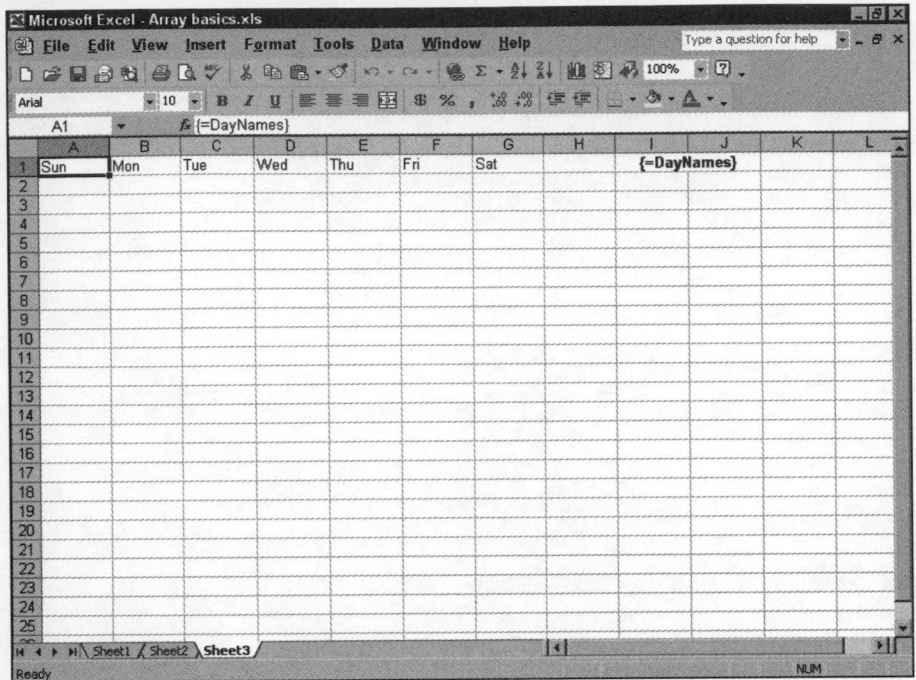

Figure 16-4: You can use a named array in an array formula.

Working with Array Formulas

This section deals with the mechanics of selecting cells that contain arrays and entering and editing array formulas. These procedures differ a bit from working with ordinary ranges and formulas.

Entering an array formula

When you enter an array formula into a cell or range, you must follow a special procedure so that Excel knows that you want an array formula rather than a normal formula. You enter a normal formula into a cell by pressing Enter. You enter an array formula into one or more cells by pressing Ctrl+Shift+Enter.

You can easily identify an array formula, because the formula is enclosed in brackets in the formula bar. The following formula, for example, is an array formula:

```
{=SUM(LEN(A1:A5))}
```

Don't enter the brackets when you create an array formula; Excel inserts them for you.

Caution   If the result of an array formula consists of more than one value, you must select all of the cells in the results range before you enter the formula. If you fail to do this, only the first element of the result is returned.

Selecting an array formula range

You can select the cells that contain a multicell array formula manually, by using the normal cell selection procedures. Or, you can use either of these methods:

✦ Activate any cell in the array formula range. Select Edit ➪ Go To (or press F5), click the Special button, and then choose the Current Array option. Click OK to close the dialog box.

✦ Activate any cell in the array formula range and press Ctrl+/ to select the entire array.

Editing an array formula

If an array formula occupies multiple cells, you must edit the entire range as though it is a single cell. The key point to remember is that you can't change just one element of an array formula. If you attempt to do so, Excel displays a message that says "you cannot change part of an array" and does not accept the edit.

The following rules apply to multicell array formulas. (If you try to do any of these things, Excel lets you know about it.)

✦ You can't change the contents of any individual cell that makes up an array formula (you must change the entire array at once).

✦ You can't move cells that make up part of an array formula (but you can move an entire array formula).

✦ You can't delete cells that form part of an array formula (but you can delete an entire array).

✦ You can't insert new cells into an array range. This rule includes inserting rows or columns that would add new cells to an array range.

To edit an array formula, select all the cells in the array range and activate the formula bar as usual (click it or press F2). Excel removes the brackets from the formula while you edit it. Edit the formula and then press Ctrl+Shift+Enter to enter the changes. All of the cells in the array now reflect your editing changes.

Caution   If you fail to press Ctrl+Shift+Enter after editing an array formula, the formula will no longer be an array formula.

You can't change any individual cell that makes up a multicell array formula. However, you can apply formatting to the entire array or to only parts of it.

Expanding or contracting a multicell array formula

You might need to expand a multicell array formula (to include more cells) or contract it (to include fewer cells). Doing so requires a few steps:

1. Select the entire range that contains the array formula.

2. Press F2 to enter Edit mode.

3. Press Ctrl+Enter. This step enters an identical (non-array) formula into each selected cell.

4. Change your range selection to include additional or fewer cells.

5. Press F2.

6. Press Ctrl+Shift+Enter.

Tip   If you contract an array, remember to remove the extra formulas you created outside of the new array in Step 3.

Creating multicell array formulas

This section contains examples that demonstrate additional features of array formulas that are entered into a range of cells. These features include creating arrays from values, performing operations, using functions, transposing arrays, and generating consecutive integers.

Creating an array from values in a range

The following array formula creates an array from a range of cells. Figure 16-5 shows a workbook with some data entered into A1:C4. The range D8:F11 contains a single array formula:

```
{=A1:C4}
```

The array in D8:F11 is linked to the range A1:C4. Change any value in A1:C4 and the corresponding cell in D8:F11 reflects that change.

Tip   You can also create an array constant from values in a range. To do so, select the cells that contain the array formula. Then press F2 to edit the array formula. Press F9 to convert the cell references to values. Press Ctrl+Shift+Enter to reenter the array formula (which now uses an array constant).

Performing operations on an array

So far, most of the examples in this chapter simply entered arrays into ranges. The following array formula creates a rectangular array and multiplies each array element by 2:

```
{={1,2,3,4;5,6,7,8;9,10,11,12}*2}
```

Array Formulas: The Downside

If you've followed along in this chapter, you probably understand some of the advantages of using array formulas. The main advantage, of course, is that an array formula enables you to perform otherwise impossible calculations. As you gain more experience with arrays, you undoubtedly will discover some disadvantages.

Array formulas are one of the least understood features of Excel. Consequently, if you plan to share a workbook with someone who may need to make modifications, you should probably avoid using array formulas. Encountering an array formula when you don't know what it is can be very confusing.

You may also discover that you can easily forget to enter an array formula by pressing Ctrl+Shift+Enter. If you edit an existing array, you still must use these keys to complete the edits. Except for logical errors, this is probably the most common problem that users have with array formulas. If you press Enter by mistake after editing an array formula, just double-click the cell to get back into Edit mode, and then press Ctrl+Shift+Enter.

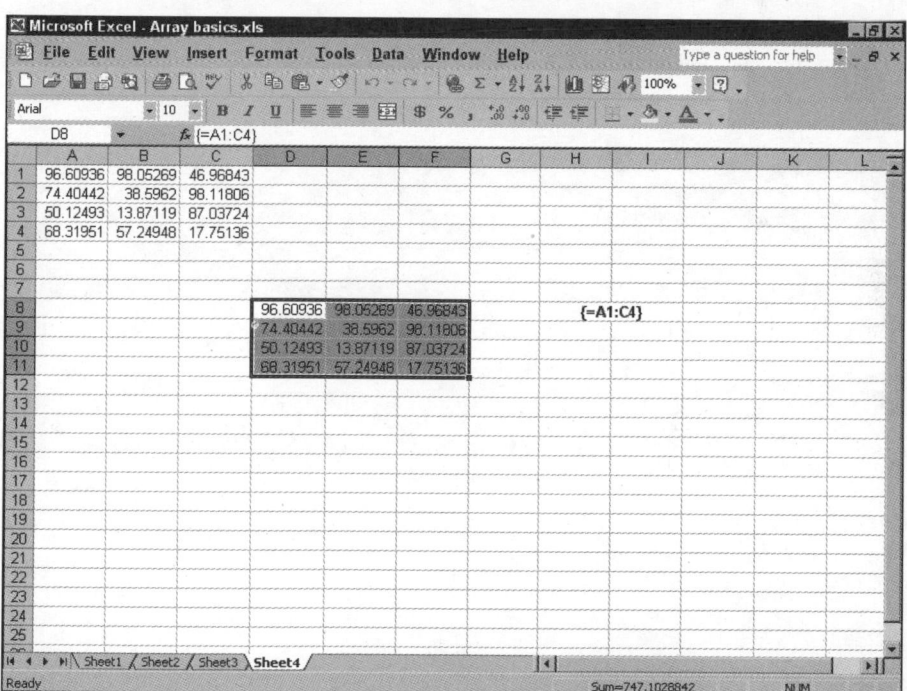

Figure 16-5: You can create an array using the values in a range.

The following array formula multiplies each array element by itself:

```
{={1,2,3,4;5,6,7,8;9,10,11,12}*{1,2,3,4;5,6,7,8;9,10,11,12}}
```

The following array formula is a simpler way of obtaining the same result:

    {={1,2,3,4;5,6,7,8;9,10,11,12}^2}

If the array is stored in a range (such as A1:C4), the array formula returns the square of each value in the range, as follows:

    {=A1:C4^2}

Figure 16-6 shows examples of several of these array formula operations.

Using functions with an array

As you might expect, you also can use functions with an array. The following array formula, which you can enter into a 10-cell vertical range, calculates the square root of each array element:

    {=SQRT({1;2;3;4;5;6;7;8;9;10})}

If the array is stored in a range, an array formula such as the one that follows returns the square root of each value in the range:

    {=SQRT(A1:A10)}

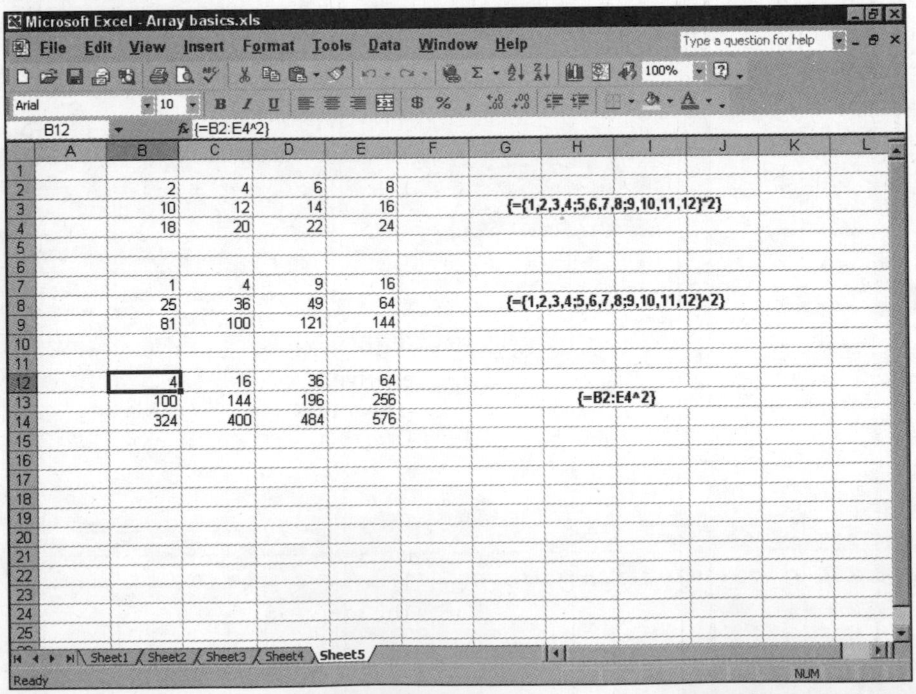

Figure 16-6: You can easily perform operations on an entire array using array formulas.

Transposing an array

When you transpose an array, you convert rows to columns and columns to rows. In other words, you can convert a horizontal array to a vertical array (and vice versa). Use Excel's TRANSPOSE function to transpose an array.

Consider the following one-dimensional horizontal array constant:

```
{1,2,3,4,5}
```

You can enter this array into a vertical range of cells by using the TRANSPOSE function. To do so, select a range of five cells that occupy five rows and one column. Then, enter the following formula and press Ctrl+Shift+Enter:

```
=TRANSPOSE({1,2,3,4,5})
```

The horizontal array is transposed, and the array elements appear in the vertical range.

Transposing a two-dimensional array works in a similar manner. Figure 16-7 shows a two-dimensional array entered into a range normally and entered into a range using the TRANSPOSE function. The formula in A1:D3 is

```
{={1,2,3,4;5,6,7,8;9,10,11,12}}
```

The formula in A6:C9 is

```
{=TRANSPOSE({1,2,3,4;5,6,7,8;9,10,11,12})}
```

You can, of course, use the TRANSPOSE function to transpose an array stored in a range. The following formula, for example, uses an array stored in A1:D3 (three rows, four columns). You can enter this array formula into a range that consists of four rows and three columns.

```
{=TRANSPOSE(A1:D3)}
```

Generating an array of consecutive integers

It's often useful to generate an array of consecutive integers for use in an array formula. Excel's ROW function, which returns a row number, is ideal for this. Consider the array formula shown here, entered into a vertical range of 12 cells:

```
{=ROW(1:12)}
```

This formula generates a 12-element array that contains integers from 1 to 12. To demonstrate, select a range that consists of 12 rows and one column, and enter the array formula into the range. You'll find that the range is filled with 12 consecutive integers.

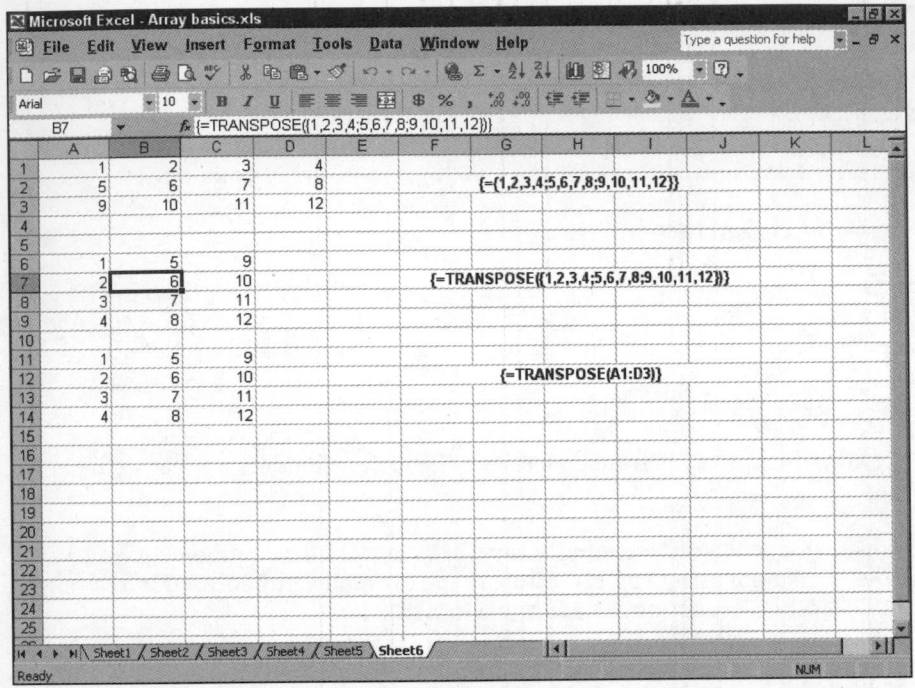

Figure 16-7: You can use the TRANSPOSE function to transpose a rectangular array.

If you want to generate an array of consecutive integers, a formula like the one shown previously is good but not perfect. To see the problem, insert a new row above the range that contains the array formula. You'll find that Excel adjusts the row references so the array formula now reads

```
{=ROW(2:13)}
```

The formula that originally generated integers from 1 to 12 now generates integers from 2 to 13.

For a better solution, use this formula:

```
{=ROW(INDIRECT("1:12"))}
```

This formula uses the INDIRECT function, which takes a text string as its argument. Excel does not adjust the references contained in the argument for the INDIRECT function. Therefore, this array formula always returns integers from 1 to 12.

Cross-Reference   Chapter 17 contains several examples that use the technique for generating consecutive integers.

Creating single-cell array formulas

The examples in the previous section all used a multicell array formula — a single array formula entered into a range of cells. The real power of using arrays becomes apparent when you use single-cell array formulas. This section contains examples of array formulas that occupy a single cell.

Counting characters in a range

Suppose you have a range of cells that contains text entries. If you need to get a count of the total number of characters in that range, the "traditional" method involves creating a formula like the one that follows and copying it down the column:

```
=LEN(A1)
```

Then, you use a SUM formula to calculate the sum of the values returned by the intermediate formulas.

The following array formula does the job without using any intermediate formulas:

```
{=SUM(LEN(A1:A14))}
```

The array formula (see Figure 16-8) uses the LEN function to create a new array (in memory) that consists of the number of characters in each cell of the range.

Summing the three smallest values in a range

Suppose you have a range of numbers and want to know the sum of the smallest three of them. The following formula returns the sum of the three smallest values in a range named Data:

```
{=SUM(SMALL(Data,{1,2,3}))}
```

The function uses an array constant as the second argument for the SMALL function. This generates a new array, which consists of the three smallest values in the range. This array is then passed to the SUM function, which returns the sum of the values in the new array.

Tip   You can easily adjust this type of array formula to suit your needs by using a different number of array elements or by using a different function such as LARGE.

Eliminating intermediate formulas

A primary benefit of using an array formula is that you can eliminate intermediate formulas in your worksheet. This makes your worksheet more compact and eliminates the need to display irrelevant calculations. Figure 16-9 shows a worksheet that contains pretest and posttest scores for students. Column D contains formulas that calculate the changes between the pretest and the posttest scores. Cell D17 contains a formula, shown here, that calculates the average of the values in column D:

```
=AVERAGE(D2:D15)
```

With an array formula, you can eliminate column D. The following array formula calculates the average of the changes, but does not require the formulas in column D:

```
{=AVERAGE(C2:C15-B2:B15)}
```

How does it work? The formula uses two arrays, the values of which are stored in two ranges (B2:B15 and C2:C15). The formula creates a new array that consists of the differences between each corresponding element in the other arrays. This new array is stored in Excel's memory, not in a range. The AVERAGE function then uses this new array as its argument and returns the result.

You can use additional array formulas to calculate other measures for the data in this example. For instance, the following array formula returns the largest change (for example, the greatest improvement):

```
{=MAX(C2:C15-B2:B15)}
```

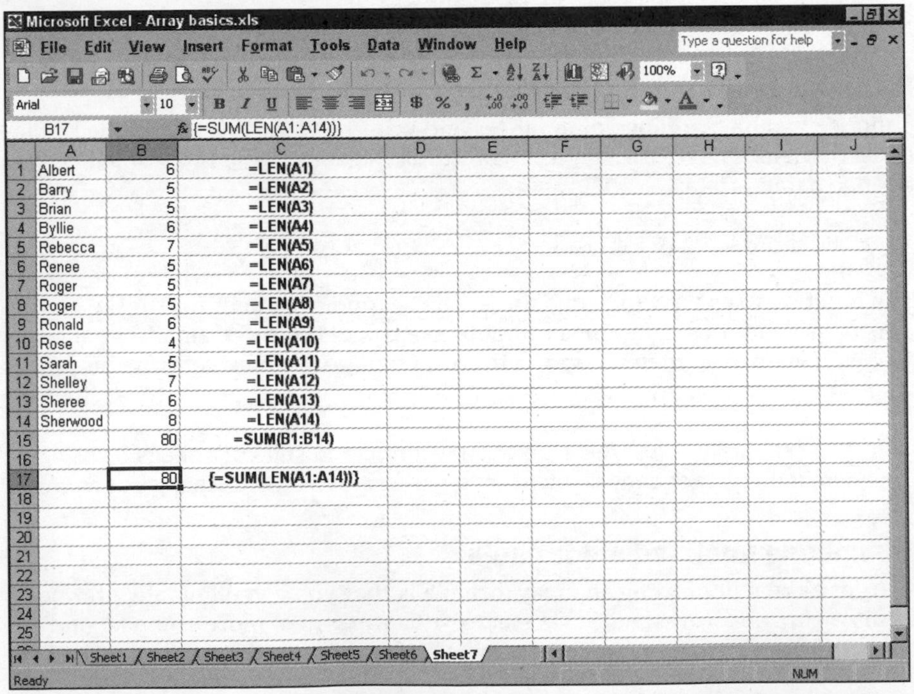

Figure 16-8: You can use a single-cell array formula to replace a whole series of individual formulas.

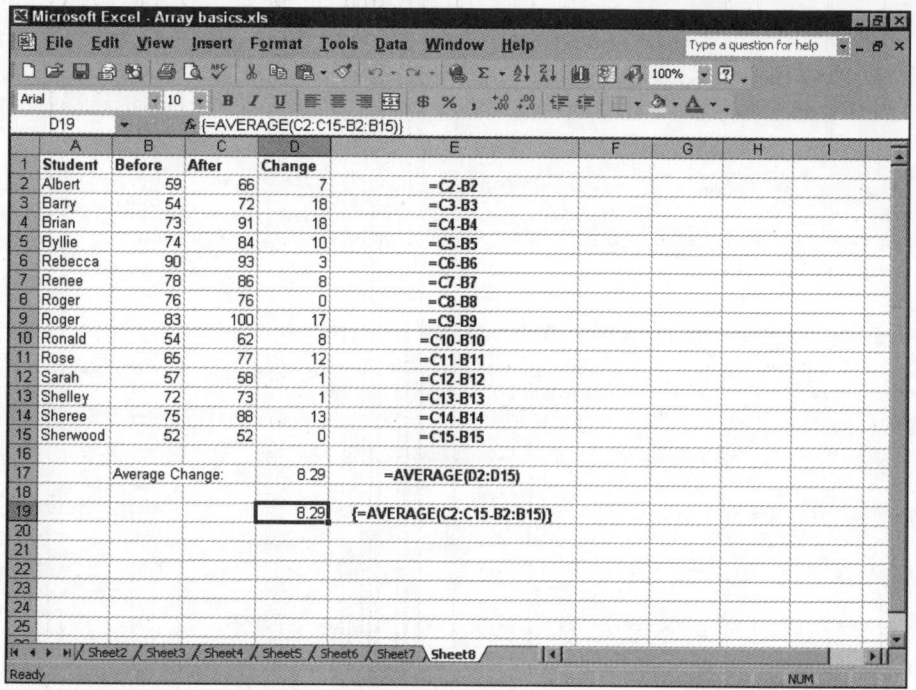

Figure 16-9: Calculating the average change requires intermediate formulas in column D unless you use an array formula.

✦   ✦   ✦

Performing Magic with Array Formulas

In the last chapter, you learned some of the basics of using arrays and array formulas in Excel. This chapter takes the subject of arrays further by showing you some advanced techniques for working with array formulas. The examples in this chapter can serve as the basis for many useful worksheets after you master the use of array formulas.

Using Some Advanced Single-Cell Array Formulas

Single-cell array formulas are ones that you enter into a single cell as opposed to returning results in a range of cells. These array formulas work with arrays contained in a range, or that exist in memory. That is, they return a single result by operating on an array. The following sections provide several interesting single-cell array formula examples.

Summing a range that contains errors

You've probably discovered that Excel's SUM function doesn't work if you attempt to sum a range that contains one or more error values (such as #DIV/0! or #NA). Figure 17-1 shows an example. The SUM formula in cell C11 returns an error value because the range that it sums (C4:C10) contains errors.

The following array formula returns a sum of the values in a range named Data, even if the range contains error values:

```
{=SUM(IF(ISERROR(Data),"",Data))}
```

Figure 17-1: You can use an array formula to sum a range of values, even if the range contains errors.

This formula works by creating a new array that contains the original values, but without the errors. The IF function effectively filters out error values by replacing them with an empty string. The SUM function then works on this "filtered" array. This technique also works with other functions, such as MIN and MAX.

> **Note**   You may want to use a function other than ISERROR. The ISERROR function returns TRUE for any error value: #N/A, #VALUE!, #REF!, #DIV/0!, #NUM!, #NAME?, or #NULL!. The ISERR function returns TRUE for any error except #N/A. The ISNA function returns TRUE only if the cell contains a #N/A.

Counting the number of error values in a range

The following array formula is similar to the previous example, but it returns a count of the number of error values in a range named Data.

```
{=SUM(IF(ISERROR(Data),1,0))}
```

This formula creates an array that consists of 1s (if the corresponding cell contains an error) and 0s (if the corresponding cell does not contain an error value).

You can simplify the formula a bit by removing the third argument for the IF function. If this argument is not specified, the IF function returns FALSE if the condition is not satisfied (that is, the cell does not contain an error value).

Actually, you can simplify the formula even more:

```
{=SUM(ISERROR(Data)*1)}
```

This version of the formula relies on the fact that

```
TRUE * 1 = 1
```

and

```
FALSE * 1 = 0
```

 **Tip** You can use this type of formula to make certain that your worksheets don't contain any of Excel's error values before you print reports. If the sum of the error values is greater than zero, you have a problem that should be corrected before printing.

Creating a conditional sum using an array formula

Often, you need to sum values based on one or more conditions. The array formula that follows, for example, returns the sum of the positive values (it excludes negative values) in a range named Data:

```
{=SUM(IF(Data>0,Data))}
```

The IF function creates a new array that consists only of positive values. This array is passed to the SUM function. The Data range can consist of any number of rows and columns.

You also can use Excel's SUMIF function for this example. The following function, which is not an array formula, returns the same result:

```
=SUMIF(Data,">0")
```

SUMIF, however, can't be used for multiple conditions. For example, if you want to sum only values that are greater than 0 and less than 5, you need an array formula. This array formula does the job:

```
{=SUM((Data>0)*(Data<=5)*Data)}
```

For an explanation of the workarounds required for using logical functions in an array formula, refer to the following sidebar, "Illogical Behavior from Logical Functions."

Illogical Behavior from Logical Functions

Excel's AND and OR functions are logical functions that return TRUE or FALSE. Unfortunately, these functions do not perform as expected when used in an array formula.

As shown in the following figure, columns A and B contain logical values. The AND function returns TRUE if all of its arguments are TRUE. Column C contains nonarray formulas that work as expected. For example, cell C3 contains the following function:

```
=AND(A3,B3)
```

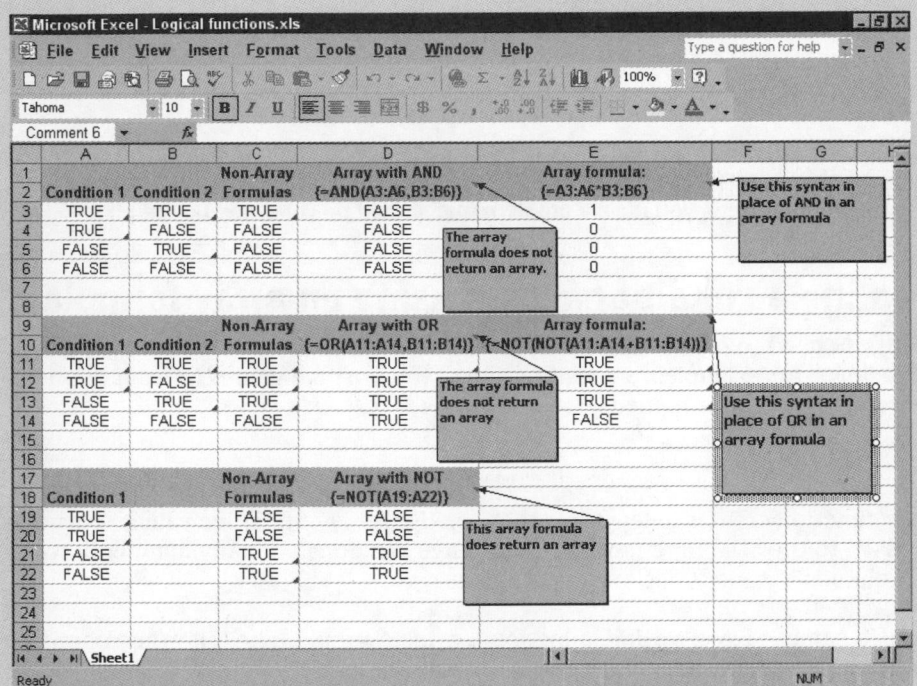

You need to use special techniques to create AND and OR conditions in array formulas.

The range D3:D6 contains this array formula:

```
{=AND(A3:A6,B3:B6)}
```

You might expect this array formula to return the following array:

```
{TRUE,FALSE,FALSE,FALSE}
```

Instead, it returns only a single item: FALSE. In fact, both the AND function and the OR function always return a single result (never an array). Even when using array constants, the AND function still returns only a single value. For example, this array formula does not return an array:

```
{=AND({TRUE,TRUE,FALSE,FALSE},{TRUE,FALSE,TRUE,FALSE})}
```

Column E contains another array formula, which follows, that returns an array of 0s and 1s. These 0s and 1s correspond to FALSE and TRUE, respectively.

```
{=A3:A6*B3:B6}
```

In array formulas, you must use this syntax in place of the AND function.

The following array formula, which uses the OR function, does not return an array (as you might expect):

```
=OR(A11:A14,B11:B14)
```

Instead, you can use a formula such as the following, which *does* return an array comprising logical OR using the corresponding elements in the ranges:

```
=NOT(NOT(A11:A14+B11:B14))
```

The NOT function works as expected: When used in an array formula, it does return an array.

Caution
Contrary to what you might expect, you cannot use the AND function in an array formula. The following array formula, while quite logical, doesn't return the correct result:

```
{=SUM(IF(AND(Data>0,Data<=5),Data))}
```

You also can combine criteria using an OR condition. For example, to sum the values that are less than 0 or greater than 5, use the following array formula:

```
{=SUM(IF(NOT(NOT((Data<0)+(Data>5))),Data))}
```

Caution
As with the AND function, you cannot use the OR function in an array formula. The following formula, for example, does not return the correct result:

```
{=SUM(IF(OR(Data<0,Data>5),Data))}
```

Summing the *n* largest values in a range

The following array formula returns the sum of the 10 largest values in a range named Data:

```
{=SUM(LARGE(Data,ROW(INDIRECT("1:10"))))}
```

The LARGE function is executed 10 times, each time with a different second argument (1, 2, 3, and so on up to 10). The results of these calculations are stored in a new array, and that array is used as the argument for the SUM function.

Tip

To sum a different number of values, replace the 10 in the argument for the INDI-RECT function with another value. To sum the *n* smallest values in a range, use the SMALL function instead of the LARGE function.

Computing an average that excludes zeros

Figure 17-2 shows a simple worksheet that calculates average sales. The formula in cell B14 is

```
=AVERAGE(Data)
```

This formula, of course, calculates the average of the values in B5:B12. Two of the sales staff had the week off, however, so this average doesn't accurately describe the average sales per representative.

Note

The AVERAGE function ignores blank cells but does not ignore cells that contain 0.

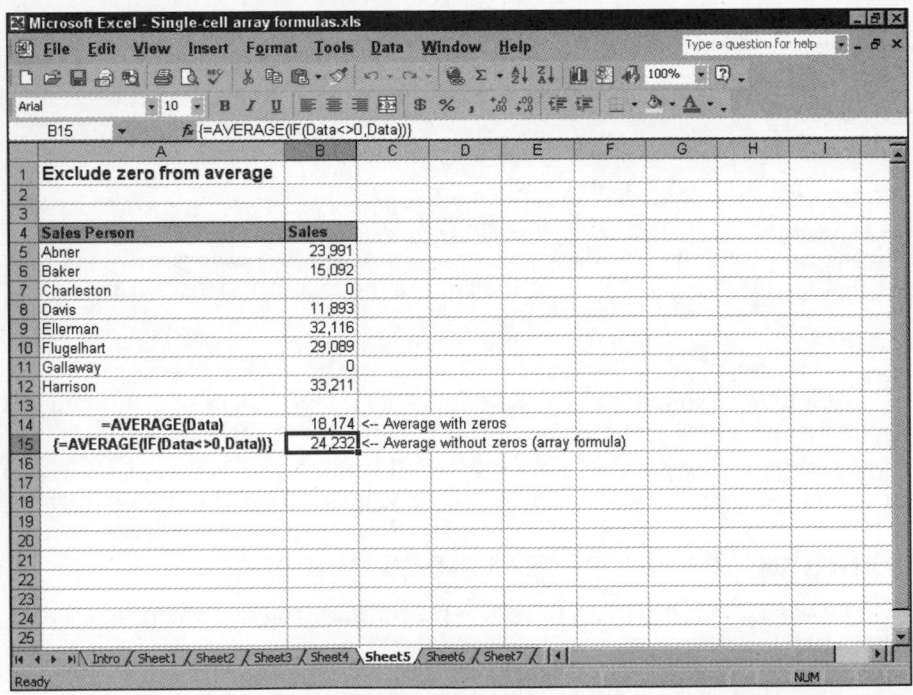

Figure 17-2: You can use an array formula to exclude values of zero from an average.

The following array formula returns the average of the range but excludes the cells that contain 0:

```
{=AVERAGE(IF(Data<>0,Data))}
```

This formula creates a new array that consists only of the nonzero values in the range. The AVERAGE function then uses this new array as its argument. You also can get the same result with a regular (nonarray) formula:

```
=SUM(Data)/COUNTIF(Data,"<>0")
```

This formula uses the COUNTIF function to count the number of nonzero values in the range. This value is divided into the sum of the values.

 **Tip**   You can, of course, use a different value for the condition. For example, you could use a condition of Data<0 to include only negative values.

Determining whether a particular value appears in a range

To determine whether a particular value appears in a range of cells, you can choose the Edit ⇨ Find command and do a search of the worksheet. However, you can also make this determination by using an array formula.

Figure 17-3 shows a worksheet with a list of names in A5:E24 (named NameList). An array formula in cell D3 checks the name entered into cell C3 (named TheName). If the name exists in the list of names, the formula displays the text Found; otherwise, it displays Not Found.

The array formula in cell D1 is

```
{=IF(OR(TheName=NameList),"Found","Not Found")}
```

This formula compares TheName to each cell in the NameList range. It builds a new array that consists of logical TRUE or FALSE values. The OR function returns TRUE if any one of the values in the new array is TRUE. The IF function uses this result to determine which message to display.

A simpler form of this formula follows. This formula displays TRUE if the name is found; otherwise it displays FALSE:

```
{=OR(TheName=NameList)}
```

Tip   Remember that TRUE is equal to 1 and FALSE is equal to 0, so you can use the results of a logical formula as 1 or 0.

Counting the number of differences in two ranges

You may want to determine how many values differ between two ranges. The following array formula compares the corresponding values in two ranges (named MyData and YourData) and returns the number of differences in the two ranges. If the contents of the two ranges are identical, the formula returns 0.

```
{=SUM(IF(MyData=YourData,0,1))}
```

The two ranges must be the same size and of the same dimensions.

Microsoft Excel - Single-cell array formulas.xls

File Edit View Insert Format Tools Data Window Help

D3   fx {=IF(OR(TheName=NameList),"Found","Not Found")}

	A	B	C	D	E	F	G	H	I	J	K
1	Is a value contained in a range?										
2											
3	Enter a Name -->		Louis	Not Found		{=IF(OR(TheName=NameList),"Found","Not Found")}					
4											
5	Al	Daniel	Harold	Lyle	Richard						
6	Allen	Dave	Ian	Maggie	Rick						
7	Andrew	David	Jack	Margaret	Robert						
8	Anthony	Dennis	James	Marilyn	Rod						
9	Arthur	Don	Jan	Mark	Roger						
10	Barbara	Donald	Jeff	Marvin	Ronald						
11	Bernard	Doug	Jeffrey	Mary	Russ						
12	Beth	Douglas	Jerry	Matt	Sandra						
13	Bill	Ed	Jim	Mel	Scott						
14	Bob	Edward	Joe	Merle	Simon						
15	Brian	Eric	John	Michael	Stacy						
16	Bruce	Fran	Joseph	Michelle	Stephen						
17	Cark	Frank	Karl	Mike	Steven						
18	Carl	Fred	Kathy	Norman	Stuart						
19	Charles	Gary	Keith	Patrick	Susan						
20	Chris	George	Kenneth	Paul	Terry						
21	Chuck	Glenn	Kevin	Peter	Thomas						
22	Clark	Gordon	Larry	Phillip	Timothy						
23	Curt	Greg	Leonard	Ray	Vincent						
24	Dan	Gregory	Louise	Rebecca	William						
25											

Intro / Sheet1 / Sheet2 / Sheet3 / Sheet4 / Sheet5 \ **Sheet6** / Sheet7 /

Ready   NUM

Figure 17-3: You can use an array formula to determine if a range contains a particular value.

This formula works by creating a new array of the same size as the ranges being compared. The IF function fills this new array with 0s and 1s (0 if a difference is found, 1 if the corresponding cells are the same). The SUM function then returns the sum of the array.

Returning the location of the maximum value in a range

Sometimes you may want to know where a particular value is located in a range. The following array formula returns the row number of the maximum value in a single-column range named Data:

```
{=MIN(IF(Data=MAX(Data),ROW(Data), ""))}
```

The IF function creates a new array that corresponds to the Data range. If the corresponding cell contains the maximum value in Data, then the array contains the row number; otherwise, it contains an empty string. The MIN function uses this new array as its second argument and returns the smallest value—the row number of the maximum value in Data.

> **Tip** If the Data range contains more than one cell that has the maximum value, the row of the first maximum cell is returned.

The following array formula is similar to the previous one, but it returns the actual cell address of the maximum value in the Data range. It uses the ADDRESS function, which takes two arguments: a row number and a column number.

```
{=ADDRESS(MIN(IF(Data=MAX(Data), ""),COLUMN(Data))}
```

> **Tip** You can easily replace the MAX function with another function to locate a different value such as the minimum or median value.

Finding the longest text string in a range

The following array formula displays the text string in a range (named Data) that has the most characters. If multiple cells contain the longest text string, the first cell is returned.

```
{=INDEX(Data,MATCH(MAX(LEN(Data)),LEN(Data),FALSE),1)}
```

This formula creates four new arrays:

✦ **Array #1:** An array that consists of the length of each cell in the Data range (created by the LEN function)

✦ **Array #2:** Another array identical to Array #1

✦ **Array #3:** An array that contains the maximum value in Array #1 (created by the MAX function)

✦ **Array #4:** An array that contains the offset of the cell that contains the maximum length (created by the MATCH function)

The INDEX function works with these arrays and returns the contents of the cell that contains the most characters. This function works only if the Data range consists of a single column.

Checking the validity of a range of values

You might have a list of items that you need to check against another list. For example, you might import a list of part numbers into a range named MyList, and you want to ensure that all of the part numbers are valid. You can do this by comparing the items in the imported list to the items in a master list of part numbers (named Master).

The following array formula returns TRUE if every item in the range named MyList is found in the range named Master. Both of these ranges must consist of a single column, but they don't need to contain the same number of rows.

```
{=ISNA(MATCH(TRUE,ISNA(MATCH(MyList,Master,0)),0))}
```

The array formula that follows returns the number of invalid items. In other words, it returns the number of items in MyList that do not appear in Master.

```
{=SUM(1*ISNA(MATCH(MyList,Master,0)))}
```

To return the first invalid item in MyList, use this array formula:

```
{=INDEX(MyList,MATCH(TRUE,ISNA(MATCH(MyList,Master,0)),0))}
```

Summing rounded values

Figure 17-4 shows a simple worksheet that demonstrates a common spreadsheet problem: rounding errors. As you can see, the grand total in cell E7 appears to display an incorrect amount (that is, it's off by a penny). The values in column E use a number format that displays two decimal places. The actual values, however, consist of additional decimal places that do not display due to rounding (as a result of the number format). The net effect of these rounding errors is a seemingly incorrect total. The total — actually $168.320997 — displays as $168.32.

The following array formula creates a new array that consists of values in column E, rounded to two decimal places:

```
{=SUM(ROUND(E4:E6,2))}
```

This formula returns $168.31.

You can also eliminate these types of rounding errors by using the ROUND function in the formula that calculates each row total in column E. This technique does not require an array formula but does require that each of the line item total formulas include the ROUND function.

Summing every *n*th value in a range

Suppose you have a range of values and you want to compute the sum of every third value in the list — the first, the fourth, the seventh, and so on. You can't accomplish this task with a standard formula, but an array formula does the job.

The following array formula returns the sum of every *n*th value in the range named Data:

```
{SUM(IF(MOD(ROW(INDIRECT("1:"&COUNT(Data)))-1,n)=0,Data,""))}
```

This formula generates an array of consecutive integers, and the MOD function uses this array as its first argument. The second argument for the MOD function is the value of *n*. The MOD function creates another array, which consists of the remainders (after each row number is divided by *n*). If the array item is 0 (for example, the row is evenly divisible by *n*), the corresponding item in the Data range will be included in the sum.

You'll find that this formula fails when *n* is 0 (for example, sums no items). The modified array formula that follows uses an IF function to handle this case:

```
{=IF(n=0,0,SUM(IF(MOD(ROW(INDIRECT("1:"&COUNT(data)))-1,n)
=0,data,"")))}
```

This formula works only when the Data range consists of a single column of values. It does not work for a rectangular range, or for a single row of values.

Microsoft Excel - Single-cell array formulas.xls

| | File | Edit | View | Insert | Format | Tools | Data | Window | Help | | Type a question for help |

| E9 | | | f_x {=SUM(ROUND(E4:E6,2))} |

	A	B	C	D	E	F	G	H	I	J
1	Summing rounded values									
2										
3	Description	Quantity	Unit Price	Discount	Total					
4	Widgets	6	$11.69	5.23%	$66.47		=B4*C4*(1-D4)			
5	Sprockets	8	$9.74	5.23%	$73.84		=B5*C5*(1-D5)			
6	Snapholytes	3	$9.85	5.23%	$28.00		=B6*C6*(1-D6)			
7	GRAND TOTAL				$168.32		=SUM(E4:E6)			
8										
9				Sum of rounded values:	$168.31		{=SUM(ROUND(E4:E6,2))}			
10										

Sheet7 / Sheet8 / Sheet9 / Sheet10 / Sheet11 / Sheet12 \ Sheet13 / Sh

Figure 17-4: You can use an array formula to correct what appear to be rounding errors.

To make the formula work with a horizontal range, you need to transpose the array of integers generated by the ROW function. The modified array formula that follows works only with a horizontal Data range:

```
{=IF(n=0,0,SUM(IF(MOD(TRANSPOSE(ROW(INDIRECT("1:"&COUNT(Data))))
)-1,n)=0,Data,"")))}
```

Determining the closest value in a range

The following array formula returns the value in a range named Data that is closest to another value (named Target):

```
{=INDEX(Data,MATCH(SMALL(ABS(Target-Data),1),ABS(Target-Data),
0))}
```

 **Tip** If two values in the Data range are equidistant from the Target value, the formula returns the first one in the list.

Figure 17-5 shows an example of this formula. In this case, the Target value is 45. The array formula in cell D5 returns 48—the value closest to 45.

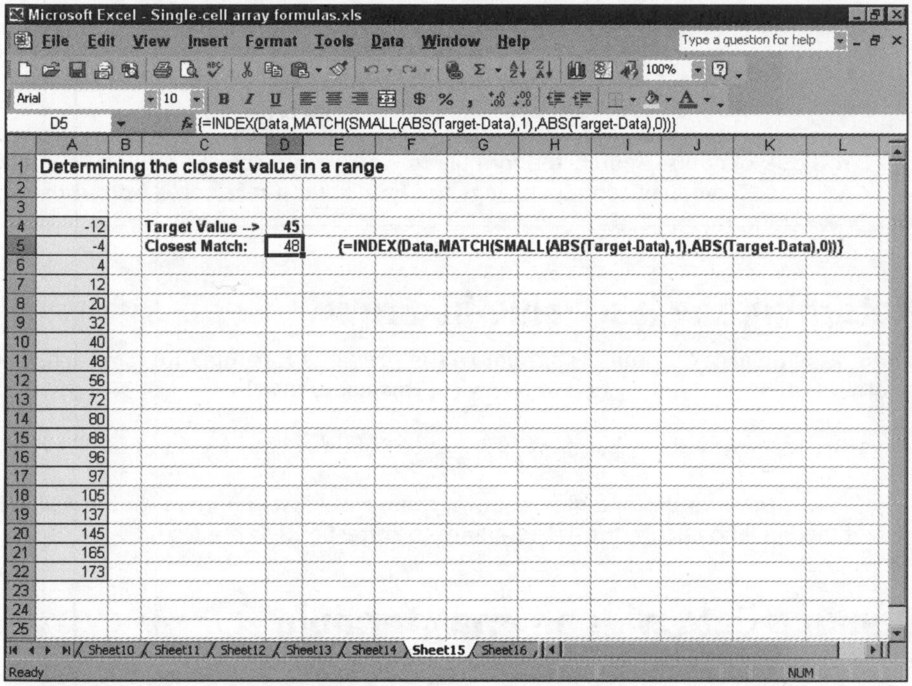

Figure 17-5: You can use an array formula to find the value that is closest to a specified value.

Returning the last value in a column

Suppose you have a worksheet that you update frequently by adding new data to columns. You might need a way to reference the last value in column A (the value most recently entered). If column A contains no empty cells, the solution is relatively simple and doesn't require an array formula:

```
=OFFSET(A1,COUNTA(A:A)-1,0)
```

This formula uses the COUNTA function to count the number of nonempty cells in column A. This value (–1) is used as the second argument for the OFFSET function. For example, if the last value is in row 100, COUNTA returns 100. The OFFSET function returns the value in the cell 99 rows down from cell A1, in the same column.

If column A has one or more empty cells interspersed the formula won't work because the COUNTA function doesn't count the empty cells.

The following array formula returns the contents of the last nonempty cell in the first 500 rows of column A:

```
{=INDIRECT(ADDRESS(MAX((ROW(1:500)*(A1:A500<>""))),COLUMN(A:A))
)}
```

Tip   You can, of course, modify the formula to work with a column other than column A. To use a different column, change the four column references from A to whatever column you need.

Returning the last value in a row

The following array formula is similar to the previous formula, but it returns the contents of last nonempty cell in a row (in this case, row 1):

```
=INDIRECT(ADDRESS(1,(MAX((TRANSPOSE(ROW(1:256))*(1:1<>""))))))
```

Tip   To use this formula for a different row, change the first argument for the ADDRESS function, and change the 1:1 reference to correspond to the row.

Ranking data with an array formula

Often, computing the rank orders for the values in a range of data is helpful. If you have a worksheet that contains the annual sales figures for 20 salespeople, for example, you may want to know how each person ranks, from highest to lowest.

If you've used Excel's RANK function, you may have noticed that the ranks produced by this function don't handle ties the way that you may like. For example, if two values are tied for third place, the RANK function gives both of them a rank of 3. You may prefer to assign each an average (or midpoint) of the ranks — in other words, a rank of 3.5 for both values tied for third place.

Figure 17-6 shows a worksheet that uses two methods to rank a column of values (named Sales). The first method (column C) uses Excel's RANK function. Column D uses array formulas to compute the ranks.

The array formula in cell D5 is

```
{=SUM(1*(B5<=Sales))-(SUM(1*(B5=Sales))-1)/2}
```

This formula copied to the cells below it.

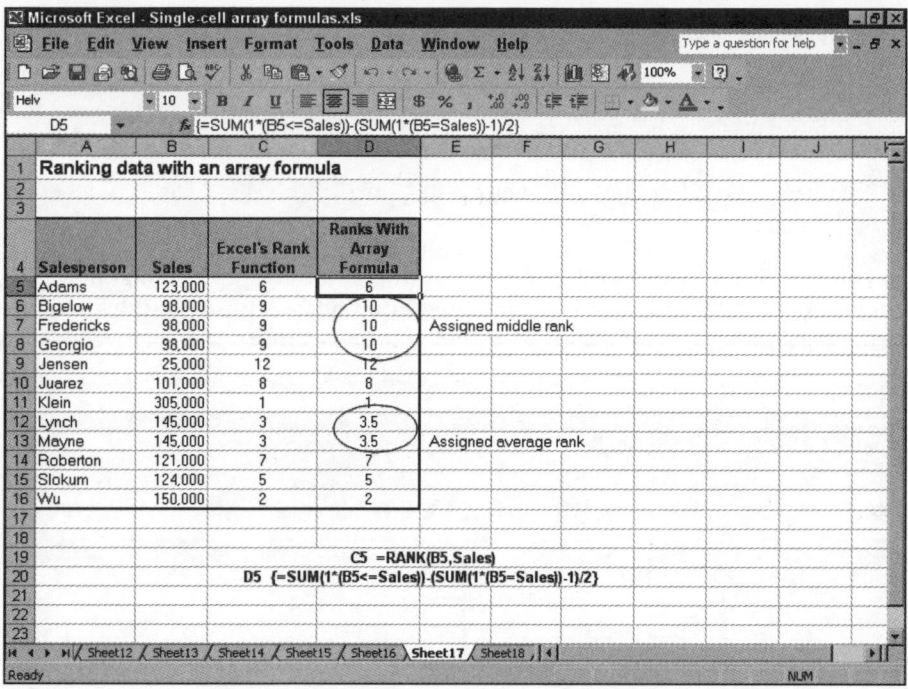

Figure 17-6: Here are two different methods of ranking data — one method uses Excel's RANK function and the other method uses array formulas.

Note   Each ranking is computed with a separate array formula, not with an array formula entered into multiple cells.

Each array function works by computing the number of higher values and subtracting one half of the number of equal values –1.

Using Some Advanced Multicell Array Formulas

The previous chapter introduced array formulas entered into multicell ranges. This section presents several more multicell array formulas. Most of these formulas return some or all of the values in a range, but the values are rearranged in some way.

Returning only positive values from a range

The following array formula works with a single-column vertical range (named Data). The array formula is entered into a range that's the same size as Data and returns only the positive values in the Data range (0s and negative numbers are ignored).

```
{=INDEX(Data,SMALL(IF(Data>0,ROW(INDIRECT("1:"&ROWS(Data)))),
ROW(INDIRECT("1:"&ROWS(Data)))))}
```

As you can see in Figure 17-7, this formula works but not perfectly. The Data range is A5:A24, and the array formula is entered into C5:C24. However, the array formula displays #NUM! error values for cells that contain a value of zero or less.

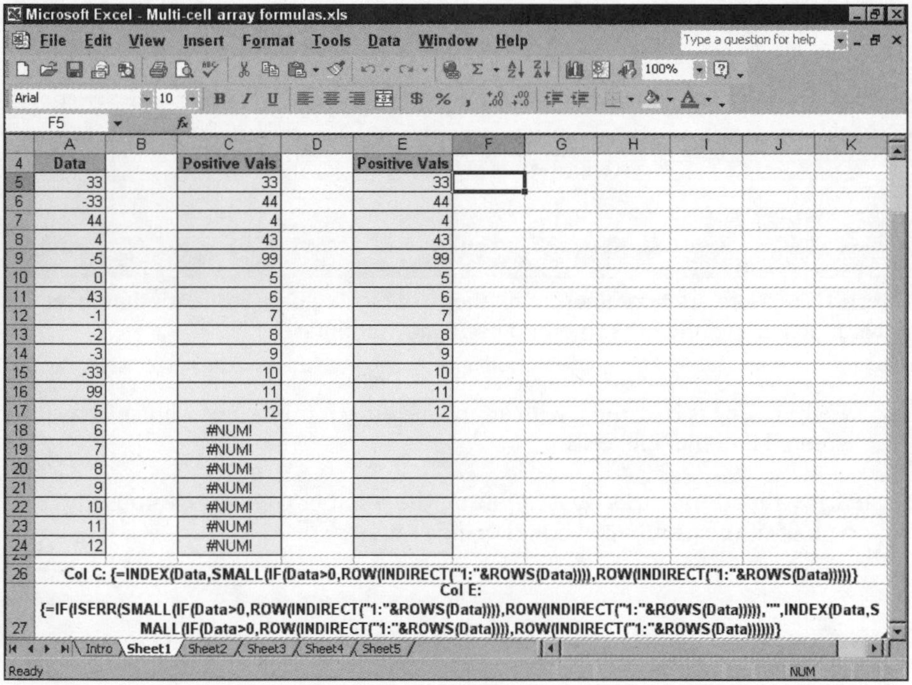

Figure 17-7: These array formulas return only the positive values that exist in a range.

This more complex array formula avoids the error value display:

```
{=IF(ISERR(SMALL(IF(Data>0,ROW(INDIRECT("1:"&ROWS(Data)))),
ROW(INDIRECT("1:"&ROWS(Data))))),"",INDEX(Data,SMALL(IF
(Data>0,ROW(INDIRECT("1:"&ROWS(Data)))),ROW(INDIRECT
("1:"&ROWS(Data)))))))}
```

Returning a list of unique items in a range

If you have a single-column range named Data, the following array formula returns a list of the unique items in the range:

```
{=INDEX(Data,SMALL(IF(MATCH(Data,Data,0)=
ROW(INDIRECT("1:"&ROWS(Data))),MATCH(Data,Data,0),""),
ROW(INDIRECT("1:"&ROWS(Data)))))}
```

This formula does not work if the Data range contains any blank cells. The unfilled cells of the array formula display #NUM!. Figure 17-8 shows an example. Range A5:A23 is named Data, and the array formula is entered into range C5:C23.

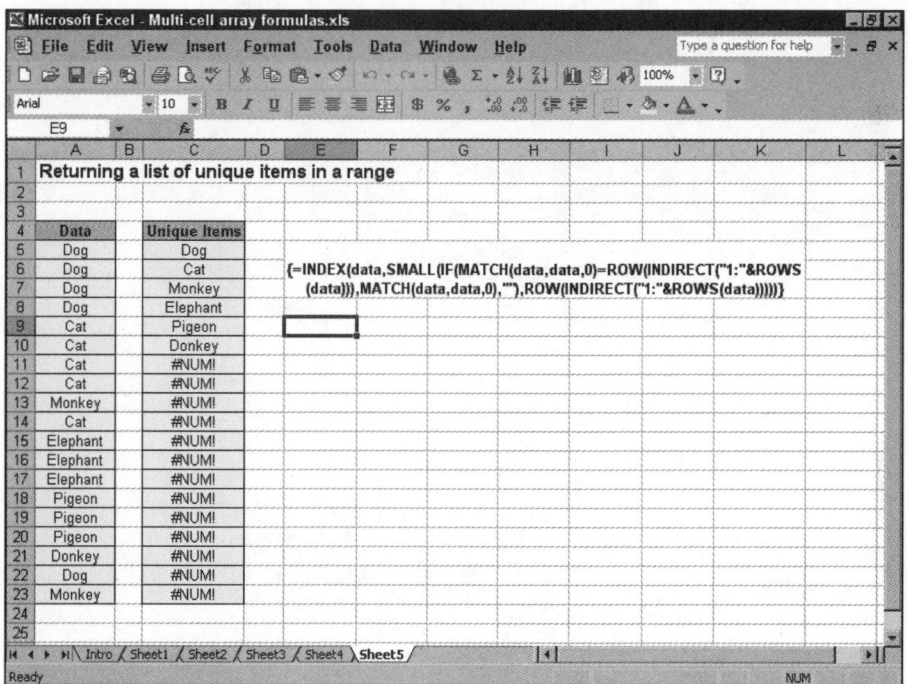

Figure 17-8: You can use an array formula to return all of the unique values in a range.

Using a Custom VBA Function to Return an Array

The chapter's final example demonstrates one course of action you can take if you can't figure out a particular array formula. If Excel doesn't provide the tools you need, you need to create your own.

For example, you can easily create an array formula that returns a sorted list of numeric values, but doing the same for text entries requires a custom VBA function. Here is an example of a custom VBA function called SORTED that handles the task:

```vba
Function SORTED(rng, Optional ascending) As Variant
    Dim SortedData() As Variant
    Dim CellCount As Long
    Dim Temp As Variant, i As Long, j As Long
    CellCount = rng.Count
    ReDim SortedData(1 To CellCount)

'   Check optional argument
    If IsMissing(ascending) Then ascending = True

'   Exit with an error if not a single column
    If rng.Columns.Count > 1 Then
        SORTED = CVErr(xlErrValue)
        Exit Function
    End If

'   Transfer data to SortedData
    For i = 1 To CellCount
        SortedData(i) = rng(i)
        If TypeName(SortedData(i)) = "Empty" _
          Then SortedData(i) = ""
    Next i
    On Error Resume Next

'   Sort the SortedData array
    For i = 1 To CellCount
        For j = i + 1 To CellCount
            If SortedData(j) <> "" Then
                If ascending Then
                    If SortedData(i) > SortedData(j) Then
                        Temp = SortedData(j)
                        SortedData(j) = SortedData(i)
                        SortedData(i) = Temp
                    End If
                Else
                    If SortedData(i) < SortedData(j) Then
                        Temp = SortedData(j)
                        SortedData(j) = SortedData(i)
                        SortedData(i) = Temp
                    End If
                End If
            End If
        Next j
    Next i

'   Transpose it
    SORTED = Application.Transpose(SortedData)
End Function
```

The SORTED function takes two arguments: a range reference and an optional second argument that specifies the sort order. The default sort order is ascending order. If you specify FALSE as the second argument, the range is returned sorted in descending order.

After the SORTED Function procedure is entered into a VBA module, you can use the SORTED function in your formulas. The following array formula, for example, returns the contents of a single-column range named Data, but sorted in ascending order. You enter this formula into a range the same size as the Data range.

```
{=SORTED(Data)}
```

As you can see, using a custom function results in a much more compact formula. Custom functions, however, are usually much slower than formulas that use Excel's built-in functions.

Figure 17-9 shows an example of this function used in an array formula. Range A2:A17 is named Data, and the array formula is entered into range C2:C17.

	A	B	C	D	E	F	G	H	I	J
1	Data Entry		Sorted Data (a)		Sorted Data (d)					
2	Ashby		Arias		Vander Wall					
3	Leyritz		Ashby		Sanders					
4	Joiner		Gomez		Rivera					
5	Hitchcock		Gwynn		Owens					
6	Gomez		Hitchcock		Leyritz					
7	Arias		Hoffman		Joiner					
8	Sanders		Jackson		Jackson					
9			Joiner		Hoffman					
10			Leyritz		Hitchcock					
11	Rivera		Owens		Gwynn					
12	Gwynn		Rivera		Gomez					
13	Vander Wall		Sanders		Ashby					
14	Owens		Vander Wall		Arias					
15	Jackson									
16	Hoffman									
17										
18										
19			{=sorted(data)}		{=sorted(data),FALSE}					
20										
21										
22										
23										
24										
25										

Figure 17-9: Sometimes you may need to create a custom VBA function to perform a task.

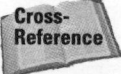

Cross-Reference   See Chapter 35 to learn more about creating custom VBA functions.

✦   ✦   ✦

Analyzing Data with Excel

Excel is a superb data analysis tool if you know how to extract the information you really need. In this part you'll learn how to obtain and analyze data in Excel. As you'll see, many of the data analysis capabilities in Excel are both surprisingly powerful and easy to use.

Importing Data from Other Sources

Excel is an excellent tool for manipulating data. Sometimes, though, the data you need to work with may not be immediately available in an Excel workbook. Fortunately, Excel has the capability to import data from many different sources, so you probably won't be faced with the task of manually reentering data that already exists in another electronic format. This chapter shows you how to import information from other programs for use in your Excel workbooks.

An Overview of Importing Data

There are a number of ways in which you can bring data into an Excel worksheet. You're probably most familiar with manual methods such as typing information into worksheet cells. Often, though, the data you need to use may already exist in another format, and you can save a lot of time — not to mention avoid a lot of input errors — by simply importing that data.

There are two primary methods of importing data into Excel. You can

✦ Copy data from another application by using the Windows clipboard

✦ Import data from another (non-Excel) file

The first method is one of the most direct methods of sharing information between different types of programs. You're probably at least somewhat familiar with Clipboard basics, but there are some subtleties you'll learn in this chapter to help make the process go just a bit smoother.

Importing data from another program's file is often the best way to deal with large amounts of information you need to bring into Excel. Generally, this method is the one you are likely to use if someone sends you a file from another program (other than Excel).

Cross-Reference   See Chapter 20 for more information on working with database files in Excel.

Although it may seem as if importing data should be simple, there is an important factor that makes the process more complicated than you might think. That factor is something known as *file formats*—the unique methods used by different pro-grams to store their data files. Different file formats evolved from the need to treat different types of data in special ways. For example, Excel needs to know which of the data in a workbook file consists of formulas, which data is simple numeric data, which data represents a date, and so on. Other programs use their own special file formats so that they can determine the contents of their data files, too.

Fortunately, Excel can import data from many different types of programs because Excel has built-in translators that help it to understand much of the information in these foreign file formats. So, if someone sends you data in a Lotus 1-2-3 spread-sheet file or in a mainframe's text file, you'll probably be able to open that file and import it into Excel.

To open any of these foreign files, choose File ➪ Open and select the file type from the drop-down list labeled Files of type (see Figure 18-1) to display only the files of the selected type in the file list. If the file is a text file, Excel's Text Import Wizard appears, to help you interpret the file. The Text Import Wizard is discussed later in this chapter.

You should understand, however, that being able to read a file and translating it perfectly are two different matters. In some cases, you may encounter one or more of the following problems while reading a foreign file into Excel:

✦ Some formulas aren't translated correctly

✦ Unsupported functions aren't translated

✦ Formatting is incorrect

✦ Column widths are incorrect

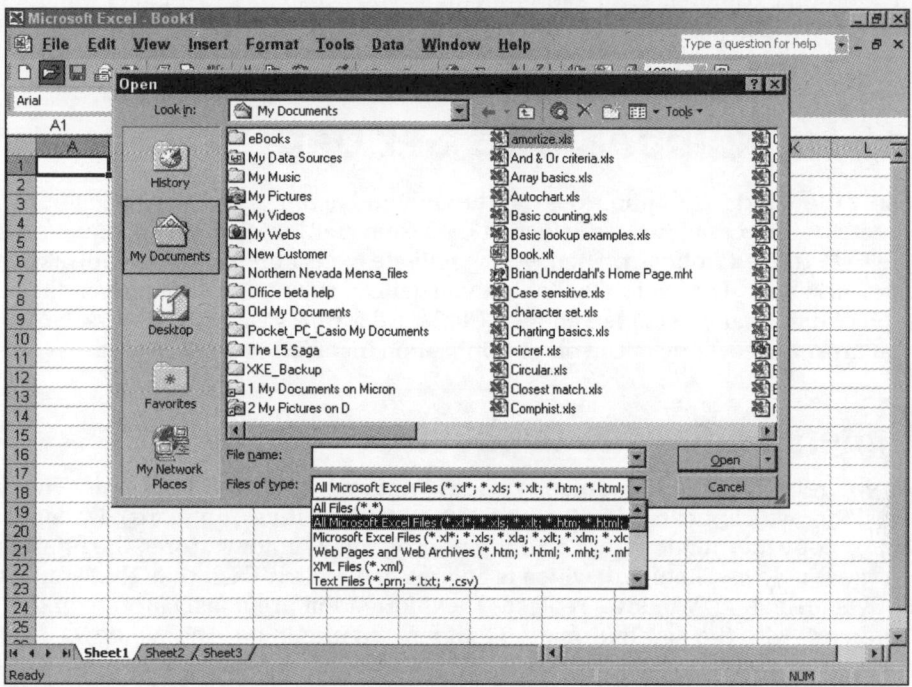

Figure 18-1: You can use the Open dialog box to import many types of foreign files into Excel.

Caution   When you open a file that wasn't produced by Excel, examine it carefully to ensure that Excel retrieved the data correctly.

If a colleague sends you a file that Excel can't open, don't give up. Simply ask your colleague to save the spreadsheet in a format that Excel can read. For example, many applications can save files in 1-2-3 format, and most applications can export to a text file format.

Tip   If the Open dialog box does not list the type of file you need to import, it may be useful to examine the installation options you used when installing Excel. Open the Add/Remove Programs dialog box in the Windows Control Panel and then open the Excel (or Microsoft Office) item. Use the Add or Remove features option and make certain that all of the converters listed under Office Shared Features are installed.

Note   If you import Lotus 1-2-3 or Quattro Pro spreadsheet files, some formulas may show #NAME? in place of the expected results. This happens when Excel's name for a function is different from the name used in the other program.

In addition to differences in a few functions, you'll also find that Excel will not run macros that are contained in Lotus 1-2-3 or Quattro Pro files.

Using the Clipboard to Get Data

Using the Windows Clipboard is another method of importing data into your worksheet. The process involves selecting data from another application and copying the data to the Clipboard. Then, you reactivate Excel and paste the information to the worksheet. The exact results that you get can vary quite a bit, depending on the type of data that you copied and the Clipboard formats that it supports. Obviously, you must have a copy of the other application installed on your system.

Understanding the Clipboards

As you read in Chapter 4, Office provides Windows with two Clipboards. The original Windows Clipboard remains (in addition to the Office Clipboard); whenever you cut or copy information from a Windows program, Windows stores the information on the Windows Clipboard, which is an area of memory. Each time that you cut or copy information, Windows replaces the information previously stored on the Clipboard with the new information that you cut or copied. The Windows Clipboard can store data in a variety of formats. Because Windows manages it, information on the Windows Clipboard can be pasted to other Windows applications, regardless of where it originated. Normally, you can't see information stored on the Windows Clipboard (nor would you want to).

Note   To view the Windows Clipboard contents, you can run the Clipboard Viewer program, which comes with Windows. The Clipboard Viewer may or may not be installed on your system (it is not installed by default). You can use the Clipboard Viewer to view only the last piece of information that you copied to the Office Clipboard. To open the Clipboard Viewer, click the Start button and choose Programs ⇨ Accessories ⇨ Clipboard Viewer.

When you copy or cut data to the Clipboard, the source application places one or more formats on the Clipboard along with the data. Different applications support different Clipboard formats. When you paste Clipboard data into another application, the destination application determines which format it can handle and typically selects the format that either provides the most information or is appropriate for where you are pasting it.

Note   In some cases, you can use the Display command in the Clipboard Viewer application to view the Clipboard data in a different format. For example, you can display a range of cells from Excel as a picture, bitmap, text, OEM text, or a DIB bitmap. Importantly, the format that you select in the Clipboard Viewer *doesn't* affect how Excel copies the data. In some cases, however, you can use Excel's Edit ⇨ Paste Special command to select alternate methods of pasting the data.

Copying data from another Windows application

Copying data from one Windows application to another is quite straightforward. The source application contains the data that you're copying, and the destination application receives the data that you're copying. Use the following steps to copy data from one application into another:

1. Activate the source document window that contains the information you want to copy.

2. Select the information that you want to copy by using the mouse or the keyboard. If Excel is the source application, this information can be a cell, range, chart, or drawing object.

3. Select Edit ➪ Copy (or any available shortcut). A copy of the information is sent to the Windows Clipboard. If you're copying from an Office application, a copy of the information is also sent to the Office Clipboard.

4. Activate the destination application. If it isn't open, you can start it without affecting the contents of the Clipboard.

5. Move to the position to which you want to paste in the destination application.

6. Select Edit ➪ Paste from the menu in the destination application. If the Clipboard contents aren't appropriate for pasting, the Paste command is grayed (not available).

Tip   In Step 3, you also can select Edit ➪ Cut from the source application menu.

Many Windows applications use a common keyboard convention for the Clipboard commands. Generally, this technique is a bit faster than using the menus, because these keys are adjacent to each other. The shortcut keys and their equivalents are

✦ Edit ➪ Copy   Ctrl+C

✦ Edit ➪ Cut   Ctrl+X

✦ Edit ➪ Paste   Ctrl+V

Tip   You can also use the right-click mouse method to display a menu that enables you to cut, copy, or paste.

You need to understand that Windows applications vary in how they respond to data that you paste from the Clipboard. If the Edit ➪ Paste command isn't available (it is grayed on the menu) in the destination application, the application can't accept the information from the Clipboard. If you copy a table from Word to Excel, the data translates into cells perfectly, complete with formatting. Copying data from other non-Office applications may not work as well; for example, you may lose the formatting, or you may end up with all the data in a single column rather than in separate columns. As discussed later in this chapter, you can use the Convert Text to Columns Wizard to convert this data into columns.

Note Some Windows programs simply don't support the Windows Clipboard. This is generally an indicator that the manufacturer is attempting to prevent you from copying information from the program, and is usually evident from the lack of an Edit menu in the program.

If you plan to do a great deal of copying and pasting between two applications, experiment until you understand how the two applications can handle each other's data.

Figure 18-2 shows an example of using the Edit ➪ Paste Special command to copy an object from another Windows program into Excel.

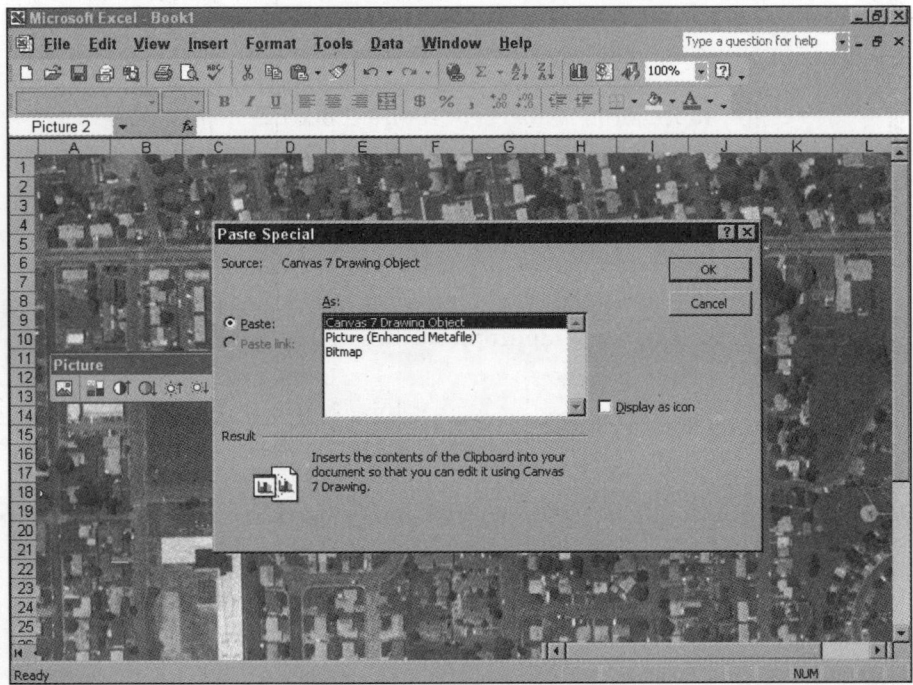

Figure 18-2: You can copy many different types of data into Excel using the Clipboard — including data that Excel would not otherwise be able to import such as in this example.

Copying data from a non-Windows application

You also can use the Windows Clipboard with non-Windows applications running in a DOS window. As you may know, you can run non-Windows programs from Windows either in a window or in full-screen mode (the application takes over the complete screen).

Note In Windows 2000 (or Windows NT 4), the DOS window is called the Command Prompt.

When you're running a non-Windows application in Windows, you can press Alt+Print Screen to copy the entire screen to the Clipboard. The screen contents can then be pasted into a Windows application (including Excel).

Caution Copying the entire screen may not result in data that can be edited in Excel. It is usually best to run the non-Windows application in a window and use the following technique to copy the data.

To copy only part of the screen, you must run the application in a window: press Alt+Enter to toggle between full-screen mode and windowed mode. You can then click the Control menu, choose Edit ➪ Mark, and select text from the window. This window may or may not have a toolbar displayed. If it does not, follow these steps:

1. Right-click the title bar and select the Toolbar option.
2. Click the Mark tool and select the text to copy.
3. Click the Copy tool to copy the selected text to the Clipboard.
4. Activate Excel.
5. Select Edit ➪ Paste to copy the Clipboard data into your worksheet.

Figure 18-3 shows a DOS window. The Mark button is depressed and some text is selected.

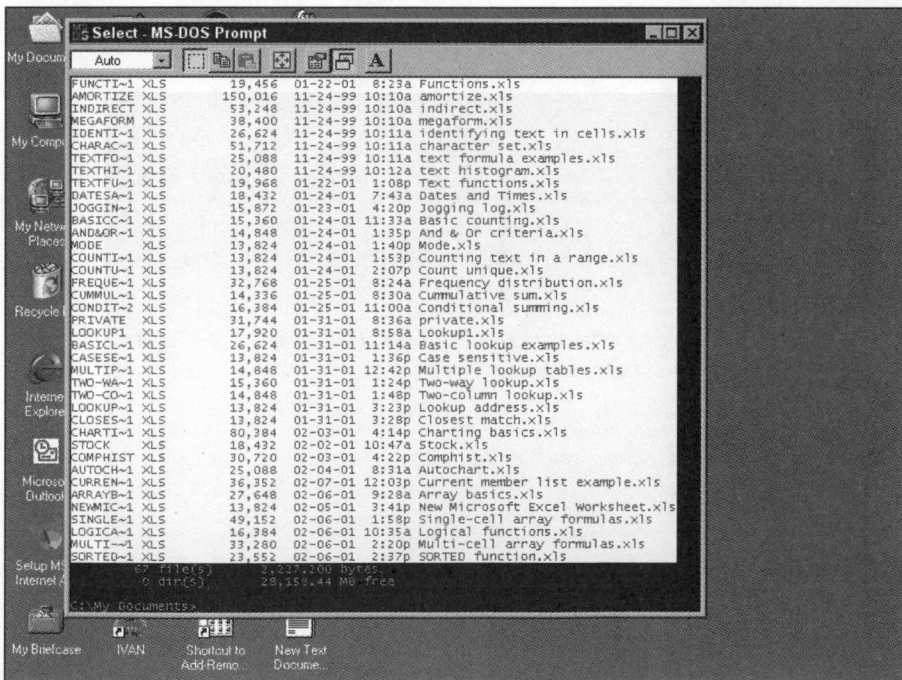

Figure 18-3: You can copy information from a DOS window and then paste it as text into Excel.

If you use this technique and copy to Excel, the information is pasted as text in a single column (see Figure 18-4). In other words, even if you copy information from neatly formatted columns, it's all pasted into a single column in Excel. But don't fret — you can use Excel's Convert Text to Columns Wizard to convert this data into columns (see the section called "Using the Text to Columns Wizard" later in this chapter).

	A	B	C	D	E	F	G	H	I	J	K	L
1	FUNCTI~1	XLS	19,456	01-22-01	8:23a	Functions.xls						
2	AMORTIZE	XLS	150,016	11-24-99	10:10a	amortize.xls						
3	INDIRECT	XLS	53,248	11-24-99	10:10a	indirect.xls						
4	MEGAFORM	XLS	38,400	11-24-99	10:10a	megaform.xls						
5	IDENTI~1	XLS	26,624	11-24-99	10:11a	identifying text in cells.xls						
6	CHARAC~1	XLS	51,712	11-24-99	10:11a	character set.xls						
7	TEXTFO~1	XLS	25,088	11-24-99	10:11a	text formula examples.xls						
8	TEXTHI~1	XLS	20,480	11-24-99	10:12a	text histogram.xls						
9	TEXTFU~1	XLS	19,968	01-22-01	1:08p	Text functions.xls						
10	DATESA~1	XLS	18,432	01-24-01	7:43a	Dates and Times.xls						
11	JOGGIN~1	XLS	15,872	01-23-01	4:20p	Jogging log.xls						
12	BASICC~1	XLS	15,360	01-24-01	11:33a	Basic counting.xls						
13	AND&OR~1	XLS	14,848	01-24-01	1:35p	And & Or criteria.xls						
14	MODE	XLS	13,824	01-24-01	1:40p	Mode.xls						
15	COUNTI~1	XLS	13,824	01-24-01	1:53p	Counting text in a range.xls						
16	COUNTU~1	XLS	13,824	01-24-01	2:07p	Count unique.xls						
17	FREQUE~1	XLS	32,768	01-25-01	8:24a	Frequency distribution.xls						
18	CUMMUL~1	XLS	14,336	01-25-01	8:30a	Cummulative sum.xls						
19	CONDIT~2	XLS	16,384	01-25-01	11:00a	Conditional summing.xls						
20	PRIVATE	XLS	31,744	01-31-01	8:36a	private.xls						
21	LOOKUP1	XLS	17,920	01-31-01	8:58a	Lookup1.xls						
22	BASICL~1	XLS	26,624	01-31-01	11:14a	Basic lookup examples.xls						
23	CASESE~1	XLS	13,824	01-31-01	1:36p	Case sensitive.xls						
24	MULTIP~1	XLS	14,848	01-31-01	12:42p	Multiple lookup tables.xls						

Figure 18-4: When you copy information from a DOS window and paste it as text into Excel, the information is pasted into a single column as shown here.

You're limited to copying one screen of information at a time — you can't scroll the DOS application while you're selecting text.

Tip   You can, however, increase the number of lines in the DOS window by clicking the Properties button when the DOS window is open and choosing the number of lines on the Screen tab. The change will take effect the next time you open the DOS window.

Importing Text Files

Text files (sometimes referred to as ASCII files) are usually considered to be the lowest-common-denominator file type. Such files contain only data, with no formatting. Consequently, most applications can read and write text files. So, if all else fails, you can probably use a text file to transfer data between two applications that don't support a common file format. Because text files are so commonly used, this entire section is devoted to discussing them and explaining how to use Excel's Text Import Wizard.

Caution Not all text files actually contain only plain text. Specifically, you may find that "text files" from a Macintosh computer often contain odd characters that show up as rectangular blocks (rather than recognizable characters) when the file is imported into a Windows program. Unfortunately, there's nothing you can do except to manually go through the imported text and delete those nontext characters.

Understanding text files

Text files simply contain data with no formatting. The following relatively standard text file formats exist, although no standard file extensions exist:

✦ **Tab-delimited files:** Each line consists of fields that are separated by tabs.

✦ **Comma-separated files:** Each line consists of fields that are separated by commas. Sometimes, text appears in quotation marks.

✦ **Nondelimited files:** Each field is a fixed length, enabling you easily to break each line of text into separate columns. These files don't contain a special field-separator character.

Tip If you want your exported text file to use a different extension, specify the complete filename and extension in quotation marks. For example, saving a workbook in comma-separated format normally uses the CSV extension. If you want your file to be named output.txt (with a TXT extension), enter "output.txt" in the File name box in the Save As dialog box.

You may find it helpful to think of some text files in terms of a database table. Each line in the text file corresponds to a database record, and each record consists of a number of fields. In Excel, each line (or record) is imported to a separate row, and each field goes into a separate column — if Excel can determine the field delimiters, that is.

If you use a proportional font, such as Arial or Times Roman, the fields of text file may appear to not line up, although they actually do. In proportional font sets, each character uses a different amount of horizontal space. For best results, use a nonproportional font, such as Courier New, when working with text files. Excel uses Courier New in its Text Import Wizard dialog box. Figure 18-5 shows the same text displayed in Arial and Courier New fonts.

Figure 18-5: It's usually best to format imported text using a nonproportional font to make it easier to identify the individual fields in the data.

Excel is quite versatile when importing text files. If each line of the text file is identically laid out, importing is usually problem-free. But if the line contains mixed information, you may need to do some additional work to make the data usable. For example, you create text files in some programs by sending a printed report to a disk file rather than to the printer. These reports often have extra information, such as page headers and footers, titles, summary lines, and so on.

Tip   You can use the Windows Notepad program to edit most plain-text files to remove extraneous information that is not needed in Excel.

Using the Text Import Wizard

The Excel Text Import Wizard makes it very easy to import information from text files. You simply follow along answering the Text Import Wizard's questions, and in a few moments you've imported the data.

Tip   Importing data from a database file is virtually identical to importing text from a text file.

Cross-Reference   For more information on Database queries, see Chapter 20. For more information on Web queries, see Chapter 28.

Note If you use the technique described in this section, you'll create a Text File Query, which you can refresh in the same way that you refresh Database and Web queries. When you want to update the Excel file that you create by importing a text file, choose Data ➪ Refresh Data. Highlight the text file that you originally imported and click the Import button. Excel automatically updates the Excel version of the file with any new data that may appear in the text file.

To import a text file into Excel, follow these steps to get started:

1. Choose Data ➪ Import External Data ➪ Import Data to open the Select Data Source dialog box.

2. In the Select Data Source dialog box, navigate to the folder containing the file that you want to import.

3. Select Text Files in the File of type list box. The dialog box then displays text files.

4. Choose the file you wish to import and click Open.

Excel displays its Text Import Wizard, a series of interactive dialog boxes in which you specify the information that Excel requires to break the lines of the text file into columns. You can truly appreciate this time-saving feature if, in a previous life, you struggled with the old data-parsing commands that are found in other spreadsheet programs and older versions of Excel.

Figure 18-6 shows the first of three Text Import Wizard dialog boxes. In the Original data type section, verify the type of data file (Excel almost always guesses correctly). You also can indicate the row that Excel should use to start importing. For example, if the file has a title in the first row, you may want to skip the first line.

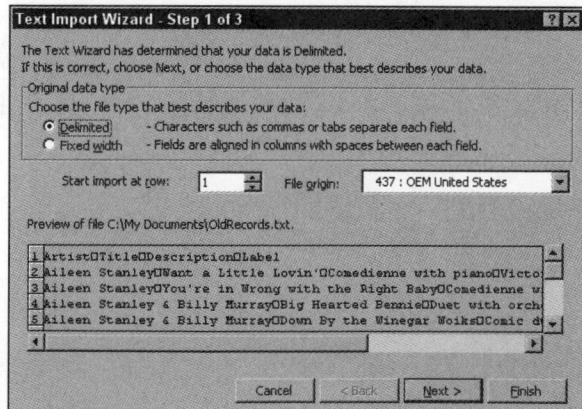

Figure 18-6: Verify that the Text Import Wizard has selected the correct type of data.

Notice that you can preview the file at the bottom of the dialog box, using the scrollbars to view more of the file. If the characters in the file don't look right, you may need to change the File Origin; this determines which character set to use (in many cases, it doesn't make any difference). After you finish with this step, click Next to move to Step 2.

The dialog box that you see for Step 2 of the Text Import Wizard varies, depending on your choice in the Original data type section in Step 1. If you selected Delimited, you see the dialog box shown in Figure 18-7. You can specify the type of delimiter, the text qualifier, and whether to treat consecutive delimiters as a single delimiter; choosing to treat consecutive delimiters as a single delimiter tells Excel to skip empty columns. The Data preview section displays vertical lines to indicate how Excel will break up the fields. The Data preview section changes as you make choices in the dialog box.

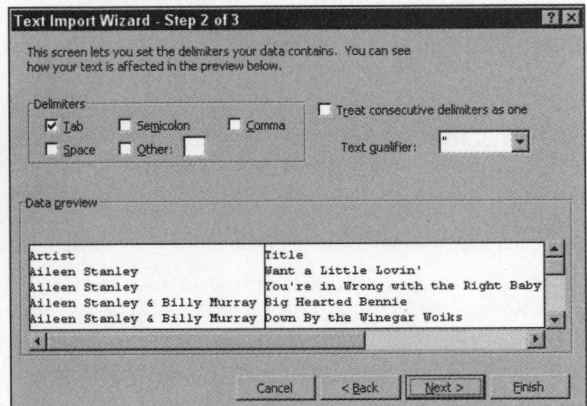

Figure 18-7: Verify that the selected delimiters correctly break down the data.

Note

If you selected Fixed width, you see a slightly different dialog box. At this point, Excel attempts to identify the column breaks and displays vertical break lines to represent how it will break fields apart into columns. If Excel guesses wrong, you can move the lines, insert new ones, or delete lines that Excel proposes. You'll see instructions in the dialog box.

If you're importing a print image file that includes page headers, you can ignore them when you specify the column indicators. Instead, base the columns on the data. When the file is imported, you can then delete the rows that contain the page headers.

Tip

You can also use the Start import at row setting in Step 1 of the Text Import Wizard to tell Excel to ignore extra rows at the beginning of the file.

When you're satisfied with how the column breaks look, click Next to move to the final step. Or, you can click Back to return to Step 1 to change the file type.

Figure 18-8 shows the last of the three Text Import Wizard dialog boxes. In this dialog box, you can select individual columns and specify the formatting to apply (General, Text, or Date). You also can specify columns to skip. If you click the Advanced button, you can specify characters to use as decimal and thousands separators. When you're satisfied with the results, click Finish. Excel prompts you for the starting cell location for the imported data; when you click OK, Excel imports the data.

 **Tip**   You may want to display the External Data toolbar, which helps you to work with the imported text file. For example, if you click the Data Range Properties tool, you see the External Data Range Properties dialog box, which you can use to change how Excel treats the imported file.

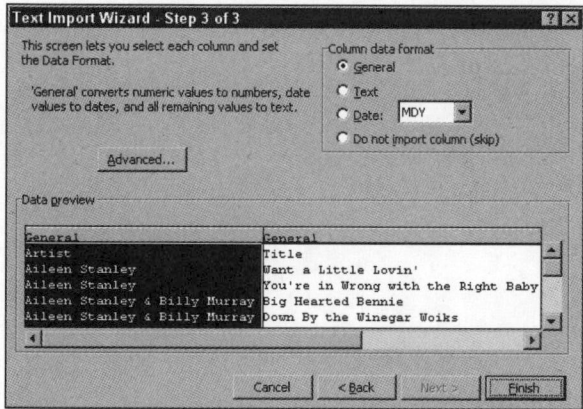

Figure 18-8: Specify the formats for the columns of data and click Finish to import the data.

If the results aren't what you expect, close the workbook and try again (text importing often involves trial and error). Don't forget that you can scroll the Data Preview window (in the Text Import Wizard dialog box) to make sure that all the data is converted properly. With some files, however, importing all the data properly is impossible. In such cases, you may want to import the file as a single column of text and then break lines into columns selectively. The procedure for doing this is discussed in the next section.

Using the Text to Columns Wizard

If you import text using the Windows Clipboard, you may find that Excel has placed all of the text into a single column without breaking it down into individual fields in separate columns. Fortunately, Excel can parse text that is stored in a column. Start by selecting the text (in a single column). Then choose Data ➪ Text to Columns; Excel displays the first of three Text to Columns Wizard dialog boxes. These dialog boxes are identical to those used for the Text Import Wizard, except that the title bar text is different.

Unfortunately, you can't use the Data ➪ Text to Columns command on a multiple selection; this would be quite handy for parsing imported files with several different layouts. Even worse, you can't use the Edit ➪ Repeat command to repeat the Text to Columns command.

✦   ✦   ✦

Working with Lists

Many users create *lists*—otherwise known as *work-sheet databases*—in Excel. In fact, since the first spreadsheet programs appeared on PCs, this has been one of the more common uses of spreadsheets. This chapter shows you how to make the most of your Excel lists and teaches you about some interesting capabilities in Excel for managing lists more effectively.

Understanding Excel Lists

A *list* is an organized collection of information that consists of a row of headers (descriptive text), followed by additional rows of data, which can be values or text. You may recognize this as a database table—which is exactly what it is.

Excel uses the term *list* to refer to a database stored in a worksheet and the term *database* to refer to a table of information stored in an external file.

External database files are discussed in Chapter 20.

Figure 19-1 shows an example of a list in a worksheet. This particular list has its headers in row 1 and includes several rows of data. The list occupies six columns. Notice that the data consists of several different types: text, values, and dates. Column D contains a formula that calculates the monthly salary from the value in column C.

	A	B	C	D	E	F	G	H	I	J
1	First_Name	Last_Name	Monthly	Annual	Location	Hired				
2	Annemarie	Andrews	$ 5,985	$ 71,820	Incline Village	12/30/2003				
3	Arthur	Bellard	$ 8,305	$ 99,660	Reno	5/7/2000				
4	Becky	Brown	$ 8,526	$102,312	Reno	12/14/2000				
5	Carole	Drews	$ 1,844	$ 22,128	Reno	8/28/1992				
6	David	Escobar	$ 3,034	$ 36,408	Sparks	12/1/1995				
7	Albert	Ferrari	$ 5,468	$ 65,616	Sparks	7/31/2002				
8	Anne-Louise	Forte	$ 3,286	$ 39,432	Olympic Valley	8/9/1996				
9	Dan	Frank	$ 7,201	$ 86,412	Reno	4/29/2007				
10	Curtis	Holt	$ 8,811	$105,732	Elko	9/25/2011				
11	Alexander	Mueller	$ 3,381	$ 40,572	Gardnerville	11/12/1996				
12	Barry	Onorato	$ 6,616	$ 79,392	Minden	9/21/2005				
13	Brian	Sax	$ 5,801	$ 69,612	Reno	6/29/2003				
14	Derrick	Smith	$ 7,520	$ 90,240	Reno	3/13/2008				
15	Clayton	Underdahl	$ 6,442	$ 77,304	Reno	3/31/2005				
16	Austin	Williams	$ 6,164	$ 73,968	Incline Village	6/26/2001				

Figure 19-1: An example of an Excel list.

People often refer to the columns in a list as *fields* and to the rows as *records*. The list shown in the figure has 6 fields (First_Name, Last_Name, Monthly, Annual, Location, and Hired) and 15 records.

Note   The size of the lists that you develop in Excel is limited by the size of a single worksheet. In other words, a list can have no more than 256 fields and can consist of no more than 65,535 records (one row contains the field names).

Understanding what can you do with a list

People use lists for a wide variety of purposes. For some users, a list is simply a way to keep track of information (for example, customer lists); others use lists to store data that ultimately will appear in a report. Common list operations include:

✦ Entering data into the list

✦ Filtering the list to display only the rows that meet certain criteria

✦ Sorting the list

✦ Inserting formulas to calculate subtotals

✦ Creating formulas to calculate results on the list filtered by certain criteria

✦ Creating a summary table of the data in the list (this is done using a pivot table; see Chapter 21).

With the exception of the last item, these operations are discussed in this chapter.

Designing a list

Although Excel is quite accommodating when it comes to the information that is stored in a list, planning the organization of your list information will pay off. The following are some guidelines to keep in mind when creating lists:

✦ Insert descriptive labels (one for each column) in the first row of the list, called the header row. If you use lengthy labels, consider using the Wrap Text format so that you don't have to widen the columns.

See Chapter 5 for information on the Wrap Text format.

Don't use more than one row for the header—Excel will recognize the header properly only if it is in a single row.

✦ Make sure each column contains the same type of information. For example, don't mix dates and text in a single column.

✦ You can use formulas that perform calculations on other fields in the same record. If you use formulas that refer to cells outside the list, make these absolute references; otherwise, you get unexpected results when you sort the list.

✦ Don't leave any empty rows within the list. For list operations, Excel determines the list boundaries automatically, and an empty row signals the end of the list.

✦ For best results, try to keep the list on a worksheet by itself.

✦ Select Window ➪ Freeze Panes to make sure that you can see the headings when you scroll the list.

See Chapter 2 for more information on controlling the view.

✦ You can preformat entire columns to ensure that the data has the same format. For example, if a column contains dates, format the entire column with the desired date format.

 **Tip**   You may want to use the Data ⇨ Validation command to make certain that only the correct type of data is entered in a column.

Lists behave no differently than any other kind of data in Excel. For example, you may create a list and then decide that it needs another column (field). If so, just insert a new column, give it a field name, and Excel expands your list. If you've ever used a database management program, you can appreciate the simplicity of this layout change.

Entering Data into a List

Of course, a list is really only useful after it actually contains your data. You can enter data into a list in three ways:

✦ Manually, using all standard data-entry techniques

✦ By importing it or copying it from another file

✦ By using a dialog box

Entering data manually

There's really nothing special about entering data into a list. You just navigate through the worksheet and enter the data into the appropriate cells.

Excel has two features that assist with repetitive data entry:

✦ **AutoComplete:** When you begin to type in a cell, Excel scans up and down the column for entries that match what you're typing. If it finds a match, Excel fills in the rest of the text automatically. Press Enter to make the entry. You can turn this feature on or off in the Edit tab of the Options dialog box.

 **Tip**   If the AutoComplete entry is not what you want, just keep typing—Excel will use your entry if you overwrite the AutoComplete entry.

✦ **Pick Lists:** You can right-click a cell and select Pick from list from the shortcut menu. Excel displays a list box that shows all entries in the column (see Figure 19-2). Click the one that you want to enter into the cell (no typing is required).

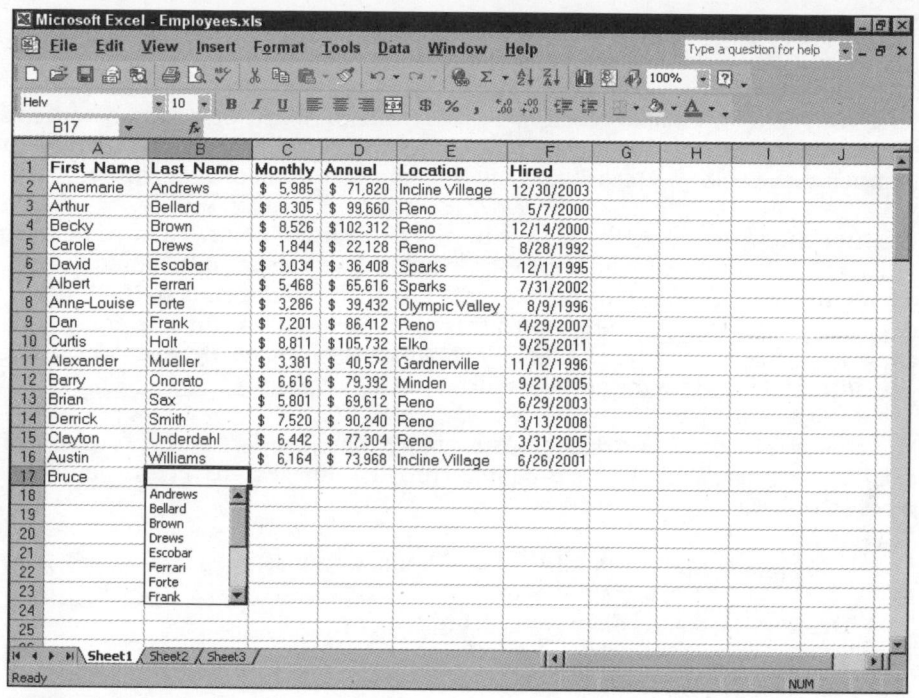

Figure 19-2: You can choose the Pick from list command on the shortcut menu to see a list of all items in the current column.

Entering data with the data form dialog box

If you prefer to use a dialog box for your data entry, Excel accommodates you. To display a data entry dialog box, move the cell pointer anywhere within the list and choose Data ⇨ Form. Excel determines the boundaries of your list and displays a dialog box showing each field in the list. Figure 19-3 is an example of such a dialog box. Fields that have a formula don't have an edit box.

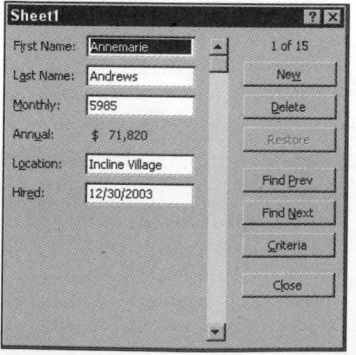

Figure 19-3: You can use the Data ⇨ Form command to display a dialog box you can use to enter and edit list data.

Note   If your list consists of more than 32 fields, you cannot use the Data ⇨ Form command. You must enter the information directly into the cells.

When the data form dialog box appears, Excel displays the first record in the list. Notice the indicator in the upper-right corner of the dialog box that tells you the number of the selected record and the total number of records in the list.

To enter a new record, click the New button to clear the fields. Then you can enter the new information into the appropriate fields. Use Tab or Shift+Tab to move among the fields. When you click New (or Close), Excel appends to the bottom of the list the data that you entered. You also can press Enter, which is equivalent to clicking on the New button. If the list contains any formulas, Excel enters them for you automatically into the new record.

You can use the data form dialog box for more than just data entry. You can edit existing data in the list, view data one record at a time, delete records, and display records that meet certain criteria.

The dialog box contains a number of additional buttons:

+ **Delete:** Deletes the displayed record.

+ **Restore:** Restores any information that you edited. You must click this button before you click the New button.

+ **Find Prev:** Displays the previous record in the list. If you entered a criterion, this button displays the previous record that matches the criterion.

+ **Find Next:** Displays the next record in the list. If you entered a criterion, this button displays the next record that matches the criterion.

+ **Criteria:** Clears the fields and lets you enter a criterion on which to search for records. For example, to locate records that have a salary greater than $50,000, enter >**50000** into the Salary field. Then you can use the Find Next and Find Prev buttons to display the qualifying records.

+ **Close:** Closes the dialog box (and enters the data that you were entering, if any).

Filtering a List

Filtering a list is the process of hiding all rows in the list except those that meet some criteria that you specify. For example, if you have a list of customers, you can filter the list to show only those who live in certain areas. Filtering is a common (and very useful) technique. Excel provides two ways to filter a list:

+ AutoFilter, for simple filtering criteria

+ Advance Filter, for more complex filtering

Using AutoFiltering

To use Excel's AutoFilter feature to filter a list, place the cell pointer anywhere within the list and then choose Data ⇨ Filter ⇨ AutoFilter. Excel analyzes your list and adds drop-down arrows to the field names in the header row, as shown in Figure 19-4. When you click the arrow in one of these drop-down lists, the list expands to show the unique items in that column. Select an item, and Excel hides all rows except those that include the selected item. In other words, Excel filters the list by the item that you selected.

	First_Nam	Last_Name	Month	Annual	Location	Hired
1	First_Nam	Last_Name	Month	Annual	Location	Hired
2	Annemarie	Andrews	$ 5,985	$ 71,820	(All)	12/30/2003
3	Arthur	Bellard	$ 8,305	$ 99,660	(Top 10...)	5/7/2000
4	Becky	Brown	$ 8,526	$102,312	(Custom...) Elko	12/14/2000
5	Carole	Drews	$ 1,844	$ 22,128	Gardnerville	8/28/1992
6	David	Escobar	$ 3,034	$ 36,408	Incline Village	12/1/1995
7	Albert	Ferrari	$ 5,468	$ 65,616	Minden	7/31/2002
8	Anne-Louise	Forte	$ 3,286	$ 39,432	Olympic Valley Reno	8/9/1996
9	Dan	Frank	$ 7,201	$ 86,412	Sparks	4/29/2007
10	Curtis	Holt	$ 8,811	$105,732	Elko	9/25/2011
11	Alexander	Mueller	$ 3,381	$ 40,572	Gardnerville	11/12/1996
12	Barry	Onorato	$ 6,616	$ 79,392	Minden	9/21/2005
13	Brian	Sax	$ 5,801	$ 69,612	Reno	6/29/2003
14	Derrick	Smith	$ 7,520	$ 90,240	Reno	3/13/2008
15	Clayton	Underdahl	$ 6,442	$ 77,304	Reno	3/31/2005
16	Austin	Williams	$ 6,164	$ 73,968	Incline Village	6/26/2001
17	Bruce	Johnson	$ 4,500	$ 54,000	Sparks	2/8/2001

Figure 19-4: You can use the Data ⇨ Filter ⇨ AutoFilter command to quickly choose criteria for displaying records.

After you filter the list, the status bar displays a message that tells you how many rows qualified. In addition, the drop-down arrow changes color to remind you that you filtered the list by a value in that column.

Note   AutoFiltering has a limit of 999 unique items that can appear in the drop-down list. If your list exceeds this limit, you can use advanced filtering, which is described later.

In addition to showing every item in the column, the drop-down list includes five other items:

+ **All:** Displays all items in the column. Use this to remove filtering for a column.

+ **Top 10:** Filters to display the "top 10" items in the list; this is discussed later.

+ **Custom:** Lets you filter the list by multiple items; this is discussed later.

+ **Blanks:** Filters the list by showing rows that contain blanks in this column.

+ **NonBlanks:** Filters the list by showing rows that contain nonblanks in this column.

 **Note**   The Blanks and NonBlanks items only appear if one or more records are missing an entry in the selected field.

To display the entire list again, click the arrow and choose All from the drop-down list. Or, you can select Data ➪ Filter ➪ Show All.

 Tip   To move out of Autofilter mode and remove the drop-down arrows from the field names, choose Data ➪ Filter ➪ AutoFilter again to remove the check mark from the AutoFilter menu item to restore the list to its normal state.

 **Caution**   If you have any formulas that refer to data in a filtered list, be aware that the formulas don't adjust to use only the visible cells. For example, if a cell contains a formula that sums values in column C, the formula continues to show the sum for *all* the values in column C — not just those in the visible rows. To solve this problem, use database functions, which are described later in this chapter.

Using AutoFiltering with multiple columns

Sometimes you may need to filter a list by values in more than one column. For example, you might want to filter a list of sales information so that it only shows your ice cream sales during February.

To create a multiple column filter, first, get into Autofilter mode. Then click the drop-down arrow in the Month field and select *Feb* to filter the list to show only records with *Feb* in the Month field. Then click the drop-down arrow in the Product field and select *Ice Cream,* filtering the filtered list to show only records that contain *Ice Cream* in the Product column — resulting in a list filtered by values in two columns.

 **Tip**   You can filter a list by any number of columns. Excel applies a different color to the drop-down arrows in the columns that have a filter applied.

Using custom AutoFiltering

Usually, AutoFiltering involves selecting a single value for one or more columns. If you choose the Custom option in a drop-down list, you gain a bit more flexibility in filtering the list; Excel displays a dialog box like the one shown in Figure 19-5.

The Custom AutoFilter dialog box lets you filter in several ways:

✦ **Values above or below a specified value:** For example, sales amounts greater than 10,000.

✦ **Values within a range:** For example, sales amounts greater than 10,000 AND sales amounts less than 50,000.

✦ **Two discrete values:** For example, state equal to New York OR state equal to New Jersey.

✦ **Approximate matches:** You can use the * and ? wildcards to filter in a number of other ways. For example, to display only those customers whose last name begins with B, use B*.

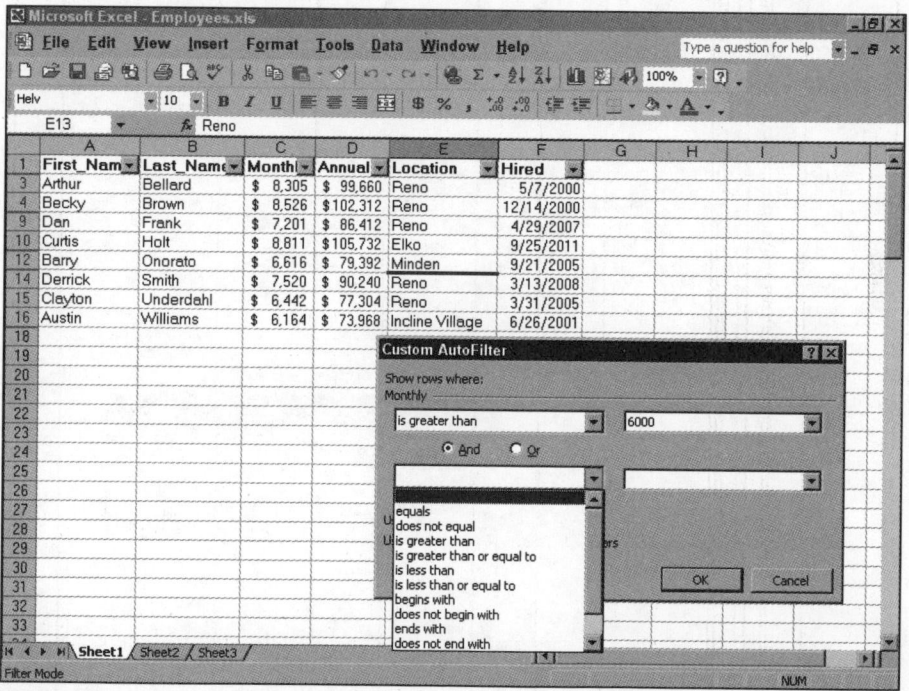

Figure 19-5: You can use the Custom AutoFilter dialog box for more control over the filtering process.

Cross-Reference   Custom AutoFiltering has limitations. For example, if you want to filter the list to show only three values in a field (such as New York or New Jersey or Connecticut), you can't do it by AutoFiltering. Such filtering tasks require the advanced filtering feature, which is discussed later in this chapter, in the section "Using Advanced Filtering."

Using Top 10 AutoFiltering

Sometimes you may want to use a filter on numerical fields to show only the highest or lowest values in the list. For example, if you have a list of employees, you may want to identify the 12 employees with the longest tenure. You could use the custom AutoFilter option, but then you must supply a cutoff date (which you may not know). The solution is to use Top 10 AutoFiltering.

Top 10 AutoFiltering is a generic term; it doesn't limit you to the top *10* items. In fact, it doesn't even limit you to the *top* items. When you choose the Top 10 option from a drop-down list, you see the Top 10 AutoFilter dialog box that is shown in Figure 19-6.

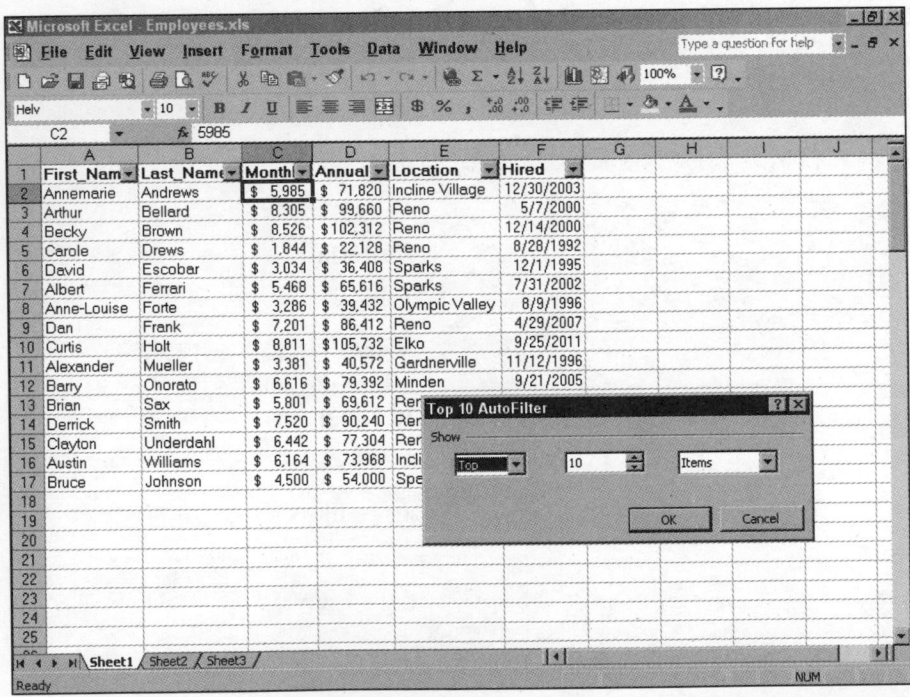

Figure 19-6: You can use the Top 10 AutoFilter dialog box to filter the list by rank or percentage.

You can choose either Top or Bottom and specify any number. Suppose that you want to see the 12 employees with the longest tenure. Choose Bottom and 12 to filter the list and show the 12 rows with the smallest values in the Hired field. You also can choose Percent or Value in this dialog box. For example, you can filter the list to show the Bottom five percent of the records.

Charting filtered list data

You can create some interesting multipurpose charts that use data in a filtered list. The technique is useful because only the visible data appears in the chart. When you change the AutoFilter criteria, the chart updates itself to show only the visible cells.

For this technique to work, select the chart and make sure that the Plot Visible Cells Only option is enabled on the Chart tab of the Options dialog box.

You can apply other filters, and the chart updates automatically. This technique lets a single chart show several different views of the data.

Using advanced filtering

In many cases, AutoFiltering does the job. But if you run up against its limitations, you need to use advanced filtering. Advanced filtering is much more flexible than AutoFiltering, but it takes a bit of upfront work to use it. Advanced filtering provides you with these capabilities:

✦ You can specify more complex filtering criteria.

✦ You can specify computed filtering criteria.

✦ You can extract to another location a copy of the rows that meet the criteria.

Setting up a criteria range for advanced filtering

Before you can use the advanced filtering feature, you must set up a *criteria range,* a designated range on a worksheet that conforms to certain requirements. The criteria range holds the information that Excel uses to filter the list. It must conform to these specifications:

✦ It must consist of at least two rows, and the first row must contain some or all field names from the list.

✦ The other rows of the criteria range must consist of your filtering criteria.

Although you can put the criteria range anywhere in the worksheet, it's a good idea not to put it in rows where you placed the list. Because Excel hides some of these rows when filtering the list, you may find that your criteria range is no longer visible after filtering. Therefore, you should generally place the criteria range above or below the list.

Figure 19-7 shows a criteria range, located in A1:F2, above the list that it uses. Only some field names need appear in the criteria range. You don't need to include field names for fields that you don't use in the selection criteria (although including all of them won't hurt anything).

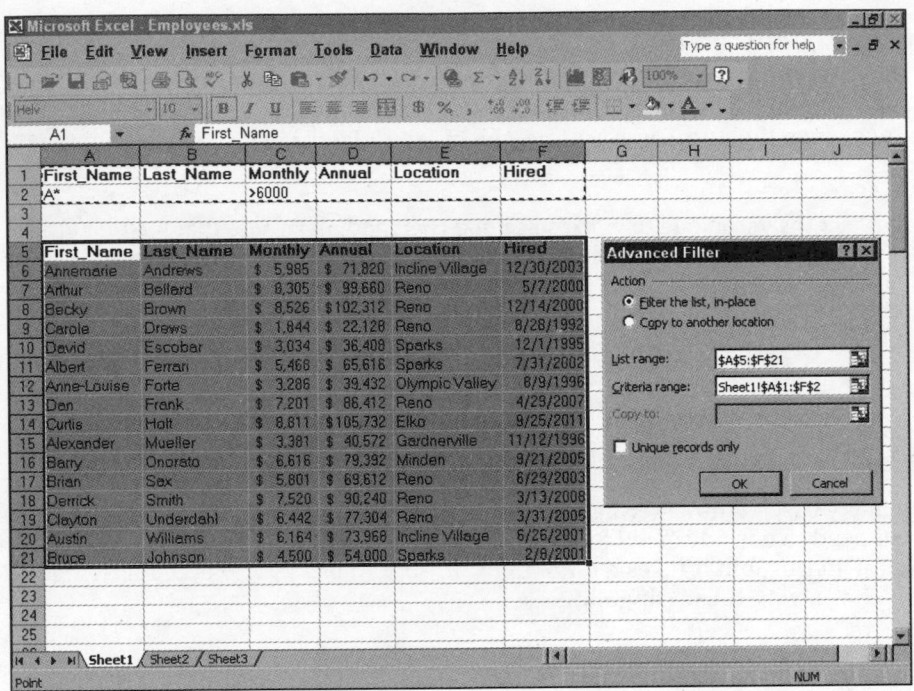

Figure 19-7: You can use advanced filtering to create a complex filter.

In this example, the criteria range has only one row of criteria where cell A2 contains "A*" and cell C2 contains ">6000". The fields in each row of the criteria range (except for the header row) are joined with an AND operator. Therefore, the filtered list will show rows in which the First_Name column begins with A AND the Monthly column is greater than 6,000. In other words, the list displays only employees whose first name begins with A and who make more than $6,000 per month.

To perform the filtering, choose Data ⇨ Filter ⇨ Advanced filter. Excel displays the Advanced Filter dialog box that is shown in Figure 19-7. Specify the list range and the criteria range, and make sure that you select the option labeled Filter the List in-place. Click OK, and Excel filters the list by the criteria that you specified.

Using multiple criteria in your filter

All the criteria you place in a single row must be met in order for a record to pass the filter. Therefore, criteria that are placed in the same row act as an AND condition.

If you use more than one row in the criteria range, the criteria in each row are joined with an OR operator. A criteria range can have any number of rows, each of which is joined to the others with an OR operator.

Tip   If you create a multiple-row criteria range, remember to make each row complete on its own. That is, if you want to see records only for employees whose first name begins with A and who make more than $6,000 per month or those whose first name begins with A and who work in the Reno location, make certain that both rows include A* in the First_Name field.

Using text or value criteria

You can use text or value criteria to specify which records pass through the filter. This type of filtering involves comparisons to a value or string, using operators such as equal (=), greater than (>), not equal to (<>), and so on.

Table 19-1 lists the comparison operators that you can use with text or value criteria.

Table 19-1 Comparison Operators	
Operator	**Comparison Type**
=	Equal to
>	Greater than
>=	Greater than or equal to
<	Less than
<=	Less than or equal to
<>	Not equal to

Table 19-2 shows examples of criteria that use strings.

	Table 19-2 Examples of String Criteria	
Criteria	**Effect**
>K	Text that begins with L through Z
<>C	All text, except text that begins with C
="January"	Text that matches January
Sm*	Text that begins with Sm
s*s	Text that begins with s and ends with s
s?s	Three-letter text that begins with s and ends with s

Note   The text comparisons are not case sensitive. For example, si* matches Simple as well as sick.

Using computed criteria

Using computed criteria can make filtering even more powerful. Computed criteria filter the list based one or more calculations. A computed criteria computes a new field for the list. Therefore, you must supply new field names in the first row of the criteria range.

Suppose you have a list that tracks your projects. In your list, you have fields for project numbers, start dates, end dates, and resources. If you want to figure out which projects will take 30 days or more, you could use a formula similar to this:

```
=End_Date-Start_Date>=30
```

This formula returns a logical value of either *True* or *False*. The result of the formula refers to cells in the first row of data in the list; it does *not* refer to the header row. When you filter the list by this criterion, the list shows only rows in which the project length (End_Date–Start_Date) is greater than or equal to 30 days. In other words, Excel bases the comparison on a computation.

Note   You could accomplish the same effect, without using a computed criterion, by adding a new column to the list that contains a formula to calculate the project length. Using a computed criterion, however, eliminates the need to add a new column.

Keep in mind these items when using computed criteria:

✦ Don't use a field name in the criteria range that appears in the list; create a new field name or just leave the cell blank.

✦ You can use any number of computed criteria and mix and match them with noncomputed criteria.

✦ Don't pay attention to the values returned by formulas in the criteria range; these refer to the first row of the list.

✦ If your computed formula refers to a value outside the list, use an absolute reference rather than a relative reference. For example, use $C$1 instead of C1.

✦ Create your computed criteria formulas using the first row of data in the list (not the field names). Make these references relative, not absolute. For example, use C5 instead of $C$5.

Using other advanced filtering operations

The Advanced Filter dialog box gives you two other options:

✦ Copy to Another Location

✦ Unique Records Only

Copying qualifying rows to another location

If you choose the Copy to Another Location option in the Advanced Filter dialog box, Excel copies the qualifying rows to another location in the worksheet or a different worksheet. You specify the location for the copied rows in the Copy to edit box. Note that the list itself is not filtered when you use this option.

Displaying only unique rows

Choosing the option labeled Unique records only hides all duplicate rows that meet the criteria that you specify. If you don't specify a criteria range, this option hides all duplicate rows in the list.

Sorting a List

In some cases, the order of the rows in your list doesn't matter. But in other cases, you want the rows to appear in a specific order. For example, in a price list, you may want the rows to appear in alphabetical order by product name. This makes the products easier to locate in the list. Or, if you have a list of accounts receivable information, you may want to sort the list so that the higher amounts appear at the top of the list (in descending order).

Rearranging the order of the rows in a list is called *sorting*. Excel is quite flexible when it comes to sorting lists, and you can often accomplish this task with the click of a mouse button.

Sorting the simple way

To quickly sort a list in ascending order, move the cell pointer into the column that you want to sort. Then click the Sort Ascending button on the Standard toolbar. The Sort Descending button works the same way, but it sorts the list in descending order. In both cases, Excel determines the extent of your list and sorts all the rows in the list.

When you sort a filtered list, Excel sorts only the visible rows. When you remove the filtering from the list, the list is no longer sorted.

Caution   Be careful if you sort a list that contains formulas. If the formulas refer to cells in the list that are in the same row, you don't have any problems. But if the formulas refer to cells in other rows in the list or to cells outside the list, the formulas will not be correct after you sort the list. If formulas in your list refer to cells outside the list, make sure that the formulas use an absolute cell reference.

Performing more complex sorting

Sometimes, you may want to sort by two or more columns. This is relevant to break ties. A tie occurs when rows with duplicate data remain unsorted. Figure 19-8 shows an example of an unsorted list. If you sort this list by Location, Excel places the rows for each month together. But you may also want to show the employees in ascending order within each month. In this case, you would need to sort by at least two columns (Location and Last_Name). You would probably also want to add a third sort by First_Name in case any employees shared the same last name and worked at the same location.

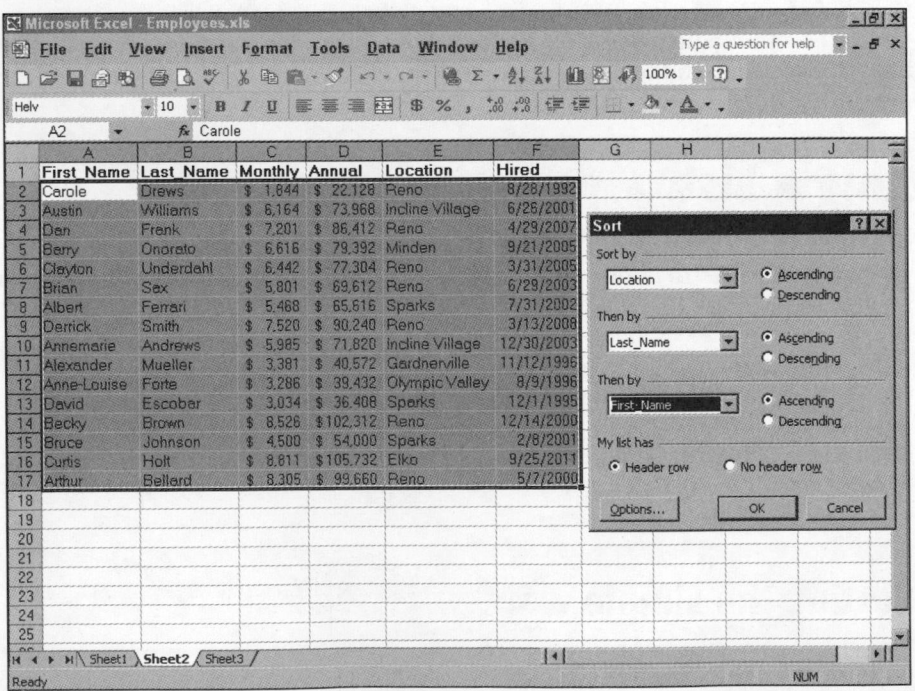

Figure 19-8: You can use the Sort dialog box to specify up to three sort keys.

If you want to sort by more than one field, choose Data ➪ Sort. Excel displays the dialog box that is shown in Figure 19-8. Simply select the first sort field from the drop-down list labeled Sort By, and specify Ascending or Descending order. Then, do the same for the second sort field. If you want to sort by a third field, specify the field in the third section. If the Header Row option is set, the first row (field names) is not affected by the sort. Click OK, and the list's rows rearrange in a flash.

> **Tip** If the sorting didn't occur as you expected, select Edit ➪ Undo (or press Ctrl+Z) to undo the sorting.

What if you need to sort your list by more than three fields? It can be done, but it takes an additional step. For example, assume that you want to sort your list by five fields: Field1, Field2, Field3, Field4, and Field5. Start by sorting by Field3, Field4, and Field5. Then resort the list by Field1 and Field2. In other words, sort the three "least important" fields first; they remain in sequence when you do the second sort.

> **Tip** Often, you want to keep the records in their original order but perform a temporary sort just to see how it looks. The solution is to add an additional column to the list with sequential numbers in it (don't use formulas to generate these numbers @md because then the numbers will change after the rows are sorted, but you can use the Fill command). Then, after you sort, you can return to the original order by resorting on the field that contains the sequential numbers. You can also use Excel's undo feature to return the list to its original order. If you use an additional column, you can perform other operations while the list is temporarily sorted (and these operations won't be undone when you undo the sort operation).

When you click the Options button in the Sort dialog box, Excel displays the Sort Options dialog box, shown in Figure 19-9.

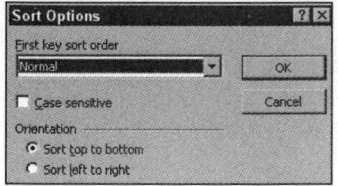 **Figure 19-9:** You can use the Sort Options dialog box to set additional sorting options.

These options are described as follows:

✦ **First key sort order:** Lets you specify a custom sort order for the sort (see the next section).

✦ **Case sensitive:** Makes the sorting case sensitive so that uppercase letters appear before lowercase letters in an ascending sort. Normally, sorting ignores the case of letters.

✦ **Orientation:** Enables you to sort by columns rather than by rows (the default).

Excel's Sorting Rules

Because cells can contain different types of information, you may be curious about how Excel sorts this information. For an ascending sort, the information appears in the following order:

1. **Values**: Excel sorts numbers from smallest negative to largest positive, and treats dates and times as values. In all cases, Excel sorts using the actual values in cells (not their formatted appearance).

2. **Text**: In alphabetical order, as follows: 0 1 2 3 4 5 6 7 8 9 (space) ! " # $ % & ' ( ) * + , – . / : ; < = > ? @ [\ ] ^ _ ` { | } ~ A B C D E F G H I J K L M N O P Q R S T U V W X Y Z.

   By default, sorting is not case-sensitive. You can change this behavior, however, in the Sort Options dialog box (described later in this chapter).

3. **Logical values**: False comes before True.

4. **Error values**: Error values (such as #VALUE! and #NA) appear in their original order; Excel does not sort them by error type.

5. **Blank cells**: Blanks cells always appear last.

Sorting in descending order reverses this sequence except that blank cells still appear last.

Using a custom sort order

Excel typically sorts either numerically or alphabetically, depending on the data being sorted. In some cases, however, you may want to sort your data in other ways. For example, if your data consists of month names, you usually want it to appear in month order rather than alphabetically. You can use the Sort Options dialog box to perform such a sort. Select the appropriate list from the drop-down list labeled First key sort order. Excel, by default, has four "custom lists," and you can define your own. Excel's custom lists are

- ✦ **Abbreviated days:** Sun, Mon, Tue, Wed, Thu, Fri, Sat
- ✦ **Days:** Sunday, Monday, Tuesday, Wednesday, Thursday, Friday, Saturday
- ✦ **Abbreviated months:** Jan, Feb, Mar, Apr, May, Jun, Jul, Aug, Sep, Oct, Nov, Dec
- ✦ **Months:** January, February, March, April, May, June, July, August, September, October, November, December

Caution

Note that the abbreviated days and months do not have periods after them. If you use periods for these abbreviations, Excel doesn't recognize them (and doesn't sort them correctly).

You may want to create a custom list. For example, your company may have several stores and you want the stores to be listed in a particular order (not alphabetically). If you create a custom list, sorting puts the items in the order that you specify in the list. You must use the Data ⇨ Sort command to sort by a custom list (click the Options button to specify the custom list).

To create a custom list, use the Custom Lists tab of the Options dialog box, as shown in Figure 19-10. Select the NEW LIST option, and make your entries (in order) in the List Entries box. Or, you can import your custom list from a range of cells by selecting the range and then clicking the Import button.

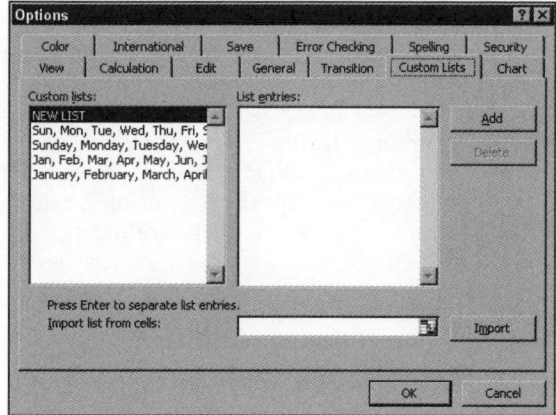

Figure 19-10: You can create custom lists to control sorting using a special sort order.

> **Tip** Custom lists also work with the AutoFill handle in cells. If you enter the first item of a custom list and then drag the cell's AutoFill handle, Excel fills in the remaining list items automatically.

Sorting nonlists

You can, of course, sort any range in a worksheet — it doesn't have to be a list. You need to be aware of a few things, however. The Sort Ascending and Sort Descending toolbar buttons may assume (erroneously) that the top row is a header row and not include these cells in the sort.

Therefore, to avoid potential errors when sorting nonlists, don't use these toolbar buttons. Instead, select the entire range and then select Data ⇨ Sort (making sure that you choose the No Header Row option).

Performing Calculations with Lists

Just like any other data in your Excel worksheets, you'll probably find that you need to perform calculations that involve the data in your lists. Excel has several tools that are designed to make this much easier.

Using database functions with lists

When you filter a list, Excel temporarily hides the rows that don't fit the filter. This might lead you to believe that filtering would be an effective way to select the values that are used in equations, but unfortunately that's not true. Excel's worksheet functions don't ignore hidden cells. Therefore, if you have a SUM formula that calculates the total of the values in a column of a list, the formula returns the same value when you filter the list.

To create formulas that return results based on filtering criteria, you need to use Excel's database worksheet functions. For example, you can create a formula that calculates the sum of values in a list that meets certain criteria. Set up a criteria range as described previously. Then enter a formula such as the following:

```
=DSUM(ListRange,FieldName,Criteria)
```

In this case, ListRange refers to the list, FieldName refers to the field name cell of the column that you are summing, and Criteria refers to the criteria range.

Excel's database functions are listed in Table 19-3.

	Table 19-3
	Excel's Database Worksheet Functions

Function	Description
DAVERAGE	Returns the average of selected database entries
DCOUNT	Counts the cells containing numbers from a specified database and criteria
DCOUNTA	Counts nonblank cells from a specified database and criteria
DGET	Extracts from a database a single record that matches the specified criteria
DMAX	Returns the maximum value from selected database entries
DMIN	Returns the minimum value from selected database entries
DPRODUCT	Multiplies the values in a particular field of records that match the criteria in a database
DSTDEV	Estimates the standard deviation based on a sample of selected database entries
DSTDEVP	Calculates the standard deviation based on the entire population of selected database entries

Function	Description
DSUM	Adds the numbers in the field column of records in the database that match the criteria
DVAR	Estimates variance based on a sample from selected database entries
DVARP	Calculates variance based on the entire population of selected database entries

Cross-Reference   Refer to Chapter 8 for general information about using worksheet functions.

Creating subtotals

Many items in most lists are related in some way. You might, for example, have a list that shows the employees who work at various locations. It could be useful to determine information such as the salary costs for each location. To do this, you can use Excel's automatic subtotals feature.

Tip   To use the automatic subtotals feature, your list must be sorted because the subtotals are inserted whenever the value in a specified field changes.

Figure 19-11 shows an example of a list, sorted by the Location field, which is appropriate for subtotals.

	A	B	C	D	E	F
1	First_Name	Last_Name	Location	Hired	Monthly	Annual
2	Curtis	Holt	Elko	9/25/2011	$ 8,811	$105,732
3	Alexander	Mueller	Gardnerville	11/12/1996	$ 3,381	$ 40,572
4	Austin	Williams	Incline Village	6/26/2001	$ 6,164	$ 73,968
5	Annemarie	Andrews	Incline Village	12/30/2003	$ 5,985	$ 71,820
6	Barry	Onorato	Minden	9/21/2005	$ 6,616	$ 79,392
7	Anne-Louise	Forte	Olympic Valley	8/9/1996	$ 3,286	$ 39,432
8	Carole	Drews	Reno	8/28/1992	$ 1,844	$ 22,128
9	Dan	Frank	Reno	4/29/2007	$ 7,201	$ 86,412
10	Clayton	Underdahl	Reno	3/31/2005	$ 6,442	$ 77,304
11	Brian	Sax	Reno	6/29/2003	$ 5,801	$ 69,612
12	Derrick	Smith	Reno	3/13/2008	$ 7,520	$ 90,240
13	Becky	Brown	Reno	12/14/2000	$ 8,526	$102,312
14	Arthur	Bellard	Reno	5/7/2000	$ 8,305	$ 99,660
15	Albert	Ferrari	Sparks	7/31/2002	$ 5,468	$ 65,616
16	David	Escobar	Sparks	12/1/1995	$ 3,034	$ 36,408
17	Bruce	Johnson	Sparks	2/8/2001	$ 4,500	$ 54,000

Figure 19-11: This list is a good candidate for subtotals, which will be inserted at each change of the location.

To insert subtotal formulas into a list automatically, move the cell pointer anywhere in the list and choose Data ⇨ Subtotals. You see the Subtotal dialog box shown in Figure 19-12.

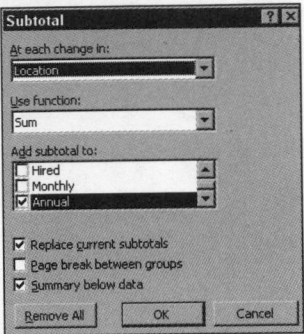

Figure 19-12: You use the Subtotal dialog box to insert subtotal formulas into a sorted list.

This dialog box offers these choices:

✦ **At each change in:** This drop-down list displays all fields in your list. You must have sorted the list by the field that you choose.

✦ **Use function:** Choose from 11 functions: You should normally use Sum (the default).

✦ **Add subtotal to:** This list box shows all the fields in your list. Place a check mark next to the field or fields that you want to subtotal.

✦ **Replace current subtotals:** If this box is checked, Excel removes any existing subtotal formulas and replaces them with the new subtotals.

✦ **Page break between groups:** If this box is checked, Excel inserts a manual page break after each subtotal.

✦ **Summary below data:** If this box is checked, Excel places the subtotals below the data (the default). Otherwise, the subtotal formulas appear above the totals.

✦ **Remove All:** This button removes all subtotal formulas in the list.

When you click OK, Excel analyzes the list and inserts formulas as specified and creates an outline for you. The formulas all use the SUBTOTAL worksheet function.

Caution

When you add subtotals to a filtered list, the subtotals may no longer be accurate when the filter is removed.

Figure 19-13 shows a worksheet after adding subtotals.

		A	B	C	D	E	F	G	H	I
	1	First_Name	Last_Name	Location	Hired	Monthly	Annual			
	2	Curtis	Holt	Elko	9/25/2011	$ 8,811	$ 105,732			
	3			Elko Total			$ 105,732			
	4	Alexander	Mueller	Gardnerville	11/12/1996	$ 3,381	$ 40,572			
	5			Gardnerville Total			$ 40,572			
	6	Austin	Williams	Incline Village	6/26/2001	$ 6,164	$ 73,968			
	7	Annemarie	Andrews	Incline Village	12/30/2003	$ 5,985	$ 71,820			
	8			Incline Village Total			$ 145,788			
	9	Barry	Onorato	Minden	9/21/2005	$ 6,616	$ 79,392			
	10			Minden Total			$ 79,392			
	11	Anne-Louise	Forte	Olympic Valley	8/9/1996	$ 3,286	$ 39,432			
	12			Olympic Valley Total			$ 39,432			
	13	Carole	Drews	Reno	8/28/1992	$ 1,844	$ 22,128			
	14	Dan	Frank	Reno	4/29/2007	$ 7,201	$ 86,412			
	15	Clayton	Underdahl	Reno	3/31/2005	$ 6,442	$ 77,304			
	16	Brian	Sax	Reno	6/29/2003	$ 5,801	$ 69,612			
	17	Derrick	Smith	Reno	3/13/2008	$ 7,520	$ 90,240			
	18	Becky	Brown	Reno	12/14/2000	$ 8,526	$ 102,312			
	19	Arthur	Bellard	Reno	5/7/2000	$ 8,305	$ 99,660			
	20			Reno Total			$ 547,668			
	21	Albert	Ferrari	Sparks	7/31/2002	$ 5,468	$ 65,616			
	22	David	Escobar	Sparks	12/1/1995	$ 3,034	$ 36,408			
	23	Bruce	Johnson	Sparks	2/8/2001	$ 4,500	$ 54,000			
	24			Sparks Total			$ 156,024			
	25			Grand Total			$1,114,608			

Formula bar: F8 = =SUBTOTAL(9,F6:F7)

Figure 19-13: Excel added the subtotal formulas to column F and created an outline.

Cross-Reference

See Chapter 25 for more information about outlining a worksheet.

✦ ✦ ✦

Using External Database Files

Although worksheet-based databases — lists, in Excel's terminology — are sufficient for many purposes, there's no denying that external database files can also be very useful. External database files offer many advantages compared to data that is stored in an Excel workbook, and this chapter shows you how to use those files with Excel.

Understanding External Database Files

When you work with an Excel workbook, the entire workbook must be loaded into memory before you can begin working. Although this provides you with immediate access to the entire file and all the data it contains, it also means that you cannot work with extremely large lists. Even if your PC has plenty of memory, Excel has limits to the amount of data that it can handle in a worksheet database.

External database files work a bit differently than Excel workbooks. When you access an external database file, you really load only a single (or sometimes several) record into memory, so external database files can contain virtually unlimited amounts of data. In fact, external database files can be as large as your operating system allows and may contain many thousands of times as many records as an Excel list.

Accessing external database files from Excel is useful when you have these situations:

+ You need to work with a very large database.

+ You share the database with others; that is, other users have access to the database and may need to work with the data at the same time.

✦ You want to work with only a subset of the data — data that meets certain criteria that you specify.

✦ The database is in a format that Excel can't import.

If you need to work with external databases, you may prefer Excel to other database programs. The advantage? After you bring the data into Excel, you can manipulate and format it by using familiar tools. Of course, real database programs, such as Access, have advantages, too. For example, it's much easier to create a complex database report in Access than it is to create it in Excel.

Note   Excel can open some database files directly. If the database has fewer than 65,535 records and no more than 255 fields, you can load the entire file into a worksheet, memory permitting. Even if you have enough memory to load such a large file, however, Excel's performance is likely to be poor.

In many cases, you may not be interested in all the records or fields in the file. Instead, you may want to bring in just the data that meets certain criteria. In other words, you want to *query* the database and load into your worksheet a subset of the external database that meets the criteria. Excel makes this type of operation relatively easy.

Note   To perform queries using external databases, Microsoft Query must be installed on your system. If Query is not installed, you will be prompted to install it when you first use the Data ⇨ Import External Data ⇨ New Database Query command.

To work with an external database file from Excel, use the Query application that is included with Excel. The general procedure is as follows:

1. Activate a worksheet.

2. Choose Data ⇨ Import External Data ⇨ New Database Query. This starts Query.

3. Specify whether you want to use Query directly or use Query Wizard.

4. Specify the database that you want to use and then create a *query* — a list of criteria that specifies which records you want.

5. Specify how you want the data returned that passes your query — either to a worksheet or as a pivot table.

You can choose to save the query in a file so that you can reuse it later. This means that modifying the query or *refreshing* it (updating it with any changed values) is a simple matter. This is particularly useful when the data resides in a shared database that is continually being updated.

Cross-Reference   Chapter 21 discusses pivot tables. You can create a pivot table using data in an external file and use Query to retrieve data.

Getting Started Using Microsoft Query

The best way to become familiar with Query is to walk through an example. In the following sections, you'll learn how to use Query to do the basics of opening a database file and importing a specified set of records.

Understanding some database terminology

People who spend their days working with databases seem to have their own special language. The following terms can help you hold your own among a group of database experts:

✦ **External database:** A collection of data that is stored in one or more files (not Excel files). Each file of a database holds a single table, and tables are composed of records and fields.

✦ **Field:** In a database table, an element of a record that corresponds to a column.

✦ **ODBC:** An acronym for Open DataBase Connectivity, a standard developed by Microsoft that uses drivers to access database files in different formats. Microsoft Query comes with drivers for Access, dBASE, FoxPro, Paradox, SQL Server, Excel workbooks, and ASCII text files. ODBC drivers for other databases are available from Microsoft and from third-party providers.

✦ **Query:** To search a database for records that meet specific criteria. This term is also used as a noun; you can write a query, for example.

✦ **Record:** In a database table, a single element that corresponds to a row.

✦ **Refresh:** To rerun a query to get the latest data. This is applicable when the database contains information that is subject to change, as in a multiuser environment.

✦ **Relational database:** A database that is stored in more than one table or file. At least one common field (sometimes called the key field) connects the tables.

✦ **Result set:** The data that is returned by a query, usually a subset of the original database. Query returns the result set to your Excel workbook or to a pivot table.

✦ **SQL:** An acronym for Structured Query Language (usually pronounced sequel). Query uses SQL to query data that is stored in ODBC databases.

✦ **Table:** A record- and field-oriented collection of data. A database consists of one or more tables.

A database file example

To use Query you'll need a database file. The type of database file isn't too important — Query can open dBASE, Access, or FoxPro files without any problem.

For this example, I'm using an Access database file that has information about an old record collection. You can use whatever database file you have handy.

Using Query to get the data

Using Query, you import only the data that's required rather than import the entire file into a worksheet. This enables you to work with any size of external database file — even one that has many more than the 65,535-record limit for an Excel list.

Starting query

Begin with an empty worksheet. Select Data ➪ Import External Data ➪ New Database Query; this action launches and activates Microsoft Query, a separate application. Excel continues to run, and you can switch back and forth between Query and Excel as needed.

Selecting a data source

When Query starts, it displays the Choose Data Source dialog box, shown in Figure 20-1.

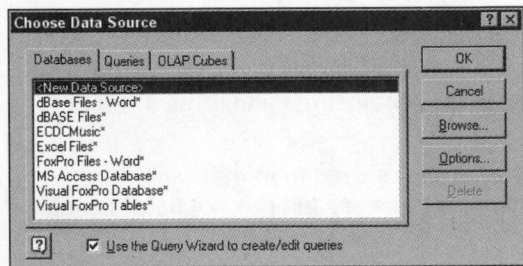

Figure 20-1: Use the Choose Data Source dialog box to select the type of database file you want to query.

This dialog box contains three tabs:

✦ **Databases:** Lists the data sources that are known to Query — this tab may be empty, depending on which data sources are defined on your system.

✦ **Queries:** Contains a list of stored queries. Again, this may or may not be empty.

✦ **OLAP Cubes:** Lists OLAP databases (see sidebar) that are available for query.

OLAP Databases

OLAP is an acronym for online analytical processing; OLAP presents a new way to organize large databases to suit the way that you analyze and manage information. In an OLAP database, data is organized by level of detail. In a business database, for example, you might want to track sales around the world for the products of a particular company. In an OLAP organization of this information, you would need to consider where and when each product was sold as well as which product was sold. Each of these aspects of the OLAP database is called a *dimension,* and each dimension is composed of several fields that can be organized hierarchically, by level of detail. You might call the "where" dimension the Location dimension, and it might contain, for example, fields for country, region, and city. The Time dimension, containing information about when the product was sold, might contain fields for month, date, day, and year.

Dimensions in an OLAP database combine to provide information about the intersecting points; because you can combine several dimensions, OLAP databases are called *cubes.*

If you've previously worked with a particular database, its name appears in the list of databases. Otherwise, you need to identify the source.

In the Databases tab, select the <New Data Source> option and click OK. This displays the Create New Data Source dialog box, shown in Figure 20-2.

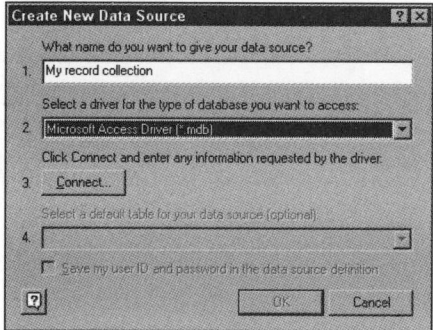

Figure 20-2: You use the Create New Data Source dialog box to specify a name and driver for the external database file.

The Create New Data Source dialog box has four numbered parts:

1. Enter a descriptive name for the data source.

2. Select a driver for the data source by selecting from the list of installed drivers.

3. The Connect button displays the ODBC Setup dialog box that asks for information specific to the driver that you select in Step 2. In this dialog box, you select the directory where the database is located.

4. Select the default data table that you want to use (this step is optional). If the database requires a password, you can also specify that the password be saved with the Data Source definition.

After you supply all the information in the Create New Data Source dialog box, click OK and Excel redisplays the Choose Data Source dialog box — which now includes the data source that you created.

You have to go through these steps only once for each data source. The next time that you access Query, any database sources that you have defined appear in the Choose Data Source dialog box.

Choosing to use the Query Wizard

The Choose Data Source dialog box has a check box at the bottom that lets you specify whether to use Query Wizard to create your query. Query Wizard walks you through the steps that are used to create your query, and if you use Query Wizard, you don't have to deal directly with Query. The examples in this chapter use this tool.

In the Choose Data Sources dialog box, make sure that you check the Use the Query Wizard to create/edit queries check box at the bottom of the dialog box and then click OK to start Query Wizard.

Choosing the columns in Query Wizard

In the first step of Query Wizard (see Figure 20-3), select the database columns that you want to appear in your query.

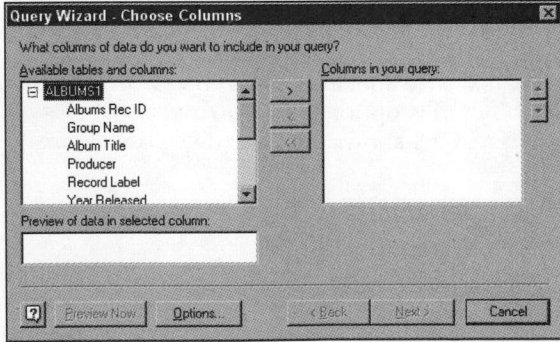

Figure 20-3: In the first step of Query Wizard, you select the columns to use in your query.

The columns that you select determine the fields from the database that Query returns to Excel. The left pane of the dialog box shows all the available columns.

To add a column to the right pane, select the column and click the > button (or you can double-click the column name). If you want to see the data for a particular column, select the column and click the Preview Now button.

Tip   If you select the table name and click >, all the fields will be added to the right pane. You can then use the < button to remove fields that you don't want included.

After you finish adding the columns, the Query Wizard dialog box looks like Figure 20-4.

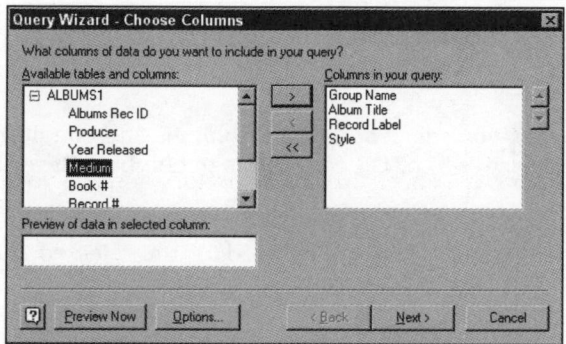

Figure 20-4: The right pane lists the columns selected for your query.

Tip   If the database contains more than one table, you can scroll down the left pane to select columns from other tables.

After you select all the columns for the query, click Next.

Filtering data in the Query Wizard

In the second Query Wizard dialog box, you specify your record selection criteria — how you want to filter the data. This step is optional. If you want to retrieve all the data, just click Next to proceed. Figure 20-5 shows the Filter Data dialog box of Query Wizard.

You enter the criteria by column. In this case, we specified one criterion by doing the following:

1. In the Column to filter column, select Record Label.

2. In the section labeled Only include rows where, select Contains from the first drop-down list.

3. In the section labeled Only include rows where, select Victor from the second drop-down list.

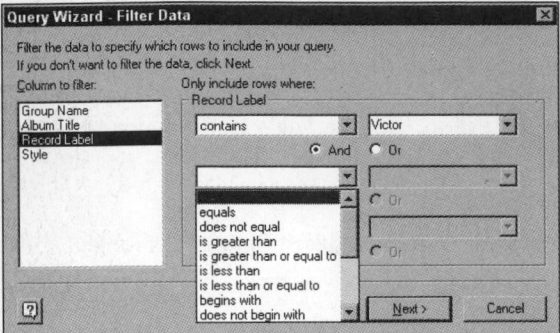

Figure 20-5: In the second step of Query Wizard, you specify how you want to filter the data.

If you want to use multiple criteria, you select additional columns and conditions and choose whether you want to use AND or OR conditions to combine the criteria.

To review the criteria that you've entered, select the column from the Column to filter list. Query Wizard displays the criteria that you entered for the selected column. After you enter all the criteria, click Next.

Table 20-1 lists and describes the operators that are available when you create a query. These operators give you complete control over which rows are returned.

Table 20-1 Query Operators	
Operator	**What It Does**
equals	Field is identical to value
does not equal	Field is not equal to value
is greater than	Field is greater than value
is greater than or equal to	Field is greater than or equal to value
is less than	Field is less than value
is less than or equal to	Field is less than or equal to value
is one of	Field is in a list of values, separated by commas
is not one of	Field is not in a list of values, separated by commas
is between	Field is between two values, separated by commas
is not between	Field is not between two values, separated by commas
begins with	Field begins with the value
does not begin with	Field does not begin with value

Operator	What It Does
ends with	Field ends with value
does not end with	Field does not end with value
contains	Field contains value
does not contain	Field does not contain value
like	Field is like value (using * and ? wildcard characters)
not like	Field is not like value (using * and ? wildcard characters)
is Null	Field is empty
is not Null	Field is not empty

Choosing the sort order in Query Wizard

The third step of the Query Wizard enables you to specify how you want the records to be sorted (see Figure 20-6). This step is optional, and you can click Next to move to the next step if you don't want the data sorted or prefer to sort it after it's returned to your worksheet.

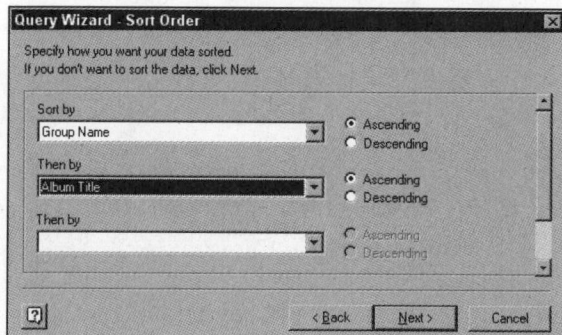

Figure 20-6: In the third step of Query Wizard, you specify the sort order.

You can specify as many sort fields as you like. Click Next to move to the next step.

Finishing with the Query Wizard

The final step of Query Wizard, shown in Figure 20-7, lets you:

✦ Give the query a name

✦ Save it to a file so that it can be reused

✦ Specify what to do with the data

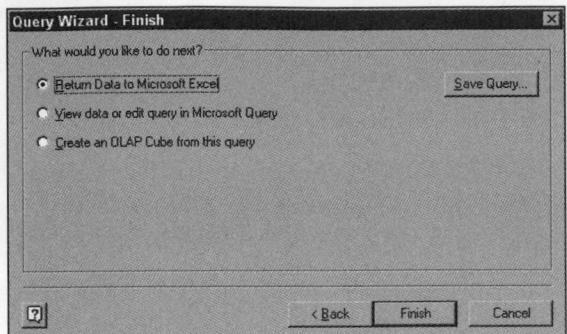

Figure 20-7: In the final step of Query Wizard, you specify what you would like to do with the extracted data.

Normally, you want to return the data to Excel. If you know how to use the Microsoft Query application, you can return the data to Query and examine it or even modify the selection criteria. Or, you can create an OLAP cube to use in a PivotTable or PivotChart report.

 See "Creating a More Advanced Query" later in this chapter for information about using Query directly.

If you plan to reuse this query, you should save it to a file. Click the Save Query button, and you are prompted for a filename. After you make your choices, click Finish.

Figure 20-8 shows the Import Data dialog box, which appears when you click the Finish button in the Query Wizard dialog box.

Your choices are:

✦ **Existing worksheet:** You can specify the upper-left cell.

✦ **New worksheet:** Excel can insert a new worksheet and insert the data beginning in cell A1.

✦ **Create a PivotTable report:** Excel can display its PivotTable Wizard so that you can specify the layout for a pivot table (see Chapter 21).

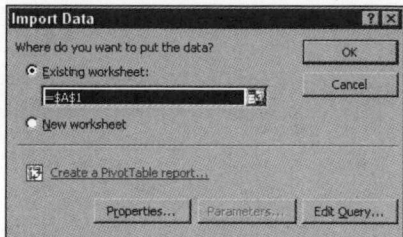

Figure 20-8: Choose where you want the imported data to appear.

Figure 20-9 shows the data that is returned to a worksheet.

	A	B	C
1	Group Name	Album Title	Record Label
2	Aileen Stanley	Want a Little Lovin'	Victor
3	Aileen Stanley	You're in Wrong with the Right Baby	Victor
4	Aileen Stanley & Billy Murray	Big Hearted Bennie	Victor
5	Aileen Stanley & Billy Murray	Down By the Winegar Woiks	Victor
6	Aileen Stanley & Billy Murray	If I Had a Girl Like You	Victor
7	Aileen Stanley & Billy Murray	Keep Your Skirts Down Mary Ann	Victor
8	Aileen Stanley & Billy Murray	Promise Me Everything, Never Get Anything Blues	Victor
9	Aileen Stanley & Billy Murray	You May be Fast but Your Mamma's Gonna' Slow You Down	Victor
10	Arthur Pryor's Band	The Boy and the Birds	Victor
11	Arthur Pryor's Band	The Lion Chase	Victor
12	Billy Murray	It's a Lotta Bologny	Victor
13	Billy Murray	Nobody Else Can Love Me Like My Old Tomato Can	Victor
14	Billy Murray	Not Here-Not There	Victor
15	Billy Murray	Oh Say! Can I See You To-night	Victor
16	Billy Murray	Roll 'Em Girls	Victor
17	Billy Murray	Three Thousand Years Ago	Victor
18	Billy Murray & Ed Smalle	Chili Bom Bom	Victor
19	Billy Murray & Ed Smalle	Happy and Go-Lucky in My Old Kentucky Home	Victor
20	Billy Murray & Ed Smalle	Oh! How She Lied to Me	Victor
21	Billy Murray & Ed Smalle	Oh! How She Lied to Me	Victor
22	Charles Hart	Pal of My Dreams	Victor
23	Criterion Quartet	Medley of Foster Songs	Victor
24	Criterion Quartet	When the Roll is Called Up Yonder	Victor
25	Edgar A. Guest	The Lost Pocket-Book	Victor

Figure 20-9: After you click OK, Query adds the results to your Excel worksheet.

Working with External Data

Excel stores the data that Query returns in either a worksheet or a pivot table. When Excel stores data in a worksheet, it stores the data in a specially named range, known as an *external data range;* Excel creates the name for this range automatically.

This section describes what you can do with the data that Excel receives from Query and stores in a worksheet.

Adjusting the external data range properties

You can adjust various properties of the external data range by using the External Data Range Properties dialog box (see Figure 20-10).

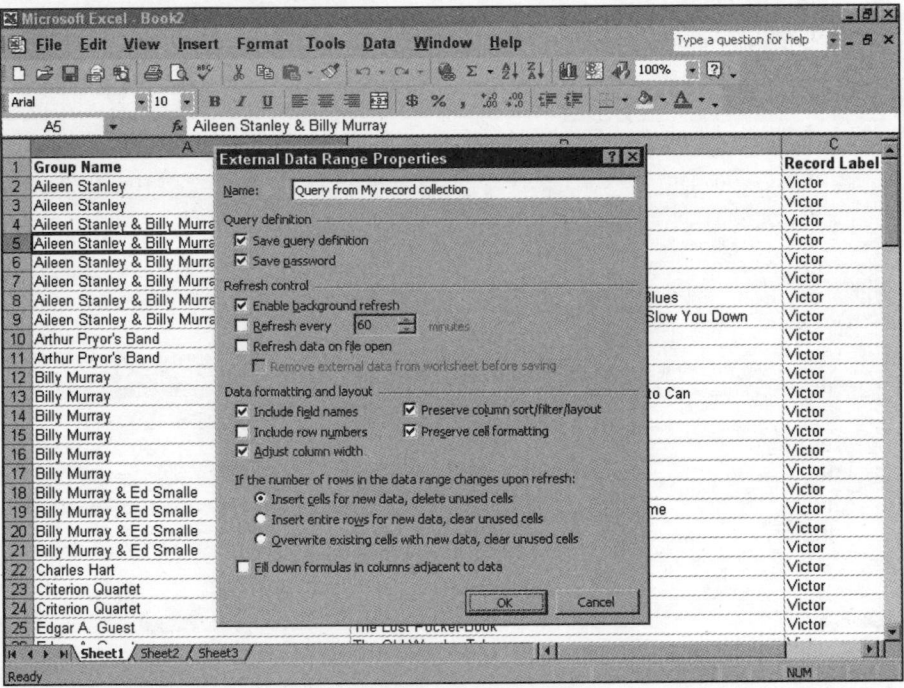

Figure 20-10: The External Data Range Properties dialog box enables you to specify various options for an external data range.

To display this dialog box, the cell pointer must be within the external data range. You can open this dialog box by using any of three methods:

✦ Right-click and select Data Range Properties from the shortcut menu.

✦ Select Data ➪ Import External Data ➪ Data Range Properties.

✦ Click the Data Range Properties tool on the External Data toolbar.

The following list describes the options in the External Data Range Properties dialog box:

✦ **Name:** The name of the external data range. You can change this name or use the default name that Excel creates. Excel substitutes, in the range name, the underscore character for any spaces that you see in the Name box of the External Data Range Properties box.

✦ **Query definition:** If you check Save query definition, Excel stores the query definition with the external data range, enabling you to refresh the data or edit the query, if necessary. If the database requires a password, you can also store the password so that you don't need to enter it when you refresh the query.

✦ **Refresh control:** Determines how and when Excel refreshes the data.

✦ **Data formatting and layout:** Determines the appearance of the external data range.

The External Data Range Properties dialog box has many options. For specific details, click the Help icon in the title bar and then click an option in the dialog box.

You can manipulate data returned from a query just like any other worksheet range. For example, you can sort the data, format it, or create formulas that use the data.

Note   Refreshing a query does not overwrite the external data range. You are free to format the external data range or insert rows and columns. You also can include formulas in those rows and columns that refer to other parts of the external data range. Your work will not be destroyed when you refresh the query.

Refreshing a query

After performing a query, you can save the file and then retrieve it later. The file contains the data that you originally retrieved from the external database. The external database may have changed, however, in the interim.

If you checked the Save query definition option in the External Data Range Properties dialog box, Excel saves the query definition with the workbook. Simply move the cell pointer anywhere within the external data table in the worksheet and then use one of the following methods to refresh the query:

✦ Right-click and select Refresh Data from the shortcut menu

✦ Select Data ➪ Refresh Data

✦ Click the Refresh Data tool on the External Data toolbar

Excel launches Query and uses your original query to bring in the current data from the external database.

Tip If you find that refreshing the query causes undesirable results, use Excel's Undo feature to "unrefresh" the data.

Note A single workbook can hold as many external data ranges as you need. Excel gives each query a unique name, and you can work with each query independently. Excel automatically keeps track of the query that produces each external data range.

Caution After performing a query, you may want to copy or move the external data range, which you can do by using the normal copy, cut, and paste techniques. However, make sure that you copy or cut the entire external data range—otherwise, the underlying query is not copied and the copied data cannot be refreshed.

Deleting a query

If you decide that you no longer need the data that is returned by a query, you can delete it by selecting the entire external data range and choosing Edit ➪ Delete.

Note If you simply press Delete, the contents of the cells are erased, but the underlying query remains. Excel displays a dialog box asking whether you want to delete the query. If you choose No, you can refresh the query, and the deleted cells appear again, including any formatting that you applied to them. When you refresh, Query returns only data that is retrieved from the external database. If you delete rows or columns that you inserted into the external data range, Query does not redisplay those rows and columns when you refresh.

Changing your query

If you bring the query results into your worksheet and discover that you don't have what you want, you can modify the query. Move the cell pointer anywhere within the external data table in the worksheet and then use one of the following methods to refresh the query:

✦ Right-click and select Edit Query from the shortcut menu

✦ Select Data ➪ Import External Data ➪ Edit Query

✦ Click the Edit Query tool on the External Data toolbar

Excel then launches (or activates) Query, and you can change the original query. After you finish, Excel reactivates, executes the modified query, and updates the external data range.

Creating a More Advanced Query

It's not always necessary—nor desirable—to use the Query Wizard. In some cases, you may want to use Query itself rather than Query Wizard.

When you select Data ➪ Import External Data ➪ New Database Query, the Choose Data Source dialog box gives you the option of whether to use Query Wizard. If you choose not to use Query Wizard, you work directly with Microsoft Query.

Creating a query manually

Before you can create a query, you must display the Criteria pane. In Query, open the View menu and confirm that a check appears next to the Criteria command. If you don't see a check, choose View ➪ Criteria to display the Criteria pane in the middle of the window. (See Figure 20-11.)

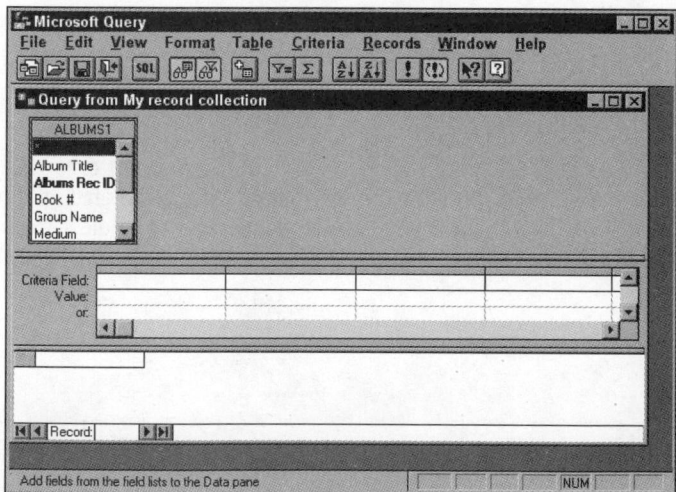

Figure 20-11: Display the Criteria pane as shown here so that you will be able to create your query.

The Query window has three panes, which are split vertically:

✦ **Tables pane:** The top pane, which holds the data tables for the database. Each data table window has a list of the fields in the table.

✦ **Criteria pane:** The middle pane, which holds the criteria that determine the rows that the query returns.

✦ **Data pane:** The bottom pane, which holds the data that passes the criteria.

Creating a query consists of the following steps:

1. Drag fields from the Tables pane to the Data pane. You can drag as many fields as you want. These fields are the columns that the query will return. You can also double-click a field instead of dragging it.

2. Enter criteria in the Criteria pane. When you activate this pane, the first row (labeled Criteria Field) displays a drop-down list that contains all the field names. Select a field and enter the criteria below it. Query updates the Data pane automatically, treating each row like an OR operator.

3. Choose File ➪ Return Data to Microsoft Excel to execute the query and place the data in a worksheet or pivot table.

Figure 20-12 shows how the query for the example presented earlier in this chapter appears in Query.

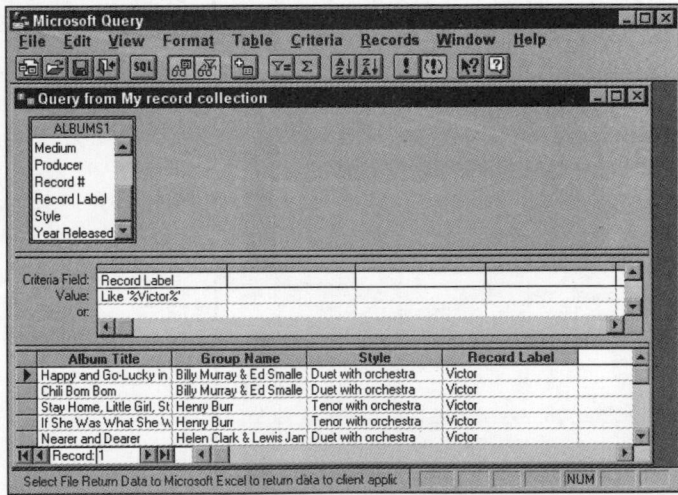

Figure 20-12: Add the fields and criteria to complete your query.

Tip

Double-click a criteria box to display the Edit Criteria dialog box. This enables you to select an operator and value.

Using multiple database tables

The example in this chapter uses only one database table. Some databases, however, use multiple tables. These databases are known as *relational databases* because a common field links the tables. Query lets you use any number of tables in your queries.

Note When you add additional tables to a query, the Tables pane in Query connects the linked fields with a line between the tables. If no links exist, the tables are not related and cannot be used together in a query.

Adding and editing records in external database tables

To add, delete, and edit data when you are using Query, make sure that a check appears next to the Records ⇨ Allow Editing command. Of course, you can't edit a database file that's set up as read-only.

Caution You need to be careful with this feature because your changes are saved to disk as soon as you move the cell pointer out of the record that you're editing (you do not need to choose File ⇨ Save).

Formatting data

If you don't like the data's appearance in the data pane, you can change the font used, by selecting Format ⇨ Font. Be aware that selective formatting isn't allowed (unlike in Excel); changing the font affects all the data in the data pane.

Tip If you need to view the data in the data pane in a different order, choose Records ⇨ Sort (or click the Sort Ascending or Sort Descending toolbar icon).

Learning more about Query

This chapter isn't intended to cover every aspect of Microsoft Query; rather, it discusses the basic features that are used most often. In fact, if you use Query Wizard, you may never need to interact with Query itself. But if you do need to use Query, you can experiment and consult the online Help to learn more. As with anything related to Excel, the best way to master Query is to use it — preferably with data that's meaningful to you.

✦　　✦　　✦

Analyzing Data with Pivot Tables

The modern versions of Excel provide many very useful
data analysis tools. One of the most interesting — yet
probably least used and understood — is the pivot table. This
chapter demonstrates this innovative feature and suggests
how you can use it to view your data in ways that you may not
have imagined.

Understanding Pivot Tables

A *pivot table* is a tool that provides a different way of looking
at your data. It provides a dynamic summary of data that is
contained in a database or list. A pivot table enables you to
create frequency distributions and cross-tabulations of several different data dimensions. In addition, you can display
subtotals and any level of detail that you want.

Just where did the name pivot table come from? Well, pivot
tables show your data in a table that has headings that you
can *pivot* from one axis to the other to display different relationships in the data.

Seeing a pivot table example

Likely the best way to understand the concept of a pivot table
is to see one. Start with Figure 21-1, which shows the data that
is being used to create the pivot table in this chapter.

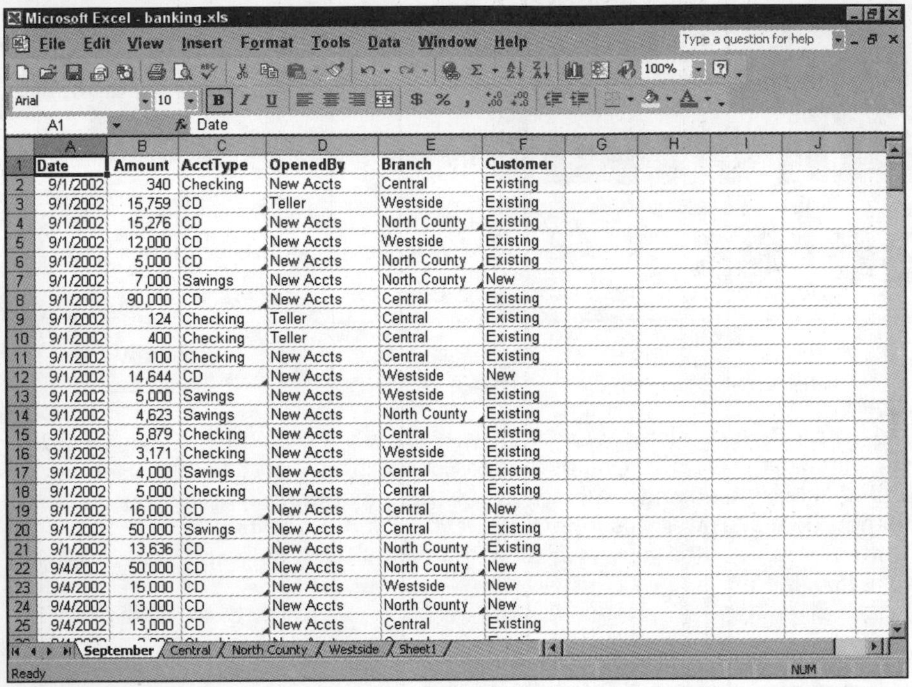

Figure 21-1: This sample database is used to create the pivot table examples for this chapter.

This database consists of daily new-account information for a three-branch bank. The database contains 350 records and tracks the following types of information:

✦ The date that each account was opened

✦ The opening amount

✦ The account type (CD, checking, savings, or IRA)

✦ Who opened the account (a teller or a new-account representative)

✦ The branch at which it was opened

✦ Whether a new customer or an existing customer opened the account

The bank database contains lots of information, but it's not all that revealing. In its present form, the information is difficult to understand. If the data were summarized, it would be more useful. Summarizing a database is essentially the process of answering questions about the data. Here are several questions that may be of interest to the bank's management:

✦ What is the total deposit amount for each branch, broken down by account type?

✦ How many accounts were opened at each branch, also broken down by account type?

✦ What's the dollar distribution of the different account types?

✦ What types of accounts do tellers most often open?

✦ How is each branch doing compared to the other two branches?

✦ Which branch opens the most accounts for new customers?

You can use a pivot table to answer questions like these. It takes only a few seconds and doesn't require a single formula.

Figure 21-2 shows a pivot table created from the database that is displayed in Figure 21-1. This pivot table shows the amount of new deposits, broken down by branch and account type. This summary is one of hundreds that you can produce from this data.

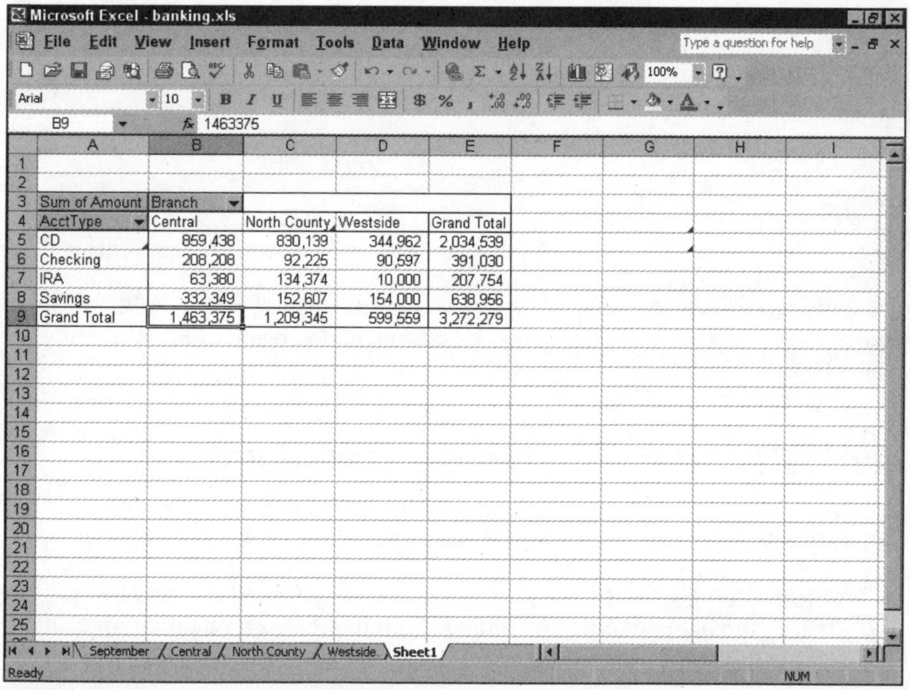

Figure 21-2: This simple pivot table displays the summary of a number of data items without using any formulas.

Figure 21-3 shows another pivot table that is generated from the bank data. This pivot table uses a page field for the Customer item. A page field enables you to display a subset of the data. In this case, the pivot table displays the data only for new customers. Notice that the orientation of the table is changed. (Branches appear in rows and AcctType appears in columns.) Changing the data orientation in a pivot table is very easy—you simply drag the fields around to change their location.

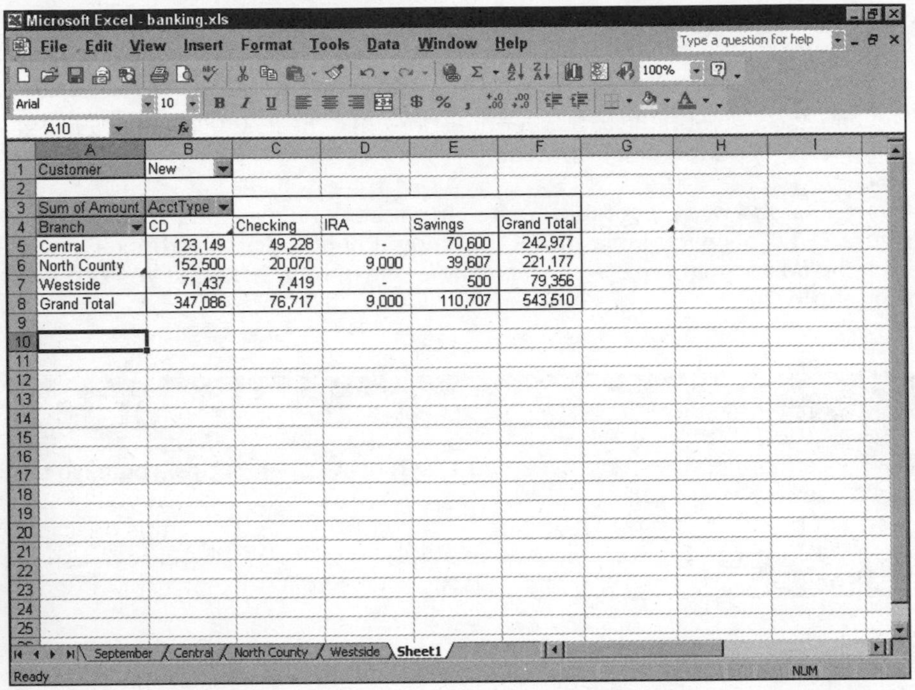

Figure 21-3: This pivot table uses a page field to limit the display to only show certain data.

Understanding pivot table terminology

If you're new to Excel, the concept of a pivot table may be a bit baffling. Understanding the terminology associated with pivot tables is important:

✦ **Column field:** A field that has a column orientation in the pivot table. Each item in the field occupies a column. Column fields can be nested.

✦ **Data area:** The cells in a pivot table that contain the summary data. Excel offers several ways to summarize the data (sum, average, count, and so on).

✦ **Grand totals:** A row or column that displays totals for all cells in a row or column in a pivot table. You can specify that grand totals be calculated for rows, columns, or both (or neither).

✦ **Group:** A collection of items that are treated as a single item. You can group items manually or automatically (group dates into months, for example).

✦ **Item:** An element in a field that appears as a row or column header in a pivot table.

✦ **Page field:** A field that has a page orientation in the pivot table — similar to a slice of a three-dimensional cube. Only one item in a page field can be displayed at one time.

✦ **Refresh:** To recalculate the pivot table after changes to the source data have been made.

✦ **Row field:** A field that has a row orientation in the pivot table. Each item in the field occupies a row. Row fields can be nested.

✦ **Source data:** The data used to create a pivot table. It can reside in a worksheet or an external database.

✦ **Subtotals:** A row or column that displays subtotals for detail cells in a row or column in a pivot table.

Choosing Appropriate Data for a Pivot Table

Before getting into the details of creating and using pivot tables, you need to understand the type of data that's relevant to this feature. The data that you're summarizing must be in the form of a database (although an exception to this does exist, which is discussed later in the chapter). You can store the database in either a worksheet or an external database file. Although Excel can convert any database to a pivot table, not all databases benefit.

Generally speaking, fields in a database table can be one of two types:

✦ **Data:** Contains a value. In Figure 21-1 for example, the Amount field is a data field.

✦ **Category:** Describes the data. In Figure 21-1 for example, the Date, AcctType, OpenedBy, Branch, and Customer fields are category fields because they describe the data in the Amount field.

A single database table can have any number of data fields and category fields. When you create a pivot table, you usually want to summarize one or more of the data fields. The values in the category fields, on the other hand, appear in the pivot table as rows, columns, or pages.

You may sometimes find that Excel's pivot table feature is useful even for databases that don't contain actual numerical data fields. For example, you might have a database that doesn't contain numerical data fields, but you can create a useful pivot table that counts fields rather than sums them. The main thing to remember is that pivot tables can be very handy at providing a different way of looking at your data, and you may need to experiment a little to see what you can find.

Creating a Pivot Table

This section walks you through the steps to create a pivot table by using the PivotTable and PivotChart Wizard. You access the PivotTable and PivotChart Wizard by choosing Data ➪ PivotTable and PivotChart Report.

Note You'll probably find it easier to follow along if you create a workbook similar to the sample shown in Figure 21-1. It's not necessary to create hundreds of rows of data, of course — all you really need are enough records so that you can see how the pivot table feature works.

Identifying your data

To start a pivot table, you must first tell Excel which data you would like to use. When you choose Data ➪ PivotTable and PivotChart Report, the first of several dialog boxes appears (see Figure 21-4).

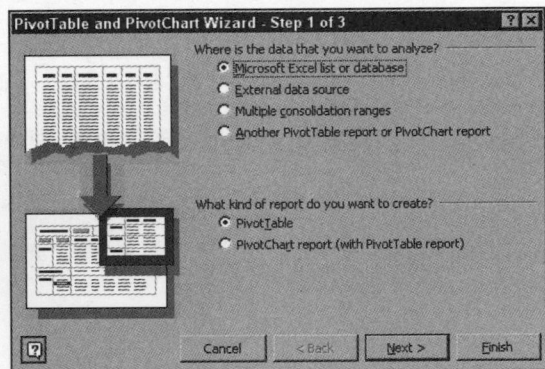

Figure 21-4: Use the first of three PivotTable and PivotChart Wizard dialog boxes to identify what you would like to analyze.

In this step, you identify the data source. The possible data sources are described in the following sections.

Note You see different dialog boxes while you work through the Wizard, depending on the location of the data that you want to analyze. The following sections present the Wizard dialog boxes for data located in an Excel list or database, in the context of describing the various possible data sources.

Using an Excel list or database

Usually, the data that you analyze is stored in a worksheet database — or *list*. Databases stored in a worksheet are limited to 65,535 records and 256 fields. Working with a database of this size isn't efficient, however (and memory may not even allow it). The first row in the database should be field names. The data can consist of values, text, or formulas.

Using an external data source

If you use the data in an external database for a pivot table, the data is retrieved by using Microsoft Query (a separate application). You can use dBASE files, SQL server data, or other data that your system is set up to access. You are prompted for the data source in Step 2 of the PivotTable and PivotChart Wizard.

Chapter 20 discusses external database access, including Query. If you plan to create a pivot table by using data in an external database, you should consult Chapter 20 before proceeding.

Using multiple consolidation ranges

You also can create a pivot table from multiple tables. This procedure is equivalent to consolidating the information in the tables. When you create a pivot table to consolidate information in tables, you have the added advantage of using all of the pivot table tools while you work with the consolidated data. (An example of this is presented later in the chapter.)

Chapter 26 discusses other consolidation techniques.

Using another pivot table

Excel enables you to create a pivot table from an existing pivot table. Actually, this is a bit of a misnomer. The pivot table that you create is based on the *data* that the first pivot table uses (not the pivot table itself). If the active workbook has no pivot tables, this option is grayed, meaning you can't choose it.

If you need to create more than one pivot table from the same set of data, the procedure is more efficient (in terms of memory usage) if you create the first pivot table and then use that pivot table as the source for subsequent pivot tables.

Specifying the location of your data

To move on to the next step of the Wizard, click Next. Step 2 of the PivotTable and PivotChart Wizard prompts you for the data. Remember that the dialog box varies, depending on your choice in the first dialog box; Figure 21-5 shows the dialog box that appears when you select an Excel list or database in Step 1.

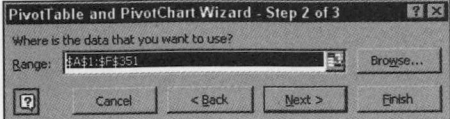

Figure 21-5: Specify the location of the data you wish to use in the pivot table.

Tip   If you place the cell pointer anywhere within the worksheet database when you select Data ➪ PivotTable and PivotChart Report, Excel identifies the database range automatically in Step 2 of the PivotTable and PivotChart Wizard.

You can use the Browse button to open a different worksheet and select a range. To move on to Step 3, click Next.

Note   If you have an existing pivot table in the workbook, Excel will ask if you want to base the new pivot table on the same data. If you have multiple pivot tables, you will need to choose one of them and then click Next to continue.

Completing the pivot table

The following sections outline how to complete the pivot table. The first step is to determine the pivot table's location. The dialog box for the final step of the PivotTable and PivotChart Wizard is shown in Figure 21-6. In this step, you specify the location for the pivot table.

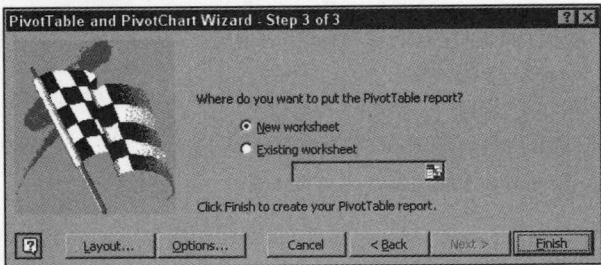

Figure 21-6: Specify where you would like the pivot table to appear.

If you select the New worksheet option, Excel inserts a new worksheet for the pivot table. If you select the Existing worksheet option, you can specify the starting cell location.

Choosing your pivot table options

In Step 3, you can click the Options button to select some options that determine how the table appears. Figure 21-7 shows the PivotTable Options dialog box.

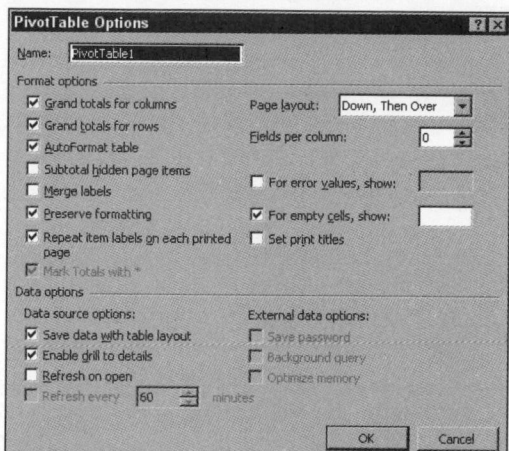

Figure 21-7: Use the PivotTable Options dialog box to select the options for your pivot table.

Tip   You can also access this dialog box after you create the pivot table. Right-click any cell in the pivot table and then select Options from the shortcut menu.

The PivotTable Options dialog box offers these choices:

✦ **Name:** You can provide a name for the pivot table. Excel provides default names in the form of PivotTable1, PivotTable2, and so on.

✦ **Grand totals for columns:** Check this box if you want Excel to calculate grand totals for items that are displayed in columns.

✦ **Grand totals for rows:** Check this box if you want Excel to calculate grand totals for items that are displayed in rows.

✦ **AutoFormat table:** Check this box if you want Excel to apply one of its AutoFormats to the pivot table. Excel uses the AutoFormat even if you rearrange the table layout.

✦ **Subtotal hidden page items:** Check this box if you want Excel to include hidden items in the page fields in the subtotals.

✦ **Merge labels:** Check this box if you want Excel to merge the cells for outer row and column labels. Doing so may make the table more readable.

✦ **Preserve formatting:** Check this box if you want Excel, when it updates the pivot table, to keep the formatting that you applied.

✦ **Repeat item labels on each printed page:** Check this box to set row titles that appear on each page when you print a PivotTable report.

✦ **Mark Totals with *:** Select this option if you want Excel to add an asterisk to totals to make them more obvious.

✦ **Page layout:** You can specify the order in which you want the page fields to appear.

✦ **Fields per column:** You can specify the number of page fields to show before starting another row of page fields.

✦ **For error values, show:** You can specify a value to show for pivot table cells that display an error.

✦ **For empty cells, show:** You can specify a value to show for pivot table cells that are empty.

✦ **Set print titles:** Check this box to set column titles that appear at the top of each page when you print a PivotTable report.

✦ **Save data with table layout:** If you check this option, Excel stores an additional copy of the data (called a pivot table cache), enabling Excel to recalculate the table more quickly when you change the layout. If memory is an issue, you should keep this option unchecked (updating is then a bit slower).

✦ **Enable drill to details:** If checked, you can double-click a cell in the pivot table to view details.

✦ **Refresh on open:** If this option is checked, the pivot table is refreshed whenever you open the workbook.

✦ **Refresh every *x* minutes:** If you are connected to an external database, you can specify how often you want the pivot table refreshed while the workbook is open.

✦ **Save password:** If you use an external database that requires a password, you can store the password as part of the query so that you don't have to reenter it.

✦ **Background query:** If this option is checked, Excel runs the external database query in the background while you continue your work.

✦ **Optimize memory:** This option reduces the amount of memory that is used when you refresh an external database query.

Setting up the layout of the pivot table

You can set up the layout of the pivot table in two different ways: by using the PivotTable and PivotChart Wizard or by using the PivotTable toolbar directly on the worksheet.

Using a dialog box to lay out a pivot table

Click the Layout button of the last Wizard dialog box to see the dialog box shown in Figure 21-8. The fields in the database appear as buttons along the right side of the dialog box. Simply drag the buttons to the appropriate area of the pivot table diagram.

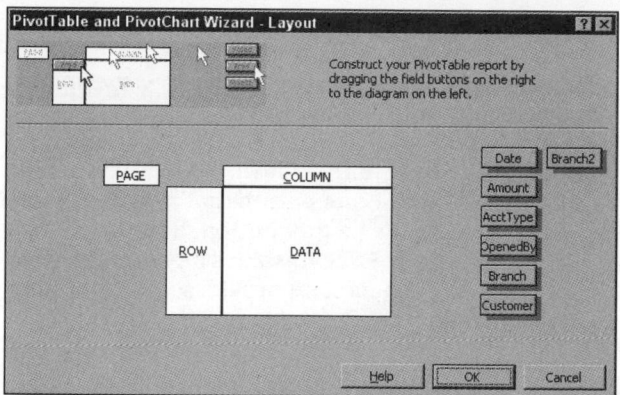

Figure 21-8: Use the Layout dialog box to specify where your data fields appear on the pivot table.

The pivot table diagram has four areas

✦ **Page:** Values in the field appear as page items in the pivot table.

✦ **Row:** Values in the field appear as row items in the pivot table.

✦ **Data:** The field is summarized in the pivot table.

✦ **Column:** Values in the field appear as column items in the pivot table.

Tip

You can drag as many field buttons as you want to any of these locations, and you don't have to use all the fields. Any fields that you don't use simply don't appear in the pivot table.

Note

When you drag a field button to the Data area, the PivotTable and PivotChart Wizard applies the SUM function if the field contains numeric values, and the COUNT function if the field contains nonnumeric values.

While you're setting up the pivot table, you can double-click a field button to customize it. You can specify, for example, that a particular field be summarized as a COUNT or other function. You also can specify which items in a field to hide or omit. You can also customize fields at any time after the pivot table is created; this is demonstrated later in this chapter.

Tip

If you drag a field button to an incorrect location, just drag it off the table diagram to get rid of it.

When you are done adding fields to the layout, click OK to redisplay the PivotTable and PivotChart Wizard – Step 3 of 3 dialog box.

Laying out a pivot table by using the PivotTable toolbar

You can also lay out a pivot table directly in a worksheet by using the PivotTable toolbar and the PivotTable Field List dialog box. The technique is very similar to the one just described, because you still drag and drop fields.

Complete the first two steps of the PivotTable and PivotChart Wizard. If you want, set options for the pivot table by using the Options button that appears in the third dialog box of the Wizard. Don't bother with the Layout button, however. Select a location for the pivot table and choose Finish. Excel displays a pivot table template similar to the one you see in Figure 21-9. The template provides you with hints about where to drop various types of fields.

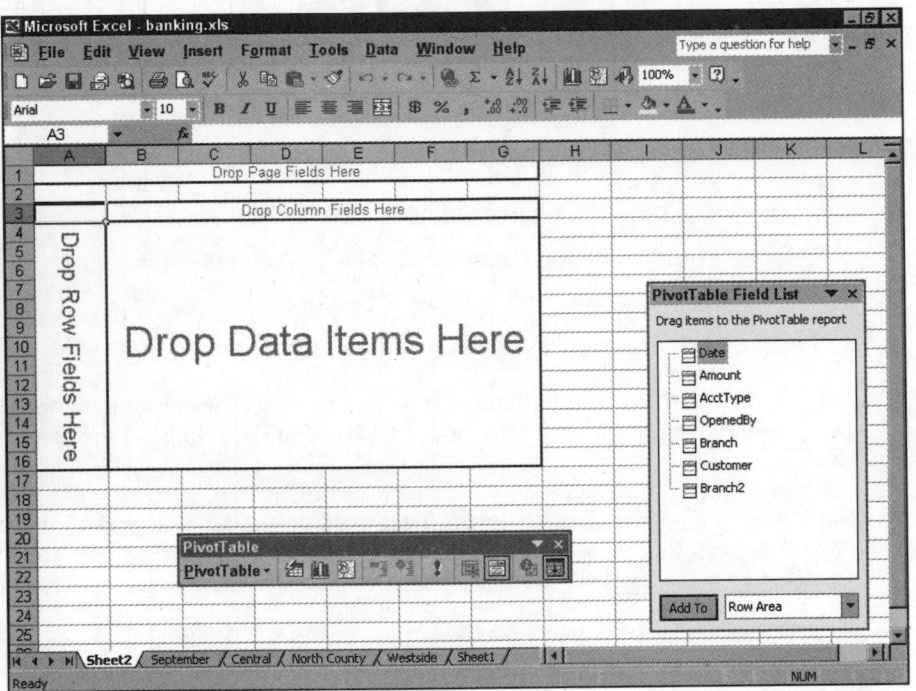

Figure 21-9: Use the PivotTable Field List dialog box to drag and drop fields onto the pivot table template that Excel displays.

Drag and drop fields from the PivotTable Field List dialog box onto the template. Excel continues to update the pivot table as you drag and drop fields. All fields remain on the PivotTable Field List dialog box, even if you use them. Fields that you've added to the pivot table are shown in bold.

Tip   If you make a mistake, simply drag the field off the template and drop it anyplace on the worksheet—Excel removes it from the pivot table template.

Note   Notice that the page field is displayed as a drop-down box. You can choose which item in the page field to display by choosing it from the list. You also can choose an item called All, which displays all the data.

Figure 21-10 shows the result of this example.

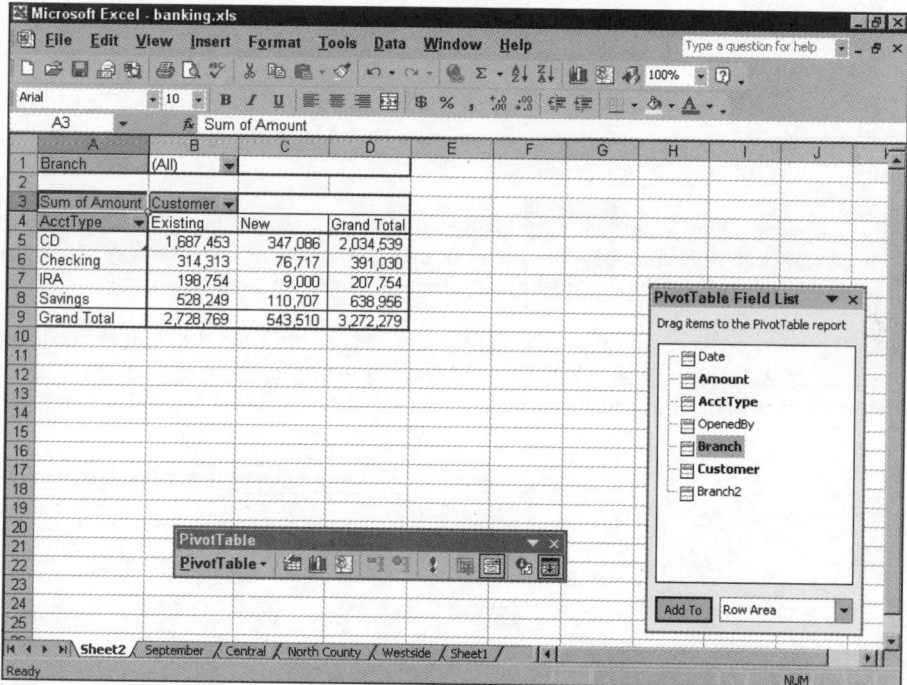

Figure 21-10: Here is the finished pivot table after the fields have been added.

Working with Pivot Tables

A pivot table is not a static object. You can continue to modify and tweak it until it looks exactly how you want it to look. This section discusses modifications that you can make to a pivot table.

You'll find the PivotTable toolbar quite useful when you work with pivot tables. This toolbar appears automatically when you activate a worksheet that contains a pivot table.

Tip   If the PivotTable toolbar does not appear automatically, select View ➪ Toolbars ➪ PivotTable.

Changing the pivot table structure

A field button identifies each of the fields on your pivot table. You can drag any of the field buttons to a new position in the pivot table (an action known as *pivoting*). For example, you can drag a column field to the row position. Excel immediately redisplays the pivot table to reflect your change. You also can change the order of the row fields or the column fields by dragging the buttons. This action affects how Excel nests the fields and can have a dramatic effect on the appearance of the table.

Figure 21-11 shows the pivot table that was created in the preceding example, after making a modification to the table's structure. The page field button (Branch) has been dragged to the row position. The pivot table now shows details for each item in the AcctType field for each branch.

Caution Dropping a field in the wrong position can produce very different results than what you expect. If your pivot table is not analyzing the data quite the way you expect, try changing the relative positions of the row or column fields.

Describing how to change the layout of a pivot table is more difficult than doing it. We suggest that you create a pivot table and experiment by dragging around field buttons to see what happens.

Figure 21-11: Dragging the Branch field to the Row area created a pivot table with two row fields.

Note   A pivot table is a special type of range, and (with a few exceptions) you can't make any changes to it. For example, you can't insert or delete rows, edit results, or move cells. If you attempt to do so, Excel displays an appropriate error message.

Removing a field

To remove a field from a pivot table, click the field button and drag it away from the pivot table. The mouse pointer changes to include a button with an X across it. Release the mouse button, and Excel updates the table to exclude the field.

Adding a new field

To add a new field to the pivot table, select any field in the pivot table. Then, drag the field that you want to add from the PivotTable Field List dialog box onto the pivot table. Excel updates the pivot table with the new field.

You also can add fields from the PivotTable and PivotChart Wizard; choose Data ➪ PivotTable and PivotChart Report to start the Wizard.

Refreshing a pivot table

Pivot tables don't contain formulas. Rather, Excel recalculates the pivot table every time that you make a change to it. If the source database is large, some delay may occur while this recalculation takes place, but for small databases, the update is virtually instantaneous.

In some cases, you may change the source data. When this happens, Excel doesn't update the pivot table automatically. Rather, you must refresh it manually. To refresh a pivot table, you can use any of these methods:

✦ Choose Data ➪ Refresh Data

✦ Right-click anywhere in the pivot table and select Refresh Data from the short-cut menu

✦ Click the Refresh Data tool on the PivotTable toolbar

Customizing a pivot table field

Several options are available for fields within a pivot table. To access these options, double-click a field button (or right-click and select Field Settings from the shortcut menu). Excel displays a PivotTable Field dialog box like the one shown in Figure 21-12.

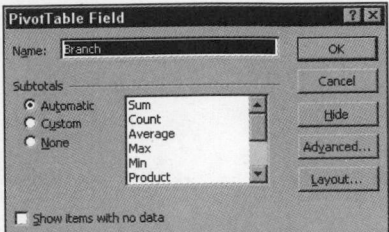

Figure 21-12: Use the PivotTable Field dialog box to modify the properties for a field.

You can modify any of these items:

✦ **Name:** Changes the name that is displayed on the field button. You can also make this change directly by editing the cell that holds the field button.

✦ **Layout:** Changes how the field's items are displayed. You can also take the more direct approach of dragging the field button to another location, as described previously.

✦ **Subtotals:** Lets you change the type of subtotaling that is displayed. Subtotaling is relevant only if you have more than one field displayed as rows or columns. You can make a multiple selection in the list box, which results in more than one line of subtotals. To eliminate subtotals, click the None option.

✦ **Hide items:** Enables you to hide (not display) one or more items from a field. Click the specific item names that you want to hide.

Excel includes some additional field options that you can specify by clicking the Advanced button in the PivotTable Field dialog box. These options let you specify how the field items are sorted and how many items to show (for example, just the top ten).

Formatting a pivot table

When you create a pivot table, Excel applies an AutoFormat to the table. If you like, you can always specify a different AutoFormat. Place the cell pointer in the pivot table and click the Format Report tool on the PivotTable toolbar. Excel displays the AutoFormat dialog box. Select an AutoFormat and click OK.

To change the number format for the pivot table data, follow this procedure:

1. Select any cell in the pivot table's Data area.

2. Right-click and choose Field Settings from the shortcut menu. Excel displays its PivotTable Field dialog box.

3. Click the Number button.

4. Select the number format that you want to use and close the dialog boxes.

Note You can also use Excel's standard techniques to assign numeric formats to the cells in the data area, but the procedure just mentioned has the advantage of applying the same formatting to all the data at the same time.

Tip If you want Excel to preserve all the formatting that you perform on individual cells, make sure that the Preserve formatting option is turned on. You do this in the PivotTable Options dialog box (right-click a cell and select Table Options from the shortcut menu). If this option is not turned on, Excel returns the formats to the default formats when you refresh the pivot table.

Grouping pivot table items

Grouping pivot table items is a handy feature that enables you to group specific items in a field. If one of the fields in your database consists of dates, for example, the pivot table displays a separate row or column for every date. You may find that grouping the dates into months or quarters and then hiding the details is more useful. Fortunately, this is easy to do.

Figure 21-13 shows a pivot table that was created using the bank database. It shows total balances for each Branch (column field) by the Date (row field). To create a report that shows weekly results, create a group for each week.

Figure 21-13: This pivot table has several weeks worth of results combined into groups.

To create the group, select the cells that you want to group—in this case, the dates in each week. Then, choose Data ➪ Group and Outline ➪ Group. Excel creates a new field called Group1. Continue with each week until you have grouped them all.

At this point, you can remove the original Date field (drag away the field button) and change the names of the field and the items (right-click the field and choose Field Settings).

Note   The new field name can't be an existing field name. If it is, Excel adds the field to the pivot table. In this example, you can't rename Branch2 to Branch.

Tip   If the items that you want to group are not adjacent to each other, you can make a multiple selection by pressing Ctrl and selecting the items that make up the group.

Viewing the details that make up pivot table results

Each cell in the Data area of a pivot table represents several records in the source database. You may be interested in seeing exactly which fields contribute to a summary value in the pivot table. To do so, double-click the appropriate summary cell in the Data area. Excel creates a new worksheet with the records that were used to create the summary. Figure 21-14 shows an example.

Figure 21-14: You can double-click a cell in the Data area of a pivot table to generate a new worksheet with the underlying data.

Note   If double-clicking a cell doesn't work, make sure that the Enable drill to details option is turned on in the PivotTable Options dialog box (right-click a pivot table cell and select Table Options from the shortcut menu).

Displaying all pages of the pivot table

If your pivot table displays a field in the Page position, you can see only one slice of the data at a time, by using the drop-down list box. Excel has an option, however, that puts each item from a page field on a separate sheet, creating a three-dimensional block of data. Click the PivotTable button on the PivotTable toolbar and choose Show Pages from the shortcut menu. Excel displays the Show Pages dialog box, which lists the page fields in your PivotTable. Select the fields that you want, and Excel inserts enough new sheets to accommodate each item in that field.

Inserting a calculated field into a pivot table

Because a pivot table is a special type of data range, you can't insert new rows or columns into a pivot table. This means that you can't insert formulas to perform calculations with the data in a pivot table. However, you can create calculated fields and calculated items for a pivot table.

A *calculated field* consists of a calculation that can involve other fields.

In the banking example, for instance, assume that management wants to increase deposits by 15 percent and wants to compare the projected deposits to the current deposits. In this situation, you can use a calculated field. Calculated fields must reside in the Data area of the pivot table (you can't use them in the Page, Row, or Column areas).

Note   You cannot create a calculated field in a pivot table that is based on an OLAP (online analytical processing) database.

Use the following procedure to create a calculated field that consists of the Amount field multiplied by 1.15 (that is, a 15 percent increase):

1. Move the cell pointer anywhere within the pivot table.
2. Click PivotTable on the PivotTable toolbar and choose Formulas ➪ Calculated Field from the menu. Excel displays the Insert Calculated Field dialog box, shown in Figure 21-15.
3. Enter a descriptive name for the field and specify the formula. The formula can use other fields, but can't use worksheet functions. For this example, the name is Projected, and the formula is the following:

```
=Amount*1.15
```

4. Click Add to add this new field.

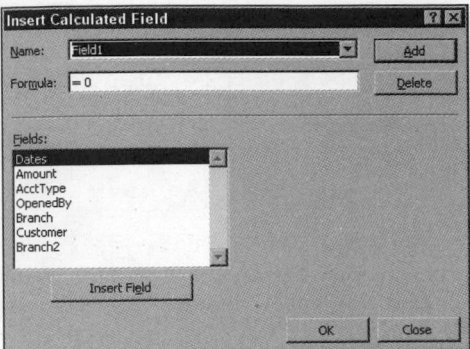

Figure 21-15: Use the Insert Calculated Field dialog box to add a calculated field to your pivot table.

5. To create additional calculated fields, repeat Steps 3 and 4. Click OK to close the dialog box.

After you create the field, Excel adds it to the Data area of the pivot table. You can treat it just like any other field, with one exception: you can't move it to the Page, Row, or Column area (it must remain in the Data area).

Tip   The formulas that you develop can also use worksheet functions, but the functions cannot refer to cells or named ranges.

Using a pivot table to consolidate sheets

Chapter 26 discusses several ways to consolidate data across different worksheets or workbooks. Excel's pivot table feature gives you yet another consolidation option. Figure 21-16 shows three worksheets, each containing monthly sales data for a store (three different stores) in a music store chain. The goal is to consolidate this information into a single pivot table. In this example, all the source data is in a single workbook, but you can consolidate data from different workbooks.

Follow these steps to create this pivot table:

1. Start with a new worksheet named Summary.

2. Choose Data ➪ PivotTable and PivotChart Report, to display the PivotTable and PivotChart Wizard.

3. Select the Multiple Consolidation Ranges option and then click Next.

4. In Step 2a of the PivotTable Wizard, select the option labeled Create a single page field for me. Click Next.

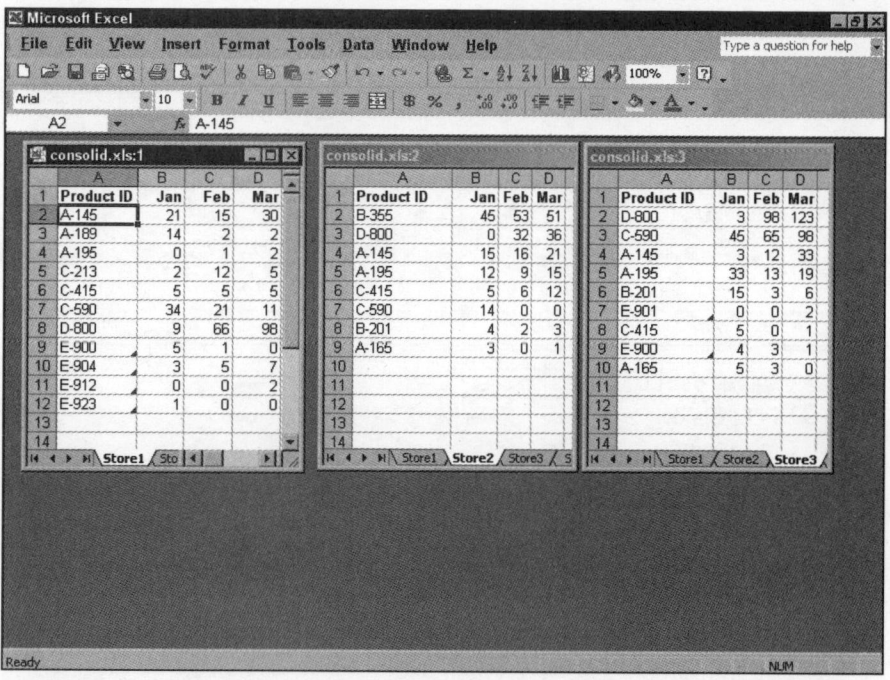

Figure 21-16: You can use a pivot table to consolidate these three worksheets.

5. In Step 2b, specify the ranges to be consolidated. The first range is Store1!$A$1:$D$12 (you can enter this directly or point to it). Click Add to add this range to the All Ranges list.

6. Repeat this for the other two ranges (see Figure 21-17). Click Next to continue to Step 3.

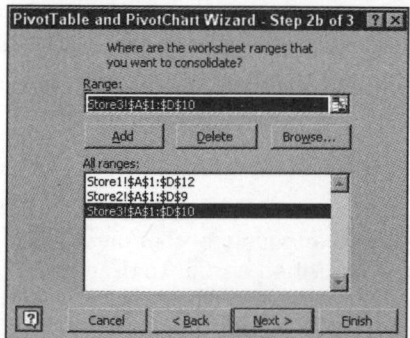

Figure 21-17: Specify all the data ranges you want to include in the pivot table.

7. Complete Step 3 of the PivotTable Wizard and click Finish.

Figure 21-18 shows the pivot table. It uses generic names, which you can change to more meaningful names.

Microsoft Excel - consolid.xls					

Figure 21-18 screenshot showing Excel pivot table:

	A	B	C	D	E
1	Page1	(All)			
2					
3	Sum of Value	Colun			
4	Row	Jan	Feb	Mar	Grand Total
5	A-145	39	43	84	166
6	A-165	8	3	1	12
7	A-189	14	2	2	18
8	A-195	45	23	36	104
9	B-201	19	5	9	33
10	B-355	45	53	51	149
11	C-213	2	12	5	19
12	C-415	15	11	18	44
13	C-590	93	86	109	288
14	D-800	12	196	257	465
15	E-900	9	4	1	14
16	E-901	0	0	2	2
17	E-904	3	5	7	15
18	E-912	0	0	2	2
19	E-923	1	0	0	1
20	Grand Total	305	443	584	1332

PivotTable Field List — Drag items to the PivotTable report: Row, Column, Value, Page1. Add To — Row Area

Figure 21-18: Here is the completed pivot table that consolidates data from three different ranges.

Tip   In Step 2a of the PivotTable Wizard, you can choose the option labeled I will create the page fields. Doing so enables you to provide an item name for each item in the page field (rather than the generic Item1, Item2, and Item3).

Creating charts from a pivot table

A *PivotChart report* is a chart that is linked to a pivot table. By using the PivotTable and PivotChart Wizard, you can create simultaneously both a pivot table and a linked chart; you can use the techniques described earlier to drag and drop fields onto the pivot chart or the pivot table. To simultaneously create a pivot table and a pivot chart, choose PivotChart (with PivotTable) in the first dialog box of the PivotTable and PivotChart Wizard. Excel creates a new worksheet and a new chart sheet; both will contain templates for the pivot table and the pivot chart, respectively. Drag fields from the PivotTable toolbar onto either the chart or the table — simply switch between the sheets in the workbook to choose the sheet with which you want to work.

Although you can create a pivot chart by using the PivotTable and PivotChart Wizard, you may find it easier to create the chart from an existing pivot table. While viewing the pivot table, click the Chart Wizard button on the PivotTable toolbar. Excel immediately creates a chart sheet in the workbook based on the pivot table. Figure 21-19 shows the pivot chart based on the banking pivot table example used throughout the chapter. Excel updates this chart whenever you make changes to the pivot table.

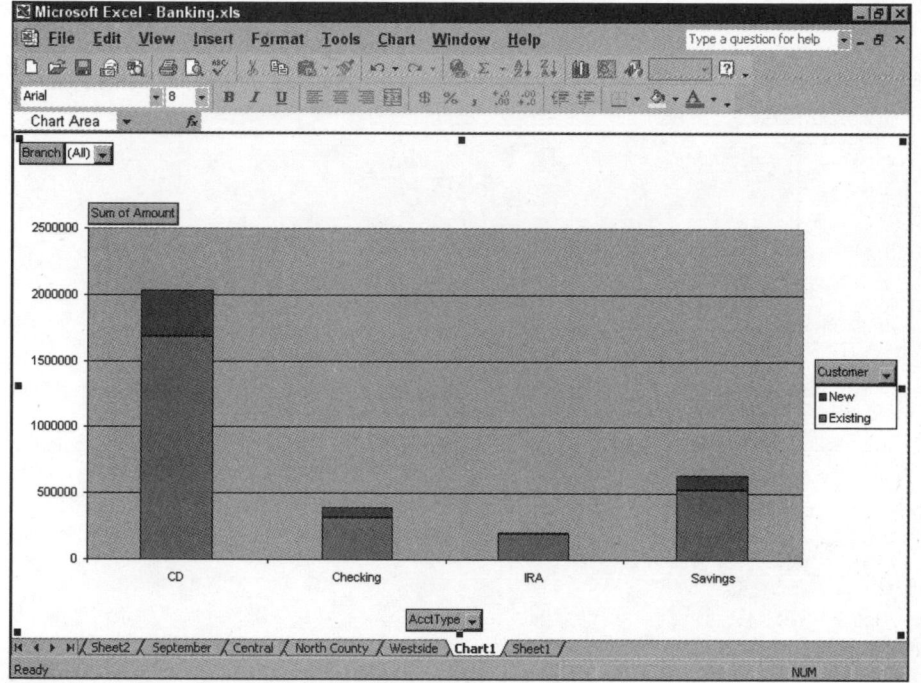

Figure 21-19: A pivot chart is based on a pivot table and changes along with the pivot table.

Tip

A pivot chart is always created on a separate Chart sheet. To convert the chart to an embedded chart on a worksheet, activate the Chart sheet and select Chart ➪ Location. Select the second option (as object in) and specify a worksheet for the chart.

✦   ✦   ✦

Performing Spreadsheet What-If Analysis

Most spreadsheet users probably realize that they have a very powerful tool for performing what-if analyses. With very little work you can easily see the effects of making changes in the assumptions that are the basis for your calculations. It's very easy to determine how a change affects the final outcome.

Of course, it helps to know the best means of performing a what-if analysis in Excel if you want to get the most value from your work. In this chapter, you'll learn how to use Excel as a very effective tool for what-if analysis.

Understanding What-If Analysis

What-if analysis is the process of determining how different input values affect the outcome of a series of calculations. For example, there might be several variables that affect the profitability of your business. In a what-if analysis, you might want to examine how changing each of those variables could influence your profit rate. That way you could determine which elements are most important to your bottom line.

Figure 22-1 shows a spreadsheet that calculates information pertaining to a mortgage loan. The worksheet is divided into two sections: the input cells and the result cells. Column D shows the formulas stored in column C.

With this worksheet, you can easily answer these what-if questions:

✦ What if I can negotiate a lower purchase price on the property?

✦ What if the lender requires a 20-percent down payment?

✦ Can I afford a 15-year mortgage?

✦ What if the interest rate decreases to 6.75 percent?

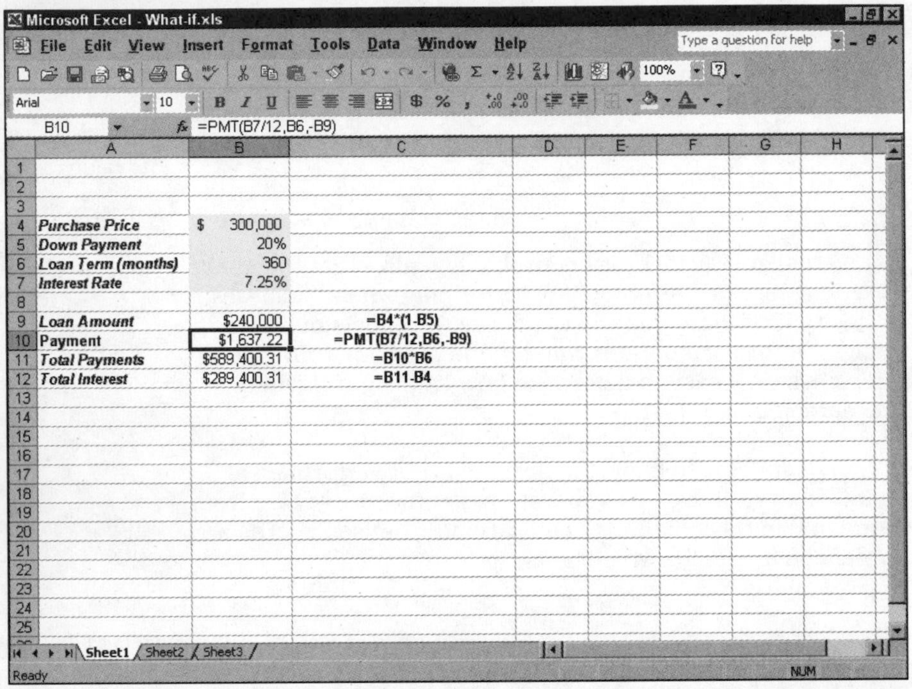

Figure 22-1: This worksheet model enables you to try different values to see the "what-if" results in the formulas.

You can answer these questions simply by changing the values in the cells in range C4:C7 and observing the effects in the dependent cells (C9:C12). You can, of course, vary any number of input cells simultaneously.

As you may expect, Excel can handle much more sophisticated models than the preceding example. To perform a what-if analysis using Excel, you have three options:

✦ **Manual what-if analysis:** Plug in new values and observe the effects on formula cells.

✦ **Data tables:** Create a table that displays the results of selected formula cells as you systematically change one or two input cells.

✦ **Scenario Manager:** Create named scenarios and generate reports that use outlines or pivot tables.

Don't Code Values

The mortgage calculation example, simple as it is, demonstrates an important point about spreadsheet design: You should always set up your worksheet so that you have maximum flexibility to make changes. Perhaps the most fundamental rule of spreadsheet design is the following:

Do not hard code (store) values in a formula. Instead, store the values in separate cells, and use cell references in the formula.

The term hard code refers to the use of actual values, or constants, in a formula. In the mortgage loan example, all the formulas use references to cells, not actual values.

You could use the value 360, for example, for the loan term argument of the PMT function in cell C10. Using a cell reference has two advantages. First, you have no doubt about the values that the formula uses (they aren't buried in the formula). Second, you can easily change the value.

Using values in formulas may not seem like much of an issue when only one formula is involved, but just imagine what would happen if this value were hard coded into several hundred formulas that were scattered throughout a worksheet.

This chapter discusses the last two options. The first of these options — manual what-if analysis — should be second nature to you by now and really doesn't need any additional explanation here.

Cross-Reference

A fourth option — macro-assisted what-if analysis — which involves creating macros to plug in variables for you, is really just a variation on the manual what-if analysis option. To learn more about automating tasks in Excel, see Part VI of this book.

Creating Data Tables for What-If Analysis

When you're working with a what-if model, Excel displays only one scenario at a time. But you can compare the results of various scenarios by using any of these techniques:

✦ Print multiple copies of the worksheet, each displaying a different scenario.

✦ Copy the model to other worksheets and set it up so that each worksheet displays a different scenario.

✦ Manually create a table that summarizes key formula cells for each scenario.

✦ Use Excel's Data ➪ Table command to create a summary table automatically.

This section discusses the Data ➪ Table command, which enables you to create a handy data table that summarizes formula cells for various values of either:

✦ A single input cell

✦ Various combinations of two input cells

For example, you may want to create a table that shows the payment details for various interest rates so that you can compare different loans directly.

You can create a data table fairly easily, but data tables have some limitations. In particular, a data table can deal with only one or two input cells at a time. In other words, you can't create a data table that uses a combination of three or more input cells.

The Scenario Manager, discussed later in this chapter, can produce a report that summarizes any number of input cells and result cells.

Creating a one-input data table

A one-input data table displays the results of one or more formulas when you use multiple values in a single input cell. You can place the table anywhere in the workbook. The left column contains various values for the single input cell. The top row contains formulas or, more often, references to formulas located elsewhere in the worksheet. You can use a single formula reference or any number of formula references. The upper-left cell of the table remains empty. Excel calculates the values that result from each level of the input cell and places them under each formula reference.

This example uses the mortgage loan worksheet shown in Figure 22-2. The goal of this example is to create a table that shows the values of the four formula cells (loan amount, monthly payment, total payments, and total interest) for various interest rates ranging from 6.00 to 8.00 percent, in 0.25 percent increments.

In Figure 22-2, row 6 consists of references to the formulas in the worksheet. For example, cell E6 contains the formula =B9. Column D contains the values of the single-input cell (interest rate) that Excel will use in the table.

Tip   When you're setting up the data table, you may want to format the data table's formula row as hidden to avoid the confusing display shown in the figure. Or you may want to start with the minimum value in the input cell.

To create the table, select the range (in this case, D6:H15) and then choose Data ➪ Table. Excel displays the Table dialog box, shown in Figure 22-3. You must specify the worksheet cell that contains the input value. Because variables for the input cell appear in a column in the data table rather than in a row, you place this cell reference in the text box called Column input cell. Enter B6 or point to the cell in the worksheet. Leave the Row input cell field blank. Click OK, and Excel fills in the table with the appropriate results.

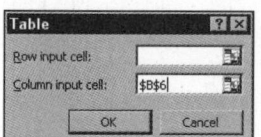

Figure 22-2: This example shows how you can use a one-input data table to view the results of a number of options at the same time.

Figure 22-3: Use the Table dialog box to specify the input cells for the data table.

Examine the contents of the cells that Excel entered as a result of this command. Notice that Excel filled in formulas — more specifically, array formulas that use the TABLE function. As discussed in Chapter 16, an array formula is a single formula that produces results in multiple cells. Because the table uses formulas, Excel updates the table that you produce if you change the cell references in the first row or if you plug in different interest rates in the first column.

Note
You can arrange a one-input table vertically (as in this example) or horizontally. If you place the values of the input cell in a row, you enter the input cell reference in the text box labeled Row input cell in the Table dialog box.

Creating a two-input data table

As the name implies, a two-input data table lets you vary *two* input cells. The two-input table has one critical difference compared to a one-input table: it can show the results of only one formula at a time. With a one-input table, you can place any number of formulas, or references to formulas, across the top row of the table. In a two-input table, this top row holds the values for the second input cell. The upper-left cell of the table contains a reference to the single result formula.

In the preceding example, you could create a two-input data table that shows the results of a formula (say, monthly payment) for various combinations of two input cells (such as interest rate and down-payment percent). To see the effects on other formulas, you simply create multiple data tables—one for each formula cell that you want to summarize.

The worksheet that is shown in Figure 22-4 demonstrates a two-input data table. In this example, the worksheet calculates the monthly payment for different combinations of interest rate and down payment.

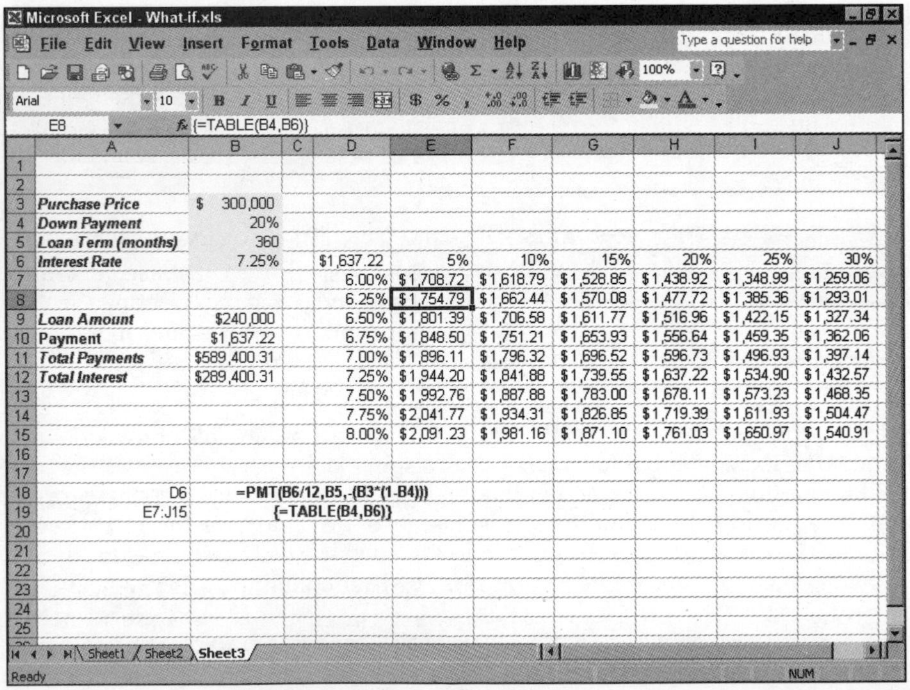

	A	B	C	D	E	F	G	H	I	J
1										
2										
3	*Purchase Price*	$ 300,000								
4	*Down Payment*	20%								
5	*Loan Term (months)*	360								
6	*Interest Rate*	7.25%		$1,637.22	5%	10%	15%	20%	25%	30%
7				6.00%	$1,708.72	$1,618.79	$1,528.85	$1,438.92	$1,348.99	$1,259.06
8				6.25%	$1,754.79	$1,662.44	$1,570.08	$1,477.72	$1,385.36	$1,293.01
9	*Loan Amount*	$240,000		6.50%	$1,801.39	$1,706.58	$1,611.77	$1,516.96	$1,422.15	$1,327.34
10	Payment	$1,637.22		6.75%	$1,848.50	$1,751.21	$1,653.93	$1,556.64	$1,459.35	$1,362.06
11	*Total Payments*	$589,400.31		7.00%	$1,896.11	$1,796.32	$1,696.52	$1,596.73	$1,496.93	$1,397.14
12	*Total Interest*	$289,400.31		7.25%	$1,944.20	$1,841.88	$1,739.55	$1,637.22	$1,534.90	$1,432.57
13				7.50%	$1,992.76	$1,887.88	$1,783.00	$1,678.11	$1,573.23	$1,468.35
14				7.75%	$2,041.77	$1,934.31	$1,826.85	$1,719.39	$1,611.93	$1,504.47
15				8.00%	$2,091.23	$1,981.16	$1,871.10	$1,761.03	$1,650.97	$1,540.91
16										
17										
18	D6	=PMT(B6/12,B5,-(B3*(1-B4)))								
19	E7:J15	{=TABLE(B4,B6)}								

Figure 22-4: This worksheet uses a two-input data table to show the results of varying two variables in a single formula.

This model uses two input cells: the interest rate and the down payment percentage.

To create the data table, select the range and choose Data ➪ Table. The Row input cell is B4, and the Column input cell is B6.

Using the Scenario Manager for What-If Analysis

Data tables are useful, but they have a few limitations:

✦ You can vary only one or two input cells at a time.

✦ The process of setting up a data table is not all that intuitive.

✦ A two-input table shows the results of only one formula cell (although you can create additional tables for more formulas).

✦ More often than not, you're interested in a few select combinations — not an entire table that shows all possible combinations of two input cells.

Excel's Scenario Manager feature makes it easy to automate your what-if models. You can store different sets of input values (called *changing cells* in the terminology of Scenario Manager) for any number of variables and give a name to each set. You can then select a set of values by name, and Excel displays the worksheet by using those values. You can also generate a summary report that shows the effect of various combinations of values on any number of result cells. These summary reports can be an outline or a pivot table.

Your sales forecast for the year, for example, may depend on several factors. Consequently, you can define three scenarios: best case, worst case, and most likely case. You then can switch to any of these scenarios by selecting the named scenario from a list. Excel substitutes the appropriate input values in your worksheet and recalculates the formulas.

Defining scenarios

To introduce you to the Scenario Manager, this section starts with a simple example: the production model shown in Figure 22-5.

This example defines three scenarios, as depicted in Table 22-1. The Best Case scenario has the lowest hourly cost and materials cost. The Worst Case scenario has high values for both the hourly cost and the materials cost. The third scenario, Most Likely Case, has intermediate values for both of these input cells (this represents the management's best estimate). The managers need to be prepared for the worst case, however — and they are interested in what would happen under the Best Case scenario.

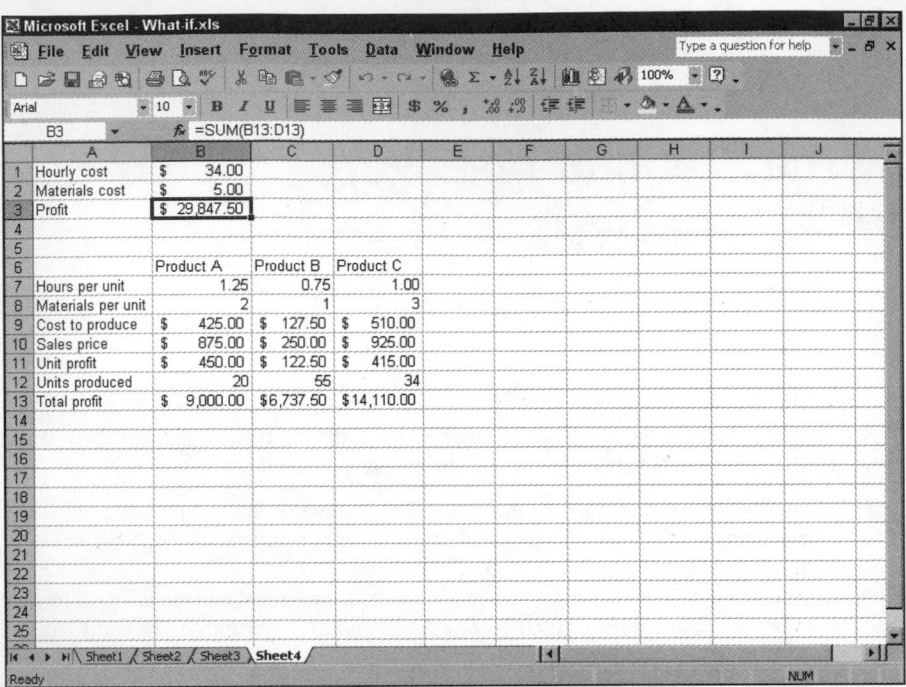

Figure 22-5: This worksheet calculates production costs for a series of products and is the basis for the scenarios in the following example.

| Table 22-1 |||
| **Three Scenarios for the Production Model** |||
Scenario	*Hourly Cost*	*Materials Cost*
Best Case	30	4
Worst Case	38	6
Most Likely Case	34	5

Access the Scenario Manager by selecting Tools ➪ Scenarios to display the Scenario Manager dialog box, shown in Figure 22-6.

When you first open this dialog box, it tells you that no scenarios are defined — which is not too surprising, because you're just starting. As you add named scenarios, they appear in this dialog box.

Tip

If you create names for the changing cells and all the result cells that you want to examine, Excel uses these names in the dialog boxes and in the reports that it generates. This makes keeping track of what's going on much easier; names also make your reports more readable.

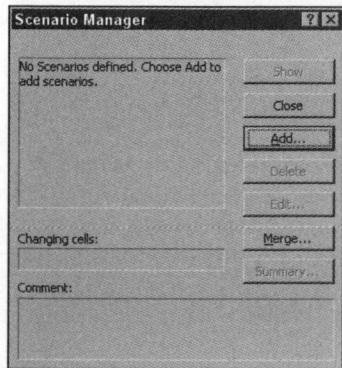

Figure 22-6: The Scenario Manager dialog box lets you assign names to different sets of assumptions.

To add a scenario, click the Add button in the Scenario Manager dialog box. Excel displays its Edit Scenario dialog box, shown in Figure 22-7.

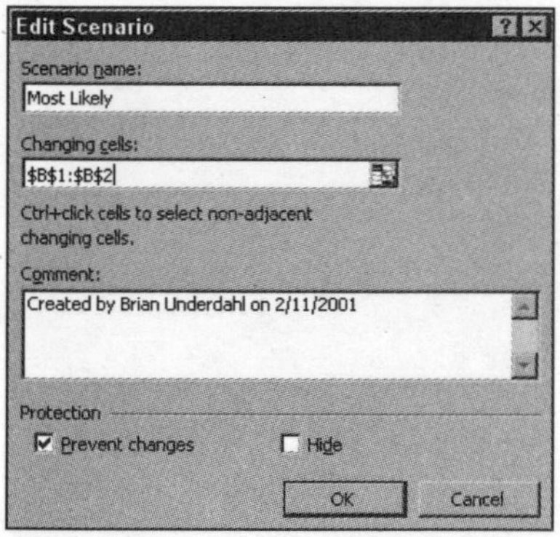

Figure 22-7: Use the Edit Scenario dialog box to create a named scenario.

This dialog box consists of four parts:

✦ **Scenario name:** The name for the scenario. You can give it any name that you like — preferably something meaningful.

✦ **Changing cells:** The input cells for the scenario. You can enter the cell addresses directly or point to them. Multiple selections are allowed, so the input cells need not be adjacent. Each named scenario can use the same set of changing cells or different changing cells. The number of changing cells for a scenario is limited to 32.

✦ **Comment:** By default, Excel displays the name of the person who created the scenario and the date that it was created. You can change this text, add new text to it, or delete it.

✦ **Protection:** The two options (preventing changes and hiding a scenario) are in effect only when you protect the worksheet and choose the Scenario option in the Protect Sheet dialog box. Protecting a scenario prevents anyone from modifying it; a hidden scenario doesn't appear in the Scenario Manager dialog box.

In this example, define the three scenarios that are listed in the preceding table. The changing cells are B1 and B2.

After you enter the information in the Add Scenario dialog box, click OK. Excel then displays the Scenario Values dialog box, shown in Figure 22-8. This dialog box displays one field for each changing cell that you specified in the previous dialog box. Enter the values for each cell in the scenario. If you click OK, you return to the Scenario Manager dialog box, which then displays your named scenario in its list. If you have more scenarios to create, click the Add button to return to the Add Scenario dialog box.

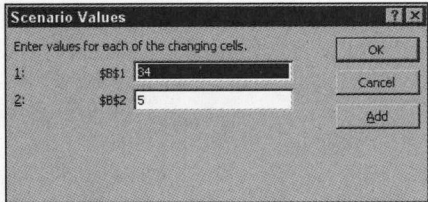

Figure 22-8: You enter the values for the scenario in the Scenario Values dialog box.

Displaying scenarios

After you define all the scenarios and return to the Scenario Manager dialog box, the dialog box displays the names of your defined scenarios. Select one of the scenarios and then click the Show button. Excel inserts the corresponding values into the changing cells and calculates the worksheet to show the results for that scenario.

Modifying scenarios

The Edit button in the Scenario Manager dialog box lets you change one or more of the values for the changing cells of a scenario. Select the scenario that you want to change, click the Edit button, choose OK to access the Scenario Values dialog box, and then make your changes. Notice that Excel automatically updates the Comments box with new text that indicates when the scenario was modified.

Merging scenarios

In workgroup situations, you may have several people working on a spreadsheet model, and several people may have defined various scenarios. The marketing department, for example, may have its opinion of what the input cells should be, the finance department may have another opinion, and your CEO may have yet another opinion.

Excel makes it easy to merge these various scenarios into a single workbook, by using the Merge button in the Scenario Manager dialog box. Clicking this button displays the Merge Scenarios dialog box, shown in Figure 22-9.

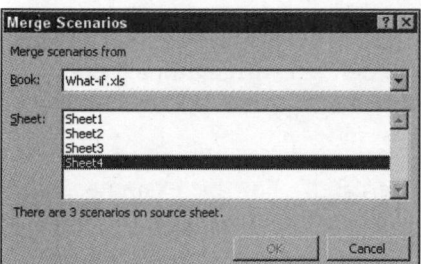

Figure 22-9: The Merge Scenarios dialog box lets you merge scenarios that are defined by others into your workbook.

Before you merge scenarios, make sure that the workbook from which you're merging is open. Then click the Merge button in the Scenario Manager dialog box. Excel displays its Merge Scenarios dialog box. Choose the workbook from which you're merging in the Book drop-down list. Then choose the sheet that contains the scenarios that you want to merge from the Sheet list box (notice that the dialog box displays the number of scenarios in each sheet as you scroll through the Sheet list box). Click OK to return to the previous dialog box, which now displays the scenario names that you merged from the other workbook.

Generating a scenario report

After you have created your scenarios, you are ready to generate a summary report. When you click the Summary button in the Scenario Manager dialog box, Excel displays the Scenario Summary dialog box, shown in Figure 22-10.

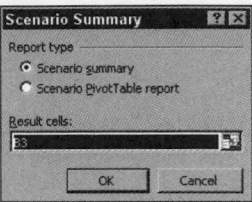

Figure 22-10: The Scenario Summary dialog box enables you to choose a report type and specify the result cells in which you're interested.

You have a choice of report types:

✦ **Scenario summary:** The summary report appears in the form of an outline.

✦ **Scenario PivotTable report:** The summary report appears in the form of a pivot table (see Chapter 21).

For simple cases of scenario management, a standard Scenario summary report is usually sufficient. If you have many scenarios defined with multiple result cells, however, you may find that a Scenario pivot table provides more flexibility.

The Scenario Summary dialog box also asks you to specify the result cells (the cells that contain the formulas in which you're interested). For this example, select B13:D13 and B3 (a multiple selection) to make the report show the profit for each product, plus the total profit.

Excel creates a new worksheet to store the summary table. Figure 22-11 shows the Scenario Summary form of the report. If you gave names to the changing cells and result cells, the table uses these names. Otherwise, it lists the cell references.

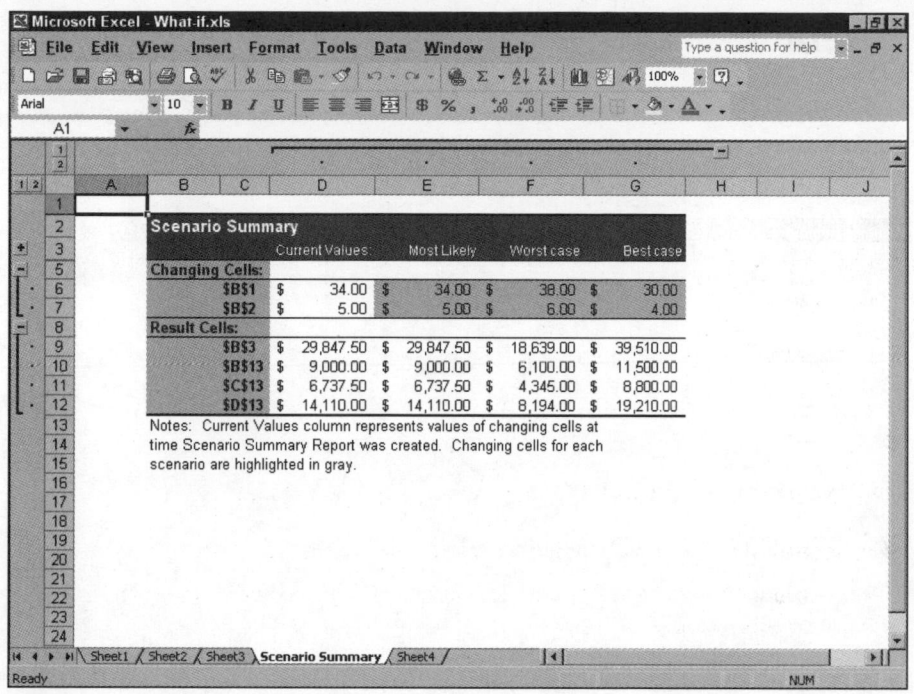

Figure 22-11: This is a summary report produced by the Scenario Manager.

Scenario Manager Limitations

As you work with the Scenario Manager, you may discover its main limitation: a scenario can use no more than 32 changing cells.

You can get around this limitation by splitting your scenarios into parts. For example, if you have a worksheet with monthly sales projections for three years (36 changing cells), you may want to define various scenarios for these projections. Because the number of changing cells exceeds the 32-cell limit, however, you can break it down into two or three scenarios — each of which uses a different set of changing cells. For example, you can define a scenario for the first 12 months, another for the second 12 months, and yet another for the third 12 months.

✦   ✦   ✦

Analyzing Data Using Goal Seeking and Solver

In the last chapter, you learned how to use Excel for what-if analysis. You saw how you could compare different outcomes that result from changing certain values in the worksheet. This chapter shows you a similar process, but in this case, you'll see how Excel can help you reach a specified goal. Rather than manually change various input cells to achieve a desired outcome, you'll see how you can tell Excel to find the best input values automatically. As you will see, Excel has the tools to greatly simplify what could otherwise be some very complicated and tedious tasks.

Understanding Goal Seeking

Consider the following what-if question: "What is the total profit if sales increase by 20 percent?" If you set up your worksheet properly, you can change the value in one cell to see what happens to the profit cell. Goal seeking takes the opposite approach. If you know what a formula result *should* be, Excel can tell you the values that you need to enter in one or more input cells to produce that result. In other words, you can ask a question such as, "How much does sales need to increase to produce a profit of $1.2 million?" Excel provides two tools that are relevant:

+ **Goal seeking:** Determines the value that you need to enter in a single-input cell to produce a result that you want in a dependent (formula) cell.

✦ **Solver:** Determines the values that you need to enter in multiple-input cells to produce a result that you want. Moreover, because you can specify certain constraints to the problem, you gain significant problem-solving capability.

Using Single-Cell Goal Seeking

Single-cell goal seeking (also known as *backsolving*) is a rather simple concept. You tell Excel the result you want to reach in a formula cell, and it determines the correct value to place in an input cell to reach that goal. The example that follows demonstrates the process.

Trying out a goal-seeking example

Figure 23-1 shows the mortgage loan worksheet that was used in Chapter 22. This worksheet has four input cells and four formula cells. Originally, this worksheet was used for a what-if analysis example. In this section, the opposite approach is taken—rather than supply different input cell values to look at the calculated formulas, this example lets Excel determine one of the input values.

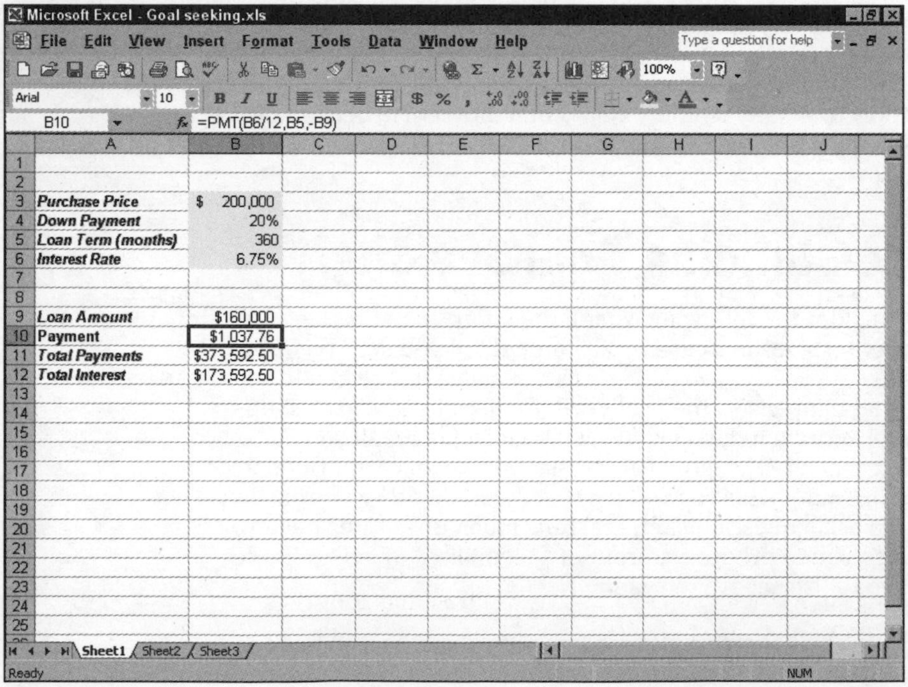

Figure 23-1: This worksheet model enables you to try using goal seeking to find the desired result.

Assume that you're in the market for a new home and you know that you can afford $1,500 per month in mortgage payments. You also know that a lender can issue a fixed-rate mortgage loan for 6.75 percent, based on an 80 percent loan-to-value ratio (that is, a 20-percent down payment). The question is, "What is the maximum purchase price I can handle?" In other words, what value in cell B3 causes the formula in cell B10 to result in $1,500? You could plug values into cell B3 until B10 displays $1,500; however, Excel can determine the answer much more efficiently.

To answer the question posed in the preceding paragraph, select Tools ⇨ Goal Seek. Excel displays the Goal Seek dialog box, shown in Figure 23-2. Completing this dialog box is similar to forming a sentence. You want to set cell B10 to 1500 by changing cell B3. Enter this information in the dialog box either by typing the cell references or by pointing with the mouse. Click OK to begin the goal-seeking process.

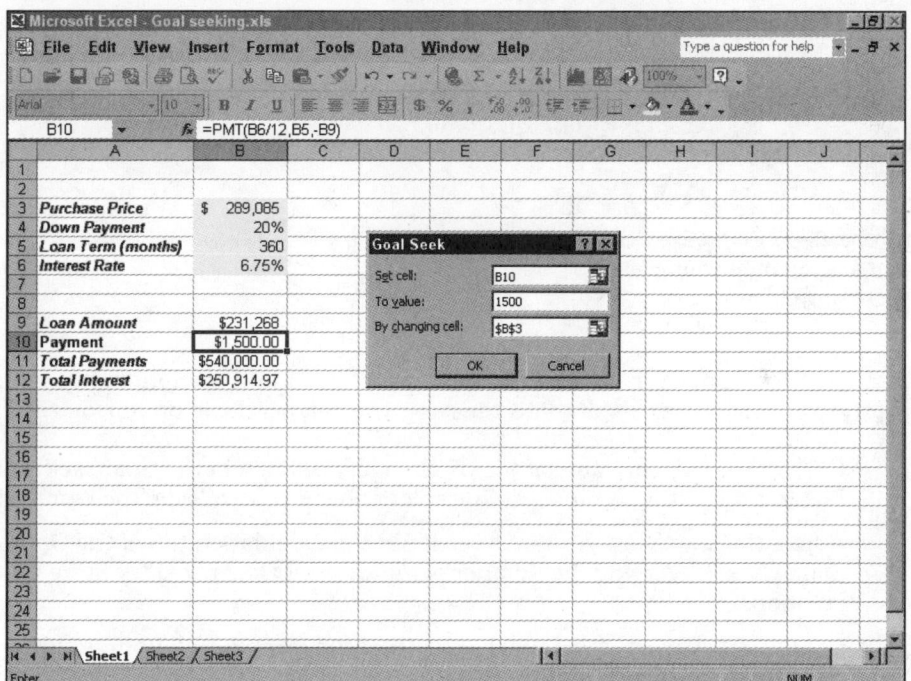

Figure 23-2: By using the Goal Seek dialog box, you can find the correct input value to reach your desired result.

In about a second, Excel announces that it has found the solution and displays the Goal Seek Status box, which shows the target value and the value that Excel calculated. In this case, Excel found an exact value. The worksheet now displays the found value in cell B3 ($289,085). As a result of this value, the monthly payment amount is $1,500. At this point, you have two options:

✦ Click OK to replace the original value with the found value.

✦ Click Cancel to restore your worksheet to the form that it had before you chose Tools ➪ Goal Seek.

Understanding a bit more about goal seeking

Some problems simply cannot be solved. For example, if you tell Excel to find a value that will produce −1 as the result when you square the value, a solution simply doesn't exist. In such a case, the Goal Seek Status box informs you of that fact (see Figure 23-3).

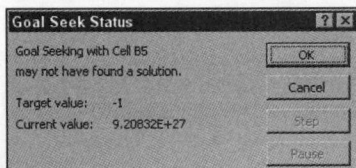

Figure 23-3: When Excel can't find a solution to your goal-seeking problem, it tells you so.

At other times, however, Excel may report that it can't find a solution, but you're pretty sure that one exists. If that's the case, you can try these options:

✦ Change the current value of the By changing cell box in the Goal Seek dialog box to a value that is closer to the solution, and then reissue the command.

✦ Adjust the Maximum iterations setting in the Calculation tab of the Options dialog box. Increasing the number of iterations makes Excel try more possible solutions.

✦ Double-check your logic to make sure that the formula cell does, indeed, depend on the specified changing cell.

Note In some cases, multiple values of the input cell produce the same desired result. For example, the formula =A1^2 returns 16 if cell A1 contains either −4 or +4. If you use goal seeking when two solutions are possible, Excel gives you the solution that has the same sign as the current value in the cell.

Perhaps the main limitation of the Tools ➪ Goal Seek command is its inability to find the value for more than one input cell. For example, it can't tell you what purchase price *and* what down-payment percent will result in a particular monthly payment. If you want to change more than one variable at a time, use Solver (discussed later in this chapter).

Graphical goal seeking

Excel provides another way to perform goal seeking — by manipulating the data series in a graph. Figure 23-4 shows a worksheet that projects sales for a startup company. The CFO knows from experience that companies in this industry can grow exponentially according to a formula such as this one:

y*(bx)

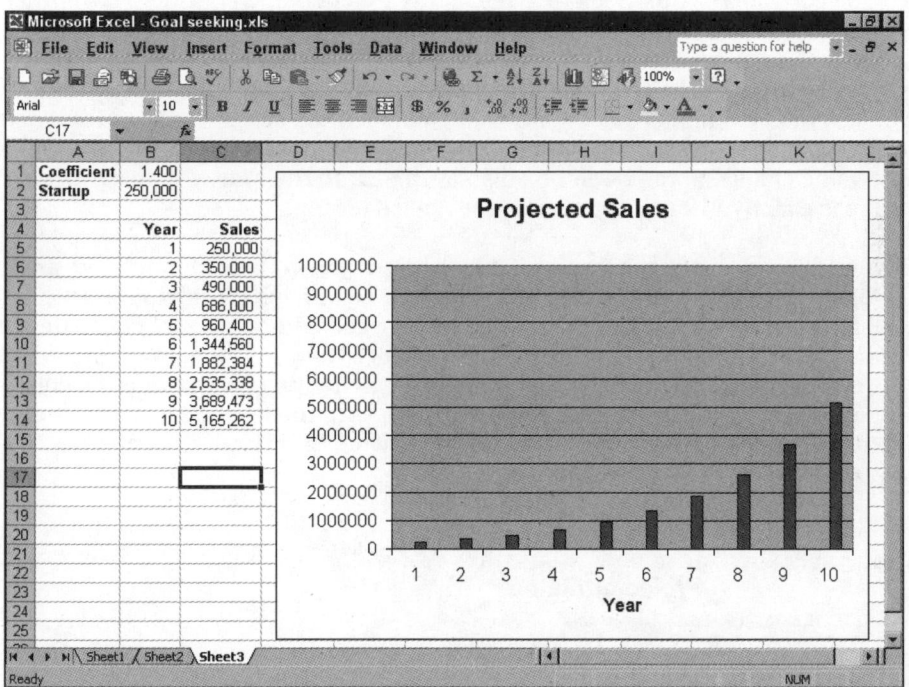

Figure 23-4: This sales projection predicts exponential growth, based on the growth coefficient in cell B1.

Table 23-1 lists and describes the variables.

Table 23-1	
Variables Used in the Sales Growth Formula	
Variable	*Description*
y	A constant equal to the first year's sales
b	A growth coefficient
x	A variable relating to time

The company managers know that sales during the first year will be $250,000, and they want to increase the company's sales to $10 million by year 10. The financial modelers want to know the exact growth coefficient that meets this goal. The worksheet that is shown in Figure 23-4 uses formulas to forecast the annual sales, based on the growth coefficient in cell B1. The worksheet has an embedded chart that plots the annual sales.

The initial guess for the growth coefficient is 1.40. As you can see, this number is too low—it results in sales of only $5.165 million for the tenth year. Although you can select Tools ➪ Goal Seek to arrive at the exact coefficient, there is another way to do it.

Click the chart so that you can edit it and then select the chart series. Now, click the last data column to select only that column in the series. Point to the top of the column, and the mouse pointer changes shape. Drag the column upward and watch the value change in the small box displayed next to the mouse pointer. When the value is exactly $10 million, release the mouse button.

Excel responds with the Goal Seek dialog box, with two fields completed, as shown in Figure 23-5. Excel just needs to know which cell to use for the input cell. Specify cell B1 or enter **Coefficient** in the By changing cell edit box. Excel calculates the value of Coefficient that is necessary to produce the result that you pointed out on the chart. If you want to keep that number (which, by the way, is 1.507), click OK. Excel replaces the current value of Coefficient with the new value, and the chart is updated automatically. It would take quite a while to arrive at this number by manually plugging in successive approximations.

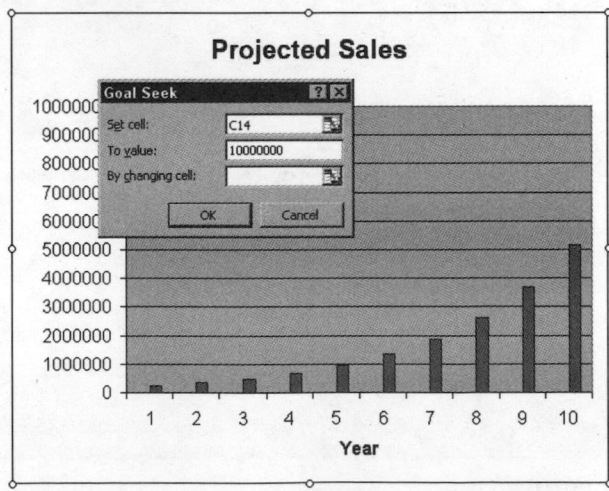

Figure 23-5: The Goal Seek dialog box appears when you directly manipulate a point on a chart that contains a formula.

Understanding Solver

Excel's goal-seeking feature is a useful tool, but it clearly has limitations. It can solve for only one adjustable cell, for example, and it returns only a single solution. Excel's powerful Solver tool extends this concept by enabling you to:

✦ Specify multiple adjustable cells.

✦ Specify constraints on the values that the adjustable cells can have.

✦ Generate a solution that maximizes or minimizes a particular worksheet cell.

✦ Generate multiple solutions to a problem.

Although goal seeking is a relatively simple operation, using Solver can be a bit more complicated. Still, having this much power is worth spending the extra time to learn about it.

Note   Frontline Systems, the original developer of Solver, offers a far more powerful version of Solver as well as tips for using Solver on their Web site at www.frontsys.com. If you find that Excel's version of Solver is too limited to handle your problem, visit the Frontline Systems Web site to download a free evaluation version of Premium Solver.

Choosing appropriate problems for Solver

Problems that are appropriate for Solver typically involve situations that meet these criteria:

✦ A target cell depends on other cells and formulas. Typically, you want to maximize or minimize this target cell or set it equal to some value.

✦ The target cell depends on a group of cells (called changing cells) that Solver can adjust to affect the target cell.

✦ The solution must adhere to certain limitations, or constraints.

After you set up your worksheet appropriately, you can use Solver to adjust the changing cells, meet the constraints that you have defined, and produce the result that you want in your target cell.

A simple Solver example

This section presents a simple example to introduce Solver. This example demonstrates how to use Solver to allocate production capacity between several products to obtain the highest overall profit.

Figure 23-6 shows a worksheet that is set up to calculate the profit for three products. Column B shows the number of units of each product, column C shows the profit per unit for each product, and column C contains formulas that calculate the profit for each product by multiplying the units by the profit per unit.

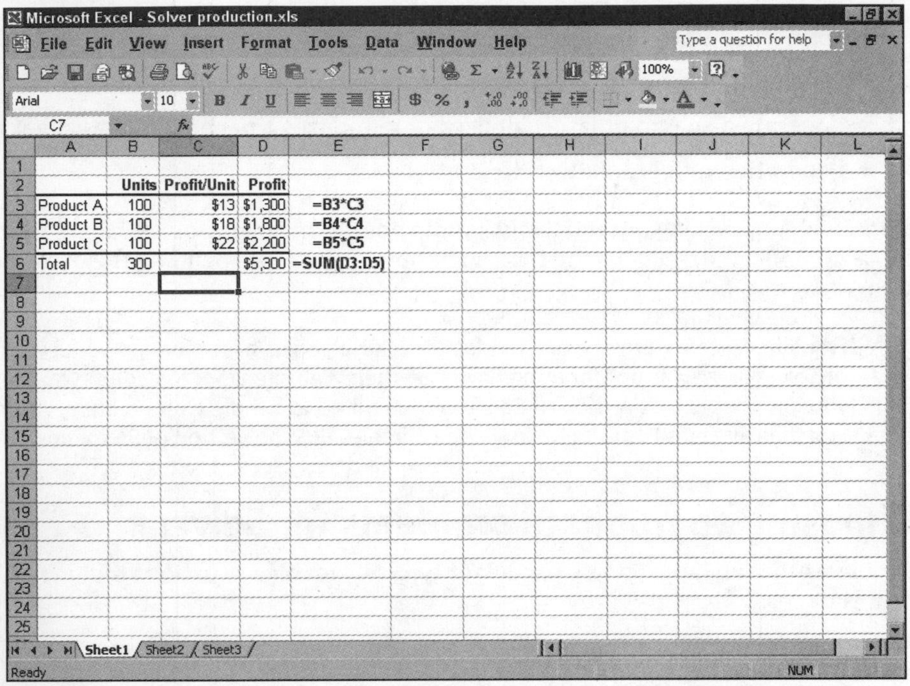

Figure 23-6: This worksheet model uses Solver to determine the optimal production mix.

It's easy to see that the greatest profit per unit comes from Product C. Therefore, the logical solution is to produce only Product C. If things were really this simple, you wouldn't need tools such as Solver. As in most situations, this company has some constraints to which it must adhere:

✦ The combined production capacity is 300 total units per day.

✦ The company needs 50 units of Product A to fill an existing order.

✦ The company needs 40 units of Product B to fill an anticipated order.

✦ Because the market for Product C is relatively limited, the company doesn't want to produce more than 40 units of this product.

These four constraints make the problem more realistic and challenging. In fact, it's a perfect problem for Solver.

The basic procedure for using Solver is as follows:

1. Set up the worksheet with values and formulas. Make sure that you format cells logically; for example, if you cannot produce portions of your products, format those cells to contain numbers with no decimal values.

2. Bring up the Solver dialog box.

3. Specify the target cell.

4. Specify the changing cells.

5. Specify the constraints.

6. Change the Solver options, if necessary.

7. Let Solver solve the problem.

To start Solver, select Tools ⇨ Solver. Excel displays its Solver Parameters dialog box, shown in Figure 23-7.

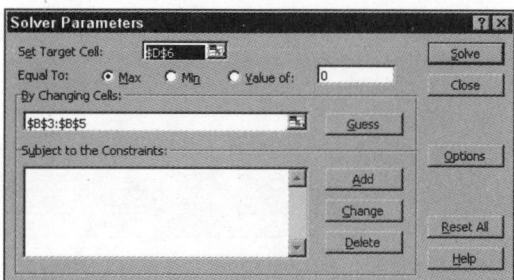

Figure 23-7: Use the Solver Parameters dialog box to set up the conditions for the problem you want Solver to solve.

Note   Solver is an add-in, so it's available only when the add-in is installed. If the Tools menu doesn't show a Solver command, you need to install the add-in before you can use it. Select Tools ⇨ Add-Ins. Excel displays its Add-Ins dialog box. Scroll down the list of add-ins and place a check mark next to the item named Solver Add-In. Click OK and Excel installs the add-in, making the Tools ⇨ Solver command available. If Solver isn't available on your computer, you'll be asked whether you want to install it.

In this example, the target cell is D6—the cell that calculates the total profit for three products. Enter (or point to) cell D6 in the Set Target Cell field of the Solver Parameters dialog box. Because the objective is to maximize this cell, click the Max option. Next, specify the changing cells, which are in the range B3:B5, in the By Changing Cells box.

The next step is to specify the constraints on the problem. The constraints are added one at a time and appear in the box labeled Subject to the Constraints. To add a constraint, click the Add button. Excel displays the Add Constraint dialog box, shown in Figure 23-8. This dialog box has three parts: a cell reference, an operator, and a value. To set the first constraint—that the total production capacity is 300 units—enter B6 as the Cell Reference, choose equal (=) from the drop-down list of operators, and enter **300** as the Constraint value. Click Add to add the remaining constraints. Table 23-2 summarizes the constraints for this problem.

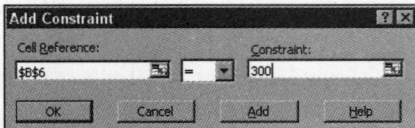

Figure 23-8: Use the Add Constraint dialog box to set up the constraints that limit the solutions to the problem.

Table 23-2	
Constraints Summary	
Constraint	**Expressed As**
Capacity is 300 units	B6=300
At least 50 units of Product A	B3>=50
At least 40 units of Product B	B4>=40
No more than 40 units of Product C	B5<=40

After you enter the last constraint, click OK to return to the Solver Parameters dialog box—which now lists the four constraints.

At this point, Solver knows everything about the problem. Click the Solver button to start the solution process. You can watch the progress onscreen, and Excel soon announces that it has found a solution, as shown in Figure 23-9.

At this point, you have these options:

✦ Replace the original changing cell values with the values that Solver found.

✦ Restore the original changing cell values.

✦ Create any or all three reports that describe what Solver did (press Shift to select multiple reports from this list).

✦ Click the Save Scenario button to save the solution as a scenario so that the Scenario Manager can use it (see Chapter 22).

If you specify any report options, Excel creates each report on a new worksheet, with an appropriate name. Figure 23-10 shows an Answer Report.

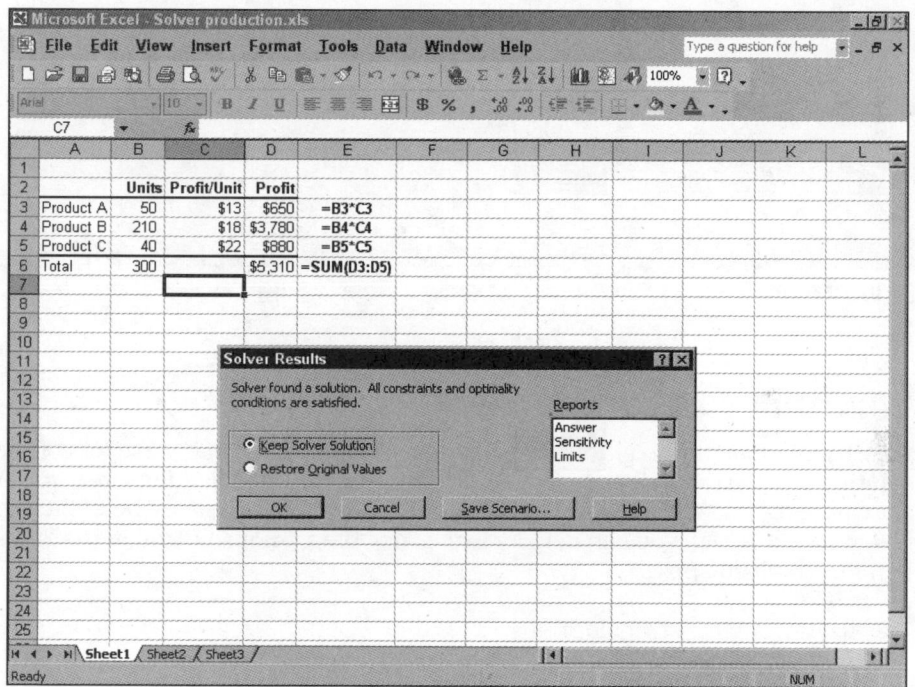

Figure 23-9: Solver informs you when it has found a solution and you can choose what action you want to take next.

Tip   Solver's reports often provide important clues that can help you optimize the solution — especially if you pay attention to which constraints are binding and which ones are not.

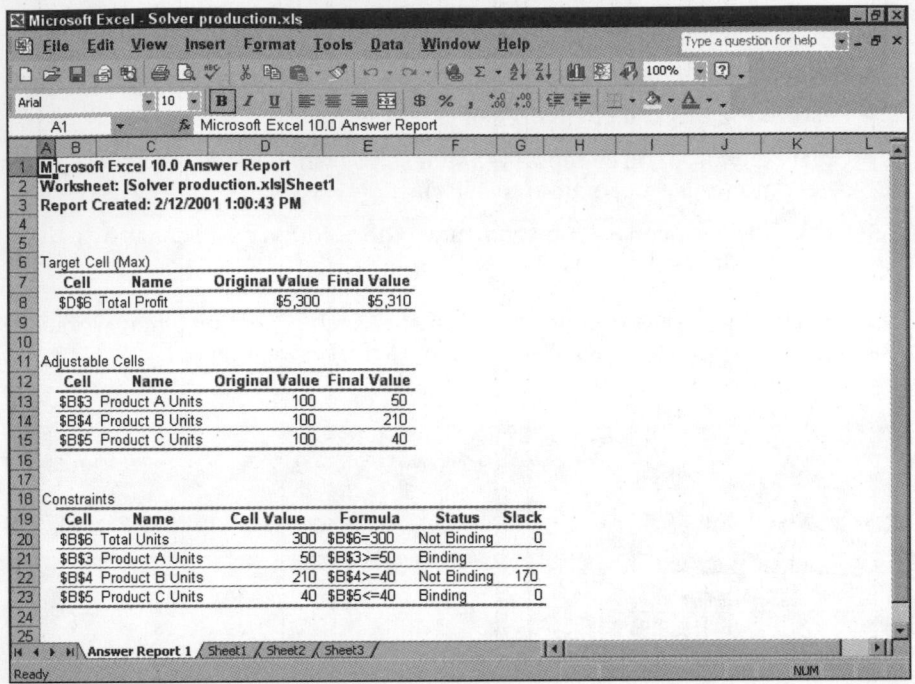

Figure 23-10: The Solver answer report shows you how Solver arrived at the answer.

Controlling the Solver options

Solver has a number of options that you can use to control many aspects of the solution process, as well as to load and to save model specifications in a worksheet range. You set these options using the Solver Options dialog box (shown in Figure 23-11), which you can display by clicking the Options button in the Solver Parameters dialog box.

This list describes Solver's options:

✦ **Max Time:** Specify the maximum amount of time (in seconds) that you want Solver to spend on a problem. If Solver reports that it exceeded the time limit, you can increase the amount of time that it spends searching for a solution.

✦ **Iterations:** Enter the maximum number of trial solutions that you want Solver to perform.

✦ **Precision:** Specify how close the Cell Reference and Constraint formulas must be to satisfy a constraint. Excel may solve the problem more quickly if you specify less precision.

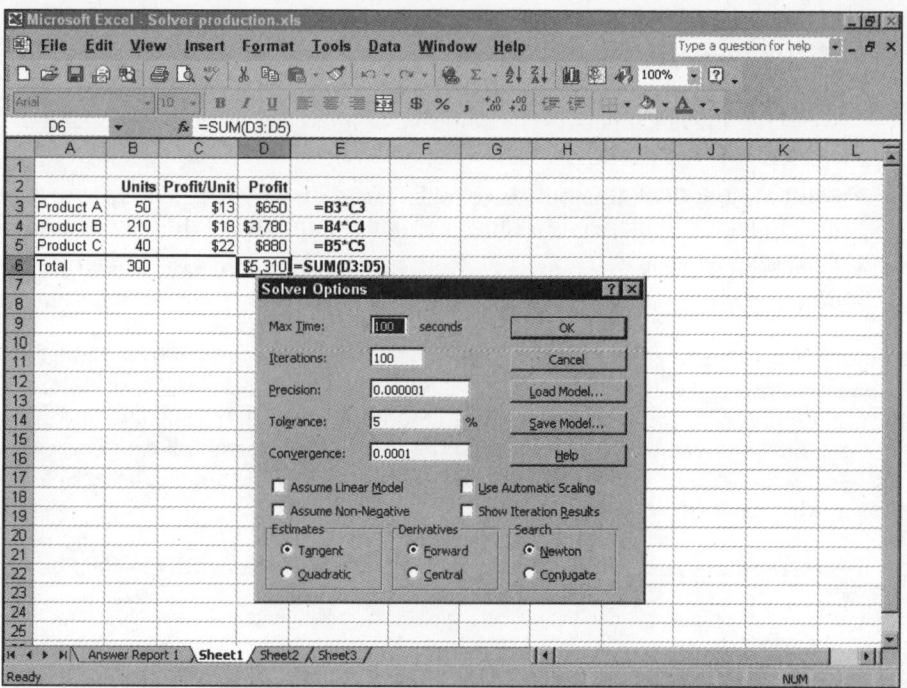

Figure 23-11: You can use these options to control many aspects of how Solver solves a problem.

✦ **Tolerance:** Designate the maximum percentage of error allowed for integer solutions (relevant only if an integer constraint is used).

✦ **Convergence:** Specify a value for when Solver should stop seeking a better solution. This value is the relative change in the target cell value for the last five iterations. Convergence applies only to nonlinear problems and must be between 0 and 1.

✦ **Assume Linear Model:** Choose this option to speed the solution process, but you can use it only if all the relationships in the model are linear. You can't use this option if the adjustable cells are multiplied or divided or if the problem uses exponents.

✦ **Assume Non-Negative:** Choose this option to assume a lower limit of zero for all adjustable cells for which you have not set a lower limit.

✦ **Use Automatic Scaling:** Use when the problem involves large differences in magnitude — when you attempt to maximize a percentage, for example, by varying cells that are very large.

✦ **Show Iteration Results:** Instruct Solver to pause and display the results after each iteration by checking this box.

✦ **Estimates, Derivatives, and Search group boxes:** Use these options to control some technical aspects of the solution. In most cases, you don't need to change these settings.

✦ **Load Model:** Click this button to make Excel display the Load Model dialog box, in which you specify a range containing the model that you want to load.

✦ **Save Model:** Click this button to make Excel display the Save Model dialog box, in which you specify a range where Excel should save the model parameters.

Usually, you want to save a model only when you're using more than one set of Solver parameters with your worksheet, because Excel saves the first Solver model automatically with your worksheet (using hidden names). If you save additional models, Excel stores the information in the form of the formulas that correspond to the specification that you make (the last cell in the saved range is an array formula that holds the options settings).

Tip   To learn more about the best settings for Solver's options, click the Help button.

Using Solver in Some Practical Examples

The remainder of this chapter consists of examples of using Solver for various types of problems.

Tip   You'll find a number of solver models on the Frontline Systems Web site at www.frontsys.com.

Minimizing shipping costs using Solver

This example involves finding alternative options for shipping materials while keeping total shipping costs at a minimum (see Figure 23-12). A company has warehouses in Los Angeles, St. Louis, and Boston. Six retail outlets throughout the United States place orders, which the company then ships from one of the warehouses. Ideally, the company wants to meet the product needs of all six retail outlets from available inventory in the warehouses and keep total shipping charges as low as possible.

This workbook is rather complicated, so each part is explained individually:

✦ **Shipping Costs Table:** This table, at the top of the worksheet, contains per-unit shipping costs from each warehouse to each retail outlet. The cost to ship a unit from Los Angeles to Denver, for example, is $58.

✦ **Product needs of each retail store:** This information appears in C12:C17. For example, Denver needs 150 units, Houston needs 225 units, and so on. C18 holds the total needed.

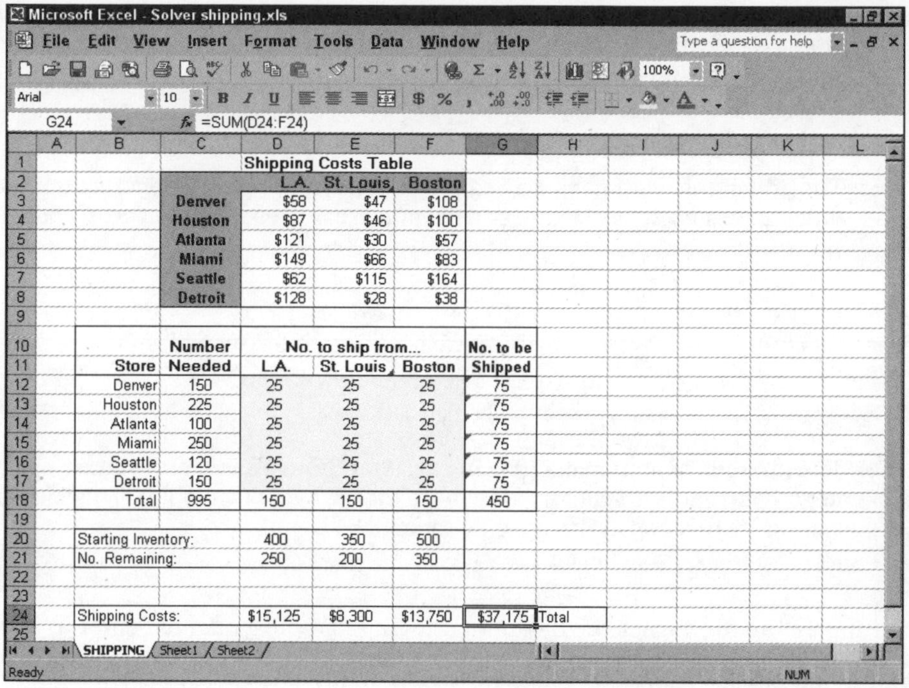

Figure 23-12: This worksheet model determines the costs to ship products from warehouses to retail outlets.

✦ **Number to ship:** The shaded range (D12:F17) holds the adjustable cells that Solver varies (they are all initialized with a value of 25, to give Solver a starting value.) Column G contains formulas that total the number of units the company needs to ship to each retail outlet.

✦ **Warehouse inventory:** Row 20 contains the amount of inventory at each warehouse, and row 21 contains formulas that subtract the amount shipped (row 18) from the inventory. For example, cell D21 contains this formula: =D20–D18.

✦ **Calculated shipping costs:** Row 24 contains formulas that calculate the shipping costs. Cell D24 contains the following formula, which is copied to the two cells to the right of Cell D24:

```
=SUMPRODUCT(D3:D8,D12:D17)
```

This formula calculates the total shipping cost from each warehouse. Cell G24 is the bottom line, the total shipping costs for all orders.

Solver fills in values in the range D12:F17 in such a way that minimizes shipping costs while still supplying each retail outlet with the desired number of units. In other words, the solution minimizes the value in cell C24 by adjusting the cells in D12:F17, subject to these constraints:

✦ The number of units needed by each retail outlet must equal the number shipped (in other words, all the orders are filled). These constraints are represented by the following specifications:

```
C12=G12     C14=G14     C16=G16
C13=G13     C15=G15     C17=G17
```

✦ The adjustable cells can't be negative because shipping a negative number of units makes no sense. These constraints are represented by these specifications:

```
D12>=0      E12>=0      F12>=0
D13>=0      E13>=0      F13>=0
D14>=0      E14>=0      F14>=0
D15>=0      E15>=0      F15>=0
D16>=0      E16>=0      F16>=0
D17>=0      E17>=0      F17>=0
```

✦ The number of units remaining in each warehouse's inventory must not be negative (that is, they can't ship more than what is available). This is represented by this constraint specifications:

```
D21>=0      E21>=0      F21>=0
```

Setting up the problem is the difficult part. For example, you must enter 37 constraints. When you have specified all the necessary information, click the Solve button to put Solver to work. Solver displays the solution that is shown in Figure 23-13.

The total shipping cost is $55,515, and all the constraints are met. Notice that shipments to Miami come from both St. Louis and Boston.

Note   Although at first glance you might think that Solver produced an incorrect result because the shipping cost total is higher than the original model, remember that the original model did not fulfill the product needs of the various stores. It's important to remember that all the problem's constraints must be met to produce an acceptable solution.

Using Solver for staff scheduling

This example deals with staff scheduling. Such problems usually involve determining the minimum number of people that satisfy staffing needs on certain days or times of the day. The constraints typically involve such details as the number of consecutive days or hours that a person can work.

Figure 23-14 shows a worksheet that is set up to analyze a simple staffing problem. The question is "What is the minimum number of employees required to meet daily staffing needs?" At this company, each person works five consecutive days. As a result, employees begin their five-day workweek on different days of the week.

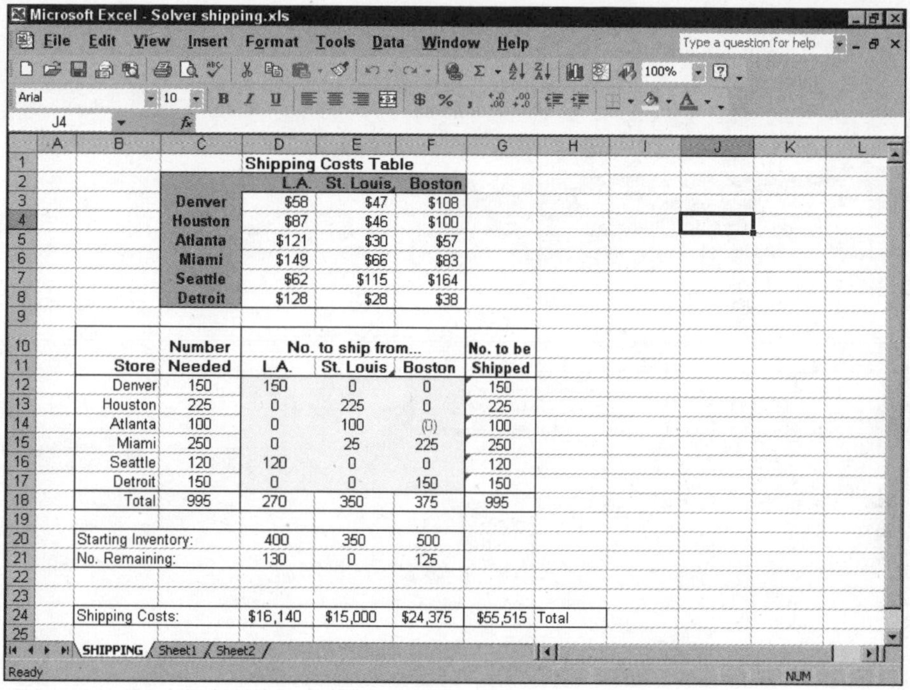

Figure 23-13: Solver produced this solution that solves the problem.

The key to this problem, as with most Solver problems, is figuring out how to set up the worksheet. This example makes it clear that setting up your worksheet properly is critical to Solver. This worksheet is laid out as follows:

✦ **Day:** Column B consists of plain text for the days of the week.

✦ **Staff Needed:** The values in column C represent the number of employees needed on each day of the week. As you see, staffing needs vary quite a bit by the day of the week.

✦ **Staff Scheduled:** Column D holds formulas that use the values in column E. Each formula adds the number of people who start on that day to the number of people who started on the preceding four days. Because the week wraps around, you can't use a single formula and copy it. Consequently, each formula in column D is different:

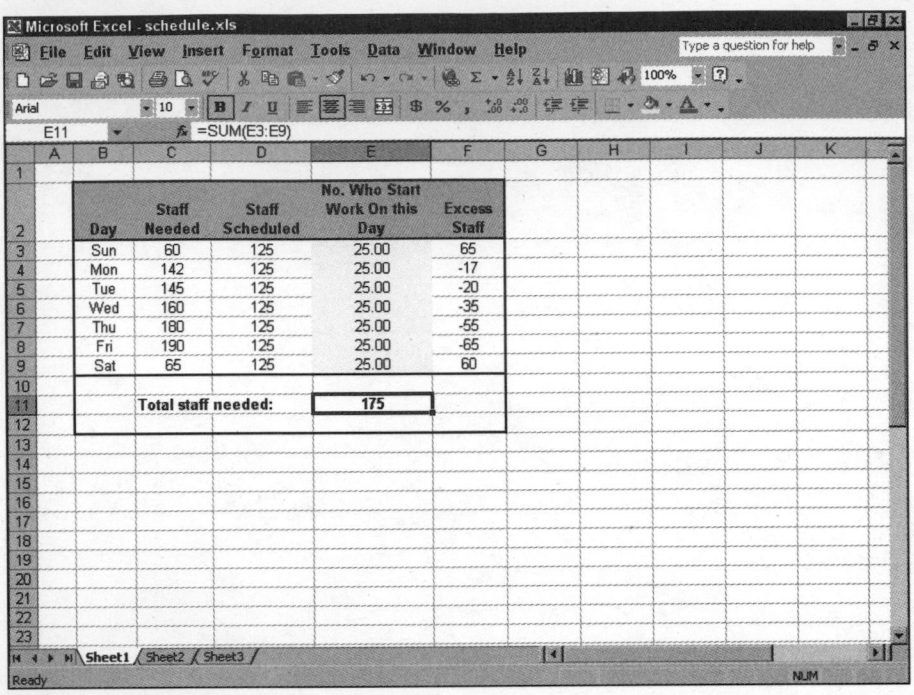

Figure 23-14: This worksheet model determines the minimum number of staff members required to meet daily staffing needs.

```
D3:   =E3+E9+E8+E7+E6
D4:   =E4+E3+E9+E8+E7
D5:   =E5+E4+E10+E9+E8
D6:   =E6+E5+E4+E10+E9
D7:   =E7+E6+E5+E4+E10
D8:   =E8+E7+E6+E5+E4
D9:   =E9+E8+E7+E6+E5
```

✦ **Adjustable cells:** Column E holds the adjustable cells — the numbers to be determined by Solver. These cells are initialized with a value of 25, to give Solver a starting value. Generally, you should initialize the changing cells to values that are as close as possible to the anticipated answer.

✦ **Excess Staff:** Column F contains formulas that subtract the number of staff members needed from the number of staff members scheduled, to determine excess staff. Cell F3 contains =D3–C3, which was copied to the six cells below it.

✦ **Total staff needed:** Cell E11 contains a formula that sums the number of people who start on each day. The formula is =SUM(E3:E9). This is the value that Solver minimizes.

This problem, of course, has constraints. The number of people scheduled each day must be greater than or equal to the number of people required. If each value in column F is greater than or equal to 0, the constraints are satisfied.

After the worksheet is set up, select Tools ➪ Solver and specify that you want to minimize cell E11 by changing cells E3:E9. Next, click Add to begin adding these constraints:

```
F3>=0
F4>=0
F5>=0
F6>=0
F7>=0
F8>=0
F9>=0
```

Click Solve to start the process. The solution that Solver finds, shown in Figure 23-15, indicates that a staff of 188 meets the staffing needs and that no excess staffing exists on any day.

If you examine the results carefully, you notice that several things are wrong:

✦ Solver's solution involves partial people—who are difficult to find. For example, 8.2 people begin their workweek on Sunday.

✦ Even more critical is the suggestion that a negative number of people should begin their workweek on Saturday.

You can easily correct both of these problems by adding more constraints. Fortunately, Solver enables you to limit the solution to integers by using the integer option in the Add Constraint dialog box. This means that you must add another constraint for each cell in E3:E9. Figure 23-16 shows how you can specify an integer constraint. Avoiding the negative people problem requires seven more constraints of the form E3>=0, one for each cell in E3:E9.

These two problems (integer solutions and negative numbers) are quite common when using Solver. They also demonstrate that checking the results is important, rather than relying only on Solver's solution.

After adding these constraints, run Solver again. This time it arrives at the solution shown in Figure 23-17. Notice that this solution requires 192 people and results in excess staffing on two days of the week. This solution is almost certainly is better than what you would arrive at manually.

```
Microsoft Excel - schedule.xls                                              _ 8 X
 File  Edit  View  Insert  Format  Tools  Data  Window  Help   Type a question for help  _ 8 X
```

	A	B	C	D	E	F	G	H	I	J	K
1											
2		Day	Staff Needed	Staff Scheduled	No. Who Start Work On this Day	Excess Staff					
3		Sun	60	60	8.20	0					
4		Mon	142	142	115.20	0					
5		Tue	145	145	13.20	0					
6		Wed	160	160	33.20	0					
7		Thu	180	180	10.20	0					
8		Fri	190	190	18.20	0					
9		Sat	65	65	-9.80	0					
10											
11			Total staff needed:		188						

E11 = SUM(E3:E9)

Figure 23-15: This solution offered by Solver isn't quite right—you have to add more constraints to correct several problems.

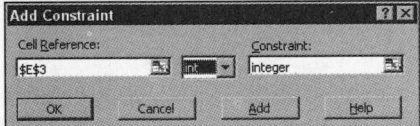

```
Add Constraint                                    ? X
Cell Reference:              Constraint:
$E$3            [int ▼]      integer

   OK       Cancel      Add       Help
```

Figure 23-16: With many problems, you have to limit the solution to integers. You can do this by selecting the integer option in the Constraint box of the Add Constraint dialog box.

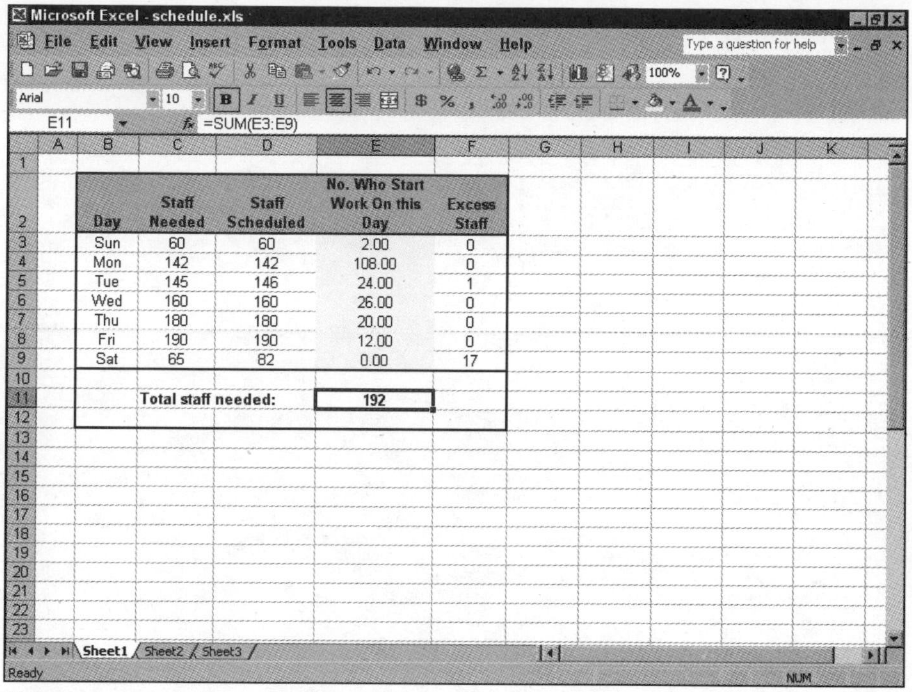

Figure 23-17: Solver produces a better solution to the staffing model problem after you add more constraints.

✦   ✦   ✦

Analyzing Data with Analysis ToolPak

As powerful as a spreadsheet program such as Excel may be, getting at that power can sometimes be a problem. One way that Excel addresses this problem is through the Analysis ToolPak add-in. This add-in enhances Excel by providing easy-to-use tools for many disciplines, including business, education, research, statistics, and engineering.

This chapter shows you both the tools and the functions that you gain access to when you install the Analysis ToolPak. You may discover that some of these features are just what you've been looking for to make your life a whole lot simpler.

Understanding the Analysis ToolPak

The Analysis ToolPak is an add-in that provides analytical capability that normally is not available in Excel. The Analysis ToolPak consists of two parts:

✦ Analytical procedures

✦ Additional worksheet functions

These analysis tools offer many features that may be useful to those in the scientific, engineering, and educational communities — not to mention business users whose needs extend beyond the normal spreadsheet fare.

Note The Analysis ToolPak is not installed by default. To make certain it is available on your system, select Tools ⇨ Add-Ins, place a check in front of the two Analysis ToolPak options and click OK. You may need your Excel (or Office) CD-ROM to complete the installation.

This section provides a quick overview of the types of analyses that you can perform with the Analysis ToolPak. Each of the following tools is discussed in detail in the course of this chapter:

✦ Analysis of variance (three types)

✦ Correlation

✦ Covariance

✦ Descriptive statistics

✦ Exponential smoothing

✦ F-test

✦ Fourier analysis

✦ Histogram

✦ Moving average

✦ Random number generation

✦ Rank and percentile

✦ Regression

✦ Sampling

✦ t-Test (three types)

✦ z-Test

As you can see, the Analysis ToolPak add-in brings a great deal of new functionality to Excel. These procedures have limitations, however, and in some cases you may prefer to create your own formulas to do some calculations.

Besides the procedures just listed, the Analysis ToolPak provides many additional worksheet functions. These functions cover mathematics, engineering, unit conversions, financial analysis, and dates. These functions are listed at the end of the chapter.

Using the analysis tools

The procedures in the Analysis ToolPak add-in are relatively straightforward. To use any of these tools, you select Tools ⇨ Data Analysis, which displays the dialog box shown in Figure 24-1. Scroll through the list until you find the analysis tool that you want to use and then click OK. Excel displays a new dialog box that's specific to the procedure that you select.

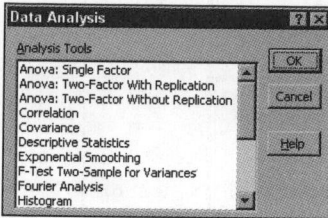

Figure 24-1: The Data Analysis dialog box enables you to select the tool in which you're interested.

Usually, you need to specify one or more input ranges plus an output range (one cell is generally sufficient). Alternatively, you can choose to place the results on a new worksheet or in a new workbook. The procedures vary in the amount of additional information that is required. In many dialog boxes, you may be able to indicate whether your data range includes labels. If so, you can specify the entire range, including the labels, and indicate to Excel that the first column (or row) contains labels. Excel then uses these labels in the tables that it produces. Most tools also provide different output options that you can select, based on your needs.

Caution

In some cases, the procedures produce their results by using formulas. Consequently, you can change your data, and the results update automatically. In other procedures, Excel stores the results as values, so if you change your data, the results don't reflect your changes. Make sure that you understand what Excel is doing.

Using the Analysis ToolPak functions

After you install the Analysis ToolPak, you have access to all the additional functions (which are described fully in the online Help system). You access these functions just like any other functions, and they appear in the Function Wizard dialog box, intermixed with Excel's standard functions.

Note

If you plan to share worksheets that use these functions, make sure that the other user has access to the add-in functions. If the other user doesn't install Analysis ToolPak add-in, formulas that use any of the Analysis ToolPak functions will return #VALUE.

Using the Analysis ToolPak Tools

This section describes each tool and provides an example. Space limitations prevent a discussion of every available option in these procedures. However, if you need to use some of these advanced analysis tools, you probably already know how to use most of the options not discussed here.

Using the Analysis of Variance tool

Analysis of variance is a statistical test that determines whether two or more samples were drawn from the same population. Using tools in the Analysis ToolPak, you can perform three types of analysis of variance:

✦ **Single-factor:** A one-way analysis of variance, with only one sample for each group of data.

✦ **Two-factor with replication:** A two-way analysis of variance, with multiple samples (or replications) for each group of data.

✦ **Two-factor without replication:** A two-way analysis of variance, with a single sample (or replication) for each group of data.

Figure 24-2 shows the dialog box for a single-factor analysis of variance. Alpha represents the statistical confidence level for the test.

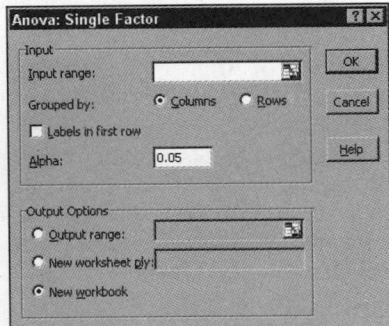

Figure 24-2: Use this dialog box to specify the parameters for a single-factor analysis of variance.

Figure 24-3 shows the results of an analysis of variance. The output for this test consists of the means and variances for each of the four samples, the value of F, the critical value of F, and the significance of F (P-value). Because the probability is greater than the Alpha value, the conclusion is that the samples were drawn from the same population.

Using the Correlation tool

Correlation is a widely used statistic that measures the degree to which two sets of data vary together. For example, if higher values in one data set are typically associated with higher values in the second data set, the two data sets have a positive correlation. The degree of correlation is expressed as a coefficient that ranges from −1.0 (a perfect negative correlation) to +1.0 (a perfect positive correlation). A correlation coefficient of 0 indicates that the two variables are not correlated.

Microsoft Excel - ATP_EXPL.XLS

File   Edit   View   Insert   Format   Tools   Data   Window   Help   Type a question for help

A19

	A	B	C	D	E	F	G	H	I	J	K	L	M
1	Low	Medium	High	Control		Anova: Single Factor							
2	34	41	32	43									
3	36	42	56	42		SUMMARY							
4	42	38	53	41		Groups	Count	Sum	Average	Variance			
5	51	53	28	37		Low	8	538	67.25	6680.214			
6	38	43	43	50		Medium	8	578	72.25	7700.214			
7	32	35	54	26		High	8	636	79.5	9397.714			
8	36	37	52	33		Control	8	544	68	6845.714			
9	269	289	318	272									
10													
11						ANOVA							
12						Source of Variation	SS	df	MS	F	P-value	F crit	
13						Between Groups	757	3	252.3333	0.032959	0.991785	2.946685	
14						Within Groups	214367	28	7655.964				
15													
16						Total	215124	31					
17													

Ready   NUM

▶ ▶ ▶ **Anova** ∕ Correlation ∕ Covariance ∕ Descriptive ∕ Exponential Smoothing ∕ F-Test ∕ Histogram

Figure 24-3: This worksheet shows the results of the analysis of variance.

Figure 24-4 shows the Correlation dialog box. Specify the input range, which can include any number of variables, arranged in rows or columns.

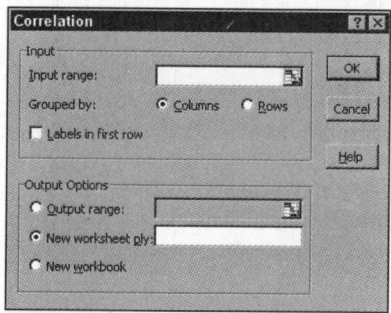

Figure 24-4: Use the Correlation dialog box to specify the ranges for the analysis.

Figure 24-5 shows the results of a correlation analysis for eight variables. The output consists of a correlation matrix that shows the correlation coefficient for each variable paired with every other variable.

	A	B	C	D	E	F	G	H	I	J	K	L	M
	Name	Height	Weight	Sex	Test1	Test2	Test3	Test4	Test5				
2	Bill	74.2	176	1	90	86	134	65	9				
3	Mike	68.5	132	1	90	87	122	31	67				
4	Carol	65.0	157	0	82	75	145	2	6				
5	Scott	73.2	199	1	90	79	109	7	92				
6	Jill	65.8	154	0	100	92	132	79	73				
7	Francis	52.4	101	0	78	89	176	18	50				
8	Helen	69.2	157	0	90	84	103	64	87				
9	Marci	69.0	148	0	65	54	123	100	32				
10	Benedict	77.0	225	1	92	85	132	74	22				
11	Hank	71.0	179	1	70	60	144	36	78				
12	John	73.5	190	1	69	58	156	12	1				
13	Susan	66.9	155	0	80	86	157	68	22				
14	Gloria	67.1	190	0	89	77	98	23	25				
15													
16		Height	Weight	Sex	Test1	Test2	Test3	Test4	Test5				
17	Height	1											
18	Weight	0.84031	1										
19	Sex	0.67077	0.51894	1									
20	Test1	0.09959	0.16347	0.00353	1								
21	Test2	-0.2805	-0.2244	-0.1533	0.83651	1							
22	Test3	-0.4374	-0.3845	-0.0136	-0.445	-0.0203	1						
23	Test4	0.22718	0.00356	-0.2127	0.07838	0.06727	-0.1515	1					
24	Test5	-0.1016	-0.1777	0.04521	0.28937	0.20994	-0.3746	0.01266	1				

Sheets: Anova \ **Correlation** \ Covariance \ Descriptive \ Exponential Smoothing \ F-Test \ Histogram

Figure 24-5: This worksheet shows the results of a correlation analysis.

Note

Notice that the resulting correlation matrix doesn't use formulas to calculate the results. Therefore, if any data changes, the correlation matrix isn't valid. You can use Excel's CORREL function to create a correlation matrix that changes automatically when you change data.

Using the Covariance tool

The Covariance tool produces a matrix that is similar to the one generated by the Correlation tool. *Covariance,* like correlation, measures the degree to which two variables vary together. Specifically, covariance is the average of the product of the deviations of each data point pair from their respective means.

Figure 24-6 shows a covariance matrix.

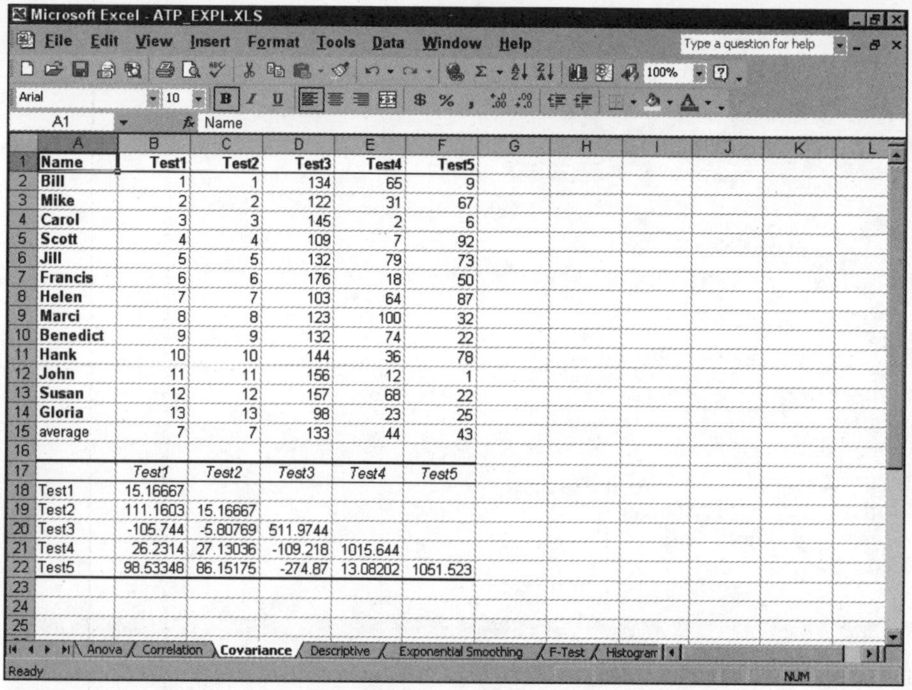

	A	B	C	D	E	F
1	Name	Test1	Test2	Test3	Test4	Test5
2	Bill	1	1	134	65	9
3	Mike	2	2	122	31	67
4	Carol	3	3	145	2	6
5	Scott	4	4	109	7	92
6	Jill	5	5	132	79	73
7	Francis	6	6	176	18	50
8	Helen	7	7	103	64	87
9	Marci	8	8	123	100	32
10	Benedict	9	9	132	74	22
11	Hank	10	10	144	36	78
12	John	11	11	156	12	1
13	Susan	12	12	157	68	22
14	Gloria	13	13	98	23	25
15	average	7	7	133	44	43
16						
17		*Test1*	*Test2*	*Test3*	*Test4*	*Test5*
18	Test1	15.16667				
19	Test2	111.1603	15.16667			
20	Test3	-105.744	-5.80769	511.9744		
21	Test4	26.2314	27.13036	-109.218	1015.644	
22	Test5	98.53348	86.15175	-274.87	13.08202	1051.523

Figure 24-6: This worksheet shows the results of a covariance analysis.

You can use the COVAR function to create a covariance matrix that uses formulas. The values that are generated by the Analysis ToolPak are *not* the same values that you would get if you used the COVAR function.

Using the Descriptive Statistics tool

This tool produces a table that describes your data with some standard statistics. It uses the dialog box shown in Figure 24-7. The Kth Largest option and Kth Smallest option each display the data value that corresponds to a rank that you specify. For example, if you check Kth Largest and specify a value of 2, the output shows the second-largest value in the input range (the standard output already includes the minimum and maximum values).

Sample output for the Descriptive Statistics tool appears in Figure 24-8. This example has three groups. Because the output for this procedure consists of values (not formulas), you should use this procedure only when you're certain that your data isn't going to change; otherwise, you will need to reexecute the procedure. You can generate all these statistics by using formulas.

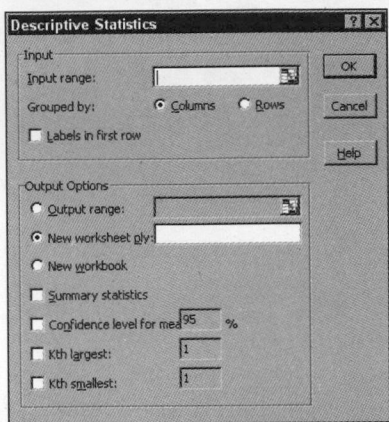

Figure 24-7: Use the Descriptive Statistics dialog box to specify the ranges and output options.

	A	B	C	D	E	F	G	H	I	J	K
1	W. Coast Sample	Midwest Sample	E. Coast Sample		W. Coast Sample		Midwest Sample		E. Coast Sample		
2	35	41	52								
3	32	35	29		Mean	39.25	Mean	46	Mean	41.35	
4	46	36	43		Standard Error	1.84801	Standard Error	2.10763	Standard Error	1.56487	
5	57	45	45		Median	37.5	Median	45.5	Median	41.5	
6	45	44	28		Mode	37	Mode	52	Mode	37	
7	28	62	35		Standard Deviation	8.26454	Standard Deviation	9.42561	Standard Deviation	6.99831	
8	60	61	37		Sample Variance	68.3026	Sample Variance	88.8421	Sample Variance	48.9763	
9	37	62	32		Kurtosis	1.47266	Kurtosis	-0.47699	Kurtosis	-0.28025	
10	34	36	37		Skewness	1.18011	Skewness	0.14121	Skewness	-0.24858	
11	33	52	41		Range	32	Range	34	Range	26	
12	37	46	54		Minimum	28	Minimum	28	Minimum	28	
13	32	52	44		Maximum	60	Maximum	62	Maximum	54	
14	38	38	42		Sum	785	Sum	920	Sum	827	
15	41	28	48		Count	20	Count	20	Count	20	
16	38	50	46		Confidence Level(95.0%)	3.86793	Confidence Level(95.0%)	4.41132	Confidence Level(95.0%)	3.27531	
17	42	52	47								
18	29	48	39								
19	40	38	40								
20	37	44	41								
21	44	50	47								
22											
23											

Figure 24-8: This worksheet shows the output from the Descriptive Statistics tool.

Using the Exponential Smoothing tool

Exponential smoothing is a technique for predicting data that is based on the previous data point and the previously predicted data point. You can specify the *damping factor* (also known as a *smoothing constant*), which can range from 0 to 1. This determines the relative weighting of the previous data point and the previously predicted data point. You also can request standard errors and a chart.

The exponential smoothing procedure generates formulas that use the damping factor that you specify. Therefore, if the data changes, Excel updates the formulas. Figure 24-9 shows sample output from the Exponential Smoothing tool.

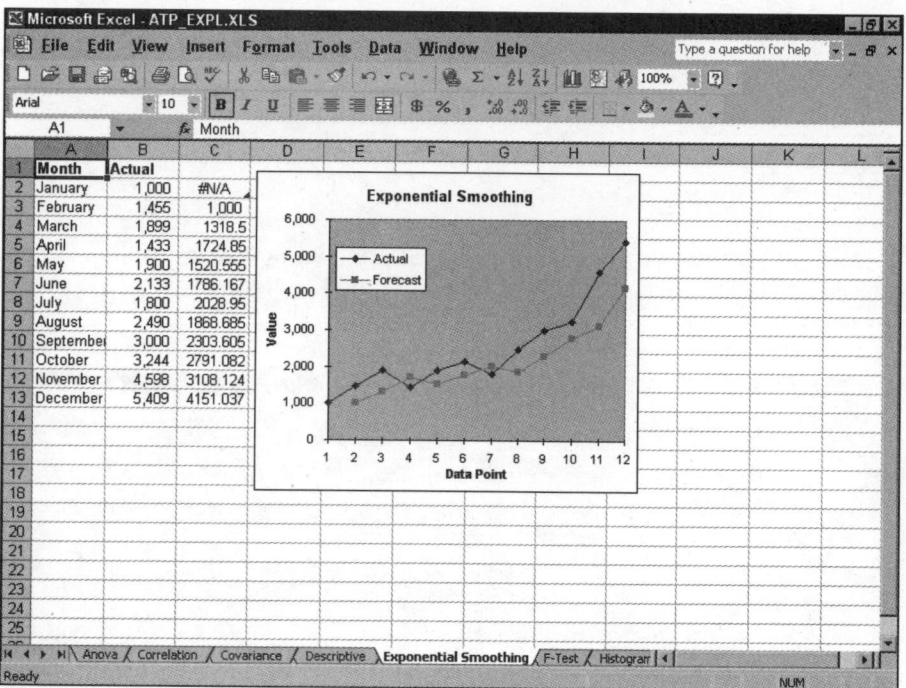

Figure 24-9: This worksheet shows the output from the Exponential Smoothing tool.

Using the F-test (two-sample test for variance) tool

The *F-test* is a commonly used statistical test that enables you to compare two population variances. Figure 24-10 shows the dialog box for this tool.

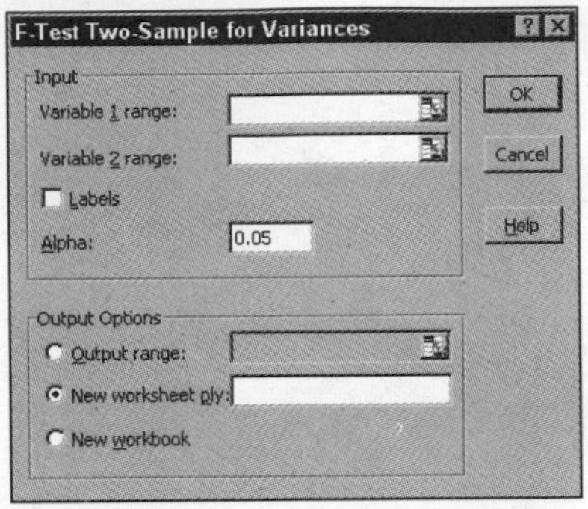

Figure 24-10: Specifying the ranges for the F-test tool

The output for this test consists of the means and variances for each of the two samples, the value of F, the critical value of F, and the significance of F. Sample output appears in Figure 24-11.

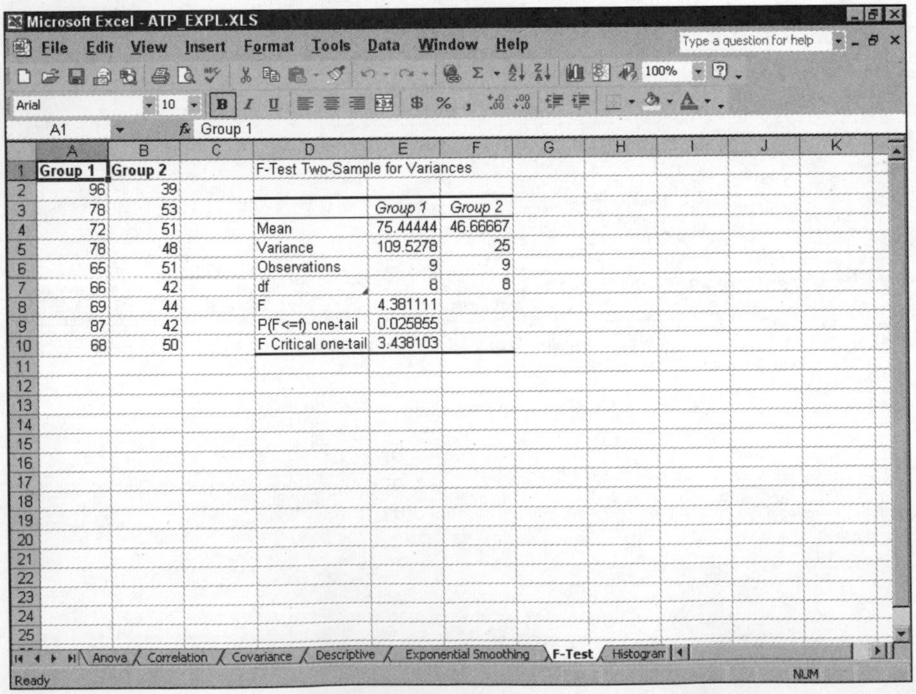

Figure 24-11: This worksheet shows the output from the F-test tool.

Using the Fourier Analysis tool

This tool performs a "fast Fourier" transformation of a range of data. Using the Fourier Analysis tool, you can transform a range limited to the following sizes: 1, 2, 4, 8, 16, 32, 64, 128, 256, 512, or 1,024 data points. This procedure accepts and generates complex numbers, which are represented as labels (not values).

Using the histogram tool

This procedure is useful for producing data distributions and histogram charts. It accepts an input range and a bin range. A *bin* range is a range of values that specifies the limits for each column of the histogram. If you omit the bin range, Excel creates ten equal-interval bins for you. The size of each bin is determined by a formula in the following form:

```
=(MAX(input_range)-MIN(input_range))/10
```

The Histogram dialog box appears in Figure 24-12. As an option, you can specify that the resulting histogram be sorted by frequency of occurrence in each bin.

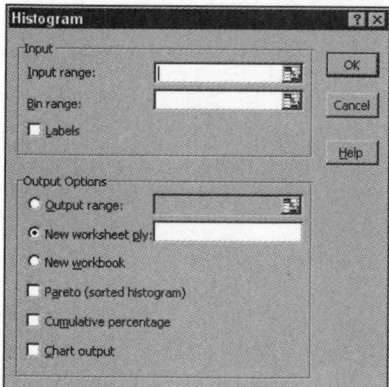

Figure 24-12: Use the Histogram tool to generate distributions and graphical output.

If you specify the Pareto (sorted histogram) option, the bin range must contain values and can't contain formulas. If formulas appear in the bin range, Excel doesn't sort properly, and your worksheet displays error values.

Figure 24-13 shows a chart generated from this procedure. The Histogram tool doesn't use formulas, so if you change any of the input data, you need to repeat the histogram procedure to update the results.

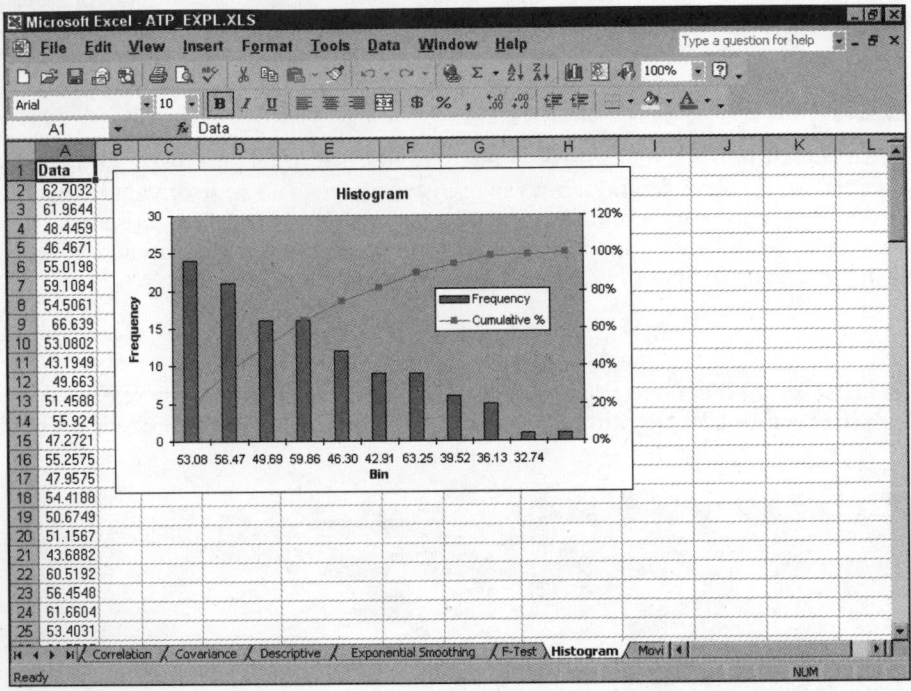

Figure 24-13: This worksheet shows the output from the Histogram tool.

Using the Moving Average tool

The Moving Average tool helps you to smooth out a data series that has lots of variability. This is best done in conjunction with a chart. Excel does the smoothing by computing a moving average of a specified number of values. In many cases, a moving average enables you to spot trends that otherwise would be obscured by noise in the data.

Figure 24-14 shows the Moving Average dialog box. You can, of course, specify the number of values that you want Excel to use for each average. If you place a check in the Standard Errors check box, Excel calculates standard errors and places formulas for these calculations next to the moving average formulas. The standard error values indicate the degree of variability between the actual values and the calculated moving averages. When you close this dialog box, Excel creates formulas that reference the input range that you specify.

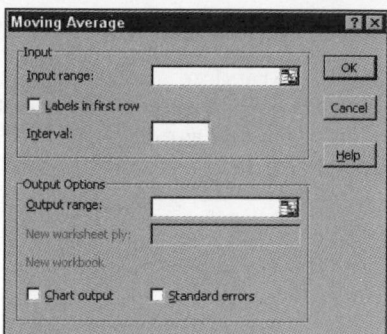

Figure 24-14: Use the Moving Average dialog box to specify the parameters for the Moving Average tool.

Figure 24-15 shows the results of using this tool. The first few cells in the output are #N/A because not enough data points exist to calculate the average for these initial values.

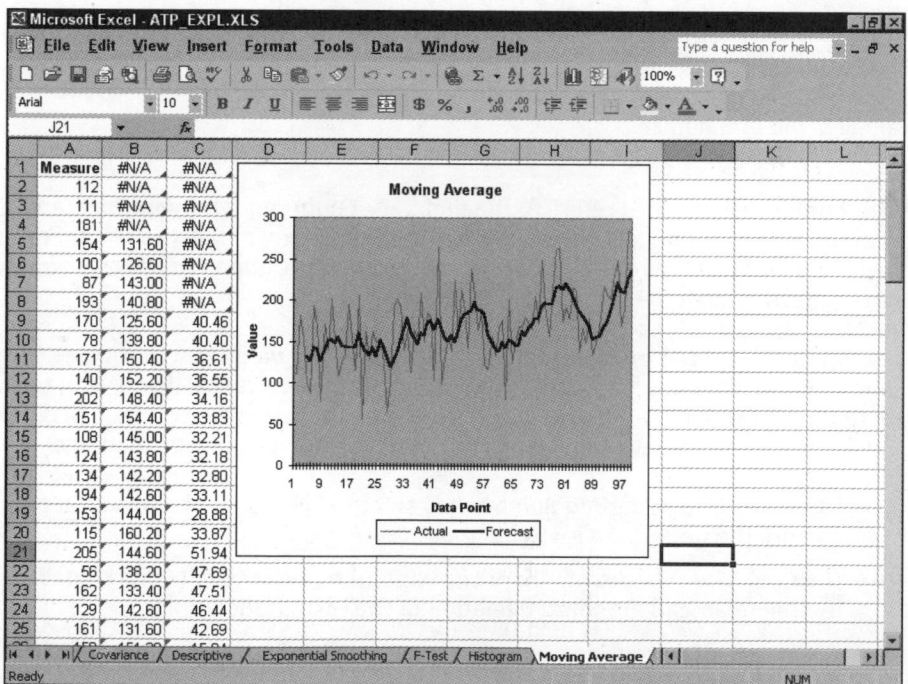

Figure 24-15: This worksheet shows the output from the Moving Average tool.

Using the Random Number Generation tool

Although Excel contains a built-in function to calculate random numbers, the Random Number Generation tool is much more flexible because you can specify what type of distribution you want the random numbers to have. Figure 24-16 shows the Random Number Generation dialog box. The dialog box varies, depending on the type of distribution that you select.

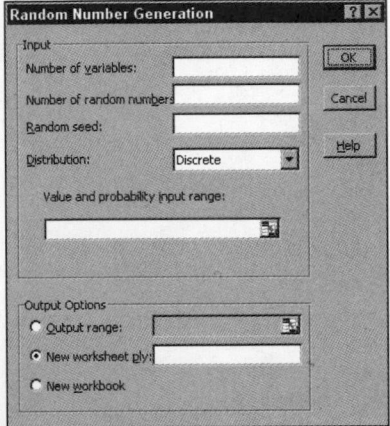

Figure 24-16: This dialog box enables you to generate a wide variety of random numbers.

The Number of variables refers to the number of columns that you want, and the Number of random numbers refers to the number of rows that you want. For example, if you want 200 random numbers arranged in 10 columns of 20 rows, you specify 10 and 20, respectively, in these text boxes.

The Random seed box enables you to specify a starting value that Excel uses in its random number-generating algorithm. Usually, you leave this blank. If you want to generate the same random number sequence, however, you can specify a seed between 1 and 32,767 (integer values only). You can create these types of distributions:

✦ **Uniform:** Every random number has an equal chance of being selected. You specify the upper and lower limits.

✦ **Normal:** The random numbers correspond to a normal distribution. You specify the mean and standard deviation of the distribution.

✦ **Bernoulli:** The random numbers are either 0 or 1, determined by the probability of success that you specify.

✦ **Binomial:** This returns random numbers based on a Bernoulli distribution over a specific number of trials, given a probability of success that you specify.

✦ **Poisson:** This option generates values in a Poisson distribution. This is characterized by discrete events that occur in an interval, where the probability of a single occurrence is proportional to the size of the interval. The lambda parameter is the expected number of occurrences in an interval. In a Poisson distribution, lambda is equal to the mean, which also is equal to the variance.

✦ **Patterned:** This option doesn't generate random numbers. Rather, it repeats a series of numbers in steps that you specify.

✦ **Discrete:** This option enables you to specify the probability that specific values are chosen. It requires a two-column input range; the first column holds the values, and the second column holds the probability of each value being chosen. The sum of the probabilities in the second column must equal 100 percent.

Using the Rank and Percentile tool

This tool creates a table that shows the ordinal and percentile ranking for each value in a range. Figure 24-17 shows the results of this procedure. You can also generate ranks and percentiles by using formulas.

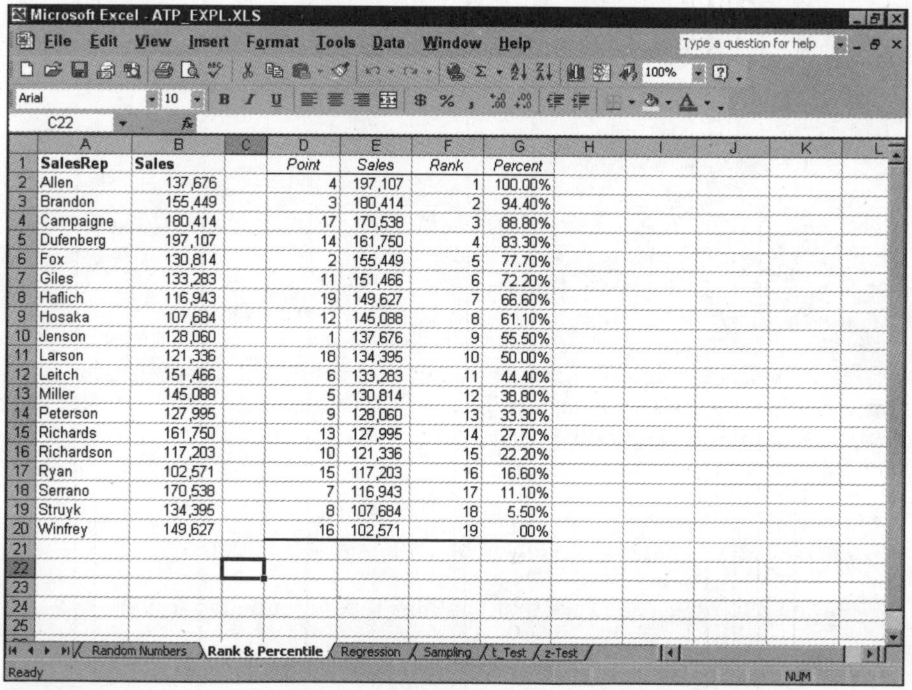

	A	B	C	D	E	F	G
1	**SalesRep**	**Sales**		*Point*	*Sales*	*Rank*	*Percent*
2	Allen	137,676		4	197,107	1	100.00%
3	Brandon	155,449		3	180,414	2	94.40%
4	Campaigne	180,414		17	170,538	3	88.80%
5	Dufenberg	197,107		14	161,750	4	83.30%
6	Fox	130,814		2	155,449	5	77.70%
7	Giles	133,283		11	151,466	6	72.20%
8	Haflich	116,943		19	149,627	7	66.60%
9	Hosaka	107,684		12	145,088	8	61.10%
10	Jenson	128,060		1	137,676	9	55.50%
11	Larson	121,336		18	134,395	10	50.00%
12	Leitch	151,466		6	133,283	11	44.40%
13	Miller	145,088		5	130,814	12	38.80%
14	Peterson	127,995		9	128,060	13	33.30%
15	Richards	161,750		13	127,995	14	27.70%
16	Richardson	117,203		10	121,336	15	22.20%
17	Ryan	102,571		15	117,203	16	16.60%
18	Serrano	170,538		7	116,943	17	11.10%
19	Struyk	134,395		8	107,684	18	5.50%
20	Winfrey	149,627		16	102,571	19	.00%

Figure 24-17: This worksheet shows the output from the rank and percentile procedure.

Using the Regression tool

The Regression tool calculates a regression analysis from worksheet data. Use regression to analyze trends, forecast the future, build predictive models, and, often, to make sense of a series of seemingly unrelated numbers.

Regression analysis enables you to determine the extent to which one range of data (the dependent variable) varies as a function of the values of one or more other ranges of data (the independent variables). This relationship is expressed mathematically, using values that Excel calculates. You can use these calculations to create a mathematical model of the data and predict the dependent variable by using different values of one or more independent variables. This tool can perform simple and multiple linear regressions and calculate and standardize residuals automatically.

Figure 24-18 shows the Regression dialog box.

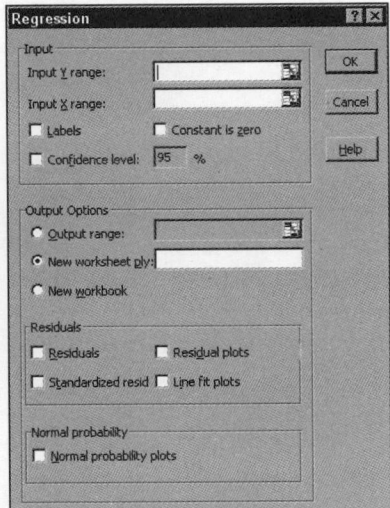

Figure 24-18: Use the Regression dialog box to specify the options for the Regression tool.

As you can see, the Regression dialog box offers many options:

✦ **Input Y Range:** The range that contains the dependent variable.

✦ **Input X Range:** One or more ranges that contain independent variables.

✦ **Confidence Level:** The confidence level for the regression.

✦ **Constant is Zero:** If checked, this forces the regression to have a constant of zero (which means that the regression line passes through the origin; when the X values are 0, the predicted Y value is 0).

- ✦ **Residuals:** These options specify whether to include residuals in the output. Residuals are the differences between observed and predicted values.
- ✦ **Normal Probability:** This generates a chart for normal probability plots.

The results of a regression analysis appear in Figure 24-19. If you understand regression analysis, the output from this procedure is familiar.

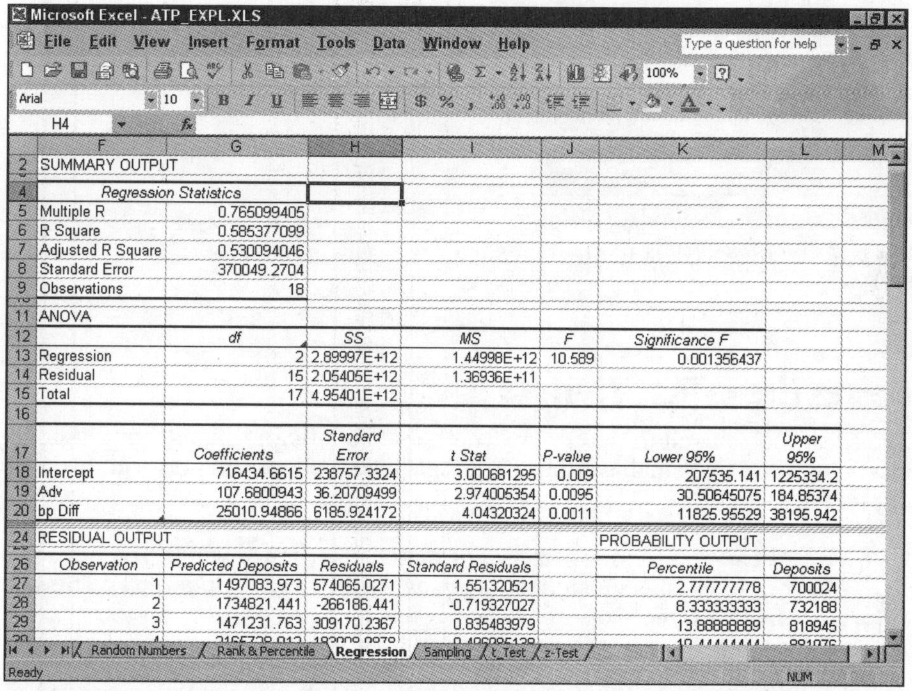

	F	G	H	I	J	K	L
2	SUMMARY OUTPUT						
4	*Regression Statistics*						
5	Multiple R	0.765099405					
6	R Square	0.585377099					
7	Adjusted R Square	0.530094046					
8	Standard Error	370049.2704					
9	Observations	18					
11	ANOVA						
12		*df*	*SS*	*MS*	*F*	*Significance F*	
13	Regression	2	2.89997E+12	1.44998E+12	10.589	0.001356437	
14	Residual	15	2.05405E+12	1.36936E+11			
15	Total	17	4.95401E+12				
16							
17		*Coefficients*	*Standard Error*	*t Stat*	*P-value*	*Lower 95%*	*Upper 95%*
18	Intercept	716434.6615	238757.3324	3.000681295	0.009	207535.141	1225334.2
19	Adv	107.6800943	36.20709499	2.974005354	0.0095	30.50645075	184.85374
20	bp Diff	25010.94866	6185.924172	4.04320324	0.0011	11825.95529	38195.942
24	RESIDUAL OUTPUT					PROBABILITY OUTPUT	
26	*Observation*	*Predicted Deposits*	*Residuals*	*Standard Residuals*		*Percentile*	*Deposits*
27	1	1497083.973	574065.0271	1.551320521		2.777777778	700024
28	2	1734821.441	-266186.441	-0.719327027		8.333333333	732188
29	3	1471231.763	309170.2367	0.835483979		13.88888889	818945

Figure 24-19: This worksheet shows the sample output from the Regression tool.

Using the Sampling tool

The Sampling tool generates a random sample from a range of input values. The Sampling tool can help you to work with a large database by creating a subset of it. The Sampling dialog box appears in Figure 24-20. This procedure has two options: periodic and random. If you choose a periodic sample, Excel selects every *n*th value from the input range, where *n* equals the period that you specify. With a random sample, you simply specify the size of the sample you want Excel to select, and every value has an equal probability of being chosen.

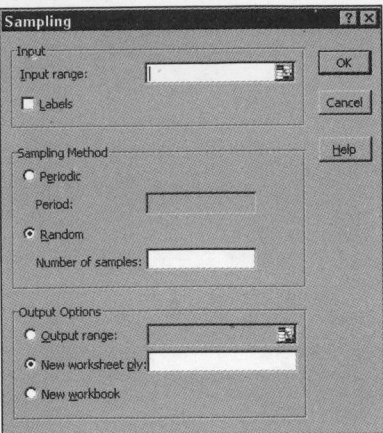

Figure 24-20: The Sampling dialog box is useful for selecting random samples.

Using the t-Test tool

The *t-Test* tool is used to determine whether a statistically significant difference exists between two small samples. The Analysis ToolPak can perform three types of t-tests:

✦ **Paired two-sample for means:** For paired samples in which you have two observations on each subject (such as a pretest and a posttest). The samples must be the same size.

✦ **Two-sample assuming equal variances:** For independent, rather than paired, samples. Excel assumes equal variances for the two samples.

✦ **Two-sample assuming unequal variances:** For independent, rather than paired, samples. Excel assumes unequal variances for the two samples.

Figure 24-21 shows the dialog box for the Paired Two Sample for Means t-test. You specify the significance level (alpha) and the hypothesized difference between the two means (that is, the *null hypothesis*).

Figure 24-22 shows sample output for the paired two-sample for means t-Test. Excel calculates *t* for both a one-tailed and two-tailed test.

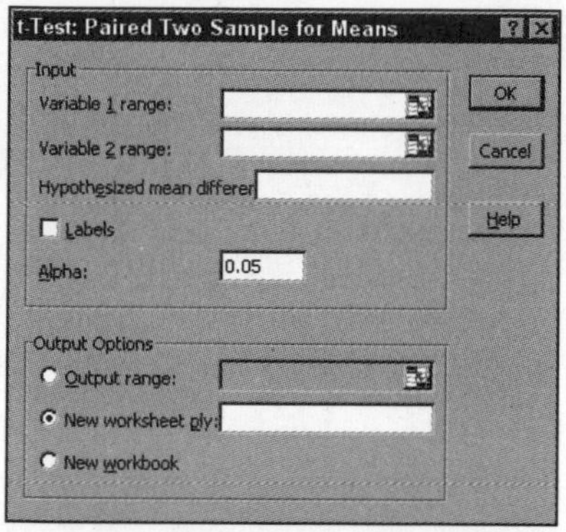

Figure 24-21: Use the t-Test Paired Two-Sample for Means dialog box to specify the ranges for the t-Test tool.

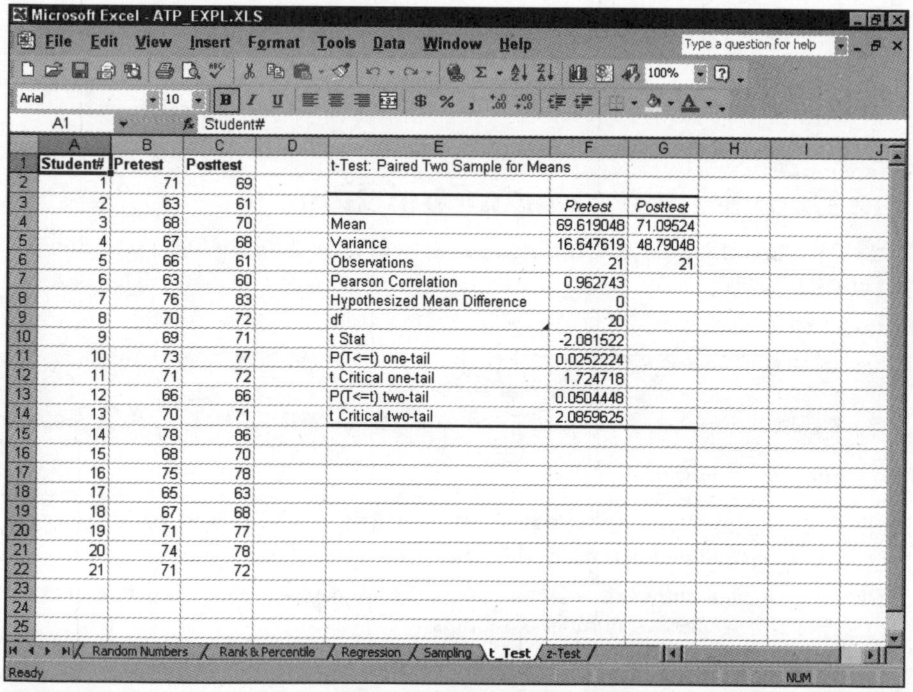

Figure 24-22: This worksheet shows the Results of a paired two-sample for means t-test.

Using the z-Test (two-sample test for means) tool

The t-test is used for small samples; the z-test is used for larger samples or populations. You must know the variances for both input ranges.

Using the Analysis ToolPak Worksheet Functions

This section lists the worksheet functions that are available in the Analysis ToolPak. For specific information about the arguments required, click the Help button in the Paste Function dialog box.

Remember, the Analysis ToolPak add-in must be installed to use these functions in your worksheet. If you use any of these functions in a workbook that you distribute to a colleague, make clear to your colleague that the workbook requires the Analysis ToolPak.

These functions appear in the Paste Function dialog box in the following categories:

✦ Date & Time

✦ Engineering

✦ Financial

✦ Information

✦ Math & Trig

The Date & Time category functions

Table 24-1 lists the Analysis ToolPak worksheet functions that you'll find in the Date & Time category.

Table 24-1 Date & Time Category Functions	
Function	**Purpose**
EDATE	Returns the serial number of the date that is the indicated number of months before or after the start date
EOMONTH	Returns the serial number of the last day of the month before or after a specified number of months
NETWORKDAYS	Returns the number of whole workdays between two dates
WEEKNUM	Returns the week number in the year
WORKDAY	Returns the serial number of the date before or after a specified number of workdays
YEARFRAC	Returns the year fraction representing the number of whole days between start_date and end_date

The Engineering category functions

Table 24-2 lists the Analysis ToolPak worksheet functions that you'll find in the Engineering category. Some of these functions are quite useful for nonengineers as well. For example, the CONVERT function converts a wide variety of measurement units.

Table 24-2	
Engineering Category Functions	
Function	*Purpose*
BESSELI	Returns the modified Bessel function In(x)
BESSELJ	Returns the Bessel function Jn(x)
BESSELK	Returns the modified Bessel function Kn(x)
BESSELY	Returns the Bessel function Yn(x)
BIN2DEC	Converts a binary number to decimal
BIN2HEX	Converts a binary number to hexadecimal
BIN2OCT	Converts a binary number to octal
COMPLEX	Converts real and imaginary coefficients into a complex number
CONVERT	Converts a number from one measurement system to another
DEC2BIN	Converts a decimal number to binary
DEC2HEX	Converts a decimal number to hexadecimal
DEC2OCT	Converts a decimal number to octal
DELTA	Tests whether two numbers are equal
ERF	Returns the error function
ERFC	Returns the complementary error function
FACTDOUBLE	Returns the double factorial of a number
GESTEP	Tests whether a number is greater than a threshold value
HEX2BIN	Converts a hexadecimal number to binary
HEX2DEC	Converts a hexadecimal number to decimal
HEX2OCT	Converts a hexadecimal number to octal
IMABS	Returns the absolute value (modulus) of a complex number
IMAGINARY	Returns the imaginary coefficient of a complex number
IMARGUMENT	Returns the argument q, an angle expressed in radians
IMCONJUGATE	Returns the complex conjugate of a complex number

Continued

Table 24-2 (continued)

Function	Purpose
IMCOS	Returns the cosine of a complex number
IMDIV	Returns the quotient of two complex numbers
IMEXP	Returns the exponential of a complex number
IMLN	Returns the natural logarithm of a complex number
IMLOG10	Returns the base-10 logarithm of a complex number
IMLOG2	Returns the base-2 logarithm of a complex number
IMPOWER	Returns a complex number raised to an integer power
IMPRODUCT	Returns the product of two complex numbers
IMREAL	Returns the real coefficient of a complex number
IMSIN	Returns the sine of a complex number
IMSQRT	Returns the square root of a complex number
IMSUB	Returns the difference of two complex numbers
IMSUM	Returns the sum of complex numbers
OCT2BIN	Converts an octal number to binary
OCT2DEC	Converts an octal number to decimal
OCT2HEX	Converts an octal number to hexadecimal

The Financial category functions

Table 24-3 lists the Analysis ToolPak worksheet functions that you'll find in the Financial category.

Table 24-3
Financial Category Functions

Function	Purpose
ACCRINT	Returns the accrued interest for a security that pays periodic interest
ACCRINTM	Returns the accrued interest for a security that pays interest at maturity
AMORDEGRC	Returns the prorated linear depreciation of an asset for each accounting period; similar to the AMORLINC function, except that this function uses a depreciation coefficient that depends on the life of the assets
AMORLINC	Returns the prorated linear depreciation of an asset for each accounting period

Function	Purpose
COUPDAYBS	Returns the number of days from the beginning of the coupon period to the settlement date
COUPDAYS	Returns the number of days in the coupon period that contain the settlement date
COUPDAYSNC	Returns the number of days from the settlement date to the next coupon date
COUPNCD	Returns the next coupon date after the settlement date
COUPNUM	Returns the number of coupons payable between the settlement date and maturity date
COUPPCD	Returns the previous coupon date before the settlement date
CUMIPMT	Returns the cumulative interest paid between two periods
CUMPRINC	Returns the cumulative principal paid on a loan between two periods
DISC	Returns the discount rate for a security
DOLLARDE	Converts a dollar price, expressed as a fraction, into a dollar price, expressed as a decimal number
DOLLARFR	Converts a dollar price, expressed as a decimal number, into a dollar price, expressed as a fraction
DURATION	Returns the annual duration of a security with periodic interest payments
EFFECT	Returns the effective annual interest rate
FVSCHEDULE	Returns the future value of an initial principal after applying a series of compound interest rates
INTRATE	Returns the interest rate for a fully invested security
MDURATION	Returns the Macauley-modified duration for a security with an assumed par value of $100
NOMINAL	Returns the annual nominal interest rate
ODDFPRICE	Returns the price per $100 face value of a security with an odd first period
ODDFYIELD	Returns the yield of a security with an odd first period
ODDLPRICE	Returns the price per $100 face value of a security with an odd last period
ODDLYIELD	Returns the yield of a security with an odd last period
PRICE	Returns the price per $100 face value of a security that pays periodic interest
PRICEDISC	Returns the price per $100 face value of a discounted security

Continued

Table 24-3 *(continued)*	
Function	**Purpose**
PRICEMAT	Returns the price per $100 face value of a security that pays interest at maturity
RECEIVED	Returns the amount received at maturity for a fully invested security
TBILLEQ	Returns the bond-equivalent yield for a Treasury bill
TBILLPRICE	Returns the price per $100 face value for a Treasury bill
TBILLYIELD	Returns the yield for a Treasury bill
XIRR	Returns the internal rate of return for a schedule of cash flows
XNPV	Returns the net present value for a schedule of cash flows
YIELD	Returns the yield on a security that pays periodic interest
YIELDDISC	Returns the annual yield for a discounted security (for example, a Treasury bill)
YIELDMAT	Returns the annual yield of a security that pays interest at maturity

The Information category functions

Table 24-4 lists the two Analysis ToolPak worksheet functions that you'll find in the Information category.

Table 24-4 **Information Category Functions**	
Function	**Purpose**
ISEVEN	Returns TRUE if the number is even
ISODD	Returns TRUE if the number is odd

The Math & Trig category functions

Table 24-5 lists the Analysis ToolPak worksheet functions that you'll find in the Math & Trig category.

Table 24-5
Math & Trig Category Functions

Function	*Purpose*
GCD	Returns the greatest common divisor
LCM	Returns the least common multiple
MROUND	Returns a number rounded to the desired multiple
MULTINOMIAL	Returns the multinomial of a set of numbers
QUOTIENT	Returns the integer portion of a division
RANDBETWEEN	Returns a random number between the numbers that you specify
SERIESSUM	Returns the sum of a power series based on the formula
SQRTPI	Returns the square root of pi

✦ ✦ ✦

Using Advanced Excel Features

A number of Excel's features can probably be fairly called advanced features if for no better reason than the ways in which they expand the definitions of what a spreadsheet program can do. In this part we show you features you may not have used in the past, but which we're sure you'll find very useful.

Creating and Using Worksheet Outlines

◆ ◆ ◆ ◆

In This Chapter

Understanding
worksheet outlining

Creating your first
outline

Using outlines
effectively

◆ ◆ ◆ ◆

Excel's worksheet outlining feature is quite similar to the outlining features you may already be familiar with from word processing. In both cases, you can easily control the level of detail that is displayed so that you can view the big picture, the complete set of details, or something in between. In many ways, outlining can be even more useful in Excel than in your word processor simply because it allows you such flexibility in reporting the contents of your worksheets. This chapter shows you how to use Excel's handy outlining features.

Understanding Worksheet Outlining

An *outline* is a document summary tool that uses different heading levels to organize the document. A book's table of contents is a familiar example of an outline. Within the table of contents you find chapters, and each chapter contains several levels of headings. To see the overall picture, you might look at just the chapter titles. To locate specific details about the subject of a chapter, you would look at the headings within the chapter. A worksheet outline functions pretty much the same way.

You can use outlines to create summary reports in which you don't want to show all the details. You'll find that some worksheets are more suitable for outlines than others. If your worksheet uses hierarchical data with subtotals, it's probably a good candidate for an outline.

Examining an outline example

The best way to understand how worksheet outlining works is to look at an example. Figure 25-1 shows a simple budget model without an outline. Subtotals are used to calculate subtotals by region and by quarter.

Figure 25-1 screenshot of Microsoft Excel - outline.xls:

	A	B	C	D	E	F	G	H	I	J	K
1	State	Jan	Feb	Mar	Q1 Total	Apr	May	Jun	Q2 Total	Jul	Aug
2	California	1118	1960	1252	4330	1271	1557	1679	4507	1218	174
3	Washington	1247	1238	1028	3513	1345	1784	1574	4703	1551	163
4	Oregon	1460	1954	1726	5140	1461	1764	1144	4369	1293	104
5	Nevada	1345	1375	1075	3795	1736	1555	1372	4663	1778	177
6	West Total	5170	6527	5081	16778	5813	6660	5769	18242	5840	620
7	New York	1429	1316	1993	4738	1832	1740	1191	4763	1106	166
8	New Jersey	1735	1406	1224	4365	1706	1320	1290	4316	1585	122
9	Massachusetts	1099	1233	1110	3442	1637	1512	1006	4155	1459	178
10	Florida	1705	1792	1225	4722	1946	1327	1357	4630	1872	198
11	East Total	5968	5747	5552	17267	7121	5899	4844	17864	6022	665
12	Kentucky	1109	1078	1155	3342	1993	1082	1551	4626	1099	184
13	Oklahoma	1309	1045	1641	3995	1924	1499	1941	5364	1529	155
14	Missouri	1511	1744	1414	4669	1243	1493	1820	4556	1228	177
15	Illinois	1539	1493	1211	4243	1165	1013	1445	3623	1833	123
16	Kansas	1973	1560	1243	4776	1495	1125	1387	4007	1357	164
17	Central Total	7441	6920	6664	17683	7820	6212	8144	17550	7046	804
18	Grand Total	18579	19194	17297	51728	20754	18771	18757	53656	18908	209

Figure 25-1: This worksheet shows a typical budget model with subtotals.

Tip   When you use the Data ➪ Subtotals command, Excel automatically creates an outline.

Figure 25-2 shows the same worksheet after the outline was created. Notice that Excel adds a new border to the left of the screen. This border contains controls that enable you to determine which level to view. This particular outline has three levels: States, Regions (each region consists of states), and Grand Total (the sum of each region's subtotal). In Figure 25-2, the outline is fully expanded so that you can see all the data.

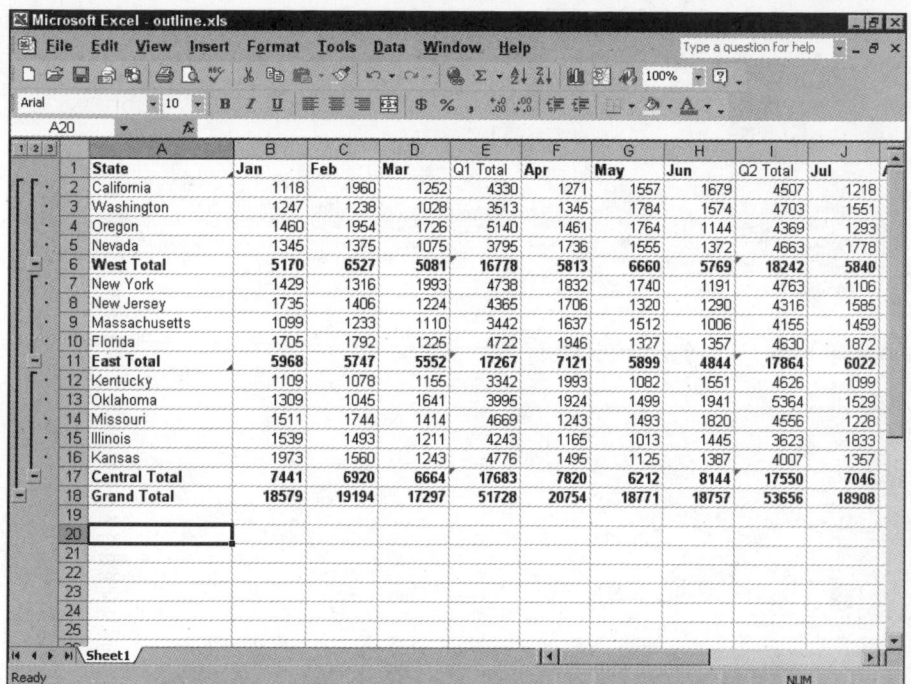

Figure 25-2: This worksheet now includes an outline that enables you to summarize the rows.

Figure 25-3 depicts the outline displayed at the second level. Now, the outline shows only the totals for the regions (the detail rows are hidden). You can partially expand the outline to show the detail for a particular region. Collapsing the outline to level 1 shows only the headers and the Grand Total row.

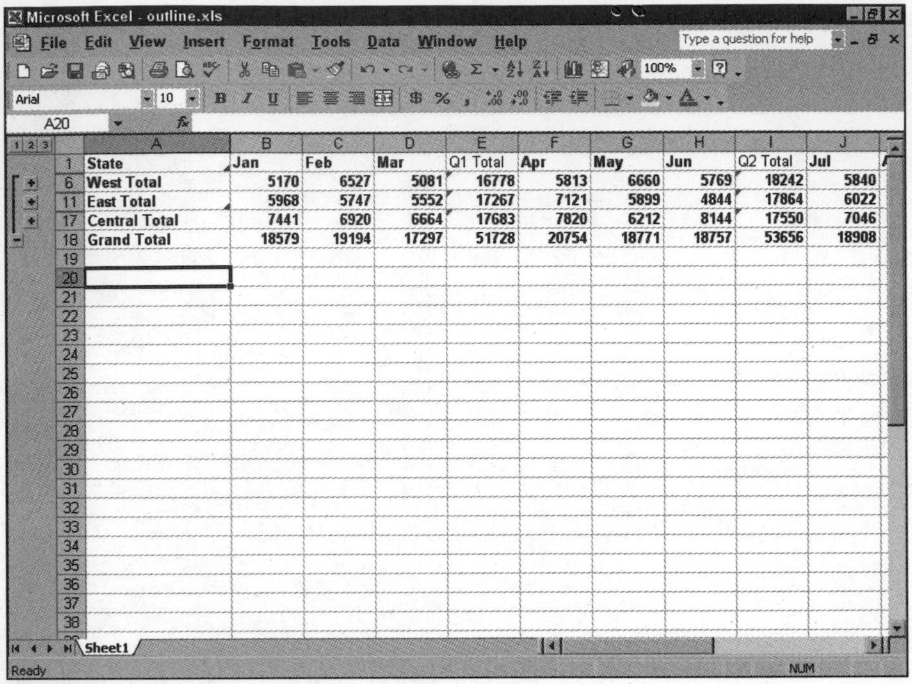

Figure 25-3: The outline has been collapsed to the second-level headings.

Excel can create outlines in both directions. In the preceding examples, the outline was a row outline. Figure 25-4 shows the same model after a column outline was added. Now, Excel displays another border at the top.

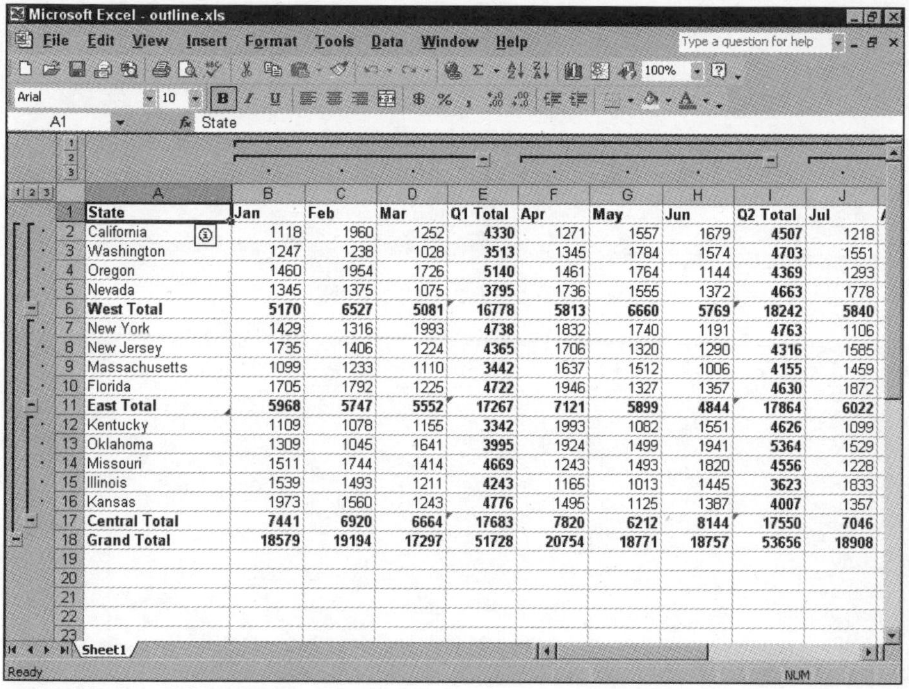

Figure 25-4: The worksheet has been fully outlined with both row and column outlines.

If you create both a row and a column outline in a worksheet, you can work with each outline independently of the other. For example, you can show the row outline at the second level and the column outline at the first level. Figure 25-5 shows the model with both outlines collapsed at the second level. The result is a nice summary table that gives regional totals by quarter.

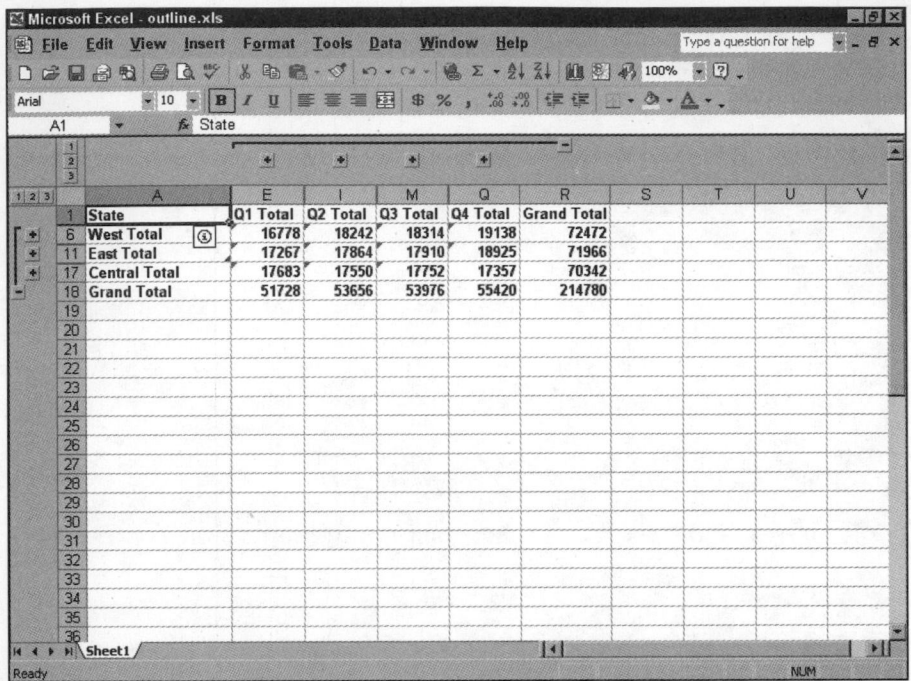

Figure 25-5: This worksheet shows how you can use the outline to display a summary report by collapsing both the row and column outlines to the second level.

Some important points about outlines

The following are points to keep in mind about worksheet outlines:

✦ A single worksheet can have only one outline (row, column, or both). If you need to create more than one outline, move the data to a new worksheet.

✦ You can either create an outline manually or have Excel do it for you automatically. If you choose the latter option, you may need to do some preparation to get the worksheet in the proper format.

✦ You can create an outline for either all data on a worksheet or just a selected data range.

✦ You can remove an outline with a single command.

 **Tip**   You can hide the outline symbols but retain the outline by pressing Ctrl+8.

✦ You can have up to eight nested levels in an outline.

Worksheet outlines can be quite useful. But if your main objective is to summarize a large amount of data, you might be better off using a pivot table. A pivot table is much more flexible and doesn't require that you create the subtotal formulas; it does the summarizing for you automatically.

Cross-Reference   Pivot tables are discussed in Chapter 21.

Creating Your First Outline

In this section, you learn the two ways to create an outline: automatically and manually. But before getting into the details of those two methods, the all-important first step is examined: getting your data ready for outlining.

Preparing your data for outlining

Before you create an outline, you need to ensure that:

✦ The data is appropriate for an outline

✦ The formulas are set up properly

Determining appropriate data

What type of data is appropriate for an outline? Generally, the data should be arranged in a hierarchy, such as a budget that consists of an arrangement similar to the following:

Company

　　　　Division

　　　　　　　　Department

　　　　　　　　　　　Budget Category

　　　　　　　　　　　　　Budget Item

In this case, each budget item (for example, airfare and hotel expenses) is part of a budget category (for example, travel expenses). Each department has its own budget, and the departments are rolled up into divisions. The divisions make up the company. This type of arrangement is well suited for a row outline—although most of your outlines probably won't have this many levels.

Tip   After the data is created, you can view (or print) the information at any level of detail that you want. When you need to create reports for different levels of management, try using an outline. Upper management may want to see only the Division totals. Division managers may want to see totals by department, and each department manager needs to see the full details for his or her department.

As demonstrated at the beginning of the chapter, you can include time-based information that is rolled up into larger units (such as months and quarters) in a column outline. Column outlines work just like row outlines, however, and the levels need not be time-based.

Setting up the formulas

Before you create an outline, you need to make sure that all the summary formulas are entered correctly and consistently. *Consistently* means that the formulas are in the same relative location. Generally, formulas that compute summary formulas (such as subtotals) are entered below the data to which they refer. In some cases, however, the summary formulas are entered above the referenced cells. Excel can handle either method, but you must be consistent throughout the range that you outline. If the summary formulas aren't consistent, automatic outlining won't produce the results that you want.

If your summary formulas aren't consistent (that is, some are above and some are below the data), you still can create an outline, but you must do it manually.

Creating an outline automatically

It's usually best to begin by having Excel create an outline rather than try to do so manually. Excel can create an outline for you automatically in a few seconds — far less time than you'll need to do it yourself!

If you don't like the results of Excel's automatic outlining, just select Data ➪ Group and Outline ➪ Clear Outline to remove the outline.

To have Excel create an outline, move the cell pointer anywhere within the range of data that you're outlining. Then, choose Data ➪ Group and Outline ➪ Auto Outline. Excel analyzes the formulas in the range and creates the outline. Depending on the formulas that you have, Excel creates a row outline, a column outline, or both.

If the worksheet already has an outline, Excel asks whether you want to modify the existing outline. Click Yes to force Excel to remove the old outline and create a new one.

Excel automatically creates an outline when you use the Data ➪ Subtotals command, which inserts subtotal formulas automatically if you set up your data as a list.

The Data ➪ Subtotals command is discussed in Chapter 19.

Creating an outline manually

When Excel creates a row outline, the summary rows all must be above the data or below the data (they can't be mixed). Similarly, for a column outline, the summary columns all must be to the right of the data or to the left of the data. If your worksheet doesn't meet these requirements, you have two choices:

✦ Rearrange the worksheet so that it does meet the requirements

✦ Create the outline manually

Usually, letting Excel create the outline is the best approach. It's much faster and less error-prone.

You also need to create an outline manually if the range doesn't contain any formulas. You may have imported a file and want to use an outline to display it better. Because Excel uses the formulas to determine how to create the outline, it is not able to make an outline without formulas.

Creating an outline manually consists of creating groups of rows (for row outlines) or groups of columns (for column outlines). To create a group of rows, click the row numbers for all the rows that you want to include in the group — but do not select the row that has the summary formulas. Then choose Data ⇨ Group and Outline ⇨ Group. Excel displays outline symbols for the group. Repeat this for each group that you want to create. When you collapse the outline, Excel hides rows in the group. But the summary row, which is not in the group, remains in view.

When creating an outline manually, always start by grouping the most detailed rows or columns first. If you want to create higher levels in the outline, do so after you've added the lower-level groupings.

If you select a range of cells (rather than entire rows or columns) before you create a group, Excel displays the Group dialog box asking what you want to group. It then groups entire rows or columns based on the range that you select.

If you realize that you grouped the wrong rows, you can ungroup the group by selecting Data ⇨ Group and Outline ⇨ Ungroup.

To speed up the process of grouping and ungrouping, you can use these keyboard shortcuts:

✦ **Alt+Shift+right arrow:** Groups selected rows or columns

✦ **Alt+Shift+left arrow:** Ungroups selected rows or columns

Outlining Tools

Excel doesn't have a toolbar devoted exclusively to outlining, but it does have tools that you can add to a customized toolbar to make outlining a little easier. Select View ➪ Toolbars ➪ Customize to display the Customize dialog box. Then add the following four items from the Data category on the Commands tab to your customized toolbar:

Button Name	What It Does
Hide Detail	Hides details of selected summary cell
Show Detail	Shows details of selected summary cell
Ungroup	Ungroups selected rows or columns
Group	Groups selected rows or columns

Using Outlines Effectively

This section discusses the basic operations that you can perform with a worksheet outline. These make your outline even more useful.

Displaying different outline levels

To display various outline levels, click the appropriate outline symbol. These symbols consist of buttons with numbers on them (1, 2, and so on) and buttons with either a plus sign (+) or a minus sign (–).

Clicking the 1 button collapses the outline so that it displays no detail, just the highest summary level of information. Clicking the 2 button expands the outline to show one level, and so on. The number of numbered buttons depends on the number of outline levels. Choosing a level number displays the detail for that level, plus any lower levels. To display all levels — the most detail — click the highest-level number.

You can expand a particular section by clicking its + button, or you can collapse a particular section by clicking its – button. In short, you have complete control over the details that Excel exposes or hides in an outline. For example, Figure 25-6 shows the outline when the only details that are displayed are the fourth-quarter results for the West region.

If you prefer, you can use the Hide Detail and Show Detail commands on the Data ➪ Group and Outline menu, to hide and show details, respectively.

	A	E	I	M	N	O	P	Q	R	S
1	State	Q1 Total	Q2 Total	Q3 Total	Oct	Nov	Dec	Q4 Total	Grand Total	
2	California	4330	4507	4722	1784	1957	1813	5554	19113	
3	Washington	3513	4703	5139	1196	1876	1649	4721	18076	
4	Oregon	5140	4369	3786	1869	1027	1343	4239	17534	
5	Nevada	3795	4663	4667	1940	1190	1494	4624	17749	
6	West Total	16778	18242	18314	6789	6050	6299	19138	72472	
11	East Total	17267	17864	17910	6632	6137	6156	18925	71966	
17	Central Total	17683	17550	17752	6598	7526	7759	17357	70342	
18	Grand Total	51728	53656	53976	20019	19713	20214	55420	214780	

Figure 25-6: You can use the outline view controls to view specific details while hiding most of the worksheet details.

Tip

If you constantly adjust the outline to show different reports, consider using the Custom Views feature to save a particular view and give it a name. Then, you can quickly switch among the named views. Use the View ➪ Custom Views command for this.

Applying styles to an outline

When you create an outline, you can have Excel automatically apply named styles to the summary rows and columns.

Cross-Reference

Chapter 5 discusses named styles.

Excel uses styles with names in the following formats (where *n* corresponds to the outline level):

✦ RowLevel_n

✦ ColLevel_n

For example, the named style that is applied to the first row level is RowLevel_1. These styles consist only of formats for the font. Using font variations makes distinguishing various parts of the outline a bit easier. You can, of course, modify the styles in any way that you want. For example, you can use the Format ➪ Style command to change the font size or color for the RowLevel_1 style. After you do so, all the RowLevel_1 cells take on the new formatting.

> **Tip**   You may prefer to use Excel's Format ➪ AutoFormat command to format an outline. Several AutoFormats use different formatting for summary cells.

You can have Excel automatically apply the styles when it creates an outline, or you can apply them after the fact. You control this in the Settings dialog box, shown in Figure 25-7. This dialog box appears when you select Data ➪ Group and Outline ➪ Settings.

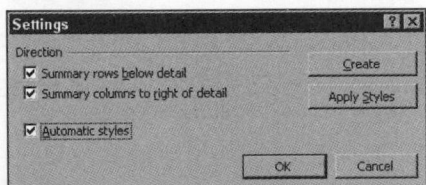

Figure 25-7: Use the Settings dialog box to select outline settings you want Excel to use.

If the Automatic styles check box contains a check mark when you create the outline, Excel automatically applies the styles. To apply styles to an existing outline, select the outline, choose Data ➪ Group and Outline ➪ Settings, and then click Apply Styles.

> **Tip**   You also can create an outline by using the Settings dialog box by clicking Create.

Adding data to an outline

You may need to add additional rows or columns to an outline. In some cases, you may be able to insert new rows or columns without disturbing the outline, and the new rows or columns become part of the outline. In other cases, you'll find that the new row or column is not part of the outline. If you create the outline automatically, just select Data ➪ Group and Outline ➪ Auto Outline again. Verify that you want to modify the existing outline.

> **Tip**   Adding additional rows or columns to the outline is much easier if you fully expand the outline before attempting to add the new rows or columns.

Removing an outline

If you no longer need an outline, you can remove it by selecting Data ⇨ Group and Outline ⇨ Clear Outline. Excel fully expands the outline by displaying all hidden rows and columns, and the outline symbols disappear. The outline styles remain in effect, however.

Caution You can't "undo" removing an outline, so make sure that you *really* want to remove the outline, before you select this command.

Tip Instead of removing the outline, consider simply hiding the outline, as discussed next.

Hiding the outline symbols

The outline symbols that Excel displays when an outline is present take up quite a bit of space (the exact amount depends on the number levels). If you want to see as much as possible onscreen, you can temporarily hide these symbols, without removing the outline. The following are the two ways to do this:

✦ Open the Options dialog box, select the View tab, and remove the check mark from the Outline Symbols check box.

✦ Press Ctrl+8.

Note When you hide the outline symbols, the outline is still in effect and the worksheet displays the data at the current outline level. That is, some rows or columns may be hidden.

Tip To quickly redisplay the outline symbols, press Ctrl+8.

The Custom Views feature, which saves named views of your outline, also saves the status of the outline symbols as part of the view, enabling you to name some views with the outline symbols and other views without them.

Creating charts from outlines

A worksheet outline also is a handy way to create summary charts. If you have a large table of data, creating a chart usually produces a confusing mess. But if you create an outline first, you can collapse the outline and select the summary data for your chart. Figure 25-8 shows an example of a chart created from a collapsed outline. When you expand an outline from which you created a chart, the chart shows the additional data.

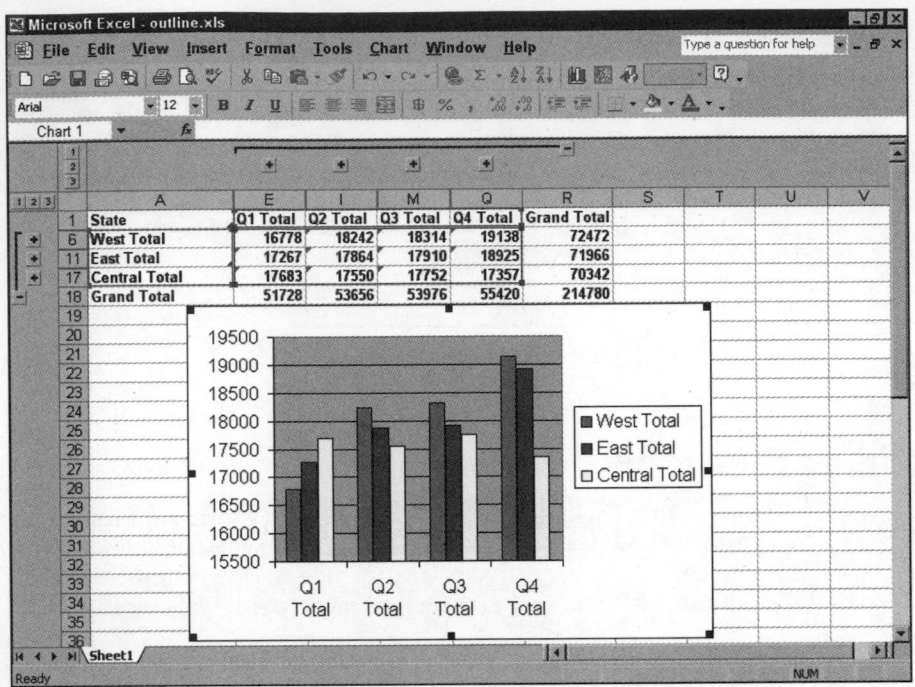

Figure 25-8: This chart was created from the summary cells in an outline.

Note   If your chart shows all the data in the outline, even when it's collapsed, remove the check mark from the Plot Visible Cells Only check box in the Chart tab in the Options dialog box.

Tip   Remember to select the data range—minus the grand totals—before you create your chart. Otherwise, Excel will create a chart that includes the grand totals as an additional data series.

✦   ✦   ✦

Linking and Consolidating Worksheets

As you use Excel, you'll probably find that it's often necessary to combine data from several different sources to obtain the results you need. This chapter discusses two procedures that help you accomplish this: linking and consolidation. *Linking* is the process of using references to cells in external workbooks to get data into your worksheet. *Consolidation* combines or summarizes information from two or more worksheets (which can be in multiple workbooks).

Linking Workbooks

Linking is the process of using formulas to combine data from two or more worksheets. When you link worksheets, you connect them in such a way that one depends on the other. The workbook that contains the link formulas (or external reference formulas) is called the *dependent* workbook. The workbook that contains the information used in the external reference formula is called the *source* workbook. Note, importantly, that you don't need to open the source workbook when you link it to the dependent workbook.

 You also can create links to data in other applications, such as a database program or a word processor. This is a completely different procedure and is the topic of Chapter 30.

Why you may want to link workbooks

When you consider linking workbooks, you might ask yourself the following question: If Workbook A needs to access data in another workbook (Workbook B), why not just enter the data into Workbook A in the first place? In some cases, you can. But the real value of linking becomes apparent when you continually update the source workbook. Creating a link in Workbook A to Workbook B means that, in Workbook A, you always have access to the most recent information in Workbook B because Workbook A is updated whenever Workbook B changes.

Linking workbooks also can be helpful if you need to consolidate different files. For example, each regional sales manager might store data in a separate workbook. You can create a summary workbook that first uses link formulas to retrieve specific data from each manager's workbook and then calculates totals across all regions.

Linking also is useful as a way to break up a large model into smaller files. You can create smaller workbook modules that are linked together with a few key external references. Often, this approach makes your model easier to deal with and uses less memory.

Linking has its downside, however. As you'll see later, external reference formulas are somewhat fragile, and accidentally severing the links that you create is relatively easy. You can prevent this from happening if you understand how linking works. Later in the chapter, some of the problems that may arise are discussed, as well as how to avoid them (see "Preventing Problems with External Reference Formulas").

Creating external reference formulas

You need to create formulas to link worksheets. These formulas are called *external* reference formulas because they are referencing data outside the worksheet.

You can create an external reference formula in these ways:

✦ **Type the cell references manually.** These references may be lengthy because they include workbook and sheet names (and, possibly, even drive and path information). The advantage of manually typing the cell references is that the source workbook doesn't have to be open.

✦ **Point to the cell references.** If the source workbook is open, you can use the standard pointing techniques to create formulas that use external references.

✦ **Copy and paste the data.** With the source workbook open, select Edit ➪ Paste Special with the Paste Link button.

✦ **Use Excel's Data ➪ Consolidate command.** This method is discussed later in the chapter (see "Consolidating Worksheets by Using Data ➪ Consolidate").

Understanding the link formula syntax

This section discusses the concept of external references. The general syntax for an external reference formula is

```
=[WorkbookName]SheetName!CellAddress
```

Precede the cell address by the workbook name (in brackets), the worksheet name, and an exclamation point. Here's an example of a formula that uses cell A1 in the Sheet1 worksheet of a workbook named Budget:

```
=[Budget.xls]Sheet1!A1
```

If the workbook name or the sheet name in the reference includes one or more spaces, you must enclose the text in single quotation marks. For example, here's a formula that refers to cell A1 on Sheet1 in a workbook named Annual Budget:

```
='[Annual Budget]Sheet1'!A1
```

When a formula refers to cells in a different workbook, that other workbook doesn't need to be open. If the workbook is closed and not in the current folder, you must add the complete path to the reference; for example:

```
='C:\My Documents\[Annual Budget]Sheet1'!A1
```

Creating a link formula by pointing

As previously mentioned, you can directly enter external reference formulas, but doing so can cause errors because you must have every bit of information exactly correct. Instead, have Excel build the formula for you, as follows:

1. Open the source workbook.

2. Select the cell in the dependent workbook that will hold the formula.

3. Enter the formula. When you get to the part that requires the external reference, activate the source workbook and select the cell or range.

4. Finish the formula and press Enter.

When you point to the cell or range, Excel automatically takes care of the details and creates a syntactically correct external reference.

 Tip

When you point to a cell reference, the cell reference is always an absolute reference (such as $A$1). If you plan to copy the formula to create additional link formulas, you can change the absolute reference to a relative reference by removing the dollar signs. See Chapter 7 for more details.

As long as the source workbook remains open, the external reference doesn't include the path to the workbook. If you close the source workbook, however, the external reference formulas change to include the full path. If you use the File ➪ Save As command to save the source workbook with a different name, Excel changes the external references to use the new filename.

Pasting links

The Paste Special command provides another way to create external reference formulas:

1. Open the source workbook.

2. Select the cell or range that you want to link and then copy it to the clipboard.

3. Activate the dependent workbook and select the cell in which you want the link formula to appear. If you're pasting a range, just select the upper-left cell.

4. Choose Edit ➪ Paste Special and then click the Paste Link button.

Working with external reference formulas

A single workbook can contain links that refer to any number of different source workbooks. This section discusses what you need to know about working with links.

Creating links to unsaved workbooks

Excel enables you to create link formulas to unsaved workbooks, and even to nonexistent workbooks. Assume that you have two workbooks open and you haven't saved either of them (they have the names Book1 and Book2). If you create a link formula to Book1 in Book2 and then save Book2, Excel displays the dialog box shown in Figure 26-1. Generally, you should avoid this situation. Simply save the source workbook first.

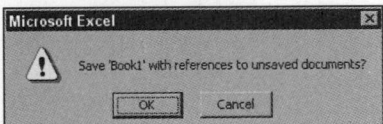

Figure 26-1: This message indicates that the workbook you're saving contains references to a workbook that you haven't yet saved.

You also can create links to documents that don't exist. You might want to do this if you'll be using a source workbook from a colleague, but the file hasn't arrived. When you enter an external reference formula that refers to a nonexistent workbook, Excel displays its Update Values dialog box, shown in Figure 26-2. If you click Cancel, the formula retains the workbook name that you entered, but it returns an error. When the source workbook becomes available, the error goes away and the formula displays its proper value.

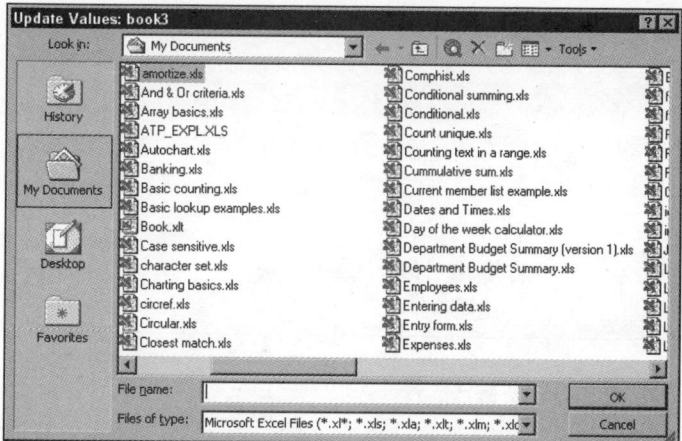

Figure 26-2: When you enter a formula that refers to a nonexistent workbook, Excel displays this dialog box to help you locate the file.

Opening a workbook with external reference formulas

When you open a workbook that contains one or more external reference formulas, Excel retrieves the current values from the source workbooks and calculates the formulas.

If Excel can't locate a source workbook that's referred to in a link formula, it displays the dialog box shown in Figure 26-3. You can either continue with undefined links or edit the links to point to existing workbooks.

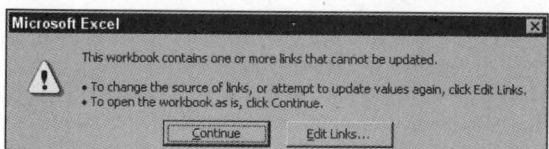

Figure 26-3: When you open a workbook with links to nonexistent workbooks, Excel displays this dialog box so that you can decide how to proceed.

Editing links

If your workbook uses several workbook links, you might want to see a list of source workbooks. To do so, choose the Edit ➪ Links command. Excel responds with the Edit Links dialog box, shown in Figure 26-4. This dialog box lists all source workbooks, plus other types of links to other documents.

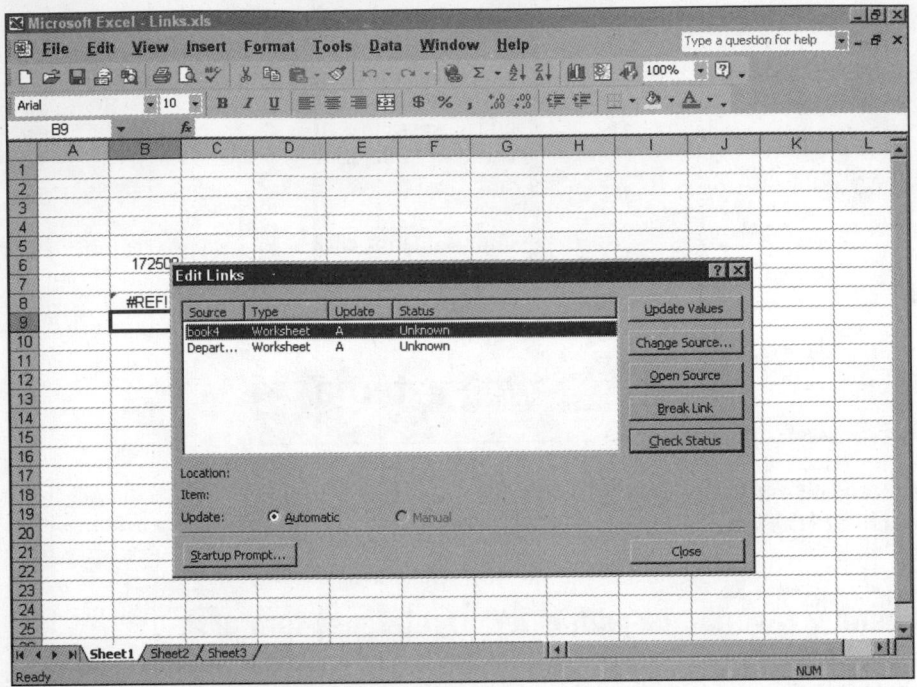

Figure 26-4: Use the Edit Links dialog box to work with the existing links in your workbook.

If you want to ensure that your link formulas have the latest values from their source workbooks, you can force an update. This step might be necessary if you just learned that someone made changes to the source workbook and saved the latest version to your network server.

To update linked formulas with their current value, click the Update Values button. Excel updates the link formulas with the latest version of the source workbook.

Note   Excel always sets worksheet links to the Automatic update option in the Links dialog box, and you can't change them to Manual. This means that Excel updates the links only when you open the workbook. Excel doesn't automatically update links when the source file changes.

A time may come when you need to change the source workbook for your external references. For example, you might have a worksheet that has links to a workbook named Preliminary Budget, but you later receive a finalized version named Final Budget.

You *could* change all the cell links manually, or you could simply change the link source. Do this in the Links dialog box. Select the source workbook that you want to change and click the Change Source button. Excel displays a dialog box that enables you to select a new source file. After you select the file, all external reference formulas are updated.

If you have external references in a workbook and then decide that you no longer need the links, you can convert the external reference formulas to values, thereby severing the links. To do so, select the link in the Edit Links dialog box and click the Break Link button. All formulas in the selected range are converted to their current values.

Tip To see which links might be causing problems, click the Check Status button. Excel immediately checks the link status of all open links and informs you of any problems by displaying a message in the Status column.

Preventing problems with external reference formulas

Using external reference formulas can be quite useful, but the links may be unintentionally severed. In almost every case, you'll be able to reestablish lost links. If you open the workbook and Excel can't locate the file, you're presented with a dialog box that enables you to specify the workbook and re-create the links. You also can change the source file by using the Change Source button in the Edit Links dialog box. The following sections discuss some points that you must remember when you use external reference formulas.

Renaming or moving a source workbook

If you rename the source document or move it to a different folder, Excel won't be able to update the links. You need to use the Edit Links dialog box to specify the new source document.

Modifying a source workbook

If you open a workbook that is a source workbook for another workbook, be extremely careful if you don't open the destination workbook at the same time. For example, if you add a new row to the source workbook, the cells all move down one row. When you open the destination workbook, it continues to use the old cell references — which are now invalid. You can avoid this problem in these ways:

✦ Open the destination workbook when you modify the source workbook. If you do so, Excel adjusts the external references in the destination workbook when you make changes to the source workbook.

✦ Use names rather than cell references in your link formula. This is the safest approach.

Avoiding intermediary links

Excel doesn't place many limitations on the complexity of your network of external references. For example, Workbook A can contain external references that refer to Workbook B, which can contain an external reference that refers to Workbook C. In this case, a value in Workbook A can ultimately depend on a value in Workbook C. Workbook B is an *intermediary* link.

Excel doesn't update external reference formulas if the workbook isn't open. In the preceding example, assume that Workbooks A and C are open. If you change a value in Workbook C, Workbook A won't reflect the change because you didn't open Workbook B (the intermediary link).

Consolidating Worksheets

The term *consolidation,* in the context of worksheets, refers to several operations that involve multiple worksheets or multiple workbook files. In some cases, consolidation involves creating link formulas. Here are two common examples of consolidation:

✦ The budget for each department in your company is stored in a separate worksheet in a single workbook. You need to consolidate the data and create a company-wide budget.

✦ Each department head submits his or her budget to you in a separate workbook. Your job is to consolidate these files into a company-wide budget.

These tasks can be difficult or easy; the tasks are easy if the information is laid out exactly the same in each worksheet (as you'll see shortly).

If the worksheets aren't laid out identically, they may be similar enough. In the second example, some budget files submitted to you may be missing categories that aren't used by a particular department. In this case, you can use a handy feature in Excel that matches data by using row and column titles. This feature is discussed later in the chapter (see "Consolidating Worksheets by Using Data ⇨ Consolidate").

If the worksheets bear little or no resemblance to each other, your best bet may be to edit the sheets so that they correspond to one another. In some cases, simply reentering the information in a standard format may be more efficient.

You can use any of the following techniques to consolidate information from multiple workbooks:

✦ Use external reference formulas

✦ Copy the data and use the Paste Special command

✦ Use Excel's Data ⇨ Consolidate command

✦ Use a pivot table (discussed in Chapter 21)

Consolidating worksheets by using formulas

Consolidating with formulas simply involves creating formulas that use references to other worksheets or other workbooks. The primary advantages to using this method of consolidation are

✦ Dynamic updating — if the values in the source worksheets change, the formulas are updated automatically.

✦ The source workbooks don't need to be open when you create the consolidation formulas.

If you are consolidating the worksheets in the same workbook and if all the worksheets are laid out identically, the consolidation task is quite simple. You can just use standard formulas to create the consolidations. For example, to compute the total for cell A1 in worksheets named Sheet2 through Sheet10, enter this formula:

```
=SUM(Sheet2:Sheet10!A1)
```

You can enter this formula manually or you can use the multisheet selection technique discussed in Chapter 4. You can then copy this formula to create summary formulas for other cells. Figure 26-5 shows this technique at work.

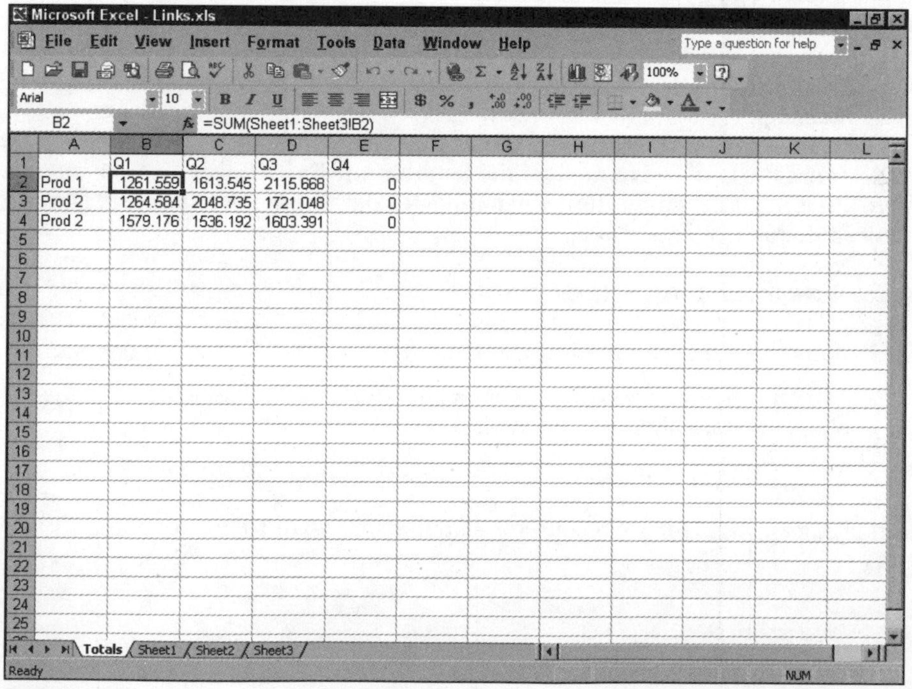

Figure 26-5: You can easily consolidate multiple worksheets by using formulas.

If the consolidation involves other workbooks, you can use external reference formulas to perform your consolidation. For example, if you want to add the values in cell A1 from Sheet1 in two workbooks (named Region1 and Region2), you can use this formula:

```
=[Region1.xls]Sheet1!A1+[Region2.xls]Sheet1!A1
```

You can include any number of external references in this formula, up to the 1,027-character limit for a formula. However, if you use many external references, such a formula can be quite lengthy and confusing, if you need to edit it.

 **Caution**   Remember that Excel expands the references to include the full path, which can increase the length of the formula. Therefore, this expansion may cause the formula to exceed the limit, thus creating an invalid formula.

 **Tip**   If the worksheets that you're consolidating aren't laid out the same, you can still use formulas but you have to ensure that each formula refers to the correct cell.

Consolidating worksheets by using Paste Special

Another method of consolidating information is to use the Edit ➪ Paste Special command. This method is applicable only when all the worksheets that you're consolidating are open.

 **Caution**   The major disadvantage to using Edit ➪ Paste Special is that the consolidation isn't dynamic. If any data that was consolidated changes, the consolidation is no longer accurate.

This technique takes advantage of the fact that the Paste Special command can perform a mathematical operation when it pastes data from the clipboard. Figure 26-6 shows the Paste Special dialog box.

Here's how to use this method:

1. Copy the data from the first source range.

2. Activate the destination workbook and select the cell in which you want to place the consolidation formula.

3. Select Edit ➪ Paste Special, click the Add option, and then click OK.

Repeat these steps for each source range that you want to consolidate.

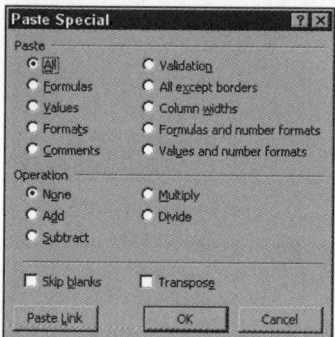

Figure 26-6: You can use the Paste Special dialog box to perform a mathematical operation as the data is consolidated into the worksheet.

Consolidating worksheets by using Data ⇨ Consolidate

For the ultimate in data consolidation, use Excel's Data ⇨ Consolidate command. This method is quite flexible, and in some cases, it even works if the source worksheets aren't laid out identically. This technique can create consolidations that are static (no link formulas) or dynamic (with link formulas). The Data ⇨ Consolidate command supports these methods of consolidation:

✦ **By position:** This method is accurate only if the worksheets are laid out identically.

✦ **By category:** Excel uses row and column labels to match data in the source worksheets. Use this option if the data is laid out differently in the source worksheets or if some source worksheets are missing rows or columns.

Figure 26-7 shows the Consolidate dialog box, which appears when you select Data ⇨ Consolidate.

The following list is a description of the controls in this dialog box:

✦ **Function list box:** Specify the type of consolidation. Usually, you use Sum, but you also can select from ten other options: Count, Average, Max, Min, Product, Count Nums, StdDev (standard deviation), StdDevp (population standard deviation), Var (variance), or Varp (population variance).

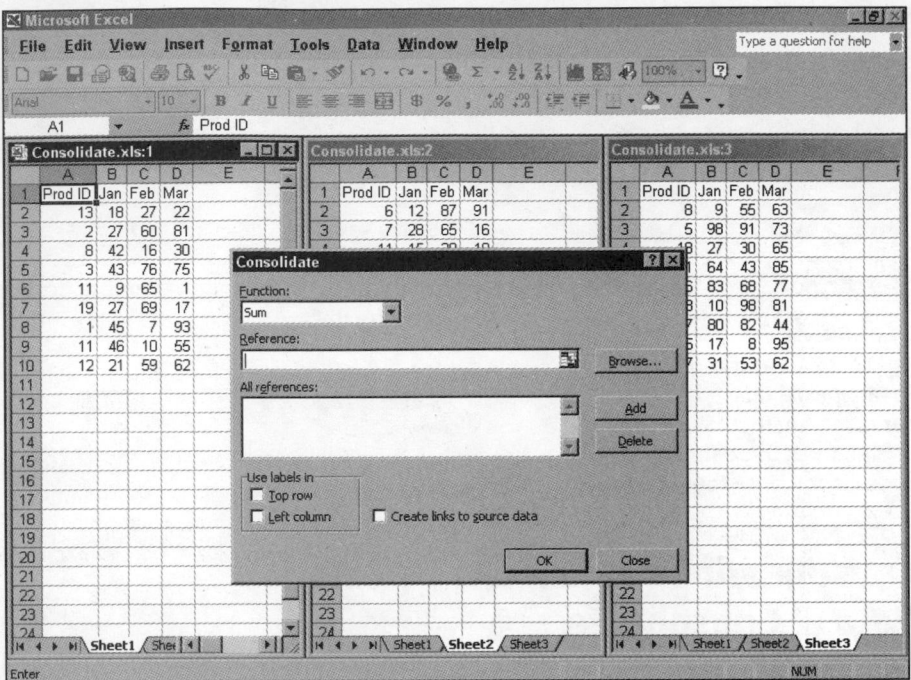

Figure 26-7: The Consolidate dialog box enables you to specify ranges to consolidate.

✦ **Reference text box:** Specify a range from a source file that you want to consolidate. You can enter the range reference manually or use any standard pointing technique (if the workbook is open). After you enter the range in this box, click the Add button to add the range to the All References list. If you consolidate by position, don't include labels in the range. If you consolidate by category, do include labels in the range.

✦ **All references list box:** Contains the list of references that you have added with the Add button.

✦ **Use labels in check boxes:** Use to instruct Excel to perform the consolidation by examining the labels in the top row, the left column, or both positions. Use these options when you consolidate by category.

✦ **Create links to source data check box:** When you select this option, Excel creates an outline that consists of external references to the destination cells in the destination worksheet. Additionally, Excel includes summary formulas in the outline. If you don't select this option, the consolidation doesn't use formulas.

✦ **Browse button:** Displays a dialog box that enables you to select a workbook to open. It inserts the filename in the Reference box, but you have to supply the range reference.

✦ **Add button:** Adds the reference in the Reference box to the All References list.

✦ **Delete button:** Deletes the selected reference from the All References list.

Looking at a consolidation example

The simple example in this section demonstrates the power of the Data ⇨ Consolidate command. Figure 26-8 shows three worksheets that will be consolidated. These worksheets report product sales for three months. Notice, however, that they don't all report on the same products. In addition, the products aren't even listed in the same order. In other words, these worksheets aren't laid out identically — which makes creating consolidation formulas difficult.

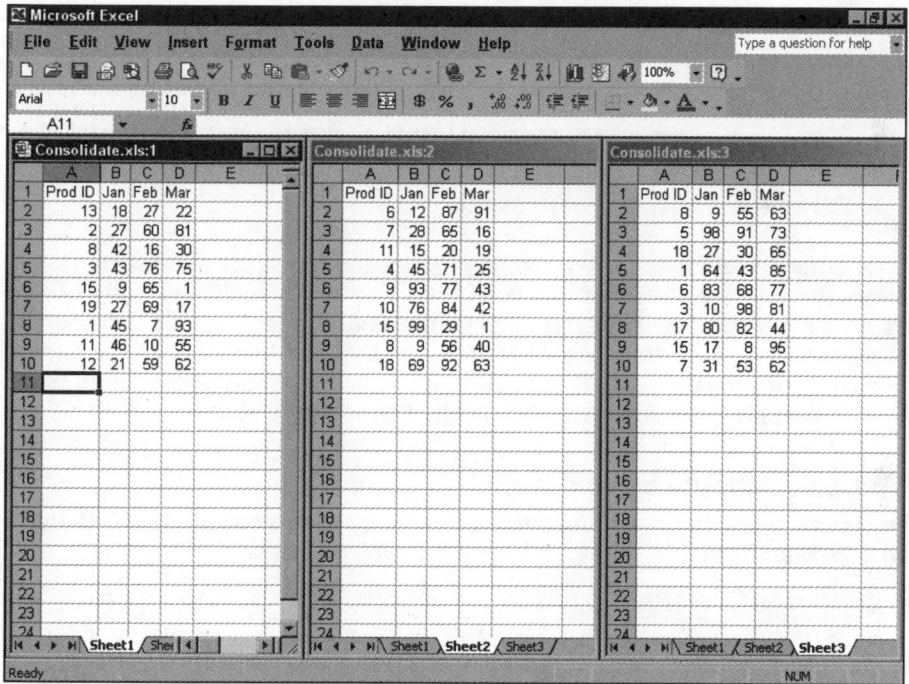

Figure 26-8: These three worksheets include data that needs to be consolidated.

To consolidate this information, start with a new workbook. The source workbooks can be open or not — it doesn't matter. Follow these steps to consolidate the workbooks:

1. Select Data ⇨ Consolidate. Excel displays its Consolidate dialog box.

2. Select the type of consolidation summary that you want to use. Use Sum for this example.

3. Enter the reference for the first worksheet to consolidate. If the workbook is open, you can point to the reference. If the workbook is not open, click the Browse button to locate the file on disk. The reference must include a range. Use A1:D100. This range is larger than the actual range to consolidate, but using this range ensures that the consolidation still works if new rows are added to the source file. When the reference in the Reference box is correct, click Add to add it to the All References list.

4. Enter the reference for the second worksheet. You can simply edit the existing reference by changing Region1 to Region2 and then clicking Add. This reference is added to the All References list.

5. Enter the reference for the third worksheet. Again, you can simply edit the existing reference by changing Region2 to Region3 and then clicking Add. This final reference is added to the All References list.

6. Because the worksheets aren't laid out the same, select the Left column and Top row check boxes to force Excel to match the data by using the labels.

7. Select the Create links to source data check box to make Excel create an outline with external references.

8. Click OK to begin the consolidation.

In seconds, Excel creates the consolidation, beginning at the active cell. Figure 26-9 shows the result. Notice that Excel created an outline, which is collapsed to show only the subtotals for each product. If you expand the outline, you can see the details. Examine it further, and you'll discover that each detail cell is an external reference formula that uses the appropriate cell in the source file. Therefore, the destination range is updated automatically if any data is changed.

A bit more about consolidation

Excel is very flexible regarding the sources that you can consolidate. You can consolidate data from:

✦ Workbooks that are open

✦ Workbooks that are closed (you have to enter the reference manually, but you can use the Browse button to get the filename part of the reference)

✦ The same workbook in which you're creating the consolidation

And, of course, you can mix and match any of the preceding choices in a single consolidation.

Note   Excel remembers the references that you entered in the Consolidate dialog box and saves them with the workbook. Therefore, if you want to refresh a consolidation later, you won't have to reenter the references.

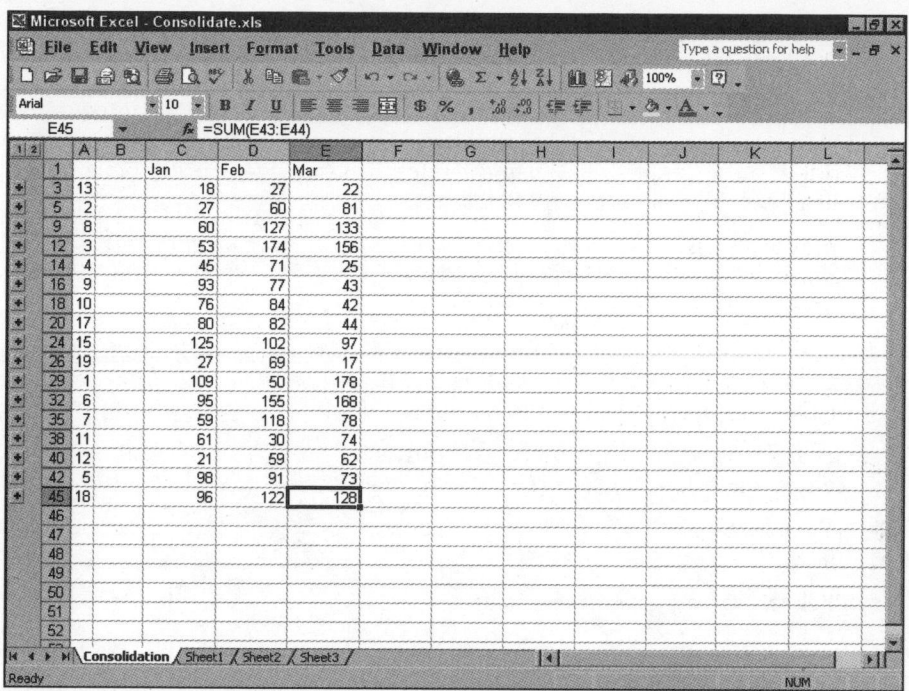

Figure 26-9: This worksheet shows the result of the consolidation.

If you perform the consolidation by matching labels, be aware that the matches must be exact. For example, *Jan* does not match *January*. The matching isn't case sensitive, however, so *April* does match *APRIL*. In addition, the labels can be in any order, and they need not be in the same order in all the source ranges.

If you don't choose the Create links to source data check box, Excel doesn't create formulas (nor an outline), which generates a static consolidation. If the data on any of the source worksheets changes, the consolidation doesn't update automatically. To update the summary information, you need to select the destination range and repeat the Data ➪ Consolidate command.

Tip

If you name the destination range **Consolidate_Area**, you don't need to select it before you update the consolidation. Consolidate_Area is a name that has special meaning to Excel.

If you choose the Create links to source data check box, Excel creates an outline. This is a standard worksheet outline, and you can manipulate it by using the techniques described in Chapter 25.

✦   ✦   ✦

Customizing Toolbars and Menus

Excel lets you modify both toolbars and menus. This chapter explains how to customize the built-in toolbars, create new toolbars, and change the menus that Excel displays. These techniques can make Excel easier to use, and they also enable you to add your own custom actions through the use of a little macro programming if you're so inclined.

Understanding How You Can Customize Toolbars

Excel's toolbars and menus enable you to control what the program does. You can, for example, click a toolbar button or select a menu command to issue a print command to print your worksheets.

 **Note**   The official term for toolbars, menu bars, and shortcut menus is a CommandBar.

Each CommandBar consists of one or more "commands." A command can take the form of an icon, of text, or both. Some of Excel's commands don't appear on any of the prebuilt toolbars.

Many users like to create custom toolbars that contain the commands that they use most often. For example, if you often use outlining in your worksheets, you may want to create a toolbar that contains the outlining tools.

 Note   Virtually no distinction exists between a menu bar and a toolbar. In fact, the menu bar that you see at the top of Excel's window is actually a toolbar that is named Worksheet Menu Bar. As with any toolbar, you can move it to a new location by dragging it.

How Excel Keeps Track of Toolbars

When you start Excel, it displays the same toolbar configuration that was in effect the last time that you used it. When you exit Excel, it updates a file named Excel.xlb in your `\Windows\Application Data\Microsoft\Excel` folder (the location may vary depending on the version of Windows you're using). This file stores your custom toolbars as well as information about which toolbars are visible and the onscreen location of each.

To restore the toolbars to their previous configuration, select File ⇨ Open to open this XLB file. This restores your toolbar configuration to the way that it was when you started Excel. You can also make a copy of the XLB file and give it a different name, which enables you to store multiple toolbar configurations that you can load at any time.

Understanding the types of customizations

The following list is a summary of the types of customizations that you can make when working with toolbars (which also include menu bars):

✦ **Move toolbars.** You can move any toolbar to another location.

✦ **Remove buttons from built-in toolbars.** You may want to do this to eliminate buttons that you never use.

✦ **Add buttons to built-in toolbars.** You can add as many buttons as you want to any toolbar.

✦ **Create new toolbars.** You can create as many new toolbars as you like, with as many buttons as you like.

✦ **Change the functionality of a button.** You make such a change by attaching your own macro to a built-in toolbar button.

✦ **Change the image that appears on any toolbar button.** A rudimentary but functional toolbar-button editor is included with Excel.

Note   The casual user cannot modify Excel's shortcut menus (the menus that appear when you right-click an object). Doing so requires the use of VBA (Visual Basic for Applications) macros.

Moving toolbars

A toolbar can be either floating or docked. A *docked* toolbar is fixed in place at the top, bottom, left, or right edge of Excel's workspace. *Floating* toolbars appear in an "always-on-top" window, and you can drag them wherever you like.

To move a toolbar, just click its border and drag it to its new position. If you drag it to one of the edges of Excel's window, it attaches itself to the edge and becomes docked. You can create several layers of docked toolbars. For example, the Standard and Formatting toolbars are (normally) both docked along the upper edge.

If a toolbar is floating, you can change its dimensions by dragging a border. For example, you can transform a horizontal toolbar to a vertical toolbar by dragging one of its corners. Figure 27-1 shows several of Excel's toolbars in various locations and sizes.

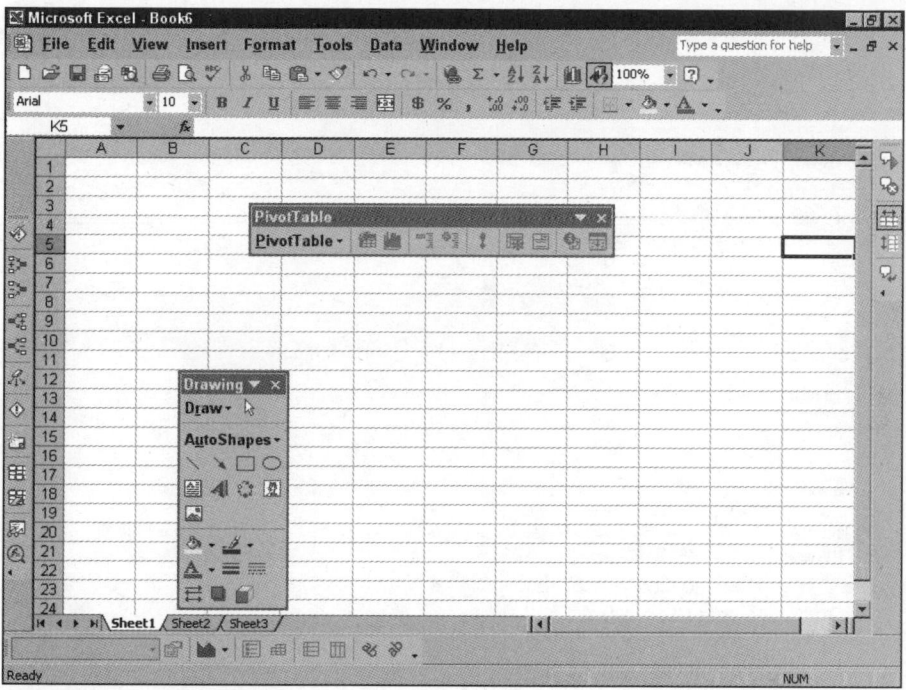

Figure 27-1: Several of Excel's toolbars (including both docked and floating toolbars) were added to this view.

Customizing Excel's Toolbars

In the following sections, you'll learn how you can easily customize any of Excel's toolbars. By doing so, you'll make Excel easier to use because you'll have immediate one-click access to the commands that you use the most.

Using the Customize dialog box

To make any changes to toolbars, you need to be in "customization mode." In customization mode, the Customize dialog box is displayed, and you can manipulate the toolbars in a number of ways. To get into customization mode, perform either of these actions:

✦ Select View ➪ Toolbars ➪ Customize

✦ Select Customize from the shortcut menu that appears when you right-click a toolbar

Either of these methods displays the Customize dialog box that is shown in Figure 27-2. This dialog box lists all the available toolbars, including custom toolbars that you have created.

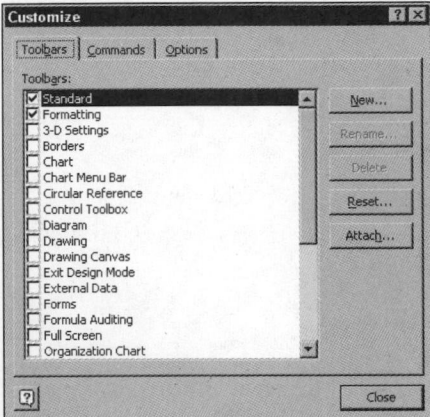

Figure 27-2: Use the Customize dialog box to modify Excel's toolbars.

The Customize dialog box has three tabs, each of which is described in the following sections.

Using the Toolbars tab

Figure 27-2 shows the Toolbars tab of the Customize dialog box. The following sections describe how to perform various procedures that involve toolbars.

Caution   Operations that you perform by using the Customize dialog box cannot be undone using the Edit ➪ Undo command.

Hiding or displaying a toolbar

The Toolbars tab displays every toolbar (built-in toolbars and custom toolbars). Add a check mark to display a toolbar; remove the check mark to hide it. The changes take effect immediately.

Tip   The Toolbars tab of the Customize dialog box includes check boxes that enable you to display some toolbars that do not appear on the list of toolbars when you select View ➪ Toolbars or when you right-click a toolbar.

Toolbar Autosensing

Normally, Excel displays a particular toolbar automatically when you change contexts; this is called *autosensing*. For example, when you activate a chart, the Chart toolbar appears. When you activate a sheet that contains a pivot table, the PivotTable toolbar appears.

You can easily defeat autosensing by hiding the toolbar. After you do so, Excel no longer displays that toolbar when you switch to its former context. You can restore this automatic behavior, however, by displaying the appropriate toolbar when you're in the appropriate context. Thereafter, Excel reverts to its normal automatic toolbar display when you switch to that context.

Creating a new toolbar

Click the New button and then enter a name in the New Toolbar dialog box. Excel creates and displays an empty toolbar. You can then add buttons to the new toolbar. See "Adding or removing toolbar buttons" later in this chapter.

Renaming a custom toolbar

Select a custom toolbar from the list and click the Rename button. Enter a new name in the Rename Toolbar dialog box. You cannot rename a built-in toolbar.

Deleting a custom toolbar

Select a custom toolbar from the list and click the Delete button. You cannot delete a built-in toolbar.

Resetting a built-in toolbar

Select a built-in toolbar from the list and click the Reset button. The toolbar is restored to its default state. If you've added any custom tools to the toolbar, they are removed. If you've removed any of the default tools, they are restored.

 Note   The Reset button is not available when a custom toolbar is selected.

Attaching a toolbar to a workbook

If you create a custom toolbar that you want to share with someone else, you can "attach" it to a workbook. To attach a custom toolbar to a workbook, click the Attach button, which presents the Attach Toolbars dialog box. Select the toolbars that you want to attach to a workbook (see Figure 27-3). You can attach any number of toolbars to a workbook.

A toolbar that's attached to a workbook appears automatically when the workbook is opened, unless the workspace already has a toolbar by the same name.

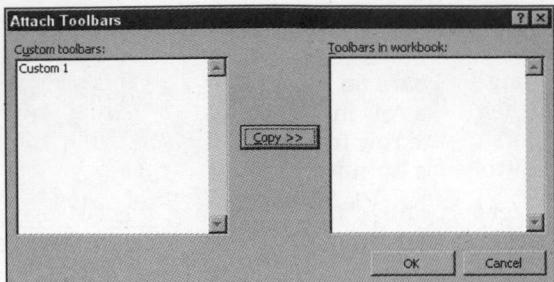

Figure 27-3: You can attach custom toolbars to a workbook in the Attach Toolbars dialog box.

Note

The toolbar that's stored in the workbook is an exact copy of the toolbar at the time that you attach it. If you modify the toolbar after attaching it, the changed version is not stored in the workbook automatically. You must manually remove the old toolbar and then add the edited toolbar.

Using the Commands tab

The Commands tab of the Customize dialog box contains a list of every tool that's available. Use this tab when you customize a toolbar. This feature is described later in the chapter (see "Adding or removing toolbar buttons").

Using the Options tab

The Options tab of the Customize dialog box, shown in Figure 27-4, offers several ways to customize your menus, toolbars, icons, and the like.

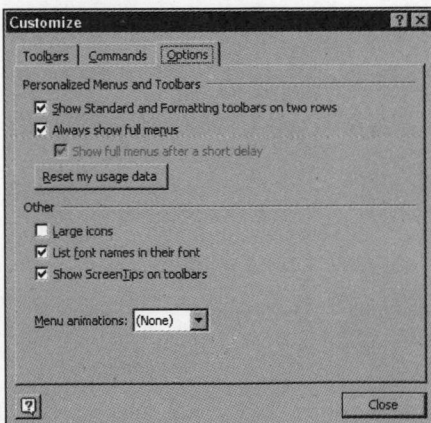

Figure 27-4: Use the Options tab of the Customize dialog box to control Excel's menus and toolbars.

The following list explains these options:

✦ **Show Standard and Formatting toolbars on two rows:** Select this option to show both these toolbars in their own row instead of in a single row. You can choose to display both toolbars in one row to save screen space, but you won't be able to see all the buttons on both toolbars.

✦ **Always show full menus:** Select this option to make certain Excel displays the complete menus rather than the "customized" menus that show only the commands you've used recently.

✦ **Show full menus after a short delay:** If you have decided to use Excel's customized menus, select this option to make certain that Excel displays the complete menus after you've floundered around for a time trying to find the commands that are supposed to be on a menu.

✦ **Reset my usage data:** If you have decided to use Excel's customized menus, click this button to make Excel forget which commands you've recently used. Doing so causes Excel to again display the full menus until it has watched for a time to see which commands you use.

✦ **Large icons:** To change the size of the icons used in toolbars, select or deselect the Large icons check box. This option affects only the images that are in buttons. Buttons that contain only text (such as buttons in a menu) don't change.

✦ **List font names in their font:** This feature displays the font names using the actual font so that you can preview the font before you select it.

✦ **Show ScreenTips on toolbar:** *ScreenTips* are the pop-up messages that display the button names when you pause the mouse pointer over a button.

✦ **Menu animations:** When you select a menu, Excel animates the display of the menu as it is dropping down. You can select the type of animation that you want.

✦ **Random:** The menu either slides or unfolds randomly.

✦ **Unfold:** The menu unfolds as it drops down.

✦ **Slide:** The menu drops down with a sliding motion

Adding or removing toolbar buttons

As noted earlier in this chapter, you can put Excel into customization mode by displaying the Customize dialog box. When Excel is in customization mode, you have access to all the commands and options in the Customize dialog box. In addition, you can

✦ Reposition a button on a toolbar

✦ Move a button to a different toolbar

✦ Copy a button from one toolbar to another

✦ Add new buttons to a toolbar by using the Commands tab of the Customize dialog box

Tip Excel provides a much simpler way to add or remove buttons from a toolbar. Just click the arrow at the end of the toolbar and select Add or Remove Buttons. You'll see a list of all the buttons for the toolbar. Buttons displayed with a check mark are visible in the toolbar; those without a check mark are not visible in the toolbar. Simply add or remove the check marks according to your preferences.

Moving and copying buttons

When the Customize dialog box is displayed, you can copy and move buttons freely among any visible toolbars. To move a button, drag it to its new location (the new location can be within the current toolbar or on a different toolbar).

To copy a button, press Ctrl as you drag the button to another toolbar. You can also copy a toolbar button within the same toolbar, but there's no real reason to have multiple copies of a button on the same toolbar.

Inserting a new button

To add a new button to a toolbar, you use the Commands tab of the Customize dialog box (see Figure 27-5).

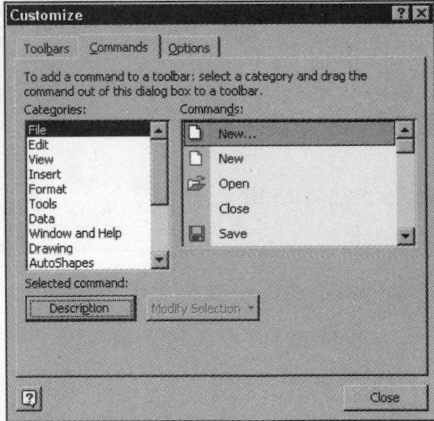

Figure 27-5: Use the Commands tab to add buttons to toolbars.

The buttons are arranged in several categories. When you select a category, the buttons in that category appear to the right in the Commands list box. To determine a button's function, select it and click the Description button.

 **Tip**   The command categories generally follow the Excel menus. If you want to add a button to perform a command that appears on a particular menu, look in the category of the same name on the Commands tab.

To add a button to a toolbar, locate it in the Commands tab and then click and drag it to the toolbar.

Performing other toolbar button operations

When Excel is in customization mode (that is, the Customize dialog box is displayed), you can right-click a toolbar button to get a shortcut menu of additional actions for the tool. Figure 27-6 shows the shortcut menu that appears when you right-click a button in customization mode.

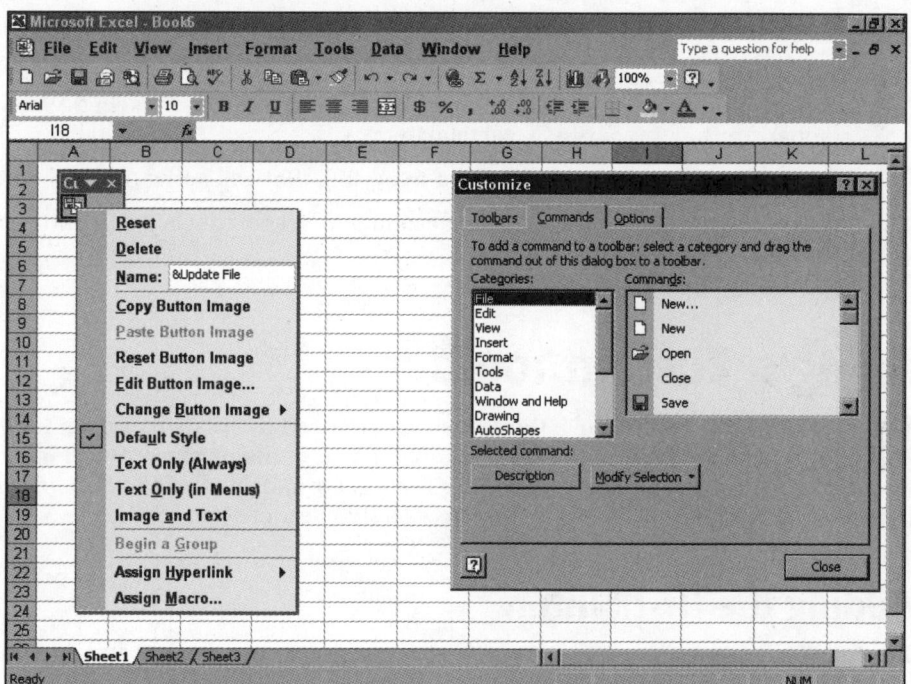

Figure 27-6: In customization mode, you can right-click a toolbar button to display this shortcut menu to give you even more customization options.

These commands are described in the following list (note that some of these commands are not available for certain toolbar tools):

✦ **Reset:** Resets the tool to its original state.

✦ **Delete:** Deletes the tool.

✦ **Name:** Lets you change the name of the tool.

✦ **Copy Button Image:** Makes a copy of the button's image and places it on the clipboard.

✦ **Paste Button Image:** Pastes the image from the clipboard to the button.

✦ **Reset Button Image:** Restores the button's original image.

✦ **Edit Button Image:** Lets you edit the button's image, using Excel's button editor.

✦ **Change Button Image:** Lets you change the image by selecting from a list of 42 button images.

✦ **Default Style:** Displays the tool with its default style (either text only or image and text).

✦ **Text Only (Always):** Always displays text (no image) for the tool.

✦ **Text Only (In Menus):** Displays text (no image) if the tool is in a menu bar.

✦ **Image and Text:** Displays the tool's image and text.

✦ **Begin a Group:** Inserts a divider in the toolbar. In a drop-down menu, a separator bar appears as a horizontal line between commands. In a toolbar, a separator bar appears as a vertical line.

✦ **Assign Hyperlink:** Lets you assign a hyperlink that will activate a Web page.

✦ **Assign Macro:** Lets you assign a macro that is executed when the button is clicked.

Creating a Custom Toolbar

This section walks you through the steps that are used to create a custom toolbar. This toolbar is an enhanced Formatting toolbar that contains many additional formatting tools that aren't found on Excel's built-in Formatting toolbar. You may want to replace the built-in Formatting toolbar with this new custom toolbar.

Adding the first button

The following steps are required in order to create this new toolbar and add one button (which has five subcommands):

1. Right-click any toolbar and select Customize from the shortcut menu to display the Customize dialog box.

2. Click the Toolbars tab and then click New to display the New Toolbar dialog box.

3. Enter a name for the toolbar: **Custom Formatting**. Click OK to create the new (empty) toolbar.

4. In the Customize dialog box, click the Commands tab.

5. In the Categories list, scroll down and select New Menu. The New Menu category has only one command (New Menu), which appears in the Commands list.

6. Drag the New Menu command from the Commands list to the new toolbar to create a menu button in the new toolbar.

7. Right-click the New Menu button in the new toolbar, select the name box on the shortcut menu, and change the name to Font.

8. In the Customize dialog box, select Format from the Categories list.

9. Scroll down through the Commands list and drag the Bold command to the Font button in your new toolbar (you'll need to add the command to the drop-down box that appears when the pointer is over the Font button). This step makes the Font button display a submenu (Bold) when the button is clicked.

10. Repeat Step 9, adding the following buttons from the Format category: Italic, Underline, Font Size, and Font.

At this point, you may want to click the Close button in the Customize dialog box to try out your new toolbar. The new toolbar contains only one button, but this button expands to show five font-related commands. Figure 27-7 shows the Custom Formatting toolbar at this stage.

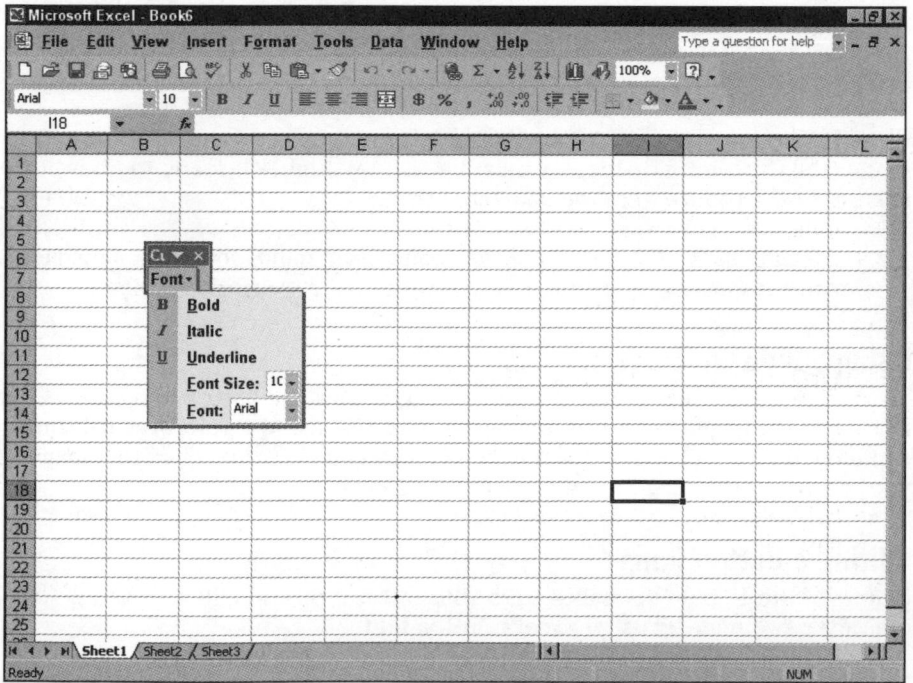

Figure 27-7: This shows the new Custom Formatting toolbar after adding a menu button with five commands.

Adding more buttons

If you followed the steps in the previous section, you should understand how tool-bar customization works, and you can now add additional buttons by following the procedures that you learned. To finish the toolbar, right-click the toolbar and select Customize. Then add additional tools.

Note   Excel doesn't have a command to save a toolbar. Instead, the new toolbar is saved when you exit Excel.

Tip   Remember that you can share your custom toolbar by attaching it to a workbook that you send to someone.

Changing a toolbar button's image

Excel offers several options to change the image that is displayed on a toolbar button. You can:

✦ Choose 1 of the 42 images that are provided by Excel.

✦ Modify or create the image by using Excel's Button Editor dialog box.

✦ Copy an image from another toolbar button.

Each method is discussed in the following sections.

To make any changes to a button image, you must be in toolbar customization mode (the Customize dialog box must be visible). Right-click any toolbar button and select Customize from the shortcut menu.

Note   You can change the image only for toolbar commands that have an icon in the commands list.

Using a built-in image

To change the image on a toolbar button, right-click the button and select Change Button Image from the shortcut menu. As you can see in Figure 27-8, this menu expands to show 42 images from which you can choose. Just click the image that you want, and the selected button's image changes.

Editing a button image

If none of the 42 built-in images suits your tastes, you can edit an existing image or create a new image by using Excel's Button Editor.

To begin editing, right-click the button that you want to edit and then choose Edit Button Image from the shortcut menu. The image appears in the Button Editor dia-log box (see Figure 27-9), in which you can change individual pixels and shift the entire image up, down, to the left, or to the right. If you've never worked with icons, you may be surprised at how difficult it is to create attractive images in such a small area.

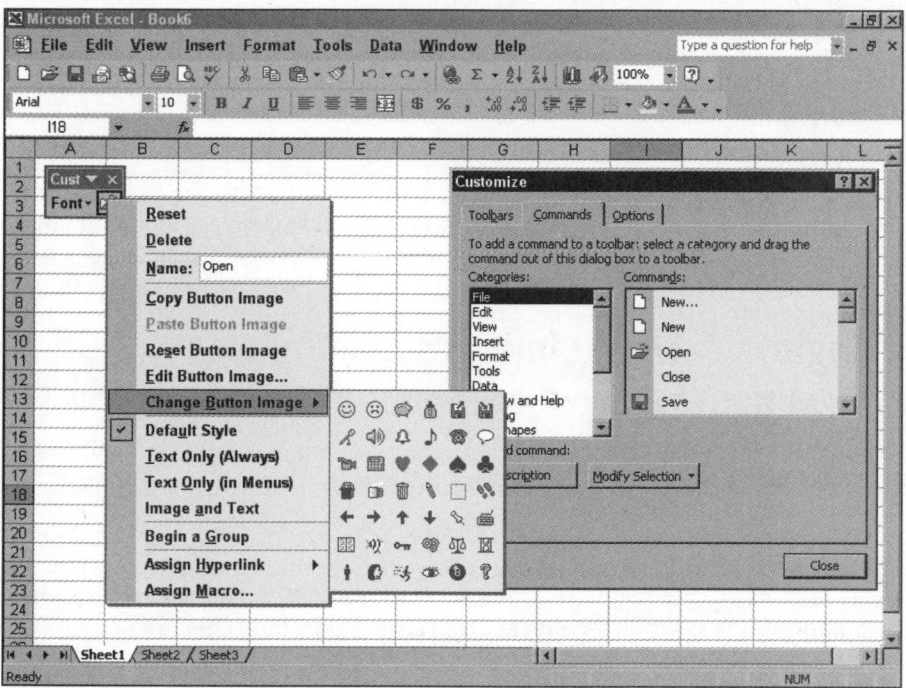

Figure 27-8: The Change Button Image option gives you 42 built-in button images to choose from.

Figure 27-9: Use the Button Editor dialog box to design your own button image or edit an existing one.

The Button Editor dialog box is straightforward. Just click a color and then click a pixel (or drag across pixels). When the image looks good, click OK. Or, if you don't like what you've done, click Cancel, and the button keeps its original image.

Caution It's always a bad idea to use a standard button image for a nonstandard purpose. For example, you probably wouldn't want to place the Save button image on a button that actually prints a copy of the worksheet.

Copying another button image

Another way to get a button image on a custom toolbar is to copy it from another toolbar button. Right-click a toolbar button, and it displays a shortcut menu that enables you to copy a button image to the clipboard. Then right-click the button where you want to use the copied image and select Paste Button Image to paste the clipboard contents to the selected button.

Activating a Web page from a toolbar button

You might want to create a button that activates your Web browser and loads a Web page.

To add a new button and to attach a hyperlink, make sure that you're in toolbar customization mode. Use the procedure previously described to add a new button and (optionally) specify a button image. Then, right-click the button and select Assign Hyperlink ➪ Open. You'll see the Assign Hyperlink: Open dialog box, shown in Figure 27-10. Type a URL or select one from the list.

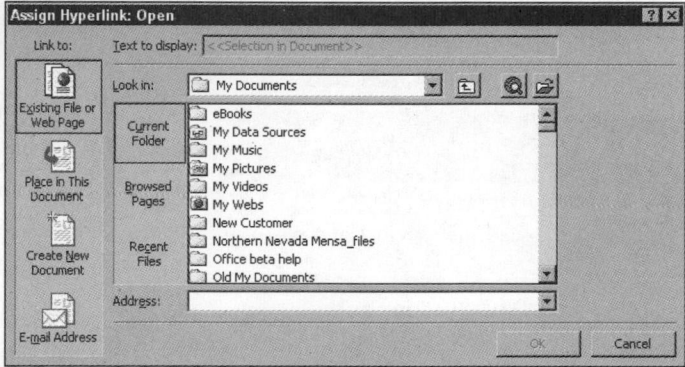

Figure 27-10: Use the Assign Hyperlink: Open dialog box to assign a hyperlink to a toolbar button.

✦   ✦   ✦

Excel and the Internet

◆ ◆ ◆ ◆

In This Chapter

Sharing your
worksheets on the
Internet

Using Excel's Internet
tools

◆ ◆ ◆ ◆

These days, virtually everyone who uses a computer is connected to the Internet. The Web has become an important way to share and gather information from a myriad of sources. To help you with these tasks, Excel has the capability to both create information that can be used on the Internet and to gather and process information that can be found on the Internet. This chapter shows you how to use Excel with the Internet.

Sharing Your Worksheets on the Internet

The Internet is a great resource when you need to share information. Excel provides several ways to share your worksheets over the Internet. The option you choose depends on your needs, as outlined in the following list:

✦ **Placing an Excel workbook on a Web server:** This option enables anyone who has access to the server to link to the workbook using standard Excel external reference formulas. This may be the best option if you need to make frequent changes in the data and need to make that data immediately available to a group of people in a number of different locations.

✦ **Publishing an Excel worksheet as a non-interactive Web page**: This option creates an HTML or XML Web page that can be viewed in any standard Web browser. The users will be able to view the data but not interact with it. This is a good option is you need to make static information widely available.

✦ **Publishing an Excel worksheet as an interactive Web page**: This option adds interactivity so that users will be able to perform actual calculations when they visit the Web page. Users must have the Office Web Components installed on their PC and must use Internet Explorer 4.01 or later.

Tip   If other people will need to open the workbook—as opposed to simply using data from it—it's best to save the workbook in Excel format rather than as a Web page. Excel can open HTML and XML files, but many features are lost when workbooks are saved in these formats.

Using Excel's Internet Tools

The remainder of this chapter describes the Internet-related features available in Excel. These features include

✦ Using HTML (or XML) as a native file format (instead of the XLS file format)

✦ Saving a worksheet as a Web page

✦ Using Excel's Web toolbar

✦ Inserting hyperlinks into a worksheet

✦ Creating and using Web queries

Using HTML as a native file format

Excel's standard file format is, of course, an XLS file. Excel, however, has the capability to use HTML (or XML) as a native file format. This means that you can create a workbook and save it in HTML format. Then, you can reopen the file without losing any information. In other words, your Excel-specific information (such as formulas, charts, pivot tables, and macros) survive the translation to HTML.

Note   XML is closely related to HTML, but there are important differences. When you save an Excel workbook in XML format, the file retains most of the features of a standard Excel XLS file. This means that the file can be opened in Excel and that it has most of the functionality you expect in an Excel workbook. Note, however, that XML is an evolving standard, and it currently is unclear whether XML offers any real advantages over Excel's other file formats.

To save a workbook in HTML format, select File ⇨ Save as Web Page. You'll see the familiar Save As dialog box—but with some new options (see Figure 28-1). In the field labeled Save as type, make sure Web Page (*.htm, *.html) is selected. Provide a filename and click Save. To reopen the file, use the normal File ⇨ Open command.

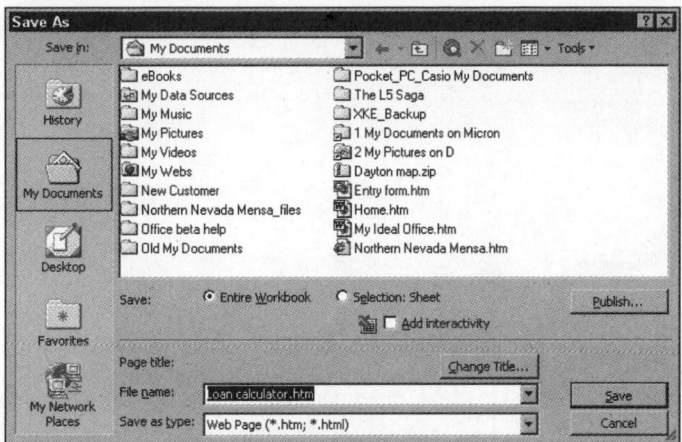

Figure 28-1: Use the Save As dialog box to save a workbook in HTML format.

Caution   Unless your workbook is very simple, saving it in HTML format generates additional "supporting" files because the HTML file format can't handle Excel-specific items, such as macros, charts, and pivot tables. The supporting files are stored in a separate subdirectory within the directory where you save the file. The directory name consists of the file's name, followed by a space and the word *files.* Therefore, if you need to transfer the file to another computer, make sure that you also transfer the supporting files in the subdirectory.

If you save your work in HTML format, you should be aware of some additional options. Select Tools ➪ Options, click the General tab, and then click the Web Options button. You'll see the Web Options dialog box, shown in Figure 28-2. Most of the time, the default settings work just fine. However, familiarizing yourself with the options available is worthwhile (these are described in the online Help). You can also access the Web Options dialog box from the Tools menu in the Save As dialog box.

When you save a workbook in HTML format, by default it will not be interactive when it's opened in a browser. The browser displays a good rendition of the worksheet, but it's essentially a "dead" workbook because the user can't change any cells. The next section describes how to save your Excel workbook in a way that provides interactivity within a Web browser.

Note   Even though the default HTML version of the workbook won't be interactive in a Web browser, it will retain most of the important Excel features — such as formulas — when opened in Excel. That's because the HTML file contains lots of proprietary tags that are ignored by browsers but that enable Excel to re-create the workbook.

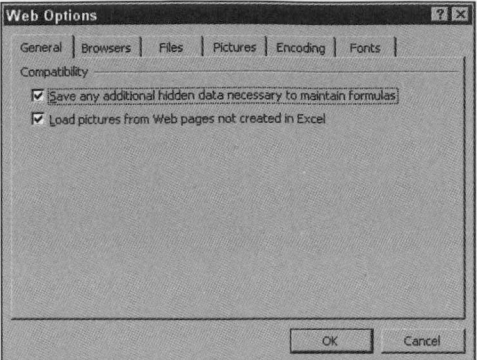

Figure 28-2: Use the Web Options dialog box to set various options for working with HTML files.

Providing interactivity in your Web documents

When you save an Excel workbook in HTML format, you can select an option that makes the file interactive within the browser. This means that the user can perform standard Excel operations directly in the browser. For example, the user can change cells or manipulate data in a pivot table.

Figure 28-3 shows an example of an Excel workbook displayed in Internet Explorer. The user can change the values, and the formulas display the calculated results.

You need to understand that the interactivity is limited. For example, you can't execute macros when an interactive Excel file is displayed in a browser.

Tip

To find the complete list of limitations that apply when an Excel worksheet is saved as a Web page, see the topic "Guidelines and limitations for saving or publishing Web pages" in the Excel online help.

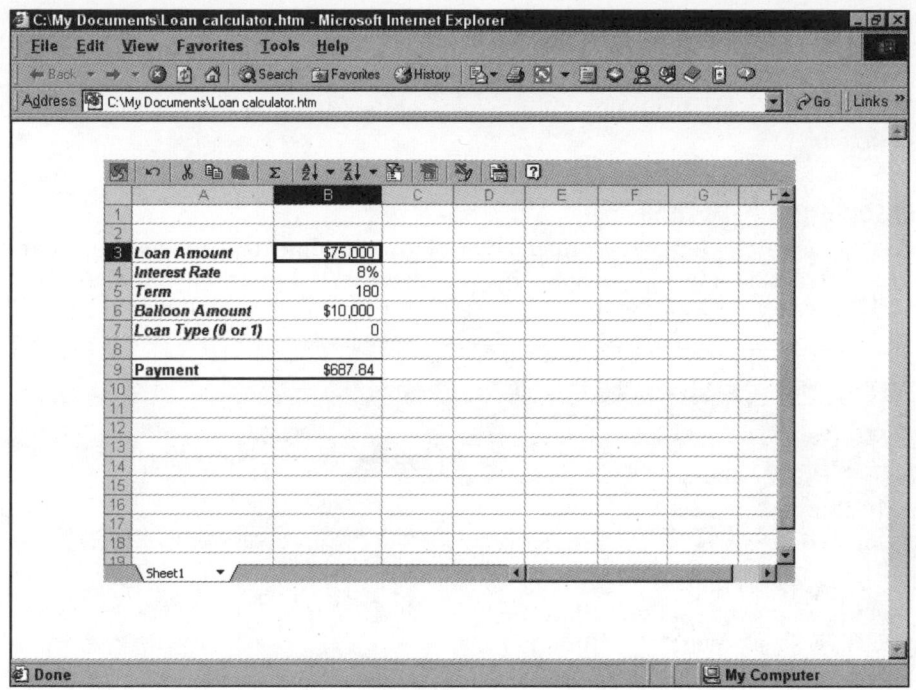

Figure 28-3: This shows an interactive Excel workbook opened in Internet Explorer.

Using the Web toolbar

You use the Web toolbar (shown in Figure 28-4) to move among files (Excel files and HTML documents); this is similar to using a Web browser. You can jump forward or backward among the workbooks and other files that you've visited and add to a "favorites" list the ones that you may use frequently.

Figure 28-4: Use the Web toolbar to browse your Excel files and HTML documents.

Working with hyperlinks

Hyperlinks are shortcuts that provide a quick way to jump to other workbooks and files. You can jump to files on your own computer, your network, and the Internet and Web.

Inserting a hyperlink

You can create hyperlinks from cell text or graphic objects, such as shapes and pictures. To create a text hyperlink, choose the Insert ➪ Hyperlink command (or press Ctrl+K). Excel responds with the Insert Hyperlink dialog box, shown in Figure 28-5.

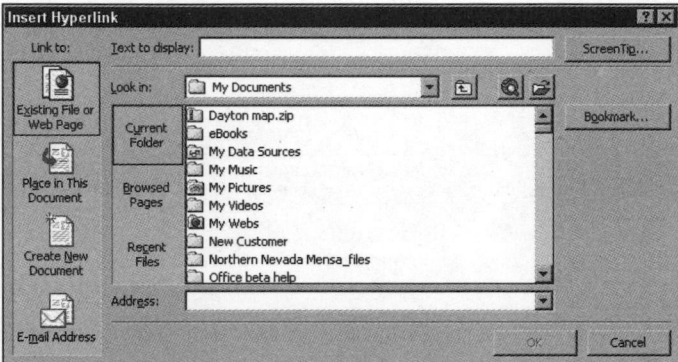

Figure 28-5: Use the Insert Hyperlink dialog box to add hyperlinks to your Excel worksheets.

Select an icon in the Link to column that represents the type of hyperlink you want to create. Then, specify the location for the file that you want to link to. The dialog box will change, depending on the icon selected. Click OK, and Excel creates the hyperlink in the active cell.

Adding a hyperlink to a graphic object works the same way. Add an object to your worksheet by using the Drawing toolbar. Select the object and then choose the Insert ➪ Hyperlink command. Specify the required information as outlined in the previous paragraph.

Using hyperlinks

When working with hyperlinks, remember that Excel attempts to mimic a Web browser. For example, when you click a hyperlink, the hyperlinked document replaces the current document — it takes on the same window size and position. The document that contains the hyperlink is hidden. You can use the Back and Forward buttons on the Web toolbar to activate the documents.

Cross-Reference   If what you really want is to link to information in an Excel workbook file stored on the Internet, use an external reference formula, as discussed in Chapter 26.

Using Web queries

Excel enables you to pull in data contained in an HTML file by performing a Web query. The data is transferred to a worksheet, where you can manipulate it any way you like.

Note Performing a Web query does not actually open the HTML file in Excel—rather, it copies the information from the HTML file.

The best part about a Web query is that Excel remembers where the data came from. Therefore, after you create a Web query, you can "refresh" the query to pull in the most recent data.

Cross-Reference The Web query feature is very similar to performing a normal database query (see Chapter 20). The only difference is that the data is coming from a Web page rather than a database file.

To create a Web query, select Data ➪ Import External Data ➪ New Web Query. Excel displays the New Web Query dialog box, shown in Figure 28-6. To begin, specify the address of the HTML file. The HTML file can be on the Internet, a corporate intranet, or on a local or network drive. Next, click to select the tables you wish to import. Click Import and you get the Import Data dialog box (see Figure 28-7), asking where you want to place the data.

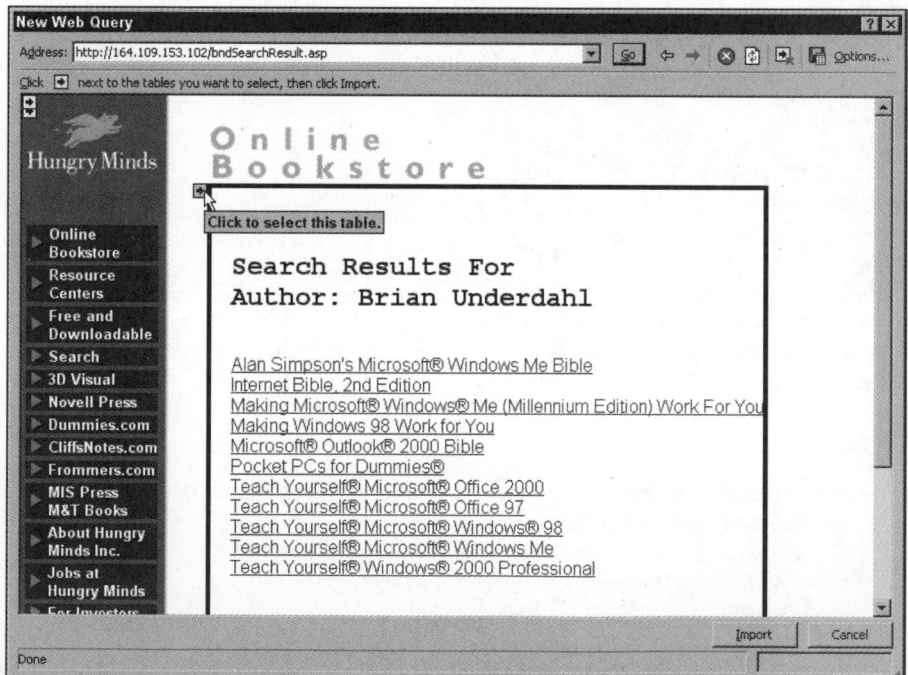

Figure 28-6: Use the New Web Query dialog box to specify the source of the data.

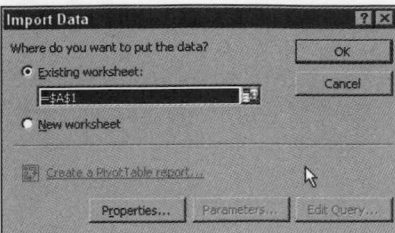

Figure 28-7: Use the Import Data dialog
box to specify the destination for the data.

After you create your Web query, you have some options. Activate any cell in the data range and select Data ➪ Import External Data ➪ Data Range Properties. Or, you can right-click and select the command from the shortcut menu. Either method displays the External Data Range Properties dialog box, shown in Figure 28-8. Adjust the settings to your liking.

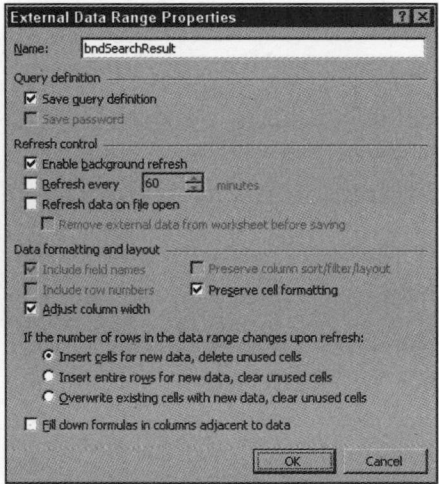

Figure 28-8: Use the External Data
Range Properties dialog box to specify
how Excel handles the imported data.

Tip   Web queries are especially useful for data that is frequently updated — such as stock market quotes.

✦   ✦   ✦

Using Excel in a Workgroup

Networks have become one of the most important productivity enhancements in the PC world. By enabling users to easily share data, networks have made it far easier for people to work together on projects. Excel has a number of features that facilitate this type of cooperation, and those features are the subject of this chapter.

Using Excel on a Network

A computer network consists of a group of PCs that are linked electronically. Users on a network can perform these tasks:

- ◆ Access files on other systems.
- ◆ Share files with other users.
- ◆ Share resources such as printers and fax modems.
- ◆ Communicate with each other electronically.

Excel has tools that enable you to work cooperatively with other Excel users on a single project. You can, for example, send an Excel workbook to other users for their review or to enable them to add their own data before returning the workbook or sending it on to the next person in a routing list. After all the additions have returned to you, Excel can easily incorporate those additions into your master copy of the workbook. In this way, a whole team of Excel users can contribute to a project effectively.

Understanding File Reservations

Networks provide users with the ability to share information stored on other computer systems. Sharing files on a network has two major advantages:

✦ It eliminates the need to have multiple copies of the files stored locally on user PCs.

✦ It ensures that the file is always up to date; for example, if everyone makes changes to the same shared copy of a customer list, there's little likelihood that the portions of the list will be correct while other portions will be obsolete.

Note   Some networks—generally known as client-server networks—designate specific computers as file servers. On these types of networks, the shared data files are normally stored on the file server. Excel doesn't care whether you are working on a client-server or peer-to-peer network (where all the PCs have essentially equal functions).

Some software applications are *multiuser applications*. Most database software applications, for example, enable multiple users to work simultaneously on the same database files. One user may be updating customer records in the database while another is extracting records. But what if a user is updating a customer record and another user wants to make a change to that same record? Multiuser database software contains record-locking safeguards which ensure that only one user at a time can modify a particular record.

Excel is *not* a multiuser application. When you open an Excel file, the entire file is loaded into memory. If the file is accessible to other users, you wouldn't want someone else to change the stored copy of a file that you've opened. If Excel allowed you to open and change a file that someone else on a network has already opened, the following scenario could happen.

Assume that your company keeps its sales information in an Excel file that is stored on a network server. Elaine wants to add this week's data to the file, so she loads it from the server and begins adding new information. A few minutes later, Albert loads the file to correct some errors that he noticed last week. Elaine finishes her work and saves the file. A while later, Albert finishes his corrections and saves the file. Albert's file overwrites the copy that Elaine saved, and her additions are gone.

This scenario *can't happen* because Excel uses a concept known as *file reservation*. When Elaine opens the sales file, she has the reservation for the file. When Albert tries to open the file, Excel informs him that Elaine is using the file. If he insists on opening it, Excel opens the file as *read-only*. In other words, Albert can open the file, but he can't save it under the same name. Figure 29-1 shows the message that Albert receives if he tries to open a file that is in use by someone else.

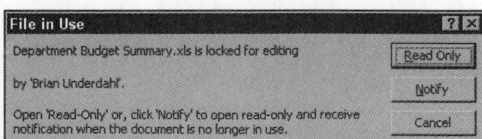

Figure 29-1: The File in Use dialog box appears if you try to open a file that someone else is using.

Albert has three choices:

✦ **Select Cancel, wait a while, and try again.** He may call Elaine and ask her when she expects to be finished.

✦ **Select Read Only.** This lets him open the file to read it, but doesn't let him save changes to the same filename.

✦ **Select Notify, which opens the file as read-only.** Excel pops up a message when Elaine is finished using the file.

Figure 29-2 shows the message that Albert receives when the file is available.

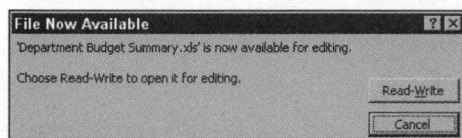

Figure 29-2: The File Now Available dialog box pops up with a new message when the file is available for editing.

> If you select Read Only, you can still save the file, but only by using the File ⇨ Save As command and specifying a different filename or a different location. You could, for example, save a local copy of the file instead of saving it back to the network drive where you opened the file.

Sharing Workbooks

Although Excel isn't a multiuser application, it does support a feature known as *shared workbooks,* which enables multiple users to work on the same workbook simultaneously. Excel keeps track of the changes and provides appropriate prompts to handle conflicts.

Understanding shared workbooks

Although you can share any Excel workbook, only certain workbooks contain information that is appropriate for sharing. The following are examples of workbooks that work well as shared workbooks:

✦ **Project tracking:** You may have a workbook that contains status information for projects. If multiple people are involved in the project, they can make changes and updates to the parts that are relevant.

✦ **Customer lists:** With customer lists, changes usually occur infrequently, but records are added and deleted.

✦ **Consolidations:** You may create a budget workbook in which each department manager is responsible for his or her department's budget. Usually, each department's budget appears on a separate sheet, with one sheet serving as the consolidation sheet.

If you plan to designate a workbook as shared, be aware that you cannot perform any of these actions while sharing the workbook:

✦ Delete worksheets or chart sheets.

✦ Insert or delete a blocks of cells. However, you can insert or delete entire rows and columns.

✦ Merge cells.

✦ Define or apply conditional formats.

✦ Set up or change data-validation restrictions and messages.

✦ Insert or change charts, pictures, drawings, objects, or hyperlinks.

✦ Assign or modify a password to protect individual worksheets or the entire workbook.

✦ Create or modify pivot tables, scenarios, outlines, or data tables.

✦ Insert automatic subtotals.

✦ Make changes to dialog boxes or menus.

✦ Write, change, view, record, or assign macros. However, you can record a macro in a shared workbook that you store in another, unshared workbook.

Tip   You may want to use the Tools ➪ Protection commands to control what users can do while working in a shared workbook.

Designating a workbook as a shared workbook

To designate a workbook as a shared workbook, select Tools ➪ Share Workbook. Excel displays the dialog box that is shown in Figure 29-3. This dialog box has two tabs: Editing and Advanced. In the Editing tab, select the check box to allow changes by multiple users and then click OK. Excel then prompts you to save the workbook.

When you open a shared workbook, the window's title bar displays [Shared]. If you no longer want other users to be able to use the workbook, remove the check mark from the Share Workbook dialog box and save the workbook.

Tip   Whenever you're working with a shared workbook, you can find out whether any other users are working on the workbook. Choose Tools ➪ Share Workbook, and the Share Workbook dialog box lists the names of the other users who have the file open as well as the time that each user opened the workbook.

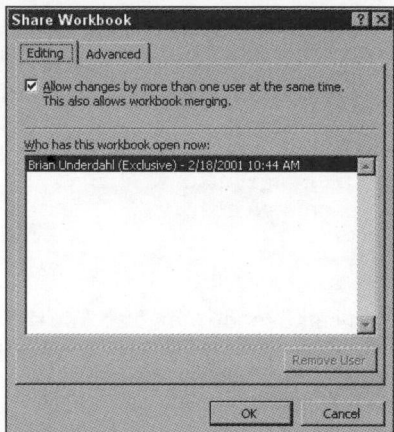

Figure 29-3: Use the Share
Workbook dialog box to control the
sharing of your workbooks.

Controlling the advanced sharing settings

Excel enables you to set options for shared workbooks. Select Tools ➪ Share
Workbook and click the Advanced tab to access these options (see Figure 29-4).

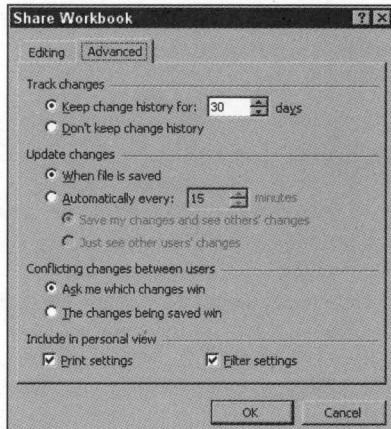

Figure 29-4: Use the Advanced tab
of the Share Workbook dialog box to
set the advanced sharing options for
your workbook.

Tracking changes

Excel can keep track of the workbook's changes — which is known as *change history*. When you designate a workbook as a shared workbook, Excel automatically turns on the change history option, enabling you to view information about previous (and perhaps conflicting) changes to the workbook. You can turn off change history by selecting the option labeled Don't keep change history. You can also specify the number of days for which Excel tracks change history.

Updating changes

While you're working on a shared workbook, you can use the standard File ➪ Save command to update the workbook with your changes. The Update changes settings determine what happens when you save a shared workbook:

✦ **When file is saved:** You receive updates from other users when you save your copy of the shared workbook.

✦ **Automatically every:** Lets you specify a time period for receiving updates from other users of the workbook. You can also specify whether Excel should save your changes automatically, too, or just show you the changes made by other users.

Resolving conflicting changes between users

As you may expect, multiple users working on the same file can result in some conflicts. For example, assume that you're working on a shared customer database workbook and another user also has the workbook open. If you and the other user both make a change to the same cell, a conflict occurs. You can specify the manner in which Excel resolves the conflicts by selecting one of two options in the Advanced tab of the Share Workbook dialog box:

✦ **Ask me which changes win:** If you select this option, Excel displays a dialog box to let you determine how to settle the conflict.

✦ **The changes being saved win:** If you select this option, your changes always take precedence.

Notice that the second option, The changes being saved win, has slightly deceptive wording. Even if the other user saves his changes, any changes you make will automatically override his changes when you save the workbook. This could result in a loss of data because you won't have any warning that you've overwritten another user's changes.

Controlling the Include in personal view settings

The final section of the Advanced tab of the Share Workbook dialog box enables you to specify settings that are specific to your view of the shared workbook. You can choose to use your own print settings and your own data-filtering settings. If you don't place check marks in these check boxes, you can't save your own print and filter settings.

Mailing and Routing Workbooks

Excel provides a few additional workgroup features. To use these features, your system must have one of these items installed:

✦ Office

✦ Microsoft Exchange

✦ A mail system that is compatible with MAPI (Messaging Application Programming Interface)

✦ Lotus cc:Mail

✦ A mail system that is compatible with VIM (Vendor Independent Messaging)

The procedures vary, depending on the mail system that you have installed; for this reason, discussions in the following sections are general in nature.

Mailing a workbook as an e-mail attachment

Electronic mail, or *e-mail,* is commonplace in most offices and is an extremely efficient means of communication. Unlike a telephone, e-mail doesn't rely on the recipient of the message being available when you want to send the message.

In addition to sending messages by e-mail, you can send complete files — including Excel workbooks. Like a growing number of software applications, Excel is *mail-enabled,* which means that you don't have to leave Excel to send a worksheet to someone by e-mail.

To send a copy of your workbook to someone, select File ➪ Send To ➪ Mail Recipient (as Attachment). Excel creates an e-mail message with a copy of the workbook attached, using your default e-mail program; in Figure 29-5, Excel opened Outlook to send the workbook. You send this e-mail message the same way that you send any message — from your e-mail program. You also can send the message to multiple recipients, the same way that you send any e-mail message to multiple recipients.

Note   When you send any file by using an e-mail program, you send a copy of the file. If the recipient makes changes to the notebook, the changes do not appear in your copy of the workbook.

In addition to sending the workbook as an e-mail attachment, you can also select the File ➪ Send To ➪ Mail Recipient command to display the E-mail dialog box, shown in Figure 29-6. When you choose this option, you can choose to send the entire workbook as an attachment or you can send just the current worksheet as the message body.

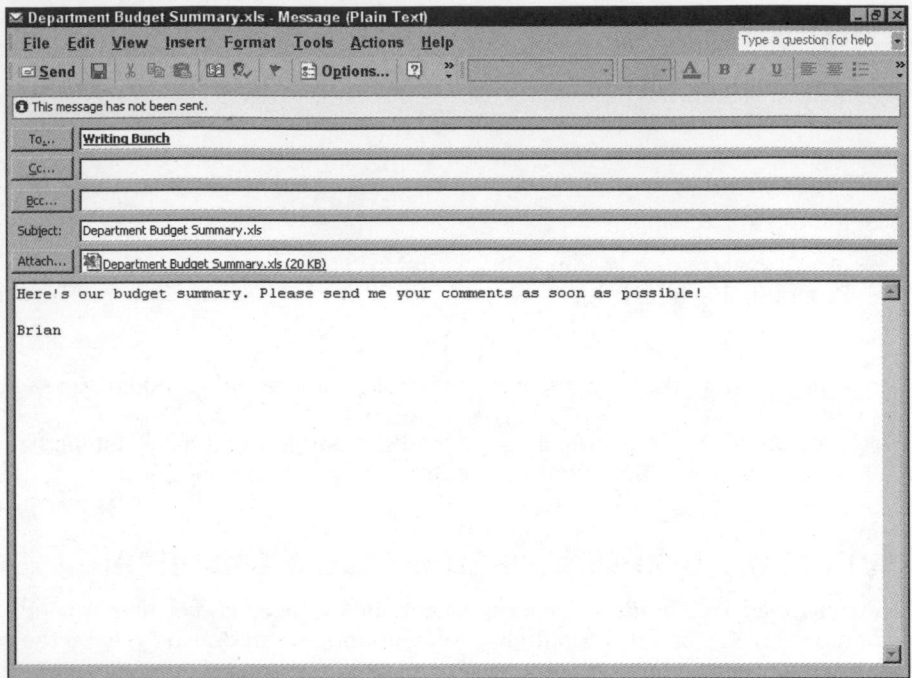

Figure 29-5: You can send a copy of your workbook as an e-mail attachment.

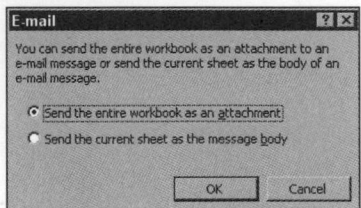

Figure 29-6: You can also send
the current worksheet as the
message body.

 **Tip**

Sending the current worksheet as the message body can be handy if the recipient just needs to do a quick review of some figures or if the recipient might not have Excel available.

In addition to the two options already mentioned, you can choose the File ➪ Send To ➪ Mail Recipient (for Review) command. This command requires that the workbook is shared, and it is intended to make it easy for you to view (and merge, if desired) any comments made by the reviewer.

Routing a workbook to others

If you choose File ➪ Send To ➪ Routing Recipient, Excel enables you to attach a routing slip to a workbook, similar to the one you see in Figure 29-7. Routing a workbook is most useful when you want the first person in the group to review (and possibly edit) the workbook and then want that person to send it to the next person on the list. For example, if you're responsible for your department's budget, you may need input from Alice, and her input may depend on Andy's input. You can set up the workbook and then route it to the others so that they can make their respective additions. When you set up the routing slip, you can tell Excel to return the workbook to you when the routing is finished.

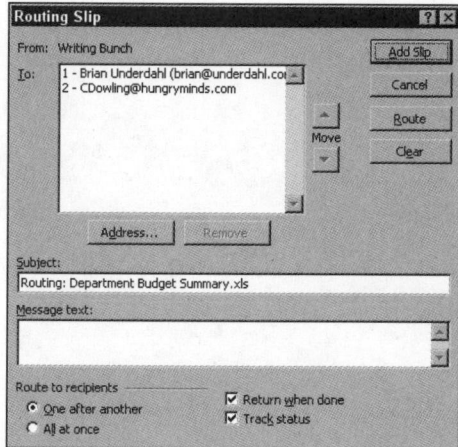

Figure 29-7: You can route a workbook to multiple recipients.

When you route a workbook, you have these two options:

✦ **Sequential routing:** Enables you to route the workbook sequentially to workgroup members. When the first recipient is finished, the workbook goes to the second recipient. When the second recipient is finished, the workbook goes to the third, and so on. When all recipients have received the workbook, it can be returned to you. Choose One after another at the bottom of the Routing Slip dialog box for this type of routing.

✦ **Simultaneous routing:** Enables you to route the workbook to all recipients at the same time. You receive a copy of the workbook from each recipient (not just one copy). This type of routing is useful if you want to solicit comments from a group of coworkers and you want the responses back quickly (you don't want to wait until a single worksheet makes the circuit). Choose All at once at the bottom of the Routing Slip dialog box for this type of routing.

Click Route to route the workbook immediately. If you don't want to route immediately, click Add Slip. Later, when you're ready to route, choose File ➪ Send To ➪ Next Routing Recipient. Either choice places the workbook in the outgoing mail folder of your e-mail program. To actually route the workbook, open your e-mail program to send the message.

Note   Whether you route or attach a workbook to an e-mail message, Excel uses your e-mail program. Because you can send a workbook to a number of people, either as an e-mail attachment or by using a routing slip, the distinction between the two methods lies in the distinction between sequential and simultaneous routing. If you choose simultaneous routing and you don't place a check mark in the Return when done check box, routing and attaching are identical because you can't guarantee a reply to e-mail.

✦   ✦   ✦

Sharing Data with Other Applications

Most Windows applications are designed to work together. The applications in Microsoft Office are an excellent example of this. These programs have a common look and feel, and sharing data among these applications is quite easy. This chapter explores some ways in which you can make use of other applications while working with Excel as well as some ways in which you can use Excel while working with other applications.

Understanding Data Sharing

Besides importing and exporting files, the following are the essential three ways in which you can transfer data to and from other Windows applications:

✦ Copy and paste, using either the Windows clipboard or the Office clipboard. Copying and pasting information creates a static copy of the data.

✦ Create a link so that changes in the source data are reflected in the destination document.

✦ Embed an entire object from one application into another application's document.

This chapter discusses these techniques and shows you how to use them.

Pasting and Linking Data

In several previous chapters, you learned how to copy data between different Excel worksheets, how to link to an external database file, and how to link Excel worksheets using external reference formulas. As useful as these options are, they are by no means the only ways in which you can paste and link data between Excel's worksheets and other types of documents.

Using the clipboards

Whenever Windows is running, you have access to the Windows clipboard—an area of your computer's memory that acts as a shared holding area for information that you have cut or copied from an application. The Windows clipboard works behind the scenes, and you usually aren't aware of it. Whenever you select data and then choose either Edit ➪ Copy or Edit ➪ Cut, the application places the selected data on the Windows clipboard. Like most other Windows applications, Excel can then access the clipboard data if you choose the Edit ➪ Paste command (or the Edit ➪ Paste Special command).

Note   If you copy or cut information while working in an Office application, the application places the copied information on both the Windows clipboard and the Office clipboard. After you copy information to the Windows clipboard, it remains on the Windows clipboard even after you paste it, so you can use it multiple times. However, because the Windows clipboard can hold only one item at a time, when you copy or cut something else, the information previously stored on the Windows clipboard is replaced. The Office clipboard, unlike the Windows clipboard, can hold up to 24 separate selections. The Office clipboard operates in all Office applications; for example, you can copy two selections from Word and three from Excel and paste any or all of them in PowerPoint.

Copying information from one Windows application to another is quite easy. The application that contains the information that you're copying is called the *source* application, and the application to which you're copying the information is called the *destination* application.

The general steps that are required to copy from one application to another are

1. Activate the source document window that contains the information that you want to copy.

2. Select the information by using the mouse or the keyboard.

3. Select Edit ➪ Copy.

4. Activate the destination application. If the program isn't running, you can start it without affecting the contents of the clipboard.

5. Move to the appropriate position in the destination application (where you want to paste the copied material).

6. Select Edit ➪ Paste from the menu in the destination application. If the clipboard contents are not appropriate for pasting, the Paste command is grayed (not available).

In Step 3 in the preceding steps, you also can select Edit ➪ Cut from the source application menu. This step erases your selection from the source application after placing the selection on the clipboard.

Note   If you repeat Step 3 in any Office application, the Office Clipboard task pane appears automatically. If it does not, select View ➪ Task Pane. You may also need to use the Task Pane selector to switch from a different task pane to the Clipboard task pane.

Tip   In Step 6 in the preceding steps, you can sometimes select the Edit ➪ Paste Special command, which displays a dialog box that presents different pasting options.

To see an example of how this works, try copying an Excel chart into a Microsoft Word report. First, select the chart in Excel by clicking it once. Then copy it to the clipboard by choosing Edit ➪ Copy. Next, activate the Word document into which you want to paste the copy of the chart, and move the insertion point to the place where you want the chart to appear. When you select Edit ➪ Paste from the Word menu bar, the chart is pasted from the clipboard and appears in your document (see Figure 30-1).

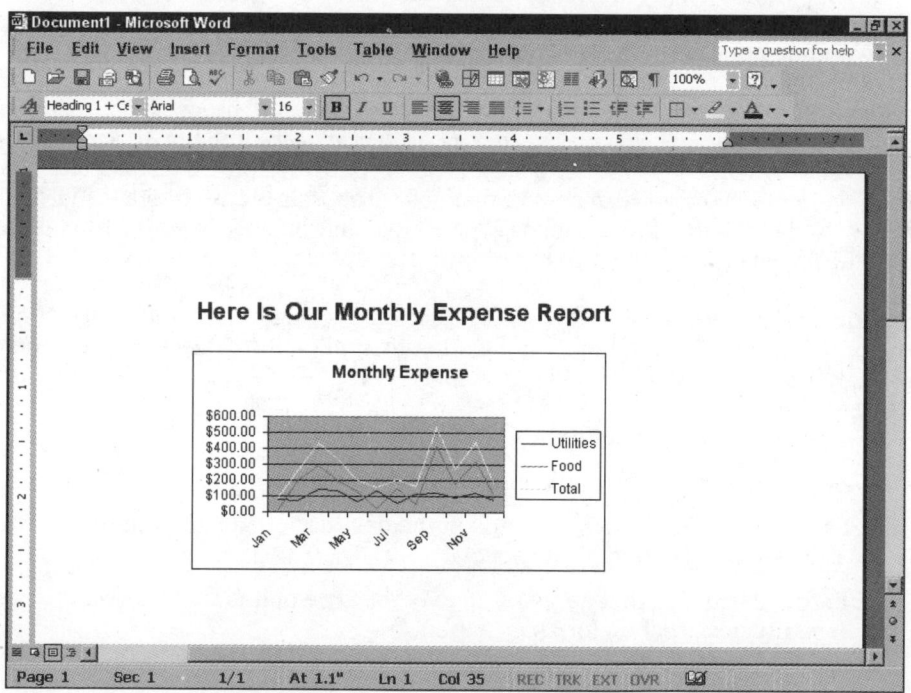

Figure 30-1: An Excel chart has been added to this Word document.

Note   Windows applications vary in the way that they respond to data that you paste from the clipboard. If the Edit ➪ Paste command is not available (is grayed on the menu) in the destination application, the application can't accept the information from the clipboard. If you copy a range of data from Excel to the clipboard and paste it into Word, Word creates a table when you paste the data. Other applications may respond differently to Excel data.

The copy-and-paste technique is static. In other words, no link exists between the information that you copy from the source application and the information that you paste into the destination application. If you're copying from Excel to a word-processing document, for example, the word-processing document *will not* reflect any subsequent changes that you make in your Excel worksheet or charts. Consequently, you have to repeat the copy-and-paste procedure to update the destination document with the source document changes. The next topic presents a way to get around this limitation.

Linking data

If you want to share data that may change, the static copy-and-paste procedure described in the preceding section isn't your best choice. Instead, you can create a dynamic link between the data that you copy from one Windows application to another. In this way, if you change the data in the source document, you don't *also* need to make the changes in the destination document because the link automatically updates the destination document.

When would you want to use this technique? If you generate proposals by using a word processor, for example, you may need to refer to pricing information that you store in an Excel worksheet. If you set up a link between your word-processing document and the Excel worksheet, you can be sure that your proposals always quote the latest prices. Not all Windows applications support dynamic linking, so you must make sure that the application to which you are copying is capable of handling such a link.

Setting up a link from one Windows application to another isn't difficult, although the process varies slightly from application to application. These are the general steps to take:

1. Copy the information to the Clipboard.

2. Switch to the destination application.

3. Select the appropriate command in the destination application to paste a link. This is usually Edit ➪ Paste Special.

4. In the dialog box that appears, specify the type of link that you want to create (see the next section for an example).

Keep in mind the following information when you're using links between two applications:

✦ Not all Windows applications support linking. Furthermore, you can link from, but not to, some programs. When in doubt, consult the documentation for the application with which you're dealing.

✦ When you save an Excel file that has a link, you save the most recent values with the document. When you reopen this document, Excel asks whether you want to update the links.

✦ Links can be broken rather easily. If you move the source document to another directory or save it under a different name, for example, the destination document's application won't be able to update the link.

✦ You can use the Edit ➪ Links command to break a link. After breaking a link, the data remains in the destination document, but is no longer linked to the source document.

✦ In Excel, external links are stored in array formulas, so you can modify a link by editing the array formula.

✦ When Excel is running, it responds to link requests from other applications, unless you have disabled remote requests. If you don't want Excel to respond to link-update requests from other applications, choose Tools ➪ Options, select the General tab, and then place a check mark in the Ignore other applications check box.

Copying Excel data to Word

One of the most frequently used software combinations is a spreadsheet and a word processor. This section discusses the types of links that you can create by using Microsoft Word to create documents that include data from Excel.

Figure 30-2 shows the Paste Special dialog box from Microsoft Word after a range of data has been copied from Excel to the clipboard. The result that you get depends on whether you select the Paste or the Paste link option and on your choice of the type of item to paste. If you select the Paste link option, you can choose to have the information pasted as an icon. If you do so, you can double-click this icon to activate the source worksheet.

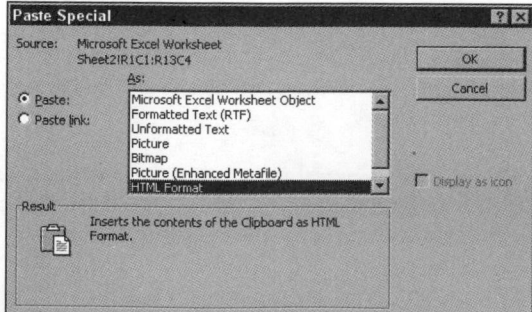

Figure 30-2: Use the Paste Special dialog box to specify the type of link to create.

Pasting without a link

Often, you don't need a link when you copy data. For example, if you're preparing a report in your word processor and you simply want to include a range of data from an Excel worksheet, you probably don't need to create a link.

If you select one of the choices in the Paste Special dialog box with the Paste option selected, the data is pasted without creating a link.

Figure 30-3 shows how a copied range from Excel appears in Word, using three of the paste special formats.

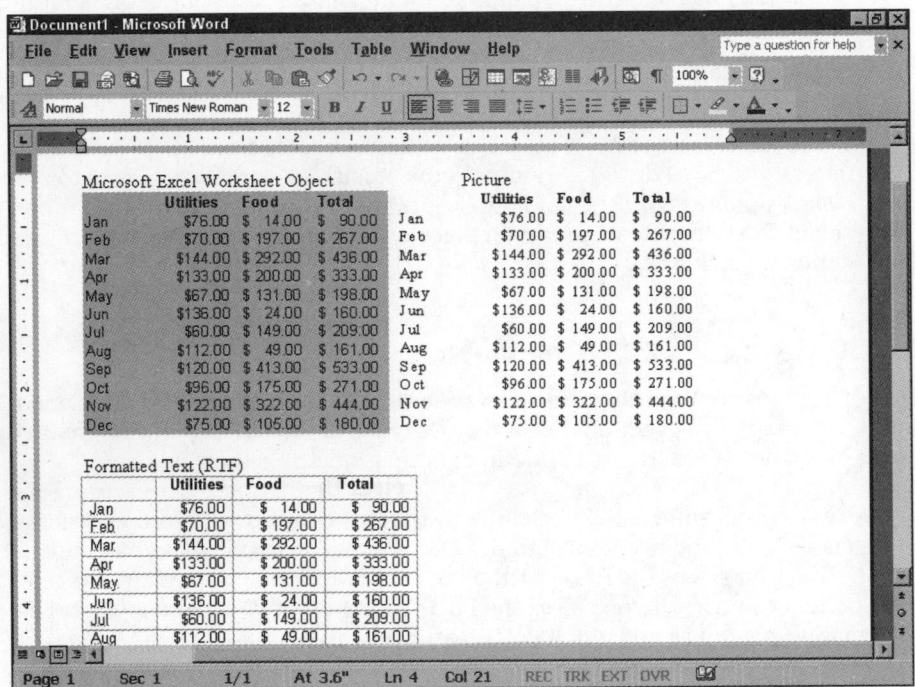

Figure 30-3: The Paste Special format option you choose determines the appearance of the pasted data.

Tip   The pasted data looks the same regardless of whether the Paste or Paste link option is selected.

Some Excel formatting does not transfer when pasted to Word as formatted text. For example, Word doesn't support vertical alignment for table cells (but you can use Word's paragraph formatting commands to apply vertical alignment).

Pasting with a link

If you think the data that you're copying will change, you may want to paste a link. If you paste the data by using the Paste link option in the Paste Special dialog box, you can make changes to the source document, and the changes appear in the destination application (a few seconds of delay may occur). You can test these changes by displaying both applications onscreen, making changes to the source document and watching for them to appear in the destination document.

Embedding Objects in Documents

Using *Object Linking and Embedding* (OLE), you can also embed an object to share information between Windows applications. This technique enables you to insert an object from another program and use that program's editing tools to manipulate it. The OLE objects can be items such as these:

✦ Text documents from other products, such as word processors

✦ Drawings or pictures from other products

✦ Information from special OLE server applications, such as Microsoft Equation

✦ Sound files

✦ Video or animation files

Most major Windows applications support OLE. You can embed an object into your document in either of two ways:

✦ Choose Edit ⇨ Paste Special and then select the "object" choice (if it's available). If you do this, select the Paste option rather than the Paste link option.

✦ Select Insert ⇨ Object.

Tip Some applications — such as those in Microsoft Office — allow you to embed an object by dragging it from one application to another.

The following sections discuss these two methods and provide a few examples using Excel and Word.

Embedding an Excel range in a Word document

This example embeds in a Word document the Excel range shown in Figure 30-4.

To start, select A1:D13 and copy the range to the clipboard. Then activate (or start) Word, open the document in which you want to embed the range, and move the insertion point to the location in the document where you want the table to appear. Choose Word's Edit ⇨ Paste Special command. Select the Paste option (not Paste link) and choose the Microsoft Excel Worksheet Object format (see Figure 30-5). Click OK and the range appears in the Word document.

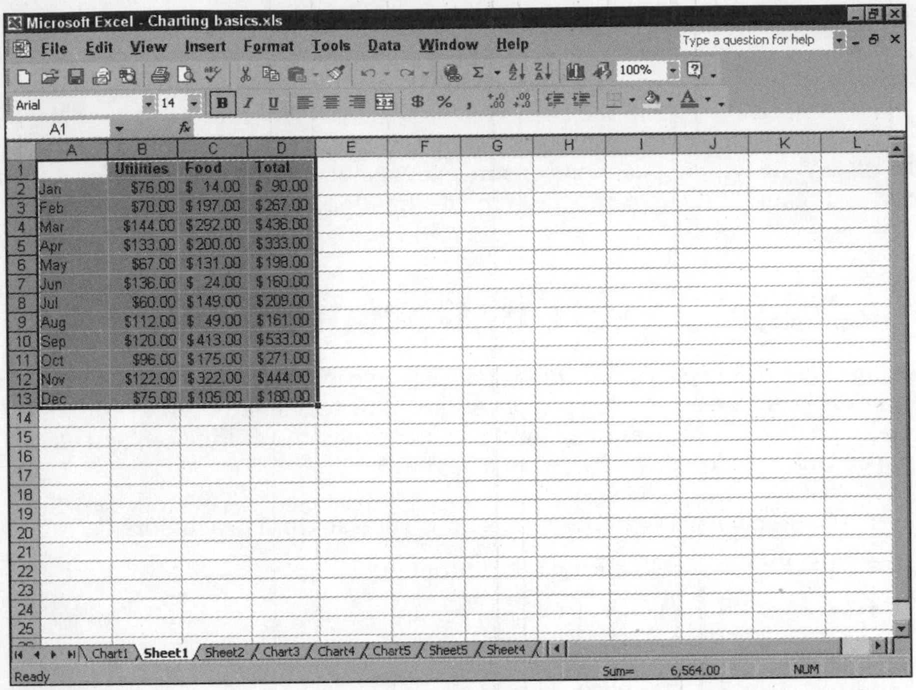

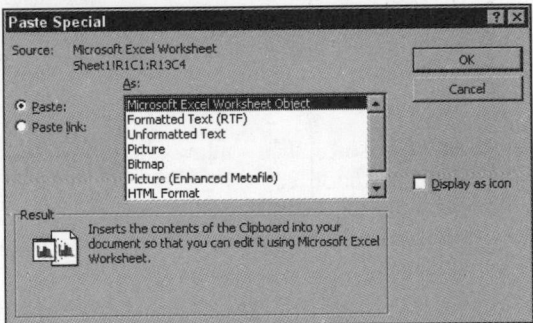

Figure 30-4: This worksheet includes a range that will be embedded in a Word document.

Figure 30-5: Choose Microsoft Excel Worksheet Object to create an embedded object in your Word document.

The pasted object is not a standard Word table. For example, you can't select or format individual cells in the table. Furthermore, it's not linked to the Excel source range. If you change a value in the Excel worksheet, the change does not appear in the embedded object in the Word document.

If you double-click the object, however, you notice something unusual: Word's menus and toolbars change to those used by Excel. In addition, the embedded object appears with Excel's familiar row and column borders. In other words, you can edit this object *in place* by using Excel's commands. Figure 30-6 shows how this looks. To return to Word, just click anywhere in the Word document.

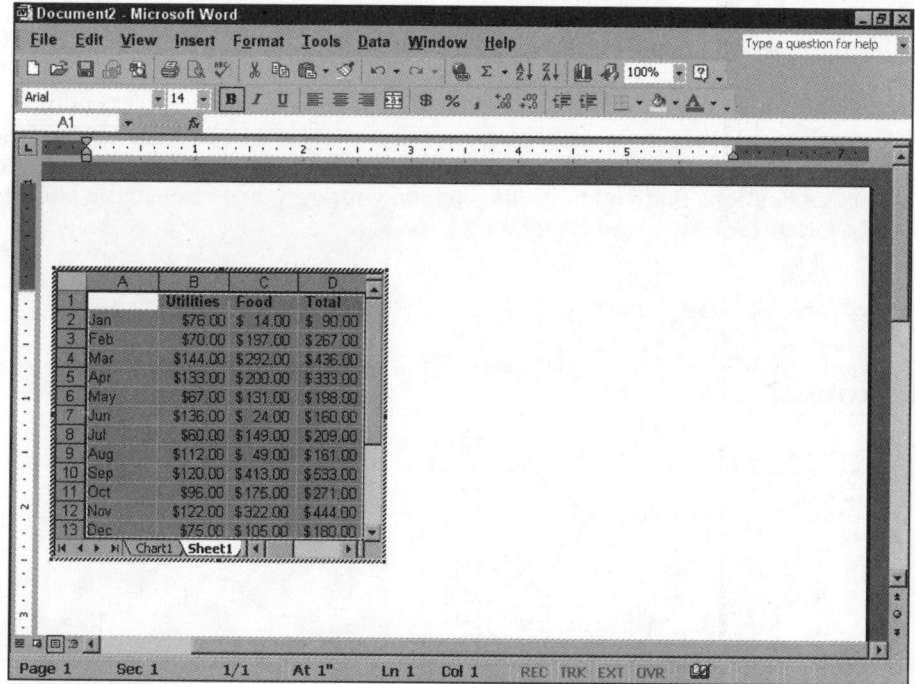

Figure 30-6: Double-clicking the embedded Excel object enables you to edit it in place. Note that Word now displays Excel's menus and toolbars.

Caution   Remember that no link is involved here. If you make changes to the embedded object in Word, these changes do not appear in the original Excel worksheet. The embedded object is completely independent from the original source.

Using this technique, you have access to all of Excel's features while you are still in Word.

Tip   You can accomplish the embedding previously described by selecting the range in Excel and then dragging it to your Word document. In fact, you can use the Windows desktop as an intermediary storage location. For example, you can drag a range from Excel to the desktop and create a scrap. Then, you can drag this scrap into your Word document. The result is an embedded Excel object.

Creating a new Excel object in Word

The preceding example embeds a range from an existing Excel worksheet into a Word document. This section demonstrates how to create a new (empty) Excel object in Word. This may be useful if you're creating a report and need to insert a table of values that doesn't exist in a worksheet.

Tip   You could insert a normal Word table, but you can take advantage of Excel's formulas and functions in an embedded Excel worksheet.

To create a new Excel object in a Word document, choose Insert ➪ Object in Word. Word responds with the Object dialog box, shown in Figure 30-7. The Create New tab lists the types of objects that you can create (the contents of the list depends on the applications that you have installed on your system). Choose the Microsoft Excel Worksheet option and click OK.

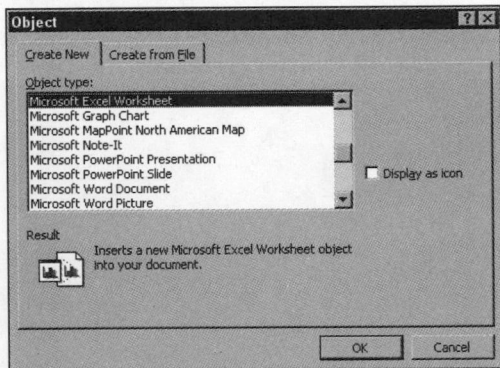

Figure 30-7: Select Microsoft Excel Worksheet to embed a blank worksheet into your Word document.

Word inserts an empty Excel worksheet object into the document and activates it for you, as shown in Figure 30-8. You have full access to Excel commands, so you can enter whatever you want into the worksheet object. After you finish, click anywhere in the Word document. You can, of course, double-click this object at any time to make changes or additions.

You can change the size of the object while it's activated by dragging any of the sizing handles that appear on the borders of the object. You also can crop the object so that when it isn't activated, the object displays only cells that contain information. To crop an object in Word, select the object so that you can see sizing handles. Then, display Word's Picture toolbar (right-click any toolbar button and choose Picture). Click the Cropping tool (it looks like a pair of plus signs), and then drag any sizing handle on the object.

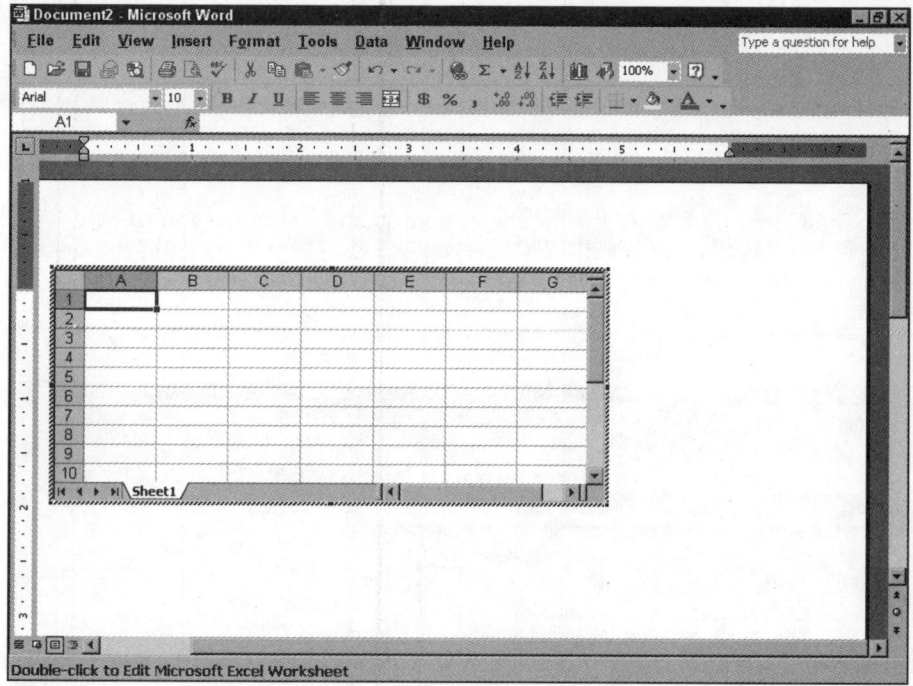

Figure 30-8: This Word document now contains an empty Excel worksheet object.

Note

Even if you crop an Excel worksheet object in Word, double-clicking the object gives you access to all rows and columns in Excel. Cropping changes only the displayed area of the object.

Tip

When you click outside the Excel worksheet object, the worksheet's scrollbars, tabs, gridlines, and so on will disappear. Any data that you have added will remain visible, however.

Embedding objects in an Excel worksheet

The preceding examples involve embedding Excel objects in a Word document. The same procedures can be used to embed other objects into an Excel worksheet.

For example, if you have an Excel workbook that requires a great amount of explanatory text, you have several choices:

✦ You can enter the text into cells. This, however, is tedious and doesn't allow much formatting.

✦ You can use a text box. This is a good alternative, but it doesn't offer many formatting features.

✦ You can embed a Word document in your worksheet. This gives you full access to all of Word's formatting features.

To embed an empty Word document into an Excel worksheet, choose Excel's Insert ⇨ Object command. In the Object dialog box, click the Create New tab and select Microsoft Word Document from the Object type list.

The result is a blank Word document, activated and ready for you to enter text. Notice that Word's menus and toolbars replace Excel's menus and toolbars. You can resize the document as you like, and the words wrap accordingly. Figure 30-9 shows an example of a Word document embedded in an Excel worksheet.

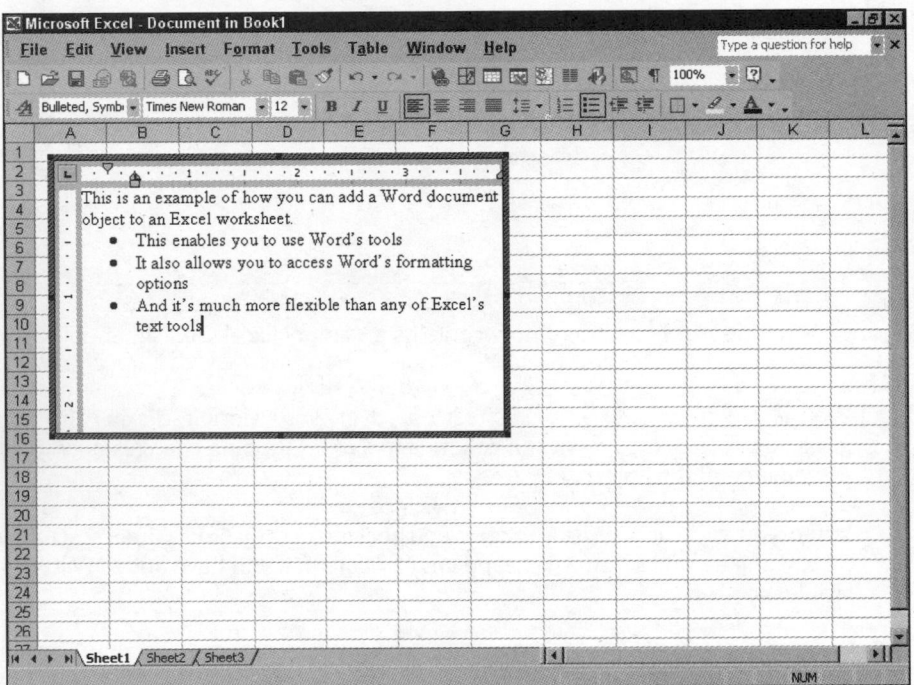

Figure 30-9: You can embed a Word document in an Excel worksheet.

You can embed many other types of objects, including audio clips, video clips, MIDI sequences, and even an entire Microsoft PowerPoint presentation.

When you embed a video clip, Excel doesn't store the actual video clip file in the Excel document. Rather, Excel stores a pointer to the original file. If, for some reason, you want to embed the complete video clip file, you can use the Object Packager application. Be aware, however, that video clip files are typically quite large, and opening and saving the workbook will take lots of time.

Microsoft Office includes several additional applications that you may find useful. For example, you can embed a Microsoft Equation object in an Excel document to graphically illustrate a formula that you use in a worksheet, or you can embed a Microsoft WordArt object to create a fancy title for an Excel report.

Tip   Some of the object types listed in the Object dialog box can result in quite useful and interesting items when inserted into an Excel worksheet. If you're not sure what an object type is, try adding the object to a blank Excel workbook to see what is available.

✦   ✦   ✦

Making Your Worksheets Error-Free

♦ ♦ ♦ ♦

In This Chapter

Understanding
worksheet problems

Using formula
AutoCorrect

Tracing cell
relationships

Checking spelling
and related features

Learning about
an unfamiliar
spreadsheet

♦ ♦ ♦ ♦

You want your Excel worksheets to produce accurate
results. Unfortunately, it can be difficult to be certain
that the results are correct — especially if you deal with large,
complex worksheets. This chapter shows you the tools and
techniques you need to help you identify and correct errors.

Understanding Worksheet Problems

When you understand what can go wrong in an Excel worksheet, it's much easier to spot and correct errors. In fact,
knowing what can cause errors makes it far easier for you to
prevent problems from happening in the first place.

Making a change in a worksheet — even a relatively minor
change — may produce a ripple effect that introduces errors
in other cells. For example, accidentally entering a value into
a cell that formerly held a formula is all too easy to do. This
can have a major impact on other formulas, and you may not
discover the problem until long after you make the change.
Or, you may *never* discover the problem.

Tip   Multicell array formulas are a little harder to accidentally
overwrite than nonarray formulas. You may want to refer to
Chapter 16 for a refresher on array formulas.

An Excel worksheet can have many types of problems. Some
problems, such as a formula that returns an error value, are
immediately apparent. Other problems are more subtle. For
example, if a formula was constructed using faulty logic, it may
never return an error value — it simply returns the wrong values. If you're lucky, you can discover the problem and correct it.

Common problems that occur in worksheets are

- ✦ Incorrect approach to a problem
- ✦ Faulty logic in a formula
- ✦ Formulas that return error values
- ✦ Circular references
- ✦ Spelling mistakes
- ✦ A worksheet is new to you, and you can't figure out how it works

Excel provides tools to help you identify and correct some of these problems. In the remaining sections, you learn about these tools.

Using Formula AutoCorrect

When you enter a formula that has a syntax error, Excel attempts to determine the problem and offers a suggested correction.

For example, if you enter the following formula (which has a syntax error), Excel displays the dialog box that is shown in Figure 31-1:

```
=SUM(A1:A12)/3B
```

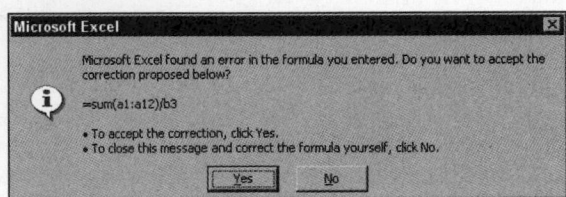

Figure 31-1: Excel can often offer a suggestion about how to correct a formula.

Caution   Be careful about accepting corrections for your formulas from Excel because it doesn't always guess correctly. For example, if you enter the following formula (which has mismatched parentheses):

```
=AVERAGE(SUM(A1:A12,SUM(B1:B12))
```

Excel proposes the following correction to the formula:

```
=AVERAGE(SUM(A1:A12,SUM(B1:B12)))
```

You may be tempted to accept the suggestion without even thinking. In this case, the proposed formula is syntactically correct—but may not be what you intended.

Tracing Cell Relationships

Excel has several useful tools that can help you track down errors and logical flaws in your worksheets. This section discusses these tools:

✦ Go To Special dialog box

✦ Excel's built-in auditing tools

These tools are useful for debugging formulas. As you probably realize by now, the formulas in a worksheet can become complicated and can refer (directly or indirectly) to hundreds or thousands of other cells. Trying to isolate a problem in a tangled web of formulas can be frustrating.

Before discussing these features, you need to be familiar with two concepts:

✦ **Cell precedents:** Applicable only to cells that contain a formula. A formula cell's precedents are all the cells that contribute to the formula's result. A *direct* precedent is a cell that you use directly in the formula. An *indirect* precedent is a cell that isn't used directly in the formula, but is used by a cell to which you refer in the formula.

✦ **Cell dependents:** Formula cells that depend on a particular cell. Again, the formula cell can be a direct dependent or an indirect dependent.

Often, identifying cell precedents for a formula cell sheds light on why the formula isn't working correctly. On the other hand, knowing which formula cells depend on a particular cell is often helpful. For example, if you're about to delete a formula, you may want to check whether it has any dependents.

Using the Go To Special dialog box

The Go To Special dialog box can be useful because it enables you to specify the type of cells that you want Excel to select. To display this dialog box, choose Edit ➪ Go To (or press Ctrl+G). The Go To dialog box appears. Click the Special button, which displays the Go To Special dialog box, as shown in Figure 31-2.

 **Note**   If you select a range before choosing Edit ➪ Go To, the command looks only at the selected cells. If only a single cell is selected, the command operates on the entire worksheet.

You can use this dialog box to select cells of a certain type—which is often helpful in identifying errors. For example, if you choose the Formulas option, Excel selects all the cells that contain a formula. If you zoom the worksheet out to a small size, you can get a good idea of the worksheet's organization (see Figure 31-3). It may also help you spot a common error: a formula that you overwrote with a value. If you find a cell that's not selected amid a group of selected formula cells, chances are good that the cell formerly contained a formula that has been replaced by a value.

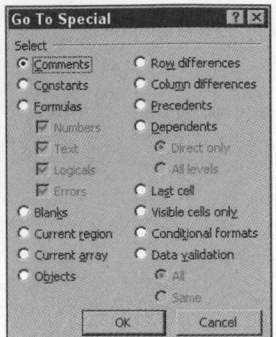

Figure 31-2: Use the Go To Special dialog box to locate specific types of cells in the worksheet.

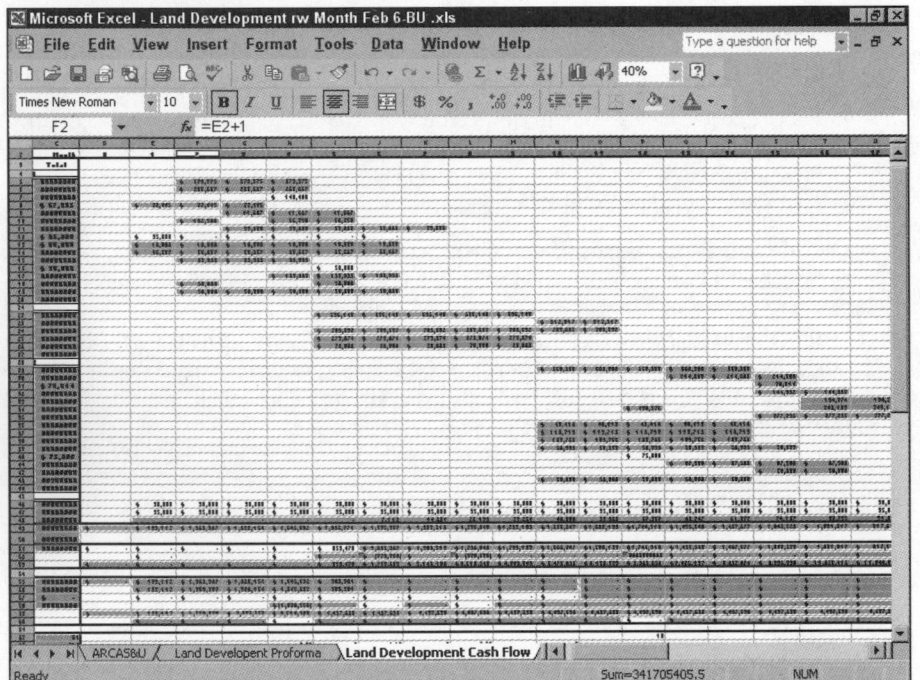

Figure 31-3: Zooming out and selecting all formula cells can give you a good overview of how the worksheet is designed.

> You can also use the Go To Special dialog box to identify cell precedents and dependents. In this case, Excel selects all cells that qualify. In either case, you can choose whether to display direct precedents or all levels.

Excel has shortcut keys that you can use to select precedents and dependents. These keys are listed in Table 31-1.

Table 31-1
Shortcut Keys to Select Precedents and Dependents

Key Combination	What It Selects
Ctrl+[	Direct precedents
Ctrl+Shift+[	All precedents
Ctrl+]	Direct dependents
Ctrl+Shift+]	All dependents

You also can select a formula cell's direct dependents by double-clicking the cell. This technique, however, works only when you turn off the Edit directly in cell option on the Edit tab of the Options dialog box.

Using Excel's Formula Auditing tools

Excel provides a set of interactive auditing tools that you may find helpful. Access these tools either by selecting Tools ➪ Formula Auditing (which results in a submenu with additional choices) or by using the Formula Auditing toolbar, shown in Figure 31-4.

Figure 31-4: Use the Formula Auditing toolbar to determine how cells in a worksheet are related.

> When you edit a cell that contains a formula, Excel color-codes the cell and range references in the formula and outlines the cells and ranges using corresponding colors. Therefore, you can see at a glance the cells that are used in the formula. You can also manipulate the colored outline to change the cell or range reference. To change the references that are used, drag the outline's border.

The tools on the Formula Auditing toolbar, from left to right, are

✦ **Error Checking:** Checks for errors in the current worksheet and displays a dialog box advising if any errors were found.

✦ **Trace Precedents:** Draws arrows to indicate a formula cell's precedents. Click this multiple times to see additional levels of precedents.

✦ **Remove Precedent Arrows:** Removes the most recently placed set of precedent arrows.

✦ **Trace Dependents:** Draws arrows to indicate a cell's dependents. Click this multiple times to see additional levels of dependents.

✦ **Remove Dependent Arrows:** Removes the most recently placed set of dependent arrows.

✦ **Remove All Arrows:** Removes all precedent and dependent arrows from the worksheet.

✦ **Trace Error:** Draws arrows from a cell that contains an error to the cells that may have caused the error.

✦ **New Comment:** Inserts a comment for the active cell. This really doesn't have much to do with auditing. It lets you attach a comment to a cell.

✦ **Circle Invalid Data:** Draws a circle around all the cells that contain invalid data. This applies only to cells that have validation criteria specified with the Data ➪ Validation command.

✦ **Clear Validation Circles:** Removes the circles that are drawn around cells that contain invalid data.

✦ **Show Watch Window:** Displays the Watch Window so that you can keep track of the value of specified cells. The Watch Window is simply a small box that allows you to see the values of cells even if those cells do not currently appear onscreen.

✦ **Evaluate Formula:** Displays the Evaluate Formula dialog box so that you can view the formula and formula results in the selected cell. If the cell contains a complex formula, you can evaluate individual sections of the formula independently.

These tools can identify precedents and dependents by drawing arrows (known as *cell tracers*) on the worksheet, as shown in Figure 31-5. In this case, cell C20 was selected and then the Trace Precedents toolbar button was clicked twice. Excel drew lines to identify the cells used by the formula in C20.

Tip   This type of interactive tracing is often more revealing when the worksheet is zoomed out to display a larger area, as shown in Figure 31-5.

The best way to learn about these tools is to use them. Start with a worksheet that has formulas and experiment with the various buttons on the Auditing toolbar.

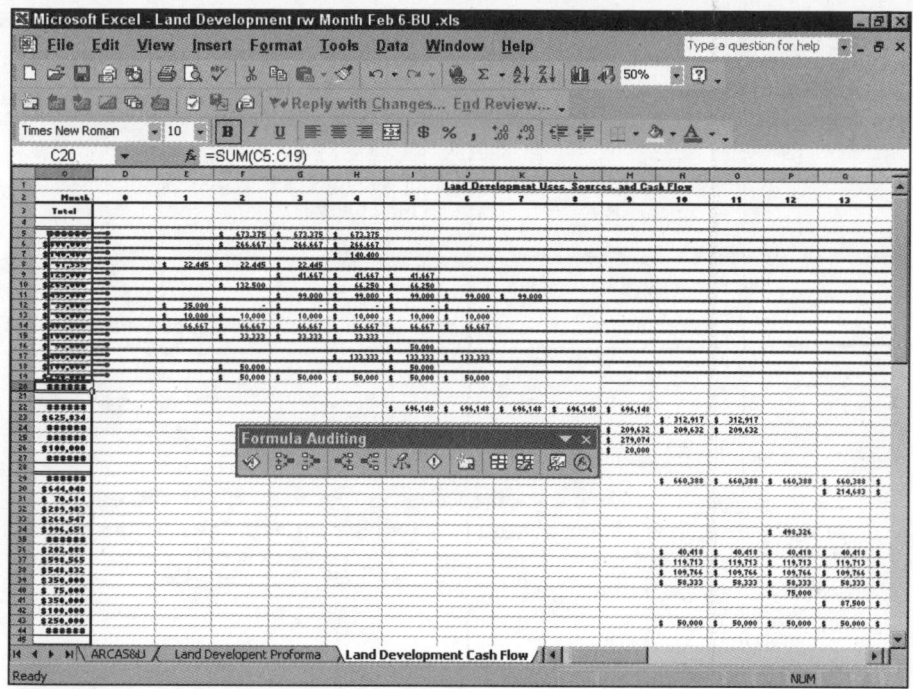

Figure 31-5: You can use the Trace Precedents toolbar button to indicate a cell's precedents.

Tracing error values

The Trace Error button on the Auditing toolbar helps you to identify the cell that is causing an error value to appear. Often, an error in one cell is the result of an error in a precedent cell. Activate a cell that contains an error and click the Trace Error button. Excel draws arrows to indicate the error source.

Table 31-2 lists the types of error values that may appear in a cell that has a formula. The Trace Error button works with all these errors.

| | Table 31-2 |
| | **Excel Error Values** |

Error Value	Explanation
#DIV/0!	The formula is trying to divide by zero. This also occurs when the formula attempts to divide by a cell that is empty.
#NAME?	The formula uses a name that Excel doesn't recognize. This can happen if you delete a name that's used in the formula or if you have unmatched quotation marks when using text.

Continued

	Table 31-2 *(continued)*
Error Value	**Explanation**
#N/A	The formula refers to an empty cell range.
#NULL!	The formula uses an intersection of two ranges that do not intersect (this concept is described later in the chapter).
#NUM!	A problem with a value exists — for example, you specified a negative number where a positive number is required.
#REF!	The formula refers to a cell that is not valid. This can happen if the cell has been deleted from the worksheet.
#VALUE!	The formula includes an argument or operand of the wrong type.

Tip Use the Watch Window to track the values in specified cells as you are correcting formula errors. This will enable you to determine when the cell no longer contains an error value — and is especially useful if the precedent cells are located a long distance from the formula cell.

Checking Spelling and Related Features

Excel includes several handy tools to help you with the nonnumeric problems — those related to spelling and words. If you also use Word, you'll find these tools quite familiar.

Spell-checking your worksheets

If you use a word processing program, you probably run its spelling checker before printing an important document. Spelling mistakes can be just as embarrassing when they appear in a spreadsheet. Fortunately, Microsoft includes a spelling checker with Excel. You can access the spelling checker by using any of these methods:

✦ Selecting Tools ➪ Spelling

✦ Clicking the Spelling button on the Standard toolbar

✦ Pressing F7

Note When you activate the spelling checker, Excel may ask you if you would like to begin at the beginning of the sheet. To avoid this prompt, you can select the range of cells you'd like to check before you activate the spelling checker.

If the spelling checker finds any words it does not recognize as correct, it will display the Spelling dialog box, as shown in Figure 31-6.

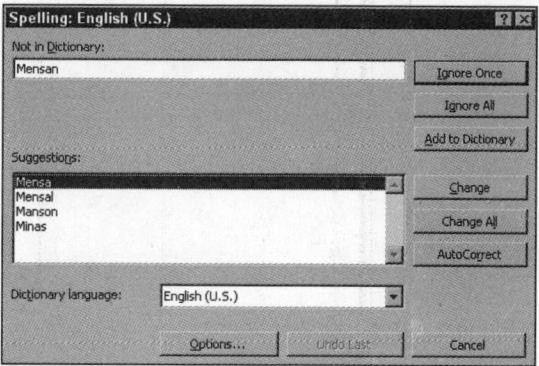

Figure 31-6: Use the Spelling dialog box to locate and correct spelling errors in your worksheets.

Note   The spell checking checks cell contents, notes, text in graphic objects and charts, and page headers and footers. Even the contents of hidden rows and columns are checked.

The Spelling dialog box works similarly to other spelling checkers with which you may be familiar. If Excel encounters a word that isn't in the current dictionary or that is misspelled, it offers a list of suggestions. You can respond by clicking one of these buttons:

✦ **Ignore Once:** Ignores the word and continues the spell check.

✦ **Ignore All:** Ignores the word and all subsequent occurrences of it.

✦ **Add to Dictionary:** Adds the word to the dictionary.

✦ **Change:** Changes the word to the selected word in the Suggestions box.

✦ **Change All:** Changes the word to the selected word in the Change to edit box and changes all subsequent occurrences of it without asking.

✦ **AutoCorrect:** Adds the misspelled word and its correct spelling to the AutoCorrect list.

Using AutoCorrect

AutoCorrect is a handy feature that automatically corrects common typing mistakes. You can also add to the list some words that Excel corrects automatically. The AutoCorrect dialog box appears in Figure 31-7. You access this feature by choosing Tools ➪ AutoCorrect Options.

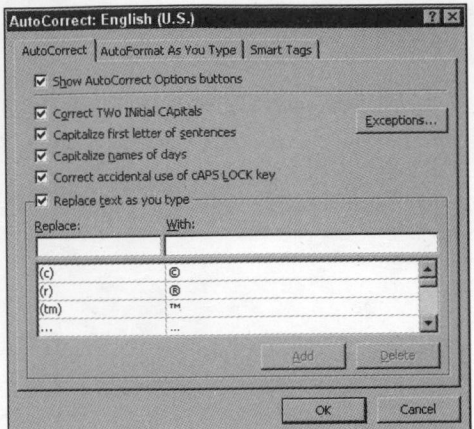

Figure 31-7: Use the AutoCorrect dialog box to control the spelling corrections Excel makes automatically.

This dialog box has several options:

✦ **Correct TWo INitial CApitals:** Automatically corrects words with two initial uppercase letters. For example, BUdget is converted to Budget. This is a common mistake among fast typists. You can click the Exceptions button to specify a list of exceptions to this rule.

✦ **Capitalize first letter of sentences:** Capitalizes the first letter in a sentence.

✦ **Capitalize names of days:** Capitalizes the days of the week. If you enter *monday,* Excel converts it to *Monday.*

✦ **Correct accidental use of cAPS LOCK key:** Corrects errors caused if you accidentally hit the CapsLock key while typing.

✦ **Replace text as you type:** AutoCorrect automatically changes incorrect words as you type them.

Excel includes a long list of AutoCorrect entries for commonly misspelled words. In addition, it has AutoCorrect entries for some symbols. For example, *(c)* is replaced with (c) and *(r)* is replaced with (r). You can also add your own AutoCorrect entries. For example, if you find that you frequently misspell the word *January* as *Janruary,* you can create an AutoCorrect entry so that it's changed automatically. To create a new AutoCorrect entry, enter the misspelled word in the Replace box and the correctly spelled word in the With box. You can also delete entries you no longer need.

Tip

You also can use the AutoCorrect feature to create shortcuts for commonly used words or phrases. For example, if you work for a company named Consolidated Data Processing Corporation, you can create an AutoCorrect entry for an abbreviation, such as cdp. Then, whenever you type cdp, Excel automatically changes it to

Consolidated Data Processing Corporation. Just make sure that you don't use a combination of characters that might normally appear in your text.

You can use the AutoFormat As You Type tab of the AutoCorrect dialog box to control how Excel treats Internet and network addresses. Use the Smart Tags tab to make Excel show Smart Tags — similar to hyperlinks — for certain types of data in your worksheets. The types of Smart Tags Excel recognizes vary depending on the types of software that are installed on your system.

Using AutoComplete

AutoComplete automatically finishes a word as soon as Excel recognizes it. For Excel to recognize the word, it must appear elsewhere in the same column. This feature is most useful when you're entering a list that contains repeated text in a column. For example, assume that you're entering customer data in a list and one of the fields is City. Whenever you start typing, Excel searches the other entries in the column. If it finds a match, it completes the entry for you. Press Enter to accept it. If Excel guesses incorrectly, keep typing to ignore the suggestion.

 **Tip** If AutoComplete isn't working, select Tools ➪ Options, click the Edit tab, and check the box labeled Enable AutoComplete for cell values.

You also can display a list of all items in a column by right-clicking and choosing Pick From List from the shortcut menu. Excel then displays a list box of all entries that are in the column. Click the one that you want, and Excel enters it into the cell for you.

Learning About an Unfamiliar Spreadsheet

When you develop a workbook yourself, you likely have a thorough understanding of how it's put together. But if you receive an unfamiliar workbook from someone else, it may be difficult to understand how it all fits together — especially if it's large.

Although every worksheet is different, a few techniques can help you become familiar with an unfamiliar workbook.

First, identify the bottom-line cell or cells. Often, a worksheet is designed to produce results in a single cell or in a range of cells. After you identify this cell or range, you should be able to use the cell-tracing techniques described earlier in this chapter to determine the cell relationships.

Zooming out for the big picture

It's often helpful to use Excel's zoom feature to zoom out to get an overview of the worksheet's layout. You can select View ➪ Zoom to display the Zoom dialog box so that you can see even more of the worksheet. When a workbook is zoomed out, you can use all the normal commands. For example, you can use the Edit ➪ Go To command to select a name range. Or, you can use the options that are available in the Go To Special dialog box (explained previously in this chapter) to select formula cells, constants, or other special cell types.

Viewing formulas

You can become familiar with an unfamiliar workbook by displaying the formulas rather than the results of the formulas. Select Tools ➪ Options, and check the box labeled Formulas on the View tab. You may want to create a new window for the workbook (Window ➪ New Window) before issuing this command. That way, you can see the formulas in one window and the results in the other.

Figure 31-8 shows an example. The window on the top shows the normal view (formula results). The window on the bottom displays the formulas.

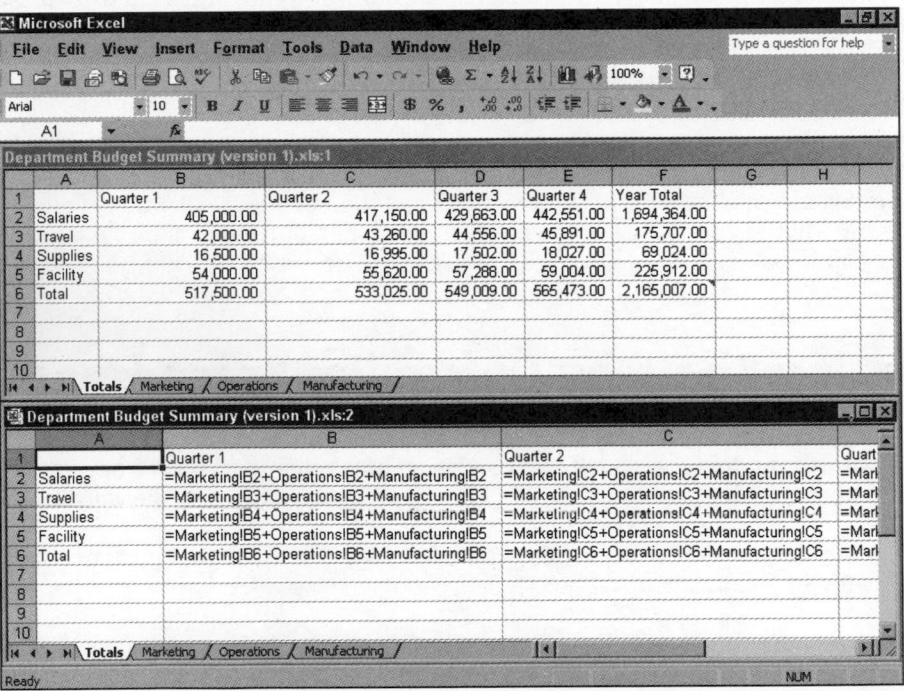

Figure 31-8: You can view the formulas in place of the formula results to learn more about a worksheet.

 **Tip**   When you print a view that is displaying the formulas rather than the results, the printout will also show the formulas.

Pasting a list of names

If the worksheet uses named ranges, you may want to create a list of the names and their references. Move the cell pointer to an empty area of the worksheet and choose Insert ⇨ Name ⇨ Paste. Excel responds with its Paste Name dialog box. Click the Paste List button to paste a list of the names and their references into the workbook.

Tip   The list of ranges names combined with a printout of the formulas can prove to be extremely valuable documentation for any important worksheet.

✦   ✦   ✦

Programming Excel with VBA

If you've ever wanted to do a bit more, or to automate routine operations so you don't always have to perform boring, repetitious tasks manually, this part is for you. This part is also aimed at those Excel users who want to develop Excel-based applications for other users. VBA — Visual Basic for Applications — is the powerful programming language that you can use for these tasks as well as for more esoteric purposes, such as developing that specialized worksheet function you simply can't find in Excel.

Introducing Visual Basic for Applications

Visual Basic for Applications (VBA) is a powerful programming language that you can use to add automation, new features, or even customized functions to your Excel workbooks. With an understanding of VBA, you have a tool at your disposal that enables you to create sophisticated applications that can be easy to use and that can save you considerable amounts of time. This chapter introduces you to the basics of VBA so that you can get even more from Excel.

Understanding Visual Basic for Applications

VBA is best thought of as Microsoft's common application scripting language; it's included with all Office applications — and even applications from other vendors. Therefore, if you master VBA using Excel, you'll be able to jump right in and write macros for other Microsoft (and non-Microsoft) products. Even better, you'll be able to create complete solutions that use features across various applications.

Following is a quick-and-dirty summary of what VBA is all about:

✦ You perform actions in VBA by executing VBA code.

✦ You write (or record) VBA code, which is stored in a VBA module.

VBA modules are stored in an Excel workbook, but you view or edit a module using the Visual Basic Editor (VBE).

Object Models

The secret to using VBA with other applications lies in understanding the object model for each application. VBA, after all, simply manipulates objects, and each product (Excel, Word, Access, PowerPoint, and so forth) has its own, unique object model. You can program an application using the objects that the application exposes.

Excel's object model, for example, exposes several very powerful data analysis objects, such as worksheets, charts, pivot tables, and scenarios, as well as numerous mathematical, financial, engineering, and general business functions. With VBA, you can work with these objects and develop automated procedures. As you work with VBA in Excel, you'll gradually build an understanding of the object model. Warning: VBA will be very confusing at first. Eventually, however, the pieces will come together, and all of a sudden you'll realize that you've mastered it!

✦ A VBA module consists of procedures.

A procedure is basically computer code that performs some action on or with objects. Here's an example of a simple procedure called Test:

```
Sub Test()
    Sum = 1 + 1
    MsgBox "The answer is " & Sum
End Sub
```

✦ A VBA module can also have function procedures.

A function procedure returns a single value. A function can be called from another VBA procedure or used in a worksheet formula. Here's an example of a function named AddTwo:

```
Function AddTwo(arg1, arg2)
    AddTwo = arg1 + arg2
End Function
```

✦ VBA manipulates objects contained in its host application (in this case, Excel).

Excel provides you with more than 100 classes of objects to manipulate. Examples of objects include a workbook, a worksheet, a range on a worksheet, a chart, and a drawn rectangle. Many, many more objects are at your disposal, and you can manipulate them using VBA code.

✦ Object classes are arranged in a hierarchy.

Objects can act as containers for other objects. For example, Excel is an object called Application, and it contains other objects, such as Workbook and CommandBar objects. The Workbook object can contain other objects, such as Worksheet objects and Chart objects. A Worksheet object can contain objects such as Range objects, PivotTable objects, and so on. The arrangement of these objects is referred to as Excel's *object model*.

✦ Like objects form a collection.

For example, the Worksheets collection consists of all the worksheets in a particular workbook. The CommandBars collection consists of all CommandBar objects. Collections are objects in themselves.

✦ When you refer to a contained or member object, you specify its position in the object hierarchy using a period as a separator between the container and the member.

For example, you can refer to a workbook named Book1.xls as:

```
Application.Workbooks("Book1.xls")
```

This refers to the Book1.xls workbook in the Workbooks collection. The Workbooks collection is contained in the Excel Application object. Extending this to another level, you can refer to Sheet1 in Book1 as:

```
Application.Workbooks("Book1.xls").Worksheets("Sheet1")
```

You can take it to still another level and refer to a specific cell as follows:

```
Application.Workbooks("Book1.xls").Worksheets("Sheet1").Range
("A1")
```

✦ If you omit a specific reference to an object, Excel uses the active objects.

If Book1 is the active workbook, the preceding reference can be simplified as:

```
Worksheets("Sheet1").Range("A1")
```

If you know that Sheet1 is the active sheet, you can simplify the reference even more:

```
Range("A1")
```

✦ Objects have properties.

A property can be thought of as a *setting* for an object. For example, a range object has properties such as Value and Name. A chart object has properties such as HasTitle and Type. You can use VBA to determine object properties and also to change them.

✦ You refer to properties by combining the object with the property, separated by a period.

For example, you can refer to the value in cell A1 on Sheet1 as:

```
Worksheets("Sheet1").Range("A1").Value
```

✦ You can assign values to VBA variables.

To assign the value in cell A1 on Sheet1 to a variable called *Interest,* use the following VBA statement:

```
Interest = Worksheets("Sheet1").Range("A1").Value
```

✦ Objects have methods.

A *method* is an action that is performed with the object. For example, one of the methods for a `Range` object is `ClearContents`. This method clears the contents of the range.

✦ You specify methods by combining the object with the method, separated by a period.

For example, to clear the contents of cell A1 on the active worksheet, use:

```
Range("A1").ClearContents
```

✦ VBA also includes all the constructs of modern programming languages, including arrays, looping, and so on.

Believe it or not, the preceding section pretty much describes VBA. Now it's just a matter of learning the details, which is the subject of the rest of this chapter.

Introducing the Visual Basic Editor

In Excel 5 and Excel 95, a VBA module appeared as a separate sheet in a workbook. Beginning with Excel 97, VBA modules no longer show up as sheets in a workbook. Instead, you use the Visual Basic Editor (VBE) to view and work with VBA modules.

Note   VBA modules are still stored with workbook files; they just aren't visible unless you activate the VBE.

The VBE is a separate application that works seamlessly with Excel. By *seamlessly*, we mean that Excel takes care of the details of opening the VBE when you need it. You can't run VBE separately; Excel must be running in order for the VBE to run.

Activating the VBE

When you're working in Excel, you can use any of these techniques to switch to the VBE:

✦ Press Alt+F11.

✦ Select Tools ➪ Macro ➪ Visual Basic Editor.

✦ Click the Visual Basic Editor button, which is located on the Visual Basic toolbar.

Note   Don't confuse the Visual Basic Editor with the Microsoft Script Editor. These are two entirely different animals. The Script Editor is used to edit HTML scripts written in VBScript or JavaScript. The Script Editor is not discussed in this book.

Figure 32-1 shows the VBE. Chances are, your VBE window won't look *exactly* like the window shown in the figure. This window is highly customizable—you can hide windows, change their sizes, "dock" them, rearrange them, and so on.

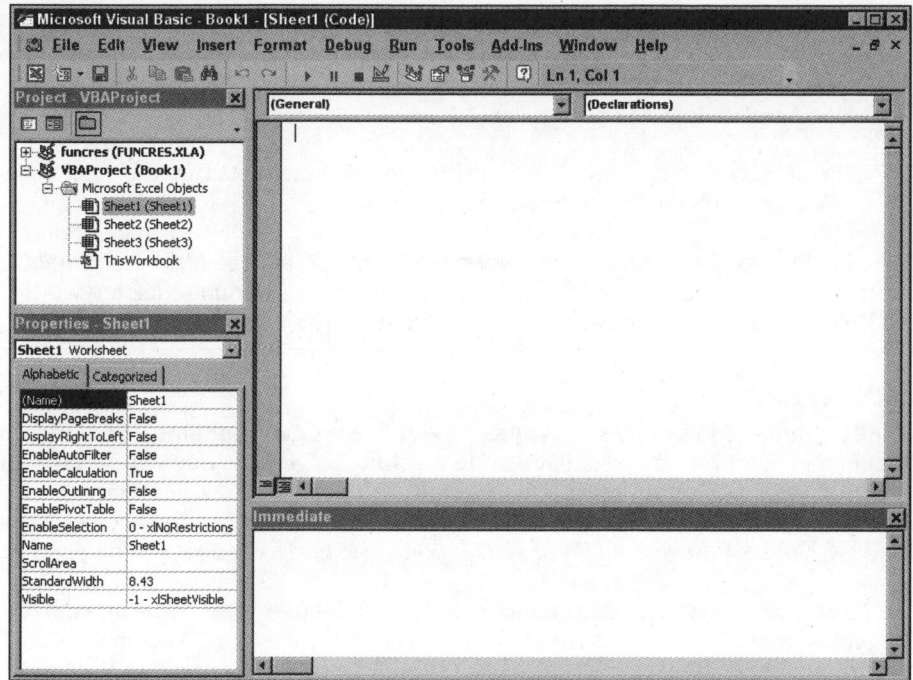

Figure 32-1: You use the Visual Basic Editor window to work with VBA code.

Identifying the VBE windows

The VBE consists of a number of parts. The sections that follow briefly describe some of the key components.

Menu bar

The VBE menu bar works like every other menu bar you've encountered. It contains commands that you use to work with the various components in the VBE. Many of the menu commands have shortcut keys associated with them. For example, the View ➪ Immediate Window command has a shortcut key of Ctrl+G.

Tip   The VBE also features shortcut menus. As you'll discover, right-clicking virtually anything in a VBE window displays a shortcut menu of common commands.

Toolbars

The Standard toolbar is directly under the menu bar by default. VBE toolbars work just like those in Excel: You can customize toolbars, move them around, display other toolbars, and so forth. Use the View ➪ Toolbars ➪ Customize command to work with VBE toolbars.

Project Explorer window

The Project Explorer window displays a tree diagram that consists of every work-book that is currently open in Excel (including add-ins and hidden workbooks). Each workbook is known as a *project*.

The Project Explorer window is discussed in more detail in the next section ("Working with the Project Explorer").

If the Project Explorer window is not visible, press Ctrl+R. To hide the Project Explorer window, click the Close button in its title bar (or right-click anywhere in the Project Explorer window, and select Hide from the shortcut menu).

Code window

A code window (sometimes known as a module window) contains VBA code. Every item in a project has an associated code window. To view a code window for an object, double-click the object in the Project Explorer window. For example, to view the code window for the Sheet1 object, double-click Sheet1 in the Project Explorer window. Unless you've added some VBA code, the code window will be empty.

Code windows are discussed later on in this chapter (see "Working with Code Windows").

Immediate window

The Immediate window is most useful for executing VBA statements directly, test-ing statements, and debugging your code. This window may or may not be visible. If the Immediate window isn't visible, press Ctrl+G. To close the Immediate window, click the Close button in its title bar (or right-click anywhere in the Immediate win-dow and select Hide from the shortcut menu).

Working with the Project Explorer

When you're working in the VBE, each Excel workbook and add-in that's currently open is considered a project. You can think of a project as a collection of objects arranged as an outline. You can "expand" a project by clicking the plus sign (+) at the left of the project's name in the Project Explorer window. You "contract" a pro-ject by clicking the minus sign (–) to the left of a project's name. Figure 32-2 shows a Project Explorer window with three projects listed (one add-in and two workbooks).

If you try to expand a project that's protected with a password, you'll be prompted to enter the password.

If you have many workbooks and add-ins loaded, the Project Explorer window may be a bit overwhelming. Unfortunately, it's not possible to hide projects in the Project Explorer window. However, you'll probably want to keep the project out-lines contracted if you're not working with them.

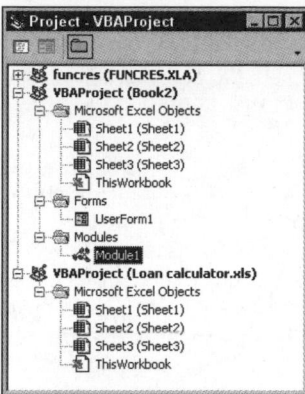

Figure 32-2: This Project Explorer window has three projects listed.

Every project expands to show at least one "node" called Microsoft Excel Objects. This node expands to show an item for each worksheet and chart sheet in the workbook (each sheet is considered an object) and another object called `ThisWorkbook` (which represents the `ActiveWorkbook` object). If the project has any VBA modules, the project listing also shows a Modules node, and the modules are listed there. A project may also contain a node called `Forms`, which contains `UserForm` objects (also known as custom dialog boxes).

Adding a new VBA module

To add a new VBA module to a project, select the project's name in the Project Explorer window, and choose Insert ⇨ Module. Or you can right-click the project's name, and choose Insert ⇨ Module from the shortcut menu.

Tip

When you record a macro, Excel automatically inserts a VBA module to hold the recorded code.

Removing a VBA module

If you need to remove a VBA module from a project, select the module's name in the Project Explorer window and choose File ⇨ Remove *xxx* (where *xxx* is the name of the module). Or you can right-click the module's name, and choose Remove *xxx* from the shortcut menu. You'll be asked whether you want to export the module before removing it. See the next section for details.

Exporting and importing objects

Every object in a project can be saved to a separate file. Saving an individual object in a project is known as *exporting*. And it stands to reason that you can also *import* objects into a project. Exporting and importing objects might be useful if you want to use a particular object (such as a VBA module or a UserForm) in a different project.

To export an object, select it in the Project Explorer window, and choose File ➪ Export File (or press Ctrl+E). You'll get a dialog box that asks for a filename. Note that the object remains in the project (only a copy of it is exported). If you export a UserForm object, any code associated with the UserForm is also exported.

To import a file into a project, select the project's name in the Explorer window, and choose File ➪ Import File. You'll get a dialog box that asks for a file. You can import only a file that has been exported using the File ➪ Export File command.

 **Tip**

If you would like to copy a module or UserForm object to another project, it's not really necessary to export and then import the object. Make sure that both projects are open. Then simply activate the Project Explorer, press Ctrl, and drag the object from one project to the other.

Working with code windows

As you become proficient with VBA, you'll be spending *lots* of time working in code windows. Each object in a project has an associated code window. To summarize, these objects can be

✦ The workbook itself (ThisWorkbook in the Project window)

✦ A worksheet or chart sheet in a workbook (for example, Sheet1 or Chart1 in the Project window)

✦ A VBA module

✦ A class module (a special type of module that lets you create new object classes)

✦ A UserForm

Minimizing and maximizing windows

At any given time, VBE may have lots of code windows. Code windows are much like worksheet windows in Excel. You can minimize them, maximize them, hide them, rearrange them, and so forth. Most people find it much easier to maximize the code window that they're working on. Doing so enables you to see more code and keeps you from getting distracted. To maximize a code window, click the maximize button in the window's title bar or just double-click the title bar. To restore a code window, making it nonmaximized, click the restore button in the window's title bar.

Minimizing a code window gets it out of the way. You can also click the Close button in a code window's title bar to close the window completely. To open it again, just double-click the appropriate object in the Project Explorer window.

The VBE doesn't let you close a workbook. You must reactivate Excel and close it from there. You can, however, use the Immediate window to close a workbook or add-in. Just activate the Immediate window, type a VBA statement similar to the following, and press Enter:

```
Workbooks("myaddin.xla").Close
```

This statement executes the `Close` method of the `Workbook` object, which closes a workbook.

Storing VBA code

In general, a code window can hold four types of code:

- ✦ **Sub procedures:** A *procedure* is a set of instructions that performs some action.

- ✦ **Function procedures:** A *function* is a set of instructions that returns a single value or an array (similar in concept to a worksheet function, such as SUM).

- ✦ **Property procedures:** These are special procedures used in class modules.

- ✦ **Declarations:** A *declaration* is information about a variable that you provide to VBA. For example, you can declare the data type for variables you plan to use.

A single VBA module can store any number of Sub procedures, function procedures, and declarations. How you organize a VBA module is completely up to you. Some people prefer to keep all their VBA code for an application in a single VBA module; others like to split up the code into several different modules.

Although you have lots of flexibility regarding where to store your VBA code, some restrictions exist. Event-handler procedures must be located in the code window for the object that responds to the event. For example, if you write a procedure that executes when the workbook is opened, that procedure must be located in the code window for the ThisWorkbook object, and the procedure must have a special name.

This concept will become clearer when we discuss events (Chapter 39) and UserForms (Chapters 37 and 38).

Entering VBA code

Before you can do anything meaningful, you must have some VBA code in a code window. You can add code to a VBA module in three ways:

- ✦ Enter the code by typing it from your keyboard.

- ✦ Use Excel's macro-recorder feature to record your actions and convert them into VBA code.

- ✦ Copy the code from another module and paste it into the module you are working in.

Entering code manually

Sometimes, the most direct route is the best. Entering code directly involves typing the code using your keyboard. Entering and editing text in a VBA module works just as you would expect. You can select text, copy it or cut it, and then paste it to another location.

 **Tip**   You can use the Tab key to indent the lines that logically belong together — for example, the conditional statements between an If and an End If statement. This isn't really necessary, but it makes the code easier to read, so it's a good habit to acquire.

A single instruction in VBA can be as long as you need it to be. For readability's sake, however, you might want to break a lengthy instruction into two or more lines. To do so, end the line with a space followed by an underscore character; then, press Enter, and continue the instruction on the following line. The following code, for example, is a single statement split over four lines:

```
MsgBox "Can't find " & UCase(SHORTCUTMENUFILE) _
    & vbCrLf & vbCrLf & "The file should be located in  _
    " & ThisWorkbook.Path & vbCrLf & vbCrLf & _
    "You may need to reinstall BudgetMan", vbCritical, APPNAME
```

Notice that the last three lines of this statement are indented. Doing so is optional, but it helps clarify the fact that these four lines are, in fact, a single statement.

 **Tip**   Like Excel, the VBE has multiple levels of Undo and Redo. Therefore, if you find that you deleted an instruction that you shouldn't have, you can click the Undo button (or press Ctrl+Z) repeatedly until the instruction comes back. After undoing, you can press F4 to redo changes that were previously undone.

Try this: Insert a VBA module into a project, and then enter the following statements into the code window of the module:

```
Sub SayHello()
    Msg = "Is your name " & Application.UserName & "?"
    Ans = MsgBox(Msg, vbYesNo)
    If Ans = vbNo Then
        MsgBox "Oh, never mind."
    Else
        MsgBox "I must be clairvoyant!"
    End If
End Sub
```

Figure 32-3 shows how this looks in a VBA module.

 **Note**   As you enter the code, you might notice that the VBE makes some adjustments to the text you enter. For example, if you omit the space before or after an equal sign (=), VBE inserts the space for you. In addition, the color of some of the text is changed. This is all perfectly normal, and you'll appreciate it later.

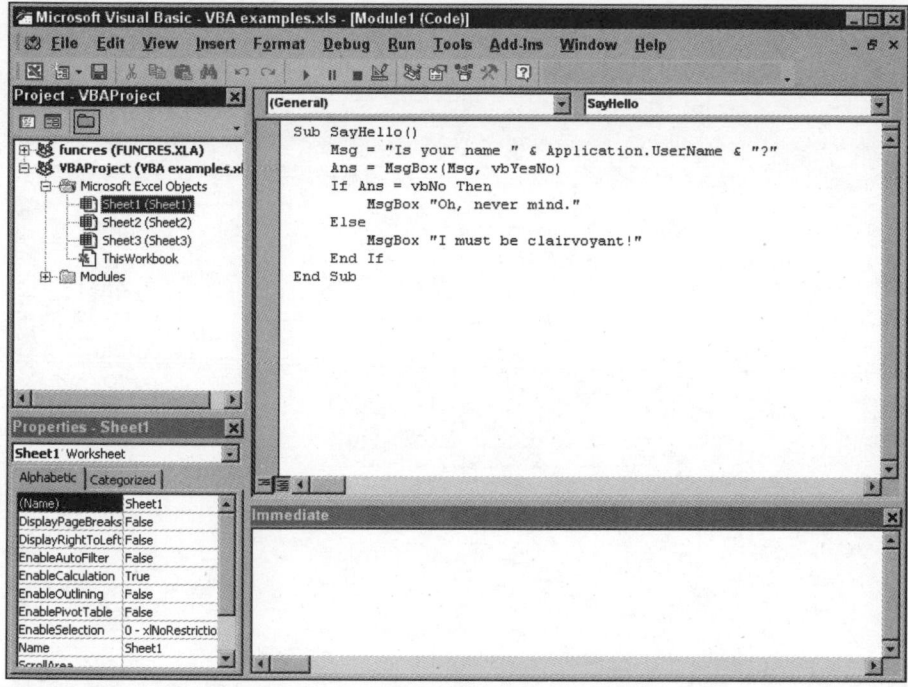

Figure 32-3: Here is an example of a simple VBA procedure.

To execute the SayHello procedure, make sure that the cursor is located anywhere within the text you typed. Then do any of the following:

✦ Press F5.

✦ Select Run ➪ Run Sub/UserForm.

✦ Click the Run Sub/UserForm button on the Standard toolbar.

If you entered the code correctly, the procedure will execute, and you can respond to a simple dialog box (see Figure 32-4). Notice that Excel is activated when the macro executes. At this point, it's not important that you understand how the code works; that becomes clear later in this chapter and in subsequent chapters.

Tip   Most of the time, you'll be executing your macros from Excel. Often, however, it's more efficient to test your macro by running it directly from the VBE.

What you did was write a VBA procedure (also known as a *macro*). When you issued the command to execute the macro, the VBE quickly compiled the code and executed it. In other words, each instruction was evaluated, and Excel simply did what it was told to do. You can execute this macro any number of times, although it tends to lose its appeal after a while.

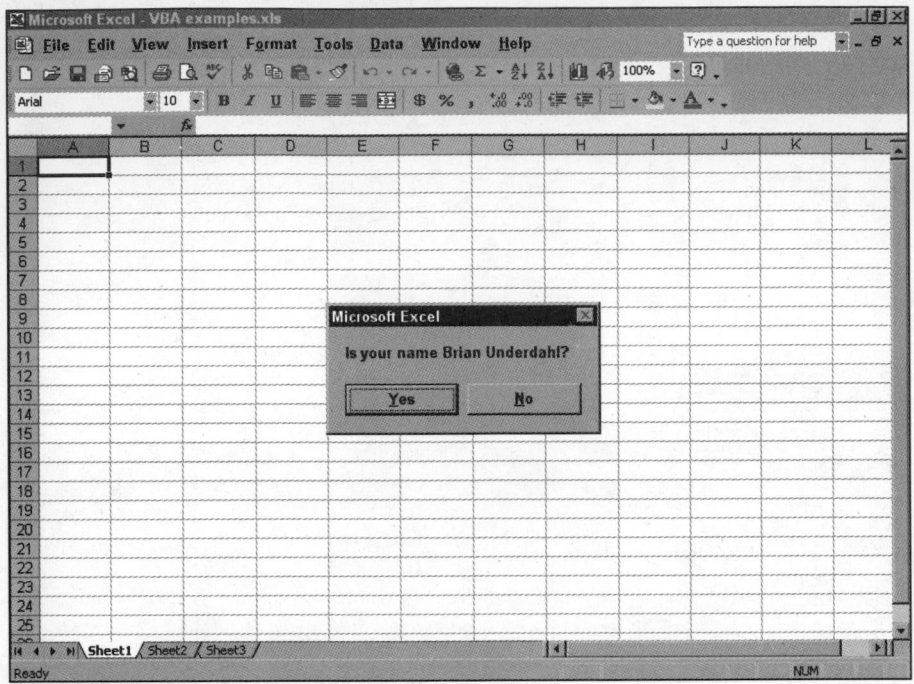

Figure 32-4: This shows the result of running the example VBA procedure.

For the record, this simple procedure uses these concepts (all of which are discussed later):

✦ Declaring a procedure (the first line)

✦ Assigning a value to variables (Msg and Ans)

✦ Concatenating strings (using the & operator)

✦ Using a built-in VBA function (MsgBox)

✦ Using built-in VBA constants (vbYesNo and vbNo)

✦ Using an If-Then-Else construct

✦ Ending a procedure (the last line)

Using the macro recorder

Another way to get code into a VBA module is to record your actions using Excel's macro recorder.

Note No matter how hard you try, you have absolutely no way to record the SayHello procedure shown previously. As you'll see, recording macros is very useful, but it has its limitations. In fact, when you record a macro you almost always need to make some adjustments or enter some code manually.

The following steps show you how to record a macro that simply changes the page setup to Landscape orientation. If you want to try this, start with a blank workbook and follow these steps:

1. Activate a worksheet in the workbook (any worksheet will do).

2. Select the Tools ⇨ Macro ⇨ Record New Macro command.

   Excel displays its Record Macro dialog box.

3. Click OK to accept the defaults.

   Excel automatically inserts a new VBA module into the project. From this point on, Excel converts your actions into VBA code. While recording, Excel displays the word *Recording* in the status bar and also displays a miniature floating toolbar that contains two toolbar buttons (Stop Recording and Relative Reference).

4. Select the File ⇨ Page Setup command.

   Excel displays its Page Setup dialog box.

5. Select the Landscape option, and click OK to close the dialog box.

6. Click the Stop Recording button on the miniature toolbar (or select Tools ⇨ Macro ⇨ Stop Recording).

   Excel stops recording your actions.

To look at the macro, activate the VBE (Alt+F11 is the easiest way) and locate the project in the Project Explorer window. Click the Modules node to expand it. Then click the Module1 item to display the code window (if the project already had a Module1, the new macro will be in Module2). The code generated by this single command is shown in Listing 32-1.

Listing 32-1: Macro for Changing Page Setup to Landscape Orientation

```
Sub Macro1()
    With ActiveSheet.PageSetup
        .PrintTitleRows = ""
        .PrintTitleColumns = ""
    End With
    ActiveSheet.PageSetup.PrintArea = ""
```

Continued

Listing 32-1 *(continued)*

```
With ActiveSheet.PageSetup
    .LeftHeader = ""
    .CenterHeader = ""
    .RightHeader = ""
    .LeftFooter = ""
    .CenterFooter = ""
    .RightFooter = ""
    .LeftMargin = Application.InchesToPoints(0.75)
    .RightMargin = Application.InchesToPoints(0.75)
    .TopMargin = Application.InchesToPoints(1)
    .BottomMargin = Application.InchesToPoints(1)
    .HeaderMargin = Application.InchesToPoints(0.5)
    .FooterMargin = Application.InchesToPoints(0.5)
    .PrintHeadings = False
    .PrintGridlines = False
    .PrintComments = xlPrintNoComments
    .PrintQuality = 600
    .CenterHorizontally = False
    .CenterVertically = False
    .Orientation = xlLandscape
    .Draft = False
    .PaperSize = xlPaperLetter
    .FirstPageNumber = xlAutomatic
    .Order = xlDownThenOver
    .BlackAndWhite = False
    .Zoom = 100
    .PrintErrors = xlPrintErrorsDisplayed
    End With
End Sub
```

You may be surprised by the amount of code generated by this single command. Although you changed only one simple setting in the Page Setup dialog box, Excel generated code that reproduced *all* the settings in the dialog box.

Note Your recorded macro may vary slightly from the above code. For example, the .PrintQuality value will depend on your printer settings.

This raises an important concept. Often, the code produced when you record a macro is overkill. If you want your macro only to switch to landscape mode, you can simplify this macro considerably by deleting the extraneous code. This makes the macro easier to read, and the macro also runs faster because it doesn't do things that are not necessary. In fact, this macro can be simplified to:

```
Sub Macro1()
    With ActiveSheet.PageSetup
        .Orientation = xlLandscape
    End With
End Sub
```

You can delete all the code except for the line that sets the `Orientation` property. Actually, this macro can be simplified even more because the `With-End With` construct isn't needed to change only one property:

```
Sub Macro1()
    ActiveSheet.PageSetup.Orientation = xlLandscape
End Sub
```

In this example, the macro changes the `Orientation` property of the `PageSetup` object on the active sheet. By the way, `xlLandscape` is a built-in constant that's provided to make things easier for you. You can use the online help to learn the relevant constants for a particular command.

You could have entered this procedure directly into a VBA module. To do so, you would have to know which objects, properties, and methods to use. Obviously, it's much faster to record the macro, and this example has a built-in bonus: You also learned that the `PageSetup` object has an `Orientation` property.

Note   Recording your actions is perhaps the *best* way to learn VBA. When in doubt, try recording. Although the result may not be exactly what you want, chances are that it will steer you in the right direction. You can use the online help to check out the objects, properties, and methods that appear in the recorded code.

Cross-Reference   The macro recorder is discussed in more detail later in this chapter.

Copying VBA code

The final way to get code into a VBA module is to copy it from another module. For example, you may have written a procedure for one project that would also be useful in your current project. Rather than reenter the code, you can simply open the workbook, activate the module, and use the normal clipboard copy-and-paste procedures to copy it into your current VBA module. After you've finished pasting, you can modify the code as necessary.

Tip   You can also import an entire module that has been exported to a file.

Customizing the VBE environment

If you're serious about becoming an Excel programmer, you'll be spending lots of time with the VBE window on your screen. To help you make things as comfortable as possible, the VBE provides quite a few customization options.

When VBE is active, choose Tools ⇨ Options. You'll see an Options dialog box with four tabs: Editor, Editor Format, General, and Docking. The sections that follow discuss some of the most useful options on these tabs.

Using the Editor tab

Figure 32-5 shows the options you access by clicking the Editor tab of the Options dialog box.

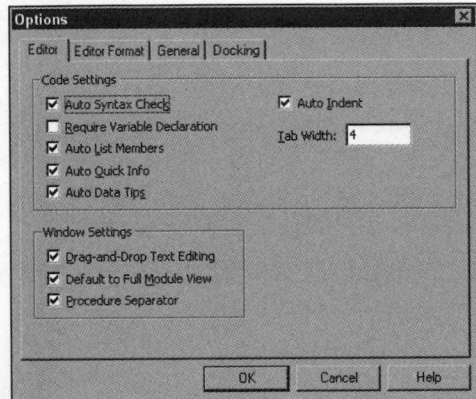

Figure 32-5: Use the Editor tab of the Options dialog box to control how the VBE functions.

Auto Syntax Check option

The Auto Syntax Check setting determines whether the VBE pops up a dialog box if it discovers a syntax error while you're entering your VBA code. The dialog box tells you roughly what the problem is. If you don't choose this setting, VBE flags syntax errors by displaying them in a different color from the rest of the code, and you don't have to deal with any dialog boxes popping up on your screen.

Require Variable Declaration option

If the Require Variable Declaration option is set, VBE inserts the following statement at the beginning of each new VBA module you insert:

```
Option Explicit
```

If this statement appears in your module, you must explicitly define each variable that you use. This is an excellent habit to get into. If you don't declare your variables, they will all be of the variant data type, which is flexible but not efficient in terms of storage or speed.

Note   Changing the Require Variable Declaration option affects only new modules, not existing modules.

Auto List Members option

If the Auto List Members option is set, VBE provides some help when you're entering your VBA code by displaying a list of member items for an object. These items include methods and properties for the object you typed.

Auto Quick Info option

If the Auto Quick Info option is set, the VBE displays information about functions and their arguments as you type. This can be very helpful, and you should probably always leave this setting on.

Auto Data Tips option

If the Auto Data Tips option is set, VBE displays the value of the variable over which your cursor is placed when you're debugging code. When you enter the wonderful world of debugging, you'll definitely appreciate this option.

Auto Indent option

The Auto Indent setting determines whether VBE automatically indents each new line of code by the same amount as the previous line.

Tip   Use the Tab key, not the spacebar, to indent your code. You can also use Shift+Tab to "unindent" a line of code.

Tip   VBE's Edit toolbar (which is hidden by default) contains two useful buttons: Indent and Outdent. These buttons let you quickly indent or "unindent" a block of code. Select the code, and then click one of these buttons to change the indenting of the block. These buttons are very useful, so you may want to copy them to your Standard toolbar.

Drag-and-Drop Text Editing option

When enabled, the Drag-and-Drop Text Editing option lets you copy and move text by dragging and dropping. You can also use keyboard shortcuts for copying and pasting.

Default to Full Module View option

The Default to Full Module View option sets the default state for new modules (it doesn't affect existing modules). If set, procedures in the code window appear as a single scrollable window. When this option is turned off, you can see only one procedure at a time.

Procedure Separator option

When the Procedure Separator option is turned on, it displays separator bars at the end of each procedure in a code window. This provides visual cues of where your procedures end.

Using the Editor Format tab

Figure 32-6 shows the Editor Format tab of the Options dialog box.

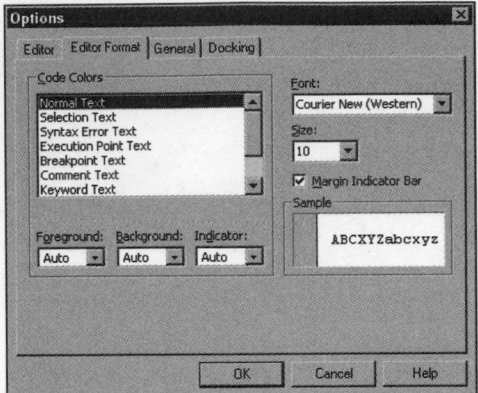

Figure 32-6: Use the Editor Format tab of the Options dialog box to control the appearance of your VBA code.

Code Colors option

The Code Colors option lets you set the text color (foreground and background) and indicator color displayed for various elements of VBA code. This is largely a matter of individual preference.

Font option

The Font option lets you select the font that's used in your VBA modules. For best results, stick with a fixed-width font, such as Courier New. In a fixed-width font, all characters are exactly the same width. This makes your code much more readable because the characters are nicely aligned vertically and you can easily distinguish multiple spaces.

Size setting

The Size setting specifies the size of the font in the VBA modules. This setting is a matter of personal preference determined by your video display resolution and your eyesight.

Margin Indicator Bar option

This option controls the display of the vertical margin indicator bar in your modules. You should keep this turned on; otherwise, you won't be able to see the helpful graphical indicators when you're debugging your code.

Using the General tab

Figure 32-7 shows the options available under the General tab in the Options dialog box. In almost every case, the default settings are just fine.

Cross-Reference

The Error Trapping setting determines what happens when an error is encountered. If you write any error-handling code, make sure that the Break on Unhandled Errors option is set. If the Break on All Errors option is set, error-handling code is ignored (which is hardly ever what you want). Error-handling techniques are discussed in Chapter 34.

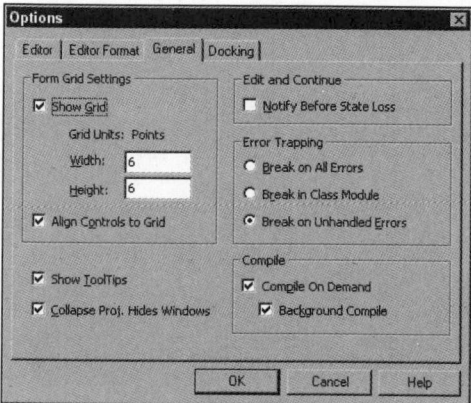

Figure 32-7: Use the General tab of the Options dialog box to control editing and error-trapping options.

Using the Docking tab

Figure 32-8 shows the Docking tab of the Options dialog box. These options determine how the various windows in the VBE behave. When a window is docked, it is fixed in place along one of the edges of the VBE window. This makes it much easier to identify and locate a particular window. If you turn off all docking, you'll have a big mess of windows that is very confusing. Generally, you'll find that the default settings work fine.

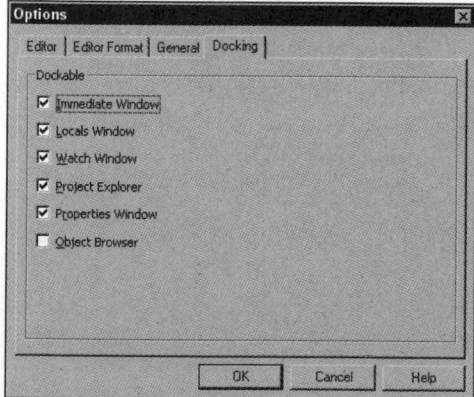

Figure 32-8: Use the Docking tab of the Options dialog box to control the positioning of the VBE windows.

Using the Macro Recorder

The macro recorder is an *extremely* useful tool, but it's important to remember these points:

✦ The macro recorder is appropriate only for simple macros or for recording a small part of a more complex macro.

✦ The macro recorder cannot generate code that performs looping (that is, repeating statements), assigns variables, executes statements conditionally, displays dialog boxes, and so on.

✦ The code that is generated depends on settings that you specify.

✦ You'll often want to clean up the recorded code to remove extraneous commands.

Tip   Excel's Visual Basic toolbar has several useful buttons for you. On this toolbar, you'll find the Run Macro, Record Macro, Stop Macro, and Visual Basic Editor buttons useful.

Understanding what is recorded

Excel's macro recorder translates your mouse and keyboard actions into VBA code. Here's an interesting way to see that code being generated:

1. Start with a blank workbook.

2. Make sure Excel's window is not maximized.

3. Press Alt+F11 to activate the VBE window, and make sure *this* window is not maximized.

4. Arrange Excel's window and the VBE window so both are visible. (For best results, minimize any other applications that are running.)

5. Activate Excel, Choose Tools ➪ Macro ➪ Record New Macro, and click OK to start the macro recorder.

   Excel inserts a new module (named Module1) and starts recording on that sheet.

6. Activate the VBE window.

7. In the Project Explorer window, double-click Module1 to display that module in the code window.

Now, move around in the worksheet and select various Excel commands. Watch as the code is generated in the window that displays the VBA module. Select cells, enter data, format cells, use the menus and toolbars, create a chart, manipulate graphic objects, and so on.

Relative or absolute?

When recording your actions, Excel normally records absolute references to cells. For example, perform these steps, and examine the code:

1. Activate a worksheet, and start the macro recorder.

2. Activate cell B1.

3. Enter Jan into cell B1.

4. Move to cell C1, and enter Feb.

5. Continue this process until you've entered the first six months of the year in B1:G1.

6. Click cell B1 to activate it again.

7. Stop the macro recorder.

Excel generates the following code:

```
Sub Macro1()
    Range("B1").Select
    ActiveCell.FormulaR1C1 = "Jan"
    Range("C1").Select
    ActiveCell.FormulaR1C1 = "Feb"
    Range("D1").Select
    ActiveCell.FormulaR1C1 = "Mar"
    Range("E1").Select
    ActiveCell.FormulaR1C1 = "Apr"
    Range("F1").Select
    ActiveCell.FormulaR1C1 = "May"
    Range("G1").Select
    ActiveCell.FormulaR1C1 = "Jun"
    Range("B1").Select
End Sub
```

To execute this macro, choose the Tools ➪ Macro ➪ Macros command (or press Alt+F8), select Macro1 (or whatever the macro is named), and click the Run button.

When executed, the macro re-creates the actions you performed when you recorded it. These same actions occur regardless of which cell is active when you execute the macro. Recording a macro using absolute references always produces the same results.

In some cases, however, you'll want your recorded macro to work with cell locations in a *relative* manner. For example, you'd probably want such a macro to start entering the month names in the active cell. In such a case, you'll want to use relative recording to record the macro.

The Stop Recording toolbar, which consists of only two buttons, is displayed when you are recording a macro. You can change the manner in which Excel records your actions by clicking the Relative Reference button on the Stop Recording toolbar. This button is a toggle. When the button appears in a pressed state, the recording mode is relative. When the button appears normally, you are recording in absolute mode. You can change the recording method at any time, even in the middle of recording.

To see how this works, erase the cells in B1:G1, and then perform these steps:

1. Activate cell B1.
2. Choose Tools ⇨ Macro ⇨ Record New Macro.
3. Name this macro Relative
4. Click OK to begin recording.
5. Click the Relative Reference button (on the Stop Recording toolbar) to change the recording mode to relative.

   When you click this button, it appears pressed.
6. Enter the first six month names in B1:G1, as in the previous example.
7. Select cell B1.
8. Stop the macro recorder.

With the recording mode set to relative, the code that Excel generates is quite different:

```
Sub Macro2()
    ActiveCell.FormulaR1C1 = "Jan"
    ActiveCell.Offset(0, 1).Range("A1").Select
    ActiveCell.FormulaR1C1 = "Feb"
    ActiveCell.Offset(0, 1).Range("A1").Select
    ActiveCell.FormulaR1C1 = "Mar"
    ActiveCell.Offset(0, 1).Range("A1").Select
    ActiveCell.FormulaR1C1 = "Apr"
    ActiveCell.Offset(0, 1).Range("A1").Select
    ActiveCell.FormulaR1C1 = "May"
    ActiveCell.Offset(0, 1).Range("A1").Select
    ActiveCell.FormulaR1C1 = "Jun"
    ActiveCell.Offset(0, -5).Range("A1").Select
End Sub
```

You can execute this macro by activating a worksheet and then choosing the Tools ⇨ Macro command. Select the macro's name, and click the Run button.

You'll also notice that the procedure varied slightly in this example: You activated the beginning cell *before* you started recording. This is an important step when you record macros that use the active cell as a base.

Although it may look strange, this macro is actually quite simple. The first statement simply enters *Jan* into the active cell. (It uses the active cell because it's not preceded by a statement that selects a cell.) The next statement uses the `Offset` method to move the selection one cell to the right. The next statement inserts more text, and so on. Finally, the original cell is selected by calculating a relative offset rather than an absolute cell. Unlike the preceding macro, this one always starts entering text in the active cell.

By the way, the code generated by Excel is much more complex than it need be, and it's not the most efficient way to code the operation. The macro that follows is a simpler and faster way to perform the same operation. This example demonstrates that VBA doesn't have to select a cell before it puts information into it — an important concept that can also speed things up considerably.

```
Sub Macro3()
    ActiveCell.Offset(0, 0) = "Jan"
    ActiveCell.Offset(0, 1) = "Feb"
    ActiveCell.Offset(0, 2) = "Mar"
    ActiveCell.Offset(0, 3) = "Apr"
    ActiveCell.Offset(0, 4) = "May"
    ActiveCell.Offset(0, 5) = "Jun"
End Sub
```

In fact, this macro can be made even more efficient by using the `With-End With` construct:

```
Sub Macro4()
    With ActiveCell
        .Offset(0, 0) = "Jan"
        .Offset(0, 1) = "Feb"
        .Offset(0, 2) = "Mar"
        .Offset(0, 3) = "Apr"
        .Offset(0, 4) = "May"
        .Offset(0, 5) = "Jun"
    End With
End Sub
```

The point here is that the recorder has two distinct modes, and you need to be aware of which mode you're recording in. Otherwise, the result will not be what you expected.

Setting the recording options

When you record your actions to create VBA code, you have several options. Recall that the Tools ➪ Macro ➪ Record New Macro command displays the Record Macro dialog box before recording begins. This dialog box gives you quite a bit of control over your macro. The following paragraphs describe your options.

Macro name

You can enter a name for the procedure that you are recording. By default, Excel uses the names Macro1, Macro2, and so on for each macro you record. You, however, may prefer to name the macro with a more descriptive name.

Shortcut key

The Shortcut key option lets you execute the macro by pressing a shortcut key combination. For example, if you enter w (lowercase), you can execute the macro by pressing Ctrl+W. If you enter W (uppercase), the macro comes alive when you press Ctrl+Shift+W.

You can add or change a shortcut key at any time, so you don't need to set this option while recording a macro.

Store macro in

The Store macro in option tells Excel where to store the macro that it records. By default, Excel puts the recorded macro in a module in the active workbook. If you prefer, you can record it in a new workbook (Excel opens a blank workbook) or in your Personal Macro Workbook.

Tip

If you create some VBA macros that you find particularly useful, you may want to store these routines on your Personal Macro Workbook. This is a workbook (Personal.xls) that is stored in your Xlstart directory. Whenever you start Excel, this workbook is loaded. It's a hidden workbook, so it's out of your way. When you record a macro, one of your options is to record it to your Personal Macro Workbook. The Personal.xls file doesn't exist until you record a macro to it.

Description

By default, Excel inserts five lines of comments (three of them blank) that list the macro name, the user's name, and the date. You can put anything you like here or nothing at all.

Cleaning up recorded macros

Earlier in this section, you saw how recording your actions while you issued a single command (the File ➪ Page Setup command) can produce an enormous amount of VBA code. In many cases, the recorded code includes extraneous commands that you can delete.

It's important to understand that the macro recorder doesn't always generate the most efficient code. If you examine the generated code, you'll see that Excel generally records what is selected (that is, an object) and then uses the `Selection` object in subsequent statements. For example, here's what is recorded if you select a range of cells and then use the buttons on the Formatting toolbar to change the numeric formatting and apply bold and italic:

```
Range("A1:C5").Select
Selection.NumberFormat = "#,##0.00"
Selection.Font.Bold = True
Selection.Font.Italic = True
```

Tip   If you use the Formatting dialog box to record this macro, you'll find that Excel records quite a bit of extraneous code. Recording toolbar button clicks often produces more efficient code.

The preceding example is just *one* way to perform these actions. You can also use the more efficient With-End With construct, as follows:

```
Range("A1:C5").Select
With Selection
 .NumberFormat = "#,##0.00"
 .Font.Bold = True
 .Font.Italic = True
End With
```

About the Code Examples

Throughout this book, you'll see many small snippets of VBA code that make a point or provide an example. This code often consists of just a single statement. In some cases, the example consists of only an expression, which isn't a valid instruction by itself.

For example, the following is an expression:

```
Range("A1").Value
```

To test an expression, you must evaluate it. The MsgBox function is a handy tool for this:

```
MsgBox Range("A1").Value
```

To try out these examples, you need to put the statement within a procedure in a VBA module, like this:

```
Sub Test()
' statement goes here
End Sub
```

Then put the cursor anywhere within the procedure, and press F5 to execute it. Make sure that the code is being executed within the proper context. For example, if a statement refers to Sheet1, make sure that the active workbook actually has a sheet named Sheet1.

If the code is just a single statement, you can use VBE's Immediate window. The Immediate window is very useful for executing a statement immediately without having to create a procedure. If the Immediate window is not displayed, press Ctrl+G in the VBE.

Just type the VBA statement and press Enter. To evaluate an expression in the Immediate window, precede the expression with a question mark (?). The question mark is a shortcut for Print. For example, you can type the following into the Immediate window:

```
? Range("A1").Value
```

The result of this expression is displayed in the next line of the Immediate window.

Or you can avoid the Select method altogether and write the code even more efficiently, like this:

```
With Range("A1:C5")
  .NumberFormat = "#,##0.00"
  .Font.Bold = True
  .Font.Italic = True
End With
```

If speed is essential in your application, you'll always want to examine any recorded VBA code closely to make sure that it's as efficient as possible.

Understanding Objects and Collections

If you've worked through the first part of this chapter, you have an overview of VBA, and you know the basics of working with VBA modules in the VBE. You've also seen some VBA code and were exposed to concepts such as objects and properties. This section gives you some additional details about objects and collections of objects.

As you work with VBA, you must understand the concept of objects and Excel's object model. It helps to think of objects in terms of a *hierarchy*. At the top of this model is the Application object — in this case, Excel itself. But if you're programming in VBA using Microsoft Word, the Application object is Word.

Exploring the object hierarchy

The Application object contains other objects. Examples of objects contained in the Application object are

> Workbooks (a collection of all Workbook objects)
>
> Windows (a collection of all Window objects)
>
> AddIns (a collection of all AddIn objects)
>
> AutoCorrect

Each of these objects can contain other objects. For example, the Workbooks collection consists of all open Workbook objects, and a Workbook object contains other objects, including:

> Worksheets (a collection of Worksheet objects)
>
> Charts (a collection of Chart objects)
>
> Names (a collection of Name objects)

Each of these objects can, in turn, contain other objects. The `Worksheets` collection consists of all `Worksheet` objects in a `Workbook`. A `Worksheet` object contains many other objects, including:

> `ChartObjects` (a collection of `ChartObject` objects)
>
> `Range`
>
> `PageSetup`
>
> `PivotTables` (a collection of `PivotTable` objects)

 **Tip**   The complete Excel object model is diagrammed in the online help system.

Understanding collections

Another key concept in VBA programming is collections. A *collection* is a group of objects of the same class (and a collection is itself an object). For example, `Workbooks` is a collection of all `Workbook` objects currently open. `Worksheets` is a collection of all `Worksheet` objects contained in a particular `Workbook` object. You can work with an entire collection of objects or with an individual object in a collection. To reference a single object from a collection, you put the object's name or index number in parentheses after the name of the collection, like this:

```
Worksheets("Sheet1")
```

If Sheet1 is the first worksheet in the collection, you may also use the following reference:

```
Worksheets(1)
```

You refer to the second worksheet in a `Workbook` as `Worksheets(2)`, and so on.

A collection also exists called `Sheets`, which is made up of all sheets in a workbook, whether they're worksheets or chart sheets. If Sheet1 is the first sheet in the workbook, you can reference it as follows:

```
Sheets(1)
```

Referencing objects

When you refer to an object using VBA, you often must qualify the object by connecting object names with a period (also known as a dot operator). What if you had two workbooks open and they both had a worksheet named Sheet1? The solution is to qualify the reference by adding the object's *container* like this:

```
Workbooks("Book1").Worksheets("Sheet1")
```

To refer to a specific range (such as cell A1) on a worksheet named Sheet1 in a workbook named Book1, you can use this expression:

```
Workbooks("Book1").Worksheets("Sheet1").Range("A1")
```

The fully qualified reference for the preceding example also includes the `Application` object:

```
Application.Workbooks("Book1").Worksheets("Sheet1").
  Range("A1")
```

Most of the time, however, you can omit the `Application` object in your references (it is assumed). If the Book1 object is the active workbook, you can even omit that object reference and use this:

```
Worksheets("Sheet1").Range("A1")
```

And if Sheet1 is the active worksheet, you can use an even simpler expression:

```
Range("A1")
```

Note Contrary to what you might expect, Excel does not have an object that refers to an individual cell that is called "Cell." A single cell is simply a Range object that happens to consist of just one element.

Simply referring to objects (as in these examples) doesn't do anything. To perform anything meaningful, you must read or modify an object's properties or specify a method to be used with an object.

Things to know about objects

The preceding sections introduced you to objects (including collections). This section adds some more concepts that are essential for would-be VBA gurus. These concepts become clearer as you work with VBA and read subsequent chapters:

✦ Objects have unique properties and methods.

   Each object has its own set of properties and methods. Some objects, however, share some properties (for example, `Name`) and some methods (such as `Delete`).

✦ You can manipulate objects without selecting them.

   This may be contrary to how you normally think about manipulating objects in Excel, especially if you've programmed XLM macros. Fact is, it's usually more efficient to perform actions on objects without selecting them first. When you record a macro, Excel generally selects the object first. This is not necessary and may actually make your macro run slower.

✦ It's important that you understand the concept of collections.

Most of the time, you'll refer to an object indirectly by referring to the collection that it's in. For example, to access a `Workbook` object named Myfile, reference the `Workbooks` collection as follows:

```
Workbooks("Myfile.xls")
```

This reference returns an object, which is the workbook with which you are concerned.

✦ Properties can return a reference to another object. For example, in the following statement, the Font property returns a Font object contained in a Range object:

```
Range("A1").Font.Bold = True
```

✦ There can be many different ways to refer to the same object.

Assume that you have a workbook named Sales and that it's the only workbook open. Then assume that this workbook has one worksheet, named Summary. You can refer to the sheet in any of these ways:

```
Workbooks("Sales.xls").Worksheets("Summary")
Workbooks(1).Worksheets(1)
Workbooks(1).Sheets(1)
Application.ActiveWorkbook.ActiveSheet
ActiveWorkbook.ActiveSheet
ActiveSheet
```

The way you choose is usually determined by how much you know about the workspace. For example, if more than one workbook is open, the second or third way is not reliable. If you want to work with the active sheet (whatever it may be), any of the last three ways would work. To be absolutely sure that you're referring to a specific sheet on a specific workbook, the first way is your best choice.

Tip

The Object Browser is a handy tool that lists every property and method for every object available. When the VBE is active, you can bring up the Object Browser by pressing F2, by choosing the View ➪ Object Browser command, or by clicking the Object Browser tool on the Standard toolbar.

Understanding Properties and Methods

It's easy to be overwhelmed with properties and methods; literally thousands are available. This section describes how to access properties and methods of objects.

Working with object properties

Every object has properties. For example, a `Range` object has a property called `Value`. You can write VBA code to display the `Value` property, or you can write VBA code to set the `Value` property to a specific value. Here's a procedure that uses VBA's `MsgBox` function to pop up a box that displays the value in cell A1 on Sheet1 of the active workbook:

```
Sub ShowValue()
    Answer = Worksheets("Sheet1").Range("A1").Value
    MsgBox Answer
End Sub
```

Tip   MsgBox is a useful keyword that you'll often use to display results while your VBA code is executing.

The code in the preceding example displays the current setting of the Value property of a specific cell: cell A1 on a worksheet named Sheet1 in the active workbook. Note that if the active workbook does not have a sheet named Sheet1, the macro will generate an error.

Now, what if you want to change the Value property? The following procedure changes the value displayed in cell A1 by changing the cell's Value property:

```
Sub ChangeValue()
    Worksheets("Sheet1").Range("A1").Value = 123
End Sub
```

After executing this routine, cell A1 on Sheet1 has the value 123. You might want to enter these procedures into a module and experiment with them.

Note   Every object has a default property. For a Range object, the default property is the Value property. Therefore, you can omit the .Value part from the preceding code, and it will have the same effect. It's usually considered good programming practice, however, to include the property, even if it's the default property.

Working with object methods

In addition to properties, objects also have methods. A *method* is an action that you perform with an object. Here's a simple example that uses the Clear method on a range object. After you execute this procedure, A1:C3 on Sheet1 will be empty.

```
Sub ZapRange()
    Worksheets("Sheet1").Range("A1:C3").Clear
End Sub
```

Most methods also take arguments to define the action further. Arguments for a method are placed in parentheses. Here's an example that copies cell A1 to cell B1 by using the Copy method of the Range object. In this example, the Copy method has one argument (the destination of the copy).

```
Sub CopyOne()
    Worksheets("Sheet1").Range("A1").Copy _
        Worksheets("Sheet1").Range("B1")
End Sub
```

Specifying Arguments for Methods and Properties

An issue that often leads to confusion among VBA programmers concerns arguments for methods and properties. Some methods use arguments to further clarify the action to be taken, and some properties use arguments to further specify the property value. In some cases, one or more of the arguments is optional.

If a method uses arguments, place the arguments after the name of the method, separated by commas. If the method uses optional arguments, you can insert blank placeholders for the optional arguments. Consider the Protect method for a workbook object. Check the online help, and you'll find that the Protect method takes three arguments: password, structure, windows. These arguments correspond to the options in the Protect Workbook dialog box.

If you want to protect a workbook named MyBook.xls, for example, you might use a statement such as this:

```
Workbooks("MyBook.xls").Protect "xyzzy", True, True
```

If you don't want to assign a password, you can use a statement such as this:

```
Workbooks("MyBook.xls").Protect , True, True
```

Notice that the first argument is omitted and that the placeholder is specified with a comma.

Another approach, which makes your code more readable, is to use named arguments. Here's an example of how you use named arguments for the preceding example:

```
Workbooks("MyBook.xls").Protect Structure:=True, Windows:=True
```

Using named arguments is a good idea, especially for methods that have lots of optional arguments, as well as when you need to use only a few of them.

For properties that use arguments, you must place the arguments in parentheses. For example, the Address property of a Range object takes five arguments, all of which are optional. The following statement is invalid because the parentheses are omitted:

```
MsgBox Range("A1").Address False    ' invalid
```

The proper syntax for such a statement requires parentheses, as follows:

```
MsgBox Range("A1").Address(False)
```

The statement could also be written using a named argument:

```
MsgBox Range("A1").Address(rowAbsolute:=False)
```

 **Tip**   Notice that this example used the line-continuation character sequence (a space followed by an underscore). You can omit the line continuation sequence and type the statement on a single line.

Trying Out a Sample Using the Comment Object

To help you better understand the properties and methods available for an object, you may want to try an example using the `Comment` object. You create a `Comment` object when you use Excel's Insert ➪ Comment command to enter a cell comment. In the sections that follow, you'll get a feel for working with objects. If you're a bit overwhelmed by the material in this section, don't fret. These concepts will become much clearer over time.

Tip   One way to learn about a particular object is to look it up in the online help system. Notice that the underlined words are "jumps" that display additional information. For example, you can click Properties to get a list of all properties for the Comment object or you can click Method to get a list of the object's methods. The easiest way to get specific help about a particular object, property, or method is to type the word in a code window and press F1.

Understanding a Comment object

The `Comment` object has six properties. Table 32-1 contains a list of these properties, along with a brief description of each. If a property is *read-only*, your VBA code can read the property but cannot change it.

Table 32-1		
Properties of a Comment Object		
Property	**Read-Only**	**Description**
Application	Yes	Returns the name of the application that created the comment (that is, Excel).
Author	Yes	Returns the name of the person who created the comment.
Creator	Yes	Returns a number that specifies the application that created the object. Not used in Excel for Windows (relevant only for Excel for Macintosh).
Parent	Yes	Returns the parent object for the comment (it is always a Range object).
Shape	Yes	Returns a Shape object that represents the shape attached to the comment.
Visible	No	Is True if the comment is visible.

Table 32-2 shows the methods that you can use with a `Comment` object. Again, these methods perform common operations that you may have performed manually with a comment at some point — but you probably never thought of these operations as methods.

Table 32-2
Methods of a Comment Object

Method	Description
Delete	Deletes a comment
Next	Returns a Comment object that represents the next comment
Previous	Returns a Comment object that represents the previous comment
Text	Sets the text in a comment (takes three arguments)

Note   You may be surprised to see that Text is a method rather than a property. This leads to an important point: The distinction between properties and methods isn't always clear-cut, and the object model isn't perfectly consistent. In fact, it's not really important that you distinguish between properties and methods. As long as you get the syntax correct, it doesn't matter if a word in your code is a property or a method.

Figure 32-9 shows the ten members of the comment class.

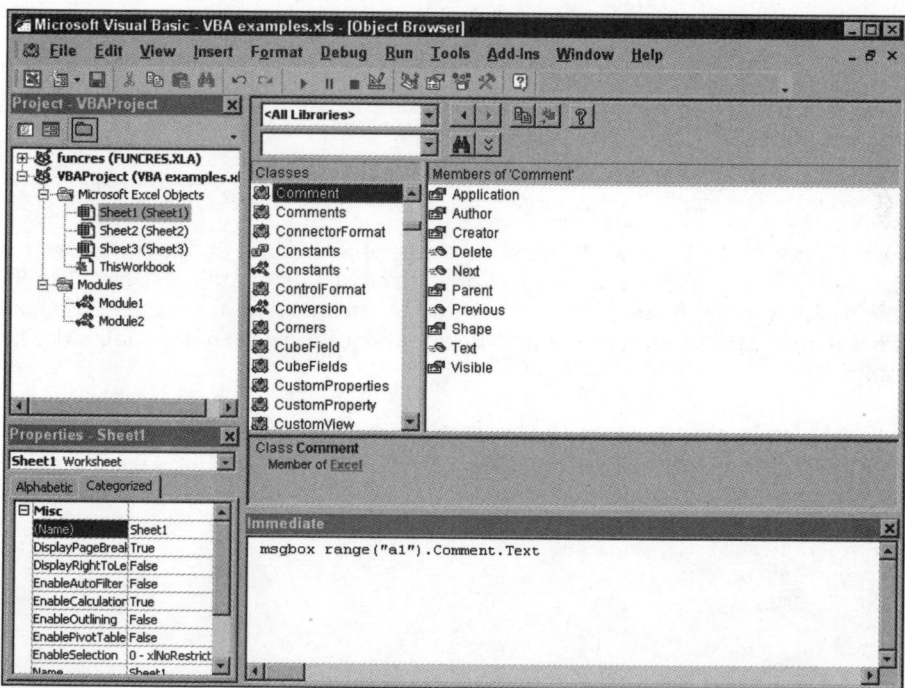

Figure 32-9: The VBE displays different icons for properties and methods so it is easier for you to identify them correctly.

Understanding the Comments collection

A *collection* is a group of like objects. Every worksheet has a Comments collection, which consists of all Comment objects on the worksheet. If the worksheet has no comments, this collection is empty.

For example, the following code refers to the first comment on Sheet1 of the active workbook:

```
Worksheets("Sheet1").Comments(1)
```

The following statement displays the text contained in the first comment on Sheet1:

```
MsgBox Worksheets("Sheet1").Comments(1).Text
```

Unlike most objects, a Comment object does not have a Name property. Therefore, to refer to a specific comment, you must use an index number or use the Comment property of a Range object to return a specific comment (keep reading, and this will make sense).

The Comments collection is also an object and has its own set of properties and methods. For example, the following example shows the total number of comments:

```
MsgBox ActiveSheet.Comments.Count
```

The Comments collection here has a Count property that stores the number of objects in the active worksheet. The next example shows which cell has the first comment:

```
MsgBox ActiveSheet.Comments(1).Parent.Address
```

Here, Comments(1) returns the first Comment object in the Comments collection. The Parent property of the Comment object returns its container, which is a Range object. The message box displays the Address property of the Range. The net effect is that the statement displays the address of the cell that contains the first comment.

You can also loop through all the comments on a sheet by using the For Each-Next construct (this is explained in Chapter 34). This example displays a separate message box for each comment on the active worksheet:

```
For Each cmt in ActiveSheet.Comments
    MsgBox cmt.Text
Next cmt
```

Understanding the Comment property

In this section, you've been learning about the Comment object. If you dig through the online help, you'll find that a Range object has a property named Comment. This property returns an object: a `Comment` object. For example, the following statement refers to the `Comment` object in cell A1:

```
Range("A1").Comment
```

If this were the first comment on the sheet, you could refer to the same `Comment` object as follows:

```
Comments(1)
```

To display the comment in cell A1 in a message box, use a statement like this:

```
MsgBox Range("A1").Comment.Text
```

Note That a property can return an object is a very important concept — a difficult one to grasp, perhaps, but critical to mastering VBA.

Working with objects within a Comment object

Working with properties is confusing at first because some properties actually return objects. Suppose that you want to determine the background color of a particular comment on Sheet1. If you look through the list of properties for a `Comment` object, you won't find anything that relates to color. Rather, you must do this:

1. Use the `Comment` object's `Shape` property to return the `Shape` object that's contained in the comment.
2. Use the `Shape` object's `Fill` property to return a `FillFormat` object.
3. Use the `FillFormat` object's `ForeColor` property to return a `ColorFormat` object.
4. Use the `ColorFormat` object's `RGB` property to set the color.

Put another way, getting at the interior color for a `Comment` object involves accessing other objects contained in the `Comment` object. Here's a look at the object hierarchy that's involved.

> Application (Excel)
>
> Workbook object
>
> Worksheet object
>
> Comment object
>
> Shape object
>
> FillFormat object
>
> ColorFormat object

This can get very confusing until you become used to "thinking" VBA. But, as an example of the "elegance" of VBA, code to change the color of a comment can be written with a single statement:

```
Worksheets("Sheet1").Comments(1).Shape.Fill.ForeColor.RGB _
    = RGB(0, 255, 0)
```

This type of referencing is certainly not intuitive and can be difficult to get used to. Fortunately, recording your actions in Excel almost always yields some insights regarding the hierarchy of the objects involved. And, if you work with this long enough, it all makes perfect sense.

Adding a new Comment object

You may have noticed that the list of methods for the Comment object doesn't include a method to add a new comment. The reason is that the AddComment method belongs to the Range object. The following statement adds a comment (an empty comment) to cell A1 on the active worksheet:

```
Range("A1").AddComment
```

If you consult the online help, you'll discover that the AddComment method takes an argument that represents the text for the comment. Therefore, you can add a comment and then add text to the comment with a single statement, like this:

```
Range("A1").AddComment "Formula developed by Brian."
```

 Note The AddComment method generates an error if the cell already contains a comment.

Some useful Application object properties

When you're working with Excel, only one workbook at a time can be active, and if the sheet is a worksheet, one cell is the active cell (even if a multicell range is selected).

VBA knows this and lets you refer to these active objects in a simplified manner. This is often useful because you won't always know the exact workbook, worksheet, or range that you want to operate on. VBA handles this by providing properties of the Application object. For example, the Application object has an ActiveCell property that returns a reference to the active cell. The following instruction assigns the value 1 to the active cell:

```
ActiveCell.Value = 1
```

Notice that the preceding example omitted the reference to the Application object (because it is assumed). This instruction will fail if the active sheet is not a worksheet. For example, if VBA executes this statement when a chart sheet is active, the procedure halts and you'll receive an error message.

If a range is selected in a worksheet, the active cell will be one of the corner cells of the range (which corner is determined by how the range was selected). In other words, the active cell is always a single cell.

The `Application` object also has a `Selection` property that returns a reference to whatever is selected, which could be a single cell (the active cell), a range of cells, or an object such as `ChartObject`, `TextBox`, or `Shape`.

Table 32-3 lists the other `Application` properties that are useful when working with cells and ranges.

Table 32-3
Some Useful Properties of the Application Object

Property	Object Returned
ActiveCell	The active cell
ActiveSheet	The active sheet (worksheet or chart)
ActiveWindow	The active window
ActiveWorkbook	The active workbook
RangeSelection	The selected cells on the worksheet in the specified window, even when a graphic object is selected
Selection	The object selected (it could be a Range, Shape, ChartObject, and so on)
ThisWorkbook	The workbook that contains the procedure being executed

The advantage of using these properties to return an object is that you don't need to know which cell, worksheet, or workbook is active or to provide a specific reference to it. For example, the following instruction clears the contents of the active cell, even though the address of the active cell is not known:

```
ActiveCell.ClearContents
```

The example that follows displays a message that tells you the name of the active sheet:

```
MsgBox ActiveSheet.Name
```

If you want to know the name of the active workbook, use a statement like this:

```
MsgBox ActiveWorkbook.Name
```

If a range on a worksheet is selected, you can fill the entire range with a value by executing a single statement. In the following example, the `Selection` property of the `Application` object returns a `Range` object that corresponds to the selected cells. The instruction simply modifies the `Value` property of this `Range` object, and the result is a range filled with a single value:

```
Selection.Value = 12
```

Note that if something other than a range is selected (such as a `ChartObject` or a `Shape`), the preceding statement will generate an error because `ChartObjects` and `Shape` objects do not have a `Value` property.

The following statement, however, enters a value of 12 into the `Range` object that was selected before a non-`Range` object was selected. If you look up the `RangeSelection` property in the online help, you'll find that this property applies to a `Window` object only.

```
ActiveWindow.RangeSelection.Value = 12
```

Working with Range Objects

Much of the work you will do in VBA involves cells and ranges in worksheets. After all, that's what spreadsheets are designed to do. The earlier discussion on relative versus absolute macro recording exposed you to working with cells in VBA, but you need to know much more.

A `Range` object is contained in a `Worksheet` object and consists of a single cell or range of cells on a single worksheet. The sections that follow discuss three ways of referring to `Range` objects in your VBA code:

✦ The Range property of a Worksheet or Range class object

✦ The Cells property of a Worksheet object

✦ The Offset property of a Range object

Working with the Range property

The `Range` property returns a `Range` object. If you consult the online help for the `Range` property, you'll learn that this property has two syntaxes:

```
object.Range(cell1)
object.Range(cell1, cell2)
```

The `Range` property applies to two types of objects: a `Worksheet` object or a `Range` object. Here, cell1 and cell2 refer to placeholders for terms that Excel will recognize as identifying the range (in the first instance) and *delineating* the range (in the second instance). Following are a few examples of using the `Range` method.

You've already seen examples like the following one earlier in the chapter. The instruction that follows simply enters a value into the specified cell. In this case, it puts a 1 into cell A1 on Sheet1 of the active workbook.

```
Worksheets("Sheet1").Range("A1").Value = 1
```

The Range property also recognizes defined names in workbooks. Therefore, if a cell is named "Input," you can use the following statement to enter a value into that named cell:

```
Worksheets("Sheet1").Range("Input").Value = 1
```

The example that follows enters the same value into a range of 20 cells on the active sheet. If the active sheet is not a worksheet, this causes an error message.

```
ActiveSheet.Range("A1:B10").Value = 2
```

The next example produces exactly the same result as the preceding example.

```
Range("A1", "B10") = 2
```

The sheet reference is omitted, however, so the active sheet is assumed. The value property is also omitted, so the default property (which is Value, for a Range object) is assumed. This example also uses the second syntax of the Range property. With this syntax, the first argument is the cell at the top left of the range and the second argument is the cell at the lower right of the range.

The following example uses Excel's range intersection operator (a space) to return the intersection of two ranges. In this case, the intersection is a single cell, C6. Therefore, this statement enters 3 into cell C6:

```
Range("C1:C10 A6:E6") = 3
```

And finally, the next example enters the value 4 into five cells; that is, a noncontiguous range. The comma serves as the union operator.

```
Range("A1,A3,A5,A7,A9") = 4
```

So far, all the examples have used the Range property on a Worksheet object. You can also use the Range property on a Range object.

Following is an example of using the Range property on a Range object (in this case, the Range object is the active cell). This example treats the Range object as if it were the upper-left cell in the worksheet and then enters a value of 5 into the cell that *would be* B2. In other words, the reference returned is relative to the upper-left corner of the Range object. Therefore, the statement that follows enters a value of 5 into the cell directly to the right and one row below the active cell:

```
ActiveCell.Range("B2") = 5
```

This may be confusing, but fortunately, you have a much clearer way to access a cell relative to a range, called the `Offset` property (which is discussed after the next section).

Working with the Cells property

Another way to reference a range is to use the `Cells` property. Like the `Range` property, you can use the `Cells` property on `Worksheet` objects and `Range` objects. Check the online help, and you'll see that the `Cells` property has three syntaxes:

```
object.Cells(rowIndex, columnIndex)
object.Cells(rowIndex)
object.Cells
```

Following are some examples that demonstrate how to use the `Cells` property. The first example enters the value 9 into cell 1 on Sheet1. This example uses the first syntax, which accepts the index number of the row (from 1 to 65,536) and the index number of the column (from 1 to 256):

```
Worksheets("Sheet1").Cells(1, 1) = 9
```

Here's an example that enters the value 7 into cell D3 (that is, row 3, column 4) in the active worksheet:

```
ActiveSheet.Cells(3, 4) = 7
```

You can also use the `Cells` property on a `Range` object. When you do so, the `Range` object returned by the `Cells` property is relative to the upper-left cell of the referenced `Range`. Confusing? Probably. An example might help clear this up. The following instruction enters the value 5 into the active cell. Remember, in this case, the active cell is treated as if it were cell A1 in the worksheet:

```
ActiveCell.Cells(1, 1) = 5
```

Cross-Reference   The real advantage of this type of cell referencing will be apparent when you use variables and looping (see Chapter 34). In most cases, you will not use actual values for the arguments. Rather, you'll use variables.

To enter a value of 5 into the cell directly below the active cell, you can use this instruction:

```
ActiveCell.Cells(2, 1) = 5
```

Think of the preceding example as if it said: "Start with the active cell and consider this cell to be cell A1. Return the cell in the second row and the first column."

The second syntax of the `Cells` method uses a single argument that can range from 1 to 16,777,216. This number is equal to the number of cells in a worksheet (65,536 rows × 256 columns). The cells are numbered starting from A1 and continuing right and then down to the next row. The 256th cell is IV1; the 257th is A2.

The next example enters the value 2 into cell H3 (which is the 520th cell in the worksheet) of the active worksheet:

```
ActiveSheet.Cells(520) = 2
```

To display the value in the last cell in a worksheet (IV65536), use this statement:

```
MsgBox ActiveSheet.Cells(16777216)
```

This syntax can also be used with a Range object. In this case, the cell returned is relative to the Range object referenced. For example, if the Range object is A1:D10 (40 cells), the Cells property can have an argument from 1 to 40 and return one of the cells in the Range object. In the following example, a value of 2000 is entered into cell A2 because A2 is the fifth cell (counting from the top and to the right and then down) in the referenced range:

```
Range("A1:D10").Cells(5) = 2000
```

Note In the preceding example, the argument for the Cells property is not limited to values between 1 and 40. If the argument exceeds the number of cells in the range, the counting continues as if the range were larger than it actually is. Therefore, the preceding statement could change the value in a cell that's outside of the range A1:D10.

The third syntax for the Cells property simply returns all cells on the referenced worksheet. Unlike the other two syntaxes, in this one, the return data is not a single cell. This example uses the ClearContents method on the range returned by using the Cells property on the active worksheet. The result is that the contents of every cell on the worksheet are cleared:

```
ActiveSheet.Cells.ClearContents
```

Working with the Offset property

The Offset property (like the Range and Cells properties) also returns a Range object. But unlike the other two methods, the Offset property applies only to a Range object and no other class. Its syntax is as follows:

```
object.Offset(rowOffset, columnOffset)
```

The Offset property takes two arguments that correspond to the relative position from the upper-left cell of the specified Range object. The arguments can be positive (down or right), negative (up or left), or zero. The example that follows enters a value of 12 into the cell directly below the active cell:

```
ActiveCell.Offset(1,0).Value = 12
```

The next example enters a value of 15 into the cell directly above the active cell:

```
ActiveCell.Offset(-1,0).Value = 15
```

By the way, if the active cell is in row 1, the Offset property in the preceding example generates an error because it cannot return a Range object that doesn't exist.

When you record a macro using the relative reference mode, Excel uses the Offset property to reference cells relative to the starting position (that is, the active cell when macro recording begins). For example, the macro recorder generated the following code. I started with the cell pointer in cell B1, entered values into B1:B3, and then returned to B1.

```
Sub Macro1()
    ActiveCell.FormulaR1C1 = "1"
    ActiveCell.Offset(1, 0).Range("A1").Select
    ActiveCell.FormulaR1C1 = "2"
    ActiveCell.Offset(1, 0).Range("A1").Select
    ActiveCell.FormulaR1C1 = "3"
    ActiveCell.Offset(-2, 0).Range("A1").Select
End Sub
```

You'll notice that the generated code references cell A1, which may seem a bit odd because that cell was not even involved in the macro. This is a quirk in the macro recording procedure that makes the code more complex than necessary. You can delete all references to Range("A1"), and the macro still works perfectly:

```
Sub Modified Macro1()
    ActiveCell.FormulaR1C1 = "1"
    ActiveCell.Offset(1, 0).Select
    ActiveCell.FormulaR1C1 = "2"
    ActiveCell.Offset(1, 0).Select
    ActiveCell.FormulaR1C1 = "3"
    ActiveCell.Offset(-2, 0).Select
End Sub
```

In fact, here's a much more efficient version of the macro that doesn't do any selecting:

```
Sub Macro1()
    ActiveCell = 1
    ActiveCell.Offset(1, 0) = 2
    ActiveCell.Offset(2, 0) = 3
End Sub
```

✦   ✦   ✦

VBA Programming Fundamentals

Chapter 32 introduced you to Visual Basic for Applications (VBA); now it's time to become better acquainted with VBA. This chapter discusses some of the key language elements and programming concepts in VBA. If you've used other programming languages, much of this information may be familiar. VBA has a few unique wrinkles, however, so even experienced programmers may find some new information.

An Overview of VBA Language Elements

Chapter 32 presented an overview of objects, properties, and methods, but it didn't tell you much about how to manipulate objects so that they do meaningful things. This chapter gently nudges you in that direction by exploring VBA's *language elements,* the keywords and control structures that you use to write VBA routines.

To get the ball rolling, the following simple procedure is stored in a VBA module and calculates the sum of the first 100 integers. When done, the procedure displays a message with the result.

```
Sub VBA_Demo()
'    This is a simple VBA Example
    Total = 0
    For i = 1 To 100
        Total = Total + i
    Next i
    MsgBox Total
End Sub
```

Entering VBA Code

VBA code, which resides in a VBA module, consists of instructions. The accepted practice is to use one instruction per line. This standard is not a requirement, however; you can use a colon to separate multiple instructions on a single line. The following example combines four instructions on one line:

```
Sub OneLine()
    x= 1: y= 2: z= 3: MsgBox x + y + z
End Sub
```

Most programmers agree that code is easier to read if you use one instruction per line:

```
Sub OneLine()
    x = 1
    y = 2
    z = 3
    MsgBox x + y + z
End Sub
```

Each line can be as long as you like; the VBA module window scrolls to the left when you reach the right side. For lengthy lines, you may want to use VBA's line continuation sequence: an underscore (_) preceded by a space. For example:

```
Sub LongLine()
    SummedValue = _
        Worksheets("Sheet1").Range("A1").Value + _
        Worksheets("Sheet2").Range("A1").Value
End Sub
```

When you record macros, Excel often uses underscores to break long statements into multiple lines.

This procedure uses some common language elements, including a comment (the line preceded by the apostrophe), a variable (Total), two assignment statements (Total = 0 and Total = Total + i), a looping structure (For-Next), and a VBA statement (MsgBox). All these are discussed in subsequent sections of this chapter.

 **Note**   VBA procedures need not manipulate any objects. The preceding procedure, for example, doesn't do anything with objects.

After you enter an instruction, VBA performs these actions to improve readability:

✦ It inserts spaces between operators. If you enter Ans=1+2 (without any spaces), for example, VBA converts it to:

```
Ans = 1 + 2
```

✦ VBA adjusts the case of the letters for keywords, properties, and methods. If you enter the following text:

```
Result=activesheet.range("a1").value=12
```

VBA converts it to:

```
Result = ActiveSheet.Range("a1").Value = 12
```

Notice that text within quotation marks (in this case, `"a1"`) is not changed.

✦ Because VBA variable names are not case sensitive, the interpreter by default adjusts the names of all variables with the same letters so that their case matches the case of letters that you most recently typed. For example, if you first specify a variable as myvalue (all lowercase) and then enter the variable as MyValue (mixed case), VBA changes all other occurrences of the variable to MyValue. An exception occurs if you declare the variable with Dim or a similar statement; in this case, the variable name always appears as it was declared.

✦ VBA scans the instruction for syntax errors. If VBA finds an error, it changes the color of the line and may display a message describing the problem. Use the VBE's Tools ⇨ Options command to display the Options dialog box, where you control the error color (use the Editor Format tab) and whether the error message is displayed (use the Auto Syntax Check option in the Editor tab).

Understanding Comments

A *comment* is descriptive text embedded within your code. The text of a comment is completely ignored by VBA. It's a good idea to use comments liberally to describe what you're doing (an instruction's purpose is not always obvious).

You can use a complete line for your comment, or you can insert a comment *after* an instruction on the same line. A comment is indicated by an apostrophe. VBA ignores any text that follows an apostrophe — except when the apostrophe is contained within quotation marks — up until the end of the line. For example, the following statement does not contain a comment, even though it has an apostrophe:

```
Msg = "Can't continue"
```

The following example shows a VBA procedure with three comments:

```
Sub Comments()
'    This procedure does nothing of value
     x = 0    'x represents nothingness
'    Display the result
     MsgBox x
End Sub
```

Although the apostrophe is the preferred comment indicator, you can also use the Rem keyword to mark a line as a comment. For example,

```
Rem — The next statement prompts the user for a filename
```

Note   The Rem keyword is essentially a holdover from old versions of BASIC; it is included in VBA for the sake of compatibility. Unlike the apostrophe, Rem can be written only at the beginning of a line, not on the same line as another instruction.

Following are a few general tips on making the best use of comments:

✦ Use comments to describe briefly the purpose of each procedure you write.

✦ Use comments to describe changes you make to a procedure.

✦ Use comments to indicate that you're using functions or constructs in an unusual or nonstandard manner.

✦ Use comments to describe the purpose of variables so that you and other people can decipher otherwise cryptic names.

✦ Use comments to describe workarounds that you develop to overcome Excel bugs.

✦ Write comments as you code rather than after.

Tip   You may want to test a procedure without including a particular instruction or group of instructions. Instead of deleting the instruction, simply turn it into a comment by inserting an apostrophe at the beginning. VBA then ignores the instruction(s) when the routine is executed. To convert the comment back to an instruction, delete the apostrophe.

Tip   Visual Basic Editor's (VBE) Edit toolbar contains two very useful buttons. Select a group of instructions, and then use the Comment Block button to convert the instructions to comments. The Uncomment Block button converts a group of comments back to instructions.

Understanding Variables, Data Types, and Constants

VBA's main purpose in life is to manipulate data. Some data resides in objects, such as worksheet ranges. Other data is stored in variables that you create.

A *variable* is simply a named storage location in your computer's memory. Variables can accommodate a wide variety of *data types* — from simple Boolean values (True or False) to large, double-precision values (see the following section). You assign a value to a variable by using the equal sign operator (more about this later).

You'll make your life easier if you get into the habit of making your variable names as descriptive as possible. VBA does, however, have a few rules regarding variable names:

✦ You can use alphabetic characters, numbers, and some punctuation characters, but the first character must be alphabetic.

✦ VBA does not distinguish between case. To make variable names more readable, programmers often use mixed case (for example, InterestRate rather than interestrate).

✦ You cannot use spaces or periods. To make variable names more readable, programmers often use the underscore character (Interest_Rate).

✦ Special type declaration characters (#, $, %, &, or !) cannot be embedded in a variable name.

✦ Variable names may have as many as 254 characters.

The following list contains some examples of assignment expressions that use various types of variables. The variable names are to the left of the equal sign. Each statement assigns the value to the right of the equal sign to the variable on the left.

```
x = 1
InterestRate = 0.075
LoanPayoffAmount = 243089
DataEntered = False
x = x + 1
MyNum = YourNum * 1.25
UserName = "Bob Johnson"
DateStarted = #3/14/94#
```

VBA has many *reserved words,* which are words that you cannot use for variable or procedure names (see the online Help files for details). If you attempt to use one of these words, you get an error message. For example, although the reserved word Next might make a very descriptive variable name, the following instruction generates a syntax error:

```
Next = 132
```

Note Unfortunately, syntax error messages aren't always very descriptive. The preceding instruction generates this error message: Compile Error: Expected: variable. So if an instruction produces a strange error message, check the online help to make sure your variable name doesn't have a special use in VBA.

Defining data types

Data type refers to how data is stored in memory—as integers, real numbers, strings, and so on. Although VBA can take care of data typing automatically, it does so at a cost: slower execution and less efficient use of memory. (There's no such thing as a free lunch.) As a result, letting VBA handle data typing may present problems when you're running large or complex applications. If you need to conserve every last byte of memory, you need to be on familiar terms with data types.

Table 33-1 lists VBA's assortment of built-in data types (note that you can also define custom data types, as described later in this chapter).

Table 33-1
VBA's Built-In Data Types

Data Type	Bytes Used	Range of Values
Byte	1 byte	0 to 255
Boolean	2 bytes	True or False
Integer	2 bytes	–32,768 to 32,767
Long	4 bytes	–2,147,483,648 to 2,147,483,647
Single	4 bytes	–3.402823E38 to –1.401298E–45 (for negative values); 1.401298E–45 to 3.402823E38 (for positive values)
Double	8 bytes	–1.79769313486232E308 to –4.94065645841247E–324 (negative values); 4.94065645841247E–324 to 1.79769313486232E308 (positive values)
Currency	8 bytes	–922,337,203,685,477.5808 to 922,337,203,685,477.5807
Decimal	14 bytes	+/–79,228,162,514,264,337, 593,543,950,335 with no decimal point; +/–7.9228162514264337593543950335 with 28 places to the right of the decimal
Date	8 bytes	January 1, 0100 to December 31, 9999
Object	4 bytes	Any object reference
String (variable-length)	10 bytes + string length	0 to approximately 2 billion
String (fixed-length)	Length of string	1 to approximately 65,400
Variant (with numbers)	16 bytes	Any numeric value up to the range of a double data type
Variant (with characters)	22 bytes + string length	0 to approximately 2 billion
User-defined	Varies	Varies by element

Note The decimal data type is a rather unusual data type because you cannot actually declare it. In fact, it is a "subtype" of a variant. You need to use VBA's CDec function to convert a variant to the decimal data type.

Generally, it's best to use the data type that uses the smallest number of bytes yet still can handle all the data assigned to it. When VBA works with data, execution speed is a function of the number of bytes VBA has at its disposal. In other words, the fewer bytes used by data, the faster VBA can access and manipulate the data.

Declaring variables

If you don't declare the data type for a variable that you use in a VBA routine, VBA uses the default data type, variant. Data stored as a variant acts like a chameleon: It changes type, depending on what you do with it. The following procedure demonstrates how a variable can assume different data types.

```
Sub VariantDemo()
    MyVar = "123"
    MyVar = MyVar / 2
    MyVar = "Answer: " & MyVar
    MsgBox MyVar
End Sub
```

In the `VariantDemo` procedure, `MyVar` starts out as a three-character string. Then this "string" is divided by two and becomes a numeric data type. Next, `MyVar` is appended to a string, converting `MyVar` back to a string. The `MsgBox` statement displays the final string: *Answer: 61.5.*

Determining a data type

You can use VBA's `TypeName` function to determine the data type of a variable. Here's a modified version of the previous procedure. This version displays the data type of `MyVar` at each step. You'll see that it starts out as a string, and then is converted to a double, and finally ends up as a string again.

```
Sub VariantDemo2()
    MyVar = "123"
    MsgBox TypeName(MyVar)
    MyVar = MyVar / 2
    MsgBox TypeName(MyVar)
    MyVar = "Answer: " & MyVar
    MsgBox TypeName(MyVar)
    MsgBox MyVar
End Sub
```

Thanks to VBA, the data type conversion of undeclared variables is automatic. This process may seem like an easy way out, but remember that you sacrifice speed and memory.

Before you use a variable in a procedure, you may want to *declare* it — that is, tell VBA its name and data type. Declaring variables provides two main benefits:

✦ Your programs run faster and use memory more efficiently. The default data type, variant, causes VBA to repeatedly perform time-consuming checks and reserve more memory than necessary. If VBA knows the data type, it doesn't have to investigate, and it can reserve just enough memory to store the data.

✦ You avoid problems involving misspelled variable names. Say that you use an undeclared variable named CurrentRate. At some point in your routine, however, you insert the statement CurentRate = .075. This misspelled variable name, which is very difficult to spot, will likely cause your routine to give incorrect results.

Forcing yourself to declare all variables

To force yourself to declare all the variables that you use, include the following as the first instruction in your VBA module:

```
Option Explicit
```

This statement causes your program to stop whenever VBA encounters a variable name that has not been declared. VBA issues an error message, and you must declare the variable before you can proceed.

Tip   To ensure that the Option Explicit statement is automatically inserted whenever you insert a new VBA module, enable the Require Variable Declaration option in the Editor tab of the VBE's Options dialog box.

Scoping variables

A variable's *scope* determines which modules and procedures the variable can be used in. A variable's scope can be any of the following:

Scope	How a Variable with This Scope Is Declared
Single procedure	Include a Dim, Static, or Private statement within the procedure.
Modulewide	Include a Dim statement before the first procedure in a module.
All modules	Include a Public statement before the first procedure in a module.

Each scope is discussed further in the following sections.

Local variables

A *local variable* is a variable declared within a procedure. Local variables can be used only in the procedure in which they are declared. When the procedure ends, the variable no longer exists, and Excel frees up its memory.

Tip   If you need the variable to retain its value, declare it as a Static variable (see "Static Variables" later in this section).

The most common way to declare a local variable is to place a Dim statement between a Sub statement and an End Sub statement (in fact, Dim statements usually are placed right after the Sub statement, before the procedure's code).

The following procedure uses six local variables declared using Dim statements:

```
Sub MySub()
    Dim x As Integer
    Dim First As Long
    Dim InterestRate As Single
    Dim TodaysDate As Date
    Dim UserName As String * 20
    Dim MyValue
'    - [The procedure's code goes here] -
End Sub
```

Notice that the last Dim statement in the preceding example doesn't declare a data type; it simply names the variable. As a result, that variable becomes a variant.

By the way, you also can declare several variables with a single Dim statement. For example,

```
Dim x As Integer, y As Integer, z As Integer
Dim First As Long, Last As Double
```

 **Caution** Unlike some languages, VBA does not let you declare a group of variables to be a particular data type by separating the variables with commas. For example, the following statement, although valid, does *not* declare all the variables as integers:

```
Dim i, j, k As Integer
```

Another Way of Data-Typing Variables

Like most other dialects of BASIC, VBA lets you append a character to a variable's name to indicate the data type. For example, you can declare the MyVar variable as an integer by tacking % onto the name:

```
Dim MyVar%
```

Type-declaration characters exist for most of VBA's data types (data types not listed don't have type-declaration characters) as the following table shows:

Data Type	Type-Declaration Character
Integer	%
Long	&
Single	!
Double	#
Currency	@
String	$

In VBA, only k is declared to be an integer; the other variables are declared variants. To declare i, j, and k as integers, use this statement:

```
Dim i As Integer, j As Integer, k As Integer
```

If a variable is declared with a local scope, other procedures in the same module can use the same variable name, but each instance of the variable is unique to its own procedure.

In general, local variables are the most efficient because VBA frees up the memory they use when the procedure ends.

Module-wide variables

Sometimes, you'll want a variable to be available to all procedures in a module. If so, just declare the variable *before* the module's first procedure outside of any procedures or functions.

In the following example, the Dim statement is the first instruction in the module. Both MySub and YourSub have access to the CurrentValue variable.

```
Dim CurrentValue as Integer

Sub MySub()
'    - [Code goes here] -
End Sub

Sub YourSub()
'    - [Code goes here] -
End Sub
```

The value of a modulewide variable does not change when a procedure ends.

Public variables

To make a variable available to all the procedures in all the VBA modules in a project, declare the variable at the module level by using the Public keyword rather than Dim. Here's an example:

```
Public CurrentRate as Long
```

The Public keyword makes the CurrentRate variable available to any procedure in the project (that is, a single workbook), even those in other modules. You must insert this statement before the first procedure in a module. This type of declaration must also appear in a standard VBA module — not in a code module for a sheet or a UserForm.

Static variables

Static variables are a special case. They are declared at the procedure level, and they retain their value when the procedure ends.

You declare static variables using the `Static` keyword:

```
Sub MySub()
    Static Counter as Integer
    - [Code goes here] -
End Sub
```

Working with constants

A variable's value may, and often does, change while a procedure is executing (that's why it's called a variable). Sometimes, you need to refer to a named value or string that never changes: a *constant*.

Declaring constants

You declare constants using the `Const` statement. Here are some examples:

```
Const NumQuarters as Integer = 4
Const Rate = .0725, Period = 12
Const ModName as String = "Budget Macros"
Public Const AppName as String = "Budget Application"
```

The second example doesn't declare a data type. Consequently, the two constants are variants.

Tip Because a constant never changes its value, you'll normally want to declare your constants as a specific data type.

Like variables, constants also have a scope. If you want a constant to be available within a single procedure only, declare it after the `Sub` or `Function` statement to make it a local constant. To make a constant available to all procedures in a module, declare it before the first procedure in the module. To make a constant available to all modules in the workbook, use the `Public` keyword and declare the constant before the first procedure in a module.

Note If you attempt to change the value of a constant in a VBA procedure, you get an error—which is what you would expect. A constant is a constant, not a variable.

Tip Using constants throughout your code in place of hard-coded values or strings is an excellent programming practice. For example, if your procedure needs to refer to a specific value, such as an interest rate, several times, it's better to declare the value as a constant and use the constant's name rather than its value in your expressions. This technique not only makes your code more readable, but it also makes it easier to change should the need arise—you have to change only one instruction rather than several.

Using predefined constants

Excel and VBA contain many predefined constants, which you can use without declaring; in fact, you don't even need to know the value of these constants to use them. The macro recorder generally uses constants rather than actual values. The following procedure uses a built-in constant (xlManual) to change the Calculation property of the Application object (that is, to change Excel's recalculation mode to manual):

```
Sub CalcManual()
    Application.Calculation = xlManual
End Sub
```

If you have the AutoList Members option turned on (Tools ➪ Options), VBA lists all the constants that can be assigned to a property. Usually, the names of the constants are self-explanatory.

Working with strings

Like Excel, VBA can manipulate both numbers and text (strings). Two types of strings exist in VBA:

✦ Fixed-length strings are declared with a specified number of characters. The maximum length is 65,535 characters.

✦ Variable-length strings theoretically can hold up to 2 billion characters.

Each character in a string takes 1 byte of storage, and a small additional amount of storage is used for the header of each string. When you declare a string variable with a Dim statement, you can specify the maximum length if you know it (that is, a fixed-length string), or you can let VBA handle it dynamically (a variable-length string). Working with fixed-length strings is slightly more efficient in terms of memory usage.

In the following example, the MyString variable is declared to be a string with a maximum length of 50 characters. YourString is also declared as a string, but its length is unfixed.

```
Dim MyString As String * 50
Dim YourString As String
```

Working with dates

A variable defined as a date uses 8 bytes of storage and can hold dates ranging from January 1, A.D. 100, to December 31, 9999. The date data type is also useful for storing time-related data. In VBA, you specify dates and times by enclosing them between two pound signs (#), as shown next.

 The range of dates that VBA can handle is much larger than Excel's own date range—which begins with January 1, 1900. Therefore, be careful that you don't attempt to use a date in a worksheet that is outside of Excel's acceptable date range.

Here are some examples of declaring variables and constants as date data types:

```
Dim Today As Date
Dim StartTime As Date
Const FirstDay As Date = #1/1/2001#
Const Noon = #12:00:00#
```

 Date variables display dates according to your system's short date format, and times appear according to your system's time format (either 12- or 24-hour). You can modify these system settings by using the Regional Settings option in the Windows Control Panel.

Using Assignment Expressions

An *assignment expression* is a VBA instruction that makes a mathematical evaluation and assigns the result to a variable or an object. Much of the work done in VBA involves developing (and debugging) expressions.

If you know how to create formulas in Excel, you'll have no trouble creating expressions in VBA. With a worksheet formula, Excel displays the result in a cell. A VBA expression, on the other hand, can be assigned to a variable or used as a property value.

VBA uses the equal sign (=) as its assignment operator. The following are examples of assignment statements (the expressions are to the right of the equal sign):

```
x = 1
x = x + 1
x = (y * 2) / (z  * 2)
FileOpen = True
FileOpen = Not FileOpen
Range("TheYear").Value = 2003
```

 Expressions can be very complex. You may want to use the continuation sequence (space followed by an underscore) to make lengthy expressions easier to read.

Often, expressions use functions — VBA's built-in functions, Excel's worksheet functions, or custom functions that you develop in VBA.

Operators play a major role in VBA. Familiar operators describe mathematical operations, including addition (+), multiplication (*), division (/), subtraction (-), exponentiation (^), and string concatenation (&). Less-familiar operators are the backslash (\), used in integer division, and the Mod operator, used in modulo arithmetic. The Mod operator returns the remainder of one number divided by another. For example, the following expression returns 2:

```
17 Mod 3
```

VBA also supports the same comparative operators used in Excel formulas: equal to (=); greater than (>); less than (<); greater than or equal to (>=); less than or equal to (<=); and not equal to (<>).

In addition, VBA provides a full set of logical operators, shown in Table 33-2.

Table 33-2 VBA's Logical Operators	
Operator	**What It Does**
Not	Performs a logical negation on an expression
And	Performs a logical conjunction on two expressions
Or	Performs a logical disjunction on two expressions
XoR	Performs a logical exclusion on two expressions
Eqv	Performs a logical equivalence on two expressions
Imp	Performs a logical implication on two expressions

The order of precedence for operators in VBA is exactly the same as in Excel. Of course, you can add parentheses to change the natural order of precedence.

The following instruction uses the Not operator to toggle the gridline display in the active window. The DisplayGridlines property takes a value of either True or False. Therefore, using the Not operator changes False to True and True to False.

```
ActiveWindow.DisplayGridlines = _
   Not ActiveWindow.DisplayGridlines
```

The following expression performs a logical And. The MsgBox statement displays True only when Sheet1 is the active sheet *and* the active cell is in row 1.

```
MsgBox ActiveSheet.Name = "Sheet1" And ActiveCell.Row = 1
```

The following expression performs a logical Or. The MsgBox statement displays True when either Sheet1 *or* Sheet2 is the active sheet.

```
MsgBox ActiveSheet.Name = _
   "Sheet1" Or ActiveSheet.Name = "Sheet1"
```

Working with Arrays

An *array* is a group of elements of the same type that have a common name; you refer to a specific element in the array using the array name and an index number. For example, you may define an array of 12 string variables so that each variable corresponds to the name of a different month. If you name the array `MonthNames`, you can refer to the first element of the array as `MonthNames(0)`, the second element as `MonthNames(1)`, and so on, up to `MonthNames(11)`.

Tip
You address array elements using a number that represents an offset from the start of the array. That's why the first array element has an index number of 0 rather than 1 — it's at the beginning of the array and you don't have to travel into the array to reach it.

Declaring arrays

You declare an array with a `Dim` or `Public` statement, just as you declare a regular variable. You can also specify the number of elements in the array. You do so by specifying the first index number, the keyword `To`, and the last index number — all inside parentheses. For example, here's how to declare an array comprising exactly 100 integers:

```
Dim MyArray(1 To 100) As Integer
```

Tip
When you declare an array, you need to specify only the upper index, in which case VBA assumes that 0 is the lower index. Therefore, the two statements that follow have the same effect:

```
Dim MyArray(0 to 100) As Integer
Dim MyArray(100) As Integer
```

In both these cases, the array consists of 101 elements.

If you would like VBA to assume that 1 is the lower index for all arrays that declare only the upper index, include the following statement before any procedures in your module:

```
Option Base 1
```

Declaring multidimensional arrays

VBA arrays can have up to 60 dimensions, although it's rare to need more than 3 dimensions (a 3D array). The following statement declares a 100-integer array with two dimensions (2D):

```
Dim MyArray(1 To 10, 1 To 10) As Integer
```

You can think of the preceding array as occupying a 10×10 matrix. To refer to a specific element in a 2D array, you need to specify two index numbers. For example, here's how you can assign a value to an element in the preceding array:

```
MyArray(3, 4) = 125
```

A *dynamic array* doesn't have a preset number of elements. You declare a dynamic array with a blank set of parentheses:

```
Dim MyArray() As Integer
```

Before you can use a dynamic array in your code, however, you must use the ReDim statement to tell VBA how many elements are in the array (or ReDim Preserve if you want to keep the existing values in the array). You can use the ReDim statement any number of times, changing the array's size as often as you need to.

Using Object Variables

An *object variable* is a variable that represents an entire object, such as a range or a worksheet. Object variables are important for two reasons:

✦ They can simplify your code significantly.

✦ They can make your code execute more quickly.

Object variables, like normal variables, are declared with the Dim or Public statement. For example, the following statement declares InputArea as a Range object.

```
Public InputArea As Range
```

To see how object variables simplify your code, examine the following procedure, which was written without using object variables:

```
Sub NoObjVar()
    Worksheets("Sheet1").Range("A1").Value = 124
    Worksheets("Sheet1").Range("A1").Font.Bold = True
    Worksheets("Sheet1").Range("A1").Font.Italic = True
End Sub
```

This routine enters a value into cell A1 of Sheet1 on the active workbook and then boldfaces and italicizes the cell's contents. That's lots of typing. To reduce wear and tear on your fingers, you can condense the routine with an object variable:

```
Sub ObjVar()
    Dim MyCell As Range
    Set MyCell = Worksheets("Sheet1").Range("A1")
    MyCell.Value = 124
    MyCell.Font.Bold = True
    MyCell.Font.Italic = True
End Sub
```

After the variable `MyCell` is declared as a `Range` object, the `Set` statement assigns an object to it. Subsequent statements can then use the simpler `MyCell` reference in place of the lengthy `Worksheets("Sheet1").Range("A1")` reference.

Tip

After an object is assigned to a variable, VBA can access it more quickly than it can access a normal lengthy reference that has to be resolved. So when speed is critical, use object variables. One way to think about this is in terms of "dot processing." Every time VBA encounters a dot, as in Sheets(1).Range("A1"), it takes time to resolve the reference. Using an object variable reduces the number of dots to be processed. The fewer the dots, the faster the processing time. Another way to improve the speed of your code is by using the With-End With construct, which also reduces the number of dots to be processed.

Creating User-Defined Data Types

VBA lets you create custom, or *user-defined,* data types (a concept much like Pascal records or C structures). A user-defined data type can ease your work with some types of data. For example, if your application deals with customer information, you may want to create a user-defined data type named `CustomerInfo,` as follows:

```
Type CustomerInfo
    Company As String * 25
    Contact As String * 15
    RegionCode As Integer
    Sales As Long
End Type
```

Note

You define custom data types outside of procedures at the top of your module.

After you create a user-defined data type, you use a `Dim` statement to declare a variable as that type. Usually, you define an array; for example:

```
Dim Customers(1 To 100) As CustomerInfo
```

Each of the 100 elements in this array consists of four components (as specified by the user-defined data type, `CustomerInfo`). You can refer to a particular component of the record as follows:

```
Customers(1).Company = "Acme Tools"
Customers(1).Contact = "Tim Robertson"
Customers(1).RegionCode = 3
Customers(1).Sales = 150677
```

You can also work with an element in the array as a whole. For example, to copy the information from `Customers(1)` to `Customers(2)`, use this instruction:

```
Customers(2) = Customers(1)
```

The preceding example is equivalent to the following instruction block:

```
Customers(2).Company = Customers(1).Company
Customers(2).Contact = Customers(1).Contact
Customers(2).RegionCode = Customers(1).RegionCode
Customers(2).Sales = Customers(1).Sales
```

Working With Built-In Functions

Like most programming languages, VBA has a variety of built-in functions that simplify calculations and operations. Often, the functions enable you to perform operations that are otherwise difficult, or even impossible. Many of VBA's functions are similar (or identical) to Excel's worksheet functions. For example, the VBA function UCase, which converts a string argument to uppercase, is equivalent to the Excel worksheet function UPPER.

 Tip To get a list of VBA functions while you're writing your code, type VBA followed by a period (.). The VBE displays a list of all functions that you can select (see Figure 33-1). If this doesn't work for you, make sure that the Auto List Members option is selected. Choose Tools ➪ Options, and click the Editor tab.

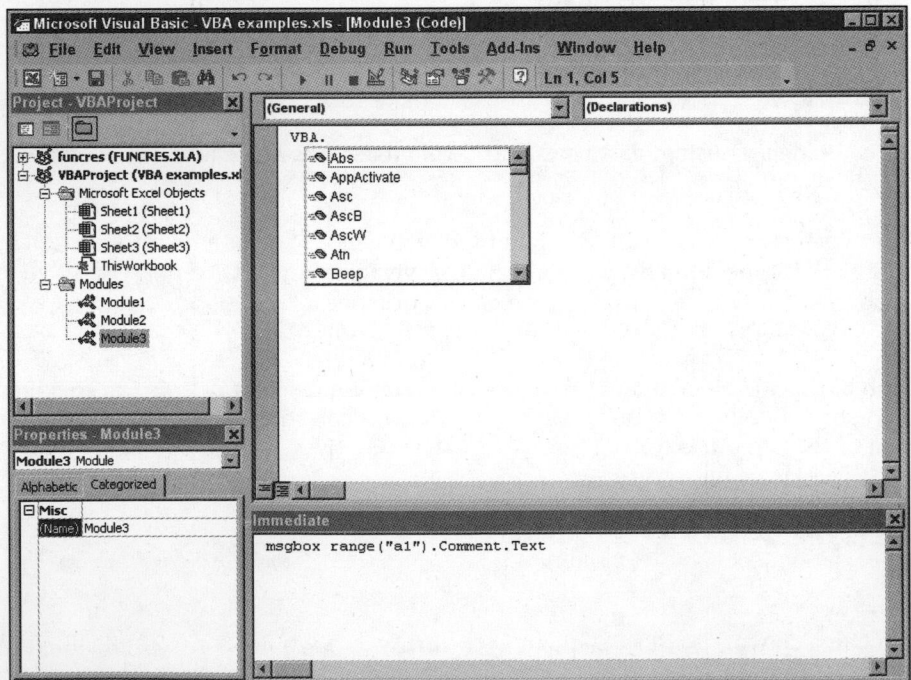

Figure 33-1: You can view a list of the VBA functions to use in your code.

You use functions in VBA expressions in much the same way that you use functions in worksheet formulas. For instance, you can nest VBA functions.

Here's a simple procedure that calculates the square root of a variable by using VBA's Sqr function. It then stores the result in another variable and displays the result:

```
Sub ShowRoot()
    MyValue = 25
    SquareRoot = Sqr(MyValue)
    MsgBox SquareRoot
End Sub
```

You can use many (but not all) of Excel's worksheet functions in your VBA code. The WorksheetFunction object, which is contained in the Application object, holds all the worksheet functions that you can call from your VBA procedures.

Tip   To use a worksheet function in a VBA statement, just precede the function name with

```
Application.WorksheetFunction
```

The following example demonstrates how to use an Excel worksheet function in a VBA procedure. Excel's infrequently used ROMAN function converts a decimal number into a Roman numeral.

```
Sub ShowRoman()
    DecValue = 1999
    RomanValue = Application.WorksheetFunction.Roman(DecValue)
    MsgBox RomanValue
End Sub
```

When you execute this procedure, the MsgBox function displays the string MCMXCIX.

You cannot use worksheet functions that have an equivalent VBA function. For example, VBA cannot access Excel's SQRT worksheet function because VBA has its own version of that function: Sqr. Thus, the following statement generates an error:

```
MsgBox Application.WorksheetFunction.Sqrt(123)    'error
```

You can use VBA to create custom worksheet functions that work just like Excel's built-in worksheet functions.

The MsgBox Function

The MsgBox function is one of VBA's most useful functions. Many examples in this chapter use this function to display the value of a variable.

This function often is a good substitute for a simple custom dialog box. It's also an excellent debugging tool because you can insert MsgBox functions at any time to pause your code and to display the result of a calculation or assignment.

Most functions return a single value, which you assign to a variable. The MsgBox function not only returns a value, but also displays a dialog box that the user can respond to. The value returned by the MsgBox function represents the user's response to the dialog box. You can use the MsgBox function even when you have no interest in the user's response but want to take advantage of the message display.

The official syntax of the MsgBox function has five arguments (those in square brackets are optional):

```
MsgBox(prompt[, buttons][, title][, helpfile, context])
```

   prompt   (Required) The message displayed in the pop-up display.

   buttons   (Optional) A value that specifies which buttons and which icon, if any, appear in the message box. Use built-in constants — for example, vbYesNo.

   title   (Optional) The text that appears in the message box's title bar. The default is Microsoft Excel.

   helpfile   (Optional) The name of the help file associated with the message box.

   context   (Optional) The context ID of the help topic. This represents a specific help topic to display.

You can assign the value returned to a variable, or you can use the function by itself without an assignment statement. The next example assigns the result to the variable Ans.

```
Ans = MsgBox("Continue?", vbYesNo + vbQuestion, "Tell me")
If Ans = vbNo Then Exit Sub
```

Notice that this example used the sum of two built-in constants (vbYesNo + vbQuestion) for the buttons argument. Using vbYesNo displays two buttons in the message box: one labeled Yes and one labeled No. Adding vbQuestion to the argument also displays a question mark icon. When the first statement is executed, Ans contains one of two values, represented by the constants vbYes or vbNo. In this example, if the user clicks the No button, the procedure ends.

For more information, refer to the online help, which lists all the constants you can use.

Manipulating Objects and Collections

As an Excel programmer, you'll spend lots of time working with objects and collections. Therefore, you'll want to know the most efficient ways to write your code to manipulate these objects and collections. VBA offers two important constructs that can simplify working with objects and collections:

✦ With-End With constructs

✦ For Each-Next constructs

Using With-End With constructs

The With-End With instruction construct enables you to perform multiple operations on a single object. To start understanding how the With-End With construct works, examine the following procedure, which modifies five properties of a selection's formatting (the selection is assumed to be a Range object):

```
Sub ChangeFont1()
    Selection.Font.Name = "Times New Roman"
    Selection.Font.FontStyle = "Bold Italic"
    Selection.Font.Size = 12
    Selection.Font.Underline = xlSingle
    Selection.Font.ColorIndex = 5
End Sub
```

This procedure can be rewritten using the With-End With construct. The following procedure performs exactly like the preceding one:

```
Sub ChangeFont2()
    With Selection.Font
        .Name = "Times New Roman"
        .FontStyle = "Bold Italic"
        .Size = 12
        .Underline = xlSingle
        .ColorIndex = 5
    End With
End Sub
```

Some people think that the second incarnation of the procedure is actually more difficult to read. Remember, though, that the objective is increased speed. Although the first version may be more straightforward and easier to understand, a procedure that uses the With-End With construct when changing several properties of an object can be significantly faster than the equivalent procedure that explicitly references the object in each statement.

Using For Each-Next constructs

A *collection* is a group of related objects. For example, the Workbooks collection is a collection of all open Workbook objects. You can work with many other collections, and you don't have to know how many elements are in a collection to use the For Each-Next construct.

Suppose that you want to perform some action on all objects in a collection. Or suppose that you want to evaluate all objects in a collection and take action under certain conditions. These are perfect occasions for the For Each-Next construct.

The syntax of the For Each-Next construct is

```
For Each element In group
    [instructions]
    [Exit For]
    [instructions]
Next [element]
```

The following procedure uses the For Each-Next construct to refer to each of the six single-precision members of a fixed-length array one at a time:

```
Sub Macro1()
    Dim MyArray(5)
    For i = 0 To 5
        MyArray(i) = Rnd
    Next i
    For Each n In MyArray
        Debug.Print n
    Next n
End Sub
```

The next procedure uses the For Each-Next construct with the Sheets collection in the active workbook. When you execute the procedure, the MsgBox function displays each sheet's Name property. (If five sheets exist in the active workbook, the MsgBox function is called five times.)

```
Sub CountSheets()
    Dim Item as WorkSheet
    For Each Item In ActiveWorkbook.Sheets
        MsgBox Item.Name
    Next Item
End Sub
```

Note   In the preceding example, Item is an object variable (more specifically, a Worksheet object). There's nothing special about the name Item; you can use any valid variable name in its place.

The next example uses For Each-Next to cycle through all objects in the Windows collection:

```
Sub HiddenWindows()
    AllVisible = True
    For Each Item In Windows
        If Item.Visible = False Then
            AllVisible = False
            Exit For
```

```
        End If
    Next Item
    MsgBox AllVisible
End Sub
```

If a window is hidden, the value of `AllVisible` is changed to False and the `For Each-Next` loop is exited. The message box displays True if all windows are visible and displays False if at least one window is hidden. The `Exit For` statement is optional. It provides a way to exit the `For Each-Next` loop early. This is generally used in conjunction with an `If-Then` statement (described later in this chapter).

Here's an example that closes all workbooks except the active workbook. This procedure uses the `If-Then` construct to evaluate each workbook in the `Workbooks` collection.

```
Sub CloseInActive()
    For Each Book In Workbooks
        If Book.Name <> ActiveWorkbook.Name Then Book.Close
    Next Book
End Sub
```

The final example of `For Each-Next` is designed to be executed after the user selects a range of cells. Here, the `Selection` object acts as a collection that consists of `Range` objects because each cell in the selection is a `Range` object. The procedure evaluates each cell and uses VBA's `UCase` function to convert its contents to uppercase (numeric cells are not affected).

```
Sub MakeUpperCase()
    For Each Cell In Selection
        Cell.Value = UCase(Cell.Value)
    Next Cell
End Sub
```

Controlling Execution

Some VBA procedures start at the top and progress line by line to the bottom. Macros that you record, for example, always work in this fashion. Often, however, you need to control the flow of your routines by skipping over some statements, executing some statements multiple times and testing conditions to determine what the routine does next.

The preceding section described the `For Each-Next` construct, which is a type of loop. This section discusses the additional ways of controlling the execution of your VBA procedures:

✦ GoTo statements

✦ If-Then constructs

✦ Select Case constructs

✦ For-Next loops

✦ Do While loops

✦ Do Until loops

Using GoTo statements

The most straightforward way to change the flow of a program is to use a GoTo statement. This statement simply transfers program execution to a new instruction, which must be preceded by a label (a text string followed by a colon). VBA procedures can contain any number of labels, and a GoTo statement cannot branch outside of a procedure.

The following procedure uses VBA's InputBox function to get the user's name. If the name is not Howard, the procedure branches to the WrongName label and ends. If the name is Howard, the procedure executes some additional code. The Exit Sub statement causes the procedure to end.

```
Sub GoToDemo()
    UserName = InputBox("Enter Your Name:")
    If UserName <> "Howard" Then GoTo WrongName
    MsgBox ("Welcome Howard...")
'   -[More code here] -
    Exit Sub
WrongName:
    MsgBox "Sorry. Only Howard can run this."
End Sub
```

This simple procedure works, but in general you should use the GoTo statement only when you have no other way to perform an action. In fact, the only time you *really* need to use a GoTo statement in VBA is for error trapping (refer to Chapter 32).

Using If-Then constructs

Perhaps the most commonly used instruction grouping in VBA is the If-Then construct. This common instruction is one way to endow your applications with decision-making capability. Good decision making is the key to writing successful programs. A successful Excel application essentially boils down to making decisions and acting on them.

The basic syntax of the If-Then construct is

```
If condition Then true_instructions [Else false_instructions]
```

The If-Then construct is used to execute one or more statements conditionally. The Else clause is optional. If included, it lets you execute one or more instructions when the condition you're testing is not true.

The following procedure demonstrates an If-Then structure without an Else clause. The example deals with time. VBA uses the same date-and-time serial number system as Excel. The time of day is expressed as a fractional value — for example, noon is represented as 0.5. VBA's Time function returns a value that represents the time of day, as reported by the system clock. In the following example, a message is displayed if the time is before noon. If the current system time is greater than or equal to 0.5, the procedure ends and nothing happens.

```
Sub GreetMe()
    If Time < 0.5 Then MsgBox "Good Morning"
End Sub
```

If you want to display a different greeting when the time of day is after noon, add another If-Then statement, like so:

```
Sub GreetMe()
    If Time < 0.5 Then MsgBox "Good Morning"
    If Time >= 0.5 Then MsgBox "Good Afternoon"
End Sub
```

Another approach is to use the Else clause of the If-Then construct; for example:

```
Sub GreetMe()
    If Time < 0.5 Then MsgBox "Good Morning" Else _
        MsgBox "Good Afternoon"
End Sub
```

Notice that this example used the line continuation sequence; If-Then-Else is actually a single statement.

If you need to expand a routine to handle three conditions (for example, morning, afternoon, and evening), you can use either three If-Then statements or a nested If-Then-Else structure.

But for more complex applications, you need another syntax:

```
If condition Then
    [true_instructions]
[ElseIf condition-n Then
    [alternate_instructions]]
[Else
    [default_instructions]]
End If
```

VBA's IIf Function

VBA offers an alternative to the If-Then construct: the IIf function. This function takes three arguments and works much like Excel's IF worksheet function. The syntax is

```
IIf(expr, truepart, falsepart)
```

expr (Required) Expression to evaluate

truepart (Required) Value or expression returned if expr is True

falsepart (Required) Value or expression returned if expr is False

The following instruction demonstrates the use of the IIf function. The message box displays Zero if cell A1 contains a zero or is empty. It displays Nonzero if cell A1 contains anything else.

```
MsgBox IIf(Range("A1") = 0, "Zero", "Nonzero")
```

Here's how you can use this syntax to rewrite the GreetMe procedure:

```
Sub GreetMe()
    If Time < 0.5 Then
        MsgBox "Good Morning"
    ElseIf Time >= 0.5 And Time < 0.75 Then
        MsgBox "Good Afternoon"
    ElseIf Time >= 0.75 Then
        MsgBox "Good Evening"
    End If
End Sub
```

With this syntax, when a condition is true, the conditional statements are executed and the If-Then construct ends. In other words, the extraneous conditions are not evaluated. Although this syntax makes for greater efficiency, some may find the code to be more difficult to understand.

Nested If-Then structures can be cumbersome. When you need to choose among three or more alternatives, the Select Case structure (covered in the following section) is often a better construct to use.

Using Select Case constructs

The Select Case construct is useful for choosing among three or more options. This construct also works with two options and is a good alternative to If-Then-Else. The syntax for Select Case is

```
Select Case testexpression
    [Case expressionlist-n
        [instructions-n]]
```

```
        [Case Else
            [default_instructions]]
    End Select
```

The following example of a Select Case construct shows another way to code the GreetMe examples presented in the preceding section:

```
Sub GreetMe()
    Select Case Time
        Case Is < 0.5
            Msg = "Good Morning"
        Case 0.5 To 0.75
            Msg = "Good Afternoon"
        Case Else
            Msg = "Good Evening"
    End Select
    MsgBox Msg
End Sub
```

Any number of instructions can be written below each Case statement, and they all are executed if that case evaluates to True. If you use only one instruction per case, as in the preceding example, you may want to put the instruction on the same line as the Case keyword (but don't forget VBA's statement-separator character, the colon). This technique makes the code more compact; for example:

```
Sub Discount3()
    Quantity = InputBox("Enter Quantity: ")
    Select Case Quantity
        Case "": Exit Sub
        Case  0 To 24: Discount = 0.1
        Case 25 To 49: Discount = 0.15
        Case 50 To 74: Discount = 0.2
        Case Is >= 75: Discount = 0.25
    End Select
    MsgBox "Discount: " & Discount
End Sub
```

Tip

VBA exits a Select Case construct as soon as a True case is found. Therefore, for maximum efficiency, you might want to check the most likely case first.

Select Case structures can also be nested. The following procedure, for example, tests for Excel's window state (maximized, minimized, or normal) and then displays a message describing the window state. If Excel's window state is normal, the procedure tests for the window state of the active window and then displays another message.

```
Sub AppWindow()
    Select Case Application.WindowState
        Case xlMaximized: MsgBox "App Maximized"
        Case xlMinimized: MsgBox "App Minimized"
        Case xlNormal: MsgBox "App Normal"
            Select Case ActiveWindow.WindowState
```

```
                    Case xlMaximized: MsgBox "Book Maximized"
                    Case xlMinimized: MsgBox "Book Minimized"
                    Case xlNormal: MsgBox "Book Normal"
                End Select
        End Select
    End Sub
```

You can nest Select Case constructs as deeply as you need, but make sure that each Select Case statement has a corresponding End Select statement.

Using looping blocks of instructions

Looping is the process of repeating a block of instructions. You may know the number of times to loop, or it may be determined by the values of variables in your program.

For-Next loops

The simplest type of *loop* is a For-Next loop, which has already been used in several previous examples. Its syntax is

```
For counter = start To end [Step stepval]
    [instructions]
    [Exit For]
    [instructions]
Next [counter]
```

Following is an example of a For-Next loop that doesn't use the optional Step value or the optional Exit For statement. This routine executes the Sum = Sum + Sqr(Count) statement 100 times and displays the result — that is, the sum of the square roots of the first 100 integers.

```
Sub SumSquareRoots()
    Sum = 0
    For Count = 1 To 100
        Sum = Sum + Sqr(Count)
    Next Count
    MsgBox Sum
End Sub
```

In this example, Count (the loop counter variable) started out as 1 and increased by 1 each time the loop repeated. The Sum variable simply accumulates the square roots of each value of Count.

You can also use a Step value to skip some values in the loop. Here's the same procedure rewritten to sum the square roots of the odd numbers between 1 and 100:

```
Sub SumOddSquareRoots()
    Sum = 0
```

```
    For Count = 1 To 100 Step 2
        Sum = Sum + Sqr(Count)
    Next Count
    MsgBox Sum
End Sub
```

In this procedure, Count starts out as 1 and then takes on values of 3, 5, 7, and so on. The final value of Count is 99.

For-Next loops can also include one or more `Exit For` statements within the loop. When this statement is encountered, the loop terminates immediately, as the following example demonstrates. This procedure determines which cell has the largest value in column A of the active worksheet.

```
Sub ExitForDemo()
    MaxVal = Application.WorksheetFunction.Max(Range("A:A"))
    For Row = 1 To 65536
        Set TheCell = Range("A1").Offset(Row - 1, 0)
        If TheCell.Value = MaxVal Then
            MsgBox "Max value is in Row " & Row
            TheCell.Activate
            Exit For
        End If
    Next Row
End Sub
```

The maximum value in the column is calculated by using Excel's MAX function. This value is then assigned to the MaxVal variable. The For-Next loop checks each cell in the column. If the cell being checked is equal to MaxVal, the Exit For statement ends the procedure. Before terminating the loop, though, the procedure informs the user of the row location and then activates the cell.

The previous examples use relatively simple loops. But you can have any number of statements in the loop, and you can even nest For-Next loops inside other For-Next loops. Here's an example that uses nested For-Next loops to initialize a 10×10×10 array with the value −1. When the procedure is finished, each of the 1,000 elements in MyArray will contain −1.

```
Sub NestedLoops()
    Dim MyArray(1 to 10, 1 to 10, 1 to 10)
    For i = 1 To 10
        For j = 1 To 10
            For k = 1 To 10
                MyArray(i, j, k) = -1
            Next k
        Next j
    Next i
End Sub
```

Do While loops

A Do While loop is another type of looping structure available in VBA. Unlike a For-Next loop, a Do While loop executes while a specified condition is met. A Do While loop can have either of two syntaxes:

```
Do [While condition]
    [instructions]
    [Exit Do]
    [instructions]
Loop
```

or

```
Do
    [instructions]
    [Exit Do]
    [instructions]
Loop [While condition]
```

As you can see, VBA lets you put the While condition at the beginning or the end of the loop. The difference between these two syntaxes involves the point in time when the condition is evaluated. In the first syntax, the contents of the loop may never be executed. In the second syntax, the contents of the loop are always executed at least once.

The following example uses a Do While loop with the first syntax.

```
Sub DoWhileDemo()
    Do While Not IsEmpty(ActiveCell)
        ActiveCell.Value = 0
        ActiveCell.Offset(1, 0).Select
    Loop
End Sub
```

This procedure uses the active cell as a starting point and then travels down the column, inserting a zero into the active cell. Each time the loop repeats, the next cell in the column becomes the active cell. The loop continues until VBA's IsEmpty function determines that the active cell is not empty.

The following procedure uses the second Do While loop syntax. The loop will always be executed at least once, even if the initial active cell is not empty.

```
Sub DoWhileDemo2()
    Do
        ActiveCell.Value = 0
        ActiveCell.Offset(1, 0).Select
    Loop While Not IsEmpty(ActiveCell)
End Sub
```

The following is another Do While loop example. This procedure opens a text file, reads each line, converts the text to uppercase, and then stores it in the active sheet, beginning with cell A1 and continuing down the column. The procedure uses VBA's EOF function, which returns True when the end of the file has been reached. The final statement closes the text file.

```
Sub DoWhileDemo1()
    Open "c:\data\textfile.txt" For Input As #1
    LineCt = 0
    Do While Not EOF(1)
      Input #1, LineOfText
      Range("A1").Offset(LineCt, 0) = UCase(LineOfText)
      LineCt = LineCt + 1
    Loop
    Close #1
End Sub
```

Do While loops can also contain one or more Exit Do statements. When an Exit Do statement is encountered, the loop ends immediately.

Do Until loops

The Do Until loop structure is very similar to the Do While structure. The difference is evident only when the condition is tested. In a Do While loop, the loop executes *while* the condition is true. In a Do Until loop, the loop executes *until* the condition is true.

Do Until also has two syntaxes:

```
Do [Until condition]
    [instructions]
    [Exit Do]
    [instructions]
Loop
```

or

```
Do
    [instructions]
    [Exit Do]
    [instructions]
Loop [Until condition]
```

The following example was originally presented for the Do While loop but has been rewritten to use a Do Until loop. The only difference is the line with the Do statement. This example makes the code a bit clearer because it avoids the negative required in the Do While example:

```
Sub DoUntilDemo1()
    Open "c:\data\textfile.txt" For Input As #1
    LineCt = 0
    Do Until EOF(1)
        Input #1, LineOfText
        Range("A1").Offset(LineCt, 0) = UCase(LineOfText)
        LineCt = LineCt + 1
    Loop
    Close #1
End Sub
```

✦   ✦   ✦

Working with VBA Sub Procedures

A *procedure* holds a group of VBA statements that accomplishes a desired task. Most VBA code is contained in procedures. This chapter focuses on *Sub procedures,* which perform tasks but do not return discrete values.

VBA also supports Function procedures, which are discussed in Chapter 34. Chapter 34 has many additional examples of procedures that you can incorporate into your work.

Understanding Procedures

A *procedure* is a series of VBA statements that resides in a VBA module, which you access in the VBE. A module can hold any number of procedures.

You have a number of ways to *call,* or execute, procedures. A procedure is executed from beginning to end (but it can also be ended prematurely).

Although there is no limit on the length of a procedure, it's usually best to write several smaller procedures, each with a single purpose. Then design a main procedure that calls those other procedures. This approach can make your code easier to maintain.

Some procedures are written to receive arguments. An *argument* is simply information that is used by the procedure that is "passed" to the procedure when it is executed. Procedure arguments work much like the arguments you use in Excel worksheet functions. Instructions within the procedure generally perform logical operations on these arguments, and the results of the procedure are usually based on those arguments.

Declaring a Sub procedure

A procedure declared with the `Sub` keyword must adhere to the following syntax:

```
[Private | Public][Static] Sub name [(arglist)]
    [instructions]
    [Exit Sub]
    [instructions]
End Sub
```

The following list explains the necessary syntax:

`Private`: (Optional) Indicates that the procedure is accessible only to other procedures in the same module.

`Public`: (Optional) Indicates that the procedure is accessible to all other procedures in all other modules in the workbook. If used in a module that contains an `Option Private` statement, the procedure is not available outside the project.

`Static`: (Optional) Indicates that the procedure's variables are preserved when the procedure ends.

`Sub`: (Required) The keyword that indicates the beginning of a procedure.

`name`: (Required) Represents any valid procedure name.

`arglist`: (Optional) Represents a list of variables, enclosed in parentheses, that receive arguments passed to the procedure. Use a comma to separate arguments.

`instructions`: (Optional) Represents valid VBA instructions.

`Exit Sub`: (Optional) A statement that forces an immediate exit from the procedure prior to its formal completion.

`End Sub`: (Required) Indicates the end of the procedure.

Note   With a few exceptions, all VBA instructions in a module must be contained in procedures. Exceptions include module-level variable declarations, user-defined data type definitions, and a few other instructions that specify module-level options (for example, Option Explicit).

Scoping a procedure

A variable's scope determines the modules and procedures in which the variable can be used. Similarly, a procedure's scope determines which other procedures can call it.

Public procedures

By default, procedures are *public* — that is, they can be called by other procedures in any module in the workbook. It's not necessary to use the `Public` keyword, but programmers often include it for clarity. The following two procedures are both public:

Naming Procedures

Every procedure must have a name. The rules governing procedure names are generally the same as for variable names. The exception is that a procedure name cannot be like a cell address. For example, you can't name a procedure J34 because J34 is a cell address.

Ideally, a procedure's name should describe what its contained processes do. A good rule of thumb is to use a name that includes a verb and a noun (for example, ProcessDate, PrintReport, Sort_Array, or CheckFilename). Avoid meaningless names such as DoIt, Update, and Fix.

Some programmers use sentence-like names that describe the procedure (for example, WriteReportToTextFile and Get_Print_Options_And_Print_Report). Although long names are very descriptive and unambiguous, they are also more difficult to type.

```
Sub First()
'    ... [code goes here] ...
End Sub

Public Sub Second()
'    ... [code goes here] ...
End Sub
```

Private procedures

Private procedures can be called by other procedures in the same module, but not by procedures in other modules.

Tip When you choose Excel's Tools ➪ Macro ➪ Macros command, the Macro dialog box displays only the public procedures. Therefore, if you have procedures that are designed to be called only by other procedures in the same module, you should make sure that the procedure is declared as Private. This prevents the user from running the procedure from the Macro dialog box.

The following example declares a private procedure, named MySub:

```
Private Sub MySub()
'    ... [code goes here] ...
End Sub
```

Tip You can force all procedures in a module to be private — even those declared with the Public keyword — by including the following statement before your first Sub statement:

```
Option Private Module
```

If you write this statement in a module, you can omit the Private keyword from your Sub declarations.

Note   Excel's macro recorder normally creates new Sub procedures called Macro1, Macro2, and so on. These procedures are all public procedures, and they will never use any arguments.

Executing Procedures

You can execute, or call, a VBA Sub procedure in many ways:

✦ With the Run ⇨ Run Sub/UserForm command (in the VBE). Or you can press the F5 shortcut key. Excel executes the procedure at the cursor position. This method doesn't work if the procedure requires one or more arguments.

✦ From Excel's Macro dialog box (which you open by choosing Tools ⇨ Macro ⇨ Macros). Or you can press the Alt+F8 shortcut key.

✦ Using the Ctrl key shortcut assigned to the procedure (assuming you assigned one).

✦ By clicking a button or a shape on a worksheet. The button or shape must have the procedure assigned to it.

✦ From another procedure you write.

✦ From a Toolbar button.

✦ From a custom menu that you develop.

✦ When an event occurs. These events include opening the workbook, saving the workbook, closing the workbook, making a change to a cell, activating a sheet, and many other things.

✦ From the Immediate window in the VBE. Just type the name of the procedure, write any arguments that may apply, and press Enter.

These methods of executing procedures are discussed in the following sections.

Note   In many cases, a procedure will not function properly unless it is in the appropriate context. For example, if a procedure is designed to work with the active worksheet, it will fail if a chart sheet is active. A good procedure incorporates code that checks for the appropriate context and exits gracefully if it can't proceed.

Executing a procedure with the Run ⇨ Run Sub/UserForm command

The Run Sub/UserForm menu command is used primarily to test a procedure while you are developing it. You would never expect a user to have to activate the VBE to execute a procedure. Use the Run ⇨ Run Sub/UserForm command (or F5) in the VBE to execute the current procedure (in other words, the procedure that contains the cursor).

If the cursor is not located within a procedure when you issue the Run ➪ Run Sub/UserForm command, VBE displays its Macro dialog box so that you can select a procedure to execute.

Executing a procedure from the Macro dialog box

Choosing Excel's Tools ➪ Macro ➪ Macros command displays the Macro dialog box, shown in Figure 34-1 (you can also press Alt+F8 to access this dialog box). The Macro dialog box lists all available procedures. Use the Macros in drop-down list box to limit the scope of the macros displayed (for example, show only the macros in the active workbook).

Tip   The Macro dialog box does not display procedures declared with the Private keyword, procedures that require one or more arguments, or procedures contained in add-ins.

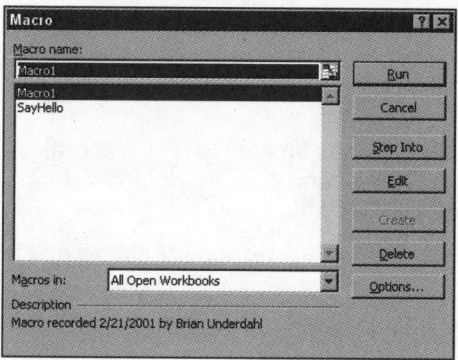

Figure 34-1: You can use the Macro dialog box to run any of the listed procedures.

Executing a procedure using a Ctrl+shortcut key combination

You can assign a Ctrl+shortcut key combination to any procedure that doesn't use any arguments. If you assign the Ctrl+T key combo to a procedure named Update, for example, pressing Ctrl+T executes the Update procedure.

Caution   If you assign one of Excel's predefined shortcut key combinations to a procedure, your key assignment takes precedence over the predefined key assignment. For example, Ctrl+S is Excel's predefined shortcut key for saving the active workbook. But if you assign Ctrl+S to a procedure, pressing Ctrl+S no longer saves the active workbook.

When you begin recording a macro, the Record Macro dialog box gives you the opportunity to assign a shortcut key. However, you can assign a shortcut key at any time. To assign a Ctrl shortcut key to a procedure (or change a procedure's shortcut key), follow these steps:

1. Activate Excel and choose the Tools ➪ Macro ➪ Macros command.

2. Select the appropriate procedure from the list box in the Macro dialog box.

3. Click the Options button to display the Macro Options dialog box (see Figure 34-2).

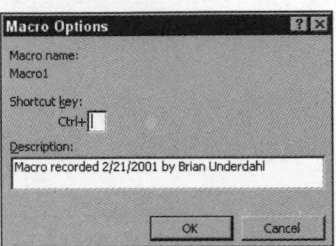

Figure 34-2: You can use the Macro Options dialog box to assign a Ctrl-key shortcut and an optional description to a procedure.

4. Enter a character into the text box labeled Ctrl+.

   The character that you enter into the text box labeled Ctrl+ is case-sensitive. If you enter a lowercase *s*, the shortcut key combo is Ctrl+S. If you enter an uppercase *S*, the shortcut key combo is Ctrl+Shift+S.

5. Enter a description (optional). If you enter a description for a macro, it is displayed in the Macro dialog box.

6. Click OK to close the Macro Options dialog box, and click Close to close the Macro dialog box.

Tip   Excel doesn't use too many Ctrl+Shift+key combinations, so using an uppercase character is a good idea. Also, remember that you can use many of the punctuation keys.

Executing a procedure from a custom menu

Excel provides two ways for you to customize its menus: using the View ➪ Toolbars ➪ Customize command or writing VBA code. The latter method is preferable, but you can use either technique to assign a macro to a new menu item.

Following are the steps required to display a new menu item on a menu and to assign a macro to the menu item. It assumes that the new menu item is on the Data menu, that the menu item text is Customer File, and that the procedure is named `OpenCustomerFile`.

1. Choose the View ➪ Toolbars ➪ Customize command. Excel displays the Customize dialog box.

Tip

When the Customize dialog box is displayed, Excel is in a special "customization" mode. The menus and toolbars are not active, but they can be customized.

2. Click the Commands tab in the Customize dialog box.

3. Scroll down and click Macros in the Categories list.

4. In the Commands list, drag the first item (labeled Custom Menu Item) to the bottom of the Data menu (after the Refresh Data item). The Data menu drops down when you click it.

5. Right-click the new menu item (which is labeled Custom Menu Item) to display a shortcut menu.

6. Enter a new name for the menu item: **&Customer File** in the text box labeled Name (see Figure 34-3).

Caution

The ampersand (&) is used to indicate which character in the menu item will be underlined (the C in this example), and therefore which character can be used to activate the command using the keyboard. If you choose to underline a character that is underlined in a command further up on the menu, Excel won't allow users to activate your new command using the underlined character. Note that you can place the ampersand within a word to choose a different underlined character.

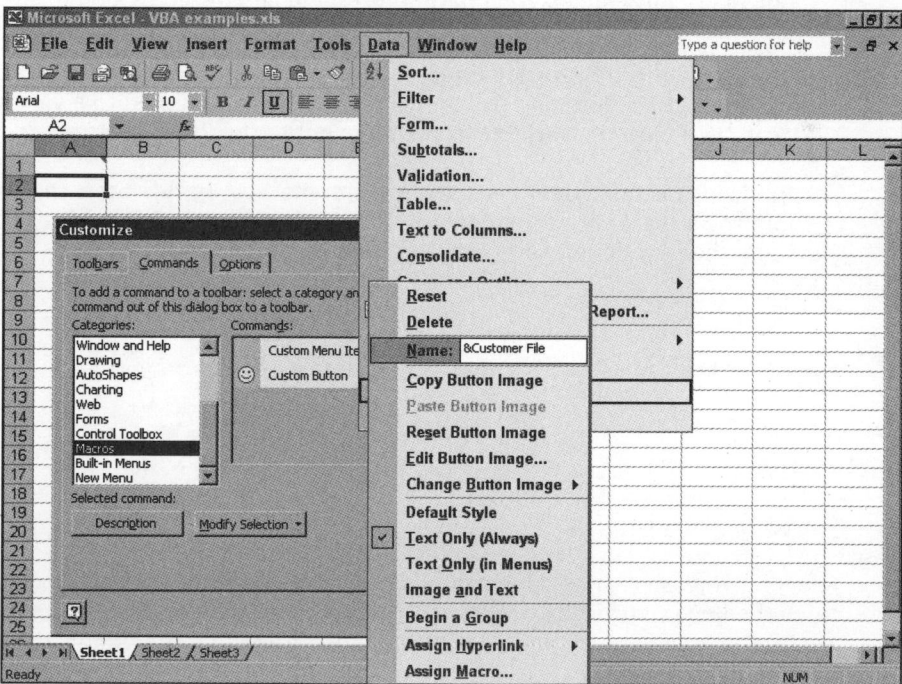

Figure 34-3: You can add a custom menu item to run your procedures.

7. Click Assign Macro on the shortcut menu.

8. In the Assign Macro dialog box, select the `OpenCustomerFile` procedure from the list of macros.

9. Click OK to close the Assign Macro dialog box, and click Close to close the Customize dialog box.

Caution

After you follow the preceding process, the new menu item always appears on Excel's menu — even when the workbook that contains the macro is not open. Selecting the new menu item opens the workbook if it's not already open.

Cross-Reference

Refer to Chapter 41 to learn how to use VBA to create menu items that are displayed only when a particular workbook is open.

Executing a procedure from another procedure

One of the most common ways to execute a procedure is from another procedure. You have three ways to do this:

✦ Enter the procedure's name followed by its arguments (if any) separated by commas.

✦ Use the `Call` keyword followed by the procedure's name and then its arguments (if any) enclosed in parentheses and separated by commas.

✦ Use the `Run` method of the `Application` object. You can use this method to execute other VBA procedures. The `Run` method is also useful when you need to run a procedure and the procedure's name is assigned to a variable. You can then pass the variable as an argument to the `Run` method.

The following example demonstrates the first method. In this case, the `MySub` procedure processes some statements (not shown), executes the `UpdateSheet` procedure, and then executes the rest of the statements.

```
Sub MySub()
'   ... [code goes here] ...
    UpdateSheet
'   ... [code goes here] ...
End Sub

Sub UpdateSheet()
'   ... [code goes here] ...
End Sub
```

The following example demonstrates the second method. The `Call` keyword executes the `Update` procedure, which requires one argument; the calling procedure passes the argument to the called procedure. Procedure arguments are discussed later in this chapter.

```
Sub MySub()
    MonthNum = InputBox("Enter the month number: ")
    Call UpdateSheet(MonthNum)
'    ... [code goes here] ...
End Sub

Sub UpdateSheet(MonthSeq)
'    ... [code goes here] ...
End Sub
```

Tip

Even though it's optional, some programmers always use the Call keyword just to make it perfectly clear that another procedure is being called.

The next example uses the Run method to execute the UpdateSheet procedure and passes MonthNum as the argument:

```
Sub MySub()
    MonthNum = InputBox("Enter the month number: ")
    Result = Application.Run("UpdateSheet", MonthNum)
'    ... [code goes here] ...
End Sub

Sub UpdateSheet(MonthSeq)
'    ... [code goes here] ...
End Sub
```

The Run method is also useful when the procedure name is assigned to a variable. In fact, it's the only way to execute a procedure in such a way. The following example demonstrates this. The Main procedure determines the day of the week (an integer between 0 and 6, beginning with Sunday). The SubToCall variable is assigned a string that represents a procedure name. The Run method then calls the appropriate procedure (either WeekEnd or Daily).

```
Sub Main()
    Select Case WeekDay(Now)
        Case 0: SubToCall = "WeekEnd"
        Case 6: SubToCall = "WeekEnd"
        Case Else: SubToCall = "Daily"
    End Select
        Application.Run SubToCall
End Sub

Sub WeekEnd()
    MsgBox "Today is a weekend"
'   Code to execute on the weekend
'   goes here
End Sub
```

```
Sub Daily()
    MsgBox "Today is not a weekend"
'    Code to execute on the weekdays
'    goes here
End Sub
```

Cross-Reference   You can also use the Run method to execute a procedure located in a different workbook. See the "Calling a Procedure in a Different Workbook" section later in this chapter.

Calling a procedure in a different module

If VBA can't locate a called procedure in the current module, it looks for public procedures in other modules in the same project.

If you need to call a private procedure from another procedure, both procedures must reside in the same module.

You can't have two procedures with the same name in the same module, but you can have identically named procedures in different modules. You can persuade VBA to execute an *ambiguously named* procedure — that is, another procedure in a different module that has the same name. To do so, precede the procedure name with the module name and a dot. For example, say that you define procedures named MySub in Module1 and Module2. If you want a procedure in Module2 to call the MySub in Module1, you can use either of the following statements:

```
Module1.MySub
Call Module1.MySub
```

If you do not differentiate between procedures that have the same name, you get an Ambiguous name detected error message.

Calling a procedure in a different workbook

In some cases, you may need your procedure to execute another procedure defined in a different workbook. To do so, you have two options: Establish a reference to the other workbook, or use the Run method and specify the workbook name explicitly.

To add a reference to another workbook, select the VBE's Tools ➪ References command. Excel displays the References dialog box (see Figure 34-4), which lists all available references, including all open workbooks. Simply check the box that corresponds to the workbook that you want to add as a reference and click OK. After you establish a reference, you can call procedures in the workbook as if they were in the same workbook as the calling procedure.

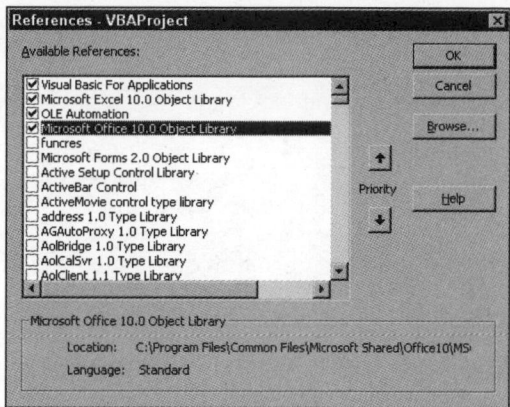

Figure 34-4: You can use the Reference dialog box to establish a reference to another workbook.

A referenced workbook does not have to be open; it is treated like a separate object library. Use the Browse button in the References dialog box to establish a reference to a workbook that isn't open. The workbook names that appear in the list of references are listed by their VBE project names. By default, every project is initially named *VBAProject*. Therefore, the list may contain several identically named items. To distinguish a project, change its name in the Properties window of the VBE. The list of references displayed in the References dialog box also includes object libraries and ActiveX controls that are registered on your system. Your Excel workbooks always include references to the following object libraries (and you can't unreference them because they are essential):

✦ Visual Basic for Applications

✦ Microsoft Excel 10.0 Object Library

✦ OLE Automation

✦ Microsoft Office 10.0 Object Library

If you've established a reference to a workbook that contains the procedure YourSub, for example, you can use either of the following statements to call YourSub:

```
YourSub
Call YourSub
```

To precisely identify a procedure in a different workbook, specify the project name, module name, and procedure name using the following syntax:

```
MyProject.MyModule.MySub
```

Why Call Other Procedures?

If you're new to programming, you may wonder why anyone would ever want to call a procedure from another procedure. You may ask, "Why not just put the code from the called procedure into the calling procedure and keep things simple?"

One reason is to clarify your code. The simpler your code, the easier it is to modify. Smaller routines are easier to decipher and then debug — especially if someone else ends up working on the project. Examine the accompanying procedure, which does nothing but call other procedures. This procedure is so easy to read, it acts like an outline.

```
Sub Main()
    Call GetUserOptions
    Call ProcessData
    Call CleanUp
    Call CloseItDown
End Sub
```

Calling other procedures also eliminates redundancy. Suppose that you need to perform an operation at ten different places in your routine. Rather than enter the code ten times, you can write a procedure to perform the operation and then simply call the procedure ten times.

Also, you may have a series of general-purpose procedures that you use frequently. If you store these in a separate module, you can import the module to your current project and then call these procedures as needed — which is much easier than copying and pasting the code into your new procedures.

Alternatively, you can use the `Call` keyword:

```
Call MyProject.MyModule.MySub
```

Another way to call a procedure in a different workbook is to use the `Run` method of the `Application` object. This technique does not require that you establish a reference. The following statement executes the `Consolidate` procedure located in a workbook named `budget macros.xls`:

```
Application.Run "'budget macros.xls'!Consolidate"
```

Executing a procedure from a toolbar button

You can customize Excel's toolbars to include buttons that execute procedures when clicked. The procedure for assigning a macro to a toolbar button is virtually identical to the procedure for assigning a macro to a menu item.

Assume that you want to assign a procedure to a toolbar button on a toolbar. Here are the steps required to do so:

1. Choose the View ⇨ Toolbars ⇨ Customize command to display the Customize dialog box.

2. Click the Commands tab in the Customize dialog box.

3. Scroll down and click Macros in the Categories list.

4. In the Commands list, drag the second item (labeled Custom Button) to the desired toolbar.

5. Right-click the new button to display a shortcut menu.

6. Enter a new name for the button in the text box labeled Name. This is the "tooltip" text that appears when the mouse pointer moves over the button. This step is optional; if you omit it, the tooltip displays *Custom*.

7. Right-click the new button, and select Assign Macro from the shortcut menu.

   Excel displays its Assign Macro dialog box.

8. Select the procedure from the list of macros.

9. Click OK to close the Assign Macro dialog box.

10. Click Close to close the Customize dialog box.

Cross-Reference   Custom toolbars are covered in Chapter 40.

Executing a procedure by clicking an object

Excel has a variety of objects that you can place on a worksheet or chart sheet, and you can attach a macro to any of these objects. These objects are available from three toolbars:

✦ The Drawing toolbar

✦ The Forms toolbar

✦ The Control Toolbox toolbar

To assign a procedure to a `Button` object (which is on the Forms toolbar), follow these steps:

1. Make sure that the Forms toolbar is displayed.

2. Click the Button tool on the Forms toolbar.

3. Drag your mouse pointer in the worksheet to create the button.

   Excel jumps right in and displays the Assign Macro dialog box.

4. Select the macro you want to assign to the button, and click OK.

Tip   To assign a macro to a shape, create a shape using the Drawing toolbar. Right-click the shape and choose Assign Macro from the shortcut menu.

Executing a procedure when an event occurs

You might want a procedure to be executed when a particular event occurs. Examples of events include opening a workbook, entering data into a worksheet, saving a workbook, and many others. A procedure that is executed when an event occurs is known as an *event-handler* procedure. Event-handler procedures are characterized by the following:

✦ They have special names that are made up of an object, an underscore, and the event name. For example, the procedure that is executed when a workbook is opened is called `Workbook_Open`.

✦ They are stored in the code window for the particular object.

Cross-Reference   Chapter 38 is devoted to event-handler procedures.

Executing a procedure from the Immediate window

You also can execute a procedure by entering its name in the Immediate window of the VBE. If the Immediate window is not visible, press Ctrl+G. The Immediate window executes VBA statements as you enter them. To execute a procedure, simply enter the name of the procedure in the Immediate window and press Enter.

This method can be quite useful when you're developing a procedure because you can insert commands to display results in the Immediate window. The following procedure demonstrates this technique:

```
Sub ChangeCase()
    MyString = "This is a test"
    MyString = UCase(MyString)
    Debug.Print MyString
End Sub
```

Figure 34-5 shows what happens when you enter ChangeCase in the Immediate window: The `Debug.Print` statement displays the result immediately.

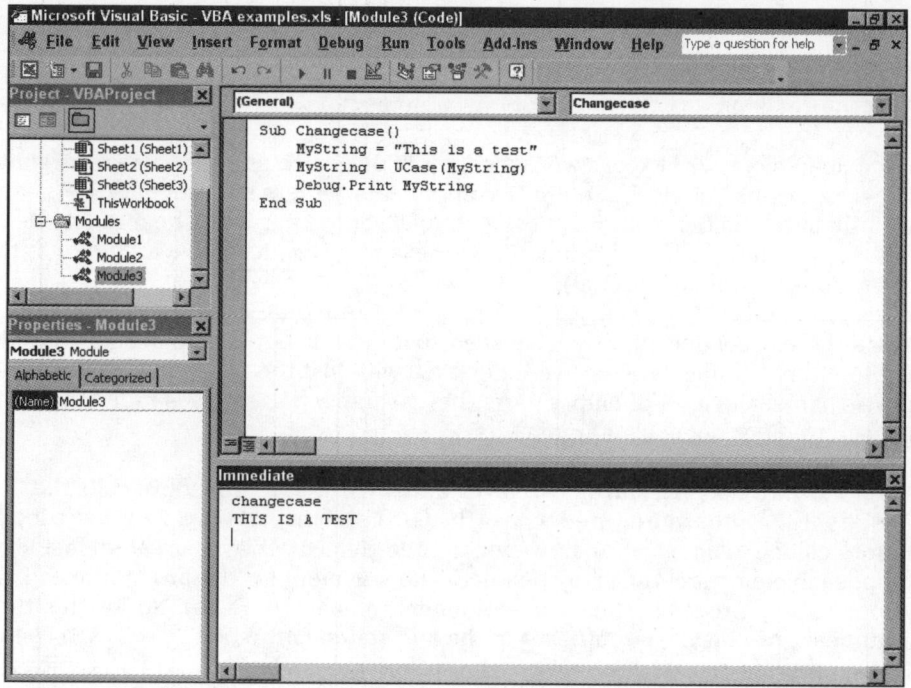

Figure 34-5: You can execute a procedure by entering its name in the Immediate window.

Passing Arguments to Procedures

A procedure's *arguments* provide it with data that it uses in its instructions. The data that's *passed* by an argument can be any of the following:

- ✦ A variable
- ✦ A constant
- ✦ A literal
- ✦ An array
- ✦ An object

With regard to arguments, procedures are very similar to worksheet functions in the following respects:

- ✦ A procedure may not require any arguments.
- ✦ A procedure may require a fixed number of arguments.

✦ A procedure may accept an indefinite number of arguments.

✦ A procedure may require some arguments, leaving others optional.

✦ A procedure may have all optional arguments.

For example, a few of Excel's worksheet functions, such as RAND, use no arguments. Others, such as COUNTIF, require two arguments. Others still, such as SUM, can use an indefinite number of arguments — up to 30. Still other worksheet functions have optional arguments. The PMT function, for example, can have five arguments (three are required, two are optional).

Most of the procedures that you've seen so far in this book have been declared without any arguments. They were declared with just the Sub keyword, the procedure's name, and a set of empty parentheses. Empty parentheses indicate that the procedure does not accept arguments.

The following example shows two procedures. The Main procedure calls the ProcessFile procedure three times (the Call statement is in a For-Next loop). Before calling ProcessFile, however, a three-element array is created. Inside the loop, each element of the array becomes the argument for the procedure call. The ProcessFile procedure takes one argument (named TheFile). Notice that the argument goes inside parentheses in the Sub statement. When ProcessFile finishes, program control continues with the statement after the Call statement.

```
Sub Main()
    File(1) = "dept1.xls"
    File(2) = "dept2.xls"
    File(3) = "dept3.xls"
    For i = 1 To 3
        Call ProcessFile(File(i))
    Next i
End Sub

Sub ProcessFile(TheFile)
    Workbooks.Open FileName:=TheFile
'   ...[more code here]...
End Sub
```

You can also, of course, pass literals (that is, not variables) to a procedure. For example,

```
Sub Main()
    Call ProcessFile("budget.xls")
End Sub
```

You can pass an argument to a procedure in two ways: by reference and by value. Passing an argument by reference (the default method) simply passes the memory address of the variable. Passing an argument by value, on the other hand, passes a copy of the original variable. Consequently, changes to the argument within the procedure are not reflected in the original variable.

The following example demonstrates this concept. The argument for the Process procedure is passed by reference (the default method). After the `Main` procedure assigns a value of 10 to `MyValue`, it calls the `Process` procedure and passes `MyValue` as the argument. The `Process` procedure multiplies the value of its argument (named `YourValue`) by 10. When `Process` ends and program control passes back to `Main`, the `MsgBox` function displays `MyValue: 100`.

```
Sub Main()
    MyValue = 10
    Call Process(MyValue)
    MsgBox MyValue
End Sub

Sub Process(YourValue)
    YourValue = YourValue * 10
End Sub
```

If you don't want the called procedure to modify any variables passed as arguments, you can modify the called procedure's argument list so that arguments are passed to it *by value* rather than *by reference*. To do so, precede the argument with the `ByVal` keyword. This technique causes the called routine to work with a copy of the passed variable's data, not the data itself. In the following procedure, for example, the changes made to `YourValue` in the `Process` procedure do not affect the `MyValue` variable in `Main`. As a result, the `MsgBox` function displays 10, not 100.

```
Sub Process(ByVal YourValue)
    YourValue = YourValue * 10
End Sub
```

In most cases, you'll be content to use the default reference method of passing arguments. However, if your procedure needs to use data passed to it in an argument and you absolutely must keep the original data intact, you'll want to pass the data by value.

A procedure's arguments can mix and match by value and by reference. Arguments preceded with `ByVal` are passed by value; all others are passed by reference.

Note   If you pass a variable defined as a user-defined data type to a procedure, it must be passed by reference. Attempting to pass it by value generates an error.

A procedure that uses arguments can define the data types directly in the argument list. The following is a `Sub` statement for a procedure with two arguments of different data types. The first is declared as an integer, and the second is declared as a string.

```
Sub Process(Iterations As Integer, TheFile As String)
```

When you pass arguments to a procedure, the data that you pass as the argument must match the argument's data type. For example, if you call Process in the preceding example and pass a string variable for the first argument, you get a *type mismatch* error.

Cross-Reference Arguments are relevant to both Sub procedures and Function procedures. Chapter 35 provides more examples of using arguments with your routines, including how to handle optional arguments.

Tip A variable declared as Public is available to all procedures in the module. In some cases, you may want to access a Public variable rather than pass the variable as an argument when calling another procedure.

Using Error-Handling Techniques

When a VBA procedure is running, errors can occur. These include either syntax errors (which you must correct before you can execute a procedure) or run-time errors (which occur while the procedure is running). This section deals with run-time errors.

Caution For error-handling procedures to work, the Break on All Errors setting *must* be turned off. In the VBE, select Tools ⇨ Options and click the General tab in the Options dialog box. If Break on All Errors is selected, VBA ignores your error-handling code. You'll usually want to use the Break on Unhandled Errors option.

Normally, a run-time error causes VBA to stop, and the user sees a dialog box that displays the error number and a description of the error. A good application doesn't make the user deal with these messages. Rather, it incorporates error-handling code to trap errors and take appropriate actions. At the very least, your error-handling code can display a more meaningful error message than the one popped up by VBA.

Trapping errors

You can use the On Error statement to specify what happens when an error occurs. Basically, you have two choices:

✦ Ignore the error, and let VBA continue. You can later poll the Err object to determine what the error was and take action if necessary.

✦ Jump to a special error-handling section of your code to take action. This section is placed at the end of the procedure and marked by a label.

To cause the VBA program to continue when an error occurs, insert the following statement in your code:

```
On Error Resume Next
```

Some errors are inconsequential, and can simply be ignored. But you may want to determine what the error was. When an error occurs, you can use the Err object to determine the error number. VBA's Error function can be used to display the text for Err.Value, which defaults to just Err. For example, the following statement displays the same information as the normal Visual Basic error dialog box (the error number and the error description):

```
MsgBox "Error" & Err & ": " & Error(Err)
```

You can, of course, make the error message a bit more meaningful to your end users by using more descriptive text.

You also use the On Error statement to specify a location in your procedure to jump to when an error occurs. You use a label to mark the location. For example,

```
On Error GoTo ErrorHandler
```

Error-handling examples

The first example demonstrates an error that can safely be ignored. The SpecialCells method selects cells that meet a certain criteria. (This method is equivalent to selecting the Edit ⇨ Go To command and clicking the Special button to select, for example, cells that contain formulas.)

In the example that follows, the SpecialCells method selects all the cells in the current range selection that contain a formula that returns a number. Normally, if no cells in the selection qualify, VBA generates an error message. Using the On Error Resume Next statement simply prevents the error message from appearing.

```
Sub SelectFormulas()
    On Error Resume Next
    Selection.SpecialCells(xlFormulas, xlNumbers).Select
End Sub
```

The following procedure uses an additional statement to determine if an error did occur.

```
Sub SelectFormulas2()
    On Error Resume Next
    Selection.SpecialCells(xlFormulas, xlNumbers).Select
    If Err <> 0 Then MsgBox "No formula cells were found."
End Sub
```

If the value of Err is not equal to 0, an error occurred, and a message box displays a notice to the user.

The next example demonstrates error handling by jumping to a label.

```
Sub ErrorDemo()
    On Error GoTo Handler
    Selection.Value = 123
    Exit Sub
Handler:
    MsgBox "Cannot assign a value to the selection."
End Sub
```

The procedure attempts to assign a value to the current selection. If a range is not selected or the sheet is protected, the assignment statement results in an error. The On Error statement specifies a jump to the Handler label if an error occurs. Notice the use of the Exit Sub statement before the label. This prevents the error-handling code from being executed if no error occurs.

Sometimes, you can take advantage of an error to get information. The example that follows simply checks to see whether a particular workbook is open:

```
Sub CheckForFile1()
    FileName = "BUDGET.XLS"
    FileExists = False

'    Cycle through all workbooks
    For Each book In Workbooks
        If UCase(book.Name) = FileName Then
            FileExists = True
        End If
    Next book

'    Display appropriate message
    If FileExists Then _
        MsgBox FileName & " is open." Else _
            MsgBox FileName & " is not open."
End Sub
```

Here, a For Each-Next loop cycles through all objects in the Workbooks collection. If the workbook is open, the FileExists variable is set to True. Finally, a message is displayed that tells the user whether the workbook is open.

The preceding routine can be rewritten to use error handling to determine whether the file is open. In the example that follows, the On Error Resume Next statement causes VBA to ignore any errors. The next instruction attempts to reference the workbook and assign its name to a variable. If the workbook is not open, an error occurs. The If-Then-Else structure checks the value property of Err and displays the appropriate message.

```
Sub CheckForFile()
    FileName = "BUDGET.XLS"
    On Error Resume Next
```

```
        x = UCase(Workbooks(FileName).Name)
        If Err = 0 Then
            MsgBox FileName & " is open."
        Else
            MsgBox FileName & " is not open."
        End If
    End Sub
```

Trying Out A Realistic Example

The remainder of this chapter is a real-life exercise that demonstrates many of the concepts covered in this and the preceding two chapters.

This section describes the development of a useful utility that qualifies as an application. More important, it demonstrates the *process* of analyzing a problem and then solving it with VBA.

Understanding the goal

The goal of this exercise is to develop a utility that rearranges a workbook by alphabetizing its sheets. If you tend to create workbooks that consist of many sheets, you know that it can be difficult to locate a particular sheet. If the sheets are ordered alphabetically, though, it's much easier to find a desired sheet.

Setting out the project requirements

Where to begin? One way to get started is to list the requirements for your application. As you develop your application, you can check your list to ensure that you're covering all the bases.

Here's the list of requirements for this example application:

1. It should sort the sheets in the active workbook in ascending order.

2. It should be easy to execute.

3. It should always be available. In other words, the user shouldn't have to open a workbook to use this utility.

4. It should work properly for any open workbook.

5. It should not display any VBA error messages.

Determining what you already know

Often, the most difficult part of a project is figuring out where to start. In this case, start by listing things that you know about Excel that may be relevant to the project requirements:

✦ Excel doesn't have a command that sorts sheets.

✦ You can move a sheet easily by dragging its sheet tab.

 **Tip**   Turn on the macro recorder and drag a sheet to a new location to find out what kind of code this action generates.

✦ You'll need to know how many sheets are in the active workbook. You can get this information with VBA.

✦ You'll need to know the names of all the sheets. Again, you can get this information with VBA.

✦ Excel has a command that sorts data in worksheet cells.

✦ Thanks to the Macro Options dialog box, assigning a shortcut key to a macro is easy.

✦ If a macro is stored in the Personal Macro Workbook, it will always be available.

✦ You need a way to test the application as you develop it. For certain, you don't want to be testing it using the same workbook in which you're developing the code.

 Tip   Create a dummy workbook for testing purposes.

Setting up your approach

Although you still may not know exactly how to proceed, you could devise a preliminary, skeleton plan that describes the general tasks required:

1. Identify the active workbook.

2. Get a list of all the sheet names in the workbook.

3. Count the sheets.

4. Sort them (somehow).

5. Rearrange the sheets in the sorted order.

Determining what you still need to know

There are still a few holes in the plan. You still need to determine the following:

✦ How to identify the active workbook

✦ How to count the sheets in the active workbook

✦ How to get a list of the sheet names

✦ How to sort the list

✦ How to rearrange the sheets according to the sorted list

Tip   When you lack critical information about specific methods or properties, you can consult this book or the online help. You may eventually discover what you need to know. Your best bet, however, is to turn on the macro recorder and see what it spits out when you perform some relevant actions.

Doing some preliminary recording

Here's an example of using the macro recorder to learn about VBA. Start with a workbook that contains three worksheets. Turn on the macro recorder and specify your Personal Macro Workbook as the destination for the macro. With the macro recorder running, drag the third worksheet to the first sheet position. Here's what the macro recorder creates:

```
Sub Macro1()
    Sheets("Sheet3").Select
    Sheets("Sheet3").Move Before:=Sheets(1)
End Sub
```

Tip   Move is a method that moves a sheet to a new location in the workbook. It also takes an argument that specifies the location for the sheet.

Next you need to find out how many sheets are in the active workbook. If you search for the word *Count* in the online help system, you'll find that it's a property of a collection. Activate the Immediate window in the VBE and type the following statement:

```
? ActiveWorkbook.Sheets.Count
```

The result is more useful information — this property shows the number of worksheets in the workbook.

What about the sheet names? Time for another test. Enter the following statement in the Immediate window:

```
? ActiveWorkbook.Sheets(1).Name
```

This tells you that the name of the first sheet is Sheet3, which is correct. More good information to keep in mind.

Next, remember something about the For Each-Next construct: It is useful for cycling through each member of a collection. Try this short procedure to test it out:

```
Sub Test()
    For Each Item In ActiveWorkbook.Sheets
        MsgBox Item.Name
    Next Item
End Sub
```

Another success. This macro displays three message boxes, each displaying a different sheet name.

Finally, it is time to think about sorting options. From the online help, you can learn that the Sort method applies to a range or a pivot table. So one option is to transfer the sheet names to a range and then sort the range, but that seems like overkill for this application. A better option is to dump the sheet names into an array of strings and then sort the array by using VBA code.

Doing your initial setup

Now you need to do some initial setup work. Follow these instructions:

1. Create an empty workbook with five worksheets, named Sheet1, Sheet2, Sheet3, Sheet4, and Sheet5.

2. Move the sheets around randomly so that they aren't in any particular order.

3. Save the workbook as Test.xls.

4. Activate the VBE and select the Personal.xls project in the Project Window.

Note   If Personal.xls doesn't appear in the Project window in the VBE, you haven't used the Personal Macro Workbook. To have Excel create this workbook for you, simply record a macro (any macro) and specify the Personal Macro Workbook as the destination for the macro.

5. Insert a new VBA module (use the Insert ⇨ Module command).

6. Create an empty procedure called SortSheets (see Figure 34-6).

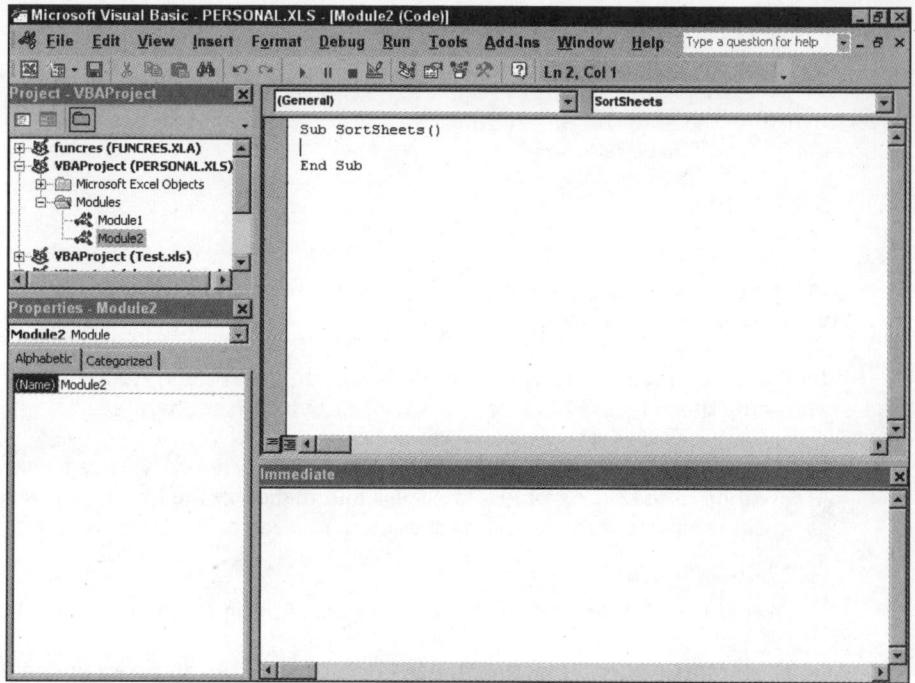

Figure 34-6: First create an empty procedure in a module located in the Personal Macro Workbook.

 **Tip** Actually, you can store this macro in any module in the Personal Macro Workbook. However, it's a good idea to keep each macro in a separate module. That way, you can easily export the module and import it into a different project later on.

7. Activate Excel. Use the Tools ⇨ Macro ⇨ Macros command (Options button) to assign a shortcut key to this macro. The Ctrl+Shift+S key combination is a good choice.

Doing some preliminary code writing

Now it's time to write some code. You need to put the sheet names into an array of strings. But because you won't know yet how many sheets are in the active workbook, you use a Dim statement with empty parentheses to declare the array. You can use ReDim afterward to redimension the array for the proper number of elements.

Enter the following code, which inserts the sheet names into the SheetNames array (and uses a MsgBox function within the loop just to assure you that the sheets' names were indeed being entered into the array).

```
Sub SortSheets()
    Dim SheetNames()
    SheetCount = ActiveWorkbook.Sheets.Count
    ReDim SheetNames(1 To SheetCount)
    For i = 1 To SheetCount
        SheetNames(i) = ActiveWorkbook.Sheets(i).Name
        MsgBox SheetNames(i)
    Next i
End Sub
```

To test the preceding code, activate the Text.xls workbook and press Ctrl+Shift+S. Five message boxes appear, each displaying the name of a corresponding sheet.

When you're convinced that your code is working correctly, remove the `MsgBox` statement (these message boxes become annoying after a while).

 **Tip**   Rather than use the MsgBox function to test your work, you can use the Print method of the Debug object to display information in the Immediate window. For this example, use the following statement in place of the MsgBox statement:

```
Debug.Print SheetNames(i)
```

You may find this technique less intrusive than using MsgBox statements.

At this point, the `SortSheets` procedure simply creates an array of sheet names in the active workbook. Two steps remain: Sort the values in the `SheetNames` array, and then rearrange the sheets to correspond to the sorted array.

Writing a sort procedure

It is time to sort the `SheetNames` array. You could place the sorting code in the `SortSheets` procedure, but a better approach is to write a general-purpose sorting procedure that you could reuse with other projects (sorting arrays is a common operation).

You may be a bit daunted by the thought of writing a sorting procedure. The good news is that it's relatively easy to find commonly used routines that you can use or adapt. The Internet, of course, is a great source for such information.

You can sort an array in many ways. For this example, we'll choose the *bubble sort* method; although it's not a particularly fast technique, it's easy to code. The bubble sort method uses a nested `For-Next` loop to evaluate each array element. If the array element is greater than the next element, the two elements swap positions. This evaluation is repeated for every pair of items (that is, n–1 times).

Here's the sorting procedure:

```
Sub BubbleSort(List())
'   Sorts the List array in ascending order
    Dim First As Integer, Last As Integer
```

```
            Dim i As Integer, j As Integer
            Dim Temp
            First = LBound(List)
            Last = UBound(List)
            For i = First To Last - 1
                For j = i + 1 To Last
                    If List(i) > List(j) Then
                        Temp = List(j)
                        List(j) = List(i)
                        List(i) = Temp
                    End If
                Next j
            Next i
    End Sub
```

This procedure accepts one argument: a one-dimensional array named List. An array passed to a procedure can be of any length. It uses the LBound and UBound functions to define the lower bound and upper bound of the array to the variables First and Last, respectively.

Next, modify SortSheets by adding a call to the BubbleSort procedure, passing the SheetNames array as an argument. At this point, you need to modify your module to look like this:

```
Sub SortSheets()
    Dim SheetNames()
    SheetCount = ActiveWorkbook.Sheets.Count
    ReDim SheetNames(1 To SheetCount)
    For i = 1 To SheetCount
        SheetNames(i) = ActiveWorkbook.Sheets(i).Name
    Next i
    Call BubbleSort(SheetNames)
End Sub

Sub BubbleSort(List() As String)
'   Sorts the List array in ascending order
    Dim First As Integer, Last As Integer
    Dim i As Integer, j As Integer
    Dim Temp

    First = LBound(List)
    Last = UBound(List)
    For i = First To Last - 1
        For j = i + 1 To Last
            If List(i) > List(j) Then
                Temp = List(j)
                List(j) = List(i)
                List(i) = Temp
            End If
        Next j
    Next i
End Sub
```

At this point, when the SheetSort procedure ends, it contains an array that consists of the sorted sheet names in the active workbook. So far, so good. Now you merely have to write some code to rearrange the sheets to correspond to the sorted items in the SheetNames array.

Rearranging the sheets

The code that you recorded earlier will again prove useful. Remember the instruction that was recorded when you moved a sheet to the first position in the workbook?

```
Sheets("Sheet1").Move Sheets(1)
```

The following For-Next loop that will go through each sheet and move it to its corresponding sheet location, specified in the SheetNames array:

```
For i = 1 To SheetCount
    Sheets(SheetNames(i)).Move Sheets(i)
Next i
```

For example, the first time through the loop, the loop counter (i) is 1. The first element in the SheetNames array is (in this example) Sheet1. Therefore, the expression for the Move method within the loop evaluates to:

```
Sheets("Sheet1").Move Sheets(1)
```

The second time through the loop, the expression evaluates to:

```
Sheets("Sheet2").Move Sheets(2)
```

Next add the new code to the SortSheets procedure:

```
Sub SortSheets()
    SheetCount = ActiveWorkbook.Sheets.Count
    ReDim SheetNames(1 To SheetCount)
    For i = 1 To SheetCount
        SheetNames(i) = ActiveWorkbook.Sheets(i).Name
    Next i
    Call BubbleSort(SheetNames)
    For i = 1 To SheetCount
        ActiveWorkbook.Sheets(SheetNames(i)).Move _
            ActiveWorkbook.Sheets(i)
    Next i
End Sub
```

Cleaning up your code

Time to clean things up. You should declare all the variables used and then add a few comments and blank lines to make the code easier to read. The SortSheets procedure now looks like the following:

```
Sub SortSheets()
'    This routine sorts the sheets of the
'    active workbook in ascending order.

    Dim SheetNames() As String
    Dim SheetCount As Integer
    Dim i As Integer

    SheetCount = ActiveWorkbook.Sheets.Count
    ReDim SheetNames(1 To SheetCount)

'   Fill array with sheet names
    For i = 1 To SheetCount
        SheetNames(i) = ActiveWorkbook.Sheets(i).Name
    Next i

'   Sort the array in ascending order
    Call BubbleSort(SheetNames)

'   Move the sheets
    For i = 1 To SheetCount
        ActiveWorkbook.Sheets(SheetNames(i)).Move _
            ActiveWorkbook.Sheets(i)
    Next i
End Sub
```

Try it out and everything should be working. To test the code further, add a few more sheets to Test.xls and change some of the sheet names.

Doing some more testing

The fact that the procedure works with the Test.xls workbook doesn't necessarily mean that it will work with all workbooks. To test it further, load a few other workbooks and retry the routine. If you do, you may discover some problems:

✦ Workbooks with many sheets takes a long time to sort because the screen is continually updated during the move operations.

✦ The sorting doesn't always work. For example, a sheet named SUMMARY (all uppercase) would appear before a sheet named Sheet1. This problem is caused by the BubbleSort procedure (an uppercase U is "greater than" a lowercase H).

✦ If there are no visible workbook windows, pressing the Ctrl+Shift+S shortcut key combo causes the macro to fail.

✦ If the workbook's structure is protected, the Move method fails.

✦ After sorting, the last sheet in the workbook becomes the active sheet. Changing the active sheet is not a good practice; it's better to keep the original sheet active.

✦ If you interrupt the macro by pressing Ctrl+Break, VBA displays an error message.

Correcting the problems

Fixing the screen-updating problem is a breeze. Insert the following instruction at the beginning of SortSheets to turn screen updating off:

```
Application.ScreenUpdating = False
```

It is also easy to fix the problem with the BubbleSort procedure: use VBA's UCase function to convert the sheet names to uppercase. That way, all the comparisons are made using uppercase versions of the sheet names. The corrected line read as follows:

```
If UCase(List(i)) > UCase(List(j)) Then
```

Tip Another way to solve the "case" problem is to add the following statement to the top of your module:

```
Option Text Compare
```

This statement causes VBA to perform string comparisons based on a case-insensitive text sort order. In other words, A is considered the same as a.

To prevent the error message that appears when no workbooks are visible, you can add some error checking. If no active workbook exists, an error occurs. You can use On Error Resume Next to ignore the error and then check the value of Err. If Err is not equal to 0, it means that an error occurred. Therefore, the procedure ends. The error-checking code is

```
On Error Resume Next
SheetCount = ActiveWorkbook.Sheets.Count
If Err <> 0 Then Exit Sub ' No active workbook
```

There's usually a good reason that a workbook's structure is protected. The best approach may be to display a message box to that effect (with a stop sign icon generated by the vbCritical constant) and then exit the procedure. (If desired, a user can unprotect the workbook and redo the sheet sorting.) Testing for a protected workbook structure is easy — the ProtectStructure property of a Workbook object returns True if a workbook is protected. Add the following block of code:

```
'   Check for protected workbook structure
   If ActiveWorkbook.ProtectStructure Then
       MsgBox ActiveWorkbook.Name & " is protected." , _
          vbCritical, "Cannot Sort Sheets."
       Exit Sub
   End If
```

To reactivate the original active sheet after the sorting is performed, you can add code that assigns the original sheet to an object variable (OldActive), and then activate that sheet when the routine is finished.

Pressing Ctrl+Break normally halts a macro, and VBA usually displays an error message. But because one of your goals is to avoid VBA error messages, you need to insert a command to prevent this situation. The Application object has an EnableCancelKey property that can disable Ctrl+Break. can add the following statement at the top of the routine:

```
Application.EnableCancelKey = xlDisabled
```

Caution   Be very careful when you disable the cancel key. If your code gets caught in an infinite loop, you can't break out of it. For best results, insert this statement only after you're sure everything is working properly.

Viewing the final product

After all these corrections, the SortSheets procedure looks like Listing 34-1.

> Listing 34-1: **The Final Build for the SortSheets Procedure**

```
Sub SortSheets()
'   This routine sorts the sheets of the
'   active workbook in ascending order.

    Dim SheetNames() As String
    Dim i As Integer
    Dim SheetCount As Integer
    Dim VisibleWins As Integer
    Dim Item As Object
    Dim OldActive As Object

    On Error Resume Next
    SheetCount = ActiveWorkbook.Sheets.Count
    If Err <> 0 Then Exit Sub ' No active workbook

'   Check for protected workbook structure
    If ActiveWorkbook.ProtectStructure Then
        MsgBox ActiveWorkbook.Name & " is protected.", _
           vbCritical, "Cannot Sort Sheets."
```

Continued

Listing 34-1 *(continued)*

```
        Exit Sub
    End If

'   Disable Ctrl+Break
    Application.EnableCancelKey = xlDisabled

'   Get the number of sheets
    SheetCount = ActiveWorkbook.Sheets.Count

'   Redimension the array
    ReDim SheetNames(1 To SheetCount)

'   Store a reference to the active sheet
    Set OldActive = ActiveSheet

'   Fill array with sheet names and hidden status
    For i = 1 To SheetCount
        SheetNames(i) = ActiveWorkbook.Sheets(i).Name
    Next i

'   Sort the array in ascending order
    Call BubbleSort(SheetNames)

'   Turn off screen updating
    Application.ScreenUpdating = False

'   Move the sheets
    For i = 1 To SheetCount
        ActiveWorkbook.Sheets(SheetNames(i)).Move _
            ActiveWorkbook.Sheets(i)
    Next i

'   Reactivate the original active sheet
    OldActive.Activate
End Sub
```

Tip   Because the SortSheets macro is stored in the Personal Macro Workbook, it is available whenever Excel is running. At this point, the macro can be executed by selecting the macro's name from the Macro dialog box (Alt+F8 displays this dialog box) or by pressing Ctrl+Shift+F8. If you like, you can also assign this macro to a new toolbar button or to a new menu item. Procedures for doing this are described earlier in this chapter.

So there you have it. The utility meets all the original project requirements: It sorts all sheets in the active workbook, it can be executed easily, it's always available, it seems to work for any workbook, and we have yet to see it display a VBA error message.

✦   ✦   ✦

Creating Custom Worksheet Functions

Custom worksheet functions are VBA procedures that enable you to enhance Excel's computational abilities. To create custom worksheet functions, you use VBA to create function procedures — the subject of this chapter.

Understanding VBA Functions

Function procedures that you write in VBA are quite versatile. You can use these functions in two situations:

✦ As part of an expression in a different VBA procedure

✦ In formulas that you create in a worksheet

In fact, you can use a function procedure anywhere that you can use an Excel worksheet function or a VBA built-in function. Custom functions also appear in the Insert Function dialog box, so they appear to be part of Excel.

With so many predefined worksheet functions from which to choose, you may be curious why anyone would need to develop additional functions. The main reason is that creating a custom function can greatly simplify your formulas by making them shorter — and shorter formulas are more readable and easier to work with. For example, you can often replace a complex formula with a single function. Another reason is that you can write functions to perform operations that would otherwise be impossible.

 **Cross-Reference** This chapter assumes that you are familiar with entering and editing VBA code in the Visual Basic Editor (VBE). Refer to Chapter 32 for an overview of the VBE.

Trying Out An Introductory Example

The process of creating custom functions is relatively easy, after you understand VBA. This section provides an example of a VBA function procedure. This function is stored in a VBA module, which is accessible from the VBE.

Creating a simple custom function

This example function, named `NumSign`, uses one argument. The function returns a text string of `Positive` if its argument is greater than zero, `Negative` if the argument is less than zero, and `Zero` if the argument is equal to zero. The function is shown in Figure 35-1.

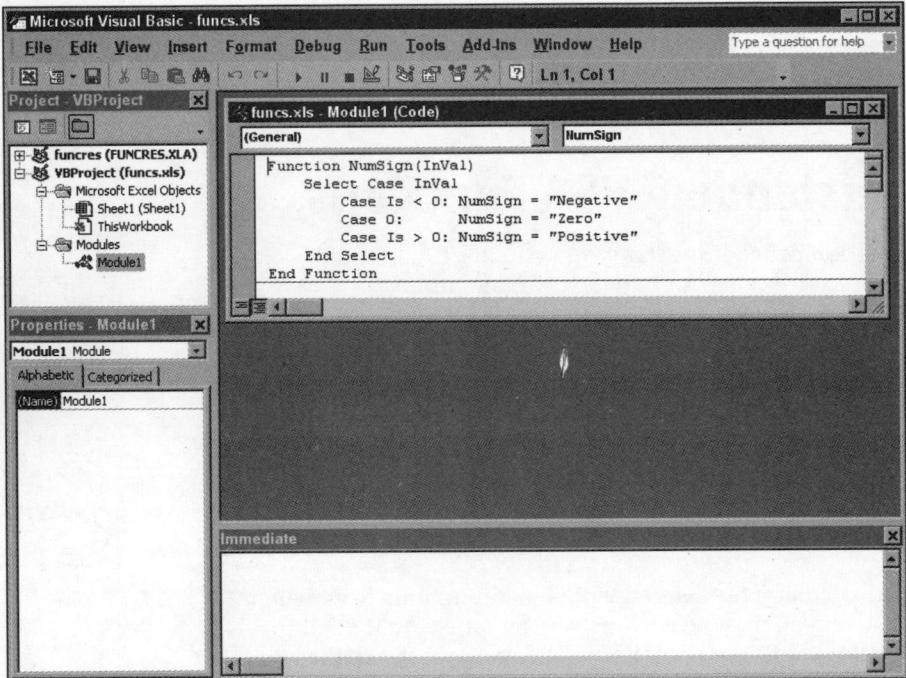

Figure 35-1: This is an example of a simple custom function you can create.

You could, of course, accomplish the same effect with the following worksheet formula, which uses a nested `IF` function:

```
=IF(A1=0,"Zero",IF(A1>0,"Positive","Negative"))
```

Many would agree that the custom function solution is easier to understand and to edit than the worksheet formula.

Using the function in a worksheet

When you enter a formula that uses the NumSign function, Excel executes the function to get the result (see Figure 35-2). This custom function works just like any built-in worksheet function. You can insert it in a formula by using the Insert ⇨ Function command, which displays the Insert Function dialog box (custom functions are located in the User Defined category). You also can nest custom functions and combine them with other elements in your formulas.

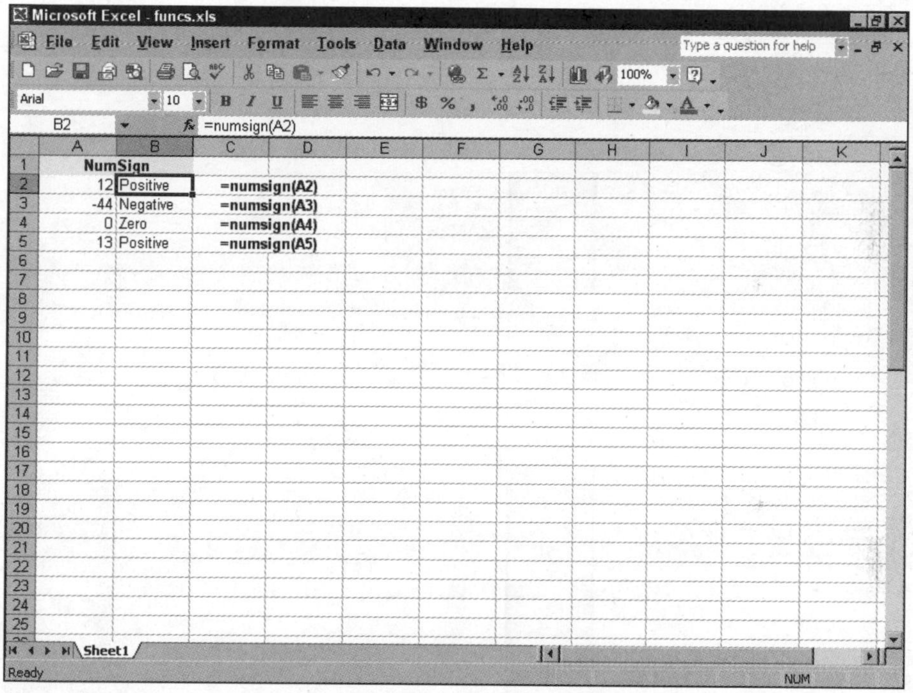

Figure 35-2: You can use the custom function in a worksheet formula.

Using the function in a VBA subroutine

You can also use your custom function in a VBA subroutine. The following VBA subroutine procedure, which is defined in the same module as the custom NumSign function, uses the built-in MsgBox function to display the result of the NumSign function:

```
Sub ShowSign()
    CellValue = ActiveCell.Value
    MsgBox NumSign(CellValue)
End Sub
```

In this example, the variable `CellValue` contains the value in the active cell (this variable could contain any value, not necessarily obtained from a cell). `CellValue` is then passed to the function as its argument. Figure 35-3 shows the result of executing the `NumSign` subroutine.

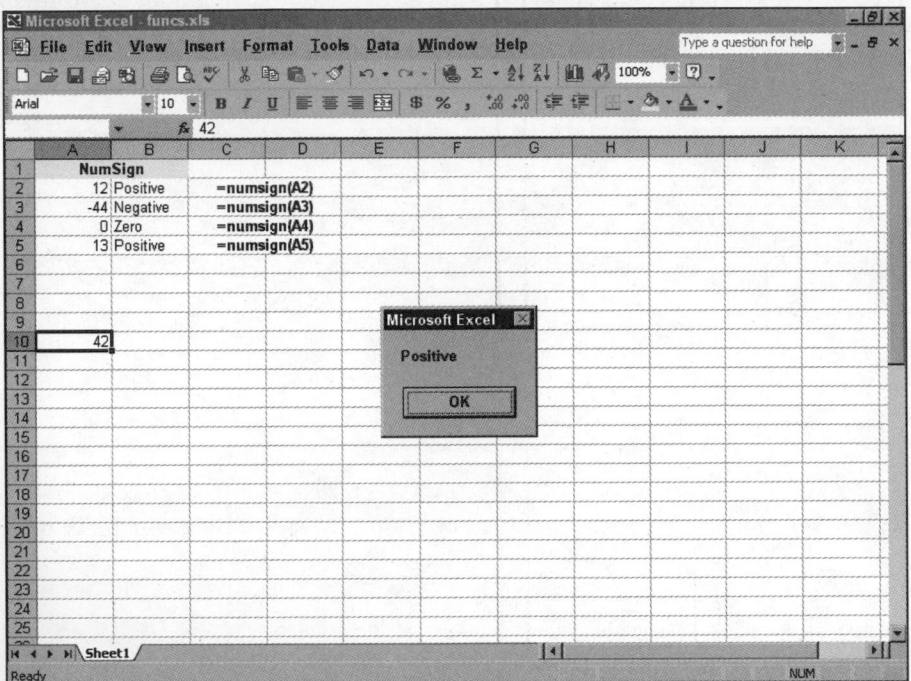

Figure 35-3: You can also use a custom function in a VBA subroutine.

Cross-Reference   See Chapter 34 to learn more about running a VBA procedure.

Analyzing the custom function

This section describes the `NumSign` function. Here again is the code:

```
Function NumSign(InVal)
    Select Case InVal
        Case Is < 0: NumSign = "Negative"
        Case 0:      NumSign = "Zero"
        Case Is > 0: NumSign = "Positive"
    End Select
End Function
```

Notice that the procedure starts with the keyword Function rather than Sub, followed by the name of the function (NumSign). This custom function uses one argument (InVal); the argument's name is enclosed in parentheses. InVal is the cell or variable that is to be processed. When the function is used in a worksheet, the argument can be a cell reference (such as A1) or a literal value (such as –123). When the function is used in another procedure, the argument can be a numeric variable, a literal number, or a value that is obtained from a cell.

The NumSign function uses the Select Case construct to take a different action, depending on the value of InVal. If InVal is less than zero, NumSign is assigned the text Negative. If InVal is equal to zero, NumSign is assigned the text Zero. If InVal is greater than zero, NumSign is assigned the text Positive. The value returned by a function is always assigned to the function's name.

The procedure ends with an End Function statement.

Cross-Reference   The Select Case construct is discussed in Chapter 33.

Creating Function Procedures

A custom function procedure has much in common with a subroutine procedure. Function procedures have some important differences, however, which are discussed in this section.

Declaring a function

The syntax for declaring a function is as follows:

```
[Public | Private][Static] Function name [(arglist)][As type]
   [statements]
   [name = expression]
   [Exit Function]
   [statements]
   [name = expression]
End Function
```

These elements are defined as follows:

✦ **Public:** Indicates that the function is accessible to all other procedures in all other modules in the workbook. (Optional)

✦ **Private:** Indicates that the function is accessible only to other procedures in the same module. Private functions can't be used in worksheet formulas and do not appear in the Insert Function dialog box. (Optional)

✦ **Static:** Indicates that the values of variables declared in the function are preserved between calls, rather than being reset. (Optional)

✦ **Function:** A keyword that indicates the beginning of a function procedure. (Required)

✦ **name:** Any valid variable name. When the function finishes, the single-value result is assigned to the function's name. (Required)

✦ **arglist:** A list (one or more) of variables that represent arguments passed to the function. The arguments are enclosed in parentheses. Use a comma to separate arguments. (Optional)

✦ **type:** The data type that is returned by the function. (Optional)

✦ **statements:** Valid VBA statements. (Optional)

✦ **Exit Function:** A statement that causes an immediate exit from the function. (Optional)

✦ **End Function:** A keyword that indicates the end of the function. (Required)

 Tip   A value is assigned to the function's name when a function is finished executing.

To create a custom function, follow these steps:

1. Activate the Visual Basic Editor (or press Alt+F11).

2. Select the workbook in the Project window.

3. Choose Insert ➪ Module to insert a VBA module (or you can use an existing module).

4. Enter the keyword Function followed by the function's name and a list of the arguments (if any) in parentheses.

5. Insert the VBA code that performs the work — and make sure that the variable corresponding to the function's name has the appropriate value (this is the value that the function returns).

6. End the function with an End Function statement.

Function names must adhere to the same rules as variable names, and you can't use a name that looks like a worksheet cell (for example, a function named J21 isn't accepted).

Executing function procedures

Although many ways exist to execute a *subroutine* procedure, you can execute a *function* procedure in just two ways:

✦ Call it from another procedure

✦ Use it in a worksheet formula

What a Function Can't Do

Almost everyone who starts creating custom worksheet functions using VBA makes a fatal mistake: They try to get the function to do more than is possible.

A worksheet function returns a value, and it must be completely "passive." In other words, the function cannot change anything on the worksheet. For example, it's impossible to develop a worksheet function that changes the formatting of a cell. If your function attempts to perform an action that is not allowed, the function simply returns an error.

VBA functions that are not used in worksheet formulas can do anything that a regular subroutine can do — including changing cell formatting.

Calling custom functions from a procedure

You can call custom functions from a procedure just as you call built-in VBA functions. For example, after you define a function called `CalcTax`, you can enter a statement such as the following:

```
Tax = CalcTax(Amount, Rate)
```

This statement executes the `CalcTax` custom function with `Amount` and `Rate` as its arguments. The function's result is assigned to the `Tax` variable.

Using custom functions in a worksheet formula

Using a custom function in a worksheet formula is like using built-in functions. You must ensure that Excel can locate the function procedure, however. If the function procedure is in the same workbook, you don't have to do anything special. If the function is defined in a different workbook, you may have to tell Excel where to find the function. The following are the three ways in which you can do this:

✦ **Precede the function's name with a file reference.** For example, if you want to use a function called `CountNames` that's defined in a workbook named MyFunctions, you can use a reference such as the following:

```
=MyFunctions.xls!CountNames(A1:A1000)
```

If you insert the function with the Insert Function dialog box, the workbook reference is inserted automatically.

✦ **Set up a reference to the workbook.** If the custom function is defined in a reference workbook, you don't need to precede the function name with the workbook name. You establish a reference to another workbook with the Tools ➪ References command (in the Visual Basic Editor). You are presented with a list of references that includes all open workbooks. Place a check mark in the item that refers to the workbook that contains the custom function (use the Browse button if the workbook isn't open).

✦ **Create an add-in.** When you create an add-in from a workbook that has function procedures, you don't need to use the file reference when you use one of the functions in a formula; the add-in must be installed, however. Chapter 39 discusses add-ins.

Note   If you plan on developing custom worksheet functions, make sure that you heed the warning in the sidebar "What a Function Can't Do."

Tip   Your function procedures don't appear in the Macros dialog box when you select Tools ➪ Macro, because you can't execute a function directly. As a result, you need to do extra, up-front work to test your functions as you're developing them. One approach is to set up a simple subroutine that calls the function. If the function is designed to be used in worksheet formulas, you can enter a simple formula to test it as you're developing the function.

Learning About Function Procedure Arguments

Here are some important points to remember about function procedure arguments:

✦ Arguments can be variables (including arrays), constants, literals, or expressions.

✦ Some functions do not have arguments.

✦ Some functions have a fixed number of required arguments (from 1 to 60).

✦ Some functions have a combination of required and optional arguments.

The following section presents a series of examples that demonstrate how to use arguments effectively with functions. Coverage of optional arguments is beyond the scope of this book.

Learning about a function with no argument

Like subroutines, functions don't necessarily have to use arguments. Excel, for example, has a few built-in worksheet functions that don't use arguments. These include RAND, TODAY, and NOW.

The following is a simple example of a function that has no arguments. This function returns the UserName property of the Application object, which is the name that appears in the Options dialog box (General tab). This example is simple, but it can be useful because no other way is available to get the user's name to appear in a worksheet formula.

```
Function User()
' Returns the name of the current user
    User = Application.UserName
End Function
```

When you enter the following formula into a worksheet cell, the cell displays the name of the current user:

```
=User()
```

Tip

As with Excel's built-in functions, when you use a function with no arguments, you must include a set of empty parentheses.

The following example is a simple subroutine that uses the User custom function as an argument for the MsgBox function. The concatenation operator (&) joins the literal string with the result of the User function.

```
Sub ShowUser()
   MsgBox ("The user is " & User())
End Sub
```

Learning about a function with one argument

This section contains a more complex function that is designed for a sales manager who needs to calculate the commissions that are earned by the sales force. The commission rate is based on the amount sold — those who sell more earn a higher commission rate. The function returns the commission amount, based on the sales made (which is the function's only argument — a required argument). The calculations in this example are based on the following table:

Monthly Sales	Commission Rate
0–$9,999	8.0%
$10,000–$19,999	10.5%
$20,000–$39,999	12.0%
$40,000+	14.0%

Several ways exist to calculate commissions for various sales amounts that are entered into a worksheet. You could write a formula such as the following:

```
=IF(AND(A1>=0,A1<=9999.99),A1*0.08,IF(AND(A1>=10000,A1<=19999.9
9), A1*0.105
,IF(AND(A1>=20000,A1<=39999.99),A1*0.12,IF(A1>=40000,A1*0.14,0)
)))
```

This is not the best approach, for a couple of reasons. First, the formula is overly complex and difficult to understand. Second, the values are hard-coded into the formula, making the formula difficult to modify if the commission structure changes.

A better approach is to use a lookup table function to compute the commissions; for example:

```
=VLOOKUP(A1,Table,2)*A1
```

Using the VLOOKUP function, however, requires that you have a table of commission rates set up in your worksheet.

An even better approach is to create a custom function, such as the following:

```
Function Commission(Sales)
' Calculates sales commissions
   Tier1 = 0.08
   Tier2 = 0.105
   Tier3 = 0.12
   Tier4 = 0.14
   Select Case Sales
       Case 0 To 9999.99: Commission = Sales * Tier1
       Case 1000 To 19999.99: Commission = Sales * Tier2
       Case 20000 To 39999.99: Commission = Sales * Tier3
       Case Is >= 40000: Commission = Sales * Tier4
   End Select
End Function
```

After you define the Commission function in a VBA module, you can use it in a worksheet formula or call it from other VBA procedures.

Entering the following formula into a cell produces a result of 3,000 (the amount, 25,000, qualifies for a commission rate of 12 percent):

```
=Commission(25000)
```

Even if you don't need custom functions in a worksheet, creating function procedures can make your VBA coding much simpler. If your VBA procedure calculates sales commissions, for example, you can use the Commission function and call it from a VBA subroutine. The following is a tiny subroutine that asks the user for a sales amount and then uses the Commission function to calculate the commission due and to display it:

```
Sub CalcComm()
    Sales = InputBox("Enter Sales:")
    MsgBox "The commission is " & Commission(Sales)
End Sub
```

The subroutine starts by displaying an input box that asks for the sales amount. Then, the procedure displays a message box with the calculated sales commission for that amount. The Commission function must be available in the active workbook; otherwise, Excel displays a message saying that the function is not defined.

Learning about a function with two arguments

This example builds on the previous one. Imagine that the sales manager implements a new policy: The total commission paid is increased by one percent for every year that the salesperson has been with the company. For this example, the custom Commission function (defined in the preceding section) has been modified so that it takes two arguments — both of which are required arguments. Call this new function `Commission2`:

```
Function Commission2(Sales, Years)
'   Calculates sales commissions based on years in service
    Tier1 = 0.08
    Tier2 = 0.105
    Tier3 = 0.12
    Tier4 = 0.14
    Select Case Sales
       Case 0 To 9999.99: Commission2 = Sales * Tier1
       Case 1000 To 19999.99: Commission2 = Sales * Tier2
       Case 20000 To 39999.99: Commission2 = Sales * Tier3
       Case Is >= 40000: Commission2 = Sales * Tier4
    End Select
    Commission2 = Commission2 + (Commission2 * Years / 100)
End Function
```

The modification was quite simple. The second argument (`Years`) was added to the `Function` statement, and an additional computation was included that adjusts the commission, before exiting the function.

The following is an example of how you write a formula by using this function (it assumes that the sales amount is in cell A1 and the number of years that the salesperson has worked is in cell B1):

```
=Commission2(A1,B1)
```

Learning about a function with a range argument

The example in this section demonstrates how to use a worksheet range as an argument. Actually, it's not at all tricky; Excel takes care of the details behind the scenes.

Assume that you want to calculate the average of the five largest values in a range named `Data`. Excel doesn't have a function that can do this, so you can write the following formula:

```
=(LARGE(Data,1)+LARGE(Data,2)+LARGE(Data,3)+LARGE(Data,4)+LARGE
(Data,5))/5
```

This formula uses Excel's `LARGE` function, which returns the nth largest value in a range. The preceding formula adds the five largest values in the range named `Data` and then divides the result by 5. The formula works fine, but it's rather unwieldy. And, what if you need to compute the average of the top *six* values? You would need to rewrite the formula and make sure that all copies of the formula also get updated.

Wouldn't it be easier if Excel had a function named `TopAvg`? For example, you could use the following (nonexistent) function to compute the average:

```
=TopAvg(Data,5)
```

This is an example of when a custom function can make things much easier for you. The following is a custom VBA function, named `TopAvg`, which returns the average of the top *n* values in a range:

```
Function TopAvg(InRange, Num)
' Returns the average of the highest Num values in InRange
   Sum = 0
   For i = 1 To Num
      Sum = Sum + WorksheetFunction.Large(InRange, i)
   Next i
   TopAvg = Sum / Num
End Function
```

This function takes two arguments: `InRange` (which is a worksheet range) and `Num` (the number of values to average). The code starts by initializing the `Sum` variable to 0. It then uses a `For-Next` loop to calculate the sum of the *n*th largest values in the range. Finally, `TopAvg` is assigned the value of `Sum` divided by `Num`.

Tip   Note that Excel's LARGE function is used within the loop. You can use an Excel worksheet function in VBA if you precede the function with WorksheetFunction and a period.

You can use all of Excel's worksheet functions in your VBA procedures, *except* those that have equivalents in VBA. For example, VBA has a `Rnd` function that returns a random number. Therefore, you can't use Excel's `RAND` function in a VBA procedure.

Debugging Custom Functions

Debugging a function procedure can be a bit more challenging than debugging a subroutine procedure. If you develop a function to use in worksheet formulas, an error in the function procedure simply results in an error display in the formula cell (usually #VALUE!). In other words, you don't receive the normal run-time error message that helps you to locate the offending statement.

When you are debugging a worksheet formula, using only one instance of the function in your worksheet is the best technique. The following are three methods that you may want to use in your debugging:

✦ Place MsgBox functions at strategic locations to monitor the value of specific variables. Fortunately, message boxes in function procedures pop up when the procedure is executed. But, make sure that you have only one formula in the worksheet that uses your function; otherwise, the message boxes appear for each formula that's evaluated.

✦ Test the procedure by calling it from a subroutine procedure. Run-time errors display normally, and you can either fix the problem (if you know what it is) or jump right into the debugger.

✦ Set a breakpoint in the function and then use Excel's debugger to step through the function. You then can access all the normal debugging tools.

Inserting Custom Functions

Excel's Insert Function dialog box is a handy tool that enables you to choose a worksheet function; you even can choose one of your custom worksheet functions. The Formula Palette prompts you for the function's arguments.

Note Function procedures that are defined with the Private keyword do not appear in the Insert Function dialog box.

You also can display a description of your custom function in the Insert Function dialog box. To do so, follow these steps:

1. Create the function in a module by using the VBE.

2. Activate Excel.

3. Choose the Tools ⇨ Macro ⇨ Macros command.

   Excel displays its Macro dialog box (see Figure 35-4).

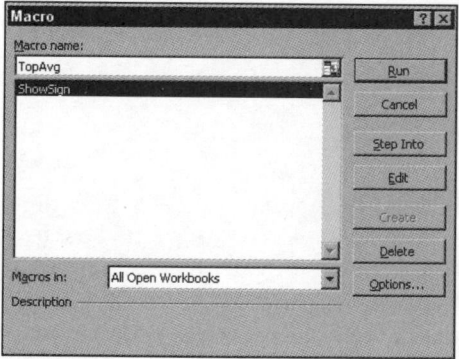

Figure 35-4: Excel's Macro dialog box doesn't list functions, so you must enter the function name yourself.

4. In the Macro dialog box, type the name of the function in the box labeled Macro Name. Notice that functions do not normally appear in this dialog box, so you must enter the function name yourself.

5. Click the Options button.

   Excel displays its Macro Options dialog box. (See Figure 35-5.)

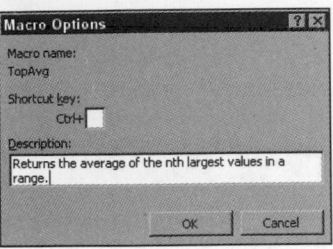

Figure 35-5: You can enter a description for a custom function. This description then appears in the Insert Function dialog box.

6. Enter a description of the function and then click OK. The Shortcut key field is irrelevant for functions.

The description that you enter appears in the Insert Function dialog box.

Custom functions are listed under the User Defined category, and no straightforward way exists to create a new function category for your custom functions.

Figure 35-6 shows the Insert Function dialog box, listing the custom functions that are in the User Defined category. In the second Function Wizard dialog box, the user is prompted to enter arguments for a custom function — just as in using a built-in worksheet function.

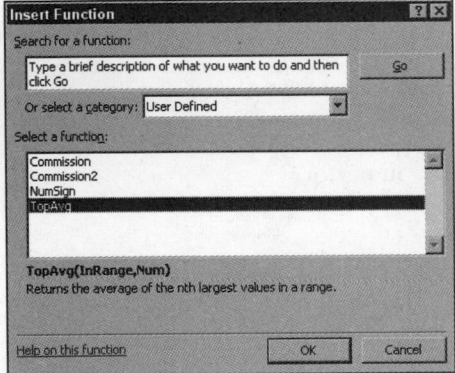

Figure 35-6: You can use the Insert Function dialog box to insert a custom function.

When you access a *built-in* function from the Insert Function dialog box, the Formula Palette displays a description of each argument. Unfortunately, you can't provide such descriptions for custom functions.

The information in this chapter only scratches the surface when it comes to creating custom functions. It should be enough to get you started, however, if you're interested in this topic. You may be able to use the examples in this chapter directly or adapt them for your needs.

✦   ✦   ✦

Introducing UserForms

Dialog boxes are perhaps the most important user inter-face element in Windows programs. Virtually every Windows program uses them, and most users understand how they work. Excel makes it relatively easy to create custom dialog boxes for your applications. In fact, you can dupli-cate the look and feel of all Excel's dialog boxes. This chapter shows you how to create your own dialog boxes — UserForms, in Excel's lingo — as well as how you can use Excel's built in dialog boxes.

Getting Started With Custom Dialog Boxes

A custom dialog box is created on a UserForm, and you access UserForms in the Visual Basic Editor.

Following is the typical sequence of steps you perform when you create a custom dialog box:

1. Insert a new UserForm into your workbook.

2. Write a procedure that displays the UserForm. This pro-cedure is located in a VBA module — not in the code module for the UserForm.

3. Add controls to the UserForm.

4. Adjust some of the properties of the controls you added.

5. Write event-handler procedures for the controls. These procedures, which are located in the code window for the UserForm, are executed when various events (such as a button click) occur.

Inserting a New UserForm

To insert a new UserForm, activate the VBE (Alt+F11), select your workbook's project from the Project window, and select Insert ⇨ UserForm. UserForms have names like UserForm1, UserForm2, and so on.

Tip   You can change the name of a UserForm to make it easier to identify. Select the form and use the Properties window to change the Name property (press F4 if the Properties window is not displayed). Figure 36-1 shows the Properties window when an empty UserForm is selected.

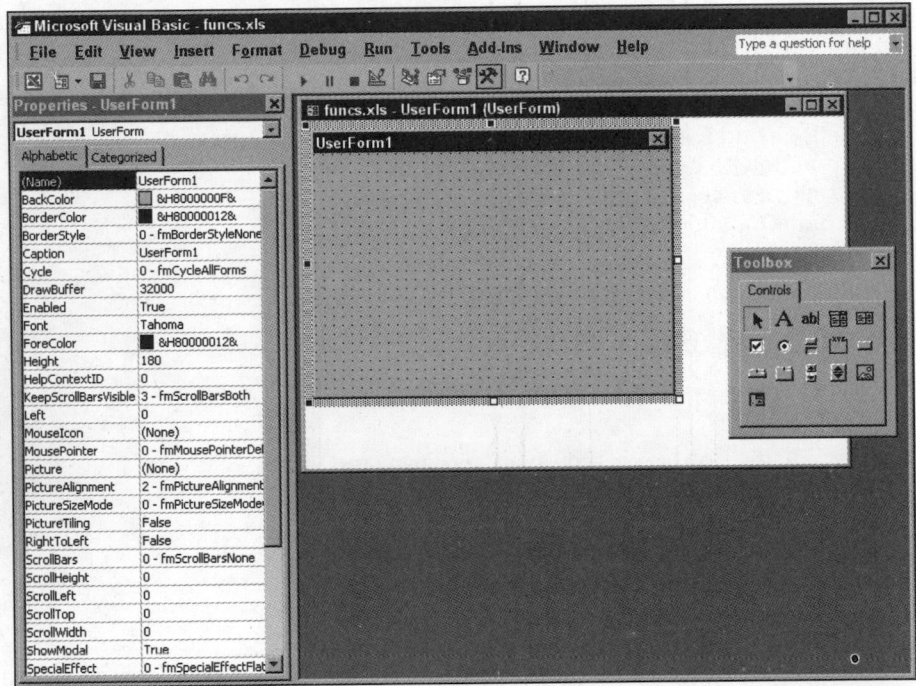

Figure 36-1: This shows the VBE immediately after you create a new UserForm.

A workbook can have any number of UserForms, and each UserForm holds a single custom dialog box.

Displaying a UserForm

To display a UserForm, use the Show method of the UserForm object. The following procedure, which is contained in a normal VBA module, displays UserForm1.

```
Sub ShowForm
    UserForm1.Show
End Sub
```

When the UserForm is displayed, it remains visible onscreen until it is dismissed. Usually, you'll add a CommandButton to the UserForm that executes a procedure that dismisses the UserForm. The procedure can either unload the UserForm (with the `Unload` statement) or hide the UserForm (with the `Hide` method of the User-Form object). This concept becomes clearer later in the chapter.

Adding Controls to a UserForm

To add controls to a custom dialog box, use the Toolbox (the VBE does not have menu commands that add controls).

 Tip   If the Toolbox is not displayed, select View ➪ Toolbox.

Just click the Toolbox button that corresponds to the control you want to add, and then click inside the dialog box. Or, you can click the control and then drag the mouse pointer in the dialog box to specify the dimensions for the control.

When you add a new control, it is assigned a name that combines the control type with the numeric sequence for that type of control. For example, if you add a CommandButton control to an empty dialog box, it is named `CommandButton1`. If you then add a second CommandButton, it is named `CommandButton2`.

 Tip   Rename all the controls that you will be manipulating with your VBA code. Doing so enables you to refer to meaningful names (such as ProductListBox) rather than generic names, such as ListBox1. To change the name of a control, use the Properties window in the VBA. Just select the object and enter a new name.

Understanding the controls that are available to you

Table 36-1 briefly describes the controls available to you in the Toolbox. You can see this toolbox in Figure 36-1.

 **Cross-Reference**   Your UserForms can also use other ActiveX controls. See "Customizing the Toolbox" later in this chapter.

Table 36-1 Controls in the Toolbox	
Name	**Description**
Label	A Label control simply displays text in your dialog box.
TextBox	A TextBox control enables the user to input text.

Continued

Table 36-1 *(continued)*

Name	Description
ComboBox	A ComboBox control is a drop-down box that displays only one item at a time. Unlike with a ListBox control, the user may be able to enter a value that does not appear in the given list of items.
ListBox	A ListBox control presents a list of items from which the user can select an item (or multiple items). You can specify a worksheet range that holds the ListBox items, or you can fill the ListBox with items using VBA.
CheckBox	A CheckBox control provides the user a binary choice: yes or no, true or false, and so on. When a CheckBox is checked, it has a value of True; otherwise, it's False.
OptionButton	OptionButtons are useful when the user needs to make exclusive selections from a small number of items. OptionButtons are always used in groups of at least two. If your dialog box contains more than one set of OptionButtons, each set of OptionButtons must have the same GroupName property value. Alternatively, you can enclose the OptionButtons in a Frame control, which automatically groups the OptionButtons contained in the frame.
ToggleButton	A ToggleButton control has two states: on and off. Clicking the button toggles between these two states, and the button changes its appearance. Its value is either True (pressed) or False (not pressed).
Frame	A Frame control is used to enclose other controls. A frame is particularly useful when the dialog box contains more than one set of OptionButton controls.
Command Button	Every dialog box that you create will probably have at least one CommandButton. Usually, you'll want to have one CommandButton labeled OK and another labeled Cancel.
TabStrip	A TabStrip control is similar to a MultiPage control.
MultiPage	A MultiPage control enables you to create tabbed dialog boxes. By default, a MultiPage control has two pages. To add additional pages, right-click a tab and select New Page from the shortcut menu.
ScrollBar	A ScrollBar control is similar to a SpinButton control. The difference is that the user can drag the ScrollBar's button to change the control's value in larger increments.
SpinButton	A SpinButton control enables the user to select a value by clicking one of two arrows; one arrow increases the value, and the other arrow decreases the value. A SpinButton is often used in conjunction with a TextBox control or a Label control, both of which display the current value of the SpinButton.
Image	An Image control is used to display a graphic image, which can come from a file or can be pasted from the clipboard.
RefEdit	A RefEdit control is used when you need to enable the user to select a range in a worksheet.

Adjusting Dialog Box Controls

After a control is placed in a dialog box, you can move and resize it using standard mouse techniques.

Tip   You can select multiple controls by Shift-clicking or by clicking and dragging the pointer to "lasso" a group of controls.

A UserForm may contain vertical and horizontal grid lines that help you align the controls you add. When you add or move a control, it *snaps* to the grid to help you line up the controls. If you don't like to see these grid lines, you can turn them off by choosing Tools ⇨ Options in the VBE. In the Options dialog box, select the General tab and set your desired options in the Form Grid Settings section.

The Format menu in the VBE window provides several commands to help you precisely align and space the controls in a dialog box. Before you use these commands, select the controls you want to work with. Figure 36-2 shows a dialog box with several OptionButton controls about to be aligned.

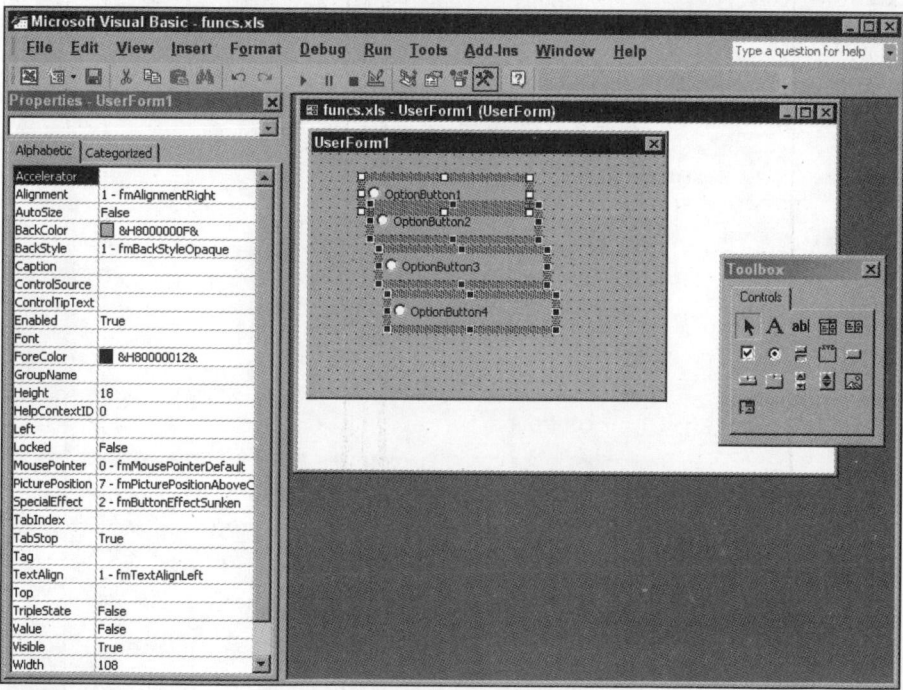

Figure 36-2: You can use the Format ⇨ Align command to change the alignment of controls.

Tip

When you select multiple controls, the last control you select appears with white handles rather than the normal black handles. The control with the white handles is used as the model against which the other black-handle controls are compared for size or position.

Adjusting a Control's Properties

You can change a control's properties at *design time* with the Properties window while you're developing the dialog box or during *run-time* when the dialog box is being displayed for the user. You use VBA instructions to change a control's properties at run-time.

Using the Properties window

In the VBE, the Properties window adjusts to display the properties of the selected item, which can be a control or the UserForm itself. In addition, you can select a control using the drop-down list at the top of the Properties window (see Figure 36-3).

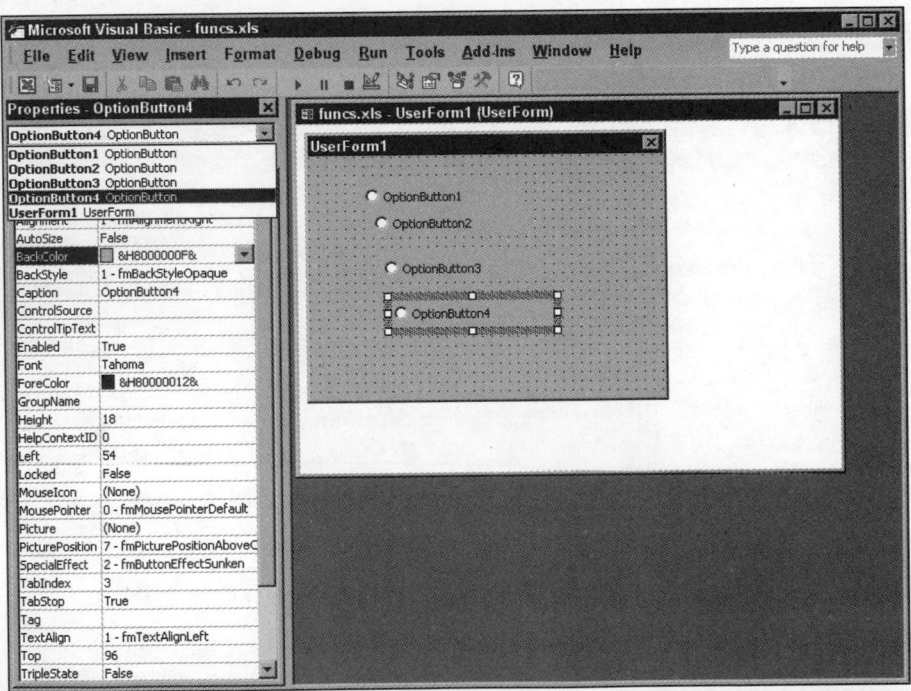

Figure 36-3: You can use the drop-down list at the top of the Properties window to select a control so that you can adjust its properties.

The Properties window has two tabs. The Alphabetic tab displays the properties for the selected object in alphabetical order. The Categorized tab displays them grouped into logical categories. Both tabs contain the same properties, but in a different order.

Using Controls on a Worksheet

Many UserForm controls can be embedded directly into a worksheet. These controls are accessible from the Control Toolbox toolbar in Excel (not VBE). Adding such controls to a worksheet requires much less effort than creating a dialog box. In addition, you may not have to create any macros because you can link a control to a worksheet cell. For example, if you insert a CheckBox control on a worksheet, you can link it to a particular cell by setting its LinkedCell property. When the CheckBox is checked, the linked cell displays TRUE. When the CheckBox is unchecked, the linked cell displays FALSE.

When you add a control to a worksheet, Excel goes into design mode. In this mode, you can adjust the properties of any controls on your worksheet, add or edit event-handler procedures for the control, or change its size or position. To display the Properties window for an ActiveX control, right-click the control and select Properties from the shortcut menu.

When Excel is in design mode, you can't try out the controls. To test the controls, you must exit design mode by clicking the Exit Design Mode button on the Control Toolbox toolbar.

To change a property, just click it and specify the new property. Some properties can take on a finite number of values, selectable from a list. If so, the Properties window displays a button with a downward-pointing arrow when you select the property. Click the button and you'll be able to select the property's value from the list. For example, the TextAlign property can have any of the following values: 1 - fmTextAlignLeft, 2 - fmTextAlignCenter, or 3 - fmTextAlignRight.

A few properties (for example, Font and Picture) display a small button with an ellipsis when selected. Click the button to display a dialog box associated with the property.

The Image control's Picture property is worth mentioning because you can either select a graphic file that contains the image or paste an image from the clipboard. When pasting an image, first copy it to the clipboard, and then select the Picture property for the Image control and press Ctrl+V to paste the clipboard contents.

Note   If you select two or more controls at once, the Properties window displays only the properties that are common to the selected controls.

Understanding common properties

Although each control has its own unique set of properties, many of those properties have the same name and often share a common purpose. For example, every control has a Name property and properties that determine its size and position (Height, Width, Left, and Right).

If you're going to manipulate a control using VBA, you may prefer to provide a meaningful name for the control. For example, the first OptionButton that you add to a UserForm has a default name of OptionButton1. You refer to this object in your code using a statement such as

```
OptionButton1.Value = True
```

But if you give the OptionButton a more meaningful name (such as `obLandscape`), you can use a statement such as

```
obLandscape.Value = True
```

Note Many people find it helpful to use a name that also identifies the type of object. The preceding example uses `ob` as the prefix to identify the fact that this control is an OptionButton.

Tip The best way to learn about the various properties for a control is to use the online help. Simply click a property in the Properties window and press F1.

Accommodating keyboard users

Many users prefer to navigate through a dialog box using the keyboard. The Tab and Shift+Tab keystrokes cycle through the controls, and pressing a hot key operates the control. To make sure that your dialog box works properly for keyboard users, you must be mindful of two issues: tab order and accelerator keys.

Changing the tab order

The tab order determines the sequence in which the controls are activated when the user presses Tab or Shift+Tab. It also determines which control has the initial *focus*. If a user enters text into a TextBox control, for example, the TextBox has the focus. If the user clicks an OptionButton, the OptionButton has the focus. The control that's first in the tab order has the focus when a dialog box is first displayed. By default, Excel sets the tab order in the same sequence as the controls were added.

Note The term tab order may be a little misleading. It has nothing to do with any tabs that are on the dialog box — only with the order in which the Tab key moves between controls.

To set the tab order of your controls, choose View ➪ Tab Order. You can also right-click the dialog box and choose Tab Order from the shortcut menu. In either case, Excel displays the Tab Order dialog box, shown in Figure 36-4. The Tab Order dialog box lists all the controls, the sequence of which corresponds to the order in which controls pass the focus between each other in the UserForm. To move a control, select it and click the arrow keys up or down. You can choose more than one control (click while pressing Shift or Ctrl) and move them all at once.

Alternatively, you can set an individual control's position in the tab order using the Properties window. The first control in the tab order has a `TabIndex` property of 0. Changing the `TabIndex` property for a control may also affect the `TabIndex` property of other controls. These adjustments are made automatically to ensure that no control has a `TabIndex` setting that is greater than the total number of controls in the UserForm. If you want to remove a control from the tab order, set its `TabStop` property to False.

Testing a UserForm

You can test a UserForm in three ways without actually calling it from a VBA procedure:

✦ Choose *the Run ➪ Run Sub/UserForm command.

✦ Press F5.

✦ Click the Run Sub/UserForm button on the Standard toolbar.

These three techniques all trigger the UserForm's `Initialize` event. When a dialog box is displayed in this test mode, you can try out the tab order and the accelerator keys.

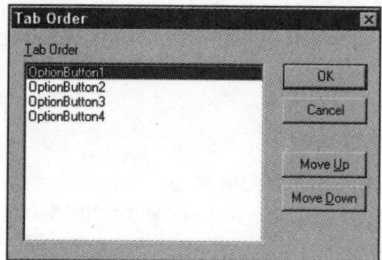

Figure 36-4: Use the Tab Order dialog box to specify the tab order of the controls.

 **Note**   Some controls, such as Frame and MultiPage, act as containers for other controls. The controls inside a container have their own tab order. To set the tab order for a group of OptionButtons inside a Frame control, select the Frame control before you choose the View ➪ Tab Order command.

Setting hot keys

You can assign an accelerator key, or *hot key,* to most dialog box controls. This enables the user to access the control by pressing Alt+the hot key. Use the `Accelerator` property in the Properties window for this purpose.

 **Note**   Some controls, such as a TextBox, don't have an Accelerator property because they don't display a Caption. You still can enable direct keyboard access to these controls using a Label control. Assign an accelerator key to the Label, and put it ahead of the TextBox in the tab order.

Manipulating UserForms with VBA

This section provides an overview of using VBA to work with custom dialog boxes.

Displaying a UserForm

To display a dialog box from VBA, you create a procedure that uses the Show method of the UserForm object. You cannot display a dialog box without using at least one line of VBA code. If your UserForm is named UserForm1, the following procedure displays the dialog box on that form:

```
Sub ShowDialog()
    UserForm1.Show
End Sub
```

This procedure must be located in a standard VBA module, not in the code module for the UserForm.

Note VBA also has a Load statement. Loading a UserForm loads it into memory, but it is not visible until you use the Show method. To load a UserForm, use a statement like this:

```
Load UserForm1
```

If you have a complex UserForm, you might want to load it into memory before it is needed so that it appears more quickly when you use the Show method. In the majority of situations, however, it's not necessary to use the Load statement.

Closing a UserForm

To close a UserForm, use the UnLoad statement. For example,

```
Unload UserForm1
```

Or, you can use the following:

```
Unload Me
```

Normally, your VBA code should include the Unload statement after the dialog box has performed its actions. For example, your dialog box may have a Command Button that serves as an OK button. Clicking this button executes a macro. One of the statements in the macro unloads the UserForm. The UserForm remains visible on the screen until the macro that contains the Unload statement finishes.

Caution When a UserForm is unloaded, its controls are reset to their original values. In other words, your code will not be able to access the user's choices after the UserForm is unloaded. If the user's choice must be used later on (after the UserForm is unloaded), you need to store the value in a global variable.

A UserForm is automatically unloaded by default when the user clicks the close button (the big *X*) in the upper-right corner. No Unload statement is necessary for the UserForm to start unloading itself. With a CommandButton marked Cancel, it's generally convenient to have an event-handler procedure that contains the Unload statement, plus whatever other instructions are necessary to perform the business of the UserForm and clean up after itself. But the close button has no event of its own. So clicking the big *X* stops VBA execution of the UserForm module, and any cleanup instructions associated with the Cancel button are skipped over. The solution to this problem is to place your cleanup instructions within the UserForm_Terminate event hander. This way, both the Cancel button and the close button initiate the cleanup process. You can then keep your Unload statement within the _Click event handler for the Cancel button. You'll see more about event-handler procedures in the next section.

The next chapter presents an example that effectively disables the close button.

UserForms also have a Hide method. When you invoke this method, the dialog box disappears, but it remains loaded in memory, so your code can still access the various properties of the controls. Here's an example of a statement that hides a UserForm:

```
UserForm1.Hide
```

Or, you can use the following:

```
Me.Hide
```

If for some reason you would like your UserForm to disappear immediately while its macro is executing, use the Hide method at the top of the procedure, and follow it with a DoEvents command. For example, in the following procedure, the UserForm disappears immediately when CommandButton1 is clicked. The last statement in the procedure unloads the UserForm.

```
Private Sub CommandButton1_Click()
    Me.Hide
    DoEvents
    For r = 1 To 10000
        Cells(r, 1) = r
    Next r
    Unload Me
End Sub
```

Understanding event-handler procedures

In official terminology, when the user interacts with the dialog box by selecting an item from a ListBox, clicking a CommandButton, and so on, he causes an *event* to occur. For example, clicking a CommandButton raises the Click event for the CommandButton. Your application needs procedures that are executed when these events occur. These procedures are sometimes known as *event-handler* procedures.

Event-handler procedures must be located in the code window for the UserForm. However, your event-handler procedure can call another procedure that's located in a standard VBA module.

Your VBA code can change the properties of the controls while the dialog box is displayed — that is, at run-time. For example, you may assign to a ListBox control a procedure that changes the text in a Label when an item is selected. This type of manipulation becomes clearer later in this chapter.

Creating a UserForm: An Example

If you've never created a custom dialog box, you may want to walk through the example in this section. The example includes step-by-step instructions for creating a simple dialog box and developing a VBA procedure to support the dialog box.

This example uses a custom dialog box to get two pieces of information: a person's name and sex. The dialog box uses a TextBox control to get the name, and three OptionButtons to get the sex (Male, Female, or Unknown). The information collected in the dialog box is then sent to the next blank row in a worksheet.

Creating the dialog box

Figure 36-5 shows the finished custom dialog box for this example.

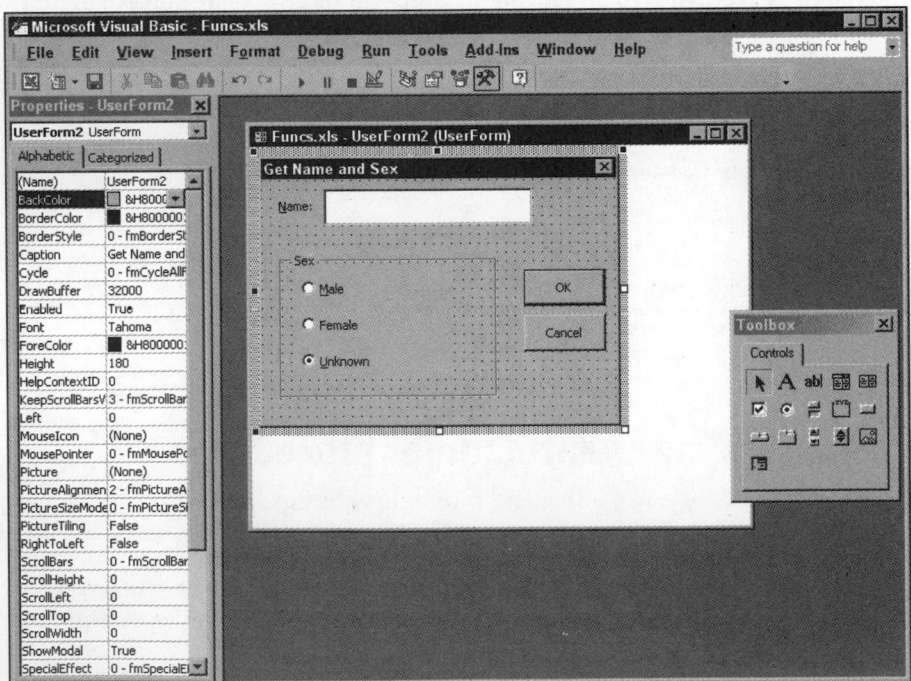

Figure 36-5: This dialog box asks the user to enter a name and a sex.

For best results, follow these steps:

1. Press Alt+F11 to activate the VBE.

2. In the Project window, select the workbook's project and choose Insert ⇨ UserForm to add an empty UserForm.

3. If the Properties window isn't visible, press F4.

4. Use the Properties window to change the UserForm's Caption property to Get Name and Sex.

5. Add a Label control and adjust the properties as follows:

Property	Value
Accelerator	N
Caption	Name:
TabIndex	0

6. Add a TextBox control and adjust the properties as follows:

Property	Value
Name	TextName
TabIndex	1

7. Add a Frame control and adjust the properties as follows:

Property	Value
Caption	Sex
TabIndex	2

8. Add an OptionButton control inside of the Frame and adjust the properties as follows:

Property	Value
Accelerator	M
Caption	Male
Name	OptionMale
TabIndex	0

9. Add another OptionButton control inside the Frame and adjust the properties as follows:

Property	Value
Accelerator	F
Caption	Female
Name	OptionFemale
TabIndex	1

10. Add yet another Option Button control inside the Frame and adjust the properties as follows:

Property	Value
Accelerator	U
Caption	Unknown
Name	OptionUnknown
TabIndex	2
Value	True

11. Add a CommandButton control outside the frame and adjust the properties as follows:

Property	Value
Caption	OK
Default	True
Name	OKButton
TabIndex	3

12. Add another CommandButton control and adjust the properties as follows:

Property	Value
Caption	Cancel
Cancel	True
Name	CancelButton
TabIndex	4

Tip   In some cases, you may find it easier to copy an existing control rather than create a new one. To copy a control, press Ctrl while you drag the control.

Writing code to display the dialog box

Next, you add a CommandButton to the worksheet. This button executes a procedure that displays the UserForm. Here's how:

1. Activate Excel.

2. Right-click any toolbar, and select Control Toolbox from the shortcut menu. Excel displays its Control Toolbox toolbar, which closely resembles the VBE Toolbox.

3. Use the Control Toolbox toolbar to add a CommandButton to the worksheet. Click the CommandButton tool, and then drag the mouse pointer in the worksheet to create the button.

   If you like, you can change the caption for the worksheet CommandButton. To do so, right-click the button and select CommandButton Object ⇨ Edit from the shortcut menu.

4. Double-click the button.

   This activates the VBE — specifically, the code module for the worksheet is displayed, with an empty event-handler procedure for the worksheet's CommandButton.

5. Enter the following statement in the `CommandButton1_Click` procedure:

   `UserForm1.Show`

   This short procedure uses the `Show` method of an object (`UserForm1`) to display the dialog box.

Note   If your UserForm has a name other than UserForm1, you'll need to substitute the correct name in step 5.

6. Return to Excel so that you can try out your command button.

Trying it out

The next step is to try out the procedure that displays the dialog box.

Note   When you click the CommandButton on the worksheet, you'll find that nothing happens. Rather, the button is selected because Excel is still in design mode, which happens automatically when you enter a control using the Control Toolbox toolbar. To exit design mode, click the Exit Design Mode button.

When you exit design mode, clicking the button displays the dialog box (see Figure 36-6).

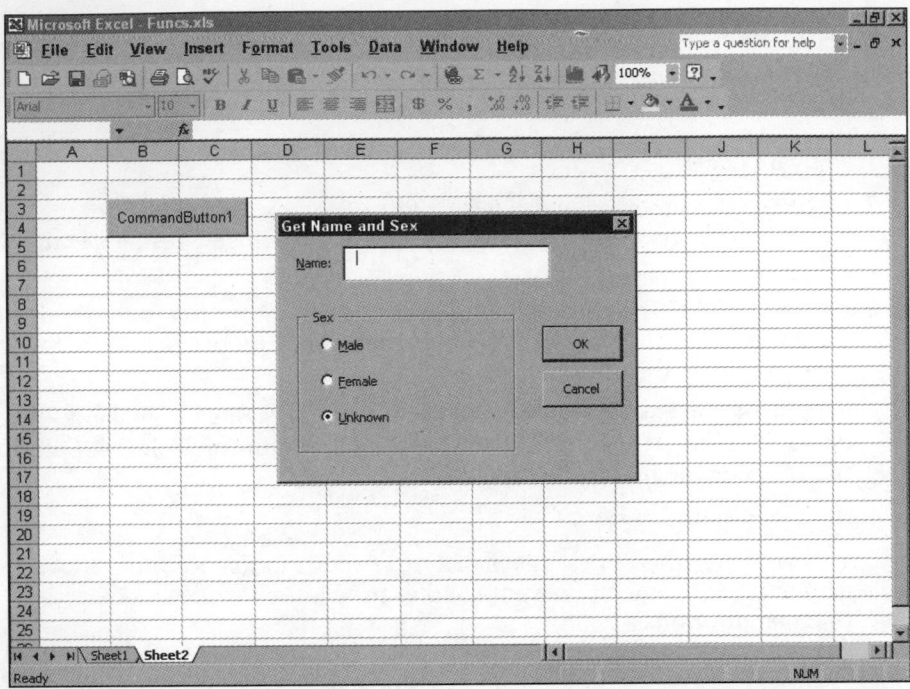

Figure 36-6: The CommandButton's Click event procedure displays the dialog box.

When the dialog box is displayed, enter some text into the TextBox and click OK. You'll find that nothing happens — this is understandable because you haven't created any event-handler procedures yet.

Note   Click the Close button in the dialog box's title bar to get rid of the dialog box.

Adding event-handler procedures

This section explains how to write the procedures that handle the events that occur when the dialog box is displayed. To continue our example, do the following:

1. Press Alt+F11 to activate the VBE.

2. Make sure the UserForm is displayed, and double-click the Cancel button. The VBE activates the Code window for the UserForm and provides an empty procedure named `CancelButton_Click`.

3. Modify the procedure as follows (this is the event handler for the CancelButton's `Click` event):

```
Private Sub CancelButton_Click()
    Unload UserForm1
End Sub
```

This procedure, which is executed when the user clicks the Cancel button, simply unloads the dialog box.

4. Double-click the OK button and enter the following procedure (this is the event handler for the OKButton's `Click` event):

```
Private Sub OKButton_Click()
'    Make sure Sheet1 is active
     Sheets("Sheet1").Activate

'    Determine the next empty row
     NextRow = _
       Application.WorksheetFunction.CountA(Range("A:A")) + 1
'    Transfer the name
     Cells(NextRow, 1) = TextName.Text

'    Transfer the sex
     If OptionMale Then Cells(NextRow, 2) = "Male"
     If OptionFemale Then Cells(NextRow, 2) = "Female"
     If OptionUnknown Then Cells(NextRow, 2) = "Unknown"

'    Clear the controls for the next entry
     TextName.Text = ""
     OptionUnknown = True
     TextName.SetFocus
End Sub
```

5. Activate Excel and click the CommandButton again to display the UserForm.

You'll find that the dialog box controls now function correctly. Figure 36-7 shows how this looks in action.

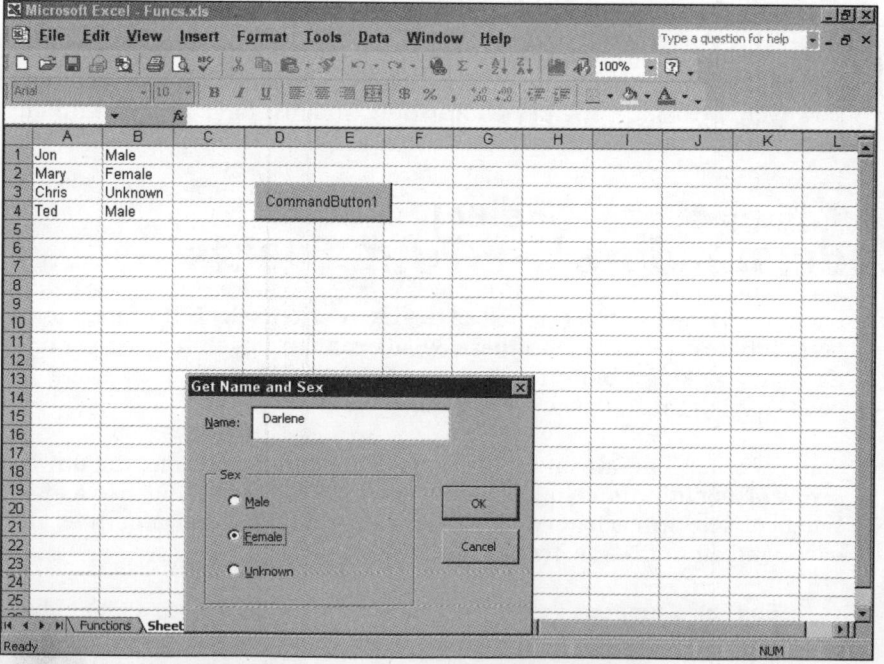

Figure 36-7: This is an example of using the custom dialog box.

Here's how the OKButton_Click procedure works: First, the procedure makes sure that the proper worksheet (Sheet1) is active. It then uses Excel's COUNTA function to determine the next blank cell in column A. Here, column A is represented by the numeral 1 in the second parameter of the Cells collection; the first parameter refers to the row number. (Column B is later represented by the numeral 2 at the same position.) Next, the procedure transfers the text from the TextBox to column A. It then uses a series of If statements to determine which OptionButton was selected and writes the appropriate text (Male, Female, or Unknown) to column B. Finally, the dialog box is reset to make it ready for the next entry. Notice that clicking OK doesn't close the dialog box. To end data entry and unload the UserForm, click the Cancel button.

Validating the data

Play around with this example some more, and you'll find that it has a small problem: It doesn't ensure that the user actually enters a name into the TextBox. The following code is inserted in the OKButton_Click procedure before the text is transferred to the worksheet. It ensures that the user enters a name (well, at least some text) in the TextBox. If the TextBox is empty, a message appears and the routine stops.

```
'    Make sure a name is entered
    If TextName.Text = "" Then
        MsgBox "You must enter a name."
        Exit Sub
    End If
```

After making all these modifications, you'll find that the dialog box works flawlessly. In real life, you probably need to collect more information than just name and sex. However, the same basic principles apply. You just have to deal with more dialog box controls.

Understanding UserForm Events

Each UserForm control (as well as the UserForm itself) is designed to respond to certain types of events, and these events can be triggered by a user or by Excel. For example, clicking a button generates a CommandButton Click event. You can write code that is executed when a particular event occurs.

Some actions generate multiple events. For example, clicking the upward-pointing arrow of a SpinButton control generates a SpinUp event and also a Change event. When a UserForm is loaded using the Show method, Excel generates an Initialize event and an Activate event.

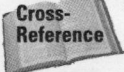

Cross-Reference Excel also supports events associated with a Sheet object, a Chart object, and the ThisWorkbook object. These types of events are discussed in Chapter 38.

Learning about events

To find out which events are supported by a particular control, perform the following steps:

1. Add a control to a UserForm.

2. Double-click the control to activate the code module for the UserForm. The VBE inserts an empty event-handler procedure for the control.

3. Click the drop-down list in the upper-right corner of the module window, and you'll see a complete list of events for the control (see Figure 36-8).

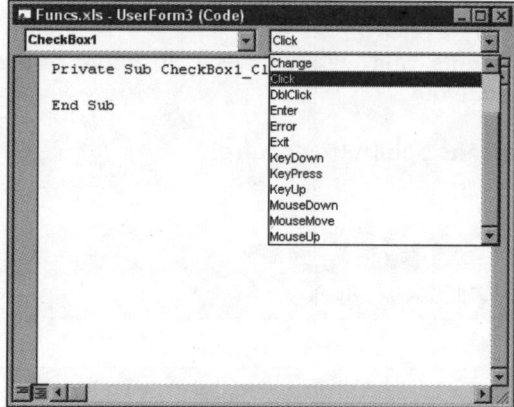

Figure 36-8: This is an example of the event list for a CheckBox control.

4. Select an event from the list, and the VBE creates an empty event-handler procedure for you.

Note To find out specific details about an event, consult the online help. The help system also lists the events available for each control.

Caution Event-handler procedures incorporate the name of the object in the procedure's name. Therefore, if you change the name of a control, you also need to make the appropriate changes to the control's event-handler procedure(s). The name changes are not performed automatically! To make things easy on yourself, provide names for your controls before you begin creating event-handler procedures.

Several events are associated with showing and unloading a UserForm:

Initialize   Occurs before a UserForm is loaded or shown

Activate   Occurs when a UserForm is activated

Deactivate	Occurs when a UserForm is deactivated
QueryClose	Occurs before a UserForm is unloaded
Terminate	Occurs after the UserForm is unloaded

Note Often, it's critical that you choose the appropriate event for your event-handler procedure and that you understand the order in which the events occur. Using the Show method invokes the Initialize and Activate events (in that order). Using the Load command invokes only the Initialize event. Using the Unload command triggers the QueryClose and Terminate events (in that order). Using the Hide method doesn't trigger either of these events.

Looking at an example: SpinButton events

To help clarify the concept of events, this section takes a close look at the events associated with a SpinButton control.

Table 36-2 lists all the events for the SpinButton control.

<table>
<tr><td colspan="2" align="center">Table 36-2
SpinButton Events</td></tr>
<tr><td>*Event*</td><td>*Description*</td></tr>
<tr><td>AfterUpdate</td><td>Occurs after the control is changed through the user interface</td></tr>
<tr><td>BeforeDragOver</td><td>Occurs when a drag-and-drop operation is in progress</td></tr>
<tr><td>BeforeUpdate</td><td>Occurs before the control is changed</td></tr>
<tr><td>Change</td><td>Occurs when the Value property changes</td></tr>
<tr><td>Enter</td><td>Occurs before the control actually receives the focus from a control on the same UserForm</td></tr>
<tr><td>Error</td><td>Occurs when the control detects an error and cannot return the error information to a calling program</td></tr>
<tr><td>Exit</td><td>Occurs immediately before a control loses the focus to another control on the same form</td></tr>
<tr><td>KeyDown</td><td>Occurs when the user presses a key and the object has the focus</td></tr>
<tr><td>KeyPress</td><td>Occurs when the user presses any key that produces a typeable character</td></tr>
<tr><td>KeyUp</td><td>Occurs when the user releases a key and the object has the focus</td></tr>
<tr><td>SpinDown</td><td>Occurs when the user clicks the lower (or left) SpinButton arrow</td></tr>
<tr><td>SpinUp</td><td>Occurs when the user clicks the upper (or right) SpinButton arrow</td></tr>
</table>

A user can operate a SpinButton control by clicking it with the mouse, or (if the control has the focus) using the up-arrow or down-arrow keys.

Mouse-initiated events

When the user clicks the upper SpinButton arrow, the following events occur in this precise order:

1. **Enter** (triggered only if the SpinButton did not already have the focus)
2. **Change**
3. **SpinUp**

Keyboard-initiated events

The user can also press Tab to set the focus to the SpinButton and then use the up-arrow key to increment the control. If so, the following events occur (in order):

1. **Enter**
2. **KeyDown**
3. **Change**
4. **SpinUp**

What about changes via code?

The SpinButton control can also be changed by VBA code, which also triggers the appropriate event(s). For example, the following instruction sets `SpinButton1`'s `Value` property to zero and also triggers the `Change` event for the SpinButton control:

```
SpinButton1.Value = 0
```

Caution   You might think that you could disable events by setting the EnableEvents property of the Application object to False. Unfortunately, this property applies only to events that involve true Excel objects: Workbooks, Worksheets, and Charts.

Pairing a SpinButton with a TextBox

A SpinButton has a `Value` property, but this control doesn't have a caption in which to display its value. In many cases, however, you will want the user to see the SpinButton's value. And sometimes you'll want the user to be able to change the SpinButton's value directly instead of clicking the SpinButton repeatedly.

The solution is to pair a SpinButton with a TextBox, which enables the user to specify a value by typing it into the TextBox directly or by clicking the SpinButton to increment or decrement the value in the TextBox.

Figure 36-9 shows a simple example. The SpinButton's `Min` property is 1, and its `Max` property is 100. Therefore, clicking the SpinButton's arrows changes its `Value` property setting to an integer between 1 and 100.

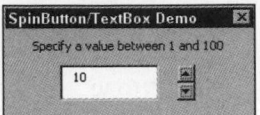

Figure 36-9: This is an example of a SpinButton paired with a TextBox.

The code required to "link" a SpinButton with a TextBox is relatively simple. It's basically a matter of writing event-handler procedures to ensure that the SpinButton's `Value` property is in sync with the TextBox's `Text` property.

The following procedure is executed whenever the SpinButton's `Change` event is triggered. That is, the procedure is executed when the user clicks the SpinButton or changes its value by pressing the up arrow or the down arrow.

```
Private Sub SpinButton1_Change()
    TextBox1.Text = SpinButton1.Value
End Sub
```

The procedure simply assigns the SpinButton's `Value` to the `Text` property of the TextBox control. Here, the controls have their default names (`SpinButton1` and `TextBox1`). If the user enters a value directly into the TextBox, its `Change` event is triggered and the following procedure is executed:

```
Private Sub TextBox1_Change()
    NewVal = Val(TextBox1.Text)
    If NewVal >= SpinButton1.Min And _
        NewVal <= SpinButton1.Max Then _
        SpinButton1.Value = NewVal
End Sub
```

This procedure starts by using VBA's `Val` function to convert the text in the TextBox to a value (if the TextBox contains a string, the `Val` function returns 0). The next statement determines if the value is within the proper range for the SpinButton. If so, the SpinButton's `Value` property is set to the value entered in the TextBox.

The example is set up so that clicking the OK button (which is named `OKButton`) transfers the SpinButton's value to the active cell. The event handler for this CommandButton's `Click` event is as follows:

```
Private Sub OKButton_Click()
'    Enter the value into the active cell
    If CStr(SpinButton1.Value) = TextBox1.Text Then
        ActiveCell = SpinButton1.Value
```

About the Tag Property

Every UserForm and control has a Tag property. This property doesn't represent anything specific, and, by default, is empty. You can use the Tag property to store information for your own use.

For example, you may have a series of TextBox controls in a UserForm. The user may be required to enter text into some, but not all of them. You can use the Tag property to identify (for your own use) which fields are required. In this case, you can set the Tag property to a string such as Required. Then, when you write code to validate the user's entries, you can refer to the Tag property.

The following example is a function that examines all TextBox controls on UserForm1 and returns the number of "required" TextBox controls that are empty:

```
Function EmptyCount()
  EmptyCount= 0
  For Each ctl In UserForm1.Controls
    If TypeName(ctl) = "TextBox" Then
      If ctl.Tag = "Required" Then
        If ctl.Text = "" Then
          EmptyCount = EmptyCount + 1
        End If
      End If
    End If
  Next ctl
End Function
```

```
        Unload Me
      Else
        MsgBox "Invalid entry.", vbCritical
        TextBox1.SetFocus
        TextBox1.SelStart = 0
        TextBox1.SelLength = Len(TextBox1.Text)
      End If
  End Sub
```

This procedure does one final check: It makes sure that the text entered in the TextBox matches the SpinButton's value. This is necessary in the case of an invalid entry. For example, if the user enters 3r into the TextBox, the SpinButton's value would not be changed, and the result placed in the active cell would not be what the user intended. Notice that the SpinButton's Value property is converted to a string using the CStr function. This ensures that the comparison does not generate an error if a value is compared to text. If the SpinButton's value does not match the TextBox's contents, a message box is displayed. Notice that the focus is set to the TextBox object, and the contents are selected (using the SelStart and SelLength properties). This makes it very easy for the user to correct the entry.

Working With UserForm Controls

When working with controls on a UserForm, the VBA code is usually contained in the code window for the UserForm. You can also refer to dialog box controls from a general VBA module. To do so, you need to *qualify* the reference to the control by specifying the UserForm name. For example, consider the following procedure, which is located in a VBA module. It simply displays the UserForm named UserForm1.

```
Sub GetData()
    UserForm1.Show
End Sub
```

Assume that you want to provide a default value for the text box named TextName. You could modify the procedure as follows:

```
Sub GetData()
    UserForm1.TextName.Value = "John Doe"
    UserForm1.Show
End Sub
```

Another way to set the default value is to take advantage of the UserForm's Initialize event. You can write code in the UserForm_Initialize procedure, which is located in the code module for the UserForm. Here's an example:

Understanding the Controls Collection

The controls on a UserForm compose a collection. For example, the following statement displays the number of controls on UserForm1:

```
MsgBox UserForm.Controls.Count
```

There is not a collection of each control type. For example, no collection of Command-Button controls exists. However, you can determine the type of control using the TypeName function. The following procedure uses a For Each-Next structure to loop through the Controls collection and then displays the number of CommandButton controls on UserForm1:

```
Sub CountButtons()
    cbCount = 0
    For Each ctl In UserForm1.Controls
        If TypeName(ctl) = "CommandButton" Then _
            cbCount = cbCount + 1
    Next ctl
    MsgBox cbCount
End Sub
```

```
Private Sub UserForm_Initialize()
    TextName.Value = "John Doe"
End Sub
```

Tip   Notice that when the control is referenced in the code module for the UserForm, no need exists to qualify the references with the UserForm name.

Customizing the Toolbox

When a UserForm is active in the VBE, the Toolbox (see Figure 36-10) displays the controls that you can add to the UserForm. This section describes ways to customize the Toolbox.

Figure 36-10: The Toolbox contains the controls that you can add to a UserForm.

Changing icons or tip text

If you would prefer a different icon or different tip text for a particular tool, right-click the tool and select Customize *xxx* from the shortcut menu (where *xxx* is the control's name). This brings up a new dialog box that enables you to change the Tool Tip Text, edit the icon, or load a new icon image from a file.

Adding new pages

The Toolbox initially contains a single tab. Right-click this tab and select New Page to add a new tab to the Toolbox. You can also change the text displayed on the tab by selecting Rename from the shortcut menu.

Customizing or combining controls

A very handy feature enables you to customize a control and then save it for future use. You can, for instance, create a CommandButton control that's set up to serve an OK button. You can set the following properties: `Width`, `Height`, `Caption`, `Default`, and `Name`. Then, drag the customized CommandButton to the Toolbox. This creates a new control. Right-click the new control to rename it or change its icon.

You can also create a new Toolbox entry that consists of multiple controls. For example, you can create two CommandButtons that represent a UserForm's OK and Cancel buttons. Customize them as you want and then select them both and drag them to the Toolbox. In this case, you can use this new Toolbox control to add two customized buttons in one fell swoop.

This also works with controls that act as containers. For example, create a Frame control and add four customized OptionButtons, neatly spaced and aligned. Then drag the Frame to the Toolbox to create a customized Frame control.

Tip   You might want to place your customized controls on a separate page in the Toolbox. This enables you to export the entire page so that you can share it with other Excel users. To export a Toolbox page (so that it may be reloaded into a later instance of the Toolbox), right-click the tab and select Export Page.

Adding new ActiveX controls

UserForms can use some other ActiveX controls developed by Microsoft or other vendors. To add an additional ActiveX control to the Toolbox, right-click the page of the Toolbox where you want the new controls to appear, and select Additional Controls. This displays the dialog box shown in Figure 36-11.

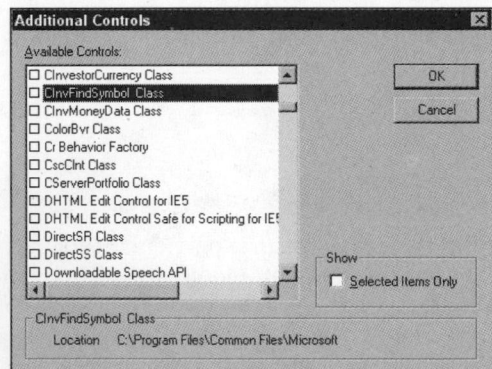

Figure 36-11: The Additional Controls dialog box enables you to add other ActiveX controls to the Toolbox.

The Additional Controls dialog box lists all ActiveX controls that are installed on your system. Select the control(s) that you want to add, and then click OK to add an icon for each selected control.

Caution   Not all ActiveX controls that are installed on your system will work in Excel UserForms. In fact, most of them probably won't work. Moreover, you need a license to use some controls in an application. If you aren't licensed to use a particular control, you'll receive an error message to that effect.

Creating UserForm "Templates"

You might find that when you design a new UserForm, you tend to add the same controls each time. For example, every UserForm might have two CommandButtons that serve as OK and Cancel buttons. The previous section described how to create a new control that combines these two (customized) buttons into a single control. Another option is to create your UserForm "template" and then export it so that it can be imported into other projects.

Start by creating a UserForm that contains all the controls and customizations that you would need to reuse in other projects. Then, make sure the UserForm is selected and choose File ⇨ Export File (or press Ctrl+E). You are prompted for a filename. When you start your next project, select File ⇨ Import File to load the saved UserForm.

A Dialog Box Checklist

Before you unleash a custom dialog box on end users, make sure that everything is working correctly. The following checklist should help you identify potential problems:

✦ Are similar controls the same size?

✦ Are the controls evenly spaced?

✦ Is the dialog box overwhelming? If so, you may want to group the controls using a MultiPage control.

✦ Can every control be accessed with a hot key?

✦ Are any of the hot keys duplicated?

✦ Is the tab order set correctly?

✦ If the dialog box will be stored in an add-in, did you test it thoroughly after creating the add-in? It's important to remember that an add-in will never be the active workbook.

✦ Will your VBA code take appropriate action if the dialog box is canceled or the user presses Esc?

✦ Are there any misspellings in the text?

✦ Does the dialog box have an appropriate caption?

✦ Will the dialog box be displayed properly at all video resolutions? Sometimes labels that display properly with a high-resolution display appear cut off in VGA display mode.

✦ Are the controls grouped logically (by function)?

✦ Do ScrollBar and SpinButton controls allow valid values only?

✦ Are ListBoxes set properly (Single, Multi, or Extended)?

Considering Alternatives to Custom Dialog Boxes

In some cases, you can save yourself the trouble of creating a custom dialog box by using one of several prebuilt dialog boxes:

✦ An input box

✦ A message box

✦ A dialog box for selecting a file to open

✦ A dialog box for specifying a filename and location for a save operation

✦ A dialog box for specifying a directory (requires a Windows API call)

These dialog boxes are described in the following sections.

Using an input box

Two InputBox functions actually exist: one from Excel and one from VBA.

VBA's InputBox function

The syntax for VBA's InputBox function is

```
InputBox(prompt[,title][,default][,xpos][,ypos][,helpfile,
context])
```

prompt	(Required) The text displayed in the input box
title	(Optional) The caption of the input box window
default	(Optional) The default value to be displayed in the dialog box
xpos, ypos	(Optional) The screen coordinates at the upper-left corner of the window
helpfile, context	(Optional) The help file and help topic

The InputBox function prompts the user for a single bit of information. The function always returns a string, so it may be necessary to convert the results to a value.

The prompt may consist of about 1,024 characters (more or less, depending on the width of the characters used). In addition, you can provide a title for the dialog box and a default value and specify its position on the screen. You can also specify a custom help topic; if you do, the input box includes a Help button. The following example uses VBA's `InputBox` function to ask the user for his full name:

```
Sub GetName()
    Do Until UserName <> ""
        UserName = InputBox("Enter your full name: ", _
            "Identify Yourself")
    Loop
    FirstSpace = InStr(UserName, " ")
    If FirstSpace <> 0 Then
        UserName = Left(UserName, FirstSpace)
    End If
    MsgBox "Hello " & UserName
End Sub
```

Notice that this `InputBox` function is written in a `Do Until` loop to ensure that something is entered when the input box appears. If the user clicks Cancel or doesn't enter any text, UserName contains an empty string and the input box reappears. The procedure then attempts to extract the first name by searching for the first space character (using the `InStr` function) and then using the `Left` function to extract all characters before the first space. If a space character is not found, the entire name is used as entered.

The `InputBox` function always returns a string. If the string returned by the `InputBox` function looks like a number, you can convert it to a value using VBA's `Val` function. Or, you can use Excel's `InputBox` method, which is described in the next section.

Excel's InputBox method

One advantage of using Excel's `InputBox` method rather than VBA's is that with Excel's you can specify the data type returned. In addition, the `InputBox` method enables the user to specify a worksheet range by dragging in the worksheet. The method's syntax is

```
object.InputBox(prompt,title,default,left,top,helpfile,context,
type)
```

prompt	(Required) The text displayed in the input box
title	(Optional) The caption in the input box window
default	(Optional) The default value to be returned by the function, if the user enters nothing
left, top	(Optional) The screen coordinates at the upper-left corner of the window
helpfile, context	(Optional) The help file and help topic
type	(Optional) A code for the data type returned, as listed in Table 36-3

	Table 36-3 Codes to Determine the Data Type Returned by Excel's InputBox Method	
Code	**Meaning**	
0	A formula	
1	A number	
2	A string (text)	
4	A logical value (True or False)	
8	A cell reference, as a Range object	
16	An error value, such as #N/A	
64	An array of values	

To specify more than one data type to be returned, use the sum of the pertinent codes. For example, to display an input box that can accept text or numbers, set type equal to 3 (that is, 1 + 2, or "number" plus "text").

Excel's InputBox method is quite versatile. For example, if you use 8 for the type argument, the user can point to a range in the worksheet. In the following code, the InputBox method returns a Range object (note the Set keyword) and then clears the values from the selected cells. The default value displayed in the input box is the current selection's address. The On Error statement ends the procedure if the input box is canceled.

```
Sub GetRange()
    Dim UserRange As Range
    Default = Selection.Address
    On Error GoTo Canceled
    Set UserRange = Application.InputBox _
        (Prompt:="Range to erase:", _
        Title:="Range Erase", _
        Default:=Default, _
        Type:=8)
    UserRange.Clear
    UserRange.Select
Canceled:
End Sub
```

Tip   Yet another advantage of using Excel's InputBox method instead of VBA's is that Excel performs input validation automatically. In the GetRange example, if you enter something other than a range address, Excel displays an informative message and enables the user to try again.

Using VBA's MsgBox function

Many of this book's examples use VBA's `MsgBox` function as an easy way to display a variable's value. The official syntax for `MsgBox` is as follows:

```
MsgBox(prompt[,buttons][,title][,helpfile, context])
```

prompt (Required) The text displayed in the message box

buttons (Optional) A numeric expression that determines which buttons and icon is displayed in the message box (see Table 36-4)

title (Optional) The caption in the message box window

helpfile, context (Optional) The help file and help topic

You can easily customize your message boxes because of the flexibility of the *buttons* argument. (Table 36-4 lists the many constants that you can use for this argument.) You can specify which buttons to display, whether an icon appears, and which button is the default.

Table 36-4
Constants Used for Buttons in the MsgBox Function

Constant	Value	Description
VbOKOnly	0	Display OK button only
VbOKCancel	1	Display OK and Cancel buttons
VbAbortRetryIgnore	2	Display Abort, Retry, and Ignore buttons
VbYesNoCancel	3	Display Yes, No, and Cancel buttons
VbYesNo	4	Display Yes and No buttons
VbRetryCancel	5	Display Retry and Cancel buttons
VbCritical	16	Display Critical Message icon
VbQuestion	32	Display Warning Query icon
VbExclamation	48	Display Warning Message icon
VbInformation	64	Display Information Message icon
VbDefaultButton1	0	First button is default
VbDefaultButton2	256	Second button is default
VbDefaultButton3	512	Third button is default
VbDefaultButton4	768	Fourth button is default
VbSystemModal	4096	All applications are suspended until the user responds to the message box (may not work under all conditions)

You can use the MsgBox function by itself (to simply display a message) or assign its result to a variable. When MsgBox does return a result, it represents the button clicked by the user. The following example displays a message and does not return a result:

```
Sub MsgBoxDemo()
    MsgBox "Click OK to continue"
End Sub
```

To get a response from a message box, you can assign the results of the MsgBox function to a variable. The following code uses some built-in constants (described in Table 36-4) to make it easier to work with the values returned by MsgBox:

```
Sub GetAnswer()
    Ans = MsgBox("Continue?", vbYesNo)
    Select Case Ans
        Case vbYes
'           ...[code if Ans is Yes]...
        Case vbNo
'           ...[code if Ans is No]...
    End Select
End Sub
```

Actually, it's not even necessary to use a variable to use the result of a message box. The following procedure displays a message box with Yes and No buttons. If the user doesn't click the Yes button, the procedure ends.

```
Sub GetAnswer2()
    If MsgBox("Continue?", vbYesNo) <> vbYes Then Exit Sub
'       ...[code if Yes button is not clicked]...
End Sub
```

The following function example uses a combination of constants to display a message box with a Yes button, a No button, and a question mark icon. The second button is designated as the default button. For simplicity, these constants are assigned to the Config variable.

```
Function ContinueProcedure() as Boolean
    Config = vbYesNo + vbQuestion + vbDefaultButton2
    Ans = MsgBox("An error occurred. Continue?", Config)
    If Ans = vbYes Then ContinueProcedure = True _
        Else ContinueProcedure = False
End Function
```

If you would like to force a line break in the message, use the vbCrLf constant in the text. The following example displays the message in three lines:

```
Sub MultiLine()
    Msg = "This is the first line" & vbCrLf
    Msg = Msg & "Second line" & vbCrLf
    Msg = Msg & "Last line"
```

```
    MsgBox Msg
End Sub
```

Using Excel's GetOpenFilename method

If your application needs to ask the user for a filename, you can use the `InputBox` function. But this approach often leads to typographical errors. A better approach is to use the `GetOpenFilename` method of the `Application` object, which ensures that your application gets a valid filename as well as its complete path.

The `GetOpenFilename` method displays the normal Open dialog box (displayed when you select the File ⇨ Open command), but does not actually open the file specified. Rather, the method returns a string that contains the path and filename selected by the user. Then you can do whatever you want with the filename. The syntax for this method is as follows (all arguments are optional):

```
object.GetOpenFilename(FileFilter, FilterIndex, Title,
ButtonText, MultiSelect)
```

The *FileFilter* argument determines what appears in the dialog box's Files of type drop-down list. The argument consists of pairs of file filter strings followed by the wildcard file filter specification, with each part and each pair separated by commas. If omitted, this argument defaults to the following:

```
"User (*.*),*.*"
```

Notice that the first part of this string (`User (*.*)`) is the text displayed in the Files of type drop-down list. The second part (`*.*`) actually determines which files are displayed.

The *FilterIndex* argument specifies which FileFilter is the default, and the title argument is text that is displayed in the title bar. If the *MultiSelect* argument is True, the user can select multiple files, all of which are returned in an array. The *ButtonText* argument is not used in Excel for Windows.

The following instruction assigns a string to a variable named `Filt`. This string can then be used as a `FileFilter` argument for the `GetOpenFilename` method. In this case, the dialog box enables the user to select from four different file types, plus an "all files" option.

```
Filt = "Text Files (*.txt),*.txt," & _
       "Lotus Files (*.prn),*.prn," & _
       "Comma Separated Files (*.csv),*.csv," & _
       "ASCII Files (*.asc),*.asc," & _
       "All Files (*.*),*.*"
```

The following example prompts the user for a filename. It defines five file filters. Notice that it uses VBA's line continuation sequence to set up the `Filter` variable; doing so makes it much easier to work with this rather complicated argument.

```
Sub GetImportFileName()
'    Set up list of file filters
    Filt = "Text Files (*.txt),*.txt," & _
           "Lotus Files (*.prn),*.prn," & _
           "Comma Separated Files (*.csv),*.csv," & _
           "ASCII Files (*.asc),*.asc," & _
           "All Files (*.*),*.*"

'    Display *.* by default
    FilterIndex = 5

'    Set the dialog box caption
    Title = "Select a File to Import"

'    Get the file name
    FileName = Application.GetOpenFilename _
        (FileFilter:=Filt, _
         FilterIndex:=FilterIndex, _
         Title:=Title)

'    Exit if dialog box canceled
    If FileName = False Then
        MsgBox "No file was selected."
        Exit Sub
    End If

'    Display full path and name of the file
    MsgBox "You selected " & FileName
End Sub
```

Figure 36-12 shows the dialog box that appears when this procedure is executed.

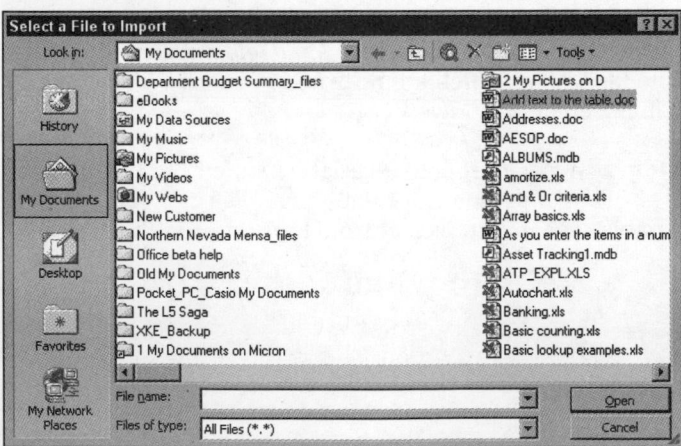

Figure 36-12: The GetOpenFilename method displays a customizable dialog box.

The following example is similar to the previous example. The difference is that the user can press Ctrl or Shift and select multiple files when the dialog box is displayed. Notice that this example checks for the Cancel button click by determining if `FileName` is an array. If the user doesn't click Cancel, the result is an array that consists of at least one element. In this example, a list of the selected files is displayed in a message box.

```
Sub GetImportFileName2()
'    Set up list of file filters
     Filt  = "Text Files (*.txt),*.txt," & _
             "Lotus Files (*.prn),*.prn," & _
             "Comma Separated Files (*.csv),*.csv," & _
             "ASCII Files (*.asc),*.asc," & _
             "All Files (*.*),*.*"

'    Display *.* by default
     FilterIndex = 5

'    Set the dialog box caption
     Title = "Select a File to Import"

'    Get the file name
     FileName = Application.GetOpenFilename _
         (FileFilter:=Filt, _
          FilterIndex:=FilterIndex, _
          Title:=Title, _
          MultiSelect:=True)

'    Exit if dialog box canceled
     If Not IsArray(FileName) Then
         MsgBox "No file was selected."
         Exit Sub
     End If

'    Display full path and name of the files
     For i = LBound(FileName) To UBound(FileName)
         Msg = Msg & FileName(i) & vbCrLf
     Next i
     MsgBox "You selected:" & vbCrLf & Msg
End Sub
```

Using Excel's GetSaveAsFilename method

Like the `GetOpenFilename` method, Excel's `GetSaveAsFilename` method returns a filename and path but doesn't take any action. The syntax for this method is

```
object.GetSaveAsFilename(InitialFilename, FileFilter,
FilterIndex, Title, ButtonText)
```

All the arguments are optional.

Prompting for a directory

If you need to get a filename, use the `GetOpenFileName` method, as described previously. But if you need to get only a directory name, you'll find that you have no direct way to do so. However, you can use a Windows API call to display a dialog box that returns a drive and directory name.

This section presents a function named `GetDirectory` that displays the Browse for Folder dialog box and returns a string that represents the selected directory. If the user clicks Cancel, the function returns an empty string.

The `GetDirectory` function takes one argument, which is optional. This argument is a string that will be displayed in the dialog box. If the argument is omitted, the dialog box displays `Select a folder` as the message.

Following are the API declarations required at the beginning of the workbook module. This function also uses a custom data type, called `BROWSEINFO`.

```
'32-bit API declarations
Declare Function SHGetPathFromIDList Lib "shell32.dll" _
  Alias "SHGetPathFromIDListA" (ByVal pidl As Long, ByVal _
  pszPath As String) As Long

Declare Function SHBrowseForFolder Lib "shell32.dll" _
  Alias "SHBrowseForFolderA" (lpBrowseInfo As BROWSEINFO) _
  As Long

Public Type BROWSEINFO
    hOwner As Long
    pidlRoot As Long
    pszDisplayName As String
    lpszTitle As String
    ulFlags As Long
    lpfn As Long
    lParam As Long
    iImage As Long
End Type
```

The `GetDirectory` function is as follows:

```
Function GetDirectory(Optional Msg) As String
    Dim bInfo As BROWSEINFO
    Dim path As String
    Dim r As Long, x As Long, pos As Integer

'    Root folder = Desktop
    bInfo.pidlRoot = 0&

'    Title in the dialog
    If IsMissing(Msg) Then
```

```
        bInfo.lpszTitle = "Select a folder."
    Else
        bInfo.lpszTitle = Msg
    End If

'   Type of directory to return
    bInfo.ulFlags = &H1

'   Display the dialog
    x = SHBrowseForFolder(bInfo)

'   Parse the result
    path = Space$(512)
    r = SHGetPathFromIDList(ByVal x, ByVal path)
    If r Then
        pos = InStr(path, Chr$(0))
        GetDirectory = Left(path, pos - 1)
    Else
        GetDirectory = ""
    End If
End Function
```

The following simple procedure demonstrates how to use the `GetDirectory` function in your code. Executing this procedure displays the dialog box. When the user clicks OK or Cancel, the `MsgBox` function displays the full path of the selected directory.

```
Sub GetAFolder()
    Dim Msg As String
    Msg = "Please select a location for the backup."
    MsgBox GetDirectory(Msg)
End Sub
```

Displaying Excel's Built-In Dialog Boxes

Code that you write in VBA can execute Excel's menu commands. And, if the command leads to a dialog box, your code can "make choices" in the dialog box — although the dialog box itself isn't displayed. For example, the following statement is equivalent to selecting the Edit ⇨ Go To command, specifying a range named `InputRange`, and clicking OK. However, the Go To dialog box never appears.

```
Application.Goto Reference:="InputRange"
```

In some cases, however, you may *want* to display one of Excel's built-in dialog boxes so that the end user can make the choices. This is easy to do, using the `Dialogs` method of the `Application` object. Here's an example:

```
Result = Application.Dialogs(xlDialogFormulaGoto).Show
```

This statement, when executed, displays the GoTo dialog box (xlDialogFormulaGoto is a predefined constant). The user can specify a named range or enter a cell address to go to. This dialog box works exactly as it does when you choose the Edit ⇨ Go To command (or press F5).

Note   Contrary to what you might think, the Result variable does not hold the range that is selected. Rather, the value assigned to Result is True if the user clicked OK, and False if the user clicked Cancel or pressed Esc.

You can get a list of all the dialog box constants using the Object Browser. Follow these steps:

1. In a VBA module, press F2 to bring up the Object Browser.

2. In the Object Browser dialog box, select Excel from the top list.

3. Type **xlDialog** in the second list.

4. Click the binoculars button.

Caution   Attempting to display a built-in dialog box in an incorrect context results in an error. For example, if you select a series in a chart and then attempt to display the xlDialogFormatFont dialog box, you'll get an error message because that dialog box is not appropriate for that selection.

Most of the built-in dialog boxes also accept arguments, which correspond to the controls on the dialog box. You can specify arguments that correspond to the defaults for the dialog box. For example, the xlDialogCellProtection dialog box uses two arguments: locked and hidden. If you want to display that dialog box with both these options checked, use the following statement:

```
Application.Dialogs(xlDialogCellProtection).Show True, True
```

Note   Normally, the dialog box used to protect cells is one "tab" in the Format Cells dialog box. If you use the preceding statement, however, the Protection tab appears in its own dialog box with no other tabs.

Tip   The arguments for each of the built-in dialog boxes are listed in the online help. To locate the help topic, search for Built-In Dialog Box Argument Lists.

✦   ✦   ✦

UserForm Techniques

CHAPTER

37

◆ ◆ ◆ ◆

In This Chapter

Selecting ranges

Creating a splash screen

Disabling a UserForm's close button

Changing a dialog box's size

Zooming and scrolling a sheet from a UserForm

Applying ListBox techniques

Using the MultiPage control

◆ ◆ ◆ ◆

In the last chapter you learned the basics of using UserForms. This chapter presents lots of useful and informative examples that introduce you to some additional techniques that involve UserForms. You may be able to adapt these techniques to your own work.

Selecting Ranges

Several of Excel's built-in dialog boxes enable the user to specify a range by pointing and clicking in a sheet. For example, the Goal Seek dialog box asks the user to select two ranges.

Your custom dialog boxes can also provide this type of functionality, thanks to the RefEdit control. The RefEdit control doesn't look exactly like the range selection control used in Excel's built-in dialog boxes, but it works the same. If the user clicks the small button on the right side of the control, the dialog box disappears temporarily and a small range selector is displayed — this is exactly what happens with Excel's built-in dialog boxes.

Figure 37-1 shows a custom dialog box that contains a RefEdit control. This dialog box performs a simple mathematical operation on all nonformula (and nonempty) cells in the selected range.

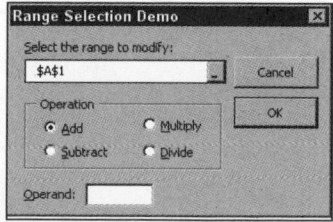

Figure 37-1: The RefEdit control here enables the user to select a range.

Following are a few things to keep in mind when using a RefEdit control:

✦ The RefEdit control returns a text string that represents a range address. You can convert this string to a `Range` object using a statement such as this:

```
Set UserRange = Range(RefEdit1.Text)
```

✦ It's a good practice to initialize the RefEdit control to display the current range selection. You can do so in the `UserForm_Initialize` procedure using a statement such as this:

```
RefEdit1.Text = ActiveWindow.RangeSelection.Address
```

✦ Don't assume that RefEdit will always return a valid range address. Pointing to a range isn't the only way get text into this control. The user can type any text and edit or delete the displayed text. Therefore, you need to make sure the range is valid. The following code snippet is an example of a way to check for a valid range:

```
On Error Resume Next
Set UserRange = Range(RefEdit1.Text)
If Err <> 0 Then
    MsgBox "Invalid range selected"
    RefEdit1.SetFocus
    On Error GoTo 0
    Exit Sub
End If
```

✦ The user can also click the worksheet tabs while selecting a range with the RefEdit control. Therefore, you can't assume that the selection is on the active sheet. However, if a different sheet is selected, the range address is preceded by a sheet name; for example:

```
Sheet2!$A$1:$C:4
```

✦ If you need to get a single cell selection from the user, you can pick out the upper-left cell of a selected range by using a statement such as this:

```
Set OneCell = Range(RefEdit1.Text).Range("A1")
```

Cross-Reference As discussed in Chapter 36, you can also use VBA's InputBox function to enable the user to select a range.

Creating a Splash Screen

Some developers like to display some introductory information when the application is opened. This is commonly known as a *splash screen*. You are undoubtedly familiar with Excel's splash screen, which appears for a few seconds as Excel is loading. You can create a splash screen for your Excel application with a UserForm. Follow these instructions to create a splash screen for your project:

Caution Keep in mind that the splash screen is not displayed until the workbook is entirely loaded. In other words, if you would like to display the splash screen to give the user something to look at while the workbook is loading, this technique won't fill the bill.

1. Create your workbook.

2. Activate the Visual Basic Editor and insert a new UserForm into the project. The code in this example assumes this form is named `UserForm1`.

3. Place any controls you like on `UserForm1`. For example, you may want to insert an Image control that has your company's logo. Figure 37-2 shows an example.

Figure 37-2: This splash screen is displayed briefly when the workbook is opened.

4. Insert the following procedure into the code module for the `ThisWorkbook` object:

```
Private Sub Workbook_Open()
    UserForm1.Show
End Sub
```

5. Insert the following procedure into the code module for `UserForm1` (this assumes a five-second delay):

```
Private Sub UserForm_Activate()
    Application.OnTime Now + _
        TimeValue("00:00:05"), "KillTheForm"
End Sub
```

6. Insert the following procedure into a general VBA module:

```
Private Sub KillTheForm()
    Unload UserForm1
End Sub
```

When the workbook is opened, the `Workbook_Open` procedure is executed. This procedure displays the UserForm. At that time, its `Activate` event occurs, which triggers the `UserForm_Activate` procedure. This procedure uses the `OnTime` method of the `Application` object to execute a procedure named `KillTheForm` at a particular time. In this case, the time is five seconds from the current time. The `KillTheForm` procedure simply unloads the UserForm.

7. As an option, you can add a small CommandButton named `CancelButton`, set its `Cancel` property to True, and insert the following event-handler procedure in the UserForm's code module:

```
Private Sub CancelButton_Click()
    KillTheForm
End Sub
```

Doing so enables the user to cancel the splash screen before the time has expired by pressing Esc. You can stash this small button behind another object so that it won't be visible.

Disabling a UserForm's Close Button

When a UserForm is displayed, clicking the close button (the *X* in the upper-right corner) unloads the form. You might have a situation in which you don't want this to happen. For example, you may require that the UserForm be closed only by clicking a particular CommandButton.

Although you can't physically remove the close button, you can prevent the user from closing a UserForm by clicking it. You can do this by monitoring the UserForm's `QueryClose` event.

The procedure that follows, which is located in the code module for the UserForm, is executed before the form is closed (that is, when the `QueryClose` event occurs):

```
Private Sub UserForm_QueryClose _
  (Cancel As Integer, CloseMode As Integer)
    If CloseMode = vbFormControlMenu Then
        MsgBox "Click the OK button to close the form."
        Cancel = True
    End If
End Sub
```

The `UserForm_QueryClose` procedure uses two arguments. The `CloseMode` argument contains a value that indicates the cause of the `QueryClose` event. If `CloseMode` is equal to `vbFormControlMenu` (a built-in constant), that means the user clicked the close button. In such a case, a message is displayed, the `Cancel` argument is set to True, and the form is not actually closed.

Changing a Dialog Box's Size

Many applications use dialog boxes that change their own size. For example, Excel's AutoFormat dialog box (displayed when you select Format ➪ AutoFormat) increases its height when the user clicks the Options button.

The example in this section demonstrates how to get a custom dialog box to change its size dynamically. Changing a dialog box's size is done by altering the Width or Height property of the UserForm object.

Figure 37-3 shows the dialog box as it is first displayed, and Figure 37-4 shows it after the user clicks the Options button. Notice that the button's caption changes, depending on the size of the UserForm.

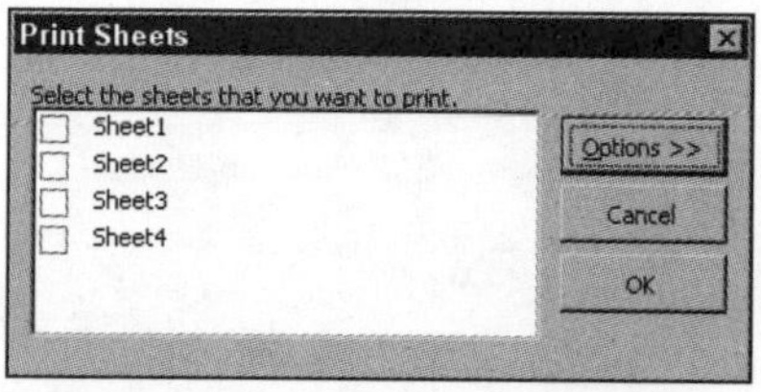

Figure 37-3: This shows a sample dialog box in its standard mode.

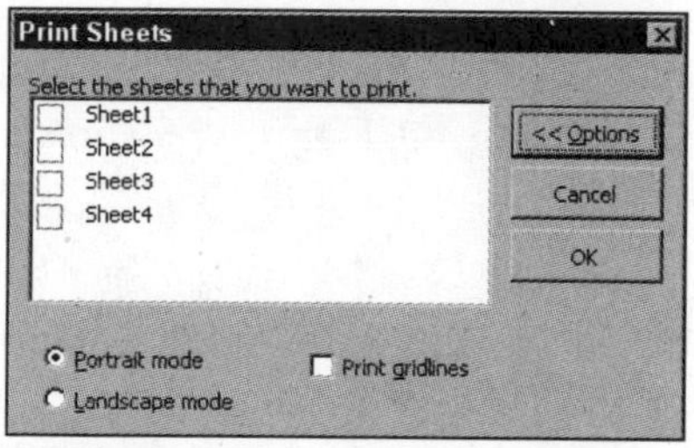

Figure 37-4: This shows the same dialog box enlarged to show some options.

As you're creating the UserForm, set it to its largest size to enable you to work with the controls. Then use the UserForm_Initialize procedure to set it to its default size.

This example displays a list of worksheets in the active workbook and enables the user to select which sheets to print. Following is the event handler that's executed when the CommandButton named OptionsButton is clicked:

```
Private Sub OptionsButton_Click()
    If OptionsButton.Caption = "Options >" Then
        UserForm1.Height = 164
        OptionsButton.Caption = "<< Options"
    Else
        UserForm1.Height = 128
        OptionsButton.Caption = "Options >"
```

```
        End If
    End Sub
```

This procedure examines the Caption of the CommandButton and sets the UserForm's Height property accordingly.

> **Note**   When controls are not displayed because they are outside the visible portion of the UserForm, the accelerator keys for such controls continue to function. To block access to nondisplayed controls, you can write code to disable the controls when they are not displayed.

Zooming and Scrolling a Sheet from a UserForm

When you display a dialog box, it's often helpful if the user can scroll through the worksheet to examine various ranges. Normally, this is impossible while a dialog box is displayed.

The example in this section demonstrates how to use ScrollBar controls to enable sheet scrolling and zooming while a dialog box is displayed. Figure 37-5 shows how the example dialog box is set up.

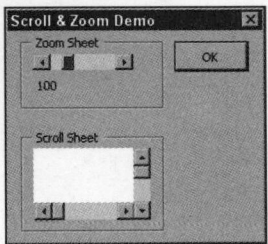

Figure 37-5: This shows ScrollBar controls that enable zooming and scrolling of the worksheet.

If you look at the code for this example, you'll see that it's remarkably simple. The controls are initialized in the UserForm_Initialize procedure.

```
    Private Sub UserForm_Initialize()
        LabelZoom.Caption = ActiveWindow.Zoom
    '   Zoom
        With ScrollBarZoom
            .Min = 10
            .Max = 400
            .SmallChange = 1
            .LargeChange = 10
```

```
                .Value = ActiveWindow.Zoom
        End With

'       Horizontally scrolling
        With ScrollBarColumns
            .Min = 1
            .Max = 256
            .Value = ActiveWindow.ScrollColumn
            .LargeChange = 25
            .SmallChange = 1
        End With

'       Vertically scrolling
        With ScrollBarRows
            .Min = 1
            .Max = ActiveSheet.Rows.Count
            .Value = ActiveWindow.ScrollRow
            .LargeChange = 25
            .SmallChange = 1
        End With
    End Sub
```

This procedure sets various properties of the ScrollBar controls using values based on the active window.

When the ScrollBarZoom control is used, the ScrollBarZoom_Change procedure is executed. This procedure sets the ScrollBar control's Value property to the ActiveWindow's Zoom property value. It also changes a label to display the current zoom factor.

```
    Private Sub ScrollBarZoom_Change()
        With ActiveWindow
            .Zoom = ScrollBarZoom.Value
            LabelZoom = .Zoom & "%"
        End With
    End Sub
```

Worksheet scrolling is accomplished by the following two procedures. These procedures set the ScrollRow or ScrollColumns property of the ActiveWindow object equal to the appropriate ScrollBar control value.

```
    Private Sub ScrollBarColumns_Change()
        ActiveWindow.ScrollColumn = ScrollBarColumns.Value
    End Sub

    Private Sub ScrollBarRows_Change()
        ActiveWindow.ScrollRow = ScrollBarRows.Value
    End Sub
```

Applying ListBox Techniques

The ListBox control is extremely versatile, but it can be a bit tricky to work with. This section consists of a number of simple examples that demonstrate common techniques involving the ListBox control.

Tip   In most cases, the techniques described in this section also work with a ComboBox control.

Understanding the ListBox control

Following are a few points to keep in mind when working with ListBox controls. Examples in the sections that follow demonstrate many of these points.

✦ The items in a ListBox can be retrieved from a range of cells (specified by the RowSource property), or they can be added using VBA code (using the AddItem method).

✦ A ListBox can be set up to enable a single selection or a multiple selection. This is determined by the MultiSelect property.

✦ It's possible to display a ListBox with no items selected (the ListIndex property is –1). However, once an item is selected, it's not possible to unselect all items.

✦ A ListBox can contain multiple columns (controlled by the ColumnCount property) and even a descriptive header (controlled by the ColumnHeads property).

✦ The vertical height of a ListBox displayed in a UserForm window isn't always the same as the vertical height when the UserForm is actually displayed.

✦ The items in a ListBox can be displayed as check boxes if multiple selection is allowed or as option buttons if a single selection is allowed. This is controlled by the ListStyle property.

Note   For complete details on the properties and methods for a ListBox control, consult the online help.

Adding items to a ListBox control

Before displaying a UserForm that uses a ListBox control, you probably need to fill the ListBox with items. You can fill a ListBox at design time using items stored in a worksheet range, or at run-time using VBA to add the items to the ListBox.

The two examples in this section presume that

✦ You have a dialog box on a UserForm named UserForm1.

✦ This dialog box contains a ListBox control named ListBox1.

✦ The workbook contains a sheet named Sheet1, and range A1:A12 contains the items to be displayed in the ListBox.

Adding items to a ListBox at design time

To add items to a ListBox at design time, the ListBox items must be stored in a worksheet range. Use the RowSource property to specify the range that contains the ListBox items. Figure 37-6 shows the Properties window for a ListBox control. The RowSource property is set to A1:A12. When the UserForm is displayed, the ListBox contains the 12 items in this range. The items appear in the ListBox at design time, as soon as you specify the range for the RowSource property.

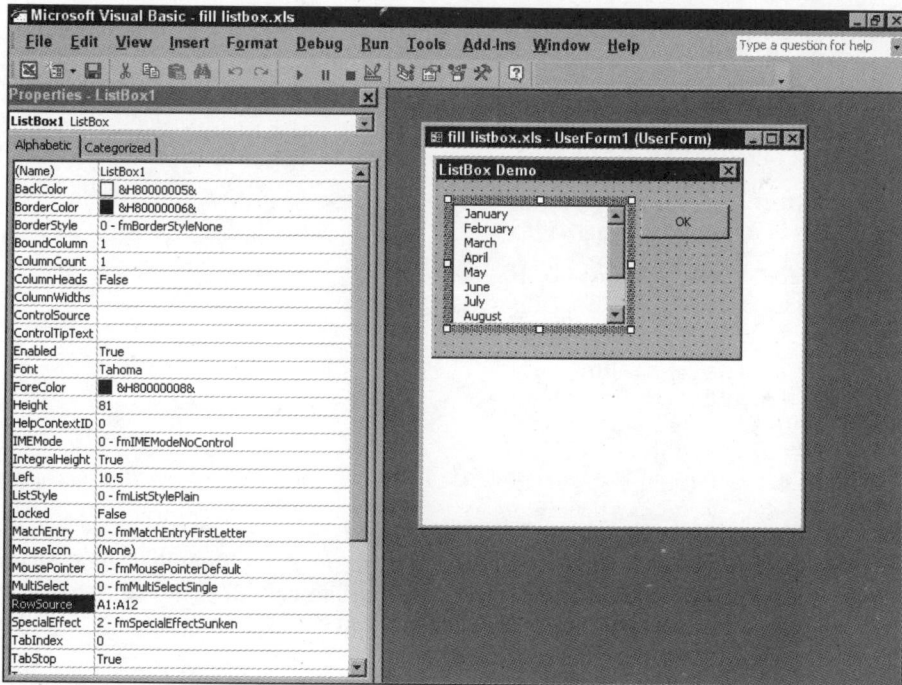

Figure 37-6: Setting the RowSource property at design time.

Note   If you don't include the worksheet name when you specify the RowSource property, the ListBox uses the specified range on the active worksheet.

Adding items to a ListBox at run-time

To add ListBox items at run-time, you have two choices:

✦ Set the RowSource property to a range address using code.

✦ Write code that uses the AddItem method to add the ListBox items.

As you might expect, you can set the RowSource property via code rather than with the Properties window. For example, the following procedure sets the RowSource property for a ListBox before displaying the UserForm. In this case, the items consist of the cell entries in a range named Categories on the Budget worksheet.

```
UserForm1.ListBox1.RowSource = "Budget!Categories"
UserForm1.Show
```

If the ListBox items are not contained in a worksheet range, you can write VBA code to fill the ListBox before the dialog box appears. The procedure fills the ListBox with the names of the months using the AddItem method.

```
Sub ShowUserForm2()
'   Fill the list box
    With UserForm2.ListBox1
        .RowSource=""
        .AddItem "January"
        .AddItem "February"
        .AddItem "March"
        .AddItem "April"
        .AddItem "May"
        .AddItem "June"
        .AddItem "July"
        .AddItem "August"
        .AddItem "September"
        .AddItem "October"
        .AddItem "November"
        .AddItem "December"
    End With
    UserForm2.Show
End Sub
```

Note   In the preceding code, notice that the RowSource property is set to an empty string. This is to avoid a potential error that occurs if the Properties window has a nonempty RowSource setting. If you try to add items to a ListBox that has a non-null RowSource setting, you'll get a "permission denied" error.

You can also use the AddItem method to retrieve ListBox items from a range. Here's an example that fills a ListBox with the contents of A1:A12 on Sheet1.

```
For Row = 1 To 12
    UserForm1.ListBox1.AddItem Sheets("Sheet1").Cells(Row, 1)
Next Row
```

If your data is stored in a one-dimensional array, you can assign the array to the ListBox with a single instruction. For example, assume you have an array named dData that contains 50 elements. The following statement creates a 50-item list in ListBox1:

```
ListBox1.List = dData
```

Adding only unique items to a ListBox

In some cases, you may need to fill a ListBox with unique (nonduplicated) items from a list. For example, assume you have a worksheet that contains customer data. One of the columns might contain the country name of each customer (see Figure 37-7). You would like to fill a ListBox with the country name of your customers, but you don't want to include duplicate state names.

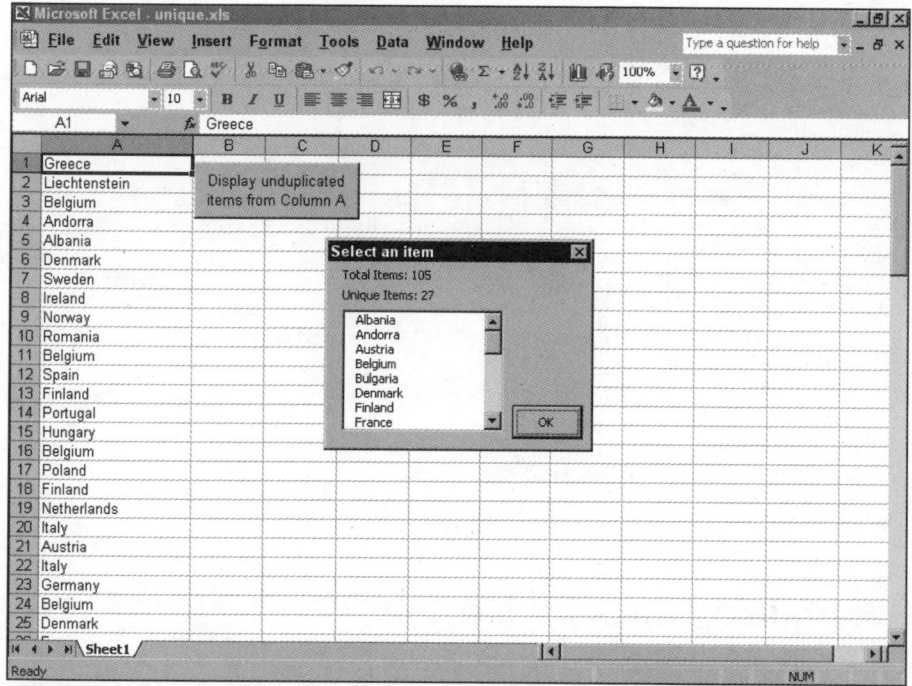

Figure 37-7: A Collection object is used to fill a ListBox with the unique items from Column A.

One technique involves using a `Collection` object. You can add items to a `Collection` object with the following syntax:

```
object.Add item, key, before, after
```

The *key* argument, if used, must be a unique text string that specifies a separate key that can be used to access a member of the collection. The important word here is *unique*. If you attempt to add a nonunique key to a collection, an error occurs and the item is not added. You can take advantage of this situation and use it to create a collection that consists of only unique items.

The following procedure demonstrates how to fill a ListBox with unique items. It starts by declaring a new Collection object named NoDupes. It assumes that range B1:B100 contains a list of items, some of which may be duplicated. The code loops through the cells in the range and attempts to add the cell's value the NoDupes collection. It also uses the cell's value (converted to a string) for the *key* argument. Using the On Error Resume Next statement causes VBA to ignore the error that occurs if the key is not unique. When an error occurs, the item is not added to the collection, which is just what you want. The procedure then transfers the items in the NoDupes collection to the ListBox.

```
Sub RemoveDuplicates1()
    Dim AllCells As Range, Cell As Range
    Dim NoDupes As New Collection

    On Error Resume Next
    For Each Cell In Range("B1:B100")
        NoDupes.Add Cell.Value, CStr(Cell.Value)
    Next Cell
    On Error GoTo 0

'   Add the nonduplicated items to a ListBox
    For Each Item In NoDupes
        UserForm1.ListBox1.AddItem Item
    Next Item

'   Show the UserForm
    UserForm1.Show
End Sub
```

Determining the selected item

The examples in previous sections merely display a UserForm with a ListBox filled with various items. These procedures omit a key point: how to determine which item or items were selected by the user.

Note This discussion assumes a "single selection" ListBox object — one whose MultiSelect property is set to 0.

To determine which item was selected, access the ListBox's Value property. The following statement, for example, displays the text of the selected item in ListBox1:

```
MsgBox ListBox1.Value
```

If you need to know the position of the selected item in the list (rather than the content of that item) you can access the ListBox's ListIndex property. The next example uses a message box to display the item number of the selected ListBox item.

```
MsgBox "You selected item #" & ListBox1.ListIndex
```

 **Note** The numbering of items in a ListBox begins with 0, not 1. Therefore, the ListIndex of the first item is 0, and the ListIndex of the last item is equivalent to the value of the ListCount property minus 1.

Determining multiple selections

Normally, a ListBox's MultiSelect property is zero, which means that the user can select only one item in the ListBox.

If the ListBox allows multiple selections (that is, if its MultiSelect property is either 1 or 2), trying to access the ListIndex, Value, or List properties results in an error. Instead, you need to use the Selected property, which returns an array whose first item has an index of 0. For example, the following statement displays True if the first item in the ListBox list is selected:

```
MsgBox ListBox1.Selected(0)
```

The following code loops through each item in the ListBox. If the item was selected, it appends the item's text to a variable called Msg. Finally, the names of all the selected items are displayed in a message box.

```
Private Sub OKButton_Click()
    Msg = ""
    For i = 0 To ListBox1.ListCount - 1
        If ListBox1.Selected(i) Then _
            Msg = Msg & ListBox1.List(i) & vbCrLf
    Next i
    MsgBox "You selected: " & vbCrLf & Msg
    Unload Me
End Sub
```

Creating a ListBox with changing contents

This example demonstrates how to create a ListBox in which the contents change depending on the user's selection from a group of OptionButtons.

Figure 37-8 shows the sample dialog box. The ListBox gets its items from a worksheet range. The procedures that handle the Click event for the OptionButton controls simply set the ListBox's RowSource property to a different range. One of these procedures is as follows:

```
Private Sub obMonths_Click()
    ListBox1.RowSource = "Sheet1!Months"
End Sub
```

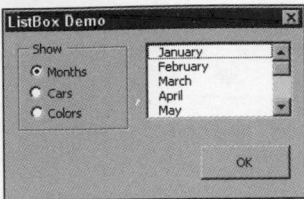

Figure 37-8: The contents of this ListBox depend on the selected OptionButton.

Clicking the OptionButton named obMonths changes the RowSource property of the ListBox to use a range named Months on Sheet1.

Building a ListBox from another list

Some applications require a user to select several items from a list. It's often useful to create a new list of the selected items. (For an example of this situation, check out the dialog box that appears when you choose the Tools ➪ Attach Toolbars command in a VBA module.)

Figure 37-9 shows a dialog box with two ListBoxes. The Add button adds the item selected in the left ListBox to the right ListBox. The Delete button removes the selected item from the list on the right. A CheckBox determines the behavior when a duplicate item is added to the list. If the *Allow duplicates* CheckBox is not checked, a message box appears if the user attempts to add an item that's already on the list.

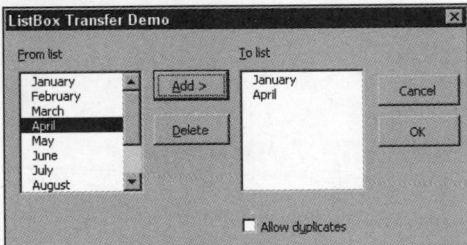

Figure 37-9: This shows a dialog box that builds a list from another list.

The code for this example is relatively simple. Here's the procedure that is executed when the user clicks the Add button:

```
Private Sub AddButton_Click()
    If ListBox1.ListIndex = -1 Then Exit Sub
    If Not cbDuplicates Then
'       See if item already exists
        For i = 0 To ListBox2.ListCount - 1
```

```
            If ListBox1.Value = ListBox2.List(i) Then
                Beep
                Exit Sub
            End If
        Next i
    End If
    ListBox2.AddItem ListBox1.Value
End Sub
```

The code for the Delete button is even simpler:

```
Private Sub DeleteButton_Click()
    If ListBox2.ListIndex = -1 Then Exit Sub
    ListBox2.RemoveItem ListBox2.ListIndex
End Sub
```

Notice that both routines check to make sure that an item is actually selected. If the ListBox's ListIndex property is -1, no items are selected and the procedure ends.

Moving items in a ListBox

The example in this section demonstrates how to enable the user to move the location of items up or down in a ListBox. The VBE uses this type of technique itself to enable you to control the tab order of the items in a UserForm.

Figure 37-10 shows a dialog box that contains a ListBox and two CommandButtons. Clicking the Move Up button moves the selected item up in the ListBox; clicking the Move Down button moves the selected item down.

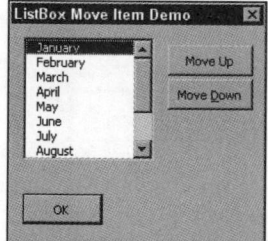

Figure 37-10: The buttons enable the user to move items up or down in the ListBox.

The event-handler procedures for the two CommandButtons are as follows:

```
Private Sub MoveUpButton_Click()
    With ListBox1
        ItemNum = .ListIndex
        If ItemNum > 0 Then
            TempItem = .List(ItemNum - 1)
            .List(ItemNum - 1) = .List(ItemNum)
```

```
            .List(ItemNum) = TempItem
            .ListIndex = .ListIndex - 1
        End If
    End With
End Sub

Private Sub MoveDownButton_Click()
    With ListBox1
        ItemNum = .ListIndex
        If ItemNum < .ListCount - 1 And ItemNum <> -1 Then
            TempItem = .List(ItemNum + 1)
            .List(ItemNum + 1) = .List(ItemNum)
            .List(ItemNum) = TempItem
            .ListIndex = .ListIndex + 1
        End If
    End With
End Sub
```

These procedures work fairly well, but you'll find that for some reason, relatively rapid clicking doesn't always register. For example, you may click the Move Down button three times in quick succession, but the item moves only one or two positions. The solution is to add a new DblClick event handler for each CommandButton. These procedures, which simply call the Click procedures, are as follows:

```
Private Sub MoveUpButton_DblClick _
  (ByVal Cancel As MSForms.ReturnBoolean)
    Call MoveUpButton_Click
End Sub

Private Sub MoveDownButton_DblClick _
  (ByVal Cancel As MSForms.ReturnBoolean)
    Call MoveDownButton_Click
End Sub
```

Using a ListBox to select rows

The example in this section is actually a useful utility. It displays a ListBox that consists of the entire used range of the active worksheet (see Figure 37-11). The user can select multiple items in the ListBox. Clicking the All button selects all items, and clicking the None button deselects all items. Clicking OK selects those corresponding rows in the worksheet. You can, of course, select multiple noncontiguous rows directly in the worksheet by pressing Ctrl as you click the row borders. However, you may find that selecting rows is easier using this method.

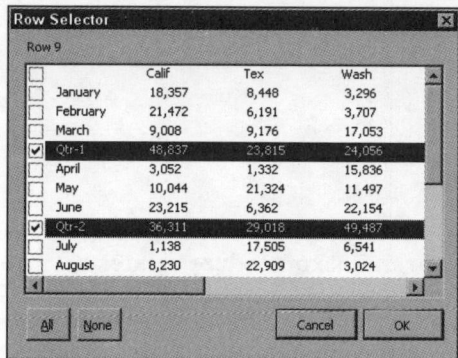

Figure 37-11: This ListBox makes it easy to select rows in a worksheet.

Selecting multiple items is possible because the ListBox's MultiSelect property is set to 1 – fmMultiSelectMulti. The "check boxes" on each item are displayed because the ListBox's ListStyle property is set to 1 – fmListStyleOption.

The UserForm's Initialize procedure is as follows. This procedure creates a Range object named rng that consists of the active sheet's used range—or more accurately, the narrowest rectangular range on the active worksheet containing data. Additional code sets the ListBox's ColumnCount and RowSource properties and adjusts the ColumnWidths property such that the ListBox columns are proportional to the column widths in the worksheet.

```
Private Sub UserForm_Initialize()
    ColCnt = ActiveSheet.UsedRange.Columns.Count
    Set rng = ActiveSheet.UsedRange
    With ListBox1
        .ColumnCount = ColCnt
        .RowSource = rng.Address
        cw = ""
        For c = 1 To .ColumnCount
            cw = cw & rng.Columns(c).Width & ";"
        Next c
        .ColumnWidths = cw
        .ListIndex = 0
    End With
End Sub
```

The All and None buttons (named SelectAllButton and SelectNoneButton, respectively) have simple event-handler procedures and are listed here:

```
Private Sub SelectAllButton_Click()
    For r = 0 To ListBox1.ListCount - 1
        ListBox1.Selected(r) = True
```

```
        Next r
    End Sub

    Private Sub SelectNoneButton_Click()
        For r = 0 To ListBox1.ListCount - 1
            ListBox1.Selected(r) = False
        Next r
    End Sub
```

The OKButton_Click procedure is listed next. This procedure creates a Range object named RowRange that consists of the rows that correspond to the selected items in the ListBox. To determine if a row was selected, the code examines the Selected property of the ListBox control. Notice that it uses the Union function to add additional ranges to the RowRange object.

```
    Private Sub OKButton_Click()
        Dim RowRange As Range
        RowCnt = 0
        For r = 0 To ListBox1.ListCount - 1
            If ListBox1.Selected(r) Then
                RowCnt = RowCnt + 1
                If RowCnt = 1 Then
                    Set RowRange = ActiveSheet.Rows(r + 1)
                Else
                    Set RowRange = _
                        Union(RowRange, ActiveSheet.Rows(r + 1))
                End If
            End If
        Next r
        If Not RowRange Is Nothing Then RowRange.Select
        Unload Me
    End Sub
```

Using a ListBox to activate a sheet

The example in this section is just as useful as it is instructive. This example uses a multicolumn ListBox to display a list of sheets within the active workbook. The columns represent

✦ The sheet's name

✦ The type of sheet (worksheet, chart, or Excel 5/95 dialog sheet)

✦ The number of nonempty cells in the sheet

✦ Whether the sheet is visible

Figure 37-12 shows an example of the dialog box.

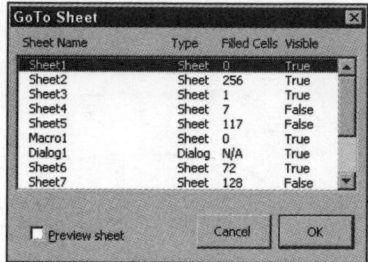

Figure 37-12: This dialog box enables
the user to activate a sheet.

The code in the following `UserForm_Initialize` procedure creates a two-dimensional array and collects the information by looping through the sheets in the active workbook. It then transfers this array to the ListBox named `ListBox1`.

```
Private Sub UserForm_Initialize()
    Dim SheetData() As String
    Set OriginalSheet = ActiveSheet
    ShtCnt = ActiveWorkbook.Sheets.Count
    ReDim SheetData(1 To ShtCnt, 1 To 4)
    ShtNum = 1
    For Each Sht In ActiveWorkbook.Sheets
        If Sht.Name = ActiveSheet.Name Then _
          ListPos = ShtNum - 1
        SheetData(ShtNum, 1) = Sht.Name
        Select Case TypeName(Sht)
            Case "Worksheet"
                SheetData(ShtNum, 2) = "Sheet"
                SheetData(ShtNum, 3) = _
                  Application.CountA(Sht.Cells)
            Case "Chart"
                SheetData(ShtNum, 2) = "Chart"
                SheetData(ShtNum, 3) = "N/A"
            Case "DialogSheet"
                SheetData(ShtNum, 2) = "Dialog"
                SheetData(ShtNum, 3) = "N/A"
        End Select
        If Sht.Visible Then
            SheetData(ShtNum, 4) = "True"
        Else
            SheetData(ShtNum, 4) = "False"
        End If
        ShtNum = ShtNum + 1
    Next Sht
    With ListBox1
        .ColumnWidths = "100 pt;30 pt;40 pt;50 pt"
        .List = SheetData
```

```
            .ListIndex = ListPos
        End With
End Sub
```

The `ListBox1_Click` procedure is as follows:

```
Private Sub ListBox1_Click()
    If cbPreview Then _
        Sheets(ListBox1.Value).Activate
End Sub
```

The value of the CheckBox control named `cbPreview` determines if the selected sheet is previewed when the user clicks an item in the ListBox.

Clicking the OK button named `OKButton` executes the `OKButton_Click` procedure, which is as follows:

```
Private Sub OKButton_Click()
    Dim UserSheet As Object
    Set UserSheet = Sheets(ListBox1.Value)
    If UserSheet.Visible Then
        UserSheet.Activate
    Else
        If MsgBox("Unhide sheet?", _
            vbQuestion + vbYesNoCancel) = vbYes Then
            UserSheet.Visible = True
            UserSheet.Activate
        Else
            OriginalSheet.Activate
        End If
    End If
    Unload Me
End Sub
```

The `OKButton_Click` procedure creates an object variable that represents the selected sheet. If the sheet is visible, it is activated. If it's not visible, the user is presented with a message box asking if the sheet should be unhidden. If the user responds in the affirmative, the sheet is unhidden and activated. Otherwise, the original sheet (stored in an object variable named `OriginalSheet`) is activated.

Double-clicking an item in the ListBox has the same result as clicking the OK button. The following `ListBox1_DblClick` procedure simply calls the `OKButton_Click` procedure:

```
Private Sub ListBox1_DblClick(ByVal Cancel As _
  MSForms.ReturnBoolean)
    Call OKButton_Click
End Sub
```

Using the MultiPage Control

The MultiPage control is very useful for custom dialog boxes that must display many controls. The MultiPage control enables you to group the choices and place each group on a separate "tab."

Figure 37-13 shows an example of a UserForm that contains a MultiPage control. In this case, the control has three pages, each with its own tab. The MultiPage control is versatile, giving you a great deal of control over its appearance and functionality.

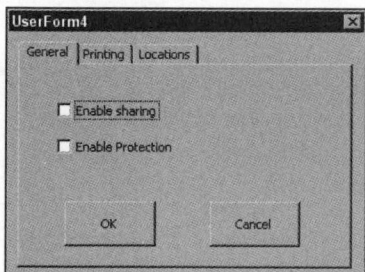

Figure 37-13: MultiPage groups your controls on pages, making them accessible from a tab.

Using a MultiPage control can be a bit tricky. Following are some things to keep in mind when using this control:

✦ The tab (or page) that's displayed up front is determined by the control's Value function. A value of 0 displays the first tab, a value of 1 displays the second tab, and so on.

✦ By default, a MultiPage control has two pages. To add a new page, right-click a tab and select New Page from the shortcut menu.

✦ When you're working with a MultiPage control, just click a tab to set the properties for that particular page. The Properties window displays the properties that you can adjust.

✦ You may find it difficult to select the actual MultiPage control because clicking the control selects a page within the control. To select the control itself, you can use the Tab key to cycle among all the controls. Or you can select the MultiPage control from the drop-down list in the Properties window.

✦ If your MultiPage control has lots of tabs, you can set its MultiRow property to True to display the tabs in more than one row.

✦ If you prefer, you can display buttons instead of tabs. Just change the `Style` property to 1. If the `Style` property value is 0, the MultiPage control won't display tabs or buttons.

✦ The `TabOrientation` property determines the location of the tabs on the MultiPage control.

✦ For each page, you can set a transition effect by changing the `TransitionEffect` property. For example, clicking a tab can cause the new page to "push" the former page out of the way. Use the `TransitionPeriod` property to set the speed of the transition effect.

The next chapter contains several examples that use the MultiPage control.

✦   ✦   ✦

Working with Excel's Events

In several recent chapters you've seen examples of VBA event-handler procedures. These procedures are the keys to making your Excel applications interactive. This chapter provides more comprehensive coverage of the concept of Excel events and includes many examples that you can adapt to meet your own needs. As you'll see, understanding and implementing events can give your Excel applications a powerful edge.

Understanding Events

Excel is capable of monitoring a wide variety of events and executing your VBA code when a particular event occurs. These events can be classified as:

- ✦ **Workbook events:** These occur for a particular workbook. Examples include `Open` (the workbook is opened or created), `BeforeSave` (the workbook is about to be saved), and `NewSheet` (a new sheet is added).

- ✦ **Worksheet events:** These occur for a particular worksheet. Examples include `Change` (a cell on the sheet is changed), `SelectionChange` (the cell pointer is moved), and `Calculate` (the worksheet is recalculated).

- ✦ **Chart events:** These occur for a particular chart. Examples include `Select` (a chart object is selected) and `SeriesChange` (a data point value in a series is changed). To monitor events for an embedded chart, use a class module.

- ✦ **Application events:** These occur for the application (Excel). Examples include `NewWorkbook` (a new workbook is created), `WorkbookBeforeClose` (any workbook is about to be closed), and `SheetChange` (a cell in any open workbook is altered).

✦ **UserForm events:** These occur for a particular UserForm or object contained on the UserForm. For example, a UserForm has an Initialize event (which occurs before the UserForm is displayed); and a CommandButton on a UserForm has a Click event (which occurs when the button is clicked).

✦ **Events not associated with objects:** The final category consists of two useful Application-level events: OnTime and OnKey. These work differently than other events.

Each of these different types of events is covered in this chapter.

Understanding event sequences

As you'll see, some actions trigger multiple events. For example, when you insert a new worksheet into a workbook, this triggers several events at the Application level:

1. SheetDeactivate event. This occurs when the active worksheet is deactivated.

2. SheetActivate event. This occurs when the newly added worksheet is activated.

3. WorkbookNewSheet event. This occurs when a new worksheet is added.

Note   Event sequencing is more complicated than you might think. The preceding events are Application-level events. When you add a new worksheet, additional events occur at the Workbook and Worksheet levels.

These three events occur in the order listed. Event sequences are not always logical. For example, you might think that the WorkbookNewSheet event occurs before the SheetActivate event, but it doesn't.

At this point, just keep in mind that events fire in a particular sequence, and knowing what the sequence is can be critical when writing event-handler procedures. Later in this chapter, you'll see how to determine the order of the events that occur for a particular action (see "Monitoring Application-Level Events").

Deciding where to put event-handler procedures

Newcomers often wonder why their event-handler procedures aren't executing when events occur. The answer almost always is that these procedures are in the wrong place.

In the Visual Basic Editor (VBE) window, each project is listed in the Project window. The project components are arranged in a collapsible list, as shown in Figure 38-1.

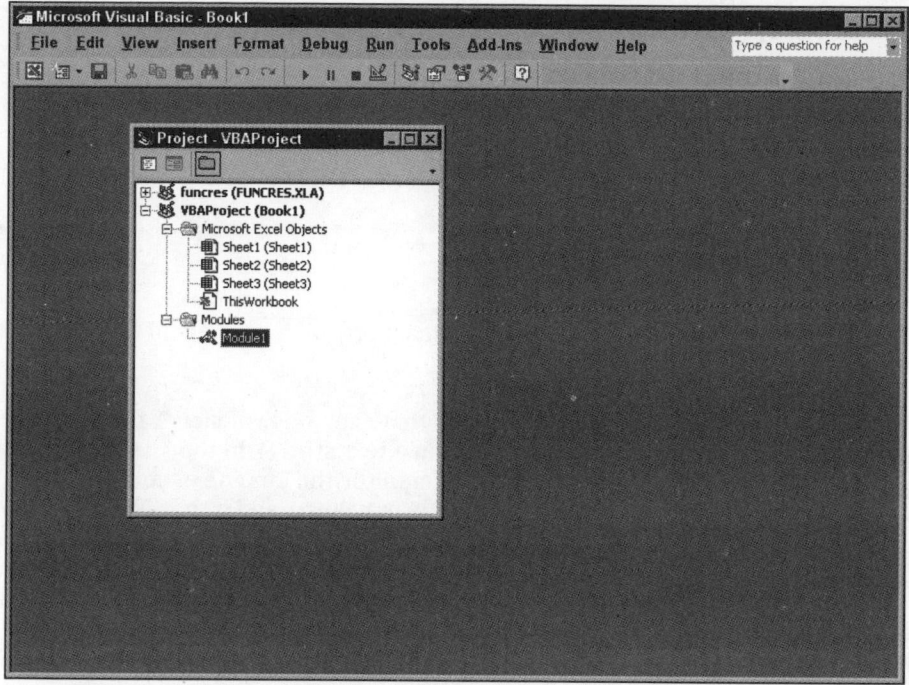

Figure 38-1: The components of each VBA project are listed in the Project window.

Each of the following components has its own code module:

- ✦ Sheet objects.
- ✦ Chart objects.
- ✦ ThisWorkbook object.
- ✦ General VBA modules. Never put event-handler procedures in a general (that is, nonobject) module.
- ✦ Class modules.

Even though the event-handler procedure must be located in the correct module, the procedure can call other standard procedures stored in other modules. For example, the following procedure, located in the module for the ThisWorkbook object, calls a procedure named WorkbookSetup stored in a general VBA module:

```
Private Sub Workbook_Open()
    Call WorkbookSetup
End Sub
```

Disabling events

By default, all events are enabled. To disable all events, execute the following VBA instruction:

```
Application.EnableEvents = False
```

To enable events, use this instruction:

```
Application.EnableEvents = True
```

Why do you need to disable events? The main reason is to prevent an infinite loop of cascading events from occurring.

For example, assume you've written code that executes whenever data is entered into a cell (this particular cell must contain a text string). In this case, you use a procedure named `Worksheet_Change` to monitor the `Change` event for a `Worksheet`. Your procedure validates the user's entry, and if that entry is not a string, it displays a message and then clears the entry. The problem is that clearing the entry with your VBA code generates a new `Change` event, so your event-handler procedure executes again. This is not the intention, so you must disable events before you clear the cell, and then enable events again so that you can monitor the user's next entry.

Another way to prevent an infinite loop of cascading events is to declare a `Static Boolean` variable at the beginning of your event-handler procedure, such as this:

```
Static AbortProc As Boolean
```

Whenever the procedure must make its own changes, set the `AbortProc` variable to True; otherwise, make sure it is set to False. Insert the following statement as the first instruction in the procedure:

```
If AbortProc Then Exit Sub
```

The event procedure is reentered, but the True state of `AbortProc` trips `Exit Sub`, sending VBA back to the preceding iteration (at the end of which `AbortProc` resets to False). `AbortProc` becomes a kind of "guard lock" mechanism.

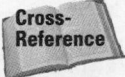 **Cross-Reference** For a practical example of validating data, see "Validating Data Entry" later in this chapter.

 **Caution** Disabling events in Excel applies to all workbooks. For example, if you disable events in your procedure and then open another workbook that has, say, a Workbook_Open procedure, that procedure will not execute.

Entering event-handler code

Every event-handler procedure has a predetermined name. You can declare the procedure by typing it, but a much better approach is to let the VBE do it for you.

Figure 38-2 shows the code module for the `ThisWorkbook` object. To insert a procedure declaration, select `Workbook` from the objects list on the left. Then select the event from the procedures list on the right. When you do this, you get a procedure "shell" that contains the procedure declaration line and an `End Sub` statement.

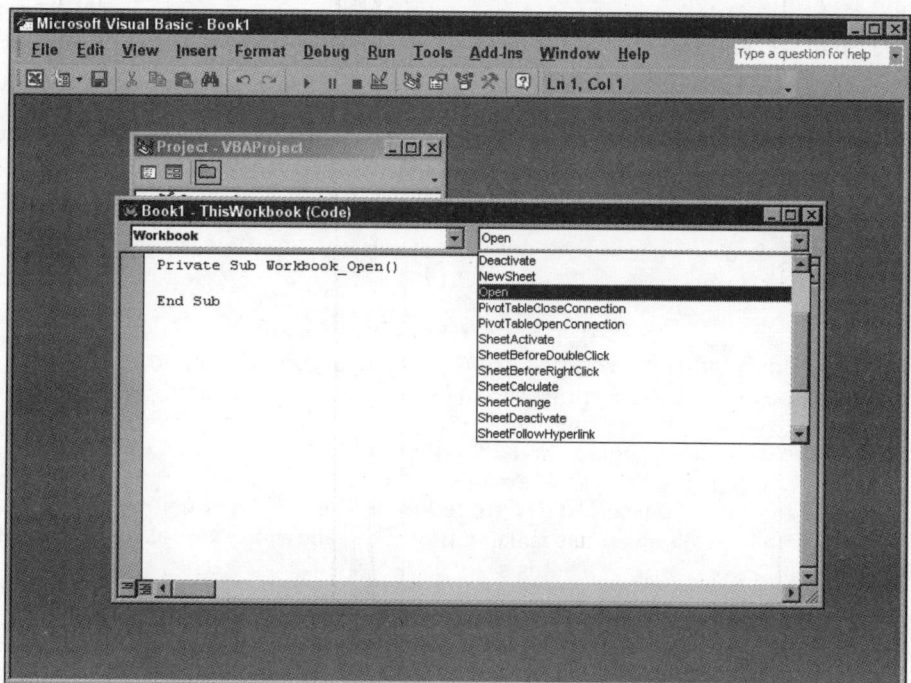

Figure 38-2: The best way to create an event procedure is to let the VBE do it for you.

For example, if you select `Workbook` from the objects list and `Open` from the procedures list, the VBE inserts the following (empty) procedure:

```
Private Sub Workbook_Open()

End Sub
```

Your code, of course, goes between these two lines.

Using event-handler procedures that take arguments

Some event-handler procedures contain an argument list. For example, you may need to create an event-handler procedure to monitor the SheetActivate event for a workbook. If you use the technique described in the previous section, the VBE creates the following procedure:

```
Private Sub Workbook_SheetActivate(ByVal Sh As Object)

End Sub
```

This procedure uses one argument (Sh), which represents the activated sheet. In this case, Sh is declared as an Object data type rather than a Worksheet data type because the activated sheet also can be a Chart sheet.

Your code can, of course, make use of data passed as an argument. The following example displays the name of the activated sheet by accessing the argument's Name property. The argument becomes either a Worksheet object or a Chart object.

```
Private Sub Workbook_SheetActivate(ByVal Sh As Object)
    MsgBox Sh.Name & " was activated."
End Sub
```

Several event-handler procedures use a Boolean argument named Cancel. For example, the declaration for a Workbook's BeforePrint event is

```
Private Sub Workbook_BeforePrint(Cancel As Boolean)
```

The value of Cancel passed to the procedure is True. However, your code can set Cancel to False, which cancels the printing. The following example demonstrates this.

```
Private Sub Workbook_BeforePrint(Cancel As Boolean)
    Msg = "Have you loaded the 5164 label stock?"
    Ans = MsgBox(Msg, vbYesNo, "About to print...")
    If Ans = vbNo Then Cancel = True
End Sub
```

The Workbook_BeforePrint procedure executes before the workbook prints. This procedure displays a message box asking the user to verify that the correct label stock is loaded. If the user clicks the No button, Cancel is set to False and nothing prints.

Using Workbook-Level Events

Workbook-level events occur for a particular workbook. Table 38-1 lists the Workbook events, along with a brief description of each. Workbook event-handler procedures are stored in the code module for the ThisWorkbook object.

Table 38-1
Workbook Events

Event	Action that Triggers the Event
Activate	A workbook is activated.
AddinInstall	A workbook is installed as an add-in.
AddinUninstall	A workbook is uninstalled as an add-in.
BeforeClose	A workbook is about to be closed.
BeforePrint	A workbook (or anything in it) is about to be printed.
BeforeSave	A workbook is about to be saved.
Deactivate	A workbook is deactivated.
NewSheet	A new sheet is created in a workbook.
Open	A workbook is opened.
PivotTableCloseConnection	A PivotTable report closes its connection to its data source.
PivotTableOpenConnection	A PivotTable report opens its connection to its data source.
SheetActivate	Any sheet is activated.
SheetBeforeDoubleClick	Any worksheet is double-clicked. This event occurs before the default double-click action.
SheetBeforeRightClick	Any worksheet is right-clicked. This event occurs before the default right-click action.
SheetCalculate	Any worksheet is calculated (or recalculated).
SheetChange	Any worksheet is changed by the user or an external link.
SheetDeactivate	Any sheet is deactivated.
SheetFollowHyperlink	Any hyperlink is clicked in Excel.
SheetPivotTableUpdate	The sheet containing a PivotTable report has been updated.
SheetSelectionChange	The selection on any worksheet is changed.
WindowActivate	Any workbook window is activated.
WindowDeactivate	Any workbook window is deactivated.
WindowResize	Any workbook window is resized.

Cross-Reference If you need to monitor events for any workbook, you must work with Application-level events (see "Monitoring Application-Level Events" later in this chapter).

The remainder of this section presents examples of using Workbook-level events.

Note   All the example procedures that follow must be located in the code module for the ThisWorkbook object. If you put them into any other type of code module, they will not work.

Using the Open event

One of the most common monitored events is a workbook's Open event. This event is triggered when the workbook (or add-in) opens, and executes the Workbook_Open procedure. A Workbook_Open procedure can do almost anything and often is used for the following tasks:

+ Displaying welcome messages

+ Opening other workbooks

+ Setting up custom menus or toolbars

+ Activating a particular sheet

+ Ensuring that certain conditions are met; for example, a workbook may require that a particular add-in is installed

Caution   If the user holds down the Shift key while opening a workbook, the workbook's Workbook_Open procedure will not execute.

The following is a simple example of a Workbook_Open procedure. It uses VBA's Weekday function to determine the day of the week. If it's Friday, a message box appears to remind the user to perform a file backup. If it's not Friday, nothing happens.

```
Private Sub Workbook_Open()
   If Weekday(Now) = 5 Then
       Msg = "Today is Friday. Make sure that you "
       Msg = Msg & "do your weekly backup!"
       MsgBox Msg, vbInformation
   End If
End Sub
```

Using the Activate event

The following procedure executes whenever the workbook is activated. This procedure simply maximizes the active window.

```
Private Sub Workbook_Activate()
    ActiveWindow.WindowState = xlMaximized
End Sub
```

Using the SheetActivate event

The following procedure executes whenever the user activates any sheet in the workbook. The code simply selects Cell A1. Including the `On Error Resume Next` construct causes the procedure to ignore the error that occurs if the activated sheet is a Chart sheet.

```
Private Sub Workbook_SheetActivate(ByVal Sh As Object)
    On Error Resume Next
    Range("A1").Select
End Sub
```

An alternative method to handle the case of a Chart sheet is to check the sheet type. Use the `Sh` argument, which is passed to the procedure.

```
Private Sub Workbook_SheetActivate(ByVal Sh As Object)
    If TypeName(Sh) = "Worksheet" Then Range("A1").Select
End Sub
```

Using the NewSheet event

The following procedure executes whenever a new sheet is added to the workbook. The sheet is passed to the procedure as an argument. Because a new sheet can be either a worksheet or a Chart sheet, this procedure determines the sheet type. If it's a worksheet, it inserts a date and time stamp in Cell A1.

```
Private Sub Workbook_NewSheet(ByVal Sh As Object)
    If TypeName(Sh) = "Worksheet" Then _
        Range("A1") = "Sheet added " & Now()
End Sub
```

Using the BeforeSave event

The `BeforeSave` event occurs before the workbook is actually saved. As you know, using the File ➪ Save command sometimes brings up the Save As dialog box. This happens if the file has never been saved or was opened in read-only mode.

When the `Workbook_BeforeSave` procedure executes, it receives an argument that enables you to identify whether the Save As dialog box will appear. The following example demonstrates this:

```
Private Sub Workbook_BeforeSave _
  (ByVal SaveAsUI As Boolean, Cancel As Boolean)
    If SaveAsUI Then
        MsgBox "Click OK to display the Save As dialog box."
    End If
End Sub
```

When the user attempts to save the workbook, the `Workbook_BeforeSave` procedure executes. If the save operation brings up the Save As dialog box, the `SaveAsUI` variable is True. The preceding procedure checks this variable and displays a message only if the Save As dialog box is displayed. If the procedure sets the `Cancel` argument to True, the file is not saved.

Using the Deactivate event

The following example demonstrates the `Deactivate` event. This procedure executes whenever the workbook is deactivated and essentially does not enable the user to deactivate the workbook. When the `Deactivate` event occurs, the code reactivates the workbook and displays a message.

```
Private Sub Workbook_Deactivate()
    Me.Windows(1).Activate
    MsgBox "Sorry, you may not leave this workbook"
End Sub
```

Caution   We do not recommend using procedures such as this one that attempt to "take over" Excel. Such events can be very frustrating and confusing for the user.

This example illustrates the importance of understanding event sequences. When you try this procedure you'll see that it works well if the user attempts to activate another workbook. However, it's important to understand that the following actions also trigger the `Workbook_Deactivate` event:

✦ Closing the workbook

✦ Opening a new workbook

✦ Minimizing the workbook

In other words, this procedure might not perform as intended. The user may not activate a different workbook, but he or she can close the workbook, open a new workbook, or minimize the workbook. The message box still appears, but the actions occur anyway.

Using the BeforeClose event

The `BeforeClose` event occurs before a workbook is closed. This event often is used in conjunction with a `Workbook_Open` event handler. For example, use the `Workbook_Open` procedure to initialize items in your workbook, and use the `Workbook_BeforeClose` procedure to "clean up" or restore settings to normal before the workbook closes.

If you attempt to close a workbook that hasn't been saved, Excel displays a prompt that asks if you want to save the workbook before it closes.

Caution   A problem can arise from this event. By the time the user sees this message, the BeforeClose event has already occurred. This means the Workbook_BeforeClose procedure has already executed.

Consider this scenario: You need to display a custom menu when a particular workbook is open. Therefore, your workbook uses a `Workbook_Open` procedure to create the menu when the workbook opens, and it uses a `Workbook_BeforeClose` procedure to remove the menu when the workbook closes. These two event-handler procedures are as follows:

```
Private Sub Workbook_Open()
    Call CreateMenu
End Sub

Private Sub Workbook_BeforeClose(Cancel As Boolean)
    Call DeleteMenu
End Sub
```

As previously noted, Excel's "save workbook before closing" prompt occurs after the `Workbook_BeforeClose` event handler runs. So when the user clicks `Cancel`, the workbook remains open, but the custom menu item is already deleted!

One solution to this problem is to bypass Excel's prompt and write your own code in the `Workbook_BeforeClose` procedure, asking the user to save the workbook. The following code demonstrates this:

```
Private Sub Workbook_BeforeClose(Cancel As Boolean)
    If Not Me.Saved Then
        Msg = "Do you want to save the changes you made to "
        Msg = Msg & Me.Name & "?"
        Ans = MsgBox(Msg, vbQuestion + vbYesNoCancel)
        Select Case Ans
            Case vbYes
                Me.Save
            Case vbNo
                Me.Saved = True
            Case vbCancel
                Cancel = True
                Exit Sub
        End Select
    End If
    Call DeleteMenu
End Sub
```

This procedure determines whether the workbook has been saved. If it has, no problem: the `DeleteMenu` procedure executes and the workbook closes. If the workbook has not been saved, the procedure displays a message box that duplicates the one Excel normally shows. If the user clicks Yes, the menu is deleted and the workbook closes. If the user clicks No, the code sets the `Saved` property of the

`Workbook` object to True (but doesn't actually save the file) and deletes the menu. If the user clicks `Cancel`, the `BeforeClose` event is canceled and the procedure ends without deleting the menu.

Working with Worksheet Events

The events for a `Worksheet` object are some of the most useful. As you'll see, monitoring these events can make your applications perform feats that otherwise would be impossible.

Table 38-2 lists the worksheet events, with a brief description of each.

Table 38-2 Worksheet Events	
Event	*Action That Triggers the Event*
Activate	A worksheet is activated.
BeforeDoubleClick	A worksheet is double-clicked.
BeforeRightClick	A worksheet is right-clicked.
Calculate	A worksheet is calculated (or recalculated).
Change	Cells on a worksheet are changed by the user or an external link.
Deactivate	A worksheet is deactivated.
FollowHyperlink	A hyperlink on the worksheet is clicked.
PivotTableUpdate	A PivotTable on the worksheet has been updated.
SelectionChange	The selection on a worksheet is changed.

Using the Change event

The `Change` event is triggered when any cell in a worksheet is changed by the user or an external link. The `Change` event is not triggered when a calculation generates a different value for a formula or when an object is added to the sheet.

When the `Worksheet_Change` procedure executes, it receives a `Range` object as its `Target` argument. This `Range` object represents the changed cell or range that triggered the event. The following example displays a message box that shows the address of the `Target` range:

```
Private Sub Worksheet_Change(ByVal Target As Excel.Range)
    MsgBox "Range " & Target.Address & " was changed."
End Sub
```

To get a feel for the types of actions that generate the Change event for a worksheet, enter the preceding procedure into the code module for a Worksheet object. After entering this procedure, activate Excel and, using various techniques, make changes to the worksheet. Every time the Change event occurs, a message box displays the address of the range that changed.

Unfortunately, the Change event doesn't always work as expected. For example:

✦ Changing the formatting of a cell does not trigger the Change event (as expected), but using the Edit ➪ Clear Formats command *does*.

✦ Filling a range using the Edit ➪ Fill command does not generate the Change event, but using AutoFill to fill the range *does*.

✦ Using the Edit ➪ Delete command does not generate the Change event, but pressing the Del key does. In fact, pressing Del generates an event even if the cell is empty at the start.

✦ Cells changed via Excel commands do not trigger the Change event. These commands include Data ➪ Form, Data ➪ Sort, Tools ➪ Spelling, and Edit ➪ Replace.

✦ If your VBA procedure changes a cell, it *does* trigger the Change event.

As you can see, it's not a good idea to rely on the Change event to detect cell changes for critical applications.

Monitoring a specific range for changes

The Change event occurs when any cell on the worksheet changes. In most cases, all that matters are changes made to a specific cell or range. When the Worksheet_Change event-handler procedure is called, it receives a Range object as its argument. This Range object represents the cell or cells that changed.

Assume your worksheet has a range named InputRange and you want to monitor changes to this range only. No Change event exists for a Range object, but you can perform a quick check within the Workhseet_Change procedure. The following procedure demonstrates this:

```
Private Sub Worksheet_Change(ByVal Target As Excel.Range)
    Dim VRange As Range
    Set VRange = Range("InputRange")
    If Union(Target, VRange).Address = VRange.Address Then
        Msgbox "The changed cell is in the input range."
    End if
End Sub
```

This example creates a range object named VRange, which represents the worksheet range that you want to monitor for changes. The procedure uses VBA's Union function to determine if VRange contains the Target range (passed to the procedure in its argument). The Union function returns an object that consists of all the cells in both of its arguments. If the range address is the same as the VRange address, then Vrange contains Target and a message box appears. Otherwise, the procedure ends and nothing happens.

The preceding procedure has a flaw. Target may consist of a cell or a range. For example, if the user changes more than one cell at a time, Target becomes a multi-cell range. Therefore, the procedure requires modification to loop through all the cells in Target. The following procedure checks each changed cell and displays a message box if the cell is within the desired range:

```
Private Sub Worksheet_Change(ByVal Target As Excel.Range)
    Set VRange = Range("InputRange")
    For Each cell In Target
        If Union(cell, VRange).Address = VRange.Address Then
            Msgbox "The changed cell is in the input range."
        End if
    Next cell
End Sub
```

Tracking cell changes in a comment

The following example adds a notation to the cell's comment each time the cell changes (as determined by the Change event). The state of a CheckBox, embedded in the worksheet, determines whether the change is added to the comment.

Because the object passed to the Worksheet_Change procedure can consist of a multicell range, the procedure loops through each cell in the Target range. If the cell doesn't contain a comment, one is added. Then, new text is appended to the existing comment text (if applicable).

```
Private Sub Worksheet_Change(ByVal Target As Excel.Range)
   If CheckBox1 Then
     For Each cell In Target
         With cell
             On Error Resume Next
             OldText = .Comment.Text
             If Err <> 0 Then .AddComment
             NewText = OldText & "Changed by " & _
               Application.UserName & " at " & Now & vbLf
             .Comment.Text NewText
             .Comment.Visible = True
             .Comment.Shape.Select
              Selection.AutoSize = True
             .Comment.Visible = False
         End With
     Next cell
   End If
End Sub
```

Note This example is primarily for instructional purposes. If you really need to track changes in a worksheet, Excel's Tools ➪ Track Changes feature does a much better job.

Validating data entry

Excel's Data Validation feature is a useful tool, but it suffers from a potentially serious problem. When you paste data to a cell that uses data validation, the pasted value not only fails to receive validation, but also deletes the validation rules associated with the cell!

This section demonstrates how to use a worksheet's Change event to create your own data validation procedure.

Listing 38-1 presents a procedure that executes when a user changes a cell. The validation is restricted to the range named InputRange. Values entered into this range must be integers between 1 and 12.

Listing 38-1: Determining whether a Cell Entry Will Be Validated

```
Private Sub Worksheet_Change(ByVal Target As Excel.Range)
    Dim VRange As Range, cell As Range
    Dim Msg As String
    Dim ValidateCode As Variant
    Set VRange = Range("InputRange")
    For Each cell In Target
        If Union(cell, VRange).Address = VRange.Address Then
            ValidateCode = EntryIsValid(cell)
            If ValidateCode = True Then
                Exit Sub
        Else
                Msg = "Cell " & cell.Address(False, False) _
                    & ":"
                Msg = Msg & vbCrLf & vbCrLf & ValidateCode
                MsgBox Msg, vbCritical, "Invalid Entry"
                Application.EnableEvents = False
                cell.ClearContents
                cell.Activate
                Application.EnableEvents = True
            End If
        End If
    Next cell
End Sub
```

The Worksheet_Change procedure creates a Range object (VRange) that repre-sents the validated worksheet range. Then it loops through each cell in the Target argument, which represents the cell or cells that changed. The code determines whether each cell is contained in the range to be validated. If it is, the code passes the cell as an argument to a custom function (EntryIsValid), which returns True if the cell is a valid entry.

If the entry is not valid, the EntryIsValid function returns a string that describes the problem and the user receives information via a message box. When the message box is dismissed, the invalid entry is cleared from the cell and the cell is activated. Notice that events are disabled before the cell is cleared. If events were not disabled, clearing the cell would produce a Change event, which causes an endless loop.

The EntryIsValid*xxxx* function procedure is presented in Listing 38-2.

Listing 38-2: Validating an Entry That Was Just Made into a Restricted Range

```
Private Function EntryIsValid(cell) As Variant
'    Returns True if cell is an integer between 1 and 12
'    Otherwise it returns a string that describes the problem

'    Blank
    If cell = "" Then
        EntryIsValid = True
        Exit Function
    End If

'    Numeric?
    If Not IsNumeric(cell) Then
        EntryIsValid = "Non-numeric entry."
        Exit Function
    End If

'    Integer?
    If CInt(cell) <> cell Then
        EntryIsValid = "Integer required."
        Exit Function
    End If

'    Between 1 and 12?
    If cell < 1 Or cell > 12 Then
        EntryIsValid = "Valid values are between 1 and 12."
        Exit Function
    End If

'    It passed all the tests
    EntryIsValid = True
End Function
```

Using the SelectionChange event

The following procedure demonstrates the SelectionChange event. It executes whenever the user makes a new selection on the worksheet.

```
Private Sub Worksheet_SelectionChange(ByVal Target _
    As Excel.Range)
        Cells.Interior.ColorIndex = xlNone
        With ActiveCell
            .EntireRow.Interior.ColorIndex = 36
            .EntireColumn.Interior.ColorIndex = 36
        End With
End Sub
```

This procedure shades the row and column of an active cell, making it easy to identify. The first statement removes the background color of all cells. Next, the entire row and column of the active cell is shaded light yellow. Figure 38-3 shows the shading.

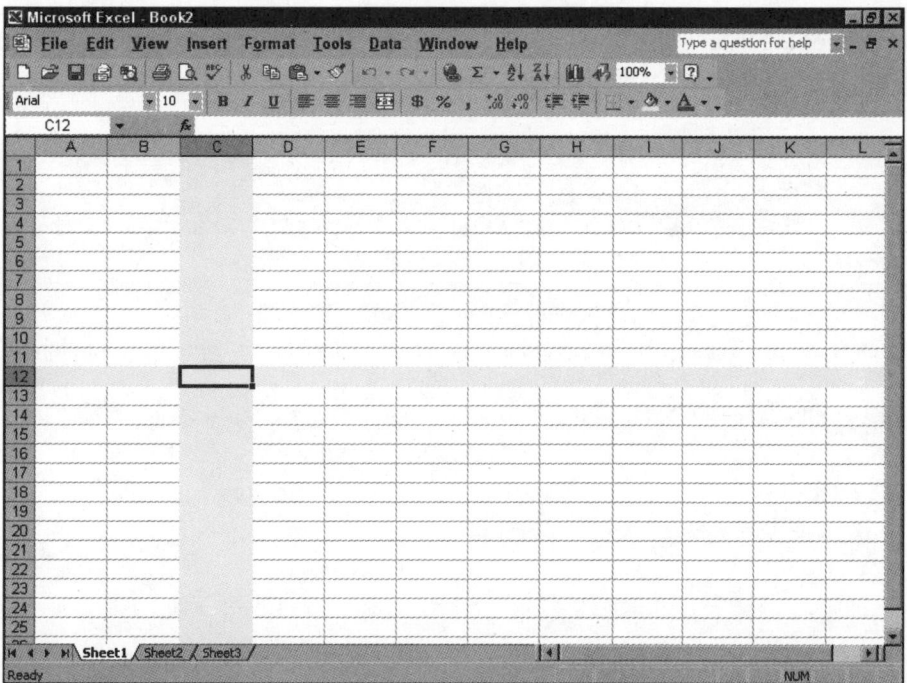

Figure 38-3: Moving the cell cursor causes the active cell's row and column to become shaded.

Caution   You won't want to use this procedure if your worksheet contains background shading because it will be wiped out.

Using the BeforeRightClick event

When the user right-clicks in a worksheet, a shortcut menu appears. If, for some reason, you want to prevent the shortcut menu from appearing, you can trap the RightClick event. The following procedure sets the Cancel argument to True, which cancels the RightClick event and, thus, the shortcut menu. Instead, a message box appears.

```
Private Sub Worksheet_BeforeRightClick _
    (ByVal Target As Excel.Range, Cancel As Boolean)
        Cancel = True
        MsgBox "The shortcut menu is not available."
End Sub
```

 **Cross-Reference**   Chapter 41 describes other ways to disable shortcut menus.

Monitoring Chart Events

By default, events are enabled only for charts that reside on a Chart sheet. To work with events for an embedded chart, you must create a class module. Table 38-3 lists the Chart events and a brief description of each.

Table 38-3		
Events Recognized by a Chart Sheet		
Event	*Action That Triggers the Event*	
Activate	A Chart sheet or embedded chart is activated.	
BeforeDoubleClick	An embedded chart is double-clicked. This event occurs before the default double-click action.	
BeforeRightClick	An embedded chart is right-clicked. The event occurs before the default right-click action.	
Calculate	New or changed data is plotted on a chart.	
Deactivate	A chart is deactivated.	
DragOver	A range of cells is dragged over a chart.	
DragPlot	A range of cells is dragged and dropped onto a chart.	
MouseDown	A mouse button is pressed while the pointer is over a chart.	
MouseMove	The position of the mouse pointer is changed over a chart.	
MouseUp	A mouse button is released while the pointer is over a chart.	
Resize	A chart is resized.	
Select	A chart element is selected.	
SeriesChange	The value of a chart data point is changed.	

Using the Object Browser to Locate Events

The Object Browser is a useful tool that can help you learn about objects and their properties and methods. It also can help you find out which objects support a particular event. For example, if you want to find out which objects support the MouseMove event, activate the VBE and press F2 to display the Object Browser window. Make sure <All Libraries> is selected, and then type MouseMove and click the binoculars icon (see the accompanying figure). (You may need to use the Tools ⇨ References command to include the MSForms library.)

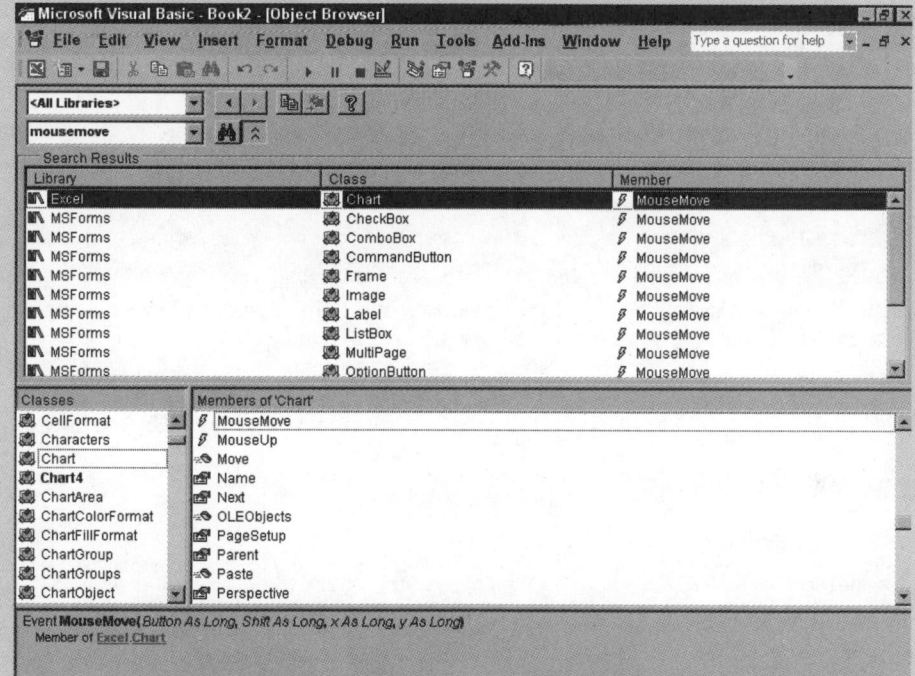

The Object Browser displays a list of matching items. Events are indicated with a small yellow lightning bolt. From this list, you can see which objects support the MouseMove event. Most of the objects are controls in the MSForms library, home of the UserForm control. But you also can see that Excel's Chart object supports the MouseMove event.

Notice how the list here is divided into three columns: Library, Class, and Member. The match for the item you're searching for may appear in any of these columns. This brings up a crucial point: The name of an event or term belonging to one library or class may be the same as that for another belonging to a different library or class, though they may not share the same meaning or functionality. In fact, you can probably bet on their being different. So be sure to click each item in the Object Browser list and check the status bar at the bottom of the list for the syntax. You might find, for instance, that one class or library treats the MouseMove event differently.

Using Application Events

Previous sections discussed Workbook and Worksheet events. These events are monitored for a particular workbook. If you want to monitor events for all open workbooks or all worksheets, use Application events.

Table 38-4 lists the Application events, with a brief description of each.

Table 38-4	
Events Recognized by the Application Object	
Event	**Action That Triggers the Event**
NewWorkbook	A new workbook is created.
SheetActivate	Any sheet is activated.
SheetBeforeDoubleClick	Any worksheet is double-clicked. This event occurs before the default double-click action.
SheetBeforeRightClick	Any worksheet is right-clicked. This event occurs before the default right-click action.
SheetCalculate	Any worksheet is calculated (or recalculated).
SheetChange	Cells in any worksheet are changed by the user or an external link.
SheetDeactivate	Any sheet is deactivated.
SheetFollowHyperlink	A hyperlink is clicked.
SheetSelectionChange	The selection is changed on any worksheet except a Chart sheet.
WindowActivate	Any workbook window is activated.
WindowDeactivate	Any workbook window is deactivated.
WindowResize	Any workbook window is resized.
WorkbookActivate	Any workbook is activated.
WorkbookAddinInstall	A workbook is installed as an add-in.
WorkbookAddinUninstall	Any add-in workbook is uninstalled.
WorkbookBeforeClose	Any open workbook is closed.
WorkbookBeforePrint	Any open workbook is printed.
WorkbookBeforeSave	Any open workbook is saved.
WorkbookDeactivate	Any open workbook is deactivated.

Event	Action That Triggers the Event
WorkbookNewSheet	A new sheet is created in any open workbook.
WorkbookOpen	A workbook is opened.
WorkbookPivotTableCloseConnection	A PivotTable report connection has been closed.
WorkbookPivotTableOpenConnection	A PivotTable report connection has been opened.

Enabling Application-level events

To make use of Application-level events, do the following:

1. Create a new class module.

2. Set a name for this class module in the Properties window under *Name*.

   By default, VBA gives each new class module a name and a number; but trying to remember which module was Class21 and which Class22 can quickly become cumbersome.

3. In the class module, declare a public Application object, using the WithEvents keyword, as in:

   ```
   Public WithEvents App as Application
   ```

4. Create a variable that you will use to refer to the declared object in the class module.

5. Write event-handler procedures in the class module.

Note   This procedure is virtually identical to the one required to use events with an embedded chart.

Determining when a workbook is opened

The example in this section stores information in a text file in order to keep track of every workbook that is opened. It starts by inserting a new class module, naming it AppClass. The code in the class module is

```
Public WithEvents AppEvents As Application

Private Sub AppEvents_WorkbookOpen _
  (ByVal Wb As Excel.Workbook)
    Call UpdateLogFile(Wb)
End Sub
```

This declares AppEvents as an Application object with events. The AppEvents_WorkbookOpen procedure is called whenever a workbook is opened. This event-handler procedure calls UpdateLogFile and passes the Wb variable, which represents the Workbook that opened. You then add a VBA module and insert the following code:

```
Dim AppObject As New AppClass

Sub Init()
'   Called by Workbook_Open
    Set AppObject.AppEvents = Application
End Sub

Sub UpdateLogFile(Wb)
    txt = Wb.FullName
    txt = txt & "," & Date & "," & Time
    txt = txt & "," & Application.UserName
    Fname = ThisWorkbook.Path & "\logfile.txt"
    Open Fname For Append As #1
    Write #1, txt
    Close #1
    MsgBox txt
End Sub
```

Notice at the top that the AppObject variable is declared as type AppClass; that is, the name of the class module. The call to Init is in the Workbook_Open procedure, which is in the code module for ThisWorkbook. Here's the procedure:

```
Private Sub Workbook_Open()
    Call Init
End Sub
```

The UpdateLogFile procedure opens a text file, or creates it if it doesn't exist. It then writes key information about the workbook that opened: filename, full path name, date, time, and username.

The Workbook_Open procedure calls the Init procedure. Therefore, when the workbook opens, the Init procedure instigates the object variable.

Caution The text file is written to the same directory as the workbook. No error handling occurs, so the code fails when the workbook is opened from a CD-ROM drive.

Monitoring Application-level events

To get a feel for the event generation process, you might find it helpful to see a list of events that are generated as you go about your work.

The workbook contains a class module with 21 defined procedures, one for each Application-level event. Here's an example:

```
Private Sub XL_NewWorkbook(ByVal Wb As Excel.Workbook)
    LogEvent "NewWorkbook: " & Wb.Name
End Sub
```

Each of these procedures calls the `LogEvent` procedure and passes an argument that consists of the event name and object. Here's the `LogEvent` procedure:

```
Sub LogEvent(txt)
    EventNum = EventNum + 1
    With UserForm1
        With .lblEvents
            .AutoSize = False
            .Caption = .Caption & vbCrLf & txt
            .Width = UserForm1.FrameEvents.Width - 20
            .AutoSize = True
        End With
        .FrameEvents.ScrollHeight = .lblEvents.Height + 20
        .FrameEvents.ScrollTop = EventNum * 20
    End With
End Sub
```

The `LogEvent` procedure updates the UserForm by modifying the `Caption` property of the `Label` control named `lblEvents`. The procedure also adjusts the `ScrollHeight` and `ScrollTop` properties of the frame named FrameEvents, which contains `Label`. Adjusting these properties causes the most recently added text to show up while older text scrolls out of view.

Trapping UserForm Events

A UserForm supports many events, and each control placed on a UserForm has its own set of events. Table 38-5 lists the UserForm events that you can trap.

Table 38-5	
Events Recognized by a UserForm	
Event	**Action That Triggers the Event**
Activate	The UserForm is activated.
AddControl	A control is added at run-time.
BeforeDragOver	A drag-and-drop operation is in progress while the pointer is over the form.
BeforeDropOrPaste	Data is about to be dropped or pasted; that is, the mouse button has been released.
Click	A mouse is clicked while the pointer is over the form.

Continued

Table 38-5 *(continued)*

Event	Action That Triggers the Event
DblClick	A mouse is double-clicked while the pointer is over the form.
Deactivate	The UserForm is deactivated.
Error	An error has occurred.
Initialize	The UserForm is about to be shown.
KeyDown	A key is pressed.
KeyPress	Any ANSI key is pressed.
KeyUp	A key is released.
Layout	The size of a UserForm or a control is changed.
MouseDown	A mouse button is pressed.
MouseMove	The mouse is moved.
MouseUp	The mouse button was released
QueryClose	This occurs before a UserForm is closed.
RemoveControl	A control is removed from the UserForm at run-time.
Resize	The UserForm was resized.
Scroll	The UserForm is scrolled.
Terminate	The UserForm is terminated.
Zoom	The UserForm is zoomed.

Cross-Reference   Many of the examples in Chapters 36 and 37 demonstrate event handling for UserForms and UserForm controls.

Using Non-Object Events

The events discussed in this chapter are associated with an object (Application, Workbook, Sheet, and so on). This section discusses two additional "rogue" events: OnTime and OnKey. These events are not associated with an object. Rather, they are accessed using methods of the Application object.

Note   Unlike the other events discussed in this chapter, you use a general VBA module to program the "On-" events in this section.

Using the OnTime event

The OnTime event occurs at a specified time. The following example demonstrates how to program Excel to beep and then display a message at 3:00 p.m.:

```
Sub SetAlarm()
    Application.OnTime 0.625, "DisplayAlarm"
End Sub

Sub DisplayAlarm()
    Beep
    MsgBox "Wake up. It's time for your afternoon break!"
End Sub
```

In this example, the SetAlarm procedure uses the OnTime method of the Application object to set up the OnTime event. This method takes two arguments: the time (0.625, or 3:00 p.m., in the example) and the procedure to execute when the time occurs (DisplayAlarm in the example). In the example, after SetAlarm executes, the DisplayAlarm procedure is called at 3:00 p.m., bringing up the message.

Most people find it difficult to think of time in terms of Excel's time numbering system. Therefore, you might want to use VBA's TimeValue function to represent the time. TimeValue converts a string that looks like a time into a value that Excel can handle. The following statement shows an easier way to program an event for 3:00 p.m.:

```
Application.OnTime TimeValue("3:00:00 pm"), "DisplayAlarm"
```

If you want to schedule an event that's relative to the current time — for example, 20 minutes from now — you can write an instruction like this:

```
Application.OnTime Now + TimeValue("00:20:00"), "DisplayAlarm"
```

You also can use the OnTime method to schedule a procedure on a particular day. Of course, you must keep your computer running and the workbook with the procedure open.

Note   The OnTime method has two additional arguments. If you plan to use this method, refer to the online help for complete details.

Using the OnKey event

While you work, Excel constantly monitors what you type. Because of this, you can set up a keystroke or a key combination that, when pressed, executes a particular procedure.

The following example uses the OnKey method to set up an OnKey event. This event essentially reassigns the PgDn and PgUp keys. After the Setup_OnKey procedure executes, pressing PgDn executes the PgDn_Sub procedure, and pressing PgUp executes the PgUp_Sub procedure. The next effect is that pressing PgDn moves down one row and pressing PgUp moves up one row.

```
Sub Setup_OnKey()
    Application.OnKey "{PgDn}", "PgDn_Sub"
    Application.OnKey "{PgUp}", "PgUp_Sub"
End Sub

Sub PgDn_Sub()
    On Error Resume Next
    ActiveCell.Offset(1, 0).Activate
End Sub

Sub PgUp_Sub()
    On Error Resume Next
    ActiveCell.Offset(-1, 0).Activate
End Sub
```

Note Notice that the key codes are enclosed in brackets, not parentheses. For a complete list of the keyboard codes, consult the online help. Search for OnKey.

Tip The preceding examples used On Error Resume Next to ignore any errors generated. For example, if the active cell is in the first row, trying to move up one row causes an error. Furthermore, if the active sheet is a Chart sheet, an error occurs because no such thing as an active cell exists in a Chart sheet.

By executing the following procedure, you cancel the OnKey events and the keys return to their normal functions.

```
Sub Cancel_OnKey()
    Application.OnKey "{PgDn}"
    Application.OnKey "{PgUp}"
End Sub
```

Caution Contrary to what you might expect, using an empty string as the second argument for the OnKey method does *not* cancel the OnKey event. Rather, it causes Excel to ignore the keystroke and do nothing. For example, the following instruction tells Excel to ignore Alt+F4 (the percent sign represents the Alt key):

```
Application.OnKey "%{F4}", ""
```

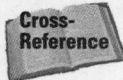

Cross-Reference Although you can use the OnKey method to assign a shortcut key for executing a macro, it's better to use the Macro Options dialog box for this task. For more details, see "Executing a Procedure Using a Ctrl+Shortcut Key Combination" in Chapter 34.

✦   ✦   ✦

Creating Custom Excel Add-Ins

For developers, one of the most useful features in Excel is
its capability to create add-ins. This chapter discusses
this concept and provides a practical example of creating an
add-in.

Understanding Add-Ins

Generally speaking, a spreadsheet *add-in* is something that's
added to the spreadsheet to give it additional functionality.
Excel includes several add-ins, including the Analysis ToolPak,
AutoSave, and Solver. Some add-ins (such as the Analysis
ToolPak, discussed in Chapter 24) provide new worksheet
functions that can be used in formulas. Usually, the new features blend in well with the original interface, so they appear
to be part of the program.

Excel's approach to add-ins is quite powerful because any
knowledgeable Excel user can create add-ins from XLS workbooks. An Excel add-in is basically a different form of an XLS
workbook file. Any XLS file can be converted into an add-in,
but not every workbook is a good candidate for an add-in.
Add-ins are always hidden, so you can't display worksheets or
chart sheets that are contained in an add-in. But you can
access its VBA subroutines and functions and display dialog
boxes that are contained on dialog sheets.

The following are some typical uses for Excel add-ins:

+ **To store one or more custom worksheet functions.**
  When the add-in is loaded, the functions can be used
  like any built-in worksheet function.

+ **To store Excel utilities.** VBA is ideal for creating general-
  purpose utilities that extend the power of Excel.

✦ **To store proprietary macros.** If you don't want end users to see (or modify) your macros, store the macros in an add-in. The macros can be used, but they can't be viewed or changed.

As previously noted, Excel ships with several useful add-ins and you can acquire other add-ins from third-party vendors or the Internet. In addition, Excel includes the tools that enable you to create your own add-ins. This process is explained later in the chapter, but first, some background is required.

Working with Add-Ins

The best way to work with add-ins is to use Excel's add-in manager, which you access by selecting Tools ⇨ Add-Ins. This command displays the Add-Ins dialog box, shown in Figure 39-1. The list box contains all the add-ins that Excel knows about. Those that are checked are open. You can open and close add-ins from this dialog box by selecting or deselecting the check boxes.

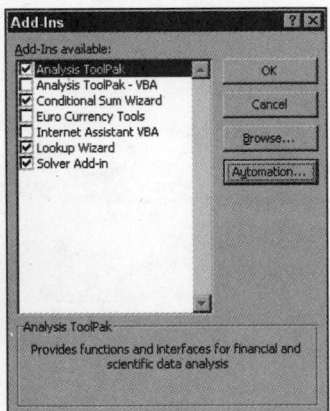

Figure 39-1: The Add-Ins dialog box lists the add-ins you can use with Excel.

Note   Most add-in files can also be opened by selecting File ⇨ Open. You'll find that after an add-in is opened, however, you can't choose File ⇨ Close to close it. The only way to remove the add-in is to exit and restart Excel or to write a macro to close the add-in.

When an add-in is opened, you may or may not notice anything different. In nearly every case, however, some change is made to the menu — either a new menu or one or more new menu items on an existing menu. For example, when you open the Analysis ToolPak add-in, a new menu item called Data Analysis appears on the Tools menu.

Why Create Add-Ins?

Most Excel users have no need to create add-ins. But if you develop spreadsheets for others — or if you simply want to get the most out of Excel — you may be interested in pursuing this topic further.

The following are several reasons why you may want to convert your XLS application to an add-in:

✦ **To prevent access to your VBA code:** When you distribute an application as an add-in, the end users can't view the sheets in the workbook. If you use proprietary techniques in your VBA code, this can prevent it from being copied (or at least make it more difficult to copy).

✦ **To avoid confusion:** If an end user loads your application as an add-in, the file is not visible and therefore is less likely to confuse novice users or get in the way. Unlike a hidden XLS workbook, an add-in can't be unhidden.

✦ **To simplify access to worksheet functions:** Custom worksheet functions that are stored in an add-in don't require the workbook name qualifier. For example, if you have a custom function named MOVAVG stored in a workbook named Newfuncs.xls, you would have to use a syntax such as the following to use this function in a different workbook:

```
=NEWFUNC.XLS!MOVAVG(A1:A50)
```

But if this function is stored in an add-in file that's open, the syntax is much simpler because you don't need to include the file reference:

```
=MOVAVG(A1:A50)
```

✦ **To provide easier access:** After you identify the location of your add-in, it appears in the Add-Ins dialog box, with a friendly name and a description of what it does.

✦ **To permit better control over loading:** Add-ins can be opened automatically when Excel starts, regardless of the directory in which they are stored.

✦ **To omit prompts when unloading:** When an add-in is closed, the user never sees the Save Change In . . .? prompt.

Creating Add-Ins

Although any workbook can be converted to an add-in, not all workbooks benefit by this. In fact, workbooks that consist only of worksheets (that is, not macros or custom dialog boxes) become unusable because add-ins are hidden.

The only types of workbooks that benefit from conversion to an add-in are those with macros. For example, you may have a workbook that consists of general-purpose macros (subroutines and functions). This type of workbook makes an ideal add-in.

Creating an add-in is quite simple. These steps describe how to create an add-in from a normal workbook file:

1. Develop your application and make sure that everything works properly. Don't forget to include a method to execute the macro or macros. You may want to add a new menu item (described later in the chapter).

2. Test the application by executing it when a *different* workbook is active. This simulates its behavior when it's an add-in because an add-in is never the active workbook. You may find that some references no longer work. For example, the following statement works fine when the code resides in the active workbook, but fails when a different workbook is active:

```
x = Worksheets("Data").Range("A1")
```

You could qualify the reference with the name of the workbook object, like this:

```
x = Workbooks("MYBOOK.XLS").Worksheets("Data").Range("A1")
```

This method is not recommended because the name of the workbook changes when it's converted to an add-in. The solution is to use the ThisWorkbook qualifier, as follows

```
x = ThisWorkbook.Worksheets("Data").Range("A1")
```

3. Select File ➪ Properties, click the Summary tab, enter a brief descriptive title in the Title field, and then enter a longer description in the Comments field. This step is not required, but it makes using the add-in easier.

4. Lock the project. This optional step protects the VBA code and UserForms from being viewed. You do this in the Visual Basic Editor, using the Tools ➪ *Projectname* Properties command. Click the Protection tab and make the appropriate choices.

5. Save the workbook as an XLA file by selecting File ➪ Save As. Select Microsoft Excel Add-In from the Save as type drop-down list (this option is at the bottom of the list).

After you create the add-in, you need to test it. Select Tools ➪ Add-Ins and use the Browse button in the Add-Ins dialog box to locate the XLA file that you created in Step 5. This installs the add-in. The Add-Ins dialog box uses the descriptive title that you provided in Step 3.

Note   You can continue to modify the macros and UserForms in the XLA version of your file and save your changes in the Visual Basic Editor. In versions prior to Excel 97, the changes have to be made to the XLS version and then the workbook has to be resaved as an add-in.

Trying Out An Add-In Example

This section discusses the steps that are used to create a useful add-in that displays a dialog box (see Figure 39-2) in which the user can quickly change several Excel settings. Although these settings can be changed in the Options dialog box, the add-in makes these changes interactively. For example, if the Grid Lines check box is deselected, the gridlines are removed immediately.

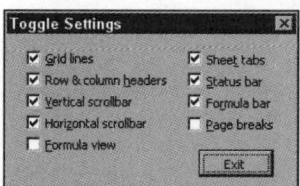

Figure 39-2: This dialog box enables the user to change various Excel settings interactively.

Setting Up the Workbook

The workbook must have at least one worksheet even if it is empty. Although the worksheet is not used, it must be present because every workbook must have at least one sheet.

Use the Visual Basic Editor to insert a VBA module (named Module1) and a UserForm (named UserForm1).

Creating Module1

The following macro is contained in the Module1 module. This subroutine ensures that a worksheet is active. If the active sheet is not a worksheet, a message box is displayed and nothing else happens. If a worksheet is active, the subroutine displays the dialog box that is contained in UserForm1.

```
Sub ShowToggleSettingsDialog()
  If TypeName(ActiveSheet) <> "Worksheet" Then
    MsgBox "A worksheet must be active.", vbInformation
  Else
    UserForm1.Show
  End If
End Sub
```

Adding the ThisWorkbook macro

The ThisWorkbook object contains a macro that adds a menu item to the Tools menu when the workbook (add-in) is opened. Another macro removes the menu item when the workbook (add-in) is closed. These two subroutines, which appear in the following syntax, are explained next:

```
Private Sub Workbook_Open()
  Set NewMenuItem = Application.CommandBars _
    ("Worksheet Menu Bar").Controls("Tools").Controls.Add
  With NewMenuItem
    .Caption = "Toggle Settings..."
    .BeginGroup = True
    .OnAction = "ShowToggleSettingsDialog"
  End With
End Sub

Private Sub Workbook_BeforeClose(Cancel As Boolean)
  On Error Resume Next
  Application.CommandBars("Worksheet Menu Bar"). _
    Controls("Tools").Controls("Toggle Settings...").Delete
End Sub
```

The Workbook_Open subroutine adds a menu item (Toggle Settings) to the bottom of the Tools menu on the Worksheet Menu Bar. This subroutine is executed when the workbook (or add-in) is opened.

The Workbook_BeforeClose subroutine is executed when the add-in is closed. This subroutine removes the Toggle Settings menu item from the Tools menu.

Creating UserForm1

Figure 39-3 shows the UserForm1 form, which has ten controls: nine check boxes and one command button. The controls have descriptive names, and the Accelerator property is set so that the controls display an accelerator key (for keyboard users).

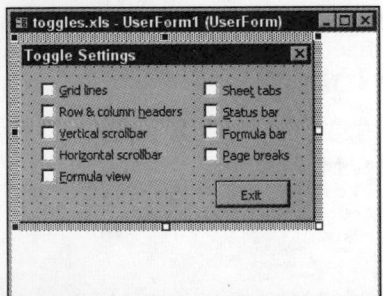

Figure 39-3: This shows the custom dialog box being created in the VBE.

The UserForm1 object contains the event-handler subroutines for the objects that are on the form. The following subroutine is executed before the dialog box is displayed:

```
Private Sub UserForm_Initialize()
  cbGridlines = ActiveWindow.DisplayGridlines
  cbHeaders = ActiveWindow.DisplayHeadings
  cbVerticalScrollbar = ActiveWindow.DisplayVerticalScrollBar
  cbHorizontalScrollbar =
ActiveWindow.DisplayHorizontalScrollBar
  cbFormulaView = ActiveWindow.DisplayFormulas
  cbSheetTabs = ActiveWindow.DisplayWorkbookTabs
  cbStatusBar = Application.DisplayStatusBar
  cbFormulaBar = Application.DisplayFormulaBar
  cbPageBreaks = ActiveSheet.DisplayPageBreaks
End Sub
```

The UserForm_Initialize subroutine adjusts the settings of the CheckBox controls in the dialog box to correspond to the current settings. For example, if the worksheet is displaying gridlines, ActiveWindow.DisplayGridlines returns True. This value is assigned to the cbGridlines CheckBox—which means that the CheckBox is displayed with a check mark.

Each CheckBox also has an event-handler subroutine, listed in the following code, that is executed when the control is clicked. Each subroutine makes the appropriate changes. For example, if the Grid lines CheckBox is selected, the DisplayGridlines property is set to correspond to the CheckBox.

```
Private Sub cbGridlines_Click on()
  ActiveWindow.DisplayGridlines = cbGridlines
End Sub

Private Sub cbHeaders_Click on()
  ActiveWindow.DisplayHeadings = cbHeaders
End Sub

Private Sub cbVerticalScrollbar_Click on()
  ActiveWindow.DisplayVerticalScrollBar = cbVerticalScrollbar
End Sub

Private Sub cbHorizontalScrollbar_Click on()
  ActiveWindow.DisplayHorizontalScrollBar =
cbHorizontalScrollbar
End Sub
```

```
Private Sub cbFormulaView_Click on()
   ActiveWindow.DisplayFormulas = cbFormulaView
End Sub

Private Sub cbSheetTabs_Click on()
   ActiveWindow.DisplayWorkbookTabs = cbSheetTabs
End Sub

Private Sub cbStatusBar_Click on()
   Application.DisplayStatusBar = cbStatusBar
End Sub

Private Sub cbFormulaBar_Click on()
   Application.DisplayFormulaBar = cbFormulaBar
End Sub

Private Sub cbPageBreaks_Click on()
   ActiveSheet.DisplayPageBreaks = cbPageBreaks
End Sub
```

The UserForm1 object has one additional event-handler subroutine for the Exit button. This subroutine, listed as follows, simply closes the dialog box:

```
Private Sub ExitButton_Click on()
   Unload UserForm1
End Sub
```

Testing the Workbook

Before you convert this workbook to an add-in, you need to test it. You should test it when a different workbook is active, to simulate what happens when the workbook is an add-in. Remember, an add-in is never the active workbook and it never displays any of its worksheets.

To test it, save the workbook, close it, and then reopen it. When the workbook reopens, the Workbook_Open subroutine is executed. This subroutine added the new menu item — Toggle Setting — to the Tools menu. Selecting Tools ➪ Toggle Setting displays the dialog box that is shown earlier, in Figure 39-2.

Adding Descriptive Information

This step is recommended but not necessary. Choose File ➪ Properties from Excel's menu to bring up the Properties dialog box. Then, click the Summary tab, as shown in Figure 39-4.

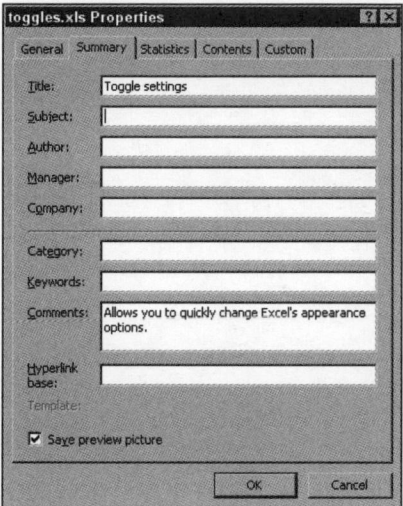

Figure 39-4: Use the Properties dialog box to enter descriptive information about your add-in.

Enter a title for the add-in in the Title field. This is the text that appears in the Add-Ins dialog box. In the Comments field, enter a description. This information appears at the bottom of the Add-Ins dialog box when the add-in is selected.

Protecting the Project

One advantage of an add-in is that it can be protected so that others can't see the source code. If you want to protect the project, follow these steps:

1. Activate the Visual Basic Editor.

2. In the Project window, click the project.

3. Select Tools ⇨ *Projectname* Properties.

   VBE displays its Project Properties dialog box.

4. Click the Protection tab (see Figure 39-5).

5. Select the Lock project for viewing check box.

6. Enter a password (twice) for the project.

7. Click OK.

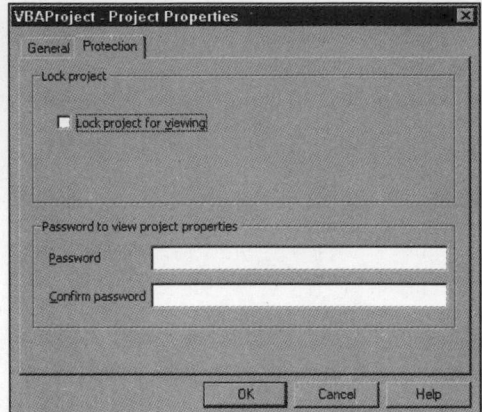

Figure 39-5: Use the Project Properties dialog box to protect your add-in.

Creating the Add-In

To save the workbook as an add-in, activate Excel, make sure the workbook is active, and then choose File ➪ Save As. Select Microsoft Excel Add-In (*.xla) from the Save as Type drop-down list. Enter a name for the add-in file and then click OK.

Opening the Add-In

To avoid confusion, close the XLS workbook before you open the add-in that was created from it. Then, select Tools ➪ Add-Ins. Excel displays its Add-Ins dialog box. Click the Browse button and locate the add-in that you just created. After you do so, the Add-Ins dialog box displays the add-in in its list. Notice that the information that you provided in the Properties dialog box appears here. Click OK to close the dialog box and open the add-in.

When the add-in is open, the Tools menu displays a new menu item (Toggle Settings) that executes the ShowToggleSettingsDialog subroutine in the add-in.

Note   If you activate the VBE window, you find that the add-in is listed in the Project window. However, you can't make any modifications unless you provide the password.

✦   ✦   ✦

Creating Custom Toolbars

◆ ◆ ◆ ◆

In This Chapter

Understanding
command bars

Manipulating
toolbars and buttons
manually

Manipulating the
CommandBars
collection

◆ ◆ ◆ ◆

Toolbars are one of the most useful elements of the modern computer program interface. Toolbars provide one-click access to commands that may be buried several levels deep in a menu system. By creating custom toolbars, you can even provide easy access to special features you've designed that may not be accessible through the standard menus. This chapter shows you how to create and modify custom toolbars.

Understanding Command Bars

Technically, a toolbar is known as a `CommandBar` object. In fact, what's commonly called a toolbar is actually one of three types of command bars:

- ✦ **Toolbar:** A floating bar with one or more clickable controls. This chapter focuses on this type of command bar.

- ✦ **Menu bar:** The two built-in menu bars are Worksheet Menu Bar and Chart Menu Bar.

- ✦ **Shortcut menu:** The menu that pops up when you right-click an object.

Cross-Reference
Because a menu bar is also a command bar, virtually all the information in this chapter also applies to menu bars. Chapter 41 discusses custom menus.

Understanding toolbar manipulations

The following list summarizes the ways in which you can customize toolbars in Excel:

✦ **Remove controls from built-in toolbars.** You can get rid of controls that you never use and free up a few pixels of screen space.

✦ **Add controls to built-in toolbars.** You can add as many controls as you want to any toolbar. These controls can be custom buttons or buttons from other toolbars, or they can come from the stock of controls that Excel provides.

✦ **Create new toolbars.** You can create as many new toolbars as you like, with toolbar controls from any source.

✦ **Change the functionality of built-in toolbar controls.** You do this by attaching your own macro to a built-in control.

✦ **Change the image that appears on any toolbar control.** Excel includes a rudimentary but functional toolbar button editor, although several other image-changing techniques are also possible.

You can perform these customizations by using the Customize dialog box that is displayed when you select the View ➪ Toolbars ➪ Customize command or by writing VBA code.

Cross-Reference

Chapter 27 covers the ways you can manipulate toolbars using the View ➪ Toolbars ➪ Customize command.

How Excel handles toolbars

Before you start working with custom toolbars, it's important to understand how Excel deals with toolbars in general. You may be surprised.

Storing toolbars

Toolbars can be attached to XLS (worksheet) or XLA (add-in) files, which makes it easy to distribute custom toolbars with your applications. You can attach any number of toolbars to a workbook. When the user opens your file, all attached toolbars automatically appear.

Excel stores toolbar information in an XLB file (the exact name and location of this file varies). Why is this XLB file important? Assume that a colleague gives you an Excel workbook that has a custom toolbar stored in it. When you open the workbook, the toolbar appears. You examine the workbook but decide that you're not interested in it. Nonetheless, when you exit Excel, the custom toolbar is added to your XLB file. If you make *any* toolbar changes — from the minor adjustment of a built-in toolbar to the introduction of a custom toolbar — the XLB file is resaved when you exit Excel.

Tip

You can delete custom toolbars that you never use. Use the View ➪ Toolbars ➪ Customize command to do this.

When toolbars don't work correctly

Excel's approach to storing toolbars can cause problems. Suppose you've developed an application that uses a custom toolbar and you've attached that toolbar to the application's workbook. The first time an end user opens the workbook, the toolbar is displayed. When the user closes Excel, your toolbar is saved in the user's XLB file. If the user alters the toolbar in any way — for example, if he accidentally removes a button — the next time your application is opened, the correct toolbar does *not* appear. Rather, the user sees the altered toolbar, which now lacks an important button. In other words, a toolbar attached to a workbook is not displayed if the user already has a toolbar with the same name. In many cases, this is *not* what you want to happen.

Fortunately, you can write VBA code to prevent this scenario. The trick is never to allow your custom toolbar to be added to the user's toolbar collection. The best way to do this is to create the toolbar on the fly every time the workbook is opened and then delete it when your application closes. With this process, the toolbar is never stored in the user's XLB file.

Manipulating Toolbars and Buttons Manually

Excel makes it easy for you to create new toolbars and modify existing toolbars. In fact, you may not even have to use VBA to work with toolbars because you can do just about all your toolbar customization without it.

 **Note**   Any customizations you make to a toolbar, either built-in or custom, are saved, so the changes remain in effect even when you restart Excel. These toolbar changes are not associated with a particular workbook. To restore a toolbar to its original state, you must reset it.

To perform any type of manual toolbar (or menu) customization, Excel needs to be in *command bar customization mode.* You can put Excel into this mode by using any of these techniques:

✦ Select View ➪ Toolbars ➪ Customize.

✦ Select Tools ➪ Customize.

✦ Right-click any toolbar or menu, and select Customize from the shortcut menu.

When Excel is in command bar customization mode, the Customize dialog box is displayed, and you can manipulate toolbars and menus any way you like. After you've made your customization, click the Close button in the Customize dialog box.

To store a toolbar in a workbook file, select View ➪ Toolbars ➪ Customize to display the Customize dialog box. Click the Attach button on the Toolbars tab to bring up the Attach Toolbars dialog box, shown in Figure 40-1. This dialog box lists all the custom toolbars in the Toolbars collection in the list box on the left. Toolbars already stored in the workbook are shown in the list box on the right.

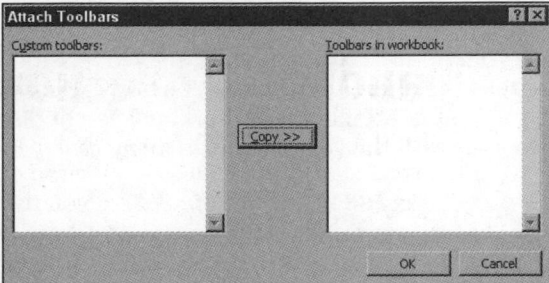

Figure 40-1: Use the Attach Toolbars dialog box to store your custom toolbars with a workbook so that you can distribute them.

To attach a toolbar, select it and click the Copy button. When a toolbar in the right list box is selected, the Copy button reads Delete; you can click it to remove a selected toolbar from a workbook. A toolbar that's attached to a workbook automatically appears when the workbook is opened, unless the workspace already has a toolbar by the same name.

Distributing a toolbar with an add-in

Distributing an application as an add-in is often the preferred method for end users. Not surprisingly, an add-in also can include one or more custom toolbars. But you need to be aware of a potential glitch.

Here's a typical scenario: You create an application that uses a custom toolbar. The buttons on that toolbar execute VBA procedures in the application's workbook. You attach the toolbar to the workbook and save the workbook. You create an add-in from the workbook. You close the XLS version of the application. You install the add-in. You click a button on the custom toolbar *and the XLS file opens!*

Your intent, of course, is to have the toolbar buttons execute procedures in the add-in, *not* the XLS file. But when you attach the toolbar to the workbook, the toolbar is saved in its current state. In that state, the workbook includes references to the macros in the XLS file. Consequently, clicking a button opens the XLS file so that the macro can be executed. You could manually (or via VBA) change the OnAction property of each toolbar button so it refers to the add-in. A better approach, though, is to write code to create the toolbar on the fly when the add-in is opened. This topic is discussed in detail later in the chapter.

Caution

The copy of the toolbar stored in the workbook always reflects its contents at the time you attach it. If you modify the toolbar after attaching it, the changed version is not automatically stored in the workbook. You must manually remove the old toolbar and then attach the edited toolbar.

Manipulating the CommandBars Collection

The `CommandBars` collection is contained in the `Application` object and is a collection of all `CommandBar` objects. Each `CommandBar` object has a collection of `Controls`. All these objects have properties and methods that enable you to control toolbars with VBA procedures.

You can write VBA code to manipulate toolbars and other types of command bars. This section provides some key background information that you should know about before you start working with toolbars. As always, a thorough understanding of the object model will make your task much easier.

You manipulate Excel command bars (including toolbars) by using objects located within the `CommandBars` collection. This collection consists of the following items:

✦ All of Excel's built-in toolbars.

✦ Any other custom toolbars that you create.

✦ A built-in menu bar named Worksheet Menu Bar. This appears when a worksheet is active.

✦ A built-in menu bar named Chart Menu Bar. This appears when a chart sheet is active.

✦ Any other custom menu bars that you create.

✦ All the built-in shortcut menus.

Understanding command bar types

As mentioned at the beginning of this chapter, three types of command bars exist, each of which is distinguished by its `Type` property. Possible settings for the `Type` property of the `CommandBars` collection are shown in the following table. VBA provides built-in constants for the command bar types.

Type	Description	Constant
0	Toolbar	msoBarTypeNormal
1	Menu Bar	msoBarTypeMenuBar
2	Shortcut Menu	msoBarTypePopUp

Listing all CommandBar objects

If you're curious about the objects in the CommandBars collection, the following procedure should be enlightening. Executing this procedure generates a list (shown in Figure 40-2) of all CommandBar objects in the CommandBars collection. For each command bar, the procedure lists its Index, Name, and Type property settings (displayed as *Toolbar, Menu Bar,* or *Shortcut*).

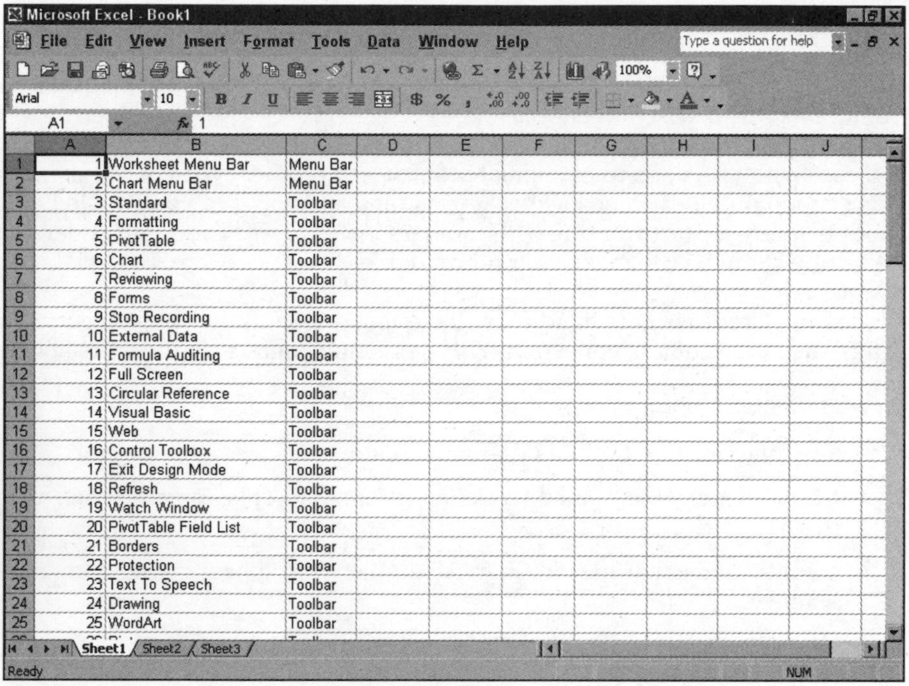

Figure 40-2: You can use a simple VBA procedure to produce a list of all CommandBar objects:

```
Sub ShowCommandBarNames()
    Cells.Clear
    Row = 1
    For Each cbar In CommandBars
        Cells(Row, 1) = cbar.Index
        Cells(Row, 2) = cbar.Name
        Select Case cbar.Type
            Case msoBarTypeNormal
                Cells(Row, 3) = "Toolbar"
            Case msoBarTypeMenuBar
                Cells(Row, 3) = "Menu Bar"
            Case msoBarTypePopUp
                Cells(Row, 3) = "Shortcut"
```

```
            End Select
            Row = Row + 1
        Next cbar
End Sub
```

Note   When you work with toolbars, you can turn on the macro recorder to see what's happening in terms of VBA code. Most (but not all) of the steps you take while customizing toolbars generate VBA code. By examining this code, you can discover how the object model for toolbars is put together. The object model is fairly simple and straightforward.

Creating a command bar

In VBA, you create a new toolbar using the Add method of the CommandBars collection. The following instruction creates a new toolbar with a default name, such as Custom 1. The created toolbar is initially empty (has no controls) and is not visible (its Visible property is False).

```
    CommandBars.Add
```

More often, you'll want to set some properties when you create a new toolbar. The following example demonstrates one way to do this:

```
    Sub CreateAToolbar()
        Dim TBar As CommandBar
        Set TBar = CommandBars.Add
        With TBar
            .Name = "MyToolbar"
            .Top = 0
            .Left = 0
            .Visible = True
        End With
    End Sub
```

The CreateAToolbar procedure uses the Add method of the CommandBars collection to add a new toolbar and create an object variable, Tbar, that represents this new toolbar. Subsequent instructions provide a name for the toolbar, set its position to the extreme upper-left corner of the screen, and make it visible. The Top and Left properties specify the position of the toolbar. Their settings represent screen coordinates, not Excel's window coordinates.

Referring to command bars

You can refer to a particular CommandBar object by its Index or its Name property. For example, the Standard toolbar has an Index property setting of 3, so you can refer to this toolbar in either of the following ways:

```
    CommandBars(3)
    CommandBars("Standard")
```

Deleting a command bar

To delete a custom toolbar, use the `Delete` method of the `CommandBar` object. You can refer to the object by its index number (if you know it) or its name. The following instruction deletes the toolbar named `MyToolbar`.

```
CommandBars("MyToolbar").Delete
```

If the toolbar doesn't exist, the instruction generates an error. To avoid the error message when you attempt to delete a toolbar that may or may not exist, the simplest solution is to ignore the error. The following code deletes `MyToolbar` if it exists. If it doesn't exist, no error message is displayed.

```
On Error Resume Next
CommandBars("MyToolbar").Delete
On Error GoTo 0
```

Another approach is to create a custom function that determines whether a particular toolbar is in the `CommandBars` collection. The following function accepts a single argument (a potential `CommandBar` object name) and returns True if the command bar exists:

```
Function CommandBarExists(n) As Boolean
    Dim cb As CommandBar
    For Each cb In CommandBars
        If UCase(cb.Name) = UCase(n) Then
            CommandBarExists = True
            Exit Function
        End If
    Next cb
    CommandBarExists = False
End Function
```

Understanding the properties of command bars

The following are some of the more useful properties of a `CommandBar` object:

`BuiltIn`	True if the object is one of Excel's built-in command bars.
`Left`	The command bar's left position in pixels.
`Name`	The command bar's display name.
`Position`	An integer that specifies the position of the command bar. Possible values are as follows:
	`msoBarLeft` — The command bar is docked on the left.
	`msoBarTop` — The command bar is docked on the top.

msoBarRight — The command bar is docked on the right.

msoBarBottom — The command bar is docked on the bottom.

msoBarFloating — The command bar isn't docked.

msoBarPopup — The command bar is a shortcut menu.

Protection	An integer that specifies the type of protection for the command bar. Possible values are as follows:

msoBarNoProtection — (Default) Not protected. The command bar can be customized by the user.

msoBarNoCustomize — Cannot be customized.

msoBarNoResize — Cannot be resized.

msoBarNoMove — Cannot be moved.

msoBarNoChangeVisible — Its visibility state cannot be changed by the user.

msoBarNoChangeDock — Cannot be docked to a different position.

msoBarNoVerticalDock — Cannot be docked along the left or right edge of the window.

msoBarNoHorizontalDock — Cannot be docked along the top or bottom edge of the window.

Top	The command bar's top position in pixels.
Type	Returns an integer that represents the type of command bar (a toolbar, a menu, or a shortcut menu).
Visible	True if the command bar is visible.

The VBA examples in the following sections demonstrate the use of some of the command bar properties.

Counting custom toolbars

The following function returns the number of custom toolbars. It loops through the CommandBars collection and increments a counter if the command bar represented by cb is a toolbar and if its BuiltIn property is False.

```
Function CustomToolbars()
    Dim cb As CommandBar
    Dim Count As Integer
    Count = 0
    For Each cb In CommandBars
        If cb.Type = msoBarTypeNormal Then
```

```
                    If Not cb.BuiltIn Then
                        Count = Count + 1
                    End If
                End If
        Next cb
        CustomToolbars = Count
    End Function
```

Preventing a toolbar from being modified

The `Protection` property of a `CommandBar` object provides you with many options for protecting a `CommandBar`. The following instruction sets the `Protection` property for a toolbar named `MyToolbar`:

```
CommandBars("MyToolbar").Protection = msoBarNoCustomize
```

After this instruction is executed, the user is unable to customize the toolbar.

The `Protection` constants are *additive,* which means that you can apply different types of protection with a single command. For example, the following instructions adjust the `MyToolbar` toolbar so that it cannot be customized or moved:

```
Set cb = CommandBars("MyToolbar")
cb.Protection = msoBarNoCustomize + msoBarNoMove
```

Animating a toolbar

The following example is quite useless, unless you're looking for a way to get the user's attention. But it does demonstrate how your VBA code can change the position of a toolbar. The following `MoveToolbar` procedure is executed when the user clicks a button on a single-button toolbar named `"Mover"`. The procedure executes a loop and randomly moves the toolbar to a different screen position each time it cycles through the loop until it ends up at its original position.

```
Sub MoveToolbar()
    With CommandBars("Mover")
        OldLeft = .Left
        OldTop = .Top
        For i = 1 To 60
            .Left = Int(vidWidth * Rnd)
            .Top = Int(vidHeight * Rnd)
            DoEvents
        Next i
        .Left = OldLeft
        .Top = OldTop
    End With
End Sub
```

In this procedure, `vidWidth` and `vidHeight` represent the width and height of the video display. These values are calculated by the `DisplayVideoInfo` procedure, which uses a Windows API function.

Creating an "autosense" toolbar

Many of Excel's built-in toolbars seem to have some intelligence; they appear when you're working in a specific context and disappear when you stop working in that context. For example, the Chart toolbar normally appears when you are working on a chart, and it disappears when you stop working on the chart.

Note To disable autosensing for a particular toolbar, just close the toolbar while you're working in the context in which it normally appears. To reenable it, make the toolbar visible again while you're working in its context.

You may want to program toolbar autosensing for your application. For example, you might want to make a toolbar visible only when a certain worksheet is activated or when a cell in a particular range is activated. Thanks to Excel's support for events, this sort of programming is relatively easy.

The procedure in Listing 40-1 creates a toolbar when the workbook is opened and uses one of its worksheets' SelectionChange events to determine whether the active cell is contained in a range named ToolbarRange. If so, the toolbar is visible; if not, the toolbar is hidden. In other words, the toolbar is visible only when the active cell is within a specific range of the worksheet.

Listing 40-1: This toolbar exists only when the cell pointer falls within a given range

```
Sub CreateToolbar()
'   Creates a demo toolbar named "AutoSense"
    Dim AutoSense As CommandBar
    Dim Button As CommandBarButton

'   Delete the existing toolbar if it exists
    Call DeleteToolbar

'   Create the toolbar
    Set AutoSense = CommandBars.Add
    For i = 1 To 4
        Set Button = AutoSense.Controls.Add(msoControlButton)
        With Button
            .OnAction = "Button" & i
            .FaceId = i + 37
        End With
    Next i
    AutoSense.Name = "AutoSense"
End Sub
```

This procedure, which is called by the `Workbook_Open` procedure, creates a simple toolbar named `AutoSense`. The four toolbar buttons are set up to execute procedures named `Button1`, `Button2`, `Button3`, and `Button4`. The DeleteToolbar procedure (not shown) simply deletes the toolbar (if it exists) before creating a new one.

Here's the event handler procedure for the `SelectionChange` event:

```
Private Sub Worksheet_SelectionChange(ByVal Target As _
  Excel.Range)
    If Union(Target, Range("ToolbarRange")).Address = _
      Range("ToolbarRange").Address Then
        CommandBars("AutoSense").Visible = True
    Else
        CommandBars("AutoSense").Visible = False
    End If
End Sub
```

This procedure checks the active cell. If it's contained within a range named `ToolbarRange`, the `AutoSense` toolbar's `Visible` property is set to True; otherwise, it is set to False.

The workbook also contains a `Workbook_BeforeClose` procedure that calls the `DeleteToolbar` procedure (which deletes the `AutoSense` toolbar) when the workbook is closed. This technique, of course, can be adapted to provide auto-sensing capability based on other criteria.

Cross-Reference   For a comprehensive discussion of the types of events Excel recognizes, see Chapter 38.

Hiding (and later restoring) all toolbars

Some developers like to "take over" Excel when their application is loaded. For example, they like to hide all toolbars, the status bar, and the formula bar. It's only proper, however, for them to clean up when their application is closed. This includes restoring the toolbars that were originally visible.

The example in this section describes a way to hide all toolbars and then restore them when the application is closed. The `HideAllToolbars` procedure is called from the `Workbook_Open` event handler, and the `RestoreToolbars` procedure is called by the `Workbook_BeforeClose` event handler.

The code keeps track of which toolbars were visible by storing their names in a worksheet named `TBSheet`. When the workbook closes, the `RestoreToolbars` subroutine reads these cells and displays the toolbars. Using a worksheet to store the toolbar names is safer than using an array. Both procedures are shown in Listing 40-2.

Listing 40-2: **Removing all toolbars and then restoring them**

```
Sub HideAllToolbars()
    Dim TB As CommandBar
    Dim TBNum As Integer
    Dim TBSheet As Worksheet
    Set TBSheet = Sheets("TBSheet")
Application.ScreenUpdating = False

'   Clear the sheet
    TBSheet.Cells.Clear

'   Hide all visible toolbars and store
'   their names
    TBNum = 0
    For Each TB In CommandBars
        If TB.Type = msoBarTypeNormal Then
            If TB.Visible Then
                TBNum = TBNum + 1
                TB.Visible = False
                TBSheet.Cells(TBNum, 1) = TB.Name
            End If
        End If
    Next TB
    Application.ScreenUpdating = True
End Sub

Sub RestoreToolbars()
    Dim TBSheet As Worksheet
    Set TBSheet = Sheets("TBSheet")
    Application.ScreenUpdating = False

'   Unhide the previously displayed toolbars
    On Error Resume Next
    For Each cell In TBSheet.Range("A:A") _
       .SpecialCells(xlCellTypeConstants)
          CommandBars(cell.Value).Visible = True
    Next cell
    Application.ScreenUpdating = True
End Sub
```

Referring to controls in a command bar

A CommandBar object, such as a toolbar, contains Control objects. These objects are mainly toolbar buttons and menu items.

The following `Test` procedure displays the `Caption` property for the first `Control` object contained in the Standard toolbar, whose index is 3:

```
Sub Test()
    MsgBox CommandBars(3).Controls(1).Caption
End Sub
```

When you execute this procedure, you'll see a message box that shows the caption property for the control. Notice the ampersand (&). The letter following the ampersand is the underlined hot key in the displayed text.

Rather than use an index number to refer to a control, you can use its `Caption` property setting. The following procedure produces the same result as the previous one:

```
Sub Test2()
    MsgBox CommandBars("Standard").Controls("New").Caption
End Sub
```

Note   In some cases, Control objects may contain other Control objects. For example, the first control on the Drawing toolbar contains other controls (this also demonstrates that you can include menu items on a toolbar). The concept of Controls within Controls will become clearer in Chapter 41.

Listing the controls on a command bar

The following procedure displays the `Caption` property for each `Control` object within a `CommandBar` object. This example uses the Standard toolbar.

```
Sub ShowControlCaptions()
    Dim Cbar as CommandBar
    Set CBar = CommandBars("Standard")
    Cells.Clear
    Row = 1
    For Each ctl In CBar.Controls
        Cells(Row, 1) = ctl.Caption
        Row = Row + 1
    Next ctl
End Sub
```

The output of the `ShowControlCaptions` procedure is shown in Figure 40-3.

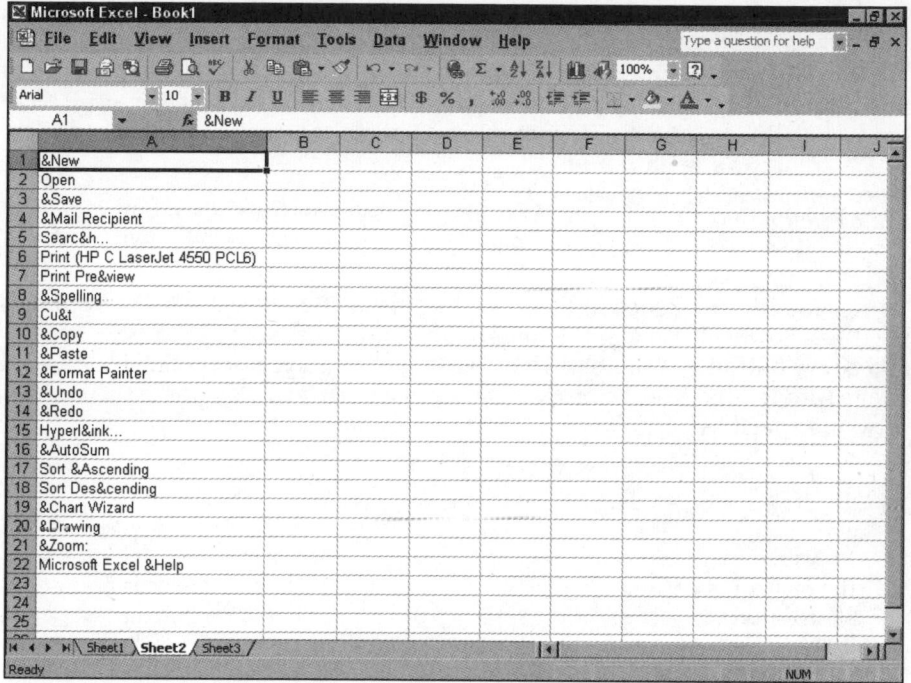

Figure 40-3: You can create a list of the captions for each control on the Standard toolbar.

Listing all controls on all toolbars

The following procedure loops through all command bars in the collection. If the command bar is a toolbar—that is, if its Type property is set to 1—another loop displays the Caption for each toolbar button.

```
Sub ShowAllToolbarControls()
    Cells.Clear
    Row = 1
    For Each Cbar In CommandBars
        If Cbar.Type = msoBarTypeNormal Then
            Cells(Row, 1) = Cbar.Name
            For Each ctl In Cbar.Controls
                Cells(Row, 2) = ctl.Caption
                Row = Row + 1
            Next ctl
        End If
    Next Cbar
End Sub
```

Adding a control to a command bar

You can add a new control to a `CommandBar` object by using the `Add` method of the `Controls` collection object. The following instruction adds a new control to a toolbar named `MyToolbar`. Its `Type` property is set to the `msoControlButton` constant, which creates a standard button.

```
CommandBars("MyToolbar").Controls.Add _
    Type:=msoControlButton
```

The toolbar button added in the preceding instruction is just a blank button; clicking it has no effect. Most of the time, you'll want to set some properties when you add a new button to a toolbar. The following code adds a new control, gives it an image through the `FaceId` property, assigns a macro by way of the `OnAction` property, and specifies a caption:

```
Sub AddButton()
    Set NewBtn = CommandBars("MyToolbar").Controls.Add _
      (Type:=msoControlButton)
    With NewBtn
        .FaceId = 300
        .OnAction = "MyMacro"
        .Caption = "Tooltip goes here"
    End With
End Sub
```

The AddButton procedure creates an object variable (NewBtn) that represents the added control. The `With-End With` construct then sets the properties for the object.

Deleting a control from a command bar

To delete a control from a `CommandBar` object, use the `Delete` method of the `Controls` collection. The following instruction deletes the first control on a toolbar named `MyToolbar`:

```
CommandBars("MyToolbar").Controls(1).Delete
```

You can also specify the control by referring to its caption. The following instruction deletes a control that has a caption of `SortButton`:

```
CommandBars("MyToolbar").Controls("SortButton").Delete
```

Using the properties of command bar controls

Command bar controls, of course, have a number of properties that determine how the controls look and work. Following is a list of a few of the more useful properties for command bar controls:

BeginGroup	True if a separator bar appears before the control.
BuiltIn	True if the control is one of Excel's built-in controls.
Caption	The text that is displayed for the control. If the control shows only an image, the caption appears when you move the mouse over the control.
Enabled	True if the control can be clicked.
FaceID	A number that represents a graphic image displayed next to the control's text.
OnAction	The name of a VBA procedure to be executed when the user clicks the control.
Style	Determines whether the button appears with a caption and/or image.
ToolTipText	Text that appears when the user moves the mouse pointer over the control.
Type	An integer that determines the type of the control.

Setting a control's Style property

The `Style` property of a command bar control determines its appearance. The `Style` property is usually specified using a built-in constant. For example, to display an image and text, set the `Style` property to `msoButtonIconandCaption`. Refer to the online help for other `Style` constants.

Tip   The text displayed on a control is the control's Caption property, and its image is determined by the value of the FaceID property.

Adjusting a toolbar button image

When you're in command bar customization mode, you can right-click any toolbar button and select Change Button Image. Doing so displays a list of 42 images from which you can select. Most of the time, none of these images is exactly what you need. Therefore, you must specify the image with VBA.

The image (if any) displayed on a toolbar control is determined by its `FaceID` property. For an image to be displayed, the control's `Style` property must *not* be `msoButtonCaption`.

The following instruction sets the `FaceId` property of the first button on the `MyToolbar` toolbar image to 45, which is the code number for a mailbox icon.

```
CommandBars("MyToolbar").Controls(1).FaceId = 45
```

Adjusting a control's Visible property

The following procedure — which causes lots of onscreen action — simply reverses the Visible property of each toolbar. Hidden toolbars are displayed, and visible toolbars are hidden. To return things to normal, execute the procedure a second time.

```
Sub ToggleAllToolbars()
    For Each cb In CommandBars
        If cb.Type = msoBarTypeNormal Then
            cb.Visible = Not cb.Visible
        End If
    Next cb
End Sub
```

Changing a control's caption dynamically

The procedure in Listing 40-3 creates a toolbar with a single button. The caption on this button displays the number format string for the active cell (see Figure 40-4). The procedure uses Worksheet events to monitor when the selection is changed. When a SelectionChange event occurs, a procedure is executed that changes the caption in the button.

Listing 40-3: **Showing the user the current cell's number format**

```
Sub MakeNumberFormatDisplay()
    Dim TBar As CommandBar
    Dim NewBtn As CommandBarButton

'   Delete existing toolbar if it exists
    On Error Resume Next
    CommandBars("Number Format").Delete
    On Error GoTo 0

'   Create a new toolbar
    Set TBar = CommandBars.Add
    With TBar
        .Name = "Number Format"
        .Visible = True
    End With

'   Add a button control
    Set NewBtn = CommandBars("Number Format").Controls.Add _
        (Type:=msoControlButton)
    With NewBtn
        .Caption = ""
        .OnAction = "ChangeNumFormat"
```

```
            .Style = msoButtonCaption
        End With
        Call UpdateToolbar
    End Sub
```

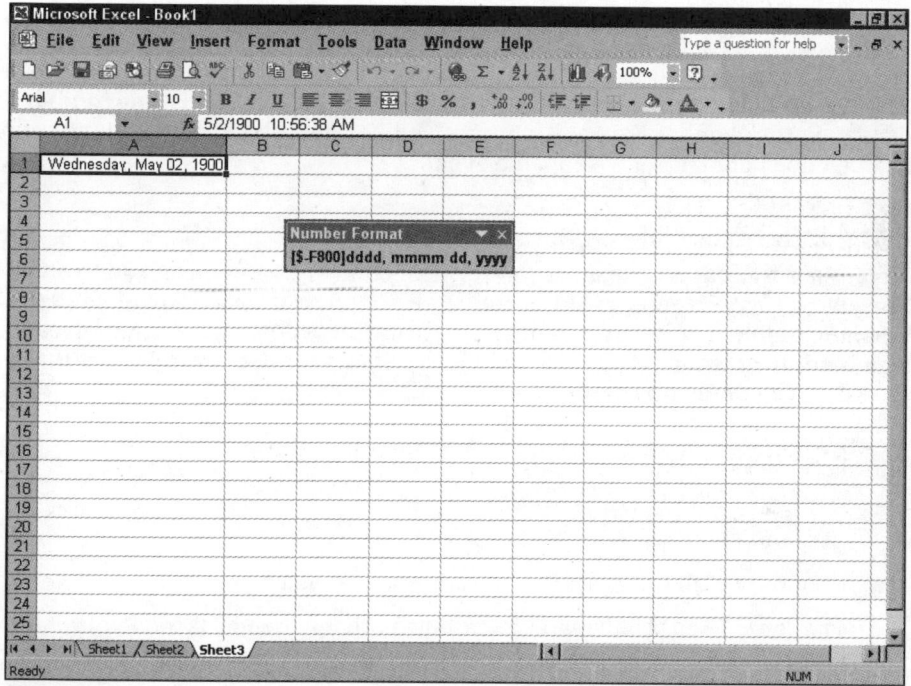

Figure 40-4: This toolbar button displays the number format for the active cell.

Cross-Reference For more information about events, see Chapter 38.

The following `UpdateToolbar` procedure simply copies the `NumberFormat` property of the `ActiveCell` to the `Caption` property of the button control:

```
    Sub UpdateToolbar()
        On Error Resume Next
        CommandBars("Number Format"). _
          Controls(1).Caption = ActiveCell.NumberFormat
        If Err <> 0 Then CommandBars("Number Format"). _
          Controls(1).Caption = ""
    End Sub
```

The button's `OnAction` property is set to a procedure named `ChangeNumFormat,` as follows:

```
Sub ChangeNumFormat()
    Application.Dialogs(xlDialogFormatNumber).Show
    Call UpdateToolbar
End Sub
```

This procedure displays the Number tab of Excel's Format Cells dialog box.

The technique described in this section works quite well, but it does have a flaw: If the user changes the number format with a button on the Formatting toolbar, the display in the Number Format is not changed because changing the number format of a cell does not trigger a trappable event.

Using other types of command bar controls

A standard toolbar button is just one type of control that you can add to a toolbar. The control type is determined by the `Type` property of the control. Besides buttons, the online help lists many other control types. Most of these, however, cannot be added to a command bar. The built-in constants for the control types that you *can* add to a command bar are as follows:

`msoControlButton`	A standard button.
`msoControlEdit`	An edit box.
`msoControlComboBox`	A combo box.
`msoControlDropdown`	A drop-down list.
`msoControlButtonPopup`	A button that, when clicked, displays other controls. Use this control to create a menu with menu items.

Note   The Type property for a Control object is a read-only property that's set when the control is created. In other words, you can't change a control's type after it has been created.

The online help lists several other `Type` constants for a command bar control. For example, you'll find `msoControlGauge`, `msoControlGraphicCombo`, and others. These controls, however, can't be used. You are limited to controls created with any of the five constants just listed.

The `MakeMonthList` procedure in Listing 40-4 creates a new toolbar, adds a drop-down list control, and fills that control with the names of each month. It also sets the `OnAction` property so that clicking the control executes a procedure named `PasteMonth`.

Listing 40-4: Attaching a drop-down list to a command bar

```
Sub MakeMonthList()
    Dim TBar As CommandBar
    Dim NewDD As CommandBarControl

'   Delete existing toolbar if it exists
    On Error Resume Next
    CommandBars("MonthList").Delete
    On Error GoTo 0

'   Create a new toolbar
    Set TBar = CommandBars.Add
    With TBar
        .Name = "MonthList"
        .Visible = True
    End With

'   Add a DropDown control
    Set NewDD = CommandBars("MonthList").Controls.Add _
        (Type:=msoControlDropdown)
    With NewDD
        .Caption = "DateDD"
        .OnAction = "PasteMonth"
        .Style = msoButtonAutomatic

'       Fill it with month name
        For i = 1 To 12
            .AddItem Format(DateSerial(1, i, 1), "mmmm")
        Next i
        .ListIndex = 1
    End With
End Sub
```

The following is the `PasteMonth` procedure:

```
Sub PasteMonth()
'   Puts the selected month in the active cell
    On Error Resume Next
    With CommandBars("MonthList").Controls("DateDD")
        ActiveCell.Value = .List(.ListIndex)
    End With
End Sub
```

The workbook has an additional twist: It uses a `Worksheet_SelectionChange` event handler. This procedure, as follows, is executed whenever the user makes a new selection on the worksheet. It determines whether the active cell contains a month name. If so, it sets the ListIndex property of the drop-down list control in the toolbar.

```
Private Sub Worksheet_SelectionChange(ByVal Target _
  As Excel.Range)
    For i = 1 To 12
        Set ActCell = Target.Range("A1")
        If ActCell.Value = Format(DateSerial(1, i, 1), _
        "mmmm") Then
            CommandBars("MonthList").Controls("DateDD") _
            .ListIndex = i
            Exit Sub
        End If
    Next i
End Sub
```

✦   ✦   ✦

Creating Custom Menus

Every Windows program has a menu system, which usually serves as the primary user interface element. The
Windows standard places the menu bar directly beneath the
application's title bar. In addition, many programs implement
another type of menu: shortcut menus. Typically, right-clicking
a selection displays a context-sensitive shortcut menu containing commands that enable you to work with the selection.

Excel uses both types of menus, and developers have almost
complete control over Excel's entire menu system, including
shortcut menus. This chapter tells you everything you need
to know about working with Excel's menus.

Understanding Excel's Menus

If you've read Chapter 40, you already know that a menu bar
(like a toolbar) is a `CommandBar` object. In fact, the techniques
described in Chapter 40 also apply to menu bars.

So how does a menu bar differ from a toolbar? In general, a
menu bar is displayed at the top of the Excel window, directly
below the title bar. When clicked, the top-level controls on a
menu bar display a drop-down list of menu items. A menu bar
may also contain three window control buttons (Minimize,
Restore (or Maximize), and Close). Toolbars, on the other
hand, usually consist of graphic icons and do not display any
control buttons. These rules are definitely not hard and fast.
You can, if desired, add traditional toolbar buttons to a menu
bar or add traditional menu items to a toolbar. You can even
move a menu bar from its traditional location and make it
free-floating.

Understanding what you can do with Excel's menus

To modify Excel's menus, you can remove elements, add elements, and change elements. In addition, you can temporarily replace Excel's standard menu bar with one of your own creation. You can change Excel's menus two ways: through the Customize dialog box or with VBA code.

When you close Excel, it saves any changes that you've made to the menu system, and these changes appear the next time you open Excel. The information about menu modifications is stored in an XLB file in your Windows directory.

See Chapter 40 for more information about the XLB file.

In most cases, you won't want your menu modifications to be saved between sessions. Generally, you'll need to write VBA code to change the menus while a particular workbook is open and then change them back when the workbook closes. Therefore, you'll need VBA code to modify the menu when the workbook is opened and more VBA code to return the menus to normal when the workbook is closed.

Learning some menu terminology

Menu terminology is often a bit confusing at first because many of the terms are similar. The following list presents the official Excel menu terminology that is referred to in this chapter:

✦ **Command bar.** An object that can function as a menu bar, a shortcut menu, or a toolbar. It is represented by the `CommandBar` object in the Office object library.

✦ **Menu bar.** The row of words that appears directly below the application's title bar. Excel has two menu bars: One is displayed when a worksheet is active, and the other is displayed when a chart sheet is active or when an embedded chart is activated.

✦ **Menu.** A single, top-level element of a menu bar. For example, both of Excel's menu bars have a File menu.

✦ **Menu item.** An element that appears in the drop-down list when you select a menu. For example, the first menu item under the File menu is New. Menu items also appear in submenus and shortcut menus.

✦ **Separator bar.** A horizontal line that appears between two menu items. The separator bar is used to group similar menu items.

✦ **Submenu.** A second-level menu that is under some menus. For example, the Edit menu has a submenu called Clear.

✦ **Submenu item.** A menu item that appears in the list when you select a submenu. For example, the Edit ⇨ Clear submenu contains the following submenu items: All, Formats, Contents, and Comments.

✦ **Shortcut menu.** The floating list of menu items that appears when you right-click a selection or an object. The shortcut menu that appears depends on the current context.

✦ **Enabled.** A menu item that can be used. If a menu item isn't enabled, its text appears grayed, and it can't be used.

✦ **Checked.** The status of a menu item that represents an on/off or True/False state. A menu item can display a graphical box that is checked or unchecked. The View ⇨ Status Bar menu item is an example.

✦ **Image.** A small graphic icon that appears next to some menu items. This icon is sometimes called a Face ID.

✦ **Shortcut key combination.** A keystroke combination that serves as an alternate method to execute a menu item. The shortcut key combination is displayed at the right side of the menu item. For example, Ctrl+S is the shortcut key combination for File ⇨ Save.

Removing menu elements

You can remove any part of Excel's menu system: menu items, menus, and entire menu bars. For example, if you don't want the end users of your application fiddling with the display, you can remove the View menu from the Worksheet Menu Bar. You can also remove one or more menu items from a menu. If you remove the New menu item from the File menu, for example, users can't use the menu to create a new workbook. Finally, you can eliminate Excel's menu bar and replace it with one that you've created. You might do this if you want your application to be completely under the control of your macros.

Caution

Remember that simply removing menu bars, menus, or menu items does not affect the alternate method of accomplishing some actions. Specifically, if corresponding shortcut keys, toolbar buttons, or shortcut menus perform the same action as a menu command, those alternate methods still work. For example, if you remove the New menu item from the File menu, the user can still use the New Workbook toolbar button, the Ctrl+N shortcut key, or the Desktop shortcut menu to create a new workbook.

Adding menu elements

You can add your own custom menus to built-in menu bars, and you can add custom menu items to a built-in menu. In fact, you can create an entirely new menu bar, if you like. For example, you might develop an application that doesn't require any of Excel's built-in menus. A simple solution is to create a new menu bar that consists of custom menus and custom menu items that execute your macros. You can hide Excel's normal menu bar and replace it with your own.

Referencing the CommandBars Collection

The `CommandBars` collection is a member of the `Application` object. When you reference this collection in a regular VBA module, you can omit the reference to the `Application` object (it is assumed). For example, the following statement (contained in a standard VBA module) displays the name of the first element of the CommandBars collection:

```
MsgBox CommandBars(1).Name
```

For some reason, when you reference the `CommandBars` collection from a code module for a `ThisWorkbook` object, you must precede it with a reference to the `Application` object, like this:

```
MsgBox Application.CommandBars(1).Name
```

Changing menu elements

If you get bored with Excel's standard menu text, you can change it to something else — for instance, you can change the Tools menu to the Stuff menu. You can also assign your own macros to built-in menu items. You have many other options for changing menu elements, including rearranging the order of the menus on a menu bar (for example, to make the Help menu appear first instead of last).

The remainder of this chapter focuses on writing VBA code to modify menus.

Trying Out Some VBA Examples

This section presents some practical examples of VBA code that manipulates Excel's menus.

Listing menu information

The following `ListMenuInfo` procedure may be instructive. It displays the caption for each item (menu, menu item, and submenu item) on the Worksheet Menu Bar.

```
Sub ListMenuInfo()
    Row = 1
    On Error Resume Next
    For Each Menu In CommandBars(1).Controls
        For Each MenuItem In Menu.Controls
            For Each SubMenuItem In MenuItem.Controls
                Cells(Row, 1) = Menu.Caption
                Cells(Row, 2) = MenuItem.Caption
                Cells(Row, 3) = SubMenuItem.Caption
```

```
                Row = Row + 1
            Next SubMenuItem
        Next MenuItem
    Next Menu
End Sub
```

Figure 41-1 shows a portion of the `ListMenuInfo` procedure's output.

	A	B	C	D	E
5	&File	Save &As...			
6	&File	Save as Web Pa&ge...			
7	&File	Save &Workspace...			
8	&File	Searc&h...			
9	&File	Ch&eck Out			
10	&File	Ch&eck In			
11	&File	We&b Page Preview			
12	&File	Page Set&up...			
13	&File	Prin&t Area	&Set Print Area		
14	&File	Prin&t Area	&Clear Print Area		
15	&File	Print Pre&view			
16	&File	&Print...			
17	&File	Sen&d To	&Mail Recipient		
18	&File	Sen&d To	Original &Sender...		
19	&File	Sen&d To	Mail Re&cipient (for Review)...		
20	&File	Sen&d To	M&ail Recipient (as Attachment)...		
21	&File	Sen&d To	&Routing Recipient...		
22	&File	Sen&d To	&Exchange Folder...		
23	&File	Sen&d To	&Online Meeting Participant		
24	&File	Propert&ies			
25	&File	&1 E:\chapters\Chap50\list menu info.xls			
26	&File	&2 \WINDOWS\Application Data\Microsof...\Excel10.xlb			
27	&File	&3 E:\chapters\Chap48\toggles.xls			
28	&File	&4 E:\chapters\Chap46\track changes.xls			
29	&File	&5 Funcs.xls			

Figure 41-1: This shows a portion of the output from the `ListMenuInfo` procedure.

Tip This procedure uses On Error Resume Next to avoid the error message that appears when the procedure attempts to access a submenu item that doesn't exist.

Adding a new menu to a menu bar

This section describes how to use VBA to add a new menu to the Worksheet Menu Bar. The Worksheet Menu Bar is the first item in the `CommandBars` collection, so you can reference it one of two ways:

```
CommandBars("Worksheet Menu Bar")
CommandBars(1)
```

In VBA terms, you use the Add method to append a new control to the
CommandBarControls collection. The new control is a "pop-up control" of type
msoControlPopup. You can specify the new control's position; if you don't, the new
menu is added to the end of the menu.

Adding a new menu is a two-step process:

1. Use the Add method to create an object variable that refers to the new control. Arguments for the Add method enable you to specify the control's type,
its ID (useful only if you're adding a built-in menu item), its position, and
whether it's a temporary control that will be deleted when Excel closes.

2. Adjust the properties of the new control. For example, you'll probably want to
specify a Caption property and an OnAction property.

Adding a menu: Take 1

In this example, the objective is to add a new Budgeting menu to the Worksheet
Menu Bar and to position this new menu to the left of the Help menu.

```
Sub AddNewMenu()
'    Get Index of Help menu
     HelpIndex = CommandBars(1).Controls("Help").Index

'    Create the menu
     Set NewMenu = CommandBars(1).Controls.Add _
       (Type:=msoControlPopup, _
         Before:=HelpIndex, _
         Temporary:=True)

'    Add a caption
     NewMenu.Caption = "&Budgeting"
End Sub
```

The preceding code is not a good example of how to add a menu, and it may or may
not insert the menu at the proper position. It suffers from two problems:

✦ It assumes that the Help menu exists, but the user may have removed the
Help menu.

✦ It assumes that the Help menu has Help as its caption, but non-English versions of Excel may have a different caption for their menus.

Adding a menu: Take 2

Listing 41-1 presents a better demonstration. It uses the FindControl method to
attempt to locate the Help menu. If the Help menu is not found, the code adds the
new menu item to the end of the Worksheet Menu Bar.

Menu-Making Conventions

You may have noticed that menus in Windows programs typically adhere to some established conventions. You should follow them if you want your applications to be easy to use. When you modify menus, keep the following points in mind:

✦ Tradition dictates that the File menu is always first and the Help menu is always last.

✦ Menu text is always proper case. The first letter of each word is uppercase, except for minor words such as *the, a,* and *and.*

✦ A menu itself does not cause any action. In other words, each menu must have at least one menu item.

✦ Menu items are usually limited to three or fewer words.

✦ Every menu item should have a hot key (underlined letter) that's unique to the menu.

✦ A menu item that displays a dialog box is followed by an ellipsis (...).

✦ Menu item lists should be kept relatively short. Sometimes, submenus provide a good alternative to long lists. If you must have a lengthy list of menu items, use separator bars to group items into logical groups.

✦ If possible, disable menu items that are not appropriate in the current context. In VBA terminology, to disable a menu item, set its Enabled property to False.

✦ Some menu items serve as toggles. When the option is on, the menu item is preceded by a check mark.

Listing 41-1: **Adding the Budgeting menu to Excel's main menu bar**

```
Sub AddNewMenu()
    Dim HelpMenu As CommandBarControl
    Dim NewMenu As CommandBarPopup

'   Find the Help Menu
    Set HelpMenu = CommandBars(1).FindControl(Id:=30010)

    If HelpMenu Is Nothing Then
'       Add the menu to the end
        Set NewMenu = CommandBars(1).Controls _
        .Add(Type:=msoControlPopup, Temporary:=True)
    Else
'       Add the menu before Help
```

Continued

Listing 41-1 *(continued)*

```
        Set NewMenu = CommandBars(1).Controls _
          .Add(Type:=msoControlPopup, Before:=HelpMenu.Index, _
        Temporary:=True)
    End If

'   Add a caption
    NewMenu.Caption = "&Budgeting"
End Sub
```

 **Cross-Reference** The preceding procedure creates an essentially worthless menu because it has no menu items. See "Adding a Menu Item to the Tools Menu" later in this chapter for an example of how to add a menu item to a menu.

To use the `FindControl` method, you must know the `Id` property of the control that you're looking for. Each of Excel's own built-in `CommandBar` controls has a unique `Id` property. For this example, determine the `Id` property of the Help menu by executing the following statement:

```
MsgBox CommandBars(1).Controls("Help").Id
```

The message box displays 30010, which is the value you use as the `Id` argument for the `FindControl` method. Table 41-1 shows the `Id` property settings for the top-level controls in Excel's menu bars.

Table 41-1
Id Property Settings for Excel's Built-in Menus

Menu	Id Setting
File	30002
Edit	30003
View	30004
Insert	30005
Format	30006
Tools	30007
Data	30011
Chart	30022
Window	30009
Help	30010

Deleting a menu from a menu bar

To delete a menu, use the `Delete` method. The following example deletes the menu in the Worksheet Menu Bar whose caption is "Budgeting." Notice that it uses `On Error Resume Next` to avoid the error message that appears if the menu does not exist.

```
Sub DeleteMenu()
    On Error Resume Next
    CommandBars(1).Controls("Budgeting").Delete
End Sub
```

Adding menu items to a menu

The example under "Adding a new menu to a menu bar" demonstrated how to add a menu to a menu bar. Listing 41-2 adds to the original procedure and, in so doing, demonstrates how to add menu items to the new menu.

Listing 41-2: Adding selections and submenu items to the Budgeting menu

```
Sub CreateMenu()
    Dim HelpMenu as CommandBarControl
    Dim NewMenu As CommandBarPopup

'   Delete the menu if it already exists
    Call DeleteMenu

'   Find the Help Menu
    Set HelpMenu = CommandBars(1).FindControl(Id:=30010)

    If HelpMenu Is Nothing Then
'       Add the menu to the end
        Set NewMenu = CommandBars(1).Controls _
         .Add(Type:=msoControlPopup, temporary:=True)
    Else
'       Add the menu before Help
        Set NewMenu = CommandBars(1).Controls _
         .Add(Type:=msoControlPopup, Before:=HelpMenu.Index, _
         temporary:=True)
    End If

'   Add a caption for the menu
    NewMenu.Caption = "&Budgeting"

'   FIRST MENU ITEM
    Set MenuItem = NewMenu.Controls.Add _
      (Type:=msoControlButton)
```

Continued

Listing 41-2 *(continued)*

```
    With MenuItem
        .Caption = "&Data Entry..."
        .FaceId = 162
        .OnAction = "Macro1"
    End With

'   SECOND MENU ITEM
    Set MenuItem = NewMenu.Controls.Add _
      (Type:=msoControlButton)
    With MenuItem
        .Caption = "&Generate Reports..."
        .FaceId = 590
        .OnAction = "Macro2"
End With
'   THIRD MENU ITEM
    Set MenuItem = NewMenu.Controls.Add _
      (Type:=msoControlPopup)
    With MenuItem
        .Caption = "View &Charts"
        .BeginGroup = True
    End With

'   FIRST SUBMENU ITEM
    Set SubMenuItem = MenuItem.Controls.Add _
      (Type:=msoControlButton)
    With SubMenuItem
        .Caption = "Monthly &Variance"
        .FaceId = 420
        .OnAction = "Macro3"
    End With
'    SECOND SUBMENU ITEM
    Set SubMenuItem = MenuItem.Controls.Add _
      (Type:=msoControlButton)
    With SubMenuItem
        .Caption = "Year-To-Date &Summary"
        .FaceId = 422
        .OnAction = "Macro4"
    End With
  End Sub
```

Specifically, the `CreateMenu` procedure builds the menu shown in Figure 41-2. This menu has three menu items, and the last menu item is a submenu with two sub-menu items.

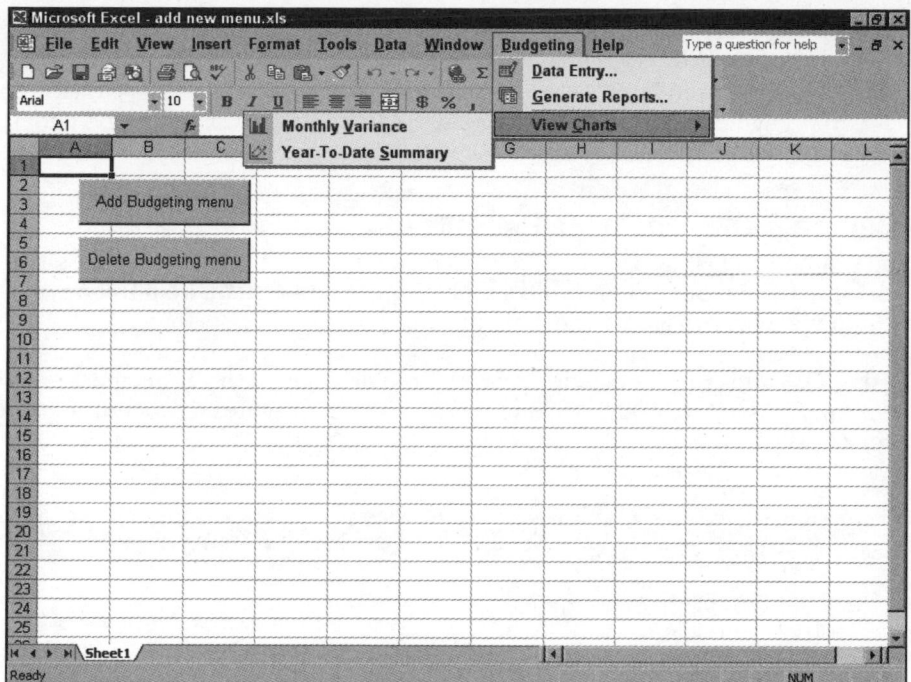

Figure 41-2: A VBA procedure created this menu and its associated menu items.

You might be wondering why the code in the preceding example deletes the menu (if it already exists) and doesn't simply exit the procedure. Rebuilding the menu ensures that the latest version is added to the menu bar. This also makes it much easier on you while you're developing the code because you don't have to delete the menu manually before testing your procedure. As you may have noticed, creating menus is very fast, so the additional time required to rebuild a menu is usually negligible.

When you examine the CreateMenu procedure, keep the following points in mind:

✦ The control type for the first two menu items is msoControlButton. The type of the third menu item, however, is msoControlPopup because the third menu item has submenu items.

✦ No OnAction property exists for controls of type msoControlPopup.

✦ The BeginGroup property of the third menu item is True, which causes a separator bar to appear before the item. The separator bar is purely cosmetic and serves to "group" similar menu items together.

✦ The `FaceID` property determines which image (if any) appears next to the menu text. The `FaceID` number represents a built-in image.

✦ The text for the `Caption` properties uses an ampersand (&) to indicate the "hot key," or accelerator key, for the menu item. The *hot key* is the underlined letter that provides keyboard access to the menu item.

Adding a menu item to the Tools menu

The example in Listing 41-2 adds several menu items to a custom menu on the Worksheet Menu Bar. Often, you'll simply want to add a menu item to one of Excel's built-in menus, such as the Tools menu.

Listing 41-3 adds the menu item Clear All But Formulas to the Tools menu — whose `Id` property is set to 30007. Clicking this menu item executes a procedure named `ClearAllButFormulas`.

Listing 41-3: **Adding a selection to Excel's Tools menu**

```
Sub AddMenuItem()
    Dim ToolsMenu As CommandBarPopup
    Dim NewMenuItem As CommandBarButton

'   Delete the menu if it already exists
    Call DeleteMenuItem

'   Find the Tools Menu
    Set ToolsMenu = CommandBars(1).FindControl(Id:=30007)
    If ToolsMenu Is Nothing Then
        MsgBox "Cannot add menu item."
        Exit Sub
    Else
        Set NewMenuItem = ToolsMenu.Controls.Add _
          (Type:=msoControlButton)
        With NewMenuItem
            .Caption = "&Clear All But Formulas"
            .FaceId = 348
            .OnAction = "ClearAllButFormulas"
            .BeginGroup = True
        End With
    End If
End Sub
```

Figure 41-3 shows the Tools menu with the new menu item.

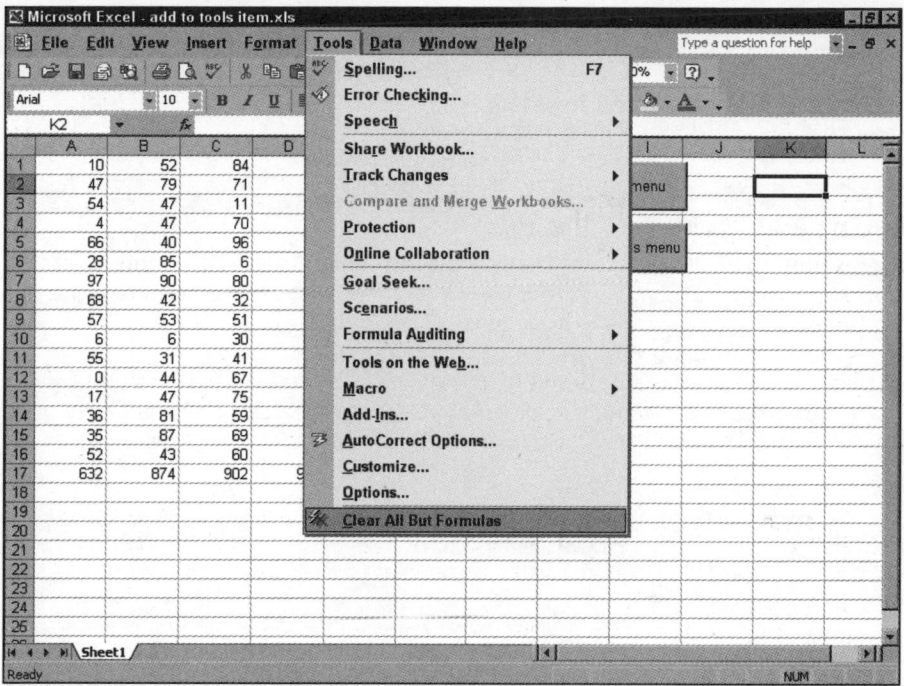

Figure 41-3: A new menu item has been added to the Tools menu.

Deleting a menu item from the Tools menu

To delete a menu item, use the `Delete` method of the `Controls` collection. The following example deletes the Clear All But Formulas menu item on the Tools menu. Note that it uses the `FindControl` method to handle the situation when the Tools menu has a different caption.

```
Sub DeleteMenuItem()
    On Error Resume Next
    CommandBars(1).FindControl(Id:=30007). _
        Controls("&Clear All But Formulas").Delete
End Sub
```

Displaying a shortcut key with a menu item

Some of Excel's built-in menu items also display a shortcut key combination that, when pressed, has the same effect as the menu command. For example, Excel's Edit menu lists several shortcut keys.

To display a shortcut key combination as part of your menu item, use the Shortcut Text property. Listing 41-4 creates a menu item Clear All But Formulas on the Tools menu. It sets the ShortcutText property to the string Ctrl+Shift+C and also uses the MacroOptions method to set up the shortcut key.

Listing 41-4: Adding a menu selection that features a shortcut key

```
Sub AddMenuItem()
    Dim ToolsMenu As CommandBarPopup
    Dim NewMenuItem As CommandBarButton

'   Delete the menu if it already exists
    Call DeleteMenuItem

'   Find the Tools Menu
    Set ToolsMenu = CommandBars(1).FindControl(Id:=30007)
    If ToolsMenu Is Nothing Then
        MsgBox "Cannot add a menu item - use Ctrl+Shift+C."
        Exit Sub
    Else
        Set NewMenuItem = ToolsMenu.Controls.Add _
          (Type:=msoControlButton)
        With NewMenuItem
            .Caption = "&Clear All But Formulas"
            .FaceId = 348
            .ShortcutText = "Ctrl+Shift+C"
            .OnAction = "ClearAllButFormulas"
            .BeginGroup = True
        End With
    End If

'   Create the shortcut key
    Application.MacroOptions _
      Macro:="ClearAllButFormulas", _
      HasShortcutKey:=True, _
      ShortcutKey:="C"
End Sub
```

After this procedure is executed, the menu item is displayed as shown in Figure 41-4.

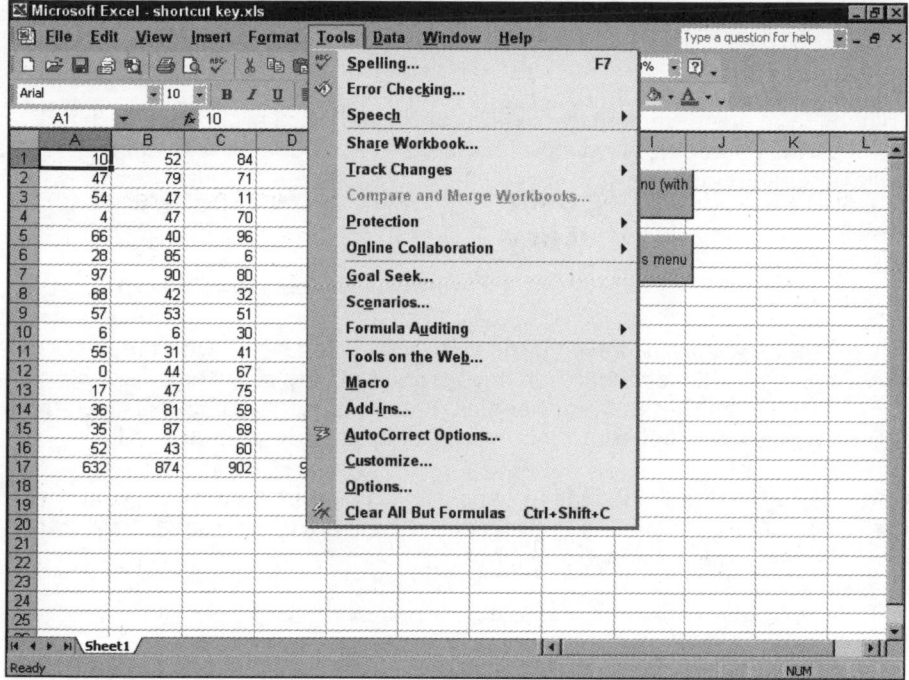

Figure 41-4: The Clear All But Formulas menu item also displays a shortcut key combination.

Working with Events

Suppose you want to create a menu when a workbook opens. You'll also want to delete the menu when the workbook closes because menu modifications remain in effect between Excel sessions. Or suppose you want a menu to be available only when a particular workbook or worksheet is active. These sorts of things are relatively easy to program, thanks to Excel's event handlers.

The examples in this section demonstrate various menu-programming techniques used in conjunction with events.

Cross-Reference   Event programming is discussed in depth in Chapter 38.

Adding and deleting menus automatically

If you need a menu to be created when a workbook is opened, use the `Workbook_Open` event. The following code, stored in the code module for the `ThisWorkbook` object, executes the `CreateMenu` procedure:

```
Private Sub Workbook_Open()
    Call CreateMenu
End Sub
```

To delete the menu when the workbook is closed, use a procedure such as the following. This procedure is executed before the workbook closes, and it executes the DeleteMenu procedure.

```
Private Sub Workbook_BeforeClose(Cancel As Boolean)
    Call DeleteMenu
End Sub
```

A problem may arise, however, if the workbook is not saved when the user closes it. Excel's "save workbook before closing" prompt occurs after the Workbook_BeforeClose event handler runs. So if the user clicks Cancel, the workbook remains open, but your custom menu has already been deleted!

One solution to this problem is to bypass Excel's prompt and write your own code in the Workbook_BeforeClose procedure to ask the user to save the workbook. The following code demonstrates how:

```
Private Sub Workbook_BeforeClose(Cancel As Boolean)
    If Not Me.Saved Then
        Msg = "Do you want to save the changes you made to "
        Msg = Msg & Me.Name & "?"
        Ans = MsgBox(Msg, vbQuestion + vbYesNoCancel)
        Select Case Ans
            Case vbYes
                Me.Save
            Case vbNo
                Me.Saved = True
            Case vbCancel
                Cancel = True
                Exit Sub
        End Select
    End If
    Call DeleteMenu
End Sub
```

This procedure determines whether the workbook has been saved. If it has, no problem; the DeleteMenu procedure is executed, and the workbook is closed. But if the workbook has not been saved, the procedure displays a message box that duplicates the one Excel normally shows. If the user clicks Yes, the workbook is saved, the menu is deleted, and the workbook is closed. If the user clicks No, the code sets the Saved property of the Workbook object to True (without actually saving the file) and deletes the menu. If the user clicks Cancel, the BeforeClose event is canceled, and the procedure ends without deleting the menu.

Disabling or hiding menus

When a menu or menu item is disabled, its text appears in a faint shade of gray, and clicking it has no effect. Excel disables its menu items when they are out of context. For example, the Links menu item on the Edit menu is disabled when the active workbook does not contain any links.

You can write VBA code to enable or disable both built-in and custom menus or menu items. Similarly, you can write code to hide menus or menu items. The key, of course, is tapping into the correct event.

The following procedures are stored in the code module for the ThisWorkbook object:

```
Private Sub Workbook_Open()
    Call AddMenu
End Sub

Private Sub Workbook_BeforeClose(Cancel As Boolean)
    Call DeleteMenu
End Sub

Private Sub Workbook_Activate()
    Call UnhideMenu
End Sub

Private Sub Workbook_Deactivate()
    Call HideMenu
End Sub
```

When the workbook is opened, the AddMenu procedure is called. When the workbook is closed, the DeleteMenu workbook is called. Two additional event-handler procedures are executed when the workbook is activated or deactivated. The UnhideMenu procedure is called when the workbook is activated, and the HideMenu procedure is called when the workbook is deactivated.

The HideMenu procedure sets the Visible property of the menu item to False, which effectively removes it from the menu bar. The UnhideMenu procedure does just the opposite. The net effect is that the menu is visible only when the workbook is active. These procedures, which assume that the Caption for the menu is "Budgeting", are as follows:

```
Sub UnhideMenu()
    CommandBars(1).Controls("Budgeting").Visible = True
End Sub

Sub HideMenu()
    CommandBars(1).Controls("Budgeting").Visible = False
End Sub
```

To disable the menu rather than hide it, simply access the `Enabled` property instead of the `Visible` property.

Working with checked menu items

Several of Excel's menu items appear with or without a check mark. For example, the View ➪ Formula Bar menu item displays a check mark if the formula bar is visible and does not display a check mark if the formula bar is hidden. When you select this menu item, the formula bar's visibility is toggled, and the check mark is either displayed or not.

You can add this type of functionality to your custom menu items. For example, you might want to add a menu item that displays a check mark only when the active sheet is displaying grid lines. Selecting this item toggles the grid-line display and also adjusts the check mark. The check mark display is determined by the `State` property of the menu item control.

The trick here is keeping the check mark in sync with the active sheet. To do so, it's necessary to update the menu item whenever a new sheet or a new workbook is activated. This is done by setting up application-level events.

Adding the menu item

The `AddMenuItem` procedure shown in Listing 41-5 is executed when the workbook is opened. It creates a new GridLines menu item on the View menu.

Listing 41-5: **Augmenting a built-in Excel menu**

```
Dim AppObject As New XLHandler

Sub AddMenuItem()
    Dim ViewMenu As CommandBarPopup
    Dim NewMenuItem As CommandBarButton

'   Delete the menu if it already exists
    Call DeleteMenuItem

'   Find the View Menu
    Set ViewMenu = CommandBars(1).FindControl(ID:=30004)
    If ViewMenu Is Nothing Then
        MsgBox "Cannot add menu item."
        Exit Sub
    Else
        Set NewMenuItem = ViewMenu.Controls.Add _
        (Type:=msoControlButton)
        With NewMenuItem
```

```
            .Caption = "&GridLines"
            .OnAction = "ToggleGridlines"
        End With
    End If

'   Set up application event handler
    Set AppObject.AppEvents = Application
End Sub
```

The `AddMenuItem` procedure adds the new menu item to the Worksheet Menu Bar, not the Chart Menu Bar. Therefore, the new menu item isn't displayed when a chart sheet is active — which is just what you want.

Notice that the final statement in the `AddMenuItem` procedure sets up the Application-level events that will be monitored. These event procedures, which are stored in a class module named `XLHandler`, are as follows:

```
Public WithEvents AppEvents As Excel.Application

Private Sub AppEvents_SheetActivate(ByVal Sh As Object)
    Call CheckGridlines
End Sub

Private Sub AppEvents_WorkbookActivate _
  (ByVal Wb As Excel.Workbook)
    Call CheckGridlines
End Sub
```

Toggling the grid-line display

The net effect is that when the user changes worksheets or workbooks, the following `CheckGridlines` procedure is executed. This procedure ensures that the check mark displayed on the GridLines menu option is in sync with the sheet.

```
Sub CheckGridlines()
    Dim TG As CommandBarButton
    On Error Resume Next
    Set TG = CommandBars(1).FindControl(Id:=30004). _
      Controls("&GridLines")
    If ActiveWindow.DisplayGridlines Then
        TG.State = msoButtonDown
    Else
        TG.State = msoButtonUp
    End If
End Sub
```

This procedure checks the active window and sets the `State` property of the menu item. If grid lines are displayed, it adds a check mark to the GridLines menu item. If grid lines are not displayed, it removes the check mark from the menu item.

Keeping the menu in sync with the sheet

When the menu item is selected, the OnAction property of that menu item triggers the following ToggleGridlines procedure:

```
Sub ToggleGridlines()
    On Error Resume Next
    ActiveWindow.DisplayGridlines = _
       Not ActiveWindow.DisplayGridlines
    Call CheckGridlines
End Sub
```

This procedure simply toggles the grid-line display of the active window. It uses On Error Resume Next to eliminate the error message that is generated if the sheet is not a worksheet.

Creating a Substitute Worksheet Menu Bar

In some cases, you may want to hide Excel's standard Worksheet Menu Bar and replace it with your own. The MakeMenuBar procedure in Listing 41-6 creates a new menu bar named MyMenuBar. This menu bar consists of two menus. The first menu is the standard File menu, copied from the Worksheet Menu Bar. The second menu contains two items: Restore Normal Menu and Help.

Listing 41-6: Replacing Excel's built-in menu with your own

```
Sub MakeMenuBar()
    Dim NewMenuBar As CommandBar

'   Delete menu bar if it exists
    Call DeleteMenuBar

'   Add a menu bar
    Set NewMenuBar = CommandBars.Add(MenuBar:=True)
    With NewMenuBar
        .Name = "MyMenuBar"
        .Visible = True
    End With

'   Copy the File menu from Worksheet Menu Bar
    CommandBars("Worksheet Menu Bar") _
      .Controls(1).Copy Bar:=CommandBars("MyMenuBar")

'   Add a new menu
    Set NewMenu = NewMenuBar.Controls.Add _
```

```
        (Type:=msoControlPopup)
    NewMenu.Caption = "&Commands"

'   Add a new menu item
    Set NewItem = NewMenu.Controls.Add(Type:=msoControlButton)
    With NewItem
        .Caption = "&Restore Normal Menu"
        .OnAction = "DeleteMenuBar"
    End With

'   Add a new menu item
    Set NewItem = NewMenu.Controls.Add(Type:=msoControlButton)
    With NewItem
        .Caption = "&Help"
        .OnAction = "ShowHelp"
    End With
End Sub
```

Figure 41-5 shows the new menu bar.

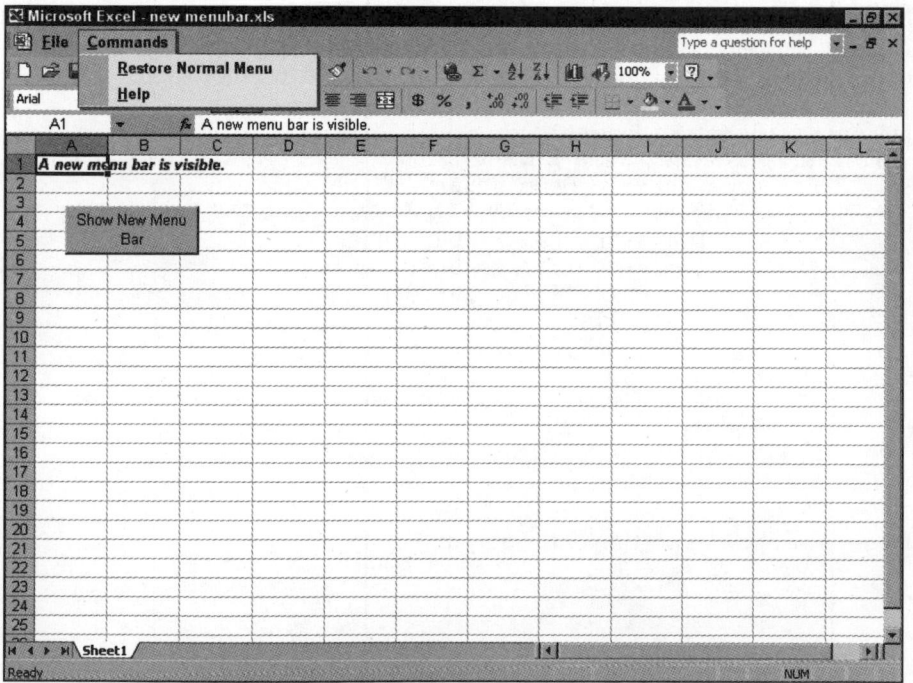

Figure 41-5: A custom menu bar replaces the standard Worksheet Menu Bar.

Notice that nothing in this procedure hides the Worksheet Menu Bar. The instruction `Set NewMenuBar = CommandBars.Add(MenuBar:=True)` adds the new command bar, and the `MenuBar` argument makes it the active menu bar. Only one menu bar can be active at a time.

Deleting the custom toolbar displays the Worksheet Menu Bar and makes it the active menu bar. The following `DeleteMenuBar` procedure returns things to normal:

```
Sub DeleteMenuBar()
    On Error Resume Next
    CommandBars("MyMenuBar").Delete
    On Error GoTo 0
End Sub
```

Working with Shortcut Menus

A *shortcut* menu is a pop-up menu that appears when you right-click virtually anything in Excel. You can't use Excel's Customize dialog box to remove or modify shortcut menus. The only way to customize shortcut menus is through VBA.

Excel has lots of shortcut menus. To work with a shortcut menu, you need to know its `Caption` property setting. You can use the following procedure to generate a list of all shortcut menus and the `Index` and `Caption` settings for each:

```
Sub ListShortCutMenus()
    Row = 1
    For Each cbar In CommandBars
        If cbar.Type = msoBarTypePopup Then
            Cells(Row, 1) = cbar.Index
            Cells(Row, 2) = cbar.Name
            For col = 1 To cbar.Controls.Count
                Cells(Row, col + 2) = _
                    cbar.Controls(col).Caption
            Next col
            Row = Row + 1
        End If
    Next cbar
End Sub
```

Figure 41-6 shows a portion of the output.

Figure 41-6: This shows part of the listing of all shortcut menus, plus the menu items in each.

6	35 Column	Cu&t	&Copy	&Paste	Paste &Special...
7	36 Row	Cu&t	&Copy	&Paste	Paste &Special...
8	37 Cell	Cu&t	&Copy	&Paste	Paste &Special...
9	38 Column	Cu&t	&Copy	&Paste	Paste &Special...
10	39 Row	Cu&t	&Copy	&Paste	Paste &Special...
11	40 Ply	&Ungroup Sheets	&Insert...	&Delete	&Rename
12	41 XLM Cell	Cu&t	&Copy	&Paste	Paste &Special...
13	42 Document	&Save	Save &As...	&Print...	Page Set&up...
14	43 Desktop	&New...	&Open...	Save &Workspace...	&Calculate Now
15	44 Nondefault Drag and Drop	&Move Here	&Copy Here	Copy Here as &Values Only	Copy Here as &F
16	45 AutoFill	&Copy Cells	Fill &Series	Fill &Formatting Only	Fill With&out Fo
17	46 Button	Cu&t	&Copy	&Paste	Clear
18	47 Dialog	&Paste	Ta&b Order...	&Run Dialog	
19	48 Series	&Selected Object	Chart T&ype...	&Source Data...	Add T&rendline...
20	49 Plot Area	&Selected Object	Chart T&ype...	&Source Data...	Chart Opt&ions...
21	50 Floor and Walls	&Selected Object	3-D &View...	Cle&ar	
22	51 Trendline	&Selected Object	Cle&ar		
23	52 Chart	&Selected Object	Cle&ar		
24	53 Format Data Series	&Selected Object	Chart T&ype...	&Source Data...	Add T&rendline...
25	54 Format Axis	&Selected Object	Cle&ar	&Hide Detail	&Show Detail
26	55 Format Legend Entry	&Selected Object	&Hide Detail	&Show Detail	Cle&ar
27	56 Formula Bar	Cu&t	&Copy	&Paste	&Format Cells...
28	57 PivotTable Context Menu	&Format Cells...	Pivot&Chart	&Wizard...	&Refresh Data
29	58 Query	Cu&t	&Copy	&Paste	Paste &Special...
30	59 Query Layout	Cu&t	&Copy	&Paste	Paste &Special...

Caution

Although you can refer to a shortcut menu by its `Index` property, this is not recommended. For some reason, `Index` values have not remained consistent between Excel versions. As a result, the same `Index` value can refer to different shortcut menus — depending on which version of Excel is in use.

Adding menu items to shortcut menus

Adding a menu item to a shortcut menu works just like adding a menu item to a regular menu. The following example demonstrates how to add a menu item to the Cell shortcut menu that appears when you right-click a cell or a row or column border. This menu item is added to the end of the shortcut menu, with a separator bar above it.

```
Sub AddItemToShortcut()
    Set NewItem = CommandBars("Cell").Controls.Add
    With NewItem
        .Caption = "Toggle Word Wrap"
        .OnAction = "ToggleWordWrap"
        .BeginGroup = True
    End With
End Sub
```

Selecting the new menu item executes a procedure named ToggleWordWrap.

Deleting menu items from shortcut menus

The following procedure uses the Delete method to remove the menu item added by the procedure in the previous section.

```
Sub RemoveItemFromShortcut()
    On Error Resume Next
    CommandBars("Cell").Controls("Toggle Word Wrap").Delete
End Sub
```

The On Error Resume Next statement avoids the error message that appears if the menu item is not on the shortcut menu.

The following procedure removes the Hide menu item from two shortcut menus: the one that appears when you right-click a row header and the one that appears for a column header:

```
Sub RemoveHideMenuItems()
    CommandBars("Column").Controls("Hide").Delete
    CommandBars("Row").Controls("Hide").Delete
End Sub
```

Disabling shortcut menu items

As an alternative to removing menu items, you may want to disable one or more items on certain shortcut menus while your application is running. When an item is disabled, it appears in a light gray color, and clicking it has no effect. The following procedure disables the Hide menu item from the Row and Column shortcut menus.

```
Sub DisableHideMenuItems()
    CommandBars("Column").Controls("Hide").Enabled = False
    CommandBars("Row").Controls("Hide").Enabled = False
End Sub
```

Disabling shortcut menus

You can also disable entire shortcut menus. For example, you may not want the user to access the commands generally made available by right-clicking a cell. The following DisableCell procedure disables the Cell shortcut menu. After the procedure is executed, right-clicking a cell has no effect.

```
Sub DisableCell()
    CommandBars("Cell").Enabled = False
End Sub
```

If you want to disable all shortcut menus, use the following procedure:

```
Sub DisableAllShortcutMenus()
    Dim cb As CommandBar
    For Each cb In CommandBars
        If cb.Type = msoBarTypePopup Then _
            cb.Enabled = False
    Next cb
End Sub
```

Caution   Disabling the shortcut menus "sticks" between sessions. Therefore, you'll probably want to restore the shortcut menus before closing Excel. To restore the shortcut menus, modify the preceding procedure to set the Enabled property to True.

Resetting shortcut menus

The Reset method restores a shortcut menu to its original condition. The following procedure resets the Cell shortcut menu to its normal state.

```
Sub ResetCellMenu()
    CommandBars("Cell").Reset
End Sub
```

Creating new shortcut menus

It's possible to create an entirely new shortcut menu. Listing 41-7 creates a shortcut menu named MyShortcut and adds six menu items to it. These menu items display one of the tabs in the Format Cells dialog box.

Listing 41-7: Creating an entirely new and separate shortcut menu

```
Sub CreateShortcut()
    Set myBar = CommandBars.Add _
      (Name:="MyShortcut", Position:=msoBarPopup, _
      Temporary:=True)

'   Add a menu item
    Set myItem = myBar.Controls.Add(Type:=msoControlButton)
    With myItem
        .Caption = "&Number Format..."
        .OnAction = "ShowFormatNumber"
        .FaceId = 1554
    End With
```

Continued

Listing 41-7 *(continued)*

```
'      Add a menu item
       Set myItem = myBar.Controls.Add(Type:=msoControlButton)
       With myItem
           .Caption = "&Alignment..."
           .OnAction = "ShowFormatAlignment"
           .FaceId = 217
       End With

'      Add a menu item
       Set myItem = myBar.Controls.Add(Type:=msoControlButton)
       With myItem
           .Caption = "&Font..."
           .OnAction = "ShowFormatFont"
           .FaceId = 291
       End With

'      Add a menu item
       Set myItem = myBar.Controls.Add(Type:=msoControlButton)
       With myItem
           .Caption = "&Borders..."
           .OnAction = "ShowFormatBorder"
           .FaceId = 149
           .BeginGroup = True
       End With

'      Add a menu item
       Set myItem = myBar.Controls.Add(Type:=msoControlButton)
       With myItem
           .Caption = "&Patterns..."
           .OnAction = "ShowFormatPatterns"
           .FaceId = 1550
       End With

'      Add a menu item
       Set myItem = myBar.Controls.Add(Type:=msoControlButton)
       With myItem
           .Caption = "Pr&otection..."
           .OnAction = "ShowFormatProtection"
           .FaceId = 2654
       End With
End Sub
```

Figure 41-7 shows how this new shortcut menu looks.

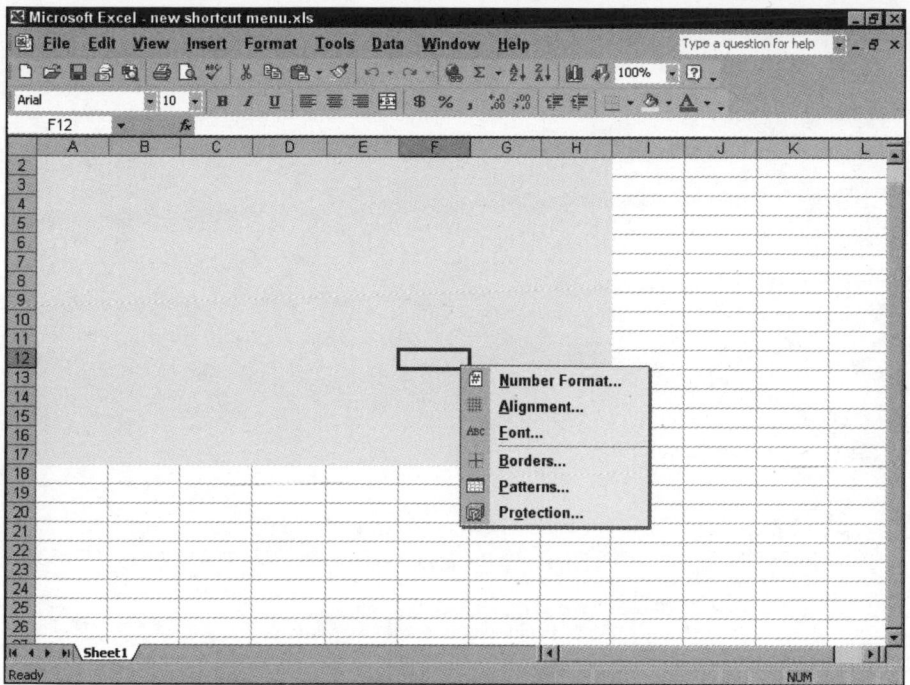

Figure 41-7: This new shortcut menu was created with VBA.

After the shortcut menu is created, you can display it with the ShowPopup method. The following procedure, located in the code module for a Worksheet object, is executed when the user right-clicks a cell.

```
Private Sub Worksheet_BeforeRightClick _
    (ByVal Target As Excel.Range, Cancel As Boolean)
      If Union(Target.Range("A1"), Range("data")).Address = _
        Range("data").Address Then
          CommandBars("MyShortcut").ShowPopup
          Cancel = True
      End If
End Sub
```

If the cell the user right-clicks is within a range named data, the MyShortcut menu appears. Setting the Cancel argument to True ensures that the normal shortcut menu is not displayed.

✦   ✦   ✦

Worksheet Function Reference

This appendix contains a complete listing of Excel's worksheet functions. The functions are arranged alphabetically by categories used by the Paste Function dialog box.

Note Some of these functions are available only when a particular add-in, such as the Analysis ToolPak, is attached.

For more information about a particular function, including its arguments, select the function in the Function Wizard and click the Help button.

Table A-1	
Database Category Functions	
Function	**What It Does**
DAVERAGE	Returns the average of selected database entries
DCOUNT	Counts the cells containing numbers from a specified database and criteria
DCOUNTA	Counts nonblank cells from a specified database and criteria
DGET	Extracts from a database a single record that matches the specified criteria
DMAX	Returns the maximum value from selected database entries
DMIN	Returns the minimum value from selected database entries

Continued

Table A-1 *(continued)*

Function	What It Does
DPRODUCT	Multiplies the values in a particular field of records that match the criteria in a database
DSTDEV	Estimates the standard deviation based on a sample of selected database entries
DSTDEVP	Calculates the standard deviation based on the entire population of selected database entries
DSUM	Adds the numbers in the field column of records in the database that match the criteria
DVAR	Estimates variance based on a sample from selected database entries
DVARP	Calculates variance based on the entire population of selected database entries

Table A-2
Date and Time Category Functions

Function	What It Does
DATE	Returns the serial number of a particular date
DATEVALUE	Converts a date in the form of text to a serial number
DAY	Converts a serial number to a day of the month
DAYS360	Calculates the number of days between two dates, based on a 360-day year
EDATE	Returns the serial number of the date that is the indicated number of months before or after the start date
EOMONTH	Returns the serial number of the last day of the month before or after a specified number of months
HOUR	Converts a serial number to an hour
MINUTE	Converts a serial number to a minute
MONTH	Converts a serial number to a month
NETWORKDAYS	Returns the number of whole workdays between two dates
NOW	Returns the serial number of the current date and time
SECOND	Converts a serial number to a second

Function	What It Does
TIME	Returns the serial number of a particular time
TIMEVALUE	Converts a time in the form of text to a serial number
TODAY	Returns the serial number of today's date
WEEKDAY	Converts a serial number to a day of the week
WEEKNUM	Returns the week number in the year
WORKDAY	Returns the serial number of the date before or after a specified number of workdays
YEAR	Converts a serial number to a year
YEARFRAC	Returns the year fraction representing the number of whole days between start_date and end_date

Table A-3
Engineering Category Functions

Function	What It Does
BESSELI	Returns the modified Bessel function In(x)
BESSELJ	Returns the Bessel function Jn(x)
BESSELK	Returns the modified Bessel function Kn(x)
BESSELY	Returns the Bessel function Yn(x)
BIN2DEC	Converts a binary number to decimal
BIN2HEX	Converts a binary number to hexadecimal
BIN2OCT	Converts a binary number to octal
COMPLEX	Converts real and imaginary coefficients into a complex number
CONVERT	Converts a number from one measurement system to another
DEC2BIN	Converts a decimal number to binary
DEC2HEX	Converts a decimal number to hexadecimal
DEC2OCT	Converts a decimal number to octal
DELTA	Tests whether two values are equal
ERF	Returns the error function

Continued

Table A-3 *(continued)*

Function	What It Does
ERFC	Returns the complementary error function
FACTDOUBLE	Returns the double factorial
GESTEP	Tests whether a number is greater than a threshold value
HEX2BIN	Converts a hexadecimal number to binary
HEX2DEC	Converts a hexadecimal number to decimal
HEX2OCT	Converts a hexadecimal number to octal
IMABS	Returns the absolute value (modulus) of a complex number
IMAGINARY	Returns the imaginary coefficient of a complex number
IMARGUMENT	Returns the argument theta, an angle expressed in radians
IMCONJUGATE	Returns the complex conjugate of a complex number
IMCOS	Returns the cosine of a complex number
IMDIV	Returns the quotient of two complex numbers
IMEXP	Returns the exponential of a complex number
IMLN	Returns the natural logarithm of a complex number
IMLOG10	Returns the base-10 logarithm of a complex number
IMLOG2	Returns the base-2 logarithm of a complex number
IMPOWER	Returns a complex number raised to an integer power
IMPRODUCT	Returns the product of two complex numbers
IMREAL	Returns the real coefficient of a complex number
IMSIN	Returns the sine of a complex number
IMSQRT	Returns the square root of a complex number
IMSUB	Returns the difference of two complex numbers
IMSUM	Returns the sum of complex numbers
OCT2BIN	Converts an octal number to binary
OCT2DEC	Converts an octal number to decimal
OCT2HEX	Converts an octal number to hexadecimal

Table A-4
Financial Category Functions

Function	What It Does
ACCRINT	Returns the accrued interest for a security that pays periodic interest
ACCRINTM	Returns the accrued interest for a security that pays interest at maturity
AMORDEGRC	Returns the depreciation for each accounting period
AMORLINC	Returns the depreciation for each accounting period
COUPDAYBS	Returns the number of days from the beginning of the coupon period to the settlement date
COUPDAYS	Returns the number of days in the coupon period that contains the settlement date
COUPDAYSNC	Returns the number of days from the settlement date to the next coupon date
COUPNCD	Returns the next coupon date after the settlement date
COUPNUM	Returns the number of coupons payable between the settlement date and maturity date
COUPPCD	Returns the previous coupon date before the settlement date
CUMIPMT	Returns the cumulative interest paid between two periods
CUMPRINC	Returns the cumulative principal paid on a loan between two periods
DB	Returns the depreciation of an asset for a specified period, using the fixed-declining balance method
DDB	Returns the depreciation of an asset for a specified period, using the double-declining balance method or some other method that you specify
DISC	Returns the discount rate for a security
DOLLARDE	Converts a dollar price, expressed as a fraction, into a dollar price, expressed as a decimal number
DOLLARFR	Converts a dollar price, expressed as a decimal number, into a dollar price, expressed as a fraction
DURATION	Returns the annual duration of a security with periodic interest payments
EFFECT	Returns the effective annual interest rate
FV	Returns the future value of an investment
FVSCHEDULE	Returns the future value of an initial principal after applying a series of compound interest rates
INTRATE	Returns the interest rate for a fully invested security

Continued

Table A-4 *(continued)*

Function	What It Does
IPMT	Returns the interest payment for an investment for a given period
IRR	Returns the internal rate of return for a series of cash flows
ISPMT	Returns the interest associated with a specific loan payment.
MDURATION	Returns the Macauley modified duration for a security with an assumed par value of $100
MIRR	Returns the internal rate of return where positive and negative cash flows are financed at different rates
NOMINAL	Returns the annual nominal interest rate
NPER	Returns the number of periods for an investment
NPV	Returns the net present value of an investment based on a series of periodic cash flows and a discount rate
ODDFPRICE	Returns the price per $100 face value of a security with an odd first period
ODDFYIELD	Returns the yield of a security with an odd first period
ODDLPRICE	Returns the price per $100 face value of a security with an odd last period
ODDLYIELD	Returns the yield of a security with an odd last period
PMT	Returns the periodic payment for an annuity
PPMT	Returns the payment on the principal for an investment for a given period
PRICE	Returns the price per $100 face value of a security that pays periodic interest
PRICEDISC	Returns the price per $100 face value of a discounted security
PRICEMAT	Returns the price per $100 face value of a security that pays interest at maturity
PV	Returns the present value of an investment
RATE	Returns the interest rate per period of an annuity
RECEIVED	Returns the amount received at maturity for a fully invested security
SLN	Returns the straight-line depreciation of an asset for one period
SYD	Returns the sum-of-years' digits depreciation of an asset for a specified period
TBILLEQ	Returns the bond-equivalent yield for a Treasury bill
TBILLPRICE	Returns the price per $100 face value for a Treasury bill
TBILLYIELD	Returns the yield for a Treasury bill
VDB	Returns the depreciation of an asset for a specified or partial period using a declining balance method

Function	What It Does
XIRR	Returns the internal rate of return for a schedule of cash flows that is not necessarily periodic
XNPV	Returns the net present value for a schedule of cash flows that is not necessarily periodic
YIELD	Returns the yield on a security that pays periodic interest
YIELDDISC	Returns the annual yield for a discounted security; for example, a Treasury bill
YIELDMAT	Returns the annual yield of a security that pays interest at maturity

Table A-5
Information Category Functions

Function	What It Does
CELL	Returns information about the formatting, location, or contents of a cell
ERROR.TYPE	Returns a number corresponding to an error type
INFO	Returns information about the current operating environment
ISBLANK	Returns TRUE if the value is blank
ISERR	Returns TRUE if the value is any error value except #N/A
ISERROR	Returns TRUE if the value is any error value
ISEVEN	Returns TRUE if the number is even
ISLOGICAL	Returns TRUE if the value is a logical value
ISNA	Returns TRUE if the value is the #N/A error value
ISNONTEXT	Returns TRUE if the value is not text
ISNUMBER	Returns TRUE if the value is a number
ISODD	Returns TRUE if the number is odd
ISREF	Returns TRUE if the value is a reference
ISTEXT	Returns TRUE if the value is text
N	Returns a value converted to a number
NA	Returns the error value #N/A
TYPE	Returns a number indicating the data type of a value

Table A-6
Logical Category Functions

Function	What It Does
AND	Returns TRUE if all its arguments are TRUE
FALSE	Returns the logical value FALSE
IF	Specifies a logical test to perform
NOT	Reverses the logic of its argument
OR	Returns TRUE if any argument is TRUE
TRUE	Returns the logical value TRUE

Table A-7
Lookup and Reference Category Functions

Function	What It Does
ADDRESS	Returns a reference as text to a single cell in a worksheet
AREAS	Returns the number of areas in a reference
CHOOSE	Chooses a value from a list of values
COLUMN	Returns the column number of a reference
COLUMNS	Returns the number of columns in a reference
GETPIVOTDATA	Returns data stored in a PivotTable
HLOOKUP	Looks in the top row of an array and returns the value of the indicated cell
HYPERLINK	Creates a shortcut that opens a document on your hard drive, a server, or the Internet
INDEX	Uses an index to choose a value from a reference or array
INDIRECT	Returns a reference indicated by a text value
LOOKUP	Looks up values in a vector or array
MATCH	Looks up values in a reference or array
OFFSET	Returns a reference offset from a given reference
ROW	Returns the row number of a reference
ROWS	Returns the number of rows in a reference
TRANSPOSE	Returns the transpose of an array
VLOOKUP	Looks in the first column of an array and moves across the row to return the value of a cell

Table A-8
Math and Trig Category Functions

Function	What It Does
ABS	Returns the absolute value of a number
ACOS	Returns the arccosine of a number
ACOSH	Returns the inverse hyperbolic cosine of a number
ASIN	Returns the arcsine of a number
ASINH	Returns the inverse hyperbolic sine of a number
ATAN	Returns the arctangent of a number
ATAN2	Returns the arctangent from x and y coordinates
ATANH	Returns the inverse hyperbolic tangent of a number
CEILING	Rounds a number to the nearest integer or to the nearest multiple of significance
COMBIN	Returns the number of combinations for a given number of objects
COS	Returns the cosine of a number
COSH	Returns the hyperbolic cosine of a number
DEGREES	Converts radians to degrees
EVEN	Rounds a number up to the nearest even integer
EXP	Returns e raised to the power of a given number
FACT	Returns the factorial of a number
FLOOR	Rounds a number down, toward 0
GCD	Returns the greatest common divisor
INT	Rounds a number down to the nearest integer
LCM	Returns the least common multiple
LN	Returns the natural logarithm of a number
LOG	Returns the logarithm of a number to a specified base
LOG10	Returns the base-10 logarithm of a number
MDETERM	Returns the matrix determinant of an array
MINVERSE	Returns the matrix inverse of an array
MMULT	Returns the matrix product of two arrays
MOD	Returns the remainder from division
MROUND	Returns a number rounded to the desired multiple

Continued

Table A-8 *(continued)*

Function	What It Does
MULTINOMIAL	Returns the multinomial of a set of numbers
ODD	Rounds a number up to the nearest odd integer
PI	Returns the value of pi
POWER	Returns the result of a number raised to a power
PRODUCT	Multiplies its arguments
QUOTIENT	Returns the integer portion of a division
RADIANS	Converts degrees to radians
RAND	Returns a random number between 0 and 1
RANDBETWEEN	Returns a random number between the numbers that you specify
ROMAN	Converts an Arabic numeral to Roman, as text
ROUND	Rounds a number to a specified number of digits
ROUNDDOWN	Rounds a number down, toward 0
ROUNDUP	Rounds a number up, away from 0
SERIESSUM	Returns the sum of a power series based on the formula
SIGN	Returns the sign of a number
SIN	Returns the sine of the given angle
SINH	Returns the hyperbolic sine of a number
SQRT	Returns a positive square root
SQRTPI	Returns the square root of (number _ pi)
SUBTOTAL	Returns a subtotal in a list or database
SUM	Adds its arguments
SUMIF	Adds the cells specified by a given criteria
SUMPRODUCT	Returns the sum of the products of corresponding array components
SUMSQ	Returns the sum of the squares of the arguments
SUMX2MY2	Returns the sum of the difference of squares of corresponding values in two arrays
SUMX2PY2	Returns the sum of the sum of squares of corresponding values in two arrays
SUMXMY2	Returns the sum of squares of differences of corresponding values in two arrays
TAN	Returns the tangent of a number
TANH	Returns the hyperbolic tangent of a number
TRUNC	Truncates a number to an integer

Table A-9
Statistical Category Functions

Function	What It Does
AVEDEV	Returns the average of the absolute deviations of data points from their mean
AVERAGE	Returns the average of its arguments
AVERAGEA	Returns the average of its arguments and includes evaluation of text and logical values
BETADIST	Returns the cumulative beta probability density function
BETAINV	Returns the inverse of the cumulative beta probability density function
BINOMDIST	Returns the individual term binomial distribution probability
CHIDIST	Returns the one-tailed probability of the chi-squared distribution
CHIINV	Returns the inverse of the one-tailed probability of the chi-squared distribution
CHITEST	Returns the test for independence
CONFIDENCE	Returns the confidence interval for a population mean
CORREL	Returns the correlation coefficient between two data sets
COUNT	Counts how many numbers are in the list of arguments
COUNTA	Counts how many values are in the list of arguments
COUNTBLANK	Counts the number of blank cells in the argument range
COUNTIF	Counts the number of cells that meet the criteria you specify in the argument
COVAR	Returns covariance, the average of the products of paired deviations
CRITBINOM	Returns the smallest value for which the cumulative binomial distribution is less than or equal to a criterion value
DEVSQ	Returns the sum of squares of deviations
EXPONDIST	Returns the exponential distribution
FDIST	Returns the F probability distribution
FINV	Returns the inverse of the F probability distribution
FISHER	Returns the Fisher transformation
FISHERINV	Returns the inverse of the Fisher transformation
FORECAST	Returns a value along a linear trend
FREQUENCY	Returns a frequency distribution as a vertical array
FTEST	Returns the result of an F-test

Continued

Table A-9 *(continued)*

Function	What It Does
GAMMADIST	Returns the gamma distribution
GAMMAINV	Returns the inverse of the gamma cumulative distribution
GAMMALN	Returns the natural logarithm of the gamma function, G(x)
GEOMEAN	Returns the geometric mean
GROWTH	Returns values along an exponential trend
HARMEAN	Returns the harmonic mean
HYPGEOMDIST	Returns the hypergeometric distribution
INTERCEPT	Returns the intercept of the linear regression line
KURT	Returns the kurtosis of a data set
LARGE	Returns the kth largest value in a data set
LINEST	Returns the parameters of a linear trend
LOGEST	Returns the parameters of an exponential trend
LOGINV	Returns the inverse of the lognormal distribution
LOGNORMDIST	Returns the cumulative lognormal distribution
MAX	Returns the maximum value in a list of arguments, ignoring logical values and text
MAXA	Returns the maximum value in a list of arguments, including logical values and text
MEDIAN	Returns the median of the given numbers
MIN	Returns the minimum value in a list of arguments, ignoring logical values and text
MINA	Returns the minimum value in a list of arguments, including logical values and text
MODE	Returns the most common value in a data set
NEGBINOMDIST	Returns the negative binomial distribution
NORMDIST	Returns the normal cumulative distribution
NORMINV	Returns the inverse of the normal cumulative distribution
NORMSDIST	Returns the standard normal cumulative distribution
NORMSINV	Returns the inverse of the standard normal cumulative distribution
PEARSON	Returns the Pearson product moment correlation coefficient
PERCENTILE	Returns the kth percentile of values in a range
PERCENTRANK	Returns the percentage rank of a value in a data set

Function	What It Does
PERMUT	Returns the number of permutations for a given number of objects
POISSON	Returns the Poisson distribution
PROB	Returns the probability that values in a range are between two limits
QUARTILE	Returns the quartile of a data set
RANK	Returns the rank of a number in a list of numbers
RSQ	Returns the square of the Pearson product moment correlation coefficient
SKEW	Returns the skewness of a distribution
SLOPE	Returns the slope of the linear regression line
SMALL	Returns the kth smallest value in a data set
STANDARDIZE	Returns a normalized value
STDEV	Estimates standard deviation based on a sample, ignoring text and logical values.
STDEVA	Estimates standard deviation based on a sample, including text and logical values
STDEVP	Calculates standard deviation based on the entire population, ignoring text and logical values.
STDEVPA	Calculates standard deviation based on the entire population, including text and logical values.
STEYX	Returns the standard error of the predicted y-value for each x in the regression
TDIST	Returns the student's t-distribution
TINV	Returns the inverse of the student's t-distribution
TREND	Returns values along a linear trend
TRIMMEAN	Returns the mean of the interior of a data set
TTEST	Returns the probability associated with a student's t-Test
VAR	Estimates variance based on a sample, ignoring logical values and text
VARA	Estimates variance based on a sample, including logical values and text
VARP	Calculates variance based on the entire population, ignoring logical values and text
VARPA	Calculates variance based on the entire population, including logical values and text
WEIBULL	Returns the Weibull distribution
ZTEST	Returns the two-tailed P-value of a z-test

Table A-10
Text Category Functions

Function	What It Does
BAHTTEXT	Converts a number to bath text
CHAR	Returns the character specified by the code number
CLEAN	Removes all nonprintable characters from text
CODE	Returns a numeric code for the first character in a text string
CONCATENATE	Joins several text items into one text item
DOLLAR	Converts a number to text, using currency format
EXACT	Checks to see whether two text values are identical
FIND	Finds one text value within another (case-sensitive)
FIXED	Formats a number as text with a fixed number of decimals
LEFT	Returns the leftmost characters from a text value
LEN	Returns the number of characters in a text string
LOWER	Converts text to lowercase
MID	Returns a specific number of characters from a text string, starting at the position you specify
PROPER	Capitalizes the first letter in each word of a text value
REPLACE	Replaces characters within text
REPT	Repeats text a given number of times
RIGHT	Returns the rightmost characters from a text value
SEARCH	Finds one text value within another (not case-sensitive)
SUBSTITUTE	Substitutes new text for old text in a text string
T	Converts its arguments to text
TEXT	Formats a number and converts it to text
TRIM	Removes spaces from text
UPPER	Converts text to uppercase
VALUE	Converts a text argument to a number

✦   ✦   ✦

Index

Numbers

Continued

Continued

Continued